Student CD Assessments

The Student CD, included with each new book, now contains questions in each chapter that help you *apply* what you've learned in each chapter to different scenarios. There are 2 modes for these quizzes. The first is the review mode, which tests your understanding of the chapter. The second is the application mode, which takes it one step further to see if you can *apply* the basic terms and concepts in the text to business scenarios. And you can count on detailed feedback on each answer, whether you answer it right or wrong.

The Student CD-ROM now includes **multi-lingual glossaries!** We know for students who speak English as their second language, the review and understanding of basic terms is critical to your success in the Introduction to Business course, so the key business terms in the text have now been translated into Spanish, Russian, and both traditional and simplified Mandarin Chinese on the Student CD-ROM.

administered distribution system
执行的发行系统
由生产商管理零售商所有行销的发行系统。

absolute advantage
абсолютное преимущество - наличие у страны монополии в определенных отраслях означает, что страна имеет возможность производить соответствующие товары или услуги с меньшими удельными издержками.

accounting
бухгалтерский учет – система сбора, классификации, обобщения и интерпретации финансовых операций на предприятии, дающая руководству и прочим заинтересованным сторонам возможность выносить обоснованные суждения и принимать экономические решения.

Getting Ready for Prime Time

This section at the beginning of the book is a fresh and friendly summary of the skills it takes to be a success in college and in business. You'll learn about business etiquette, and develop study and time management skills. There's also a primer on surfing the Web, and advice about how to get a rewarding job that will lead to a successful career. In fact, we think it's worth reading, even if your professor doesn't assign it.

"a solid grasp of the basic terminology and chapter concepts can only help you in this and future business courses"

Edition 7

Understanding Business

WILLIAM G. NICKELS

University of Maryland

JAMES M. McHUGH

St. Louis Community College at Forest Park

SUSAN M. McHUGH

Applied Learning Systems

McGraw-Hill Irwin

Boston Burr Ridge, IL Dubuque, IA Madison, WI New York San Francisco St. Louis
Bangkok Bogotá Caracas Kuala Lumpur Lisbon London Madrid Mexico City
Milan Montreal New Delhi Santiago Seoul Singapore Sydney Taipei Toronto

McGraw-Hill Irwin

UNDERSTANDING BUSINESS

Published by McGraw-Hill/Irwin, a business unit of The McGraw-Hill Companies, Inc., 1221 Avenue of the Americas, New York, NY, 10020.

This book is printed on acid-free paper.

4 5 6 7 8 9 0 DOW/DOW 0 9 8 7 6
ISBN-13: 978-0-07-253876-2 (student edition)
ISBN-10: 0-07-253876-7 (student edition)
ISBN-13: 978-0-07-288441-8 (annotated instructor's edition)
ISBN-10: 0-07-288441-X (annotated instructor's edition)
Vice president and editor-in-chief: *Robin J. Zwettler*
Editorial director: *John E. Biernat*
Executive editor: *John Weimeister*
Senior development editor: *Sarah Reed*
Developmental editor: *Burrston House*
Executive marketing manager: *Ellen Cleary*
Producer, Media technology: *Mark Molsky*
Lead project manager: *Mary Conzachi*
Manager, New book production: *Heather D. Burbridge*
Lead designer: *Matthew Baldwin*
Photo research coordinator: *Jeremy Cheshareck*
Photo researcher: *Burrston House*
Senior supplement producer: *Susan Lombardi*
Senior digital content specialist: *Brian Nacik*
Cover design: *Andrew Byrom, Keith McPherson*
Interior design: *Diane Beasley*
Typeface: *10/12 New Aster*
Compositor: *Carlisle Communications, Ltd.*
Printer: *R. R. Donnelley*

Icons and images on the cover represent some of the key features and themes found in this edition of *Understanding Business*. In addition, actual screen shots from our new video series are included to highlight companies or individuals that take you on a "field trip" to various real life businesses. Such images on the cover are from The Container Store, The Motley Fool, and Mini.

Library of Congress Cataloging-in-Publication Data

Nickels, William G.
Understanding business / William G. Nickels, James M. McHugh, Susan M. McHugh.—7th ed.
p. cm.
Includes bibliographical references and indexes.
ISBN 0-07-253876-7 (student ed. : alk. paper)—ISBN 0-07-288441-X (AIE : alk. paper)
1. Industrial management. 2. Business. 3. Business—Vocational guidance. I. McHugh, James M. II. McHugh, Susan M. III. Title.
HD31.N4897 2005
650—dc22

2003060256

www.mhhe.com

Dedication

To all the entrepreneurs who provide us with everything

we need and want,

To those brave men and women who defend our freedoms,

and

To friends and family who bring us joy.

Brief Contents

Contents

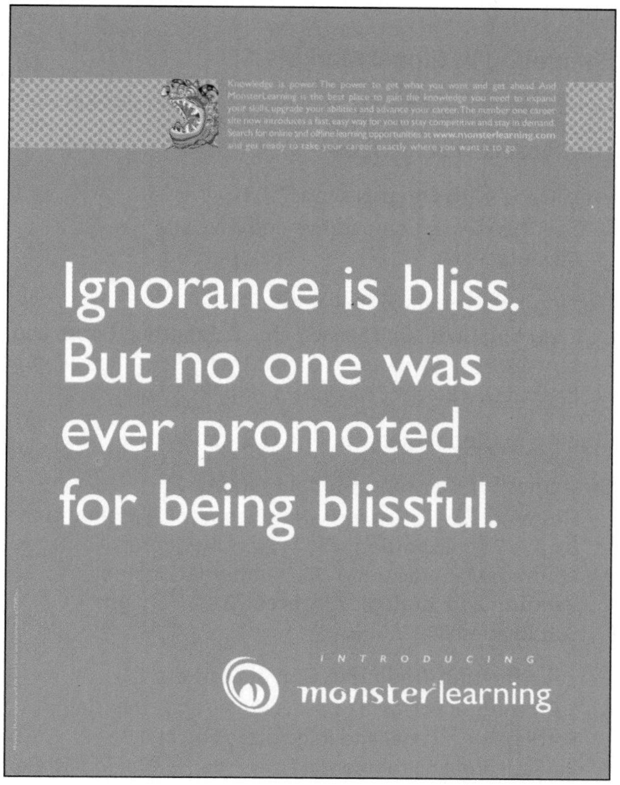
Ignorance is bliss.
But no one was
ever promoted
for being blissful.
INTRODUCING
monsterlearning

A college degree typically increases your earning power by 60 percent to 70 percent when compared to a high school diploma, and business is one of the most dynamic and practical areas of study.

A clash of economic philosophies? Perhaps. When the reunification of Germany took place residents of Chemnitz, formerly known as Karl Marx City and located in what was once East Germany, opted to retain this statue of Karl Marx while at the same time embracing one of capitalism's best known symbols, the Golden Arches of McDonald's.

Joining and giving to New York City's Learning Leaders organization is one way the Big Apple's movers and shakers are giving business a *good* name.

Operating out of one of their bedrooms Ronald and June Stein, owners of Principal Technical Services of Lake Forest, California, have fashioned a home-based business with $14 million in annual sales! They specialize in technical staffing and currently have over 200 employees, only a small percentage of whom have ever set foot in Lake Forest.

Is the goal of personalized, responsive customer service too often sacrificed to cost containment or reduction in many of today's businesses?

One of the key elements in today's global competition is labor cost. These white-collar workers at Wipro Spectramind in New Delhi, India, are 60 percent cheaper than their counterparts in the United States. How will U.S. workers meet this challenge?

With a population in excess of 1 billion, China is predicted by some experts to vault to the world's third largest car market by 2010, behind only the United States and Japan. What does this forecast mean to U.S. car manufacturers, U.S. oil companies, and potentially the world's environment?

Does advertising really sell? In a word, yes! And firms such as Hauling Ads Inc. are always searching for new ways to bring you their clients' messages.

As large as four tennis courts, the Earth Simulator is now the world's fastest computer. Built by NEC of Japan, it can process raw data approximately five times faster than IBM's ASCI, the previous speed champion.

Want to start a cyberbank? According to many of those who have, such as Walter Tillman of Earthstar Bank in Southampton, Pennsylvania, you may need to offer traditional brick-and-mortar branches as well in order to be profitable. For now, many customers are still uncomfortable with Internet banking.

Obtaining a credit card is frequently much easier than managing it. Financial independence depends on consistently sound decision making—both in terms of your choice of investments and career.

About the Authors

The *Understanding Business (UB)* author team possesses a unique blend of university, community college, industry, public service, small business, and curriculum development experience that helps them breathe life into the dynamic business concepts presented in the text. As instructors who use the *UB* text and supplements in their own classrooms, Bill Nickels and Jim McHugh have a personal stake in the quality of the entire project. As a curriculum specialist, Susan McHugh is committed to making certain that Bill and Jim (and all of the other *UB* users) have the best materials possible for creating interesting and useful classes that make learning business an exciting experience.

BILL NICKELS is an associate professor of business at the University of Maryland, College Park. With over 30 years of teaching experience, he teaches introduction to business in large sections (250 students) every semester. He teaches smaller sections in the summer. He also teaches the marketing principles course to large sections (500 students). Bill has won the Outstanding Teacher on Campus Award four times. He received his M.B.A. degree from Western Reserve University and his Ph.D. from The Ohio State University. He has written a marketing communications text and two marketing principles texts in addition to many articles in business publications. He believes in living a balanced life and wrote a book called *Win the Happiness Game* to share his secrets with others. Bill gives marketing and general business lectures to a variety of business and nonprofit organizations. Bill and his wife, Marsha, proudly anticipate the impending graduation of their son, Joel, who will become the third Dr. Nickels in the family.

JIM McHUGH is an associate professor of business at St. Louis Community College/Forest Park. He holds an M.B.A. degree from Lindenwood University and had broad experience in education, business, and government. In addition to teaching several sections of introduction to business each semester for 20 years, Jim maintains an adjunct professorship at Lindenwood University, teaching in the marketing and management areas at both the undergraduate and graduate levels. Jim has conducted numerous seminars in business, and maintains several consulting positions with small and large business enterprises. He is also actively involved in the public service sector.

SUSAN McHUGH is a learning specialist with extensive training and experience in adult learning and curriculum development. She holds a M.Ed. degree from the University of Missouri and has completed her course work for a Ph.D. in education administration with a specialty in adult learning theory. As a professional curriculum developer, she has directed numerous curriculum projects and educator training programs. She has worked in the public and private sector as a consultant in training and employee development. While Jim and Susan treasure their participation in the *UB* project, their greatest accomplishment is their collaboration on their three children, Casey, Molly, and Michael, who have all grown up regarding *UB* as a fourth sibling. Casey was a fervent user of the 4th edition, Molly eagerly used the 6th edition, and Michael will have his chance with this edition.

Preface

As authors, it is thrilling to see the results of the work we love be embraced by colleagues in hundreds of colleges and universities throughout the U.S. and around the world. Not only is *Understanding Business* the most widely used text in introduction to business courses across the country, but it is also the text we use day-in and day-out in our own intro classes. When you use the materials yourself, you have a strong vested interest in making the text and supplements the very best possible.

While we did play a significant role in the development of this text, the greatest joy we find in performing this task comes from working with the many people who deserve credit for the evolution of this remarkable project. Over 200 faculty who teach the course and hundreds of students who have used the book and its supplements were formally involved in various stages of our research and writing of this edition. We continue to hear informally from students and faculty throughout the country who call and e-mail us with comments and suggestions. We encourage you to do the same. We enjoy the interaction.

Prior to writing this edition, we held 10 close-to-the-customer focus groups in cities around the country. Discussions with over 100 instructors and students in these sessions helped us define, clarify, and test the needs of the diverse group who teach and take this course.

Additionally, more than 20 instructors provided us with in-depth evaluations of the sixth edition, providing insights for the improvements that you will encounter on every page of this edition. Once the first draft was written, another group of instructors critiqued our initial effort, which led to many more important refinements.

Many consider this process the most extensive product development process ever implemented for a text of this type. While that's probably true, we consider this talking and sharing of ideas with our colleagues and students across the country as one of the greatest perks of our jobs.

Keeping Up with What's New

Users of *Understanding Business* have always appreciated the currency of the material and the large number of examples from companies of *all* sizes and industries (e.g., service, manufacturing, profit and nonprofit) in the United States and around the world. A glance at the Chapter Notes will show you that most of them are from 2002 or 2003. Accordingly, this edition features the latest business practices and other developments affecting business, including:

- Effects of attacks of September 11, 2001, and other forms of terrorism.
- Homeland security.
- Privacy and security issues with information technology.
- Stock market decline of 2000–2002.
- Corporate scandals.
- The latest changes in the euro.
- Fall of companies such as Enron and WorldCom.

- The Sarbanes-Oxley Act.
- Enterprise portals.
- E-commerce's impact on the role of intermediaries.
- The rise, and fall, of B2C and B2B firms.
- The latest population trends.
- Internet2.
- Broadband technology.
- Online banking and smart cards.
- Alan Greenspan's endorsement by President George W. Bush.
- Radio-Frequency Identification Tags (RFID).
- Viral marketing.
- Issues regarding the World Bank and IMF.
- Latest quality standards.
- Storing and mining data.
- and much, much more.

We firmly believe that no course in college is more important than the introduction to business course. That's why we enjoy teaching it so much and why we are willing to spend so much time helping others make this the best course on campus. We are proud of the text and the integrated teaching and testing system that you have helped us develop over the years. We thank the many text and supplements users who have supported us through the years and welcome new instructors to the team. We look forward to a continuing relationship with all of you and to sharing what we consider the most exciting classroom experience possible: teaching introduction to business.

Bill Nickels
Jim McHugh
Susan McHugh

Acknowledgments

We have been blessed to work with a remarkable group of talented people at McGraw-Hill/Irwin. As executive editor, John Weimeister approached this project with a respect for what it had already achieved, and infused it with a fresh vision of what it could become. We appreciate his dedication and thank him for enlisting and guiding such a talented team of professionals.

Glenn Turner of Burrston House has been a major force on *Understanding Business* and has influenced its development since its inception. He continues to prod us and keep us focused on the needs of the market. We thank him for his loyalty and for sharing his wisdom with us through the years. Glenn and Meg Turner conducted the focus groups and managed the text reviews that have proved so helpful in revising the text and the supplements.

Every project has a "go-to" person, and we thank Sarah Reed for assuming that role for us. As development editor, Sarah juggled all of the pieces of this complex project masterfully.

Rosemary Hedger and Cherie Anderer of Burrston House carried out the extensive photo research that was necessary to effectively reflect the concepts presented in the text. The striking cover was designed by Andrew Byrom and Keith McPherson. The exceptionally inviting interior design was done by Diane Beasley. Kim Hooker and Mary Conzachi did a splendid job of keeping the production of the text on schedule. Manufacturing was kept on time under the watchful eye of Heather Burbridge. Copyeditor Janet Renard continues to amaze us with her ability to improve the text. We thank Michael Hannon for his tremendous help in preparing the first draft of the manuscript and for contributing many of the new Lecture Links. Susan Lombardi helped manage the supplements schedule for the huge ancillary package. Chris and Jennifer Cole created the fabulous new video series for this edition.

Many dedicated educators made extraordinary contributions to the quality and utility of this text and package. Barbara Barrett of St. Louis Community College at Meramec has continued her excellent work preparing a student assessment and learning guide that truly assists students in mastering the course concepts. Dennis Shannon and Jim McGowen of Southwestern Illinois College again did an exceptional job in revising the Test Bank and creating the quizzes for the Concept Mastery Toolkit CD. Gayle Ross of Ross Publishing continued to achieve miracles for us with her contributions to and management of the various resources that eventually come together to form the Instructor's Manual and Annotated Instructor's Edition (AIE). Chuck Bowles of Pikes Peak Community College did another superb job of creating the PowerPoint slides and transparency acetates. Tom Bilyeu enhanced the teaching value of the transparency acetates by preparing insightful lecture notes that accompany the acetates. Stephanie Bibb of Chicago State University prepared the handy media resource guide that adds instructional value to the video package. Mark Brookshire, founder of Stock-Trak, Inc., brought the challenging world of Wall Street to students in creating the new McGraw-Hill Investments Trader. Amit Shah of Frostburg State University prepared the manual to accompany this stock market project. Richard Drury of Northern Virginia Community College developed the new Business Plan exercises to assist aspiring entrepreneurs in building their future businesses. Many students would not be happy without the audio CD-ROMs prepared by Digital Excellence. Chia-Lang Barker and

DongWa Hu translated the glossary into traditional and simplified Chinese for the Student CD. Viatcheslav Boitchenko of Hudson-Neva Translations translated the glossary into Russian. Jim Paradiso of College of Lake County developed the content for the Online Learning Center. And many more people than we can ever acknowledge worked behind the scenes to translate our manuscript into the text you see; we thank them all.

Some said it couldn't be done, but our outstanding marketing manager, Ellen Cleary, continues to lead every edition to record-breaking sales. We appreciate the renowned service and commitment of the dedicated McGraw-Hill/Irwin sales reps as much as you do.

We want to thank the many instructors who contributed to the development of *Understanding Business.* An exceptional group of reviewers dedicated many long hours to critiquing the previous edition and subsequent drafts of this edition, and attending our focus groups. As we have stated previously in this Preface, their recommendations and contributions were invaluable in making this edition a stronger instructional tool. Our sincere thanks go to the following reviewers.

Reviewers of the Seventh Edition

We would like to thank the following instructors and students who generously provided the input and advice on which the refinements and enhancements to the Seventh Edition of the text and supplements are based.

Dave Aiken, *Hocking College*

Mohammed Alabbassi, *University of Northern Florida–Jacksonville*

Sylvia Allen, *Los Angeles Valley College*

Kenneth Anderson, *CUNY-Boro of Manhattan Community College*

Marilyn Anderson, *Phoenix College*

Robert Ash, *Santiago Canyon College*

Harold Babson, *Columbus State Community College*

Mike Baran, *South Puget Sound Community College*

Robert Barker, *Daytona Beach Community College*

Cora Barnhart, *Palm Beach Atlantic College*

Charles Beavin, *Miami Dade/North Campus*

Lori Bennett, *Moorpark College*

Robert Bennett, *Delaware County Community College*

Michael Bento, *Owens Community College*

Bill Bettencourt, *Edmonds Community College*

Carol Bibly, *Triton College*

Chris Bjornson, *Indiana University Southeast*

Margaret Black, *San Jacinto College, North Campus*

Mary Jo Boehms, *Jackson State Community College*

Steve Bradley, *Austin Community College*

Harvey Bronstein, *Oakland Community College*

Joe Brum, *Fayetteville Tech Community College*

Judy Bulin, *Monroe Community College*

Cathleen Burns, *University of Missouri–Columbia*

John Burns, *Tomball College*

Paul Callahan, *Cincinnati State Tech Community College*

Nate Calloway, *University of Maryland–Metro University College*

Marilyn Carlson, *Clark State Community College*

Ron Cereola, *James Madison University*

Kevin Chandler, *DeVry Institute of Technology–Orlando*

Glen Chapuis, *St. Charles Community College*

Bonnie Chavez, *Santa Barbara City College*

Michael Cicero, *Highline Community College*

Cindy Cloud, *Phoenix College*

Paul Coakley, *Community College of Baltimore County–Catonsville*

Barbara Connelly, *DeVry Institute–Phoenix*

Elijah Cooks, *Prince Georges Community College*

Yolanda Cooper, *Collin County Community College*

Bobbie Corbett, *North Virginia Community College–Annandale*

Amy Daniel, *Saddleback College*

Dean Danielson, *San Joaquin Delta College*

Cory Dobbs, *Rio Salado College*

Ron Dolch, *Wor-Wi Community College*

Richard Drury, *North Virginia Community College–Annandale*

Linda Durkin, *Delaware County Community College*

James Eason, *Coastal Carolina University*

Nancy Evans, *Heartland Community College*

Joyce Fairchild, *North Virginia Community College–Alexandria*

Janice Feldbauer, *Austin Community College*

Ivan Figueroa, *Miami Dade College–Kendall*

Ronald E. Foshee, *North Harris College*

Dennis Foster, *Northern Arizona University*

John Foster, *Montgomery College–Rockville*

Sofia Gill, *Palm Beach Community College–Palm Beach Gardens*

Al Gomez, *Broward Community College*

Mary Gorman, *University of Cincinnati*

Chris W. Grevesen, *DeVry College of New Jersey*

Carnella Hardin, *Glendale Community College*

Rowland Harvey, *DeVry Institute–Houston*

Carolyn Hatton, *Cincinnati State University*

Karen Hawkins, *Miami Dade College–Kendall*

Jack Heinsius, *Modesto Junior College*

Dave Hickman, *Frederick Community College*

Nathan Himelstein, *Essex Community College*

Merrily Hoffman, *San Jacinto College–Central*

Richard Hunting, *Montgomery College–Houston*

Bill Jackson, *Green River Community College*

Charlotte Jacobsen, *Montgomery College–Rockville*

Andrew Johnson, *Bellevue Community College*

Jack Johnson, *Consumnes River College*

Marie Johnson, *Skagit Valley College*

Edgar Joya, *St. Augustine College*

Jehan Kavoosi, *Clarion University*

Donald Kelley, *Francis Marion University*

Ann Kelly, *Georgia Southern University*

Marce Kelly, *Santa Monica College*

Tom Knoll, *DeVry Institute of Technology–Houston*

Steve Kober, *Pierce College*

Barbara Kriechbaum, *Hagerstown Business College*

Gary Langdale, *Saddleback College*

Michael LaSala, *Westchester Business Institute*

Dane Leonard, *Chabot College*

Harry Lepinske, *Purdue/Calumet–Hammond*

Rich Lewis, *Lansing Community College*

Ellen Ligons, *Pasadena City College*

Bryon Lilly, *DeAnza College*

Beverly Loach, *Central Piedmont Community College*

Terry Lovell, *Yavapai College*

Richard Lyons, *Indian River Community College*

Ashford Marahaja, *Berkeley College–White Plains*

Larry Martin, *Community College of Southern Nevada*

Randy Martin, *Germanna Community College*

Robert Matthews, *Oakton Community College*

Pat McMahon, *Palm Beach Community College*

Lasche McRorey, *Southwest Texas Junior College*

Herbert L. Meyer, *Scott Community College*

Bob Meyers, *Palm Beach Atlantic Community College*

Jacqueline Middleton, *Montgomery College–Germantown*

Rebecca Miles, *Delaware Tech Community College*

Willie Minor, *Rio Salado College*

Ed Mitchell, *Hillsborough Community College*

Alison Mukweyi, *Midland College*

Jerry Myers, *Stark State College*

Tom Nagle, *Northland Pioneer College*

Andrew Nelson, *Montgomery College–Germantown*

Linda Newell, *Saddleback College*

Ken Newgren, *Illinois State University*

Janet Nichols, *Northeastern University*

Ed O'Brien, *Scottsdale Community College*

Tibor Osztreicher, *Baltimore County Community College–Baltimore Campus*

Norman Pacula, *College of Marin*

Roger Pae, *Cuyahoga Community College*

Richard Paradiso, *Thomas Nelson Community College*

Jack Partlow, *North Virginia Community College–Annandale*

Steven Peters, *Walla Walla Community College*

Jim Pfister, *St. Petersburg Junior College*

John Phillips, *North Virginia Community College–Manassas*

Anita Pinkston, *Vincennes University*

Michael Potter, *DeVry Institute–Phoenix*

Lana Powell, *Valencia Community College–West*

Mark Preising, *Florida Metro University*
Ian Priestman, *Linn Benton Community College*
Kathy Pullins, *Columbus State Community College*
Michael Quinn, *James Madison University*
Gregg Rapp, *Portland Community College–Sylvania*
Robert Reck, *Western Michigan University*
Phil Reffitt, *Florida Metro University*
Levi Richard, *Citrus College*
Karen Richardson, *Tarrant County Community College–Northeast*
Dan Ricica, *Sinclair Community College*
Denver Riffe, *National College of Business & Technology*
Pollis Robertson, *Kellogg Community College*
Harriett Rojas, *Indiana Wesleyan*
Carol Rowey, *Community College of Rhode Island*
Joan Ryan, *Clackamas Community College*
Ron Schloemer, *Miami University*
Lewis Schlossinger, *Community College of Aurora*
Marcianna Schusler, *Prairie State College*
Tom Secrest, *Coastal Carolina University*
Patty Serrano, *Clark College*
Pat Setlik, *William Rainey Harper College*
Martin Shapiro, *Berkeley College–White Plains*
Dick Sharman, *Montgomery College*
Richard Sherer, *Los Angeles Trade–Tech College*
Charlie Shi, *Diablo Valley College*
Lynette Shishido, *Santa Monica College*
Gerald Silver, *Purdue/Calumet–Hammond*
Cynthia Singer, *Union City College*
Leon Singleton, *Santa Monica College*
Steven Skaggs, *Waubonsee Community College*
Noel Smith, *Palm Beach Community College–South*
Ray Sparks, *Pima Community College–East Campus*
Rieann Spence-Gale, *North Virginia Community College–Alexandria*
Sandra Spencer, *DeAnza College*
Camille Stallings, *Pima Community College–Downtown*
Vernon Stauble, *San Bernardino Valley College*
Leo Stevenson, *Western Michigan University*
Edith Strickland, *Tallahassee Community College*
David Stringer, *De Anza College*
Lynn Suksdorf, *Salt Lake Community College*
Dottie Sutherland, *Pima Community College–East Campus*
Verna Swanljung, *North Seattle Community College*
Susan Thompson, *Palm Beach Community College–Lake Worth*
Tom Thompson, *University of Maryland–University College*
Frank Titlow, *St. Petersburg College*
Shafi Ullah, *Broward Community College–South*
Vern Urlacher, *Colorado Technical University*
Margie Vance, *Albuquerque Vo-Tech Institute*
Michael Vijuk, *William Rainey Harper College*
Nancy Waldron, *Lasell College*
Tom Walker, *Seminole Community College*
Carl Wall, *Broward Community College–North*
Roger Waller, *San Joaquin Delta College*
Joyce Walsh-Portillo, *Broward Community College–Central*
Louis Watanabe, *Bellevue Community College*
Gregor Weiss, *Prince Georges Community College*
Dick Westfall, *Cabrillo College*
Jay Whitelock, *Community College of Baltimore County–Catonsville*
Jean Wicks, *Bowie State University*
Timothy Wiedman, *Thomas Nelson Community College*
Paul Wilcox, *DeVry Institute of Technology–Orlando*
Lynn Wilson, *Saint Leo University*
Greg Winter, *Barry University*
Nathaniel Woods, *Columbus State Community College*
Ron Young, *Kalamazoo Valley Community College*

The *Understanding Business* product is more than just a textbook. It includes a treasure trove of supplementary materials that play a major role in our instructional programs. Three key supplements, the test bank, the study guide, and the instructor's manual, were reviewed in order to ensure the highest quality *UB* instructors have grown to depend on. Every test bank question was reviewed by the text authors along with Robert Bennett, Delaware County

Community College; Dave Hickman, Frederick Community College; Janet Nichols, Northeastern University; Pat Selik, William Rainey Harper College; and Sandra Spencer, DeAnza College. The study guide was comprehensively reviewed by the text authors along with Mark Preising, Florida Metro University; and Louis Watanabe, Bellevue Community College. The Instructor's Manual was reviewed by the text authors along with Gordon Frank, Karl Schindl, and Jim Reinemann. Chapter 18 was carefully reviewed for accuracy by Jutta Green and Robert Smolin.

The seventh edition is all the stronger due to involvement of these committed instructors and students. We thank them all for their help, support, and friendship.

Bill Nickels **Jim McHugh** **Susan McHugh**

Reviewers and Other Participants in the Development of Previous Editions

Larry Aaronson, *Catonsville Community College;* Milton Alderfer, *Miami-Dade Community College;* Dennis G. Allen, *Grand Rapids Community College;* Dan Anderson, *Sullivan Jr. College;* Kenneth Anderson, *Charles S. Mott Community College;* Kenneth F. Anderson, *CUNY–Borough of Manhattan Community College;* Lydia E. Anderson, *Fresno City College;* John Anstey, *University of Nebraska–Omaha;* Maria Zak Aria, *Camden County College;* Glenann Arnold, *Pueblo Community College;* Ed Aronson, *Golden West College;* Larry Arp, *University of Southern Indiana;* Doug Ashby, *Lewis & Clark;* Hal Babson, *Columbus State Community College;* Harold Babson, *Columbus State Community College;* Chani Badrian, *CUNY–Baruch College;* Herm Baine, *Broward Community College;* Morris Baird, *The Community College of Baltimore County;* Russell Baker, *Florida Metropolitan University;* Xenia Balabkins, *Middlesex County College;* Michael Baldigo, *Sonoma State University;* Lee R. Baldwin, *Mt. San Antonio College;* John Balek, *Morton College;* Fran Ballard, *Florida Community College;* Barbara Barrett, *St. Louis Community College;* Richard Bartlett, *Muskigan Area Technical College;* Lorraine Bassette, *Prince George's Community College;* Robert Bennett, *Delaware County Community College;* Ellen Benowitz, *Mercer County Community College;* Alec Beudoin, *Triton College;* Jade Beavers, *Jefferson State Community College;* Charles Beavin, *Miami-Dade–North;* John Beem, *College of DuPage;* Michael Bejtlich, *Cape Cod Community College;* Larry Benke, *Sacramento City College;* Marcel Berard, *Community College of Rhode Island;* Janet L. Bernard, *Tampa College;* Patricia Bernson, *County College of Morris;* John Berry, *Antelope Valley College;* Carol Bibly, *Triton College;* Dean Bittick, *East Central College;* John Blackburn, *Ohio State University;* Jane Bloom, *Palm Beach Community College;* James H. Boeger, *Rock Valley College;* Mary Jo Boehms, *Jackson State Community College;* Jessee Bolton, *Charles County Community College;* Robert Bouck, *Lansing Community College;* John Bowdidge, *Southwest Missouri State University;* Barbara Ann Boyington, *Brookdale Community College;* Steven E. Bradley, *Austin Community College–Riverside;* Stephen Branz, *Triton College;* Robert Brechner, *Miami-Dade Community College;* Sonya Brett, *Macomb Community College;* Harvey Bronstein, *Oakland Community College;* Richard Brooke, *Florida Community College at Jacksonville;* Deborah M. Brown, *Santa Fe Community College;* Joseph Brum, *Fayetteville Technical Community College;* Thomas Buchl, *Northern Michigan University;* Howard Budner, *CUNY–Borough of Manhattan Community College;* Albert Bundons, *Johnson County Community College;* Nichole Burnes, *FMU–Tampa College;* Barrett R. Burns, *Houston Community College;* William F. Burtis, *DeAnza College;* Dennis

Butler, *Orange Coast Community College;* Ron Bytnar, *South Suburban College;* Willie Caldwell, *Houston Community College;* J. Callahan, *Florida Institute of Technology;* Nathaniel Calloway, *University of Maryland–University College;* Nathaniel R. Calloway, *University of Maryland–University College;* B. J. Campsey, *San Jose State University;* Michele Lynn Carver, *The Community College of Baltimore County;* Lesley Casula, *Lord Fairfax Community College;* Mary Margaret Cavera, *Davenport College;* Sandra Cece, *Triton College;* Sam Chapman, *Diablo Valley College;* Bruce Charnov, *Hofstra University;* Bonnie Chavez, *Santa Barbara City College;* Barbara Ching, *Los Angeles City College;* William Chittenden, *Texas Tech University;* Larry Chonko, *Baylor University;* Jill Chown, *Mankato State University;* Nancy Christenson, *Brevard Community College;* Peter D. Churchill, *Diablo Valley College;* Gary Ciampa, *Wayne County Community College;* Michael Cicero, *Highline Community College;* J. Cicheberger, *Hillsborough Community College;* Monico Cisneros, *Austin Community College;* Robert Clobes, *St. Charles County Community College;* Paul Coakley, *The Community College of Baltimore County;* James Cocke, *Pima County Community College;* Jerry Cohen, *Raritan Valley Community College;* Jeffrey Conte, *Westchester Community College;* Ron Cooley, *South Suburban College;* Allen Coon, *Robert Morris College;* Doug Copeland, *Johnson County Community College;* John Coppage, *Saginaw Valley State University;* Bobbie Corbett, *Northern Virginia Community College–Annandale;* John Courtney, *University of Maryland, University College;* James Cox, *Jefferson Community College;* William Crandall, *College of San Mateo;* Susan Cremins, *Westchester Community College;* Bruce Cudney, *Middlesex Community College;* C. Culbreth, *Brevard Community College;* Rex Cutshall, *Vincennes University;* Lawrence Danks, *Camden County College;* Clifford Davis, *SUNY–Cobleskill;* R.K. Davis, *University of Akron;* Burton V. Dean, *San Jose State University;* Cindy Del Medico, *Oakton Community College;* Evelyn Delaney, *Daytona Beach Community College;* Peter DelPiano, *Florida Metropolitan University;* Vincent Deni, *Oakland Community College;* Kathleen Denisco, *SUNY–Buffalo;* S. Desai, *Cedar Valley College;* Jack Dilbeck, *Ivy Tech State College;* Katherine Dillon, *Ocean County College;* Samuel DiRoberto, *Penn State University–Ogontz;* Steve Dolvin, *Pensacola Christian College;* Frank Dumas, *Baker College–Flint;* Dana Dye, *Gulf Coast Community College;* Shannon M. Ebersol, *Hagerstown Community College;* Ronald Eggers, *Barton College;* Pat Ellsberg, *Lower Columbia College;* Frank Emory, *Northern Virginia Community College–Woodbridge;* Warren Enos, *Ohlone College;* David Erickson, *College of Lake County;* Ted Erickson, *Normandale Community College;* Alton Evans, *Tarrant County Community College;* John Evans, *New Hampshire College;* C. S. Everett, *Des Moines Area Community College;* Shad Ewart, *Anne Arundel Community College;* Al Fabian, *IVY Tech;* Karen Fager, *Umpqua Community College;* Frank Falcetta, *Middlesex Community College;* S. Fante, *Central Florida Community College;* Bob Farris, *Mt. San Antonio College;* James Fatina, *College of Lake County–Harper College;* Edward Fay, *Canton College of Technology;* Janice Feldbauer, *Austin Community College;* Kevin Feldt, *University of Akron;* David Felt, *Northern Virginia Community College–Manassas;* Bob Ferrentino, *Lansing Community College;* Ivan Figueroa, *Miami-Dade Community College;* Robert Fineran, *East-West University;* Robert Fishco, *Middlesex County Community College;* Charles FitzPatrick, *Central Michigan University;* Joseph L. Flack, *Washtenaw Community College;* Jane Flagello, *DeVry Institute of Technology–Lombard;* H. Steven Floyd, *Manatee Community College;* Ronald E. Foshee, *North Harris College;* John Foster, *Montgomery College;* Robin Frazee, *Anne Arundel Community College;* Barry Freeman, *Bergen Community College;* Leatrice Freer, *Pitt Community College;* Roger Fremier, *Monterey Peninsula College;* Edward Friese, *Okaloosa Walton Community College;* John Frith, *Central Texas College;* Michael Fritz, *Portland Community College;* Thomas Frizzel,

Massasoit Community College; J. Pat Fuller, *Brevard Community College;* Arlen Gastineau, *Valencia Community College;* Alan Gbur, *Richard J. Daley College;* Michael Geary, *Pensacola Christian College;* Lucille S. Genduso, *Nova Southeastern University;* James George, Jr., *Seminole Community College;* Tom Gilbertson, *Baker College;* Julie Giles, *DeVry Institute of Technology DuPage Campus;* Peter Giuliani, *Franklin University;* Eileen Baker Glassman, *Montgomery College;* Bernette Glover, *Olive Harvey College;* Don Gordon, *Illinois Central College;* Ron Gordon, *Florida Metropolitan University;* Donald Gordon, *Illinois Central College;* Mary E. Gorman, *Bellevue Community College;* Kay Gough, *Bellevue Community College;* Patricia Graber, *Middlesex Country College;* Mike Graves, *Portland Community College;* Joe Gray, *Nassau Community College;* Gary Greene, *Manatee Community College;* Roberta Greene, *Central Piedmont Community College;* Stephen Griffin, *Tarrant County Junior College;* John Gubbay, *Moraine Valley Community College;* Jonathan Gueverra, *Newbury College;* Paula Gulbicki, *Middlesex Community College;* Bill Hafer, *South Suburban College;* James Hagel, *Davenport College;* Jim Hagen, *Cornell University;* Dan Hall, *East Central College;* Daniel Hallock, *St. Edward's University;* Clark Hallpike, *Elgin Community College;* Ron Halsac, *Community College Allegheny North;* Maurice Hamington, *Lane Community College;* E. Hamm, *Tidewater Community College;* Crystal Hance, *Charles County Community College;* Dennis L. Hansen, *Des Moines Area Community College;* Paula W. Hansen, *Des Moines Area Community College;* Jean Harlan, *Glendale College;* Bob Harmel, *Midwestern State University;* Karen Harris, *Montgomery College;* Gene Hastings, *Portland Community College;* Frederic Hawkins, *Westchester Business Institute;* Lewis Jerome Healy, *Chesapeake College;* Joseph Hecht, *Montclair State College;* Douglas Heeter, *Ferris State University;* Linda Hefferin, *Elgin Community College;* Michael Heim, *Lakewood Community College;* Sanford B. Helman, *Middlesex County College;* Tim Helton, *Juliet Junior College;* Edward Henn, *Broward Community College;* Charles P. Hiatt, *Central Florida Community College;* Dave Hickman, *Frederick Community College;* David Hickman, *Frederick Community College;* Leslie Hickman, *Frederick Community College;* George Hicks, *Muskigan Area Technical College;* George M. Hihn, III, *University of Akron;* Nathan Himelstein, *Essex County College;* Kevin Hofert, *Elgin Community College;* Stacey Hofert, *Elgin Community College;* Merrily Hoffman, *San Jacinto College–Central;* William Leigh Holt, *Mercer County Community College;* Cheryl Lynn Holliday, *Calvert County Community College;* Trinh Hong Hoang, *Mt. San Antonio College;* B. Hoover, *Brevard Community College;* Vince Howe, *University of North Carolina–Wilmington;* Joseph Hrebenak, *Community College Allegheny County;* Tom Humphrey, *Palomar College;* Howard Hunnius, *John Tyler Community College;* Curtis W. Hwang, *Mt. San Antonio College;* Robert Ironside, *North Lake College;* Jim Isherwood, *Community College of Rhode Island;* Gary Izumo, *Moorpark College;* Gloria Jackson, *San Antonio College;* Henry Jackson, *Delaware County Community College;* Ralph Jagodka, *Mt. San Antonio College;* Paloma Jalife, *SUNY–Oswego;* Bill Jedlicka, *Harper College;* William Jedlicka, *William Rainey Harper College;* Paul Jenner, *Southwest Missouri State University;* Velma Jesser, *Lane Community College;* Lauren Jeweler, *Frederick Community College;* Constance Johnson, *Tampa College;* Gene Johnson, *Clarke College;* Herbert J. Johnson, *Blinn College;* M. E. "Micki" Johnson, *Nova Southeastern University;* M. Gwen Johnson, *Black Hawk College;* Mike Johnson, *Delaware County Community College;* Michael Johnson, *Delaware County Community College;* Wallace Johnston, *Virginia Commonwealth University;* Valerie Jones, *Kalamazoo Valley Community College;* John Kalaras, *DeVry Institute of Technology;* Alan Kardoff, *Northern Illinois University;* Norman Karl, *Johnson County Community College;* Janice Karlen, *LaGuardia Community College;* Allen Kartchner, *Utah State University;* Bob Kegel, *Cypress College;* Warren

Keller, *Grossmont College;* Roland Kelley, *Tarrant County Junior College–NE Campus;* Jim Kennedy, *Angelina College;* Daniel Kent, *Northern Kentucky University;* Robert Kersten, *St. Louis Community College–Florissant Valley;* Scott Key, *Pensacola Junior College;* Emogene King, *Tyler Junior College;* James H. King, *McLennan Community College;* Jerry Kinskey, *Sinclair Community College;* Betty Ann Kirk, *Tallahassee Community College;* Gregory Kishel, *Fullerton College;* Patricia Kishel, *Cypress College;* Charles C. Kitzmiller, *Indian River Community College;* Karl Kleiner, *Ocean County College;* John A.Knarr, *University of Maryland–European Division;* Anna Kostorizos, *Middlesex Community College;* Pat Laidler, *Massasoit Community College;* Barbara G. Kreichbaum, *Hagerstown Business College;* Patrick C. Kumpf, *University of Cincinnati;* Kenneth Lacho, *University of New Orleans;* Micheale LaFalce, *Tampa College;* Fay Lamphear, *San Antonio College;* Keith Lane, *Fresno City College;* Jennifer Landig, *Saddleback Valley Community College;* Roger Lattanza, *University of New Mexico;* Amy J. Lee, *Parkland College;* Donna Lees, *Butte College;* Jay LeGregs, *Tyler Junior College;* Jim Lentz, *Moraine Valley Community College;* George Leonard, *St. Petersburg Junior College;* Bruce Leppien, *Delta College;* Dawn Lerman, *CUNY–Bernard Baruch College;* Thomas Lerra, *Quinsigamond Community College;* Murray Levy, *Glendale Community College;* Richard Lewis, *Lansing Community College;* Joseph Liebreich, *Reading Area Community College;* Tom Lifvendahl, *Cardinal Stritch College;* Ellen Reynolds Ligons, *Pasadena City College;* Yet Mee Lim, *Alabama State University;* Stephen Lindsey, *Citrus College;* Telissa K. Lindsey, *Peirce College;* Donald Linner, *Essex County College;* Corinne B. Linton, *Valencia Community College;* John Lloyd, *Monroe Community College;* Thomas Lloyd, *Westmoreland County Community College;* Paul Londrigan, *Charles S. Mott Community College;* Hanh Long, *DeAnza College;* Patricia Long, *Tarrant Junior College;* Anthony Lucas, *Allegheny Community College;* Barbara Luck, *Jackson Community College;* Joyce Luckman, *Jackson Community College;* Carmelo Luna, *DeVry–DuPage;* Judith Lyles, *Illinois State University;* Jerry Lunch, *Purdue University;* Richard Lyons, *Indian River Community College;* Rippy Madan, *Frostburg State University;* James W. Marco, *Wake Technical Community College;* Richard Maringer, *University of Akron–Wayne College;* Leon E. Markowicz, *Lebanon Valley College;* Alan Marks, *DeVry Institute of Technology;* Larry Martin, *Community College of Southern Nevada;* Travaul Martin, *East-West University;* Randolph L. Martin, *Germanna Community College;* Thomas Mason, *Brookdale Community College;* Bob Mathews, *Oakton Community College;* Jane Mattes, *Community College of Baltimore College–Dundalk Campus;* Stacy McAfee, *College of Southern Maryland;* Christine McCallum, *University of Akron–Wayne College;* Diana McCann, *Kentucky College of Business;* Mark M. McCarthy, *Davenport College;* Paul McClure, *Mt. San Antonio College;* Tom McFarland, *Mt. San Antonio College;* Jimmy McKenzie, *Tarrant County Junior College;* Noel McKeon, *Florida Community College;* Pat McMahon, *Palm Beach Community College–Glades;* Michael McNutt, *Orlando College South/FL Metropolitan Univ.;* Carl Meskimen, *Sinclair Community College;* Athena Miklos, *The College of Southern Maryland;* Duane Miller, *SUNY–Cobleskill;* Herbert Miller, *Indiana University–Kokomo;* Terrance Mitchell, *South Suburban College;* Kimberly Montney, *Kellogg Community College;* Joyce Mooneyhan, *Pasadena City College;* Willy Morris, *Northwestern Business College;* Richard Morrison, *Northeastern University;* William Morrison, *San Jose State University;* Ed Mosher, *Laramie County Community College;* William Motz, *Lansing Community College;* Carolyn Mueller, *Ball State University;* Micah Mukabi, *Essex County College;* Gary R. Murray, *Rose State College;* Winford C. Naylor, *Santa Barbara City College;* Herschel Nelson, *Polk Community College;* Linda Newell, *Saddleback College;* Joe Newton, *Bakersfield College;* Janet Nichols, *Northeastern University;* Sharon J. Nickels, *St. Petersburg Junior*

College; Carolyn Nickeson, *Del Mar College;* Elaine Novak, *San Jacinto College;* Phil Nufrio, *Essex County College;* Edward O'Brien, *Scotsdale Community College;* Eugene O'Connor, *California Polytechnical University–San Luis Obispo;* Marie D. O'Dell, *Anne Arundel Community College;* Cletus O'Drobinak, *South Suburban College;* Ron O'Neal, *Pierce College;* Susan Ockert, *Charles County Community College;* Susan Oleson, *Central Piedmont Community College;* David Oliver, *Edison Community College;* Katherine Olson, *Northern Virginia Community College;* Kenneth A. Olson, *County College of Morris;* J. Ashton Oravetz, *Tyler Junior College;* George Otto, *Truman College;* Nikki Paahana, *DeVry Institute of Technology;* Robert A. Pacheco, *Massasoit Community College;* Richard Packard, *City College–Richard J. Daley;* Mike Padbury, *Arapahoe Community College;* Teresa Palmer, *Illinois State University;* Dennis Pappas, *Columbus State Community College;* Dennis Pappas, *Columbus Technical Institute;* Knowles Parker, *Wake Technical Community College;* Patricia Parker, *Maryville University;* Jack Partlow, *Northern Virginia Comm. College;* Janis Pasquali, *University of California–Riverside;* Charlotte A. Patterson, *Tampa College;* Don Paxton, *Pasadena City College;* Darlene Raney Perry, *Columbus State;* Stephen Peters, *Walla Walla Community College;* Melinda Philabaum, *Indiana University–Kelley School of Business;* John P. Phillips, *Northern Virginia Community College–Manassas;* Marie Pietak, *Bucks County Community College;* Warren Pitcher, *Des Moines Area Community College;* Alison Adderley-Pittman, *Brevard Community College–Melbourn;* Joseph Platts, *Miami-Dade Community College;* Wayne Podgorski, *University of Memphis;* Raymond Pokhon, *MATC;* Robert Pollero, *Anne Arundel Community College;* Geraldine Powers, *Northern Essex Community College;* Roderick Powers, *Iowa State University;* Fred Pragasam, *University of North Florida;* Renee Prim, *Central Piedmont Community College;* Marva Pryor, *Valencia Community College;* Brokke Quigg, *Pierce College;* Charles C. Quinn, *Austin Community College–Northridge;* Donald Radtke, *Richard J. Daley College;* Anne Ranczuch, *Monroe Community College;* Richard Randall, *Nassau Community College;* Richard J. Randolph, *Johnson County Community College;* Mary E. Ray, *Indiana Business College;* Robert A. Redick, *Lincoln Land Community College;* Scott Reedy, *Brookes College;* Robert O. Reichl, *Morton College;* James Reinemann, *College of Lake County;* Dominic Rella, *Polk Community College;* Carla Rich, *Pensacola Junior College;* John Rich, *Illinois State University;* Doug Richardson, *Eastfield College;* Karen Richardson, *Tarrant County Junior College;* Al Rieger, *Burlington County College;* Kathryn Roberts, *Chipola Junior College;* Pollis Robertson, *Kellogg Community College;* Paul Rompala, *Triton College;* Ali Roodsari, *Baltimore City Community College;* Barbara Rosenthal, *Miami-Dade Community College;* Bob Roswell, *Jackson Community College;* Linda Roy, *Evergreen Valley College;* Jeri Rubin, *University of Alaska;* Bonnie S. Rucks, *DeVry Institute–DuPage;* Jill Russell, *Camden County College;* Karl Rutkowski, *Pierce Jr. College;* Tom Rutkowski, *SUNY–Cobleskill;* Maurice M. Sampson, *Community College of Philadelphia;* Roy Sanchez, *San Jacinto College;* Cathy Sanders, *San Antonio College;* Joseph C. Santora, *Essex County College;* Nicholas Sarantakes, *Austin Community College;* Billie Sargent, *National College;* Quinn Sasaki, *Mt. San Antonio College;* Jim (Wallace) Satchell, *St. Philips College;* Gordon Saul, *National Business College;* Larry Saville, *Des Moines Area Community College;* Robert R. Schaller, *Charles County Community College;* Kurt Schindler, *Wilbur Wright College;* Lance Schmeidler, *Northern Virginia Community College;* Linda Schmitigal, *Lake Superior State University;* Dennis Schmitt, *Emporia State University;* Marilyn Schwartz, *College of Marin;* Jim Seeck, *Harper College;* Daniel C. Segebath, *South Suburban College;* Justin Selden, *The University of Akron;* Patricia A. Serraro, *Clark College;* Greg Service, *Broward Community College–North;* Guy Sessions, *Spokane Falls Community College;* Phyllis T. Shafer, *Brookdale*

Community College; Dennis Shannon, *Belleville Area College;* Richard Shapiro, *Cuyahoga Community College;* Charles Shatzer, *Solano Community College;* Mark Sheehan, *Bunker Hill Community College;* Nora Jo Sherman, *Houston Community College;* Donald Shifter, *Fontbonne College;* Lynette Shishido, *Santa Monica College;* Leon Singleton, *Santa Monica College;* Jerry Sitek, *Southern Illinois University;* Michelle Slagle, *The George Washington University;* James A. Smalley, *DeVry–DuPage;* Noel Smith, *Palm Beach Community College;* Bill Snider, *Cuesta College;* Paul Solomon, *San Jose State University;* Sol A. Solomon, *Community College of Rhode Island;* Carl Sonntag, *Pikes Peak Community College;* Melinda Soto, *Mt. San Antonio Community College;* Russell W. Southall, *Laney College;* Rieann Spence-Gale, *Northern Virginia Community College;* Sandra Spencer, *DeAnza College;* Richard Stanish, *Tulsa Junior College;* Elizabeth Stanley, *Northern Virginia Community College;* Lynda St. Clair, *Bryant College;* Emanual Stein, *Queensborough Community College;* Scott Steinkamp, *Northwestern Business College;* Kenneth Steinkruger, *DeVry Institute of Technology–Chicago;* Carl Stem, *Texas Tech University;* Richard Stewart, *Gulf Coast Community College;* Robert Stivender, *Wake Technical Community College;* David Stringer, *DeAnza College;* Charles I. Stubbart, *Southern Illinois University;* Jacinto Suarez, *Bronx Community College;* Paul Sunko, *Olive Harvey College;* George Sutcliffe, *Central Piedmont Community College;* Lorraine Suzuki, *University of Maryland–Asian Division;* Carl Swartz, *Three Rivers Community College;* William Syvertsen, *Fresno City College;* James Taggart, *University of Akron;* Robert Tansky, *St. Clair County Community College;* Daryl Taylor, *Pasadena City College;* Merle E. Taylor, *Santa Barbara City College;* Verna Teasdale, *Prince George's Community College;* Ray Tewell, *American River College;* Gary W. Thomas, *Anne Arundel Community College;* Bill Thompson, *Foothill Community College;* Darrell Thompson, *Mountain View College;* Linda Thompson, *Massasoit Community College;* Susan Thompson, *Palm Beach Community College;* Tom Thompson, *University of Maryland University College;* Linda Tibbetts, *Sinclair Community College;* Darlene Tickle, *Southern Arkansas University–Magnolia;* Vern Timmer, *SUNY–Alfred;* Patricia Torpey, *National American University;* Amy Toth, *Northampton County Area Community College;* Jane A. Treptow, *Broward Community College;* Bonnie Luck-Yan Tsang, *DeAnza College;* Stephen Tsih, *San Jose City College;* Chuck Tychsen, *Northern Virginia Community College;* J. Robert Ulbrich, *Parkland College;* Pablo Ulloa, *El Paso Community College;* Robert Vandellen, *Baker College–Cadillac;* Richard Van Ness, *Schenectady County Community College;* Sal Veas, *Santa Monica College;* Heidi Vernon-Wortzel, *Northeastern University;* Julie C.Verrati, *Montgomery College;* Janna P. Vice, *Eastern Kentucky University;* Michael Vijuk, *William Rainey Harper College;* Martha Villarreal, *San Joaquin Delta College;* William Vincent, *Santa Barbara City College;* Douglas S. Viska, *William Rainey Harper College;* Cortez Walker, *Baltimore City Community College;* Steve Walker, *Midwestern State University;* Christopher Walsh, *Hagerstown Community College;* W. J. Waters, *Central Piedmont Community College;* Philip Weatherford, *Embry-Riddle Aeronautical University;* Connie Wedemeyer, *McLennan Community College;* Ron Weidenfeller, *Grand Rapids Community College;* Pete Weiksner, *Lehigh County Community College;* Henry Weiman, *Bronx Community College;* Bernard Weinrich, *St. Louis Community College–Forest Park;* Bill Weisgerber, *Saddleback College;* Martin Welc, *Saddleback College;* William A. Weller, *Modesto Junior College;* James H. Wells, *Daytona Beach Community College;* Sally Wells, *Columbia College;* Michael David Wentz, *Hagerstown Community College;* Richard Westfall, *Cabrillo College;* Aimee Wheaton, *Regis University;* Cammie White, *Santa Monica College;* Donald White, *Prince Georges Community College;* Frederick D. White, *Indian River Community College;* John Whitlock, *Community College of Baltimore County–Cantonsville;* Jean Wicks, *Bowie*

State University; Walter Wilfong, *Florida Technical College;* Dick Williams, *Laramie County Community College;* Mary E. Williams, *University of Central Oklahoma;* Paul Williams, *Mott Community College;* Stanley Williams, *Pensacola Christian College;* Gayla Jo Wilson, *Mesa State College;* Wallace Wirth, *South Suburban Community College;* Amy Wojciechowski, *West Shore Community College;* Judy Eng Woo, *Bellevue Community College;* Joyce Wood, *Northern Virginia Community College;* Bennie Woods, *Burlington County College;* Greg Worosz, *Schoolcraft College;* William Wright, *Mt. Hood Community College;* Merv Yeagle, *Hagerstown Junior College;* C. Yin, *DeVry Institute of Technology;* Ned Young, *Sinclair Community College;* Ron Young, *Kalamazoo Valley Community College;* Charles D. Zarubba, *Florida Metropolitan University–Tampa College;* C. Zarycki, *Hillsborough Community College;* John Ziegler, *Hagerstown Community College;* Richard Zollinger, *Central Piedmont College.*

Presenting a Special Visual Tour of

Understanding Business

7th edition

In the ever-changing world of business and business education, the author team of Bill Nickels, Jim McHugh, and Susan McHugh has consistently developed wildly successful new editions of their text. They haven't done it all alone, though. All past revisions of *Understanding Business* have relied on the comments and feedback from instructors and past students.

The seventh edition is no different.

Before your students can begin to understand today's business world, you'll have to provide them the most up-to-date and relevant material. With help from countless reviews and focus groups, *Understanding Business* provides a unified collection of educational tools. This combination of text, CD-ROM, and visual media work together to teach students everything they should know before entering the real world of business.

This special walkthrough section was developed to highlight the new and retained features that have made this text the clear market leader. After reading through this material, if you still have questions, please contact your local McGraw-Hill/Irwin sales representative.

"the most up-to-date and relevant material"

Maintaining Currency

Users and reviewers of *Understanding Business* made one thing clear: "Do not change the organization of the text; it works great for our classes the way it is." Heeding their collective request, this new edition features current examples and coverage of recent events within the text's existing framework. The highly praised structure is intact, but your students will also benefit from coverage of such current items as:

- Homeland security.
- Privacy and security issues with information technology.
- Stock market decline of 2000–2002.
- Corporate scandals and the "good guys."
- Effects of the September 11, 2001, attack and other forms of terrorism.
- The latest changes in the euro.
- The latest population trends.
- And much more!

Video Field Trips

Do you wish that you could assign your students to work on the marketing campaign for the Mini Cooper? Would you like to have Todd McFarlane, creator of the Spawn comic and toy industry, speak with your class about starting up a new business? Now you can. These special videos, developed exclusively for *Understanding Business*, help your students explore the text's chapter topics in an engaging manner.

Each video brings important concepts to life by taking viewers on a "field trip" to companies like Auntie Anne's Pretzels, MiniUSA, The Container Store, McFarlane Toys, Hoffman Bikes, and Motley Fool.

By watching, viewers will explore these companies and hear from the individuals who make these organizations such dynamic examples of modern business.

Integration of Important Concepts throughout the Text

Based on research and the preferences expressed by both users and nonusers of *Understanding Business*, the following key topics are incorporated as themes throughout the text:

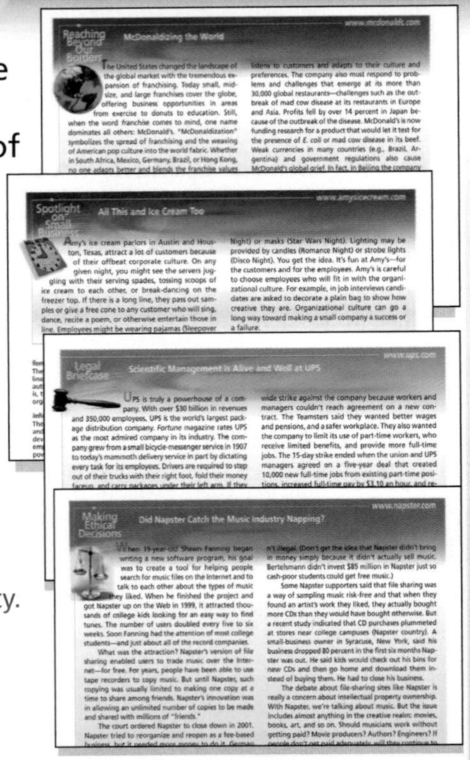
www.mcdonalds.com

Reaching Beyond Our Borders — McDonaldizing the World

The United States changed the landscape of the global market with the tremendous expansion of franchising. Today small, midsize, and large franchises cover the globe, offering business opportunities in areas from exercise to donuts to education. Still, when the word *franchise* comes to mind, one name dominates all others: McDonald's. "McDonaldization" symbolizes the spread of franchising and the weaving of American pop culture into the world fabric. Whether in South Africa, Mexico, Germany, Brazil, or Hong Kong,

listens to customers and adapts to their culture and preferences. The company also must respond to problems and challenges that emerge at its more than 30,000 global restaurants—challenges such as the outbreak of mad cow disease at its restaurants in Europe and Asia. Profits fell by over 14 percent in Japan because of the outbreak of the disease. McDonald's is now funding research for a product that would let it test for the presence of *E. coli* or mad cow disease in its beef. Weak currencies in many countries (e.g., Brazil, Argentina) and government regulations also cause

www.amysicecream.com

Spotlight on Small Business — All This and Ice Cream Too

Amy's ice cream parlors in Austin and Houston, Texas, attract a lot of customers because of their offbeat corporate culture. On any given night, you might see the servers juggling with their serving spades, tossing scoops of ice cream to each other, or break-dancing on the freezer top. If there is a long line, they pass out samples or give a free cone to any customer who will sing, dance, recite a poem, or otherwise entertain those in

Night) or masks (Star Wars Night). Lighting may be provided by candles (Romance Night) or strobe lights (Disco Night). You get the idea. It's fun at Amy's—for the customers and for the employees. Amy's is careful to choose employees who will fit in with the organizational culture. For example, in job interviews candidates are asked to decorate a plain bag to show how creative they are. Organizational culture can go a long way toward making a small company a success or a failure.

www.ups.com

Legal Briefcase — Scientific Management Is Alive and Well at UPS

UPS is truly a powerhouse of a company. With over $30 billion in revenues and 350,000 employees, UPS is the world's largest package distribution company. *Fortune* magazine rates UPS as the most admired company in its industry. The company grew from a small bicycle-messenger service in 1907 to today's mammoth delivery service in part by dictating every task for its employees. Drivers are required to step out of their trucks with their right foot, fold their money

wide strike against the company because workers and managers couldn't reach agreement on a new contract. The Teamsters said they wanted better wages and pensions, and a safer workplace. They also wanted the company to limit its use of part-time workers, who receive limited benefits, and provide more full-time jobs. The 15-day strike ended when the union and UPS managers agreed on a five-year deal that created 10,000 new full-time jobs from existing part-time posi-

www.napster.com

Making Ethical Decisions — Did Napster Catch the Music Industry Napping?

When 19-year-old Shawn Fanning began writing a new software program, his goal was to create a tool for helping people search for music files on the Internet and to talk to each other about the types of music they liked. When he finished the project and got Napster up on the Web in 1999, it attracted thousands of college kids looking for an easy way to find tunes. The number of users doubled every five to six weeks. Soon Fanning had the attention of most college students—and just about all of the record companies.

What was the attraction? Napster's version of file sharing enabled users to trade music over the Internet—for free. For years, people have been able to use tape recorders to copy music. But until Napster, such copying was usually limited to making one copy at a time to share among friends. Napster's innovation was in allowing an unlimited number of copies to be made and shared with millions of "friends."

The court ordered Napster to close down in 2001. Napster tried to reorganize and reopen as a fee-based

n't illegal. (Don't get the idea that Napster didn't bring in money simply because it didn't actually sell music. Bertelsmann didn't invest $85 million in Napster just so cash-poor students could get free music.)

Some Napster supporters said that file sharing was a way of sampling music risk-free and that when they found an artist's work they liked, they actually bought more CDs than they would have bought otherwise. But a recent study indicated that CD purchases plummeted at stores near college campuses (Napster country). A small-business owner in Syracuse, New York, said his business dropped 80 percent in the first six months Napster was out. He said kids would check out his bins for new CDs and then go home and download them instead of buying them. He had to close his business.

The debate about file-sharing sites like Napster is really a concern about intellectual property ownership. With Napster, we're talking about music. But the issue includes almost anything in the creative realm: movies, books, art, and so on. Should musicians work without getting paid? Movie producers? Authors? Engineers? If

- Constant change.
- Small business and entrepreneurship.
- Global business.
- Technology and change.
- Pleasing customers.
- Ethics and social responsibility.
- Teams.
- Quality.
- E-commerce.
- Cultural diversity.

These themes reflect a strong consensus among introduction to business instructors that certain topics deserve and need special emphasis. Among these, they encouraged us to add particular focus in the areas of small business/entrepreneurship, ethics, global business, and e-commerce. In response, this edition includes many small business, global, and Internet examples throughout. And it continues to feature boxes titled "Spotlight on Small Business" (p.260), "Making Ethical Decisions" (p.103), "Legal Briefcase" (p.302), and "Reaching Beyond Our Borders" (p.73) in every chapter. And…

ENTREPRENEURSHIP READINESS QUESTIONNAIRE

The text's emphasis on entrepreneurship is maintained with an Entrepreneurship Readiness Questionnaire and an entire chapter on entrepreneurship and the challenge of starting a business. No other introduction to business text offers as much coverage of small business and entrepreneurship as does *Understanding Business*, and since the great majority of students taking this course currently work or will work in small companies, reviewers agree that this emphasis is well placed. (pp. 203–205)

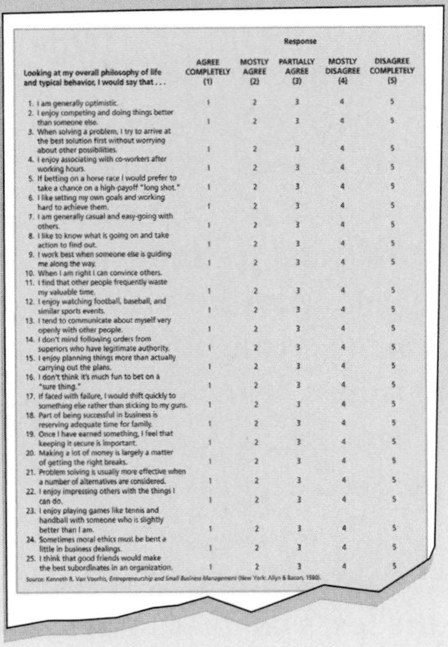

	Response				
Looking at my overall philosophy of life and typical behavior, I would say that . . .	AGREE COMPLETELY (1)	MOSTLY AGREE (2)	PARTIALLY AGREE (3)	MOSTLY DISAGREE (4)	DISAGREE COMPLETELY (5)
1. I am generally optimistic.	1	2	3	4	5
2. I enjoy competing and doing things better than someone else.	1	2	3	4	5
3. When solving a problem, I try to arrive at the best solution first without worrying about other possibilities.	1	2	3	4	5
4. I enjoy associating with co-workers after working hours.	1	2	3	4	5
5. If betting on a horse race I would prefer to take a chance on a high-payoff "long shot."	1	2	3	4	5
6. I like setting my own goals and working hard to achieve them.	1	2	3	4	5
7. I am generally casual and easy-going with others.	1	2	3	4	5
8. I like to know what is going on and take action to find out.	1	2	3	4	5
9. I work best when someone else is guiding me along the way.	1	2	3	4	5
10. When I am right I can convince others.					
11. I find that other people frequently waste my valuable time.	1	2	3	4	5
12. I enjoy watching football, baseball, and similar sports events.	1	2	3	4	5
13. I tend to communicate about myself very openly with other people.	1	2	3	4	5
14. I don't mind following orders from superiors who have legitimate authority.	1	2	3	4	5
15. I enjoy planning things more than actually carrying out the plans.	1	2	3	4	5
16. I don't think it's much fun to bet on a "sure thing."	1	2	3	4	5
17. If faced with failure, I would shift quickly to something else rather than sticking to my guns.	1	2	3	4	5
18. Part of being successful in business is reserving adequate time for family.	1	2	3	4	5
19. Once I have earned something, I feel that keeping it secure is important.	1	2	3	4	5
20. Making a lot of money is largely a matter of getting the right breaks.	1	2	3	4	5
21. Problem solving is usually more effective when a number of alternatives are considered.	1	2	3	4	5
22. I enjoy impressing others with the things I can do.	1	2	3	4	5
23. I enjoy playing games like tennis and handball with someone who is slightly better than I am.	1	2	3	4	5
24. Sometimes moral ethics must be bent a little in business dealings.	1	2	3	4	5
25. I think that good friends would make the best subordinates in an organization.	1	2	3	4	5

Source: Kenneth R. Van Voorhis, *Entrepreneurship and Small Business Management* (New York: Allyn & Bacon, 1980).

…A NEW box has been added called "Dealing with Change." This feature emphasizes the importance of the dynamic nature of business.
(pp. 229, 523)

www.webex.com

Dealing with Change — The Next Best Thing to Being There

In the days following September 11, 2001, countless U.S. businesses grounded many of their employees. Fear of flying as well as the need to cut costs drastically reduced the amount of face time between businesspeople and their out-of-town colleagues and clients—at least in-the-flesh face time, that is. Web conferencing has skyrocketed since 9/11 because the technology allows customers to see each other; talk; share PowerPoint presentations, animation, and video; and record and play back meetings—all from their own desks. In fact, one of the few technology companies to flourish since the dot-com bubble burst is the Web-conferencing services company WebEx. In 2002, WebEx's revenue climbed over 80 percent from a year earlier.

BusinessWeek

Some people might think that Web conferencing is a second choice, that if companies had unlimited time and money, they would choose face-to-face meetings first. Not always. For example, Texas Instruments (TI) found that virtual meetings not only reduce travel costs and save time but are also helpful in generating feedback from international participants. Some foreign participants find it easier to use the online chat feature that allows them to type in English, which they find easier than speaking it.

Even on a local level, many people are finding Web connectivity beneficial. If you've ever crowded around a PC screen with a few other people, you know how difficult it can be to see what is going on. It is much easier if everyone brings his or her own laptop to a meeting, makes a wireless connection, turns on WebEx, and gets a personal view. Not only can everyone see but everyone also shares control of the screen and can enter comments and revisions. When the meeting is over, everyone has the same version of the document and there is no confusion about what decisions were made. It looks like virtual work has finally become a business reality.

Sources: Olga Kharif, "Subrah Iyar and Min Zhu: Meetings on the Web," *Business Week*, October 1, 2002; and Timothy J. Mullaney, "Break Out the Black Ink," *Business Week*, May 13, 2002.

The BusinessWeek Connection

BusinessWeek

It's no secret that reading *BusinessWeek* articles helps students stay current, but the typical subscription rate makes it difficult for students to afford to read the articles regularly. McGraw-Hill/Irwin, in cooperation, with our sister company BusinessWeek, make it possible for students to receive the magazine for 15 weeks at a special price—substantially less than the lowest subscription rate.

Dealing with Change — **Applying the Four Ps** — www.autobytel.com

You can see the four Ps of marketing in action if you closely follow changes that are occurring in the automobile industry. New products are being designed to meet market niches. There are, for example, sports cars designed to compete with the Porsche Boxster and appeal to successful young executives, and sport-utility vehicles (SUVs) for nearly every taste. Pickup trucks have features like four-wheel drive, grocery-bag hooks, and center armrests that double as laptop workstations.

Never before have there been more choices in cars—from small personal cars to large vans to "green" cars that run on a combination of gas and battery power. And in those cars is every conceivable convenience from phones to CD players, cup holders, and global positioning systems. Automobile companies truly seem to be listening to customers and trying to meet their needs. This is the *product* part of the four Ps.

BusinessWeek

When it comes to *pricing,* there is a whole new revolution going on in this industry. On the Web, sites such as Autobytel.com and Autoweb.com provide product and price information and dealer referrals. ... from anywhere in the world via the Internet. The car will be shipped to a nearby port, and all paperwork is handled with ease.

Promotion for new and used cars is also changing. Dealers are trying low-pressure salesmanship because they know that customers are now armed with much more information than in the past. More and more power is being shifted to consumers. They can go on the Internet; learn about various cars and their features, including safety features; pick which features they want; get the best price available; and order the car—all without leaving their homes. In such an atmosphere the marketing task shifts from helping the seller sell to helping the buyer buy. Internet sellers make every effort to help buyers find the car that best meets their needs and minimize the hassle involved in getting that car.

In the future, the real difference among dealers may be in postpurchase (after-sale) service. Those dealers who treat customers best through relationship marketing (discussed later in this chapter) may develop loyalty that can't be matched in any other way. Such rela-

Additionally, throughout the text, special boxes feature *BusinessWeek* articles to help emphasize the importance of reading and staying current. (p. 401)

"students to receive the magazine for 15 weeks at a special price"

Passcode ISBN 0-07-251530-9

Learning Business Skills That Will Last a Lifetime

The Secretary of Labor appointed a commission, the Secretary's Commission on Achieving Necessary Skills (SCANS), to identify the skills people need to succeed in the workplace. SCANS's fundamental purpose is to encourage a high-performance economy characterized by high-skill, high-wage employment. To help your students connect what they learn in class to the world outside, it is important that they understand five workplace competencies:

1. Resource skills.
2. Interpersonal skills.
3. Information ability.
4. Systems understanding.
5. Technology ability.

Throughout the seventh edition of *Understanding Business*, several pedagogical devices are used to help students master these skills.

Learning Goals

Tied directly to the summaries at the end of the chapter and to the test questions, the Learning Goals help students preview what they should know after reading the chapter, and then test that knowledge by answering the questions in the summary. (p. 100)

Developing Workplace Skills

The Developing Workplace Skills section has activities designed to increase student involvement in the learning process. Some of these miniprojects require library or Internet searches, while others can be used as team activities either in or out of the classroom. (p. 325)

Cross-Reference System

This system, unique to this text, refers students back to the primary discussion and examples of key concepts. A specific page reference appears when a key concept occurs in a chapter subsequent to its original discussion, which eliminates the need to continuously revisit and restate key concepts, thus reducing overall text length. (pp. 36, 214)

Getting to Know Business Professionals

Each chapter begins with a profile of a person whose career relates closely to the material covered in the chapter. Not all the personalities are famous since many of them work in small businesses and nonprofit organizations. Getting to know these business professionals provides the perfect transition to the text material. (pp. 141, 211)

Profile

www.auntiannes.com

Getting to Know Anne Beiler of Auntie Anne's Pretzels

Anne Beiler of Auntie Anne's Pretzels twisted a stand at a farmers' market into one of the fastest-growing franchises in the United States. Raised Amish-Mennonite in Pennsylvania, Beiler made her first attempt at entrepreneurship at age 12 when she baked cakes and pies for the family to sell at area farmers' markets.

In 1987, Beiler was working as a manager in a market concession stand in order to earn enough money to support her family and make it possible for her husband, Jonas, to open a free family counseling service in their home. When another booth in the market became available for sale, Beiler and her husband borrowed $6,000 to buy it to start their own business. They wanted to make enough money to keep the free clinic open to the local Amish and Mennonite families in their community.

Anne Beiler had been working for three months to perfect her pretzel recipe when a supplier accidentally delivered the wrong ingredients. The result was a very disappointing pretzel. But Beiler experimented and added a few more ingredients at her husband's suggestion. Her customers were amazed—the new

"better than the best" products and services, their goal was to exceed the expectations of all of their customers. They achieved one of their major goals in 1992 when Jonas Beiler opened the Family Resource and Counseling Center. Six years later, the couple created the Angela Foundation, a nonprofit organization named after their daughter that serves as the giving arm of the company. The franchise system also sponsors Children's Miracle Network.

As their company was growing, the Beilers were tempted to seek additional funding through venture capitalists (you will learn about venture capitalists in Chapter 6) and/or by going public (selling stock in the company, which we will discuss in Chapter 20). "We needed a cash infusion to grow. But I decided it wasn't right," said Anne Beiler. "Had we gone public, the pressure to perform financially would have been greater than our feelings about supporting our employees and franchisees. It was difficult enough to keep the personal touch adding 60 stores a year. Service would have become a problem, the quality would have become a problem, money would have outweighed caring, and that

"Had we gone public [sold stock], the pressure to perform financially would have been greater than our feelings about supporting our employees and franchisees. It was difficult enough to keep the personal touch adding 60 stores a year."

"increase student involvement in the learning process"

Video Cases

Video cases are provided for each chapter—and all of them are new to this edition. They feature companies, processes, practices, and managers that highlight and bring to life the key concepts, and especially the themes, of the seventh edition.
(pp. 31, 326)

Casing the Web

Each chapter concludes by referencing a short case to allow students to practice managerial decision making. They are intentionally brief and meant to be discussion starters rather than comprehensive cases that could require the entire class period. These cases are found on the text website at www.mhhe.com/ub7e.
(p. 326)

Progress Assessments

If students are not understanding and retaining the material, Progress Assessments will stop them and show them that they need to review before proceeding. Progress Assessments are a proven learning tool that helps students comprehend and retain the material. (p. 148)

Photo and Illustration Essays

More and more students have expressed that they are visually oriented learners; therefore, this increased emphasis on the pedagogical value of the illustrations is essential. Each photo and illustration in the text is accompanied by a short essay that highlights the relevance of the visuals to the material in the text.

The Business Cycle

Many people were caught off guard by the rapid decline of the stock market in 2001–2003. Investors lost $7.7 trillion in value between March 2000 and July 2002, at which point the market fell another 400 points in one day![26] The people most taken by surprise believed that the stock market would continue the rapid rise that occurred during the 1990s. Those people must not have been familiar with the concept of business cycles. **Business cycles** are the periodic rises and falls that occur in economies over time. Economists look at a number of types of cycles, from seasonal cycles that occur within a year to cycles that occur every 48–60 years.

Business cycles demonstrate that over time the stock market is likely to rise *or* fall by significant amounts. Such cycles have shown to be rather consistent; that is, long periods of growth are typically followed by periods of decline. Investing, therefore, always involves a certain degree of risk, but usually the greater the risk the higher the payoff. Can you see why investors may be wise to study past trends before putting their

Economist Joseph Schumpeter identified the four phases of long-term business cycles as boom–recession–depression–recovery:

1. An economic boom is just what it sounds like—business is booming.
2. **Recession** is two or more consecutive quarters of decline in the GDP. In a recession prices fall, people purchase fewer products, and businesses fail. A recession has many negative consequences for an economy: high unemployment, increased business failures, and an overall drop in living standards.
3. A **depression** is a severe recession usually accompanied by deflation. Business cycles rarely go through a depression phase. In fact, while there were many business cycles during the 20th century, there was only one severe depression (1929–1933).
4. A recovery occurs when the economy stabilizes and starts to grow. This eventually leads to an economic boom, starting the cycle all over again

Critical Thinking Questions

Found in each chapter, Critical Thinking Questions ask students to pause and think about how the material they are reading applies to their own lives.
(p. 286)

Interactive Summaries

The end-of-chapter summaries are directly tied with the learning goals and are written in a unique question-and-answer format. (p. 234)

Getting Ready for Prime Time

The Getting Ready for Prime Time minibooklet, found at the front of the text, introduces students to the skills needed to succeed in college and beyond. Material covered includes a unique and popular business etiquette discussion, study skills and time management guidance, a primer to surfing the Internet, and advice about how to get a rewarding job that will lead to a successful career.

The Latest in Technology

Perhaps the fastest-changing and most dynamic element of business today is the use of the Internet. Many new e-businesses have already come and gone, but even in failure they have left in their wake a new way of doing business. Although the business-to-business market is in a state of flux, use of the Internet as a dynamic business tool has resulted in the rethinking and restructuring of traditional business relationships, redesign of supply chains, and many other new ways of conducting and facilitating customer interaction.

The seventh edition of *Understanding Business* integrates Web material throughout the text along with useful components that work flawlessly with the text.

Taking It to the Net Exercises

Each chapter contains optional Taking It to the Net exercises that allow students to research topics and issues on the Web and make decisions based on their research. (pp. 169, 456)

Lecture Links

New!

Lecture Links, which are identified in the margin of the Annotated Instructor's Edition, provide detailed concept coverage from Internet articles as well as interesting discussions that instructors can use to embellish their lectures.

UB7E Online Learning Center

www.mhhe.com/ub7e

The McGraw-Hill Online Learning Center is an interactive site that includes such features as links to professional resources and other exciting instructor support tools as well as Web-based projects. Some features include website addresses for all companies referenced in the text; URLs for all Taking It to the Net exercises; crossword puzzles that help review key terms; additional chapter quizzes; threaded discussion questions for instructors; and conceptual assessment questions.

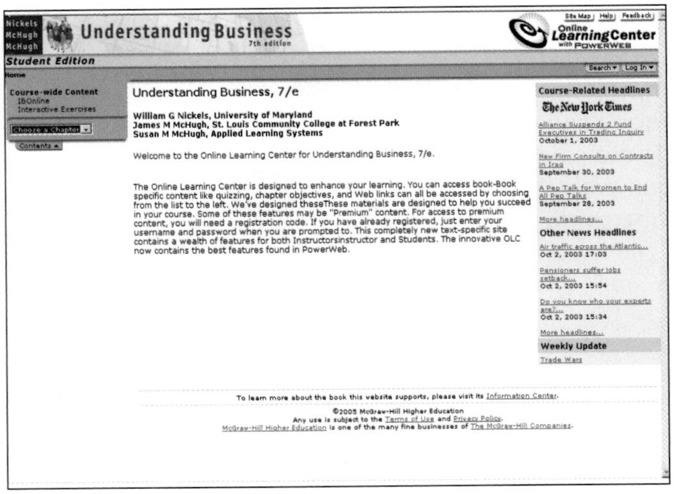

KEEPING IN TOUCH VIA THE WEB

Bill Nickels, Jim McHugh, and Susan McHugh read the latest business journals and keep up to date with the latest developments to use in their classes, and through their attention to detail, they have come to understand the value of the Internet for sharing information. For that reason, the Internet is an important educational component for ***Understanding Business*** students to gather and use information.

Business Plan Software and Manual

New!

ISBN: 0072953225

For those who include business planning as part of their course, this business planning CD is available with the text along with a user manual. This new manual includes exercises based on the modules in the software, as well as a semester-long project. The new Business Mentor leads students through the sections of the feasibility and business plans.

PowerWeb Helps Keep Your Course Up to Date

Enhanced!

PowerWeb provides the easiest way to integrate current real-world content with this latest edition of *Understanding Business*. Experienced instructors have culled articles and essays from a wide range of periodicals including *The Wall Street Journal*, *USA Today*, the *New York Times*, *Business Week*, *Forbes*, and many others.

Now you can access PowerWeb articles and updates specifically created to accompany *Understanding Business* through the text's Online Learning Center (www.mhhe.com/ub7e) and see firsthand what PowerWeb can mean to your course.

PowerWeb to Go is new and allows you to download PowerWeb content to your PDA for a minimal price.

Create an Online Course Today!

Blackboard www.blackboard.com WebCT

If you are interested in educating students online, McGraw-Hill/Irwin offers *Understanding Business* content for complete online courses. We have joined forces with the most popular delivery platforms available, such as WebCT and Blackboard. These platforms have been designed for instructors who want complete control over course content and how it is presented to their students. You can customize the Understanding Business Online Learning Center content or author your own course materials—it's entirely up to you. Remember, the content of *Understanding Business* is flexible enough to use with any platform currently available (and it's free). If your department or school is already using a platform, we can certainly help.

PageOut is the easiest way to create a website for your introductory business course. There's no need for HTML coding, graphic design, or a thick how-to book. Just fill in a series of boxes and click on one of our professional designs. In no time at all, your course is online.

If you need assistance in preparing your course website, our team of product specialists is ready to help you take your course materials and build

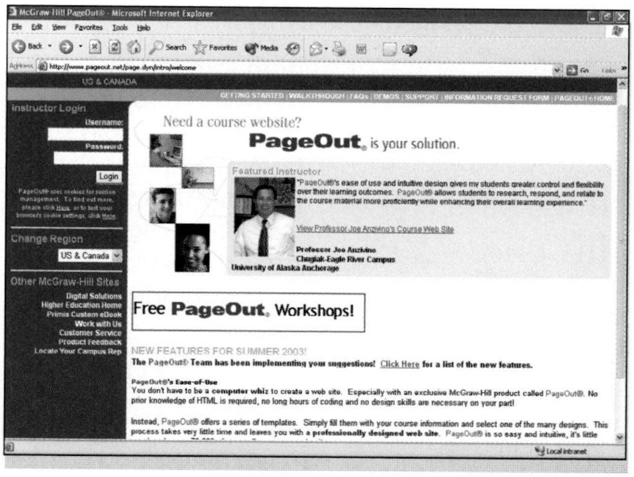

a custom website. Simply contact a McGraw-Hill/Irwin PageOut specialist to start the process. Best of all, PageOut is free when you adopt *Understanding Business*! To learn more, please visit www.pageout.net.

The Best Instructional Materials

All the supplements that are available with the seventh edition of *Understanding Business* were originally developed by the authors to help instructors use their class time more effectively and make this course more practical and interesting for students. Users say that no introductory business text package is as market responsive, easy to use, and fully integrated as this one.

Preparation

Instructor's Manual

Vol. 1 ISBN 0072884428
Vol. 2 ISBN 0072884436

All material in the Instructor's Manual (IM) is easy to use and has been widely praised by new instructors, adjunct instructors, and experienced educators alike. Many instructors tell us that the IM is a valuable time-saver. The IM is unique in its thorough integration with both the text and package. Detailed lecture outlines contain marginal notes recommending where to use PowerPoint slides, acetates, supplementary cases, Lecture Links, and Critical Thinking exercises. The IM also features Lecture Link content (see page xxxvi), supplementary cases, Critical Thinking exercises, and much more.

Annotated Instructor's Edition

ISBN: 0072922982

The AIE is a reproduction of the student edition of the text with the addition of marginal notes that suggest where to use various instructional tools such as the overhead transparencies, PowerPoint presentation slides, supplementary cases, and Lecture Links. It also identifies the activities that facilitate the SCANS competencies.

Instructor's Presentation CD-ROM

ISBN: 0072921145

The Instructor's Manual, the PowerPoint slides, video clips, Test Bank, and more are compiled in electronic format on a CD for your convenience in customizing multimedia lectures.

Testing

Test Bank

Vol. 1 ISBN 0072884339
Vol. 2 ISBN 0072884398

The Nickels/McHugh/McHugh Test Bank is like no other on the market. It is designed to test three levels of learning:

1. Knowledge of key terms.
2. Understanding of concepts and principles.
3. Application of principles.

A rationale for the correct answer and the corresponding text page add to the uniqueness of the 4,500+ question Test Bank, as does the fact that the Test Bank asks questions about the boxed material in the text. Each chapter also includes a Test Table organizing the questions by learning objective and level of learning. A quick quiz is also provided in each chapter as an easy handout.

Diploma (Windows/Mac)

ISBN: 0072538805

The Test Bank also comes in a computerized version that allows users to add and edit questions; save and reload multiple test versions; select questions based on type, difficulty, or key word; and utilize password protection.

Teletest

For those who prefer not to use the computerized test-generator, McGraw-Hill/Irwin provides a Teletest Service. A master copy of the exam, with answer key, is sent first-class mail the same day it is requested. Fax is also available within 30 minutes of the request. Please call 1-800-338-3987 (prompt #3).

Presentation Tools

Videos

New!

VHS ISBN 0072538791
DVD ISBN 007292117X

Companies and individuals profiled in our new Video Field Trips include Auntie Anne's Pretzels, HotJobs.com, SAS, Southwest Airlines, MiniUSA, Hoffman Bikes, Motley Fool, Delta Force, Digital Domain, The Container Store, and more.

Most segments are 8 to 15 minutes in length and are suitable for classroom, home, or lab viewing.

New!

The video package is also available in DVD format for those professors who have access to a DVD player in their classroom. This allows for easy selection of the video you'd like to watch through a simple menu. The DVD videos are also closed captioned.

Media Resource Guide

ISBN: 0072884347

Puzzled about incorporating media in the classroom? This guide provides helpful instruction on how to use all media components along with a manual that contains teaching notes and discussion questions for each of the videos.

Telecourse Guide

ISBN: 007288438X

The Telecourse Instructor's Manual to accompany the "It's Strictly Business" telecourse makes your job easier by presenting lesson overviews and questions from the Test Bank organized by the Telecourse videos.

"easy to use, and fully integrated"

PowerPoint CD-ROM

ISBN: 0072538783

Over 600 "slides" keyed to the text are available and include the transparency acetate images as well as many additional slides that support and expand the text discussion. These slides can be modified with PowerPoint and are also available on the Instructor's CD and the Online Learning Center.

Acetates with Lecture Notes

ISBN: 0072884363

Over 275 acetates augment the concepts and examples presented in the text while also enabling you to illustrate your lectures with colorful visual aids. Detailed lecture notes accompany each of the acetates.

Instructor's Orientation Video on CD

This simple instruction video walks you through each supplement—a perfect tool for part-time faculty or as an orientation to effective use of classroom supplements for anyone. This CD is included with each copy of the Annotated Instructor's Edition.

Key Supplements for Today's Students

Concept Mastery Toolkit CD-ROM

ISBN: 0072884371

Free with each new copy of the text, this new software by Interactive Learning LLC adds another dimension to the text's lessons for your students. Approximately 25 practice exam questions for every chapter, modeled on but not taken from the Test Bank, are included. The presented assessment questions test your students' ability to apply the

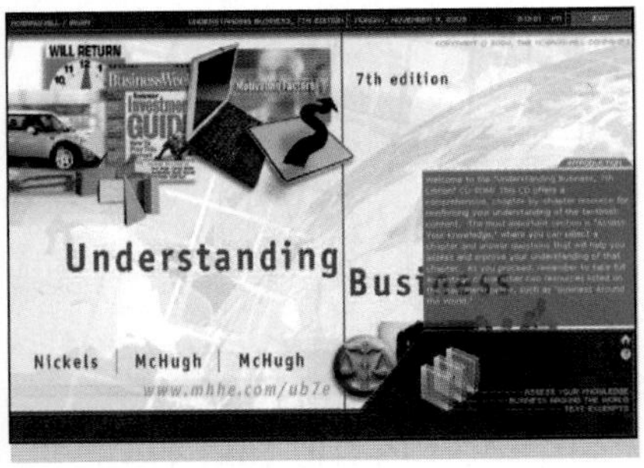

concepts they've learned in the chapter to different situations. They receive detailed feedback for each answer whether they answer correctly or not, and they can click each answer and go directly to screen shots of the actual page in the text, where the relevant passage is highlighted.

To help many of our ESL students understand the key term definitions, the CD now contains glossary translations not only in Spanish, but in Russian and in both Traditional and Simplified Mandarin Chinese.

Student Assessment and Learning Guide

ISBN: 0072884355

The Student Assessment and Learning Guide contains various forms of open-ended questions, key term review, practice test and answers, and Internet excercises to help them be successful in the introduction to business course.

McGraw-Hill Investments Trader

New to this edition, students now are able to access the McGraw-Hill Investments Trader. Students will have access to a hypothetical $100,000 account to buy and sell stocks and mutual funds. They will be using real company data in conjunction with the text content on investments to compete with students around the world. An accompanying manual is available on the Student CD. For more information and access, visit the Online Learning Center at www.mhhe.com/ub7e.

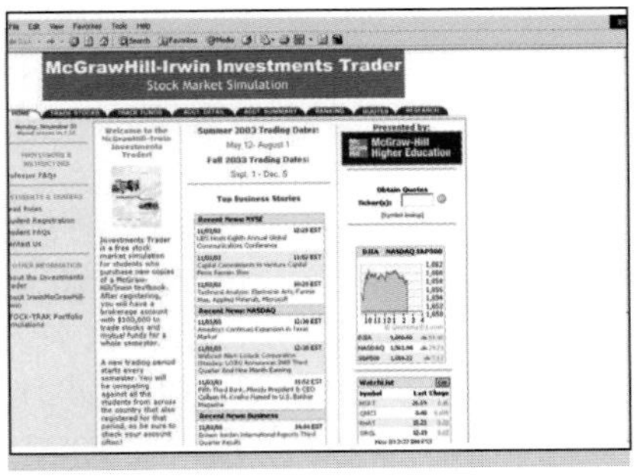

Audio Text on CD

ISBN: 0072921161

The text is now available in an audio format to allow your students to brush up on business concepts while commuting in their cars, jogging, or wherever and whenever they like! Sight-impaired students and non-native English speakers will also find these CDs extremely useful in exploring the contents of *Understanding Business*.

Study to Go

Study to Go is a fun new PDA feature. Students can download (for free) digital content from the Understanding Business website onto their Pocket PC or PDA. There they'll have mobile access to flashcards, quizzes, and key terms from the book. With Study to Go you can study anytime, anywhere.

To Our Fellow Introduction to Business Instructors,

We firmly believe that no course in college is more important than the introduction to business course. That's why we enjoy teaching it so much and why we are willing to spend so much time helping others make this the best course on campus.

We are proud of the seventh edition of *Understanding Business* and its integrated teaching and testing system. We are also proud of the fact that we have built such a relationship with our users that they aren't afraid to come to us with their thoughts and feedback on previous editions. Every comment is taken into consideration.

We thank the many text and supplements users who have worked with us through the years and welcome new instructors to the team. We look forward to a continuing relationship with all of you and to sharing what we consider the most exciting classroom experience possible: teaching Introduction to Business.

Bill Nickels
Jim McHugh
Susan McHugh

"We firmly believe that no course in college is more important than the introduction to business course."

Prologue

Getting Ready for Prime Time

Top 10 Reasons to Read This Introduction

(Even if it isn't assigned)

10 You don't want the only time you get a raise to be when the government increases the minimum wage.

9 What the heck—you already bought the book, you might as well get your money's worth.

8 You can learn what professional behavior is all about so you don't suddenly find yourself in a section of the classroom all alone.

7 You need to know that "Point and Click" is not a new music group.

6 You need to know that a time management course is not a class on clock repair.

5 Not many job-producing résumés and interviews start with "Like, you know, this is, like, what I want to, like, do you know."

4 Getting off to a good start in the course can improve your chances of getting a higher grade, and your Uncle Ernie will send you a quarter for every A you get.

3 It must be important because the authors spent so much time writing it.

2 You want to run with the big dogs someday.

And the number one reason for reading this introductory section is . . .

1 It could be on a test.

Learning the Skills Needed to Succeed Today and Tomorrow

Your life is full. You're starting a new semester, probably even beginning your college career, and you're feeling pulled in many directions. Why take time to read this introductory section? We lightheartedly offer our top 10 reasons to read it on page P-1, but the real importance of this section to your success is no joking matter. The purpose of this introduction and of the entire text is to help you learn principles, strategies, and skills for success that will help you not only in this course but also in your career and entire life. Whether or not you learn these skills is up to you. Learning them won't guarantee success, but not learning them—well, you get the picture.

We hope you invest the time to read the entire Getting Ready for Prime Time section. However, we realize that some parts of the material may be more relevant to your individual needs at a particular time than others. To help you focus on the most important information for your needs, we've divided the material into three major categories:

1. **Succeeding in This Course.** An overview of the skills you'll need to succeed in this course and throughout college as well as the skills needed to succeed in your career after you earn your diploma. READ THIS SECTION BEFORE YOUR FIRST CLASS and make a great first impression!
2. **Surfing the Internet.** A quick and easy overview of how to surf the Internet. This section is designed for newbies (new users), so if you are an experienced surfer you may just want to skim the titles in this section to see if there is anything you would like to know more about. However if you are new to the Internet, this is an excellent place to start.
3. **Getting the Job You Want.** Guidelines to finding and getting the job you want with an emphasis on job search, résumé writing, and interviewing skills.

This is an exciting and challenging time. Never before have there been more opportunities to become successful. And never before have there been more challenges. Success in any venture comes from understanding basic principles and having the skills to apply those principles effectively. What you learn now could help you be a success—for the rest of your life.

Begin applying these skills now to gain an edge on the competition. Good luck. We wish you the best.

Bill Nickels **Jim McHugh** **Susan McHugh**

SUCCEEDING IN THIS COURSE

Since you've signed up for this course, we're guessing you already know the value of a college education. But just to give you some numerical backup, you should know that the gap between the earnings of high school graduates and college graduates, which is growing every year, now ranges from 60 to 70 percent. According to the U.S. Census Bureau, the holders of bachelor's degrees will make an average of $40,478 per year as opposed to just $22,895 for high school graduates.[1] That's a whopping additional $17,583 a year. Thus, what you invest in a college education is likely to pay you back many times. See Figure P.1 to get an idea of how much salary difference a college degree makes by the end of a 30-year career. That doesn't mean there aren't good careers available to non–college graduates. It just means that those with an education are more likely to have higher earnings over their lifetime.

The value of a college education is more than just a larger paycheck. Other benefits include increasing your ability to think critically and communicate your ideas to others, improving your ability to use technology, and preparing yourself to live in a diverse world.[2] Knowing you've met your goals and earned a college degree also gives you the self-confidence to continue to strive to meet your future goals.

Experts say it is likely that today's college graduates will hold seven or eight different jobs (often in several different careers) in their lifetime. There are many returning students in college today who are changing their careers and their plans for life. In fact, 41 percent of the people enrolled in college today are 25 or older. More than 1.6 million students are over 40.[3] Talk to them and learn from their successes and mistakes. You too may want to change careers someday. Often that is the path to long-term happiness and success. That means you will have to be flexible and adjust your strengths and talents to new opportunities. Many of the best jobs of the future don't even exist today. Learning has become a lifelong job. You will have to constantly update your skills if you want to achieve and remain competitive.

If you're typical of many college students, you may not have any idea what career you'd like to pursue. That isn't necessarily a big disadvantage in today's fast-changing job market. There are no perfect or certain ways to prepare for the most interesting and challenging jobs of tomorrow. Rather, you should continue your college education, develop strong computer skills, improve your verbal and written communication skills, and remain flexible while you explore the job market.

FIGURE P.1

SALARY COMPARISON OF HIGH SCHOOL VERSUS COLLEGE GRADUATES

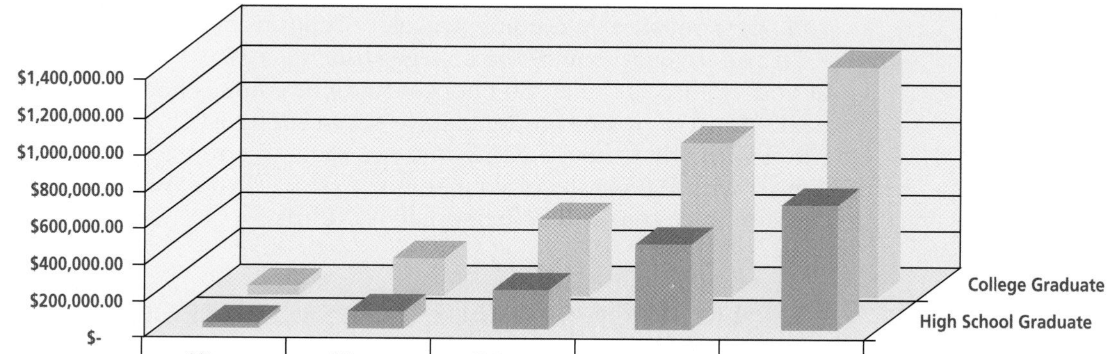

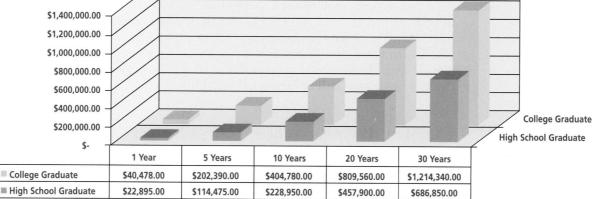

	1 Year	5 Years	10 Years	20 Years	30 Years
College Graduate	$40,478.00	$202,390.00	$404,780.00	$809,560.00	$1,214,340.00
High School Graduate	$22,895.00	$114,475.00	$228,950.00	$457,900.00	$686,850.00

Graduation from college brings smiles all around and for a good reason; today's businesses seek knowledgeable workers to fill jobs in a changing workplace. For students willing to assume the challenge, the rewards are worth the effort. College graduates earn 60 percent to 70 percent more than high school graduates. What additional benefits do you see from earning a college degree?

USING THIS COURSE TO PREPARE FOR YOUR CAREER

One of the objectives of this class is to help you choose an area in which you might enjoy working and in which you might succeed. This book and this course together may be one of your most important learning experiences ever. They're meant to help you understand business so that you can use business principles throughout your life. You'll learn about production, marketing, finance, accounting, management, economics, and more. At the end of the course, you should have a much better idea about what careers would be best for you and what careers you would not enjoy.

But you don't have to be in business to use business principles. You can use marketing principles to get a job and to sell your ideas to others. You can use your knowledge of investments to make money in the stock market. Similarly, you'll be able to use management skills and general business knowledge wherever you go and in whatever career you pursue—including government agencies, charities, and social causes.

ASSESSING YOUR SKILLS AND PERSONALITY

The earlier you can do a personal assessment of your interests, skills, and values, the better it will be for you in finding some career direction. In recognition of this need, many colleges offer self-assessment programs. Hundreds of schools use a software exercise called the System for Interactive Guidance and Information (SIGI). A different version, called DISCOVER, is used at hundreds of other schools. Both SIGI and DISCOVER feature self-assessment exercises, create personalized lists of occupations based on your interests and skills, and provide information about different careers and the preparation each requires. Visit your college's placement center, career lab, or library and learn what programs are available for you.

It would be helpful to use one or more self-assessment programs early in this course so you can determine, while you're learning about the different business fields, which ones most closely fit your interests and skills. Self-assessment will help you determine the kind of work environment you'd prefer (e.g., technical, social service, or business); what values you seek to fulfill in a career (e.g., security, variety, or independence); what abilities you have (e.g., creative/artistic, numerical, or sales); and what important job characteristics you stress most (e.g., income, travel, or amount of job pressure).

Even if you're one of the college students over 30 years old, an assessment of your skills will help you choose the right courses and career path to follow next. Many returning students have taken such tests because they are not satisfied with what they're doing and are seeking a more rewarding occupation. Armed with the results of your self-assessment, you are more likely to make a career choice that will be personally fulfilling.

LEARNING PROFESSIONAL BUSINESS STRATEGIES

Business professionals have learned the importance of networking and of keeping files on subjects that are important to them. These are two secrets to success that students should begin practicing now: retention of knowledge and keeping contacts. One thing that links students in all colleges is the need to retain what they learn. You need a strategy to help you meet this need. It's also extremely important to keep the names of contact people at various organizations. In addition, you may want to keep facts and figures of all kinds about the economy and business-related subjects. These are all reasons why you should develop resource files.

An effective way to become an expert on almost any business subject is to set up your own information system. Eventually you may want to store data on computer disks for retrieval on your personal computer and to access professional databases as businesspeople do. Meanwhile, it's effective to establish a comprehensive filing system on paper.

If you start now, you'll soon have at your fingertips information that will prove invaluable for use in term papers and throughout your career. Few college students do this filing; those who don't lose much of the information they read in college or thereafter. Developing this habit is one of the most effective ways of educating yourself and having the information available when you need it. The only space you'll need to start is a 12-inch-square corner of your room to hold a portable file box. The box should hold hanging folders in which you can place a number of tabbed file folders. To start filling these files, you might put your course notes in them with the names of your professors and the books you used. You may need this information later for employment references. Also, be sure to keep all the notes you make when talking with people about careers, including salary information, courses needed, and contacts.

Each time you read a story about a firm that interests you, either cut it out of the publication or photocopy it and then place it in an appropriate file. You might begin with files labeled Careers, Small Business, Economics, Management, and Resource People. You might summarize the article on a Post-it note and stick this summary on the front for later reference. Today, it is possible to find the latest data on almost any subject on the Internet. Good students know, or quickly learn, how to find such information efficiently. The best students know the importance of keeping such information in files so that it is readily accessible. Those files may be in their computers or on their desktops, ready for easy access.

You definitely want to have a personal data file titled Credentials for My Résumé or something similar. In that file, you'll place all reference letters and other information about jobs you may have held. Soon you'll have a tremendous amount of information available to you. You can add to these initial files until you have your own comprehensive information system.

Businesspeople are constantly seeking ways to increase their knowledge of the business world and to increase their investment returns. One way they do so is by watching television shows such as *Wall $treet Week* and *Nightly Business Report*. Watching such programs is like getting a free graduate education in business. Try viewing some of these shows or listening to similar shows on the radio, and see which ones you like best. Take notes and put them in your files. Another way, one of the best, to increase your business knowledge is to read your local newspaper. Keep up with the business news in your local area so you know what jobs are available and where. You may also want to join local business groups to begin networking with

Ever looked for something you know you read, but cannot find it when you need it? A simple file system can ensure that articles, class assignments, important contacts, and so on are at your fingertips. Technology today simplifies the process even further by making such information instantly accessible. What other information would you keep in your file system?

people and learning the secrets of the local business scene. Many business groups and professional societies accept student members.

Learning to Behave Like a Professional

Good manners are back, and for a good reason. As the world becomes increasingly competitive, the gold goes to the individuals and the teams that have an extra bit of polish. The person who makes a good impression will be the one who gets the job, wins the promotion, or clinches the deal. Manners and professionalism must become second nature to anyone who wants to achieve and maintain a competitive edge.[4]

Often, students focus on becoming experts in their particular field and neglect other concerns, including proper attire and etiquette. Their résumés look great, and they may get through the interview process, but then they get in the workplace and may not succeed. Their behavior, including their verbal behavior, is so unacceptable that they are rejected by their peers.[5]

The lesson is this: You can have good credentials, but a good presentation is everything. You can't neglect etiquette, or somewhere in your career you will be at a competitive disadvantage because of your inability to use good manners or to maintain your composure in tense situations. You must constantly practice the basics until they become second nature to you. Such basics include saying "Please" and "Thank you" when you ask for something. They also include opening doors for others, standing when an older person enters the room, and using a polite tone of voice. You may want to take a class in etiquette to learn the proper way to eat in a nice restaurant and handle the various utensils, the proper way to act at a formal party, and so on. Of course, it is critical that you are honest, reliable, dependable, and ethical at all times.

You can probably think of sports stars who have earned a bad reputation by not acting professionally (e.g., spitting, swearing, and criticizing teammates in front of others). People in professional sports are fined if they are late to meetings or refuse to follow the rules established by the team and coach. Business professionals also must follow set rules. Many of these rules are not formally written anywhere, but every successful businessperson learns them through experience.

Good grooming in business does not always mean wearing a suit. Growing numbers of businesses have adopted business casual as the proper attire. The key to remember is casual does not mean sloppy. It's also important to recognize how your appearance impacts both you and the company. What do you think proper business casual means?

You can begin the habits now while you are in college so that you will have the skills needed for success when you start your career.[6] Those habits include the following:

1. **Making a good first impression.** An old saying goes, "You never get a second chance to make a good first impression." You have just a few seconds to make an impression. Therefore, how you dress and look is important.[7] Take a clue as to what is appropriate at any specific company by studying the people there who are most successful. What do they wear? How do they act?
2. **Focusing on good grooming.** Be aware of your appearance and its impact on those around you. Consistency is essential—you can't project a good image by dressing up a few times a week and then showing up looking like you're getting ready to mow a lawn. Wear appropriate, clean clothing and acces-

sories. For example, revealing shirts, nose rings, and such may not be appropriate in a work setting. It is not appropriate for men to wear hats inside buildings. It is also not appropriate, usually, to wear wrinkled clothing or to have shirttails hanging out of your pants. Many businesses are adopting "business casual" policies, but others still require traditional attire, so it may be helpful to ask what the organization's policies are and choose your wardrobe accordingly.

What is business casual to some may not be acceptable to others, but there are a few guidelines most organizations accept.[8] First, casual doesn't mean sloppy or shabby. For women, business casual attire includes simple skirts and slacks (no jeans), cotton shirts, sweaters (not too tight), blazers, low-heeled shoes or boots (always with socks or stockings). For men, acceptable business casual attire includes khaki trousers, sport shirts with collars, sweaters or sport jackets, casual loafers or lace-up shoes (no athletic shoes).[9]

3. **Being on time.** When you don't come to class or to work on time, you're sending a message to your teacher or boss. You're saying, "My time is more important than your time. I have more important things to do than be here." In addition to the lack of respect tardiness shows to your teacher or boss, it rudely disrupts the work of your colleagues. Promptness may not be a priority in some circles, but in the workplace promptness is essential. But being punctual doesn't always mean just being on time. You have to pay attention to the corporate culture. Sometimes you have to come earlier than others and leave later to get that promotion you desire. To develop good work habits and get good grades, it is important to get to class on time and not leave early.
4. **Practicing considerate behavior.** Considerate behavior includes listening when others are talking—for example, not reading the newspaper or eating in class. Don't interrupt others when they are speaking. Wait for your turn to present your views in classroom or workplace discussions. Of course, eliminate all words of profanity from your vocabulary. Use appropriate body language by sitting up attentively and not slouching. Sitting up has the added bonus of helping you stay awake! Professors and managers get a favorable impression from those who look and act alert. That may help your grades in school and your advancement at work.
5. **Practicing good "netiquette."** Computer technology, particularly e-mail, can be a great productivity tool. The basic courtesy rules of face-to-face communication also apply to e-mail exchanges. As in writing a letter, you should introduce yourself at the beginning of your first e-mail message. Next, you should let your recipients know how you got their names and e-mail addresses. Then you can proceed with your clear but succinct message, and finally close the e-mail with a signature. Do not send an attachment (files of text or graphics attached to an e-mail message) with your e-mail unless your correspondent has indicated that he or she will accept it. Ask first! You can find much more information about proper Internet etiquette (netiquette) on the Internet. For example, Onlinenetiquette.com offers netiquette advice.
6. **Practicing good cell phone manners.** Cellular phones are a vital part of today's world, but it is important to be polite when using the phone. Turn off the phone when you are in class or a business meeting unless you are expecting a critical call. Your Introduction to Business class is not the place to be arranging a date for tonight. If you are expecting a critical call, turn off the audible phone ring and use the vibrating ring if your phone has that feature. If you do have to have your

cellular phone turned on, sit by the aisle and near the door to leave if the phone rings. Leave the room before answering the call. Apologize to the professor after class and explain the nature of the emergency. Most professors will be sympathetic when you explain why you left the room abruptly.

7. **Being prepared.** A businessperson would never show up for a meeting without reading the materials assigned for that meeting and being prepared to discuss the topics of the day. To become a professional, you must practice acting like a professional. For students, that means reading assigned materials before class, asking questions and responding to questions in class, and discussing the material with fellow students.

From the minute you enter your first job interview until the day you retire, people will notice whether you follow the proper business etiquette. Just as traffic laws enable people to drive more safely, business etiquette allows people to conduct business with the appropriate amount of dignity. How you talk, how you eat, and how you dress all create an impression on others. We encourage you to add a course or seminar on etiquette to your college curriculum. Many businesses today require their employees to complete such a course.[10] Taking the initiative to do so on your own will help sharpen your competitive edge.

Business etiquette may encompass different rules in different countries. It is important, therefore, to learn the proper business etiquette for each country you visit. Areas that require proper etiquette include greeting people (shaking hands is not always appropriate); eating (Europeans, for example, often hold their knives and forks the whole time they are eating); giving gifts; presenting and receiving business cards; and conducting business in general. Honesty, high ethical standards, and good character (e.g., reliability and trustworthiness) are important ingredients to success in any country. Having a reputation for integrity will enable you to be proud of who you are and will contribute a great deal to your business success. Unethical behavior can ruin your reputation, so think carefully before you act. When in doubt, don't! Ethics is so important to success that we include ethics discussions throughout the text.

It is crucial that people learn business etiquette appropriate for the countries in which they do business. Behavior taken for granted in the United States can be insulting in other cultures. Here an American businesswoman greets a Chinese counterpart. What are some of the cultural differences that might affect her business behavior in China?

DOING YOUR BEST IN SCHOOL

The skills you need to succeed in college are the same skills you need to succeed in life after college. Career, family, and hobbies all involve the same organizational and time management skills. Applying these skills during your college years will ensure that you will have the life skills you need for a successful career. We will try to help you hone your skills by offering hints for improving your study habits, taking tests, and managing your time.

Study Hints

Studying is your business now. When you fill out a form you write "Student" in the occupation box, right? So until you get out of school and into a full-time job, studying is your business. Like any good businessperson, you aim for success. Let us suggest some strategies for success:

1. **Go to class.** It is often tempting to cut a class on a nice day or when there are other things to do. But nothing is more important to doing well in school than going to class every time. If possible, sit in the front near the instructor. This will help you focus more on what is being said and less on distractions in the room.
2. **Listen well.** It's not enough to show up for class if you use the time for a siesta. Make eye contact with the instructor. In your mind, form a picture of what is discussed. Try to include past experiences in your picture. This ties new knowledge to what you already know.
3. **Take careful notes.** Make two columns in your notebook and use one side to write down the important concepts and the other side to write examples or more detailed explanations. Use abbreviations and symbols whenever possible. Use wide spacing to make the notes easier to read. Rewrite the notes after class because hastily written notes are often difficult to decipher much later. Rereading and rewriting notes also helps store the information in your long-term memory. You learn the concepts in the course the same way you learn the words to your favorite song: through repetition and review.

Effective listening and note taking is critical to success in college. Some students prefer to enter class notes directly into their computers ,especially since many laptop computers are so light and manageable; others prefer to write them down by hand. Which method do you think is most useful and why?

4. **Find a good place to study.** Find a place with good lighting and a quiet atmosphere. Some students do well with classical music or other music without lyrics playing in the background. Keep your study place equipped with extra supplies such as pens, pencils, calculator, folders, and paper so that you don't have to interrupt study time to hunt for what you need.
5. **Read the text using a strategy such as "survey, question, read, recite, review" (SQ3R).**
   a. *Survey* or scan the chapter first to see what it is all about. This means looking over the table of contents, learning goals, headings,

photo captions, and charts so you get a broad idea of the content. Scanning will provide an introduction and help get your mind in a learning mode.

b. Write *questions,* first by changing the headings into questions. For example, you could change the heading of this section to: "What hints can I use to study better?" Read the questions that appear throughout each chapter in the Progress Assessment and Critical Thinking sections. The Progress Assessment questions give you a chance to recall what you've read. The Critical Thinking questions help you relate the material to your own experiences. Research has shown that it is easier to retain information and concepts if you can relate to them personally.

c. *Read* the chapter to find the answers to your questions. Be sure to read the boxes throughout the text as well. They offer extended examples or discussions of the concepts in the text. You've probably asked, "Will the stuff in the boxes be on the tests?" Even if your instructor chooses not to test over them directly, they are often the most interesting parts and will help you retain the concepts.

d. *Recite* your answers to yourself or to others in a study group. Make sure you say the answers in your own words so that you clearly understand the concepts. Research has shown that saying things is a more effective way to learn them than seeing, hearing, or reading about them. Used in study groups, recitation is also good practice for working in teams in the work world.

e. *Review* by rereading and recapping the information. The chapter summaries are written in a question-and-answer form, much like a classroom dialogue. Cover the written answers and see if you can answer the questions yourself first. The summaries are directly tied to the learning goals so you can see whether you've accomplished the chapter's objectives.

6. **Use the study guide.** The Student Assessment Learning Guide gives you the chance to practice thinking through answers and writing them down. It also includes practice multiple-choice tests.
7. **Use flash cards.** Much of the material in this course consists of terminology. The key terms in the book are highlighted in boldface type, and their definitions appear in the margins. Page references to these terms are provided at the end of each chapter. Write the terms you don't know on index cards and go through them between classes and when you have other free time.
8. **Use the Concept Mastery Toolkit CD-ROM.** Using the computer software in the pocket on the inside back cover of the book is a great way to practice your test-taking skills. The software contains sample test questions. It will analyze your achievement and tell you not only if you were correct or incorrect, but also why. Then it will provide page references to concepts you have trouble understanding and even pop up a picture of the appropriate text page so you don't have to fumble through your text while you are at the computer.
9. **Go over old exams, if possible.** Sometimes a professor will make old exams available so that you can see the style of the exam. If such exams are not available, ask your professor exactly how the exam will be given. That is, ask how many multiple-choice questions and how many true–false and essay questions there will be. It is not unethical to ask your professor's former students what kind of questions are given and what material is usually emphasized. It is unethical, though, to go over illegally obtained exams.

10. **Use as many of your senses in learning as possible.** If you're an auditory learner—that is, if you learn best by hearing—record yourself reading your notes and answering the questions you've written. Listen to the tape while you're dressing in the morning. You can also benefit from reading or studying aloud. Use the text on tape (a set of audiotapes) that is available with this book. If you're a visual learner, you should use pictures, charts, colors, and graphs. Your professor has a set of videotapes that illustrate the concepts in this text. If you're a kinesthetic learner, you remember best by doing, touching, and experiencing. You can benefit from doing some of the Developing Workplace Skills and Taking It to the Net exercises at the end of each chapter.

Test-Taking Hints

Often students will say, "I know this stuff, but I'm just no good at taking multiple-choice (or essay) tests." Other students find test-taking relatively easy. A survey of such students reveals the following test-taking hints:

1. **Get plenty of sleep and a good meal.** It is better to be alert and awake during an exam than to study all night and be groggy. If you keep up with your reading and your reviews, there is no need to pull an all-nighter just before the exam. Proper nutrition plays an important part in your brain's ability to function.
2. **Bring all you need for the exam.** Sometimes you will need number 2 pencils, erasers, and a calculator. Ask beforehand what you'll need.
3. **Relax.** Begin at home before the test. Take deep, slow breaths. Picture yourself in the testing session, relaxed and confident. Get to class early to settle down. If you start to get nervous during the test, stop and take deep breaths. Turn the test over and write down information you remember. Sometimes this helps you connect the information you know to the questions on the test.
4. **Read the directions on the exam carefully.** You don't want to miss anything or do something you are not supposed to do.
5. **Read all the answers in multiple-choice questions.** Often there is more than one correct-sounding answer to a multiple-choice question, but one is clearly better. Be sure to read them all to be sure that the one you pick is best. A technique that may help you is to cover up the choices while reading the question. If the answer you think of is one of the choices, it is probably the correct answer. If you are still unsure of the answer, start eliminating options you know are wrong. Narrowing the choices to two or three improves your odds.

Because life really *is* mostly essay questions, developing critical thinking skills is vital to this course and to your success in business. That's why you will encounter critical thinking exercises in each chapter of the text. Take time and generate your own thoughts about the issues raised in the chapter. It will pay off in real life.

FRANK & ERNEST® by Bob Thaves

6. **Answer all the questions.** Unless your instructor takes off more for an incorrect answer than no answer at all, you have nothing to lose by guessing. Also, skipping a question can lead to inadvertently misaligning your answers on a scan sheet. You could end up with all of your subsequent answers scored wrong!
7. **Read true–false questions carefully.** All parts of the statement must be true or the entire statement is false. Watch out for absolutes such as never, always, or none. These most likely make a statement false.
8. **Organize your thoughts before answering essay questions.** Think of the sequence you intend to use to present what you want to say. Use complete sentences with correct grammar and punctuation. Explain or defend your answers.
9. **Go over the test at the end.** Make sure you have answered all the questions and that you have put your name on the exam and followed all the other directions.

"Time is money" the saying goes. Some, however, would argue that time is more valuable than money. If your bank account balance falls, you might be able to build it back up by finding a better paying job, taking on a second job, or even selling something you own. But you only have a limited amount of time and there is no way to make more. Don't steal someone else's valuable time by being late for class or appointments. If you do, what message are you sending?

Time Management Hints

Throughout your life, the most important management skill you will learn is to manage your time. Now is as good a time to learn as any. Here are some hints that other students have learned—often the hard way:

1. **Write weekly goals for yourself.** Make certain your goals are realistic and attainable. Write the steps you will use to achieve each goal. Reward yourself when you reach a goal.
2. **Keep a "to do" list.** It is easy to forget things unless you have them written down. Jot tasks down the first time you think of them so that you don't "rediscover" chores when you think of them again. Writing them down gives you one less thing to do: remembering what you have to do.

3. **Prepare a daily schedule.** Use a commercial daily planner or create your own. Write the days of the week across the top of the page. Write the hours of the day from the time you get up until the time you go to bed down the left side. Draw lines to form columns and rows and fill in all the activities you have planned in each hour. Hopefully, you will be surprised to see how many slots of time you have available for studying.
4. **Prepare for the next day the night before.** Having everything ready to go will help you make a quick, unfrenzied start in the morning.
5. **Prepare weekly and monthly schedules.** Use a calendar to fill in activities and upcoming assignments. Include both academic and social activities so you can balance your work and fun.
6. **Space out your work.** Don't wait until the last week of the course to write all your papers and study for your exams. If you do a few pages a day, you can do a 20-page paper in a couple of weeks with little effort. It is really difficult to push out 20 pages in a day or two.

7. **Defend your study time.** Fraternities and sororities often set aside time for everyone to study. It is important to study some every day. Use the time between classes to go over your flash cards and read the next day's assignments. Make it a habit to defend your study time so you don't slip.
8. **Take time for fun.** If you have some fun every day, life will be full. But if you don't have fun, life can be a real drag. Schedule your fun times along with your study schedule so that you have balance.

MAKING THE MOST OF THE RESOURCES FOR THIS COURSE

College courses are best at teaching you concepts and ways of thinking about business. However, to learn firsthand about real-world applications, you will need to explore and interact with actual businesses. Textbooks are like comprehensive tour guides in that they tell you what to look for and where to look, but they can never replace experience.

This text, then, isn't meant to be the only resource for this class. In fact, it's not even the primary resource. Your professor will be much better than the text at responding to your specific questions and needs. This book is just one of the resources he or she can use with you to satisfy your desire to understand what the business world is all about. There are seven basic resources for the class in addition to the text and study guide:

1. **The professor.** One of the most valuable facets of college is the chance to study with experienced professors. Your instructor is more than a teacher of facts and concepts. As mentioned above, he or she is a resource who's there to answer questions and guide you to the answers for others. It's important for you to develop a friendly relationship with all of your professors. One reason for doing so is that many professors get job leads they can pass on to you. Professors are also excellent references for future jobs. By following the rules of dress and etiquette outlined above, you can create a good impression, which will be valuable should you ask a professor to write a good letter of recommendation for you. Finally, your professor is one more experienced person who can help you find and access resource materials, both at your college and in the business world.
2. **The supplements that come with this text: the Concept Mastery Toolkit software, the Student Assessment Learning Guide, and the audiotapes.** The exam prep disk and study guide will help you review and interpret key material and give you practice answering test questions. Even if your professor does not assign the study guide and exam prep disk, you may want to use them anyhow. Doing so will improve your test scores and help you compete successfully with the other students. If you are an auditory learner (you learn best by listening) or if you have a long commute to class, you'll find the audiotaped version of this text to be a great resource.
3. **Outside readings.** We recommend that you review the following magazines and newspapers as well as other resources during the course and throughout your career: *The Wall Street Journal, Forbes, Business Week, Fortune, Money, Smart Money, Harvard Business Review, Black Enterprise,* and *Entrepreneur.* You may also want to read your local newspaper's business section and national news magazines such as *Time* and *Newsweek* to keep up with current issues. If you're not familiar with these sources, it's time to get to know them. You don't necessarily have to become a regular subscriber, but you should learn

what information is available in these sources over time. All of these sources are probably available free of charge in your school's learning resource center or the local public library. One secret to success in business is staying current, and these magazines will help you do so.

4. **Your own experience and that of your classmates.** Many college students have had experience working in business or nonprofit organizations. Talking together about those experiences exposes you to many real-life examples that are invaluable for understanding business. Don't rely totally on the professor for answers to the cases and other exercises in this book. Often there is no single "right" answer, and your classmates may open up new ways of looking at things for you.

   Part of being a successful businessperson is knowing how to work with others. College classrooms are excellent places to practice this skill. Some professors provide opportunities for their students to work together in small groups. Such exercises build teamwork as well as presentation and analytical skills. If you have students from other countries in your class, working with them can help you learn about different cultures and different approaches to handling business problems. There is strength in diversity, so seek out people different from yourself to work with on teams.

5. **Outside contacts.** One of the best ways to learn about different businesses is to visit them in person. Who can tell you more about what it's like to start a career in accounting than someone who's doing it now? The same is true of other jobs. The world can be your classroom if you let it. When you go shopping, for example, think about whether you would enjoy working in and managing a store. Talk with the clerks and the manager to see how they feel about the job. Think about the possibilities of owning or managing a restaurant, an auto body shop, a

Business changes day by day. That is why it's important to keep current by staying up to date with business publications like the ones pictured here. If class schedules or job duties limit your library time, you can find links for many of the resources shown here at our website, www.mhhe.com/ub7e.

health club, a print shop, or any other establishment you visit. If something looks interesting, talk to the employees and learn more about their jobs and the industry. Soon you may discover fascinating careers in places such as the zoo or a health club or in industries such as travel or computer sales. In short, be constantly on the alert to find career possibilities, and don't hesitate to talk with people about their careers. Typically, they'll be pleased to give you their time.

6. **The Internet.** Never before have students had access to information as easily as they do today. What makes information gathering so easy now is the Internet. In fact, you will find more material than you could use in a lifetime. On the Internet you can search through library catalogs all over the world, find articles from leading business journals, view paintings from leading museums, and more—much more. Throughout this text we will present information and exercises that require you to use the Internet. This resource will become even more important in the future. Information changes rapidly, and it is up to you to stay current. If you don't already know how to use the Internet, learn to do so now! Reading the Surfing the Internet skills section beginning on page P-17 will get you started.
7. **PowerWeb.** To help you keep up with the constant changes occurring throughout the world, this text is accompanied by a very powerful new Internet tool called PowerWeb. PowerWeb gathers information about changes as they relate to each chapter in the text. Use it to find current articles, interactive exercises, daily news, study tips, and Web research. You can access PowerWeb with the CD included with each new text. Or you can simply go to www.dushkin.com/powerweb and register using your passcode on the card included with your new text. You can also access PowerWeb through the text website or www.mhhe.com/nickelsme.
8. **The library or learning resource center.** The library is a great complement to the Internet as a valuable resource. Work with your librarian to learn how to best access the information you need.

Getting the Most from This Text

Many learning aids appear throughout this text to help you understand the concepts:

1. **List of Learning Goals at the beginning of each chapter.** Reading through these goals will help you set the framework and focus for the chapter material. Since every student at one time or other has found it difficult to get into studying, the Learning Goals are there to provide an introduction and to get your mind into a learning mode.
2. **Self-test questions.** Periodically, within each chapter, you'll encounter set-off lists of questions called Progress Assessment or Critical Thinking. These questions give you a chance to pause, think carefully about, and recall what you've just read.
3. **Key terms.** Developing a strong business vocabulary is one of the most important and useful aspects of this course. To assist you, all key terms in the book are highlighted in boldface type. Key terms are also defined in the margins, and page references to these terms are given at the end of each chapter. A full glossary is located in the back of the book. You should rely heavily on these learning aids in adding these terms to your vocabulary.

4. **Boxes.** Each chapter contains a number of boxes that offer extended examples or discussions of concepts in the text. This material is designed to highlight key concepts and to make the book more interesting to read. The boxes cover major themes of the book: (*a*) ethics (Making Ethical Decisions); (*b*) small business (Spotlight on Small Business); (*c*) legal environment of business (Legal Briefcase); (*d*) global business (Reaching Beyond Our Borders); and (*e*) constant change (Dealing with Change).
5. **End-of-chapter summaries.** The summaries are directly tied to the Learning Goals so you can see whether you've accomplished the chapter's objectives.
6. **Developing Workplace Skills exercises.** Regardless of how hard we try to make learning easier, the truth is that students tend to forget most of what they read and hear. To really remember something, it's best to do it. That's why there are Developing Workplace Skills sections at the end of each chapter. The purpose of Developing Workplace Skills questions is to suggest small projects that reinforce what you've read and help you develop the skills you need to succeed in the workplace. These activities will help you develop skills in using resources, interpersonal skills, skills in managing information, skills in understanding systems, and computer skills.
7. **Taking It to the Net exercises.** These exercises not only give you practice surfing the Internet but, more important, they direct you to dynamic outside resources that reinforce the concepts introduced in the text.
8. **Casing the Web cases.** These cases give you another chance to think about the material and apply it in real-life situations. These cases are referenced at the end of each chapter and can be found on the text's website at www.mhhe.com/ub7e.
9. **Cross-reference system.** Cross-reference citations refer you back to the primary discussion and examples of all key concepts. Specific page references are given each time key concepts appear after their original discussions. Going back to the pages referenced allows you to quickly review or study a concept in context in order to improve your comprehension of the material.

Studying business involves many concepts, theories, applications, and, yes, terms to remember. To help you recall many of these terms, your text provides a page-specific cross-referencing system that highlights page numbers for the location of primary discussions of terms defined earlier in the book.

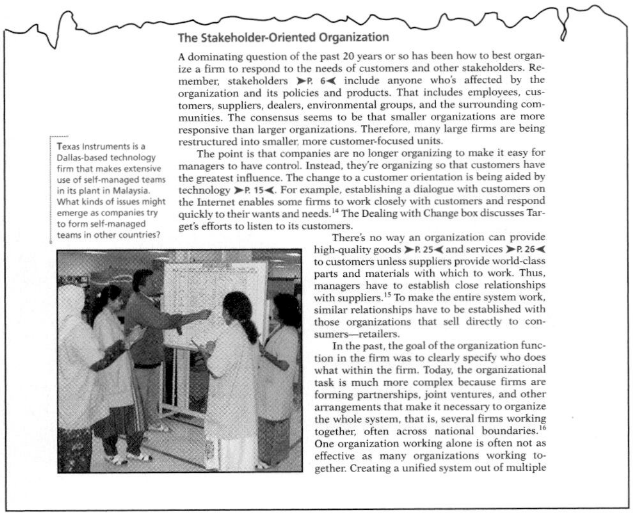

The Stakeholder-Oriented Organization

A dominating question of the past 20 years or so has been how to best organize a firm to respond to the needs of customers and other stakeholders. Remember, stakeholders ➤P. 6◀ include anyone who's affected by the organization and its policies and products. That includes employees, customers, suppliers, dealers, environmental groups, and the surrounding communities. The consensus seems to be that smaller organizations are more responsive than larger organizations. Therefore, many large firms are being restructured into smaller, more customer-focused units.

The point is that companies are no longer organizing to make it easy for managers to have control. Instead, they're organizing so that customers have the greatest influence. The change to a customer orientation is being aided by technology ➤P. 15◀. For example, establishing a dialogue with customers on the Internet enables some firms to work closely with customers and respond quickly to their wants and needs.[14] The Dealing with Change box discusses Target's efforts to listen to its customers.

Texas Instruments is a Dallas-based technology firm that makes extensive use of self-managed teams in its plant in Malaysia. What kinds of issues might emerge as companies try to form self-managed teams in other countries?

There's no way an organization can provide high-quality goods ➤P. 25◀ and services ➤P. 26◀ to customers unless suppliers provide world-class parts and materials with which to work. Thus, managers have to establish close relationships with suppliers.[15] To make the entire system work, similar relationships have to be established with those organizations that sell directly to consumers—retailers.

In the past, the goal of the organization function in the firm was to clearly specify who does what within the firm. Today, the organizational task is much more complex because firms are forming partnerships, joint ventures, and other arrangements that make it necessary to organize the whole system, that is, several firms working together, often across national boundaries.[16] One organization working alone is often not as effective as many organizations working together. Creating a unified system out of multiple

If you use the suggestions we've presented here, you will not simply "take a course in business." Instead, you will actively participate in a learning experience that will help you greatly in your chosen career. The most important secret to success may be to enjoy what you are doing and to do your best in everything. You can't do your best without taking advantage of all the learning aids that are available to you.

SURFING THE INTERNET

Most students today have had many opportunities to explore the Internet, but if you aren't one of them this section is for you. The purpose of this section is to help ease novices toward the on-ramp to the information superhighway. The material is arranged in a question-and-answer format so that you can easily jump to a topic you would like to know more about. Don't worry if you have never so much as pressed an Enter key—we won't get too technical for you. You don't have to understand the technical complexities of the Internet to travel on the information superhighway. But, as in learning to drive, it's usually a good idea to learn where the gas pedal is.

Technology changes so quickly that writing about how to use the Internet is like washing the windows of the Empire State Building—as soon as you're finished it's time to start over again. For this reason we've tried to keep the discussion as general as possible and not give too many specific steps that may be out of date by the time you read this. The important thing to remember is that you can't break anything on the information superhighway, so just jump right in, explore the online world, and have fun!

WHAT IS THE INTERNET?

The Internet is a network of networks. It involves tens of thousands of interconnected computer networks that include millions of host computers. The Internet is certainly not new. The Pentagon began the network in 1969 when the world feared that a nuclear war would paralyze communications. The computer network was developed to reach far-flung terminals, even if some connections were broken. The system took on a life of its own, however, and grew as scientists and other academics used it to share data and electronic mail. No one owns the Internet. There is no central computer; each message you send from your computer has an address code that lets any other computer on the Internet forward it to its destination. There is no Internet manager. The closest thing to a governing body is the Internet Society in Reston, Virginia. This is a volunteer organization of individuals and corporate members who promote Internet use and oversee development of new communication software. See Figure P.2 for a description of how the Internet works.

If even the idea of learning how to use the Internet is enough to make your head spin, relax. We'll show you how easy it is to use this powerful business tool. How can the Internet help you simplify many of your everyday tasks, such as communicating with instructors and colleagues and gathering information?

WHAT IS THE WORLD WIDE WEB, AND HOW IS IT DIFFERENT FROM THE INTERNET?

The World Wide Web (WWW, or the Web) is a means of accessing, organizing, and moving through the information in the Internet. Therefore, the Web is part of the Internet. Think of the Internet as a gigantic library and the Web as the Dewey Decimal System. Until the creation of the World Wide Web in 1993, it was as though that gigantic library simply threw all of its books and other materials into mountainous piles. If you wanted to

The Internet is a network of networks that connects an estimated 606 million users worldwide. Historically, the primary users were scientists, researchers, students, and academics who tapped in from their personal computers, terminals, or workstations. Today Internet use is widespread.

In some cases, users pull information directly from one of the desired computers. To reach certain desired computers a user may have to travel through other computers.

If a user is not at an institution with a direct connection to a desired computer that is part of the Internet, that person will dial into an intermediary computer, known as an Internet service provider (ISP).

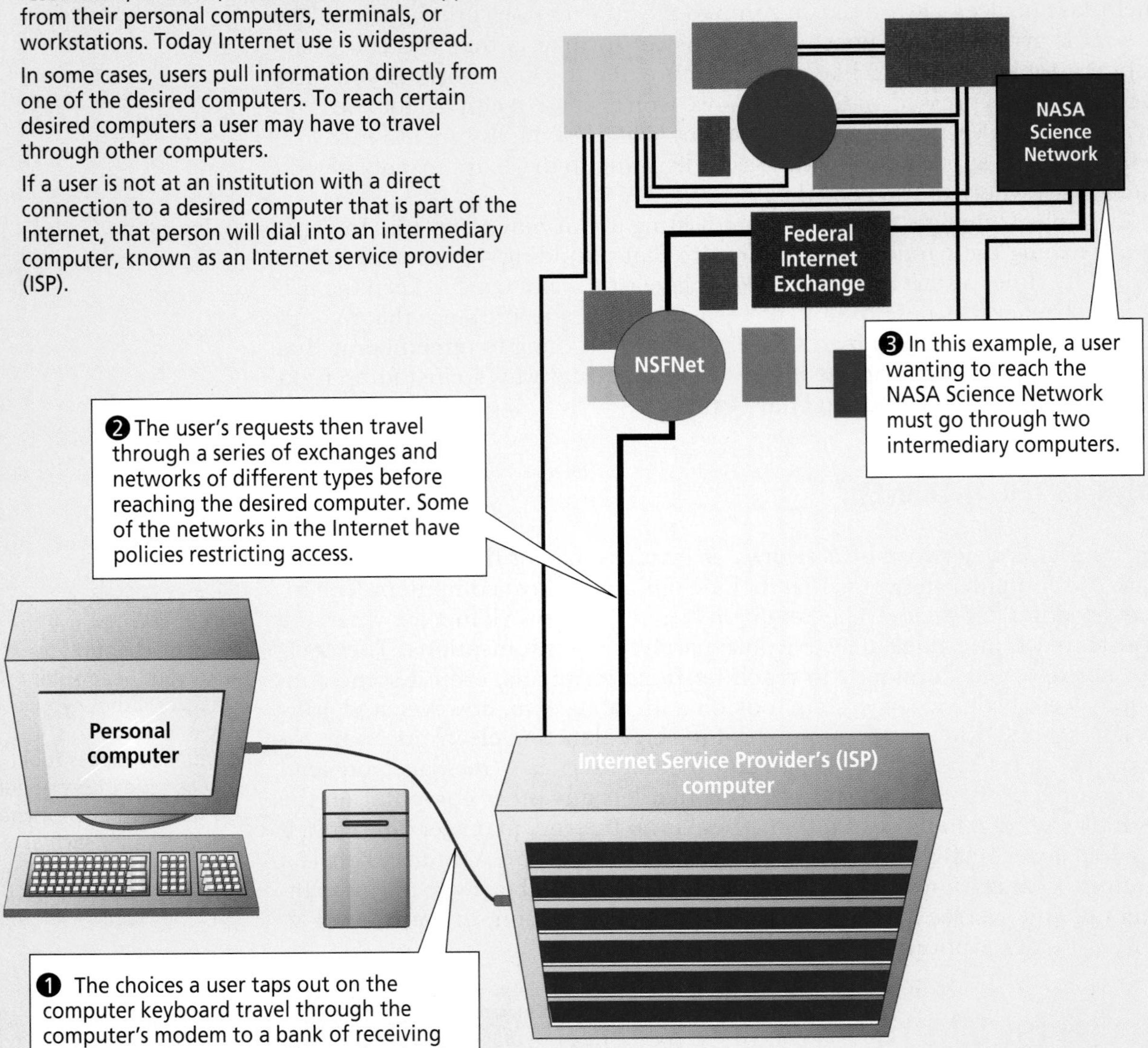
NASA Science Network
Federal Internet Exchange
NSFNet
❸ In this example, a user wanting to reach the NASA Science Network must go through two intermediary computers.
❷ The user's requests then travel through a series of exchanges and networks of different types before reaching the desired computer. Some of the networks in the Internet have policies restricting access.
Personal computer
Internet Service Provider's (ISP) computer
❶ The choices a user taps out on the computer keyboard travel through the computer's modem to a bank of receiving modems at the ISP's site. The modem bank connects to a terminal server, which allows multiple modems to connect into the ISP's computer. Now the user has access to the Internet.

Examples of providers that offer dial-up connections to the Internet include Earthlink and Mindspring. General online services such as America Online provide varying levels of access to the Internet, from a gateway for sending and receiving electronic mail to file retrieval and access to bulletin board–type discussion groups.

FIGURE P.2

HOW THE INTERNET WORKS

FIGURE P.3

HYPERTEXT LINKS AND A URL

find something on the Internet, you needed to type in a complex code representing the exact address of the site you wanted.

The basic difficulty of navigating the Internet without the Web is twofold: (1) the traffic signs on the Internet are written in Unix, and (2) there is no defined structure for organizing information. Unix is an operating system that was designed long before anyone thought of the term *user-friendly*. And, since the Internet does not require a prescribed structure for entering information, even experienced users have difficulty retrieving information without a tool like the Web.

When the Web evolved, the game changed. Not only did the Web add graphics and sound, which breathed life into the dreary text-only Internet, but it also made navigating parts of the Internet easy—even for beginners. Now Web cruisers don't need to know Unix in order to travel the Net. You can go from place to place on the Web simply by clicking on a word or a picture in a format called hypertext. Hypertext allows any part of any document to be linked to any other document, no matter where it is, allowing you to jump around from place to place with a click of the mouse. Hypertext links are usually shown in a contrasting color on the computer screen (see Figure P.3). *Cruising* or *surfing* means following hypertext links from page to page on the Web.

What Do I Need to Be Able to Get on the Web?

The first thing you need in order to cruise the information superhighway is a computer with a modem (a device that connects your computer with other computers via phone lines) and a Web browser. There are other ways to connect to the Internet (through special telephone lines, cable lines, or satellites), but until they become more widely available, many of us will use modems and standard phone lines to access the Net.

If cable Internet or digital subscriber line (DSL) service is available in your area, you may be interested in the comparison of these services that appears in Figure P.4. Keep in mind that your Internet connection is the pipeline used

FIGURE P.4

PICK A PIPE

	ADVANTAGES	DISADVANTAGES
Cable	• Theoretically, cable has the most bandwidth and therefore the fastest speed—as much as 4,000 Kbps, compared to the mere 56k of traditional phone modems. • Uses same cable lines used to deliver TV. • Not limited by distance from a central office. • Time to download 10Mb file: 1 minute	• Speed will decrease as more users sign up since all users on the network share the available bandwidth. • Not available in older, high-density areas (like cities), since it is expensive to dig up concrete to bury cables.
Digital subscriber line (DSL)	• Downloading speed can be as high as 4,000 Kbps (most of the bandwidth is used for incoming data, with only a small amount used for outgoing). • Uses telephone lines already in place. • Can use the same phone line for voice even while you're online so there's no need for a separate phone line for computer connection. • Time to download 10Mb file: 1 minute	• Limited to locations within 20,000 feet of telephone central office. • Good for downloading, but not for two-way communication like videoconferencing or Web hosting that requires the same bandwidth for incoming and outgoing data.
Satellite	• Download speed can be 400Kbps. Not nearly as fast as cable or DSL, but much better than the traditional 56 Kbps. • Time to download 10Mb file: 10 minutes	• Most satellite services can only push data to you. Two-way services may be available soon. • Since data are beamed from a satellite in space, you need to place an 18-inch dish in the line of sight to the satellite. Weather conditions can affect reception.
Analog modem	• Download speed ranges from 28.8 to 56 Kbps • Time to download 10Mb file: 1–2 hours	• Widely available.

to move data to your computer. The bigger the pipe, the faster the flow. Whether your connection is by cable modem, telephone lines, DSL, satellite, or fixed wireless, the impact is much the same. Data can reach you more than 50 times as fast as with traditional 56k modems and normal phone lines (the kind that came with most computers in the late 1990s and early 2000s).

Many schools offer students Internet service, so check out what is available at your school. You may have already paid computer-service fees that include Internet connection, so get your money's worth and get online now. If you can't connect through your school, you can connect to the Net by signing up with an Internet service provider (ISP). Your ISP will give you the phone number and a set of directions for connecting your computer to the Net. At this time, most ISPs provide unlimited access to the Internet for a flat monthly fee. Some ISPs offer "free" Internet access, but you must be willing to share private information about yourself and to give up a great deal of screen space to advertising messages.

What Is a Web Browser?

A Web browser is a program or application that provides you with a way to access the World Wide Web. The first graphical Web browser that allowed pointing and clicking was Mosaic, developed by Eric Bina and Marc Andreessen at the National Center for Supercomputing Applications. Andreessen, an undergraduate at the time, later went on to fame and fortune as the developer of Netscape Navigator.[11] Mosaic was based on a code written by Tim Berners-Lee of CERN, the European laboratory for particle physics.

Which Is the Best Browser?

Currently, the two most popular Web browsers are Netscape Navigator (now owned by America Online) and Microsoft Internet Explorer. At the time of this writing, the best browser is the one you have access to—in other words, neither one has a clear advantage over the other. (While it may not have a functional advantage, Microsoft Explorer is now more widely used since it is packaged with the Windows operating system that comes loaded on most new PCs. You can read about Netscape's lawsuit against Microsoft regarding this practice in the appendix to Chapter 4.)

The power of the browsers has increased greatly in the last 10 years. For example, Netscape version 1.1 fit on a standard floppy disk. Today, the download of Netscape 7.0.2 takes 19.4 megabytes (about 17 floppies)—and that's for the compressed disk image.[12] If we had to predict the future, we would have to say that both Netscape and Microsoft will continue to improve their browsers and that Web users will benefit from the competition as the browsers become more powerful and easier to use.

WHERE DO I GO WHEN I CLICK ON SOMETHING?

When you're navigating the Net, you can go from a Web page in Paris to one in Peru. What happens? When you click on a link, your computer sends out a request for information to another server. That server, which may be next door or across the planet, interprets your request, finds the information (text, graphics, or entire Web pages), and then breaks it up into packets. The server sends the packets to your computer, where your browser puts them back together and you see the Web page, all in the blink of an eye (or an eternity—they don't call it the World Wide Wait for nothing).

Why Does It Take So Long to Move from One Place to Another on the Web?

The speed with which you reach other Internet sites depends not only on the speed and size of your phone line and computer but also on the speed and size of phone lines and computers at the other site. You won't get to class any faster in a Ferrari than in a bus if you're locked in a traffic jam. The same is true on the information superhighway. Sometimes your computer will seem to take forever to get to a site or to open an image. If this happens, you can click the Stop button on your menu bar and try again later when the Internet may be less busy.

Why Would I Want to Surf the Internet?

You can use the Internet to:

1. **Communicate online.** Internet communication is discussed in more detail in the pages that follow. Here, though, is a brief list of communication options:
   a. *Newsgroups.* These are special-interest groups in which you can get advice or just share thoughts with people.
   b. *Electronic mail (e-mail).* E-mail lets you stay in touch with friends, trade files, and do business, all from the comfort of your computer desktop.
   c. *Internet relay chat (IRC).* IRCs allow you to chat with other people all over the world in real time (that is, talk with someone else while you are both online rather than sending messages to be read later). Live and uncensored, IRC can sometimes sound like a junior high school locker room, so choose your chats wisely.
   d. *Instant messaging.* Instant messaging allows you to know when other people on your contact list are online and available to chat with you.
2. **Gather information.** Internet users can tap into such diverse institutions as the Federal Reserve and the Library of Congress. Some websites offer news headlines, stock market information, access to encyclopedias, and other databases. Search engines can help you find the sites that have the information you need. There are special websites that offer push technology that makes gathering information automatic: After you tell it what you are interested in, the program searches the Web periodically and then pushes the information to you without your having to ask for it.[13]
3. **Shop.** Forgot your mom's birthday? No problem. Get online and order roses to be delivered to her door before she disinherits you. Or, if things get too bad, book a flight out of town with a few mouse clicks and a credit card number. Note, however, that credit card security is a concern that is getting lots of attention as more and more people shop on the Internet.
4. **Play games (after you finish studying, of course).** You can play games against another person or against the computer while you're online.

Do I Have to Be a Computer Major to Surf the Web?

There are only four simple things you need to know about to navigate the Web: (1) Web addresses, (2) directories and search engines, (3) links, and (4) the Back Page button.

What Are Web Addresses?

Every website has an address called a uniform resource locator (URL). Go back to Figure P.3 and look at the top of the browser window. See the line that starts with http://? That's the URL for the page. To get to any website, you just type its address in the space for the URL entry in your Web browser. To do this, of course, you have to know the exact URL. It is important to know that the Web is constantly evolving and therefore URLs often change as new sites are added and old ones dropped. Sometimes a new URL is supplied when you visit an old site, but often it is not, in which case you reach a dead end.

What If I Don't Know Which Site I Need, Much Less Its URL?

You can use a search engine such as Google to find information on topics that interest you. The more specifically you define your topic, the more successful your search will be. Using an extremely general term, such as the word "search" used here, will result in too many matches to be useful. How many matches did Google find in this illustration?

To find topics that interest you, you can use one of several Web directories or search engines. Once you are at the search engine's home page, all you have to do is to enter the keywords for the topic you want and you will quickly receive a list of links to sites related to your request. Some of the most popular directories and search engines are Google, Alta Vista, and Ask Jeeves.[14]

You'll always get better results from a search engine if you define what you're searching for as specifically as possible. The easiest way to narrow your search is to add or subtract terms from your search string. Let's say you want to buy a new stereo and you aren't sure which brands have the best sound. If you search Google using the word *stereo*, you'll get more than 6 million site matches. However, you can focus the search a little more by adding another search word. Just typing in the word itself isn't good enough, though. In order to receive only sites that contain both *stereo* and the other word, you have to place the search term in quotation marks. If you search for "stereo and review" you get around 50 matches—many of which are sites that review stereo equipment.

Don't worry about remembering all these surfing tips. Most search engines have an Advanced Options menu that provides a form you can use to narrow or broaden your search. Also, many search engines offer specific instructions on how to make the most of your search on their site.

If you try different search engines to look for the same topic, you'll get different results. That's because each search engine uses its own program (called a bot or crawler) to search the Web. Not only do these programs use different methods of searching and indexing, but they start from different points on the Web. You probably will also get different results if you search on a directory rather than a search engine, again because of the different approach to indexing sites. You can search on multiple search engines all at once by using a metasearch engine such as MetaCrawler (www.metacrawler.com) or Dogpile (www.dogpile.com).[15] MetaCrawler returns answers to queries from nine popular search engines, 10 search channels, forums, and links to major e-commerce sites. Dogpile returns query results from other Web search engines, Usenet, and file transfer protocol (ftp) sites. It also supplies stock quotes and news from wire services.

What Do I Need to Know about Links?

Once you're at a site, the two main ways to cruise around are by clicking on an icon button link or on a text link. One way to tell if something is a link is to place your cursor over the graphic icon or text. If the cursor changes into a hand, then you know it is a live link. When you click on a link, you will be sent to another website or to another page on the current website.

What If I Want to Get Back to Someplace I've Been?

If you want to go back to a site you have left recently, you can just click on the Back Page button in your browser. This will lead you back through the exact same page route you traveled before. Or you can enter the desired site's URL. If you are on the same website, you can choose the home-page link or one of the section icons to take you back to the home page or another section.

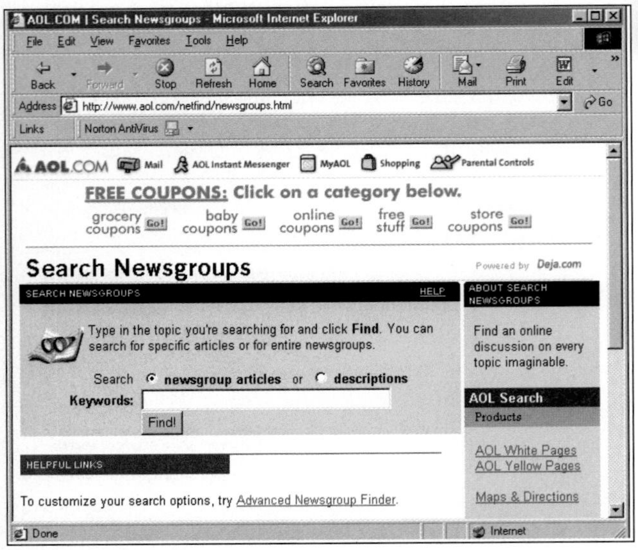

Newsgroups are collections of discussions from people all over the world. They are divided into categories such as computers, recreation, and society. You can use newsgroup search features like AOL's to find newsgroups that interest you.

How Can I Communicate with Others Online?

You can reach out and touch your fellow Internet surfers via newsgroups, e-mail, an IRC, or instant messaging.

What Are Newsgroups?

The Usenet is a global network of discussion groups known as newsgroups.[16] Newsgroups are collections of messages from people all over the world on any subject you can imagine (and some you'd rather not imagine). Newsgroups are divided into categories indicated by the first letters of their name. There are many different category prefixes, but the main ones you will see are comp (computer), sci (science), rec (recreation), soc (society), and alt (alternative). Under these headings are thousands of subcategories from alt.alien.visitors to za.humour.

How Do I Join a Newsgroup?

Web browsers have built-in newsreading capabilities. You first need to go to the Mail and News options menu and enter your server information, which is usually something like "news.myserver.com" (contact your Internet service provider to find out exactly what it is). There are also options for organizing how you read your messages. Some people like their messages "threaded" (meaning all postings on a particular topic are grouped together), while others prefer to sort their messages by date.

When you find a group you like, don't jump into the conversation right away. Take time to read the frequently asked questions (FAQ) list for that group first. The FAQ list includes the questions that most newcomers ask. After you read the FAQs, you should read at least a week's worth of postings to get a feel for the group and what kinds of discussions its members have. Remember, you may be joining discussions that have been going on for a year or more, so you may feel like the new kid on the block for a while. But most newsgroups are quite friendly if you use basic netiquette.

How Do I Send E-mail?

As with "snail mail," or letters delivered by the U.S. postal system, e-mail is delivered to its recipient by an address. An Internet e-mail address has two parts: the user name and the name of the computer on which that user has an account. For example, Professor Ulysses R. Smart's e-mail address at Ignatius Quinius University may be ursmart @iqu.edu. The symbol @ is pronounced "at." The suffix *.edu* indicates that the address is one of an educational institution.

There are several e-mail software packages available. Netscape and Internet Explorer include e-mail capabilities. To compose a message, click on the Mail button (see Figure P.5). Enter the e-mail address of the person to whom you are writing in the *To:* field. Enter the subject of your message in the *Subject:* field. If you want others to receive the message, enter their e-mail addresses in the *CC:* field and separate each e-mail address with a comma. Next, enter the body of the message in the large space. When you have completed your message, click on the Send button. To check for new messages received, simply click on the Get Mail button. If you have received new mail,

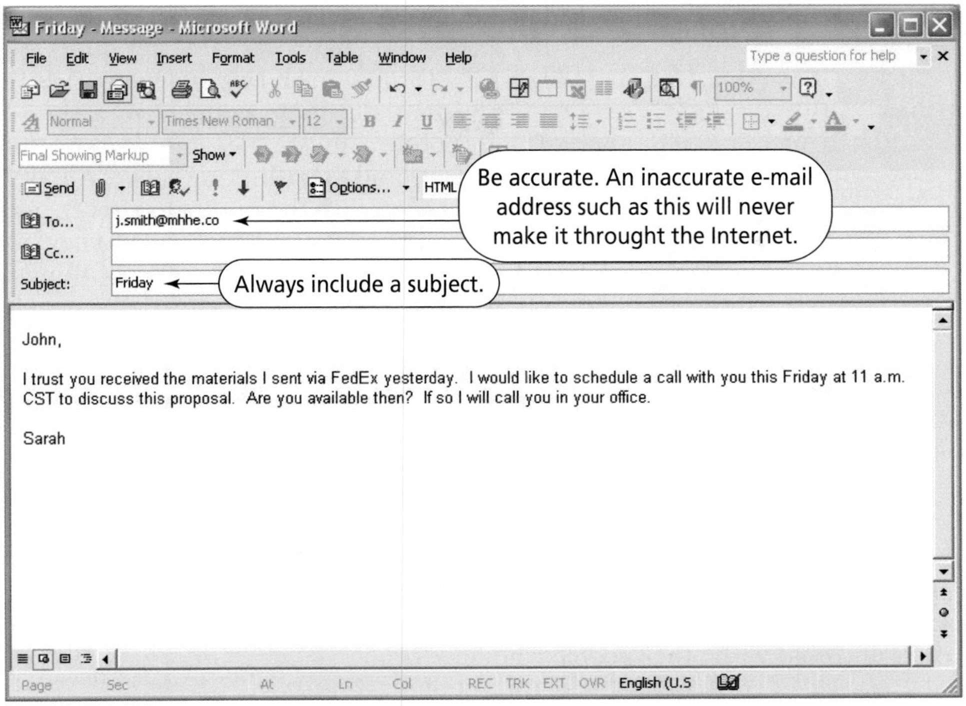

FIGURE P.5

E-MAIL FORM

the subject and sender will be displayed in a window. Click on a message to display its contents.

You can also send files with your e-mail. To send files from a graphics program or word processor, simply choose Attach File and navigate your hard drive to find the file you want to send. Double-click on that file to attach it. Before you send an attached file, make sure that the person you are sending it to can receive it. Some people have slow connections that come to a near halt if their system receives a large attachment. Others have mailboxes that fill too quickly if they receive a number of large files, so always ask before the first time you send someone attachments.

One of the more interesting ways to take advantage of e-mail is to join one or more mailing lists (or listservs, to use the technical term).

What Are Listservs?

Listservs, or mailing lists, are similar to Usenet newsgroups. Unlike newsgroups, though, listserv discussions are delivered to your in-box as e-mail, and responding can be as easy as punching your Reply button (which sends the message to everyone on the mailing list). (Some listservs do not provide a response feature since they are designed to dispense information rather than facilitate discussions. You should be able to find out the listserv's capabilities in its FAQs file.) To find a mailing list that piques your interest, try the mailing list directory Listz at www.listz.com. Be careful, though; mailing lists can quickly jam your in-box.

What Is IRC?

Internet relay chat (IRC) is an Internet protocol that allows you to have real-time conversations with other people around the world. As with newsgroups, it's best at first to observe, or "lurk," and see how the others on the IRC channel interact. To use an IRC channel you must have a chat "client" or program. The two most popular freeware chat clients are PIRCH for Windows and Ircle

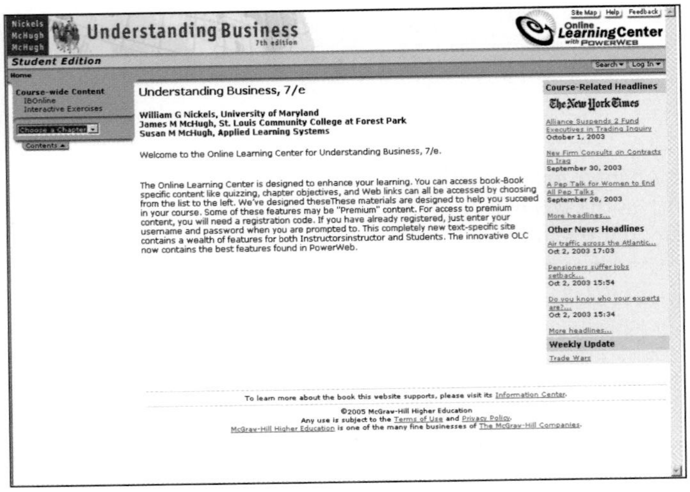

The welcome mat is always out at our website, www.mhhe.com/ub7e. UB7E Online Learning Center contains Casing the Web cases for each chapter, a stock market project, links to professional resources, Internet exercises, glossary, career resources, crossword puzzles, and support tools. It also contains special e-commerce coverage in case you would like to know more about how the Internet has changed the way we do business.

for the Mac. DALnet (www.dal.net) is one of the largest IRC networks. DALnet offers extensive information on IRC and how to use it.

The first step is to connect to a server. Then choose a nickname, join a room (or "channel"), and start lurking away. All IRC channels start with the number sign (#), and most servers have a channel called #newbie where you can ease into the swing of things.

Not all IRC is idle chat. Many people have discovered ways to use IRC to help one another by developing virtual support groups online. Talk City is one example of an online community that uses IRC as a vehicle for people to draw support in a safe and friendly environment.

Although IRC is one of the most popular uses for the Internet, it could easily be replaced by Internet phones, or more advanced Web chat, like America Online's Virtual Places (VP). VP's attraction is that you create an on-screen avatar, or 3-D representation of yourself. Then you can go to designated Web pages and chat with other people who have VP.

What Is Instant Messaging?

Instant messaging is software that allows you to chat in real time with individuals you've added to a contact list. Using popular instant messaging software from AOL, MSN, or another provider allows you to know when your friends are online and available for chatting. Of course, it also allows you and your friends to set the software so that you can go online without others knowing it so you aren't constantly interrupted. To learn more about instant messaging check out AOL at www.aim.com/index.adp or MSN at http://messenger.msn.com.

Where Can I Go to Learn More about the Web?

The best way to learn how to do something is by doing it, so the best place to learn about the Web is on the Web. It's time for you to put the pedal to the metal and get yourself onto the information superhighway. To learn more about the Web go to Learn the Net at www.learnthenet.com.

GETTING THE JOB YOU WANT

One of the more important objectives of this text is to help you get the job you want. First, you have to decide what you want to do. We'll help you explore this decision by explaining what people do in the various business functions: accounting, marketing, human resource management, finance, and so on. There are many good books about finding the job you want, so we can only introduce the subject here to get you thinking about careers as you read the various chapters.

If you are a returning student, you have both blessings and handicaps that younger students do not have. First, you may have had a full-time job already. Second, you are more likely to know what kind of job you don't want. That is a real advantage. By exploring the various business careers in depth, you should be able to choose a career path that will meet your objectives. If you have a full-time job right now, you've already discovered that working while going to school is exhausting. Many older students must juggle family responsibilities in addition to the responsibilities of school and work. But take heart. You have also acquired many skills from these experiences. Even if they were acquired in unrelated fields, these skills will be invaluable as you enter your new career. You should have no trouble competing with younger students because you have more focus and experience. We enjoy having both kinds of students in class because of the different perspectives they have.

So, whether you're beginning your first career or your latest career, it's time to develop a strategy for finding and obtaining a personally satisfying job.

JOB SEARCH STRATEGY

It is never too early to begin thinking about a future career or careers. The following strategies will give you some guidance in that pursuit:

1. **Begin with self-analysis.** You might begin your career quest by completing a self-analysis inventory. You can refer to Figure P.6 for a sample of a simple assessment.

"I got the job" are the words students look forward to saying after years of college study. Job fairs are among the many resources students can use to help find the right match. Here Doris Onwunumali meets with a representative of Cemex S.A. at the Drexel University job fair. Do you think it's ever too early to start thinking about your career?

Interests

1. How do I like to spend my time?
2. Do I enjoy being with people?
3. Do I like working with mechanical things?
4. Do I enjoy working with numbers?
5. Am I a member of many organizations?
6. Do I enjoy physical activities?
7. Do I like to read?

Abilities

1. Am I adept at working with numbers?
2. Am I adept at working with mechanical things?
3. Do I have good verbal and written communication skills?
4. What special talents do I have?
5. In which abilities do I wish I were more adept?

Education

1. Have I taken certain courses that have prepared me for a particular job?
2. In which subjects did I perform the best? The worst?
3. Which subjects did I enjoy the most? The least?
4. How have my extracurricular activities prepared me for a particular job?
5. Is my GPA an accurate picture of my academic ability? Why?
6. Do I want a graduate degree? Do I want to earn it before beginning my job?
7. Why did I choose my major?

Experience

1. What previous jobs have I held? What were my responsibilities in each?
2. Were any of my jobs applicable to positions I may be seeking? How?
3. What did I like the most about my previous jobs? Like the least?
4. Why did I work in the jobs I did?
5. If I had to do it over again, would I work in these jobs? Why?

Personality

1. What are my good and bad traits?
2. Am I competitive?
3. Do I work well with others?
4. Am I outspoken?
5. Am I a leader or a follower?
6. Do I work well under pressure?
7. Do I work quickly, or am I methodical?
8. Do I get along well with others?
9. Am I ambitious?
10. Do I work well independently of others?

Desired job environment

1. Am I willing to relocate? Why?
2. Do I have a geographic preference? Why?
3. Would I mind traveling in my job?
4. Do I have to work for a large, nationally known firm to be satisfied?
5. Must I have a job that initially offers a high salary?
6. Must the job I assume offer rapid promotion opportunities?
7. In what kind of job environment would I feel most comfortable?
8. If I could design my own job, what characteristics would it have?

Personal goals

1. What are my short- and long-term goals? Why?
2. Am I career-oriented, or do I have broader interests?
3. What are my career goals?
4. What jobs are likely to help me achieve my goals?
5. What do I hope to be doing in 5 years? In 10 years?
6. What do I want out of life?

FIGURE P.6

A PERSONAL ASSESSMENT

2. **Search for jobs you would enjoy.** Begin at your college's career planning office or placement office, if your school has one. Keep interviewing people in various careers, even after you've found a job. Career progress demands continuous research.
3. **Begin the networking process.** According to a Manhattan-based job placement firm, two-thirds of people get jobs through networking.[17] You can start with your fellow students, family, relatives, neighbors, friends, professors, and local businesspeople. Be sure to keep a file with the names, addresses, and phone numbers of contacts—where they work, the person who recommended them to you, and the relationship between the source person and the contact. A great way to make contacts and a good impression on employers is to do part-time work and summer internships at those firms you find interesting.

4. **Go to the Internet for help.** You will find details about finding jobs on a variety of websites. Many of these sites can help you write your résumé as well as help you search for jobs that meet your interests and skills. Later we'll list a number of these sites.

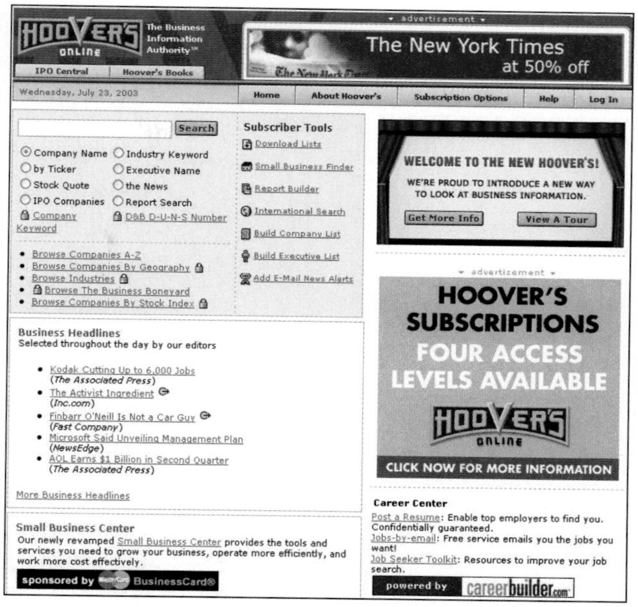

A job interview often determines if you get the position you want. That is why it's important to learn as much as you can about a prospective employer before an interview. Hoover's Online is a valuable website containing information about specific companies you may be considering. How do you think such information could help you get the job?

5. **Prepare a good cover letter and résumé.** Once you know what you want to do and where you would like to work, you need to develop a good résumé and cover letter. Your résumé lists your education, work experience, and activities. We'll talk about these key job search tools in more detail.
6. **Develop interviewing skills.** Interviewers will be checking your appearance (clothes, haircut, fingernails, shoes); your attitude (friendliness is desired); your verbal ability (speak loud enough to be heard clearly); and your motivation (be enthusiastic). Note also that interviewers want you to have been active in clubs and activities and to have set goals. Have someone evaluate you on these scales now to see if you have any weak points. You can then work on those points before you have any actual job interviews. We'll give you some clues on how to do this later.
7. **Follow up.** Write a thank-you note after interviews, even if you think they didn't go well. You have a chance to make a lasting impression with a follow-up note. Keep in touch with companies in which you have an interest. Show your interest by calling periodically or sending e-mail and letting the company know you are still interested. Indicate your willingness to travel to various parts of the country or the world to be interviewed. Get to know people in the company and learn from them whom to contact and what qualifications to emphasize.

More Hints on the Job Search

The placement bureau at your school is a good place to begin reading about potential employers. On-campus interviewing is by far the number one source of jobs (see Figure P.7). Another good source of jobs involves writing to companies and sending a good cover letter and résumé. You can identify companies to contact in your library or on the Internet. Check such sources as the *Million Dollar Directory* or the *Standard Directory of Advertisers.* Your library and the Internet may also have annual reports that will give you even more information about your selected companies.

Other good sources of jobs include the want ads, job fairs, summer and other internship programs, placement bureaus, and sometimes walking into firms that appeal to you and asking for an interview. The *Occupational Outlook Quarterly,* produced by the U.S. Department of Labor, says this about job hunting:

> The skills that make a person employable are not so much the ones needed on the job as the ones needed to get the job, skills like the ability to find a job opening, complete an application, prepare the résumé, and survive an interview.

FIGURE P.7

WHERE COLLEGE STUDENTS FIND JOBS

SOURCE OF JOB	PERCENTAGE OF NEW EMPLOYEES
On-campus interviewing	49.3%
Write-ins	9.8
Current employee referrals	7.2
Job listings with placement office	6.5
Responses from want ads	5.6
Walk-ins	5.5
Cooperative education programs	4.8
Summer employment	4.7
College faculty/staff referrals	4.5
Internship programs	4.5
High-demand major programs	4.4
Minority career programs	2.9
Part-time employment	2.4
Unsolicited referrals from placement	2.1
Women's career programs	2.1
Job listings with employment agencies	1.9
Referrals from campus organizations	1.8

Here are a few printed sources you can use for finding out about jobs and other career choices:

Occupational Outlook Handbook (Washington, DC: U.S. Department of Labor, 2002–2003 edition).

The Big Book of Jobs (New York: VGM Career Books, 2003–2004 edition).

Adams Internet Job Search Almanac, 6th ed. (Avon, MA: Adams Media Corporation, 2002).

Les Krantz, *The Job Finder's Guide*, 4th ed. (Fort Lee, NJ: Barricade Books, 2002).

Kathryn Kraemer Troutman, *Ten Steps to a Federal Job* (Baltimore, MD: The Resume Place, 2002).

Michael Farr, *America's Top Jobs for People Without a Four-Year Degree*, 6th ed. (Indianapolis, IN: JIST Publishing, 2003).

Richard Nelson Bolles, *What Color Is Your Parachute*? (Berkeley, CA: Ten Speed Press, 2003 edition).

Martin Yate, *Knock 'Em Dead 2003* (Holbrook, MA: Adams Media Corporation, 2003).

Martin Yate, *Cover Letters That Knock 'Em Dead* (Holbrook, MA: Adams Media Corporation, 2003).

Caryl Krannich and Ron Krannich, *Interview for Success*, 8th ed. (Manassas Park, VA: Impact Publications, 2003).

Jean Erickson Walker, *The Age Advantage: Making the Most of Your Midlife Career Transition* (New York: Berkeley Publishing Group, 2000).

The Directory of Executive Recruiters (Peterborough, NH: Kennedy Information, 2003).

You can also use the Internet to search for job information. To find information about careers or internships try these sites (though keep in mind that addresses on the Internet are subject to sudden and frequent change):

Monstertrak: www.jobtrak.com
CareerBuilder: www.careerbuilder.com
Hoover's: www.hoovers.com
Monster: www.monster.com
America's Job Bank: www.ajb.dni.us
Yahoo! Classifieds: www.classifieds.yahoo.com
Student Advantage: www.studentadvantage.com
National Assembly of Voluntary Health and Social Welfare Organizations: www.nassembly.org

It's never too early in your career to begin designing a résumé and thinking of cover letters. Preparing such documents reveals your strengths and weaknesses more clearly than most other techniques. By preparing a résumé now, you may discover that you haven't been involved in enough outside activities to impress an employer. That information may prompt you to join some student groups, to become a volunteer, or to otherwise enhance your social skills.

You may also discover that you're weak on experience, and seek an internship or part-time job to fill in that gap. In any event, it's not too soon to prepare a résumé. It will certainly help you decide what you'd like to see in the area marked Education and, if you haven't already done so, help you choose a major and other coursework. Given that background, let's discuss how to prepare these materials.

Travel and tourism represents the largest nongovernmental industry in the United States and is vital to many state economies. Although the terrorist attacks on September 11, 2001, hurt the industry as Americans became apprehensive about traveling, the future looks bright. As the population of the United States ages and more and more people are retired, there will be greater demand for recreation, travel, and tourism services. What types of career preparation would be desirable or necessary to pursue a career in this diverse field?

Writing Your Résumé

A résumé is a document that lists information an employer would need to evaluate you and your background. It explains your immediate goals and career objectives. This information is followed by an explanation of your educational background, experience, interests, and other relevant data. Be sure to use industry buzzwords in your résumé (see Figure P.8) because companies use keywords to scan such résumés. Having experience working in teams, for example, is important to many companies. For online résumé help, go to www1.umn.edu/ohr/ecep/resume.

If you have exceptional abilities but your résumé doesn't communicate them to the employer, those abilities aren't part of the person he or she will evaluate. You must be comprehensive and clear in your résumé if you are to communicate all your attributes.

FIGURE P.8

SAMPLE ACTION WORDS

Managed	Wrote	Budgeted	Improved
Planned	Produced	Designed	Increased
Organized	Scheduled	Directed	Investigated
Coordinated	Operated	Developed	Teamed
Supervised	Conducted	Established	Served
Trained	Administered	Implemented	Handled

Your résumé is an advertisement for yourself. If your ad is better than the other person's ad, you're more likely to get the interview. In this case, "better" means that your ad highlights your attributes attractively. In discussing your education, for example, be sure to highlight your extracurricular activities such as part-time jobs, sports, clubs, and other such activities. If you did well in school, include your grades. The idea is to make yourself look as good on paper as you are in reality.

The same is true for your job experience. Be sure to describe what you did, any special projects in which you participated, and any responsibilities you had. For the interests section, if you include one, don't just list your interests, but describe how deeply you were involved. If you organized the club, volunteered your time, or participated more often than usual in an organization, make sure to say so in the résumé. See Figure P.9 for a sample résumé. Most companies prefer that you keep your résumé to one page unless you have many years of experience.

Putting Your Résumé on the Internet

You might want to post your résumé on the Internet because many larger firms seek candidates on the Net. While Internet résumés allow you to cast a wide net by allowing you to reach the greatest number of potential employers with the least amount of effort, the Internet is not always the most effective job search tool. It may have been more effective a couple of years ago, but today thousands of other eager job hunters send résumés online and the volume can overwhelm recruiters. In fact, in 2001, Drake Beam Morin, a leader in the outplacement service field, found that only 5 percent of its clients found jobs through the Internet.[18] That doesn't mean you shouldn't post your résumé online; it does mean, though, that you can't just send a few hundred résumés into cyberspace and then sit back and wait for the phone to ring. Include online résumés as a tool in your job search process, but continue to use the more traditional tools such as networking.

An Internet résumé is different from a standard one because the elimination process is done by computer. Thus, you must understand what the computer is programmed to look for. It wants nouns, not verbs. Whereas the traditional résumé is built on verbs like *managed* and *supervised,* résumés on the Internet are built around nouns like *program management* and *teams.* They also emphasize software programs you have mastered, like Microsoft Word. Listing jobs chronologically is no longer the best thing to do. Instead, emphasize knowledge, skills, and abilities. At the beginning of your résumé or after the Experience section, you may write a new section called Key Skills or Functional Expertise and list all the nouns that fit your experience.

FIGURE P.9

SAMPLE RÉSUMÉ

Yann Ng
345 Big Bend Boulevard
Kirkwood, Missouri, 63122
314-555-5385
YNG@AOL.COM

Job objective: Sales representative in business-to-business marketing

Education:

St. Louis Community College at Meramec
A.A. in Business (3.6 grade point average)
Served on Student Representative Board

University of Missouri, St. Louis
B.S. in Business: Marketing major (3.2 grade point average, 3.5 in major)
Earned 100 percent of college expenses working 35 hours a week.
Member of Student American Marketing Association
Vice President of Student Government Association
Dean's List for two semesters

Work experience:
Schnuck's Supermarket: Worked checkout evenings and weekends for four years while in school. Learned to respond to customer requests quickly, and communicate with customers in a friendly and helpful manner.

Mary Tuttle's Flowers: For two summers, made flower arrangements, managed sales transactions, and acted as assistant to the manager. Also trained and supervised three employees. Often handled customer inquiries and complaints.

Special skills:
Fluent in Vietnamese, French, and English. Proficient at using WordPerfect and Word. Developed my own website (www.yan@stilnet.com) and use the Internet often to do research for papers and for personal interests.

Other interests:
Cooking: often prepare meals for my family and friends. Reading, especially the classics. Piano playing and aerobics. Traveling: Asia, Europe, and America. Doing research on the Internet.

For example, a salesperson might put terms that apply to selling such as *prospect, approach, presentations, close sale, follow up, focus groups,* and *service.*

Here are some hints on preparing your résumé for the Internet:

- Keep it simple. Use text only. Put a summary of your skills and your objective at the top so that the reader can capture as much as possible in the first 30 seconds.
- If you e-mail your résumé, send it in the text of the message; don't put it as an attachment. It takes too long for the receiver to open an attachment.
- Customize each mailing to that specific company. You may use a standard résumé, but add data to customize it and to introduce it.

Competition for good jobs is always tough; in slow growth times, like the early 2000s, it has often been downright painful. A thorough and professional résumé can be an important first step in a successful search. Members of the National Résumé Writers' Association like Global Career Strategies can and want to help. Visit their site at www.resumecompass.com.

- Put your cover letter and résumé in one file.
- Use any advertised job title as the subject of your e-mail message, citing any relevant job numbers. (Note that some companies don't want you to e-mail them your résumé and cover letter, preferring letters or faxes instead.)

Posting résumés to Internet job sites can cause privacy nightmares for job seekers, resulting in everything from identity theft to losing their current job when their employers, who use the same job search services, find out that they are looking for new jobs. Sometimes posted résumés are sold to other sites or individuals willing to pay for them. Scam artists posing as recruiters, meanwhile, also can download all the résumés they want and do virtually whatever they want with them. At worst, online résumés can give identity thieves a starting point to steal personal information. Here are tips to protect your résumé and your identity:[19]

- *Never* include highly private information, such as Social Security numbers and birthdays.
- Check job boards' privacy policies to see how information is used and resold.
- Post résumés directly to employers if possible.
- Date résumés and remove them promptly after finding a job.
- If possible, withhold confidential information such as telephone numbers and your name and use temporary e-mail addresses for contacts.

You can find more details about applying for jobs on the Internet in Margaret Riley Dikel and Frances E. Roehm's 2002–2003 edition of *The Guide to Internet Job Searching.* See Figure P.10 for a sample Internet résumé.

Writing a Cover Letter

A cover letter is used to announce your availability and to introduce the résumé. The cover letter is probably one of the most important advertisements anyone will write in a lifetime—so it should be done right.

First, the cover letter should indicate that you've researched the organization in question and are interested in a job there. Let the organization know what sources you used and what you know about it in the first paragraph to get the attention of the reader and show your interest.

You may have heard people say, "what counts is not what you know, but whom you know." This is only partly true—because both knowledge and personal contacts are necessary—but it's important nonetheless. If you don't know someone, you can get to know someone. You do this by calling the organization (or better yet, visiting its offices) and talking to people who already have the kind of job you're hoping to get. Ask about training, salary, and other relevant issues. Then, in your cover letter, mention that you've talked with some of the firm's employees and that this discussion increased your interest. You thereby show the letter reader that you "know someone,"

FIGURE P.10

SAMPLE INTERNET RÉSUMÉ

Yann Ng
345 Big Bend Boulevard
Kirkwood, Missouri, 63122
314-555-5385
YNG@AOL.COM

Job objective: Sales representative in business-to-business marketing

Education:
St. Louis Community College at Meramec
A.A. in Business (3.6 grade point average)
Service on Student Representative Board
Courses included introduction to business, accounting, and marketing.

University of Missouri, St. Louis
B.S. in Business: Marketing major (3.2. grade point average, 3.5 in major)
Earned 100 percent of college expenses working 35 hours a week.
Member of Student American Marketing Association
Vice President of Student Government Association
Dean's List for two semesters

Work experience:
Schnuck's Supermarket: Worked checkout evenings and weekends for four years while in school. Learned to respond to customer requests quickly, and communicate with customers in a friendly and helpful manner.

Mary Tuttle's Flowers: For two summers, made flower arrangements, managed sales transactions, and acted as assistant to the manager. Also trained and supervised three employees. Often handled customer inquiries and complaints.

Special skills: Fluent in Vietnamese, French, and English. Proficient at using MS Word 2000, MS Excel 2000, and MS PowerPoint 2000. Developed my own website (www.yan@stilnet.com) and use the Internet often to do research for papers and for personal interests. Sales skills include conducting focus groups, prospecting, making presentations, and customer service.

Other interests: Cooking: often prepare meals for my family and friends. Reading, especially the classics. Piano playing and aerobics. Traveling: Asia, Europe, and America. Doing research on the Internet.

if only casually, and that you're interested enough to actively pursue the organization. This is all part of networking.

Second, in the description of yourself, be sure to say how your attributes will benefit the organization. For example, don't just say, "I will be graduating with a degree in marketing." Say, "You will find that my college training in marketing and marketing research has prepared me to learn your marketing system quickly and begin making a contribution right away." The sample cover letter in Figure P.11 will give you a better feel for how this looks.

Third, be sure to "ask for the order." That is, say in your final paragraph that you're available for an interview at a time and place convenient for the in-

FIGURE P.11

SAMPLE COVER LETTER

345 Big Bend Blvd.
Kirkwood, MO 63122
October 10, 2004

Mr. Carl Karlinski
Premier Designs
45 Apple Court
Chicago, Illinois 60536

Dear Mr. Karlinski: [Note that it's best to know whom to write by name.]

Recent articles in *Inc.* and *Success* have praised your company for its innovative products and strong customer orientation. I'm familiar with your creative display materials. In fact, we've used them at Mary Tuttle's Flower Shop—my employer for the last two summers. Christie Bouchard, your local sales representative, told me all about your products and your training program at Premier Designs.

Christie mentioned the kind of salespeople you are seeking. Here's what she said and my qualifications.

Requirement: Men and women with proven sales ability.

Qualifications: Success making and selling flower arrangements at Mary Tuttle's and practicing customer relations at Schnuck's Supermarket. As you know, Schnuck's has one of the best customer-oriented training programs in the food industry.

Requirement: Self-motivated people with leadership ability.

Qualifications: Paid my way through college working nights and summers. Selected to be on the Student Representative Board at St. Louis Community College at Meramec and active in student government at the University of Missouri. Paid my own way to Asia, Europe, and the Americas.

Could you use such a successful salesperson at Premier Designs? I will be in the Chicago area the week of January 4–9. What time and date would be most convenient for us to discuss career opportunities at Premier? I'll phone your secretary to set up an appointment.

Sincerely,

Yann Ng

terviewer. Again, see the sample cover letter in Figure P.11 for guidance. Notice in this letter how the writer subtly shows that she reads business publications and draws attention to her résumé.

Principles to follow in writing a cover letter and preparing your résumé include the following:

- Be confident. List all your good qualities and attributes.
- Don't be apologetic or negative. Write as one professional to another, not as a humble student begging for a job.
- Describe how your experience and education can add value to the organization.

- Research every prospective employer thoroughly before writing anything. Use a rifle approach rather than a shotgun approach. That is, write effective marketing-oriented letters to a few select companies rather than to a general list.
- Have your materials prepared by an experienced keyboarder if you are not highly skilled yourself. If you have access to a word processing system with a letter-quality laser printer, you can produce individualized letters efficiently.
- Have someone edit your materials for spelling, grammar, and style. Don't be like the student who sent out a second résumé to correct "some mixtakes." Or another who said, "I am acurite with numbers."
- Don't send the names of references until asked.

Preparing for Job Interviews

Companies usually don't conduct job interviews unless they're somewhat certain that the candidate has the requirements for the job. The interview, therefore, is pretty much a make-or-break situation. If it goes well, you have a greater chance of being hired. That's why you must be prepared for your interviews. There are five stages of interview preparation:

1. **Do research about the prospective employers.** Learn what industry the firm is in, its competitors, the products or services it produces and their acceptance in the market, and the title of your desired position. You can find such information in the firm's annual reports, in Standard & Poor's, Hoover's, Moody's manuals, and various business publications such as *Fortune, Business Week,* and *Forbes.* Ask your librarian for help or search the Internet. You can look in the *Reader's Guide to Business Literature* to locate the company name and to look for articles about it. This important first step shows you have initiative and interest in the firm.
2. **Practice the interview.** Figure P.12 lists some of the more frequently asked questions in an interview. Practice answering these questions and more at the placement office and with your roommate, parents, or friends. Don't memorize your answers, but be prepared—know what you're going to say. Interviewers will be impressed if you thought enough to prepare questions for them about the products, job, company culture, etc. Figure P.13 shows sample questions you might ask. Be sure you know whom to contact, and write down the

FIGURE P.12

FREQUENTLY ASKED QUESTIONS

- How would you describe yourself?
- What are your greatest strengths and weaknesses?
- How did you choose this company?
- What do you know about the company?
- What are your long-range career goals?
- What courses did you like best? Least?
- What are your hobbies?
- Do you prefer a specific geographic location?
- Are you willing to travel (or move)?
- Which accomplishments have given you the most satisfaction?
- What things are most important to you in a job?
- Why should I hire you?
- What experience have you had in this type of work?
- How much do you expect to earn?

- Who are your major competitors, and how would you rate their products and marketing relative to yours?
- How long does the training program last, and what is included?
- How soon after school would I be expected to start?
- What are the advantages of working for this firm?
- How much travel is normally expected?
- What managerial style should I expect in my area?
- How would you describe the working environment in my area?
- How would I be evaluated?
- What is the company's promotion policy?
- What is the corporate culture?
- What is the next step in the selection procedures?
- How soon should I expect to hear from you?
- What other information would you like about my background, experience, or education?
- What is your highest priority in the next six months and how could someone like me help?

FIGURE P.13

SAMPLE QUESTIONS TO ASK THE INTERVIEWER

names of everyone you meet. Review the action words in Figure P.8 and try to fit them into your answers.

3. **Be professional during the interview.** You should look and sound professional throughout the interview. Do your homework and find out how managers dress at the firm. Make sure you wear an appropriate outfit. When you meet the interviewers, greet them by name, smile, and maintain good eye contact. Sit up straight in your chair and be alert and enthusiastic. If you have practiced, you should be able to relax and be confident. Other than that, be yourself, answer questions, and be friendly and responsive. (You will learn more about what types of questions job interviewers are legally allowed to ask you in Chapter 11.) Remember, the interview is not one-way communication; don't forget to ask the questions you've prepared before the interview. Do *not* ask about salary, however, until you've been offered a job. When you leave, thank the interviewers and, if you're still interested in the job, tell them so. If they don't tell you, ask them what the next step is. Maintain a positive attitude. Figures P.14 and P.15 outline what the interviewers will be evaluating.
4. **Follow up on the interview.** First, write down what you can remember from the interview: names of the interviewers and their titles, dates for training, and so on. Put the information in your career file. You can send a follow-up letter thanking each interviewer for his or her time. You can also send a letter of recommendation or some other piece of added information to keep their interest. "The squeaky wheel gets the grease" is the operating slogan. Your enthusiasm for working for the company could be a major factor in hiring you.
5. **Be prepared to act.** Know what you want to say if you do get a job offer. You may not want the job once you know all the information. Don't expect to receive a job offer from everyone you meet, but do expect to learn something from every interview. With some practice and persistence, you should find a rewarding and challenging job.

Be Prepared to Change Careers

If you're like most people, you'll find that you'll follow several different career paths over your lifetime. This is a good thing in that it enables you to try different jobs and stay fresh and enthusiastic. The key to moving forward in your

FIGURE P.14

TRAITS RECRUITERS SEEK IN JOB PROSPECTS

1. **Ability to communicate.** Do you have the ability to organize your thoughts and ideas effectively? Can you express them clearly when speaking or writing? Can you present your ideas to others in a persuasive way?
2. **Intelligence.** Do you have the ability to understand the job assignment? Learn the details of operation? Contribute original ideas to your work?
3. **Self-confidence.** Do you demonstrate a sense of maturity that enables you to deal positively and effectively with situations and people?
4. **Willingness to accept responsibility.** Are you someone who recognizes what needs to be done and is willing to do it?
5. **Initiative.** Do you have the ability to identify the purpose for work and to take action?
6. **Leadership.** Can you guide and direct others to obtain the recognized objectives?
7. **Energy level.** Do you demonstrate a forcefulness and capacity to make things move ahead? Can you maintain your work effort at an above-average rate?
8. **Imagination.** Can you confront and deal with problems that may not have standard solutions?
9. **Flexibility.** Are you capable of changing and being receptive to new situations and ideas?
10. **Interpersonal skills.** Can you bring out the best efforts of individuals so they become effective, enthusiastic members of a team?
11. **Self-knowledge.** Can you realistically assess your own capabilities? See yourself as others see you? Clearly recognize your strengths and weaknesses?
12. **Ability to handle conflict.** Can you successfully contend with stress situations and antagonism?
13. **Competitiveness.** Do you have the capacity to compete with others and the willingness to be measured by your performance in relation to that of others?
14. **Goal achievement.** Do you have the ability to identify and work toward specific goals? Do such goals challenge your abilities?
15. **Vocational skills.** Do you possess the positive combination of education and skills required for the position you are seeking?
16. **Direction.** Have you defined your basic personal needs? Have you determined what type of position will satisfy your knowledge, skills, and goals?

Source: "So You're Looking for a Job?" The College Placement Council.

career is a willingness to change jobs, always searching for the career that will bring the most personal satisfaction and growth. This means that you'll have to write many cover letters and résumés and go through many interviews. Each time you change jobs, go through the steps in this section of the Prologue to be sure you're fully prepared. Good luck!

FIGURE P.15

INTERVIEW RATING SHEET

Candidate: "For each characteristic listed below there is a rating scale of 1 through 7, where '1' is generally the most unfavorable rating of the characteristic and '7' the most favorable. Rate each characteristic by *circling* just one number to represent the impression you gave in the interview that you have just completed."

Name of Candidate ___________

1. Appearance								
Sloppy	1	2	3	4	5	6	7	Neat
2. Attitude								
Unfriendly	1	2	3	4	5	6	7	Friendly
3. Assertiveness/Verbal Ability								
a. Responded completely to questions asked								
Poor	1	2	3	4	5	6	7	Excellent
b. Clarified personal background and related it to job opening and description								
Poor	1	2	3	4	5	6	7	Excellent
c. Able to explain and sell job abilities								
Poor	1	2	3	4	5	6	7	Excellent
d. Initiated questions regarding position and firm								
Poor	1	2	3	4	5	6	7	Excellent
e. Expressed thorough knowledge of personal goals and abilities								
Poor	1	2	3	4	5	6	7	Excellent
4. Motivation								
Poor	1	2	3	4	5	6	7	High
5. Subject/Academic Knowledge								
Poor	1	2	3	4	5	6	7	Good
6. Stability								
Poor	1	2	3	4	5	6	7	Good
7. Composure								
Ill at ease	1	2	3	4	5	6	7	Relaxed
8. Personal Involvement/Activities, Clubs, Etc.								
Low	1	2	3	4	5	6	7	Very high
9. Mental Impression								
Dull	1	2	3	4	5	6	7	Alert
10. Adaptability								
Poor	1	2	3	4	5	6	7	Good
11. Speech Pronunciation								
Poor	1	2	3	4	5	6	7	Good
12. Overall Impression								
Unsatisfactory	1	2	3	4	5	6	7	Highly satisfactory

13. Would you hire this individual if you were permitted to make a decision right now?

Yes No

Video Case

HOTJOBS.com

When you were a child you were probably asked that age-old question, "What do you want to be when you grow up?" Your response might have been a movie star, professional athlete, or even president of the United States. Today, as you face the challenge of college, you may still dream of those glamourous jobs even though they seem a bit more remote than they did as a youngster. As a college student, you realize it's time to start taking that question more seriously. A goal of this video series and your textbook is to help you answer this longstanding question.

Christopher Jones of HotJobs.com says that a career is really a patchwork of jobs. Today, college graduates are likely to experience many different jobs that may lead to several different careers. This is a major change from your grandparent's days when a person generally stayed with a particular job or company for their entire work career. Because of such changes, each video in this series asks the businesspeople interviewed two specific questions:

1. How did you get to where you are today?
2. What advice do you have for college students?

This opening video reveals the answers of the businesspeople you will meet in the later videos. For example, Jones suggests diligence and the ability to accept rejection as needed traits in finding the right career. Garrett Boone, cofounder of The Container Store, is a true believer in passion and patience. He stresses a long-term perspective in searching for the right career. He also advises job seekers that attention to detail is critical in the competitive job market of the 21st century. Matt Hoffman of Hoffman Sports Association and Todd McFarlane of the McFarlane companies are two entrepreneurs you will meet in the videos who personify these characteristics.

There is no better time to learn to act like a businessperson than the present. Learning the positive business behaviors suggested in the videos will go a long way in preparing you for your career search. For example, practicing good "netiquette" will help you send an e-mail to recruiters that may get answered. Posting a résumé that is carefully constructed and proofread may get employers to come to you. Your résumé, remember, is really your calling card. Networking, both online and offline, is also an effective way of finding the right job. Companies such as HotJobs.com strongly encourage networking and offer assistance to job seekers and employers looking to find the right match.

Success in your career is often related to the satisfaction and enjoyment you get from your job. Elizabeth Bryant from Southwest Airlines and Sharon Larking of Abbott Laboratories attest to this fact in videos profiling their companies. Being prepared to change jobs and careers also helps keep you fresh and enthusiastic. Scott Ross of Digital Domain left a secure job to follow his dream. As you move on that path toward determining your career, perhaps the best advice to follow was offered over 2,500 years ago by the Chinese philosopher Confucius who said, "Choose a job you love, and you will never have to work a day in your life." Enjoy the video series and good career hunting!

Thinking It Over

1. What do you feel is the most important factor to consider in searching for the right career? Why?
2. Why are factors such as good grooming and being on time important behaviors in an effective job search?
3. Do you have a career path in mind at the present time? If so, what do you believe will be the key factors involved in your succeeding in attaining your career goals? If not, what tools will you use to help find the right career?

Chapter 1

Managing within the Dynamic Business Environment: Taking Risks and Making Profits

Learning Goals

After you have read and studied this chapter, you should be able to

1. Describe the relationship of businesses' profit to risk assumption and discuss how businesses and nonprofit organizations add to the standard of living and quality of life for all.
2. Explain the importance of entrepreneurship to the wealth of an economy.
3. Examine how the economic environment and taxes affect businesses.
4. Illustrate how the technological environment has affected businesses.
5. Identify various ways in which businesses can meet and beat competition.
6. Demonstrate how the social environment has changed and tell what the reaction of the business community has been.
7. Analyze what businesses must do to meet the global challenge, which includes war and terrorism.
8. Review how trends from the past are being repeated in the present and what such trends will mean for the service sector.

Getting to Know Meg Whitman from eBay

Going, going, gone! Turning an online auction site into one of the world's biggest dot-com success stories will keep Meg Whitman, president and chief executive officer (CEO) of eBay, in the spotlight for some time to come. Few people know more about meeting the challenges of today's dynamic business environment than Whitman. When she took over eBay, it had $6 million in revenue. Today, revenue is about $476 million a year and is growing rapidly. It is no wonder, then, that *Worth* magazine chose her as number 5 on its list of best CEOs.

How did Whitman get to such a lofty position? She began her career in product management at Procter & Gamble. That experience led to 10 years in consulting with Bain & Company. From there, Whitman went to Disney, where, among her other accomplishments, she opened the first Disney store in Japan. She then moved on to Stride Rite, where she added to her reputation by revising the Keds brand. Her successes led to her becoming the CEO of Florists' Transworld Delivery (FTD) and launching FTD's Internet strategy. That experience proved invaluable to her long-term career. In the interim, she went to Hasbro's Playskool division—which you may know as the maker of Mr. Potato Head.

Few people know more about meeting the challenges of today's dynamic business environment than Whitman.

With such a successful career, not to mention two children, Whitman did not need any new challenges. When eBay asked her to come to California, she hesitated. But the potential was too much to deny, so she moved her family and took up the daunting task of running eBay.

EBay began as an Internet auction company that resembled an online garage sale. The process involved bidding for items—mostly used goods—and waiting to see if others outbid you. It turned out to be a wonderful way of selling stuff that was cluttering up the house. It also became a great way to find collectors' items and goods of all kinds. Suddenly people had a way of buying and selling used goods as well as new but unneeded items they received for weddings, birthdays, and other events. Today customers are so devoted to the site that they don't consider themselves "bidding" for items as much as "winning" them. But just how did Meg Whitman turn an online auction process into a profitable business?

Whitman has expanded available goods from garage-sale-type items to more expensive goods such as homes, antiques, automobiles, boats, and computers. The company adjusts to the wants and needs of the market very quickly. The question becomes, Where does it stop? Whitman's goal is to make overseas sales reach half of eBay's total sales.

You can see that eBay faces all kinds of environmental challenges: technological, competitive, economic, social, and political. For example, the technological system can fail, and has. One time the company was offline for 20 hours. Whitman immediately responded by refunding fees and making sure customers were satisfied with any adjustments they had to make. Competition is also a major issue. America Online, Amazon.com, Yahoo, and Lycos have all tried to capture the same market. Whitman has successfully maintained eBay's leadership position but must constantly adapt her offerings to stay ahead of the competition. Major changes in economic conditions also affect the firm.

The purpose of this text is to introduce you to the exciting and challenging world of business. Each chapter will begin with a story like this one. You will meet more successful managers like Meg Whitman, and entrepreneurs who have started businesses of all kinds. You will learn about all aspects of business: management, human resource management, marketing, accounting, finance, and more. You will also learn about businesses of all sizes, from hot-dog vendors in a local street market to huge global concerns like eBay. We begin by looking at some key terms and exploring the rapidly changing business environment so that you can start preparing to meet tomorrow's challenges today.

Sources: Hillary Johnson, "Meg Whitman," *Worth,* June 2002, pp. 60–61; Melanie Wells, "D-Day for eBay," *Business 2.0,* June 2002, pp. 68–70; Alynda Wheat and Matthew Schuerman, "The Power," *Fortune,* October 14, 2002, p. 107; Annie Groer, "Furnishing the eBay Way," *The Washington Post,* March 27, 2003, pp. HI & H6; and David Kirkpatrick, "Tech: Where the Action Is," *Fortune,* May 12, 2003, pp. 78–84.

Business and Entrepreneurship: Revenues, Profits, and Losses

business
Any activity that seeks to provide goods and services to others while operating at a profit.

profit
The amount of money a business earns above and beyond what it spends for salaries and other expenses.

entrepreneur
A person who risks time and money to start and manage a business.

One of the ways to become a success in the United States, or almost anywhere else in the world, is to start a business. A **business** is any activity that seeks to provide goods and services to others while operating at a profit. **Profit** is the amount of money a business earns above and beyond what it spends for salaries and other expenses.

Since not all businesses make a profit, starting a business can be a risky proposition. An **entrepreneur** is a person who risks time and money to start and manage a business. Once an entrepreneur has started a business, there is usually a need for good managers and other workers to keep the business going. Not all entrepreneurs are skilled at being managers.

Businesses provide people with the opportunity to become wealthy. Sam Walton of Wal-Mart began by opening one store in Arkansas and, over time, became the richest person in America; his heirs now have billions of dollars. Bill Gates started Microsoft and is now the richest person in the world. He is said to be worth about $36 billion (that's billion with a *b,* not million with an *m*). There are about 497 billionaires in the world today.[1] Furthermore, there are about 11 million millionaires in the world, and that number is expected to be about 30 million in 2025. There are some 3.3 million millionaires in the United States.[2] That's about 1 millionaire per 100 people. Maybe you will be one of them some day if you start your own business.

Businesses don't just make money for entrepreneurs. Businesses provide us with necessities such as food, clothing, housing, medical care, and transportation, as well as other goods and services that make our lives easier and better.

Matching Risk with Profit

Profit, remember, is the amount of money a business earns *above and beyond* what it pays out for salaries and other expenses. For example, if you were to start a business selling hot dogs in the summer, you would have to pay for the cart rental, for the hot dogs and other materials, and for someone to run the cart while you were away. After you paid your employee and yourself, paid for the food and materials you used, paid the rent on the cart, and paid your taxes,

No occupation in the world is more diverse than entrepreneurship. Robert L. Johnson started Black Entertainment Television (BET) in 1980 and built it into a major success. Viacom purchased BET for about $3 billion in 2000, making Johnson a billionaire. He recently bought an NBA expansion team in Charlotte for $300 million. How diverse are the entrepreneurs who own the retail shops and other businesses in your town?

any money left over would be profit. Keep in mind that profit is over and above the money you pay yourself in salary. You could use any profit you make to rent or buy a second cart and hire other employees. After a few summers, you might have a dozen carts employing dozens of workers.

Revenue is the total amount of money a business takes in during a given period by selling goods and services. A **loss** occurs when a business's expenses are more than its revenues. If a business loses money over time, it will likely have to close, putting its employees out of work. In fact, approximately 80,000 businesses in the United States fail each year. Some people, though, think this number is an overstatement. Some owners close down one business to start another one or retire; even though such closings are not failures, they are reported as such in the statistics. Still, most business failures are due to poor management or problems associated with cash flow (which we discuss later in this book). You will learn more about terms such as *revenue* and *expenses* when you read the accounting chapter (Chapter 18).

revenue
The total amount of money a business takes in during a given period by selling goods and services.

loss
When a business's expenses are more than its revenues.

Starting a business involves risk. Steve Forbes of *Forbes* magazine says, "Risk-taking is the critical element for improving our standard of living."[3] **Risk** is the chance an entrepreneur takes of losing time and money on a business that may not prove profitable. Even among companies that do make a profit, not all make the same amount. Those companies that take the most risk may make the most profit. There is a lot of risk involved, for example, in making a movie. Even one James Bond film, *Casino Royale,* lost money. Of course, some movies make a huge profit. *My Big Fat Greek Wedding,* for example, cost only $5 million to make and brought in about $210 million.[4] Similarly, it may involve some risk to open a fast-food franchise in the inner city because insurance and land costs there are usually higher than in suburban areas, but the chance of making substantial profits in the inner city is also good because there's often less competition there than in other areas.

risk
The chance an entrepreneur takes of losing time and money on a business that may not prove profitable.

As a potential business owner, you need to do research (e.g., talk to other businesspeople, read business publications) to find the right balance between risk and profit for you. Different individuals have different tolerances for risk. To decide which is the best choice for you, you have to calculate the risks and the potential rewards of each decision. The more risks you take, the higher the rewards may be. In Chapter 6, you will learn more about the risks and the rewards that come with starting a business. The box titled Spotlight on Small Business shows you some of the reasons for the growth of entrepreneurship today.

Businesses Add to the Standard of Living and Quality of Life

Entrepreneurs such as Sam Walton (Wal-Mart) and Bill Gates (Microsoft) not only became wealthy themselves by starting successful businesses; they also provided employment for other people. Wal-Mart is currently the nation's largest private employer. Employees pay taxes that the federal government and local communities use to build hospitals, schools, playgrounds, and other facilities. Taxes are also used to keep the environment clean and to support people in need. Businesses, too, pay taxes to the federal government and local communities. That money can be used for schools, libraries, hospitals, and other such facilities. Thus, the wealth businesses generate and the taxes they pay may help everyone in their communities. A nation's businesses are part of an economic system that contributes to the standard of living and quality of life for everyone in the country.

The term **standard of living** refers to the amount of goods and services people can buy with the money they have. For example, the United States has one of the highest standards of living in the world, even though a few workers in some other countries, such as Germany and Japan, make more money per hour. How can that be? Prices for goods and services in Germany and Japan are higher than in the United States, so what a person can buy in those countries is less than what a person in the United States can buy with the same amount of

standard of living
The amount of goods and services people can buy with the money they have.

Spotlight on Small Business

www.emkf.org

The Environment for Small Businesses

A study by the Kauffman Center for Entrepreneurial Leadership in Kansas City, Missouri, revealed that of 10 industrialized countries, the United States had the most people trying to start a business. About 1 in 12 U.S. citizens a year tries to start a business; this means that about 900,000 new businesses are being created annually, and that total doesn't count self-employed consultants and other one-person firms. Since this is a chapter on the environment of business, we list here some of what is happening in the United States that promotes such interest in starting small businesses:

- The fallen stock market has led people to search for alternative ways of investing their money, and that includes investing in their own businesses.
- Compared to other countries, there are more public and private groups teaching entrepreneurs how to build a business, so more try and fewer fail.
- Fabulous rags-to-riches success stories lure others to follow suit.
- Technology enables growth and opens a host of its own business opportunities—such as Internet-related companies.
- As corporations cut the number of managers through programs designed to empower employees, skilled managers are available to start their own businesses.
- There is a strong cultural need for independence.
- There is more risk in starting a business than there is in opening a new outlet of a successful franchise, but the rewards may be greater as well.
- The challenge of the New Economy (that is, economic growth spurred by the growth of Internet commerce) endows business with an irresistible calling, and an air of romance and bravado.
- People can use their businesses to help their communities by creating jobs and providing needed goods and services while making a living for themselves.

Sources: Margaret Webb Pressler, "So You Want to Start Your Own Business?" *Washington Post,* June 27, 1999, pp. H1, H8; Paulette Thomas, "Rewriting the Rules," *The Wall Street Journal,* May 22, 2000, p. R4; Elizabeth Corcoran, "The Dual Bottom Line," *Forbes,* November 25, 2002, pp. 130–32; and Norm Brodsky, "Street Smarts," *Inc.,* April 2003, pp. 53–58.

money. For example, a bottle of beer that in Japan may cost $7 may in the United States cost less than $1. A pound of rice may be five times more expensive in Japan than in the United States.[5] Often, the reasons goods cost more in one country versus another include higher taxes and stricter government regulations. Finding the right level of taxes and regulation is an important step toward making a country (or a city) prosperous. We'll explore that issue more deeply in Chapter 2. At this point, it is enough to understand that the United States has such a high standard of living largely because of the wealth created by its businesses. Here are some statistics about the high standard of living enjoyed by people in the United States: 68 percent own their own homes, 75 percent drive their own cars, 98 percent have a color TV, 94 percent have a videocassette recorder, and 90 percent have a microwave oven.[6]

quality of life
The general well-being of a society in terms of political freedom, a clean natural environment, education, health care, safety, free time, and everything else that leads to satisfaction and joy.

The term **quality of life** refers to the general well-being of a society in terms of political freedom, a clean natural environment, education, health care, safety, free time, and everything else that leads to satisfaction and joy. Maintaining a high quality of life requires the combined efforts of businesses, nonprofit organizations, and government agencies. The more money businesses create, the more is potentially available to improve the quality of life for everyone.

Responding to the Various Business Stakeholders

stakeholders
All the people who stand to gain or lose by the policies and activities of a business.

Stakeholders are all the people who stand to gain or lose by the policies and activities of a business. Stakeholders include customers, employees, stockholders, suppliers, dealers, bankers, people in the surrounding community (e.g., community interest groups), environmentalists, and elected government leaders (see Figure 1.1). All of these groups are affected by the products, policies, and practices of businesses, and their concerns need to be addressed.

The challenge of the 21st century will be for organizations to balance, as much as possible, the needs of all stakeholders. For example, the need for the business to make profits may be balanced against the needs of employees for sufficient income. The need to stay competitive may call for moving a business overseas, but that might do great harm to the community because many jobs would be lost. It may be legal to move, but would moving be best for everyone? Business leaders must make a decision based on all factors, including the need to make a profit. As you can see, pleasing all stakeholders is not easy and calls for trade-offs that are not always pleasing to one or another stakeholder.

In the past, many businesses acted on the premise that "corporations exist to maximize shareholder value."[7] This premise implies that other concerns are less worthy of managers' attention than profit is. Others say that, rather than giving shareholders special privilege, businesses have an equal obligation to all their stakeholders. A major challenge for businesses is to stay profitable while trying to maintain a balance between the wants and needs of all the stakeholders. Here is how a 2002 article reported that the CEOs of the 200 largest companies in the United States viewed their responsibilities:

> *Balancing the shareholder's expectations of maximum return against other priorities is one of the fundamental problems confronting corporate management. The shareholder must receive a good return, but the legitimate concerns of other constituents (customers, employees, communities, suppliers, and society at large) also must have the appropriate attention.*[8]

Not all businesses adhere to that statement; nonetheless, in their rush to give consumers what they want and need—and to make a profit for shareholders—managers must be careful to balance those needs against the needs of the community. This means, for one thing, that their businesses cause minimal damage to the natural environment. Business and government leaders throughout the coming years will be discussing issues such as the potential benefits and hazards of nuclear power, recycling, the management of forests, the ethical treatment of animals, and the protection of the air we breathe and the water we drink.

Typically, the standard of living in a country is measured by how many things we own: homes, cars, TV sets, and the like. Standing outside of Saks Fifth Avenue one can't help but be impressed by the standard of living achieved by some citizens. Measuring the quality of life is something else. Measures include whether the air and water are clean and pure, and whether people have leisure time for family and fun. In your opinion, have too many people sacrificed their quality of life to have a higher standard of living?

Critical Thinking

Imagine that you are thinking of starting a restaurant in your community. Who would be the various stakeholders of your business? What are some of the things you could do to benefit your community other than providing jobs and tax revenue? How could you establish good relationships with your suppliers? With your employees? Do you see any conflict between your desire to be as profitable as possible and your desire to pay employees a living wage?

Using Business Principles in Nonprofit Organizations

Despite their efforts to satisfy all their stakeholders, businesses cannot do everything that is needed to make a community all it can be. Nonprofit organizations—such as public schools, civic associations, charities, and groups devoted to social causes—also make a major contribution to the welfare of society. A **nonprofit organization** is an organization whose goals do not

nonprofit organization
An organization whose goals do not include making a personal profit for its owners or organizers.

FIGURE 1.1

A BUSINESS AND ITS STAKEHOLDERS

Often the needs of a firm's various stakeholders will conflict. For example, paying employees more may cut into stockholders' profits. Balancing such demands is a major role of business managers.

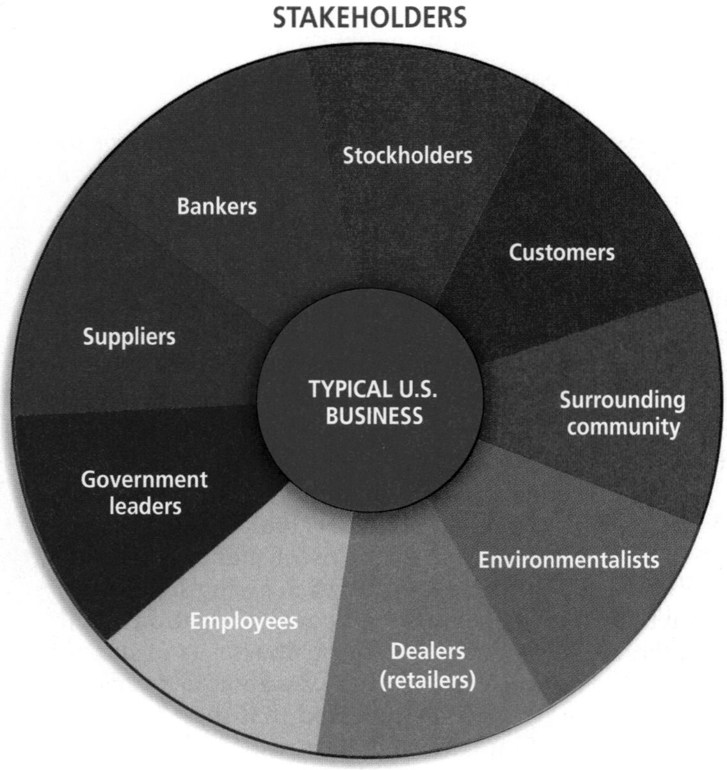

include making a personal profit for its owners or organizers. Nonprofit organizations often do strive for financial gains, but such gains are used to meet the stated social or educational goals of the organization rather than profit.

You may prefer to work for a nonprofit organization. This doesn't mean, however, that you shouldn't study business. If you want to start or work in a nonprofit organization, you'll need to learn business skills such as information management, leadership, marketing, and financial management. Therefore, the knowledge and skills you acquire in this and other business courses will be useful for careers in any organization, including a nonprofit one.

Because such transfer of skills is possible, many businesspeople volunteer their expertise in nonprofit organizations. Others change careers to run nonprofit organizations that require the same skills they had been using in the business world. Melissa Bradley, for example, started a profitable consulting firm her first year out of college. When she was 23, revenues reached $1 million. Seeing the opportunity that entrepreneurship offers, Bradley sold her consulting firm to launch The Entrepreneurial Development Institute (TEDI), a nonprofit organization that teaches entrepreneurship to at-risk young people.

Businesses, nonprofit organizations, and volunteer groups often strive to accomplish the same objectives.[9] All such groups can help feed people, provide them with clothing and housing, clean up the environment and keep it clean, and improve the standard of living and quality of life for all. To accomplish such objectives, however, businesses in the United States must remain competitive with the best businesses in the rest of the world by offering quality goods and services.

Progress Assessment

- What is the difference between *revenue* and *profit*?
- What is the difference between *standard of living* and *quality of life*?
- What is risk, and how is it related to profit?
- What does the term *stakeholders* mean?

ENTREPRENEURSHIP VERSUS WORKING FOR OTHERS

There are two ways to succeed in business. One way, the way chosen by Meg Whitman, is to rise up through the ranks of large companies like Hasbro or eBay. The advantage of working for others is that somebody else assumes the entrepreneurial risk and provides you with benefits such as paid vacation time and health insurance. Most people choose that option. It is a very good option and can lead to a happy and prosperous life. Businesses need good managers to succeed, and all workers contribute to producing and marketing the goods and services that increase the quality of life and standard of living for others.

The other, more risky path is to start your own business. The national anthem, "The Star Spangled Banner," says that the United States is the "land of the free and the home of the brave." Part of being free is being able to own your own business and to reap the profits from that business. But freedom to succeed also means freedom to fail, and many small businesses fail each year. Thus, it takes a brave person to start a small business. Furthermore, as an entrepreneur you don't receive any benefits such as paid vacation time and health insurance. You have to provide them for yourself!

Before you take on the challenge of entrepreneurship it makes sense to study those who have succeeded to learn the process. Very few entrepreneurs have had more successes in the United States than Wu-Fu Chen. He has started 11 companies (e.g., Communications Equipment Corporation, Cascade Communications, and Ardent Communications) and is a multimillionaire as a result. Chen is the 10th child of Taiwanese farmers. He rose above his humble background by going to school and working hard. After earning a bachelor's degree in engineering, Chen began working for a producer of computerized financial systems. While on the job, he saw the income potential that comes from being an entrepreneur rather than an employee. He worked for several different firms to learn different technologies and took business courses at night. Finally, he felt it was time to start his own business. That business became so successful that he sold it four years later for $7 million. Chen repeated this process of starting and selling businesses several times; recently, he sold a company for $156 million.

What you can learn from successful entrepreneurs like Chen is that you often start by getting a good education. Then you get a job working for a firm in which you can learn all about a certain business. Eventually, however, if you want to become a huge success, you might want to start your own business.

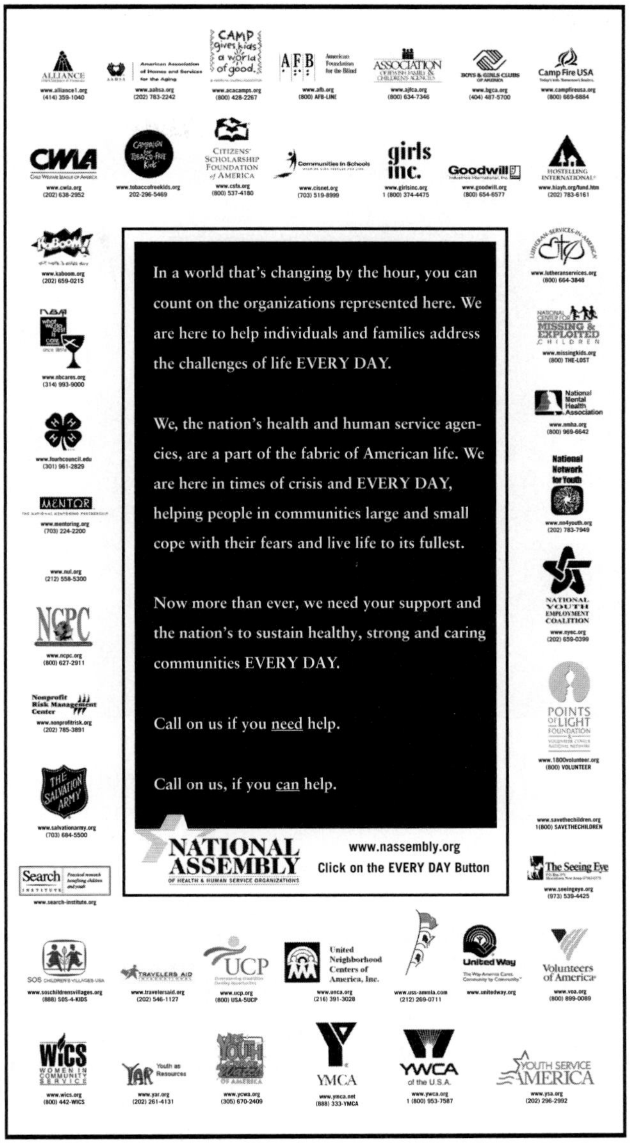

Nonprofit organizations, like those shown in this ad, can use business principles to operate effectively. One business practice they use is advertising, as this ad demonstrates. Additionally, nonprofit organizations need people to handle accounting, finance, human resource management, and other business functions. Would you prefer to work in a profit-oriented business or a nonprofit organization like those pictured? What do you think would be the key differences?

Opportunities for Entrepreneurs

The United States provides opportunities for all. Often the most attractive opportunity for many people is that of owning and managing their own businesses. Millions of people from all over the world have taken the entrepreneurial

Some of the most successful entrepreneurs in the United States are immigrants who began with almost nothing. Juan Gallicchio, for example, came to Philadelphia from Argentina with his family, $1,000, and no knowledge of English. Now he and his family own a thriving food-distribution system (candy). Theirs is the 73rd largest Latino-owned business in the United States. Is this an unusual success story or typical of U.S. entrepreneurship?

challenge and succeeded. The number of Hispanic-owned businesses in the United States has grown dramatically. The same is true of businesses owned by Asians, Pacific Islanders, Native Americans, and Alaskan Natives. Some 30 percent of Koreans who immigrated to the United States now own their own businesses. Other Asians are also prospering in business.

Top African American business leaders include David L. Steward of World Wide Technology, Inc.; Houston L. Williams of Pacific Network Supply; J. Bruce Llewellyn of the Philadelphia Coca-Cola Bottling Company; John H. Johnson of Johnson Publishing; Charlie W. Johnson of Active Transportation Company; and Dave Bing of the Bing Group. Among *Black Enterprise* magazine's top 100 firms in 2001, 23 industrial/service firms and auto dealerships grossed more than $200 million in revenues.[10]

Tremendous opportunities exist for all men and women willing to take the risk of starting a business. Notice that we said *men and women.* The number of women business owners has dramatically increased in the last 20 years. In 1980, there were about 3 million women business owners; by 2000, there were over 8 million. Women now own over a third of all businesses. Names you may be familiar with include Oprah Winfrey, Donna Karan, and Lillian Vernon. Women also make great managers, as you can see from the opening profile of Meg Whitman.[11]

The Importance of Entrepreneurs to the Creation of Wealth

Have you ever wondered why some countries are relatively wealthy and others poor? Economists have been studying the issue of wealth creation for many years. They began the process by studying potential sources of wealth to determine which are the most important. Over time, they came up with five factors that seemed to contribute to wealth. They called them **factors of production**. Figure 1.2 shows those five factors. They are:

factors of production
The resources used to create wealth: land, labor, capital, entrepreneurship, and knowledge.

1. Land (or natural resources).
2. Labor (workers).
3. Capital (This includes machines, tools, buildings, or whatever else is used in the production of goods. It does *not* include money; money is used to buy factors of production—it is not a factor itself.)
4. Entrepreneurship.
5. Knowledge.

Traditionally, business and economic textbooks have emphasized only four factors of production: land, labor, capital, and entrepreneurship. But management expert and business consultant Peter Drucker says that the most important factor of production in our economy is and always will be knowledge. The young workers in the high-tech industries in the Silicon Valley area of California are sometimes called knowledge workers. Many became millionaires while still in their 20s during the booming 1990s. When high-tech businesses began to fail in the early 2000s, a lot of knowledge workers

FIGURE 1.2

THE FIVE FACTORS OF PRODUCTION

Land:	Land and other natural resources are used to make homes, cars, and other products.
Labor:	People have always been an important resource in producing goods and services, but many people are now being replaced by technology.
Capital:	Capital includes machines, tools, buildings, and other means of manufacturing.
Entrepreneurship:	All the resources in the world have little value unless entrepreneurs are willing to take the risk of starting businesses to use those resources.
Knowledge:	Information technology has revolutionized business, making it possible to quickly determine wants and needs and to respond with desired goods and services.

had to find new jobs in other parts of the country, but their education and experience made the transition easier.

Such results should motivate today's college students to get as much education as possible to prepare themselves for knowledge-oriented jobs and to be prepared to change jobs as the economy demands.[12] Note that information is not the same as knowledge. There is often too much information available and the management of information (information management) is critical. We will study this topic in depth in Chapter 17.

If you were to analyze rich countries versus poor countries to see what causes the differences in the levels of wealth, you'd have to look at the factors of production in each country. Such analyses have revealed that some relatively poor countries often have plenty of land and natural resources. Russia and China, for example, both have vast areas of land with many resources, but they are not rich countries. In contrast, Japan and Hong Kong are relatively rich countries but are poor in land and other natural resources. Therefore, land isn't the critical element for wealth creation.

Most poor countries have many laborers, so it's not labor that's the primary source of wealth today. Laborers need to find work to make a contribution; that is, they need entrepreneurs to provide jobs for them. Furthermore, capital—machinery and tools—is now becoming available in world markets, so capital isn't the missing ingredient. Capital is not productive without entrepreneurs to put it to use.

Clearly, then, what makes rich countries rich today is a combination of entrepreneurship and the effective use of knowledge. Together, lack of entrepreneurship and the absence of knowledge among workers, along with the lack of freedom, contribute to keeping poor countries poor. The box called Reaching Beyond Our Borders discusses the importance of freedom to economic development.

Entrepreneurship also makes some states and cities in the United States rich while others remain relatively poor. The business environment either encourages or discourages entrepreneurship. In the following section, we'll explore what makes up the business environment and how to build an environment that encourages growth and job creation.

Progress Assessment

- What are some of the advantages of working for others?
- Why is the United States called the land of opportunity?
- What are the five factors of production? Which factors are the key to wealth?

Reaching Beyond Our Borders

www.heritage.org

Freedom and Protective Laws Equal Prosperity

Recent studies have found that the freer a country is, the wealthier its citizens are. Freedom includes freedom from excess taxation, government regulations, and restrictions on trade. The average per capita gross domestic product (GDP)—the total value of all final goods and services produced divided by the number of people in the country—for the freest countries in the early 2000s was over $21,000. The freest countries are Hong Kong, Singapore, and New Zealand. The United States was tied for fourth with Ireland, the Netherlands, Luxembourg, and Estonia. For the least free, per capita GDP was under $3,000. The least free countries include North Korea, Iraq, Libya, Cuba, and Zimbabwe. As a country introduces more freedom, its economy also begins to grow.

The economic and legal environment therefore has much to do with a country's economic prosperity. More freedom equals more prosperity for all. Recently, for example, the Heritage Foundation (a conservative think tank) prepared an index that measures the impact of laws, regulations, and government policies on the economy. This index classifies the governments of Singapore and the United States as among the least restrictive and those of Russia and Cuba as the most restrictive. It may not be a coincidence, then, that Singapore and the United States are relatively wealthy countries and Russia and Cuba are not. Such figures show why businesses must work closely with government to minimize taxes, maximize economic freedom, and establish laws that protect businesspeople.

The legal environment of business is a critical part of any economic growth plan. That is why this text focuses on legal issues throughout. By reading about such issues in the context of various business functions, you will see how important the legal system is to business.

Sources: www.heritage.org/index/2001/chapters/execsum.html; "Profiles in Prosperity," *World,* June 15, 2002, pp. 70–71; Arch Puddington, "The Resilience of Global Freedom," *The Washington Times,* December 27, 2002, p. A21; and Steve Chapman, "Hopeful Signs in a Year That Was," *The Washington Times,* December 29, 2002, p. B1.

The Business Environment

business environment The surrounding factors that either help or hinder the development of businesses.

The **business environment** consists of the surrounding factors that either help or hinder the development of businesses. Figure 1.3 shows the five elements in the business environment:

1. The economic and legal environment.
2. The technological environment.
3. The competitive environment.
4. The social environment.
5. The global business environment.

Businesses grow and prosper in a healthy environment. The results are job growth and the wealth that makes it possible to have both a high standard of living and a high quality of life. The wrong environmental conditions, in contrast, lead to business failure, loss of jobs, and a low standard of living and quality of life. In short, creating the right business environment is the foundation for social progress of all kinds, including good schools, clean air and water, good health care, and low rates of crime.

The Economic and Legal Environment

People are willing to start new businesses if they believe that the risk of losing their money isn't too great. Part of that risk involves the economic system and how government works with or against businesses. Government can do a lot

FIGURE 1.3

TODAY'S DYNAMIC BUSINESS ENVIRONMENT

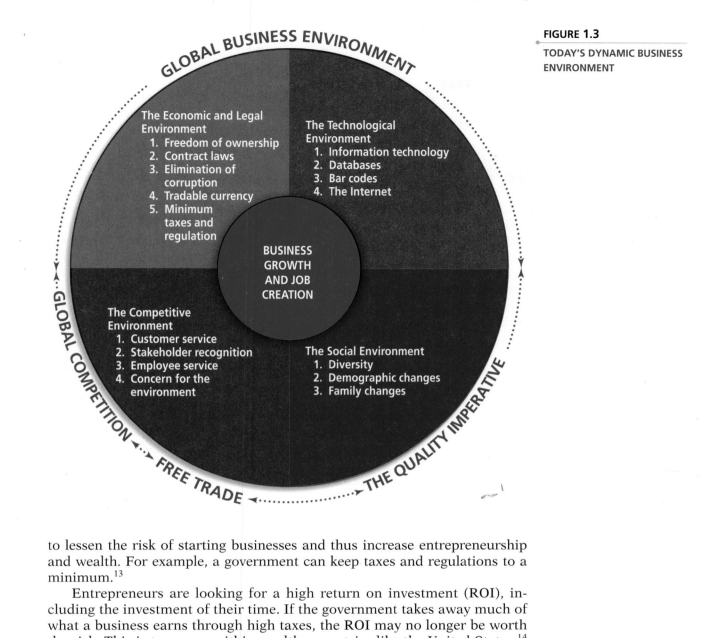

to lessen the risk of starting businesses and thus increase entrepreneurship and wealth. For example, a government can keep taxes and regulations to a minimum.[13]

Entrepreneurs are looking for a high return on investment (ROI), including the investment of their time. If the government takes away much of what a business earns through high taxes, the ROI may no longer be worth the risk. This is true even within wealthy countries like the United States.[14] States and cities that have high taxes and restrictive regulations tend to drive entrepreneurs out, while states and cities with low taxes and less restrictive regulations attract entrepreneurs. Laws that encourage entrepreneurship have been enacted all across the United States and the world. Some of the tax laws that help small businesses include the provisions for deducting home office expenses, business travel and meals, and other business expenses.

One way for government to actively promote entrepreneurship is to allow private ownership of businesses. In some countries, the government owns most businesses and thus there's little incentive for people to work hard or create profit. All around the world today, however, various countries in which the government formerly owned most businesses are selling those businesses to private individuals to create more wealth. One of the best things the governments of developing countries can do is to minimize the interference with the free exchange of goods and services. We shall discuss that issue in more depth in Chapter 2. Let's explore what else the government in developing countries can do to foster entrepreneurial growth.

Starting a business in some countries is much harder than in others. In India, for example, a person has to go through an extraordinary and time-consuming bureaucratic process to get permission to start a business—and with no certainty of success. Nonetheless, those businesses that do get started can become a major source of wealth and employment. This jewelry business is one small example. Can you imagine the opportunities and wealth that might be created with just a little more freedom in this country of over a billion people?

The government can lessen the risks of entrepreneurship by passing laws that enable businesspeople to write contracts that are enforceable in court. The Universal Commercial Code, for example, covers things like contracts and warranties. You will read more about such laws in the appendix to Chapter 4. In countries that don't yet have such laws, the risks of starting a business are that much greater.

The government can also establish a currency that's tradable in world markets. That is, you can buy and sell goods and services anywhere in the world using that currency.

The government can help minimize corruption in business and in its own ranks. It's hard to do business in many poor countries because the governments are so corrupt.[15] It's very difficult in such countries to get permission to build a factory or open a store without a government permit, which is obtained largely through bribery of public officials. Among businesses themselves, leaders can threaten competitors and minimize competition.

There are many laws in the United States to minimize corruption, and businesses can flourish as a result. Nonetheless, corrupt and illegal activities at some companies do negatively affect the business community and the economy as a whole. Examples include the Enron, Adelphia, WorldCom, Tyco, and ImClone scandals of recent years. The Enron scandal destroyed the company (and the pension funds of many who worked there), its accounting firm (Arthur Andersen), and other companies that had questionable accounting practices.

Bloomberg Personal Finance magazine reported that "one of the greatest threats to the U.S. economy . . . is the wholesale undermining of investor confidence in the stock market as a result of corporate deceptions like those of Enron." The box called Reaching Beyond Our Borders on p. 15 illustrates that these moral and ethical issues are global, not confined to the United States. Lapses in the ethical environment have placed new emphasis on laws restraining businesspeople from committing unethical and/or illegal acts. We will explore business ethics in depth in Chapter 4.

The capitalist system relies heavily on honesty, integrity, and high ethical standards.[16] Failure of those fundamentals can weaken the whole system; the faltering economy of the early 2000s was due in part to such failure. It is easy to see the damage caused by the poor moral and ethical behavior of some businesspeople. What is not so obvious is the damage caused by the moral and ethical lapses of the everyday consumer—that is, you and me. The Making Ethical Decisions box on p. 16 discusses that issue in more depth. We will be discussing ethics, morality, and related issues throughout the text, but we believe that the place to start is by reviewing our own personal behavior.

The Technological Environment

Since prehistoric times, humans have felt the need to create tools that make their jobs easier. Various tools and machines developed throughout history have changed the business environment tremendously, but few technological changes have had a more comprehensive and lasting impact on businesses than the emergence of information technology (IT): computers, modems, cellular phones, and so on. Chief among these developments is the Internet. Although many Internet firms have failed in recent years, the Internet will prove to be a major force in business in the coming years.[17] The Internet is such a major force in business today that we discuss its impact on businesses through-

Reaching Beyond Our Borders

www.bsr.org/

Ethics Lapses Are Global

So much is being reported about the legal and ethical problems among U.S. firms that one may think that the issues are largely domestic and don't extend to other countries. The truth is, however, that businesses throughout the world are facing the same examination and legislative reaction that has been occurring in the United States. Just about everywhere, the cry is for more clarity in accounting. This means making accounting records easier to read for the average investor. There is also a need for more checks and balances between management and boards of directors.

BusinessWeek

In Switzerland, major financial institutions such as UBS and Zurich Financial Services have suffered from questionable behavior attributed to the unchecked power of their executives and their indifference to shareholder rights. Scandinavian corporate practices have been scrutinized since ABB (an engineering firm) paid $89 million to its chief executive officer (CEO) when he left the firm. The collapse of many German firms, including the Kirsh media empire, is forcing a new look at corporate governance in Germany. French companies, including TotalFinaElf, are appointing independent directors and separating the duties of chairpeople and CEOs, as is being done in the United States.

In Hong Kong for the first time, certain types of financial wrongdoing, such as insider trading, are becoming criminal offenses. Again, similar changes are happening in the United States. Japan, Italy, and other countries could also be mentioned, but you get the idea. All over the world companies are being held to a higher standard because of some companies' lapses in corporate responsibility and behavior. The rules and regulations differ from country to country, but the goal is the same: to protect investors from questionable accounting practices and to force businesses to become more responsive to the public and more responsible for corporate behavior. *Business Week* issued a special report on corporate responsibility on May 6, 2002. We'll have *Business Week* boxes throughout the text to help tie what you learn in the classroom to what you can learn on your own from reading business periodicals.

Source: John Rossant, Jack Ewing, and Brian Bremmer, "The Corporate Cleanup Goes Global," *Business Week,* May 6, 2002, pp. 80–81.

out the text. In addition, we provide Internet exercises at the end of each chapter to give you some hands-on experience with various Internet uses.

How Technology Benefits Workers and You One of the advantages of working for others is that the company often provides the tools and technology to make your job more productive. **Technology** means everything from phones and copiers to computers, medical imaging devices, personal digital assistants, and the various software programs that make business processes more efficient and productive.[18] *Efficiency* means producing items using the least amount of resources. **Productivity** is the amount of output you generate given the amount of input (e.g., hours worked). The more you can produce in any given period of time, the more money you are worth to companies. Tools and technology greatly improve productivity. Such tools vary from hammers and saws to computer-aided design and computer-aided manufacturing machines and artificial intelligence.

technology
Everything from phones and copiers to computers, medical imaging devices, personal digital assistants, and the various software programs that make business processes more efficient and productive.

productivity
The amount of output you generate given the amount of input (e.g., hours worked).

Technology affects people in all industries. Take Barry Sonnenfeld, for example. He was the director of the movie *Men in Black 2.* He also was involved with films like *The Addams Family* and *Get Shorty.* Sonnenfeld does a lot of his work on the road. Therefore, he carries three cell phones, a Palm VII, a Palm V with wireless service, an IBM Thinkpad, and a pager that he also uses for e-mail. All these devices keep Sonnenfeld in contact with people all over the world and enable him to do other work whenever there is a break in the production process.[19]

Making Ethical Decisions

Ethics Begin with You

Television, movies, and the print media all paint a dismal picture of ethics among businesspeople, government officials, and citizens in general. It is easy to criticize the ethics of people whose names appear in the headlines. It is more difficult to see the moral and ethical misbehavior of your own social group. Do you find some of the behaviors of your friends morally or ethically questionable?

One of the major trends in business today is that many companies are creating ethics codes to guide their employees' behavior. We believe that this trend toward improving ethical behavior is so important that we've made it a major theme of this book. Throughout the text you'll see boxes, like this one, called Making Ethical Decisions. The boxes contain short descriptions of situations that pose ethical dilemmas and ask what you would do to resolve them. The idea is for you to think about the moral and ethical dimensions of every decision you make.

Here is your first ethical dilemma: Soon you will be taking exams in this course. Suppose you didn't prepare for one of the tests as thoroughly as you should have. As luck would have it, on exam day you are sitting in the desk right in front of the instructor, who has just happened to leave the answer key sticking out of her book. The instructor is called out of the room and everyone else is concentrating intently on his or her own work. No one will know if your eyes wander toward the answer key. A good grade on this test will certainly help your grade point average. What is the problem in this situation? What are your alternatives? What are the consequences of each alternative? Which alternative will you choose? Is your choice ethical?

Source: "What You Can Do to Help America," *Bottom Line Personal,* January 1, 2003, p. 2; and Walter B. Wriston, "A Code of Your Own," *The Wall Street Journal,* January 16, 2003, p. A12.

Farmers also are big on high tech. Don Glenn is a farmer in Decatur, Alabama. He uses his personal computer to compare data from last year's harvest with infrared satellite photos of his farm that show which crops are flourishing. He has a desktop terminal called a DTN that allows him to check the latest grain prices, and he uses AgTalk, a Web-based bulletin board, to converse with other farmers from all over the world. He also bids for bulk fertilizer on XSAg.com, an online agricultural exchange. High-tech equipment tells Glenn how and where to spread fertilizer and seed, tracks yields yard by yard, and allows him to maintain high profit margins.[20]

One reason that workers make more money in the United States than in most other countries is that they have access to the technologies that make them more productive. Other countries may have less expensive labor, but that labor is not always as productive as it could be. Top management should make sure that the company has the latest in technology and that its employees are trained to use it in order to stay competitive not only in the domestic market but in global markets as well.

e-commerce
The buying and selling of goods over the Internet.

The Growth of E-Commerce One of the major themes of this text is managing change.[21] There are special boxes called Dealing with Change throughout the text that discuss the rapidly changing business environment and the need to adjust to these changes. One of the more important changes of recent years is the growth of **e-commerce**, the buying and selling of goods over the Internet. There are two major types of e-commerce transactions: business-to-consumer (B2C) and business-to-business (B2B). As important as the Internet has been in the consumer market, it has become even more important in the B2B market, which consists of selling goods and services from one business to another, such as IBM selling consulting services to a local bank. B2B e-commerce is already at least five times as big as B2C e-commerce. While the potential of the B2C e-commerce market is measured in billions, B2B E-commerce is said to be measured in trillions of dollars.

Timken Company succeeded in the United States by building a highly sophisticated plant in Asheboro, North Carolina. The plant can manufacture small batches of industrial bearings without refitting machine tools between operations. High technology enables the company to stay in the United States and compete globally. That preserves jobs and helps create wealth for the local community. Are jobs in such plants likely to pay more or less than those in less sophisticated manufacturing plants?

The rise of Internet marketing came so fast and furious that it drew hundreds of competitors into the fray. Many of the new Internet companies failed. Companies such as Pets.com, CDnow, Internet Capital Group, Peapod, eToys, and Drkoop.com have failed entirely or seen their stock prices drop dramatically. Many B2B stocks experienced similar failures. There is no question that some Internet businesses will grow and prosper, but along the way there will continue to be lots of failures, just as there have been in traditional businesses.[22] Traditional businesses will have to learn how to deal with the new competition from B2B and B2C firms. See the Dealing with Change box on p. 19 for more about how businesses have adapted to e-commerce change. We will be discussing e-commerce throughout the text.

There once were dozens of automobile companies; almost all of them failed, and only a few large companies now dominate the auto industry. Similarly, success will come to those e-commerce businesses that offer quality products at good prices with great service. Many of those companies, such as Sears and General Electric, have combined their traditional brick-and-mortar operations with new Internet sites that make them more competitive.[23]

Using Technology to Be Responsive to Customers One of the major themes of this text is that businesses succeed or fail largely because of the way they treat their customers. The businesses that are most responsive to customer wants and needs will succeed, and those that do not respond to customers will not be as successful. One way traditional retailers can respond to the Internet revolution is to use technology to become much more responsive to customers. For example, businesses mark goods with Universal Product Codes (bar codes)—those series of lines and numbers that you see on most consumer packaged goods. Bar codes can be used to tell retailers what product you bought, in what size and color, and at what price. A scanner at the checkout counter can read that information and put it into a database.

A **database** is an electronic storage file where information is kept. One use of databases is to store vast amounts of information about consumers. For example, a retailer may ask for your name, address, and telephone number so that it can put you on its mailing list. The information you give the retailer is added to the database. Because companies routinely trade database information, many retailers know what you buy and from whom you buy it. Using that information, companies can send you catalogs and other direct mail advertising that offers the kind of products you might want, as indicated by your past purchases. The use of databases enables stores to carry only the merchandise that the local population wants. It also enables stores

database
An electronic storage file where information is kept; one use of databases is to store vast amounts of information about consumers.

Webvan like many other Internet firms, failed during the dot-com explosion in 2000–2002. It's not that the Internet does not provide an excellent opportunity to sell things. It does. But the cost of setting up distribution centers and delivery systems and satisfying customer concerns of not being able to see, touch, and examine products has proven too difficult for some businesses to overcome. Do you think most customers will eventually change their preference for shopping in stores?

to carry less inventory, saving them money. We will talk more about how technology helps identify and meet the needs of target markets in Chapters 13 and 15.

The Competitive Environment

Competition among businesses has never been greater than it is today. Some companies have found a competitive edge by focusing on quality. The goal for many companies is zero defects—no mistakes in making the product. Some companies, such as Motorola in the United States and Toyota in Japan, have come close to meeting that standard. However, simply making a high-quality product isn't enough to allow a company to stay competitive in world markets. Companies now have to offer both high-quality products and outstanding service at competitive prices (value). That is why General Motors (GM) is building automobile plants in Argentina, Poland, China, and Thailand. The strategies of combining excellence with low-cost labor and minimizing distribution costs have resulted in larger markets and potential long-term growth for GM. Figure 1.4 shows how competition has changed businesses from the traditional model to a new, world-class model.

Competing by Exceeding Customer Expectations Manufacturers and service organizations throughout the world have learned that today's customers are very demanding. Not only do they want good quality at low prices, but they want great service as well. In fact, some products in the 21st century will be designed to fascinate, bewitch, and delight customers, exceeding their expectations. Every manufacturing and service organization in the world should have a sign over its door telling its workers that the customer is king. Business is becoming customer-driven, not management-driven as in the past. This means that customers' wants and needs must come first.

FIGURE 1.4

HOW COMPETITION HAS CHANGED BUSINESS

TRADITIONAL BUSINESSES	WORLD-CLASS BUSINESSES
Customer satisfaction	Delighting the customer[1]
Customer orientation	Customer and stakeholder orientation[2]
Profit orientation	Profit and social orientation[3]
Reactive ethics	Proactive ethics[4]
Product orientation	Quality and service orientation
Managerial focus	Customer focus

[1] *Delight* is a term from total quality management. *Bewitch* and *fascinate* are alternative terms.

[2] Stakeholders include employees, stockholders, suppliers, dealers (retailers), and the community; the goal is to please *all* stakeholders.

[3] A social orientation goes beyond profit to do what is right and good for others.

[4] *Proactive* means doing the right thing before anyone tells you to do it. *Reactive* means responding to criticism after it happens.

Dealing with Change

www.ecommercetimes.com

Adjusting to the E-Commerce Era

One of the more significant changes occurring today is the movement toward doing business on the Internet. Many businesses are finding the new competition overwhelming. That includes, for example, traditional bookstores that now have to compete with eBay and Amazon.com. Who would have thought that garage sales would be done over the Internet? Or that cars or homes could be sold online? What is this e-commerce revolution and why is it happening now? That is, what are the advantages of e-commerce that other businesses have to accept and incorporate into their long-term strategies?

Businesses are lured to e-commerce by a number of factors, including, but not limited to:

- *Less investment in land, buildings, and equipment.* E-commerce firms can usually sell things for less because they don't have to invest as much in buildings (bricks), and can reach people inexpensively over the Internet (clicks).
- *Low transaction costs.* The automation of customer service lowers costs, which may make it possible for a company to offer products at a lower price. Also, there are no sales taxes (yet) on the Internet, so everything is a little less expensive than in stores.
- *Large purchases per transaction.* Online stores like Amazon.com often make personalized recommendations to customers that increase their order size.
- *Integration of business processes.* The Internet offers companies the ability to make more information available to customers than ever before. For example, a computer company that tracks each unit through the manufacturing and shipping process can allow customers to see exactly where the order is at any time. This is what overnight package delivery company Federal Express did when it introduced online package tracking.
- *Larger catalogs.* Amazon.com offers a catalog of 3 million books on the Internet. Imagine fitting a paper catalog that size in your mailbox!
- *Flexibility.* Successful websites are not just glorified mail-order catalogs. The Internet offers companies the ability to configure products and build custom orders, to compare prices between multiple vendors easily, and to search large catalogs quickly.
- *Improved customer interactions.* Online tools allow businesses to interact with customers in ways unheard of before, and at almost instant speeds. For example, customers can receive automatic e-mails to confirm orders and to notify them when orders are shipped.

Despite these many benefits, Internet-based companies have not captured the retail market as expected. Instead, traditional retail stores have adapted to the changing environment and have used the Internet to supplement their traditional stores. The combination of e-commerce with traditional stores is called click-and-brick retailing, for obvious reasons. The top 20 online sellers are names that are quite familiar to most students. They include Dell, Sears, Best Buy, Office Depot, QVC, JCPenney, Staples, and Victoria's Secret. Four years after going online, Victoria's Secret sold about a third of its goods on the Internet.

Two companies have done quite well as Web-only firms: eBay and Amazon.com. We chose Meg Whitman of eBay for the opening profile in this chapter because of her outstanding success in this field.

Sources: "Cornering the Retail Market," *Washington Post,* June 6, 2002, pp. E1, E6; Don Steinberg, "The Ultimate Technology Survival Guide," *SmartBusiness,* February 2002, pp. 37–49; Ruth P. Stevens, "On e*Sale Here," *1to1 Magazine,* September 2002, pp. 43–46; and Maryanne Murray Buechner, "Cruising the Online Mall," *Time,* April 2003.

Customer-driven organizations include Nordstrom department stores (they have a very generous return policy, for example) and Disney amusement parks (the parks are kept clean and appeal to all ages). Moto Photo does its best to please customers with fast, friendly service. Such companies can successfully compete against Internet firms if they continue to offer better and friendlier service. Successful organizations must now listen more closely to customers to determine their wants and needs, then adjust the firm's products, policies, and practices to meet those demands. We will explore these concepts in more depth in Chapter 13.

One company that competes with speed is Sterling Autobody Centers. Chief executive officer John McNeill (the man pictured) once had to wait two months to get his damaged car repaired. Rather than get angry, he saw an opportunity and opened a chain of car-repair centers that guaranteed fast service. His concept and company was so successful that Allstate, the nation's second largest insurer, recently purchased it. What businesses in your area could you challenge by providing faster, better service?

Competing with Speed Have you noticed how everyone seems to be in more of a hurry today? Well, the truth is that most people do live at a fast pace, and businesses need to respond or risk losing their business. For example, companies used to say, "Allow six weeks for delivery." Today, many customers want things delivered in two days or less. That's why FedEx and other high-speed delivery firms are doing so well. Most of today's consumers want fast food, fast delivery, fast responses to Internet searches, and so on. Usually, the companies that provide speedy service are those that are winning. Speed isn't everything, however. It has to be accompanied by good quality and reasonable prices, for example. Some consumers may prefer less speed and more helpful service or less speed and lower prices.

Businesses are demanding fast service from other businesses. The old saying "Time is money" has taken on new importance. The *Harvard Business Review* reports that not since the Industrial Revolution have the stakes of dealing with change been so high. In a marketplace that wants things to happen faster every day, the battle more often than not is going to the swiftest competitor, not necessarily the biggest, strongest, or even the shrewdest. Some small companies have made speedy response the core of their business. That means coming up with new products faster than before and producing those products faster as well. It also means speedy service. We'll explore production and operations management further in Chapter 9.

To keep up in such a dynamic business environment, people have to return to school periodically over their lifetime to learn the latest concepts, strategies, and tools. In response, schools have made it easier to take courses at night and on weekends. Master of business administration (MBA) programs have been shortened and businesspeople are being given credit for on-the-job experience so that completion of the program goes faster. Community colleges have been very responsive to the needs of students at all stages of their careers, offering courses and schedules that fit the lifestyle of today's busy workers. That includes courses on the Internet and distance learning courses students can take from remote sites.

Competing by Restructuring and Empowerment To meet the needs of customers, firms must give their frontline workers (office clerks, front-desk people at hotels, salespeople, etc.) the responsibility, authority, freedom, training, and equipment they need to respond quickly to customer requests and to make other decisions essential to producing quality goods and providing good service. This is called **empowerment**, and we'll be talking about that process throughout this book. To

empowerment
Giving frontline workers the responsibility, authority, and freedom to respond quickly to customer requests.

implement a policy of empowerment, managers must train frontline people to make decisions without the need to consult managers. The new role of supervisors, then, is to support frontline people with training and the technology to do their jobs well, including handling customer complaints quickly and satisfactorily.

In this chapter, we simply want to acknowledge that many businesses must reorganize to make their employees more effective than they are now. Many firms have done so by forming cross-functional teams—that is, teams made up of people from various departments, such as design, production, and marketing. These teams have learned to work without close supervision; thus, they are often called self-managed cross-functional teams.

One aspect of empowerment has been the elimination of managers. Companies that have implemented self-managed teams expect a lot more from their lower-level workers than they did in the past and can therefore do without various levels of managers. Because they have less management oversight, such workers need more education. Furthermore, empowered employees need to be treated more as partners in the firm. Increasingly, managers' jobs will be to train, support, coach, and motivate lower-level employees. As many companies have discovered, it sometimes takes years to restructure an organization so that managers are willing to give up some of their authority and employees are willing to assume more responsibility.

Employees with increased responsibility are likely to demand increased compensation based on performance. Often, in larger firms, that will mean giving employees not only higher pay but partial ownership of the firm as well. It will also mean developing entirely new organizational structures to meet the changing needs of customers and employees. We'll discuss such organizational changes and models in Chapter 8.

Progress Assessment

- What are four ways the government can foster entrepreneurship?
- What is productivity and how does technology enhance it?
- How can companies compete with speed?

The Social Environment

Demography is the statistical study of the human population with regard to its size, density, and other characteristics such as age, race, gender, and income. In this book, we're particularly interested in the demographic trends that most affect businesses and career choices. The U.S. population is going through major changes that are dramatically affecting how people live, where they live, what they buy, and how they spend their time. Furthermore, tremendous population shifts are leading to new opportunities for some firms and to declining opportunities for others.

demography
The statistical study of the human population with regard to its size, density, and other characteristics such as age, race, gender, and income.

Managing Diversity An increasing percentage of the U.S. population in the future will be minorities—by the year 2050, non-Hispanic whites will be a slim majority. Over 24 percent will be Hispanic.[24] In 2000, there were about 10.6 million citizens of Asian descent in the United States; by 2006, that number should increase to about 12.8 million. The equivalent change for whites will be from about 197 million to 199 million; for African Americans, from about 36.2 million to 38 million; and for Hispanics, from about 37 million to 39.3 million.[25]

Companies have responded to this diverse customer base by hiring a more diverse workforce to serve them. Texas-based SBC Communications Inc., for example, is one of the largest data communications companies in the world.

One of the strengths of the United States is its ability to welcome people from all over the world and help them prosper. Most of them would support the notion that the United States is still "the land of opportunity" for all. This photo shows a diversity conference. Such conferences often help people with different backgrounds and opinions to be heard and to listen to and learn from others. What are some of the diversity issues in your community?

The company's workforce is 51 percent female and 34 percent people of color; people of color represent 26 percent of SBC's management team. The company also spends over 21 percent of its procurement dollars with diversity suppliers (that is, suppliers owned by minorities).[26] More than 75 percent of Fortune 1000 companies have some sort of diversity initiative. Some, like BellSouth and Kodak, have a chief diversity officer (CDO) in the executive suite. In short, companies are taking diversity management seriously.

Diversity has come to mean much more than recruiting and keeping minorities and women. Many more groups are now included in diversity efforts. The list of 26 diversity groups identified by Federated Department Stores includes seniors, the disabled, homosexuals, atheists, extroverts, introverts, married people, singles, and the devout.[27] Sometimes the issue is a difference in ages.[28] In the book *Generations at Work,* the authors state, "The boomers [those people born between 1946 and 1964] say the Generation Xers [those born between 1965 and 1980] are slackers, whiners; they're rude, they lack social skills, and they always want to buck the system, and they don't want to spend time in the ranks. And the Xers say the boomers are self-righteous: they're workaholics, they're more interested in politics than results, they talk a good talk but don't practice what they preach."[29] You can imagine the conflicts that may develop between these two groups at work. The management of diverse groups—whether they are different because of race, sex, age, sexual orientation, country of origin, religion, or some other classification—can be difficult. It gets even more difficult as managers go overseas and must respond to all the cultural, political, and social issues that are peculiar to each country. Nonetheless, companies such as IBM, Continental Airlines, Ford, and Hyatt all believe that they are more successful and more profitable because of their diversity initiatives.

The Increase in the Number of Older Americans By 2030, the baby boomers will be senior citizens. People ages 45 to 54 are currently the richest group in U.S. society. They have a median income of $55,917.[30] They spend more than others on everything except health care and thus represent a lucrative market for restaurants, transportation, entertainment, education, and so on.

There are now nearly 46 million citizens ages 60 and above. By 2010, that number will increase to about 56 million, and by 2020, there will be more than 74 million people over the age of 60 (23 percent of the total population).[31] What do such demographics mean for you and for businesses in the future? Think of the products and services the middle-aged and elderly will need—travel, medicine,

Entrepreneurship is an exciting way to make a living, but working for a big company can be equally rewarding. These employees of SAS, a software design firm located in North Carolina, are enjoying the company swimming pool—just one of the many employee benefits the company sponsors. Other firms provide indoor tracks, weight rooms, employee cafeterias, and corporate retreats. Which would you prefer: starting your own business or working for a larger firm with an employee benefits program?

nursing homes, assisted-living facilities, adult day care, home health care, recreation, and the like—and you'll see opportunities for successful businesses of the 21st century. Businesses that cater to the aging baby boomers will have the opportunity for exceptional growth in the near future. For example, there are lots of computer games for young people, but senior citizens may enjoy playing games and doing other things on the computer as well. The market could be huge.

Two-Income Families Several factors have led to a dramatic growth in two-income families in the United States. The high costs of housing and of maintaining a comfortable lifestyle, the high level of taxes, and the cultural emphasis on "having it all" have made it difficult if not impossible for many households to live on just one income. Furthermore, many women today simply want a career outside the home.

One result of this trend is a host of programs that companies have implemented in response to the demands of busy two-income families. IBM and Procter & Gamble, for example, each offer employees pregnancy benefits, parental leave, flexible work schedules, and elder care programs. Some companies offer referral services that provide counseling to parents in search of child care or elder care. Such trends are creating many new opportunities for graduates in human resource management.[32]

Many employers provide child care benefits of some type; some of these programs, such as the one at S. C. Johnson & Son, are on-site. Corporate day care centers are expensive to operate and often cause resentment from employees who don't use the benefits. The resentment has led companies to offer what are called cafeteria-style benefits packages, which enable families to choose from a menu of benefits. A couple may choose day care instead of a dental plan, for instance.

Many companies are increasing the number of part-time workers. This enables mothers and fathers to stay home part of the day with children and still earn income. Some companies allow workers to telecommute, which means they work from home and keep in touch with the company through telecommunications (telephone, fax, e-mail, etc.). This lowers the company's cost for office space and also makes it possible for parents to meet the demands of both job and family.

Workplace changes due to the rise of two-income families create many job opportunities in day care, counseling, and other related fields. You'll learn more about what's happening in human resource management in Chapter 11.

Single Parents The rapid growth of single-parent households has had a major effect on businesses as well. It is a tremendous task to work full-time and raise a family. Welfare rules force single parents to work after a certain period. Single parents have encouraged businesses to implement programs such as family leave (where workers can take time off to attend to a sick child) and flextime (where workers can come in or leave at selected times). Again, you will be able to read about such programs in more detail in Chapter 11.

The Global Environment

The global environment of business is so important that we show it as surrounding all other environmental influences (see again Figure 1.3). Two important environmental changes in recent years have been the growth of international competition and the increase of free trade among nations. Japanese manufacturers like Honda, Mitsubishi, and Sony won much of the market for automobiles, videocassette recorders, digital video disk players, television sets, and other products by offering global consumers products of higher quality than those made by U.S. manufacturers. This competition hurt many U.S. industries, and many jobs were lost. Recently, U.S. businesses have become more competitive and Japan's economy is now suffering.

Today, manufacturers in countries such as China, India, South Korea, and Mexico can produce high-quality goods at low prices because their workers are paid less money than U.S. workers and because they've learned quality concepts from Japanese, German, and U.S. producers. Late in the 1990s, however, Thailand, Malaysia, Hong Kong, Japan, South Korea, and other Asian countries had banking problems that caused a major upheaval in global markets. These problems affected all nations, showing the interdependence of countries around the world today.

Better technology, machinery, tools, education, and training enable each worker to be more productive. U.S. companies such as Disney, FedEx, Intel, and Microsoft, as well as many smaller companies, are as good or better than competing organizations anywhere in the world. But some businesses have gone beyond simply competing with organizations in other countries by learning to cooperate with international firms. Cooperation among businesses has the potential to create rapidly growing world markets that can generate prosperity beyond most people's expectations. The challenge is tremendous, but so is the will to achieve. You'll read much more about the importance of global business in Chapter 3.

War and Terrorism Few recent events have had a bigger effect on U.S. businesses than the terrorist attacks on the World Trade Center and the Pentagon on September 11, 2001 (now known as 9/11). One of the obvious effects was on the travel industry; after 9/11 some people were afraid to fly, and this fear affected not only the airlines but also hotels, amusement parks, restaurants, and more. The impact was even felt by companies like Boeing, which sells planes to the airline industry.[33] Prior to 9/11, the stock market had already suffered a decline; the drop-off in business that followed the attacks only added to the woes.

The threat of terrorism adds greatly to organizational costs, including the cost of security personnel, security equipment, and insurance (firms are finding it difficult to get insurance against terrorist attacks). Airlines, for example, have had to install stronger cockpit doors, buy more security equipment, and hire new security personnel. The U.S. government has also experienced huge cost increases because of homeland security issues.[34]

The war in Iraq that began in March 2003 and ongoing threats of war in various parts of the world have had a major impact on businesses everywhere. Some businesses, like the defense industry (i.e., businesses that make bombs and other war materials), stand to gain profits. Others will suffer losses. Since

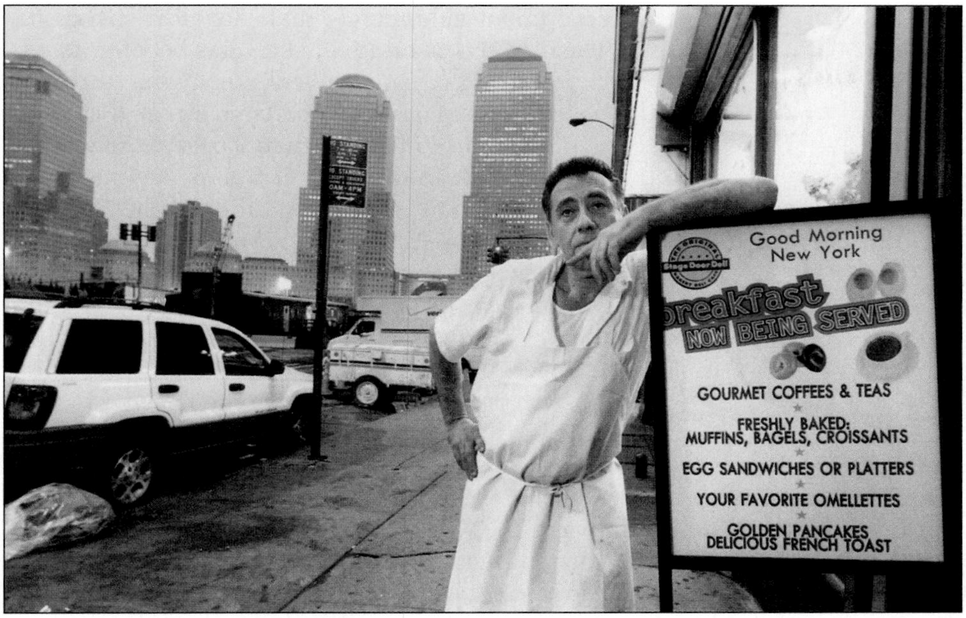

Pete Travos came to the United States from the Greek island of Kefalonia. He opened a deli in New York across from the World Trade Center. When terrorists destroyed the Center they impacted hundreds of businesses that catered to its workers. By closing earlier and making other cutbacks, Travos hopes to survive and serve the tenants when the new buildings are finished, but that's a long way off. As this example illustrates, entrepreneurship is fraught with some unforeseen challenges.

President George W. Bush said that the war on terrorism will last a long time, there is some doubt whether the U.S. business sector will experience growth comparable to that of the 1990s for many years to come. Only time will tell.

How Global Changes Affect You In the long run, there is every hope for a resurgence of global trade. As businesses expand to serve global markets, new jobs will be created in both manufacturing and service industries. U.S. exports are expected to continue to increase under new trade agreements that will lead to expansion of the job market both in the United States and globally. Global trade also means global competition. The students who will prosper are those who are prepared for the markets of tomorrow. That means that you must prepare yourself now to compete in a rapidly changing worldwide environment. Rapid changes create a need for continuous learning. In other words, be prepared to continue your education throughout your career. Colleges will offer updated courses in computer technology, telecommunications, language skills, and other subjects you'll need to stay competitive. Students have every reason to be optimistic about job opportunities in the future if they prepare themselves well.

The Evolution of American Business

Many managers and workers are losing their jobs in major manufacturing firms. Businesses in the United States have become so productive that, compared to the past, fewer workers are needed in industries that produce goods. **Goods** are tangible products such as computers, food, clothing, cars, and appliances. Due to the increasing impact of technology and global competition, shouldn't we be concerned about the prospect of high unemployment rates and low incomes? Where will the jobs be when you graduate? These important questions force us all to look briefly at the U.S. economy and its future.

goods
Tangible products such as computers, food, clothing, cars, and appliances.

Progress in the Agricultural and Manufacturing Industries

The United States has seen strong economic development since the 1800s. The agricultural industry led the way, providing food for the United States and much of the world. Cyrus McCormick's invention of the harvester in 1834 and other inventions, such as the cotton gin, and modern improvements on such

Agriculture is one of the largest and most important industries in the United States. Use of technology has led to increased productivity and made farmers more efficient, resulting in larger farms. This trend has meant less expensive food for us, but a continual reduction in the number of small, family-run farms. Is it still possible for small farms to be successful, and if so, how?

equipment did much to make farming successful. The modern farming industry has become so efficient through the use of technology that the number of farmers has dropped from about 33 percent of the population to less than 2 percent. The number of farms in the United States declined from some 5.7 million at the beginning of the 20th century to under 2 million today. However, average farm size is now about 455 acres versus 160 acres in the past. In other words, agriculture is still a major industry in the United States. What has changed is that the millions of small farms that existed previously have been replaced by some huge farms, some merely large farms, and some small but highly specialized farms. The loss of farmworkers over the past century is not a negative sign. It is instead an indication that U.S. agricultural workers are the most productive in the world.

Most farmers who lost their jobs went to work in factories. The manufacturing industry, much like agriculture, used technology to become more productive. As you read earlier, that productivity was due to tools and machines. The consequence, as in farming, was the elimination of many jobs. Again, the loss to society is minimal if the wealth created by increased productivity and efficiency creates new jobs elsewhere—and that's exactly what has happened over the past 50 years. Many workers in the industrial sector found jobs in the service sector. Most of those who can't find work today are people who need retraining and education to become qualified for jobs that now exist. We'll discuss the manufacturing sector and production in more detail in Chapter 9.

Progress in Service Industries

services
Intangible products (i.e., products that can't be held in your hand) such as education, health care, insurance, recreation, and travel and tourism.

As noted above, many workers who could no longer find employment in manufacturing were able to find jobs in the service industry. **Services** are intangible products (i.e., products that can't be held in your hand) such as education, health care, insurance, recreation, and travel and tourism. In the past, the dominant industries in the United States produced goods (steel, railroads, machine tools, etc.). Today, the leading firms are in services (legal, health, telecommunications, entertainment, financial, etc.). Together, services make up more than half of the American economy.[35] Since the mid-1980s, the service industry has generated almost all of the U.S. economy's increases in employment. Although service-sector growth has slowed, it remains the largest area of growth. Chances are very high that you'll work in a service job at some point in your career. Figure 1.5 lists many service-sector jobs; look it over to see where the careers of the future are likely to be. Retailers like Gap are part of the service sector. Each new retail store creates many managerial jobs for college graduates.

Another bit of good news is that there are more high-paying jobs in the service sector than in the goods-producing sector. High-paying service-sector jobs can be found in health care, accounting, finance, entertainment, telecommunications, architecture, law, and software engineering. Projections are that some areas of the service sector will grow rapidly, while others may have much slower growth. The strategy for college graduates is to remain flexible, to find out where the jobs are being created, and to move when appropriate.

Your Future in Business

Despite the growth in the service sector described above, the service era now seems to be coming to a close as a new era is beginning. We're now in the midst of an information-based global revolution that will alter all sectors of

There's much talk about the service sector, but few discussions actually list what it includes. Here's a representative list of services as classified by the government:

LODGING SERVICES

Hotels, rooming houses, and other lodging places
Sporting and recreation camps
Trailer parks and camp sites for transients

PERSONAL SERVICES

Laundries	Child care
Linen supply	Shoe repair
Diaper service	Funeral homes
Carpet cleaning	Tax preparation
Photographic studios	Beauty shops
Health clubs	

BUSINESS SERVICES

Accounting	Exterminating
Ad agencies	Employment agencies
Collection agencies	Computer programming
Commercial photography	Research and development labs
Commercial art	Management services
Stenographic services	Public relations
Window cleaning	Detective agencies
Consulting	Interior design
Equipment rental	

AUTOMOTIVE REPAIR SERVICES AND GARAGES

Auto rental	Tire retreading
Truck rental	Exhaust system shops
Parking lots	Car washes
Paint shops	Transmission repair

MISCELLANEOUS REPAIR SERVICES

Radio and television	Welding
Watch	Sharpening
Reupholstery	Septic tank cleaning

MOTION PICTURE INDUSTRY

Production	Theaters
Distribution	Drive-ins

AMUSEMENT AND RECREATION SERVICES

Dance halls	Racetracks
Symphony orchestras	Golf courses
Pool halls	Amusement parks
Bowling alleys	Carnivals
Fairs	Ice skating rinks
Botanical gardens	Circuses
Video rentals	Infotainment

HEALTH SERVICES

Physicians	Nursery care
Dentists	Medical labs
Chiropractors	Dental labs

LEGAL SERVICES

EDUCATIONAL SERVICES

Libraries	Correspondence schools
Schools	Data processing schools

SOCIAL SERVICES

Child care	Family services
Job training	

NONCOMMERCIAL MUSEUMS, ART GALLERIES, AND BOTANICAL AND ZOOLOGICAL GARDENS

SELECTED MEMBERSHIP ORGANIZATIONS

Business associations	Civic associations

FINANCIAL SERVICES

Banking	Real estate agencies
Insurance	Investment firms (brokers)

MISCELLANEOUS SERVICES

Architectural	Surveying
Engineering	Utilities
Telecommunications	

FIGURE 1.5

WHAT IS THE SERVICE SECTOR?

the economy: agricultural, industrial, and service. It's exciting to think about the role you'll play in that revolution. You may be a leader; that is, you may be one of the people who will implement the changes and accept the challenges of world competition based on world quality standards. This book will introduce you to some of the concepts that will make such leadership possible.

Remember that most of the concepts and principles that make businesses more effective and efficient are applicable in government agencies and nonprofit organizations as well. This is an introductory business text, so we'll tend to focus on business. Nonetheless, we'll remind you periodically that you can apply these concepts in other areas. Business can't prosper in the future without the cooperation of government and social leaders throughout the world.

Progress Assessment

- What are some of the diverse groups of people that managers must manage?
- What are the factors that have led to two-income families?
- What is the major factor that caused people to move from farming to industry and from industry to the service sector?

Summary

1. Describe the relationship of businesses' profit to risk assumption and discuss how businesses and nonprofit organizations add to the standard of living and quality of life for all.

1. A business is any activity that seeks to provide goods and services to others while operating at a profit.
   - ***What are the relationships between risk, profit, and loss?***

   Profit is money a business earns above and beyond the money that it spends for salaries and other expenses. Businesspeople make profits by taking risks. *Risk* is the chance an entrepreneur takes of losing time and money on a business that may not prove profitable. A loss occurs when a business's costs and expenses are more than its revenues.

   How do businesses add to the standard of living and quality of life of a community?

   Businesses and their employees create the wealth that people use to buy goods and services. Businesses, through taxes, also are the source of funds for government agencies and nonprofit organizations that help improve the quality of life of society. *Quality of life* refers to the general well-being of a country's people in terms of political freedom, a clean natural environment, safety, education, health care, free time, and other things that lead to satisfaction and joy. Thus, businesses may add to both the quality of life and standard of living of society by creating the wealth needed to fund progress in those areas.
   - ***What groups are considered stakeholders, and which stakeholders are most important to a business?***

   Stakeholders include customers, employees, stockholders, suppliers, dealers, bankers, people in the local community, environmentalists, and elected government leaders. The goal of business leaders is to try to balance the needs of all these stakeholders and still make a profit. Some businesses put the needs of stockholders above the other interests, but most businesses today seek a balance among the needs of the various stakeholders.

2. Explain the importance of entrepreneurship to the wealth of an economy.

2. Entrepreneurs are people who risk time and money to start and manage a business.
   - ***What importance does entrepreneurship hold in the list of the five factors of production?***

   Businesses use five factors of production: land (natural resources), labor (workers), capital (buildings and machinery), entrepreneurship, and knowledge. Of these, the most important are entrepreneurship and knowledge (managed information) because without them land, labor, and capital are not of much use.

3. Economic factors affect business by increasing or decreasing the risks of starting a business.
   - ***What are some things that the government in developing countries can do to lessen the risk of starting businesses?***

   The government may allow private ownership of businesses, pass laws that enable businesspeople to write contracts that are enforceable in court, establish a currency that's tradable in world markets, help to lessen corruption in business and government, and keep taxes and regulations to a minimum. From a business perspective, lower taxes mean lower risks, more growth, and thus more money for workers and the government.

3. Examine how the economic environment and taxes affect businesses.

4. Adapting to technological change is one of the most important tasks of management.
   - ***How has technology benefited workers, businesses, and consumers?***

   Technology enables workers to be more productive. For example, computer-aided design and computer-aided manufacturing makes design and manufacturing workers much more productive (that is, they produce more per hour of work). Information technology (computers, modems, cellular phones, etc.) is used by business to monitor the business environment so that firms can quickly adapt to changing conditions. Technology has also made it possible for businesses to become much more responsive to consumers.

4. Illustrate how the technological environment has affected businesses.

5. Competition among businesses has never been greater than it is today.
   - ***What are some ways in which businesses meet and beat competition?***

   Some companies found a competitive edge in the 1980s by focusing on making high-quality products. By the early 1990s, meeting the challenge of making a quality product was not enough to stay competitive in world markets. Companies had to offer quality products and outstanding service at competitive prices (value). The speed of new product development, production, delivery, and service is also critical. Companies aim to exceed customer expectations. Often that means empowering frontline workers by giving them more training and more responsibility and authority. It also means restructuring the firm to create more teams.

5. Identify various ways in which businesses can meet and beat competition.

6. The United States is going through a social revolution that's having a dramatic impact on how people live, where they live, what they buy, and how they spend their time.
   - ***How have such social changes affected businesses?***

   Changes in society are resulting in new opportunities for some firms and declining opportunities for others. Moreover, a diverse population challenges businesses to manage a diverse workforce. Diversity groups include minorities, women, homosexuals, single people, older people, and young new hires. As more women have entered the labor force, companies have implemented a variety of programs to assist two-income and single-parent families. Many employers provide child care benefits of some type to keep their valued employees. The biggest threat to business may be the loss of trust caused by scandals such as the Enron case and the mistrust of the accounting firms responsible for monitoring the books of companies.

6. Demonstrate how the social environment has changed and tell what the reaction of the business community has been.

7. War and terrorism have changed the international environment of business tremendously.
   - ***What will be the impacts of such threats?***

   Some businesses, such as those that produce bombs and other war materials, may prosper. Others, such as tourism, may suffer.

7. Analyze what businesses must do to meet the global challenge, which includes war and terrorism.

8. Review how trends from the past are being repeated in the present and what such trends will mean for the service sector.

8. The United States has matured from an economy based on industry to one based on services and from one dominated by domestic issues to one dominated by global issues.
   - ***What do these trends mean for tomorrow's graduates?***

   Check over Figure 1.5, which outlines the service sector. That is where you are most likely to find the fast-growing firms of the future.
   - ***What is the history of our economic development in the United States, and what does it tell us about the future?***

   What has sustained the United States as the world's economic leader is the development and use of technology to improve productivity. The agricultural sector, for example, has been able to produce more food with fewer workers. Displaced agricultural workers eventually went to work in factories, producing more industrial goods. Improved productivity resulting from technology and increased competition from foreign firms combined to reduce the need for factory workers and contributed to the development of a service economy in the United States. The service era is now giving way to an information-based global revolution that will affect all sectors of the economy. The secret to long-term success in such an economy is flexibility and continuing education to be prepared for the opportunities that are sure to arise.

Key Terms

business 4
business environment 12
database 17
demography 21
e-commerce 16
empowerment 20
entrepreneur 4
factors of production 10
goods 25
loss 5
nonprofit organization 7
productivity 15
profit 4
quality of life 6
revenue 5
risk 5
services 26
stakeholders 6
standard of living 5
technology 15

Developing Workplace Skills

1. This text describes the growth trend in the numbers of businesses in the service sector. Look through your local Yellow Pages or go on the Internet to find and list five businesses that provide services in your area. This text also describes how certain demographic and social changes affect businesses. For each of the local service businesses on your list, describe how social trends might affect it. Include both negative effects and positive effects. Be prepared to explain your answers.

2. What are some of the signs that people in the United States have a high standard of living? What are some signs that such a high standard of living may be negatively affecting their quality of life?

3. Make a list of nonprofit organizations in your community that might offer you a chance to learn some of the skills you'll need in the job you hope to have when you graduate. How could you make time in your schedule to volunteer or work at one or more of those organizations? Write a letter to a nonprofit organization to inquire about such opportunities.

4. Use a computer word processing program to write a one-page report on how technology will change society in the next 10 years. Use a computer graphics program to create a chart (or draw a chart by hand) that illustrates the increased use of personal computers in American homes since 1980.

5. Form into teams of four or five and discuss the technological and e-commerce revolutions. How many students now shop for goods and services online? What have been their experiences? What other high-tech equipment do they use (e.g., cell phones, pagers, laptop computers, desktop computers, personal digital assistants, portable music players)?

Taking It To The Net

This exercise requires using the Internet. If you do not know how to navigate this powerful computer network, you need to read "Surfing the Internet" in the Getting Ready for Prime Time section.

Purpose

To gather data regarding trends in population and the social environment and to analyze how these changes affect American businesses.

Exercise

1. Select the Population Clock from the Census Bureau's homepage at www.census.gov. Record the time and population for the United States.
2. The U.S. Commerce Department conducts an economic census every five years (in years ending with 2 and 7). How do businesses use the information gathered in this census? To help answer this question, click on Economic Census, then click on Slide Shows. There you'll find a slide show that reviews the scope and use of the economic census. (Hint: Be sure to scroll down to read the notes that explain each slide). What are the three major ways businesses use the economic census data explained in the slide show?
3. Return to the U.S. Census Bureau's homepage. What is the population of the nation right now? Has the population changed since you started this exercise? If so, how? What does this tell you about the U.S. population? How could businesses use this information?

Casing The Web

To access the case "Moving Up the Corporate Ladder," visit

www.mhhe.com/ub7e

Video Case

Toying with Success: The McFarlane Companies

In his school days, Todd McFarlane had dreams of playing major league baseball. Unfortunately, his dream didn't come true. So like most of us, he put his dreams aside and decided that he had to get a job and make a living. But McFarlane did not want to just go to "work" every day; he wanted to do something he enjoyed. As a teen, he liked to draw superheroes. He developed his drawing skill throughout high school and college and began to send out samples of his work, lots of samples. Alas, he got lots of rejections until finally someone offered him a job.

McFarlane's first job was working freelance on obscure comic books for Marvel Comics, the biggest name in the comic book industry. By working relentlessly and turning his high-quality work in on time, McFarlane earned a reputation as a good worker. That reputation earned him the right to work a little on well-known comics like Batman, the Hulk, and Spiderman. He brought

Spiderman from relative obscurity to the number one book with record sales. Over time, he became the highest paid comic book artist at Marvel.

McFarlane began to feel a bit cramped and held back by the way things were done at Marvel. He had many ideas he wanted to try, but was discouraged by the lack of excitement at the company. He decided it was time to quit and start his own comic book business. He was able to persuade several of his best co-workers to come with him.

Many insiders in the comic book industry gave his new company one year at best. McFarlane believed failure was out of the question and he did anything but fail. His first comic, Spawn, sold 1.7 million copies—the rest was history. Today, when it comes to creating comics, producing movies, directing music videos, and running one of the most successful toy companies in the world, McFarlane has done it all. His path to success was similar to other entrepreneurs who learned about their business working for a large company. Chapter 1 shows that the energy and the risk-taking these entrepreneurs apply to the task is what creates jobs and wealth.

Entrepreneurs like McFarlane, however, face many challenges in the business environment: economic, technological, competitive, social, and global. For example, he owes some of his success to a legal system that protects his intellectual property and allows him to make contracts that are enforceable. He also takes advantage of the latest in technology to push creativity forward in making toys, movies, and video games. The Internet provides a means to reach the young people who are his key customers. Competitively, McFarlane loves to see competitors turn out shoddy goods because it provides an opportunity for him to make high-quality toys and other products that may cost more, but are well worth the extra few cents. It's impossible to avoid social issues like dock strikes and global problems like diseases that hold up production. The key is to keep focused and keep business going.

What about his major league dreams? Part of McFarlane's dream started coming true when he bought Mark McGuire's record-breaking 70th home run ball. It cost him a cool $3 million! To his chagrin the record was broken the next year by Barry Bonds. But McFarlane did not give up. Combining it with other McGuire and Sammy Sosa balls he had purchased, he formed the McFarlane collection and sent it on a tour of every major league stadium. The payoff was good public relations for his firm and the development of a relationship with people in professional sports and management that led to licensing rights to produce major league toys. The $3 million ball may lead to $20 million in profit. Did his dreams come true? He doesn't have a baseball career, but every toy contract with a major league team includes what you might call a signing bonus: the right for McFarlane to hit batting practice in every ballpark that shows his collection. That's not the same as being a player, but McFarlane's not complaining.

Thinking It Over

1. What lessons can you take from Todd McFarlane about how to be a success in life?
2. What dreams do you have, and where could you work where you may be able to fulfill at least a major part of your dream?
3. What skills can you develop working for a larger firm before you go out on your own to become a successful entrepreneur?
4. What are some of the challenges you see in today's dynamic business environment and what are some of the opportunities?

Joy A. Baggett's Simple Success Marketing, Inc.

Name: Joy A. Baggett

Age: 27

Position/title: President

Salary range: $50,000–$100,000

Time in this position: 6 years; founder of firm

Major factors in the decision to take this position: My experience with several South Florida advertising agencies was enough to allow me solid working knowledge of the operational side of the business. As just an account executive, however, in charge of administrative details, I was unable to "run the firm," make the important decisions for a client's marketing directives, and my salary potential was limited.

Company's Web address: *www.simplesuccess.com*

Company description: Simple Success Marketing, Inc., is a full-service marketing and advertising firm. With one phone call, a client is able to have all of their marketing needs met in a professional, timely, and cost-effective manner. Services include consulting and management of public relations, special events, graphic design, media buying, advertising, direct mail, and collateral material production.

Job description: Find new accounts and guide clients in their marketing decisions as it pertains to their budget allocation, image design, and business development.

Career paths: Raised in the Colorado Rockies, I longed for the sunny, ocean-side therapy of South Florida for my college education and for life. After obtaining my bachelor's degree in marketing, I was able to obtain several account executive positions with area advertising agencies. Quickly realizing that my talent was to lead, not follow, I formed Simple Success Marketing, Inc., in 1996, now a 10-person, full-service marketing firm.

Ideal next job: I would seek a consulting position with a large corporation on strategy only and avoid the daily pressure of artwork decisions and deadlines.

Best part of your job: Helping a client succeed in growing their sales as a direct result of our marketing efforts.

Worst part of your job: Having to meet a campaign deadline no matter what—nights, weekends, whatever it takes. Timing is everything with marketing. Period.

Educational background: I have a Bachelor's degree in Marketing with a minor in Business Administration from Palm Beach Atlantic College.

Favorite course: Consumer Behavior

Best course for your career: All of the statistics courses that I was required to take.

Recommended by Robert Myers, Palm Beach Atlantic College

Chapter 2

How Economics Affects Business: The Creation and Distribution of Wealth

Learning Goals

After you have read and studied this chapter, you should be able to

1. Compare and contrast the economics of despair with the economics of growth.
2. Explain what capitalism is and how free markets work.
3. Discuss the major differences between socialism and communism.
4. Explain the trend toward mixed economies.
5. Discuss the economic system of the United States, including the significance of key economic indicators, productivity, and the business cycle.
6. Define *fiscal policy* and *monetary policy,* and explain how each affects the economy.

Profile

www.hersheys.com

Getting to Know Milton Hershey of Hershey's Chocolate

Every kid deserves a hug and kiss. At least that's what Milton Hershey, founder of the Hershey Chocolate Company (now Hershey Foods Corporation), thought. Way back in 1907, when Hershey first introduced Hershey's Kisses, each little chocolate was hand-wrapped. Today's wrapping machines can wrap up to 33 million Kisses a day—that's more than 12 billion a year! As sweet as a Hershey Kiss is, it is only one of dozens of types of candy produced and distributed by Hershey Foods today.

Milton Hershey's love for candy making started early in his life. After a brief apprenticeship with a candy maker, Hershey opened his own candy shop in Philadelphia when he was only 18. That shop failed after six years. Hershey knew he needed to learn a lot more about candy making and quality in order to succeed. He traveled to Denver, Colorado, to work in a caramel factory where he learned about the benefits of using fresh milk in the candy-making process.

Hershey was renowned for supporting his workers. During the Great Depression of the 1930s, Hershey kept people at work building a grand hotel, a community building, a sports arena, and a new office building for the factory.

Soon Hershey thought he was ready to try it on his own again. He first set up shop in Chicago, then New Orleans, and then New York City. Eventually he ended up in Lancaster, Pennsylvania, where he was finally successful in forming the Lancaster Caramel Company. Hershey discovered some equipment to cover the caramel with chocolate and, as they say, the rest is history. Hershey sold the caramel company but kept the chocolate-making equipment and the rights to make chocolate. Hershey returned to his birthplace, Derry Church, Pennslyvania, and built a chocolate manufacturing plant near the heart of dairy country, where he could get the fresh milk needed to make the finest milk chocolate.

Hershey built a new community, Hershey, Pennsylvania, around his chocolate plant. Soon the town sported a bank, a department store, a school, a park, several churches, a golf course, a zoo, and a trolley system (to bring in workers from nearby towns). The town remains very much a company town. The streets have names such as Chocolate and Cocoa. The bank gives its customers Hershey's Kisses. The street lamps are shaped like Kisses.

Hershey was renowned for supporting his workers. During the Great Depression of the 1930s, Hershey kept people at work building a grand hotel, a community building, a sports arena, and a new office building for the factory. During World War II, when Hershey had to stop production of Kisses because the foil wrappers were needed for the war effort, Hershey used his chocolate molding department to make over 3 billion chocolate rations for the military troops.

Milton Hershey and his wife, Catherine, believed that people are morally obligated to share the fruits of their success. They established the Hershey Industrial School, now called the Milton Hershey School. The school houses, feeds, clothes, and educates some 1,300 disadvantaged children. The school still owns a substantial share of Hershey Foods. In fact, the school's endowment fund, now valued at over $5.4 billion, is larger than the endowments of most Ivy League colleges.

Milton Hershey was both a dreamer and a builder. He had the genius to develop his chocolate business in the right place at the right time. His personal convictions about the obligations of wealth and the quality of life in the town he founded have made the company, the community, and the school his living legacy. It is important to study people like Milton Hershey—business leaders who strive for the finest quality in the goods they produce and do everything they can to support their workers and their communities. Such people help offset the impression, created by recent business scandals, that all or most businesspeople are dishonest and unethical, and have no feelings toward the community or workers.

This chapter explores economics and, in particular, the free-market system that makes it possible for entrepreneurs like Milton Hershey to thrive. It also explores the economic systems of other countries so you can see the direct effect that economic systems have on the wealth and the happiness of communities throughout the world.

Sources: http://hersheys.com/about/milton.shtml; Shelly Branch, "Sale of Hershey to Be Contested by School Alumni," *The Wall Street Journal,* July 29, 2002, p. B10; and Stacey Hirsh, "Will H[illegible] Kiss Town Goodbye?" *Newsday,* August 10, 2002, p. A15.

How Economic Conditions Affect Businesses

Why is South Korea comparatively wealthy and North Korea suffering economically? Annual income per capita (per person) is $8,900 in South Korea, but only $706 in North Korea.[1] Why is China's per capita annual income about $800 while Taiwan's is over $15,000? Such questions are part of the subject of economics. In this chapter, we explore the various economic systems of the world and how they either promote or hinder business growth, the creation of wealth, and a higher quality of life ➤P. 6◄ for all.

A major part of America's business success is due to an economic and social climate that allows businesses to operate freely. People are free to start a business anywhere and are just as free to fail, as Milton Hershey's story illustrates. The freedom to fail and start again motivates people to try until they succeed because the rewards are often so great, as Hershey's story also illustrates. Any change in the U.S. economic or political system has a major influence on the success of the business system. Global economics and politics also have a major influence on businesses in the United States. Therefore, to understand business, you must also understand basic economics and politics.

Milton Hershey is just one of millions of men and women who have created wealth for their families and their countries when given the chance. That chance comes when a free market (one not controlled by government) is introduced and people can find a little money to get started. The Reaching Beyond Our Borders box will give you an idea of how small businesses can grow and help whole communities prosper anywhere in the world.

economics
The study of how society chooses to employ resources to produce goods and services and distribute them for consumption among various competing groups and individuals.

macroeconomics
The part of economics study that looks at the operation of a nation's economy as a whole.

microeconomics
The part of economics study that looks at the behavior of people and organizations in particular markets.

What Is Economics?

Economics is the study of how society chooses to employ resources to produce goods and services and distribute them for consumption among various competing groups and individuals. Remember from Chapter 1 that these resources (land, labor, capital, entrepreneurship, and knowledge) are called factors of production ➤P. 10◄.

Economists usually work from one of two perspectives: **macroeconomics** looks at the operation of a nation's economy as a whole and **microeconomics**

The economic contrast is remarkable. Business is booming in Seoul (pictured on left). But North Korea, a communist country, is not doing well, as the picture on the right of thousands of workers using old fashioned tools in a work-for-food program shows. South Korea has 110 telephones per 100 residents while North Korea has just 5. The annual income per person in the South is $8,900 versus $706 in the North. What do you think accounts for the dramatic differences in the economies of these two neighboring countries?

www.infomanage.com

Reaching Beyond Our Borders

Entrepreneurs in El Salvador and Brazil

When Pablo Tesak came to El Salvador, he noticed that the majority of consumer products there were imported from the United States and Europe. Tesak decided to develop a line of snack products that would be produced in El Salvador and be made available to the poor people there. By setting up a factory to make simple and cheap snack items, Tesak prospered. Later, a civil war in the country caused dissent among his workers. In order to stabilize his workforce Tesak raised salaries, but he discovered that his employees needed still more compensation.

To keep his workers and increase their productivity, Tesak opened a "price club." He arranged to buy local products from nearby factories and make them available to employees at cost, with interest-free monthly payments. The club now sells beds, refrigerators, and other household goods to Tesak's employees and provides them with services such as medical care, English courses, and a summer camp for children. Tesak also set up a $500,000 home credit line so that his employees could borrow money to buy homes. As a result of these new benefits, employee morale and productivity increased substantially. Tesak learned that even when hunger, war, poverty, and disease are constant threats, entrepreneurship can flourish and can improve conditions for everyone involved.

Samuel Kline took another approach to helping the poor in Brazil. He opened a chain of stores that provides credit to poor people so they can buy goods with small payments over time. Casas Bahia is Brazil's largest nonfood retailer. Ninety percent of its customers buy on credit. Most of them couldn't afford to buy goods elsewhere. Some people have criticized Kline, saying that he exploits the poor, but he points out that Casas Bahia's customers wouldn't be able to buy what they want and need if he weren't there. Also, the people who patronize his stores don't complain. They make their payments regularly and buy more goods when they come. One important benefit Kline provides is employment for almost 17,000 workers. Also, he locates his stores in the poorest areas of town to make access easier to those who don't have transportation.

Source: Miriam Jordan, "Down Market," *The Wall Street Journal,* June 11, 2002, pp. A1, A8.

looks at the behavior of people and organizations in particular markets. For example, while macroeconomics looks at how many jobs exist in the whole economy, microeconomics examines how many people will be hired in a particular industry or a particular region of the country. Topics discussed in this chapter that are part of macroeconomics include gross domestic product, unemployment rate, and price indexes. Chapter topics that deal with microeconomic issues include pricing and supply and demand.

Some economists define economics as the allocation of "scarce" resources. They believe that resources are scarce and need to be carefully divided among people, usually by the government. There's no way to maintain peace and prosperity in the world by merely dividing the resources we have today among the existing nations. There aren't enough known resources available to do that. **Resource development** is the study of how to increase resources and to create the conditions that will make better use of those resources. Outside of government, businesses may contribute to an economic system by inventing products that greatly increase available resources. For example, businesses may discover new energy sources, new ways of growing food, and new ways of creating needed goods and services.[2] The Dealing with Change box on p. 38 will give you some good news about macroeconomic conditions in the world today.

resource development
The study of how to increase resources and to create the conditions that will make better use of those resources.

Why Economics Was Known as "the Dismal Science"

Imagine the world when kings and other landowners had most of the wealth and the majority of the people were peasants. The peasants had many children, and it may have seemed a natural conclusion that there would soon be too many people and not enough food and other resources. English economist Thomas www.rich.frb.org/pubs/macro/

Dealing with Change

Some Good Macroeconomic News

Macroeconomics examines world economies including world poverty levels. The good news is that world poverty has fallen dramatically in the past 30 years. The number of people in "extreme" poverty (that is, people who make about $500 a year) fell from 550 million to 350 million. Note, however, that there are more people in the world who make $500 a year than there are people in the United States (the population of the United States is about 290 million). If you were to look at the people in the world who make less than $1,000 a year, the decline was from 41 percent of the world's population to 19 percent. Rising incomes in China and India, the world's most populous nations, account for most of the improvement.

On the one hand, the world has a long way to go to raise the income of the very poorest people. On the other hand, progress is being made, and as more countries learn about the benefits of economic freedom, the news should only get better.

BusinessWeek

Sources: Robert J. Barnes, "The U.N. Is Dead Wrong on Poverty and Inequality," *Business Week,* May 6, 2002, p. 24; Peter Coy, "Economic Trends," *Business Week,* June 17, 2002; and Aung San Suu Kyi, "All We Want Is Our Freedom," *Parade Magazine,* March 9, 2003, pp. 4–5.

Malthus made this argument in the late 1700s and early 1800s. In response to such views, Scottish writer and thinker Thomas Carlyle called economics "the dismal science." Followers of Malthus today (who are called neo-Malthusians) still believe that there are too many people in the world and that the solution to poverty is birth control, which includes such measures as forced abortions and forced sterilization.[3] The latest statistics, however, show that the world population is growing more slowly than was expected, and in some industrial countries (Japan, Germany, Italy, Russia) may be so slow so that there will be too many old people and too few young people to care for them. In the developing world, on the other hand, population will continue to climb relatively quickly. Countries such as Iraq, Pakistan, Yemen, and Colombia will see population increases that may lead to greater poverty and more unrest.[4] Such studies about the effects of population growth on the economy are part of macroeconomics.

Some macroeconomists believe that a large population can be a valuable resource, especially if the people are educated. They believe that one of the keys to economic growth throughout the world is to better educate people. You've probably heard or read the saying "Give a man a fish and you feed him for a day, but teach a man to fish and you feed him for a lifetime." You can add to that: "Teach a person to start a fish farm and he or she will be able to feed a village for a lifetime." *The secret to economic development is contained in this last statement.* Business owners provide jobs and economic growth for their employees and communities as well as for themselves.

If there were no way to increase resources faster than population growth, we would all be in big trouble. But, thankfully, technological advances in many countries have provided the means to increase production of food and other resources so that people in many areas of the world are much better off than in Malthus's time. You have only to compare the world today with the world in the 18th and 19th centuries to see the differences—countries such as the United States, Canada, and most of Europe are much richer now, and most people live much better lives.

The challenge for macroeconomists is to determine what makes some countries relatively wealthy and other countries relatively poor, and then to implement policies and programs that lead to increased prosperity for everyone in all countries. One way to begin understanding this challenge is to consider the theories of Adam Smith.

Growth Economics and Adam Smith

Adam Smith developed a theory of wealth creation more than 200 years ago. His theory relied on entrepreneurs working to improve their lives. To make money, they would provide goods and services, as well as jobs, for others. What countries have adopted the ideas of Adam Smith?

The Scottish economist Adam Smith was one of the first people to imagine a system for creating wealth and improving the lives of everyone. Rather than believing that fixed resources had to be divided among competing groups and individuals, Smith envisioned creating more resources so that everyone could become wealthier. The year was 1776. Adam Smith's book *An Inquiry into the Nature and Causes of the Wealth of Nations* often is called simply *The Wealth of Nations*.

Adam Smith believed that freedom was vital to the survival of any economy, especially the freedom to own land or property and the freedom to keep the profits ➤P. 4◄ from working the land or running a business. He believed that people will work hard if they have incentives for doing so—that is, if they know they will be rewarded.

He made the desire for improving one's condition in life the basis of his theory. According to Smith, as long as farmers, laborers, and businesspeople (entrepreneurs) could see economic reward for their efforts (i.e., receive enough money in the form of profits to support their families), they would work long hours and work hard. As a result of those efforts, the economy would prosper—with plenty of food and all kinds of products available to everyone. Smith's ideas were later challenged by Malthus and others who believed that economic conditions would only get worse, but it is Smith, not Malthus, who is considered by some to be the father of modern economics.

How Businesses Benefit the Community

Under Adam Smith's theory, businesspeople don't necessarily deliberately set out to help others. They work primarily for their own prosperity and growth. Yet as people try to improve their own situation in life, Smith said, their efforts serve as an "invisible hand" that helps the economy grow and prosper through the production of needed goods, services, and ideas. Thus, the **invisible hand** turns self-directed gain into social and economic benefits for all.[5]

invisible hand
A phrase coined by Adam Smith to describe the process that turns self-directed gain into social and economic benefits for all.

How is it that people working in their own self-interest produce goods, services, and wealth for others? The only way farmers in a given area can become wealthy is to sell some of their crops to others. To become even wealthier, farmers would have to hire workers to produce more food. As a consequence, people in that area would have plenty of food available and some would have jobs on the farms. So the farmers' self-centered efforts to become wealthy lead to jobs for some and food for almost all. Stop and envision that process for a minute because it is critical to your understanding of economic growth in the United States and other free countries.

The same principles apply to other products as well—everything from clothing to houses to cellular phones. To increase wealth for their families, manufacturers would work long and hard, and hire others. As a consequence, nearly everyone in the area would have access to clothes, homes, phones, and so on, and almost everyone who was willing and able to work would have a job. That is how Adam Smith felt wealth would be created. Experience in some countries has shown that he was right.

Smith assumed that as people became wealthier, they would naturally reach out to help the less fortunate in the community, as Milton Hershey did in the United States and Pablo Tesak and Samuel Kline did in other countries (review the Reaching Beyond Our Borders box on page 37). That has not always happened. Today, however, many U.S. businesspeople are becoming more concerned about social issues and their obligation to return to society some of

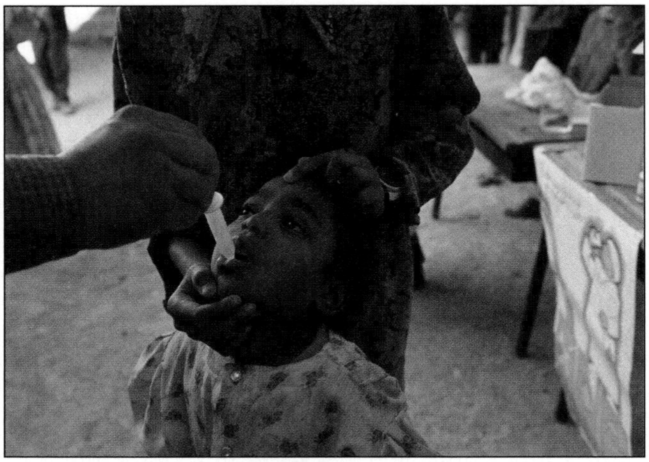

The Bill and Melinda Gates Foundation is just one of many foundations that provide needed funds for nonprofit organizations operating everywhere. Making use of a Gates Foundation grant, this photo shows a Moroccan student receiving a dose of Zithromax to prevent trachoma, a leading cause of blindness in developing nations. Do you think economically prosperous nations should be more giving to the peoples of developing nations?

what they've earned. For example, Bill Gates (the cofounder of Microsoft) and his wife, Melinda, set up the largest foundation in history, worth some $24 billion. The Bill and Melinda Gates Foundation works to improve schools; wire libraries to the Internet; and improve world health by providing vaccines, training people in health matters, and more. Ninety percent of U.S. business owners contribute money to charities, compared with 70 percent of U.S. households.[6]

Critical Thinking

Many people say that businesspeople do not do enough for society. Some students choose to go into the public sector instead of business because they "want to help others." However, businesspeople say that they do more to help others than nonprofit groups do because they provide jobs for people rather than giving them charity, which often precludes them from searching for work. Furthermore, they believe that businesses create all the wealth that nonprofit groups distribute. Can you find some middle ground in this debate that would show that both businesspeople and those who work for nonprofit organizations contribute to society and need to work together more closely to help people? Could you use the concepts of Adam Smith to help illustrate your position?

Progress Assessment

- What is the difference between macroeconomics and microeconomics?
- Why was economics known as "the dismal science"?
- What is better than teaching a man to fish?
- What does Adam Smith's term *invisible hand* mean? How does the invisible hand create wealth for a country?

UNDERSTANDING FREE-MARKET CAPITALISM

Basing their ideas on free-market principles, such as those of Adam Smith, businesspeople in the United States, Europe, Japan, Canada, and other countries began to create more wealth than had ever been created before. They hired others to work on their farms and in their factories, and their nations began to prosper as a result. Businesspeople soon became the wealthiest people in society.

Great disparities in wealth remained or even increased. Many businesspeople owned large homes and fancy carriages, while most workers lived in humble surroundings. Nonetheless, there was always the promise of better times. One way to be really wealthy was to start a successful business of your own. Of course, it wasn't that easy—it never has been. Then and now, you have to accumulate some money to buy or start a business, and you have to work long hours to make it grow. But the opportunities are there.

The economic system that has led to wealth creation in much of the world is known as capitalism. **Capitalism** is an economic system in which all or most of the factors of production and distribution (e.g., land, factories, railroads, and stores) are privately owned (not owned by the government) and are operated for profit. In capitalist countries, businesspeople decide what to produce; how much to pay workers; how much to charge for goods and services; whether to produce certain goods in their own countries, import those goods, or have them made in other countries; and so on. No country is purely capitalist, however. Often the government gets involved in issues such as determining minimum wages and setting farm prices, as it does in the United States. But the *foundation* of the U.S. economic system is capitalism. Similarly, capitalism is the foundation for the economies of England, Canada, Australia, and most other developed nations.

capitalism
An economic system in which all or most of the factors of production and distribution are privately owned and operated for profit.

The Foundations of Capitalism

Some people don't understand how the free-market system works or what rights it confers. As a result, they can't determine what the best economic system is. You should learn how the U.S. economy works and what mechanisms exist to promote economic growth. People under free-market capitalism have four basic rights:

1. *The right to private property.* This is the most fundamental of all rights under capitalism. It means that individuals can buy, sell, and use land, buildings, machinery, inventions, and other forms of property. They can also pass property on to their children.
2. *The right to own a business and to keep all of that business's profits.* Recall from Chapter 1 that profits equal revenues minus expenses (salaries, materials, taxes). Profits act as important incentives for business owners.
3. *The right to freedom of competition.* Within certain guidelines established by the government, individuals are free to compete with other individuals or businesses by offering new products and promotions. To survive and grow, businesses need laws and regulations, such as the laws of contracts, which ensure that people will do what they say they'll do.
4. *The right to freedom of choice.* People are free to choose where they want to work and what career they want to follow. Other freedoms of choice include where to live and what to buy or sell.

One benefit of such rights and freedoms is that people are willing to take more risks than they would

The people of Poland have learned that moving from a communist to a capitalist system is not easy. However, some entrepreneurs flourished. Wala Lukaszuk, for example, enjoyed early success with her own salad bar, but she is now experiencing competition from larger businesses. Capitalism does not guarantee success; it only affords the opportunity to try. Have you talked with someone familiar with socialism or communism to compare the advantages and disadvantages with capitalism?

www.vacationspot.com

Spotlight on Small Business

Starting a Small Business in the United States versus Elsewhere

The chances for success when starting a business vary from country to country depending on the social and economic conditions. Few stories illustrate this concept better than the following one about competition between a team of entrepreneurs in Europe and a team in the United States.

The European entrepreneurs are friends: Peter Ingelbrecht and Laurent Coppieters from Belgium. When they had trouble finding a house for a vacation on Spain's Costa del Sol, Ingelbrecht and Coppieters decided to start an online vacation-home booking agency called Rent-a-Holiday. The pair sought financial help from venture capitalists (people who lend money to new businesses for a share of the ownership). At first, Belgian financiers refused to help them. More cautious than many U.S. financiers, the Belgian venture capitalists wanted to see evidence of Rent-a-Holiday's success. Ingelbrecht and Coppieters were frustrated. Yet, determined to succeed, they were able to gather $400,000 from their families and eventually they found a venture capitalist firm willing to lend them $850,000.

In addition to having difficulty in finding the money to start their business, Ingelbrecht and Coppieters had difficulty in finding people in Europe who were eager to work for a start-up Internet company. Potential employees considered the risks of working for a start-up company too great compared with working for established firms.

In the United States, Greg Slyngstad and Steve Murch had a similar idea about starting their own online vacation business, which they eventually called VacationSpot.com. They, too, sought financing but had much better success than the Belgian entrepreneurs. In fact, several companies wanted to finance the venture. Slyngstad and Murch accepted venture capitalist Technology Crossover's offer of $5 million and an additional $4 million from a variety of other investors. "It's heaven for entrepreneurs now in America," Slyngstad said during his company's start-up phase. Furthermore, people with master of business administration (MBA) degrees were eager to join the new venture. They were more willing than their European counterparts to take a risk in working for a new business.

The American venture was also more successful in finding customers for its Internet site. The European entrepreneurs used real estate agents to complete transactions by phone or fax. The Americans did the same, but they also built a full-service website that allowed people to book a holiday villa online. The site also supplied reviews of the vacation homes written by previous guests.

The end of the story is this: The American firm eventually bought the European firm and gave the European entrepreneurs a little over 20 percent ownership of the new combined firm, which retained the name VacationSpot.com. Then in 2000, Microsoft bought the company for nearly $71 million.

Sources: William Echikson, "Home Field Advantage," *Business Week, e.biz,* December 13, 1999, pp. 72–74; Kate Pocock, "Send Your Mouse Shopping in Paris," *Toronto Sun,* May 25, 2000; Craig Stoltz, "Internet Travel: Shakeout Time," *Washington Post,* May 14, 2000; and Villapolis.com, 2003.

otherwise. The Spotlight on Small Business box illustrates that point dramatically. Now that you know those rights, let's explore how the free market works. What role do consumers play in the process? How do businesses learn what consumers need and want? These questions and more are answered next.

How Free Markets Work

The free market is one in which decisions about what to produce and in what quantities are made by the market—that is, by buyers and sellers negotiating prices for goods and services. You and I and other consumers in the United States and in other free-market countries send signals to tell producers what to make, how many, in what color, and so on. We do that by choosing to buy (or not to buy) certain products and services.

For example, if all of us decided we wanted T-shirts from our favorite sports teams, the clothing industry would respond in certain ways. Manufacturers and retailers would increase the price of T-shirts, because they know people are willing to pay more than before. People in the clothing industry would also realize they could make more money by making more T-shirts. Thus, they would have incentive to pay workers to start work earlier and end later. Furthermore, the number of clothing companies making T-shirts would increase. How many T-shirts they make depends on how many we request or buy in the stores. The prices and quantities would continue to change as the amount of T-shirts we buy changed.

The same process occurs with most other products. The price tells producers how much to produce. As a consequence, there's rarely a long-term shortage of goods in the United States. If something is wanted but isn't available, the price tends to go up until someone begins making more of that product, sells the ones already on hand, or makes a substitute.

Various factors affect the demand for specific kinds of T-shirts; thus the supply needs to change as well. Following the attack on the World Trade Center, this T-shirt shop in New York's Chinatown experienced increased demand for shirts featuring a New York icon. As tourists began returning to New York they wanted a reminder of their trip. How much does price factor into your decision when considering the purchase of things like a souvenir T-shirt?

How Prices Are Determined

How free markets work is an important part of economics. The main point is that, in a free market, prices are not determined by sellers; they are determined by buyers and sellers negotiating in the marketplace. A seller may want to receive $50 for a T-shirt, but the quantity demanded at that price may be quite low. If the seller lowers the price, the quantity demanded is likely to increase. How is a price determined that is acceptable to both buyers and sellers? The answer is found in the microeconomic concepts of supply and demand. We shall explore both next.

The Economic Concept of Supply

Supply refers to the quantity of products that manufacturers or owners are willing to sell at different prices at a specific time. Generally speaking, the amount supplied will increase as the price increases because sellers can make more money with a higher price.

Economists show this relationship between quantity supplied and price on a graph. Figure 2.1 on p. 44 shows a simple supply curve for T-shirts. The price of the shirts in dollars is shown vertically on the left of the graph. The quantity of shirts sellers are willing to supply is shown horizontally at the bottom of the graph. The various points on the curve indicate how many T-shirts sellers would provide at different prices. For example, at a price of $5 a shirt, a T-shirt vendor would provide only 5 T-shirts, but at $50 a shirt the vendor would supply 50 shirts. The supply curve indicates the relationship between the price and the quantity supplied. All things being equal, the higher the price, the more the vendor will be willing to supply.

The Economic Concept of Demand

Demand refers to the quantity of products that people are willing to buy at different prices at a specific time. Generally speaking, the quantity demanded will increase as the price decreases. Again, the relationship between price and quantity demanded can be shown in a graph. Figure 2.2 on p. 44 shows a simple demand curve for T-shirts. The various points on the graph indicate the quantity demanded at various prices. For example, at a price of $45, the quantity demanded is just 5 shirts; but if the price were $5, the quantity demanded would increase to 35 shirts. The line connecting the dots is called a demand curve. It shows the relationship between quantity demanded and price.

supply
The quantity of products that manufacturers or owners are willing to sell at different prices at a specific time.

demand
The quantity of products that people are willing to buy at different prices at a specific time.

FIGURE 2.1

THE SUPPLY CURVE AT VARIOUS PRICES

The supply curve rises from left to right. Think it through. The higher the price of T-shirts goes (the vertical axis), the more sellers will be willing to supply.

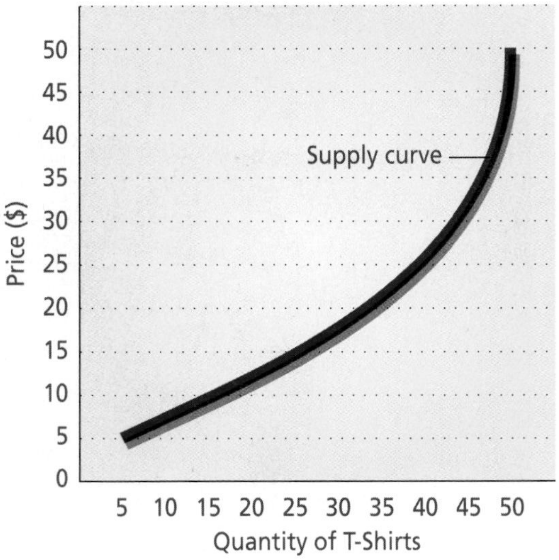

FIGURE 2.2

THE DEMAND CURVE AT VARIOUS PRICES

This is a simple demand curve showing the quantity of T-shirts demanded at different prices. The demand curve falls from left to right. It is easy to understand why. The lower the price of T-shirts, the higher the quantity demanded.

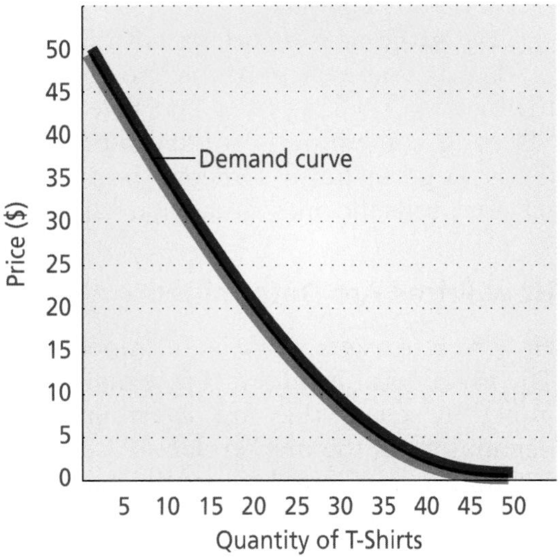

The Equilibrium Point or Market Price

It should be clear to you after reviewing Figures 2.1 and 2.2 that the key factor in determining the quantity supplied and the quantity demanded is *price*. Sellers prefer a high price, and buyers prefer a low price. If you were to lay one of the two graphs on top of the other, the supply curve and the demand curve would cross. At that crossing point, the quantity demanded and the quantity supplied would be equal. Figure 2.3 illustrates that point. At a price of $15, the quantity of T-shirts demanded and the quantity supplied are equal (25 shirts). That crossing point is known as the equilibrium point or the equilibrium price. In the long run, that price would become the market price. **Market price**, then, is determined by supply and demand.

market price
The price determined by supply and demand.

Proponents of a free market would argue that, because supply and demand interactions determine prices, there is no need for government involvement or government planning. If surpluses develop (i.e., if quantity supplied exceeds quantity demanded), a signal is sent to sellers to lower the price. If shortages develop (i.e., if quantity supplied is less than quantity demanded), a signal is sent to sellers to increase the price. Eventually, supply will again equal demand if nothing interferes with market forces.

In countries without a free market, there is no such mechanism to reveal to businesses (via price) what to produce and in what amounts, so there are often shortages (not enough products) or surpluses (too many products). In such countries, the government decides what to produce and in what quantity, but the government has no way of knowing what the proper quantities are. Furthermore, when the government interferes in otherwise free markets, such as when it subsidizes farm goods, surpluses and shortages may also develop.

One benefit of the free market is that it allows open competition among companies. Businesses must provide customers with quality products at fair prices with good service; otherwise, they will lose customers to those businesses that do provide good products, good prices, and good service. Who, for

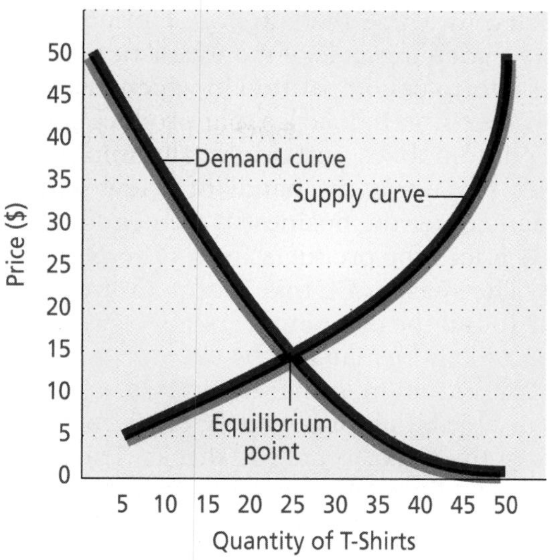

FIGURE 2.3

THE EQUILIBRIUM POINT

The place where quantity demanded and supplied meet is called the equilibrium point. When we put both the supply and demand curves on the same graph, we find that they intersect at a price where the quantity supplied and the quantity demanded are equal. In the long run, the market price will tend toward the equilibrium point.

example, are some of the competitors that Hershey Foods must compete with today? We'll discuss the nature of competition next, right after pausing for the Critical Thinking exercise.

Critical Thinking

Recently, the U.S. Supreme Court ruled that cities could have voucher programs that give money directly to parents, and the parents can then choose between competing schools: public and private. The idea for promoting such a ruling was to create competition among schools. As with businesses, schools were expected to improve their products (how effectively they teach) to win students from competitors. Supposedly, that would mean an improvement in all schools, private and public, and would benefit many students. Do you believe that such economic principles apply in both private and public organizations? Are there other public functions that might benefit from more competition, including competition from private firms?

Competition within Free Markets

Economists generally agree that four different degrees of competition exist: (1) perfect competition, (2) monopolistic competition, (3) oligopoly, and (4) monopoly.

Perfect competition exists when there are many sellers in a market and no seller is large enough to dictate the price of a product. Under perfect competition, sellers produce products that appear to be identical. Agricultural products (e.g., apples, corn, potatoes) are often considered to be the closest examples of such products. You should know, however, that there are no true examples of perfect competition. Today, government price supports and drastic reductions in the number of farms make it hard to argue that even farming is an example of perfect competition.

perfect competition
The market situation in which there are many sellers in a market and no seller is large enough to dictate the price of a product.

Monopolistic competition exists when a large number of sellers produce products that are very similar but are perceived by buyers as different (e.g., hot dogs, candy, personal computers, T-shirts). Under monopolistic competition, product differentiation (the attempt to make buyers think similar products are different in some way) is a key to success. Think about what that means for just a moment. Through tactics such as advertising, branding, and packaging, sellers try to convince buyers that their products are different from those of competitors. Actually, the competing products may be similar or even interchangeable.

monopolistic competition
The market situation in which a large number of sellers produce products that are very similar but that are perceived by buyers as different.

The fast-food industry, in which there are often pricing battles between hamburger places, offers a good example of monopolistic competition.

oligopoly
A form of competition in which just a few sellers dominate the market.

An **oligopoly** is a form of competition in which just a few sellers dominate a market. Oligopolies exist in industries that produce products such as breakfast cereal, tobacco, automobiles, soft drinks, aluminum, and aircraft. One reason some industries remain in the hands of a few sellers is that the initial investment required to enter the business is tremendous.

In an oligopoly, prices for products from different companies tend to be close to the same. The reason for this is simple. Intense price competition would lower profits for all the competitors, since a price cut on the part of one producer would most likely be matched by the others. As in monopolistic competition, product differentiation, rather than price, is usually the major factor in market success in a situation of oligopoly. Note, for example, that most cereals are priced about the same, as are soft drinks. Thus, advertising is a major factor in which of the few available brands consumers buy because often it is advertising that creates the perceived differences.

monopoly
A market in which there is only one seller for a product or service.

A **monopoly** occurs when there is only one seller for a product or service. That is, one seller controls the total supply of a product and the price. In the United States, laws prohibit the creation of monopolies. That is one reason Microsoft got into trouble with the law: It appeared to have monopoly power in the market for computer operating systems.

The U.S. legal system has permitted monopolies in the markets for public utilities that sell natural gas, water, and electric power. These utility companies' prices and profits usually have been monitored and controlled by public service commissions that are supposed to protect the interest of buyers. For example, the Florida Public Service Commission is the administering agency over the Florida Power and Light utility company. New legislation has ended the monopoly status of utilities in some areas, and consumers in those areas are able to choose among utility providers. The intention of this deregulation is to increase competition among utility companies and, ultimately, lower prices for consumers. We will discuss deregulation in more detail in the appendix following Chapter 4.

Benefits and Limitations of Free Markets

The free market—with its competition and incentives—was a major factor in creating the wealth that industrialized countries now enjoy.[7] Some people even talk of the free market as an economic miracle. Free-market capitalism, more than any other economic system, provides opportunities for poor people to work their way out of poverty. For example, one study that tracked more than 50,000 American workers found the income gains of those in the bottom 20 percent to be four times the gains of the top 20 percent.[8] Capitalism also encourages businesses to be more efficient so they can successfully compete on price and quality.

Yet even as free-market capitalism has brought prosperity to the United States and to much of the rest of the world, it has brought inequality as well. Business owners and managers make more money and have more wealth than workers. Similarly, people who are old, disabled, or sick may not be able to start and manage a business. Others may not have the talent or the drive to start and manage a business or farm. What should society do about such inequality? Not all business owners are as generous to their employees as Milton Hershey was. In fact, the de-

Deregulation of the electric utilities industry in some states has given consumers both a choice of suppliers and sources. In Pennsylvania, for example, by paying a little extra each month you can have your electrical supply generated by 100 percent renewable sources, one of which is wind. Would you be willing to pay more for "green" products that produce less pollution and fewer troublesome byproducts? If so, why?

sire to produce as much as possible and to create as much wealth as possible has led some businesspeople (throughout history and even in some places still today) to use such practices as slavery and child labor.

The greatest danger of free markets is that businesspeople and others may let greed dictate how they act. Recent charges made against some big businesses—oil companies, accounting firms, telecommunications firms, drug companies, and others—indicate the scope of this danger. Such corruption has been called the worm at the core of business.[9] Some businesspeople deceived the public about their products and others deceived their stockholders about the value of their stock. All this was done in order to increase the executives' personal assets.[10]

Clearly, some government rules and regulations are necessary to make sure that all of businesses' stakeholders ➤P. 6◀ are protected and that people who are unable to work get the basic care they need. To overcome the limitations of capitalism, some countries have adopted an economic system called socialism. It, too, has its good and bad points. We explore the advantages and disadvantages of socialism after the Progress Assessment questions.

Progress Assessment

- What are the four basic rights that people have under free-market capitalism?
- How do businesspeople know what to produce and in what quantity?
- How are prices determined?
- What are some of the limitations of free markets?

Understanding Socialism

Socialism is an economic system based on the premise that some, if not most, basic businesses—such as steel mills, coal mines, and utilities—should be owned by the government so that profits can be evenly distributed among the people. For example, France owns 75 percent of the communications company France Telecom and over 44 percent of the automaker Renault. Entrepreneurs often own and run the smaller businesses, but private businesses and individuals are taxed relatively steeply to pay for social programs.[11] The top federal personal income tax rate in the United States, for example, is 35 percent, but in more socialist countries, such as Denmark and the Netherlands, the top rate is 60 percent; in Finland the top rate is 57 percent, and in Belgium it is 55 percent.[12] While people in the United States pay sales taxes of about 5 percent, more or less (more in California, less—in fact, nothing—in Delaware), socialist countries charge a value-added tax (which is something like a sales tax) of 15 to 20 percent.[13] Socialists acknowledge the major benefit of capitalism—wealth creation—but believe that wealth should be more evenly distributed than occurs in free-market capitalism. They believe that the government should be the agency that carries out the distribution.

socialism
An economic system based on the premise that some, if not most, basic businesses should be owned by the government so that profits can be evenly distributed among the people.

Socialism has become the guiding economic platform for many countries in Europe (such as Sweden, Finland, and Belgium), much of Africa, India, and much of the rest of the world. Socialist nations tend to rely heavily on the government to provide education, health care, retirement benefits, unemployment benefits, and other social services. Some countries, such as France, are leaning more to the center (between capitalism and socialism) to get their economies moving faster.[14] In France, for example, President Jacques Chirac has promised to cut income taxes by a third, lower the value-added tax, and cut government bureaucracy. The top tax rate in France was cut by 2.5 percent, from 55 percent to 52.5 percent.[15]

Socialism has been much more successful in some countries than others. The photo on the left of Denmark's modern and clean public transportation system reflects the relative prosperity of that country. Per capita GDP is very high ($22,800). India (right photo) is not doing nearly as well, but it is beginning to experience economic growth as a result of a move away from agriculture toward more services and industrial firms. What factors could account for this disparity in the economic success of these two socialist countries?

brain drain
The loss of the best and brightest people to other countries.

The Benefits of Socialism

The major benefit of socialism is supposed to be social equality. There is more equality of outcome in socialism than in capitalism because income is taken from the wealthier people, in the form of taxes, and redistributed to the poorer members of the population through various government programs. Free education (even through the college level), free health care, and free child care are some of the benefits socialist governments distribute to their people (using the money from taxes). Workers in socialist countries usually get longer vacations than workers in capitalist countries. They also tend to work fewer hours per week and have more employee benefits, such as generous sick leave.

The Negative Consequences of Socialism

Socialism may create more equality than capitalism, but it takes away some of businesspeople's incentives to start work early and leave work late. For example, tax rates in some nations once reached 85 percent. Today, doctors, lawyers, business owners, and others who earn a lot of money have very high tax rates (usually over 50 percent). As a consequence, many of them leave socialist countries for more capitalistic countries with lower taxes, such as the United States. This loss of the best and brightest people to other countries is called a **brain drain**.

Imagine an experiment in socialism in your own class: Say that after the first exam, those with grades of 90 and above have to give some of their points to those who make 70 and below so that everyone ends up with grades in the 80s. What would happen to the incentive of those who got As on the first exam? Would they study as hard for the second exam, knowing that they would have to give away any points above 90? What about those who got 70s? Would they work less hard if they knew that they would get extra points if they didn't do well? Can you see why workers may not work as hard or as well if they all get the same benefits regardless of how hard they work?

Capitalism results in the freedom of opportunity, which is the freedom to keep whatever you earn. That creates incentives to work hard, but it also results in an unequal distribution of outcomes. In contrast, socialism strives for equality of outcomes. Socialist systems, therefore, tend to discourage the best from working as hard as they can. In the business world, socialism also results in fewer inventions and less innovation because those who come up with new ideas usually don't receive as much reward as they would in a capitalist system. Over the past decade or so, most socialist countries have simply not kept up with the United States in new inventions, job creation, or wealth creation. It is important, however, not to confuse socialism with communism. We shall explore that system next.

UNDERSTANDING COMMUNISM

The 19th-century German political philosopher Karl Marx saw the wealth created by capitalism, but he also noted the poor working and living conditions of laborers in his time. He decided that workers should take over ownership of businesses and share in the wealth. In 1848 he wrote *The Communist Manifesto,* outlining the process. Marx thus became the father of communism. **Communism** is an economic and political system in which the state (the government) makes almost all economic decisions and owns almost all the major factors of production. It intrudes further into the lives of people than socialism does. For example, some communist countries do not allow their citizens to practice certain religions, change jobs, or move to the town of their choice.

communism
An economic and political system in which the state (the government) makes all economic decisions and owns almost all the major factors of production.

One problem with communism is that the government has no way of knowing what to produce because prices don't reflect supply and demand as they do in free markets. The government must guess what the economic needs of the people are. As a result, shortages of many items may develop, including shortages of food and basic clothing. Another problem with communism is that it doesn't inspire businesspeople to work hard because the government takes most of their earnings. Therefore, although communists once held power in many nations around the world, communism is slowly disappearing as an economic form.

Most communist countries today are now suffering severe economic depression, and some people (for example, in North Korea) are starving.[16] The people in Cuba are suffering from the lack of goods and services readily available in most other countries. Some parts of the former Soviet Union remain under communist concepts, but the movement there is toward free markets. In fact, Russia now has a flat tax of 13 percent, much lower than the tax rate in the United States. When Russia introduced that low rate, tax revenues jumped by nearly 30 percent.[17] With such low tax rates, people no longer did whatever they could to avoid paying them. The trend toward free markets is also appearing in Vietnam and parts of China. The regions in China that are most free have prospered greatly while the rest of the country has grown relatively slowly.

THE TREND TOWARD MIXED ECONOMIES

The nations of the world have largely been divided between those that followed the concepts of capitalism and those that adopted the concepts of communism or socialism. Thus, to sum up the preceding discussion, the two major economic systems vying for dominance in the world today can be defined as follows:

1. **Free-market economies** exist when the market largely determines what goods and services get produced, who gets them, and how the economy grows. *Capitalism* is the popular term used to describe this economic system.
2. **Command economies** exist when the government largely decides what goods and services will be produced, who will get them, and how the economy will grow. *Socialism* and *communism* are the popular terms used to describe variations of this economic system.

free-market economies
Economic systems in which the market largely determines what goods and services get produced, who gets them, and how the economy grows.

command economies
Economic systems in which the government largely decides what goods and services will be produced, who will get them, and how the economy will grow.

The experience of the world has been that neither free-market nor command economies have resulted in optimum economic conditions. Free-market mechanisms haven't been responsive enough to the needs of the poor, the old, or the disabled. Some people also believe that businesses in free-market economies have not done enough to protect the environment. Over time, voters in free-market countries, such as the United States, have therefore elected officials who have adopted many social and environmental programs such as Social Security, welfare, unemployment compensation, and various clean air and water acts.

Socialism and communism, for their part, haven't always created enough jobs or wealth to keep economies growing fast enough. As a consequence, communist governments are disappearing and socialist governments have been cutting back on social programs and lowering taxes on businesses and workers. The idea is to generate more business growth and thus generate more revenue.

The trend, then, has been for so-called capitalist countries to move toward more socialism and for so-called socialist countries to move toward more capitalism. We say "so-called" because no country in the world is purely capitalist or purely socialist. All countries have some mix of the two systems. Thus, the long-term global trend is toward a blend of capitalism and socialism. This trend likely will increase with the opening of global markets caused by the Internet. The net effect of capitalist systems moving toward socialism and socialist systems moving toward capitalism is the emergence throughout the world of mixed economies.

mixed economies
Economic systems in which some allocation of resources is made by the market and some by the government.

Mixed economies exist where some allocation of resources is made by the market and some by the government. Most countries don't have a name for such a system. If the dominant way of allocating resources is by free-market mechanisms, then the leaders of such countries still call their system capitalism. If the dominant way of allocating resources is by the government, then the leaders call their system socialism. Figure 2.4 compares the various economic systems.

Like most other nations of the world, the United States has a mixed economy. The degree of government involvement in the economy today is a matter of some debate, as it has been at various times in the past.[18] The government has now become the largest employer in the United States, which means that the number of workers in the public sector is more than the number in the entire manufacturing sector. There's much debate about the role of government in health care, education, business regulation, and other parts of the economy. The government's perceived goal is to grow the economy while maintaining some measure of social equality. That goal is very hard to attain. Nonetheless, the basic principles of freedom and opportunity should lead to economic growth that is sustainable.

Governments have a great effect on businesses in the United States and throughout the world. Later in the chapter, we'll explore several issues having to do with the U.S. government and the economy. Keep in mind as you read this material that the foundation of the U.S. economy is capitalism. The government serves as a means to *supplement* that basic system as it tries to promote both economic growth and social equality.

This is an interesting time to monitor the relationship between business and government in the United States. This is also an interesting time to watch how the Internet affects other such relationships worldwide. The Internet is expected to unite businesses around the world in one electronic mall in which the economic systems of the individual countries involved will be less critical to business success than they ever have been before. The Dealing with Change box on p. 52 explores that development further.

Progress Assessment

- What led to the emergence of socialism?
- What are the benefits and drawbacks of socialism?
- What countries still practice communism?
- What are the characteristics of a mixed economy?

	CAPITALISM	SOCIALISM	COMMUNISM	MIXED ECONOMY
Social and economic goals	Private ownership of land and business. Liberty and the pursuit of happiness. Free trade. Emphasis on freedom and the profit motive for economic growth.	Public ownership of major businesses. Some private ownership of smaller businesses and shops. Government control of education, health care, utilities, mining, transportation, and media. Very high taxation. Emphasis on equality.	Public ownership of all businesses. Government-run education and health care. Emphasis on equality. Many limitations on freedom, including freedom to own businesses, change jobs, buy and sell homes, and to assemble to protest government actions.	Private ownership of land and business with government regulation. Government control of some institutions (e.g., mail). High taxation for defense and the common welfare. Emphasis on a balance between freedom and equality.
Motivation of workers	Much incentive to work efficiently and hard because profits are retained by owners. Workers are rewarded for high productivity.	Capitalist incentives exist in private businesses. Government control of wages in public institutions limits incentives.	Very little incentive to work hard or to produce quality goods or services.	Incentives are similar to capitalism except in government-owned enterprises, which may have few incentives. High marginal taxes can discourage overtime work.
Control over markets	Complete freedom of trade within and among nations. No government control of markets.	Some markets are controlled by the government and some are free. Trade restrictions among nations vary and include some free-trade agreements.	Total government control over markets except for illegal transactions.	Some government control of trade within and among nations (trade protectionism). Government regulation to ensure fair trade within the country.
Choices in the market	A wide variety of goods and services is available. Almost no scarcity or oversupply exists for long because supply and demand control the market.	Variety in the marketplace varies considerably from country to country. Choice is directly related to government involvement in markets.	Very little choice among competing goods.	Similar to capitalism, but scarcity and oversupply may be caused by government involvement in the market (e.g., subsidies for farms).
Social freedoms	Freedom of speech, press, assembly, religion, job choice, movement, and elections.	Similar to mixed economy. Governments may restrict job choice, movement among countries, and who may attend upper-level schools (i.e., college).	Very limited freedom to protest the government, practice religion, or change houses or jobs.	Some restrictions on freedoms of assembly and speech. Separation of church and state may limit religious practices in schools.

FIGURE 2.4

COMPARISONS OF KEY ECONOMIC SYSTEMS

www.woodcam.com

Dealing with Change

The Internet Integrates World Markets

One of the most important changes of our time in business, especially small business, has been the globalization of markets. In the past, a small business was fairly confined in its market reach. It couldn't afford to advertise nationally, much less globally. Given such constraints, it was possible for the government to regulate businesses closely and for a country to stay isolated from other countries. Today, however, even small businesses have established websites that allow them to reach global markets quickly and easily.

Woodmere Camera in Lynbrook, New York, for example, sells rare cameras. The market for such cameras is global, but in the past Woodmere had no way to reach beyond its local clientele. Today, however, Woodmere has established a website (www.woodcam.com) that provides customers an online catalog and allows them to request information by e-mail and place orders by filling out an electronic order form. ArtSelect LLC (www.artselect.com) sells reproductions of paintings by great artists like Monet and Picasso out of its offices in Fairfield, Iowa. CDnow (www.cdnow.com) has teamed with Amazon.com and sells a good percentage of its music outside the United States.

Catalog retailers are still the masters of selling online. With their established warehouse, shipping, and call-center facilities, catalog companies were poised to use the Internet quickly and effectively.

Once traditional retailers learned to get onto the Web to reach other countries, they began bringing the Web into their retail stores. Many stores now have kiosks at which consumers can access the Web and find a wider variety of goods and services than in the store. The question is not clicks *or* bricks now but rather how best to combine clicks *and* bricks.

People in one country can also work for people in another country—over the Internet. For example, a software developer in India can work for a California company and send his or her programs to the company over the Internet as quickly and efficiently as someone from, say, Oklahoma could.

Where people live therefore no longer always determines where they work. What has developed because of the Internet is a global market with global workers making global products. Some questions that such changes raise are: To whom shall the small-business worker in India pay income taxes—India, the United States, or both? Who pays worker benefits? When someone is unemployed in India, should he or she be counted in the unemployment figures in the United States? Such questions will be important in an era when workers can live anywhere in the world. The World Wide Web will have a profound effect on all the economies of the world and will likely force countries to adopt similar economic systems or risk becoming social isolates in the world economy. What will that world economic system be? What will the rights of workers be? What union and environmental rules will apply? As you can see, the next few years will present tremendous challenges and opportunities to those who understand economics and business, especially small businesses that have whole new worlds to conquer.

Sources: Jay Krall, "Coming Soon to Stores: Wireless Shopping," *The Wall Street Journal,* July 15, 2002, p. R7; "Kings of E-Commerce," *Business 2.0,* November 2002, p. 38; and Tim Hanrahan, "When Worlds Collide," *The Wall Street Journal,* April 28, 2003, pp. R1–R4.

Understanding the Economic System of the United States

Over the past few years, while many countries around the world have moved toward free-market economies, the United States has been moving toward having more social programs. Furthermore, there has been much conflict between business leaders and government leaders. Some business leaders believe that taxes are too high and there are too many government regulations.[19] Government leaders have been divided on the direction the government should take. Some believe that the government should become more involved than it has been in health care, education, and environmental issues. Others believe there should be less involvement. Those subjects dominated political debate throughout the latter half of the 20th century and are likely to continue throughout the 21st century.

Because of such uncertainty, the U.S. economic system is in a state of flux and keeping up with issues and events can be a challenge. The following sections will introduce the terms and concepts you'll need to understand the issues facing government and business leaders today. As an informed citizen, you can then become a leader in helping to create a world economy that is best for all.

Deregulation of the airline industry in the 1970s has led to many new carriers and lower fares for passengers, but financial woes and bankruptcies for many airlines. Competition is one of the driving forces that keeps economies growing and improving. Today, much of the competition among airlines is focused on price, so much so that passengers are now getting fewer rather than new and improved services. For example, many airlines don't provide any food on flights. With the majority of U.S. airlines now losing money, what are your thoughts about the positives and negatives of deregulation?

Key Economic Indicators

Three major indicators of economic conditions are (1) the gross domestic product (GDP), (2) the unemployment rate, and (3) the price indexes. Another important statistic is the increase or decrease in productivity. When you read business literature, you'll see these terms used again and again. It will greatly increase your understanding if you learn the terms now.

Gross Domestic Product **Gross domestic product (GDP)** is the total value of final goods and services produced in a country in a given year. Either a domestic company or a foreign-owned company may produce the goods and services included in the GDP as long as the companies are located within the country's boundaries. For example, production values from Japanese automaker Honda's factory in Ohio would be included in the U.S. GDP. Likewise, revenue generated by the Ford car factory in Mexico would be included in Mexico's GDP, even though Ford is a U.S. company. Before 1991, GDP was reported as gross national product (GNP). The major difference was that the earnings of a multinational firm were attributed to the country where the firm was owned. More nations used GDP than GNP as a measure, so the United States changed to GDP as well so that economies could be compared using the same statistics.

If GDP growth slows or declines, there are often many negative effects on businesses. A major influence on the growth of GDP is how productive the workforce is, that is, how much output workers create with a given amount of input.

gross domestic product (GDP)
The total value of goods and services produced in a country in a given year.

Almost every discussion about a nation's economy is based on GDP. The total U.S. GDP in the early 2000s was about $10 trillion. The level of U.S. economic activity is actually larger than the GDP figures show because the figures don't take into account illegal activities (e.g., sales of illegal drugs). The high GDP in the United States is what enables Americans to enjoy such a high standard of living ➤P. 5◄.

The Unemployment Rate The **unemployment rate** refers to the number of civilians at least 16 years old who are unemployed and tried to find a job within the prior four weeks. In 2000 the U.S. unemployment rate reached its lowest point in over 30 years, falling as low as 3.9 percent, but the rate rose rapidly to over 6 percent as a result of the economic slowdown of 2002–2003. Figure 2.5 describes the four types of unemployment: frictional, structural, cyclical, and seasonal. The United States tries to protect those who are unemployed because of recessions, industry shifts, and other cyclical factors. Nonetheless, for a variety of reasons, many of these individuals do not receive unemployment benefits.

unemployment rate
The number of civilians at least 16 years old who are unemployed and tried to find a job within the prior four weeks.

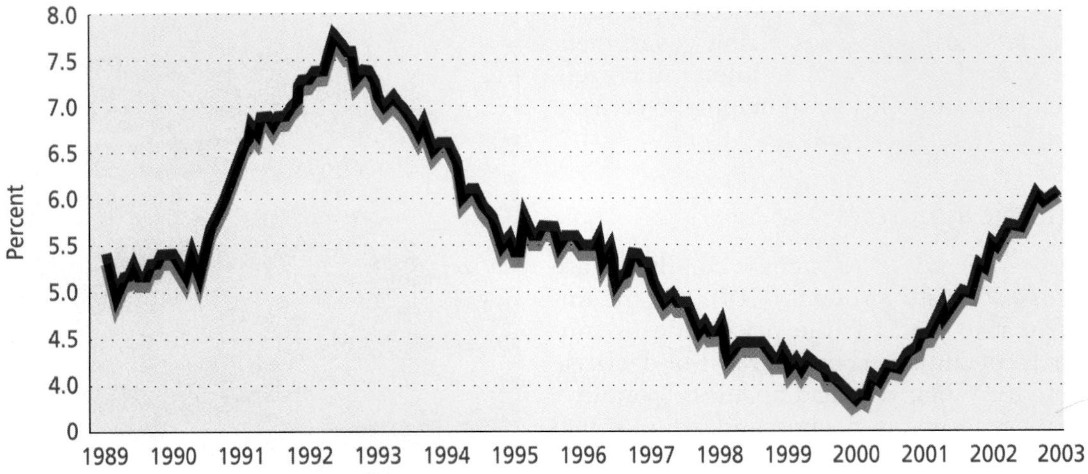

There are several kinds of unemployment:

- *Frictional unemployment* refers to those people who have quit work because they didn't like the job, the boss, or the working conditions and who haven't yet found a new job. It also refers to those people who are entering the labor force for the first time (e.g., new graduates) or are returning to the labor force after significant time away (e.g., parents who reared children). There will always be some frictional unemployment because it takes some time to find a first job or a new job.
- *Structural unemployment* refers to unemployment caused by the restructuring of firms or by a mismatch between the skills (or location) of job seekers and the requirements (or location) of available jobs (e.g., coal miners in an area where mines have been closed).
- *Cyclical unemployment* occurs because of a recession or a similar downturn in the business cycle (the ups and downs of business growth and decline over time). This type of unemployment is the most serious.
- *Seasonal unemployment* occurs where demand for labor varies over the year, as with the harvesting of crops.

FIGURE 2.5

U.S. UNEMPLOYMENT RATE, 1989–2003

inflation
A general rise in the prices of goods and services over time.

disinflation
A situation in which price increases are slowing (the inflation rate is declining).

deflation
A situation in which prices are declining.

consumer price index (CPI)
Monthly statistics that measure the pace of inflation or deflation.

producer price index (PPI)
An index that measures prices at the wholesale level.

The Price Indexes The price indexes help to measure the health of the economy by measuring the levels of inflation, disinflation, deflation, and stagflation. **Inflation** refers to a general rise in the prices of goods and services over time. Rapid inflation is scary. If the cost of goods and services goes up by just 7 percent a year, everything would double in cost in just 10 years or so. You can read more about such numbers in the Practicing Management Decisions Case at www.mhhe.com/ub7e. **Disinflation** describes a condition where price increases are slowing (the inflation rate is declining). That was the situation in the United States throughout the 1990s. **Deflation** means that prices are actually declining.[20] It occurs when countries produce so many goods that people cannot afford to buy them all (too few dollars are chasing too many goods). *Stagflation* occurs when the economy is slowing but prices are going up anyhow.[21]

The **consumer price index (CPI)** consists of monthly statistics that measure the pace of inflation or deflation. Costs of about 400 goods and services—including housing, food, apparel, and medical care—are computed to see if they are going up or down. The CPI is an important figure because some wages and salaries, rents and leases, tax brackets, government benefits, and interest rates are based on it.

The **producer price index (PPI)** measures prices at the wholesale level. Other indicators of the economy's condition include housing starts, retail sales, and changes in personal income. You can learn more about such indicators by reading business periodicals, listening to business broadcasts on radio and television, and exploring the Internet.

How does the unemployment rate in your area differ from that of other regions in the country? You may want to search the Internet to find out. Do the prices you pay for everyday goods and services seem to be rising or falling, or can't you tell? What are some of the factors that affect the economic condition of your state?

Critical Thinking

Productivity in the United States

An increase in productivity ➤P. 15◄ means that a worker can produce more goods and services in the same period of time than before. Productivity in the United States has gone up in recent years because computers and other technology have made the process of production faster and easier for many workers.[22] The higher productivity is, the lower costs are in producing goods and services, and the lower prices can be. Therefore, businesspeople are eager to increase productivity. The United States isn't a wealthy country because it has jobs that pay well; rather, jobs pay well because U.S. workers are very productive.[23] Compared to the United States, Europe is more sluggish because the European countries spend less on increasing productivity.[24]

At the beginning of the 20th century in the United States, more than 30 out of 100 workers were needed to produce enough food to feed everyone and create some surplus for world use. Today it takes fewer than 2 out of 100 workers to produce far greater quantities of food that contribute a much larger share to world production. What made the difference? The answer is that the use of tractors, chemical fertilizers, combines, silos, and other machines and resources (capital) raised farmers' productivity.

Now that the U.S. economy is a service economy, productivity is an issue, because service firms are so labor intensive.[25] Spurred by foreign competition, productivity in the manufacturing sector is rising rapidly. In the service sector, productivity is growing more slowly because there are fewer new technologies available to assist service workers (e.g., teachers, clerks, lawyers, and personal service providers like barbers) than there are for factory workers.

Productivity in the Service Sector

In the service sector, computers, word processors, and other technological innovations are beginning to make workers more productive. The United States is ahead of much of the world in service productivity. However, one problem with the service industry is that an influx of machinery may add to the *quality* of the service provided but not to the *output per worker* (productivity).

For example, you've probably noticed how many computers have been installed on college campuses. They add to the quality of education but don't necessarily boost professors' productivity. The same is true of some new equipment in hospitals, such as CAT scanners and PET scanners (more modern versions of the X-ray machine). They improve patient care but don't necessarily increase the number of patients that can be seen. In other words, today's productivity measures fail to capture the increase in quality caused by new technology.

The United States and other countries need to develop new measures of productivity for the service economy, measures that include quality as well as quantity of output. Otherwise, it will appear that the United States isn't making much progress toward improving the standard of living when, in fact, it's likely that the standard of living is continuing to improve. New measures would prove the case one way or the other. Despite productivity improvement, the economy is likely to go through a series of ups and downs, much as it has over the past few years.

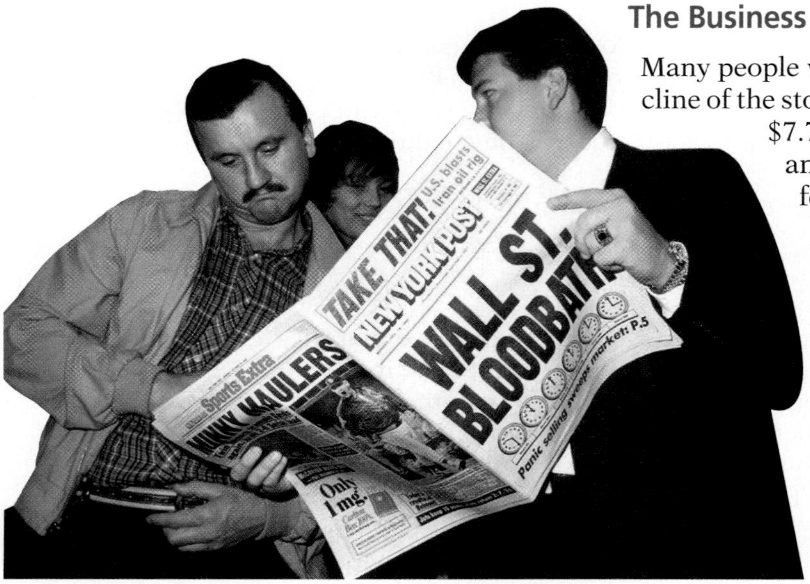

Business cycles demonstrate that over time the stock market is likely to rise *or* fall by significant amounts. Such cycles have shown to be rather consistent; that is, long periods of growth are typically followed by periods of decline. Investing, therefore, always involves a certain degree of risk, but usually the greater the risk the higher the payoff. Can you see why investors may be wise to study past trends before putting their money into stocks?

The Business Cycle

Many people were caught off guard by the rapid decline of the stock market in 2001–2003. Investors lost \$7.7 trillion in value between March 2000 and July 2002, at which point the market fell another 400 points in one day![26] The people most taken by surprise believed that the stock market would continue the rapid rise that occurred during the 1990s. Those people must not have been familiar with the concept of business cycles. **Business cycles** are the periodic rises and falls that occur in economies over time. Economists look at a number of types of cycles, from seasonal cycles that occur within a year to cycles that occur every 48–60 years.

Economist Joseph Schumpeter identified the four phases of long-term business cycles as boom–recession–depression–recovery:

1. An economic boom is just what it sounds like—business is booming.
2. **Recession** is two or more consecutive quarters of decline in the GDP. In a recession prices fall, people purchase fewer products, and businesses fail. A recession has many negative consequences for an economy: high unemployment, increased business failures, and an overall drop in living standards.
3. A **depression** is a severe recession usually accompanied by deflation. Business cycles rarely go through a depression phase. In fact, while there were many business cycles during the 20th century, there was only one severe depression (1929–1933).
4. A recovery occurs when the economy stabilizes and starts to grow. This eventually leads to an economic boom, starting the cycle all over again.

The goal of economists is to predict such ups and downs. That is very difficult to do. Business cycles are based on facts, but what those facts describe can be explained only by using theories. Therefore, one cannot say with certainty what will happen next. One can only theorize. But one thing is for sure: The economy and the stock market will rise and fall.

Since dramatic swings up and down in the economy cause all kinds of disruptions to businesses, the government tries to minimize such changes. The government uses fiscal policy and monetary policy to try to keep the economy from slowing too much or growing too rapidly.

business cycles
The periodic rises and falls that occur in all economies over time.

recession
Two or more consecutive quarters of decline in the GDP.

depression
A severe recession.

fiscal policy
The federal government's efforts to keep the economy stable by increasing or decreasing taxes or government spending.

Stabilizing the Economy through Fiscal Policy

Fiscal policy refers to the federal government's efforts to keep the economy stable by increasing or decreasing taxes or government spending.

The first half of fiscal policy involves taxation. Theoretically, high tax rates tend to slow the economy because they draw money away from the private sector and put it into the government. High tax rates may discourage small-business ownership because they decrease the profits businesses can make and make the effort less rewarding. It follows, then, that—theoretically—low tax rates would tend to give the economy a boost.[27]

FIGURE 2.6

GOVERNMENT REVENUES AND EXPENDITURES

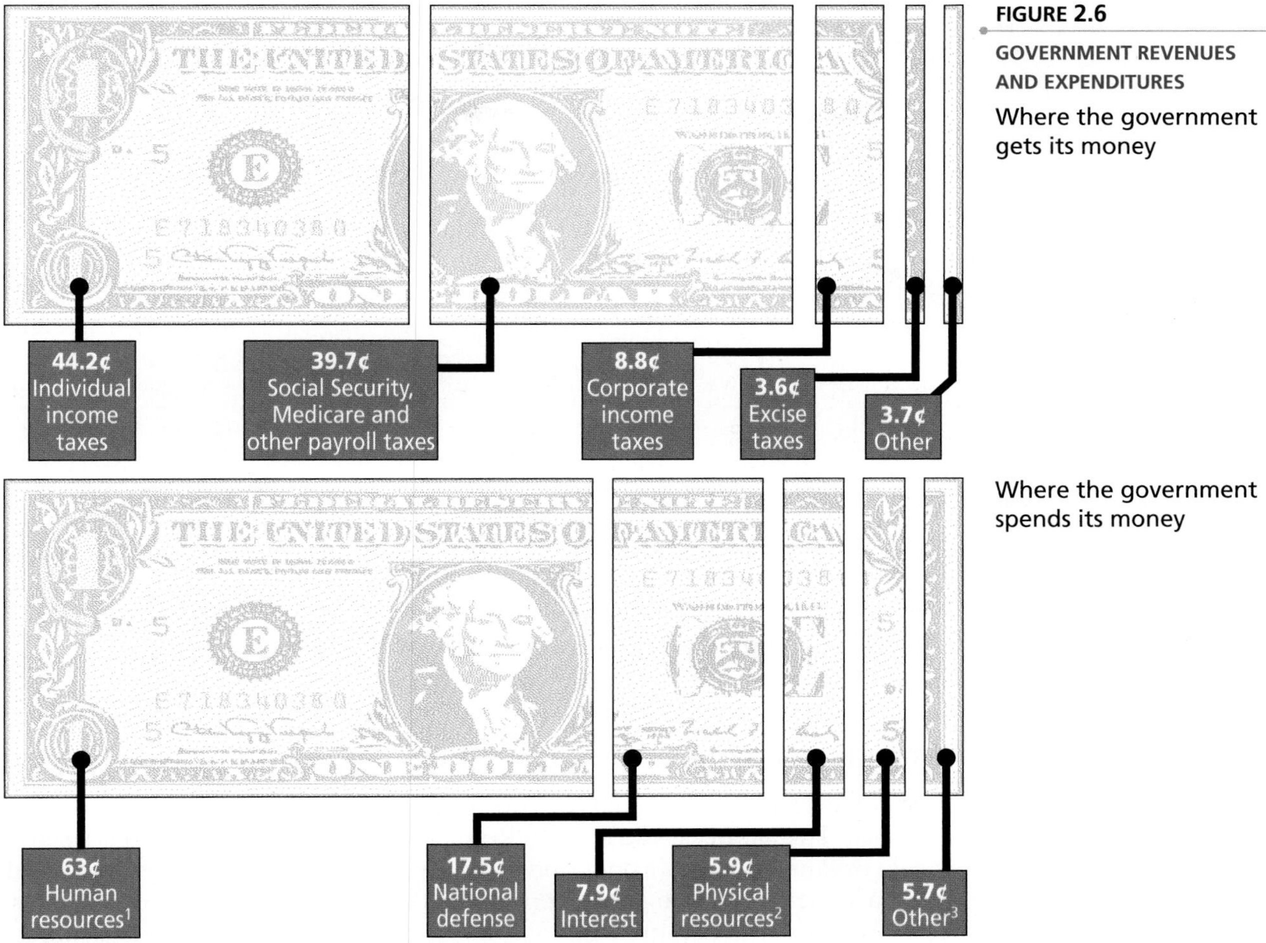

[1]Includes Social Security, education, health, income security, and veterans.
[2]Includes commerce, housing, transportation, and environment.
[3]Includes international affairs, agriculture, science and space, and justice.

In the United States, the percentage of GDP taken by the government through taxes at all levels (federal, state, and local) was about 20.7 percent in 1995. That rate had fallen to 18.4 percent by 2001, but it has been going up since then.[28] Figure 2.6 shows you where the government gets its money and where the money is spent. When you count all fees, sales taxes, and more, taxes on the highest-earning citizens could, until the recent tax cuts, exceed 50 percent. Is that figure too high or not high enough?

The second half of fiscal policy involves government spending. The government spends money on highways, social programs, education, defense, and so on. The national deficit is the amount of money that the federal government spends over and above the amount it gathers in taxes for a specific period of time (namely a fiscal year). Over time, such deficits increase the national debt. The **national debt** is the sum of government deficits over time. Recently, the national debt was a little over $6 trillion (see Figure 2.7). That's over $21,000 for every man, woman, and child in the United States, or over $80,000 for a family of four. (You can see what your current share of the national debt is by checking out the National Debt Clock at www.brillig.com/debt_clock.)

national debt
The sum of government deficits over time.

One way to lessen the annual deficits is to cut government spending. Many presidents have promised to make the government "smaller," that is, to lower government spending—but that doesn't happen very often. There seems to be

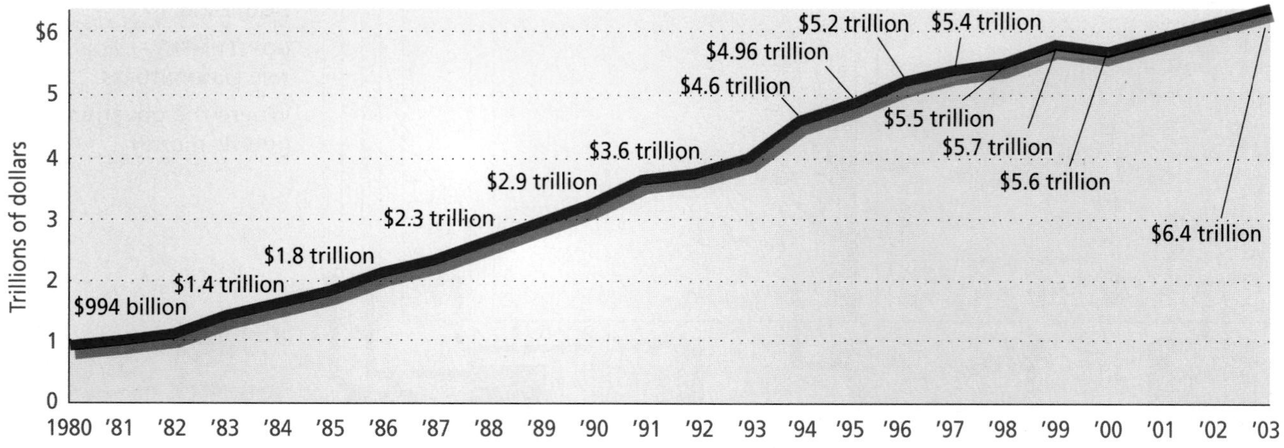

FIGURE 2.7

THE NATIONAL DEBT

Source: Government data.

a need for more social programs or more defense spending each year, and thus the deficits continue and add to the national debt. Some people believe that spending by the government helps the economy to grow. Others believe that the money the government spends comes out of the pockets of consumers and businesspeople and thus slows growth. What do you think?

Using Monetary Policy to Keep the Economy Growing

Have you ever wondered what organization adds or subtracts money from the economy? The answer is the Federal Reserve Bank (the Fed). The Fed is a semiprivate organization that is not under the direct control of the government but does have members who are appointed by the president of the United States. We will discuss the Fed in detail later in the book when we look at the subject of banking in Chapter 21. Our goal in this chapter is to simply introduce you to the concept of monetary policy and the role of the Fed in controlling the economy.

How much money should be spent on aircraft carriers and the planes and expensive weapons they carry? Should we cut back on defense or homeland security in order to increase funding for education or Medicare, or should we increase expenditures in each of these areas? How high should the national debt be? What are some of the reasons that businesses should be concerned with such issues?

Making Ethical Decisions

www.nolo.com/chunktax/tax8.html

Exploring the Tax Laws

Imagine that you've been out of school for a while and you and your spouse together are now earning $80,000 a year. To get to that point, you both paid your way through college. You look forward to buying a home, cars, and other goods and services that you postponed to get your education.

You decide to buy a nice home. The federal government allows you to deduct from your taxable income both the mortgage interest charges on that home and the local property taxes. That makes the payments much easier at first. In fact, almost all the money you're paying into the home the first few years is tax deductible.

You also feel that you should give some money to your religious group and other charities. The money you give these nonprofit organizations is also tax deductible if you itemize such deductions. You read in the paper that you and other people who buy homes and give money to charity are receiving unfair tax breaks. After all, poor people can't get deductions for the rent they pay and they can't afford to give to charity. Some people feel that you shouldn't receive a "government subsidy" to buy your home. You, on the other hand, feel that you're paying enough in taxes, but you want to give your fair share. You also know that some people can buy tax-free bonds and others get tax breaks to rent out a second home. Businesspeople can write off some entertainment and travel expenses, and more.

Should the tax laws of the United States be changed to eliminate certain deductions? What percentage of a person's income should go to the government? Should everyone pay equally, or should the rich pay more? What are the moral and ethical reasons for your position?

Monetary policy is the management of the money supply and interest rates. That policy is controlled by the Federal Reserve System. The most obvious role of the Federal Reserve is the raising and lowering of interest rates.[29] When the economy is booming, the Fed tends to raise interest rates. This makes money more expensive to borrow. Businesses thus borrow less, and the economy slows as businesspeople spend less money on everything they need to grow, including labor and machinery. The opposite is true when the Fed lowers interest rates. Businesses tend to borrow more, and the economy takes off. Raising and lowering interest rates should therefore help control the rapid ups and downs of the economy.

monetary policy
The management of the money supply and interest rates.

The Federal Reserve also controls the money supply. A simple explanation is that the more money that the Fed makes available to businesspeople and others, the faster the economy grows. To slow the economy, the Fed lowers the money supply. If you are eager to learn more about the Fed and the money supply, you can turn to Chapter 21 now. You don't need to know all the details, however, to understand that there are two major efforts being made to control the economy of the United States: fiscal policy (taxes and spending) and monetary policy (control over interest rates and the money supply).

The economic goal is to keep the economy growing so that more people can rise up the economic ladder and enjoy a satisfying quality of life.

Progress Assessment

- Name the three economic indicators and describe how well the United States is doing based on each indicator.
- What's the difference between a recession and a depression?
- How does the government manage the economy using fiscal policy?
- What does the term *monetary policy* mean? What organization is responsible for monetary policy?

Summary

1. Compare and contrast the economics of despair with the economics of growth.

1. Economics is the study of how society chooses to employ resources to produce various goods and services and to distribute them for consumption among various competing groups and individuals.
   - ***Why was economics known as "the dismal science"?***
   In the late 1700s and early 1800s, Thomas Malthus theorized that the human population would grow so fast that resources could not keep up. On the basis of his theories, some countries today have placed severe restrictions on population, including forced sterilization and forced abortions. The economic outlook for the long run was and is considered dismal in some countries.
   - ***How does the government create a climate for economic growth?***
   In 1776, Adam Smith called the mechanism for creating wealth and jobs an invisible hand. Under his system (capitalism), businesspeople don't deliberately set out to help others. In fact, they work mostly for their own prosperity and growth. Yet people's efforts to improve their own situation in life act like an invisible hand to help the economy grow and prosper through the production of needed goods, services, and ideas.

2. Explain what capitalism is and how free markets work.

2. Capitalism is an economic system in which all or most of the means of production and distribution (e.g., land, factories, railroads, and stores) are privately owned and operated for profit.
   - ***Who decides what to produce under capitalism?***
   In capitalist countries, businesspeople decide what to produce; how much to pay workers; how much to charge for goods and services; whether to produce certain goods in their own countries, import those goods, or have them made in other countries; and so on.
   - ***What are the basic rights people have under capitalism?***
   The four basic rights under capitalism are (1) the right to private property, (2) the right to own a business and to keep all of that business's profits after taxes, (3) the right to freedom of competition, and (4) the right to freedom of choice.
   - ***How does the free market work?***
   The free market is one in which decisions about what to produce and in what quantities are made by the market—that is, by buyers and sellers negotiating prices for goods and services. Buyers' decisions in the marketplace tell sellers what to produce and in what quantity. When buyers demand more goods, the price goes up, signaling suppliers to produce more. The higher the price, the more goods and services suppliers are willing to produce. Price, then, is the mechanism that allows free markets to work.

3. Discuss the major differences between socialism and communism.

3. Socialism is an economic system based on the premise that some businesses should be owned by the government.
   - ***What are the advantages and disadvantages of socialism?***
   Socialism creates more social equity. Compared to workers in capitalist countries, workers in socialist countries not only receive more free education and health care benefits but also work fewer hours, have longer vacations, and receive more free benefits in general, such as child care. The major disadvantage of socialism is that it lowers the profits of owners and managers, thus cutting the incentive to start a business or to work hard. Socialist economies tend to have a higher unemployment rate and a slower growth rate than capitalist economies.

- ***How does socialism differ from communism?***

Under communism, the government owns almost all major production facilities and dictates what gets produced and by whom. Communism is also more restrictive when it comes to personal freedoms, such as religious freedom. While there are many countries practicing socialism, there are only a couple (e.g., North Korea, Cuba) still practicing communism.

4. Explain the trend toward mixed economies.

4. A mixed economy is one that is part capitalist and part socialist. That is, some businesses are privately owned, but taxes tend to be high to distribute income more evenly among the population.

- ***What countries have mixed economies?***

The United States has a mixed economy, as do most other countries of the world.

- ***What are the benefits of mixed economies?***

A mixed economy has most of the benefits of wealth creation that free markets bring plus the benefits of greater social equality and concern for the environment that socialism offers.

5. Discuss the economic system of the United States, including the significance of key economic indicators, productivity, and the business cycle.

5. Three major indicators of economic conditions are (1) the gross domestic product (GDP), (2) the unemployment rate, and (3) the price indexes.

- ***What are the key terms used to describe the U.S. economic system?***

Gross domestic product (GDP) is the total value of final goods and services produced in a country in a given year. The unemployment rate refers to the number of civilians at least 16 years old who are unemployed and who tried to find a job within the most recent four weeks. The consumer price index (CPI) measures changes in the prices of about 400 goods and services that consumers buy. It contains monthly statistics that measure the pace of inflation (consumer prices going up) or deflation (consumer prices going down). Productivity is the total volume of goods and services one worker can produce in a given period. Productivity in the United States has increased due to the use of machinery and other technology.

- ***What are the four phases of business cycles?***

In an economic boom, businesses do well. A recession occurs when two or more quarters show declines in the GDP, prices fall, people purchase fewer products, and businesses fail. A depression is a severe recession. Recovery occurs when the economy stabilizes and starts to grow.

6. Define *fiscal policy* and *monetary policy,* and explain how each affects the economy.

6. Fiscal policy consists of government efforts to keep the economy stable by increasing or decreasing taxes or government spending. The search is for a good balance between taxes and spending so that the economy can grow and the government can fund its various programs.

- ***What is the importance of monetary policy to the economy?***

Monetary policy is the management of the money supply and interest rates. When unemployment gets too high, the Federal Reserve System may put more money into the economy and lower interest rates. That provides a boost to the economy as businesses borrow and spend more money and hire more people.

Key Terms

brain drain 48
business cycles 56
capitalism 41
command economies 49
communism 49
consumer price index (CPI) 54
deflation 54
demand 43
depression 56
disinflation 54
economics 36

fiscal policy 56
free-market economies 49
gross domestic product (GDP) 53
inflation 54
invisible hand 39
macroeconomics 36
market price 44
microeconomics 36
mixed economies 50
monetary policy 59
monopolistic competition 45
monopoly 46
national debt 57
oligopoly 46
perfect competition 45
producer price index (PPI) 54
recession 56
resource development 37
socialism 47
supply 43
unemployment rate 53

Developing Workplace Skills

1. In teams, develop a list of the advantages of living in a capitalist society. Then develop lists headed "What are the disadvantages?" and "How could such disadvantages be minimized?" Describe why a poor person in a socialist country might reject capitalism and prefer a socialist state. How could the United States overcome this situation to broaden the base of the free market?

2. Show your understanding of the principles of supply and demand by looking at the employment market today. Explain, for example, the high salaries that computer scientists are getting at Microsoft. Also explain why some PhDs aren't getting better pay than computer scientists who only have undergraduate degrees. Why do some librarians make less than some garbage collectors, even though the librarians may have a better education?

3. This exercise will help you understand socialism from different perspectives. Form four groups. Each group should adopt a different role in a socialist economy: One group will be the business owners, another group will be workers, and another will be government leaders. Within your group discuss and list the advantages and disadvantages to you of lowering taxes on businesses. Then have each group choose a representative to go to the front of the class and debate the tax issue with the representatives from the other groups.

4. Draw a line and mark one end "free-market capitalism" and the other end "central planning." Mark where on the line the United States is now. Explain why you marked the spot you chose. Students from other countries may want to do this exercise for their own countries and explain the differences to the class.

5. Break into small groups. In your group discuss how the following changes have affected people's purchasing behavior and attitudes toward the U.S. and its economy: September 11, 2001; the war in Iraq in March–April 2003; new illnesses such as SARS; the growth of the Internet; and the numerous charges against big business behaving illegally, unethically, and immorally. Have a group member prepare a short summary for the class.

Taking It To The Net 1

Purpose

To compare the value of the dollar based on variances in the consumer price index.

Exercise

Do your parents ever tire of telling you how much things cost back in their day? Sure, things were cheaper then, but the value of a dollar was different too. Think about something you bought today (shoes, soda, candy bar, haircut—whatever). How much did the good or service you bought today cost your parents when they were your age? Find out by using the handy tool on the Federal Reserve Bank of Minneapolis's Woodrow website (http://woodrow.mpls.frb.fed.us/research/data/us/calc). The calculator uses the consumer price index to compare the value of the dollar in different years. Enter the cost of the item you bought today, the year you would like to compare it with, and—presto—you'll find out how Mom and Pop could get along on such a small paycheck. (For an even bigger shock, compare the current dollar to the dollar in your grandparents' day!)

1. How much would a $50 pair of jeans bought today have cost the year you were born?
2. How much would a job paying $6 an hour today have paid in 1970?
3. How much would a new car costing $18,000 today have cost the year your mother first got her driver's license?

Taking It To The Net 2

Purpose

To familiarize you with the sources of economic information that are important to business decision makers.

Exercise

Imagine your boss asked you to help her in preparing the company's sales forecast for the next two years. In the past she felt that the trend in the nation's GDP, the employment trends in U.S. manufacturing, and in manufacturing in Illinois were especially helpful in forecasting sales. She would like you to do the following:

1. Go to the Bureau of Economic Analysis website (www.bea.doc.gov) and locate the gross domestic product data. Compute an annual figure for the last four years by averaging the quarterly data. Plot this on graph paper or a spreadsheet. Leave enough space for six years so that you can draw a projection line for the next two years.
2. On the Bureau of Labor Statistics (BLS) website (www.bls.gov) go to the page with the information about the manufacturing industry. What is the employment trend in that industry over the last four years?
3. On the BLS website, find the manufacturing employment for the state of Illinois. Using the data from July, plot the trend in manufacturing employment in Illinois over the last four years.
4. If sales in your company tend to increase as the GDP increases and as employment in manufacturing in the United States and Illinois remains stable or increases, what do you think is going to happen to your company's sales?

Casing The Web

To access the case "The Rule of 72," visit

www.mhhe.com/ub7e

Video Case

La Baguette

The differences between capitalism and socialism become apparent when you compare opening and managing a restaurant in the United States, which is largely a capitalist country, and France, which is largely a socialist country. Michel Buthion, owner of La Baguette, a French restaurant in Oklahoma, notes some of the differences when he says, "In France, you have to deal with high taxes, incredible labor costs, the chamber of commerce, inspectors, an inspector just for the pipes, bribes or you can't buy a new liquor license, luxury tax. If you live in the south of France, you have to deal with mobsters. They are not called that. It is called 'buying insurance,' but it is the same thing." In socialist countries, the government runs many of the largest businesses and is very active in regulating the rest.

In the United States, on the other hand, starting a business is a lot easier. Labor costs are lower, taxes are lower, and, of course, competition from other French restaurants is much lower. Labor makes up about 15 percent of cost in the United States versus 50 percent in France. One reason for the higher labor cost is French workers get 5 weeks of vacation right from the start.

Starting a business in a communist country is even harder. The government runs most of the larger businesses and makes it difficult to start your own. The government in communist countries is not as responsive to supply and demand conditions, so there are likely to be shortages of some goods and surpluses in others. In the United States, Michel can get whatever he needs for his restaurant easily, including wine from France.

In the United States, Michel and his brother Alain enjoy four basic rights: the right to own their own store (private property), the right to keep all the profits from the business (minus taxes), the right to freedom of competition, and the right to choose what to sell in their restaurant and what to charge. The brothers feel free to offer new products (such as tapas) and to remodel their restaurant whenever they please. The must follow certain regulations, but they don't find them as onerous as similar ones in France—or even similar ones in cities like New York or San Francisco. The United States is a mixed economy, and one must expect some governmental control over all businesses.

The competitive situation for La Baguette is called monopolistic competition. That means that there are other restaurants with similar food offerings, but the restaurants differentiate themselves in some way. For La Baguette, that means offering high quality food and a French atmosphere that attracts the local community.

The law of supply and demand affected the restaurant a little when the French government did not support the U.S. war in Iraq. People stopped coming to the restaurant for a while, and Michel and Alain had to consider whether or not to lower prices. As demand falls for a product, one usually lowers prices to increase demand again. In this case, however, the public came back to the restaurant rather quickly and the brothers did not have to lay off many workers or to cut prices.

In both socialist and capitalist countries, businesses are subject to economic slowdowns. The recent economic slowdown did not have a big effect on the restaurant, however, because Oklahoma came out of the recession better than some states and the customers of the restaurant are relatively wealthy and can afford to eat out, even during an economic decline. So, even within the United States, there are differences in economic situations and different levels of free-market capitalism. The federal government's fiscal policy (e.g., cutting taxes when the economy slows) and the Federal Reserve's monetary policy (cutting interest rates when the economy slows) keep the economy moving ahead, and keep business booming at La Baguette.

Thinking It Over

1. What would be the advantages and disadvantages to the *employees* of La Baguette if the United States were fundamentally a socialist country versus a largely capitalist country?
2. Can you list four advantages that La Baguette experiences by being in Oklahoma that it wouldn't have in Paris?
3. If a French restaurant can succeed in Oklahoma, might an American-style steak house do well in southern France? What problems might a steak house face in trying to operate in France?

Chapter 3

Competing in Global Markets

Learning Goals

After you have read and studied this chapter, you should be able to

1. Discuss the growing importance of the global market and the roles of comparative advantage and absolute advantage in global trade.
2. Explain the importance of importing and exporting, and understand key terms used in global business.
3. Illustrate the strategies used in reaching global markets and explain the role of multinational corporations in global markets.
4. Evaluate the forces that affect trading in global markets.
5. Debate the advantages and disadvantages of trade protectionism.
6. Explain how e-commerce is affecting global trade.

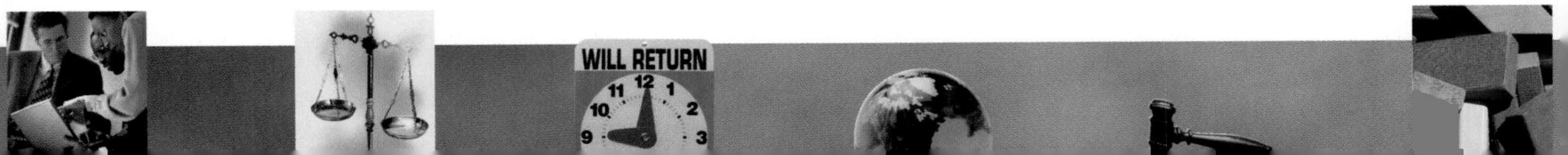

Getting to Know Li Yifei of MTV Networks China

If asked to think of a company with tremendous influence on the music, style, innovation, and attitude of the teenage and 20-plus population, three letters could come to mind: M-T-V. Imagine bringing MTV's marketing power to China, the most populous nation on earth and a country with not only emerging economic potential but also increasing demand among its teenagers and 20-somethings. Viacom, the owner of MTV, envisions such a future and has entrusted Li Yifei, general manager of MTV Networks China, to make it happen.

It would be an understatement to call Li's job a challenge. Traditional media regulators in China are very conservative and not typically receptive to broadcasting attractive, sometimes scantily clad vee-jays who work for a foreign network. When dealing with her mostly male Chinese business associates, Li has to rein in her usual straightforward, confident business style. As she knows well, Chinese culture expects a woman to be soft and humble when conducting business. What she is doing is obviously working. MTV is now on air in China, even if it is currently limited to four hours of programming a day.

In 2001, Li persuaded CCTV, China's state-owned national TV network, to air the Chinese version of the MTV awards. While the awards did not garner huge ratings, the 7.9 percent rating translated to a viewership of 150 million—more than half the size of the U.S. population. Li promises that future telecasts will attract even larger numbers of viewers. She also has committed herself to gaining more market access for MTV in China by seeking a local partner. She knows it's easier to gain access to markets in China if you have the support of a Chinese partner. To date, Li has cultivated an audience that is growing 40 percent each year, with MTV currently in 60 million Chinese households.

Viacom is counting on Li Yifei's judgment. She brings an interesting background and credentials to the job. A native of Beijing (China's capital city), Li was a national champion in tai chi (a form of martial arts) at 13. A good student, she earned the opportunity to attend the most elite foreign-language university in Beijing. In 1985, at age 21, she left China to come to the United States after receiving a scholarship to attend Baylor University in Waco, Texas. Li earned a master's degree in political science at Baylor and also observed firsthand the differences between the U.S. and Chinese cultures.

When dealing with her mostly male Chinese business associates, Li Yifei has to rein in her usual straightforward, confident business style. As she knows well, Chinese culture expects a woman to be soft and humble when conducting business.

After graduation, she was one of 40 students selected for a prestigious internship at the United Nations. There she had the opportunity to produce the television program *U.N. Calling Asia.* After deciding diplomacy was not her career calling, Li became manager of the Beijing office of Burson-Marsteller, a large public relations company. She assisted the firm's clients in business dealings with the Chinese bureaucracy, helped handle complicated paperwork the government required, and assisted with cultural details involved with trade contacts of all kinds. Her work caught the eye of Viacom, and in 1999 she was hired as the general manager of MTV Networks China.

Li Yifei is a vivid example of an emerging global businessperson, that is, a person who speaks different languages, understands cultural events and situations that affect business, and visualizes the vast potential and challenges of global markets in the new millennium. The future of U.S. economic growth and the continued economic expansion of developing nations such as China are tied to open markets and global trade. This chapter will explain the opportunities that exist in global markets and the challenges businesspeople must face to succeed globally.

Sources: Jonah Greenberg, "Asia Wants to Rock All Day, All Night in China," Reuters, May 9, 2002; Jennifer Kent, "MTV Exec Tells Baylor U. Students How to Do Business in China," University Wire, April 30, 2002; and "Viacom Invested in China," AsiaInfo Services, May 8, 2002.

THE DYNAMIC GLOBAL MARKET

Have you ever dreamed of traveling to exotic cities like Paris, Tokyo, Rio de Janeiro, or Cairo? In times past, the closest most Americans ever got to working in such cities was in their dreams. Today, the situation has changed. It's hard to find a major U.S. company that does not cite global expansion as a link to its future growth. A recent study noted that 91 percent of the companies doing business globally believe it's important to send employees on assignments in other countries.

Has the possibility of a career in global business ever crossed your mind? Maybe a few facts will make evaluating such a career more interesting: The United States is a market of about 290 million people, but there are over 6 billion potential customers in the 193 countries that make up the global market. (See Figure 3.1 for a map of the world and important statistics about world population.) Perhaps more interesting is that approximately 75 percent of the world's population lives in developing areas where technology, education, and per capita income still lag considerably behind those of developed (or industrialized) nations such as the United States.

Today Americans buy billions of dollars worth of goods from China.[1] American Express credit card usage is on the rise in Germany, Saudi Arabia, and other global markets. Major league baseball teams, the National Basketball Association, and the National Football League play games in Mexico, Italy, Japan, and elsewhere. In fact, Yao Ming of the People's Republic of China was the Houston Rockets' first pick in the National Basketball Association's draft in 2002.[2] Mel Gibson, Will Smith, and Harrison Ford continuously draw crowds to movie theaters around the globe as American movies take center stage in the global entertainment market.[3]

exporting
Selling products to another country.

importing
Buying products from another country.

The United States is the largest exporting nation in the world. It is the largest importing nation as well. **Exporting** is selling products to another country. **Importing** is buying products from another country. Competition in exporting is very intense. U.S. companies face aggressive competition from exporters such as Germany, Japan, and China.

These facts show that global trade is big business today and will become increasingly important throughout the 21st century. Therefore, it would be wise to prepare yourself for the global challenge. Stop for just a moment and ask yourself the following questions: Are you studying a foreign language in school? Have you talked with anyone about the excitement and rewards of trav-

FIGURE 3.1

WORLD POPULATION BY CONTINENT

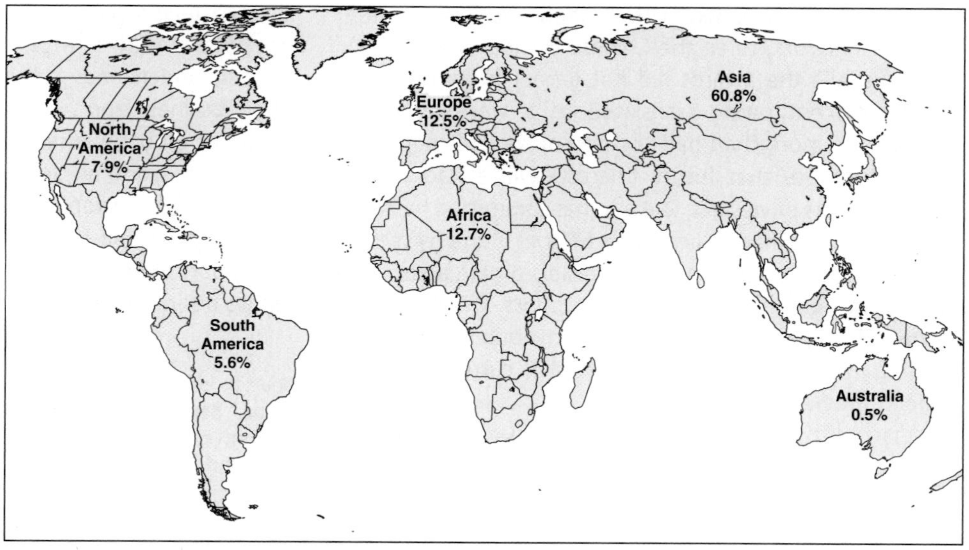

eling to and trading with other countries? Does your college offer students the opportunity to study abroad? To find out more about how your school can help you with any of these questions, talk with your instructor, meet with a guidance counselor, or visit your college website.

The purpose of this chapter is to familiarize you with the potential of global business, including its many challenges. The demand for students with training in global business is almost certain to grow as the number of businesses competing in the global market continues to increase. You might even decide that a career in global business is your long-term goal. If you make that choice, prepare yourself to work hard and always be ready for new challenges.

Why Trade with Other Nations?

There are several reasons why countries trade with other countries. First, no nation, not even a technologically advanced one, can produce all of the products that its people want and need. Second, even if a country did become self-sufficient, other nations would seek to trade with that country in order to meet the needs of their own people. Third, some nations (e.g., China, Russia) have an abundance of natural resources and a lack of technological know-how, while other countries (e.g., Japan, Taiwan, Switzerland) have sophisticated technology but few natural resources. Trade relations enable each nation to produce what it is most capable of producing and to buy what it needs in a mutually beneficial exchange relationship. This happens through the process of free trade.[4] **Free trade** is the movement of goods and services among nations without political or economic trade barriers. It is often a hotly debated concept.[5] Figure 3.2 offers some of the pros and cons of free trade.

free trade
The movement of goods and services among nations without political or economic trade barriers.

The Theories of Comparative and Absolute Advantage

Global trade is the exchange of goods and services across national borders.[6] Exchanges between and among countries involve more than goods and services, however.[7] Countries also exchange art, sports, cultural events, medical advances, space exploration, and labor. Comparative advantage theory, suggested in the early 19th century by English economist David Ricardo, was the guiding principle that supported this idea of free economic exchange.[8] **Comparative advantage theory** states that a country should sell to other countries those products that it produces most effectively and efficiently, and buy from other countries those products it cannot produce as effectively or efficiently.

comparative advantage theory
Theory that states that a country should sell to other countries those products that it produces most effectively and efficiently, and buy from other countries those products that it cannot produce as effectively or efficiently.

FIGURE 3.2

THE PROS AND CONS OF FREE TRADE

PROS	CONS
• The global market contains over 6 billion potential customers for goods and services. • Productivity grows when countries produce goods and services in which they have a comparative advantage. • Global competition and less-costly imports keep prices down, so inflation does not curtail economic growth. • Free trade inspires innovation for new products and keeps firms competitively challenged. • Uninterrupted flow of capital gives countries access to foreign investments, which help keep interest rates low.	• Domestic workers (particularly in manufacturing-based jobs) can lose their jobs due to increased imports or production shifts to low-wage global markets. • Workers may be forced to accept pay cuts from employers, who can threaten to move their jobs to lower-cost global markets. • Moving operations overseas because of intense competitive pressure often means the loss of service jobs and growing numbers of white-collar jobs. • Domestic companies can lose their comparative advantage when competitors build advanced production operations in low-wage countries.

The United States has a comparative advantage in producing goods and services, such as computer chips, software, and engineering services. In contrast, the United States does not have a comparative advantage in growing coffee or making shoes. Coffee beans, shoes, and many other products are imported. Through specialization and trade, the United States and its trading partners can realize mutually beneficial exchanges.[9]

absolute advantage
The advantage that exists when a country has a monopoly on producing a specific product or is able to produce it more efficiently than all other countries.

A country has an **absolute advantage** if it has a monopoly on producing a specific product or is able to produce it more efficiently than all other countries. For instance, South Africa once had an absolute advantage in diamond production. Today there are very few instances of absolute advantage in global markets.

Critical Thinking

Countries like the United States that have a high standard of living ➤P. 5◄ are referred to as *industrialized nations;* countries with a low standard of living and quality of life ➤P. 6◄ are called *developing countries* (former terms used were *underdeveloped* or *less-developed countries*). What's the reason why developing nations are not fully industrialized? Is it because they lack natural resources? If so, how do you explain the success of industrialized nations like Japan and Singapore, which have few natural resources?

Getting Involved in Global Trade

People interested in finding a job in global business often think of firms like Boeing, Ford, IBM, and Intel, which have large multinational accounts. The real job potential, however, may be with small businesses. Today in the United States, small businesses account for only about 20 percent of exports, while generating about half of the private-sector commerce, but they are becoming more involved in global markets with the help of the U.S. Department of Commerce.

Getting started globally is often a matter of observation, determination, and risk. What does that mean? First, it is important to observe and study global markets. The college library, the Internet, and your classmates are good starting points for doing your research. Second, if you have the opportunity, traveling to different countries is a great way to observe foreign cultures and lifestyles and see if doing business globally appeals to you.

Three generations of Irish Eyes are always smiling at Tullycross Fine Irish Imports of Philadelphia. Owner Marjorie Filmyer and family regularly meet with sellers of Irish handcrafts and attend international trade shows to find the latest jewels from the Emerald Isle. Does an importing or exporting career sound appealing to you?

For example, years ago an American traveler in an African country noticed that there was no ice available for drinks, for keeping foods fresh, and so on. Further research showed that, in fact, there was no ice factory for hundreds of miles, yet the market seemed huge. The man returned to the United States, found some willing investors, and returned to Africa to build an ice-making plant. The job was not easy though. Much negotiation was necessary with the local authorities (negotiation often best done by local citizens and businesspeople who know the system), and the plant was built. This forward-thinking entrepreneur gained a considerable return on his idea, and the people in that country gained a needed product.

Importing Goods and Services

Foreign students attending U.S. colleges and universities often notice that some products widely available in their countries are not available in the United States, or are

Howard Schultz found his "caffeine high" while visiting the neighborhood coffee and espresso bars in Italy. He returned home to the United States and purchased the Starbucks coffee shop in Seattle and built it into an international phenomenon. Here Schultz tips his cup to the newly opened Starbucks in Vienna, Austria, the birthplace of the coffeehouse tradition in 1683. In Vienna, coffee is practically a sacred tradition. Do you think Vienna represents a good opportunity or a competitive challenge for a newcomer like Starbucks?

more expensive here. By working with producers in their native country, finding some start-up financing, and putting in many hours of hard work, many students have become major importers while still in school.

Howard Schultz, CEO of Starbucks, found his opportunity while traveling in Italy.[10] Schultz became enthralled with the neighborhood coffee and espresso bars he frequented there. He loved the ambiance, the aroma, and especially the sense of community he saw and wondered why we lacked such great gathering places in the United States. Schultz saw an opportunity and in 1987 bought the original Starbucks coffee shop in Seattle, from which grew a national phenomenon.[11] Because the Italian coffee bars caught the attention of Howard Schultz, people across America now know what a "grande latte" is.

Exporting Goods and Services

You may be surprised at what you can sell in other countries. Who would think, for example, that U.S. firms could sell beer in Germany, the home of so many good beers? Well, right around the corner from a famous beer hall in Munich you can buy Samuel Adams Boston Lager. Thousands of cases have been sold, and a local licensing agreement (licensing will be discussed later in this chapter) assures more sales to come.

American brewing giant Anheuser-Busch also noted the opportunities. It purchased part ownership in Tsingtao Brewing, the largest brewing company in central China.[12] The company also sells its flagship Budweiser product in major Chinese cities.[13] If these company moves surprise you, well, you haven't heard anything yet. Can you imagine selling sand to countries in the Middle East? Meridan Group exports a special kind of sand used in swimming pool filters that sells well.

The fact is, you can sell just about any good or service that is used in the United States to other countries—and often the competition is not nearly as intense for producers in global markets as it is at home. You can, for example, sell snowplows to the Saudi Arabians. They use them to plow sand off their driveways. Tropical Blossom Honey Company in Edgewater, Florida, was pleasantly surprised to find that Saudis are significant consumers of

When Gert Boyle's husband died in 1970, her bankers gave her little chance of successfully running Columbia Sportswear Company. Today, Columbia is one of the world's largest outdoor apparel manufacturers thanks to the "Mother Boyle" ads that Gert and son Tim began in 1984, and to the company's expansion into global markets. What challenges does a company like Columbia Sportswear face in exporting products to global markets?

honey. Why honey? Because the Koran (the Muslim holy book) suggests that it has healing properties. GlobalSight Corporation, a small global consulting and software company in San Jose, California, found expanded opportunities for its clients in e-commerce by adapting websites to the cultural and linguistic needs of a particular country or region.[14] The possibilities seem almost limitless.

It's important for businesses to be aware of these great opportunities. It's also important to note that exporting is a terrific boost to the U.S. economy. The U.S. Department of Commerce estimates that every $1 billion in U.S. exports generates 25,000 jobs at home. But don't be misled: Selling in global markets is not by any means easy. Adapting products to specific global markets is potentially profitable but can be very difficult. We shall discuss a number of forces that affect global trading later in this chapter. For now, read how McDonald's attempts to face global challenges in the Reaching Beyond Our Borders box.

If you are interested in exporting, write for "The Basic Guide to Exporting," available from the U.S. Government Printing Office; Superintendent of Documents; Washington, D.C. 20402. More advice can be found at the U.S Department of Commerce's website (www.doc.gov) or in *Business America,* a trade magazine published by the Department of Commerce's International Trade Administration. The magazine can be ordered from the U.S. Government Printing Office as well. The Bureau of Export Administration (www.bea.gov) also offers key exporting advice available through the Department of Commerce website. The Small Business Administration also has information available on its website (www.sba.gov).

Measuring Global Trade

balance of trade
A nation's ratio of exports to imports.

trade deficit
An unfavorable balance of trade; occurs when the value of a country's imports exceeds that of its exports

balance of payments
The difference between money coming into a country (from exports) and money leaving the country (for imports) plus money flows from other factors such as tourism, foreign aid, military expenditures, and foreign investment.

In measuring the effectiveness of global trade, nations carefully follow two key indicators: balance of trade and balance of payments. The **balance of trade** is a nation's ratio of exports to imports. A *favorable* balance of trade, or trade surplus, occurs when the value of the country's exports exceeds that of its imports. An *unfavorable* balance of trade, or **trade deficit,** occurs when the value of the country's imports exceeds that of its exports. It is easy to understand why countries prefer to export more than they import. If I sell you $200 worth of goods and buy only $100 worth, I have an extra $100 available to buy other things. However, I'm in an unfavorable position if I buy $200 worth of goods from you and sell you only $100.

The **balance of payments** is the difference between money coming into a country (from exports) and money leaving the country (for imports) plus money flows coming into or leaving a country from other factors such as tourism, foreign aid, military expenditures, and foreign investment. The goal is always to have more money flowing into the country than flowing out of the country; in other words a *favorable* balance of payments. Conversely, an *unfavorable* balance of payments exists when more money is flowing out of a country than coming in.

Reaching Beyond Our Borders

www.mcdonalds.com

McDonaldizing the World

The United States changed the landscape of the global market with the tremendous expansion of franchising. Today small, midsize, and large franchises cover the globe, offering business opportunities in areas from exercise to donuts to education. Still, when the word *franchise* comes to mind, one name dominates all others: McDonald's. "McDonaldization" symbolizes the spread of franchising and the weaving of American pop culture into the world fabric. Whether in South Africa, Mexico, Germany, Brazil, or Hong Kong, no one adapts better and blends the franchise values into the local culture better than McDonald's.

For example, after setting up its first franchises in Hong Kong in 1975, McDonald's altered the breakfast menu after realizing that customers there liked burgers for breakfast, then preferred chicken or fish for the rest of the day. The company also offers unique products such as curry potato pie and red bean sundaes for its Hong Kong customers. In Israel, all meat served in McDonald's restaurants is 100 percent kosher beef. The company also closes its restaurants on the Sabbath and on religious holidays. However, the company also operates nonkosher restaurants for Israelis who don't keep a strict kosher diet and desire to visit McDonald's on the Sabbath and religious holidays. To meet the unique challenge in India and respect the religious sentiments of the population, the company did not introduce beef or pork into the menu.

In Hong Kong, Israel, India, and all other markets in which McDonald's operates, the company continuously listens to customers and adapts to their culture and preferences. The company also must respond to problems and challenges that emerge at its more than 30,000 global restaurants—challenges such as the outbreak of mad cow disease at its restaurants in Europe and Asia. Profits fell by over 14 percent in Japan because of the outbreak of the disease. McDonald's is now funding research for a product that would let it test for the presence of *E. coli* or mad cow disease in its beef. Weak currencies in many countries (e.g., Brazil, Argentina) and government regulations also cause McDonald's global grief. In fact, in Beijing the company was told to remove 30 of its large landmark golden arches in the city because they don't fit with the surrounding architecture. In 2003, the company closed 600 restaurants globally due to poor market conditions.

Yet, with all its problems and challenges, McDonald's is the leading restaurant in the world, serving over 46 million customers worldwide per day. By using such adaptive strategies in global markets, the company has reaped a large payoff. Today, McDonald's derives more than half of its sales from abroad. Still, the challenge goes on. Some critics even ask whether the golden arches are doomed to fall. It seems the key question is: Can Ronald McDonald make meals all around the globe "happy meals"? Time will tell.

Sources: Carol Matlack and Pallavi Gogoi, "What's This? The French Love McDonald's?" *Business Week,* January 13, 2003, p. 50; and "Big Mac Dips into Giant Loss," *The Mirror* (UK), January 24, 2003, p. 2.

For many years, the United States exported more goods and services to other countries than it imported. Every year since 1985, however, the United States has bought more goods from other nations than it has sold to other nations.[15] Remember, this is called a trade deficit or unfavorable balance of trade. In the early 2000s, the United States ran its highest trade deficits with Japan and China.[16] Still, the fact remains that the United States historically has never focused significantly on exporting compared to other nations. How then, you may ask, is the United States the world's largest exporting nation? Good question; let's look at the answer.

Even though the United States exports the largest *volume* of goods globally, it exports a much lower *percentage* of its products than other countries do. (Figure 3.3 lists the major trading countries in the world.) In the early 1980s, for example, no more than 10 percent of American businesses exported products. However, slow economic growth in the United States and other economic factors lured more businesses to global markets beginning in the late 1980s. Today, most large businesses are involved in global trade, and growing numbers of small and medium-sized businesses are going global as well.

FIGURE 3.3

THE LARGEST TRADING COUNTRIES IN THE WORLD

United States
Germany
Japan
France
Britain
China/Hong Kong
Canada
Italy
Netherlands

Source: World Trade Organization, 2003.

International competition is widespread, even in airline manufacturing. Brazilians huddle around the ERJ 170 jet produced by Embraer, the leading exporter in South America's largest country. The company hopes the jet will surpass the 717 made by Boeing (U.S.) and the Airbus A318 produced in Europe as the aircraft of choice in global markets. Exports such as aircraft are critical to a country's effectiveness in global trade. Why do countries generally seek a favorable balance of trade?

TRADING IN GLOBAL MARKETS: THE U.S. EXPERIENCE

As we discussed in the preceding section, since 1985 the United States has experienced a trade deficit, or an unfavorable balance of trade. During the mid-1980s, reports showed that the United States had become a debtor nation, that is, a country that owes more money to other nations than other nations owe to it. As you might suspect, this information caused quite a stir when it was first reported. Some doomsayers even predicted the United States was on the road to economic ruin. Let's examine this controversy a bit further.

foreign direct investment The buying of permanent property and businesses in foreign nations.

Economists measure a nation's economic strength by comparing several factors. They calculate the amount of money a nation owes to foreign creditors and the value of what foreign creditors own in a particular country, referred to as foreign direct investment. **Foreign direct investment** is the buying of permanent property and businesses in foreign nations. This information is compared to how much money foreign creditors owe to a nation and the value of what a nation owns in other countries. Increasingly, economists and trade analysts have come to agree that a high amount of foreign direct investment in a nation is not necessarily a bad sign. In fact, the amount of foreign direct investment in a country means that other nations perceive that country as a strong economic leader. The U.S. Department of Commerce has reported that foreign direct investment in the United States grew steadily in the 1990s and continues on in the early 2000s. Even though the United States has run trade deficits, it still is viewed as a favorable venue for foreign direct investment and private investment.[17] Figure 3.4 lists the five nations and the five companies with the largest direct foreign investment in the United States.

dumping Selling products in a foreign country at lower prices than those charged in the producing country.

In supporting free trade, the United States, like other nations, wants to make certain that global trade is conducted fairly.[18] To ensure this level playing field, countries enforce laws to prohibit unfair practices such as dumping.[19] **Dumping** is the practice of selling products in a foreign country at lower prices than those charged in the producing country. Companies sometimes use this tactic to reduce surplus products in foreign markets or to gain a foothold in a new market by offering products for lower prices than domestic competitors do. Japan and Russia, for example, have been accused of dumping steel in the United States, Canada of dumping softwood lumber.[20] U.S. laws against dumping are specific and require that foreign firms must price their products to include 10 percent overhead costs plus an 8 percent profit margin. It can take time to prove accusations of dump-

COUNTRY	TOTAL INVESTMENT (BILLIONS)
United Kingdom	$196
Japan	157
Germany	134
France	118
Netherlands	114

COMPANY	COUNTRY	PRODUCT
BP	United Kingdom	Petroleum
DaimlerChrysler	Germany	Automobiles
Ahold	Netherlands	Food Stores
Royal Dutch/Shell	United Kingdom/Netherlands	Petroleum
Toyota Motors	Japan	Automobiles

Sources: U.S. Department of Commerce; www.bea.gov.ail.htm; *Forbes.*

FIGURE 3.4

LEADING COUNTRIES AND COMPANIES WITH FOREIGN DIRECT INVESTMENT IN THE UNITED STATES

ing, however. There's also evidence that some governments offer financial incentives to certain industries to sell goods in global markets for less than they sell them at home. Dumping promises to remain a difficult trade issue in the 2000s.

Now that you understand some of the basic terms used in global business, we can begin to discuss this topic more deeply. We'll begin by looking at different strategies a business can use to enter global markets. Before doing so, however, let's assess your progress so far.

Progress Assessment

- How do world population and market statistics support the expansion of U.S. businesses into global markets?
- What is comparative advantage, and what are some examples of this concept in actual global markets?
- How are a nation's balance of trade and balance of payments determined?
- What is dumping?

Critical Thinking

About 95 percent of the world's population lives outside the United States but many U.S. companies, especially small businesses, still do not engage in global trade. Why is that? What does this indicate about the potential for increasing U.S. exports? What does it say about career opportunities in global business?

STRATEGIES FOR REACHING GLOBAL MARKETS

The many ways in which an organization may participate in global trade include licensing, exporting, franchising, contract manufacturing, creating international joint ventures and strategic alliances, creating foreign subsidiaries, and engaging in foreign direct investment. Each of these strategies provides opportunities for becoming involved in global markets, along with specific commitments and risks. Figure 3.5 places the strategies discussed in the following sections (as well as foreign direct investment, discussed earlier) on a

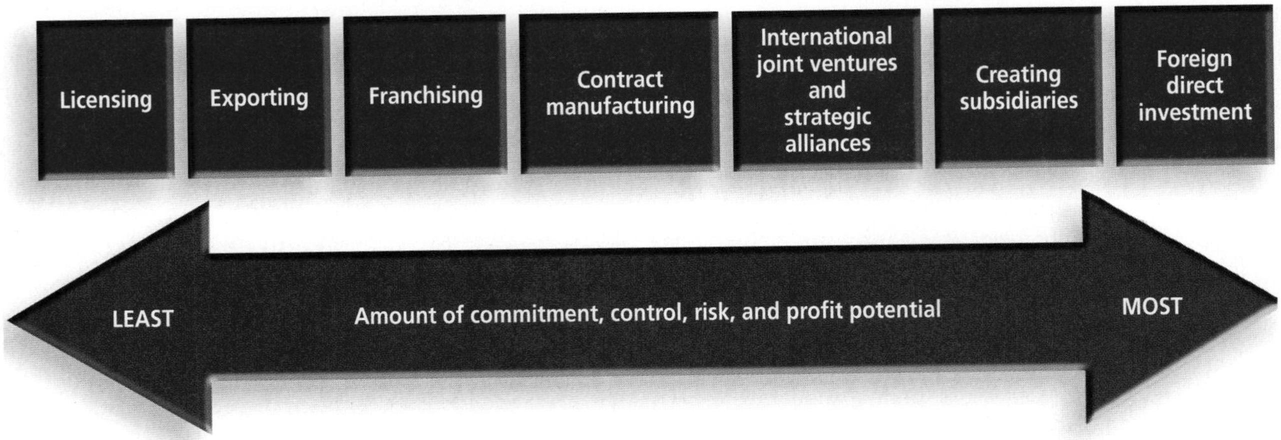

FIGURE 3.5

STRATEGIES FOR REACHING GLOBAL MARKETS

continuum showing the amount of commitment, control, risk, and profit potential associated with each one. Take a few minutes to look over Figure 3.5 before you continue.

Licensing

licensing
A global strategy in which a firm (the licensor) allows a foreign company (the licensee) to produce its product in exchange for a fee (a royalty).

A firm (the licensor) may decide to compete in a global market by **licensing** the right to manufacture its product or use its trademark to a foreign company (the licensee) for a fee (a royalty). A company with an interest in licensing generally needs to send company representatives to the foreign producer to help set up the production process. The licensor may also assist or work with a licensee in such areas as distribution, promotion, and consulting.

A licensing agreement can be beneficial to a firm in several different ways. Through licensing, an organization can gain additional revenues from a product that it normally would not have generated in its home market. In addition, foreign licensees often must purchase start-up supplies, component materials, and consulting services from the licensing firm. Such agreements have been very profitable for companies like Disney, Coca-Cola, and PepsiCo. These firms often enter foreign markets through licensing agreements that typically extend into long-term service contracts. For example, Oriental Land Company and the Hong Kong government have licensing agreements with Walt Disney Company. Oriental Land Company owns and operates Tokyo Disneyland and Tokyo Disney Sea Park under a licensing agreement.[21]

Tokyo Disneyland celebrated its 20th anniversary in 2003.[22] The taxpayers of Hong Kong will mostly finance the $3.5 billion to build Hong Kong Disneyland, which is expected to open in 2005.[23] Disney collects management and consulting fees from both. A final advantage of licensing worth noting is that licensors spend little or no money to produce and market their products. These costs come from the licensee's pocket. Therefore, licensees generally work very hard to see that the product they license succeeds in their market.

However, companies that enter into licensing agreements may also experience some problems. One major problem is that often a firm must grant licensing rights to its product for an extended period, maybe 20 years or longer. If a product experiences remarkable growth and success in the foreign market, the bulk of the revenues earned belong to the licensee. Perhaps even more threatening is that a licensing firm is actually selling its expertise in a product area. If a foreign licensee learns the company's technology or product secrets, it may break the agreement and begin to produce a similar product on its own. If legal remedies are not available, the licensing firm may lose its trade secrets, not to mention the agreed-on royalties.

www.wellsfargo.com/com/ceo/ilc

Dealing with Change

Like Money in the Bank

Getting paid is a key concern of exporters when shipping goods to global buyers. Naturally, an exporting firm would like to be paid immediately when goods are shipped. Conversely, importers want to know that the exact goods they ordered have in fact been the ones that are shipped (and are in good condition) before they commit payment. In essence, neither side in a transaction wants to take the risk of the others not following through fully in the agreement. What's an exporter to do? Look to its local bank and the use of a letter of credit.

Letters of credit have been a key part of global trade for centuries. To make a long and sometimes complicated explanation as concise as possible, a letter-of-credit transaction works something like this:

1. After signing a contract, an importer requests its bank to issue a letter of credit to pay for the shipment of goods it is buying from an exporter.
2. The importer's bank issues the letter of credit to the exporter's bank; the bank then informs the exporter it has received the letter. The exporter is now assured that it's safe to ship the goods to the foreign buyer.
3. The exporter then signs over title to the goods to its bank and receives a draft from the bank that instructs the importer's bank to send payment for the goods. Acceptance by the importer's bank generally means the exporter will get its money immediately from its bank, and that the bank will take the risk of collecting the money from the importer's bank. Both banks, of course, receive fees for their services.

Again, this is a simplified explanation. If you would like to learn more about letter-of-credit systems, contact a local bank for information.

Also, technology is hard at work to assist would-be exporters in getting their money promptly. The international trade acceptance draft is becoming a faster, less paper-intensive way of ensuring payment for global shipments. Who knows, maybe someday we will bid adieu to the letter of credit.

Sources: Erika Morphy, "Once Again, a Slew of Electronic Products Is Taking Aim at the Venerable Letter of Credit. This Time, They May Finally Prevail," *Global Finance,* May 2001, pp. 36–39; and Russ Banham, "Maiden Voyage," *CFO,* November 2002, pp. 71–76.

Exporting

As global competition has intensified, the U.S. government has created Export Assistance Centers (EACs) to provide hands-on exporting assistance and trade-finance support for small and medium-sized businesses that choose to directly export goods and services. A nationwide network of EACs now exists in over 100 U.S. cities, with further expansion planned.[24] In 2002, over 50,000 small and medium-sized businesses were helped by EACs. This activity is critical because it's estimated that over 95 percent of the exporters in the United States are small and medium-sized businesses.[25] EACs represent a strong source of future federal export promotion efforts.

Thirsty Iranians unload the world's best-selling soft drink enjoyed by billions of customers daily around the globe. Coca-Cola generates approximately 80 percent of its business from global markets primarily through licensing agreements between the company and local bottling companies. What advantages do companies receive from licensing agreements? What disadvantages?

Still, even with the help of EACs available, many U.S. firms are reluctant to go through the trouble of establishing foreign trading relationships. In such cases specialists called export-trading companies (or export-management companies) are available to step in to negotiate and establish the trading relationships desired.[26] An export-trading company not only matches buyers and sellers from different countries but also provides needed services (such as dealing with foreign customs offices, documentation requirements, even weights and measures) to ease the process of entering global markets. Export-trading companies also help exporters with a key and risky element of doing business globally: getting paid. The Dealing with Change box on p. 77 highlights one of the oldest methods of obtaining payment from global business, with a new technology twist.

Companies that work with export-trading companies are involved in indirect exporting. If you are considering career opportunities in global business, you should know that export-trading companies often provide internships or part-time opportunities for students.

Been reading too long and need a food break? How about a hot Domino's pizza with squid and sweet mayonnaise or a duck gizzard with sprouts pizza to satisfy your craving? Domino's serves pizza around the world that appeals to different tastes. Franchises like Domino's and McDonald's know the world is a big place and preferences in food, even pizza, can vary considerably. What do franchises have to do to ensure their products are appropriate for global markets they hope to serve?

Franchising

Franchising is an arrangement whereby someone with a good idea for a business sells the rights to use the business name and sell a product or service to others in a given territory. Franchising is popular both domestically and internationally and will be discussed in depth in Chapter 5. U.S. franchisors such as McDonald's, 7-Eleven, and Dunkin' Donuts have many global units operated by foreign franchisees. However, global franchising is not limited to only the large franchisors. For example, Rocky Mountain Chocolate Factory, a Colorado-based producer of premium chocolate candies with 235 retail stores worldwide, entered into a franchising agreement with the Muhairy Group of the United Arab Emirates. The Muhairy Group will open stores in Saudi Arabia, Oman, Kuwait, Bahrain, and Qatar, where chocolate is considered a gourmet luxury much like caviar is in the United States.[27]

Franchisors, however, have to be careful to adapt their product or service to the countries they serve. For example, KFC's first 11 Hong Kong outlets failed within two years. Apparently the chicken was too greasy, and eating with fingers was too messy for the fastidious people of Hong Kong. McDonald's made a similar mistake when entering the Netherlands market. It originally set up operations in the suburbs, as it does in the United States, but soon learned that the Dutch mostly live in the cities. Pizza Hut originally approached the global market using a strategy of one-pie-fits-all. The company found out the hard way that Germans like small individual pizzas, not the large pies preferred in the United States. Preferences in pizza toppings also differ globally. Japanese customers, for example, enjoy squid and sweet mayonnaise pizza.

Contract Manufacturing

contract manufacturing
A foreign country's production of private-label goods to which a domestic company then attaches its brand name or trademark; also called *outsourcing*.

Contract manufacturing involves a foreign company's production of private-label goods to which a domestic company then attaches its own brand name or trademark. The practice is also known as *outsourcing*. For example, Dell Computer contracts with Quanta Computer of Taiwan to make notebook PCs, on which it then puts the Dell brand name. Many other well-known U.S. firms, such as Levi-Strauss and Nike, practice contract manufacturing. Cisco Systems, the world leader in Internet-routing gear, depends heavily on contract manufacturers such as Solectron and Flextronics.[28] Contract manufacturing also enables a company to experiment in a new market without incurring heavy start-up costs such as a manufacturing plant. If the brand name becomes a success, the company has penetrated a new market with relatively low risk. A firm can also use contract manufacturing temporarily to meet an unexpected increase in orders.

Competition has fueled the growth of long-term partnerships called strategic alliances in global markets. Airbus Industries, a European consortium, is an example of such an alliance. Started by government backing from Britain, France, Germany, and Spain, Airbus is currently involved in the $10 billion A380 project that it sees as a key to future growth in its ongoing market battle with Boeing Corporation. Do you think the U.S. government should subsidize a company such as Boeing to enhance its competitive position in global markets?

International Joint Ventures and Strategic Alliances

A **joint venture** is basically a partnership in which two or more companies (often from different countries) join to undertake a major project. According to Coopers & Lybrand, a New York–based international professional services firm, companies that participate in such partnerships grow much faster than their counterpart companies that are not participating. Joint ventures can even be mandated by governments as a condition of doing business in their country. It's often hard to gain entry into a country like China, but agreeing to a joint venture with a Chinese firm can help a company gain such entry. For example, Volkswagen and General Motors entered into joint ventures with Shanghai Automotive Industrial Corporation, China's largest domestic car company, to build cars in China.[29]

joint venture
A partnership in which two or more companies (often from different countries) join to undertake a major project.

Joint ventures are developed for other business reasons as well. Campbell Soup Company formed joint ventures with Japan's Nakano Vinegar Company and Malaysia's Cheong Chan Company to expand its rather low share of the soup market in both countries. Global Engine Alliance, a combination of DaimlerChrysler, Mitsubishi Motors, and Hyundai Motor Company, is a joint venture that will develop aluminum engines that will be used by both Asian manufacturers and DaimlerChrysler's U.S. Chrysler unit.[30] Joint ventures can also bring together unique partners. For example, a few years ago, the University of Pittsburgh and the Italian government entered a joint venture to bring a new medical transplant center to Sicily.

The benefits of international joint ventures are clear:

1. Shared technology.
2. Shared marketing and management expertise.
3. Entry into markets where foreign companies are often not allowed unless their goods are produced locally.
4. Shared risk.

The drawbacks are not so obvious. An important one, however, is that one partner can learn the other's technology and practices, and then go off on its own and use what it has learned. Also, over time, a shared technology may become obsolete or the joint venture may become too large to be as flexible as needed.

Global market potential is also fueling the growth of strategic alliances. A **strategic alliance** is a long-term partnership between two or more companies

strategic alliance
A long-term partnership between two or more companies established to help each company build competitive market advantages.

established to help each company build competitive market advantages. Such alliances can provide access to markets, capital, and technical expertise.[31] Unlike joint ventures, however, they do not typically involve sharing costs, risks, management, or even profits. Many executives and management consultants predict that few companies in the 21st century will succeed in the global market by going it alone; most will need strategic alliances.[32] Strategic alliances can be flexible, and they can be effective between firms of vastly different sizes. Motorola, a large communications equipment manufacturer, once entered a strategic alliance with a small Canadian firm with only six employees. Oracle Corporation, a leader in computer software, has alliances with 15,000 different partners that range from giant companies like Ford Motor Company and Chevron to emerging firms like Nantucket Nectars (a maker of juice-based beverages).

foreign subsidiary
A company owned in a foreign country by another company (called the *parent company*).

multinational corporation
An organization that manufactures and markets products in many different countries and has multinational stock ownership and multinational management.

Foreign Subsidiaries

As you recall, foreign direct investment is the buying of permanent property and businesses in foreign nations. As the size of a foreign market expands, many firms increase foreign direct investment and establish a foreign subsidiary. A **foreign subsidiary** is a company that is owned in a foreign country by another company (called the *parent company*). Such a subsidiary would operate much like a domestic firm, with production, distribution, promotion, pricing, and other business functions under the control of the foreign subsidiary's management.

The legal requirements of both the country where the parent firm is located (called the *home country*) and the foreign country where the subsidiary is located (called the *host country*) have to be observed. The primary advantage of a subsidiary is that the company maintains complete control over any technology or expertise it may possess. The major shortcoming associated with creating a subsidiary is that the parent company is committing a large amount of funds and technology within foreign boundaries. Should relations with the host country falter, the firm's assets could be taken over by the foreign government. Such a takeover is called an *expropriation*.

Do you know that if you purchase fuel at any of the 1,300 Getty stations in the United States today, you are buying gas from a subsidiary of a Russian-owned company called Lukoil? Lukoil bought Getty Oil to give the firm a foothold in the United States. Are there U.S. companies in your community that are subsidiaries of foreign corporations?

Consumer products giant Nestlé is an example of a major firm with many foreign subsidiaries. The Swiss-based company spent billions of dollars acquiring foreign subsidiaries such as Ralston Purina, Chef America (maker of Hot Pockets), and Dreyer's Ice Cream in the United States as well as Perrier in France. The company continues to look for opportunities around the globe.[33] Nestlé is also an example of a multinational corporation. A **multinational corporation** is an organization that manufactures and markets products in many different countries; it has multinational stock ownership and multinational management. Multinational corporations are typically extremely large corporations, but not all large firms involved in global business are multinationals. For example, a business could literally be exporting everything it produces, thus deriving 100 percent of its sales and profits globally, and still not be considered a multinational corporation. Only firms that have *manufacturing capacity* or some other physical presence in different nations can truly be called multinational.

There has been much discussion about the economic power of multinational corporations such as General Motors, Siemens, and Royal Dutch/Shell. It may be hard to imagine, but the annual sales of just one multinational company can be larger than the gross domestic product (GDP) of a nation such as Pakistan, Venezuela, or Turkey. If you are thinking about a career in global business, you will need an understanding of what multinational corporations are and what they mean for global business. Multinational businesses offer great career opportunities in global

FIGURE 3.6

THE LARGEST MULTINATIONAL CORPORATIONS IN THE WORLD

COMPANY	COUNTRY	SALES (BILLION)
Wal-Mart	United States	$217
Exxon Mobil	United States	213
General Motors	United States	175
BP	United Kingdom	174
Ford Motor	United States	162
DaimlerChrysler	Germany	136
Royal Dutch/Shell	United Kingdom/Netherlands	135
General Electric	United States	125
Toyota Motor	Japan	121
Mitsubishi	Japan	112

Sources: *Business Week;* Morgan Stanley Capital International; and S&P Compustat.

business. They are also excellent training grounds for entrepreneurs who want to build their own global business. Figure 3.6 lists the 10 largest multinational corporations in the world.

Becoming involved in global business requires selecting a strategy to enter a market that best fits the goals of the business.[34] As you can see, the different strategies discussed reflect different levels of ownership, financial commitment, and risk that a company can assume. However, this is just the beginning. It's important to be aware of key market forces that affect a business's ability to trade in global markets. After the Progress Assessment, we'll discuss these forces.

Progress Assessment

- What are the advantages to a firm of using licensing as a method of entry in global markets? What are the disadvantages?
- What services are usually provided by an export-trading company?
- What is the key difference between a joint venture and a strategic alliance?
- What is a multinational corporation? Can you name at least three multinational corporations?

FORCES AFFECTING TRADING IN GLOBAL MARKETS

Succeeding in any business takes work and effort, due to the many challenges that exist in all markets. Unfortunately, the hurdles are higher and more complex in global markets than in domestic ones. This is particularly true when dealing with differences in sociocultural forces, economic and financial forces, legal and regulatory forces, and physical and environmental forces. Let's take a look at each of these global market forces to see how they challenge even the most established global businesses.

Sociocultural Forces

As we stated in Chapter 1, the United States is a multicultural nation, yet understanding cultural diversity in America remains one of the true business challenges of the 21st century. The word *culture* refers to the set of values, beliefs, rules, and institutions held by a specific group of people.[35] Primary components of a culture can include social structures, religion, manners and customs, values and attitudes, language, and personal communication. If you hope to get involved in global trade, it's critical to be aware of the cultural differences among nations.

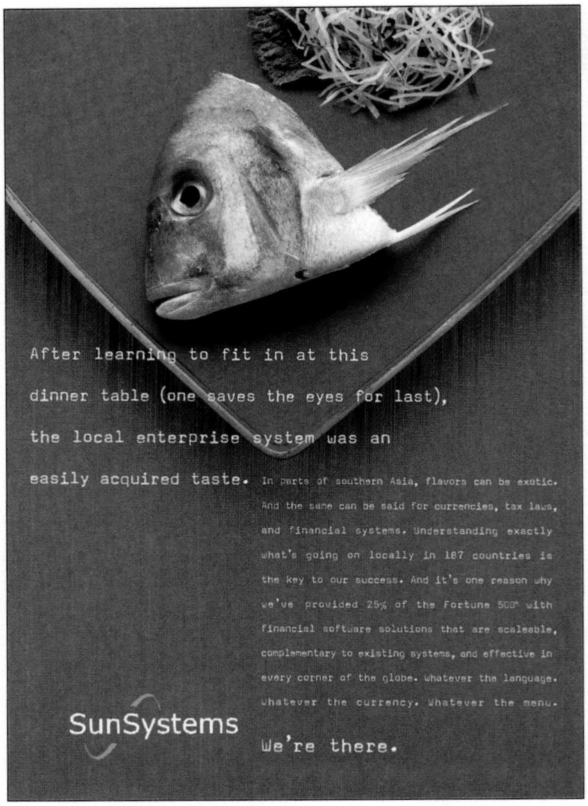
After learning to fit in at this dinner table (one saves the eyes for last), the local enterprise system was an easily acquired taste.
In parts of southern Asia, flavors can be exotic. And the same can be said for currencies, tax laws, and financial systems. Understanding exactly what's going on locally in 187 countries is the key to our success. And it's one reason why we've provided 25% of the Fortune 500® with financial software solutions that are scaleable, complementary to existing systems, and effective in every corner of the globe. Whatever the language. Whatever the currency. Whatever the menu.
SunSystems
We're there.

Can you think of anything more appetizing than a tasty fish head? No? Well, the cheeseburgers and "finger-licking-good" chicken we devour in the United States often get similar reactions in other cultures. Understanding different sociocultural perspectives related to time, change, natural resources, even food can be important in succeeding in global markets. How do you think companies can help employees being assigned to global markets adapt to the different cultures they will encounter and help them avoid "culture shock"?

Different nations have very different ways of conducting business, and unfortunately American businesspeople are notoriously bad at adapting to those ways. In fact, American businesspeople have consistently been accused of *ethnocentricity,* which is an attitude that one's own culture is superior to all others. In contrast, foreign businesspeople are very good at adapting to U.S. culture. Think of how effectively German and Japanese carmakers have adapted to Americans' wants and needs in the auto industry. Japanese manufacturer Toyota sold more vehicles in the United States than in Japan in 2002. Its Camry model was the best-selling car in the United States that year.[36] Let's look at experiences American businesses have faced in adapting to some of the important sociocultural (societal and cultural) differences in global markets.

Religion is an important part of any society's culture and can have a significant impact on business operations. Consider the violent clashes between religious communities in India, Pakistan, Northern Ireland, and the Middle East—clashes that have wounded these areas' economies. Unfortunately, companies at times do not consider the religious implications of business decisions. Both McDonald's and Coca-Cola offended Muslims in Saudi Arabia by putting the Saudi Arabian flag on their packaging. The flag's design contains a passage from the Koran (Islam's sacred scripture), and Muslims feel their holy writ should never be wadded up and thrown away. In another example, an American manager in Islamic Pakistan toured a new plant under his control. While the plant was in full operation, he went to his office to make some preliminary forecasts of production. As he was working, suddenly all the machinery in the plant stopped. He rushed out, suspecting a power failure, only to find his production workers on their prayer rugs. Upon learning that Muslims are required to pray five times a day, the manager returned to his office and proceeded to lower his production estimates.

Sociocultural differences can also affect important business decisions involving human resource management. In Latin American countries, workers believe that managers are placed in positions of authority to make decisions and be responsible for the well-being of the workers under their control. Consider what happened to one American manager in Peru who was unaware of this important cultural characteristic and believed workers should participate in managerial functions. This manager was convinced he could motivate his workers to higher levels of productivity by instituting a more democratic decision-making style than the style already in place. Soon workers began quitting their jobs in droves. When asked why, the Peruvian workers said the new production manager and supervisors did not know their jobs and were asking the workers what to do. All stated they wanted to find new jobs, since obviously this company was doomed because of incompetent managers.

Learning about additional sociocultural perspectives related to time factors, change, competition, natural resources, achievement, and even work itself can be of great assistance in global markets. Today, before managers and their families are sent on a global assignment, firms often give them training on how to adapt to different cultures. For you as a student, taking courses in cultural variations and anthropology can help you gain a better understanding of foreign cultures.

- PepsiCo attempted a Chinese translation of "Come Alive, You're in the Pepsi Generation" that read to Chinese customers as "Pepsi Brings Your Ancestors Back from the Dead."
- Coors Brewing Company put its slogan "Turn It Loose" into Spanish and found it translated as "Suffer from Diarrhea."
- Perdue Chicken used the slogan "It Takes a Strong Man to Make a Chicken Tender," which was interpreted in Spanish as "It Takes an Aroused Man to Make a Chicken Affectionate."
- KFC's patented slogan "finger-lickin' good" was understood in Japanese as "Bite Your Fingers Off."
- On the other side of the translation glitch, Electrolux, a Scandinavian vacuum manufacturer, tried to sell its products in the U.S. market with the slogan "Nothing Sucks Like an Electrolux."

FIGURE 3.7

OOPS, DID WE SAY THAT?

A global marketing strategy can be very difficult to implement. Look at the problems these well-known companies encountered in global markets.

Sociocultural differences affect not only management behaviors but also global marketing strategies. *Global marketing* is the term used to describe selling the same product in essentially the same way everywhere in the world. Some companies have developed brand names—such as Intel, Nike, IBM, Sony, Ford, Dell, and Toyota—with widespread global appeal and recognition. However, even these successful global marketers often face difficulties. For example, translating an advertising theme into a different language can be disastrous. To get an idea of the problems companies have faced with translations, take a look at Figure 3.7.

A sound philosophy to adopt in global markets is this: *Never assume that what works in one country will work in another.* Take for example Kids "R" Us, the clothing subsidiary of Toys "R" Us. Several years ago, the company missed its profit projections in Puerto Rico by banking heavily on back-to-school sales. Toys "R" Us planners failed to understand that Puerto Rican kids wear uniforms to school. They wrongly assumed that Puerto Rico's being a territory of the United States made the Puerto Rican market almost identical to the U.S. market. Thousands of similar stories could be told. The truth is that many U.S. companies often fail to think globally. For many years U.S. auto producers didn't adapt automobiles to drive on the left side of the road, as is done in many countries, and they printed owner's manuals only in English. Also, the United States is one of only five nations in the world that still refuse to conform to the metric system.

Since global marketing works only in limited cases, it's critical that U.S. exporters thoroughly research their objectives before attempting to penetrate global markets. "Think global, act local" is a valuable motto to follow.

Economic and Financial Forces

Economic differences can also muddy the water in global markets. Surely it's hard for us to imagine buying chewing gum by the stick instead of by the package. Yet this buying behavior is commonplace in economically depressed nations like Haiti, because customers there have only enough money to buy small quantities. You might suspect that with over 1 billion people, India would be a dream market for companies like Coca-Cola and PepsiCo.[37] However, Indians annually consume an average of only three soft drinks per person, compared to the 50-plus *gallons* per person Americans consume each year. While it's true some of this uneven consumption may be due to cultural differences, it's also clearly related to the low per capita income level of Indian consumers. Thus, what might seem like the global opportunity of a lifetime may not be a viable opportunity at all due to economic conditions.

Global financial markets unfortunately do not have a worldwide currency. Mexicans shop with pesos, South Koreans with won, Japanese with yen, and Americans with dollars. Globally, the U.S. dollar is considered the world's dominant and most stable form of currency.[38] This doesn't mean, however, that the dollar always retains the same market value or that foreign currency such as the euro may not someday replace or challenge the U.S. dollar's dominance.[39] Since 2002, the euro is the official currency of the European Union (EU). It replaced currencies such as the German deutschmark, the French franc, and the Italian lira. We will discuss the EU and the euro later in this chapter.

In an international transaction today, one dollar may be exchanged for eight pesos; tomorrow, however, you may only get seven pesos for the same dollar. The **exchange rate** is the value of one nation's currency relative to the currencies of other countries. Changes in a nation's exchange rates can have important implications in global markets. A *high value of the dollar* means that a dollar would be traded for more foreign currency than previously. The products of foreign producers would be cheaper because it takes fewer dollars to buy them, but the cost of U.S.-produced goods would become more expensive to foreign purchasers because of the dollar's high value. Conversely, a *low value of the dollar* means that a dollar is traded for less foreign currency. Therefore, foreign goods become more expensive because it takes more dollars to buy them, but American goods become cheaper to foreign buyers because it takes less foreign currency to buy American goods.[40]

exchange rate
The value of one nation's currency relative to the currencies of other countries.

Global financial markets operate under a system called *floating exchange rates,* in which currencies "float" according to the supply and demand in the global market for the currency. This supply and demand for currencies is created by global currency traders, who form a market for a nation's currency based on the perceived trade and investment potential of the country. At certain times, however, a country itself will intervene and adjust the value of its currency, often to increase the export potential of its products. **Devaluation** is lowering the value of a nation's currency relative to other currencies. Both Argentina and Venezuela devalued their currencies in the early 2000s.[41]

devaluation
Lowering the value of a nation's currency relative to other currencies

Changes in currency values cause many problems globally. Consider a multinational corporation like Nestlé, which has factories in 479 countries and employs over 220,000 workers around the world.[42] Labor costs can vary considerably as currency values shift. Or consider a medium-sized company

Happy birthday to "euro"! These Irish misses are dressed as euro coins to celebrate the big day in the history of the European Union (EU). The euro officially became the common currency of 12 of the members of the EU on January 1, 2002, replacing the mark, franc, lira, peseta, and other former currencies. Do you think the euro will challenge the American dollar for leadership among the world's currencies?

like the H. B. Fuller Company headquartered in St. Paul, Minnesota. Fuller has direct operations in 36 countries in North America, Latin America, Europe, and Asia, making paints, adhesives, and coatings. Company president Al Stroucken believed that the most dramatic problem Fuller faced was in dealing with currency fluctuations. The company learned to use currency fluctuations to its advantage by buying raw materials from sources with currencies lowered in value.

Currency valuation problems can be especially harsh on developing economies. Often, the only possibility of trade in many developing nations is through one of the oldest forms of trade: *bartering,* which is the exchange of merchandise for merchandise or service for service with no money involved.[43] **Countertrading** is a complex form of bartering in which several countries may be involved, each trading goods for goods or services for services. It has been estimated that countertrading accounts for over 20 percent of all global exchanges, especially deals involving developing countries. For example, let's say that a developing country such as Jamaica wants to buy vehicles from Ford Motor Company in exchange for Jamaican bauxite. Ford, however, does not have a need for Jamaican bauxite but does have a need for computer monitors. In a countertrade agreement, Ford may trade vehicles to Jamaica, which then trades bauxite to another country, say India, which then exchanges computer monitors with Ford. This countertrade is thus beneficial to all three parties. With many countries still in the developing stage, there is no question that countertrading will continue in global markets through much of the 21st century. Trading products for products helps businesses avoid some of the financial problems and currency constraints that exist in global markets.

countertrading
A complex form of bartering in which several countries may be involved, each trading goods for goods or services for services.

Understanding economic conditions, currency fluctuations, and countertrade opportunities is vital to a company's success in the global market. In financing export operations in the United States, banks have traditionally been the best source of the capital needed for global investment. However, when U.S. banks are not willing to provide export financing, exporters often turn to foreign banks and other sources for financing. This is especially true for small and medium-sized businesses. These companies must be creative in scouring the globe for financing.

Legal and Regulatory Forces

In any economy, both the conduct and direction of business are firmly tied to the legal and regulatory environment. In the United States, for example, federal, state, and local laws, and other government regulations heavily impact business practices. (You will read more about U.S. laws and regulations in the appendix to Chapter 4.) In global markets, no central system of law exists, so several groups of laws and regulations may apply. This makes the task of conducting global business extremely difficult as businesspeople find myriad laws and regulations in global markets that are often inconsistent. Important legal questions related to antitrust rules, labor relations, patents, copyrights, trade practices, taxes, product liability, child labor, prison labor, and other issues are written and interpreted differently country by country.[44]

American businesspeople are required to follow U.S. laws and regulations in conducting business globally. U.S. legislation, such as the Foreign Corrupt Practices Act of 1978, often creates competitive disadvantages for American businesspeople when competing with foreign competitors. This law specifically prohibits "questionable" or "dubious" payments to foreign officials to secure business contracts. The problem is that this law runs contrary to beliefs and practices in many countries, where corporate or government bribery is not only acceptable but also perhaps the only way to secure a lucrative contract.[45]

FIGURE 3.8

COUNTRIES MOST LIKELY TO DEMAND A BRIBE

1. Cameroon
2. Nigeria
3. Indonesia
4. Azerbaijan
5. Uzbekistan
6. Honduras
7. Tanzania

Source: Transparency International.

For a partial list of countries where bribery or other unethical business practices are most common see Figure 3.8. Fortunately for U.S. companies, the Organization for Economic Cooperation and Development (OECD) is leading a global effort to fight corruption and bribery in foreign markets.[46] We will discuss the efforts of the OECD further in Chapter 4.

To be successful in global markets, it's often important to contact local businesspeople in the host countries and gain their cooperation and sponsorship. Such local contacts can help a company penetrate the market and deal with what can be imposing bureaucratic barriers. Local businesspeople are also familiar with laws and regulations that could have an important impact on a foreign firm's business in their country. Beyond legal questions are those concerning ethics; the Making Ethical Decisions box gives an example of one company's dilemma.

Physical and Environmental Forces

Certain physical and environmental forces can also have an important impact on a company's ability to conduct business in global markets. In fact, technological constraints may make it difficult or perhaps impossible to build a large global market. For example, some developing countries have such primitive transportation and storage systems that international distribution is ineffective, if not impossible. This is especially true with regard to food, which is often spoiled by the time it reaches the market in certain countries. Compound this fact with unclean water and the lack of effective sewer systems, and you can sense the intensity of the problem.

American exporters must also be aware that certain technological differences affect the nature of exportable products. For example, houses in most developing countries do not have electrical systems that match those of U.S. homes, in kind or capacity. How would the differences in electricity available (110 versus 220 volts) affect an American appliance manufacturer wishing to export? Also, computer and Internet usage in many developing countries is very thin or nonexistent. You can see how this would make for a tough business environment in general and would make e-commerce difficult, if not nearly impossible.

Not all Americans see free trade as an economic benefit to our country. The members of the United Steelworkers Union believe the U.S. government should provide protection from global competition to the steel industry and its workers. The union claims it has lost almost 70 percent of its membership over the past 20 years because of the growth of imported steel. President Bush responded by putting temporary 30 percent tariffs on imported steel. Should governments protect industries from foreign competition? Why or why not?

Making Ethical Decisions

www.spu.edu/depts/sbe/ethics

Doing Bad by Trying to Do Good

The CEO of a major pharmaceutical manufacturer decided to set up what she considered to be a generous program to fight the growing AIDS epidemic in developing countries. She decided her company would give its expensive AIDS-related drug for free to government clinics in several of the poor countries. To her surprise, the decision was roundly booed by many humanitarian groups, which complained the company should instead lower the price of the drug so that everyone could afford it rather than give it away to only part of the affected population. The company currently charges regular customers approximately $8 for one pill. Critics claim that the company could lower the price to 40 cents per pill (a few cents over cost) and really help fight the dreaded disease. Puzzled by the reaction, the CEO said, "We are doing more than anyone else and are still criticized. We should work together to fix this problem." What are the CEO's alternatives? What are the consequences of each alternative? What would you do?

TRADE PROTECTIONISM

As we discussed in the previous section, sociocultural, economic and financial, legal and regulatory, and physical and environmental forces are all challenges to trading globally. What is often a much greater barrier to global trade, however, is the political atmosphere between nations. **Trade protectionism** is the use of government regulations to limit the import of goods and services. Advocates of trade protectionism believe it allows domestic producers to survive and grow, producing more jobs. Countries often use protectionist measures to guard against such practices as dumping; many are wary of foreign competition in general. To understand how this political climate affects global business, let's briefly review some global economic history.

trade protectionism
The use of government regulations to limit the import of goods and services. Advocates of trade protectionism believe that it allows domestic producers to survive and grow, producing more jobs.

Business, economics, and politics have always been closely linked. In fact, what we now call economics was once referred to as *political economy,* indicating the close ties between politics (government) and economics. In the 17th and 18th centuries, businesspeople and government leaders advocated an economic principle called *mercantilism.* The overriding idea of mercantilism was for a nation to sell more goods to other nations than it bought from them, that is, to have a favorable balance of trade.[47] According to the mercantilists, this condition would result in a flow of money to the country that sold the most globally. This philosophy led governments to assist in this process by charging a **tariff,** basically a tax on imports, thus making imported goods more expensive to buy.

tariff
A tax imposed on imports.

Generally, there are two different kinds of tariffs: protective and revenue. *Protective tariffs* (import taxes) are designed to raise the retail price of imported products so that domestic goods will be more competitively priced. These tariffs are meant to save jobs for domestic workers and to keep industries (especially *infant industries,* which consist of new companies in the early stages of growth) from closing down entirely because of foreign competition. *Revenue tariffs* are designed to raise money for the government. Revenue tariffs are also commonly used by developing countries to help infant industries compete in global markets. Today there is still considerable debate about the degree of protectionism a government should practice.

An **import quota** limits the number of products in certain categories that a nation can import. The United States has import quotas on a number of products, including beef and sugar. The Legal Briefcase box highlights a few other interesting import quotas imposed by the United States. Overall, the goal is to

import quota
A limit on the number of products in certain categories that a nation can import.

www.plustariff.com

Legal Briefcase

When Is a Fish Not a Fish?

If it looks like a catfish, swims like a catfish, and tastes like a catfish, the odds are it's a catfish. Well, according to the U.S. Congress and the Bush administration, you may have to think again. The U.S. government blocked low-cost Vietnamese catfish importers from increasing their market share of the growing catfish market. The Vietnamese were taking considerable business away from catfish farms in several southern U.S. states. Five senators from the region added language to an agriculture appropriations bill that stated the whiskered fish from the Mekong Delta in Vietnam cannot be imported under the name *catfish,* even though the whiskered fish is very similar to the species raised in U.S. farm ponds. Vietnamese exporters were required to label their fish *basa* or *tra* to sell in the American market.

U.S. catfish farmers applauded the decision and said it was only fair to their industry. They noted that, in 2001, Vietnam exported 29.7 million pounds of frozen fish fillets, mostly catfish; in 2002 the number jumped to 40.3 million pounds. The aqua farmers complained that the Vietnamese were unjustly marketing a fish that was not a "real" catfish. They also charged that the Vietnamese exploited cheap labor and weak regulatory laws in their country to produce the fish. In early 2003, the U.S. Commerce Department ruled that the Vietnamese had sold catfish at below-market prices (a practice, as explained in the text, called dumping) and recommended that import duties—fees ranging from 38 percent to 64 percent—be charged on the imported frozen fish fillets. The Vietnamese stated that their fish met health standards and that they were competing fairly, meeting the requirements of free trade. Vietnam fish farmers denounced the Commerce Department decision as irresponsible and unfair.

Critics conclude that such decisions not only hurt countries, like Vietnam, that are slowly moving toward market economies but also increase the possibilities of trade wars or retaliation from other trading nations. Daniel Tarullo, a Georgetown University law professor, advises, "If there is enough firing on both sides of the trade issue, sometimes it can get out of control." Let's watch and see.

Sources: Tini Tran, "Vietnamese Catfish Producers Slam U.S. Ruling of Dumping as Irresponsible," AP Worldstream, January 28, 2003; "Vietnam Requests 'Just' Ruling on Catfish," AP Online, January 23, 2003; and George Hager, "Bush Plays Free-Trade Game," *USA Today,* May 2, 2002, p. 1C.

embargo
A complete ban on the import or export of a certain product or stopping all trade with a particular country.

protect U.S. companies in order to preserve jobs. An **embargo** is a complete ban on the import or export of a certain product or the stopping of all trade with a particular country. Political disagreements have caused many countries to establish embargoes. Such hostilities provoked embargoes against Cuba and Iraq.[48] The United States also prohibits the export of specific products globally. The Export Administration Act of 1979 prohibits the exporting of goods (e.g., high-tech weapons) that would endanger national security.[49]

Nontariff barriers are not as specific or formal as tariffs, import quotas, and embargoes but can be as detrimental to free trade. It's common for countries to set restrictive standards that detail exactly how a product must be sold in a country. For example, Denmark requires companies to sell butter in cubes, not tubs. J. W. Kisling of Multiplex Company—a medium-sized U.S. maker of beverage-dispensing equipment with offices in Germany, France, Taiwan, England, and Canada—feels that a good deal of trade is stifled by nontariff barriers.

Japan, for instance, steadfastly argued that it had some of the lowest tariffs in the world and welcomed foreign exporters, yet for many years American businesses found it difficult to establish trade relationships with the Japanese. Observers insisted that a Japanese tradition, called *keiretsu* (pronounced "care-yet-sue") was the root of the problem. Under keiretsu, major companies (like Mitsui and Mitsubishi) built "corporate families" that forged semipermanent ties with suppliers, customers, and distributors with full support of the government.[50] The Japanese believed such huge corporate alliances would provide economic payoffs by nurturing long-term strategic thinking and mutually beneficial cooperation. As the Japanese economy has faltered, so has keiretsu. U.S. businesses are now finding Japan a friendlier place for imports.

Anti-globalization protests in Seattle, Prague, and Genoa (pictured here) have pitted activists against the World Trade Organization (WTO). The demonstrators vented their fears and distrust of globalization being controlled by multinational corporations and international financial entities that have worked to their own benefit and have not addressed the needs of the world's developing countries. What do you believe the role of an organization like the WTO should be in dealing with global trade issues?

It would be easy for would-be exporters to view the trade barriers discussed above as good reasons to avoid global trade. Still, wherever you stand on the tariff issue, it's obvious that overcoming trade constraints creates a tremendous business opportunity. In the next sections, we look at organizations and agreements that attempt to eliminate trade barriers and facilitate trade among nations.

The General Agreement on Tariffs and Trade, and the World Trade Organization

In 1948, government leaders from 23 nations throughout the world formed the **General Agreement on Tariffs and Trade (GATT),** which established an international forum for negotiating mutual reductions in trade restrictions. In short, the countries agreed to negotiate to create monetary and trade agreements that might facilitate the exchange of goods, services, ideas, and cultural programs. In 1986, the Uruguay Round of the GATT was convened to specifically deal with the renegotiation of trade agreements. After eight years of meetings, 124 nations at the Uruguay Round voted to modify the GATT. The U.S. House of Representatives and Senate approved the new agreement in 1994. Under the agreement, tariffs were lowered an average of 38 percent worldwide, and new trade rules were expanded to areas such as agriculture, services, and the protection of patents.

General Agreement on Tariffs and Trade (GATT)
A 1948 agreement that established an international forum for negotiating mutual reductions in trade restrictions.

The Uruguay Round also established the **World Trade Organization (WTO),** which on January 1, 1995, assumed the primary task of mediating future trade disputes. The WTO, headquartered in Geneva, Switzerland, and comprising 144 member nations, acts as an independent entity that oversees key cross-border trade issues and global business practices. It's the world's first attempt at establishing a global mediation center. Trade issues are expected to be resolved within 12 to 15 months instead of languishing for years, as was the case in the past.

World Trade Organization (WTO)
The international organization that replaced the General Agreement on Tariffs and Trade, and was assigned the duty to mediate trade disputes among nations.

However, before you get the impression that all's well in global trade, it's important to note the formation of the WTO did not totally eliminate the internal national laws that impede trade expansion. Therefore, in November 2001, a new round of talks (this time called the WTO Round) took place at Doha, Qatar, in the Persian Gulf.[51] Key topics discussed included dismantling protection of manufactured goods, eliminating subsidies on agricultural products, and overturning temporary protectionist measures that impede global trade. While the efforts of the WTO are admirable, many tough decisions lie ahead.[52] The admission of China to the WTO in December 2001, along with the Chinese commitment to free trade, promises to stir differing emotions within the WTO.[53] Also, the desire of Russia to gain prompt acceptance into the WTO promises to heighten debate among WTO member nations.[54]

Common Markets

common market
A regional group of countries that have a common external tariff, no internal tariffs, and a coordination of laws to facilitate exchange; also called a *trading bloc*. An example is the European Union.

One of the issues not resolved by the GATT rounds or at the WTO is whether common markets will create regional alliances at the expense of global expansion. A **common market** (also called a *trading bloc*) is a regional group of countries that have a common external tariff, no internal tariffs, and the coordination of laws to facilitate exchange among member countries. Two such common markets, the European Union (EU) and the South American Common Market (called Mercosur), are worth looking at briefly (see Figure 3.9).

The EU began in the late 1950s as an alliance of six trading partners (then known as the Common Market and later the European Economic Community). Today the EU is a group of 15 nations that united economically in the early 1990s. The objective was to make Europe, the world's second largest economy (behind the United States)—with almost 20 percent of the world's GDP and representing some 360 million people—an even stronger competitor in global commerce. Europeans see economic integration as the major way to compete for global business, particularly with the United States. The EU will grow to 25 nations by May 2004 as new members are accepted from the Mediterranean region and Eastern Europe.[55]

The path to European unification, however, was not easy. A significant step was taken on January 1, 1999, when the EU officially launched its joint cur-

FIGURE 3.9

MEMBERS OF THE EUROPEAN UNION

Current EU members are highlighted in dark blue. Countries to be added in May 2004 are in light blue.

rency, the euro. The formal transition occurred three years later on January 1, 2002, when the separate currencies of 12 of the EU nations were transformed into a single monetary unit. EU members Great Britian, Sweden, and Denmark elected not to convert to the euro at that time. European businesses expected to save billions each year on currency conversions that had to be made prior to the introduction of the euro.

The EU clearly hopes that having a unified currency will bring its member nations more economic clout, as well as more buying power and greater economic and political stability. C. Fred Bergsten, director of the Washington-based Institute for International Economics, suggests that the euro will certainly be a worthy challenger to the U.S. dollar in global markets due to the economic strength and size of the EU. In late 2002 and early 2003, his words rang true as the dollar fell below the euro in value for the first time.[56]

Mercosur is a common market that groups Brazil, Argentina, Paraguay, Uruguay, and associate members Chile and Bolivia. Like the EU, Mercosur had ambitious economic goals that included a single currency. There was even talk of an agreement combining Mercosur and the Andean Pact (which includes Venezuela, Colombia, Peru, and Ecuador) that would pave the way for an economic free-trade zone spanning South America. However, more than a decade after its formation, the Mercosur trade bloc seems to be on shaky ground. With currency problems in Brazil and a financial crisis in Argentina, Mercosur partners such as Chile are looking for better economic prospects elsewhere. The Mercosur has work to do if it wants to attain its objectives.

The North American Free Trade Agreement (NAFTA)

North American Free Trade Agreement (NAFTA)
Agreement that created a free-trade area among the United States, Canada, and Mexico.

A widely debated issue of the early 1990s was the ratification of the **North American Free Trade Agreement (NAFTA),** which created a free-trade area among the United States, Canada, and Mexico. The objectives of NAFTA were to (1) eliminate trade barriers and facilitate cross-border movement of goods and services among the three countries; (2) promote conditions of fair competition in this free-trade area; (3) increase investment opportunities in the territories of the three nations; (4) provide effective protection and enforcement of intellectual property rights (patents, copyrights, etc.) in each nation's territory; and (5) establish a framework for further regional trade cooperation.[57]

Opponents—led primarily by organized labor, and businessman and former presidential candidate Ross Perot—warned of serious economic consequences if the U.S. Congress passed this agreement. Their primary concerns focused on the loss of U.S. jobs and significant amounts of capital leaving the United States. In contrast, supporters predicted that NAFTA would open a vast new market for U.S. exports that would create jobs and market opportunities in the long term. In 1994, Congress approved NAFTA and President Bill Clinton signed it into law. Today, the three NAFTA countries have a combined population of 417 million people and a gross domestic product (GDP) of more than $11 trillion.[58] According to the agreement, the United States, Canada, and Mexico can lower trade barriers with one another while maintaining independent trade agreements with nonmember countries.

Since its approval, NAFTA has experienced both success and difficulties. On the positive side, U.S. exports to the NAFTA partners increased approximately 85 percent since the agreement was signed. Mexico has fared even better; it has experienced a 225 percent increase in trade flows and has replaced Japan as America's number two trading partner (behind Canada).[59] On the downside, the devaluation of the Mexican peso in 1995 forced the United States to commit $30 billion in aid to Mexico. Also, it's estimated that the United States has lost almost 1 million jobs since the signing of NAFTA.[60]

Furthermore, annual per capita income in Mexico (about $9,000) still lags considerably behind that of the United States ($35,900) and Canada ($28,900), causing illegal immigration to remain a major problem. Other concerns—such as child-labor laws, sweatshop violations, and environmental concerns—promise to keep NAFTA a much-debated topic.

Like other economic trade agreements, NAFTA has changed the landscape of global trade. Possible expansion of NAFTA into a Free Trade Area of the Americas (FTAA) would create a free-trade area of 800 million people and range in scope from Patagonia to Alaska. Advocates say that FTAA could be operational by 2005; others argue that the U.S. political environment could stall its implementation.[61] Strong free-trade supporters even suggest that a Transatlantic Free Trade Area aligned with the European Union is possible. Economists are somewhat divided on this issue. Some resoundingly praise such suggestions while others express concern that, as the world divides itself into major trading blocs (EU, NAFTA, etc.), poor countries that don't fit in the plans of the common markets will suffer. The issues surrounding common markets and free-trade areas will extend far into the 21st century.

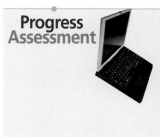

Progress Assessment

- What are the major hurdles to successful global trade?
- What does *ethnocentricity* mean?
- Which cultural and societal differences are most likely to affect global trade efforts? (Name at least two.)
- What are the advantages and disadvantages of trade protectionism and of tariffs?

The Future of Global Trade: Global E-Commerce

Global trade opportunities grow more interesting each day. New and expanding markets present great potential for trade and development. Changes in technology also have changed the landscape of global trade, as businesses find that many foreign markets are often no farther than a mouse click away. Let's look briefly at issues certain to influence global markets in the 21st century.

Advanced communication has made distant global markets instantly accessible. Also, the lure of over 6 billion customers is hard to pass up. Nowhere is the lure of global markets keener than in the developing countries in Asia, and particularly in the world's most populous country, the People's Republic of China. With more than 1.2 billion people, China is a fast-growing economy that's shifting its economic philosophy from central planning to free markets.

Multinational companies such as General Motors, Caterpillar, and Levi-Strauss have invested heavily in China's future. Not long ago, such investments in China were considered too risky and not worth the effort. Today, however, U.S. companies are flocking to China and are eager to trade with the Chinese. Economists suggest that soon U.S. foreign direct investment could surpass exports as the primary means by which U.S. companies deliver goods to China. Concerns remain about China's one-party political system, its human rights policies, the growing trade imbalance, and difficulties in China's financial markets. Yet in 2000 the U.S. Congress granted China permanent normal trading rights, paving the way for China's acceptance into the World Trade Organization (WTO) in 2001. Still, many analysts warn that profits will take a long time to materialize for companies doing business with China.[62]

Russia is also a prize coveted by global traders. Like China, Russia presents enormous opportunities. Philip Morris, Bristol-Myers Squibb, and Gillette are multinational firms with manufacturing facilities in Russia. PepsiCo has been doing business with Russia for many years. Chevron/Texaco and Exxon Mobil are hard at work in the Caspian Sea area looking to develop vast oil reserves. However, severe political and social problems still persist in Russia and in many of the former states of the Soviet Union. Even so, Russia's 150 million potential customers, craving American goods, represent an opportunity too good to pass up.

While China, Russia, and Japan attract most of the attention in Asia, U.S. businesses are not forgetting the rest of the continent. Add India (now also with over 1 billion people), Taiwan, Indonesia, Thailand, Singapore, the Philippines, Korea, and Malaysia to the growing list of developing countries in Asia, and it's easy to see the great potential the Asian market holds for U.S. business—and possibly for you.

As technology continues its unprecedented growth, markets not only in Asia but also in the rest of the world are instantly accessible. The growth of the Internet and advances in e-commerce enable companies worldwide to bypass normally required distribution channels to reach a large market. Take New England Pottery Company, for example. Adopting Internet technology helped the company become the world's largest vendor in the garden pottery industry. By speeding up the flow of information between buyers and its manufacturing partners in Europe, South America, and Asia, the company increased its sales by 20 percent a year. Autobytel, an Irvine, California, company, took its e-commerce system into Scandinavia and the United Kingdom. The company lets consumers buy, lease, and insure new cars and trucks online. Such attention to global potential and the ability to react quickly often gives emerging companies like Autobytel an advantage over their larger counterparts in penetrating global markets.

It's important, though, to remember that obstacles and problems with technology still exist in global trade. For example, American Express Foreign Exchange Services and International Strategies Inc. reported that 43 percent of the small businesses they polled could not find information on the Web that could help them do business globally. Many of the companies polled also stated that communication with companies in Asia still needed to be carried out by faxing hard copies of documents—a process now seen as almost old-fashioned in comparison to Internet communication. In addition, some developing nations fear that e-commerce will lead to the erosion of their local and national languages and cultures. Overcoming such technological and social obstacles is one of the key challenges facing business in the 21st century. Yet despite these hurdles, technology has the potential to radically change industries and create opportunities for all businesses in global trade, regardless of size.

Globalization and You

Whether you aspire to be an entrepreneur, a manager, or some other type of business leader, it's becoming increasingly important to think globally as you plan your career. As this chapter points out, global markets offer many opportunities, yet they are laced with significant challenges and complexities. By studying foreign languages, learning about foreign cultures through courses in anthropology and world literature, and taking business courses (including a course in global business), you can develop a global perspective on your future.

As we have emphasized, the potential of global markets does not belong only to the multinational corporations. Small and medium-sized businesses are often better prepared to take the leap into global markets than are large, cumbersome corporations saddled with bureaucracies. It's the ability of small and medium-sized businesses to react quickly to opportunities that gives them an advantage. Don't forget to think about using that advantage. Also don't forget the potential of franchising, which we will examine in more detail in Chapter 5.

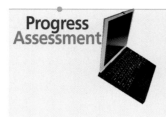

Progress Assessment

- What are the economic risks of doing business in countries like the People's Republic of China or Russia?
- What might be some important factors that will have an impact on global trading?

Summary

1. Discuss the growing importance of the global market and the roles of comparative advantage and absolute advantage in global trade.

1. The world market for trade is huge. Some 95 percent of the people in the world live outside the United States. Major U.S. companies routinely cite expansion to global markets as a route to future growth.
   - ***Why should nations trade with other nations?***

   (1) No country is self-sufficient, (2) other countries need products that prosperous countries produce, and (3) natural resources and technological skills are not distributed evenly around the world.
   - ***What is the theory of comparative advantage?***

   The theory of comparative advantage contends that a country should make and then sell those products it produces most efficiently but buy those it cannot produce as efficiently.
   - ***What is absolute advantage?***

   Absolute advantage means that a country has a monopoly on a certain product or can produce the product more efficiently than any other country can. There are few examples of absolute advantage.

2. Explain the importance of importing and exporting, and understand key terms used in global business.

2. Anyone, students included, can get involved in world trade through importing and exporting. Businesspeople do not have to work for big multinational corporations.
   - ***What kinds of products can be imported and exported?***

   Just about any kind of product can be imported and exported. Companies can sometimes find surprising ways to succeed in either activity. Selling in global markets is not necessarily easy, though.
   - ***What terms are important in understanding world trade?***

   Exporting is selling products to other countries. *Importing* is buying products from other countries. The *balance of trade* is the relationship of exports to imports. The *balance of payments* is the balance of trade plus other money flows such as tourism and foreign aid. *Dumping* is selling products for less in a foreign country than in your own country. *Trade protectionism* is the use of government regulations to limit the importation of products. See the Key Terms list at the end of this chapter to be sure you know the other important terms.

3. Illustrate the strategies used in reaching global markets and explain the role of multinational corporations in global markets.

3. A company can participate in world trade in a number of ways.
   - ***What are some ways in which a company can get involved in global business?***

   Ways of entering world trade include licensing, exporting, franchising, contract manufacturing, joint ventures and strategic alliances, foreign subsidiaries, and direct foreign investment.
   - ***How do multinational corporations differ from other companies that participate in global business?***

   Unlike other companies that are involved in exporting or importing, multinational corporations also have manufacturing facilities or some other type of physical presence in different nations.

4. Evaluate the forces that affect trading in global markets.

4. There are many restrictions on foreign trade.
   - ***What are some of the forces that can discourage participation in global business?***

   Potential stumbling blocks to world trade include sociocultural forces, economic and financial forces, legal and regulatory forces, and physical and environmental forces.

5. Debate the advantages and disadvantages of trade protectionism.

5. Political differences are often the most difficult hurdles to global trade.
   - ***What is trade protectionism?***

   Trade protectionism is the use of government regulations to limit the import of goods and services; advocates believe that it allows domestic producers to survive and grow, producing more jobs. The key tools of protectionism are tariffs, import quotas, and embargoes.
   - ***What are tariffs?***

   Tariffs are taxes on foreign products. There are two kinds of tariffs: (1) protective tariffs, which are used to raise the price of foreign products, and (2) revenue tariffs, which are used to raise money for the government.
   - ***What is an embargo?***

   An embargo prohibits the importing or exporting of certain products.
   - ***Is trade protectionism good for domestic producers?***

   That is debatable. Trade protectionism offers pluses and minuses.
   - ***Why do governments continue such practices?***

   The theory of mercantilism started the practice of trade protectionism and it has persisted, though in a lesser form, ever since.

6. Explain how e-commerce is affecting global trade.

6. Technology is changing the way businesses communicate around the globe.
   - ***How is e-commerce affecting global trade?***

   The Internet has made distant global markets instantly accessible. E-commerce enables companies to bypass normal distribution channels to reach large global markets quickly.

Key Terms

absolute advantage 70
balance of payments 72
balance of trade 72
common market 90
comparative advantage theory 69
contract manufacturing 78
countertrading 85
devaluation 84
dumping 74
embargo 88
exchange rate 84
exporting 68
foreign direct investment 74
foreign subsidiary 80
free trade 69
General Agreement on Tariffs and Trade (GATT) 89
importing 68
import quota 87
joint venture 79
licensing 76
multinational corporation 80
North American Free Trade Agreement (NAFTA) 91
strategic alliance 79
tariff 87
trade deficit 72
trade protectionism 87
World Trade Organization (WTO) 89

Developing Workplace Skills

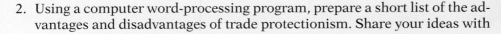

1. Call or visit a business involved with importing foreign goods (such as a wine importer). Talk with the owner or manager about the problems and joys of being involved in global trade. Compile a list of advantages and disadvantages. Then get together with others in the class and compare notes.

2. Using a computer word-processing program, prepare a short list of the advantages and disadvantages of trade protectionism. Share your ideas with

others in the class and debate the following statement: The United States should increase trade protection to save American jobs and American companies.

3. Many U.S. firms have made embarrassing mistakes when trying to sell products overseas. Sometimes the product is not adapted to the needs of the country, sometimes the advertising makes no sense, sometimes the color or packaging is wrong, and so forth. Find an example of such a marketing mistake and suggest how the company could have been more responsive to the needs of foreign markets. If possible, use a graphics program to illustrate a more appropriate advertisement or packaging option.

4. I. M. Windy is a candidate for the U.S. House of Representatives from your district. He just delivered an excellent speech at your college. He spoke at great length on the topic of tariffs. His major arguments were that we need tariffs to

   a. Provide revenues.
   b. Protect our young industries.
   c. Encourage Americans to buy U.S.-made products because doing so is patriotic.
   d. Keep our military strong.
   e. Protect American workers and wages.
   f. Help us maintain a favorable balance of trade.
   g. Create a favorable balance of payments.

   Do you agree with Mr. Windy? Evaluate each of the candidate's major points by indicating whether you consider it valid or invalid. Justify your position.

5. Choose a good, service, or idea that you would like to market to a specific country. Identify the benefits of supplying the product to this market. Identify the sociocultural, economic and financial, legal and regulatory, and physical and environmental forces you might encounter. Provide alternatives you can use to address these forces. Form your own joint venture with three classmates to deal with this exercise. Have each member make a list of the strengths and weaknesses he or she would bring to such an assignment. Decide among yourselves whether a joint venture would be worthwhile to achieve your market objectives or whether you each would be better off choosing another strategy in entering this market. Explain why your group decided to organize the way it did.

Taking It To The Net 1

Purpose

To compare the shifting exchange rates of various countries and to predict the effects of such exchange shifts on global trade.

Exercise

One of the difficulties of engaging in global trade is the constant shift in exchange rates. How much do exchange rates change over a 30-day period? Research this by choosing five currencies (the euro, the British pound, Japan's yen, Mexico's peso, etc.) and recording their exchange rates relative to the U.S. dollar for 30 days. The rates are available on the Internet at www.washingtonpost.com/wp-srv/business/longterm/stocks/currency.htm.

At the end of the tracking period, choose a company and describe what effects the currency shifts you noted might have on this company's trade with each of the countries or areas whose currency you chose.

Taking It To The Net 2

Purpose

To identify those nations with high export potential and those with low export potential (except for basic goods, such as food).

Exercise

Imagine your company is ready to expand its products to foreign countries. Which countries are most likely to buy your products? The potential to export to a specific country is based on a number of factors, including the size of its population and the strength of its GDP.

1. From the population data given on the United Nations Population Information Network website (www.un.org/popin), prepare a list of the 20 countries with the largest population.
2. Go to the InfoNation section of the UN's Cyber School Bus website (www.un.org/Pubs/CyberSchoolBus) and find the GDP per person for each of the nations on your population list. Rate each of the nations in your population list for its export potential. Using the GDP per capita and the population size, place each of those nations into the following categories:
   a. High export potential (those nations whose population is one of the 10 largest and whose GDP per capita is greater than $20,000).
   b. Medium-high export potential (those nations whose population is ranked 11 to 21 and whose GDP per capita is greater than $20,000).
   c. Medium export potential (those nations whose population is one of the 10 largest and whose GDP per capita is between $3,000 and $20,000).
   d. Low export potential (those nations whose population is ranked 11 to 21 and whose GDP per capita is less than $3,000).

Casing The Web

To access the case "Cooling Off the Sweatshops," visit

www.mhhe.com/ub7e

Video Case

Six Billion Customers and Counting—IBM

When choosing a company to illustrate global business, it's not a bad idea to choose one that has about 315,000 employees around the world. It would also be helpful if about half of the firm's employees called the United States home and half were spread among 160 countries or so. The company that fits this global description is IBM.

The company was known as *International* Business Machines long before IBM finally reached its goal of becoming a global powerhouse. (It's first business machine was a scale for weighing meat.) IBM's brand name is now the third most valuable name in the world, after Coke and Microsoft. The brand name alone is said to be worth some $50 billion.

The person responsible for marketing the IBM brand is Lee Green, who is featured in this video. Lee's work includes those funny commercials for which IBM has become well known. IBM tries to maintain a global image by using the same themes in every country where it does business. The ad may change a little to adapt to the culture and the times, but the themes are the same.

A company may reach global markets in various ways, ranging from licensing to foreign direct investment. You can read about each option and the risks and rewards in this chapter. IBM tends to do a great deal of foreign direct investment. That makes it a multinational firm. IBM's annual revenue is greater than many countries' entire GDP.

IBM recognizes the fact that the United States has a population of about 290 million people, while the worldwide population is over 6 billion. Simple arithmetic tells us that some 95 percent of the total world population is outside the U.S. As a result, the company has to adapt to a variety of environmental forces: socio-cultural, economic, political and legal, and so forth. IBM's global network of employees, research facilities, and offices help create a cohesive company message that reaches customers around the globe. The company mission is to help people in other countries develop their own products by using their own people to develop products specific to their own markets.

IBM clearly has a comparative advantage in producing some goods. It maintains that advantage by changing its product offers over time to match the changing needs of a global economy. It's interesting to note that IBM works with both small and large businesses and that they recognize that there is a huge potential for small businesses to do more globally, especially using the Internet. IBM's strength is to help businesses of all kinds to integrate their operations to become global in scope. The company is trying to "invent the future" not only for themselves, but for other companies as well. To do that, it has to maintain its corporate image through advertising and through providing excellent service with every contact, whether that contact is over the Internet, on the phone, or in person.

How could you prepare for a job in global business? You could study a foreign language, sign up for overseas program at your college, or simply make it a matter of researching the topic in as many ways as possible, including talking with those now involved in global business. Lee Green has been in over 100 countries because of his work. If that kind of life sounds glamorous and exciting to you, global business is the thing to study.

Thinking It Over

1. What did you learn from this video that might help you to more effectively pursue a career in global business?
2. From what you have read in this chapter and seen in the video, does it seem that the opportunities in global business are greater in small or large businesses? Why?
3. What impression do you have of multinational firms that have operations in multiple countries? Do they seem to be a major benefit to the world or are there some negatives that you see? Discuss.

Chapter 4

Demonstrating Ethical Behavior and Social Responsibility

Learning Goals

After you have read and studied this chapter, you should be able to

1 Explain why legality is only the first step in behaving ethically.

2 Ask the three questions one should answer when faced with a potentially unethical action.

3 Describe management's role in setting ethical standards.

4 Distinguish between compliance-based and integrity-based ethics codes, and list the six steps in setting up a corporate ethics code.

5 Define *corporate social responsibility* and examine corporate responsibility to various stakeholders.

6 Analyze the role of American businesses in influencing ethical behavior and social responsibility in global markets.

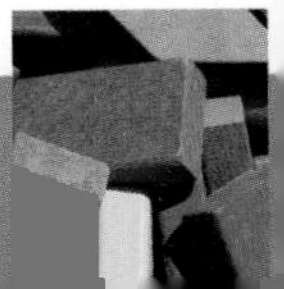

Getting to Know Dean Jernigan, CEO of Storage USA and Founder of the Memphis Redbirds

Name just about any professional sports organization (NFL, NBA, ABA, Arena Football, CFL, USFL) and it probably promised the folks in Memphis, Tennessee, a team. Well, the promised teams either never showed up or showed up but left town faster than an Elvis fanatic hearing the King was spotted crossing the state line. So you can imagine the skepticism when Dean Jernigan, the founder and former CEO of Storage USA, the country's second largest self-storage company, announced that he wanted to buy a minor-league team and build a new $80.5 million major-league-class stadium in the troubled Memphis downtown. He would involve the community and hire minorities in proportion to the city's population—and (here's the punch line) he said he would not take a penny of the profits for himself. Every cent made on tickets, souvenirs, refreshments, parking—everything—would go to the community to fund sports activities for area kids through two new charities. Jernigan wouldn't even accept a salary for running the team. What's the catch? There is none.

"Baseball is different [from a traditional business] . . . It's a monopoly, like an airport. I think that if you are the holder of a monopoly, of a community asset like that, then you have an obligation not to run it just for the benefit of yourself."

So why would a successful businessman like Dean Jernigan want to do something like this? Because he believes that a ball team is an essential part of the town to which it belongs and should thrive to the benefit—not to the expense—of its community.

Such ethical action begins at home. When seventh-grader Dean Jernigan moved to Memphis with his parents, the family was poor by most standards. Jernigan had only three shirts to wear to school the entire year. Both parents worked, his father as a carpenter and his mother as a saleswoman in a store. Jernigan and his four siblings often had to take care of themselves as they grew up. It was baseball that gave Jernigan a place to go, a community.

It may sound like Jernigan is lost in nostalgia, but the truth is that he is modern and technologically skilled. His former company, Storage USA, outperformed its competitors in large part because it's more wired and more up-to-date than any other self-storage company. The company was recently sold to GE for $2.4 billion. Jernigan also wants the Memphis Redbirds, a part of the St. Louis Cardinals training system, to be as businesslike as possible. Jernigan believes that although the Redbirds isn't a traditional business it still can be run like a business. He just wants every penny to go back into the town. "Baseball is different [from a traditional business]," he said. "It's a monopoly, like an airport. I think that if you are the holder of a monopoly, of a community asset like that, then you have an obligation not to run it just for the benefit of yourself."

In 2000, the Redbirds drew 850,000 fans and did about $20 million in business. Had Dean Jernigan followed conventional wisdom and built the new stadium in Memphis's suburban sprawl, the park probably would have been a success, but it would have had little more impact on its community than a new shopping mall. By putting the stadium in the heart of downtown Memphis, Jernigan and his Redbirds have stimulated a central-Memphis revitalization.

With the media saturated by stories of high-profile business scandals, why do we open this chapter on ethics with a story about a man few people have heard of? Because we want you to know that not all businesspeople let greed guide their actions, that there are honest, ethical people in the business world. In this chapter, we explore the responsibility of businesses to all of their stakeholders: customers, investors, employees, and society. We look at the responsibilities of individuals as well. After all, responsible business behavior depends on responsible behavior of each individual in the business.

Sources: Geoff Calkins, "We've Taken the Greed Out of Sports," *Fast Company,* November 1, 2000, p. 170; Jeff Pearlman, "St. Louis Cardinals: Memphis Belle Community Spirit and Spiffy New Ballpark Make the Cardinals' Triple A Club the Class of the Minors," *Sports Illustrated,* July 3, 2000, p. 52; and Dan O'Neill, "5 Questions Keith McDonald, Catcher for the Memphis Redbirds," *St. Louis Post-Dispatch,* May 25, 2002, p. D7.

Ethics Is More Than Legality

The American public was shocked when it learned in 2001 that Enron, the now bankrupt energy-trading company, created off-the-books partnerships to hide debts and losses. When Enron's auditor, the venerable Arthur Andersen, was found guilty of obstructing justice by shredding documents related to its audit of Enron, the public became even more worried about widespread corporate dishonesty. The Enron disgrace soon was followed by more scandals at major companies like Xerox, WorldCom, Tyco International, and ImClone.

Given the ethical lapses that are so prevalent today, what can be done to restore trust in the free-market system and leaders in general? First, those who have broken the law need to be punished accordingly. Arresting business leaders, putting them in handcuffs, and carting them off to jail may seem harsh, but it is a first step toward showing the public that it is time to get serious about legal and ethical behavior in business. No one should be above the law: not religious people, not government people, and not businesspeople. New laws making accounting records more transparent (easy to read and understand) and more laws making businesspeople and others more accountable may help. But laws don't make people honest, reliable, or truthful. If laws alone were a big deterrent, there would be much less crime than exists today.

ethics
Standards of moral behavior, that is, behavior that is accepted by society as right versus wrong.

The danger in writing new laws to correct behavior is that people may begin to think that any behavior that is within the law is also acceptable. The measure of behavior, then, becomes, "Is it legal?" A society gets in trouble when it considers ethics and legality to be the same. Ethics and legality are two very different things. Although following the law is an important first step, ethical behavior requires more than that. Ethics reflects people's proper relations with one another: How should people treat others? What responsibility should they feel for others? Legality is more narrow. It refers to laws we have written to protect ourselves from fraud, theft, and violence. Many immoral and unethical acts fall well within our laws.[1] You can learn more about the fine line between legality and ethics by reading the Making Ethical Decisions box.

Ethical Standards Are Fundamental

We define **ethics** as the standards of moral behavior, that is, behavior that is accepted by society as right versus wrong. Many Americans today have few moral absolutes. Many decide situationally whether it's OK to steal, lie, or drink and drive. They seem to think that what is right is whatever works best for the individual, that each person has to work out for himself or herself the difference between right and wrong. That is the kind of thinking that has led to the recent scandals in government and business.

This isn't the way it always was. When Thomas Jefferson wrote that all men have the right to life, liberty, and the pursuit of happiness, he declared it to be a self-evident truth. Going back even further in time, the Ten Commandments were not called the "The Ten Highly Tentative Suggestions."

After an ethics scandal shocked a worldwide audience, Russian skaters Elena Berezhnaya and Anton Sikharulidze had to share the gold medal in the 2002 Winter Olympics pairs event with their Canadian competitors Jamie Sale and David Pelletier. French figure skating judge Marie-Reine Le Gougne admitted she was pressured to inflate the Russian scores. What messages do such actions send to young people watching these competitions?

Making Ethical Decisions

www.napster.com

Did Napster Catch the Music Industry Napping?

When 19-year-old Shawn Fanning began writing a new software program, his goal was to create a tool for helping people search for music files on the Internet and to talk to each other about the types of music they liked. When he finished the project and got Napster up on the Web in 1999, it attracted thousands of college kids looking for an easy way to find tunes. The number of users doubled every five to six weeks. Soon Fanning had the attention of most college students—and just about all of the record companies.

What was the attraction? Napster's version of file sharing enabled users to trade music over the Internet—for free. For years, people have been able to use tape recorders to copy music. But until Napster, such copying was usually limited to making one copy at a time to share among friends. Napster's innovation was in allowing an unlimited number of copies to be made and shared with millions of "friends."

The court ordered Napster to close down in 2001. Napster tried to reorganize and reopen as a fee-based business, but it needed more money to do it. German media giant Bertelsmann, which had already invested $85 million in Napster, offered to buy the site outright for $15 million. The deal fell through in September 2002, and Napster filed Chapter 7 bankruptcy and liquidated its few assets. Interestingly, CD-burning software-maker Roxio paid $5 million for the Napster name and technology in May 2003. Roxio will combine Napster with an online music service by Vivendi Universal and Sony Corp., two of the record labels that forced Napster out of business.

Through all of this Napster claimed that it never did anything illegal. Much of the music industry felt otherwise. People were reproducing compact discs and other products for free. To record companies, that's like walking into music stores and stealing CDs. But Napster argued that since no one was selling the music, it wasn't illegal. (Don't get the idea that Napster didn't bring in money simply because it didn't actually sell music. Bertelsmann didn't invest $85 million in Napster just so cash-poor students could get free music.)

Some Napster supporters said that file sharing was a way of sampling music risk-free and that when they found an artist's work they liked, they actually bought more CDs than they would have bought otherwise. But a recent study indicated that CD purchases plummeted at stores near college campuses (Napster country). A small-business owner in Syracuse, New York, said his business dropped 80 percent in the first six months Napster was out. He said kids would check out his bins for new CDs and then go home and download them instead of buying them. He had to close his business.

The debate about file-sharing sites like Napster is really a concern about intellectual property ownership. With Napster, we're talking about music. But the issue includes almost anything in the creative realm: movies, books, art, and so on. Should musicians work without getting paid? Movie producers? Authors? Engineers? If people don't get paid adequately, will they continue to work to produce high-quality music, software, books? Would you work if you didn't get paid fairly?

Technology changes so rapidly that as soon as Napster and the similar sites that had followed it were forced out of business, others took their place. It's more difficult now, but it is still possible to find free music online. Remember, too, that just because something is legal doesn't mean it is ethical. How will you respond to these ethical challenges? Are you willing to pass up the opportunity to get free music if you think that Napster-style file sharing is unethical?

Sources: Frank Ahrens, "Judge Blocks Napster's Sale to Bertelsmann," *Washington Post,* September 4, 2002, p. E1; "Music Label Sues Napster's Money Backers," *APonline,* April 23, 2003; and "Napster Makes a Comeback, but It's Not Free," *Philadelphia Inquirer,* May 20, 2003, p. B3.

In a country like the United States, with so many diverse cultures, you might think it is impossible to identify common standards of ethical behavior. However, among sources from many different times and places—such as the Bible, Aristotle's *Ethics,* William Shakespeare's *King Lear,* the Koran, and the *Analects* of Confucius—you'll find the following basic moral values: Integrity, respect for human life, self-control, honesty, courage, and self-sacrifice are right; cheating, cowardice, and cruelty are wrong. Furthermore, all of the world's major religions support a version of the Golden Rule, even if it is stated only in the negative form: Do not do unto others as you would not have them do unto you.[2]

Ethics Begins with Each of Us

It is easy to criticize business and political leaders for their moral and ethical shortcomings, but we must be careful in our criticism to note that Americans in general are not always as honest and honorable as they should be. A recent study revealed that two-thirds of the American population reported never giving any time to the community in which they live. Nearly one-third said they never contributed to a charity. Both managers and workers cited low managerial ethics as a major cause of American business's competitive woes. Employees reported that they often violate safety standards and goof off as much as seven hours a week.

Young people learn from such behavior. In one recent study, 50 percent of college students, 70 percent of high school students, and 54 percent of middle school students said they had cheated on an exam in the past 12 months.[3] When someone tipped off a San Diego State University instructor that one of his classes was getting the answer keys to his quizzes from classes held earlier in the day, he tested the students' honesty by scrambling the questions. A full third of the students simply wrote the answers from the pirated test key. Some of the dishonest students, who subsequently flunked the course, said the instructor should have shared the blame because giving the same test to different classes was "negligent and stupid." Apparently they thought they didn't have a choice but to cheat since the teacher didn't make it impossible for them to do so. What course was it? Business Ethics.[4]

It is always healthy when discussing moral and ethical issues to remember that ethical behavior begins with you and me. We cannot expect society to become more moral and ethical unless we as individuals commit to becoming more moral and ethical ourselves.

The purpose of the Making Ethical Decisions boxes you see throughout the text is to demonstrate to you that it is important to keep ethics in mind whenever you are making a business decision. The choices are not always easy. Sometimes the obvious solution from an ethical point of view has drawbacks from a personal or professional point of view. For example, imagine that your supervisor at work has asked you to do something you feel is unethical. You have just taken out a mortgage on a new house to make room for your first baby, due in two months. Not carrying out your supervisor's request may get you fired. What would you do? Sometimes there is no desirable alternative. Such situations are called ethical dilemmas because you must choose between equally unsatisfactory alternatives. It can be very difficult to maintain a balance between ethics and other goals such as pleasing stakeholders or advancing in your career. It is helpful to ask yourself the following questions when facing an ethical dilemma:[5]

1. *Is it legal?* Am I violating any law or company policy? Whether you are thinking about having a drink and then driving home, gathering marketing intelligence, designing a product, hiring or firing employees, planning on how to get rid of waste, or using a questionable nickname for an employee, it is necessary to think about the legal implications of what you do. This question is the most basic one in behaving ethically in business, but it is only the first.
2. *Is it balanced?* Am I acting fairly? Would I want to be treated this way? Will I win everything at the expense of another party? Win–lose situations often end up as lose–lose situations. There is nothing like a major loss to generate retaliation from the loser. You can see that in the stock market today. Many companies that were merely suspected of wrongdoing have seen their stock drop dramatically. Not every situation can be completely balanced, but it is important to the health of our rela-

tionships that we avoid major imbalances over time. An ethical businessperson has a win–win attitude. In other words, such a person tries to make decisions that benefit all parties involved.

3. *How will it make me feel about myself?* Would I feel proud if my family learned of my decision? My friends? Would I be able to discuss the proposed situation or action with my immediate supervisor? The company's clients? How would I feel if my decision were announced on the evening news? Will I have to hide my actions or keep them secret? Has someone warned me not to disclose my actions? Am I feeling unusually nervous? Decisions that go against our sense of right and wrong make us feel bad—they corrode our self-esteem. That is why an ethical businessperson does what is proper as well as what is profitable.

There are no easy solutions to ethical dilemmas. Individuals and companies that develop a strong ethics code and use the three ethics-check questions just presented have a better chance than most of behaving ethically. If you would like to know which style of recognizing and resolving ethical dilemmas you favor, fill out the ethical orientation questionnaire in Figure 4.1.

Critical Thinking

Think of a situation you have been involved in that tested your ethical behavior. For example, maybe your best friend forgot about a term paper due the next day and asked you if he could copy and hand in a paper you wrote for another instructor last semester. What are your alternatives, and what are the consequences of each one? Would it have been easier to resolve the dilemma if you had asked yourself the three questions listed on p. 104? Try answering them now and see if you would have made a different choice.

Managing Businesses Ethically and Responsibly

Organizational ethics begin at the top. Ethics is caught more than it is taught. That is, people learn their standards and values from observing what others do, not from hearing what they say. This is as true in business as it is at home. The leadership and example of strong top managers can help instill corporate values in employees. The majority of CEOs surveyed recently attributed unethical employee conduct to the "failure of the organization's leadership in establishing ethical standards and culture."[6]

Any trust and cooperation between workers and managers must be based on fairness, honesty, openness, and moral integrity. The same can be said about relationships among businesses and among nations. A business should be managed ethically for many reasons: to maintain a good reputation; to keep existing customers; to attract new customers; to avoid lawsuits; to reduce employee turnover; to avoid government intervention (the passage of new laws and regulations controlling business activities); to please customers, employees, and society; and simply to do the right thing.

Some managers think that ethics is a personal matter—that either individuals have ethical principles or they don't.[7] These managers feel that they are not responsible for an individual's misdeeds and that ethics has nothing to do with management. But a growing number of people think that ethics has everything to do with management. Individuals do not usually act alone; they need the implied, if not the direct, cooperation of others to behave unethically in a corporation.

FIGURE 4.1

ETHICAL ORIENTATION QUESTIONNAIRE

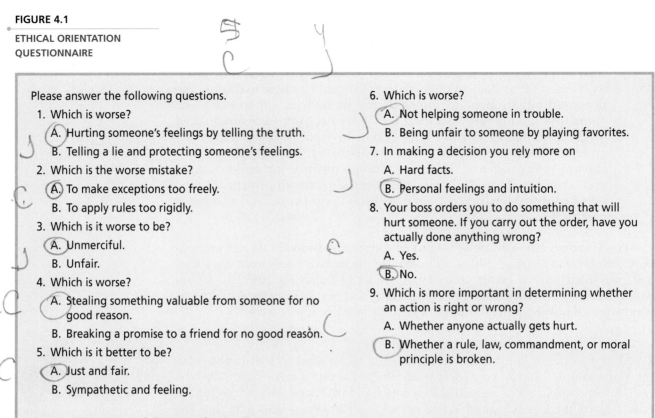

Please answer the following questions.

1. Which is worse?
   A. Hurting someone's feelings by telling the truth.
   B. Telling a lie and protecting someone's feelings.
2. Which is the worse mistake?
   A. To make exceptions too freely.
   B. To apply rules too rigidly.
3. Which is it worse to be?
   A. Unmerciful.
   B. Unfair.
4. Which is worse?
   A. Stealing something valuable from someone for no good reason.
   B. Breaking a promise to a friend for no good reason.
5. Which is it better to be?
   A. Just and fair.
   B. Sympathetic and feeling.
6. Which is worse?
   A. Not helping someone in trouble.
   B. Being unfair to someone by playing favorites.
7. In making a decision you rely more on
   A. Hard facts.
   B. Personal feelings and intuition.
8. Your boss orders you to do something that will hurt someone. If you carry out the order, have you actually done anything wrong?
   A. Yes.
   B. No.
9. Which is more important in determining whether an action is right or wrong?
   A. Whether anyone actually gets hurt.
   B. Whether a rule, law, commandment, or moral principle is broken.

To score: The answers fall in one of two categories, J or C. Count your number of J and C answers using this key: 1. A = J, B = C; 2. A = C, B = J; 3. A = J, B = C; 4. A = C, B = J; 5. A = C, B = J; 6. A = J, B = C; 7:A = C, B = J; 8. A = J, B = C; 9. A = J, B = C

What your score means: The higher your J score, the more you rely on an ethic of *justice.* The higher your C score, the more you prefer an ethic of *care.* Neither style is better than the other, but they are different. Because they appear so different they may seem opposed to one another, but they're actually complementary. In fact, your score probably shows you rely on each style to a greater or lesser degree. (Few people end up with a score of 9 to 0.) The more you can appreciate both approaches, the better you'll be able to resolve ethical dilemmas and to understand and communicate with people who prefer the other style.

An ethic of justice is based on principles like justice, fairness, equality, or authority. People who prefer this style see ethical dilemmas as conflicts of rights that can be solved by the impartial application of some general principle. The advantage of this approach is that it looks at a problem logically and impartially. People with this style try to be objective and fair, hoping to make a decision according to some standard that's higher than any specific individual's interests. The disadvantage of this approach is that people who rely on it might lose sight of the immediate interests of particular individuals. They may unintentionally ride roughshod over the people around them in favor of some abstract ideal or policy. This style is more common for men than women.

An ethic of care is based on a sense of responsibility to reduce actual harm or suffering. People who prefer this style see moral dilemmas as conflicts of duties or responsibilities. They believe that solutions must be tailored to the special details of individual circumstances. They tend to feel constrained by policies that are supposed to be enforced without exception. The advantage of this approach is that it is responsive to immediate suffering and harm. The disadvantage is that, when carried to an extreme, this style can produce decisions that seem not simply subjective, but arbitrary. This style is more common for women than men.

To learn more about these styles and how they might relate to gender, go to www.ethicsandbusiness.org/kg1.htm.

Source: Center for Ethics and Business (www.ethicsandbusiness.org).

Written in 1943 by long-time Chairman General Robert Wood Johnson, the Johnson & Johnson Credo serves as a conscious plan that represents and encourages a unique set of values. Our Credo sums up the responsibilities we have to the four important groups we serve:

- Our customers—We have a responsibility to provide high-quality products they can trust, offered at a fair price.
- Our employees—We have a responsibility to treat them with respect and dignity, pay them fairly and help them develop and thrive personally and professionally.
- Our communities—We have a responsibility to be good corporate citizens, support good works, encourage better health and protect the environment.
- Our stockholders—We have a responsibility to provide a fair return on their investment.

The deliberate ordering of these groups—customers first, stockholders last— proclaims a bold business philosophy: If we meet our first three responsibilities, the fourth will take care of itself . . . To ensure our adherence to Credo values, we periodically ask every employee to evaluate the company's performance in living up to them. We believe that by monitoring our actions against the ethical framework of Our Credo, we will best ensure that we make responsible decisions as a company.

FIGURE 4.2

OVERVIEW OF JOHNSON & JOHNSON'S CODE OF ETHICS

This is an overview of Johnson & Johnson's code of ethics, what it calls its Credo. To see the company's complete Credo, go to its website at www.jnj.com/careers/ourcredo.html.

For example, when Sears, Roebuck & Company was besieged with complaints about its automotive services, Sears management introduced new goals and incentives for its auto center employees. The increased pressure on the Sears employees to meet service quotas caused them to become careless and to exaggerate to customers the need for repairs. Did the managers say directly, "Deceive the customers"? No, but the message was clear anyway. The goals and incentives created an environment in which mistakes did occur and managers did not make efforts to correct the mistakes. Sears settled pending lawsuits by offering coupons to customers who had paid for unnecessary repairs. The estimated cost to Sears was $60 million.[8] Such misbehavior does not reflect a management philosophy that intends to deceive. It does, however, show an insensitivity or indifference to ethical considerations. In an effort to remedy this insensitivity, Sears replaced 23,000 pages of policies and procedures with a simple booklet called "Freedoms & Obligations," which discusses the company's code of business conduct from a commonsense approach.

As Vice President for Corporate Development at Enron, Sherron Watkins sensed that something was rotten with the financial reporting at the company. She "blew the whistle" on her bosses who hid billions of dollars of debt and operating losses from investors and employees. The Sarbanes-Oxley Act now protects whistleblowers like Watkins from any company retaliation. What penalties should be imposed on corporate executives who knowingly cheat investors and employees?

Setting Corporate Ethical Standards

Formal corporate ethics codes are popular these days. Eighty percent of the organizations surveyed recently by the Ethics Resource Center have written codes of ethics. Whether or not a business has a written ethics code seems to be determined by the size of the company. Ninety percent of the organizations with more than 500 employees have written standards.[9] Figure 4.2 offers a sample from one company's code of ethics.

Although ethics codes vary greatly, they can be classified into two major categories: compliance-

compliance-based ethics codes
Ethical standards that emphasize preventing unlawful behavior by increasing control and by penalizing wrongdoers.

integrity-based ethics codes
Ethical standards that define the organization's guiding values, create an environment that supports ethically sound behavior, and stress a shared accountability among employees.

based and integrity-based. **Compliance-based ethics codes** emphasize preventing unlawful behavior by increasing control and by penalizing wrongdoers. Whereas compliance-based ethics codes are based on avoiding legal punishment, **integrity-based ethics codes** define the organization's guiding values, create an environment that supports ethically sound behavior, and stress a shared accountability among employees. See Figure 4.3 for a comparison of compliance-based and integrity-based ethics codes.

The following six-step process can help improve America's business ethics:

1. Top management must adopt and unconditionally support an explicit corporate code of conduct.
2. Employees must understand that expectations for ethical behavior begin at the top and that senior management expects all employees to act accordingly.
3. Managers and others must be trained to consider the ethical implications of all business decisions.
4. An ethics office must be set up. Phone lines to the office should be established so that employees who don't necessarily want to be seen with an ethics officer can inquire about ethical matters anonymously. **Whistleblowers** (people who report illegal or unethical behavior) must feel protected from retaliation. In 2002, President George W. Bush signed the Corporate and Criminal Fraud Accountability (Sarbanes-Oxley) Act. The act contains historic protections for corporate whistleblowers.[10]
5. Outsiders such as suppliers, subcontractors, distributors, and customers must be told about the ethics program. Pressure to put aside ethical considerations often comes from the outside, and it helps employees resist such pressure when everyone knows what the ethical standards are.
6. The ethics code must be enforced. It is important to back any ethics program with timely action if any rules are broken. That is the best way to communicate to all employees that the code is serious.[11]

whistleblowers
People who report illegal or unethical behavior.

This last step is perhaps the most critical. No matter how well intended a company's ethics code is, it is worthless if it is not enforced. (Well, maybe not

FIGURE 4.3

STRATEGIES FOR ETHICS MANAGEMENT

Integrity-based ethics codes move beyond legal compliance to create a "do-it-right" climate that emphasizes core values such as honesty, fair play, good service to customers, a commitment to diversity, and involvement in the community. These values are ethically desirable, but not necessarily legally mandatory.

FEATURES OF COMPLIANCE-BASED ETHICS CODES		FEATURES OF INTEGRITY-BASED ETHICS CODES	
Ideal:	Conform to outside standards (laws and regulations)	Ideal:	Conform to outside standards (laws and regulations) and chosen internal standards
Objective:	Avoid criminal misconduct	Objective:	Enable responsible employee conduct
Leaders:	Lawyers	Leaders:	Managers with aid of lawyers and others
Methods:	Education, reduced employee discretion, controls, penalties	Methods:	Education, leadership, accountability, decision processes, controls, and penalties

www.enron.com

Dealing with Change

Enron: From Ethics Poster Child to Wanted Poster

Can you think of a company worthy of inclusion in the respected Domini 400 Social Index; the socially minded Calvert Group index; and the country's oldest socially responsible fund, Pax World Balanced Fund? Would you believe Enron? The managers of these socially responsible investment funds certainly had difficulty believing the company they once rated so highly (Enron was the Pax fund's top holding) was capable of such socially irresponsible behavior. The case is still under investigation at the time of this writing, but it is alleged (and one executive has confessed) that Enron committed accounting fraud and that the executives sold millions of dollars' worth of stock just before the fraud became public while the company's pension regulations prohibited regular employees from selling their stock. The result was that the executives who bankrupted the company made millions while the employees and other small investors lost millions.

How did the professional managers of Domini, Calvert, and Pax choose such an unethical company? Part of the answer is that Enron's kind of fraud is difficult to detect. The accounting system as it stood was not transparent; that is, it did not require full disclosure. Many people believe that accounting rules need to be changed; others think that dishonest businesses aren't going to reveal their hidden transactions no matter what the disclosure rules are. Socially responsible investing experts believe there are really two areas of special concern: auditors and board members.

Many large accounting firms such as Arthur Andersen, Enron's accounting firm, make more money from consulting with businesses than from auditing them. A conflict of interest arises when an accounting firm audits a company to which it provides consulting services. How can the firm possibly be independent? Arthur Andersen showed that it certainly couldn't be independent—the company was found guilty of shredding Enron documents that could have been evidence in the case. Before the Enron scandal came to light, Pax World would vote against hiring an accounting firm at a holding's annual meeting if the firm made more than 75 percent of its revenues from consulting. It is now considering lowering the acceptable percentage.

Independence of the corporate board is the other major problem. While it is difficult for investors to influence who is on the company's board of directors, experts believe that, at the very least, the board's auditing committee should be managed by a truly independent board member.

There is much more that can be learned from the Enron fiasco—so much that the University of California in Irvine offers a whole course focused on the ethics of Enron. The ex-Enron employee who blew the whistle on the company's scandals was invited to be the star speaker for the course. The class will focus on issues such as what effect incentives have on the management of a company. As the Enron executives go on trial, the students will have ample resources for term papers.

Sources: Laurent Belsie, "Enron's Ex-Role: Model of Ethics," *Christian Science Monitor,* March 4, 2002, p. 20; "Andersen's Bad Experience Yields Sobering Lessons," *USA Today,* April 12, 2002, p. 13A; and "Enron to Become Business Course at California University," Xinhua News Agency, July 9, 2002.

completely worthless—a copy of Enron's code of ethics was recently offered for auction on eBay for around $10. No bidders though.)[12] By ignoring its written code of ethics, both Enron's board and management sent employees the message that rules could be shelved when inconvenient.[13] Read the Dealing with Change box for more about the Enron case.

An important factor to the success of enforcing an ethics code is the selection of the ethics officer. The most effective ethics officers set a positive tone, communicate effectively, and relate well with employees at every level of the company. They are equally comfortable serving as counselors or as investigators. An ethics director's background or functional area seems to be unimportant. For example, the head of Texas Instruments' ethics office came from operations, whereas another of the company's ethics officers has a background in public relations.

- When faced with ethical dilemmas, what questions can you ask yourself that might help you make ethical decisions?
- What are the six steps to follow in establishing an effective ethics program in a business?

Corporate Social Responsibility

corporate social responsibility A business's concern for the welfare of society.

corporate philanthropy Dimension of social responsibility that includes charitable donations.

corporate responsibility Dimension of social responsibility that includes everything from hiring minority workers to making safe products.

corporate policy Dimension of social responsibility that refers to the position a firm takes on social and political issues.

Corporate social responsibility is the concern businesses have for the welfare of society. It goes well beyond merely being ethical. Just as you and I need to be good citizens, contributing what we can to society, corporations need to be good citizens as well. The social performance of a company has several dimensions:

- **Corporate philanthropy** includes charitable donations to nonprofit groups of all kinds. Corporate charitable donations amounted to $9.1 billion in 2001.[14] Strategic philanthropy involves companies making long-term commitments to one cause, such as McDonald's founding and support of Ronald McDonald Houses, which house families whose critically ill children require treatment away from home. Philanthropy isn't limited to large corporations. The Spotlight on Small Business box describes how small businesses can become involved in such generous giving.
- **Corporate responsibility** includes everything from hiring minority workers to making safe products, minimizing pollution, using energy wisely, and providing a safe work environment—that is, everything that has to do with acting responsibly within society.
- **Corporate policy** refers to the position a firm takes on social and political issues.

The Xerox Corporation has had a long-standing commitment to community service. Shown here are Xerox employees breaking ground on the construction site of a new home they are about to build for Habitat for Humanity. Through the company's Social Service Leave program over 80 Xerox employees volunteered to help build the simple house that will be purchased by a family in need at no profit and through no-interest loans.

So much news coverage has been devoted to the problems caused by corporations that people tend to get a negative view of the impact that companies have on society. If the news were more balanced, much more could be said about the positive contributions that businesses make. Few people know, for example, that Xerox has a program called Social Service Leave, which allows employees to leave for up to a year and work for a nonprofit organization. While on Social Leave, the Xerox employee gets full salary and benefits, including job security. IBM and Wells-Fargo Bank have similar programs. In fact, many companies are jumping on the volunteerism bandwagon by allowing employees to give part-time help to social agencies of all kinds. In 2002, President Bush signed an executive order establishing the USA Freedom Corps to oversee Citizen Corps, a new program designed to strengthen homeland security efforts through the help of volunteers. Volunteers handle administrative work at local police departments and spread antiterrorism information as part of expanded Neighborhood Watch programs. Some donate their professional health care

Spotlight on Small Business

www.giftsinkind.org

Myths about Small-Business Philanthropy

Many entrepreneurs have a hard time determining how to start a charitable-giving program in their businesses. Often this is because of misconceptions.

Myth 1: Charities need cash, so struggling small businesses can't help them without jeopardizing their own cash flow.

Reality: Sure, charities need money. But they also need equipment (such as used computers), food, clothing, and volunteers. Pat Heffron, a franchisee of Chem-Dry (which specializes in carpet and upholstery cleaning), found a way to train his employees and help the community at the same time. New Chem-Dry employees learn how to do their jobs by cleaning discarded furniture, which Heffron then donates to local shelters for battered women and the homeless. Another way a small business can contribute to charities without taking a penny out of the cash register is to shop for business supplies through Internet charity sites such as Greatergood.com. Companies listed on such sites donate between 2 and 20 percent of their revenues to the buyer's charity of choice. One extra click—no extra money.

Myth 2: If your business is small, you can't make a significant difference.

Reality: If you target your involvement to small programs within your community, you'll be able to have a notable impact. For instance, one Chicago manufacturer invested just $1,500 in a new local early-childhood literacy program that rewarded inner-city parents with grocery money when they read to their children.

Myth 3: Charity organizers will pay attention only to large contributors with well-known names.

Reality: Nonprofits look for ways to form partnerships with both large and small companies. For example, Dine Across America, a fund-raising effort for a national antihunger organization, received funding for administrative expenses from American Express. But more important, it was small businesses—restaurants and food wholesalers—that donated the food and labor.

Business owners who don't know how to locate nonprofit organizations that need donations can call Gifts in Kind International (703–836–2121), which serves as an intermediary by collecting clothing, office equipment, and other useful materials and distributing them to more than 50,000 nonprofit organizations and schools across the nation.

Sources: Robert Franklin, "Still Helping Out," *Minneapolis Star Tribune,* November 13, 2002, p. 1D; "Online Philanthropy Can Be Big Business," *Europemedia,* July 6, 2002; and Kathy Doellefeld-Clancy, "The Gift of Giving," *St. Louis Post-Dispatch,* December 23, 2002, p. B7.

skills to support emergency medical efforts, and some train others in disaster response and emergency preparedness.[15] Volunteerconnections.org, NetworkforGood.org, and VolunteerMatch.org are Web-based services that link volunteers with nonprofit and public sector organizations around the country. Volunteers enter a zip code or indicate the geographic area in which they'd like to work and the programs list organizations that could use their help.[16]

Two-thirds of the MBA students surveyed by a group called Students for Responsible Business said they would take a lower salary to work for a socially responsible company. But when the same students were asked to define a socially responsible company, things got complicated. It appears that even those who want to be socially responsible can't agree on what it involves. Maybe it would be easier to understand social responsibility if we looked at the concept through the eyes of the stakeholders to whom businesses are responsible: customers, investors, employees, and society in general.

Responsibility to Customers

One responsibility of business is to satisfy customers by offering them goods and services of real value. A recurring theme of this book is the importance of pleasing customers. This responsibility is not as easy to meet as it seems. Keep in mind

Which way to the beach? Rhino Entertainment employees joined Heal the Bay, a nonprofit environmental organization dedicated to cleaning up the Santa Monica Bay, in their 2002 Bay Days Festival. Companies like Rhino are committed to serving their community by helping to protect its environment. Do companies have responsibilities to the environment beyond obeying environmental laws?

that three out of five new businesses fail—perhaps because their owners failed to please their customers. One of the surest ways of failing to please customers is not being totally honest with them. For example, in 1988 a consumer magazine reported that the Suzuki Samurai was likely to roll over if a driver swerved violently in an emergency. When Suzuki executives denied there was a problem, sales plummeted.

In contrast, Daimler-Benz suffered a similar problem in 1997 during a test simulating a swerve around a wayward elk, when its new A-class Baby Benz rolled over. The company quickly admitted a problem, came up with a solution, and committed the money necessary to put that solution into action. In addition, company representatives continued to answer questions in spite of aggressive press coverage. Daimler took out full-page ads that read: "We should like to thank our customers most warmly for their loyalty. You have given us the chance to remedy a mistake." Since the test flip, only 2 percent of the orders for the vehicle were canceled. The solution cost the company $59 million in 1997 and $118 million each year thereafter. Analysts say those costs probably eliminate any profit on the vehicle. However, the quick resolution of the problem protected the company's reputation, thus allowing its other models to become such hits that Daimler's net earnings remained the same.[17]

The payoff for socially conscious behavior could result in new business as customers switch from rival companies simply because they admire the company's social efforts—a powerful competitive edge. Consumer behavior studies show that, all else being equal, a socially conscious company is likely to be viewed more favorably than less socially responsible companies. The important point to remember is that customers prefer to do business with companies they trust and, even more important, do not want to do business with companies they don't trust.

Responsibility to Investors

American economist Milton Friedman made a classic statement when he said that corporate social responsibility means making money for stockholders. Ethical behavior is good for shareholder wealth. It doesn't subtract from the bottom line; it adds to it.[18] Those cheated by financial wrongdoing are the shareholders themselves. Unethical behavior may seem to work for the short term, but it guarantees eventual failure. For example, in just 11 business days in June 2002, 44 CEOs left American corporations amid accusations of wrongdoing and plummeting stock prices.[19]

Some people believe that before you can do good you must do well (i.e., make a lot of money); others believe that by doing good, you can also do well. For example, Bagel Works, a New England–based chain of bagel stores, has a dual-bottom-line approach that focuses on the well-being of the planet as well as profits. Bagel Works has received national recognition for social responsibility. Its mission involves commitments to the environment and to community service. In addition to employing environmentally protective practices such as in-store recycling, composting, using organically grown ingredients, and using nontoxic cleaners, each store includes donations for community causes in its budget. The company donates 10 percent of its pretax profits to charities each year.

Many people believe that it makes financial as well as moral sense to invest in companies that are planning ahead to create a better environment. By

Bernie Ebbers, former CEO of No. 2 long-distance company WorldCom, appears before the House Financial Services Committee in 2002. After disclosing it hid billions of dollars in expenses, WorldCom filed bankruptcy in July 2002. With assets of approximately $107 billion, its collapse was almost twice the size of Enron's. In fact, it was the largest bankruptcy filing in U.S. history. Contrast this news with the headlines in 1997 that heralded the WorldCom and MCI $37 billion merger as the largest merger yet.

choosing to put their money into companies whose goods and services benefit the community and the environment, investors can improve their own financial health while improving society's health.

A few investors, known as inside traders, have chosen unethical means to improve their own financial health. **Insider trading** involves insiders using private company information to further their own fortunes or those of their family and friends. A recent high-profile case of insider trading involved home-style diva Martha Stewart. It was alleged that Stewart sold her 3,000 shares in ImClone, a pharmaceutical company, just before the government announced it would not approve a promising drug and the company's stock price fell dramatically. Stewart says it was just a coincidence and that she didn't know about the drug's rejection, but her phone records indicate that she made repeated calls that day to her broker, who happened also to be the broker for the ImClone CEO's daughter (who dumped her stock the same day as Stewart and is facing insider-trading charges). Stewart's phone records also indicate that she was in close contact with the CEO himself in the days preceding the announcement.[20] The case is, as of this writing, not yet resolved, but it has been costly. Stewart has lost several million dollars as a result of charges against her.

insider trading
An unethical activity in which insiders use private company information to further their own fortunes or those of their family and friends.

Insider trading isn't limited to company executives and their friends. For example, before it was publicly known that IBM was going to take over Lotus Development, an IBM secretary told her husband, who told two co-workers, who told friends, relatives, business associates, and even a pizza delivery man. A total of 25 people received the information and traded illegally on the insider tip within a six-hour period. When the deal was announced publicly, the stock soared 89 percent. One of the inside traders, a stockbroker who passed the information to a few of his customers, made $468,000 in profits. The U.S. Securities and Exchange Commission filed charges against the secretary, her husband, and 23 others. Four of the defendants settled out of court by paying penalties that equaled twice their profit. Prosecutors are placing increased emphasis on the prosecution of insider trading cases in order to ensure that the public is able to conduct business in a securities market that is fair and equally accessible to all.

Companies can misuse information for their own benefit at investors' expense as well. In the case of WorldCom, the company admitted in June 2002 that intentional accounting irregularities made the company look almost $4 billion more profitable than it was. The stock plummeted and the company filed for bankruptcy a month later. This led to more scrutiny of the company's books. It now looks like WorldCom's practice of counting revenue twice dated back as far as 1999, that additional debt continued to be undisclosed, and that revenue that was not received was entered in the books—pushing the irregularities to more than $5 billion.[21] Investors who purchased stock on the basis of the company's false financial reports saw share prices free-fall from the midteens in January 2002 to less than a dime by the following July. The pain was even greater for long-term investors who bought the stock at around $60 in 1999.

Responsibility to Employees

Businesses have several responsibilities to employees. First, they have a responsibility to create jobs if they want to grow. It's been said that the best social program in the world is a job. Once a company creates jobs, it has an obligation to see to it that hard work and talent are fairly rewarded. Employees need realistic hope of a better future, which comes only through a chance for upward mobility. People need to see that integrity, hard work, goodwill, ingenuity, and talent pay off. Studies have shown that the factor that most influences a company's effectiveness and financial performance is human resource management. We will discuss human resource management in Chapter 11.

If a company treats employees with respect, they usually will respect the company as well. For example, Fel-Pro, an Illinois manufacturer of gaskets and other engine parts, established a summer camp for children of employees. Those who used this company benefit were more productive than they had been before because they felt their children were safe. Employees who made the most of Fel-Pro's corporate social responsibility programs were its highest performers. In addition, the increased benefits reduced employee turnover. Given that the U.S. Department of Labor estimates that replacing employees costs between 150 and 250 percent of their annual salaries, retaining workers is good for business as well as for morale.[22]

When employees feel they've been treated unfairly, they often strike back. Getting even is one of the most powerful incentives for good people to do bad things. Not many disgruntled workers are desperate enough to resort to violence in the workplace, but a great number do relieve their frustrations in more subtle ways, such as blaming mistakes on others, not accepting responsibility for decision making, manipulating budgets and expenses, making commitments they intend to ignore, hoarding resources, doing the minimum needed to get by, and making results look better than they are. The loss of employee commitment, confidence, and trust in the company and its management can be very costly indeed. A recent survey revealed that employee theft more than doubled from 1994 to 2000. Today employee theft costs companies about five times more than shoplifting does.[23] You will read more about issues that affect employee–management relations in Chapter 12.

Crickey, crocodile hunter Steve Irwin is crazy about those crocs! Irwin, the owner and director of the Australia Zoo in Queensland, Australia, is so passionate about animals that he has contributed all of the profits from his successful feature film, *The Crocodile Hunter: Collision Course,* to wildlife preservation programs.

Responsibility to Society and the Environment

One of business's major responsibilities to society is to create new wealth. If businesses don't do it, who will? More than a third of working Americans receive their salaries from nonprofit organizations that in turn receive their funding from others, who in turn receive their money from business. Foundations, universities, and other nonprofit organizations own billions of shares in publicly held companies. As those stock prices increase, more funds are available to benefit society.

Businesses are also partially responsible for promoting social justice. Business is perhaps the most crucial institution of civil society. For its own well-being, business depends on its employees being active in politics, law, churches and temples, arts, charities, and so on. Rhino Entertainment, a vintage music and video distributor, has a simple mission: "To put out some great stuff, have some fun, make some money, learn from each other, and make a difference wherever we can." Individual staff members are assigned to oversee community and environmental activities. The company has bins for can and paper recycling and for clothing donations spread throughout its offices. Employees receive extra vacation days each year in exchange for 16 hours of community service. They regularly participate in monthly activities at a local youth center. The company budgets a percentage of its revenues to go to charities that empower groups to help themselves.[24]

In its Philadelphia-area locations, Kinko's exhibits social responsibility through its use of electricity generated from renewable sources such as biomass, hydroelectric, and wind power. The switch from generic system power to cleaner electricity is a way for Kinko's to reduce the pollution that comes from its electricity use by avoiding the release of approximately 160 tons of CO_2 pollution annually. Would you be more likely to do business with Kinko's than with a competitor who isn't as friendly to the environment?

Many companies believe that business has a role in building a community that goes well beyond giving back. To them, charity is not enough. Their social contributions include cleaning up the environment, building community toilets, providing computer lessons, caring for the elderly, and supporting children from low-income families. Samsung, a Korean electronics conglomerate, emphasizes volunteer involvement. For example, a busload of Samsung employees and managers are transported each month to a city park, where they spread out to pick up garbage, pull weeds, and plant saplings. Managers even volunteer to help spruce up employee homes. Local employees feel such loyalty to the company that in the height of the 1999 unrest that destroyed many businesses in Indonesia, local employees and their neighbors pulled together to protect Samsung's refrigerator factory there and shielded foreign managers from violence. With the help of relatives in the countryside, the local employees set up a food supply network that helped protect their colleagues from skyrocketing prices for food staples such as rice and palm oil.[25]

Businesses are clearly taking responsibility for helping to make their own environment a better place. Environmental efforts may increase the company's costs, but they also may allow the company to charge higher prices, to increase market share, or both. For example, Ciba Specialty Chemicals, a Swiss textile-dye manufacturer, developed dyes that require less salt than traditional dyes. Since used dye solutions must be treated before they are released into rivers or streams, having less salt and unfixed dye in the solution means having lower water-treatment costs. Patents protect Ciba's low-salt dyes, so the company can charge more for its dyes than other companies can charge for theirs. Ciba's experience illustrates that, just as a new machine enhances labor productivity, lowering environmental costs can add value to a business.

Not all environmental strategies prove to be as financially beneficial to the company as Ciba's, however. For instance, in the early 1990s StarKist responded to consumer concerns about dolphins dying in the process of tuna fishing because the nets meant to capture tuna also caught dolphins swimming over the yellowfin tuna schools in the eastern Pacific. The company announced that it would sell only tuna from the western Pacific, where the skipjack tuna do not swim underneath dolphins. Unfortunately, the company found that customers were unwilling to pay a premium for the dolphin-safe tuna and that they considered the taste of the skipjack inferior to that of yellowfin tuna. In addition, it turned out that there was no clear environmental gain: In exchange for every dolphin saved by not fishing in the eastern Pacific, thousands of immature tuna and dozens of sharks, turtles, and other marine animals died in the western Pacific fishing process.

Environmental quality is a public good; that is, everyone gets to enjoy it regardless of who pays for it. The trick for companies is to find the right public good that will appeal to their target market. Many corporations are publishing reports that document their net social contribution. To do that, a company must measure its positive social contributions and subtract its negative social impacts. We shall discuss that process next.

At Ford Motor Company the future is now. Here Ford shows off its hydrogen fuel cell electric engine. Implementing hydrogen fuel cells would make the United States less dependent on foreign oil and help preserve our environment. President Bush proposed spending $1.2 billion on a program called "Freedom Fuel" to speed the development of hydrogen fuel cells. Should the government fully subsidize automobile manufacturers to produce nonpolluting hydrogen-fueled cars? Why or why not?

Social Auditing

It is nice to talk about having organizations become more socially responsible. It is also encouraging to see some efforts made toward creating safer products, cleaning up the environment, designing more honest advertising, and treating women and minorities fairly. But is there any way to measure whether organizations are making social responsibility an integral part of top management's decision making? The answer is yes, and the term that represents that measurement is *social auditing*.

social audit
A systematic evaluation of an organization's progress toward implementing programs that are socially responsible and responsive.

A **social audit** is a systematic evaluation of an organization's progress toward implementing programs that are socially responsible and responsive. One of the major problems of conducting a social audit is establishing procedures for measuring a firm's activities and their effects on society. What should be measured? See Figure 4.4 for an outline of business activities that could be considered socially responsible.

There is some question as to whether positive actions should be added (e.g., charitable donations, pollution control efforts) and then negative effects

FIGURE 4.4

SOCIALLY RESPONSIBLE BUSINESS ACTIVITIES

- Community-related activities such as participating in local fund-raising campaigns, donating executive time to various nonprofit organizations (including local government), and participating in urban planning and development.
- Employee-related activities such as establishing equal opportunity programs, offering flextime and other benefits, promoting job enrichment, ensuring job safety, and conducting employee development programs. (You'll learn more about these activities in Chapters 11 and 12.)
- Political activities such as taking a position on nuclear safety, gun control, pollution control, consumer protection, and other social issues; and working more closely with local, state, and federal government officials.
- Support for higher education, the arts, and other nonprofit social agencies.
- Consumer activities such as ensuring product safety, creating truthful advertising, handling complaints promptly, setting fair prices, and conducting extensive consumer education programs.

subtracted (e.g., layoffs, overall pollution levels) to get a net social contribution. Or should just positive actions be recorded? In general, social responsibility is becoming one of the aspects of corporate success that business evaluates, measures, and develops.

In addition to the social audits conducted by the companies themselves, there are four types of groups that serve as watchdogs regarding how well companies enforce their ethical and social responsibility policies:[26]

1. *Socially conscious investors* who insist that a company extend its own high standards to all its suppliers.
2. *Environmentalists* who apply pressure by naming names of companies that don't abide by the environmentalists' standards.
3. *Union officials* who hunt down violations and force companies to comply to avoid negative publicity.
4. *Customers* who take their business elsewhere if a company demonstrates unethical or socially irresponsible practices.

What these groups look for constantly changes as the worldview changes. For example, until September 11, 2001, no group formally screened publicly traded companies to determine potential links to terrorism or the spread of weapons of mass destruction. Now some groups have begun to look at companies that may be even peripherally linked as the U.S. focuses on terrorism.[27] One important thing to remember is that it isn't enough for a company to be right when it comes to ethics and social responsibility. It also has to convince its customers and society that it's right.

INTERNATIONAL ETHICS AND SOCIAL RESPONSIBILITY

Ethical problems and issues of social responsibility are not unique to the United States. Top business and government leaders in Japan were caught in a major "influence-peddling" (read bribery) scheme in Japan. Similar charges have been brought against top officials in South Korea, the People's Republic of China, Italy, Brazil, Pakistan, and Zaire. What is new about the moral and ethical standards by which government leaders are being judged? They are much stricter than in previous years. Top leaders are now being held to a higher standard.

Government leaders are not the only ones being held to higher standards. Many American businesses are demanding socially responsible behavior from their international suppliers by making sure their suppliers do not violate U.S. human rights and environmental standards. For example, Sears will not import ➤P. 68◄ products made by Chinese prison labor. The clothing manufacturer Phillips–Van Heusen said it would cancel orders from suppliers that violate its ethical, environmental, and human rights code. Dow Chemical expects its suppliers to conform to tough American pollution and safety laws rather than just to local laws of their respective countries. McDonald's denied rumors that one of its suppliers grazes cattle on cleared rain forest land but wrote a ban on the practice anyway.

In contrast to companies that demand that their suppliers demonstrate socially responsible behavior are those that have been criticized for exploiting workers in less developed countries. Nike, the world's largest athletic shoe company, has been accused by human rights and labor groups of treating its workers poorly while lavishing millions of dollars on star athletes to endorse its products. Cartoonist Garry Trudeau featured an anti-Nike campaign in his popular syndicated series *Doonesbury*. An Ernst & Young report on Nike's operations in Asia indicated that thousands of young women labored over 10 hours a day, six days a week, in excessive heat, noise, and foul air, for slightly

The Hershey School was established by chocolate magnate Milton Hershey to house, feed, clothe, and educate orphans and economically disadvantaged children he considered "his kids." The school still owns a substantial share of Hershey Foods. In fact, the school's endowment fund is now valued over $5.4 billion, which is more than those of most Ivy League colleges.

more than $10 a week. The report also found that workers with skin or breathing problems caused by the factory conditions had not been transferred to departments free of chemicals. More than half the workers who dealt with dangerous chemicals did not wear protective masks or gloves. Haryanto, a native of Jakarta, travels the globe speaking on college campuses to advocate workers' rights. He describes how he lost two fingers of his right hand making soles for Nike sneakers and how seven of his friends also lost fingers in the same machine. He says that Nike refused to fix the machine's broken switches.

Nike officials say they are working to improve conditions, but their critics say they are not doing enough quickly enough.[28] While customers still seem to favor brand, price, and quality over their perception of a company's humane treatment and social responsibility, surveys show that the vast majority of respondents would pay an extra few dollars for a garment that had been made in a worker-friendly environment.

The justness of requiring international suppliers to adhere to American ethical standards is not as clear-cut as you might think. Is it always ethical for companies to demand compliance with the standards of their own countries? What about countries where child labor is an accepted part of the society and families depend on the children's salaries for survival? What about foreign companies doing business in the United States? Should they expect American companies to comply with their ethical standards? What about multinational corporations? Since they span different societies, do they not have to conform to any one society's standards? Why is Sears applauded for not importing goods made in Chinese prisons when there are many prison-based enterprises in the United States? None of these questions are easy to answer, but they give you some idea of the complexity of social responsibility issues in international markets. (See the Reaching Beyond Our Borders box for an example of an ethical culture clash.)

In an effort to identify some form of common global ethic and to fight corruption in global markets, the partners in the Organization of American States signed the Inter-American Convention Against Corruption. A similar anticorruption convention was signed by 29 member states of the Organization for Economic Cooperation and Development (OECD) and five other states that are home to nearly all of the major multinational corporations. The OECD convention covers only those companies and governments that offer bribes and not the individuals who accept them. However, such loopholes are expected to be eliminated in the years ahead.[29] In many places "Fight corruption" remains just a slogan, but even a slogan is a start.

Progress Assessment

- What is corporate social responsibility, and how does it relate to each of business's major stakeholders?
- What is a social audit, and what kinds of activities does it monitor?

Reaching Beyond Our Borders

www.pathfinder.com

Ethical Culture Clash

Communications and electronics giant Motorola describes itself as dedicated to "uncompromising integrity." Robert W. Galvin, Motorola's board chairman, says that the company's ethical values and standards are an "indispensable foundation" for the company's work, relationships, and business success. Almost half of Motorola's employees are non-American, and more than half of its revenues come from non-American markets. Is it difficult for Motorola employees to adhere to the company's ethical values while at the same time respecting the values of the host countries in which Motorola manufactures and markets its products?

Here's an example of how corporate ethics can clash with cultural ethics. Joe, the oldest son of a poor South American cloth peddler, managed to move to the United States, earn an engineering degree, and get a job with Motorola. After five years, Joe seemed to have bought into the Motorola culture and was happy to have been granted a transfer back to his home country. Joe was told that the company expected him to live there in a safe and presentable home of his choice. To help him afford such a residence, Motorola agreed to reimburse him a maximum of $2,000 a month for the cost of his rent and servants. Each month Joe submitted rental receipts for exactly $2,000. The company later found out that Joe was living in what was, by Western standards, a shack in a dangerous slum area of town. Such a humble home could not have cost more than a couple hundred dollars a month. The company was concerned for Joe's safety as well as for the effect the employee's unseemly residence would have on Motorola's image. The human resource manager was ultimately concerned about Joe's lack of integrity, given that he had submitted false receipts for reimbursement.

Joe was upset with what he considered the company's invasion of his privacy. He argued that he should receive the full $2,000 monthly reimbursement that all of the other Motorola employees received. He explained his choice of housing by saying that he was making sacrifices so he could send the extra money to his family and put his younger siblings through school. This was especially important since his father had died and his family had no one else to depend on but Joe. "Look, my family is poor," Joe said, "so poor that most Westerners wouldn't believe our poverty even if they saw it. This money means the difference between hope and despair for all of us. For me to do anything less for my family would be to defile the honor of my late father. Can't you understand?"

Often it is difficult to understand what others perceive as being ethical. Different situations often turn the clear waters of "rightness" downright muddy. In Joe's case, one could see that Joe was trying to do the honorable thing for his family. One could also argue that Motorola's wish to have its higher-level people live in safe housing is not unreasonable, given the dangerous conditions of the city in which Joe lived. The policy of housing reimbursement supports Motorola's intent to make its employees' stay in the country reasonably comfortable and safe, not to increase their salaries. If Joe worked in the United States, where he would not receive a housing supplement, it would clearly be unethical for him to falsify expense reports in order to receive more money to send to his family. In South America, though, the issue is not so clear.

Sources: R. S. Moorthy, Robert C. Solomon, William J. Ellos, and Richard T. De George, "Friendship or Bribery?" *Across the Board,* January 1999, pp. 43–47; and "Motorola Emphasizes 'People Development in the Information Age' at the Asia Society/Dow Jones Conference in Shanghai, China," news release, May 10, 2000.

Summary

1. Ethics goes beyond obeying laws. It also involves abiding by the moral standards accepted by society.
   - ***How is legality different from ethics?***

   Ethics reflects people's proper relations with one another. Legality is more limiting; it refers only to laws written to protect people from fraud, theft, and violence.

1. Explain why legality is only the first step in behaving ethically.

2. Ask the three questions one should answer when faced with a potentially unethical action.

2. It is often difficult to know when a decision is ethical.
   - ***How can we tell if our business decisions are ethical?***

   Our business decisions can be put through an ethics check by asking three questions: (1) Is it legal? (2) Is it balanced? and (3) How will it make me feel?

3. Describe management's role in setting ethical standards.

3. Some managers think ethics is an individual issue that has nothing to do with management, while others believe ethics has everything to do with management.
   - ***What is management's role in setting ethical standards?***

   Managers often set formal ethical standards, but more important are the messages they send through their actions. Management's tolerance or intolerance of ethical misconduct influences employees more than any written ethics codes do.

4. Distinguish between compliance-based and integrity-based ethics codes, and list the six steps in setting up a corporate ethics code.

4. Ethics codes can be classified as compliance-based or integrity-based.
   - ***What's the difference between compliance-based and integrity-based ethics codes?***

   Whereas compliance-based ethics codes are concerned with avoiding legal punishment, integrity-based ethics codes define the organization's guiding values, create an environment that supports ethically sound behavior, and stress a shared accountability among employees.

5. Define *corporate social responsibility* and examine corporate responsibility to various stakeholders.

5. Corporate social responsibility is the concern businesses have for society.
   - ***How do businesses demonstrate corporate responsibility toward stakeholders?***

   Business is responsible to four types of stakeholders: (1) business's responsibility to customers is to satisfy them with goods and services of real value; (2) business is responsible for making money for its investors; (3) business has several responsibilities to employees: to create jobs, to maintain job security, and to see that hard work and talent are fairly rewarded; and (4) business has several responsibilities to society: to create new wealth, to promote social justice, and to contribute to making its own environment a better place.
   - ***How are a company's social responsibility efforts measured?***

   A corporate social audit measures an organization's progress toward social responsibility. Some people believe that the audit should add together the organization's positive actions and then subtract the negative effects of business to get a net social benefit.

6. Analyze the role of American businesses in influencing ethical behavior and social responsibility in global markets.

6. Many customers are demanding that companies deal only with other companies that share a commitment to environmental and human rights issues.
   - ***How can American companies influence ethical behavior and social responsibility in global markets?***

   Companies like Sears, Phillips–Van Heusen, and Dow Chemical will not import products from companies that do not meet their ethical and social responsibility standards.

Key Terms

compliance-based ethics codes 108
corporate philanthropy 110
corporate policy 110
corporate responsibility 110
corporate social responsibility 110
ethics 102
insider trading 113
integrity-based ethics codes 108
social audit 116
whistleblowers 108

1. What sources have helped shape your personal code of ethics and morality? What influences, if any, have ever pressured you to compromise those standards? Think of an experience you had at work or school that tested your ethical standards. What did you decide to do to resolve your dilemma? Now that time has passed, are you comfortable with the decision you made? If not, what would you do differently?

2. Newspapers and magazines are full of stories about individuals and businesses that are not socially responsible. What about those individuals and organizations that do take social responsibility seriously? We don't normally read or hear about them. Do a little investigative reporting of your own. Identify a public interest group in your community and identify its officers, objectives, sources and amount of financial support, and size and characteristics of membership. List some examples of its recent actions and/or accomplishments. You should be able to choose from environmental groups, animal protection groups, political action committees, and so on. Call the local chamber of commerce, the Better Business Bureau, or local government agencies for help. Try using one of the Internet search engines to help you find more information.

3. You are manager of a coffeehouse called the Morning Cup. One of your best employees desires to be promoted to a managerial position; however, the owner is grooming his slow-thinking son for the promotion your employee seeks. The owner's act of nepotism may hurt a valuable employee's chances for advancement, but complaining may hurt your own chances for promotion. What do you do?

4. Contact a local corporation and ask for a copy of its written ethics code. Would you classify its code as compliance-based or integrity-based? Explain.

5. What effects have the new laws protecting whistleblowers had on the business environment? Use the Internet or the library to research individuals who reported their employers' illegal and/or unethical behavior. Did the companies change their policies? If so, what effect have these policies had on the companies' stakeholders? What effect did reporting the problems have on the whistleblowers themselves?

Purpose

To illustrate that ethical behavior is complex and that even efforts to be socially responsible can create ethical dilemmas.

Exercise

Few other events have pierced the hearts of so many people, American or otherwise, than the terrorist attacks of September 11, 2001. People's desire to unite and do whatever possible to help the victims was a driving force in generating both governmental and charitable assistance of unheard-of magnitude. Gathering the resources was the easy part; deciding how they should be distributed was the unimaginably difficult part. In an effort to distribute relief funds fairly, the U.S. government devised a method of calculating the value of individual lives. Log on to www.usdoj.gov/victimcompensation to calculate yours. For the curious, a single 30-year-old earning $25,000: $470,878. A married 40-year-old earning $225,000 with two children: $3,246,723. Your initial impulse might be to divide the money evenly, but ask yourself the following questions and then decide how you would compensate the families of the September 11 victims if it were up to you:

1. Does the widowed mother of four need more than the widowed father of one? If so, how do you decide how much?
2. Should a family previously living on an income of $25,000 a year receive the same as a family whose breadwinner earned $250,000?
3. The government calculations contain a deduction if the family received insurance benefits. Is it ethical to penalize a family for having the foresight to pay for life insurance policies?
4. The plan provides for pain and suffering. Who suffered more, a widower married 35 years or a widow married six months? How do you place a dollar value on such suffering even if you could determine it? The government decided to pay a flat $250,000. Do you agree that this is the best ethical answer?
5. Families of the Oklahoma City bombing victims questioned why the victims of one attack are more worthy of such a fund than others. Do you have an answer for them?

Taking It To The Net 2

Purpose

To demonstrate the level of commitment one business has to social responsibility.

Exercise

Richard Foos of Rhino Records built a multimillion-dollar entertainment experience out of a pile of dusty old records, and did it by sticking to his ideals. Foos fosters ethical practices in Rhino's day-to-day business, supporting numerous charitable groups and promoting community service by Rhino employees. See for yourself how Foos responds to social and environmental issues by going to Rhino's website at www.rhino.com. Then answer the following questions:

1. What is the social mission of Rhino Records?
2. What does the Social and Environmental Responsibility Team (SERT) do to implement this mission?
3. How does Rhino Records encourage its employees to get involved in community service?
4. How do Rhino employees communicate the company's social mission to their customers?

Casing The Web

To access the case "Got a Deadline? Click Here," visit

www.mhhe.com/ub/7e

Video Case

Doing Unto Others—Abbott Laboratories

Why should a company establish ethical standards? For Abbott Laboratories, the answer is: "Because it is the right thing to do." It's also important for business reasons because a pharmaceutical company needs to establish trust with all its stakeholders: employees, customers, regulators, shareholders, and so on.

Abbott has been in business for over 100 years. It now employs some 70,000 people around the world and operates in 130 countries. The company makes and distributes pharmaceuticals, medical devices, and nutritional aids. You can imagine the challenge the company faces in meeting the legal, moral, and ethical codes of so many different countries. This is especially true in the pharmaceutical industry because it is involved in numerous issues, like kickbacks, overpricing, and unethical promotions. Only an effort by top management is enough to even begin tackling such major issues.

Abbott has had a compliance-based ethics code for many years. But it's one thing to talk about establishing a strong ethics program and quite another to implement one. That's why the company appointed Charlie Brock as Abbott's chief ethics and compliance officer. Each division has an ethics staff, and Brock is the coordinator over them all. One of Brock's first steps in implementing Abbott's ethics program was to let everyone in the company know what the firm's ethical standards are. But the company did not stop with employees; suppliers, distributors, and customers also needed to know that Abbott has such standards and intends to apply them rigorously. That meant establishing a program based on specific standards that are communicated clearly and are enforced with penalties for noncompliance. Abbott uses the latest technology to train employees in ethical standards. Interactive software developed by California-based LRN presents difficult ethical cases and teaches employees what to do when tough ethical issues arise.

Abbott goes beyond just compliance-based ethics to integrity-based ethics. That is, it has a broad program of "global citizenship" that covers everything from how the company reports information to stockholders to how it treats its employees, to how it manufactures goods, to how it tries to minimize environmental effects. The company has been very generous to many nonprofit groups, but takes special pride in its efforts to conquer AIDS in the world, including developing products to treat and hopefully cure the disease. This effort also means teaching people in developing countries how to test themselves for HIV to prevent spreading AIDS to their children. All told, Abbott will spend over $100 million on such efforts over the next five years. That includes building partnerships with other firms to make a difference in the world.

Abbott is truly a company to be admired for its corporate citizenship and its active involvement in self-regulation. Not only has the company established an ethics office and set clear ethics codes; it vigorously applies those codes. Its community outreach, including a strong commitment to ending the AIDS crisis, sets a model for other companies to benchmark. Most important, the company does it all for the right reason: It is the morally right thing to do!

Thinking It Over

1. Do you think Abbott's ethics program will succeed in creating the trust the company is striving to maintain? Why or why not?
2. Would you be more or less interested in working for a company with such a strong commitment to ethics and community involvement? What does your answer say about the value of such programs?
3. What are some issues involved in manufacturing and selling drugs in countries around the world? How does an ethics code address most of these issues?
4. One way a company like Abbott could make a difference in developing countries might be to sell a treatment for AIDS at or below cost. What would be the long-term consequences of such a decision to the company?

Appendix

Working within the Legal Environment of Business

THE NEED FOR LAWS

Imagine a society without laws. Just think, no speed limits to control how fast we drive, no age restrictions on the consumption of alcoholic beverages, no limitations on who can practice medicine—a society in which people are free to do whatever they choose, with no interference. Obviously, the more we consider this possibility, the more unrealistic we realize it is. Laws are an essential part of a civilized nation. Over time, though, the depth and scope of the body of laws must change to reflect the needs and changes in society. The **judiciary** is the branch of government chosen to oversee the legal system through the court system.

judiciary
The branch of government chosen to oversee the legal system through the court system.

The court system in the United States is organized at the federal, state, and local levels. At both the federal and state levels, trial courts hear cases involving criminal and civil law. Criminal law defines crimes, establishes punishments, and regulates the investigation and prosecution of people accused of committing crimes. Civil law involves legal proceedings that do not involve criminal acts; it includes laws regulating marriage, payment for personal injury, and so on. Both federal and state systems have appellate courts. Such courts hear appeals of decisions made at the trial-court level brought by the losing party in the case. Appellate courts can review and overturn decisions made at the trial-court level.

A curious observer looks at what's left of a Ford Explorer that was equipped with faulty Bridgestone/Firestone tires. The wrecked vehicle was used in a lawsuit against both companies. Overall, 6.5 million tires were recalled due to complaints about the tires coming apart at high speeds. Do you think both companies should be liable for the faulty tires or just Bridgestone/Firestone? Why?

The judiciary also governs the activities and operations of business. In fact, businesspeople often complain that the government is stepping in more and more to govern the behavior of business. Thus, you see laws and regulations regarding sexual harassment on the job, hiring and firing practices, unpaid leave for family emergencies, environmental protection, safety, and more. As you may suspect, businesspeople prefer to set their own standards of behavior. However, the U.S. business community has not been perceived as implementing acceptable practices fast enough. To hasten the process, the federal government has expanded its control and enforcement procedures. In this appendix we will look at some of the laws and regulations now in place and how they affect business.

Business law refers to rules, statutes, codes, and regulations that are established to provide a legal framework within which business may be conducted and that are enforceable by court action. A businessperson should be familiar with laws regarding product liability, sales, contracts, fair competition, consumer protection, taxes, and bankruptcy. Let's start at the beginning and discuss the foundations of the law. It's hard to understand the law unless you know what the law is.

business law
Rules, statutes, codes, and regulations that are established to provide a legal framework within which business may be conducted and that are enforceable by court action.

Statutory and Common Law

There are two major kinds of law: statutory law and common law. Both are important for businesspeople.

Statutory law includes state and federal constitutions, legislative enactments, treaties of the federal government, and ordinances—in short, written law. You can read the statutes that make up this body of law, but they are often written in language whose meaning must be determined in court. That's one reason why there are more than 900,000 lawyers in the United States.

Common law is the body of law that comes from decisions handed down by judges. Common law is often referred to as *unwritten law* because it does not appear in any legislative enactment, treaty, or other such document. Under common law principles, what judges have decided in previous cases is very important to today's cases. Such decisions are called **precedent**, and they guide judges in the handling of new cases. Common law evolves through decisions made in trial courts, appellate courts, and special courts. Lower courts (trial courts) must abide by the precedents set by higher courts (appellate courts) such as the U.S. Supreme Court. In law classes, therefore, students study case after case to learn about common law as well as statutory law.

statutory law
State and federal constitutions, legislative enactments, treaties of the federal government, and ordinances—in short, written law.

common law
The body of law that comes from decisions handed down by judges; also referred to as *unwritten law*.

precedent
Decisions judges have made in earlier cases that guide the handling of new cases.

Administrative Agencies

Different organizations within the government issue many rules, regulations, and orders. **Administrative agencies** are federal or state institutions and other government organizations created by Congress or state legislatures with delegated power to pass rules and regulations within their mandated area of authority. Legislative bodies can not only create administrative agencies but also terminate them. Some administrative agencies hold quasi-legislative, quasi-executive, and quasi-judicial powers. This means an agency is allowed to pass rules and regulations within its area of authority, conduct investigations in cases of suspected rules violations, and hold hearings when it feels the rules and regulations have been violated. Administrative agencies actually issue more rulings affecting business and settle more disputes than courts do. We will look in depth at agencies like the Securities and Exchange Commission (SEC) and the Equal Employment Opportunity Commission (EEOC) later in the text. Figure A.1 lists and describes the powers and functions of several administrative agencies at the federal, state, and local levels of government. How many of these agencies have you heard about?

administrative agencies
Federal or state institutions and other government organizations created by Congress or state legislatures with delegated power to pass rules and regulations within their mandated area of authority.

FIGURE A.1

EXAMPLES OF FEDERAL, STATE, AND LOCAL ADMINISTRATIVE AGENCIES

EXAMPLES	POWERS AND FUNCTIONS
FEDERAL AGENCIES	
Federal Trade Commission	Enforces laws and guidelines regarding unfair business practices and acts to stop false and deceptive advertising and labeling
Food and Drug Administration	Enforces laws and regulations to prevent distribution of adulterated or misbranded foods, drugs, medical devices, cosmetics, and veterinary products, as well as any hazardous consumer products
STATE AGENCIES	
Public utility commissions	Set rates that can be charged by various public utilities to prevent unfair pricing by regulated monopolies (e.g., natural gas, electric power companies)
State licensing boards	License various trades and professions within a state (e.g., state cosmetology board, state real estate commission)
LOCAL AGENCIES	
Maricopa County Planning Commission	Oversees land-use proposals, long-term development objectives, and other long-range issues in Maricopa County, Arizona
City of Chesterfield Zoning Board	Sets policy regarding zoning of commercial and residential property in the city of Chesterfield, Missouri

TORT LAW

tort
A wrongful act that causes injury to another person's body, property, or reputation.

negligence
In tort law, behavior that causes unintentional harm or injury.

The tort system is an example of common law at work. A **tort** is a wrongful act that causes injury to another person's body, property, or reputation. Although torts often are noncriminal acts, victims can be awarded compensation. This is especially true if the conduct that caused harm is considered intentional. An intentional tort is a willful act that results in injury. The question of intent was a major factor in the tobacco industry lawsuits. Courts investigated whether cigarette makers willfully withheld from the public information about the harmful effects of their products.[1] **Negligence**, in tort law, deals with behavior that causes unintentional harm or injury. Decisions involving negligence can often lead to huge judgments against businesses. In a highly publicized case, McDonald's lost a lawsuit to a person severely burned by its hot coffee. The jury felt the company failed to provide an adequate warning on the cup.[2] Product liability is another example of tort law that's often very controversial. This is especially true regarding torts related to business actions. Let's look briefly at this issue.

Product Liability

product liability
Part of tort law that holds businesses liable for harm that results from the production, design, sale, or use of products they market.

strict product liability
Legal responsibility for harm or injury caused by a product regardless of fault.

Few issues in business law raise as much debate as product liability. Critics believe product liability laws have gone too far and deter product development.[3] Others feel these laws should be expanded to include products such as software and fast foods.[4] **Product liability**, covered under tort law, holds businesses liable for harm that results from the production, design, sale, or use of products they market. At one time the legal standard for measuring product liability was whether a producer knowingly placed a hazardous product on the market. Today, many states have extended product liability to the level of **strict product liability**.[5] Legally, this means without regard to fault. Thus, a

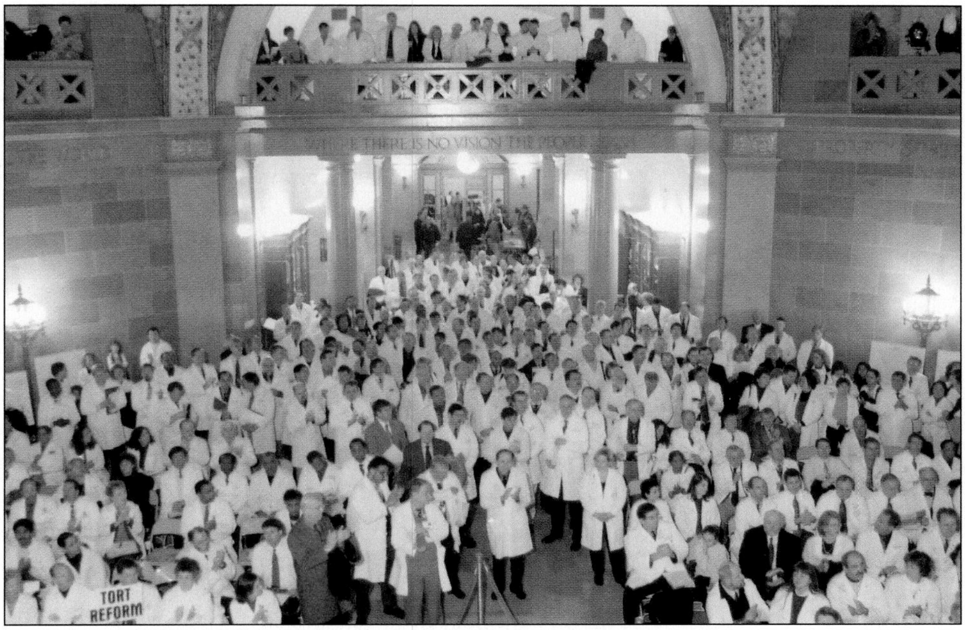

These physicians are not attending a medical convention; they are preparing to join a rally supporting tort reform in the state capital rotunda in Jefferson City, Missouri. Like other doctors across the nation, they are appealing the state legislature to enact major legal reforms that would reduce their fast-growing malpractice insurance rates.

company could be held liable for damages caused by placing a defective product on the market even if the company did not know of the defect at the time of sale. In such cases, the company is required to compensate the injured party financially.

The rule of strict liability has caused serious problems for businesses.[6] It's estimated that more than 50 companies have been forced into bankruptcy due to asbestos litigation.[7] Companies that produced lead-based paint could also be subjected to expensive legal liabilities even though lead paint has been banned in the United States for nearly three decades.[8] The manufacturers of chemicals and drugs are also often susceptible to lawsuits under strict product liability. A producer may place a drug or chemical on the market that everyone agrees is safe. Years later, a side effect or other health problem could emerge. Under the doctrine of strict liability, the manufacturer can be held liable.

In an interesting liability case, the gun industry has been accused of damages under the rules of strict product liability. Cities such as Newark, Philadelphia, Chicago, New Orleans, and Miami filed lawsuits against gun manufacturers seeking financial payments to cover the costs of police work and medical care necessitated by gun violence.[9] Lawsuits have also been filed on behalf of private individuals affected by gun violence.[10] Those who support the plaintiffs contend the industry is liable because it does nothing to enhance the safety or prevent the criminal misuse of its products. The gun industry has strongly refuted such charges and denied liability. Thus far, several of the lawsuits have been dropped and others have been dismissed by courts, but the issue still lingers.[11] Fast food was also on the strict liability front burner. McDonald's was the subject of a liability suit charging that its food caused obesity, diabetes, and other health problems in children.[12] The initial lawsuit against the company was dismissed by the trial judge.[13] However, many expect the issue to resurface in other lawsuits.[14]

Businesses and insurance companies have called for legal relief from huge losses that are often awarded in strict product liability suits.[15] They have lobbied Congress to set limits on the amounts of damages for which they are liable should their products harm consumers. Figure A.2 highlights several major product liability awards that cost companies dearly.

FIGURE A.2

MAJOR PRODUCT LIABILITY CASES

COMPANY	YEAR	SETTLEMENT
Ford Motor Company	1978	$125 million in punitive damages awarded in the case of a 13-year-old boy severely burned in a rear-end collision involving a Ford Pinto
A. H. Robins	1987	Dalkon Shield intrauterine birth-control devices recalled after eight separate punitive-damage awards
Playtex Company	1988	Considered liable and suffered a $10 million damage award in the case of a toxic shock syndrome fatality in Kansas; removed certain types of tampons from the market
Jack in the Box	1993	Assessed large damages after a two-year-old child who ate at Jack in the Box died of *E. coli* poisoning and others became ill
Sara Lee Corporation	1998	Costly company recall necessitated when tainted hot dogs caused food-poisoning death of 15 people
General Motors	1999	Suffered $4.8 billion punitive award in faulty fuel-tank case
Major Tobacco Firms	2000	$145 billion punitive judgment in Florida case (on appeal)

Sources: U.S. Department of Justice; American Trial Lawyers Association.

LAWS PROTECTING IDEAS: PATENTS, COPYRIGHTS, AND TRADEMARKS

patent
A document that gives inventors exclusive rights to their inventions for 20 years.

Many people, including you perhaps, have invented products that are assumed to have commercial value. The question that obviously surfaces is what to do next. One step may be to apply for a patent. A **patent** is a document that gives inventors exclusive rights to their inventions for 20 years from the date they file the patent applications.[16] The U.S. Patent and Trademark Office (USPTO) grants approximately 190,000 patents a year.[17] In addition to filing forms, the inventor must make sure the product is truly unique. Since patent applicants are usually recommended to seek the advice of a lawyer, less than 2 percent of product inventors file on their own.

Patent owners have the right to sell or license the use of a patent to others. Foreign companies are also eligible to file for U.S. patents and account for nearly half the U.S. patents issued. The penalties for violating a patent can be very severe. The USPTO, however, cannot take action on behalf of patent holders if infringement of a patent occurs. The defense of patent rights is solely the job of the patent holder. In a rather famous case, the camera and film company Polaroid was able to force Kodak to recall all of its instant cameras because Polaroid had several patents that Kodak violated. Kodak lost millions of dollars, and Polaroid maintained market leadership in instant cameras for many years. In another case inventor Robert Kearns won millions of dollars from Ford and Chrysler by proving that both companies violated his patent on intermittent windshield wipers.

How good are your chances of receiving a patent if you file for one? More than 60 percent of patent applications are approved, each at a minimum cost to the inventor of $6,600 in fees over the life of the patent. The time it takes to process a patent is close to two years.[18] That time has increased since the growth in patents requested is outstripping the number of examiners in the

USPTO.[19] This is especially true in the growth of what are called business-method patents (such as Amazon.com's famous patent on a one-click online purchase system), which involve different business applications using the Internet.[20] The USPTO has agreed to take steps to tighten the issuing of such patents.[21]

In 1999, the U.S. Congress passed changes to current patent law through the American Inventor's Protection Act, which requires patent applications to be made public after 18 months regardless of whether a patent has been granted. This law was passed in part to address critics who argued that some inventors would intentionally delay or drag out a patent application because they expected others to develop similar products or technology. When someone else did file for a similar patent, the inventor surfaced to claim the patent—referred to as a *submarine patent*—and demand large fees for its use.[22] The late engineer Jerome Lemelson, for example, reportedly collected more than a billion dollars in patent royalties for a series of long-delayed patents, including forerunners of the fax machine, the Walkman, and the bar-code scanner.[23]

EAT IN, CARRY OUT, OR LOG-ON.
TM
Heads up people. Your next visit to McDonald's® could take you all the way to the Internet. Intel® Centrino™ mobile technology and McDonald's are working together to get you connected without wires. Now when you come into a participating McDonald's restaurant displaying on the door, you'll find easy, convenient, high speed wireless LAN access. Visit www.mcdwireless.com for an up to the minute list of participating locations and other important details.
centrino
MOBILE TECHNOLOGY
smile

From the desert sands of Saudi Arabia to the beaches of Miami, Florida, the golden arches of McDonald's are one of the most recognized trademarks in the world. McDonald's has the exclusive legal protection to use this symbol. Look closely at the "TM" to the right of the arches. This signifies the logo is a trademark.

Just as a patent protects an inventor's right to a product or process, a **copyright** protects a creator's rights to materials such as books, articles, photos, paintings, and cartoons. Copyrights are filed with the Library of Congress and involve a minimum of paperwork. They last for the lifetime of the author or artist plus 70 years, and can be passed on to the creator's heirs.[24] The Copyright Act of 1978, however, gives a special term of 75 years from publication to works published before January 1, 1978, whose copyrights had not expired by that date. The holder of an exclusive copyright may charge a fee to anyone who wishes to use the copyrighted material. If a work is created by an employee in the normal course of a job, the copyright belongs to the employer and lasts 95 years from publication or 120 years from creation, whichever comes first.[25]

A **trademark** is a legally protected name, symbol, or design (or combination of these) that identifies the goods or services of one seller and distinguishes them from those of competitors. Trademarks generally belong to the owner forever, as long as they are properly registered and renewed every 10 years. Some well-known trademarks include the Pillsbury Doughboy, the Disney Company's Mickey Mouse, the Nike swoosh, and the golden arches of McDonald's. Like a patent, a trademark is protected from infringement.[26] Companies fight hard to protect trademarks, especially in global markets where pirating can be extensive.[27] We will discuss trademarks in more detail in Chapter 14.

copyright
A document that protects a creator's rights to materials such as books, articles, photos, and cartoons.

trademark
A legally protected name, symbol, or design (or combination of these) that identifies the goods or services of one seller and distinguishes them from those of competitors.

SALES LAW: THE UNIFORM COMMERCIAL CODE

At one time, laws involving businesses varied from state to state, making interstate trade extremely complicated. Today, all states have adopted the same commercial law. The **Uniform Commercial Code (UCC)** is a comprehensive commercial law that covers sales laws and other commercial laws. Since all 50 states have adopted the law (although it does not apply in certain sections of Louisiana), the UCC simplifies trading across state lines.[28]

Uniform Commercial Code (UCC)
A comprehensive commercial law, adopted by every state in the United States, that covers sales laws and other commercial laws.

The UCC has 11 articles, which contain laws covering sales; commercial paper such as promissory notes and checks; bank deposits and collections; letters of credit; bulk transfers; warehouse receipts, bills of lading, and other documents of title; investment securities; and secured transactions. We do not have space to discuss all 11 articles, but we would like to discuss two of them: Article 2, which contains laws regarding warranties, and Article 3, which covers negotiable instruments.

Warranties

express warranties
Specific representations by the seller that buyers rely on regarding the goods they purchase.

implied warranties
Guarantees legally imposed on the seller.

A warranty guarantees that the product sold will be acceptable for the purpose for which the buyer intends to use it. There are two types of warranties. **Express warranties** are specific representations by the seller that buyers rely on regarding the goods they purchase. The warranty you receive in the box with a clock, toaster, or DVD player is the express warranty. It spells out the seller's warranty agreement. **Implied warranties** are legally imposed on the seller. It is implied, for example, that the product will conform to the customary standards of the trade or industry in which it competes. For example, it's expected that a toaster will toast your bread to your desired degree (light, medium, dark) or that food bought for consumption off an establishment's premises is fit to eat.

Warranties offered by sellers can be either full or limited. A full warranty requires a seller to replace or repair a product at no charge if the product is defective, whereas a limited warranty typically limits the defects or mechanical problems that are covered. Many of the rights of buyers, including the acceptance and rejection of goods, are spelled out in Article 2 of the UCC. Both buyers and sellers should become familiar with the UCC. You can read more about it on the Internet or in business law books in the library.

Negotiable Instruments

negotiable instruments
Forms of commercial paper (such as checks) that are transferable among businesses and individuals and represent a promise to pay a specified amount.

Negotiable instruments are forms of commercial paper (such as checks) that are transferable among businesses and individuals and represent a promise to pay a specified amount. Article 3 of the Uniform Commercial Code requires negotiable instruments to follow four conditions. They must (1) be written and signed by the maker or drawer, (2) be made payable on demand or at a certain time, (3) be made payable to the bearer (the person holding the instrument) or to specific order, and (4) contain an unconditional promise to pay a specified amount of money. Checks or other forms of negotiable instruments are transferred (negotiated for payment) when the payee signs the back. The payee's signature is referred to as an *endorsement*.

Contract Law

If I offer to sell you my bike for $35 and later change my mind, can you force me to sell the bike, saying we had a contract? If I lose $120 to you in a poker game, can you sue in court to get your money? If I agree to sing at your wedding for free and back out at the last minute, can you claim I violated a contract? These are the kinds of questions that contract law answers.

contract
A legally enforceable agreement between two or more parties.

contract law
Set of laws that specify what constitutes a legally enforceable agreement.

A **contract** is a legally enforceable agreement between two or more parties. **Contract law** specifies what constitutes a legally enforceable agreement. Basically, a contract is legally binding if the following conditions are met:

1. *An offer is made.* An offer to do something or sell something can be oral or written. If I agree to sell you my bike for $35, I have made an offer. That offer is not legally binding, however, until other conditions are met.

2. *There is a voluntary acceptance of the offer.* The principle of mutual acceptance means that both parties to a contract must agree on the terms. If I use duress in getting you to agree to buy my bike, the contract would not be legal. Duress occurs if there is coercion through force or threat of force. You couldn't use duress to get me to sell my bike, either. Even if we both agree, though, the contract is still not legally binding without the next four conditions.
3. *Both parties give consideration.* **Consideration** means something of value. If I agree to sell you my bike for $35, the bike and the $35 are consideration, and we have a legally binding contract. If I agree to sing at your wedding and you do not give me anything in return (consideration), we have no contract.

consideration
Something of value; consideration is one of the requirements of a legal contract.

4. *Both parties are competent.* A person under the influence of alcohol or drugs, or a person of unsound mind (one who has been legally declared incompetent), cannot be held to a contract. In many cases, a minor may not be held to a contract either. For example, if a 15-year-old agrees to pay $10,000 for a car, the seller will not be able to enforce the contract due to the buyer's lack of competence.
5. *The contract must be legal.* A contract covering the sale of illegal drugs or stolen merchandise would be unenforceable since both types of sales are violations of criminal law.
6. *The contract is in proper form.* An agreement for the sale of goods worth $500 or more must be in writing. Contracts that cannot be fulfilled within one year also must be put in writing. Contracts regarding real property (land and everything attached to it) must be in writing.

Breach of Contract

Breach of contract occurs when one party fails to follow the terms of a contract. Both parties may voluntarily agree to end a contract; but if one person violates the contract, the following may occur:

breach of contract
When one party fails to follow the terms of a contract.

1. *Specific performance.* The person who violated the contract may be required to live up to the agreement if money damages would not be adequate. For example, if I legally offered to sell you a rare painting, I would have to sell you that painting.
2. *Payment of damages.* The term **damages** refers to the monetary settlement awarded to a person who is injured by a breach of contract. If I fail to live up to a contract, you can sue me for damages, usually the amount you would lose from my nonperformance. If we had a legally binding contract for me to sing at your wedding, for example, and I failed to come, you could sue me for the cost of hiring a new singer.
3. *Discharge of obligation.* If I fail to live up to my end of a contract, you could agree to drop the matter. Generally you would not have to live up to your end of the agreement either.

damages
The monetary settlement awarded to a person who is injured by a breach of contract.

Lawyers would not be paid so handsomely if the law were as simple as implied in these rules of contracts. In fact, it is always best to have a contract in writing even if not required under law. The offer and consideration in a contract should be clearly specified, and the contract should be signed and dated. A contract does not have to be complicated as long as it has these elements: (1) It is in writing, (2) mutual consideration is specified, and (3) there is a clear offer and agreement.

Laws to Promote Fair and Competitive Practices

One objective of legislators is to pass laws that the judiciary will enforce to ensure a competitive atmosphere among businesses and promote fair business practices. Chapter 2 explained how competition is a cornerstone of the free-market system. In the United States, the Justice Department's antitrust division and other government agencies serve as watchdogs to ensure that competition among sellers flows freely and that new competitors have open access to the market. The scope of the government is broad and extensive. The Justice Department's antitrust division has tackled the competitive practices of market giants such as Microsoft, Visa, and MasterCard.[29] Figure A.3 highlights key high-profile antitrust cases.

There was, however, a time when big businesses were able to drive smaller competitors out of business with little resistance. The following discussion shows how government responded to these troubling situations in the past and how business must deal with new challenges facing them today.

The History of Antitrust Legislation

In the late 19th century, big oil companies, railroads, steel companies, and other industrial firms dominated the U.S. economy. The fear was that such large and powerful companies would be able to crush any competitors and then charge high prices. It was in that atmosphere that Congress passed the Sherman Antitrust Act in 1890. The Sherman Act was designed to prevent large organizations from stifling the competition of smaller or newer firms. The Sherman Act forbids the following: (1) contracts, combinations, or conspiracies in restraint of trade, and (2) actual monopolies ➤P. 46◄ or attempts to monopolize any part of trade or commerce.

Because of the act's vague language, there was some doubt about just what practices it prohibited. The following laws were passed later to clarify some of the legal concepts in the Sherman Act:

- **The Clayton Act of 1914.** The Clayton Act prohibits exclusive dealing, tying contracts, interlocking directorates, and buying large amounts of stock in competing corporations. *Exclusive dealing* is selling goods with the condition that the buyer will not buy goods from a competitor

FIGURE A.3
HISTORY OF HIGH-PROFILE ANTITRUST CASES

CASE	OUTCOME
United States v. *Standard Oil* 1911	Standard Oil broken up into 34 companies; Amoco, Chevron, and Exxon-Mobil are results of the breakup
United States v. *American Tobacco* 1911	American Tobacco split into 16 companies; British Tobacco and R. J. Reynolds are results of the breakup
United States v. *E.I. du Pont de Nemours* 1961	DuPont ordered to divest its 23 percent ownership stake in General Motors
United States v. *AT&T* 1982	Settled after Ma Bell agreed to spin off its local telephone operations into seven regional operating companies
United States v. *Microsoft* 2000	Microsoft ordered to halt prior anticompetitive practices

Source: U.S. Department of Justice.

(when the effect lessens competition). A *tying contract* requires a buyer to purchase unwanted items in order to purchase desired items. For example, let's say I wanted to purchase 20 cases of Pepsi Cola per week to sell in my restaurant. Pepsi, however, says it will sell me the 20 cases only if I also agree to buy 10 cases each of its Mountain Dew and Diet Pepsi products. My purchase of Pepsi Cola would be *tied* to the purchase of the other two products. An *interlocking directorate* occurs when a board of directors includes members of the board of competing corporations.

- **The Federal Trade Commission Act of 1914**. The Federal Trade Commission Act prohibits unfair methods of competition in commerce. This legislation set up the five-member Federal Trade Commission (FTC) to enforce compliance with this act. The FTC deals with wide-ranging competitive issues—everything from preventing companies from making misleading "Made in the USA" claims and regulating telemarketers' practices, to insisting that funeral providers give consumers accurate, itemized price information about funeral goods and services.[30] The involvement and activity of the FTC typically depends on the members serving on the board at the time. For example, the FTC conducted three times as many investigations and brought twice as many cases of unfair competition in the 1990s as it did during the 1980s. In the early 2000s, the FTC's antitrust authority was expanded by the Bush administration. The FTC is now responsible for overseeing mergers and acquisitions in the health care, energy, computer hardware, automotive, and biotechnology industries.[31] We will discuss mergers and acquisitions in depth in Chapter 5. The Wheeler-Lea Amendment of 1938 gave the FTC additional jurisdiction over false or misleading advertising. It also gave the FTC power to increase fines if its requirements are not met within 60 days.
- **The Robinson-Patman Act of 1936.** The Robinson-Patman Act prohibits price discrimination. An interesting aspect of the Robinson-Patman Act is that it applies to both sellers and buyers who "knowingly" induce or receive an unlawful discrimination in price. It also stipulates that certain types of price cutting are criminal offenses punishable by fine and imprisonment. Specifically, the legislation outlaws price differences that "substantially" weaken competition unless these differences can be justified by lower selling costs associated with larger purchases. It also prohibits advertising and promotional allowances unless they are offered to all retailers, large and small. This act applies to business-to-business transactions and does not apply to consumers in business transactions.

February 23, 2003, is a day that will be long remembered in West Warwick, Rhode Island. Ninety-six people died and 187 were injured at the Station nightclub when a band's pyrotechnics display started a deadly fire. The nightclub's highly flammable soundproofing engulfed the club in flames in less than three minutes. Do you think the consumers' right to safety was violated in this tragic fire?

The changing nature of business from manufacturing to knowledge technology has called for new levels of regulation on the part of federal agencies. For example, Microsoft's competitive practices have been the focus of intense investigation. One of the major accusations against the computer software giant was that it hindered competition by refusing to sell the Windows operating system to computer manufacturers who did not agree to sell Windows-based computers exclusively.[32] Computer manufacturers had a choice of buying only Windows or buying no Windows at all.[33] Given that many consumers wanted Windows, the computer companies had little choice but to agree. Read the description of the Clayton Act again. Do you think Microsoft violated the law? The trial court in the case said it did; however, most of the conclusions of the trial court were overturned at the appeals court level.[34] Some say the case is not over yet; three states continue to appeal the decision, so stay tuned to legal developments.[35]

Laws to Protect Consumers

consumerism
A social movement that seeks to increase and strengthen the rights and powers of buyers in relation to sellers.

taxes
How the government (federal, state, and local) raises money.

Consumerism is a social movement that seeks to increase and strengthen the rights and powers of buyers in relation to sellers. Although consumerism is not a new movement, it has taken on new vigor and direction in the early 2000s because of the corporate scandals and greed involving companies such as Enron, Global Crossing, and WorldCom. Consumers have been particularly critical of federal agencies such as the Securities and Exchange Commission (SEC) for their lack of oversight and action in the securities markets.[36] (We discuss the SEC in depth in Chapters 18 and 20.) To help allay consumer fears concerning falsifying financial statements (such as WorldCom's $4 billion "mistake"), as of 2002, CEOs have to verify the accuracy of their firms' financial statements to the SEC.[37]

Consumerism is the people's way of getting a fair share in marketing exchanges. It's vital that businesses recognize consumer needs and interests in making important decisions. In the 1960s, President John F. Kennedy proposed four basic rights of consumers: (1) the right to safety, (2) the right to be informed, (3) the right to choose, and (4) the right to be heard. These rights will not be maintained if consumers passively wait for organizations to recognize them; they will come partially from consumer action in the marketplace. Figure A.4 lists several major consumer protection laws.

A Stanley Works machinist joined his fellow workers dressed as Uncle Sam in a protest of the company's plan to reincorporate in Bermuda to avoid paying U.S. taxes. Such tax avoidance could cost the United States an estimated $4 billion in lost taxes over the next 10 years. While it's legal to incorporate offshore, critics say that in addition to being unpatriotic, the zero tax rate gives these companies an unfair advantage. What do you think?

Tax Laws

Mention the word *taxes* and most people frown. That's because taxes affect almost every individual and business in the United States. **Taxes** are how the government (federal, state, and local) raises money. Traditionally, taxes have been used primarily as a source of funding for government operations and programs. They have also been used as a method of encouraging or discouraging taxpayers from doing something. For example, if the government wishes to reduce the use of certain classes of products (cigarettes, liquor, etc.), it passes what are referred to as *sin taxes*.[38] The additional cost of the product from increased taxes perhaps discourages additional consumption. In other situations, the government may encourage businesses to hire new employees or purchase new equipment by offering a tax credit. A tax credit is an amount that can be deducted from a tax bill.

LEGISLATION	PURPOSE
Pure Food and Drug Act (1906)	Protects against the adulteration and misbranding of foods and drugs sold in interstate commerce.
Food, Drug, and Cosmetic Act (1938)	Protects against the adulteration and sale of foods, drugs, cosmetics, or therapeutic devices and allows the Food and Drug Administration to set minimum standards and guidelines for food products.
Wool Products Labeling Act (1940)	Protects manufacturers, distributors, and consumers from undisclosed substitutes and mixtures in manufactured wool products.
Fur Products Labeling Act (1951)	Protects consumers from misbranding, false advertising, and false invoicing of furs and fur products.
Flammable Fabrics Act (1953)	Prohibits the interstate transportation of dangerously flammable wearing apparel and fabrics.
Automobile Information Disclosure Act (1958)	Requires auto manufacturers to put suggested retail prices on all new passenger vehicles.
Textile Fiber Products Identification Act (1958)	Protects producers and consumers against misbranding and false advertising of fiber content of textile fiber products.
Cigarette Labeling Act (1965)	Requires cigarette manufacturers to label cigarettes as hazardous to health.
Fair Packaging and Labeling Act (1966)	Makes unfair or deceptive packaging or labeling of certain consumer commodities illegal.
Child Protection Act (1966)	Removes from sale potentially harmful toys and allows the FDA to pull dangerous products from the market.
Truth-in-Lending Act (1968)	Requires full disclosure of all finance charges on consumer credit agreements and in advertisements of credit plans.
Child Protection and Toy Safety Act (1969)	Protects children from toys and other products that contain thermal, electrical, or mechanical hazards.
Fair Credit Reporting Act (1970)	Requires that consumer credit reports contain only accurate, relevant, and recent information and are confidential unless a proper party requests them for an appropriate reason.
Consumer Product Safety Act (1972)	Created an independent agency to protect consumers from unreasonable risk of injury arising from consumer products and to set safety standards.
Magnuson–Moss Warranty–Federal Trade Commission Improvement Act (1975)	Provides for minimum disclosure standards for written consumer products warranties and allows the FTC to prescribe interpretive rules and policy statements regarding unfair or deceptive practices.
Alcohol Labeling Legislation (1988)	Provides for warning labels on liquor saying that women shouldn't drink when pregnant and that alcohol impairs a person's abilities.
Nutrition Labeling and Education Act (1990)	Requires truthful and uniform nutritional labeling on every food the FDA regulates.

FIGURE A.4

CONSUMER PROTECTION LAWS

Taxes are levied from a variety of sources. Income (personal and business), sales, and property are the major bases of tax revenue. The federal government receives its largest share of taxes from income. States and local communities often make extensive use of sales taxes. School districts are generally dependent on property taxes. The tax policies of states and cities are taken into consideration when businesses seek to locate operations. Tax policies also affect personal decisions such as retirement. A key tax issue sure to reappear in the 21st century involves Internet taxation, especially taxing Internet transactions (e-commerce).[39] The European Union has already decided to levy certain Internet taxes.[40] Expect this issue to be debated fiercely in the years ahead. Figure A.5 highlights the primary types of taxes levied on individuals and businesses.

FIGURE A.5
TYPES OF TAXES

TYPE	PURPOSE
Income taxes	Taxes paid on the income received by businesses and individuals. Income taxes are the largest source of tax income received by the federal government.
Property taxes	Taxes paid on real and personal property. *Real property* is real estate owned by individuals and businesses. *Personal property* is a broader category that includes any movable property such as tangible items (wedding rings, equipment, etc.) or intangible items (stocks, checks, mortgages, etc.). Taxes are based on their assessed value.
Sales taxes	Taxes paid on merchandise sold at the retail level.
Excise taxes	Taxes paid on selected items such as tobacco, alcoholic beverages, airline travel, gasoline, and firearms. These are often referred to as *sin taxes.* Income generated from the tax goes toward a specifically designated purpose. For example, gasoline taxes often help the federal government and state governments pay for highway construction or improvements.

BANKRUPTCY LAWS

bankruptcy
The legal process by which a person, business, or government entity unable to meet financial obligations is relieved of those obligations by a court that divides any assets among creditors, allowing creditors to get at least part of their money and freeing the debtor to begin anew.

Bankruptcy is the legal process by which a person, business, or government entity unable to meet financial obligations is relieved of those debts by a court. The court divides any assets among creditors, allowing creditors to get at least part of their money and freeing the debtor to begin anew. The U.S. Constitution gives Congress the power to establish bankruptcy laws, and there has been bankruptcy legislation since the 1890s. Two major amendments to the bankruptcy code include the Bankruptcy Amendments and Federal Judgeships Act of 1984 and the Bankruptcy Reform Act of 1994. The 1984 legislation allows a person who is bankrupt to keep part of the equity (ownership) in a house, $1,200 in a car, and some other personal property. The Bankruptcy Reform Act of 1994 amended more than 45 sections of the bankruptcy code and created reforms to speed up and simplify the process.

In 2002, a record 1.5 million Americans filed for bankruptcy.[41] By contrast, only 172,000 Americans filed for bankruptcy in 1978, and fewer than 800,000 did so in 1990.[42] Interestingly, business bankruptcies were down 4 percent in 2002, to 38,540.[43] The number of bankruptcies began to increase in the late 1980s and grew tremendously in the 1990s. While high-profile bankruptcies such as those of Kmart, United Airlines, Polaroid, and WorldCom sometimes dominate the news, over 90 percent of bankruptcy filings each year are by individuals.[44] Bankruptcy attorneys say the increase in filings is due to a lessening of the stigma of bankruptcy, the changing economy, an increase in understanding of bankruptcy law and the protection it offers, increased advertising by bankruptcy attorneys, and the ease with which some consumers can get credit.[45] However, all that may be changing. In 2002, the U.S. Congress declined to act on bankruptcy legislation that makes it more difficult to escape overwhelming debt through bankruptcy protection. The new legislation would have forced a debtor with sufficient income to repay at least 25 percent of his or her debt over five years. It's possible the legislation may reappear in the next Congress.[46]

voluntary bankruptcy
Legal procedures initiated by a debtor.

involuntary bankruptcy
Bankruptcy procedures filed by a debtor's creditors.

Bankruptcy can be either voluntary or involuntary. In **voluntary bankruptcy** cases the debtor applies for bankruptcy, whereas in **involuntary bankruptcy** cases the creditors start legal procedures against the debtor. Most bankruptcies today are voluntary because creditors usually want to wait in hopes that they will be paid all of the money due them rather than settle for only part of it.

Bankruptcy procedures begin when a petition is filed with the court under one of the following sections of the Bankruptcy Code:

Chapter 7—"straight bankruptcy" or liquidation (used by businesses and individuals).

Chapter 11—reorganization (used by businesses and some individuals).

Chapter 13—repayment (used by individuals).

"Say it isn't so, Kermit!" Unfortunately, even the disappointment of young customers and many others could not stop the bankruptcy of famed toy retailer FAO Schwartz. The company filed for bankruptcy under Chapter 11 and plans to close stores and reorganize operations. Are bankruptcy laws that permit a firm to declare bankruptcy and still operate under a reorganization plan fair to creditors and lenders?

Chapter 7 calls for straight bankruptcy, which requires the sale of nonexempt assets of debtors. Under federal exemption statutes, a debtor may be able to retain up to $7,500 of equity in a home ($15,000 in a joint case); up to $1,200 of equity in an automobile; up to $4,000 in household furnishings, apparel, and musical instruments; and up to $500 in jewelry. States may have different exemption statutes. When the sale of assets is over, the resulting cash is divided among creditors, including the government. Almost 70 percent of bankruptcies follow Chapter 7 procedures. Chapter 7 stipulates the order in which the assets are to be distributed among the creditors. First, creditors with secured claims receive the collateral for their claims or repossess the claimed asset (such as an automobile). Then unsecured claims are paid in this order:

1. Costs involved in the bankruptcy case.
2. Any business costs incurred after bankruptcy was filed.
3. Wages, salaries, or commissions (limited to $2,000 per person).
4. Contributions to employee benefit plans.
5. Refunds to consumers who paid for products that weren't delivered (limited to $900 per claimant).
6. Federal and state taxes.

The remainder (if any) is divided among unsecured creditors in proportion to their claims. See Figure A.6 for the steps used in liquidating assets under Chapter 7.

Chapter 11 bankruptcy allows a company to reorganize and continue operations while paying only a limited proportion of its debts. The company does not have to be insolvent in order to file for relief under Chapter 11. The Bankruptcy Reform Act of 1994 extends a fast-track procedure for small businesses filing under Chapter 11. Under certain conditions, the company can sell assets, borrow money, and change officers to strengthen its market position. A trustee appointed by the court to protect the interests of creditors usually supervises all such matters. Chapter 11 is designed to help both debtors and creditors find the best solution.

Under Chapter 11, a company continues to operate but has court protection against creditors' lawsuits while it tries to work out a plan for paying off its debts. In theory, Chapter 11 is a way for sick companies to recover. In reality, less than 33 percent of Chapter 11 companies survive—usually only the big ones with lots of cash available.[47] In 1991, the U.S. Supreme Court gave individuals the right to file bankruptcy under Chapter 11.

Chapter 13 bankruptcy permits individuals, including small-business owners, to pay back creditors over a period of three to five years. Chapter 13 proceedings are less complicated and less expensive than Chapter 7 proceedings. The debtor files a proposed plan for paying off debts to the court. If the plan is approved, the debtor pays a court-appointed trustee in monthly installments as

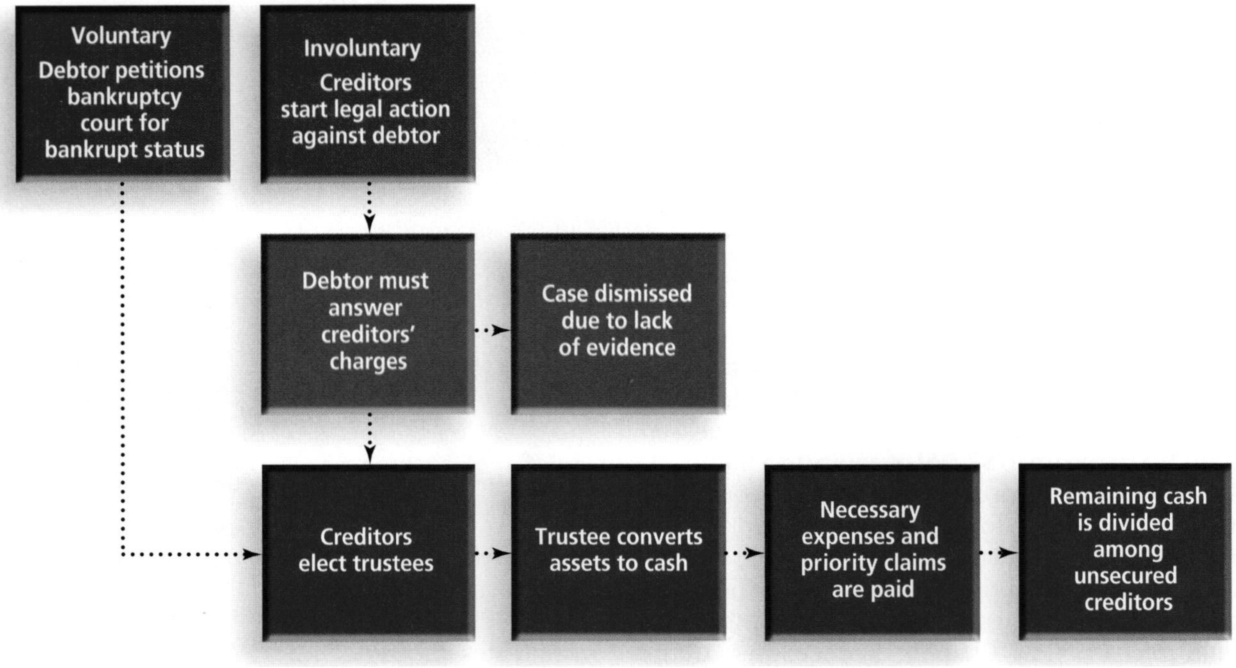

FIGURE A.6

HOW ASSETS ARE DIVIDED IN BANKRUPTCY

This figure shows that the creditor (the person owed money) selects the trustee (the person or organization that handles the sale of assets). Note that the process may be started by the debtor or the creditors.

deregulation
Government withdrawal of certain laws and regulations that seem to hinder competition.

agreed on in the repayment plan. The trustee then pays each creditor. In bankruptcy legislation proposed by the U.S. Congress in 2002, more debtors would have been required to file bankruptcy under Chapter 13.

DEREGULATION

By 1980, the United States had developed laws and regulations covering almost every aspect of business. There was concern that there were too many laws and regulations, and that these laws and regulations were costing the public money (see Figure A.7). Thus began the movement toward deregulation. **Deregulation** means that the government withdraws certain laws and regulations that seem to hinder competition. Perhaps the most publicized examples of deregulation were those in the airlines and the telecommunications industry. At one time, the government restricted airlines with regard to where they could land and fly. When such restrictions were lifted, the airlines began competing for different routes and charging lower prices. This was a clear benefit to consumers, but it put tremendous pressure on the airlines to be more competitive. Airlines such as Southwest Airlines were born to take advantage of the opportunities. Southwest, now a major competitor, has the highest market capitalization in the airline industry.[48] After passage of the Telecommunications Act in 1996, similar deregulation in telecommunications gave consumers a flood of options in the telephone service market.[49] Companies like WorldCom, Qwest, and Global Crossing jumped headfirst into the competitive market and gained significant support from investors. Today, WorldCom and Global Crossing have filed for bankruptcy and Qwest is under federal investigation. Telecom investors have suffered $2 trillion in market losses to date.[50]

The electric power industry and other utilities also became targets of deregulation. In 1999, California became the first state to deregulate the electric power industry. Since then, the state has experienced significant problems with deregulation of electric power.[51] In response to California's problems, several states halted deregulation programs. In addition, accusations of phony transactions from companies such as Enron have soured some states on deregulation. Still, not everyone is endorsing a move back to

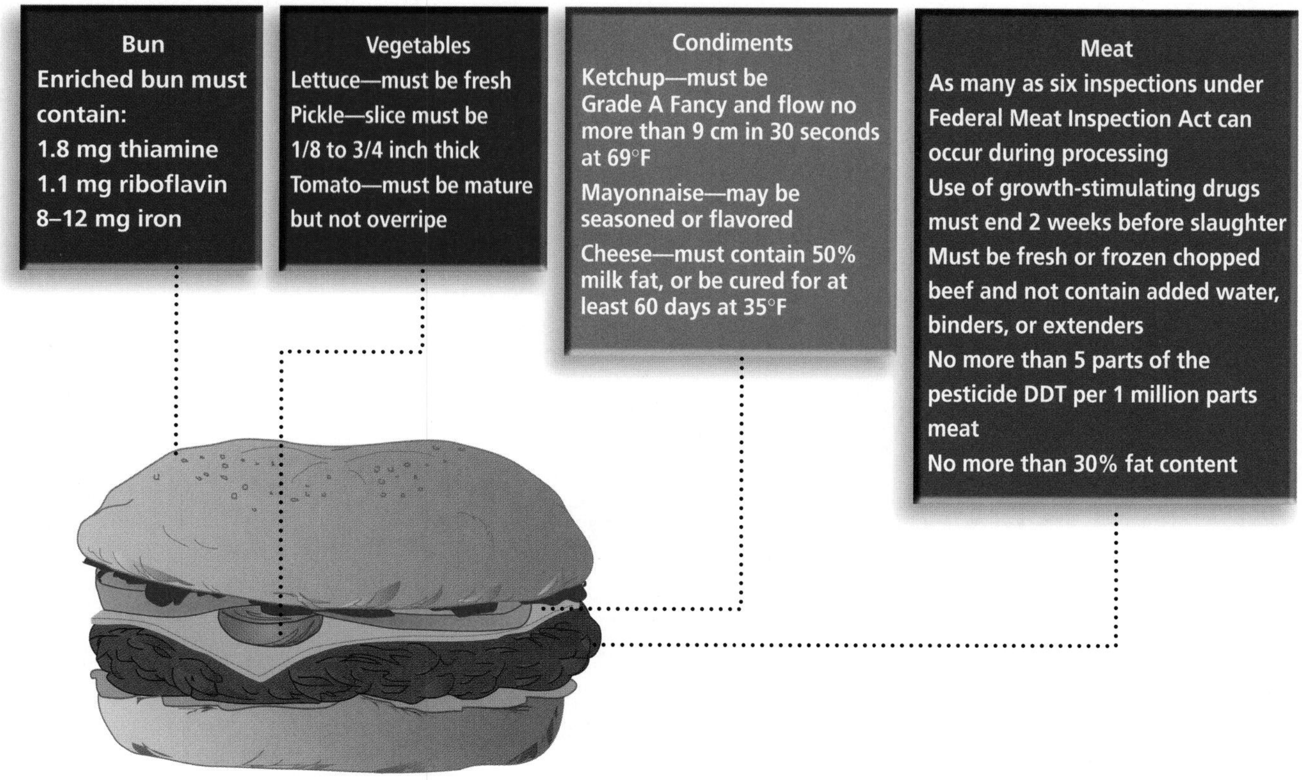

Bun
Enriched bun must contain:
1.8 mg thiamine
1.1 mg riboflavin
8–12 mg iron
Vegetables
Lettuce—must be fresh
Pickle—slice must be 1/8 to 3/4 inch thick
Tomato—must be mature but not overripe
Condiments
Ketchup—must be Grade A Fancy and flow no more than 9 cm in 30 seconds at 69°F
Mayonnaise—may be seasoned or flavored
Cheese—must contain 50% milk fat, or be cured for at least 60 days at 35°F
Meat
As many as six inspections under Federal Meat Inspection Act can occur during processing
Use of growth-stimulating drugs must end 2 weeks before slaughter
Must be fresh or frozen chopped beef and not contain added water, binders, or extenders
No more than 5 parts of the pesticide DDT per 1 million parts meat
No more than 30% fat content

FIGURE A.7

HAMBURGER REGULATIONS

Does this amount of regulation seem just right, too little, or too much for you?

government-controlled regulation in utilities. In Texas and New York, deregulation programs have been somewhat successful.[52] Time will tell if utility deregulation will survive. There is also a call for new regulations in the banking and investments industries that would change the nature of financial markets and make them more competitive.

It seems some regulation of business is necessary to ensure fair and honest dealings with the public. Still, businesses have adapted to the laws and regulations, and have done much toward producing safer, more effective products. However, corporate scandals in 2002 soured what appeared to be better dialogue and cooperation between business and government. Many in government and society called for even more government regulation and control of business operations to protect investors and workers. With global competition increasing and small and medium-sized businesses striving to capture selected markets, business and government need to continue to work together to create a competitive environment that is fair and open. If businesses do not want additional regulation, they must accept their responsibilities to all their stakeholders.

Key Terms

administrative agencies 125
bankruptcy 136
breach of contract 131
business law 125
common law 125
consideration 131
consumerism 134
contract 130
contract law 130
copyright 129
damages 131
deregulation 138
express warranties 130
implied warranties 130
involuntary bankruptcy 136
judiciary 124
negligence 126
negotiable instruments 130
patent 128
precedent 125
product liability 126
statutory law 125
strict product liability 126
taxes 134
tort 126
trademark 129
Uniform Commercial Code (UCC) 129
voluntary bankruptcy 136

Chapter 5

Choosing a Form of Business Ownership

Learning Goals

After you have read and studied this chapter, you should be able to

1. Compare the advantages and disadvantages of sole proprietorships.
2. Describe the differences between general and limited partners, and compare the advantages and disadvantages of partnerships.
3. Compare the advantages and disadvantages of corporations, and summarize the differences between C corporations, S corporations, and limited liability companies.
4. Define and give examples of three types of corporate mergers, and explain the role of leveraged buyouts and taking a firm private.
5. Outline the advantages and disadvantages of franchises, and discuss the opportunities for diversity in franchising and the challenges of global franchising.
6. Explain the role of cooperatives.

Getting to Know Anne Beiler of Auntie Anne's Pretzels

Anne Beiler of Auntie Anne's Pretzels twisted a stand at a farmers' market into one of the fastest-growing franchises in the United States. Raised Amish-Mennonite in Pennsylvania, Beiler made her first attempt at entrepreneurship at age 12 when she baked cakes and pies for the family to sell at area farmers' markets.

In 1987, Beiler was working as a manager in a market concession stand in order to earn enough money to support her family and make it possible for her husband, Jonas, to open a free family counseling service in their home. When another booth in the market became available for sale, Beiler and her husband borrowed $6,000 to buy it to start their own business. They wanted to make enough money to keep the free clinic open to the local Amish and Mennonite families in their community.

Anne Beiler had been working for three months to perfect her pretzel recipe when a supplier accidentally delivered the wrong ingredients. The result was a very disappointing pretzel. But Beiler experimented and added a few more ingredients at her husband's suggestion. Her customers were amazed—the new creation was the best pretzel they had ever tasted. The new twist gave Beiler a recipe for success as the demand for her pretzels grew so much that she eliminated the other snacks on the menu at her booth and concentrated on pretzels.

"Had we gone public [sold stock], the pressure to perform financially would have been greater than our feelings about supporting our employees and franchisees. It was difficult enough to keep the personal touch adding 60 stores a year."

Beiler named her store Auntie Anne's Hand-Rolled Soft Pretzels. When word of mouth increased the popularity of her pretzels, she opened more stores and incorporated her business under the name Auntie Anne's, Inc. As the company grew, Anne went from bagging the pretzel mix in the garage to overseeing a corporate staff of more than 100 employees and supporting a franchise system of more than 700 stores. The franchise employs more than 8,000 store owners, managers, and crew members in 43 states and 13 countries. Auntie Anne's even expanded into frozen custard with the opening of Auntie Anne's Cre-ámo Classic Cones in 2001.

The Beilers tried to guide Auntie Anne's where they felt it should go. Committed to providing customers with "better than the best" products and services, their goal was to exceed the expectations of all of their customers. They achieved one of their major goals in 1992 when Jonas Beiler opened the Family Resource and Counseling Center. Six years later, the couple created the Angela Foundation, a nonprofit organization named after their daughter that serves as the giving arm of the company. The franchise system also sponsors Children's Miracle Network.

As their company was growing, the Beilers were tempted to seek additional funding through venture capitalists (you will learn about venture capitalists in Chapter 6) and/or by going public (selling stock in the company, which we will discuss in Chapter 20). "We needed a cash infusion to grow. But I decided it wasn't right," said Anne Beiler. "Had we gone public, the pressure to perform financially would have been greater than our feelings about supporting our employees and franchisees. It was difficult enough to keep the personal touch adding 60 stores a year. Service would have become a problem, the quality would have become a problem, money would have outweighed caring, and that would have carried out to the customer."

To solve the cash problem, the Beilers decided to slow the increase of company-owned stores, close unprofitable stores, and become very cost conscious. To them, a cash infusion from selling stock would have been a quick fix that would have put their values at risk, and it wasn't worth it. Just like the Beilers, all business owners must decide for themselves which form of business is best for them. Whether you dream of going into business for yourself, starting a business with a friend, or someday leading a major corporation, it's important to know that each form of ownership has its advantages and disadvantages. You will learn about them in this chapter.

Sources: Devlin Smith, "Law & Pretzels," *Entrepreneur,* December 2001; Ilan Mochari, "In a Former Life: Anne Beiler," *Inc.*, September 1, 2000; and Ken Park, "Fastest-Growing U.S. Franchises in 2000," in *The World Almanac and Book of Facts 2002,* ed. Ken Park (New York: World Almanac Books, 2001).

Basic Forms of Business Ownership

Like Anne Beiler, hundreds of thousands of people start new businesses in the United States every year. In fact, the number of new U.S. businesses started each year currently stands at 800,000—triple the number of start-ups from the 1960s.[1] Chances are, you have thought of owning your own business or know someone who has. One key to success in starting a new business is understanding how to get the resources you need. You may have to take on partners or find other ways of obtaining money. To stay in business, you may need help from someone with more expertise than you have in certain areas, or you may need to raise more money to expand. How you form your business can make a tremendous difference in your long-term success. You can form a business in one of several ways. The three major forms of business ownership are (1) sole proprietorships, (2) partnerships, and (3) corporations.

It can be easy to get started in your own business. You can begin a word processing service out of your home, open a car repair center, start a restaurant, develop a website, or go about meeting other wants and needs of your community. A business that is owned, and usually managed, by one person is called a **sole proprietorship.** That is the most common form of business ownership.

sole proprietorship
A business that is owned, and usually managed, by one person.

Many people do not have the money, time, or desire to run a business on their own. They prefer to have someone else or some group of people get together to form the business. When two or more people legally agree to become co-owners of a business, the organization is called a **partnership.**

partnership
A legal form of business with two or more owners.

There are advantages to creating a business that is separate and distinct from the owners. A legal entity with authority to act and have liability separate from its owners is called a **corporation.** The almost 5 million corporations in the United States comprise only 20 percent of all businesses, but they earn 81 percent of the total receipts (see Figure 5.1).[2]

corporation
A legal entity with authority to act and have liability separate from its owners.

As you will learn in this chapter, each form of business ownership has its advantages—and disadvantages. It is important to understand these advantages and disadvantages before attempting to start a business. Keep in mind that just because a business starts in one form of ownership, it doesn't have to stay in that form. Many companies start out in one form, then add (or drop) a partner or two, and eventually become corporations, limited liability companies, or franchisors. Let's begin our discussion by looking at the most basic form of ownership—the sole proprietorship.

FIGURE 5.1

FORMS OF BUSINESS OWNERSHIP

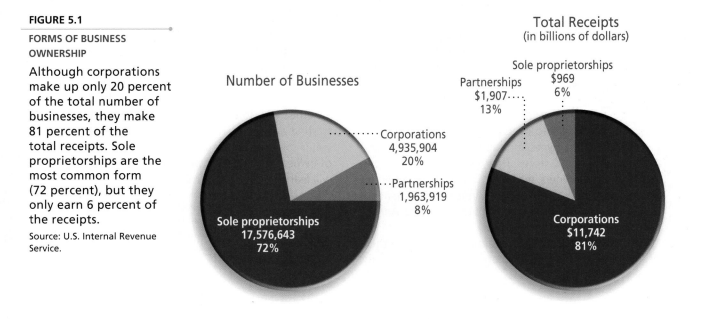

Although corporations make up only 20 percent of the total number of businesses, they make 81 percent of the total receipts. Sole proprietorships are the most common form (72 percent), but they only earn 6 percent of the receipts.

Source: U.S. Internal Revenue Service.

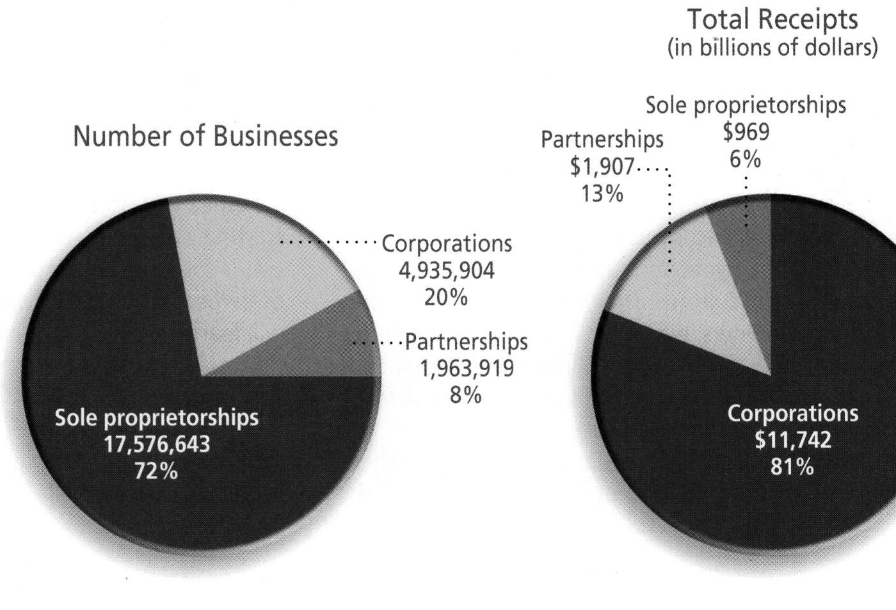

SOLE PROPRIETORSHIPS

Advantages of Sole Proprietorships

Sole proprietorships are the easiest kind of businesses for you to explore in your quest for an interesting career. Every town has sole proprietors you can visit. Talk with some of these businesspeople about the joys and frustrations of being on their own. Most will mention the benefits of being their own boss and setting their own hours. Other advantages they mention may include the following:

Many of the nation's largest firms started out as sole proprietorships. Jessica Nam of Jessica's Wonders plans to be one of those success stories. Nam started her baked goodies business in her dorm at Brown University. Today, she rings up sales close to $500,000 in the New England area. Have you ever thought about starting your own business?

1. **Ease of starting and ending the business.** All you have to do to start a sole proprietorship is buy or lease the needed equipment (e.g., a saw, a word processor, a tractor, a lawn mower) and put up some announcements saying you are in business. It is just as easy to get out of business; you simply stop. There is no one to consult or to disagree with about such decisions. You may have to get a permit or license from the local government, but often that is no problem.
2. **Being your own boss.** Working for others simply does not have the same excitement as working for yourself—at least, that's the way sole proprietors feel. You may make mistakes, but they are your mistakes—and so are the many small victories each day.
3. **Pride of ownership.** People who own and manage their own businesses are rightfully proud of their work. They deserve all the credit for taking the risks and providing needed goods or services.
4. **Leaving a legacy.** Business owners have something to leave behind for future generations.
5. **Retention of company profit.** Other than the joy of being your own boss, there is nothing like the pleasure of knowing that you can earn as much as possible and not have to share that money with anyone else (except the government, in taxes).
6. **No special taxes.** All the profits of a sole proprietorship are taxed as the personal income of the owner, and the owner pays the normal income tax on that money. (However, owners do have to estimate their taxes and make quarterly payments to the government or suffer penalties for nonpayment.)

Disadvantages of Sole Proprietorships

Not everyone is equipped to own and manage a business. Often it is difficult to save enough money to start a business and keep it going. The costs of inventory, supplies, insurance, advertising, rent, computers, utilities, and so on may be too much to cover alone. There are other disadvantages of owning your own business:

1. **Unlimited liability—the risk of personal losses.** When you work for others, it is their problem if the business is not profitable. When you own your own business, you and the business are considered one. You have **unlimited liability;** that is, any debts or damages in-

unlimited liability
The responsibility of business owners for all of the debts of the business.

curred by the business are your debts and you must pay them, even if it means selling your home, your car, or whatever else you own. This is a serious risk, and one that requires not only thought but also discussion with a lawyer, an insurance agent, an accountant, and others.[3]

2. **Limited financial resources.** Funds available to the business are limited to the funds that the one (sole) owner can gather. Since there are serious limits to how much money one person can raise, partnerships and corporations have a greater probability of obtaining the needed financial backing to start a business and keep it going.
3. **Management difficulties.** All businesses need management; that is, someone must keep inventory records, accounting records, tax records, and so forth. Many people who are skilled at selling things or providing a service are not so skilled in keeping records. Sole proprietors often find it difficult to attract good, qualified employees to help run the business because they cannot compete with the salary and fringe benefits offered by larger companies.
4. **Overwhelming time commitment.** Though sole proprietors may say they set their own hours, it's hard to own a business, manage it, train people, and have time for anything else in life. This is true of any business, but a sole proprietor has no one with whom to share the burden. The owner often must spend long hours working. The owner of a store, for example, may put in 12 hours a day, at least six days a week—almost twice the hours worked by a nonsupervisory employee in a large company. Imagine how this time commitment affects the sole proprietor's family life. Tim DeMello, founder of the successful company Wall Street Games Inc., echoes countless other sole proprietors when he says, "It's not a job, it's not a career, it's a way of life."
5. **Few fringe benefits.** If you are your own boss, you lose the fringe benefits that often come from working for others. You have no paid health insurance, no paid disability insurance, no sick leave, and no vacation pay. These and other benefits may add up to approximately 30 percent of a worker's income.[4]
6. **Limited growth.** Expansion is often slow since a sole proprietorship relies on its owner for most of its creativity, business know-how, and funding.
7. **Limited life span.** If the sole proprietor dies, is incapacitated, or retires, the business no longer exists (unless it is sold or taken over by the sole proprietor's heirs).[5]

Don't forget to talk with a few local sole proprietors about the problems they have faced in being on their own. They are likely to have many interesting stories to tell about problems getting loans from the bank, problems with theft, problems simply keeping up with the business, and so on. These problems are also reasons why many sole proprietors choose to find partners to share the load.

Critical Thinking

Have you ever dreamed of opening your own business? If you did, what kind of business was it? What talents or skills do you have that you could use? Could you start such a business in your own home? How much would it cost to start? Could you begin part-time while you worked elsewhere? What satisfaction and profit could you get from owning your own business? What could you lose?

PARTNERSHIPS

A partnership is a legal form of business with two or more owners. There are several types of partnerships: (1) general partnerships, (2) limited partnerships, and (3) master limited partnerships. A **general partnership** is a partnership in which all owners share in operating the business and in assuming liability for the business's debts. A **limited partnership** is a partnership with one or more general partners and one or more limited partners. A **general partner** is an owner (partner) who has unlimited liability and is active in managing the firm. Every partnership must have at least one general partner. A **limited partner** is an owner who invests money in the business but does not have any management responsibility or liability for losses beyond the investment. **Limited liability** means that limited partners are not responsible for the debts of the business beyond the amount of their investment—their liability is *limited* to the amount they put into the company; their personal assets are not at risk.

A newer form of partnership, the **master limited partnership (MLP),** looks much like a corporation (which we discuss next) in that it acts like a corporation and is traded on the stock exchanges like a corporation, but it is taxed like a partnership and thus avoids the corporate income tax.[6] For example, Sunoco, Inc., formed MLP Sunoco Logistics (SXL) to acquire, own, and operate a group of crude oil and refined product pipelines and storage facilities. SXL began trading on the New York Stock Exchange in 2002. Income received by SXL is not taxed before it is passed on to investors in the form of dividends as it would have been if SXL were a corporation.

Another newer type of partnership was created to limit the disadvantage of unlimited liability. Many states are now allowing partners to form what is called a **limited liability partnership (LLP)**. LLPs limit partners' risk of losing their personal assets to only their own acts and omissions and to the acts and omissions of people under their supervision.[7] See the Dealing with Change box to see how the partners' actions in one LLP are being investigated and how the results may influence future LLP regulations.

All states except Louisiana have adopted the Uniform Partnership Act (UPA) to replace laws relating to partnerships. The UPA defines the three key elements of any general partnership as (1) common ownership, (2) shared profits and losses, and (3) the right to participate in managing the operations of the business.

general partnership
A partnership in which all owners share in operating the business and in assuming liability for the business's debts.

limited partnership
A partnership with one or more general partners and one or more limited partners.

general partner
An owner (partner) who has unlimited liability and is active in managing the firm.

limited partner
An owner who invests money in the business but does not have any management responsibility or liability for losses beyond the investment.

limited liability
The responsibility of a business's owners for losses only up to the amount they invest; limited partners and shareholders have limited liability.

master limited partnership (MLP)
A partnership that looks much like a corporation (in that it acts like a corporation and is traded on a stock exchange) but is taxed like a partnership and thus avoids the corporate income tax.

limited liability partnership (LLP)
A partnership that limits partners' risk of losing their personal assets to only their own acts and omissions and to the acts and omissions of people under their supervision.

Advantages of Partnerships

There are many advantages to having one or more partners in a business. Often, it is much easier to own and manage a business with one or more partners. Your partner can cover for you when you are sick or go on vacation. Your partner may be skilled at inventory control and accounting, while you do the selling or servicing. A partner can also provide additional money, support, and expertise. Some of the professionals who are enjoying the advantages of partnerships today are doctors, lawyers, dentists, and accountants. Partnerships usually have the following advantages:

1. **More financial resources.** When two or more people pool their money and credit, it is easier to pay the rent, utilities, and other bills incurred by a business. A limited partnership is specially designed to help raise money. As mentioned earlier, a limited partner invests money in the business but cannot legally have any management responsibility and has limited liability.
2. **Shared management and pooled/complementary skills and knowledge.** It is simply much easier to manage the day-to-day activities of a business with carefully chosen partners. Partners give each other free

www.andersen.com

Dealing with Change

Testing the Limits of Limited Liability Partnerships

To the partners of Arthur Andersen LLP, limited liability partnership status sounded good. In an LLP, each partner's liability is limited to his or her own acts and omissions and to the acts and omissions of people under his or her supervision—not to the actions of others in the business. Now regulators are wondering if this new business form is too good of a thing for the Illinois-based Andersen. You see, Andersen is the now-bankrupt auditor that faces a bevy of lawsuits related not only to the Enron fiasco but also to many other flawed audits. Andersen has been found guilty of obstruction of justice for shredding documents that may have proved it helped Enron deceive the public about Enron's financial problems.

Obviously, most Andersen partners were not involved in supervising the Enron account. As part of an LLP, these partners might expect to be exempt from losses incurred by the guilty partners. Theoretically, as long as they didn't know about illegal activities themselves, they are liable only for the assets they contributed to the firm. However, there have been very few court cases, and certainly none of this magnitude, that have tested the LLP protection. It is yet unclear how much insulation the structure will provide. Under Illinois law, all of the partners may have to pay more than their original investment if that total investment isn't enough to pay for claims such as real estate leases. This means that all of the partners risk losing their homes and all their other assets to pay for the wrongdoings of the guilty partners. The lesson: Limited liability partnerships are not a risk-free form of ownership. You still need to choose your partners wisely.

Sources: Joseph Weber, "Why Andersen Is Making a Last Stand," *Business Week,* May 13, 2002, p. 100; Joseph Weber and Mike McNamee, "Accounting: Andersen, Now You See It . . ." *Business Week,* April 15, 2002, p. 45; and Wendy Zellner, "Scandals in Corporate America: The Price of Victory over Andersen," *Business Week,* July 1, 2002, p. 38.

time from the business and provide different skills and perspectives. Some people find that the best partner is a spouse. That is why you see so many husband-and-wife teams managing restaurants, service shops, and other businesses.

3. **Longer survival.** One study that examined 2,000 businesses started since 1960 reported that partnerships were four times as likely to succeed as sole proprietorships. Being watched by a partner can help a businessperson become more disciplined.
4. **No special taxes.** As with sole proprietorships, all profits of partnerships are taxed as the personal income of the owners, and the owners pay the normal income tax on that money. Similarly, partners must estimate their taxes and make quarterly payments or suffer penalties for nonpayment.

Disadvantages of Partnerships

Anytime two people must agree, there is the possibility of conflict and tension. Partnerships have caused splits among families, friends, and marriages. Let's explore the disadvantages of partnerships:

1. **Unlimited liability.** Each *general* partner is liable for the debts of the firm, no matter who was responsible for causing those debts. You are liable for your partners' mistakes as well as your own. Like sole proprietors, general partners can lose their homes, cars, and everything else they own if the business loses a lawsuit or goes bankrupt.
2. **Division of profits.** Sharing risk means sharing profits, and that can cause conflicts. There is no set system for dividing profits in a partnership, so profits are not always divided evenly. For example, two people form a partnership in which one puts in more money and the other

Spotlight on Small Business — Choose Your Partner

www.entrepreneur.com

Suppose you need money and want help running your business, and you decide to take on a partner. You know that partnerships are like marriages and that you won't really know the other person until after you live together. How do you choose the right partner? Before you plunge into a partnership, do three things:

1. Talk to people who have been in successful—and unsuccessful—partnerships. Find out what worked and what didn't. Ask them how conflicts were resolved and how decisions were made.
2. Interview your prospective partner very carefully. What skills does the person have? Are they the same as yours, or do they complement your skills? What contacts, resources, or special attributes will the person bring to the business? Do you both feel the same about family members working for the business? Do you share the same vision for the company's future?
3. Evaluate your prospective partner as a decision maker. Ask yourself, "Is this someone with whom I could happily share authority for all major business decisions?"

As in a good marriage, the best way to avoid major conflicts is to begin with an honest communication of what each partner expects to give and get from the partnership.

Sources: Kim T. Gordon, "Partner Power," *Entrepreneur,* August 2001; and Cliff Ennico, "Picking the Right Partner," *Entrepreneur,* April 8, 2002.

puts in more hours working the business. Each may feel justified in asking for a bigger share of the profits. Imagine the resulting conflicts.

3. **Disagreements among partners.** Disagreements over money are just one example of potential conflict in a partnership. Who has final authority over employees? Who hires and fires employees? Who works what hours? What if one partner wants to buy expensive equipment for the firm and the other partner disagrees? Potential conflicts are many. Because of such problems, all terms of partnership should be spelled out in writing to protect all parties and to minimize misunderstandings.[8] The Spotlight on Small Business box offers a few tips about choosing a partner.
4. **Difficult to terminate.** Once you have committed yourself to a partnership, it is not easy to get out of it (other than by death, which immediately terminates the partnership). Sure, you can end a partnership just by quitting. However, questions about who gets what and what happens next are often very difficult to solve when the partnership ends. Surprisingly, law firms often have faulty partnership agreements and find that breaking up is hard to do. How do you get rid of a partner you don't like? It is best to decide such questions up front in the partnership agreement. Figure 5.2 gives you more ideas about what should be included in partnership agreements.

The best way to learn about the advantages and disadvantages of partnerships is to interview several people who have experience with such agreements. They will give you insights and hints on how to avoid problems.

One common fear of owning your own business or having a partner is the fear of losing everything you own if the business loses a lot of money or someone sues the business. Many businesspeople

John and Angela Day started their partnership from the back of a car on the streets in Prince George's County, Maryland. Today, the Days operate a clothing store called the H.O.B.O. Shop (Helping Our Brothas Out) in an urban neighborhood. What do you think is the most important criteria to use in selecting a potential partner for a business?

FIGURE 5.2

HOW TO FORM A PARTNERSHIP

It's not hard to form a partnership, but it's wise for each prospective partner to get the counsel of a lawyer experienced with such agreements. Lawyers' services are usually expensive, so would-be partners should read all about partnerships and reach some basic agreements before calling a lawyer.

For your protection, be sure to put your partnership agreement in writing. The Model Business Corporation Act recommends including the following in a written partnership agreement:

1. The name of the business. Many states require the firm's name to be registered with state and/or county officials if the firm's name is different from the name of any of the partners.
2. The names and addresses of all partners.
3. The purpose and nature of the business, the location of the principal offices, and any other locations where business will be conducted.
4. The date the partnership will start and how long it will last. Will it exist for a specific length of time, or will it stop when one of the partners dies or when the partners agree to discontinue?
5. The contributions made by each partner. Will some partners contribute money, while others provide real estate, personal property, expertise, or labor? When are the contributions due?
6. The management responsibilities. Will all partners have equal voices in management, or will there be senior and junior partners?
7. The duties of each partner.
8. The salaries and drawing accounts of each partner.
9. Provision for sharing of profits or losses.
10. Provision for accounting procedures. Who'll keep the accounts? What bookkeeping and accounting methods will be used? Where will the books be kept?
11. The requirements for taking in new partners.
12. Any special restrictions, rights, or duties of any partner.
13. Provision for a retiring partner.
14. Provision for the purchase of a deceased or retiring partner's share of the business.
15. Provision for how grievances will be handled.
16. Provision for how to dissolve the partnership and distribute the assets to the partners.

try to avoid this and the other disadvantages of sole proprietorships and partnerships by forming corporations. We discuss this basic form of business ownership in the following section.

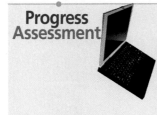

Progress Assessment

- Most people who start businesses in the United States are sole proprietors. What are the advantages and disadvantages of sole proprietorships?
- What are some of the advantages of partnerships over sole proprietorships?
- Why would unlimited liability be considered a major drawback to sole proprietorships and general partnerships?
- What is the difference between a limited partner and a general partner?

CORPORATIONS

Although the word *corporation* makes people think of big businesses like General Motors, IBM, Ford, Exxon, General Electric, Microsoft, and Wal-Mart, it is not necessary to be big in order to incorporate. Obviously, many corporations are big and contribute substantially to the U.S. economy. However, incorporating may be beneficial for small businesses as well.

A **conventional (C) corporation** is a state-chartered legal entity with authority to act and have liability separate from its owners (the corporation's stockholders are its owners). What this means for the owners is that they are not liable for the debts or any other problems of the corporation beyond the money they invest. Owners no longer have to worry about losing personal belongings such as their house, car, or other property because of some business problem—a significant benefit. A corporation not only limits the liability of owners but often enables many people to share in the ownership (and profits) of a business without working there or having other commitments to it. Corporations can choose whether to offer such ownership to outside investors or whether to remain privately held. (We will discuss stock ownership in Chapter 20.) Figure 5.3 describes various types of corporations.

The Andersen name is lowered from its lofty place atop the Center City building in Philadelphia after the company suffered severe losses from its part in the Enron scandal. Since retired Andersen partners' pensions are based on the company's current earnings, retirees' monthly checks fell as the *current* partners lost business. And if Andersen should stop doing business altogether, the pension checks to its retirees or their widows stop too. That's a painful lesson on the importance of choosing your partners wisely.

Advantages of Corporations

Most people are not willing to risk everything to go into business. Yet for a business to grow and prosper and create economic opportunity, many people would have to be willing to invest their money in it. One way to solve this problem is to create an artificial being, an entity that exists only in the eyes of the law—a corporation. Let's explore some of the advantages of corporations:

conventional (C) corporation
A state-chartered legal entity with authority to act and have the liability separate from its owners.

1. **Limited liability.** A major advantage of corporations is the limited liability of owners. Corporations in England and Canada have the letters *Ltd.* after their name, as in British Motors, Ltd. The *Ltd.* stands for

You may find some confusing types of corporations when reading about them. Here are a few of the more widely used terms:

An *alien corporation* does business in the United States but is chartered (incorporated) in another country.

A *domestic corporation* does business in the state in which it's chartered (incorporated).

A *foreign corporation* does business in one state but is chartered in another. About one-third of all corporations are chartered in Delaware because of its relatively attractive rules for incorporation. A foreign corporation must register in states where it operates.

A *closed (private) corporation* is one whose stock is held by a few people and isn't available to the general public.

An *open (public) corporation* sells stock to the general public. General Motors and Exxon/Mobil are examples of public corporations.

A *quasi-public corporation* is a corporation chartered by the government as an approved monopoly to perform services to the general public. Public utilities are examples of quasi-public corporations.

A *professional corporation* is one whose owners offer professional services (doctors, lawyers, etc.). Shares in professional corporations aren't publicly traded.

A *nonprofit corporation* is one that doesn't seek personal profit for its owners.

A *multinational corporation* is a firm that operates in several countries.

FIGURE 5.3

CORPORATE TYPES

Corporations can fit in more than one category.

When neighborhood pet owners sniffed the all-natural treats Mark Beckloff and Dan Dye baked for their dogs, they came begging for biscuits. Thinking they could take a bite out of the specialized pet food market, Mark and Dan decided to open a bakery just for dogs. Twelve years later, they had 28 stores around the country, one in Japan, and converted their partnership into a corporation. Can you think of other innovative products that fit a specialized market niche?

"limited liability," probably the most significant advantage of corporations. Remember, limited liability means that the owners of a business are responsible for losses only up to the amount they invest.

2. **More money for investment.** To raise money, a corporation can sell ownership (stock) to anyone who is interested. This means that millions of people can own part of major companies like IBM, Xerox, and General Motors and smaller companies as well. If a company sold 10 million shares for $50 each, it would have $500 million available to build plants, buy materials, hire people, manufacture products, and so on. Such a large amount of money would be difficult to raise any other way.

   Corporations can also borrow money from individual investors through issuing bonds. Corporations may also find it easier to obtain loans from financial institutions, since lenders find it easier to place a value on the company when they can review how the stock is trading. Many small or individually owned corporations that do not trade actively may not have such opportunities, however. You can read about how corporations raise funds through the sale of stocks and bonds in Chapter 20.

3. **Size.** That one word summarizes many of the advantages of some corporations. Because they have the ability to raise large amounts of money to work with, corporations can build modern factories or software development facilities with the latest equipment. They can also hire experts or specialists in all areas of operation. Furthermore, they can buy other corporations in other fields to diversify their risk. (What this means is that a corporation can be involved in many businesses at once so that if one fails, the effect on the total corporation is lessened.) In short, a large corporation with numerous resources can take advantage of opportunities anywhere in the world.

   Remember, however, that corporations do not have to be large to enjoy the benefits of incorporating. Many doctors, lawyers, and individuals, as well as partners in a variety of businesses, have incorporated. The vast majority of corporations in the United States are small businesses.

4. **Perpetual life.** Because corporations are separate from those who own them, the death of one or more owners does not terminate the corporation.

5. **Ease of ownership change.** It is easy to change the owners of a corporation. All that is necessary is to sell the stock to someone else.

6. **Ease of drawing talented employees.** Corporations can attract skilled employees by offering such benefits as stock options (the right to purchase shares of the corporation for a fixed price).

7. **Separation of ownership from management.** Corporations are able to raise money from many different investors without getting them involved in management. A corporate hierarchy is shown in Figure 5.4.

The pyramid in Figure 5.4 shows that the owners/stockholders are separate from the managers and employees. The owners/stockholders elect a board of directors. The directors hire the officers of the corporation and oversee major policy issues. The owners/stockholders thus have some say in who runs the corporation, but they have no control over the daily operations.

Disadvantages of Corporations

There are so many sole proprietorships and partnerships in the United States that clearly there must be some disadvantages to incorporating. Otherwise, more people would incorporate their businesses. The following are a few of the disadvantages:

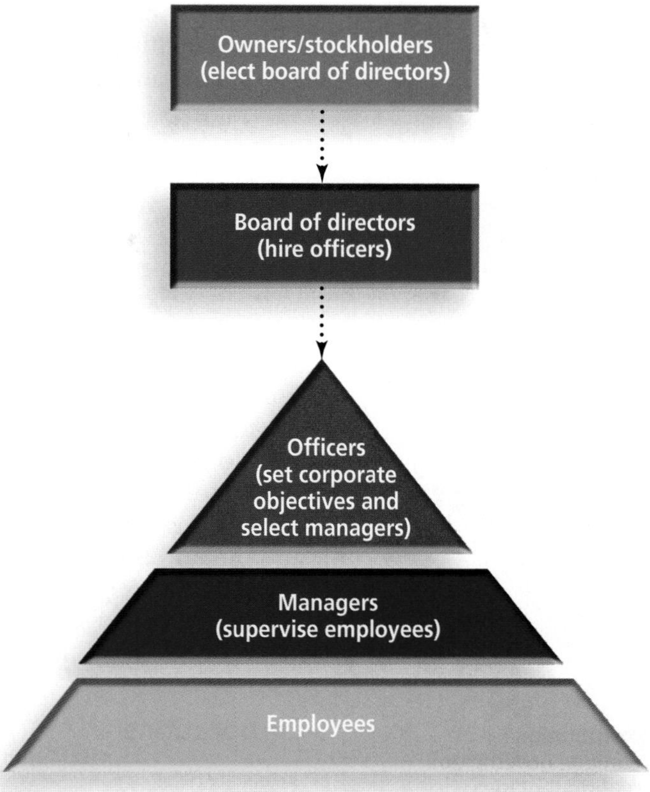

FIGURE 5.4

HOW OWNERS AFFECT MANAGEMENT

Owners have an influence on how business is managed by electing a board of directors. The board hires the top managers (or fires them). It also sets the pay for top managers. Top managers then select other managers and employees with the help of the human resources department.

1. **Extensive paperwork.** The paperwork filed to start a corporation is just the beginning. Tax laws demand that a corporation prove that all its expenses and deductions are legitimate. Corporations must therefore process many forms. A sole proprietor or a partnership may keep rather broad accounting records; a corporation, in contrast, must keep detailed financial records, the minutes of meetings, and more.
2. **Double taxation.** Corporate income is taxed twice. First the corporation pays tax on income before it can distribute any to stockholders. Then the stockholders pay tax on the income (dividends) they receive from the corporation. States often tax corporations more harshly than they tax other enterprises. Sometimes they levy special taxes that apply to corporations but not to other forms of business.
3. **Two tax returns.** If an individual incorporates, he or she must file both a corporate tax return and an individual tax return. Depending on the size of the corporation, a corporate return can be quite complex and require the assistance of a certified public accountant (CPA).
4. **Size.** Size may be one advantage of corporations, but it can be a disadvantage as well. Large corporations sometimes become too inflexible and too tied down in red tape to respond quickly to market changes.
5. **Difficulty of termination.** Once a corporation is started, it's relatively hard to end.
6. **Possible conflict with stockholders and board of directors.** Some conflict may brew if the stockholders elect a board of directors that disagrees with the present management. Since the board of directors chooses the company's officers, entrepreneurs could find themselves forced out of the very company they founded. This is what happened to Rod Canion, one of the founders of Compaq Computer, and Steve Jobs, a founder of Apple Computer (Jobs has since returned to the company).
7. **Initial cost.** Incorporation may cost thousands of dollars and involve expensive lawyers and accountants. There are less expensive ways of incorporating in certain states (see the next subsection in this chapter), but many people do not have the time or confidence to go through this procedure without the help of a lawyer.

Many people are discouraged by the costs, paperwork, and special taxes corporations must pay. However, many other businesspeople believe the hassles of incorporation outweigh the advantages.[9]

Individuals Can Incorporate

Not all corporations are large organizations with hundreds of employees or thousands of stockholders. Individuals (e.g., truckers, doctors, lawyers, plumbers, athletes, and movie stars) can also incorporate. Normally, individuals who incorporate do not issue stock to outsiders; therefore, they do not share all of the same advantages and disadvantages of large corporations (such as more money for investment and size). Their major advantage is limited liability and possible tax benefits. As noted in Figure 5.3, many firms incorporate in Delaware because it is relatively easy to do so there.[10] Although you are not required to file for incorporation through a lawyer, it is usually wise to consult one. In addition to lawyers' fees, the secretary of state's office charges a fee for incorporating a business. Such fees vary widely by state, from a low of $40 in Maryland and South Dakota to a high of $300 in Texas. Like the fee, the length of time it will take to actually have your business incorporated will vary widely by state. The average time is approximately 30 days from the date of application. Figure 5.5 outlines how to incorporate.

S Corporations

S corporation
A unique government creation that looks like a corporation but is taxed like sole proprietorships and partnerships.

One issue that has received much attention in recent years is the formation of S corporations. An **S corporation** is a unique government creation that looks like a corporation but is taxed like sole proprietorships and partnerships. The paperwork and details of S corporations are similar to those of conventional

FIGURE 5.5

HOW TO INCORPORATE

The process of forming a corporation varies somewhat from state to state. The articles of incorporation are usually filed with the secretary of state's office in the state in which the company incorporates. The articles contain

- The corporation's name.
- The names of the people who incorporated it.
- Its purposes.
- Its duration (usually perpetual).
- The number of shares that can be issued, their voting rights, and any other rights the shareholders have.
- The corporation's minimum capital.
- The address of the corporation's office.
- The name and address of the person responsible for the corporation's legal service.
- The names and addresses of the first directors.
- Any other public information the incorporators wish to include.

Before a business can so much as open a bank account or hire employees, it needs a federal tax identification number. To apply for one, get an SS-4 form from the IRS.

In addition to the articles of incorporation listed, a corporation has bylaws. These describe how the firm is to be operated from both legal and managerial points of view. The bylaws include

- How, when, and where shareholders' and directors' meetings are held, and how long directors are to serve.
- Directors' authority.
- Duties and responsibilities of officers, and the length of their service.
- How stock is issued.
- Other matters, including employment contracts.

(C) corporations. S corporations have shareholders, directors, and employees and have the benefit of limited liability, but their profits are taxed as the personal income of the shareholders—thus avoiding the double taxation of C corporations.

Avoiding double taxation is reason enough for more than 2 million U.S. companies to operate as S corporations.[11] Yet not all businesses can become S corporations. In order to qualify, a company must:

1. Have no more than 75 (or 150, including spouses) shareholders.
2. Have shareholders that are individuals or estates and are citizens or permanent residents of the United States.
3. Have only one class of outstanding stock.
4. Not have more than 25 percent of income derived from passive sources (rents, royalties, interest, etc.).

An S corporation that loses its status as such may not reelect S corporation status for a minimum of five years. The tax structure of S corporations isn't attractive to all businesses. It's important to note that the benefits of S corporations change every time the tax rules change. The best way to learn all the benefits or shortcomings for a specific business is to go over the tax advantages and liability differences with a lawyer, an accountant, or both.[12]

Limited Liability Companies

Many businesses are being attracted to the newest form of business ownership: the limited liability company (LLC). Billed as the "business entity of the future," a **limited liability company (LLC)** is similar to an S corporation but without the special eligibility requirements. LLCs were introduced in Wyoming in 1977 and were recognized by the Internal Revenue Service as a partnership for federal income tax purposes in 1988. In 1995 the National Conference of Commissioners on Uniform State Laws approved the final version of the Uniform Limited Liability Company Act. By 1996, all 50 states and the District of Columbia recognized LLCs. The number of LLCs has risen dramatically since 1988, when there were fewer than 100 filings. Today nearly one in every six new business registrations in the country is an LLC.[13] LLCs are particularly attractive to professionals such as doctors, accountants, attorneys, and contractors.

limited liability company (LLC)
A company similar to an S corporation but without the special eligibility requirements.

Why the drive toward forming LLCs? LLCs offer businesses the best of all corporate worlds. Advantages include:[14]

1. **Limited liability.** Personal assets are protected. Limited liability was previously available only to limited partners and shareholders of C corporations.
2. **Choice of taxation.** LLCs can choose to be taxed as partnerships or as corporations. Partnership-level taxation was previously a benefit normally reserved for partners or S corporation owners.
3. **Flexible ownership rules.** LLCs do not have to comply with ownership restrictions as S corporations do. Owners can be a person, partnership, or corporation.
4. **Flexible distribution of profit and losses.** Profit and losses don't have to be distributed in proportion to the money each person invests. LLC members agree on the percentage to be distributed to each member. Regular and S corporations must distribute profits and losses in proportion to shares held.

5. **Operating flexibility.** LLCs do have to submit articles of organization, which are similar to articles of incorporation, but they are not required to keep minutes, file written resolutions, or hold annual meetings. An LLC also submits a written operating agreement, similar to a partnership agreement, describing how the company is to be operated.

Of course, LLCs have their disadvantages as well. These include:

1. **No stock.** LLC ownership is nontransferable. LLC members need the approval of the other members in order to sell their interests. In contrast, regular and S corporation stockholders can sell their shares as they wish.
2. **Limited life span.** LLCs are required to identify dissolution dates in the articles of organization (no more than 30 years in some states). The death of a member can cause LLCs to dissolve automatically. Members may choose to reconstitute the LLC after it dissolves.
3. **Fewer incentives.** Unlike corporations, LLCs can't deduct the cost of fringe benefits. Since there's no stock, you can't use stock options as incentives to employees.
4. **Taxes.** LLC members must pay self-employment taxes—the Medicare/Social Security taxes paid by sole proprietors and partnerships—on profits. In contrast, S corporations pay self-employment tax on salary but not on the entire profits.
5. **Paperwork.** While the paperwork required of LLCs is not as great as that required of corporations, it is more than what is required of sole proprietors.

The start-up cost for an LLC is approximately $2,500, with annual charges of $1,500 for tax-return preparation and legal fees. Information about LLCs is available from the Association of Limited Liability Companies in Washington, D.C. The Commerce Clearinghouse also has a user-friendly introduction called *A Guide to Limited Liability Companies;* call 800–835–5224 for information. Another recommended guidebook on LLCs is *The Essential Limited Liability Company Handbook* (Entrepreneur Media Incorporated, 800-833-3324). You can also find LLC information on the Small Business Administration's website at www.onlinewbc.gov/docs/growing/llcs.html. Figure 5.6 lists the advantages and disadvantages of the major forms of business ownership.

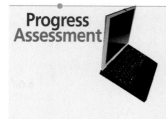

Progress Assessment

- What are the major advantages and disadvantages of incorporating a business?
- What is the role of owners (stockholders) in the corporate hierarchy?
- If you buy stock in a corporation and someone gets injured by one of the corporation's products, can you be sued? Why or why not? Could you be sued if you were a general partner in a partnership?

Critical Thinking

In the past, forming a corporation was the only way to achieve limited liability. Why in the future would most sole proprietors and partners be expected to form limited liability companies (LLCs) rather than corporations?

		Partnerships		Corporations		
	SOLE PROPRIETORSHIP	**GENERAL PARTNERSHIP**	**LIMITED PARTNERSHIP**	**CONVENTIONAL CORPORATION**	**S CORPORATION**	**LIMITED LIABILITY COMPANY**
Documents needed to start business	None, may need permit or license	Partnership agreement (oral or written)	Written agreement; must file certificate of limited partnership	Articles of incorporation, bylaws	Articles of incorporation, bylaws, must meet criteria	Articles of organization and operating agreement; no eligibility requirements
Ease of termination	Easy to terminate: just pay debts and quit	May be hard to terminate, depending on the partnership agreement	Same as general partnership	Hard and expensive to terminate	Same as conventional corporation	May be difficult, depending upon operating agreement
Length of life	Terminates on the death of owner	Terminates on the death or withdrawal of partner	Same as general partnership	Perpetual life	Same as conventional corporation	Varies according to dissolution dates in articles of organization
Transfer of ownership	Business can be sold to qualified buyer	Must have other partner(s)' agreement	Same as general partnership	Easy to change owners; just sell stock	Can sell stock, but with restrictions	Can't sell stock
Financial resources	Limited to owner's capital and loans	Limited to partners' capital and loans	Same as general partnership	More money to start and operate; may sell stocks and bonds	Same as conventional corporation	Same as partnership
Risk of losses	Unlimited liability	Unlimited liability	Limited liability	Limited liability	Limited liability	Limited liability
Taxes	Taxed as personal income	Taxed as personal income	Same as general partnership	Corporate, double taxation	Taxed as personal income	Varies
Management responsibilities	Owner manages *all* areas of the business	Partners share management	Can't participate in management	Separate management from ownership	Same as conventional corporation	Varies
Employee benefits	Usually fewer benefits and lower wages	Often fewer benefits and lower wages; promising employee could become a partner	Same as general partnership	Usually better benefits and wages, advancement opportunities	Same as conventional corporation	Varies, but are not tax deductible

FIGURE 5.6

COMPARISON OF FORMS OF BUSINESS OWNERSHIP

CORPORATE EXPANSION: MERGERS AND ACQUISITIONS

The merger mania of the late 1990s reached its peak in 2000, when the total spent on mergers and acquisitions hit a stunning $3.4 trillion and a new deal was being struck every 17 minutes.[15] It seemed as though each deal made was intended to top the one before. In 1998 there was the $1.75 billion World-Com/MCI merger, which was quickly dwarfed in 1999 with the record-breaking www.aoltimewarner.com

Dealing with Change: Falling Giants

If history repeats itself, and in this case it appears to be doing so, then approximately two-thirds of the youngest merged giants will fail to meet their goals. The greatest merger mania in history seems to be unraveling before our eyes. These failing corporate giants lost around $2 trillion in market value in 2000 alone. The once high-flying WorldCom filed for bankruptcy. AOL Time Warner executives admitted that combining the two companies hasn't worked out the way they had hoped (Time couldn't even get its AOL e-mail to work right). Manufacturing conglomerate Tyco International used its stock to buy more than 20 companies a year only to end up in trouble in 2001 due to the creative accounting involved in purchasing those companies. Tyco's market cap (the total worth of all of the company's stock) plunged $90 billion in just the first six months of 2002.

Why did CEOs have the urge to merge if so many land mines lay in the way? The booming markets in the mid-1990s convinced many CEOs that they needed to beef up in order to compete and to achieve the double-digit growth Wall Street expected. Deregulation in telecommunications and banking primed the merger pump, and the flow of mergers quickly spread to other industries. The remarkable upward spiral of the stock market gave dot-com entrepreneurs rising stock prices. They used that high-priced stock to buy other companies, which increased their earnings, which raised their stock prices higher, which allowed them to buy more and bigger businesses. Of course, if the CEOs got a big bonus for merger deals no matter what happened to the share price, they were even more eager to merge. Joseph Nacchio, CEO of Qwest Communications, received a $26 million "growth payment" when Qwest bought US West in 1999, and Solomon Trujillo of US West got $15 million for selling. In 2000, Qwest's value was down $20–$30 billion.

Some economists see merger waves in terms of games CEOs play. When one company merges with another, its competitors ask themselves what their next move should be in order to get not the best outcome, but the least bad outcome. Since they fear being left behind, the first deal inspires others. For example, after Daimler bought Chrylser, Ford and GM each bought other carmakers. But which carmakers have remained the most profitable? BMW, Porsche, and Toyota—all of which stayed out of the mania.

Change is constant, of course, so every merger wave is followed by a counterwave. A recent survey revealed that more than a third of the largest international mergers completed in the preceding decade are now being "demerged." For example, luxury goods giant LVMH is selling bits of the empire it accumulated in the 1990s. As of this writing, AOL Time Warner's critics are calling for a breakup.

Sources: Karen Lowery Miller, "The Giants Stumble," *Newsweek,* July 8, 2002, p. 14; Stephanie N. Mehta, "Calling WorldCom's Woes," *Fortune,* July 22, 2002; and Stephanie N. Mehta, "AOL: You Got Mauled!" *Fortune,* August 12, 2002.

$77 billion merger of Exxon and Mobil. That record was broken yet again in 2000 when America Online and Time Warner announced that they would merge to form a company with a combined net worth of a staggering $270 billion. Mergers involving financial institutions and telecommunications companies led the corporate consolidation parade. Most of the new deals involved companies trying to expand within their own fields to save costs, enter new markets, position for international competition, or adapt to changing technologies or regulations.[16] The Dealing with Change box reviews how well some of these newly merged giants have met these goals.

merger
The result of two firms forming one company.

acquisition
One company's purchase of the property and obligations of another company.

vertical merger
The joining of two companies involved in different stages of related businesses.

What's the difference between mergers and acquisitions? A **merger** is the result of two firms forming one company. It is similar to a marriage joining two individuals as one. An **acquisition** is one company's purchase of the property and obligations of another company. It is more like buying a house than entering a marriage.

There are three major types of corporate mergers: vertical, horizontal, and conglomerate. A **vertical merger** is the joining of two firms involved in different stages of related businesses. Think of a merger between a bicycle company and a company that produces bike wheels. Such a merger would ensure a constant supply of wheels needed by the bicycle manufacturer. It could also help ensure quality control of the bicycle company's products. A **horizontal merger** joins two firms in the same industry and allows them to diversify or expand their products. An example of a horizontal merger is the merger of a bicycle company and a tricycle company. The business can now supply a variety of cycling products. A **conglomerate merger** unites firms in completely unrelated industries. The primary purpose of a conglomerate merger is to diversify business operations and investments. The acquisition of a restaurant chain by a bicycle company would be an example of a conglomerate merger. Figure 5.7 illustrates the differences in the three types of mergers.

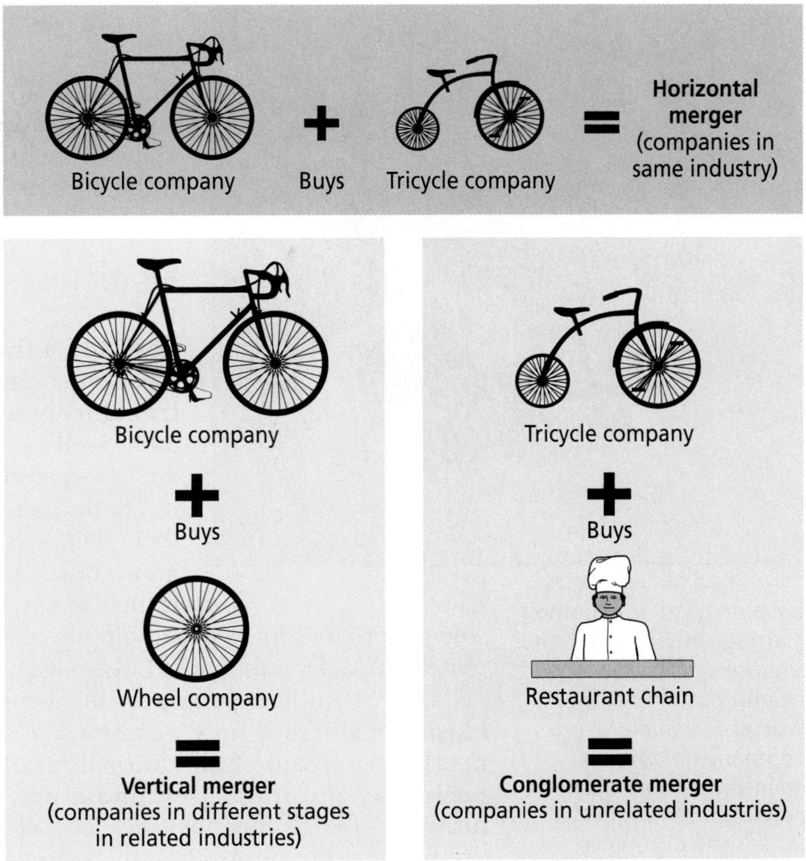

FIGURE 5.7
TYPES OF MERGERS

Rather than merge or sell to another company, some corporations decide to maintain control, or in some cases regain control, of a firm internally. For example, Steve Stavro, the majority owner and head of a group that invested in the Maple Leaf Gardens Ltd. (owners of the Toronto Maple Leafs hockey team), decided to take the firm private. *Taking a firm private* involves the efforts of a group of stockholders or management to obtain all the firm's stock for themselves. In the Maple Leaf Gardens situation, Stavro's investors group successfully gained total control of the company by buying all of the company's stock. For the first time in 65 years, investors in the open market could no longer purchase stock in the Maple Leafs.[17]

Suppose the employees in an organization feel there is a good possibility they may lose their jobs. Or what if the managers believe that corporate performance could be enhanced if they owned the company? Do either of these groups have an opportunity of taking ownership of the company? Yes—they might attempt a leveraged buyout. A **leveraged buyout (LBO)** is an attempt by employees, management, or a group of investors to purchase an organization primarily through borrowing. The funds borrowed are used to buy out the stockholders in the company. The employees, managers, or investors now become the owners of the firm. LBOs have ranged in size from $50 million to $6 billion and have involved everything from small family businesses to giant corporations like R. J. Reynolds and Northwest Airlines.

Today, merger mania isn't restricted to American companies. Foreign companies are gobbling up U.S. companies. The $41 billion merger of Stuttgart, Germany–based Daimler-Benz and U.S. automaker Chrysler in 1998 created a global automotive giant, DaimlerChrysler.[18] Foreign companies have found that often the quickest way to grow is to buy an established operation and bring the brands and technology back to their home countries. In 2001 alone, foreign companies paid approximately $133 billion to buy U.S. companies.[19]

horizontal merger
The joining of two firms in the same industry.

conglomerate merger
The joining of firms in completely unrelated industries.

leveraged buyout (LBO)
An attempt by employees, management, or a group of investors to purchase an organization primarily through borrowing.

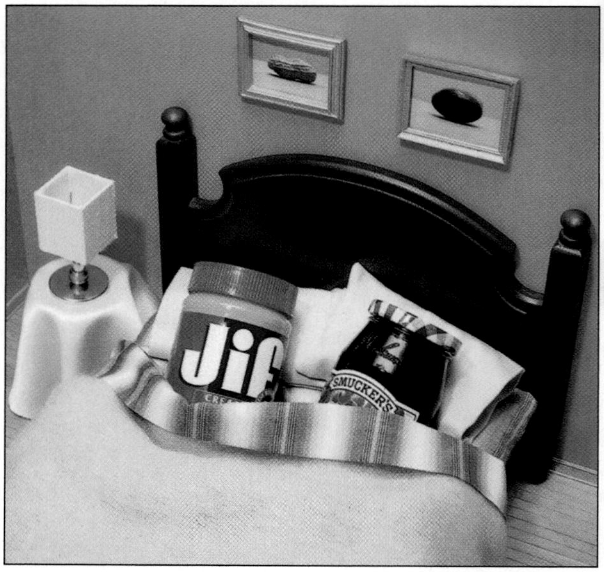

Some may call it a business marriage made in heaven. Smuckers' acquisition of Jif peanut butter from the Procter & Gamble Company united two mainstays of American life: peanut butter and jelly. What's the difference between a merger and an acquisition?

Special Forms of Ownership

In addition to the three basic forms of business ownership, we shall discuss two special forms of ownership: franchises and cooperatives. Let's look at franchises first.

Franchises

Basically, a **franchise agreement** is an arrangement whereby someone with a good idea for a business (the **franchisor**) sells the rights to use the business name and to sell a product or service (the **franchise**) to others (the **franchisee**) in a given territory.

Some people are more comfortable not starting their own business from scratch. They would rather join a business with a proven track record through a franchise agreement. A franchise can be formed as a sole proprietorship, partnership, or corporation. Some of the best-known franchises are McDonald's, Jiffy Lube, 7-Eleven, Weight Watchers, and Holiday Inn.[20]

Over 8 million people in the United States work in a franchise. Franchised businesses now account for approximately $1 trillion in sales, or nearly 50 percent of all national retail sales.[21] In fact, 1 out of 12 American businesses are franchises, and a new franchise opens every six and a half minutes of each business day. The most popular businesses for franchising are restaurants (more than 80 percent of all franchises), retail stores, hotels and motels, and automotive parts and service centers. Subway Restaurants recently surpassed McDonald's as the largest restaurant chain in the United States. However, even though Subway has approximately 150 more outlets than McDonald's, Mickey D's still outsells Subway.[22]

franchise agreement
An arrangement whereby someone with a good idea for a business sells the rights to use the business name and sell a product or service to others in a given territory.

franchisor
A company that develops a product concept and sells others the rights to make and sell the products.

franchise
The right to use a specific business's name and sell its products or services in a given territory.

franchisee
A person who buys a franchise.

Advantages of Franchises

Franchising has penetrated every aspect of American and global business life by offering products and services that are reliable, convenient, and competitively priced. The worldwide growth of franchising could not have been accomplished by accident. Franchising clearly has some advantages:

1. **Management and marketing assistance.** Compared with someone who starts a business from scratch, a franchisee (the person who buys a franchise) has a much greater chance of succeeding because he or she has an established product (e.g., Wendy's hamburgers, Domino's pizza); help with choosing a location and promotion; and assistance in all phases of operation. It is like having your own store with full-time consultants available when you need them. Franchisors provide intensive training. For example, McDonald's sends all new franchisees and managers to Hamburger University in Oak Brook, Illinois. Some franchisors are helping their franchisees succeed by helping with local marketing efforts rather than having them depend solely on national advertising. Furthermore, franchisees have a whole network of fellow franchisees who are facing similar problems and can share their experiences. For example, The UPS Store provides its 3,600 franchisees with a software program that helps them build data

This may look like the set of *Camelot*, but it is actually the Holiday Inn in downtown Edinburgh, Scotland. Holiday Inn franchises try to complement the environment of the areas they serve. What do you think the local reaction would have been if the franchise tried to build the typical American-style hotel in this area?

banks of customer names and addresses. The company also provides one-on-one phone support and quick e-mail access through its help desk. The help desk focuses on personalizing contact with the company's franchisees by immediately addressing their questions and concerns.

2. **Personal ownership.** A franchise operation is still your store, and you enjoy much of the incentives and profit of any sole proprietor. You are still your own boss, although you must follow more rules, regulations, and procedures than you would with your own privately owned store.
3. **Nationally recognized name.** It is one thing to open a gift shop or ice cream store. It is quite another to open a new Hallmark store or a Baskin-Robbins. With an established franchise, you get instant recognition and support from a product group with established customers from around the world.
4. **Financial advice and assistance.** A major problem with small businesses is arranging financing and learning to keep good records. Franchisees get valuable assistance and periodic advice from people with expertise in these areas. In fact, some franchisors will even provide financing to potential franchisees they feel will be valuable parts of the franchise system. For example, SRA International Inc., an executive-recruiting franchise, eases entry for selected new franchisees by allowing $20,000 of the $35,000 initiation fee to be paid from revenue over a period of two years or more.
5. **Lower failure rate.** Historically, the failure rate for franchises has been lower than that of other business ventures. According to the International Franchise Association, a Washington, D.C.–based trade group, franchises have a 66 percent higher success rate than independent businesses.[23] However, franchising has grown so rapidly that many weak franchises have entered the field, so you need to be careful and invest wisely.

Disadvantages of Franchises

It almost sounds like franchising is too good to be true. There are, however, some potential pitfalls. You must be sure to check out any such arrangement with present franchisees and possibly discuss the idea with an attorney and an accountant. Disadvantages of franchises include the following:

1. *Large start-up costs.* Most franchises will demand a fee just for the rights to the franchise. Fees for franchises can vary considerably. Start-up costs for a Jazzercise franchise, for example, range from $2,000 to $3,000; but if it's Krispy Kreme you're after, you'd better have a lot more dough. An average Krispy Kreme store will cost you approximately $2 million.[24]
2. *Shared profit.* The franchisor often demands either a large share of the profits in addition to the start-up fees or a percentage commission based on sales, not profit. This share demanded by the franchisor is generally referred to as a *royalty.* For example, if a franchisor demands a 10 percent royalty on a franchise's net sales, 10 cents of every dollar collected at the franchise (before taxes and other expenses) must be paid to the franchisor.
3. *Management regulation.* Management "assistance" has a way of becoming managerial orders, directives, and limitations. Franchisees feeling burdened by the company's rules and regulations may lose the spirit and incentive of being their own boss with their own business. One of the biggest changes in franchising in recent years has been the banding together of franchisees to resolve their grievances with franchisors rather than each fighting their battles alone. For example, franchisees joined forces to sue franchisor Meineke Discount Muffler Shops, Inc., for fraudulently pocketing money they gave the company for advertising. The franchisees won an initial judgment of $390 million against the company, but the award was overturned on appeal.
4. *Coattail effects.* What happens to your franchise if fellow franchisees fail? Quite possibly you could be forced out of business even if your particular franchise has been profitable. This is often referred to as a *coattail effect.* The actions of other franchisees clearly have an impact on your future growth and level of profitability. Franchisees must also look out for competition from fellow franchisees. For example, TCBY franchisees' love for frozen yogurt melted as the market became flooded with new TCBY stores. McDonald's franchisees complain that due to the McDonald's Corporation's relentless growth formula, some of the new stores have cannibalized business at existing locations, squeezing franchisees' profits per outlet.
5. *Restrictions on selling.* Unlike owners of private businesses, who can sell their companies to whomever they choose on their own terms, many franchisees face restrictions in the reselling of their franchises. In order to control the quality of their franchisees, franchisors often insist on approving the new owner, who must meet their standards.
6. *Fraudulent franchisors.* Contrary to common belief, most franchisors are not large systems like McDonald's and Subway. Many are small, rather obscure companies that prospective franchisees may know little about. Most franchisors are honest, but there has been an increase in complaints to the Federal Trade Commission ➤P. 126◄

www.ftc.gov/bcp/conline/pubs/invest/homewrk.htm

Legal Briefcase

Franchising Fraud

It's a story we've all heard before. Uncle Dick, Aunt Jane, or some enterprising person down the street dips into his or her life savings, retirement accounts, or other personal funds to invest in a new franchise opportunity. The next thing we hear is that the franchisee is basking on a beach on the French Riviera. Sounds like we better get to the bank pronto and then make a quick stop to pick up some suntan lotion.

Actually, you'd better not move too fast. It's true that a franchise is often a quick and efficient way for people who lack experience or detailed business training to grow a business. The lure of some franchises can almost be seductive. It's important to remember, though, that not all franchises have fairytale endings. In fact, investors lose hundreds of millions of dollars a year to ill-conceived franchises and, worse, franchise scams.

Many fraudulent franchise schemes are advertised at business opportunity and franchise shows, in newspaper ads, and by e-mail. For example, one e-mail ad for a business distributing music albums promised, "We will show you step by step how to earn $150,000 per year just working a few hours per week. Imagine that!" Bob Keith, 54, of Philadelphia, said he lost $13,000 after signing up and being promised a supply of current popular music to sell. "I got recordings from artists that have been dead for 30 years," he said. Other customers said they were sent CDs of whale songs.

Sleazy salespersons peddle franchise opportunities to wide-eyed would-be millionaires, yet the businesses are clearly destined to flop. Fatty Arburgers might sound like the next McDonald's, and Kelly's Coffee & Fudge Factory the next Starbucks, but be sure the franchise has stores up and operating before putting your money on the table. The important thing to remember is this: Beware of business opportunities that sound too good to be true—they probably are. To protect yourself against franchise fraud, do your homework and don't be afraid to ask questions.

Sources: Boris Worrall, "Victims Lured by a Bright Idea," *Evening Mail,* January 12, 2001; and David Ho, "Charges Filed vs. Work-at-Home Scams," AP Online, June 20, 2002.

about franchisors that delivered little or nothing of what they promised. See the Legal Briefcase box for advice about avoiding fraudulent practices.

Figure 5.8 also gives you some tips on becoming a franchisee.

Diversity in Franchising

Today there is a gap between female business owners (80 percent of all new businesses in 2000) and the number of female franchise owners (only 24 percent of the U.S. franchises). The private consulting firm Women in Franchising (WIF) found that female franchise ownership decreases as franchise cost increases. "There's not so much of a glass ceiling keeping women from purchasing a franchise as there is a green ceiling—money," says Samuel Crawford, a WIF senior franchise consultant and author of the study. According to reports by the National Foundation for Women Business Owners (NFWBO), while women own 38 percent of all U.S. companies, they receive less than 2 percent of venture capital. And although access to capital is increasing, NFWBO found the amount of credit granted to women still trails that granted to men.[25]

In an effort to promote diversity in business, some franchisors actively recruit women to be franchisees. For example, Church's Chicken coordinated a year-long community-based effort entitled Church's Professional Mentoring Program (Church's PMP). The support program, led by the company's president Hala Moddelmog, provided tools for success in franchising, maintained ongoing online chats by franchise experts, and partnered each new franchisee with a successful franchisee. "We've found that almost half of all suc-

Since buying a franchise is a major investment, be sure to check out a company's financial strength before you get involved. Watch out for scams, too. Scams called *bust-outs* usually involve people coming to town, renting nice offices, taking out ads, and persuading people to invest. Then they disappear with the investors' money. For example, in San Francisco a company called T.B.S. Inc. sold distributorships for in-home AIDS tests. It promised an enormous market and potential profits of $3,000 for an investment of less than $200. The test turned out to be nothing more than a mail-order questionnaire about lifestyle.

A good source of information about franchise possibilities is available from Franchise Watchdog in Burlington, Vermont. It compares what franchisors have to offer, including fees and support services, and also rates franchisors by sampling franchisees. Another good resource for evaluating a franchise deal is the handbook *Investigate before Investing,* available from International Franchise Association Publications.

CHECKLIST FOR EVALUATING A FRANCHISE

The franchise

Did your lawyer approve the franchise contract you're considering after he or she studied it paragraph by paragraph?

Does the franchise give you an exclusive territory for the length of the franchise?

Under what circumstances can you terminate the franchise contract and at what cost to you?

If you sell your franchise, will you be compensated for your goodwill (the value of your business's reputation and other intangibles)?

If the franchisor sells the company, will your investment be protected?

The franchisor

How many years has the firm offering you a franchise been in operation?

Does it have a reputation for honesty and fair dealing among the local firms holding its franchise?

Has the franchisor shown you any certified figures indicating exact net profits of one or more going firms that you personally checked yourself with the franchisee? Ask for the company's disclosure statement.

Will the firm assist you with
- A management training program?
- An employee training program?
- A public relations program?
- Capital?
- Credit?
- Merchandising ideas?

Will the firm help you find a good location for your new business?

Has the franchisor investigated you carefully enough to assure itself that you can successfully operate one of its franchises at a profit both to itself and to you?

You, the franchisee

How much equity capital will you need to purchase the franchise and operate it until your income equals your expenses?

Does the franchisor offer financing for a portion of the franchising fees? On what terms?

Are you prepared to give up some independence of action to secure the advantages offered by the franchise? Do you have your family's support?

Does the industry appeal to you? Are you ready to spend much or all of the remainder of your business life with this franchisor, offering its product or service to the public?

Your market

Have you made any study to determine whether the product or service that you propose to sell under the franchise has a market in your territory at the prices you'll have to charge?

Will the population in the territory given to you increase, remain static, or decrease over the next five years?

Will demand for the product or service you're considering be greater, about the same, or less five years from now than it is today?

What competition already exists in your territory for the product or service you contemplate selling?

Sources: U.S Department of Commerce, *Franchise Opportunities Handbook;* and Rhonda Adams, "Franchising Is No Simple Endeavor," Gannett News Services, March 14, 2002.

FIGURE 5.8

BUYING A FRANCHISE

cessful women business owners have relied on a female mentor, especially in the beginning stages," said Moddelmog. By sponsoring the program, Church's hopes to demonstrate that franchising can be a profitable and rewarding choice for women.[26]

A growing number of women are getting the message. In fact, women aren't just franchisees anymore either; they are becoming franchisors as well. When women have difficulty obtaining financing for expanding their businesses, they often turn to finding franchisees to sidestep expansion costs. For example, the top-rated franchise companies Auntie Anne's, Decorating Den, and Jazzercise are owned by women. Marilyn Ounijan, founder and CEO of Ca-

Running a home-based business is tough work, especially for parents of young children. Pat Cobe and Ellen Pariapiano, founders of "Mompreneurs," developed ways of running businesses at home while raising families. The two now write and lecture to would-be entrepreneurs on work-from-home and time management topics. What do you think would be the hardest part of working from home?

reers USA, claims that having franchisees pay for inventory and other costs of growing a business allowed the company to grow from her office in her home to 23 locations throughout the country. Franchising provided Careers USA a cost-effective way to enter new markets.[27]

Minority franchise ownership is not growing as quickly as franchise ownership in general, largely because of the significant start-up capital needed to purchase a franchise. However, *Black Enterprise* magazine publisher Earl Graves encourages African Americans to look for opportunities in franchising in his book *How to Succeed in Business without Being White.* Franchising opportunities seem perfectly attuned to the needs of aspiring minority businesspeople.[28] The U.S. Commerce Department's Federal Minority Business Development Agency provides minorities with training in how to run franchises.

Home-Based Franchises

Home-based businesses offer many obvious advantages, including relief from the stress of commuting, extra time for family activities, and low overhead expenses. But one of the disadvantages of owning a business based at home is the feeling of isolation. Compared to home-based entrepreneurs, home-based franchisees feel less isolated. Experienced franchisors share their knowledge of building a profitable enterprise with franchisees. For example, when Henry and Paula Feldman decided to quit sales jobs that kept them on the road for weeks, they wanted to find a business to run at home together.

The Feldmans started their home-based franchise, Money Mailer, Inc. (a direct mail advertiser), with nothing more than a table and a telephone. Five years later, they owned 15 territories, which they ran from an office full of state-of-the-art equipment. They grossed more than $600,000 during their fifth year. Henry says that the real value of being in a franchise is that the systems are in place: "You don't have to develop them yourself. Just be willing to work hard, listen, and learn. There's no greater magic than that." See the Taking It to the Net exercise at the end of this chapter for a website that will help you explore home-based franchise opportunities.

E-Commerce in Franchising

We've already talked about how e-commerce is revolutionizing the way we do business. Online business is not limited to those with technical knowledge and the risk tolerance to start their own businesses from scratch. Today, Internet

Buying a franchise takes time and research. Harness the power of the Internet to find information about specific franchises. A good place to start is by doing the Taking It to the Net exercise at the end of this chapter.

users everywhere are able to obtain franchises to open online retail stores stocked with merchandise made in all parts of the world. For example, Click Point exports Colombian goods and services to the United States via Web-based franchises.[29] Before you jump online and buy a Web-based franchise, however, make certain you check out the facts fully. The saying "You get what you pay for" may be old, but it's not old-fashioned.

Many franchisees with existing brick-and-mortar stores are expanding their businesses online. Franchisees that started with a limited territory are now branching out globally. For example, Carole Shutts owns a Rocky Mountain Chocolate Factory franchise in Galena, Illinois. Her website generates 15 percent of her sales. Other Rocky Mountain franchisees have competing websites. Right now, Shutts isn't concerned about the competition from her colleagues because she thinks multiple sites will build brand awareness.[30]

Many franchisors prohibit franchisee-sponsored websites. Conflicts between franchisors and franchisees can erupt if the franchisor then creates its own website. The franchisees may be concerned that the site will pull sales from their brick-and-mortar locations. Sometimes the franchisors send "reverse royalties" to outlet owners who feel their sales were hurt by the franchisor's Internet sales, but that doesn't always bring about peace. Before buying a franchise, you would be wise to read the small print regarding online sales.

Using Technology in Franchising

Franchisors are speeding onto the information superhighway in an effort to meet the needs of both their customers and their franchisees. For example, U.S. Web Corporation set up its website to streamline processes of effective communication for its employees, customers, and vendors. It built a computer network to allow communication among its 50 franchisees, almost eliminating paperwork. Using the website, every franchisee has immediate access to every subject that involves the franchise operation, even the forms to fill out. There is a chat room where franchisees can discuss issues with each other. All franchisees are kept up-to-date on company news via e-mail. The company has found that the Internet is a great way of disseminating information and is revolutionizing franchisor support and franchisee communications.[31]

Franchising in International Markets

The attraction of global markets has carried over into franchising. Today, American franchisors are counting their profits in pesos, won, euros, krona, baht, yen, and many other currencies. More than 450 of America's 3,000 franchisors have outlets overseas. For example, McDonald's has more than 30,000 restaurants in 121 countries serving 46 million customers.[32]

Because of proximity and language, Canada is by far the most popular target for U.S.-based franchises. Many other franchisors are finding it surprisingly easy to move into South Africa and the Philippines. Even though franchisors find the costs of franchising high in these markets, the costs are counterbalanced by less competition and a rapidly expanding consumer base.

Newer, smaller franchises are going international as well. Smaller franchises such as SpeeDee Oil Change & Tune-Up, Rug Doctor Pro, and Merry

Maids have all ventured into the international market. Long Island–based Nathan's Famous Inc. sells hot dogs in the Caribbean and the Middle East. Auntie Anne sells hand-rolled pretzels in Indonesia, Malaysia, the Philippines, Singapore, Japan, Venezuela, and Thailand.

What makes franchising successful in international markets is what makes it successful in the United States: convenience and a predictable level of service and quality. Franchisors, though, must be careful to adapt to the region. In France, people thought a furniture-stripping place called Dip 'N' Strip was a bar that featured strippers. In general, however, U.S. franchises are doing well all over the world and are adapting to the local customs and desires of consumers.

International franchising travels both ways. Just as McDonald's and Starbucks have exported the golden arches and the longhaired mermaid symbols worldwide, foreign franchises are changing tastes here. For example, Maria's Bakery customers in the United States enjoy sweet pastries made from the recipes perfected by franchisor Maria Lee, who is considered the Martha Stewart of Hong Kong. Asian franchisors have added stores throughout the entire United States, whereas businesses from Latin America more often focus only on California, Texas, and Florida. Just as U.S. franchisors must adapt to their foreign markets, foreign franchisors must tinker with menus and store layouts to better fit the U.S. market. For example, Maria's Bakery franchises in the United States carry milk tea drinks and ice cream, products the Hong Kong stores never sold because there was so much competition from other food vendors there.[33]

COOPERATIVES

Some people dislike the notion of having owners, managers, workers, and buyers as separate individuals with separate goals. These people have formed a different kind of organization to meet their needs for things such as electricity, child care, housing, health care, food, and financial services. Such an organization, called a **cooperative,** is owned and controlled by the people who use it—producers, consumers, or workers with similar needs who pool their resources for mutual gain. In many rural parts of the country, for example, electrical power is sold through cooperatives. The government sells wholesale power to electric cooperatives at rates that are, on average, from 40 to 50 percent below the rates nonfederal utilities charge.[34]

cooperative
A business owned and controlled by the people who use it—producers, consumers, or workers with similar needs who pool their resources for mutual gain.

There are 47,000 cooperatives in the United States today. Some co-ops ask members/customers to work at the cooperative for a number of hours a month as part of their duties. Members democratically control these businesses by electing a board of directors that hires professional management. You may have one of the country's 4,000 food cooperatives near you. If so, stop by and chat with the people there to learn more about this growing aspect of the U.S. economy. If you are interested in knowing more about cooperatives, contact the National Cooperative Business Association (800-636-6222).

There is another kind of cooperative in the United States, set up for different reasons. These cooperatives are formed to give members more economic power as a group than they would have as individuals. The best example of such cooperatives is a farm cooperative. The idea at first was for farmers to join together to get better prices for their food products. Eventually, however, the organization expanded so that farm cooperatives now buy and sell fertilizer, farm equipment, seed, and other products needed on the farm.[35] This has become a multibillion-dollar industry. The cooperatives now own many manufacturing facilities. Farm cooperatives do not pay the same kind of taxes that corporations do and thus have an advantage in the marketplace.

In spite of debt and mergers, cooperatives are still a major force in agriculture today. Some top co-ops have familiar names such as Land O Lakes,

Sunkist, Ocean Spray, Blue Diamond, Associated Press, Ace Hardware, True Value Hardware, Riceland Foods, and Welch's.

WHICH FORM OF OWNERSHIP IS FOR YOU?

As you can see, you may participate in the business world in a variety of ways. You can start your own sole proprietorship, partnership, corporation, or cooperative—or you can buy a franchise and be part of a larger corporation. There are advantages and disadvantages to each. However, there are risks no matter which form you choose. Before you decide which form is for you, you need to evaluate all the alternatives carefully.

The miracle of free enterprise is that the freedom and incentives of capitalism make risks acceptable to many people, who go on to create the great corporations of America. You know many of their names: J. C. Penney, Malcolm Forbes, Richard Warren Sears and Alvah C. Roebuck, Levi Strauss, Henry Ford, Thomas Edison, and so on. They started small, accumulated capital, grew, and became industrial leaders. Could you do the same?

Progress Assessment

- What are some of the factors to consider before buying a franchise?
- What opportunities are available for starting a global franchise?
- What is a cooperative?

Summary

1. Compare the advantages and disadvantages of sole proprietorships.

1. The major forms of business ownership are sole proprietorships, partnerships, and corporations.
   - ***What are the advantages and disadvantages of sole proprietorships?***
   The advantages of sole proprietorships include ease of starting and ending, being your own boss, pride of ownership, retention of profit, and no special taxes. The disadvantages include unlimited liability, limited financial resources, difficulty in management, overwhelming time commitment, few fringe benefits, limited growth, and limited life span.

2. Describe the differences between general and limited partners, and compare the advantages and disadvantages of partnerships.

2. The three key elements of a general partnership are common ownership, shared profits and losses, and the right to participate in managing the operations of the business.
   - ***What are the main differences between general and limited partners?***
   General partners are owners (partners) who have unlimited liability and are active in managing the company. Limited partners are owners (partners) who have limited liability and are not active in the company.
   - ***What does unlimited liability mean?***
   Unlimited liability means that sole proprietors and general partners must pay all debts and damages caused by their business. They may have to sell their houses, cars, or other personal possessions to pay business debts.
   - ***What does limited liability mean?***
   Limited liability means that corporate owners (stockholders) and limited partners are responsible for losses only up to the amount they invest. Their other personal property is not at risk.

- ***What is a master limited partnership?***

A master limited partnership is a partnership that acts like a corporation but is taxed like a partnership.

- ***What are the advantages and disadvantages of partnerships?***

The advantages include more financial resources, shared management and pooled knowledge, and longer survival. The disadvantages include unlimited liability, division of profits, disagreements among partners, and difficulty of termination.

3. A corporation is a state-chartered legal entity with authority to act and have liability separate from its owners.

3. Compare the advantages and disadvantages of corporations, and summarize the differences between C corporations, S corporations, and limited liability companies.

- ***What are the advantages and disadvantages of corporations?***

The advantages include more money for investment, limited liability, size, perpetual life, ease of ownership change, ease of drawing talented employees, and separation of ownership from management. The disadvantages include initial cost, paperwork, size, difficulty of termination, double taxation, and possible conflict with a board of directors.

- ***Why do people incorporate?***

Two important reasons for incorporating are special tax advantages and limited liability.

- ***What are the advantages of S corporations?***

S corporations have the advantages of limited liability (like a corporation) and simpler taxes (like a partnership). In order to qualify for S corporation status, a company must have fewer than 75 stockholders; its stockholders must be individuals or estates and U.S. citizens or permanent residents; and the company cannot have more than 25 percent of its income derived from passive sources.

- ***What are the advantages of limited liability companies?***

Limited liability companies have the advantage of limited liability without the hassles of forming a corporation or the limitations imposed by S corporations. LLCs may choose whether to be taxed as partnerships or corporations.

4. The number of mergers reached a peak at the start of the new millennium.

4. Define and give examples of three types of corporate mergers, and explain the role of leveraged buyouts and taking a firm private.

- ***What is a merger?***

A merger is the result of two firms forming one company. The three major types of mergers are vertical mergers, horizontal mergers, and conglomerate mergers.

- ***What are leveraged buyouts, and what does it mean to take a company private?***

Leveraged buyouts are attempts by managers and employees to borrow money and purchase the company. Individuals who, together or alone, buy all of the stock for themselves are said to take the company private.

5. A person can participate in the entrepreneurial age by buying the rights to market a new product innovation in his or her area.

5. Outline the advantages and disadvantages of franchises and discuss the opportunities for diversity in franchising and the challenges of global franchising.

- ***What is this arrangement called?***

An arrangement to buy the rights to use the business name and sell its products or services in a given territory is called a franchise.

- ***What is a franchisee?***

A franchisee is a person who buys a franchise.

- ***What are the benefits and drawbacks of being a franchisee?***

The benefits include a nationally recognized name and reputation, a proven management system, promotional assistance, and pride of ownership. Drawbacks include high franchise fees, managerial regulation, shared profits, and transfer of adverse effects if other franchisees fail.

- ***What are the opportunities for women and minorities in franchising?***

Women now own 24 percent of the nation's franchises. Minority franchise ownership is not growing as quickly as franchise ownership in general, largely because of the significant start-up capital needed to purchase a franchise.

- ***What is the major challenge to global franchises?***

It is often difficult to transfer an idea or product that worked well in the United States to another culture. It is essential to adapt to the region.

6. Explain the role of cooperatives.

6. People who dislike organizations in which owners, managers, workers, and buyers have separate goals often form cooperatives.

- ***What is the role of a cooperative?***

Cooperatives are organizations that are owned by members/customers. Some people form cooperatives to give members more economic power than they would have as individuals. Small businesses often form cooperatives to give them more purchasing, marketing, or product development strength.

Key Terms

acquisition 156
conglomerate merger 157
conventional (C) corporation 149
cooperative 165
corporation 142
franchise 158
franchise agreement 158
franchisee 158
franchisor 158
general partner 145
general partnership 145
horizontal merger 157
leveraged buyout (LBO) 157
limited liability 145
limited liability company (LLC) 153
limited liability partnership (LLP) 145
limited partner 145
limited partnership 145
master limited partnership (MLP) 145
merger 156
partnership 142
S corporation 152
sole proprietorship 142
unlimited liability 143
vertical merger 156

Developing Workplace Skills

1. Research businesses in your area and identify companies that use each of the following forms of ownership: sole proprietorship, partnership, corporation, and franchise. Arrange interviews with managers from each form of ownership and get their impressions, hints, and warnings. (If you are able to work with a team of fellow students, divide the interviews among team members.) How much does it cost to start? How many hours do they work? What are the specific benefits? Share the results with your class.

2. Have you thought about starting your own business? What opportunities seem attractive? Think of a friend or friends whom you might want for a partner or partners in the business. List all the financial resources and personal skills you will need to launch the business. Then make separate lists of the personal skills and the financial resources that you and your friend(s) might bring to your new venture. How much capital and what personal skills do you need but neither of you have? Develop an action plan to obtain them.

3. Let's assume you want to open one of the following new businesses. What form of business ownership would you choose for each business? Why?

   a. Video game rental store.

   b. Wedding planning service.

c. Software development firm.
d. Computer hardware manufacturing company.
e. Online bookstore.

4. Successful businesses continually change. Methods of change discussed in this chapter include mergers, acquisitions, taking a firm private, and leveraged buyouts. Find an article in the library or on the Internet that illustrates how one of these methods changed an organization. What led to the change? How will this change affect the company's stakeholders? What benefits does the change provide? What new challenges does it create?

5. Go on the Internet and find information about a business cooperative. Find out how it was formed, who can belong to it, and how it operates.

Taking It To The Net

Purpose

To explore current franchising opportunities and to evaluate the strengths and weaknesses of a selected franchise.

Exercise

Go to Be the Boss: The Virtual Franchise Expo (www.betheboss.com).

1. Take the self-test to see if franchising is a good personal choice for you. Find the test by clicking on Franchising, then on Franchising—An Interactive Self-Test under Franchising Basics.
2. Go back to the home page and use the search tool to find a franchise that has the potential of fulfilling your entrepreneurial dreams. Navigate to the profile of the franchise you selected. Explore the franchise's website if such a link is available. Refer to the questions listed in Figure 5.8 on p. 162 in this chapter and assess the strengths and weaknesses of your selected franchise. (Hint: The website also contains tips for evaluating a franchise listing.)
3. Did your search give you enough information to answer most of the questions in Figure 5.8? If not, what other information do you need, and where can you obtain it?

Casing The Web

To access the case "Keeping the Air in Blimpie," visit

www.mhhe.com/ub7e

Video Case

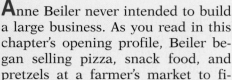

Making Profits with a Twist—Auntie Anne's Pretzels

Anne Beiler never intended to build a large business. As you read in this chapter's opening profile, Beiler began selling pizza, snack food, and pretzels at a farmer's market to finance her husband's free counseling center. Her success encouraged friends and relatives to want to open their own pretzel shops at farmer's markets. Jonas (Beiler's husband) began building booths in the barn, and they soon had 40 locations. What they did not have was a form of business ownership. They explored the idea of a sole proprietorship (because of the ease of starting up and so on) and also considered a partnership or a corporation. (The advantages and disadvantages of each type are covered in this chapter.)

The Beilers contacted a lawyer to look at their business and make a recommendation. They decided franchising was an excellent way to expand. The company now owns 30 of its stores and the rest are franchises. Auntie Anne's currently operates 746 stores and is opening some 40 to 50 additional locations a year.

Franchisees find that franchising is not exactly like being an entrepreneur. They still enjoy the thrill of ownership, but their freedom to do what they please is limited by the franchisor's rules. On the other hand, franchisees have the advantage of marketing assistance. The assurance that franchisors like Auntie Anne's know how to do things right can reduce the franchisee's risk, which means fewer failures.

Unfortunately, franchises have disadvantages as well. One is the cost (sometimes huge) of buying the franchise. Often, however, the franchisor will help with financing to make the purchase easier. Franchising provides some ease of expansion (by using OPM—other people's money), but franchisors have to deal with scores of different owners who have diverse needs. Maintaining consistent quality control when working with so many different people can be a challenge for franchisors.

Auntie Anne's began with a philosophy that stresses customer service, cleanliness, and quality. Establishing good relationships with franchisees solved many potential problems. The company's success, however, has not made Auntie Anne's complacent. The firm works continuously to improve relations with franchisees and has had few problems. In fact, Auntie Anne's focuses so thoroughly on its relationships that the company has had only two cases of litigation with franchisees in 15 years.

Anne Beiler has not forgotten why she went into business in the first place: to help her husband do good in the community. She once considered seeking venture capital investment, but found that venture capitalists didn't share her values. Beiler believes when you give, you get, and then you give some more. She is proud of creating opportunities for women to become franchise owners and proud that a diverse group of people found good jobs in a community-minded company.

Thus far, Auntie Anne's has not done much selling over the Internet, but that may change. Expanding overseas has its challenges as well. Cultural variations are always present. For example, eating on the run is acceptable in the United States but frowned on in other countries. People in some countries have never heard of pretzels. Still, with stores in over 13 countries, Auntie Anne's is slowly but surely doing its famous twist around the world.

Thinking It Over

1. What lessons can you take from this case that you could apply in starting or buying your own franchise?
2. What are the advantages of franchising versus incorporating when a company wants to expand?
3. Is it a good idea for a company to have an attitude of "giving to the community" when it starts? What conflicts might arise?
4. How do the advantages and disadvantages of franchising compare to other forms of business?

Chapter 6

Entrepreneurship and Starting a Small Business

Learning Goals

After you have read and studied this chapter, you should be able to

1. Explain why people are willing to take the risks of entrepreneurship, list the attributes of successful entrepreneurs, describe the benefits of entrepreneurial teams and intrapreneurs, and explain the growth of home-based and Web-based businesses.
2. Discuss the importance of small business to the American economy and summarize the major causes of small-business failure.
3. Summarize ways to learn about how small businesses operate.
4. Analyze what it takes to start and run a small business.
5. Outline the advantages and disadvantages small businesses have in entering global markets.

www.amooregroup.org

Getting to Know Renee Amoore, Founder of the Amoore Group

Renee Amoore has come a long way from her roots in Bryn Mawr, Pennsylvania. While her parents only made it through school as far as the eighth grade, they instilled in Amoore and her seven sisters the importance of a good education. Her mother cleaned houses and her father drove school buses so that the eight girls could go to college. Amoore graduated from the Harlem School of Nursing and served as head emergency room nurse at New York's Harlem Hospital. While working as evening and night program coordinator at the Philadelphia Child Guidance Clinic, Amoore earned a bachelor's degree in human services at Antioch College in 1979. She went on to earn her master's degree in administration from the same school in 1982.

Amoore soon earned a reputation for innovative treatment approaches for people with mental illnesses and addictive disorders. She eventually became CEO of Growth Horizons, Inc., an organization that serves people with substance abuse problems. In 1995, Amoore started her own health care management and consulting business called The Amoore Group (TAG). TAG includes three separate companies: Amoore Health Systems, Inc., a local service provider and health care consultant; 521 Management Group, Inc., a public relations and governmental liaison business; and Ramsey Educational and Development Institute, Inc., an organization that provides programs that help welfare recipients find jobs. Amoore started her businesses with $35,000 of her own money. Today TAG generates $15 million a year and has 100 employees in the United States and 20 in South Africa. TAG ranked 6th in the *Philadelphia Business Journal*'s list of Top 25 Minority-Owned Businesses.

Amoore's parents didn't just teach her about the importance of a good education. They also emphasized the importance of self-reliance, responsibility, and accountability. Amoore interprets those values as the responsibility to serve others. That is why one of her companies (Ramsey) is a nonprofit company that provides physical and speech therapy for children with disabilities. It is also why Amoore is actively involved in politics. As she works to spread her message of individual empowerment, she also works on raising money to help less affluent African Americans become part of the political process.

Amoore started her businesses with $35,000 of her own money. Today TAG generates $15 million a year and has 100 employees in the United States and 20 in South Africa.

In 2002 the U.S. Department of Labor appointed Amoore to the Secretary's Committee on 21st Century Skills Gaps, of the President's Council on the 21st Century Workforce. Amoore's business success and community involvement have earned her numerous awards, including the 2003 Paradigm Award for the Pennsylvania region's most outstanding businesswoman. Stories about people who take risks, like Renee Amoore, are commonplace in this age of the entrepreneur. As you read about such risk takers in this chapter, maybe you'll be inspired to take the risk to become an entrepreneur yourself.

Sources: Thomas J. Brady, "2003 Paradigm Winner Named," *Philadelphia Enquirer,* January 20, 2003, p. C3; and www.amooregroup.org/amoore/president.html.

The Age of the Entrepreneur

entrepreneurship
Accepting the risk of starting and running a business.

A poll of college seniors showed that 56 percent of them were more attracted to starting their own businesses than to joining the corporate ranks.[1] Generation X people (now in their 20s and early 30s) seem to share the pragmatic view that in this time of post-downsized America it doesn't make sense to work in a company where your reward can just as easily be a pink slip as a promotion or bonus. Why not get a piece of the action by working in your own company? Of the 5 million or so Americans going into business for themselves each year, almost a third are 30 or younger.[2] Colleges around the country are responding to this trend by offering more courses on the subject of entrepreneurship. **Entrepreneurship** is accepting the risk of starting and running a business. Explore this chapter and think about the possibility of entrepreneurship in your future.

The Job-Creating Power of Entrepreneurs in the United States

One of the major issues in the United States today is the need to create more jobs. You can get some idea about the job-creating power of entrepreneurs when you look at some of the great American entrepreneurs from the past and the present. The history of the United States is the history of its entrepreneurs. Consider just a few of the many entrepreneurs who have helped shape the American economy:

- Du Pont, which manufactures thousands of products under such brand names as Teflon and Lycra, was started in 1802 by French immigrant Éleuthère Irénée du Pont de Nemours. Some 18 shareholders provided $36,000 in start-up money.
- Avon started in 1886 on $500 David McConnell borrowed from a friend.
- George Eastman launched Kodak in 1880 with a $3,000 investment.
- Procter & Gamble was formed in 1837 by William Procter and James Gamble with a total of $7,000 in capital.

Attention all sports fanatics! Chris Bevilacqua and Steve Greenberg, co-founders of College Sports Television (CSTV), need you to help their new 24/7 college sports channel thrive. The partners raised $100 million to start the network with a little help from media financier Paul Allen, the NBA's Kevin Garnett, the NFL's Tiki Barber and Brian Urlacher, and former star Joe Namath. If you desire to become an entrepreneur, do you know where to look for start-up funds?

- Ford Motor Company began with an investment of $28,000 by Henry Ford and 11 associates.
- Amazon.com began with investments by founder Jeff Bezos's family and friends. Bezos's parents invested $300,000, a huge portion of their retirement account. Today they are billionaires.

The stories are all about the same. One entrepreneur or a couple of entrepreneurs had a good idea, borrowed some money from friends and family, and started a business. That business now employs thousands of people and helps the country prosper.

The United States still has plenty of entrepreneurial talent. Names such as Steve Jobs (Apple Computer), Ross Perot (Electronic Data Systems), Michael Dell (Dell Computer), Bill Gates (Microsoft), Howard Schultz (Starbucks), Scott Cook (Intuit), and Ted Turner (Cable News Network) have become as familiar as those of the great entrepreneurs of the past.

Why People Take the Entrepreneurial Challenge

Taking the risks of starting a business can be scary and thrilling at the same time. One entrepreneur described it as almost like bungee jumping. You might be scared, but if you watch six other people do it and they survive, you're then able to do it yourself. The following are some of the many reasons people are willing to take the risks of starting a business:

- **Opportunity.** The opportunity to share in the American dream is a tremendous lure. Many people, including those new to this country, may not have the necessary skills for working in today's complex organizations. However, they may have the initiative and drive to work the long hours demanded by entrepreneurship. The same is true of many corporate managers who left the security of the corporate life (either by choice or as a result of corporate downsizing) to run businesses of their own.[3] Other people, including an increasing number of people with disabilities, find that starting their own businesses offers them more opportunities than working for others.[4]

Ray Lemire (a.k.a. Big Parmesan) may not be Italian, but he loves pasta. In 1995 Lemire combined his knowledge of direct mail and his passion for pasta to cook up a gourmet pasta business called the Flying Noodle. Sales from the firm's website quickly boiled to over 75 percent of the company's $400,000 in revenue. Do you think the Web will continue to change the way we do business?

- **Profit.** Profit is another important reason to become an entrepreneur. At one time the richest person in America was Sam Walton, the entrepreneur who started Wal-Mart. Now the richest person in America is Bill Gates, the entrepreneur who founded Microsoft Corporation.[5]
- **Independence.** Many entrepreneurs simply do not enjoy working for someone else. Many lawyers, for example, do not like the stress and demands of big law firms. Some have found enjoyment and self-satisfaction in starting their own businesses.[6]
- **Challenge.** Some people believe that entrepreneurs are excitement junkies who flourish on taking risks. Nancy Flexman and Thomas Scanlan, however, in their book *Running Your Own Business,* contend that entrepreneurs take moderate, calculated risks; they are not just gambling. In general, though, entrepreneurs seek achievement more than power.[7]

What Does It Take to Be an Entrepreneur?

Would you succeed as an entrepreneur? You can learn about the managerial and leadership skills needed to run a firm. However, you may not have the personality to assume the risks, take the initiative, create the vision, and rally others to follow your lead. Those traits are harder to learn or acquire. A list of entrepreneurial attributes you would look for in yourself includes the following:[8]

- **Self-directed.** You should be thoroughly comfortable and thoroughly self-disciplined even though you are your own boss. You will be responsible for your success or possible failure.
- **Self-nurturing.** You must believe in your idea even when no one else does, and be able to replenish your own enthusiasm. When Walt Disney suggested the possibility of a full-length animated feature film, *Snow White,* the industry laughed. His personal commitment and enthusiasm caused the Bank of America to back his venture. The rest is history.
- **Action-oriented.** Great business ideas are not enough. The most important thing is a burning desire to realize, actualize, and build your dream into reality.
- **Highly energetic.** It's your business, and you must be emotionally, mentally, and physically able to work long and hard. For example, Tabitha Mageto and Remi Pageon, co-owners of Artisan Bakery in Virginia, often spend 18 hours a day in their shop. During the Christmas season, each pulls a 48-hour shift. "But that is better than working 18-hour days for someone else," says Mageto.[9]
- **Tolerant of uncertainty.** Successful entrepreneurs take only calculated risks (if they can help it). Still, they must be able to take some risks. Remember, entrepreneurship is not for anyone who is squeamish or bent on security.

It is important to know that most entrepreneurs don't get the ideas for their products and services from some flash of inspiration. Rather than a flash, the source of innovation is more like a flash*light.* Imagine a search party, walking around in the dark, shining lights, looking around, asking questions, and looking some more. The late Sam Walton used such a flashlight approach. He visited his stores and those of competitors and took notes. He'd see a good idea on Monday, and by Tuesday every Wal-Mart manager in the country knew about it. He expected his managers to use flashlighting too. Every time they traveled on business, they were expected to come back with at least one idea worth more than the cost of their trip. "That's how most creativity happens,"

FIGURE 6.1

ADVICE FOR POTENTIAL ENTREPRENEURS

- Work for other people first and learn on their money.
- Research your market, but don't take too long to act.
- Start your business when you have a customer. Maybe try your venture as a sideline at first.
- Set specific objectives, but don't set your goals too high. Remember, there's no easy money.
- Plan your objectives within specific time frames.
- Surround yourself with people who are smarter than you—including an accountant and an outside board of directors who are interested in your well-being and who'll give you straight answers.
- Don't be afraid to fail. Former football coach Vince Lombardi summarized the entrepreneurial philosophy when he said, "We didn't lose any games this season, we just ran out of time twice." New entrepreneurs must be ready to run out of time a few times before they succeed.

Sources: Kathleen Lynn, "Entrepreneurs Get Tips on Weathering Recession," *Bergen County (New Jersey) Record*, March 5, 2002, p. I5; and Keith Lowe, "Setting Clear Goals," Entrepreneur.com, August 5, 2002.

says business author Dale Dauten. "Calling around, asking questions, saying 'What if?' till you get blisters on your tongue."

Keep in mind that necessity isn't always the mother of invention. Entrepreneurs don't always look for what customers need—they look for what they *don't* need as well. Aaron Lapin thought we didn't need the hassles of the touchy process of whipping heavy cream to top our pies. He made millions selling his invention: Reddi Wip. Although we'd rather reach for a can in the refrigerator than whip our own cream, Reddi Wip isn't a necessity. If you think you may have the entrepreneurial spirit in your blood, complete the Entrepreneurial Readiness Questionnaire in the appendix to this chapter. There is also some advice for would-be entrepreneurs in Figure 6.1.

Critical Thinking

Do you know anyone who seems to have the entrepreneurial spirit? What about him or her makes you say that? Are there any similarities between the characteristics demanded of an entrepreneur and those of a professional athlete? Would an athlete be a good prospect for entrepreneurship? Why or why not? Could teamwork be important in an entrepreneurial effort?

Entrepreneurial Teams

An **entrepreneurial team** is a group of experienced people from different areas of business who join together to form a managerial team with the skills needed to develop, make, and market a new product. A team may be better than an individual entrepreneur because team members can combine creative skills with production and marketing skills right from the start. Having a team also can ensure more cooperation and coordination among functions.

entrepreneurial team
A group of experienced people from different areas of business who join together to form a managerial team with the skills needed to develop, make, and market a new product.

One of the exciting companies begun in the 1980s was Compaq Computer. It was started by three senior managers at Texas Instruments: Bill Murto, Jim Harris, and Rod Canion. All three were bitten by the entrepreneurial bug and decided to go out on their own. They debated what industry to enter but finally decided to build a portable personal computer that was compatible with the IBM PC.

The key to Compaq's early success was that the company was built around this "smart team" of experienced managers. The team wanted to combine the discipline of a big company with an environment where people could feel they were participating in a successful venture. The trio of corporate entrepreneurs recruited seasoned managers with similar desires. All the managers worked as a team. For example, the company's treasurer and top engineer contributed to production and marketing decisions. Everyone worked together to conceive, develop, and market products.

Compaq, now the second largest PC maker in the United States, merged with Hewlett-Packard in 2002. Entrepreneurs such as the three from Compaq often turn their companies over to professional managers once the companies reach a certain size. Frequently, such a change is good for the firm because the professionals introduce new ideas and instill new entrepreneurial spirit.

Micropreneurs and Home-Based Businesses

Not every person who starts a business has the goal of growing it into a mammoth corporation. Some are interested in simply enjoying a balanced lifestyle while doing the kind of work they want to do. Business writer Michael LeBoeuf calls such business owners **micropreneurs.** While other entrepreneurs are committed to the quest for growth, micropreneurs know they can be happy even if their companies never appear on a list of top-ranked businesses.

micropreneurs
Entrepreneurs willing to accept the risk of starting and managing the type of business that remains small, lets them do the kind of work they want to do, and offers them a balanced lifestyle.

Many micropreneurs are home-based business owners. More than 20 million small businesses in the United States are run out of the owner's home.[10] Nearly half of those home-based businesses are in service industries. Micropreneurs include writers, consultants, video producers, architects, bookkeepers, and such. In fact, the development of this textbook involved many home-based business owners. The authors, the developmental editors, the copy editor, and even the text designer operate home-based businesses.

Many home-based businesses are owned by people who are trying to combine career and family. Don't misunderstand and picture home-based workers as female child-care givers; nearly 50 percent are men.[11] In addition to helping business owners balance work and family, other reasons for the growth of home-based businesses include the following:

- Computer technology has leveled the competitive playing field, allowing home-based businesses to look and act as big as their corporate competitors. Broadband Internet connections, fax machines, and other

When Maria and Jay Seneses started 1 Cent CDs, their home-based auction business on eBay, they hoped to sell enough CDs to earn a living while spending more time with their young son. They discovered that the same technology that gave them the freedom to run a successful business from home made them feel trapped at work. As Maria says, "At the end of the day you don't get to go home. You're already there and so is the work." What are other advantages and disadvantages of working at home?

technologies are so affordable that setting up a business takes a much smaller initial investment than it used to.

- Corporate downsizing has made workers aware that there is no such thing as job security, leading many to venture out on their own. Meanwhile, the work of the downsized employees still needs to be done and corporations are outsourcing much of the work to smaller companies; that is, they are contracting with small companies to temporarily fill their needs. (We'll talk more about outsourcing in Chapter 8.)
- Social attitudes have changed. Whereas home-based entrepreneurs used to be asked when they were going to get a "real" job, they are now likely to be asked instead for how-to-do-it advice.
- New tax laws have loosened the restrictions regarding deductions for home offices.[12]

Working at home has its challenges, of course. In setting up a home-based business, you could expect the following major challenges:

- **Getting new customers.** Getting the word out can be difficult because you don't have signs or a storefront.
- **Managing time.** Of course, you save time by not commuting, but it takes self-discipline to use that time wisely.
- **Keeping work and family tasks separate.** Often it is difficult to separate work and family tasks. It's great to be able to throw a load of laundry in the washer in the middle of the workday if you need to, but you have to keep such distractions to a minimum. It is also difficult to leave your work at the office if the office is at home. Again, it takes self-discipline to keep work from trickling out of the home office and into the family room.[13]
- **Abiding by city ordinances.** Government ordinances restrict such things as the types of businesses that are allowed in certain parts of the community and how much traffic a home-based business can attract to the neighborhood.[14]
- **Managing risk.** Home-based entrepreneurs should review their homeowner's insurance policy since not all policies cover business-related claims. Some even void the coverage if there is a business in the home.

Those who wish to get out of an office building and into a home office should focus on finding opportunity instead of accepting security, getting results instead of following routines, earning a profit instead of earning a paycheck, trying new ideas instead of avoiding mistakes, and creating a long-term vision instead of seeking a short-term payoff. Figure 6.2 lists 10 ideas for potentially successful home-based businesses, and Figure 6.3 on p. 181 highlights clues to avoiding home-based business scams. You can find a wealth of online information about starting a home-based business at www.entrepreneur.com.

One picture may be worth a thousand words, but a picture online is worth much more than that to businesses such as KEH.com. Before going online KEH used printed catalogs to reach potential customers. What advantages does doing business online offer small businesses?

FIGURE 6.2

POTENTIAL HOME-BASED BUSINESSES

Many businesses can be started at home. Listed below are 10 businesses that have low start-up costs, don't require an abundance of administrative tasks, and are in relatively high demand and easy to sell:

1. Cleaning service.
2. Gift-basket business.
3. Web merchant.
4. Mailing list service.
5. Microfarming (small plots of land for such high-value crops as mushrooms, edible flowers, or sprouts).
6. Tutoring.
7. Résumé service.
8. Web design.
9. Medical claims assistance.
10. Personal coaching.

Look for a business that meets these important criteria: (1) The job is something you truly enjoy doing; (2) you know enough to do the job well or you are willing to spend time learning it while you have another job; and (3) you can identify a market for your product or service.

Source: "Hundreds of Home Based Business Ideas," YourHomeBiz.com, September 2002.

Web-Based Businesses

The Internet has sprouted a world of small Web-based businesses that sell everything from staplers to refrigerator magnets to wedding dresses. Online sales amounted to over $33 billion in 2001, more than double the $15 billion in sales just two years earlier.[15]

Atlanta's KEH Camera Brokers began as a hobby, grew into a mail-order business, and is now a flourishing Web-based business (www.keh.com). More than 57 percent of the store's sales are made online. Customers have found that the website is an efficient pipeline for buying and selling cameras. The far reach of the Web was a natural fit for the company. "The Web is a so much better vehicle for our customers [compared with a mail-order catalog]," store manager Pat Mulherin said. "They want to be able to see our inventory." When KEH's first Web page went active, it was an immediate success. "Within two months it was accounting for 35 percent of our business, then quickly went up." Prior to the Web the small store produced mail-order catalogs listing used cameras for sale. Creating and mailing the catalogs was a slow process; by the time a customer saw a product and tried to order it, another customer could have already purchased it. The KEH website's listing of available cameras is updated every four hours. A used camera is listed for sale on the website a few hours after it enters KEH's inventory.[16]

The Internet community has numerous sites that lend entrepreneurs a helping hand in setting up their online stores:

- DistributorMatch.com plays matchmaker between manufacturers and distributors. If you're looking for ideas about what you might like to sell online, this site may get you started.
- Hypermart.com offers full e-commerce capability that allows small businesses to build their own security or electronic shopping carts.
- Microsoft's LinkExchange can get your advertising banners on key sites.
- The E-Commerce Research Room (www.wilsonweb.com) offers reports and resources about e-commerce.
- Sitecritique.net offers constructive criticism of your website by other users, a resource directory, a Web design and usability magazine, and Web design products and services.

Figure 6.4 on p. 182 offers tips on setting up a Web-based business.

FIGURE 6.3

WATCH OUT FOR SCAMS

You've probably read many newspaper and magazine ads selling home-based businesses. You may have even received unsolicited e-mail messages touting the glory of particular work-at-home opportunities. Beware of work-at-home scams! Here are a few clues that tell you a home business opportunity is a scam:

1. The ad promises that you can earn hundreds or even thousands of dollars a week working at home.
2. No experience is needed.
3. You only need to work a few hours a week.
4. There are loads of CAPITAL LETTERS and exclamation points!!!!!
5. You need to call a 900 number for more information.
6. You're asked to send in some money to receive a list of home-based business opportunities.
7. You're pressured to make a decision NOW!!!!

Do your homework before investing in a business opportunity. Call and ask for references. Contact the Better Business Bureau (www.bbb.org), county and state departments of consumer affairs, and the state attorney general's office. Conduct an Internet search and ask people in chat rooms, Usenet discussion groups, or bulletin boards if they've dealt with the company. Visit websites such as www.friendsinbusiness.com to find advice on specific online scams. Most important, don't pay a great deal of money for a business opportunity until you've talked to an attorney.

Don't get the idea that a Web-based business is always a fast road to success. It can sometimes be a shortcut to failure. Hundreds of high-flying dot-coms crashed after promising to revolutionize the way we shop. That's the bad news. The good news is that you can learn from someone else's failure and spare yourself some pain. Startupfailures.com serves as a community for those who have tried and failed. The site bills itself as "The place for bouncing back!" It offers job listings, a feature called "Ask the Coach," and a story reminding site visitors that failing doesn't make you a failure, only failing to learn from your mistakes does. If you would like to learn more about the pitfalls of Web-based businesses, the "Lessons Learned" tab on the Startupfailures.com site provides an archive of stories by Internet hopefuls who have been there, done that.

Entrepreneurship within Firms

Entrepreneurship in a large organization is often reflected in the efforts and achievements of intrapreneurs. **Intrapreneurs** are creative people who work as entrepreneurs within corporations. The idea is to use a company's existing resources—human, financial, and physical—to launch new products and generate new profits. At 3M, which produces a wide array of products from adhesives (Scotch tape) to nonwoven materials for industrial use, managers are expected to devote 15 percent of their time to thinking up new products or services.[17] You know those bright-colored Post-it Notes people use to write messages on just about everything? That product was developed by Art Fry, a 3M employee. He needed to mark the pages of a hymnal in a way that wouldn't damage the book or fall out. He came up with the idea of the self-stick, repositionable paper. The 3M labs soon produced a sample, but distributors thought the product wasn't important and market surveys were inconclusive. Nonetheless, 3M kept sending samples to secretaries of top executives. Eventually, after launching a major sales and marketing program, the orders began pouring in, and Post-it Notes became a big winner. The company continues to update the product; making the notes from recycled paper is just one of the many innovations. Post-it Notes

intrapreneurs
Creative people who work as entrepreneurs within corporations.

FIGURE 6.4

TIPS FOR OPENING A WEB-BASED BUSINESS

Web-based businesses are still in their infancy. Much of their early success could be due to the novelty of shopping online. In order to stand out in the crowd of e-commerce businesses and still be around now that the novelty has faded, you need to build a loyal and ever-growing customer base by providing first-class customer care.

Here are some tips for attracting and retaining online customers:

1. *Keep it simple.* Avoid unnecessary graphics and special effects. If your site requires a specific browser add-on, your customers may move on to another site rather than stop to upgrade their browsers.
2. *Provide added value.* The more information you provide about your products or services, the more likely customers will buy. Examples of well-designed sites are those of Landsend.com. and Homedepot.com.
3. *Make buying easy.* Make it easy for customers to drop items into a cart while browsing. For good examples of this feature, see Amazon.com and REI.com.
4. *Display certification.* You will gain credibility if you display a seal of approval from an organization such as VeriSign (www.verisign.com) that identifies your site as secure for online credit card purchases.
5. *Post a privacy policy.* Assure customers that you will not pass personal information on to others.
6. *Deliver low prices.* Online shoppers expect good value.
7. *Be accessible.* Provide a phone number, an e-mail address, a fax number, and a physical address.
8. *Add a toll-free number.* If customers become frustrated, they want to speak to a live person.
9. *Get it right the first time.* Customers who receive their entire order on time are more likely to buy from you again.
10. *Respond quickly.* Immediate response gives the customer a sense of support and service.
11. *Use an autoresponder.* Sending out automatic e-mail responses to specific types of e-mail questions helps to reduce your online support load and costs.
12. *Provide inexpensive shipping.* Break even on shipping.
13. *Guarantee satisfaction.* If customers aren't happy with a product, assure them they can return it at no cost.
14. *Keep track of what's selling.* You learn a little bit more about your business every time a customer buys something. E-commerce products gather sales statistics that let you analyze buying trends and customer habits that help you plan your inventory.
15. *Build a support network.* You can build relationships with other Web-based entrepreneurs by participating in business chat rooms and by subscribing to different professional associations' websites.

Sources: Karen E. Klein, "Hitting the Right Note Online," *Business Week,* August 9, 2002; "What Makes a Web Site Credible?" Entrepreneur.com, July 8, 2002; and "Fresh from Site Judging, Web Makeover Author Reveals the Five Most Commonly Encountered E-Commerce Errors," M2 Presswire, May 5, 2002.

have gone international as well—the notepads sent to Japan are long and narrow to accommodate vertical writing. Now you can even use Post-it Notes electronically—the software program Post-it Software Notes allows you to type messages onto brightly colored notes and store them on memo boards, embed them in documents, or send them through e-mail.

Hewlett-Packard calls its intrapreneurial approach the Triad Development Process. The idea is to link the design engineer, the manufacturer, and the marketer (the Triad) in a cross-functional team from the design phase on. Everything, even the assembly line, shuts down if the Triad team wants to test an innovation.

The classic intrapreneurial venture is the Skunkworks of Lockheed Martin Corporation. The Skunkworks is a top-secret research and development center that turned out such monumental products as America's first fighter jet in 1943 and the Stealth fighter in 1991.

Encouraging Entrepreneurship—What Government Can Do

Part of the Immigration Act passed by Congress in 1990 was intended to encourage more entrepreneurs to come to the United States. The act created a category of "investor visas" that allows 10,000 people to come to the United States each year if they invest $1 million in an enterprise that creates or preserves 10 jobs. Some people are promoting the idea of increasing the number of such immigrants. They believe the more entrepreneurs that can be lured to the United States, the more jobs will be created and the more the economy will grow.

One way to encourage entrepreneurship is through enterprise zones. **Enterprise zones** are specific geographic areas to which governments try to attract private business investment by offering lower taxes and other government support. The government could have a significant effect on entrepreneurship by offering investment tax credits that would give tax breaks to businesses that make the kind of investments that would create jobs. To learn more about the benefits of enterprise zones and to see a map of their locations throughout the United States, go to www.ezec.gov.

Got a craving for some delicious gado-gado and green curry or just want to munch on some krupuk? If so, Kalustyan's is the place to go. Located in New York City (Manhattan), this spice, grocery, and cookware store is popular with customers, who enjoy the friendly atmosphere and the Indian and Middle Eastern food fare sold there. Kalustyan is yet another example of entrepreneurial success achieved by immigrants—in this case Aziz Osmani and Sayedul Alam, who came from Bangladesh. Can you think of products from other countries that might be successful in your area?

States are becoming stronger supporters of entrepreneurs as they create programs that invest directly in new businesses. Often, state commerce departments serve as clearinghouses for such investment programs. States are also creating incubators and technology centers to reduce start-up capital needs. **Incubators** are centers that offer new businesses low-cost offices with basic business services such as accounting, legal advice, and secretarial help. The number of incubators in the United States now exceeds 1,000.[18] Incubators help companies survive because they provide assistance in the critical stage of early development. One incubator graduate, Visual Networks, grew so rapidly that it displaced the incubator that housed it, forcing the Maryland Technology Development Center to move elsewhere. According to a recent study conducted by the National Business Incubator Association (NBIA), 87 percent of incubator graduates remain in business. To learn more about what incubators offer and to find links to incubators in your area, visit NBIA's website at www.nbia.org.

enterprise zones
Specific geographic areas to which governments try to attract private business investment by offering lower taxes and other government support.

incubators
Centers that offer new businesses low-cost offices with basic business services.

Progress Assessment

- Why are people willing to take the risks of entrepreneurship?
- What are the advantages of entrepreneurial teams?
- How do micropreneurs differ from other entrepreneurs?
- What are some of the opportunities and risks of Web-based businesses?

GETTING STARTED IN SMALL BUSINESS

Let's suppose you have a great idea for a new business, you have the attributes of an entrepreneur, and you are ready to take the leap into business for yourself. How do you start a business? How much paperwork is involved? That is what the rest of this chapter is about. We will explore small businesses, their role in the economy, and small-business management. It may be easier to identify with a small neighborhood business than with a giant global firm, yet the principles of management are similar. The management of charities, government agencies, churches, schools, and unions is much the same as the management of small and large businesses. So, as you learn about small-business management, you will make a giant step toward understanding management in general. All organizations demand capital, good ideas, planning, information management, budgets (and financial management in general), accounting, marketing, good employee relations, and good overall managerial know-how. We shall explore these areas as they relate to small businesses and then, later in the book, apply the concepts to large firms, even global organizations.

Small versus Big Business

small business
A business that is independently owned and operated, is not dominant in its field of operation, and meets certain standards of size (set by the Small Business Administration) in terms of employees or annual receipts.

The Small Business Administration (SBA) defines a **small business** as one that is independently owned and operated, is not dominant in its field of operation, and meets certain standards of size in terms of employees or annual receipts (e.g., less than $2 million a year for service businesses). A small business is considered "small" only in relation to other businesses in its industry. A wholesaler may sell up to $22 million and still be considered a small business by the SBA. In manufacturing, a plant can have 1,500 employees and still be considered small. Let's look at some interesting statistics about small businesses:[19]

- There are about 20 million full- and part-time home-based businesses in the United States.
- Nearly 750,000 tax-paying, employee-hiring businesses are started every year.
- Small businesses create 75 percent of the new jobs in the United States.
- Of all nonfarm businesses in the United States, almost 97 percent are considered small by SBA standards.
- Small businesses account for about 45 percent of the gross domestic product (GDP).
- The total number of U.S. employees who work in small business is greater than the populations of Australia and Canada combined.
- About 80 percent of Americans find their first jobs in small businesses.
- The number of women owning small businesses has increased rapidly. Women now own nearly 6 million small businesses. That's more than one-third of all small businesses and a 43 percent increase from 4.1 million in 1987.
- Minority-owned businesses are one of the fastest-growing segments of the U.S. economy. In the past decade, the number of small businesses owned by Asians has grown 463 percent, Hispanics 417 percent, and African Americans 108 percent.

As you can see, small business is really a big part of the U.S. economy. How big a part? We'll explore that question next.

Importance of Small Businesses

Since 75 percent of the nation's new jobs are in small businesses, there is a very good chance that you will either work in a small business someday or start one. A quarter of the small businesses list "lack of qualified workers" as one of their biggest obstacles to growth.

Vegetarian living is not only nutritious, it can also be healthy financially. Vicki Slotnick and Jeremy Paige used what they learned in 20 years of vegetarian living to start Organica Foods. By the end of their first year in business, Organica cookies were in 600 7-Eleven stores in southern California. How important is it to know your product before starting a business?

In addition to providing employment opportunities, small firms believe they offer other advantages that larger companies do not. Owners of small companies report that their greatest advantages over big companies are their more personal customer service and their ability to respond quickly to opportunities.

Bigger is not always better. Picture a hole in the ground. If you fill it with big boulders, there are many empty spaces between them. However, if you fill it with sand, there is no space between the grains. That's how it is in business. Big businesses don't serve all the needs of the market. There is plenty of room for small companies to make a profit filling those niches.

Small-Business Success and Failure

You can't be naive about business practices, or you'll go broke. There is some debate about how many new small businesses fail each year. Conventional wisdom says that half of all small businesses fail in their first four years, and the SBA reports a 60 percent death rate within six years.[20] Yet a study by economist Bruce Kirchhoff shows that the failure rate is only 18 percent over the first eight years. Kirchhoff contends that the other failure rates are the result of misinterpretations of Dun & Bradstreet statistics. When small-business owners went out of business to start new and different businesses, they were included in the "business failure" category when obviously that was not the case. Similarly, when a business changed its form of ownership from partnership to corporation, it was counted as a failure. Retirements of sole owners were also included as business failures. All in all, the good news for entrepreneurs is that business failures are much lower than has traditionally been reported.

Although the chances of business survival may be greater than some used to think, keep in mind that even the most optimistic interpretation of the statistics shows that nearly one out of five businesses that cease operations is left owing money to creditors. Figure 6.5 on p. 186 lists reasons for small-business failures, among which are managerial incompetence and inadequate financial planning.

Choosing the right type of business is critical. Many of the businesses with the lowest failure rates require advanced training to start—veterinary services, dental practices, medical practices, and so on. While training and degrees may

FIGURE 6.5

CAUSES OF SMALL-BUSINESS FAILURE

The following are some of the causes of small-business failure:

- Plunging in without first testing the waters on a small scale.
- Underpricing or overpricing goods or services.
- Underestimating how much time it will take to build a market.
- Starting with too little capital.
- Starting with too much capital and being careless in its use.
- Going into business with little or no experience and without first learning something about the industry or market.
- Borrowing money without planning just how and when to pay it back.
- Attempting to do too much business with too little capital.
- Not allowing for setbacks and unexpected expenses.
- Buying too much on credit.
- Extending credit too freely.
- Expanding credit too rapidly.
- Failing to keep complete, accurate records, so that the owners drift into trouble without realizing it.
- Carrying habits of personal extravagance into the business.
- Not understanding business cycles.
- Forgetting about taxes, insurance, and other costs of doing business.
- Mistaking the freedom of being in business for oneself for the liberty to work or not, according to whim.

buy security, they do not tend to produce much growth. If you want to be both independent and rich, you need to go after growth. Often high-growth businesses, such as technology firms, are not easy to start and are even more difficult to keep going.

In general it seems that the easiest businesses to start are the ones that tend to have the least growth and the greatest failure rate (e.g., restaurants).[21] The easiest businesses to keep alive are difficult ones to get started (e.g., manufacturing). And the ones that can make you rich are the ones that are both hard to start and hard to keep going (e.g., automobile assembly). See Figure 6.6 to get an idea of the business situations that are most likely to lead to success.

When you decide to start your own business, you must think carefully about what kind of business you want. You are not likely to find everything you want in one business—easy entry, security, and reward. Choose those characteristics that matter the most to you; accept the absence of the others; plan, plan, plan; and then go for it!

FIGURE 6.6

SITUATIONS FOR SMALL-BUSINESS SUCCESS

The following factors increase the chances of small-business success:

- The customer requires a lot of personal attention, as in a beauty parlor.
- The product is not easily made by mass-production techniques (e.g., custom-tailored clothes or custom auto-body work).
- Sales are not large enough to appeal to a large firm (e.g., a novelty shop).
- The neighborhood is not attractive because of crime or poverty. This provides a unique opportunity for small grocery stores and laundries.
- A large business sells a franchise operation to local buyers. (Don't forget franchising as an excellent way to enter the world of small business.)
- The owner pays attention to new competitors.
- The business is in a growth industry (e.g., computer services or Web design).

Critical Thinking

Imagine yourself starting a small business. What kind of business would it be? How much competition is there? What could you do to make your business more attractive than those of competitors? Would you be willing to work 60 to 70 hours a week?

Learning about Small-Business Operations

Hundreds of would-be entrepreneurs of all ages have asked the same question: "How can I learn to run my own business?" Many of these people had no idea what kind of business they wanted to start; they simply wanted to be in business for themselves. That seems to be a major trend among students today. Therefore, here are some hints for learning about small business.

Learn from Others

Your search for small-business knowledge might begin by investigating your local community college for classes on the subject. There are more than 1,400 entrepreneurship programs in postsecondary schools throughout the United States.[22] One of the best things about such courses is that they bring together entrepreneurs from diverse backgrounds. (Many entrepreneurs have started businesses as students—see the Spotlight on Small Business box on p. 188.) An excellent way to learn how to run a small business is to talk to others who have already done it. They will tell you that location is critical. They will caution you not to be undercapitalized, that is, not to start without enough money. They will warn you about the problems of finding and retaining good workers. And, most of all, they will tell you to keep good records and hire a good accountant and lawyer before you start. Free advice like this is invaluable.

Get Some Experience

There is no better way to learn small-business management than by becoming an apprentice or working for a successful entrepreneur. Many small-business owners got the idea for their businesses from their prior jobs. The rule of thumb is: Have three years' experience in a comparable business.

Many new entrepreneurs come from corporate management. They are tired of the big-business life or are being laid off because of corporate downsizing. Such managers bring their managerial expertise and enthusiasm with them.

Getting experience before you start your own business isn't a new concept. In fact, way back in 1818, Cornelius Vanderbilt sold his own sailing vessels and went to work for a steamboat company so he could learn the rules of the new game of steam. After learning what he needed to know, he quit, started his own steamship company, and became the first American to accumulate $100 million.

By running a small business part-time, during your off hours or on weekends, you can experience the rewards of working for yourself while still enjoying a regular paycheck. Learning a business while working for someone else may also save you money because you are less likely to make "rookie mistakes" when you start your own business.

Take Over a Successful Firm

Small-business management takes time, dedication, and determination. Owners work long hours and rarely take vacations. After many years, they may feel stuck in their business. They may think they can't get out because they have too

Spotlight on Small Business

www.sba.gov

Making the Grade in Business

What do Bill Gates, Michael Dell, and Steven Jobs have in common? They all started their companies (Microsoft, Dell Computer, and Apple) while they were still in college.

Today, various programs challenge you to do the same thing. *Success* magazine declared University of St. Thomas in Minneapolis one of the highest-ranked entrepreneurship programs in the country. Every year, 15 to 20 St. Thomas students run their own part-time businesses, ranging from property management to electronics wiring to deck restoration. Senior Joe Keeley is founder of College Summer Nannies Inc., a child care placement service with an inventive educational twist. Keeley came up with the idea for his business when he worked as a summer nanny after his freshman year. He learned that many parents face child care problems in the summer. "People in the neighborhood started asking me if I had any college friends who would do what I was doing," said Keeley. "That's when I started thinking there might be an opportunity here." A lawyer helped him draw up contracts and incorporation papers. Keeley's referral service recruits only college students who are highly motivated. These students are mature enough to do the job, but young enough to connect well with kids. Keeley added a customized educational element to the business: "I start out by interviewing the family to determine the child's interests or needs. Maybe the kids need help with math or reading, or they're simply into baseball or hockey. Then I recruit nannies with strengths in those areas." The strategy seems to work: Keeley has arranged a dozen placements and collected about $8,500 in fees each summer.

It's never too early to think about making that business opportunity of your dreams a reality. Aron Leifer started MultiMedia Audiotext, a company that designs computer software, when he was 16. Soon he was bringing in an impressive $50,000 a month. Not bad for a teenager who still lived with his parents. He sold the company three years later for $800,000. He used those funds to start iVerify, a company that offers a security-based software service that checks phone numbers and confirms user identities before credit card orders initiate. Now, at 20, he is chairman, CEO, and president of his own corporation and manages over 30 employees. Leifer received the Fleet Youth Entrepreneur of the Year Award and was nominated for the Ernst & Young Entrepreneur of the Year Award.

"The idea of growing in a field is called networking, [and it's] all about talking with people about your product," Leifer advises. "The goal is to team up with semicompetitive people. You have to do this to get anywhere in the world, as you are forced to team up with others in the industry. You might be scared, but by talking with people who have done it already, the more people you involve."

To learn more online about starting your own business, check out the lessons in the SBA Classroom at www.sba.gov or go to Quicken's small-business advice site at www.quicken.com/small_business. Who knows? Someday your name may be on the great entrepreneurs list along with Gates, Dell, and Jobs.

Sources: Christina McCarroll, "Beyond Babysitting," *Christian Science Monitor,* June 24, 2002, p. 15; and Dick Youngblood, "Start-up Upstarts of St. Thomas," *Minneapolis Star Tribune,* July 1, 2002, p. 3D.

much time and effort invested. Consequently, there are millions of small-business owners out there eager to get away, at least for a long vacation.

This is where you come in. Find a successful businessperson who owns a small business. Tell him or her that you are eager to learn the business and would like to serve an apprenticeship, that is, a training period. Say that at the end of the training period (one year or so), you would like to help the owner or manager by becoming assistant manager. As assistant manager, you would free the owner to take off weekends and holidays, and to take a long vacation—a good deal for him or her. For another year or so, work very hard to learn all about the business—suppliers, inventory, bookkeeping, customers, promotion, and so on. At the end of two years, make the owner this offer: He or she can retire or work only part-time, and you will take over the business. You can establish a profit-sharing plan for yourself plus a salary. Be generous with yourself; you will earn it if you manage the business. You can even ask for 40 percent or more of the profits.

The owner benefits by keeping ownership in the business and making 60 percent of what he or she earned before—without having to work. You benefit by making 40 percent of the profits of a successful firm. This is an excellent deal for an owner about to retire—he or she is able to keep the firm and a healthy profit flow. It is also a clever and successful way to share in the profits of a successful small business without any personal money investment.

If profit sharing doesn't appeal to the owner, you may want to buy the business outright. How do you determine a fair price for a business? Value is based on (1) what the business owns, (2) what it earns, and (3) what makes it unique. Naturally, your accountant will need to help you determine the business's value.

If your efforts to take over the business through either profit sharing or buying fail, you can quit and start your own business fully trained.

Mamas, don't let your daughters grow up to be cowgirls. Instead, let them be CEOs. Tami Longaberger, CEO of Longaberger Basket Company, is an example of the growing number of daughters that are taking over family businesses. The number of women starting new businesses and assuming top management roles is also growing each year. What qualities do women have that help them become successful entrepreneurs and managers?

MANAGING A SMALL BUSINESS

The Small Business Administration has reported that 90 percent of all small-business failures are a result of poor management. Keep in mind, though, that the term *poor management* covers a number of faults. It could mean poor planning, poor record keeping, poor inventory control, poor promotion, or poor employee relations. Most likely it would include poor capitalization. To help you succeed as a business owner, in the following sections we explore the functions of business in a small-business setting:

- Planning your business.
- Financing your business.
- Knowing your customers (marketing).
- Managing your employees (human resource development).
- Keeping records (accounting).

Although all of the functions are important in both the start-up and management phases of the business, the first two functions—planning and financing—are the primary concerns when you start your business. The remaining functions are the heart of the actual operations once the business is started.

Begin with Planning

It is amazing how many people are eager to start a small business but have only a vague notion of what they want to do. Eventually, they come up with an idea for a business and begin discussing the idea with professors, friends, and other businesspeople. It is at this stage that the entrepreneur needs a business plan. A **business plan** is a detailed written statement that describes the nature of the business, the target market, the advantages the business will have in relation to competition, and the resources and qualifications of the owner(s). A business plan forces potential owners of small businesses to be quite specific about the products or services they intend to offer. They must analyze the competition, calculate how much money they need to start, and cover other details of operation. A business plan is also mandatory for talking with bankers or other investors.

business plan
A detailed written statement that describes the nature of the business, the target market, the advantages the business will have in relation to competition, and the resources and qualifications of the owner(s).

In the late 1990s, adding dot-com to a business was a sure fire path to success. Well, things changed. Entrepreneurs learned it's not enough for a company to "sound" innovative; experience, knowledge, and a solid business plan are the hallmarks of building a start-up company into a long-lasting business success. What current trends seem most helpful to budding entrepreneurs?

Michael Celello, president of the People's Commercial Bank, says that fewer than 10 percent of prospective borrowers come to a bank adequately prepared. He offers several tips to small-business owners, including picking a bank that serves businesses the size of yours, having a good accountant prepare a complete set of financial statements and a personal balance sheet, making an appointment before going to the bank, going to the bank with an accountant and all the necessary financial information, and demonstrating to the banker that you're a person of good character: civic minded and respected in business and community circles. Finally, he says to ask for all the money you need, be specific, and be prepared to personally guarantee the loan.

Writing a Business Plan

A good business plan takes a long time to write, but you've got to convince your readers in five minutes not to throw the plan away. While there is no such thing as a perfect business plan, prospective entrepreneurs do think out the smallest details. Jerrold Carrington of Inroads Capital Partners advises that one of the most important parts of the business plan is the executive summary. The summary has to catch the reader's interest. Bankers receive many business plans every day. "You better grab me up front," says Carrington. The box on page 191 gives you an outline of a comprehensive business plan.

Sometimes one of the most difficult tasks in undertaking complex projects, such as writing a business plan, is knowing where to start. There are many computer software programs on the market now to help you get organized. One highly rated business-plan program is Business Plan Pro by Palo Alto Software. You can find online help with the MiniPlan (www.miniplan.com), a free interactive Web tool that guides you through the business-plan writing process.

Getting the completed business plan into the right hands is almost as important as getting the right information in the plan. Finding funding requires research. Next we will discuss some of the many sources of money available to new business ventures. All of them call for a comprehensive business plan. The time and effort you invest before starting a business will pay off many times later. With small businesses, the big payoff is survival.

Getting Money to Fund a Small Business

An entrepreneur has several potential sources of capital: personal savings, relatives, former employers, banks, finance companies, venture capitalists, government agencies such as the Small Business Administration (SBA), the Farmers Home Administration, and the Economic Development Authority. You may even want to consider borrowing from a potential supplier to your future business. Helping you get started may be in the supplier's interest if there is a chance you will be a big customer later. It's usually not a good idea to ask such an investor for money at the outset. Begin by asking for advice; if the supplier likes your plan, he or she may be willing to help you with funding.

OUTLINE OF A COMPREHENSIVE BUSINESS PLAN

A good business plan is between 25 and 50 pages long and takes at least six months to write.

Cover letter

Only one thing is certain when you go hunting for money to start a business: You won't be the only hunter out there. You need to make potential funders want to read *your* business plan instead of the hundreds of others on their desks. Your cover letter should summarize the most attractive points of your project in as few words as possible. Be sure to address the letter to the potential investor by name. "To whom it may concern" or "Dear Sir" is not the best way to win an investor's support.

Section 1—Executive Summary

Begin with a two-page or three-page management summary of the proposed venture. Include a short description of the business, and discuss major goals and objectives.

Section 2—Company Background

Describe company operations to date (if any), potential legal considerations, and areas of risk and opportunity. Summarize the firm's financial condition, and include past and current balance sheets, income and cash flow statements, and other relevant financial records (you will read about these financial statements in Chapter 18). It is also wise to include a description of insurance coverage. Investors want to be assured that death or other mishaps do not pose major threats to the company.

Section 3—Management Team

Include an organization chart, job descriptions of listed positions, and detailed résumés of the current and proposed executives. A mediocre idea with a proven management team is funded more often than a great idea with an inexperienced team. Managers should have expertise in all disciplines necessary to start and run a business. If not, mention outside consultants who will serve in these roles and describe their qualifications.

Section 4—Financial Plan

Provide five-year projections for income, expenses, and funding sources. Don't assume the business will grow in a straight line. Adjust your planning to allow for funding at various stages of the company's growth. Explain the rationale and assumptions used to determine the estimates. Assumptions should be reasonable and based on industry/historical trends. Make sure all totals add up and are consistent throughout the plan. If necessary, hire a professional accountant or financial analyst to prepare these statements.

Stay clear of excessively ambitious sales projections; rather, offer best-case, expected, and worst-case scenarios. These not only reveal how sensitive the bottom line is to sales fluctuations but also serve as good management guides.

Section 5—Capital Required

Indicate the amount of capital needed to commence or continue operations, and describe how these funds are to be used. Make sure the totals are the same as the ones on the cash-flow statement. This area will receive a great deal of review from potential investors, so it must be clear and concise.

Section 6—Marketing Plan

Don't underestimate the competition. Review industry size, trends, and the target market segment. Sources like *American Demographics* magazine and the *Rand McNally Commercial Atlas and Marketing Guide* can help you put a plan together. Discuss strengths and weaknesses of the product or service. The most important things investors want to know are what makes the product more desirable than what's already available and whether the product can be patented. Compare pricing to the competition's. Forecast sales in dollars and units. Outline sales, advertising, promotion, and public relations programs. Make sure the costs agree with those projected in the financial statements.

Section 7—Location Analysis

In retailing and certain other industries, the location of the business is one of the most important factors. Provide a comprehensive demographic analysis of consumers in the area of the proposed business as well as a traffic-pattern analysis and vehicular and pedestrian counts.

Section 8—Manufacturing Plan

Describe minimum plant size, machinery required, production capacity, inventory and inventory-control methods, quality control, plant personnel requirements, and so on. Estimates of product costs should be based on primary research.

Section 9—Appendix

Include all marketing research on the product or service (off-the-shelf reports, article reprints, etc.) and other information about the product concept or market size. Provide a bibliography of all the reference materials you consulted. This section should demonstrate that the proposed company won't be entering a declining industry or market segment.

If you would like to see sample business plans that successfully secured funding, go to the sample business plan resource center at www.bplans.com/samples. You can also learn more about writing business plans on the SBA website at www.sba.gov/starting.

Employees at Concurrent Pharmaceuticals hope the infusion of $16 million in venture capital will help the firm follow in the footsteps of market giants like Intel and Cisco that used venture capital financing to grow their businesses. Venture capitalists can be a source of start-up funds for a small business, but they generally require an ownership stake in the firm.

Other than personal savings, individual investors are the primary source of capital for most entrepreneurs. *Angel investors* are private individuals who invest their own money in potentially hot new companies before they go public.[23] Websites are now available that link entrepreneurs with potential investors; examples are www.financehub.com and www.garage.com.

Investors known as **venture capitalists** may finance your project—for a price. Venture capitalists may ask for a hefty stake (as much as 60 percent) in your company in exchange for the cash to start your business. If the venture capitalist demands too large a stake, you could lose control of the business. Since the burst of the dot-com bubble, venture capitalists have tightened the purse strings on how much they are willing to invest in a business (down from $5–$30 million to $2–$10 million) and have multiplied the return they expect on their investment if the new company is sold (from the cost of the total investment to three or more times the investment before anyone else gets paid).[24] Therefore, if you're a very small company, you don't have a very good chance getting venture capital. You'd have a better chance finding an angel investor.

If your proposed venture does require millions of dollars to start, experts recommend that you talk with at least five investment firms and their clients in order to find the right venture capitalist. You can get a list of venture capitalists from the Small Business Administration. Ask for the brochure called "Directory of Operating Small Business Investment Companies." Or visit the National Venture Capital Association at www.nvca.org. You can also follow the ups and downs of venture capital availability in *Inc.* magazine.

The Small Business Administration (SBA)

venture capitalists
Individuals or companies that invest in new businesses in exchange for partial ownership of those businesses.

Small Business Administration (SBA)
A U.S. government agency that advises and assists small businesses by providing management training and financial advice and loans.

Small Business Investment Company (SBIC) Program
A program through which private investment companies licensed by the Small Business Administration lend money to small businesses.

The **Small Business Administration (SBA)** is a U.S. government agency that advises and assists small businesses by providing management training and financial advice and loans (see Figure 6.7). The SBA started a microloan demonstration program in 1991. The program provides very small loans (up to $35,000) and technical assistance to "prebankable" small-business owners. The program is administered through a nationwide network of 170 nonprofit organizations chosen by the SBA.[25] Rather than base the awarding of loans on collateral, credit history, or previous business success, these programs decide worthiness on the basis of belief in the borrowers' integrity and the soundness of their business ideas.

The SBA microloan program helps people like Karla Brown start their own businesses. Newly divorced and facing a mountain of debt, Brown needed to find a way to support her daughter. She bought two buckets of flowers and headed to the subway to sell them. Continuing the process, she made enough money to keep a steady inventory, but she needed help from her friends to pay her bills. She thought she could make a living if she could take her flowers out of the subway and into a store. She obtained a $19,000 SBA microloan and rented a store in the heart of Boston; soon after, Brown's flower shop brought in $100,000 in sales.

You may also want to consider requesting funds from the **Small Business Investment Company (SBIC) Program.** SBICs are private investment com-

FIGURE 6.7

TYPES OF SBA FINANCIAL ASSISTANCE

The SBA may provide the following types of financial assistance:

- *Guaranteed loans*—loans made by a financial institution that the government will repay if the borrower stops making payments. The maximum individual loan guarantee is capped at $1 million.
- *Microloans*—amounts ranging from $100 to $35,000 (average $10,500) to people such as single mothers and public housing tenants.
- *Export Express*—loans made to small businesses wishing to export. The maximum guaranteed loan amount is $250,000.
- *Community Adjustment and Investment Program (CAIP)*—loans to businesses to create new, sustainable jobs or to preserve existing jobs in eligible communities that have lost jobs due to changing trade patterns with Mexico and Canada following the adoption of NAFTA.
- *Pollution control loans*—loans to eligible small businesses for the financing of the planning, design, or installation of a pollution control facility. This facility must prevent, reduce, abate, or control any form of pollution, including recycling. The maximum guaranteed loan amount is $1 million.
- *504 certified development company (CDC) loans*—loans for purchasing major fixed assets, such as land and buildings for businesses in eligible communities, typically rural communities or urban areas needing revitalization. The program's goal is to expand business ownership by minorities, women, and veterans. The maximum guaranteed loan amount is $1.3 million.

panies licensed by the Small Business Administration to lend money to small businesses. An SBIC must have a minimum of $1 million in capital and can borrow up to $4 from the SBA for each $1 of capital it has. It lends to or invests in small businesses that meet its criteria. Often SBICs are able to keep defaults to a minimum by identifying a business's trouble spots early, giving entrepreneurs advice, and in some cases rescheduling payments.[26]

Perhaps the best place for young entrepreneurs to start shopping for an SBA loan is a Small Business Development Center (SBDC). SBDCs are funded jointly by the federal government and individual states and are usually associated with state universities. SBDCs can help you evaluate the feasibility of your idea, develop your business plan, and complete your funding application—all for free. The SBA recently reduced the size of its application from 150 pages to 1 page for loans under $50,000.

You may want to go to the SBA's website (www.sba.gov) for the latest information about SBA programs. The SBA site gives detailed information on the agency and other business services.

Obtaining money from banks, venture capitalists, and government sources is very difficult for most small businesses. (You will learn more about financing in Chapter 19.) Those who do survive the planning and financing of their new ventures are eager to get their businesses up and running. Your success in running a business depends on many factors. Three important factors for success are knowing your customers, managing your employees, and keeping efficient records.

Progress Assessment

- A business plan is probably the most important document a small-business owner will ever create. There are nine sections in the business plan outline on page 191. Can you describe at least five of those sections now?
- What are three of the reasons given by the SBA for why small businesses fail financially?

Knowing Your Customers

market
People with unsatisfied wants and needs who have both the resources and the willingness to buy.

One of the most important elements of small-business success is knowing the market. In business, a **market** consists of people with unsatisfied wants and needs who have both the resources and the willingness to buy. For example, we can confidently state that most of our students have the willingness to take a Caribbean cruise during their spring break. However, few of them have the resources necessary to satisfy this want. Would they be considered a good market for the local travel agency to pursue?

Once you have identified your market and its needs, you must set out to fill those needs. The way to meet your customers' needs is to offer top quality at a fair price with great service. Remember it isn't enough to get customers—you have to keep them. As Victoria Jackson, founder of the $50 million Victoria Jackson Cosmetics Company, says of the stars who push her products on television infomercials, "All the glamorous faces in the world wouldn't mean a thing if my customers weren't happy with the product and didn't come back for more." Everything must be geared to bring customers the satisfaction they deserve.

One of the greatest advantages that small businesses have over larger ones is the ability to know their customers better and to adapt quickly to their ever-changing needs. You will gain more insights about markets in Chapters 13–16. Now let's consider the importance of effectively managing the employees who help you serve your market.

Managing Employees

As a business grows, it becomes impossible for an entrepreneur to oversee every detail, even if he or she is putting in 60 hours per week. This means that hiring, training, and motivating employees is critical.

It is not easy to find good, qualified help when you offer less money, skimpier benefits, and less room for advancement than larger firms do. That is one reason employee relations is such an important part of small-business management. Employees of small companies are often more satisfied with their jobs than are their counterparts in big business. Why? Quite often they find their jobs more challenging, their ideas more accepted, and their bosses more respectful.

Often entrepreneurs reluctantly face the reality that to keep growing, they must delegate authority to others. Nagging questions such as "Who should be delegated authority?" and "How much control should they have?" create perplexing problems.

This can be a particularly touchy issue in small businesses with long-term employees, and in family businesses. As you might expect, entrepreneurs who have built their companies from scratch often feel compelled to promote employees who have been with them from the start—even when those employees aren't qualified to serve as managers. Common sense probably tells you this could be detrimental to the business.

The same can be true of family-run businesses that are expanding. Attitudes such as "You can't fire family" or you must promote certain workers because "they're family" can hinder growth. Entrepreneurs can best serve themselves and the business if they gradually recruit and groom employees for management positions. By doing this, entrepreneurs can enhance trust and support of the manager among other employees and themselves.

When Heida Thurlow of Chantal Cookware suffered an extended illness, she let her employees handle the work she once had insisted on doing herself. The experience transformed her company from an entrepreneurial company into a managerial one. She says, "Over the long run that makes us stronger than we were." You'll learn more about managing employees in Chapters 7–12.

Keeping Records

Not all small businesses stay small; some become business superstars. Take Staples, for example, the office supply chain with over 1,400 stores worldwide. Staples started with the help of an SBA loan in 1986 and is now an $11.6 billion retailer. The government, acting through the Small Business Administration, is a great supporter of entrepreneurship. Have you contacted the SBA for information about starting a small business?

Small-business owners often say that the most important assistance they received in starting and managing their business involved accounting. A businessperson who sets up an effective accounting system early will save much grief later. Computers simplify record keeping and enable a small-business owner to follow the progress of the business (sales, expenses, profits) on a daily basis. An inexpensive computer system can also help owners with other record-keeping chores, such as inventory control, customer records, and payroll.

A good accountant is invaluable in setting up such systems and showing you how to keep the system operating smoothly. Many business failures are caused by poor accounting practices. A good accountant can help make decisions such as whether to buy or lease equipment and whether to own or rent the building. Help may also be provided for tax planning, financial forecasting, choosing sources of financing, and writing up requests for funds.[27]

Other small-business owners may tell you where to find an accountant experienced in small business. It pays to shop around for advice. You'll learn more about accounting in Chapter 18.

Looking for Help

Small-business owners have learned, sometimes the hard way, that they need outside consulting advice early in the process. This is especially true of legal, tax, and accounting advice but may also be true of marketing, finance, and other areas. Most small and medium-sized firms cannot afford to hire such experts as employees, so they must turn to outside assistance.

A necessary and invaluable aide is a competent, experienced lawyer—one who knows and understands small businesses.[28] Partners have a way of forgetting agreements unless the contract is written by a lawyer and signed. Lawyers can help with a variety of matters, including leases, contracts, and protection against liabilities. Lawyers don't have to be expensive. In fact, there are several prepaid legal plans that offer services (such as drafting legal documents) for an annual rate of $150 to $350. Of course, you can find plenty of legal services online. For example, the SBA's BusinessLaw.com offers plain-English guides and minitutorials that will help you gain a basic understanding of the laws that affect each phase of the life of a small business. Findforms.com offers a search tool that helps you find free legal forms from all over the Web as well as advice, links, books, and more. Remember "free" isn't a bargain if the information isn't correct, so check the sources carefully and double-check any legal actions with an attorney.

Marketing decisions should be made long before a product is produced or a store opened. An inexpensive marketing research study may help you determine where to locate, whom to select as your target market, and what would be an effective strategy for reaching those people. Thus, a marketing consultant with small-business experience can be of great help to you.

Given the marketing power of the Internet, your business will benefit from a presence on the Internet even if you do not sell products or services directly from the Web. For example, Brandt's, a small restaurant in St. Louis, has a website that features the day's menu and specials, highlights the

Tune in to improve your competitive advantage. Jim Blasingame, award-winning host of *The Small Business Advocate Show* and best-selling author, is the voice of small business. He covers the small-business landscape with interviews of experts and entrepreneurs on his nationally syndicated weekday radio show. Blasingame also simulcasts on the Internet at www.jbsba.com. What are some other sources of advice for entrepreneurs?

credentials of the head chef, and displays photos of the restaurant. It also includes an interactive calendar that lists the scheduled live entertainment. Click on the names of the entertainers to learn what kind of music they play. Some entertainers even include audio samples of their work for you to preview. Websites such as Workz.com give you access to tools to build your own website, including sources for Web graphic design and search engine submission tactics.

Two other invaluable experts are a commercial loan officer and an insurance agent. The commercial loan officer can help you design an acceptable business plan and give you valuable financial advice as well as lend you money when you need it.[29] An insurance agent will explain all the risks associated with a small business and how to cover them most efficiently with insurance and other means (e.g., safety devices and sprinkler systems).

Service Corps of Retired Executives (SCORE)
An SBA office with volunteers from industry, trade associations, and education who counsel small businesses at no cost (except for expenses).

An important source of information for small businesses is the **Service Corps of Retired Executives (SCORE).** This SBA office has volunteers from industry, trade associations, and education who counsel small businesses at no cost (except for expenses).[30] You can find a SCORE counselor by calling (800) 634–0245 or logging on to www.score.org. The SBA also offers a free, comprehensive online entrepreneurship course for aspiring entrepreneurs.[31]

Often local colleges have business professors who will advise small-business owners for a small fee or for free. Some universities have clubs or programs that provide consulting services by master of business administration (MBA) candidates for a nominal fee. For example, the University of Maryland and Virginia Tech have internship programs that pair MBA students with budding companies in local incubator programs. The incubator companies pay half of the intern's salary, which is around $20 an hour.[32]

It also is wise to seek the counsel of other small-business owners. Other sources of counsel include local chambers of commerce, the Better Business Bureau, national and local trade associations, the business reference section of your library, and many small-business-related sites on the Internet. There are websites that can help you find the help you need by matching your consulting needs with the proper consultant. Such sites include National Consultant Referrals Inc. at www.4consulting-services.com.

Going International: Small-Business Prospects

As we noted in Chapter 3, there are only about 290 million people in the United States but more than 6 billion people in the world. Obviously, the world market is potentially a much larger, much more lucrative market for small businesses than the United States alone. In spite of that potential, most small businesses still do not think internationally. According to the U.S. Department of Commerce, only a small percentage of small businesses export even though the number of small exporters has tripled in the last decade. In fact in the past five years, the value of small-business exports has increased 300 percent. Despite this surge in export activity, many small businesses continue to have difficulty getting started in global business.

Why are so many companies missing the boat to the huge global markets? Primarily because the voyage involves a few major hurdles: (1) Financing is often difficult to find, (2) many would-be exporters don't know how to get started, (3) potential global businesspeople do not understand the cultural differences of prospective markets, and (4) the bureaucratic paperwork can threaten to bury a small business.

Besides the fact that most of the world's market lies outside the United States, there are other good reasons for going international. For instance, exporting products can absorb excess inventory, soften downturns in the domestic market, and extend product lives. It can also spice up dull routines.

Small businesses have several advantages over large businesses in international trade:

- Overseas buyers enjoy dealing with individuals rather than with large corporate bureaucracies.
- Small companies can usually begin shipping much faster.
- Small companies provide a wide variety of suppliers.
- Small companies can give more personal service and more undivided attention, because each overseas account is a major source of business to them.

The growth potential of small businesses overseas is phenomenal. For example, John Stollenwerk found customers for his Wisconsin-made shoes in Italy, and Ohio's Andrew Bohnengel opened his tape company to the rest of the world by adopting the metric standard. Web-based business applications are helping small businesses cross boundaries like never before. CPI Process Systems Inc., a six-employee import/export oil-field equipment company in Houston, Texas, won a contract away from Swiss giant ABB to build a power station in China. CPI won the deal thanks to a strong relationship with small overseas suppliers—a relationship facilitated by frequent e-mail. Dave Hammond, inventor and founder of Wizard Vending, began to push his gum-ball machines into the international market via a website. In the site's first year, Hammond sold machines in Austria, Belgium, and Germany, and Internet sales accounted for 10 percent of the company's revenues. See the Reaching Beyond Our Borders box for another small business's Internet success story.

There is an abundance of information about exporting on the Internet. A good place to start is with the Department of Commerce's Bureau of Industry and Security (www.bxa.doc.gov). Other sources of information include the SBA's list of international business resources (www.sba.gov/hotlist/internat.html). The SBA's Export Express loan program provides export financing opportunities for small businesses. The program is designed to www.thaigem.com

Reaching Beyond Our Borders

Sparkling Success in Cyberspace

Texan Don Kogen went on a backpacking adventure in Asia a decade ago and ended up becoming Thailand's leading Internet entrepreneur at age 26. Kogen was enthralled by the market in Chanthaburi, eastern Thailand, a town where gemstones define the town's way of life. Traders sort sapphires and rubies the way others handle fruits and vegetables. When Kogen first decided to extend his Thai visit, he had to work two jobs to meet his $60-a-month rent. After weeks of begging, he finally talked a local gem trader into paying him a quarter of the already low local wage to cut sapphires into finished jewels. After chipping off too much from a couple of stones, Kogen moved into gem sorting. On his off hours, Kogen learned to speak Thai and sat around the city's market watching traders haggle over stones.

After three years of watching, Kogen decided to try the business himself. He bought low-grade stones from traders who arrived at the market early and then resold them to later-arriving dealers for pennies more. He took out an ad in an American trade magazine and soon had more than 800 mail-order customers in the United States. A new fax machine allowed Kogen to increase orders, reduce delivery times, and save $25,000. He used that money to travel to the gem districts in New York City, Chicago, and San Francisco. Four years later he was earning $250,000.

The business changed dramatically when Kogen began to sell gems over the Internet a month after buying his first PC in 1998. Until the Internet, layers of intermediaries multiplied the price of a gem as much as 1,000 percent from original prices to final retail prices. Kogen's website, Thaigem.com, cut through all those layers so that stones traded only once from wholesaler to final customer. While 60 percent of his sales are to dealers, 40 percent are to individuals. Thaigem's 2002 revenues were almost $10 million, up from $4.3 million the year before. Online sales accounted for 85 percent of his 2002 revenue.

Kogen sells 200 items a day on eBay and 2,000 a day on Thaigem.com. Kogen isn't the only one selling jewels on the Internet, but he does have certain competitive advantages. He has a worldwide customer base of 68,000 and has earned an excellent reputation (99 percent of his eBay feedback is positive). Another advantage is that the low Thai labor costs are difficult for competitors in more developed countries to beat. "The lesson here is you must know the territory," says Linda Lim, a professor of international business at the University of Michigan. "You'd be surprised how many highfalutin dot-commers ignore this."

Although it's a long way from New York City and Washington, D.C., Chanthaburi suffered a serious blow after the terrorist attacks of September 11, 2001. Since America is the end market for many gemstones, the collapse in consumer confidence in the United States hurt Chanthaburi's businesses. In addition the halt in travel to the gem markets left many of the skilled stonecutters without work. However, Kogen was able to fight this trend. Although Thaigem did suffer lower sales in September like most other businesses, demand climbed again shortly thereafter, proving to Kogen at least that cyberspace can live up to its potential. Kogen is now hoping to grow even larger by supplying big customers like Wal-Mart, QVC, and JCPenney. Looks like Thaigem won't lose its luster anytime soon.

Sources: Robyn Meredith, "From Rocks to Riches," *Forbes,* August 12, 2002, p. 101; and Paul Kangas and Susie Gharib, "Nightly Business Report," *Nightly Business Report,* April 5, 2002.

finance a variety of needs of small-business exporters, including participation in foreign trade shows, catalog translations for use in foreign markets, lines of credit for export purposes, and real estate and equipment for the production of goods or services to be exported.[33]

Progress Assessment

- Why do many small businesses avoid doing business overseas?
- What are some of the advantages small businesses have over large businesses in selling in global markets?

Summary

1. There are many reasons people are willing to take the risks of entrepreneurship.

1. Explain why people are willing to take the risks of entrepreneurship, list the attributes of successful entrepreneurs, describe the benefits of entrepreneurial teams and intrapreneurs, and explain the growth of home-based and Web-based businesses.

- ***What are a few of the reasons people start their own businesses?***

Reasons include profit, independence, opportunity, and challenge.

- ***What are the attributes of successful entrepreneurs?***

Successful entrepreneurs are self-directed, self-nurturing, action-oriented, highly energetic, and tolerant of uncertainty.

- ***What have modern entrepreneurs done to ensure longer terms of management?***

They have formed entrepreneurial teams that have expertise in the many different skills needed to start and manage a business.

- ***What is a micropreneur?***

Micropreneurs are people willing to accept the risk of starting and managing the type of business that remains small, lets them do the kind of work they want to do, and offers them a balanced lifestyle.

- ***What is intrapreneuring?***

Intrapreneuring is the establishment of entrepreneurial centers within a larger firm where people can innovate and develop new product ideas internally.

- ***Why has there been such an increase in the number of home-based and Web-based businesses in the last few years?***

The increase in power and decrease in price of computer technology has leveled the field and made it possible for small businesses to compete against larger companies—regardless of location.

2. Of all the nonfarm businesses in the United States, almost 97 percent are considered small by the Small Business Administration.

2. Discuss the importance of small business to the American economy and summarize the major causes of small-business failure.

- ***Why are* small *businesses important to the U.S. economy?***

Small business accounts for almost 45 percent of gross domestic product (GDP). Perhaps more important to tomorrow's graduates, 80 percent of American workers' first jobs are in small businesses.

- ***What does the small in small business mean?***

The Small Business Administration defines a small business as one that is independently owned and operated, not dominant in its field of operation, and meets certain standards of size in terms of employees or sales (depending on the size of others in the industry).

- ***Why do many small businesses fail?***

Many small businesses fail because of managerial incompetence and inadequate financial planning. See Figure 6.5 (p. 186) for a list of causes of business failure.

3. Most people have no idea how to go about starting a small business.

3. Summarize ways to learn about how small businesses operate.

- ***What hints would you give someone who wants to learn about starting a small business?***

First, learn from others. Take courses and talk with some small-business owners. Second, get some experience working for others. Third, take over a successful firm. Finally, study the latest in small-business management techniques, including the use of computers for things like payroll, inventory control, and mailing lists.

4. Writing a business plan is the first step in organizing a business.

4. Analyze what it takes to start and run a small business.

- ***What goes into a business plan?***

See the box on page 191.

- ***What sources of funds should someone wanting to start a new business consider investigating?***

A new entrepreneur has several sources of capital: personal savings, relatives, former employers, banks, finance companies, venture capital organizations, government agencies, and more.

- ***What are some of the special problems that small-business owners have in dealing with employees?***

Small-business owners often have difficulty finding competent employees and grooming employees for management responsibilities.

- ***Where can budding entrepreneurs find help in starting their businesses?***

Help can be found from many sources: accountants, lawyers, marketing researchers, loan officers, insurance agents, the SBA, SBDCs, SBICs, and even college professors.

5. Outline the advantages and disadvantages small businesses have in entering global markets.

5. The future growth of some small businesses is in foreign markets.

- ***What are some advantages small businesses have over large businesses in global markets?***

Foreign buyers enjoy dealing with individuals rather than large corporations because (1) small companies provide a wider variety of suppliers and can ship products more quickly and (2) small companies give more personal service.

- ***Why don't more small businesses start trading internationally?***

There are several reasons: (1) Financing is often difficult to find, (2) many people don't know how to get started, (3) many do not understand the cultural differences in foreign markets, and (4) the bureaucratic red tape is often overwhelming.

Key Terms

business plan 189
enterprise zones 183
entrepreneurial team 177
entrepreneurship 174
incubators 183
intrapreneurs 181
market 194
micropreneurs 178
Service Corps of Retired Executives (SCORE) 196
small business 184
Small Business Administration (SBA) 192
Small Business Investment Company (SBIC) Program 192
venture capitalists 192

Developing Workplace Skills

1. Find issues of *Entrepreneur, Success,* and *Inc.* magazines in the library or on the Internet. Read about the entrepreneurs who are heading today's dynamic new businesses. Write a profile about one entrepreneur.

2. Select a small business that looks attractive as a career possibility for you. Talk to at least one person who manages such a business. Ask how he or she started the business. Ask about financing; personnel problems (hiring, firing, training, scheduling); accounting problems; and other managerial matters. Prepare a summary of your findings, including whether the job was rewarding, interesting, and challenging—and why or why not.

3. Contact the Small Business Administration by visiting a local office or by going to the organization's website at www.sba.gov. Write a brief summary of the services the SBA offers.

4. Select a small business in your area that has failed. List the factors you think led to its failure. Compile a list of actions the business owners might have taken to keep the company in business.

5. Choose a partner from among your classmates and put together a list of factors that might mean the difference between success and failure of a new company entering the business software industry. Can small start-ups realistically hope to compete with companies such as Microsoft and Intel? Discuss the list and your conclusions in class.

Taking It To The Net

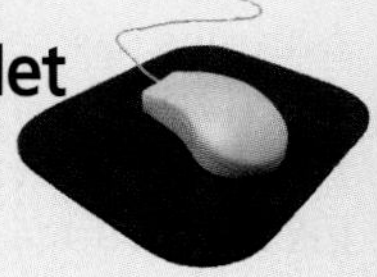

Purpose

To assess your potential to succeed as an entrepreneur and to evaluate a sample business plan.

Exercise

1. Go to www.bizmove.com/other/quiz.htm and take the interactive entrepreneurial quiz to find out if you have the qualities to be a successful entrepreneur.
2. If you have entrepreneurial traits and decide you would like to start your own business, you will need to develop a business plan. Go to www.quicken.com/small_business/cch/tools/retailer.rtf and review the business plan for Joe's Redhots. Although Joe's plan does not follow the same format as the business plan outline on page 191, does it contain all of the necessary information listed in the outline? If not, what is missing?

Casing The Web

To access the case "BMOC: Starting a Small Business at School," visit

www.mhhe.com/'ub7e

Video Case

It's In the Bag: Joe-to-Go

Jerry Andrews was a typical soccer dad: hauling kids to games, bringing snacks, and cheering on the sidelines. One day he volunteered to bring coffee to an early morning game. Later he realized that it wasn't going to be easy getting a dozen cups of hot coffee to the game, especially for Jerry, who was a polio victim since childhood. That night Andrews and his friends talked about the problem of carrying the hot coffee. The idea of a disposable thermos bag came up, and led to a major entrepreneurial idea. Why not call the bag Joe-to-Go? (Joe is a slang term for coffee.) Fortunately, special challenges call for creative solutions and creative solutions are what entrepreneurship is all about. Entrepreneurship has many pitfalls and roadblocks. You have to be passionate and realistic to overcome such barriers. You may have a good idea, but is it marketable? Where will you get the money to start? To be a successful entrepreneur it helps to be self-directed, action-oriented, highly energetic, and self-nurturing. You have to be your own cheerleader. You also have to be tolerant of uncertainty since there are no guarantees in entrepreneurship. On the other hand, it is rewarding to work for yourself and to be your own boss. With the right amount of planning, including a good business plan, you just might succeed.

Andrews knew intuitively who his customers were. Still he needed to find help in turning this idea into a viable product. Outside design and production people helped Andrews find just the right product. He also sought advice from accountants, lawyers, marketing researchers, insurance agents, and small-business advisors. Retailers who could reach those customers and tell them about the benefits of a bag that would keep coffee hot were vital. Luckily, his only investor was a salesperson who was eager to find businesses that would promote the Joe-to-Go bags in their stores.

Andrews learned one way to reach coffee retailers was to go to coffee shows where Joe-to-Go samples were displayed prominently. Everyone loved them, but nobody was buying them. Although sales were slow, retailers agreed this was a great product. It even made the cover of *Dupont Magazine*. One company that saw the potential of Joe-to-Go was Dunkin' Donuts. The company saw the potential of selling more coffee to go and felt customers may even buy a few extra donuts to go too.

Other companies soon followed Dunkin' Donuts' lead. Andrews decided to license his product. Therefore, he gets so much a box for every box sold—box after box after box. Companies are free to label the box anything they like. Some call it Joe-to-Go, others add their own name. Dunkin' Donuts, for example, calls it Box of Joe. A major victory for Andrews was getting Starbucks to carry the product. When Andrews would go to a Starbucks that didn't have the product, he would haul one out and show them one. They would be impressed and orders would pour in.

It took a great deal of patience and persistence to make Joe-to-Go pay off. There's freedom in owning your own business, but little security. Thankfully, there are always new opportunities and new challenges. Being an entrepreneur makes it exciting to get up each morning to see what the day will bring. And that by itself is a kind of success.

Thinking It Over

1. Have you or anyone you know thought of an innovative solution to a problem that could be turned into a successful product like Joe-to-Go? Did it make it to market? If so, what kind of help was needed to move the solution from the idea stage to reality? If it did not make it to market, why not? What could have been done differently to make it a success?
2. Do you have what is takes to become an entrepreneur? Why not take a minute to fill out the entrepreneurial questionnaire on page 204?
3. Often people with disabilities have challenges that are not readily apparent to others. What opportunities does that present for new entrepreneurs?
4. Does Jerry Andrews' success make you more interested in becoming an entrepreneur? What are the advantages of working for yourself rather than for someone else?

Appendix

Entrepreneur Readiness Questionnaire

Not everyone is cut out to be an entrepreneur. The fact is, though, that all kinds of people with all kinds of personalities have succeeded in starting small and large businesses. There are certain traits, however, that seem to separate those who'll be successful as entrepreneurs from those who may not be. The following questionnaire will help you determine in which category you fit. Take a couple of minutes to answer the questions and then score yourself at the end. Making a low score doesn't mean you won't succeed as an entrepreneur. It does indicate, however, that you may be happier working for someone else.

Each of the following items describes something that you may or may not feel represents your personality or other characteristics about you. Read each item and then circle the response (1, 2, 3, 4, or 5) that most nearly reflects the extent to which you agree or disagree that the item seems to fit you.

	Response				
Looking at my overall philosophy of life and typical behavior, I would say that . . .	**AGREE COMPLETELY (1)**	**MOSTLY AGREE (2)**	**PARTIALLY AGREE (3)**	**MOSTLY DISAGREE (4)**	**DISAGREE COMPLETELY (5)**
1. I am generally optimistic.	1	2	3	4	5
2. I enjoy competing and doing things better than someone else.	1	2	3	4	5
3. When solving a problem, I try to arrive at the best solution first without worrying about other possibilities.	1	2	3	4	5
4. I enjoy associating with co-workers after working hours.	1	2	3	4	5
5. If betting on a horse race I would prefer to take a chance on a high-payoff "long shot."	1	2	3	4	5
6. I like setting my own goals and working hard to achieve them.	1	2	3	4	5
7. I am generally casual and easy-going with others.	1	2	3	4	5
8. I like to know what is going on and take action to find out.	1	2	3	4	5
9. I work best when someone else is guiding me along the way.	1	2	3	4	5
10. When I am right I can convince others.					
11. I find that other people frequently waste my valuable time.	1	2	3	4	5
12. I enjoy watching football, baseball, and similar sports events.	1	2	3	4	5
13. I tend to communicate about myself very openly with other people.	1	2	3	4	5
14. I don't mind following orders from superiors who have legitimate authority.	1	2	3	4	5
15. I enjoy planning things more than actually carrying out the plans.	1	2	3	4	5
16. I don't think it's much fun to bet on a "sure thing."	1	2	3	4	5
17. If faced with failure, I would shift quickly to something else rather than sticking to my guns.	1	2	3	4	5
18. Part of being successful in business is reserving adequate time for family.	1	2	3	4	5
19. Once I have earned something, I feel that keeping it secure is important.	1	2	3	4	5
20. Making a lot of money is largely a matter of getting the right breaks.	1	2	3	4	5
21. Problem solving is usually more effective when a number of alternatives are considered.	1	2	3	4	5
22. I enjoy impressing others with the things I can do.	1	2	3	4	5
23. I enjoy playing games like tennis and handball with someone who is slightly better than I am.	1	2	3	4	5
24. Sometimes moral ethics must be bent a little in business dealings.	1	2	3	4	5
25. I think that good friends would make the best subordinates in an organization.	1	2	3	4	5

Source: Kenneth R. Van Voorhis, *Entrepreneurship and Small Business Management* (New York: Allyn & Bacon, 1980).

Scoring:

Give yourself one point for each 1 or 2 response you circled for questions 1, 2, 6, 8, 10, 11, 16, 17, 21, 22, 23.

Give yourself one point for each 4 or 5 response you circled for questions 3, 4, 5, 7, 9, 12, 13, 14, 15, 18, 19, 20, 24, 25.

Add your points and see how you rate in the following categories:

21–25	Your entrepreneurial potential looks great if you have a suitable opportunity to use it. What are you waiting for?
16–20	This is close to the high entrepreneurial range. You could be quite successful if your other talents and resources are right.
11–15	Your score is in the transitional range. With some serious work you can probably develop the outlook you need for running your own business.
6–10	Things look pretty doubtful for you as an entrepreneur. It would take considerable rearranging of your life philosophy and behavior to make it.
0–5	Let's face it. Entrepreneurship isn't really for you. Still, learning what it's all about won't hurt anything.

Part 2

Business Ownership

Career Portfolio

When you drive through any town or city, you see dozens, often hundreds and thousands, of small businesses. The kinds of businesses are as varied as the people who own and operate them. If you were to interview the owners, you would also find a great variety of reasons for choosing a specific business, for settling in a certain location, and for choosing business ownership as a way of life.

Many people become entrepreneurs ➤P. 4◄ today because they see the risks as similar to working for someone else—but the rewards much greater. The workplace as a whole is becoming increasingly risk-intensive. Many jobs are riskier propositions than they would have been 10 years ago. Downsizing and restructuring are just two reasons that job security assumptions are changing. The incentive for some risk taking with a payoff of independence, high job satisfaction, and possible high profits just might be more enticing to you in the future than it already is now.

One of the first objections people often have when encouraged to start their own business is: "Everything has already been tried." That simply isn't true. You have probably seen ideas of your own that were put into practice by someone else—someone else who made all the profits. Although the number of possibilities seems smaller than, say, 50 years ago, the opportunities for new, creative business ideas are still lurking in a veiled reality somewhere, awaiting discovery by an innovative entrepreneur—maybe you.

Skills

You will need certain qualities to succeed, no matter what type of business you choose to start.

1. You must be willing to take risks ➤P. 5◄. This doesn't mean being reckless; it means being comfortable with trying things that could possible fail. It means feeling that you control your own fate—that you affect circumstances at least as much as they affect you.
2. You must be able to see the possibilities in new ways of doing things. You need to be able to see the big picture with both creativity and practicality. An entrepreneur cannot be too set in the old ways of doing things—or of perceiving reality.
3. You need to be a self-starter—someone who doesn't need to have others tell you what to do and when. An entrepreneur should be motivated. Getting up in the morning should be exciting and challenging rather than threatening or depressing.
4. You need to be ambitious and competitive. Entrepreneurs often have to work hard and long hours, especially in the first few years in business. A successful entrepreneur sees himself or herself as a winner and *expects* to win. You also need the health and physical stamina to work long hours day after day.
5. You need to be someone who is not easily discouraged. Many successful businesspeople have experienced setback after setback, but they refuse to see setbacks as failures. An entrepreneur should see setbacks as lessons that won't have to be learned again.

Career Paths

Entrepreneurs get started in many ways. One way is to purchase an existing business. Another is to get involved with a franchise operation. Still another is to create an original idea and develop it on your own. Whatever starting point you choose, remember that entrepreneurship usually offers rewards that are commensurate with the energy you are willing to put into the enterprise. Beyond that, the career path is up to you, the entrepreneur.

SOME POSSIBLE POSITIONS FOR WOULD-BE ENTREPRENEURS

OPPORTUNITY	EARNINGS	INVESTMENT	TASKS AND RESPONSIBILITIES/ CAREER PATH	GROWTH POSSIBILITIES
Home-based, owner-run businesses	Low at first, but great potential.	Will vary; usually very low compared with other entrepreneurial ventures.	Bookkeeping, marketing, customer relations, organization of business. Must be self-motivated and able to see opportunities.	Home-based businesses promise to be a fast-growing trend.
Franchising	Considerably higher than nonfranchise operations from the first month of operation.	Varies roughly from $10,000 to several million, depending on size and scope of franchise.	Most franchisors provide considerable training and support for the beginning of operations. Owner must accept less freedom, but trades that for a greater chance of success. Opportunities in fast foods, office backup, auto repair, and many others.	Franchising will continue to be popular. One of 12 businesses is a franchise.
Small-business consultant	Earnings vary greatly, based on number of contacts and ability to market the service.	Can work for large consulting firms and thus not actually be in business. Operating on one's own; very little investment necessary.	Act as adviser to businesses in various stages of success or failure. A degree in business will help your credibility greatly. Should have a background of both experience and education. Eventually should have master's degree in business (MBA).	The demands for consultants will continue to grow, especially in the areas of international business and high technology.
Franchise director	Usually depends on the number of franchises in the territory and the size and scope of the overall operation.	Once on its feet, your business can grow using mostly the investment of others (franchisees).	Provide direction for the franchisee, provide training, and help the franchisee become successful. Many franchisors start by working first for another franchise to learn the strategies necessary for success.	Franchising will continue to be popular.

Maria F. Escamilla's Cristina's Cake Design

Name: Maria F. Escamilla

Age: 34

Position/title: Owner/Marketing/Sales Manager

Salary range: $20,000

Time in this position: 2½ years

Major factors in the decision to start your own business: I am a risk-taker

Company name: Cristina's Cake Design

Company's Web address: not available

Company description: We specialize in wedding cakes and cakes for any occasion.

Job description: I develop packages and proposals for new, current, and prospective customers.

Career paths: I always have the feeling of going beyond, the extra mile. I was a manager at a small company and then decided to open my own business.

Ideal next job: Make the business grow and maybe in the long run, start a franchise or open another one.

Best part of your job: The freedom of using my ideas and talent to make the business grow.

Worst part of your job: Being the owner is a great risk and responsibility, therefore, the extra time and effort required are bigger than being just an employee.

Educational background: I obtained my Associate's Degree in business from Palm Beach Community College in December 2002. At this time, I am pursuing my bachelor's in business management and two minors in marketing and advertising from Florida Atlantic University.

Favorite course: Marketing, Introduction to Business

Best course for your career: Marketing and Advertising

Recommended by Susan Thompson, Palm Beach Community College

Chapter 7

Management, Leadership, and Employee Empowerment

Learning Goals

After you have read and studied this chapter, you should be able to

1. Explain how the changes that are occurring in the business environment are affecting the management function.
2. Describe the four functions of management.
3. Relate the planning process and decision making to the accomplishment of company goals.
4. Describe the organizing function of management.
5. Explain the differences between leaders and managers, and describe the various leadership styles.
6. Summarize the five steps of the control function of management.

www.sirlinksalot.net/oprah

Getting to Know Oprah Winfrey: Businesswoman and TV Personality

Her name was supposed to be Orpah, after the daughter-in-law of Naomi in the Bible. It turned out that her name was spelled wrong on her birth certificate, so it became Oprah. Now Oprah is much more famous than Orpah. In fact, Oprah Winfrey is one of the most famous women in the world. She was born and reared in Mississippi. When she was young, she lived in a home with no electricity or running water. Educated in Mississippi, she began her TV career in Baltimore, Maryland. The station bosses wanted her to change her hair, nose, and just about everything else. Not surprisingly, she wanted very much to leave Baltimore and do the morning Chicago show. She applied for the job, and not only did they hire her, but they let Oprah be Oprah. The rest, as they say, is history.

Oprah's biggest source of wealth is Harpo, Inc. (*Harpo* is *Oprah* spelled backward). The company is worth about $575 million. The *Oprah Winfrey Show* reaches about 22 million viewers and is the number one daytime talk show in the United States. *O*, the Oprah magazine, has over 2.5 million readers and was the most successful magazine launch ever.

So, what is Oprah's management style? How does she stay so successful? If you were to ask Oprah what her management style is, she would hesitate to say because she just tries to be herself and trusts others to manage her affairs. In many ways, Oprah displays the characteristics of today's progressive managers. She is more a leader than a manager. She sets the tone and direction of her enterprises. She is flexible and sees opportunities as they arise. She doesn't believe much in long-range planning but is quick to seize an opportunity when it comes. Her message is "You are responsible for your own life." Few people model that belief system better than Oprah herself. Although Oprah tends to use a manage-by-instinct style herself, she works closely with others—like Jeff Jacobs, the president of Harpo—who have a more traditional managerial style.

In many ways, Oprah displays the characteristics of today's progressive managers. She is more a leader than a manager. She sets the tone and direction of her enterprises. She is flexible and sees opportunities as they arise.

Harpo, Inc., has about 220 employees (68 percent are women). Pay and benefits are exceptional, so her employees are pretty loyal. While Oprah enables others to make operational decisions, she is very involved in the content of her shows and her magazine. She reads every word in the magazine before it comes out and looks closely at every photo.

Oprah has donated 10 percent of her annual income to charity most of her adult life. Most of her giving is done anonymously. She focuses on three causes: women, children, and education. In everything she does, Oprah's goal is to do better. Her rise to success has been so rapid that she hasn't had much time to sit down and create a vision for her future, but she has had an internal vision that has suited her well so far.

In this chapter, you will read about management and the changes occurring in that area. Like Oprah, most managers today are flexible and open to new ideas. They see opportunity and act much faster than they did in the past. They tend to give their workers more responsibility and authority and act more like leaders (visionaries) than hands-on managers who tell people what to do and how to do it.

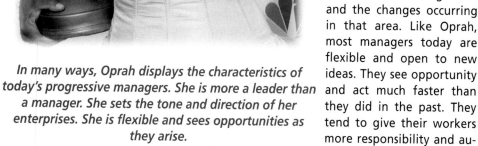

Sources: Diane Brady, "Can Oprah Keep 'Em Glued to the Glossy Pages?" *Business Week*, April 18, 2000; Patricia Sellers, "The Business of Being Oprah," *Fortune*, April 1, 2001, pp. 50 ff.; and "Mel's Useless Trivia Center," at www.angelfire.com, February 2003.

Managerial Challenges

The business scandals of the early 2000s put managers under as much scrutiny as they faced at the end of the 19th century, when they were criticized as "robber barons" because of their questionable competitive tactics.[1] Responding to public criticism adds new challenges to already pressure-filled jobs.[2]

Another current source of pressure on managers is the constant change occurring in most industries.[3] For example, THQ Inc., an interactive entertainment publisher, was recently listed as the third fastest growing company in America. THQ used to stand for Toy Head-Quarters, reflecting the company's earlier days as a toy manufacturer. Today THQ focuses exclusively on developing and publishing video games.[4] In a little more than five years, it went from 43 employees to 300. It is the fourth largest video game maker behind Nintendo, Sony PlayStation, and Electronic Arts. The company went from a small informal group of workers who knew each other well and communicated freely to a larger corporation in which knowledge-sharing is a real problem. Such rapid change makes it more important than ever to have a clear goal that enables a company to stay focused.[5]

The need to manage change has become increasingly important in light of today's emphasis on speed in the global marketplace. Global competition is just a click away. National borders mean much less now than ever before, and cooperation and integration among companies have greatly increased.

As we noted in Chapter 1, the acceleration of technological change has increased the need for a new breed of worker, one who is more educated and more skilled than workers in the past. These new workers (sometimes called knowledge workers) demand more freedom of operation and different managerial styles. The increasing diversity of the workforce is creating additional challenges. Furthermore, because the workforce is becoming more educated and self-directed, many managerial jobs are being eliminated. The corporate term for this is *downsizing* or *rightsizing,* but for the managers, a better term would be *shocking loss of jobs and income.*

Maine is a state full of trees: birch, maple, ash, and oak. It has many small, family-owned firms that make products like clothes pins, dowels, and popsicle sticks. However, many such firms have closed because of competition from less expensive labor in other countries. One of those firms is C.B. Cummings & Sons. A few years ago, Cummings had 200 employees and sales of more than $7 million. What can businesses like Cummings do to recapture markets from foreign competition?

Managers' Roles Are Changing

Managers must practice the art of getting things done through organizational resources (e.g., workers, financial resources, information, and equipment). At one time, managers were called bosses, and their job consisted of telling people what to do and watching over them to be sure they did it. Bosses tended to reprimand those who didn't do things correctly and generally acted stern. Many managers still behave that way. Perhaps you've witnessed such behavior.

Today, management is becoming more progressive. Many managers are being educated to guide, train, support, motivate, and coach employees rather than to tell them what to do. Managers of high-tech firms realize that workers often know much more about technology than they do. Thus, most modern managers emphasize teamwork and cooperation rather than discipline and order giving.[6] Managers in some high-tech firms and in progressive firms of all kinds tend to be friendly and generally treat employees as partners rather than unruly workers; many even dress more casually than before.

In the past, a worker would expect to work for the same company for many years, maybe even a lifetime. Similarly, companies would hire people and keep them for a long time. Today, many companies don't hesitate to lay off employees, and employees don't hesitate to leave if their needs are not being met. Traditional long-term contracts between management and employees—and the accompanying trust—are often no longer there. This increases the difficulty of the management task because managers must earn the trust of their employees, which includes rewarding them and finding other ways to encourage them to stay in the firm.[7]

In general, management is experiencing a revolution. Managers in the future are likely to be working in teams and to be assuming completely new roles in the firm. We'll discuss these roles and the differences between managers and leaders in detail later in the chapter.

What this means for you and other graduates of tomorrow is that management will demand a new kind of person: a skilled communicator and team player as well as a planner, coordinator, organizer, and supervisor. These trends will be addressed in the next few chapters to help you decide whether management is the kind of career you would like.

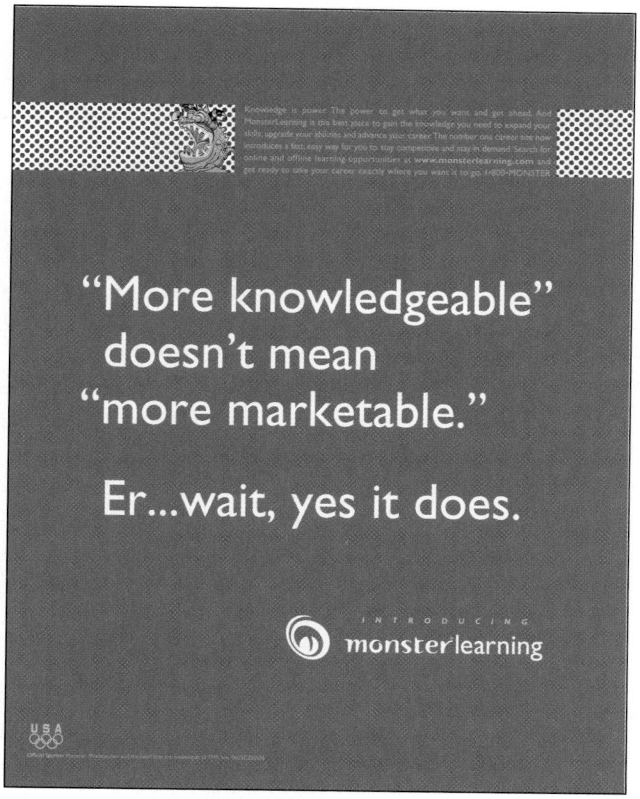

Many of today's workers are called "knowledge workers" because they have the education and skill to compete with companies anywhere in the world. Much of that learning comes from community colleges, universities, and online learning centers of all kinds. What skills will make you more competitive in tomorrow's job market?

FUNCTIONS OF MANAGEMENT

Well-known management consultant Peter Drucker says managers give direction to their organizations, provide leadership, and decide how to use organizational resources to accomplish goals. Such descriptions give you some idea of what managers do. In addition to those tasks, managers today must deal with conflict resolution, create trust in an atmosphere where trust has been badly shaken, and help create balance between work lives and family lives.[8] Managers must also effectively and efficiently use organizational resources such as buildings, equipment, and supplies. Managers look at the big picture, and their decisions make a major difference in organizations. The following definition of management provides the outline of this chapter: **Management** is the process used to accomplish organizational goals through planning, organizing, leading, and controlling people and other organizational resources (see Figure 7.1 on p. 214).

Planning includes anticipating trends and determining the best strategies and tactics to achieve organizational goals and objectives. One of those objectives is to please customers. The trend today is to have planning teams to help monitor the environment, find business opportunities, and watch for challenges. Planning is a key management function because the other functions depend heavily on having a good plan.

Organizing includes designing the structure of the organization and creating conditions and systems in which everyone and everything work together to achieve the organization's goals and objectives. Many of today's organizations are being designed around the customer. The idea is to design the firm so that everyone is working to please the customer at a profit. Thus, organizations must remain flexible and adaptable because customer needs change, and organizations must either change along with them or risk losing their business. For example, traditional bookstores had to go on the Internet to keep from losing business to Amazon.com and other Internet booksellers.

management
The process used to accomplish organizational goals through planning, organizing, leading, and controlling people and other organizational resources.

planning
A management function that includes anticipating trends and determining the best strategies and tactics to achieve organizational goals and objectives.

organizing
A management function that includes designing the structure of the organization and creating conditions and systems in which everyone and everything work together to achieve the organization's goals and objectives.

FIGURE 7.1

WHAT MANAGERS DO

Some modern managers perform all of these tasks with the full cooperation and participation of workers. Empowering employees means allowing them to participate more fully in decision making.

Planning
- Setting organizational goals.
- Developing strategies to reach those goals.
- Determining resources needed.
- Setting precise standards.

Organizing
- Allocating resources, assigning tasks, and establishing procedures for accomplishing goals.
- Preparing a structure (organization chart) showing lines of authority and responsibility.
- Recruiting, selecting, training, and developing employees.
- Placing employees where they'll be most effective.

Leading
- Guiding and motivating employees to work effectively to accomplish organizational goals and objectives.
- Giving assignments.
- Explaining routines.
- Clarifying policies.
- Providing feedback on performance.

Controlling
- Measuring results against corporate objectives.
- Monitoring performance relative to standards.
- Rewarding outstanding performance.
- Taking corrective action when necessary.

leading
Creating a vision for the organization and guiding, training, coaching, and motivating others to work effectively to achieve the organization's goals and objectives.

Leading means creating a vision for the organization and communicating, guiding, training, coaching, and motivating others to work effectively to achieve the organization's goals and objectives. The trend is to empower ➤P. 20◄ employees, giving them as much freedom as possible to become self-directed and self-motivated. This function was once known as directing; that is, telling employees exactly what to do. In many smaller firms, that is still the role of managers. In most large modern firms, however, managers no longer tell people exactly what to do because knowledge workers and others often know how to do their jobs better than the manager. Nonetheless, leadership is necessary to keep employees focused on the right tasks at the right time along with training, coaching, motivating, and the other leadership tasks. One key to success is for workers to trust the decision-making skills of their boss.[9]

controlling
A management function that involves establishing clear standards to determine whether or not an organization is progressing toward its goals and objectives, rewarding people for doing a good job, and taking corrective action if they are not.

Controlling involves establishing clear standards to determine whether an organization is progressing toward its goals and objectives, rewarding people for doing a good job, and taking corrective action if they are not. Basically, it means measuring whether what actually occurs meets the organization's goals.

The four functions just addressed—planning, organizing, leading, and controlling—are the heart of management, so let's explore them in more detail. The process begins with planning; we'll look at that right after the Progress Assessment.

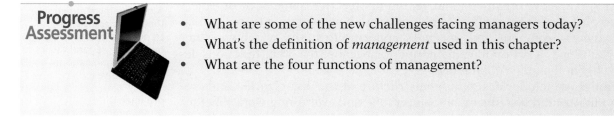

Progress Assessment

- What are some of the new challenges facing managers today?
- What's the definition of *management* used in this chapter?
- What are the four functions of management?

PLANNING: CREATING A VISION BASED ON VALUES

Planning, the first managerial function, involves setting the organizational vision, goals, and objectives. Executives rate planning as the most valuable tool in their workbench—80 percent of respondents to a managerial survey said they used it.[10] Part of the planning process involves the creation of a vision for the organization. A **vision** is more than a goal; it's an encompassing explanation of why the organization exists and where it's trying to head. A vision gives the organization a sense of purpose and a set of values that, together, unite workers in a common destiny. Managing an organization without first establishing a vision can be counterproductive. It's like motivating everyone in a rowboat to get really excited about going somewhere, but not telling them exactly where. As a result, the boat will just keep changing directions rather than speeding toward an agreed-on goal.

vision
An encompassing explanation of why the organization exists and where it's trying to head.

Usually employees work with managers to design a **mission statement,** which is an outline of the organization's fundamental purposes. A meaningful mission statement should address:

mission statement
An outline of the fundamental purposes of an organization.

- The organization's self-concept.
- Company philosophy and goals.
- Long-term survival.
- Customer needs.
- Social responsibility.
- The nature of the company's product or service.

Figure 7.2 contains Starbucks' mission statement. How well does Starbucks address all of the issues listed above?

The mission statement becomes the foundation for setting specific goals and selecting and motivating employees. **Goals** are the broad, long-term accomplishments an organization wishes to attain. Goals need to be mutually agreed on by workers and management. Thus, goal setting is often a team process.

goals
The broad, long-term accomplishments an organization wishes to attain.

Objectives are specific, short-term statements detailing how to achieve the organization's goals. One of your goals for reading this chapter, for example, may be to learn basic concepts of management. An objective you could use to achieve this goal is to answer correctly the chapter's Progress Assessment questions. Objectives must be measurable. For example, you can measure your progress in answering questions by determining what percentage you answer correctly over time.

objectives
Specific, short-term statements detailing how to achieve the organization's goals.

Planning is a continuous process. It's unlikely that a plan that worked yesterday would be successful in today's market. Most planning follows a pattern. The procedure you would follow in planning your life and career is basically the same as that used by businesses for their plans. Planning answers several fundamental questions for businesses:

1. What is the situation now? What is the state of the economy and other environments? What opportunities exist for meeting people's needs?

FIGURE 7.2
STARBUCKS' MISSION STATEMENT

To establish Starbucks as the premier purveyor of the finest coffee in the world while maintaining our uncompromising principles as we grow. The following six guiding principles will help us measure the appropriateness of our decisions:

- Provide a great work environment and treat each other with dignity and respect.
- Embrace diversity as an essential component in the way we do business.
- Apply the highest of standards in excellence to the purchasing, roasting and fresh delivery of our coffee.
- Develop enthusiastically satisfied customers all of the time.
- Contribute positively to our community and our environment.
- Recognize that profitability is essential to our future success.

FIGURE 7.3

SWOT MATRIX

This matrix identifies potential strengths, weaknesses, opportunities, and threats organizations may consider in a SWOT analysis.

Potential Internal **STRENGTHS**	Potential Internal **WEAKNESSES**
• Core competencies in key areas • An acknowledged market leader • Well-conceived functional area strategies • Proven management • Cost advantages • Better advertising campaigns	• No clear strategic direction • Obsolete facilities • Subpar profitability • Lack of managerial depth and talent • Weak market image • Too narrow a product line
Potential External **OPPORTUNITIES** • Ability to serve additional customer groups • Expand product lines • Ability to transfer skills/technology to new products • Falling trade barriers in attractive foreign markets • Complacency among rival firms • Ability to grow due to increases in market demand	Potential External **THREATS** • Entry of lower-cost foreign competitors • Rising sales of substitute products • Slower market growth • Costly regulatory requirements • Vulnerability to recession and business cycles • Changing buyer needs and tastes

What products and customers are most profitable? Why do people buy (or not buy) our products? Who are our major competitors? What threats are they to our business? These questions are part of what is called **SWOT analysis,** which is an analysis of the organization's **s**trengths, **w**eaknesses, **o**pportunities, and **t**hreats. The company begins such a process with an analysis of the business environment in general. Then it identifies strengths and weaknesses. These are internal to the firm and can be studied relatively easily. Finally, as a result of the environmental analysis, it identifies opportunities and threats. These are often external to the firm and cannot always be anticipated. Figure 7.3 lists some of the potential issues companies consider when conducting a SWOT analysis. The Spotlight on Small Business box gives you examples of SWOT analyses in action.

SWOT analysis
A planning tool used to analyze an organization's strengths, weaknesses, opportunities, and threats.

2. Where do we want to go? How much growth do we want? What is our profit goal? What are our social objectives? What are our personal development objectives?
3. How can we get there from here? This is the most important part of planning. It takes four forms: strategic, tactical, operational, and contingency (see Figure 7.4).

strategic planning
The process of determining the major goals of the organization and the policies and strategies for obtaining and using resources to achieve those goals.

Strategic planning determines the major goals of the organization. It provides the foundation for the policies, procedures, and strategies for obtaining and using resources to achieve those goals. In this definition, policies are broad guides to action, and strategies determine the best way to use resources. At the strategic planning stage, the company decides which customers to serve, what products or services to sell, and the geographic areas in which the firm will compete. Often an opportunity will arise that doesn't fit into the strategy. New customers may emerge and new product ideas may be introduced. But if those customers or products don't fit into the long-term strategy, the company can ignore them to maintain a clear focus. Every firm faces unique challenges that influence what the strategic plans must be. Some firms, for example, need to cut costs, while others need to improve performance, and still others need to increase their profits.

In today's rapidly changing environment, strategic planning is becoming more difficult because changes are occurring so fast that plans—even those set

Spotlight on Small Business

www.alumiplate.com

Taking a SWOT at the Competition

David Dayton is the CEO of AlumiPlate, a small metal-coating company in Minneapolis. As part of the company's annual strategic planning process, Dayton did a SWOT analysis. SWOT, remember, stands for strengths, weaknesses, opportunities, and threats. The analysis gave Dayton a few areas to focus on for the next year. For example, he found that one strength of the company was the high barrier to competition; that is, it is not easy to get into the metal-coating business. Dayton also found that the company's proprietary aluminum-coating technology was its best opportunity. A weakness was the company's lack of high-volume production, and a threat was the set of heavy demands on key personnel.

Some other strengths that CEOs like Dayton might look for include special skills, motivations, technology, or financial capacities. Weaknesses may include lack of capital, shortages of skilled workers, or unproven products. Opportunities are positive circumstances that, if exploited, may boost the company's success. They include things like untapped markets, promising customer relationships, and weak competitors. Threats include both clearly visible threats (such as pending regulations) and potential threats (such as new competitors or changes in consumer tastes). Certainly, the emergence of the Internet has proved to be a threat to almost all businesses, from those selling automobiles to those selling zoo equipment. But the chance to go on the Internet and sell products almost anywhere is a real opportunity.

Sources: Mark Henricks, "Analyze This," *Entrepreneur,* June 1999, pp. 72–75; Steve Glickman, "SWOT Analysis Worthwhile," *London Free Press,* September 28, 2002; "Department of Energy Awards $345,000 to the Eight Northern Indian Pueblos Council Community Reuse Organization," *Regulatory Intelligence Data,* August 28, 2002; and Fred L. Fry, Charles R. Stoner and Richard E. Hattwick, *Business: An Integrative Approach,* 3rd Ed. (Burr Ridge, IL.: McGraw-Hill/Irwin, 2004), pp. 300–301.

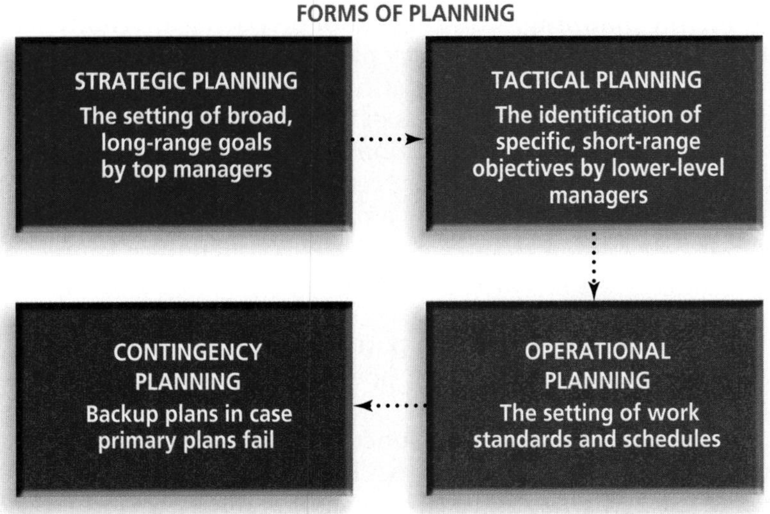

FIGURE 7.4

PLANNING FUNCTIONS

Very few firms bother to make contingency plans. If something changes the market, such companies may be slow to respond. Most organizations do strategic, tactical, and operational planning.

for just months into the future—may soon be obsolete.[11] Therefore, some companies are making shorter-term plans that allow for quick responses to customer needs and requests. The goal is to be flexible and responsive to the market. For example, Yahoo records every click made by every visitor, accumulating some 400 billion pieces of data every day—the equivalent of 800,000 books. Why do Yahoo's managers do it? So they can determine what consumers are interested in and adapt their offerings accordingly.

tactical planning
The process of developing detailed, short-term statements about what is to be done, who is to do it, and how it is to be done.

Tactical planning is the process of developing detailed, short-term statements about what is to be done, who is to do it, and how it is to be done. Tactical planning is normally done by managers or teams of managers at *lower* levels of the organization, whereas strategic planning is done by the *top* managers of

Cities, as well as companies, must do SWOT analyses. One possible threat to cities in the post-9/11/01 environment is that of a "dirty bomb" (made from nuclear waste products). Seattle recognized this new threat and staged this mock attack to see if emergency crews and equipment could handle such a disaster. What new challenges must executives prepare for as a result of potential terrorist attacks?

the firm (e.g., the president and vice presidents of the organization). Tactical planning, for example, involves setting annual budgets and deciding on other details and activities necessary to meet the strategic objectives. If the strategic plan of a truck manufacturer, for example, is to sell more trucks in the South, the tactical plan might be to fund more research of southern truck drivers' wants and needs, and to plan advertising to reach those people.

Operational planning is the process of setting work standards and schedules necessary to implement the company's tactical objectives. Whereas strategic planning looks at the organization as a whole, operational planning focuses on specific supervisors, department managers, and individual employees. The operational plan is the department manager's tool for daily and weekly operations. An operational plan may include, say, the specific dates for certain truck parts to be completed and the quality specifications those parts must meet. You will read about operations management in more detail in Chapter 9.

operational planning
The process of setting work standards and schedules necessary to implement the company's tactical objectives.

contingency planning
The process of preparing alternative courses of action that may be used if the primary plans don't achieve the organization's objectives.

Contingency planning is the process of preparing alternative courses of action that may be used if the primary plans don't achieve the organization's objectives. The economic and competitive environments change so rapidly that it's wise to have alternative plans of action ready in anticipation of such changes. For example, if an organization doesn't meet its sales goals by a certain date, the contingency plan may call for more advertising or a cut in prices at that time. Crisis planning is a part of contingency planning that involves reacting to sudden changes in the environment. For example, almost every firm in New York City had to make sudden changes to adapt to the September 11, 2001, terrorist attack on the World Trade Center. Many cities are now developing plans to respond to potential attacks. You can imagine how important such plans would be to hospitals, the police, and other such organizations.

Planning is a key management function because the other management functions depend on having good plans. Instead of creating detailed strategic plans, the leaders of market-based companies (companies that respond quickly to changes in competition or to other environmental changes) set direction. The idea is to stay flexible, listen to customers, and seize opportunities when they come, whether or not those opportunities were expected. The opportunities, however, must fit into the company's overall goals and objectives or the company could lose its focus. Clearly, then, much of management and planning involves decision making.

Decision Making: Finding the Best Alternative

decision making
Choosing among two or more alternatives.

All management functions involve some kind of decision making. **Decision making** is choosing among two or more alternatives. It sounds easier here than it is in practice. In fact, decision making is the heart of all the management functions. The rational decision-making model is a series of steps managers often follow to make logical, intelligent, and well-founded decisions. These steps can be thought of as the seven Ds of decision making:

1. Define the situation.
2. Describe and collect needed information.
3. Develop alternatives.
4. Develop agreement among those involved.
5. Decide which alternative is best.
6. Do what is indicated (begin implementation).
7. Determine whether the decision was a good one and follow up.

The best decisions are based on sound information. Managers often have computer terminals at their desks so that they can easily retrieve internal records and look up external data of all kinds. But all the data in the world can't replace a creative manager who makes brilliant decisions. Decision making is more an art than a science. It's the one skill most needed by managers and leaders in that all the other functions depend on it.

Sometimes decisions have to be made on the spot—with little information available. Managers must make good decisions in all such circumstances. **Problem solving** is the process of solving the everyday problems that occur. It is less formal than the decision-making process and usually calls for quicker action. Problem-solving teams are made up of two or more workers who are given an assignment to solve a specific problem (e.g., Why are customers not using our service policies?). Problem-solving techniques that companies use include **brainstorming** (i.e., coming up with as many solutions as possible in a short period of time with no censoring of ideas)[12] and **PMI** (i.e., listing all the **p**luses for a solution in one column, all the **m**inuses in another, and the **i**mplications in a third column). For more on these and other tools, see the list of problem-solving analytical techniques on the Mind Tools website at www.psywww.com/mtsite/page2.html.

problem solving
The process of solving the everyday problems that occur. Problem solving is less formal than decision making and usually calls for quicker action.

brainstorming
Coming up with as many solutions to a problem as possible in a short period of time with no censoring of ideas.

PMI
Listing all the pluses for a solution in one column, all the minuses in another, and the implications in a third column.

Progress Assessment

- What's the difference between goals and objectives?
- What does a company analyze when it does a SWOT analysis?
- What's the difference between strategic, tactical, and operational planning?
- What are the seven Ds in decision making?

ORGANIZING: CREATING A UNIFIED SYSTEM

After managers have planned a course of action, they must organize the firm to accomplish their goals.[13] Operationally, organizing means allocating resources (such as funds for various departments), assigning tasks, and establishing procedures for accomplishing the organizational objectives. An **organization chart** is a visual device that shows relationships among people and divides the organization's work; it shows who is accountable for the completion of specific work and who reports to whom. The problems involved in developing an organization structure will be discussed in more detail in Chapter 8. For now, it's important to know that the corporate hierarchy may include top, middle, and first-line managers (see Figure 7.5 on p. 220).

Top management (the highest level of management) consists of the president and other key company executives who develop strategic plans. Terms

organization chart
A visual device that shows relationships among people and divides the organization's work; it shows who is accountable for the completion of specific work and who reports to whom.

top management
Highest level of management, consisting of the president and other key company executives who develop strategic plans.

FIGURE 7.5

LEVELS OF MANAGEMENT

This figure shows the three levels of management. In many firms, there are several levels of middle management. Recently, however, firms have been eliminating middle-level managers because fewer are needed to oversee self-managed teams of employees.

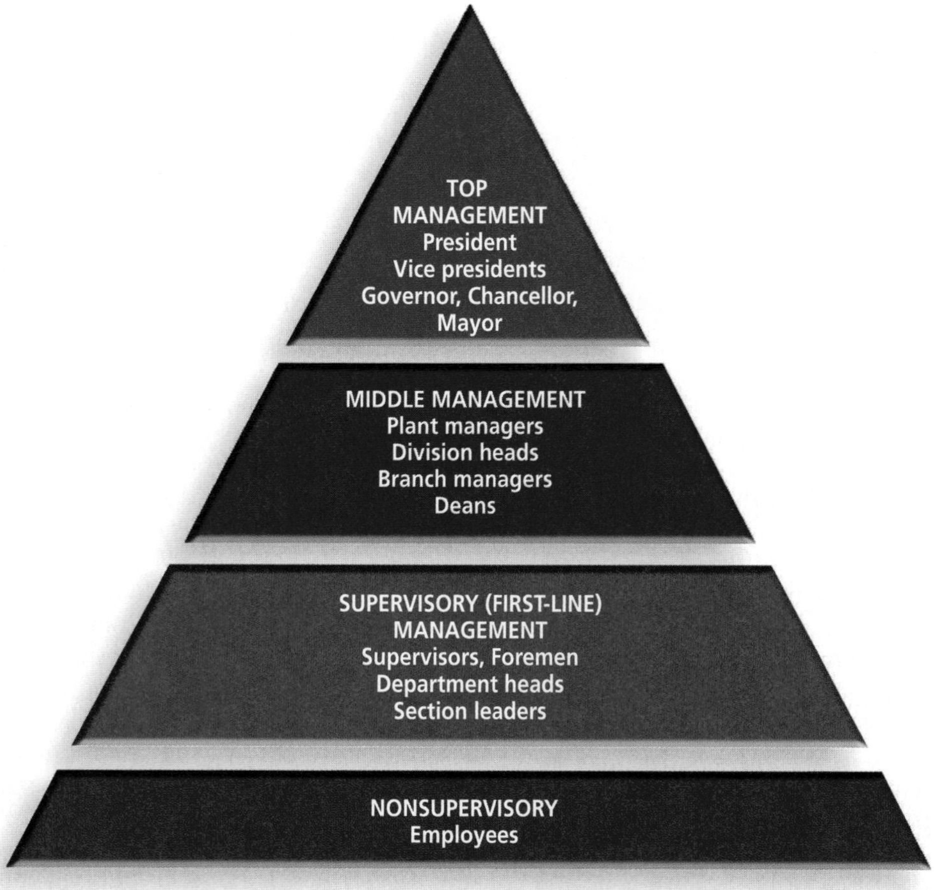

you're likely to see often are chief executive officer (CEO), chief operating officer (COO), chief financial officer (CFO), and chief information officer (CIO) or (in some companies) chief knowledge officer (CKO). The CEO is often the president of the firm and is responsible for all top-level decisions in the firm. CEOs are responsible for introducing change into an organization. The COO is responsible for putting those changes into effect. His or her tasks include structuring work, controlling operations, and rewarding people to ensure that everyone strives to carry out the leader's vision. The CFO is responsible for obtaining funds, planning budgets, collecting funds, and so on. The CIO or CKO is responsible for getting the right information to other managers so they can make correct decisions.

middle management
The level of management that includes general managers, division managers, and branch and plant managers who are responsible for tactical planning and controlling.

Middle management includes general managers, division managers, and branch and plant managers (in colleges, deans and department heads) who are responsible for tactical planning and controlling. Many firms have eliminated some middle managers through downsizing because fewer are needed when employees work in self-managed teams (discussed later in this chapter).

supervisory management
Managers who are directly responsible for supervising workers and evaluating their daily performance.

Supervisory management includes those who are directly responsible for supervising workers and evaluating their daily performance; they're often known as first-line managers (or supervisors) because they're the first level above workers.

Tasks and Skills at Different Levels of Management

Few people are trained to be good managers. Usually a person learns how to be a skilled accountant or sales representative or production-line worker, and then—because of his or her skill—is selected to be a manager. The tendency is

Frank and Ernest

What title would the person at the top of an organization chart have? What about the people at the bottom? Who are the people in the middle? Why would a company need such a chart? If this were a food chain, would you have the skills to move toward the top?

for such managers to become deeply involved in showing others how to do things, helping them, supervising them, and generally being very active in the operating task.

The further up the managerial ladder a person moves, the less important his or her original job skills become. At the top of the ladder, the need is for people who are visionaries, planners, organizers, coordinators, communicators, morale builders, and motivators. Figure 7.6 shows that a manager must have three categories of skills:

1. **Technical skills** involve the ability to perform tasks in a specific discipline (such as selling a product or developing software) or department (such as marketing or information systems).
2. **Human relations skills** involve communication and motivation; they enable managers to work through and with people. Such skills also include those associated with leadership, coaching, morale building, delegating, training and development, and help and supportiveness.
3. **Conceptual skills** involve the ability to picture the organization as a whole and the relationships among its various parts. Conceptual skills are needed in planning, organizing, controlling, systems development, problem analysis, decision making, coordinating, and delegating.

technical skills
Skills that involve the ability to perform tasks in a specific discipline or department.

human relations skills
Skills that involve communication and motivation; they enable managers to work through and with people.

conceptual skills
Skills that involve the ability to picture the organization as a whole and the relationship among its various parts.

Looking at Figure 7.6, you'll notice that first-line managers need to be skilled in all three areas. However, most of their time is spent on technical and human relations tasks (assisting operating personnel, giving directions, etc.). First-line managers spend little time on conceptual tasks. Top managers, in contrast, need to use few technical skills. Instead, almost all of their time is devoted to human relations and conceptual tasks. A person who is competent at

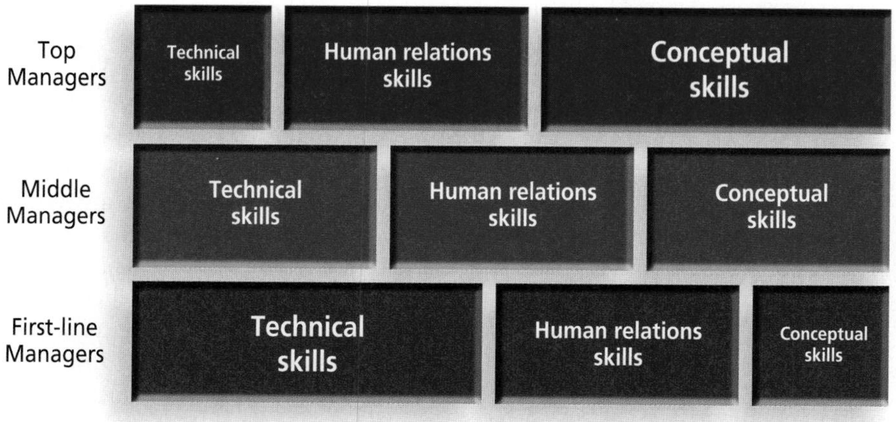

FIGURE 7.6

SKILLS NEEDED AT VARIOUS LEVELS OF MANAGEMENT

All managers need human relation skills. At the top, managers need strong conceptual skills and rely less on technical skills. First-line managers need strong technical skills and rely less on conceptual skills. Middle managers need to have a balance between technical and conceptual skills.

a low level of management may not be competent at higher levels, and vice versa. The skills needed are different at different levels.

The Trend toward Self-Managed Teams

One trend in the United States, especially in larger firms, is toward placing workers on cross-functional teams composed of people from various departments of the firm, such as marketing, finance, and distribution. Many of these teams are self-managed. This means that more planning, organizing, and controlling are being delegated to lower-level managers. What does this trend mean for managers and leaders in the 21st century? It means developing and training employees to assume greater responsibility in planning, teamwork, and problem solving.

Teamwork usually aids communication, improves cooperation, reduces internal competition, and maximizes the talents of all employees on a project. Companies such as BellSouth, Qwest Communications, and Ryder Systems use cross-functional teams to explore ways to make their companies operate faster and become more responsive to customers and other stakeholders, such as suppliers and the community. You'll read more about such teams in Chapter 8.

The Stakeholder-Oriented Organization

A dominating question of the past 20 years or so has been how to best organize a firm to respond to the needs of customers and other stakeholders. Remember, stakeholders ➤P. 6◄ include anyone who's affected by the organization and its policies and products. That includes employees, customers, suppliers, dealers, environmental groups, and the surrounding communities. The consensus seems to be that smaller organizations are more responsive than larger organizations. Therefore, many large firms are being restructured into smaller, more customer-focused units.

The point is that companies are no longer organizing to make it easy for managers to have control. Instead, they're organizing so that customers have the greatest influence. The change to a customer orientation is being aided by technology ➤P. 15◄. For example, establishing a dialogue with customers on the Internet enables some firms to work closely with customers and respond quickly to their wants and needs.[14] The Dealing with Change box discusses Target's efforts to listen to its customers.

Texas Instruments is a Dallas-based technology firm that makes extensive use of self-managed teams in its plant in Malaysia. What kinds of issues might emerge as companies try to form self-managed teams in other countries?

There's no way an organization can provide high-quality goods ➤P. 25◄ and services ➤P. 26◄ to customers unless suppliers provide world-class parts and materials with which to work. Thus, managers have to establish close relationships with suppliers.[15] To make the entire system work, similar relationships have to be established with those organizations that sell directly to consumers—retailers.

In the past, the goal of the organization function in the firm was to clearly specify who does what within the firm. Today, the organizational task is much more complex because firms are forming partnerships, joint ventures, and other arrangements that make it necessary to organize the whole system, that is, several firms working together, often across national boundaries.[16] One organization working alone is often not as effective as many organizations working together. Creating a unified system out of multiple

Dealing with Change

www.target.com

Is Target on Target for the Future?

Target is certainly one of the success stories of the recent past. It has the reputation that Sears, Kmart, and other large retailers once had. As the competition slows, Target seems to be finding the right path to success. For one thing, Target has found a market niche for its online sales. Stores are good for buying items for yourself, but websites are often better for finding gifts for someone else. Therefore, Target.com aims its website at people who need to buy gifts. One fall, for example, Target sold thousands of "Student Survival Kits" to parents and other relatives of returning students. Some 22 percent of the site's sales come from bridal and baby registries. Responding quickly to such market opportunities can keep Target in the vanguard. Soon it will add its sister stores, Mervyn's and Marshall Field, to its website. Target is also on Amazon.com's website. In short, Target seems to be on target when it comes to adapting to the Internet challenge. In this area, Target's success seems comparable to that of Wal-Mart.

What about the challenge of Wal-Mart in the area of superstores? Here Target has been less successful. Target's superstores are less productive than its regular stores. Conventional Targets average $635 per square foot in annual sales, while SuperTargets average only $500. Furthermore, groceries in the SuperTargets drag down profit margins. Target is estimated to make about 9 percent profit on nonfood items and only 2 percent on food items. Was it a mistake to go after Wal-Mart's supercenters? Wal-Mart has its own grocery warehouses, giving it a cost advantage. Target could create its own distribution centers to become more competitive, but that is dangerous ground. Such centers are costly. Adapting to change is never easy, but adapting to Wal-Mart is truly daunting. Target has its own image and its own customer base. Sometimes change is good and sometimes it's not. Listening to its customer base will enable Target to expand and profit. That may mean sticking to what Target knows best and not venturing out into Wal-Mart's strengths. It may not. That's the future challenge for Target's managers.

Sources: Chana R. Schoenberger, "Bull's Eye," *Forbes*, September 2, 2002, p. 76; Kemp Powers, "Kitchen-Sink Retailing," *Forbes*, September 2, 2002, p. 78; and Jim Collins, "Bigger, Better, Faster," *Fast Company*, June 2003, pp. 74–78.

organizations will be one of the greatest management challenges of the 21st century.[17] We'll discuss this issue in more depth in Chapter 8.

Staffing: Getting and Keeping the Right People

staffing
A management function that includes hiring, motivating, and retaining the best people available to accomplish the company's objectives.

Staffing involves recruiting, hiring, motivating, and retaining the best people available to accomplish the company's objectives. Recruiting good employees has always been an important part of organizational success. Today, however, it is critical, especially in the Internet and high-tech areas. At most high-tech companies, like IBM, Sony, and Microsoft, the primary capital equipment is brainpower. One day the company may be selling books (Amazon.com) and suddenly an employee comes up with the idea of selling music or having auctions online or whatever. Any of these opportunities may prove profitable in the long run. The opportunities seem almost limitless. Thus the firms with the most innovative and creative workers can go from start-up to major competitor with leading companies in just a year or two.

John Featherstone, U.S. employment director at Sun Microsystems, says that his company hires about 6,000 people a year, and competition among companies for the best new hires is incredibly intense. To win, Sun has developed an online recruiting program. The company pays bonuses of $1,500 to current employees who provide good leads for new workers. Sun's home page is easy to use and has an employment button that puts employment data a mouse click away.

Once they are hired, good people must be retained. Many people are not willing to work at companies unless they are treated well and get fair pay. Employees may leave to find companies that offer them a better balance between work and home. Staffing is becoming a greater part of each manager's assignment, and all managers need to cooperate with human resource management to win and keep good workers.

Staffing is such an important subject that we cannot cover it fully in this chapter. It is enough for now to understand that staffing is becoming more and more important as companies search for skilled and talented workers.[18] All of Chapter 11 will be devoted to human resource issues, including staffing. All managers must also become more aware of diversity, another human resource area, because of today's diverse workforce. We'll explore that important topic next.

managing diversity
Building systems and a climate that unite different people in a common pursuit without undermining their individual strengths.

Managing Diversity

Managing diversity means building systems and a climate that unite different people in a common pursuit without undermining their individual strengths. Diversity includes but also goes beyond differences in race, gender, ethnicity, sexual orientation, abilities, and religious affiliation. At least a third of Silicon Valley's scientists and engineers are immigrants. The mixing of people is central to the success of businesses in that area.

Kodak says in this ad that "Diversity determines a company's success." Diversity helps the company to adapt to the needs of its customers, suppliers, employees, and the community. What advantages and disadvantages do you see in such diversity programs?

Diversity determines a company's success.
Eastman Kodak Company is committed to becoming a truly diverse corporation. Embracing the ideals of diversity enables us to better meet the needs of our customers, employees, suppliers, and the communities in which we live and work. All of which ensures our continued success in the global marketplace.
Picture what we can do together!
Kodak
Interested suppliers please go to: www.kodak.com/go/supplierdiversity
© Eastman Kodak Company, 2002

If people are to work on teams, they have to learn to work together with people who have different personalities, different priorities, and different lifestyles. In the past, firms tended to look for people much like those who were already working at the firm. Today, such recruiting would probably be illegal, and it certainly would be less than optimal.

Managing and working with a diverse group of people often causes difficulties in a firm. For example, young people don't always understand the traditional values and the work ethic of older workers. Nonetheless, research has shown that heterogeneous (mixed) groups are often more productive than homogeneous (similar) groups in the workplace. Men and women, young and old, and all other mixes of people not only can learn to work together but also can do so successfully. Furthermore, it is often quite profitable to have employees who match the diversity of customers so that the company as a whole can understand cultural differences and match them effectively.[19] Managers must learn how to work with people from many different cultures, and many will also be asked to work in foreign countries. The more you can do now to learn other languages and work with diverse cultural groups, the better off you'll be when you become a manager.

Managing diversity can also mean working with minority business enterprises (MBEs) to maintain a strong and diverse supplier network. Companies such as the Chase Manhattan Bank, Ford Motor Company, JCPenney, and Pitney Bowes have built strong relationships with minority suppliers. American Airlines has demonstrated its awareness of the need to manage diversity by running ads that say, "At American, we believe our success comes from diversity. If you are a diversified supplier and would like to explore opportunities with us, we'd like to hear from you." Likewise, aircraft manufacturer Boeing says in one of its ads, "Working with women- and minority-owned companies, we have been able to build business with superior products."

LEADING: PROVIDING CONTINUOUS VISION AND VALUES

In business literature there's a trend toward separating the notion of management from that of leadership. One person might be a good manager but not a good leader. Another might be a good leader without being a good manager. One difference between managers and leaders is that managers strive to produce order and stability whereas leaders embrace and manage change. Leadership is creating a vision for others to follow, establishing corporate values and ethics, and transforming the way the organization does business in order to improve its effectiveness and efficiency. Good leaders motivate workers and create the environment for workers to motivate themselves. *Management is the carrying out of the leadership's vision.* Can you see how Oprah Winfrey (the subject of this chapter's opening profile) might be considered more of a leader than a manager?

Now and in the future, all organizations will need leaders who can supply the vision as well as the moral and ethical foundation for growth. You don't have to be a manager to be a leader. All employees can lead. That is, any employee can contribute to producing order and stability and can motivate others to work well. All employees can also add to a company's ethical environment and report ethical lapses when they occur.

Organizations will need workers and managers who share a vision and know how to get things done cooperatively. The workplace is changing from an environment in which a few dictate the rules to others to an environment in which all employees work together to accomplish common goals. Furthermore, managers must lead by doing, not just by saying.

In summary, leaders must:

- **Communicate a vision and rally others around that vision.** In doing so, the leader should be openly sensitive to the concerns of followers, give them responsibility, and win their trust.
- **Establish corporate values.** These values include a concern for employees, for customers, for the environment, and for the quality of the company's products. When companies set their business goals today, they're defining the values of the company as well.
- **Promote corporate ethics.** Ethics ➤P. 102◀ include an unfailing demand for honesty and an insistence that everyone in the company gets treated fairly. That's why we stress ethical decision making throughout this text. Many businesspeople are now making the news by giving away huge amounts to charity, thus setting a model of social concern for their employees and others (See the Making Ethical Decisions box on p. 226).
- **Embrace change.** A leader's most important job may be to transform the way the company does business so that it's more effective (does things better) and efficient (uses fewer resources to accomplish the same objectives).

Leadership Styles

Nothing has challenged researchers in the area of management more than the search for the "best" leadership traits, behaviors, or styles. Thousands of studies have been made just to find leadership traits, that is, characteristics that make leaders different from other people. Intuitively, you would conclude about the same thing that researchers have found: Leadership traits are hard to pin down. In fact, results of most studies on leadership have been neither statistically significant nor reliable. Some leaders are well groomed and tactful, www.pgdc.net/TCFI

Making Ethical Decisions

Leading by Example

Many business leaders believe that part of business success involves sharing the benefits of what we earn with others. Such a rule is not written into business ethics codes; it has been and will remain a moral obligation of being a citizen and a fellow human being. At least, that's what many businesspeople believe. Therefore, many businesspeople are quite generous with what they give to others. John Huntsman, for example, is in the chemical business. He also has both mouth and prostate cancer. To help others with similar problems, Huntsman gave $225 million to the Huntsman Cancer Institute in Salt Lake City. Similarly, Bill Gates has created a fund of more than $24 billion to save the poorest from disease.

Dan David made a fortune inventing, patenting, developing, and marketing photographic technologies, including automatic photo booths. He set up a $100 million endowment to give away million-dollar grants to people who, among other things, "help people live better today." The winners of the grants must give $100,000 to young researchers who, in turn, are encouraged to help others.

Robert Krieble made millions as the founder of Loctite, which produces high-tech sealants, adhesives, and coatings. When people asked him why he drove a Ford Fiesta, he said, "The less money I spend on myself, the more I have to give away." Home Depot chairman Bernard Marcus has pledged some $850 million to the Marcus Foundation, which supports education and the disabled.

Giving their money to others is not new to businesspeople. Steel magnate Andrew Carnegie gave away the equivalent of $3.5 billion in today's dollars to libraries and other cultural institutions. By being so generous with their money, such business leaders set an example for their employees and for the rest of us.

Are you willing to make a commitment now to donate 10 percent of your after-tax income to charitable causes? What would be the consequence of such a decision?

Sources: Phyllis Berman, "A Motivated Philanthropist," *Forbes*, September 30, 2002, pp. 90–94; Geoffrey Cowley, "Bill's Biggest Bet Yet," *Newsweek*, February 4, 2002, pp. 44–52; Frances D'Emilio, "Sowing the Seed of Genius," *Washington Times*, July 8, 2002, p. A15; and "Biology and Bill Gates," *Business Week*, May 5, 2003, pp. 76–77.

---

while others are unkempt and abrasive—yet the latter may be just as effective as the former.

Just as there's no one set of traits that can describe a leader, there's also no one style of leadership that works best in all situations. Even so, we can look at a few of the most commonly recognized leadership styles and see how they may be effective (see Figure 7.7):

autocratic leadership
Leadership style that involves making managerial decisions without consulting others.

1. **Autocratic leadership** involves making managerial decisions without consulting others. Such a style is effective in emergencies and when absolute followership is needed—for example, when fighting fires. Autocratic leadership is also effective sometimes with new, relatively unskilled workers who need clear direction and guidance. Coach Phil Jackson used an autocratic leadership style to take the Los Angeles Lakers to three consecutive National Basketball Association championships. By following his leadership, a group of highly skilled individuals became a winning team.

participative (democratic) leadership
Leadership style that consists of managers and employees working together to make decisions..

2. **Participative (democratic) leadership** consists of managers and employees working together to make decisions. Research has found that employee participation in decisions may not always increase effectiveness, but it usually increases job satisfaction. Many progressive organizations are highly successful at using a democratic style of leadership that values traits such as flexibility, good listening skills, and empathy.

   Organizations that have successfully used this style include Wal-Mart, FedEx, IBM, Cisco, AT&T, and most smaller firms. At meetings

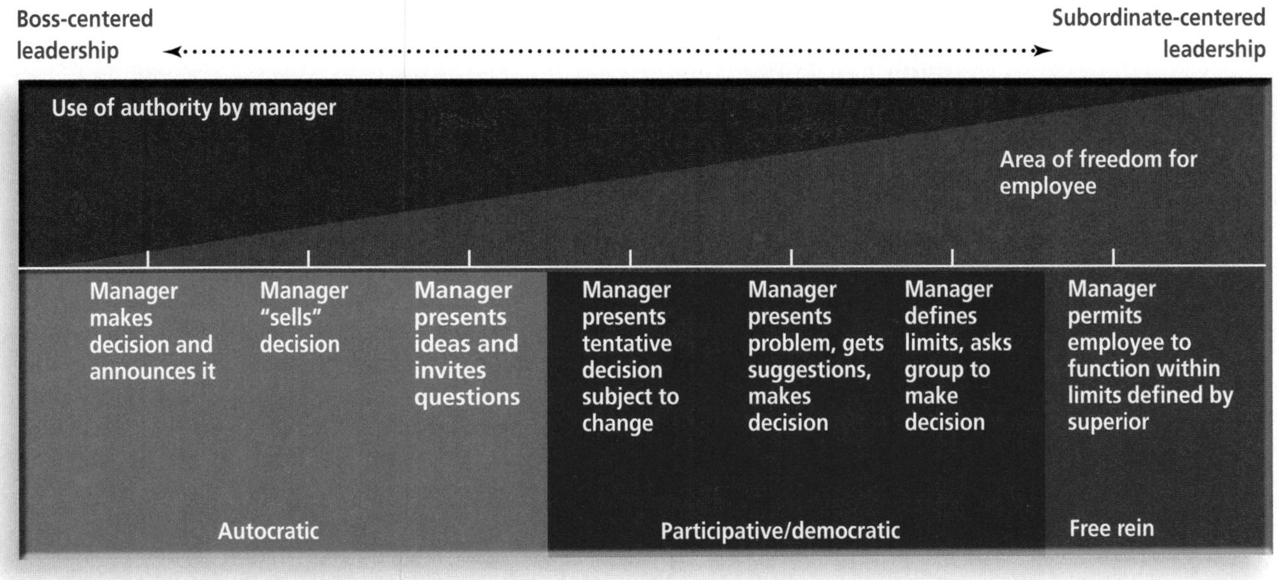

FIGURE 7.7

VARIOUS LEADERSHIP STYLES

Source: Reprinted by permission of the *Harvard Business Review.* An exhibit from "How to Choose a Leadership Pattern" by Robert Tannenbaum and Warren Schmidt (May/June 1973). Copyright © 1973 by the President and Fellows of Harvard College, all rights reserved.

in such firms, employees discuss management issues and resolve those issues together in a democratic manner. That is, everyone has some opportunity to contribute to decisions. Many firms have placed meeting rooms throughout the company and allow all employees the right to request a meeting. The Dealing with Change box explores this managerial style at Cisco.

3. **Free-rein leadership** involves managers setting objectives and employees being relatively free to do whatever it takes to accomplish those objectives. In certain organizations, where managers deal with doctors, engineers, or other professionals, often the most successful leadership style is free rein. The traits needed by managers in such organizations include warmth, friendliness, and understanding. More and more firms are adopting this style of leadership with at least some of their employees.

free-rein leadership Leadership style that involves managers setting objectives and employees being relatively free to do whatever it takes to accomplish those objectives

Individual leaders rarely fit neatly into just one of these categories. Researchers illustrate leadership as a continuum with varying amounts of employee participation, ranging from purely boss-centered leadership to subordinate-centered leadership.

Which leadership style is best? Research tells us that successful leadership depends largely on what the goals and values of the firm are, who's being led, and in what situations. It also supports the notion that any leadership style, ranging from autocratic to free-rein, may be successful depending on the people and the situation. In fact, a manager may use a variety of leadership styles, depending on a given situation. A manager may be autocratic but friendly with a new trainee; democratic with an experienced employee who has many good ideas that can only be fostered by a flexible manager who's a good listener; and free-rein with a trusted, long-term supervisor who probably knows more about operations than the manager does.

There's no such thing as a leadership trait that is effective in all situations, or a leadership style that always works best. A truly successful leader has the ability to use the leadership style most appropriate to the situation and the employees involved (see Figure 7.8).

Dealing with Change

www.cisco.com

John Chambers Uses Participative Management at Cisco

Few managers have faced more perils of the stock market than John Chambers of Cisco Systems. Not too long ago, people considered John Chambers to be the number one business leader in the United States. He's the CEO of Cisco Systems. Despite the stock market's ups and downs, Cisco keeps chugging along. Its fiscal-year revenues in 2002 were $4.8 billion, up from $4.3 billion in 2001. Cisco's stock could make a big comeback if and when the stock market turns upward again.

What does Cisco do? Cisco changes so quickly that one cannot easily define everything that it does. Put simply, it is involved in computer networking—providing the equipment that ties computers together into complex, integrated systems. It is a leading company of the Internet age. More than 75 percent of all Net traffic travels over products from Cisco.

One way Chambers ensures that Cisco remains an Internet leader is by acquiring other companies that develop improved technology. Cisco has bought not just dozens of companies but dozens of companies *per year.* Altogether, it has bought 55 companies, for a combined total of over $20 billion. In the fiscal fourth quarter of 2002, Cisco bought both Hammerhead Networks, Inc., and Navaro Networks, Inc.

Acquiring businesses is a good way of acquiring better technology. It is also a clever way to acquire top engineering talent. Competition for Internet engineers is intense; buying another company and retaining its top engineers is one way Chambers succeeds in building a superior staff.

Getting talented people through an acquisition is one thing; keeping them is another. Chambers is a good manager in that respect as well. Howard Charney, a Cisco senior vice president, could be a CEO in some other company, but he stays at Cisco, he says, because of Chambers: "John treats us like peers . . . He asks our advice. He gives us power and resources, then sets the sales targets incredibly high, which keeps us challenged." A true leader, Chambers has a participative managerial style that brings out the best in people.

BusinessWeek

The keys to Chambers's success at managing change include providing the best products by acquiring the best companies, retaining the best employees by motivating and compensating them well (and seeking their input using a participative managerial style), and focusing relentlessly on customer needs. Chambers says of Cisco, "Everything we do here is based on four principles: our customers' success, the quality of our team, our own aggressive use of information technology, and all of that applied to our overall strategy."

Source: "The Top 25 Managers to Watch," *Business Week,* January 8, 2001, p. 77.

Empowering Workers

Historically, many leaders gave explicit instructions to workers, telling them what to do to meet the goals and objectives of the organization. The term for such a process is *directing.* In traditional organizations, directing involves giving assignments, explaining routines, clarifying policies, and providing feedback on performance. Many organizations still follow this model, especially in firms like fast-food restaurants and small retail establishments where the employees don't have the skill and experience needed to work on their own, at least at first.

Progressive leaders, such as those in many high-tech firms and Internet companies, are less likely than traditional leaders to give specific instructions to employees. Rather, they're more likely to empower employees to make decisions on their own. Empowerment ➤P. 20◀ means giving employees the authority (the right to make a decision without consulting the manager) and responsibility (the requirement to accept the consequences of one's actions) to respond quickly to customer requests. Managers are often reluctant to give up the power they have to make such decisions; thus, empowerment is often resisted. In those firms that are able to implement the concept, the manager's role is becoming less that of a boss and director and more that of a coach, assistant,

THE 12 GOLDEN RULES OF LEADERSHIP	THE SEVEN SINS OF LEADERSHIP

THE 12 GOLDEN RULES OF LEADERSHIP

1. *Set a good example.* Your subordinates will take their cue from you. If your work habits are good, theirs are likely to be too.
2. *Give your people a set of objectives and a sense of direction.* Good people seldom like to work aimlessly from day to day. They want to know not only what they're doing but why.
3. *Keep your people informed of new developments of the company and how they'll affect them.* Let people know where they stand with you. Let your close assistants in on your plans at an early stage. Let people know as early as possible of any changes that will affect them. Let them know of changes that won't affect them but about which they may be worrying.
4. *Ask your people for advice.* Let them know that they have a say in your decisions whenever possible. Make them feel a problem is their problem too. Encourage individual thinking.
5. *Let your people know that you support them.* There's no greater morale killer than a boss who resents a subordinate's ambition.
6. *Don't give orders.* Suggest, direct, and request.
7. *Emphasize skills, not rules.* Judge results, not methods. Give a person a job to do and let him or her do it. Let an employee improve his or her own job methods.
8. *Give credit where credit is due.* Appreciation for a job well done is the most appreciated of fringe benefits.
9. *Praise in public.* This is where it will do the most good.
10. *Criticize in private.*
11. *Criticize constructively.* Concentrate on correction, not blame. Allow a person to retain his or her dignity. Suggest specific steps to prevent recurrence of the mistake. Forgive and encourage desired results.
12. *Make it known that you welcome new ideas.* No idea is too small for a hearing or too wild for consideration. Make it easy for them to communicate their ideas to you. Follow through on their ideas.

THE SEVEN SINS OF LEADERSHIP

On the other hand, these items can cancel any constructive image you might try to establish.

1. *Trying to be liked rather than respected.* Don't accept favors from your subordinates. Don't do special favors in trying to be liked. Don't try for popular decisions. Don't be soft about discipline. Have a sense of humor. Don't give up.
2. *Failing to ask subordinates for their advice and help.*
3. *Failing to develop a sense of responsibility in subordinates.* Allow freedom of expression. Give each person a chance to learn his or her superior's job. When you give responsibility, give authority too. Hold subordinates accountable for results.
4. *Emphasizing rules rather than skill.*
5. *Failing to keep criticism constructive.* When something goes wrong, do you tend to assume who's at fault? Do you do your best to get all the facts first? Do you control your temper? Do you praise before you criticize? Do you listen to the other side of the story?
6. *Not paying attention to employee gripes and complaints.* Make it easy for them to come to you. Get rid of red tape. Explain the grievance machinery. Help a person voice his or her complaint. Always grant a hearing. Practice patience. Ask a complainant what he or she wants to do. Don't render a hasty or biased judgment. Get all the facts. Let the complainant know what your decision is. Double-check your results. Be concerned.
7. *Failing to keep people informed.*

Sources: "To Become an Effective Executive: Develop Leadership and Other Skills," *Marketing News,* April 1984, p. 1; and Brian Biro, *Beyond Success* (New York: Berkley, 2001).

FIGURE 7.8

RULES OF LEADERSHIP

counselor, or team member. **Enabling** is the term used to describe giving workers the education and tools they need to make decisions. Clearly, enabling is the key to the success of empowerment. Without the right education, training, coaching, and tools, workers cannot assume the responsibilities and decision-making roles that make empowerment work.

enabling
Giving workers the education and tools they need to make decisions.

Empowering workers enables leaders to respond more quickly to constant changes in the business environment. The Reaching Beyond Our Borders box explores the need for leadership in today's competitive global market.

Reaching Beyond Our Borders

www.steel.org

Strong as Steel

Business leaders are faced with constant change, including changes instituted by the government. These changes may look great to some businesses but may have dire consequences for others. For example, President George W. Bush imposed tariffs (read *taxes*) of up to 30 percent on steel. The idea was to help large U.S. steel companies to consolidate into a few, large globally competitive companies. The result was not consolidation but rather the revival of struggling companies, like Gulf States Steel of Gadsden, Alabama, which was going bankrupt. Using the protection of tariffs, investors have revitalized the company. The same is true of Cleveland-based LTV steel, which is reopening under a new name. Pittsburgh's Bethlehem Steel and National Steel of Michawaka, Indiana, were seen as acquisition targets before the imposition of foreign tariffs.

On the one hand, such protections for the steel industry enable less productive firms to survive, thus further glutting the market with steel. This would tend to lower prices. On the other hand, keeping out foreign competition hurts the customers of big steel companies. Steel prices have risen by 30 to 50 percent since the tariffs. Workers in steel-consuming industries outnumber those in the steel-producing industry by more than 55 to 1. Trilla Steel Drum of Chicago, for example, employs 70 people. It makes 55-gallon steel drums. The domestic steel it must buy today costs 54 percent more than it did before the tariffs, making its drum prices rise by 20 percent. The companies that buy these drums must pay more too.

Similar issues have been raised about farm subsidies in the United States. Farmers in other countries simply can't compete with the subsidized food coming from the United States. Whether they consist of setting tariffs for foreign goods or subsidies for U.S. goods, government actions often have unintended consequences. Nonetheless, business leaders must learn to adapt to such changes as they occur. This doesn't mean, however, that they don't lobby their congressional representatives and others to change government policies, rules, and regulations. The rapid increase in global business will make such issues even more important in the coming years.

Sources: Pete Du Pont, "Paying a Price for Steel Tariffs," *Washington Times,* August 15, 2002, p. A16; Carter Dougherty, "Steel Mill Renewal," *Washington Times,* September 11, 2002, p. C8; James Dettmer, "EU, United States Engaged in Trade Tussle," *Insight,* September 2, 2002, p. 8; and Rich Miller, Paul Magnusson, and David Fairlamb, "A World of Hurt," *Business Week,* June 2, 2003, pp. 23–26.

Managing Knowledge

There's an old saying that still holds true today: "Knowledge is power." Empowering employees means giving them knowledge—that is, getting them the information they need to do the best job they can. Finding the right information, keeping the information in a readily accessible place, and making the information known to everyone in the firm together constitute **knowledge management.**[20]

knowledge management Finding the right information, keeping the information in a readily accessible place, and making the information known to everyone in the firm.

The first step to developing a knowledge management system is determining what knowledge is most important. Do you want to know more about your customers? Do you want to know more about competitors? What kind of information would make the company more effective or more efficient or more responsive to the marketplace? Once you have decided what you need to know, you set out to find answers to those questions.

Knowledge management tries to keep people from reinventing the wheel—that is, duplicating the work of gathering information—every time a decision needs to be made. A company really progresses when each person in the firm asks continually, "What do I still not know?" and "Whom should I be asking?" It's as important to know what's not working as what is working. Employees and managers now have e-mail, fax machines, intranets, and other means of keeping in touch with each other, with customers, and with other stakeholders. The key to success is learning how to process that information effectively and turn it into knowledge that everyone can use to improve processes and procedures. That is one way to enable workers to be more effective. We'll discuss information technology and knowledge management in much more detail in Chapter 17.

Critical Thinking

Do you see any problems with a democratic managerial style? Can you see a manager getting frustrated when he or she can't control others? Can someone who's trained to give orders (e.g., a military sergeant) be retrained to be a democratic manager? What problems may emerge? What kind of manager would you be? Do you have evidence to show that?

CONTROLLING: MAKING SURE IT WORKS

The control function involves measuring performance relative to the planned objectives and standards, rewarding people for work well done, and then taking corrective action when necessary. Thus, the control process (see Figure 7.9) is the heart of the management system because it provides the feedback that enables managers and workers to adjust to any deviations from plans and to changes in the environment that have affected performance. Controlling consists of five steps:

1. Establishing clear performance standards. This ties the planning function to the control function. Without clear standards, control is impossible.
2. Monitoring and recording actual performance (results).
3. Comparing results against plans and standards.
4. Communicating results and deviations to the employees involved.
5. Taking corrective action when needed and providing positive feedback for work well done.

As indicated, the control system's weakest link tends to be the setting of standards. To measure results against standards, the standards must be spe-

FIGURE 7.9

THE CONTROL PROCESS

The whole control process is based on clear standards. Without such standards, the other steps are difficult, if not impossible. With clear standards, performance measurement is relatively easy and the proper action can be taken.

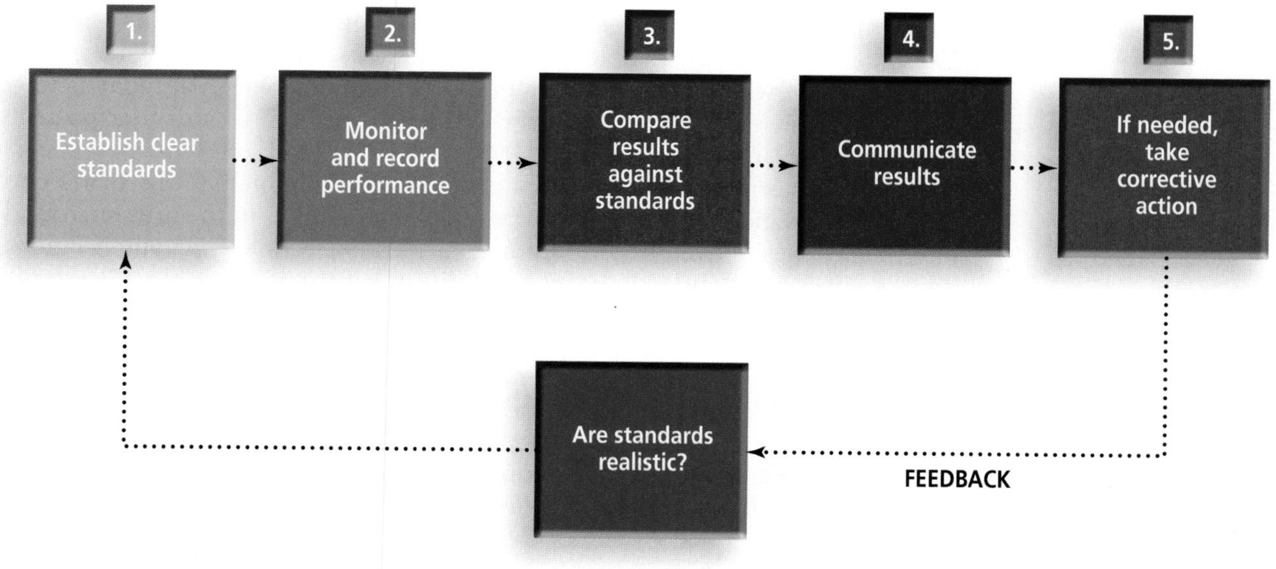

"WILSON, WHAT EXACTLY IS A KNOWLEDGE WORKER AND DO WE HAVE ANY ON THE STAFF?"

New management concepts come and go over time. One that is important at this time is knowledge management and the idea of knowledge workers. This cartoon suggests that management is not always aware of the latest techniques and how they are applied. What exactly is "knowledge management"? Does it seem like a passing fad or do you think it will be an important part of management for a long time?

cific, attainable, and measurable. Setting such clear standards is part of the planning function. Vague goals and standards such as "better quality," "more efficiency," and "improved performance" aren't sufficient because they don't describe in enough detail what you're trying to achieve. For example, let's say you're a runner and you have made the following statement: "My goal is to improve my distance." When you started your improvement plan last year, you ran 2 miles a day; now you run 2.1 miles a day. Did you meet your goal? Well, you did increase your distance, but certainly not by very much. A more appropriate statement would be "My goal is to increase my running distance from two miles a day to four miles a day by January 1." It's important to establish a time period for reaching goals. The following examples of goals and standards meet these criteria:

- Cutting the number of finished product rejects from 10 per 1,000 to 5 per 1,000 by March 31.
- Increasing the number of times managers praise employees from 3 per week to 12 per week by the end of the quarter.
- Increasing sales of product X from 10,000 per month to 12,000 per month by July.

One way to make control systems work is to establish clear procedures for monitoring performance. Accounting and finance are often the foundations for control systems because they provide the numbers management needs to evaluate progress. We shall explore both accounting and finance in detail later in the text.

A New Criterion for Measurement: Customer Satisfaction

external customers
Dealers, who buy products to sell to others, and ultimate customers (or end users), who buy products for their own personal use.

internal customers
Individuals and units within the firm that receive services from other individuals or units.

The criterion for measuring success in a customer-oriented firm is customer satisfaction. This includes satisfaction of both external and internal customers. **External customers** include dealers, who buy products to sell to others, and ultimate customers (also known as end users) such as you and me, who buy products for their own personal use. **Internal customers** are individuals and units within the firm that receive services from other individuals or units. For example, the field salespeople are the internal customers of the marketing research people who prepare research reports for them. One goal today is to go beyond simply satisfying customers to "delighting" them with unexpectedly good products and services.

Other criteria of organizational effectiveness may include the firm's contribution to society and its environmental responsibility in the area surrounding the business.[21] The traditional measures of success are usually financial; that is, success is defined in terms of profits or return on investment. Certainly these measures are still important, but they're not the whole purpose of the firm. The purpose of the firm today is to please employees, customers, and other stakeholders. Thus, measurements of success must take all these groups into account. Firms have to ask questions such as these: Do we have good relations with our employees, our suppliers, our dealers, our community leaders, the local media, our stockholders, and our bankers? What more could we do to please these groups? Are the corporate needs (such as making a profit) being met as well?

The Corporate Scorecard

A broad measurement tool that has grown in popularity in the last few years is the corporate scorecard. In addition to measuring customer satisfaction, the corporate scorecard measures financial progress, return on investment, and all else that needs to be managed for the firm to reach its final destination—profits. One scorecard, for example, might simultaneously follow customer service (Is it getting better or worse?) and product defects (Are there fewer or more?). Some companies use software that enables everyone in the firm to see the results of the corporate scorecard and work together to improve them. Some companies, like Shell Oil, use strictly financial measures of success. Others, like Motorola, use a more balanced approach. That is, they measure both financial progress and other, softer issues, such as employee and customer satisfaction. Most companies would do better by having a balanced approach that measures both financial growth and employee and customer satisfaction.

Management will be discussed in more detail in the next few chapters. Let's pause now, review, and do some exercises. Management is doing, not just reading.

Critical Thinking

What kind of management are you best suited for: human resource, marketing, finance, accounting, production, or what? Why do you feel this area is most appropriate? Would you like to work for a large firm or a small business? Private or public? In an office or out in the field? Would you like being a manager? If you aren't sure, read the following chapters and see what's involved.

Progress Assessment

- How does enabling help empowerment?
- What are the five steps in the control process?
- What's the difference between internal and external customers?
- What is a corporate scorecard?

Summary

1. Explain how the changes that are occurring in the business environment are affecting the management function.

1. Many managers are changing their approach to corporate management.
   - ***What reasons can you give to account for these changes in management?***

   Businesspeople are being challenged to be more ethical and to make their accounting practices more visible to investors and the general public. Change is now happening faster than ever, and global competition is just a click away. Managing change is an important element of success, particularly in light of today's emphasis on speed in the global marketplace. National borders mean much less now than ever before, and cooperation and integration among companies have greatly increased. Within companies, knowledge workers are demanding managerial styles that allow for freedom, and the workforce is becoming increasingly diverse, educated, and self-directed.
   - ***How are managers' roles changing?***

   Managers are being educated to guide, train, support, and teach employees rather than tell them what to do. Before employees can be empowered, they must receive extensive training and development.

2. Describe the four functions of management.

2. Managers perform a variety of functions.
   - ***What are the four primary functions of management?***

   The four primary functions are (1) planning, (2) organizing, (3) leading, and (4) controlling.

3. Relate the planning process and decision making to the accomplishment of company goals.

3. The planning function involves the process of setting objectives to meet the organizational goals.
   - ***What's the difference between goals and objectives?***

   Goals are broad, long-term achievements that organizations aim to accomplish, whereas objectives are specific, short-term plans made to help reach the goals.
   - ***What is a SWOT analysis?***

   Managers look at the strengths, weaknesses, opportunities, and threats facing the firm.
   - ***What are the four types of planning, and how are they related to the organization's goals and objectives?***

   Strategic planning is broad, long-range planning that outlines the goals of the organization. Tactical planning is specific, short-term planning that lists organizational objectives. Operational planning is part of tactical planning and involves setting specific timetables and standards. Contingency planning involves developing an alternative set of plans in case the first set doesn't work out.
   - ***What are the steps involved in decision making?***

   The seven Ds of decision making are (1) define the situation, (2) describe and collect needed information, (3) develop alternatives, (4) develop agreement among those involved, (5) decide which alternative is best, (6) do what is indicated (begin implementation), and (7) determine whether the decision was a good one and follow up.

4. Describe the organizing function of management.

4. Organizing means allocating resources (such as funds for various departments), assigning tasks, and establishing procedures for accomplishing the organizational objectives.
   - ***What are the three levels of management in the corporate hierarchy?***

   The three levels of management are (1) top management (highest level consisting of the president and other key company executives who develop strategic plans); (2) middle management (general managers, division managers, and plant managers who are responsible for tactical planning and controlling); and (3) supervisory management (first-line managers/supervisors who evaluate workers' daily performance).
   - ***What skills do managers need?***

   Managers must have three categories of skills: (1) technical skills (ability to perform specific tasks such as selling products or developing software), (2) human relations skills (ability to communicate and motivate), and (3) conceptual skills (ability to see organizations as a whole and how all the parts fit together).
   - ***Are these skills equally important at all management levels?***

   Managers at different levels need different skills. Top managers rely heavily on human relations and conceptual skills and rarely use technical skills, while first-line supervisors need strong technical and human relations skills but use conceptual skills less often. Middle managers need to have a balance of all three skills (see Figure 7.6).
   - ***What are some of the latest trends in organizational management?***

   Many firms are creating self-managed teams. In those firms, managers tend to do more coaching and training than telling people what to do. Another trend is toward stakeholder-oriented management. In those cases, management tries to satisfy the needs of all stakeholders, including employees, customers, suppliers, dealers, environmental groups, and the surrounding communities.

- ***What changes in the marketplace have made staffing more important?***
E-commerce CEOs must spend a lot of time recruiting because their companies grow so fast and run on the knowledge of mostly young workers. Keeping people is also critical because there are lots of companies seeking new talent and people feel free today to go where the action is fastest (and pays the most in dollars or stock options).

5. Executives today must be more than just managers; they must be leaders as well.
   - ***What's the difference between a manager and a leader?***
   A manager plans, organizes, and controls functions within an organization. A leader has vision and inspires others to grasp that vision, establishes corporate values, emphasizes corporate ethics, and doesn't fear change.
   - ***Describe the various leadership styles.***
   Figure 7.7 shows a continuum of leadership styles ranging from boss-centered to subordinate-centered leadership.
   - ***Which leadership style is best?***
   The best (most effective) leadership style depends on the people being led and the situation. The challenge of the future will be to empower self-managed teams to manage themselves. This is a move away from autocratic leadership.
   - ***What does empowerment mean?***
   Empowerment means giving employees the authority and responsibility to respond quickly to customer requests. Enabling is the term used to describe giving workers the education and tools they need to assume their new decision-making powers. Knowledge management involves finding the right information, keeping the information in a readily accessible place, and making the information known to everyone in the firm. Knowledge management is another way of enabling workers to do the best job they can.

5. Explain the differences between leaders and managers, and describe the various leadership styles.

6. The control function of management involves measuring employee performance against objectives and standards, rewarding people for a job well done, and taking corrective action if necessary.
   - ***What are the five steps of the control function?***
   Controlling incorporates (1) setting clear standards, (2) monitoring and recording performance, (3) comparing performance with plans and standards, (4) communicating results and deviations to employees, and (5) providing positive feedback for a job well done and taking corrective action if necessary.
   - ***What qualities must standards possess to be used to measure performance results?***
   Standards must be specific, attainable, and measurable.
   - ***What are the latest performance standards?***
   Modern companies consider customer satisfaction to be a key measure of success. A corporate scorecard enables a company to measure customer satisfaction as well as traditional standards of success, such as profit and return on investment.

6. Summarize the five steps of the control function of management.

Key Terms

leading 214
management 213
managing diversity 224
middle management 220
mission statement 215
objectives 215
operational planning 218
organization chart 219
organizing 213
participative (democratic) leadership 226
planning 213
PMI 219
problem solving 219
staffing 223
strategic planning 216
supervisory management 220
SWOT analysis 216
tactical planning 217
technical skills 221
top management 219
vision 215

Developing Workplace Skills

1. Allocate some time to do some career planning by doing a SWOT analysis of your present situation. What does the marketplace for your chosen career(s) look like today? What skills do you have that will make you a winner in that type of career? What weaknesses might you target to improve? What are the threats to that career choice? What are the opportunites? Prepare a two-minute presentation to the class.

2. Bring several decks of cards to class and have the class break up into teams of four or so members. Each team should then elect a leader. Each leader should be assigned a leadership style: autocratic, participative (democratic), or free-rein. Have each team try to build a house of cards by stacking them on top of each other. The team with the highest house wins. Each team member should then report his or her experience under that style of leadership.

3. In class, discuss the advantages and disadvantages of becoming a manager. Does the size of the business make a difference? What are the advantages of a career in a profit-seeking business versus a career in a nonprofit organization?

4. Review Figure 7.7 and discuss managers you have known, worked for, or read about who have practiced each style. Students from other countries may have interesting experiences to add. Which managerial style did you like best? Why? Which were most effective? Why?

5. Because of the illegal and unethical behavior of a few managers, managers in general are under suspicion for being greedy and dishonest. Discuss the fairness of such charges, given the thousands of honest and ethical managers, and what could be done to improve the opinion of managers among the students in your class.

Taking It To The Net

Purpose

To perform a simple SWOT analysis.

Exercise

Go to www.marketingteacher.com/Lessons/lesson_swot.htm. Click on [Exercise] and complete the SWOT analysis for the Highly Brill Leisure Center.

1. What are the center's strengths, weakness, opportunities, and threats?
2. Analyze the center's weaknesses. How do you think the company's strengths might be used to overcome some of its weaknesses?
3. Analyze the center's opportunities and threats. What additional opportunities can you suggest? What additional threats can you identify?

Casing The Web

To access the case "Leading in a Leaderless Company," visit

www.mhhe.com/ub7e

Video Case

Leading America's Team: Delta Force

Colonel Lee Van Arsdale is a West Point graduate who served 25 years in the Army, 18 of them in Special Operations. Van Arsdale believes good leadership is good leadership, in the Army or any other organization. He knows the fundamental principles are the same because he has managed a private business as well as a military team. Van Arsdale served in Operation Just Cause in Panama and was a member of a Delta Force team in Somalia. Because of his background, he was chosen as the technical advisor for the movie *Black Hawk Down*. The movie is about the rescue of downed pilots in Somalia and the brave men who attempted that rescue. The two men featured in this video died in that attempt.

Like business teams, Special Forces teams have a mission statement. Both businesses and the military provide services and need good people to carry out the mission. Both need the proper equipment to do the job. Enabling means giving people the education, tools, and training they need to do their jobs properly. Members of Special Forces are volunteers and trained to be engineers, communications specialists, weapons specialists, medics, and so on. The teams are trained to operate in certain regions of the world. That includes learning the language and the culture. Those who pass the training are self-motivated, mature, and confident. Businesses operating globally need to do similar training so managers can adapt to the different countries. Strategically, Special Forces soldiers are playing a more prominent role in our military, as seen following September 11, 2001, in Afghanistan and in the 2003 Gulf War.

Special Forces are on call 24/7, 365 days a year. They operate in some 60 to 70 countries and must be ready to go on a moment's notice. This creates a strain on families and on personnel. Because operatives must blend in with the peoples of other countries, military dress regulations are relaxed. They are given an assignment, and planning is done from the bottom up. The team, which may consist of just a few operatives or as many as a dozen, is free to decide how to carry out the mission. An empowered business may operate in a similar manner.

Why do Special Forces illustrate management principles? Because planning, organizing, leading and controlling are universal management principles. *Management* is defined as the process used to accomplish organizational goals through planning, organizing, leading, and controlling people and other organizational resources. Students who plan to enter the government, the military, charities, or associations need to understand these principles as much as those who enter businesses.

Leaders can adopt several different managerial styles. In battle, a military leader may have to be autocratic and demand the unquestioning obedience of followers. At other times, a military leader may be quite democratic and rely heavily on teams to provide input and suggestions. A good leader has to be a good listener. Therefore, the control function is critical to any operation. Feedback from the control function helps in future planning by determining what went right and what went wrong. A constant reassessment of the team's strengths, weaknesses, opportunities, and threats is called a SWOT analysis.

Working with a dedicated, focused, and fun-loving team develops a camaraderie that holds the team together and allows them to work effectively. This is true in the military, in sports, and in business. That's why many companies are moving toward the team approach to management.

Thinking It Over

1. What attracts recruits to the rigors of becoming a member of Special Forces? Would such people be less attracted to other organizations? Why or why not?
2. Planning, organizing, leading, and controlling are important to all organizations. How do they apply to a charity?
3. As one advances in the military, do the skills needed at various levels of management change from emphasis on technical to human relations to conceptual as they do in business firms? Why or why not?

Chapter 8

Adapting Organizations to Today's Markets

Learning Goals

After you have read and studied this chapter, you should be able to

1. Explain the historical organizational theories of Fayol and Weber.
2. Explain the various issues involved in structuring organizations.
3. Describe and differentiate the various organizational models.
4. Discuss the concepts involved in interfirm cooperation and coordination.
5. Explain how restructuring, organizational culture, and informal organizations can help businesses adapt to change.

Profile

www.hp.com

Getting to Know Carly Fiorina of Hewlett-Packard

Few managers have received more attention in the last few years than Carleton (Carly) Fiorina. She led the fight to unite her company, Hewlett-Packard (HP), with Compaq Computer. The news media and the stock market experts all expected the attempt to fail, but the integration took place and Fiorina now has the task of reorganizing the two companies into one. Again, many people are betting against her long-term success, but time will tell whether Fiorina will be able to successfully accomplish this huge task over the long run. Her background would indicate that she has a fighting chance.

Fiorina earned her MBA in marketing from the University of Maryland in 1980. She started her career in AT&T's government sales office and then moved into network systems. When Lucent Technologies split off from AT&T to focus on wireless products, Fiorina followed. Using her organizational skills, she was instrumental in making the firm a leading Internet company. She became president of Lucent's global service-provider business in 1998. Lucent's stock market fall came after she left.

When Hewlett-Packard began searching for a new CEO, it was looking for someone who could restructure the firm to make it a leader in e-commerce. Fiorina was selected from some 300 candidates. At her first major presentation to Wall Street analysts, Fiorina announced a major reorganization of HP's business structure. She merged HP's four product companies into two and put a high degree of focus on customer relations. Fiorina slashed bloated operating costs, reorganized divisions, and changed the sales compensation plan.

When HP joined with Compaq, Fiorina had new challenges. She had to get rid of duplicate products and eliminate some employees to realize the cost savings that the integration made available. She hoped to cut costs by $3 billion annually. The 2002 stock market crash occurred right in the middle of her reorganization attempt, and made the whole process more difficult. But Fiorina is ready to tackle all the steps necessary to make the merged companies a major force in the computer/printer industry.

She had to get rid of duplicate products and eliminate some employees to realize the cost savings that the integration made available. She hoped to cut costs by $3 billion annually.

The goal of this chapter is to introduce you to the terms and concepts involved in organizing companies (and reorganizing them as well). Few challenges in business are greater than moving an established company from the slow-moving, management-oriented style of the past to the fast-moving, team-oriented, Internet-based, and customer-based firms that most of today's markets demand.

Sources: "She Can Turn Anything into Gold," *Success,* December/January 2001, p. 30; Cliff Edwards and Andrew Park, "HP and Compaq: It's Showtime," *Business Week,* June 17, 2002, pp. 76–77; Brad Stone, "The Carly Way," *Newsweek,* May 20, 2002, pp. 50–51; and George Anders, "The Carly Chronicles," *Fast Company,* February 2003, pp. 66–72.

BUILDING AN ORGANIZATION FROM THE BOTTOM UP

Management, as you learned in Chapter 7, begins with planning. Let's say, for example, that you and two of your friends plan to start a lawn-mowing business. One of the first steps is to organize your business. Organizing, or structuring, begins with determining what work needs to be done (mowing, edging, trimming, etc.) and then dividing up tasks among the three of you; this is called a *division of labor.* One of you, for example, might have a special talent for trimming bushes, while another is better at mowing. Dividing tasks into smaller jobs is called *job specialization.* The success of a firm often depends on management's ability to identify each worker's strengths and assign the right tasks to the right person. Often a job can be done quickly and well when each person specializes.

If your business is successful, you will probably hire more workers to help. You might then organize them into teams or departments to do the various tasks. One team, for example, might mow the lawn while another team uses blowers to clean up the leaves and grass. If you are really successful over time, you might hire an accountant to keep records for you, various people to do your marketing (e.g., advertising), and repair people to keep the equipment in good shape. You can see how your business might evolve into a company with several departments: production (mowing the lawns and everything related to that), marketing, accounting, and repair. The process of setting up individual departments to do specialized tasks is called *departmentalization.* Finally, you would need to assign authority and responsibility to people so that you could control the whole process. If something went wrong in the accounting department, for example, you would know who was responsible.

Structuring an organization, then, consists of devising a division of labor (sometimes resulting in specialization); setting up teams or departments to do specific tasks (e.g., production and accounting); and assigning responsibility and authority to people. Part of the process would include allocating resources (such as funds for various departments), assigning specific tasks, and establishing procedures for accomplishing the organizational objectives. Right from the start, you have to make some ethical decisions about how you will treat your workers (see the Making Ethical Decisions box). Finally, as you learned in Chapter 7, you may develop an organization chart ➤P. 219◄ that shows relationships among people: It shows who is accountable for the completion of specific work and who reports to whom.

The Changing Organization

Never before in the history of business has so much change been introduced so quickly—sometimes too quickly.[1] As you learned in earlier chapters, much of that change is due to the changing business environment, including more global competition and faster technological change. Equally important to many businesses is the change in customer expectations.[2] Consumers today expect high-quality products and fast, friendly service—at a reasonable cost. Managing change, then, has become a critical managerial function. That sometimes includes changing the whole organizational structure. Many organizations in the past were designed more to facilitate management than to please the customer. Companies designed many rules and regulations to give managers control over employees.

We shall explore in brief the history of organizational design so that you can see what the foundations are. Then we shall explore the newest forms of organization, forms that are being designed to better serve today's customer. Though often dramatic and disruptive, such changes keep companies competitive in today's dynamic business environment.

Making Ethical Decisions

Safety versus Profit

Imagine that you have begun a successful lawn-mowing service in your neighborhood.

You observe other lawn-mowing services in the area. Several seem to hire untrained workers, many of them from other countries. The companies pay the workers minimum wage or slightly more. Most obviously, however, the owners often provide no safety equipment. Workers don't have ear protection against the loud mowers and blowers. Most don't wear goggles when operating the shredder. Very few workers wear masks when spraying potentially harmful fertilizers.

You are aware that there are many hazards connected with yardwork. You also know that safety gear can be expensive and that workers often prefer to work without such protection. You are interested in making as much money as possible, but you also are somewhat concerned about the safety and welfare of your workers. Furthermore, you are aware of the noise pollution caused by blowers and other equipment and would like to keep noise levels down, but quiet equipment is expensive.

Clearly, most other lawn services don't seem too concerned about safety and the environment. On the one hand, you know that the corporate culture you create as you begin your service will last for a long time. If you emphasize safety and environmental concern from the start, your workers will adopt your values. On the other hand, you can see the potential for making faster profits by ignoring as many safety rules as you can and by paying as little attention as you can to the environment. What are the consequences of each choice? Which would you choose?

The Historical Development of Organizational Design

To understand what is happening in organizations today, it is best to begin with a firm foundation of organizational principles. Many principles of traditional organizational design are still important today. However, some have lost importance and others may no longer apply at all—and organizational leaders need to understand which principles are still important and which are not.

Until the 20th century, most businesses were rather small, the processes for producing goods were relatively simple, and organizing workers was fairly easy. Organizing workers is still not too hard in most small firms, such as a lawn-mowing service or a small shop that produces custom-made boats. Not until the 1900s and the introduction of *mass production* (efficiently producing large quantities of goods) did business production processes and organization become complex. Usually, the bigger the plant, the more efficient production became.

Business growth led to what was called **economies of scale.** This term refers to the fact that companies can reduce their production costs if they can purchase raw materials in bulk; the average cost of goods goes down as production levels increase. The cost of building a car, for example, got much cheaper when the automobile companies went to mass production. You may have noticed the same benefits of mass production with houses and computers.

economies of scale
The situation in which companies can reduce their production costs if they can purchase raw materials in bulk; the average cost of goods goes down as production levels increase.

During the era of mass production, organization theorists emerged. In France, Henri Fayol published his book *Administration industrielle et générale* in 1919. It was popularized in the United States in 1949 under the title *General and Industrial Management*. Sociologist Max Weber (pronounced "Vay-ber") was writing about organization theory in Germany about the same time Fayol was writing his books in France. Note that it was less than 60 years ago that organization theory became popular in the United States.

Fayol's Principles of Organization Fayol introduced such principles as the following:

- **Unity of command.** Each worker is to report to one, and only one, boss. The benefits of this principle are obvious. What happens if two different bosses give you two different assignments? Which one should you follow? To prevent such confusion, each person is to report to only one manager.

- **Hierarchy of authority.** All workers should know to whom they should report. Managers should have the right to give orders and expect others to follow.
- **Division of labor.** Functions are to be divided into areas of specialization such as production, marketing, and finance. This principle, as you will read later, is now being questioned or modified.
- **Subordination of individual interests to the general interest.** Workers are to think of themselves as a coordinated team. The goals of the team are more important than the goals of individual workers.
- **Authority.** Managers have the right to give orders and the power to enforce obedience. Authority and responsibility are related: Whenever authority is exercised, responsibility arises. This principle is also being modified as managers are beginning to empower employees.
- **Degree of centralization.** The amount of decision-making power vested in top management should vary by circumstances. In a small organization, it's possible to centralize all decision-making power in the top manager. In a larger organization, however, some decision-making power should be delegated to lower-level managers and employees on both major and minor issues.
- **Clear communication channels.** All workers should be able to reach others in the firm quickly and easily.
- **Order.** Materials and people should be placed and maintained in the proper location.
- **Equity.** A manager should treat employees and peers with respect and justice.
- **Esprit de corps.** A spirit of pride and loyalty should be created among people in the firm.

Management courses in colleges throughout the world taught these principles for years, and they became synonymous with the concept of management. Organizations were designed so that no person had more than one boss, lines of authority were clear, and everyone knew to whom they were to report. Naturally, these principles tended to be written down as rules, policies, and regulations as organizations grew larger. That process of rule making often led to rather rigid organizations that didn't always respond quickly to consumer requests. For example, the Department of Motor Vehicles (DMV) in various cities and auto repair facilities have often been cited as relatively slow to adapt to the needs of their customers.[3]

These women are waiting in line at the Department of Motor Vehicles in Vienna, Virginia. Virginia and several other states have cut funding to their DMVs, thus making the waits longer and more intolerable. By cutting such funds, governors and legislators often hope that taxpayers will accept higher taxes to prevent such waits and inconvenience. Does this seem like a good management strategy to you?

Many customers expect to wait in long lines at the DMV, only to speak to employees who are not empowered to be flexible when responding to their unique needs. Some DMVs are still organized that way, but others have reorganized; some even allow customers to conduct their business over the Internet. Why do you suppose the government-run DMVs were slower to adapt to customer needs than were private businesses?

Max Weber and Organizational Theory Max Weber's book *The Theory of Social and Economic Organizations,* like Fayol's, also appeared in the United States in the late 1940s. It was Weber who promoted the pyramid-shaped organization structure that became so popular in large firms. Weber put great trust in managers and felt that the firm would do well if employees simply did what they were told. The less decision making employees had to do, the better. Clearly, this is a reasonable way to operate if you're dealing with relatively uneducated and untrained workers. Often, such workers were the only ones available at the time Weber was writing; most employees did not have the kind of educational background and technical skills that today's workers generally have.

Max Weber promoted an organizational structure composed of middle managers who implement the orders of top managers. He believed that less educated workers were best managed by having them follow strict rules and regulations monitored by managers or supervisors. What industries or businesses today would benefit by using such controls?

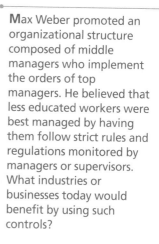

Weber's principles of organization were similar to Fayol's. In addition, Weber emphasized

- Job descriptions.
- Written rules, decision guidelines, and detailed records.
- Consistent procedures, regulations, and policies.
- Staffing and promotion based on qualifications.

Weber believed that large organizations demanded clearly established rules and guidelines that were to be followed precisely. In other words, he was in favor of bureaucracy. Although his principles made a great deal of sense at the time, the practice of establishing rules and procedures sometimes became so rigid in some companies that they became counterproductive.[4] However, some organizations today still thrive on Weber's theories. United Parcel Service (UPS), for example, still has written rules and decision guidelines that enable the firm to deliver packages quickly because employees don't have to pause to make decisions. The procedures to follow are clearly spelled out for them.

Turning Principles into Organizational Design

Following the concepts of theorists like Fayol and Weber, managers in the latter part of the 1900s began designing organizations so that managers could control workers. Most organizations are still organized that way, with everything set up in a hierarchy. A **hierarchy** is a system in which one person is at the top of the organization and there is a ranked or sequential ordering from the top down of managers and others who are responsible to that person. Since one person can't keep track of thousands of workers, the top manager needs many lower-level managers to help. The **chain of command** is the line of authority that moves from the top of the hierarchy to the lowest level. Figure 8.1 ➤P. 244◄ shows a typical hierarchical organization structure.

Some organizations have a dozen or more layers of management between the chief executive officer (CEO) and the lowest-level employees. If employees want to introduce work changes, they ask a supervisor (the first level of management), who asks his or her manager, who asks a manager at the next level up, and so on. Eventually a decision is made and passed down from manager to manager until it reaches the employees. Such decisions can take weeks or months to be made. Max Weber used the word *bureaucrat* to describe a middle manager whose function was to implement top management's orders. Thus, **bureaucracy** came to be the term used for an organization with many layers of managers who set rules and regulations and oversee all decisions.

hierarchy
A system in which one person is at the top of the organization and there is a ranked or sequential ordering from the top down of managers who are responsible to that person.

chain of command
The line of authority that moves from the top of a hierarchy to the lowest level.

bureaucracy
An organization with many layers of managers who set rules and regulations and oversee all decisions.

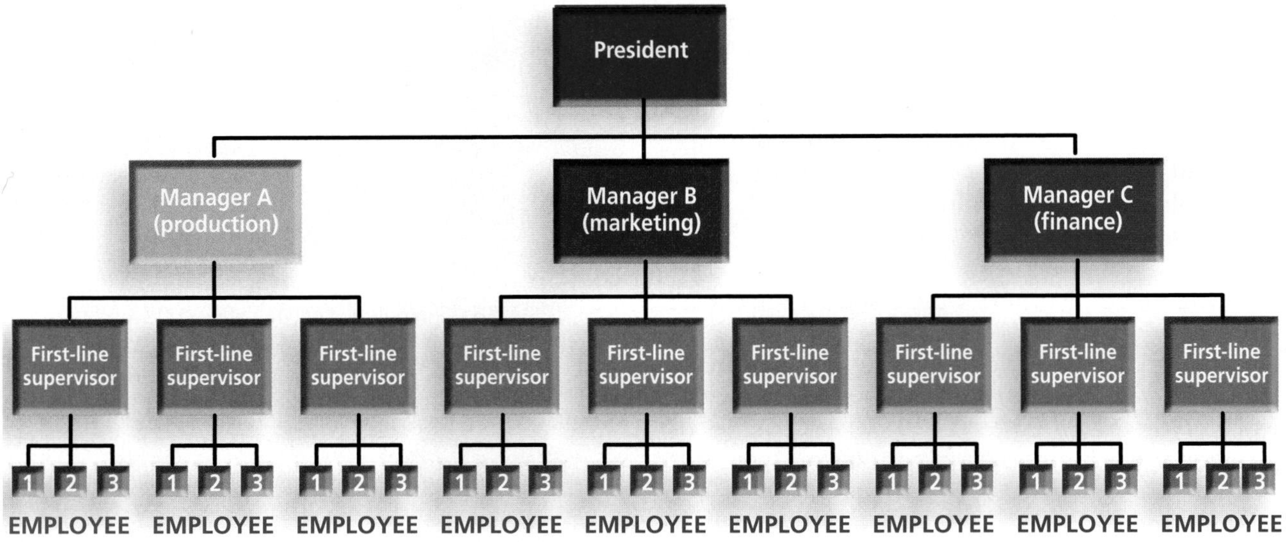

FIGURE 8.1

TYPICAL ORGANIZATION CHART

This is a rather standard chart with managers for major functions and supervisors reporting to the managers. Each supervisor manages three employees.

When employees have to ask their managers for permission to make a change, the process may take so long that customers become annoyed. Such consumer discontent may happen either in a small organization such as a flower shop or in a major organization such as an automobile dealership or a large construction firm. The employee has to find the manager, get permission to make the requested change, come back to the customer, explain what the management decision was, and so on. Has this happened to you in a department store or some other organization? Since many customers want efficient service—and they want it now—slow service is simply not acceptable in many of today's competitive firms.[5]

To make customers happier, some companies are reorganizing to give employees power to make more decisions on their own. Rather than always having to follow strict rules and regulations, they are encouraged to please the customer no matter what. For example, at Nordstrom, a chain of upscale department stores, an employee can accept a return from a customer without seeking managerial approval, even if the garment was not originally sold at that store. As you read earlier, giving employees such authority and responsibility to make decisions and please customers is called empowerment ➤P. 20◄ Remember that empowerment works only when employees are given the proper training and resources to respond.

Progress Assessment

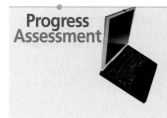

- What do the terms *division of labor* and *specialization* mean?
- What are the principles of management outlined by Fayol?
- What did Weber add to the principles of Fayol?

Critical Thinking

Now that you have learned some of the basic principles of organization, pause and think of where you have already applied such concepts yourself or have been involved with an organization that did. Did you find that a division of labor was necessary and helpful? Were you assigned specific tasks or were you left on your own to decide what to do? Were promotions based strictly on qualifications, as Weber suggested? What other factors may have been considered? What problems seem to emerge when an organization gets larger?

Issues Involved in Structuring Organizations

When designing responsive organizations, firms have had to deal with several organizational issues: (1) centralization versus decentralization, (2) span of control, (3) tall versus flat organization structures, and (4) departmentalization.

Nordstrom is a store widely known for its outstanding customer service. For example, you can return any item purchased at a Nordstrom store and the customer-service people will be friendly and responsive. What stores in your area provide outstanding service? What things do they do differently from other less customer-oriented businesses?

Centralization versus Decentralization of Authority

Imagine for a minute that you're a top manager for a retail company such as JCPenney. Your temptation may be to preserve control over all your stores in order to maintain a uniform image and merchandise. You've noticed that such control works well for McDonald's; why not JCPenney? The degree to which an organization allows managers at the lower levels of the managerial hierarchy to make decisions determines the degree of decentralization that an organization practices.

Centralized authority occurs when decision-making authority is maintained at the top level of management at the company's headquarters. **Decentralized authority** occurs when decision-making authority is delegated to lower-level managers and employees who are more familiar with local conditions than headquarter's management could be. Figure 8.2 lists some advantages and disadvantages of centralized versus decentralized authority.

centralized authority
An organization structure in which decision-making authority is maintained at the top level of management at the company's headquarters.

decentralized authority
An organization structure in which decision-making authority is delegated to lower-level managers more familiar with local conditions than headquarters management could be.

JCPenney customers in California, for example, are likely to demand clothing styles different from those demanded in Minnesota or Maine. It makes sense, therefore, to give store managers in various cities the authority to buy, price, and promote merchandise appropriate for each area. Such a delegation of authority is an example of decentralized management.

In contrast, McDonald's feels that purchasing, promotion, and other such decisions are best handled centrally. There's usually little need for each McDonald's restaurant to carry different food products. McDonald's would therefore lean toward centralized authority. However, today's rapidly changing markets, added to global differences in consumer tastes, tend to favor more de-

FIGURE 8.2

ADVANTAGES AND DISADVANTAGES OF CENTRALIZED VERSUS DECENTRALIZED MANAGEMENT

ADVANTAGES	DISADVANTAGES
Centralized	
• Greater top-management control	• Less responsiveness to customers
• More efficiency	• Less empowerment
• Simpler distribution system	• Interorganizational conflict
• Stronger brand/corporate image	• Lower morale away from headquarters
Decentralized	
• Better adaptation to customer wants	• Less efficiency
• More empowerment of workers	• Complex distribution system
• Faster decision making	• Less top-management control
• Higher morale	• Weakened corporate image

Reaching Beyond Our Borders

www.ford.com

The Internet Makes the World Smaller

The CEO of Ford Motor Company says that traditional companies have to become more nimble and more closely attuned to consumers. One source at Ford says, "You've got to break down the business into the smallest possible units to give the employees in them authority and accountability." (Throughout this text, we call that empowerment.) In the past, Ford centralized worldwide responsibility for functions such as product development, purchasing, design, and manufacturing. The new model decentralizes such decisions so that managers in Europe and South America can readily adapt to consumers in those markets.

Did you know that Ford now owns Volvo? And Mazda? And Jaguar? And Land Rover? Did you also know that, to appeal to environmentalists, Ford has developed a car that runs on fuel cells? At first, fuel-cell cars will go to fleet customers (people who buy Fords in volume), but they will be available to the public soon as well. You can see how the company is trying to make cars that will appeal to almost everyone everywhere.

How does a company keep in touch with such widespread manufacturing and customer bases? By the Internet. You can read more about Ford's new developments on its website (www.ford.com/en/default.htm).

Sources: Kathleen Kerwin and Jack Ewing, "Nasser: Ford Be Nimble," *Business Week,* September 27, 1999, pp. 42–43; "Ambitious Ford Aims High as It Sets Targets," *Birmingham Post,* January 12, 2001, p. 22; and John D. Wolpert, "Breaking Out of the Innovation Box," *Harvard Business Review,* August 2002, pp. 77–83.

centralization and thus more delegation of authority, even at McDonald's. Its restaurants in England offer tea, those in France offer a Croque McDo (a hot ham-and-cheese sandwich), those in Japan offer rice, and so on.[6] Rosenbluth International is a service organization in the travel industry. It too has decentralized so that its separate units can offer the kinds of services demanded in each region while still getting needed resources from corporate headquarters. The Reaching Beyond Our Borders box describes how Ford Motor Company used the Internet to decentralize decision making.

Choosing the Appropriate Span of Control

span of control
The optimum number of subordinates a manager supervises or should supervise.

Span of control refers to the optimum number of subordinates a manager supervises or should supervise. There are many factors to consider when determining span of control. At lower levels, where work is standardized, it's possible to implement a wide span of control (15 to 40 workers). For example, one supervisor can be responsible for 20 or more workers who are assembling computers or cleaning up movie theaters. However, the number gradually narrows at higher levels of the organization because work is less standardized and there's more need for face-to-face communication. Variables in span of control include the following:

- **Capabilities of the manager.** The more experienced and capable a manager is, the broader the span of control can be. (A large number of workers can report to that manager.)
- **Capabilities of the subordinates.** The more the subordinates need supervision, the narrower the span of control should be. Employee turnover at fast-food restaurants, for example, is often so high that managers must constantly be training new people and thus need a narrow span of control.
- **Geographical closeness.** The more concentrated the work area is, the broader the span of control can be.
- **Functional similarity.** The more similar the functions are, the broader the span of control can be.

- **Need for coordination.** The greater the need for coordination, the narrower the span of control might be.
- **Planning demands.** The more involved the plan, the narrower the span of control might be.
- **Functional complexity.** The more complex the functions are, the narrower the span of control might be.

Other factors to consider include the professionalism of superiors and subordinates and the number of new problems that occur in a day.

In business, the span of control varies widely. The number of people reporting to a company president may range from 1 to 80 or more. The trend is to expand the span of control as organizations reduce the number of middle managers and hire more educated and talented lower-level employees. That is all included in the idea of empowerment. It's possible to increase the span of control as employees become more professional, as information technology makes it possible for managers to handle more information, and as employees take on more responsibility for self-management. At Rowe Furniture in Salem, Virginia, for example, the manufacturing chief dismantled the assembly line and gave the people who had previously performed limited functions (sewing, gluing, stapling) the freedom to make sofas as they saw fit. That is, the chief empowered the company's workers. Productivity and quality soared. More companies could expand the span of control if they trained their employees better and were willing to trust them more.

Tall versus Flat Organization Structures

In the early 20th century, organizations grew bigger and bigger, adding layer after layer of management until they came to have what are called tall organization structures. A **tall organization structure** is one in which the pyramidal organization chart would be quite tall because of the various levels of management. Some organizations had as many as 14 levels, and the span of control was small (that is, there were few people reporting to each manager). You can imagine how a message would be distorted as it moved up the organization from manager to manager and then back down. When viewing such a tall organization, you saw a huge complex of managers, management assistants, secretaries, assistant secretaries, supervisors, trainers, and so on. The cost of keeping all these managers and support people was quite high. The paperwork they generated was enormous, and the inefficiencies in communication and decision making often became intolerable.

tall organization structure
An organizational structure in which the pyramidal organization chart would be quite tall because of the various levels of management.

The result was the movement toward flatter organizations. A **flat organization structure** is one that has few layers of management (see Figure 8.3) and a broad span of control (that is, there are many people reporting to each manager). Such structures can be highly responsive to customer demands because authority and responsibility for making decisions may be given to lower-level employees and managers can be spared from certain day-to-day tasks. In a bookstore that has a flat organization structure, employees may have the authority to

flat organization structure
An organization structure that has few layers of management and a broad span of control.

FIGURE 8.3

A FLAT ORGANIZATION STRUCTURE

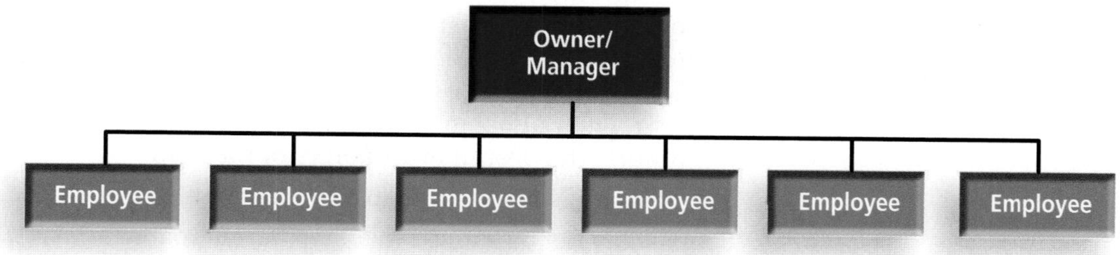

FIGURE 8.4

ADVANTAGES AND DISADVANTAGES OF A NARROW VERSUS A BROAD SPAN OF CONTROL

The flatter the organization, the broader the span of control.

ADVANTAGES	DISADVANTAGES
Narrow	
• More control by top management	• Less empowerment
• More chances for advancement	• Higher costs
• Greater specialization	• Delayed decision making
• Closer supervision	• Less responsiveness to customers
Broad	
• Reduced costs	• Fewer chances for advancement
• More responsiveness to customers	• Overworked managers
• Faster decision making	• Loss of control
• More empowerment	• Less management expertise

arrange shelves by category, process special orders for customers, and so on. In many ways, large organizations were trying to match the friendliness of small firms, whose workers often knew the customers by name. The flatter organizations became, the broader the span of control became for most managers, and many managers lost their jobs. Figure 8.4 lists some advantages and disadvantages of a narrow versus a broad span of control.

Advantages and Disadvantages of Departmentalization

departmentalization The dividing of organizational functions into separate units.

Departmentalization is the dividing of organizational functions (design, marketing, etc.) into separate units. The traditional way to departmentalize organizations is by function. Functional structure is the grouping of workers into departments based on similar skills, expertise, or resource use. A company might have, for example, a production department, a transportation department, and a finance department. Departmentalization by function enables employees to specialize and work together efficiently. It may also save costs. Other advantages include the following:

1. Employees can develop skills in depth and can progress within a department as they master those skills.
2. The company can achieve economies of scale in that it can centralize all the resources it needs and locate various experts in that area.
3. There's good coordination within the function, and top management can easily direct and control various departments' activities.

As for disadvantages of departmentalization by function,

1. There may be a lack of communication among the different departments. For example, production may be so isolated from marketing that the people making the product do not get the proper feedback from customers.
2. Individual employees may begin to identify with their department and its goals rather than with the goals of the organization as a whole. For example, the purchasing department may find a good value somewhere and buy a huge volume of goods that have to be stored at a high cost to the firm. Such a deal may make the purchasing department look good, but it hurts the overall profitability of the firm.
3. The company's response to external changes may be slow.
4. People may not be trained to take different managerial responsibilities; rather, they tend to become narrow specialists.

5. People in the same department tend to think alike (engage in groupthink) and may need input from outside the department to become more creative.

Alternative Ways to Departmentalize Functional separation isn't always the most responsive form of organization. So what are the alternatives? Figure 8.5 shows five ways a firm can departmentalize. One form of departmentalization is by product. A book publisher might have a trade book department (books sold to the general public), a textbook department, and a technical book department. Customers for each type of book are different, so separate development and marketing processes must be created for each product. Such product-focused departmentalization usually results in good customer relations.

It makes more sense in some organizations to departmentalize by customer group. A pharmaceutical company, for example, might have one department that focuses on the consumer market, another that calls on hospitals (the institutional market), and another that targets doctors. You can see how the customer groups might benefit from having specialists satisfying their needs.

Expedia.com is one Internet business that has been very successful by interacting with customers. Its website offers you great deals on flights, rental cars, hotels, vacation packages, and more. You can even print out maps to help you get to where you are going. If you have tried such a travel site for your vacation plans, were you happy with the services provided? Did you give them feedback?

Some firms group their units by geographic location because customers vary so greatly by region. Japan, Europe, and Korea may involve separate departments. Again, the benefits are rather obvious.

The decision about which way to departmentalize depends greatly on the nature of the product and the customers served. A few firms find that it's most efficient to separate activities by process. For example, a firm that makes leather coats may have one department cut the leather, another dye it, and a third sew the coat together. Such specialization enables employees to do a better job because they can focus on a few, critical skills.

Some firms use a combination of departmentalization techniques; they would be called hybrid forms. For example, a company could departmentalize simultaneously among the different layers by function, by geography, and by customers.

The development of the Internet has created whole new opportunities for reaching customers. Not only can you sell to customers directly over the Internet, but you can also interact with them, ask them questions, and provide them with any information they may want. Companies must now learn to coordinate the efforts made by their traditional departments and their Internet people to create a friendly, easy-to-use process for accessing information and buying goods and services.[7] The firms that have implemented such coordinated systems for meeting customer needs are winning market share.

Progress Assessment

- Why are organizations becoming flatter?
- What are some reasons for having a narrow span of control in an organization?
- What are the advantages and disadvantages of departmentalization?
- What are the various ways a firm can departmentalize?

FIGURE 8.5

WAYS TO DEPARTMENTALIZE

A computer company may want to departmentalize by geographic location (countries), a manufacturer by function, a pharmaceutical company by customer group, a leather manufacturer by process, and a publisher by product. In each case the structure must fit the firm's goals.

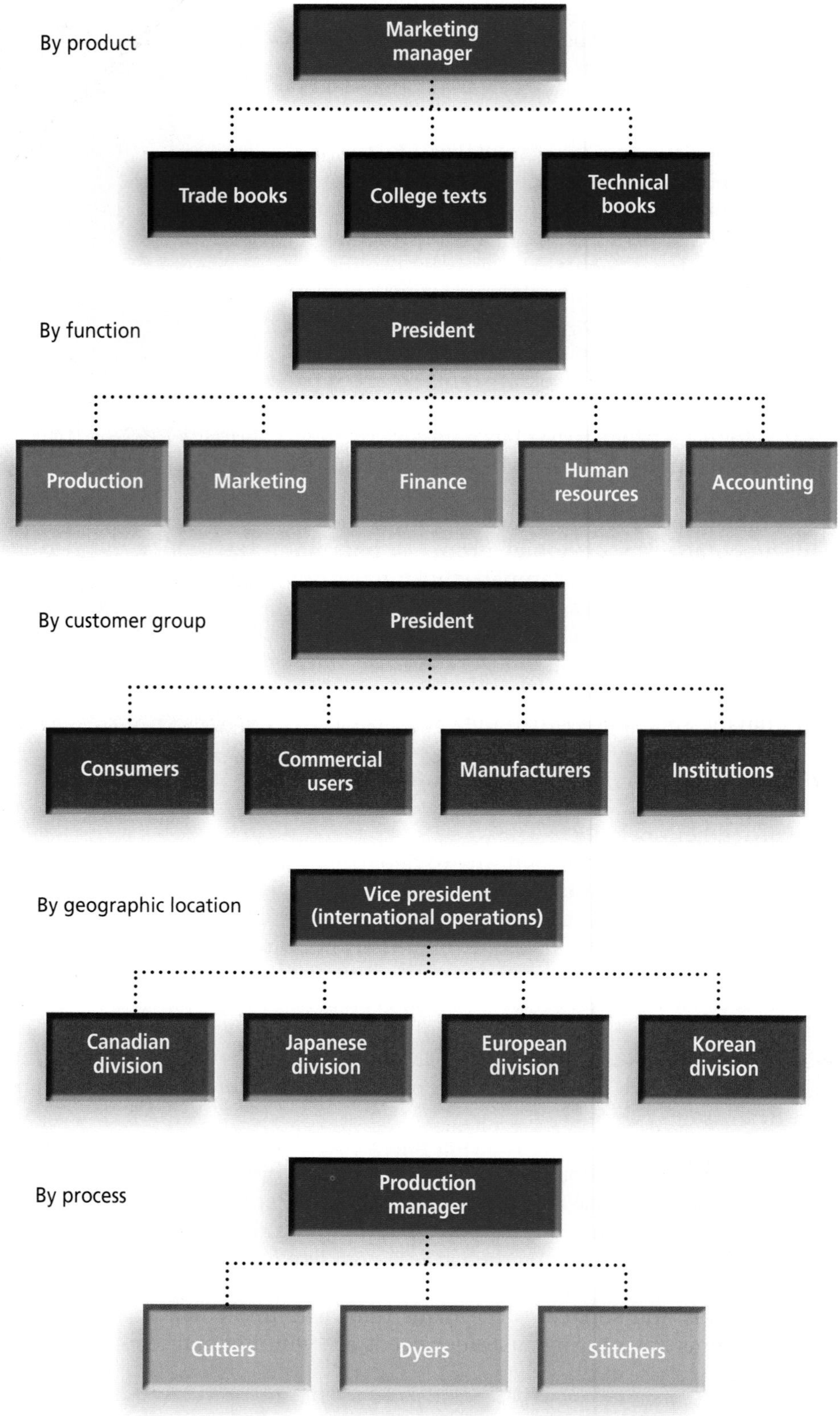

Critical Thinking

Given the limitations of departmentalization, businesses are now trying to redesign their structures to optimize skill development while increasing communication among employees in different departments. The goal, remember, is to better serve customers and to win their loyalty. What kind of skills and attributes might you need to prepare yourself to work in such an organization?

Organization Models

Now that we've explored the basic issues of organizational design, we can explore in depth the various ways to structure an organization. We'll look at four models: (1) line organizations, (2) line-and-staff organizations, (3) matrix-style organizations, and (4) cross-functional self-managed teams. You'll see that some of these models violate traditional management principles. The business community is in a period of transition, with some traditional organizational models giving way to new structures. Such transitions not only can be painful but can also be fraught with problems and errors. It will be easier for you to understand the issues involved after you have learned the basics of organizational modeling.

Line Organizations

A **line organization** has direct two-way lines of responsibility, authority, and communication running from the top to the bottom of the organization, with all people reporting to only one supervisor. The military and many small businesses are organized this way. For example, Mario's Pizza Parlor has a general manager and a shift manager. All the general employees report to the shift manager, and he or she reports to the general manager or owner. A line organization does not have any specialists who provide managerial support. For example, there would be no legal department, no accounting department, no personnel department, and no information technology (IT) department. Such organizations follow all of Fayol's traditional management rules. Line managers can issue orders, enforce discipline, and adjust the organization as conditions change.

line organization
An organization that has direct two-way lines of responsibility, authority, and communication running from the top to the bottom of the organization, with all people reporting to only one supervisor.

In large businesses, a line organization may have the disadvantages of being too inflexible, of having few specialists or experts to advise people along the line, of having lines of communication that are too long, and of being unable to handle the complex decisions involved in an organization with thousands of sometimes unrelated products and literally tons of paperwork. Such organizations usually turn to a line-and-staff form of organization.

Line-and-Staff Organizations

To minimize the disadvantages of simple line organizations, many organizations today have both line and staff personnel. A couple of definitions will help. **Line personnel** are part of the chain of command that is responsible for achieving organizational goals. Included are production workers, distribution people, and marketing personnel. **Staff personnel** advise and assist line personnel in meeting their goals (e.g., marketing research, legal advising, information technology, and human resource management). See Figure 8.6 for a diagram of a line-and-staff organization. One important difference between line and staff personnel is authority. Line personnel have formal authority to make policy decisions. Staff personnel have the authority to *advise* the line personnel and make suggestions that might influence those decisions, but they

line personnel
Employees who are part of the chain of command that is responsible for achieving organizational goals.

staff personnel
Employees who advise and assist line personnel in meeting their goals.

FIGURE 8.6

A SAMPLE LINE-AND-STAFF ORGANIZATION

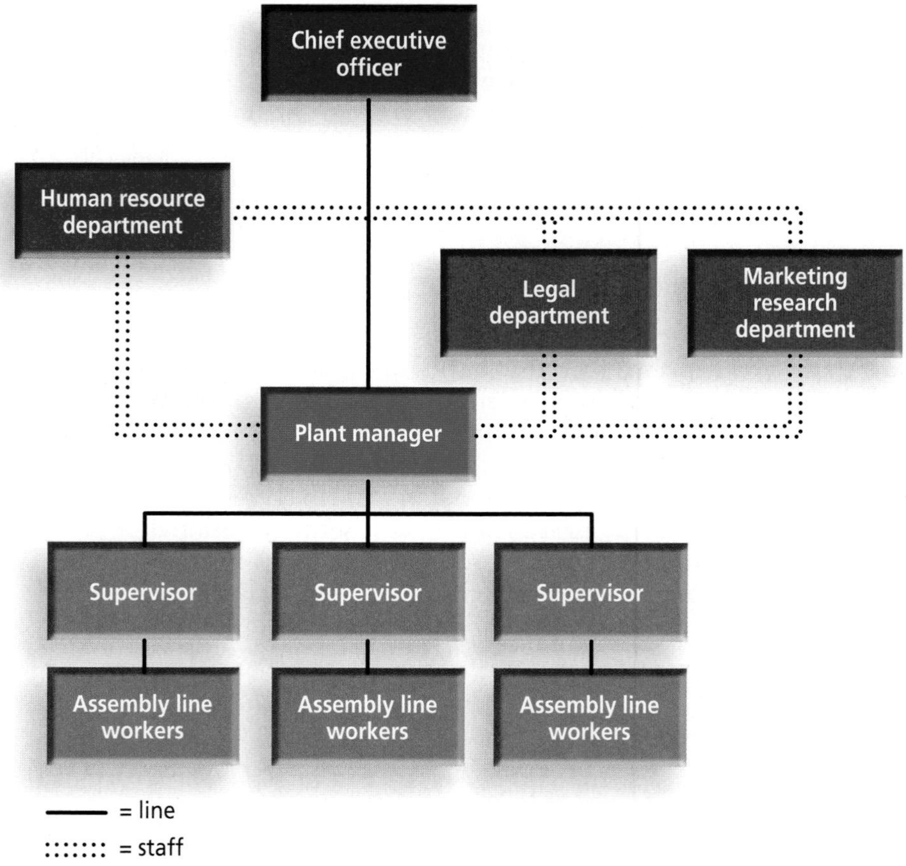

can't make policy changes themselves. The line manager may choose to seek or to ignore the advice from staff personnel.

Many organizations have benefited from the expert advice of staff assistants in areas such as safety, legal issues, quality control, database management, motivation, and investing. Staff positions strengthen the line positions and are not inferior or lower-paid. Having people in staff positions is like having well-paid consultants on the organization's payroll.

Matrix-Style Organizations

Both line and line-and-staff organization structures suffer from a certain inflexibility. Both allow for established lines of authority and communication, and both work well in organizations with a relatively unchanging environment and slow product development, such as firms selling consumer products like toasters and refrigerators. In such firms, clear lines of authority and relatively fixed organization structures are assets that ensure efficient operations.

Today's economic scene, however, is dominated by high-growth industries (e.g., telecommunications, nanotechnology, robotics, biotechnology, and aerospace) unlike anything seen in the past. In such industries, competition is stiff and the life cycle of new ideas is short. Emphasis is on product development, creativity, special projects, rapid communication, and interdepartmental teamwork. The economic, technological, and competitive environments are rapidly changing.

matrix organization
An organization in which specialists from different parts of the organization are brought together to work on specific projects but still remain part of a line-and-staff structure.

From those changes grew the popularity of the matrix organization. In a **matrix organization**, specialists from different parts of the organization are brought together to work on specific projects but still remain part of a line-and-staff structure. (See Figure 8.7 for a diagram of a matrix organization.) In other words, a project manager can borrow people from different departments to help design and market new product ideas.

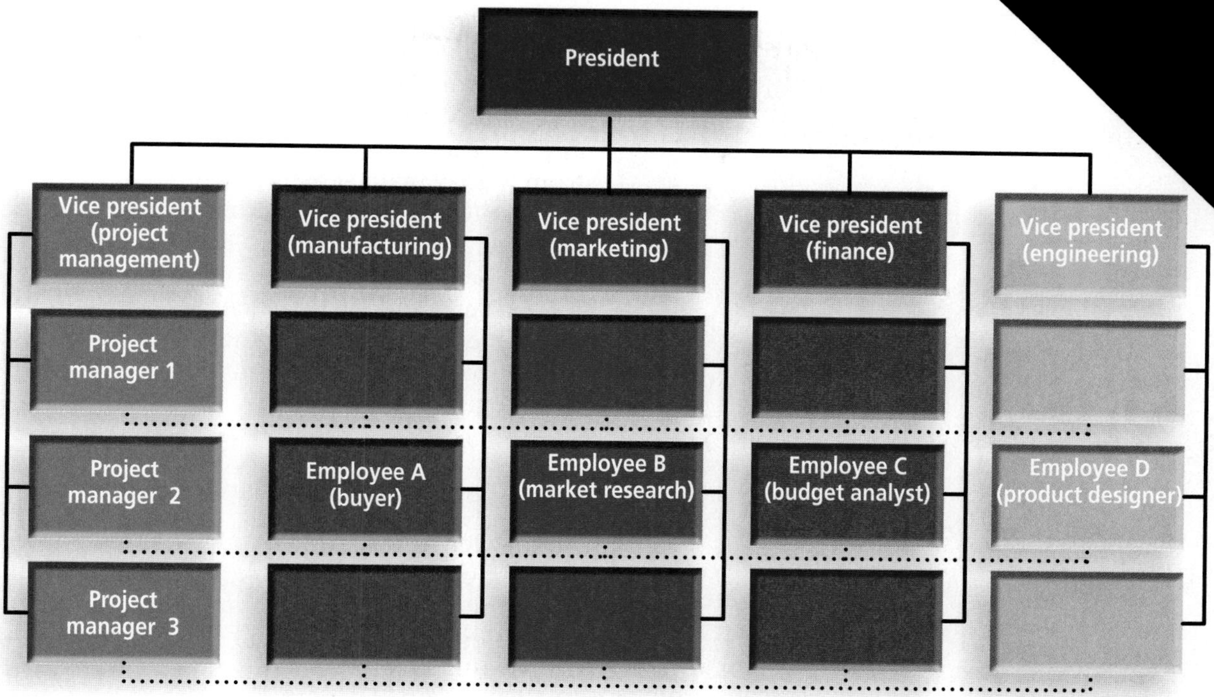

FIGURE 8.7

A MATRIX ORGANIZATION

In a matrix organization, project managers are in charge of teams made up of members of several departments. In this case, project manager 2 supervises employees A, B, C, and D. These employees are accountable not only to project manager 2 but also to the head of their individual departments. For example, employee B, a market researcher, reports to project manager 2 *and* to the vice president of marketing.

Matrix organization structures were first developed in the aerospace industry at firms such as Boeing and Lockheed Martin. The structure is now used in banking, management consulting firms, accounting firms, ad agencies, and school systems. Advantages of a matrix organization structure include the following:

- It gives flexibility to managers in assigning people to projects.
- It encourages interorganizational cooperation and teamwork.
- It can result in creative solutions to problems such as those associated with product development.
- It provides for efficient use of organizational resources.

Although it works well in some organizations, the matrix style doesn't work well in others. As for disadvantages,

- It's costly and complex.
- It can cause confusion among employees as to where their loyalty belongs—to the project manager or to their functional unit.
- It requires good interpersonal skills and cooperative employees and managers; communication problems can emerge.
- It may be only a temporary solution to a long-term problem.

If it seems to you that matrix organizations violate some traditional managerial principles, you're right. Normally a person can't work effectively for two bosses. Who has the real authority? Which directive has the first priority: the one from the project manager or the one from the employee's immediate supervisor? In reality, however, the system functions more effectively than you might imagine. To develop a new product, a project manager may be given temporary authority to "borrow" line personnel from production, marketing, and other line functions.[8] Together, the employees work to complete the project and then return to their regular positions. Thus, no one really reports to more than one manager at a time. The effectiveness of matrix organizations

Rubbermaid creates new products at a fast clip, sometimes as fast as one a day. This photo shows one of their new products that organizes sports equipment, reducing household clutter. Cross-functional teams at Rubbermaid help create new products and get them to market quickly. What are some of the advantages and challenges of working with people from various departments on new-product development?

in high-tech firms has led to the adoption of similar concepts in many firms, including such traditional firms as Rubbermaid. During the past decade, Rubbermaid turned out an average of one new product every day using the team concept from matrix management.

A potential problem with matrix management, however, is that the project teams are not permanent. They are formed to solve a problem or develop a new product, and then they break up. There is little chance for cross-functional learning because experts from each function are together for so little time.

Cross-Functional Self-Managed Teams

An answer to the disadvantage of the temporary teams created by matrix management is to establish long-lived teams and to empower them to work closely with suppliers, customers, and others to quickly and efficiently bring out new, high-quality products while giving great service. **Cross-functional self-managed teams** are groups of employees from different departments who work together on a long-term basis (as opposed to the temporary teams established in matrix-style organizations). Usually the teams are empowered to make decisions on their own without having to seek the approval of management. That's why the teams are called self-managed. The barriers between design, engineering, marketing, distribution, and other functions fall when interdepartmental teams are created.

Sometimes the teams are interfirm. Hummer, for example, has become one of the hottest divisions at General Motors (GM). A cross-functional team from GM designs, engineers, and markets Hummers, but AM General manufactures the vehicles in a plant built with a loan from GM.[9]

cross-functional self-managed teams
Groups of employees from different departments who work together on a long-term basis.

For empowerment and cross-functional self-managed teams to work effectively, the organization has to change. Moving from a manager-driven to an employee-driven or team-driven company isn't easy. Managers often resist giving up their authority over workers, while workers often resist the responsibility that comes with self-management. Nonetheless, many of the world's leading organizations are moving in that direction. They're trying to develop an organizational design that best serves the needs of all stakeholders ➤P. 6◄— employees, customers, stockholders, and the community.

Going Beyond Organizational Boundaries Cross-functional teams work best when the voice of the customer is brought into organizations. Customer input is especially valuable to product development teams. Suppliers and distributors should be included on the team as well. A cross-functional team that includes customers, suppliers, and distributors goes beyond organizational boundaries.

Some firms' suppliers and distributors are in other countries. Thus, cross-functional teams may share market information across national boundaries. The government may encourage the networking of teams, and government coordinators may assist such projects. In that case, cross-functional teams break the barriers between government and business. The use of cross-functional teams is only one way in which businesses have changed to interact with other companies. In the next section of this chapter we look at other ways that organizations manage their various interactions.

Mike DiGiovanni wanted General Motors to buy the rights to the Hummer, a military vehicle, with the idea of creating a smaller, friendlier version—the H2. He wanted a team made up of veterans who knew what they were doing. Hummer became a top-selling vehicle for GM. How important are a committed team leader and team members to the success of such an operation?

Progress Assessment

- What is the difference between line and staff personnel?
- What management principle does a matrix-style organization challenge?
- What may hinder the development of cross-functional teams?

Managing the Interactions among Firms

Whether it involves customers, suppliers and distributors, or the government, **networking** is using communications technology and other means to link organizations and allow them to work together on common objectives. Organizations are so closely linked by the Internet that each can find out what the others are doing in real time. **Real time** simply means the present moment or the actual time in which something takes place. Internet data are available in real time because they are sent instantly to various organizational partners as they are developed or collected. The net effect is a rather new concept called transparency. **Transparency** occurs when a company is so open to other companies working with it that the once-solid barriers between them become see-through and electronic information is shared as if the companies were one. Because of this integration, two companies can now work as closely together as two departments once did in traditional firms.

networking
Using communications technology and other means to link organizations and allow them to work together on common objectives.

real time
The present moment or the actual time in which something takes place.

transparency
A concept that describes a company being so open to other companies working with it that the once-solid barriers between them become see-through and electronic information is shared as if the companies were one.

Can you see the implications for organizational design? Most organizations are no longer self-sufficient or self-contained. Rather, many modern organizations are part of a vast network of global businesses that work closely together. An organization chart showing what people do within any one organization is simply not complete because the organization is part of a much larger system of firms. A modern organization chart would show people in different organizations and indicate how they are networked. This is a relatively new concept, however, so few such charts are yet available.

The organization structures tend to be flexible and changing. That is, one company may work with a design expert from a different company in Italy for a year and then not need that person anymore. Another expert from another company in another country may be hired next time for another project. Such a temporary networked organization, made up of replaceable firms that join

FIGURE 8.8

A VIRTUAL CORPORATION

A virtual corporation has no permanent ties to the firms that do its production, distribution, legal, and other work. Such firms are very flexible and can adapt to changes in the market quickly.

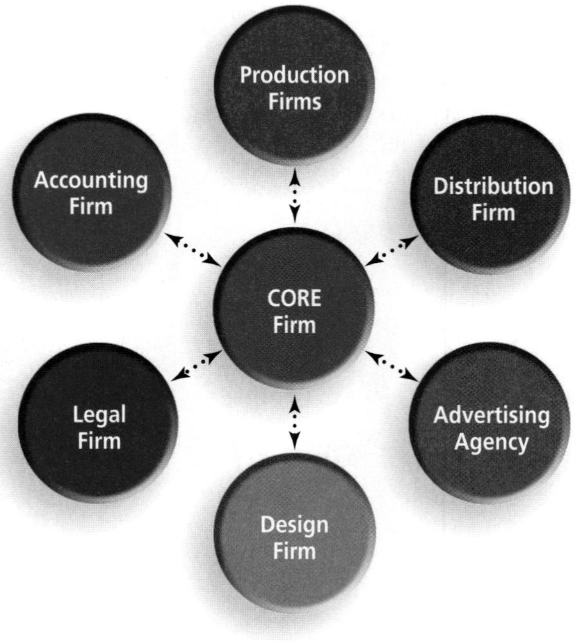

virtual corporation
A temporary networked organization made up of replaceable firms that join and leave as needed.

benchmarking
Comparing an organization's practices, processes, and products against the world's best.

and leave as needed, is called a **virtual corporation** (see Figure 8.8). This may sound confusing because it is so different from traditional organization structure, and in fact, traditional managers do often have trouble adapting to the speed of change and the impermanence of relationships that have come about in the age of networking. We discuss adaptation to change in the final section of this chapter; first, though, we describe how organizations are using benchmarking and outsourcing to manage their interactions with other firms.

Benchmarking and Outsourcing

Traditionally, organizations have tried to do all functions themselves. That is, each organization had a separate department for accounting, finance, marketing, production, and so on. Today's organizations are looking to other organizations to help them in areas where they are not able to generate world-class quality.[10] **Benchmarking** involves comparing an organization's practices, processes, and products against the world's best. For example, K2 is a company that makes skis, snowboards, in-line skates, and related products. It studied the compact-disc industry and learned to use ultraviolet inks to print graphics on skis. It went to the aerospace industry to get Piezo technology to reduce vibration in its snowboards (the aerospace industry uses the technology for wings on planes). And, finally, it learned from the cable-TV industry how to braid layers of fiberglass and carbon, and adapted that knowledge to make skis.

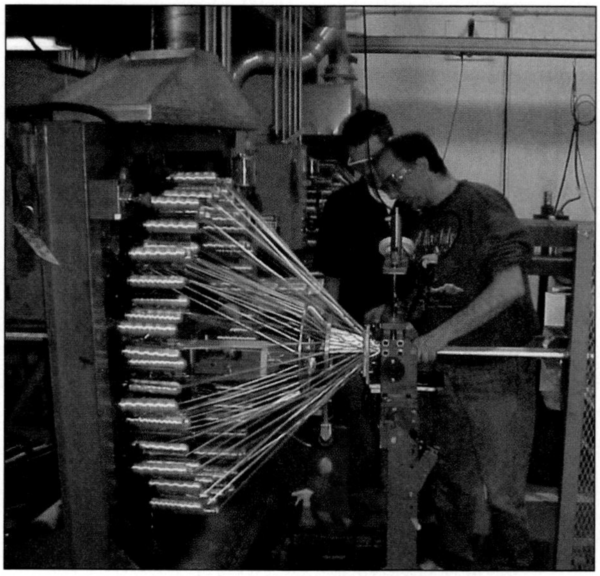

Knowledge is increasing and technology is developing so fast that companies can only maintain a leading edge by benchmarking everything they do against the best in all industries. That's how K-2 was able to find the best materials and processes for making its skis. Whom might you study to learn the best way to prepare for classes and exams?

Benchmarking is also used in a more directly competitive way. For example, Target may compare itself to Wal-Mart to see what, if anything, Wal-Mart does better. Target would then try to improve its practices or processes to become even better than Wal-Mart. Sam Walton used to do competitive benchmarking regularly. He would visit the stores of competitors and see what, if anything, the competitor was doing better. When he found something better—say, a pricing program—he would come back to Wal-Mart and make the appropriate changes.

If an organization can't do as well as the best in any particular area, such as shipping, it often will try to outsource the function to an organization that *is* the best (e.g., UPS or FedEx).[11] **Outsourcing** is assigning various functions, such as accounting, production, security, maintenance, and legal work, to outside organizations.[12] Some functions, such as information management and marketing, may be too important to assign to outside firms.[13] In that case, the organization should benchmark on the best firms and restructure its departments to try to be equally good.

When a firm has completed its outsourcing process, the remaining functions are the firm's core competencies. **Core competencies** are those functions that the organization can do as well as or better than any other organization in the world. For example, Nike is great at designing and marketing athletic shoes. Those are its core competencies. It outsources the manufacturing of those shoes, however, to other companies that can make shoes better and less expensively than Nike itself can. Similarly, Dell is best at marketing computers and outsources most other functions, including manufacturing and distribution, to others.[14] IBM has also outsourced most of its manufacturing functions.[15]

Mike Goldston, CEO of United Online (an Internet service provider), has been able to use outsourcing to significantly reduce costs, thus enabling his much smaller company to compete and take market share from industry giants like AOL. What have been your experiences with successful Internet companies such as Google, eBay, E-Trade, and Yahoo?

Adapting to Change

Once you have structured an organization, you must be prepared to adapt that structure to changes in the market. That is not always easy to do. Over a number of years, it is easy for an organization to become stuck in its ways. Employees have a tendency to say, "That's the way we've always done things. If it isn't broken, don't fix it." Managers also get stuck in their ways. Managers may say that they have 20 years' experience when the truth is that they've had one year's experience 20 times. Introducing change into an organization is thus one of the hardest challenges facing any manager.[16] Several companies have been cited in the business literature as having difficulty reinventing themselves in response to changes in the competitive environment. They include Kmart, Polaroid, and Xerox.[17] New cameras (digital) and new kinds of film brought about the downfall of Polaroid, which filed for bankruptcy and was later sold. Xerox can't seem to match competition from overseas. Kmart was unable to manage the competition from Wal-Mart, Sears, and Target, and filed for bankruptcy. New managers at these firms face tremendous hurdles as they try to revive them.

Mergers and acquisitions pose special challenges in adapting to change. That's why so many mergers of big corporations fail and why so many people were skeptical about Carly Fiorina's decision to link Hewlett-Packard and Compaq (discussed in this chapter's opening profile).

Restructuring for Empowerment

To implement the empowerment of employees, firms often must reorganize dramatically. Sometimes that may mean restructuring the firm to make frontline workers the most important people in the organization. **Restructuring** is

outsourcing
Assigning various functions, such as accounting, production, security, maintenance, and legal work, to outside organizations.

core competencies
Those functions that the organization can do as well as or better than any other organization in the world.

restructuring
Redesigning an organization so that it can more effectively and efficiently serve its customers.

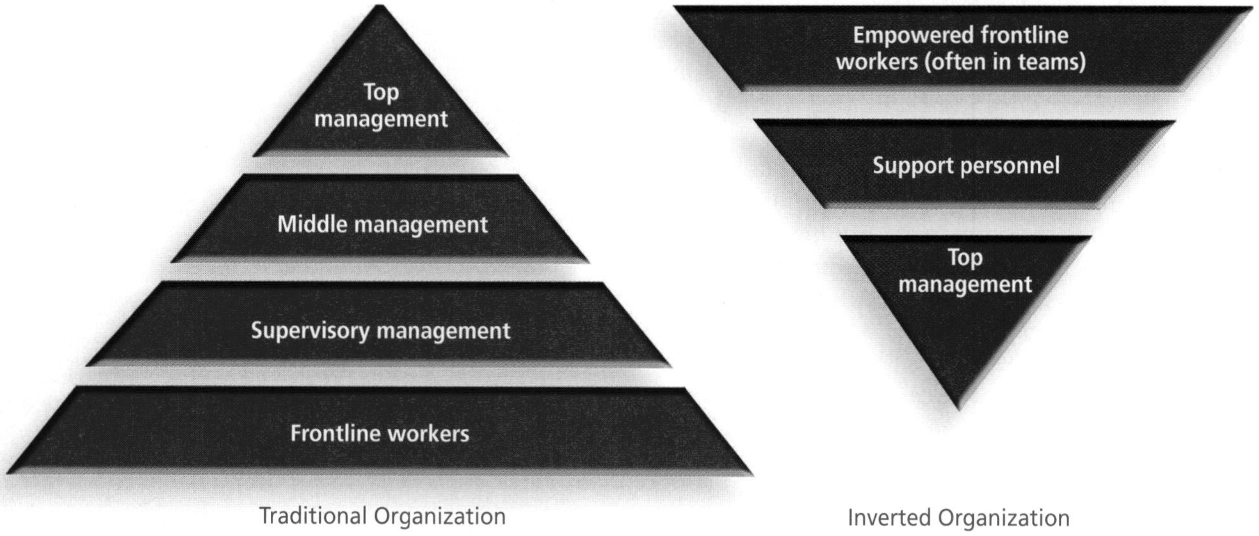

FIGURE 8.9

COMPARISON OF AN INVERTED ORGANIZATION STRUCTURE AND A TRADITIONAL ORGANIZATION STRUCTURE

redesigning an organization so that it can more effectively and efficiently serve its customers. Until recently, front-desk people in hotels, clerks in department stores, and tellers in banks hadn't been considered the key personnel. Instead, managers were considered the key people, and they were responsible for directing the work of the front-line people. The organization chart in a typical firm looked something like the organization pyramid shown in Figure 8.1 on p. 244.

inverted organization
An organization that has contact people at the top and the chief executive officer at the bottom of the organization chart.

A few service-oriented organizations have turned the traditional organization structure upside down. An **inverted organization** has contact people at the top and the chief executive officer at the bottom. There are few layers of management, and the manager's job is to assist and support front-line people, not boss them around. Figure 8.9 illustrates the difference between an inverted and a traditional organizational structure.

A good example of an inverted organization is NovaCare, a provider of rehabilitation care. At its top are some 5,000 physical, occupational, and speech therapists. The rest of the organization is structured to serve those therapists. Managers consider the therapists to be their bosses, and the manager's job is to support the therapists by arranging contacts with nursing homes, handling accounting and credit activities, and providing training.

Companies based on this organization structure support frontline personnel with internal and external databases, advanced communication systems, and professional assistance. Naturally, this means that frontline people have to be better educated, better trained, and better paid than in the past. It takes a lot of trust for top managers to implement such a system—but when they do, the payoff in customer satisfaction and in profits is often well worth the effort. In the past, managers controlled information—and that gave them power. In more progressive organizations, everyone shares information, often through an elaborate database system.

Radical Reorganization

reengineering
The fundamental rethinking and radical redesign of organizational processes to achieve dramatic improvements in critical measures of performance.

Reengineering is the fundamental rethinking and radical redesign of organizational processes to achieve dramatic improvements in critical measures of performance. Note the words *radical redesign* and *dramatic improvements.* At IBM's credit organization, for example, the process for handling a customer's request for credit once went through a five-step process that took an average of six days. By completely reengineering the customer-request process, IBM cut its credit request processing time from six days to four hours! In reengineering, narrow, task-oriented jobs become multidimensional. Employees who once did as they were told now make decisions on their own. Functional departments lose their reason for being. Managers stop acting like supervisors and instead behave like coaches. Workers focus more on the customers' needs and less on their bosses' needs. Attitudes and values change in response to new incentives. Practically every aspect of the organization is transformed, often beyond recognition.

Can you see how reengineering is often necessary to change a firm from a managerial orientation to one based on cross-functional self-managed teams? Reengineering may also be necessary to adapt an organization to fit into a virtual network. Remember, reengineering involves *radical* redesign and *dramatic* improvements. Not all organizations need such dramatic change. In fact, because of the complexity of the process, many reengineering efforts fail. In firms where reengineering is not feasible, restructuring may do. As discussed earlier in this chapter, restructuring involves making relatively minor changes to an organization in response to a changing environment. For example, a firm might add an Internet marketing component to the marketing department. That is a restructuring move, but it is not drastic enough to be called reengineering.

Reengineering guru Michael Hammer symbolically uses a megaphone to get his points across. His newest book titled *The Agenda: What Every Business Must Do to Dominate the Decade* says that reengineering processes are as important now as ever. Have you noticed that some companies are slow to change unless they are pushed hard by new competition?

Creating a Change-Oriented Organizational Culture

Any organizational change is bound to cause some stress and resistance among members of the firm. Firms adapt best when they have a change-oriented culture. **Organizational (or corporate) culture** may be defined as widely shared values within an organization that provide unity and cooperation to achieve common goals. Usually the culture of an organization is reflected in stories, traditions, and myths. Carly Fiorina, for example, has advertised the story about how Bill Hewlett and Dave Packard started their business in a Palo Alto garage. She hopes to maintain the entrepreneurial spirit of HP as symbolized by the garage.[18]

organizational (or corporate) culture
Widely shared values within an organization that provide unity and cooperation to achieve common goals.

It's obvious from visiting any McDonald's restaurant that effort has been made to maintain a culture that emphasizes quality, service, cleanliness, and value. Each restaurant has the same feel, the same look, the same atmosphere. In short, each has a similar organizational culture.

An organizational culture can also be negative. Have you ever been in an organization where you feel that no one cares about service or quality? The clerks may seem uniformly glum, indifferent, and testy. The mood seems to pervade the atmosphere so that patrons become unhappy or upset. It may be hard to believe that an organization, especially a profit-making one, can be run so badly and still survive. Are there examples in your area?

The very best organizations have cultures that emphasize service to others, especially customers.[19] The atmosphere is one of friendly, concerned, caring people who enjoy working together to provide a good product at a reasonable price. Those companies that have such cultures have less need for close supervision of employees, not to mention policy manuals; organization charts; and formal rules, procedures, and controls. The key to a productive culture is mutual trust. You get such trust by giving it.[20] The very best companies stress high moral and ethical values such as honesty, reliability, fairness, environmental protection, and social involvement. The Spotlight on Small Business box looks at how one small organization successfully implemented a customer-oriented culture.

Spotlight on Small Business

www.amysicecream.com

All This and Ice Cream Too

Amy's ice cream parlors in Austin and Houston, Texas, attract a lot of customers because of their offbeat corporate culture. On any given night, you might see the servers juggling with their serving spades, tossing scoops of ice cream to each other, or break-dancing on the freezer top. If there is a long line, they pass out samples or give a free cone to any customer who will sing, dance, recite a poem, or otherwise entertain those in line. Employees might be wearing pajamas (Sleepover Night) or masks (Star Wars Night). Lighting may be provided by candles (Romance Night) or strobe lights (Disco Night). You get the idea. It's fun at Amy's—for the customers and for the employees. Amy's is careful to choose employees who will fit in with the organizational culture. For example, in job interviews candidates are asked to decorate a plain bag to show how creative they are. Organizational culture can go a long way toward making a small company a success or a failure.

formal organization
The structure that details lines of responsibility, authority, and position; that is, the structure shown on organization charts.

informal organization
The system of relationships and lines of authority that develops spontaneously as employees meet and form power centers; that is, the human side of the organization that does not appear on any organization chart.

Thus far, we've been talking as if organizational matters were mostly controllable by management. The fact is that the formal organization structure is just one element of the total organizational system. In the creation of organizational culture, the informal organization is of equal or even greater importance. Let's explore this notion next.

The Informal Organization

All organizations have two organizational systems. One is the **formal organization**, which is the structure that details lines of responsibility, authority, and position. It's the structure shown on organization charts. The other is the **informal organization**, which is the system of relationships that develop spontaneously as employees meet and form power centers. It consists of the various cliques, relationships, and lines of authority that develop outside the formal organization. It's the human side of the organization that doesn't show on any organization chart.

Richard Tait (left) calls himself the grand poo-bah for Cranium, producer of the highly successful board game of that name. Whit Alexander, who does product development and manufacturing, is called the chief noodler. Their criteria for decision making are clever, high quality, innovative, friendly, and fun (CHIFF). What kind of leadership style and company culture might you expect in a company that is so casual?

No organization can operate effectively without both types of organization. The formal system is often too slow and bureaucratic to enable the organization to adapt quickly. However, the formal organization does provide helpful guides and lines of authority to follow in routine situations.

The informal organization is often too unstructured and emotional to allow careful, reasoned decision making on critical matters. It's extremely effective, however, in generating creative solutions to short-term problems and providing a feeling of camaraderie and teamwork among employees.

In any organization, it's wise to learn quickly who the important people are in the informal organization. Typically, there are formal rules and procedures to follow for getting certain supplies or equipment, but those procedures may take days. Who in the organization knows how to obtain supplies immediately without following the normal procedures? Which administrative assistants should you see if you want your work given first priority? These are the questions to answer to work effectively in many organizations.

The informal organization's nerve center is the *grapevine* (the system through which unofficial information flows between and among managers and employees). The key people in the grapevine usually have considerable influence in the organization.

In the old "us-versus-them" system of organizations, where managers and employees were often at odds, the informal system often hindered effective management. In the new, more open organizations, where managers and employees work together to set objectives and design procedures, the informal organization can be an invaluable managerial asset that often promotes harmony among workers and establishes the corporate culture. That's a major advantage, for example, of self-managed teams.

As effective as the informal organization may be in creating group cooperation, it can still be equally powerful in resisting management directives. Employees may form unions, go on strike together, and generally disrupt operations.[21] Learning to create the right corporate culture and to work within the informal organization is a key to managerial success.

Progress Assessment

- What is an inverted organization?
- What is reengineering?
- Why do organizations outsource functions?
- What is organizational culture?

Summary

1. Explain the historical organizational theories of Fayol and Weber.

1. The 20th century saw the introduction of the concept of economies of scale. Economies of scale exist when companies can reduce their production costs by purchasing raw materials in bulk; the average cost of each item goes down as production levels increase.
   - ***What concepts did Fayol and Weber contribute?***

   Fayol introduced principles such as unity of command, hierarchy of authority, division of labor, subordination of individual interests to the general interest, authority, clear communication channels, order, and equity. Weber added principles of bureaucracy such as job descriptions, written rules and decision guidelines, consistent procedures, and staffing and promotions based on qualifications.

2. Explain the various issues involved in structuring organizations.

2. Issues involved in structuring and restructuring organizations include (1) centralization versus decentralization, (2) span of control, and (3) tall versus flat organization structures.
   - ***What are the basics of each?***

   Departments are often being replaced or supplemented by matrix organizations and cross-functional teams. Use of cross-functional teams results in decentralization of authority. The span of control becomes larger as employees become self-directed. The problem with tall organizations is that they slow communications. The trend is to eliminate managers and flatten organizations.

3. Describe and differentiate the various organizational models.

3. Organizational design is the coordinating of workers so that they can best accomplish the firm's goals. New forms of organization are emerging that enable firms to be more responsive to customers.
   - ***What are the traditional forms of organization and their advantages?***

   The two traditional forms of organization explored in the text are (1) line organizations and (2) line-and-staff organizations. A line organization has the advantages of having clearly defined responsibility and authority, being easy to understand, and providing one supervisor for each person. Most organizations have benefited from the expert advice of staff assistants in areas such as safety, quality control, computer technology, human resource management, and investing.
   - ***What are the new forms of organization?***

   Matrix organizations and cross-functional self-managed teams.
   - ***How do they differ?***

   Matrix organizations involve *temporary* assignments (projects) that give flexibility to managers in assigning people to projects and encourage interorganizational cooperation and teamwork. Cross-functional self-managed teams are *long term* and have all the benefits of the matrix style.

4. Discuss the concepts involved in interfirm cooperation and coordination.

4. Networking is using communications technology and other means to link organizations and allow them to work together on common objectives.
   - ***What is a virtual corporation?***

   A virtual corporation is a networked organization made up of replaceable firms that join the network and leave it as needed.
   - ***Why do firms outsource some of their functions?***

   Some firms are very good at one function: for example, marketing. Competitive benchmarking tells them that they are not as good as some companies at production or distribution. The company may then outsource those functions to companies that can perform those functions more effectively and efficiently. The functions left are called the firm's core competencies.

5. Explain how restructuring, organizational culture, and informal organizations can help businesses adapt to change.

5. Organizational culture may be defined as widely shared values within an organization that provide coherence and cooperation to achieve common goals.
   - ***What's the difference between restructuring and reengineering?***

   It's basically a matter of degree. Restructuring is making needed changes in the firm so that it can more effectively and efficiently serve its customers. For example, a firm may add more computers or change how they process orders. Reengineering is the fundamental rethinking and radical redesign of organizational processes to achieve dramatic improvements in critical measures of performance.
   - ***How do inverted organizations fit into these concepts?***

   An inverted organization usually results from a major reengineering effort because the changes are dramatic in that employees are placed at the top of the hierarchy and are given much training and support while managers are at the bottom and are there to train and assist employees.
   - ***How can organizational culture and the informal organization hinder or assist organizational change?***

   The very best organizations have cultures that emphasize service to others, especially customers. The atmosphere is one of friendly, concerned, caring people who enjoy working together to provide a good product at a reasonable price. Companies with such cultures have less need than other companies for close supervision of employees; policy manuals; organization charts; and formal rules, procedures, and controls. This opens the way for self-managed teams.

Key Terms

Developing Workplace Skills

1. There is no way to better understand the effects of having many layers of management on communication accuracy than to play the game of Message Relay. Choose seven or more members of the class and have them leave the classroom. Then choose one person to read the following paragraph and another student to listen. Call in one of the students from outside and have the "listener" tell him or her what information was in the paragraph. Then bring in another student and have the new listener repeat the information to him or her. Continue the process with all those who left the room. Do not allow anyone in the class to offer corrections as each listener becomes the storyteller in turn. In this way, all the students can hear how the facts become distorted over time. The distortions and mistakes are often quite humorous, but they are not so funny in organizations such as Ford, which once had 22 layers of management.

   Here's the paragraph:

   Dealers in the Midwest region have received over 130 complaints about steering on the new Commander and Roadhandler models of our minivans. Apparently, the front suspension system is weak and the ball joints are wearing too fast. This causes slippage in the linkage and results in oversteering. Mr. Berenstein has been notified, but so far only 213 out of 4,300 dealers have received repair kits.

2. Describe some informal groups within an organization with which you are familiar (at school, at work, etc.). What have you noticed about how those groups help or hinder progress in the organization?

3. Imagine you are working for Kitchen Magic, an appliance manufacturer that produces, among other things, dishwashers for the home. Imagine further that a competitor introduces a new dishwasher that uses sound waves to clean dishes. The result is a dishwasher that cleans even the worst burnt-on food and sterilizes the dishes and silverware as well. You need to develop a similar offering fast, or your company will lose the market. Write an e-mail to management outlining the problem and explaining your rationale for recommending use of a cross-functional team to respond quickly.

4. Divide the class into teams of five. Imagine that your firm has been asked to join a virtual network. You are a producer of athletic shoes. What might

you do to minimize the potential problems of being involved with a virtual corporation? Begin by defining a virtual corporation and listing the potential problems. Also, list the benefits of being part of such a system.

5. As discussed in this chapter, many of the work groups of the future, including management, will be cross-functional and self-managed. To practice working in such an organization, break your class up into groups of five or so students. (Try to find students with different backgrounds and interests.) Each group must work together to prepare a report on the advantages and disadvantages of working in teams. Many of the problems and advantages should emerge in your group as you try to complete this assignment.

Taking It To The Net

Purpose

To describe Ford Motor Company's formal and informal organizational structures.

Exercise

When you think of how Ford Motor Company is organized, you may think of it in terms of its brands (Mazda, Mercury, Lincoln, Aston Martin, Jaguar, Land Rover, Volvo) or its businesses (Automotive Operations, Ford Financial, Hertz). However, the company serves all of its brands and businesses through what it calls hiring organizations. Learn more about it by going to www.mycareer.ford.com/OurCompany.asp.

1. How are Ford's hiring organizations organized?
2. Click on the link of one of the hiring organizations. What types of positions does this function provide? What are the preferred qualifications of the candidates Ford would like to find to fill these positions?
3. Describe Ford's unique hiring process. If you've applied for jobs before, how does Ford's hiring process differ from what you've experienced? What could this process tell you about Ford's organizational culture? How does the process help Ford find employees who will fit in its culture?

Casing The Web

To access the case "IBM Is Both an Outsourcer and a Major Outsource for Others," visit

www.mhhe.com/ub7e

Video Case

One Smooth Stone

David slew Goliath with one smooth stone, and thus was born the name of the company One Smooth Stone (OSS). It's an unusual name for an unusually interesting company. The company is in the business of providing materials for big corporate events: sales meetings, client meetings, and product presentations. Most people in the industry have attended many such meetings, so to keep them entertained is a major challenge. And that's where OSS comes in: It uses project teams to come up with original and captivating presentations for its customers.

You read about the history of organizational design in this chapter. You learned, for example, about Fayol and his principles of organization. The first principle is unity of command (every worker is to report to one, and only one, boss). Other principles include order, equity, and esprit de corps. This video shows that OSS is one company that understands the importance of esprit de corps. It is a fun and interesting place to work, and turnover is very low. The company does not follow many of Weber's principles dealing with written rules and consistent procedures. Quite the contrary: OSS is structured to be flexible and responsive to its clients. There are no set rules, and the company is certainly not consistent with its projects. Everything is custom made to the needs of each client.

OSS uses a flat organization structure. There are a few project managers, who have workers under them, but they don't look over the employees' shoulders telling them what to do or how to do it. That means there is decentralized authority. Whereas many companies are structured by department—design, engineering, marketing, finance, accounting, and so forth—OSS is structured using project teams. Each team is structured to meet the needs of an individual client. For example, the company will go out and hire people with specific skills as they are needed. The term for this is *outsourcing,* and OSS outsources many of its tasks to freelance professionals. Together, they work as self-managed teams. The focus of the team is on client needs. There are some staff workers to help with personnel, legal, and other such services.

The company is not keen on making strategic plans because its environment changes so rapidly that such plans are obsolete as soon as they are made. So the company does what is calls "strategic improvising." Although OSS sounds less structured and more informal than most companies, it still focuses on total quality and it practices continuous improvement.

In addition, the company is particularly concerned about its corporate culture. It has three values: smart, fast, and kind. It works smart, responds quickly, and is always kind to others, including its own workers. Because of its culture and responsiveness, the company has been able to capture big accounts like Motorola, Sun Microsystems, and International Truck and Engine.

The long-run success of the firm, however, is based on its project management teams. They carefully listen to what clients are trying to accomplish and then come up with solutions to their problems. You can see the creativity in this video. Clearly, OSS has been able to impress the Goliaths of big business with its presentations.

Thinking It Over

1. What have you learned from this video about the use of teams as an organizational tool versus the traditional line or line-and-staff forms of organization?
2. Does working at OSS look like more or less fun than working for a company with a more traditional approach to organizational structure and operations? Why?
3. From what you saw in the video, what do you think the core competencies of the company might be?

Chapter 9

Producing World-Class Goods and Services

Learning Goals

After you have read and studied this chapter, you should be able to

1 Define operations management and describe the evolution of manufacturing in the United States.

2 Describe the operations management planning issues involved in both the manufacturing and service sectors, including facility location, facility layout, and quality control.

3 Discuss the problem of measuring productivity in the service sector, and tell how new technology is leading to productivity gains in service companies.

4 Explain manufacturing processes, MRP, and ERP.

5 Describe the seven new manufacturing techniques that have improved the productivity of U.S. companies: just-in-time inventory control, Internet purchasing, flexible manufacturing, lean manufacturing, mass customization, competing in time, and computer-aided design and manufacturing.

6 Explain the use of PERT and Gantt charts.

Getting to Know Dain Hancock of Lockheed Martin

Can you imagine how hard it would be to manage the construction of a combat jet airplane? Now try to imagine how hard it would be if the plane was being built by 80 different suppliers in 187 different locations. Furthermore, while the plane is being constructed, the U.S. Air Force, Navy, and Marines; the British Defense Ministry; and eight other U.S. allies will be watching the progress, making comments, and changing the plans if necessary. What kind of person could pull all of that together?

The man responsible for this huge project is Dain Hancock of Lockheed Martin. Hancock was reared in Peekskill, New York. He got his bachelor's and master's degrees in mechanical engineering at Texas Tech University. He then went to work for General Dynamics in Fort Worth, Texas, where he held a number of different jobs varying from research and engineering to program management and marketing. At General Dynamics, he was responsible for the development of the F-16B aircraft.

Hancock is now president of Lockheed Martin Aeronautics Company. One of his successes at Lockheed was to consolidate three operating units into a single company. Now he has the responsibility, with the help of others, of uniting some 80 companies into a single production unit. To do that, Lockheed and its partner companies will be using a system of 90 Web software tools to share designs, track the exchange of documents, and keep an eye on progress. The Net enables people from different companies with incompatible computer systems to meet on websites and speak a common language. They will be able to talk via their computers while looking at shared documents. They can also use electronic white boards on which two or more people can draw pictures or charts, in real time, as others watch and comment.

Hancock and other managers are taking operations management beyond the control of one plant to the control of multiple plants in multiple locations, often in multiple countries. The Internet has changed business in many ways, but none other may be as dramatic as this.

Hancock and other managers are taking operations management beyond the control of one plant to the control of multiple plants in multiple locations, often in multiple countries. The Internet has changed business in many ways, but none other may be as dramatic as this. In this chapter, you will learn some basics about production and operations management. You will then be better prepared to understand the dramatic changes taking place in that area.

Sources: Faith Keenan and Spencer E. Ante, "The New Teamwork," *BusinessWeek e.biz,* February 18, 2002, pp. 12–16; and www.sae.org/technicalcommittees/navigator/hancock.htm.

AMERICA'S EVOLVING MANUFACTURING AND SERVICES BASE

During the 1970s and 1980s, foreign manufacturers captured huge chunks of the U.S. market for basic products such as steel, cement, machinery, and farm equipment using the latest in production techniques. That competition forced U.S. companies to greatly alter their production techniques and managerial styles. Many U.S. firms are now as good as or better than competitors anywhere in the world. What have American manufacturers done to regain a competitive edge? They've emphasized the following:

- Focusing on customers.
- Maintaining close relationships with suppliers and other companies to satisfy customer needs.
- Practicing continuous improvement.
- Focusing on quality.
- Saving on costs through site selection.
- Relying on the Internet to unite companies.
- Adopting new manufacturing techniques such as enterprise resource planning, computer-integrated manufacturing, flexible manufacturing, and lean manufacturing.

production
The creation of finished goods and services using the factors of production: land, labor, capital, entrepreneurship, and knowledge.

We'll discuss these developments in detail in this chapter. You'll see that operations management has become a challenging and vital element of American business. It is the implementation phase of management. Tomorrow's college graduates will face tremendous challenges (and career opportunities) in redesigning and rebuilding America's manufacturing base.

The service sector of the economy will also continue to get attention as it becomes a larger and larger part of the overall economy. Service productivity is a real issue, as is the blending of service and manufacturing through the Internet. This chapter will devote major attention to operations management in both the service and the manufacturing sectors. Since the majority of tomorrow's graduates will likely find jobs in the service sector, it is important to understand the latest operations management concepts for this sector.

Each year companies discover new ways of automating that eliminate the need for human labor. This photo shows a new, automated apparatus known as a Flipper. It can pour a dozen pancakes and flip them when needed on one griddle while, at the same time, flipping burgers on another grill. Are McDonald's or any other restaurants in your area already using equipment like this?

From Production to Operations Management

Production is the creation of goods ➤P. 25◄ and services ➤P. 26◄ using the factors of production ➤P. 10◄: land, labor, capital, entrepreneurship ➤P. 174◄, and knowledge. Production has historically been associated with manufacturing, but the nature of business has changed significantly in the last 20 years or so. The service sector, including Internet services, has grown dramatically, and the manufacturing sector has not grown much at all. The United States now has what is called a service economy—that is, one dominated by the service sector. This can be a benefit to future college graduates because many of the top-paying jobs are in legal services;

medical services; entertainment; broadcasting; and business services such as accounting, finance, and management consulting.

Production management has been the term used to describe all the activities managers do to help their firms create goods. To reflect the change in importance from manufacturing to services, the term *production* often has been replaced by *operations* to reflect both goods and services production. **Operations management**, then, is a specialized area in management that converts or transforms resources (including human resources) into goods and services. It includes inventory management, quality control, production scheduling, follow-up services, and more. In an automobile plant, operations management transforms raw materials, human resources, parts, supplies, paints, tools, and other resources into automobiles. It does this through the processes of fabrication and assembly. In a college, operations management takes inputs—such as information, professors, supplies, buildings, offices, and computer systems—and creates services that transform students into educated people. It does this through a process called education.

production management
The term used to describe all the activities managers do to help their firms create goods.

operations management
A specialized area in management that converts or transforms resources (including human resources) into goods and services.

Some organizations—such as factories, farms, and mines—produce mostly goods. Others—such as hospitals, schools, and government agencies—produce mostly services. Still others produce a combination of goods and services. For example, an automobile manufacturer not only makes cars but also provides services such as repairs, financing, and insurance. And at Wendy's you get goods such as hamburgers and fries, but you also get services such as order taking, order filling, and cleanup.

Operations Management in Action

Large companies can afford to hire specialists who study the latest in production techniques and can set up world-class systems. What can a smaller business do to stay competitive with such sophisticated companies? The answer is to hire a consultant who will provide the needed services. Demetria Giannisis is one of those consultants. She provides productivity and technology services to manufacturers in the Chicago region. By reading about one of her clients, you will learn a lot about the practice of operations management.

At Allied Tube & Conduit in Harvey, Illinois, it once took more than five hours for employees to shift from making one size of tube to another. Giannisis and her team of productivity experts helped the company streamline its processes. The team videotaped a typical mill changeover. The workers then watched the tape and saw themselves wasting time looking for tools, goofing off, asking questions, performing activities out of sequence, and operating in poor lighting. It turned out that there were four and three-quarters hours of wasted time in each six-hour changeover. Following the productivity experts' advice, activities were resequenced, tools were stocked close by, parts were given correct labels, and jobs were reassigned. There was also a period of training so that each team member understood his job better. As a result of these basic changes, the company can save some $2.5 million in labor costs. This example demonstrates that operations management can have a significant effect on profits. This is true in both manufacturing plants and service companies, for large and small organizations alike.[1]

Demetria Giannisis is the consultant who helped Allied Tube and Conduit to streamline its processes and increase productivity and profits. She filmed the company in operation to see how effective (or inefficient) the workers were. How do you think you and your friends would look if someone were to film you while you were studying or doing some of your projects? Can you see why companies frequently consult with an operations specialist?

Manufacturers Turn to a Customer Orientation and Services for Profit

Most traditional large manufacturers in the United States have had slow profit growth for the past decade despite spending an enormous amount of money on productivity and quality initiatives. Companies that have prospered and grown—General Electric and Dell, just to name a couple—have all taken a similar road to success. They've expanded operations management out of the factory and moved it closer to the customer, providing services such as custom manufacturing, fast delivery, credit, installation, and repair.[2]

Take the automobile industry, for example. While new-car sales have been rather flat in recent years, at some 17 million a year, the number of used-car sales has grown to about 200 million a year. Thus, car companies can potentially increase their revenues by providing parts and service for used cars rather than selling new ones.

Another example of the growing importance of services is in the area of corporate computing. The average company spends only one-fifth of its annual personal computer budget on purchasing the hardware. The rest (80 percent) goes to technical support, administration, and other maintenance activities. Because of this, IBM has shifted from its dependence on selling computer hardware to becoming a major supplier of computer services, software, and technology components.[3] It recently bought PricewaterhouseCoopers' tech consulting affiliate to increase its presence in the service sector. General Electric is doing the same; it generates more than $5 billion a year in worldwide revenues from Internet transactions.[4]

Companies such as Bank of America, Boeing, and Ford have outsourced ➤P. 257◄ much of their production processes and are focusing more on building customer relationships and brand images.[5] As you can see, operations management has become much more focused on services because that's where the growth and profits are.

OPERATIONS MANAGEMENT PLANNING

Operations management planning in the service sector involves many of the same issues as operations management planning in the manufacturing sector. Overlapping issues include facility location, facility layout, and quality control. The resources used may be different, but the management issues are similar.

Facility Location

facility location
The process of selecting a geographic location for a company's operations.

Facility location is the process of selecting a geographic location for a company's operations. In keeping with the need to focus on customers, one strategy in facility location is to find a site that makes it easy for consumers to access the company's service and to maintain a dialogue about their needs. Thus flower shops and banks are putting facilities in supermarkets so that their products and services are more accessible than they are in freestanding facilities. You can find a McDonald's inside some Wal-Mart stores. There are even McDonald's outlets in some gas stations now. Customers can order and pay for their meals at the pumps and by the time they are finished filling their tanks, they go to the window to pick up their food orders. Of course, the ultimate in convenience is never having to leave home at all to get services. That's why there is so much interest in Internet banking, Internet car shopping, Internet education, and so on.[6] For brick-and-mortar businesses (e.g., retail stores) to beat such competition, they have to choose good locations and offer outstanding service to those who do come. Study the location of service-sector businesses—such as hotels, banks, athletic clubs, and supermarkets—and you will see that the most successful are conveniently located.

Facility Location for Manufacturers A major issue of the recent past has been the shift of manufacturing organizations from one city or state to another in the United States or to foreign sites. Such shifts sometimes result in pockets of unemployment in some geographic areas and lead to tremendous economic growth in others.

Why would companies spend millions of dollars to move their facilities from one location to another? Issues that influence site selection include labor costs; availability of resources, such as labor; access to transportation that can reduce time to market; proximity to suppliers; proximity to customers; low crime rates; quality of life for employees; cost of living; and the ability to train or retrain the local workforce.

One of the most common reasons for a business move is the availability of inexpensive labor or the right kind of skilled labor. Even though labor cost is becoming a smaller percentage of total cost in some highly automated industries, the low cost of labor remains a key reason many producers move their plants. For example, low-cost labor is one reason why some firms are moving to Malaysia, Mexico, and other countries with low wage rates. Some of these firms have been charged with providing substandard working conditions and/or exploiting children in the countries where they have set up factories. Others, such as Grupo Moraira (Grupo M), a real estate construction and sales company in the Dominican Republic, are being used as role models for global manufacturing. Grupo M provides its employees with higher pay relative to local businesses, transportation to and from work, day care centers, discounted food, and health clinics. Its operations are so efficient that it can compete in world markets and provide world-class services to its employees.[7]

Inexpensive resources are another major reason for moving production facilities. Companies usually need water, electricity, wood, coal, and other basic resources. By moving to areas where natural resources are inexpensive and plentiful, firms can significantly lower costs—not only the cost of buying such resources but also the cost of shipping finished products. Often the

Briggs & Stratton moved many of its operations from a huge factory outside Milwaukee to a series of new factories in America's rural South. The new facilities are all nonunion. Unionized workers in the plant outside of Milwaukee would not concede to pay and benefit concessions, and the company felt it needed to cut costs to remain competitive. Besides cheaper labor, what other factors may influence companies like Briggs & Stratton to relocate?

www.ethics.ubc.ca/resources/business

Making Ethical Decisions

Stay or Leave?

Suppose that the hypothetical company ChildrenWear Industries has long been the economic foundation for its hometown. Most of the area's small businesses and schools support ChildrenWear, either by supplying the materials needed for production or by training its employees. ChildrenWear learned that if it moved its production facilities to Asia, it could increase its profits by half. Closing operations in the company's hometown would cause many of the town's other businesses to fail and schools to close, leaving a great percentage of the town unemployed, with no options for reemployment there. As a top manager at ChildrenWear, you must help decide whether the plant should be moved and, if so, when to tell the employees about the move. The law says that you must tell them at least 60 days before closing. What alternatives do you have? What are the consequences of each? Which will you choose?

most important resource is people, so companies tend to cluster where smart and talented people are. Witness Silicon Valley in California and similar areas in Colorado, Massachusetts, Virginia, Texas, Maryland, and other states.

Reducing time-to-market is another decision-making factor. As manufacturers attempt to compete globally, they need sites that allow products to move through the system quickly, at the lowest costs, so that they can be delivered rapidly to customers.[8] Access to various modes of transportation (i.e., highways, rail lines, airports, and the like) is thus critical. Information technology (IT) is also important to quicken response time, so many firms are seeking countries with the most advanced information systems.

Another way to work closely with suppliers to satisfy your customers' needs is to locate your production facilities near supplier facilities. That cuts the cost of distribution and makes communication easier.

Many businesses are building factories in foreign countries to get closer to their international customers. That's a major reason why the Japanese automaker Honda builds cars in Ohio and the German company Mercedes builds them in Alabama.[9] When U.S. firms select foreign sites, they consider whether they are near airports, waterways, and highways so that raw materials and finished goods can be moved quickly and easily.

Businesses also study the quality of life for workers and managers. Quality-of-life questions include these: Are there good schools nearby? Is the weather nice? Is the crime rate low? Does the local community welcome new businesses? Do the chief executive and other key managers want to live there? Sometimes a region with a high quality of life is also an expensive one, which complicates the decision. In short, facility location has become a critical issue in operations management. The Making Ethical Decisions box explores one of the major ethical issues involved.

Taking Operations Management to the Internet Many of today's rapidly growing companies do very little production themselves. Instead, they outsource engineering, design, manufacturing, and other tasks to other companies, such as Solectron, Flextronics, and SCI Systems, that specialize in those functions.[10] Furthermore, companies are creating whole new relationships with suppliers over the Internet so that operations management is becoming an interfirm process in which companies work together to design, produce, and ship products to customers. You read about such cooperation in the chapter opening profile about Dain Hancock at Lockheed Martin.

Coordination among companies today can be as close as coordination among departments in a single firm was in the past.

Many of the major manufacturing companies (e.g., Microsoft) are developing new Internet-focused strategies that will enable them and others to compete more effectively in the future. These changes are having a dramatic effect on operations managers as they adjust from a one-firm system to an interfirm environment and from a relatively stable environment to one that is constantly changing and evolving. This linking of firms is called supply chain management. You will learn more about it in Chapter 15.

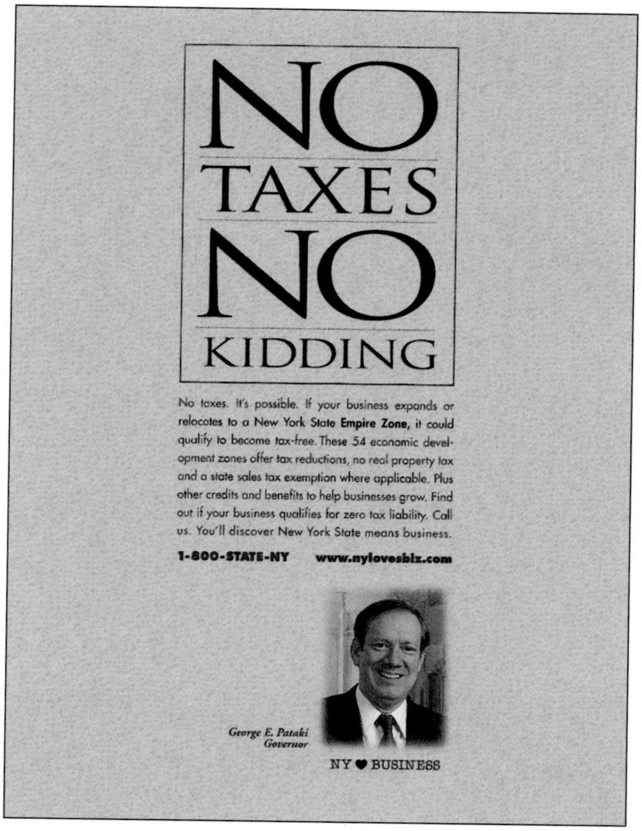

States like New York are engaged in vigorous competition to attract new businesses to their locales. This ad stresses "No taxes. No kidding" to show companies that they could significantly cut costs by moving to one of New York's many Empire Zones where there are many state funded credits and benefits and no property taxes! What are the benefits to the state of having new businesses locate there?

Facility Location in the Future New developments in information technology (computers, modems, e-mail, voice mail, teleconferencing, etc.) are giving firms and employees more flexibility than ever before in choosing locations while staying in the competitive mainstream.[11] As we noted in Chapter 1, telecommuting (working from home via computer and modem) is a major trend in business. Companies that no longer need to locate near sources of labor will be able to move to areas where land is less expensive and the quality of life may be nicer. The Reaching Beyond Our Borders box discusses living in Hawaii and doing business throughout the world.

One big incentive to locate or relocate in a particular city or state is the tax situation and degree of government support. Some states and local governments have higher taxes than others, yet many engage in fierce competition by giving tax reductions and other support, such as zoning changes and financial aid, so that businesses will locate there. Recently, for example, there has been a major revival of neighborhoods in downtown Los Angeles, in part because the city government is giving companies tax breaks and helping them find new market opportunities.

Facility Layout

facility layout
The physical arrangement of resources (including people) in the production process.

Facility layout is the physical arrangement of resources (including people) in the production process. The idea is to have offices, machines, storage areas, and other items in the best possible position to enable workers to produce goods and provide services for customers. Facility layout depends greatly on the processes that are to be performed. For services, the layout is usually designed to help the consumer find and buy things.[12] More and more, that means helping consumers find and buy things on the Internet.[13] Some stores have added kiosks that enable customers to search for goods on the Internet and then place orders in the store. The store also handles returns and other customer-contact functions. In short, services are becoming more and more customer oriented in how they design their stores and their Internet services. Some service-oriented organizations, such as hospitals, use layouts that improve the efficiency of the production process, just as manufacturers do.

For manufacturing plants, facilities layout has become critical because the possible cost savings are enormous. The Delphi Automotive Systems plant in Oak Creek, Wisconsin, is huge—a walk around the outside would be more than

Reaching Beyond Our Borders

www.origin.to

Why Not Live in Hawaii and Do Business Globally?

With Internet technology, you can work almost anywhere and telecommute. Chelsea Hill, for example, moved from Seattle, Washington, to the Hawaiian island of Maui to start a Web-based business called Origin—The Language Agency. Her company has offices in Seattle; Victoria, British Columbia; and Bristol, England. Her workers consist of freelance translators from all over the world. One of Maui's new entrepreneurs says, "When you are as physically isolated as we are on this island, you become aware of the importance of connectivity—not just broadband, but with fellow professionals."

In 1988, Hawaii passed an important telecommunications act that provided for enough funding for infrastructure upgrades and made the islands a great place for Pacific Rim telecom investors. Another act offers incentives for high-tech small businesses to relocate their research and development operations in the state. Hawaii is now one of the three most networked states in the country. If you can operate a business from anywhere, why not in a beautiful paradise like Hawaii?

Sources: Kevin Voight, "For 'Extreme Telecomuters,' Remote Work Means Really Remote," *The Wall Street Journal,* January 31, 2001, p. B1; and Allison Overholt, "Want to Web the Surf?," *Fast Company,* September 2002, p. 42.

The Igus manufacturing plant in Cologne, Germany, can shrink or expand in a flash. Its flexible design keeps it competitive in a fast-changing market. Because the layout of the plant changes so often, some employees use scooters in order to more efficiently provide needed skills, supplies, and services to multiple workstations. A fast-changing plant needs a fast-moving employee base to achieve maximum productivity.

a mile. Delphi makes catalytic converters for 40 different automobile manufacturers. Catalytic converters are stainless-steel pollution strainers in automobile exhaust systems. Delphi has a history that goes back almost 100 years. Its facility layout was typical of older plants—an assembly line that made all of the converters. The plant floor is now organized around modular, portable customer-focused work cells. Product delivery once took 21 days, but with today's more modern layout, delivery takes less than a week. The plant was redesigned to reduce cost, to increase productivity ➤P. 15◄, to simplify the process, and to speed things up. Compared to the old plant, the new plant uses only half of the space, 2 percent of its powered conveyor system, and 230 fewer processes. Productivity increased by over 25 percent, and the plant is now more profitable.[14]

Many companies like Delphi are moving from an *assembly line layout,* in which workers do only a few tasks at a time, to a *modular layout,* in which teams of workers combine to produce more complex units of the final product. For example, there may have been a dozen or more workstations on an assembly line to complete an automobile engine in the past, but all of that work may be done in one module today. A *process layout* is one in which similar equipment and functions are grouped together. The order in which the product visits a function depends on the design of the item. This allows for flexibility. When working on a major project, such as a bridge or an airplane, companies use a *fixed-position layout* that allows workers to congregate around the product to be completed. Figure 9.1 illustrates typical layout designs.

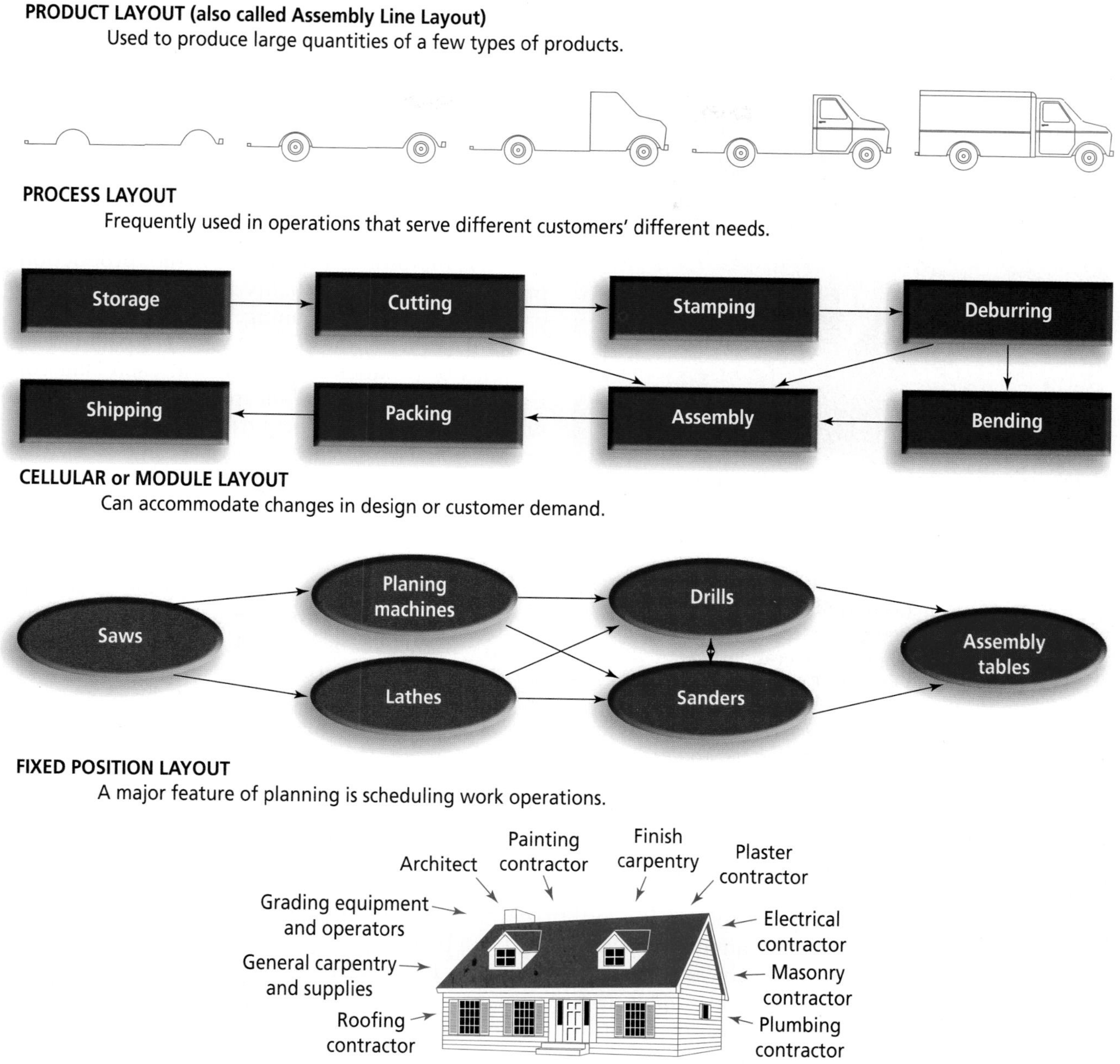

FIGURE 9.1

TYPICAL LAYOUT DESIGNS

Quality Control

quality
Consistently producing what the customer wants while reducing errors before and after delivery to the customer.

Quality is consistently producing what the customer wants while reducing errors before and after delivery to the customer. Earlier in the United States, quality control was often done by quality control departments at the end of the production line. Products were completed *and then tested.* This resulted in several problems:

1. There was a need to inspect other people's work. This took extra people and resources.
2. If an error was found, someone would have to correct the mistake or scrap the product. This, of course, was costly.
3. If the customer found the mistake, he or she might be dissatisfied and might even buy from someone else thereafter.

Such problems led to the realization that quality is not an outcome; it is a never-ending process of continually improving what a company produces.

What happens when you combine the zeal of Silicon Valley with the six sigma discipline of a large company like General Electric? You get a medical breakthrough. Janet Burki and her 280-person operations team developed the world's fastest CT scanner. It works 10 times faster than other systems and produces clear 3-D images of the beating heart. Can you see how efforts to build in quality lead to better (and faster) products?

Therefore, quality control should be part of the operations management planning process rather than simply an end-of-the-line inspection.

Companies have turned to the use of modern quality control standards, such as six sigma. **Six sigma quality** (just 3.4 defects per million opportunities) detects potential problems to prevent their occurrence. **Statistical quality control (SQC)** is the process some managers use to continually monitor all phases of the production process to assure that quality is being built into the product from the beginning. **Statistical process control (SPC)** is the process of taking statistical samples of product components at each stage of the production process and plotting those results on a graph.[15] Any variances from quality standards are recognized and can be corrected if beyond the set standards. Making sure products meet standards all along the production process eliminates or minimizes the need for having a quality control inspection at the end. Any mistakes would have been caught much earlier in the process. SQC and SPC thus save companies much time and many dollars. Some companies call such an approach to quality control the Deming cycle (after the late W. Edwards Deming, the father of the movement toward quality). It consists of Plan, Do, Check, Act (PDCA). Again, the idea is to find potential errors *before* they happen.

six sigma quality
A quality measure that allows only 3.4 defects per million opportunities.

statistical quality control (SQC)
The process some managers use to continually monitor all phases of the production process to assure that quality is being built into the product from the beginning.

statistical process control (SPC)
The process of taking statistical samples of product components at each stage of the production process and plotting those results on a graph. Any variances from quality standards are recognized and can be corrected if beyond the set standards.

Quality, as you can see, has become a major issue in operations management. The following are examples of how quality is being introduced into service and manufacturing firms:

- Holiday Inn authorized its hotel staff to do almost anything to satisfy an unhappy customer, from handing out gift certificates to eliminating charges for certain services. Empowerment ➤P. 20◀ gives managers and employees the authority to waive charges for the night's stay if the customer is still unhappy. Hampton Inns (owned by Hilton) has a similar policy.
- Motorola set a goal of attaining six sigma quality. The Spotlight on Small Business box discusses how small businesses are also using this standard.
- In the past, Xerox found 97 defects for every 100 copiers coming off the assembly line. Now it finds only 12.

Dozens of other manufacturers and service organizations could be discussed here, but you get the idea: The customer is ultimately the one who determines what the standard for quality should be. American businesses are getting serious about providing top customer service, and many are already doing it. Service organizations are finding it difficult to provide outstanding service every time because the process is so labor intensive. Physical goods (e.g., a gold ring) can be designed and manufactured to near perfection. However, it is hard to reach such perfection when designing and providing a service experience such as a dance on a cruise ship or a cab drive through New York City.

Spotlight on Small Business

www.sixsigmasystems.com

Meeting the Six Sigma Standard

Six sigma is a quality measure that allows only 3.4 defects per million opportunities. It is one thing for Motorola or GE to reach for such standards, but what about a small company like Dolan Industries? Dolan is a 41-person manufacturer of fasteners. It spent a few years trying to meet ISO 9000 standards, which are comparable to six sigma.

Once the company was able to achieve six sigma quality itself, it turned to its suppliers and demanded six sigma quality from them as well. It had to do that because its customers were demanding that level of quality. Companies such as General Electric, Honeywell, and Motorola are all seeking six sigma quality. The benefits include increases in product performance and, more important, happy customers—and profit growth.

Here is how six sigma works: If you can make it to the level of one sigma, two out of three products will meet specifications. If you can reach the two sigma level, then more than 95 percent of products will qualify. But when you meet six sigma quality, as we've said, you have only 3.4 defects in a million opportunities (which means that 99.99966 percent of your products will qualify). The bottom line is that small businesses are being held to a higher standard, one that reaches near perfection. Service organizations are also adopting six sigma standards.

Sources: Mark Henricks, "Is It Greek to You?" *Entrepreneur,* July 1999, pp. 65–67; and Thomas Pyzdek, "Six Sigma: Needs Standardization," *Quality Digest,* March 2001, p. 20; Michael Arndt, "Quality Isn't Just for Widgets," *Business Week,* July 22, 2002, pp. 72–73; and Kennedy Smith, "Six Sigma for the Service Sector," *Quality Digest,* May 2003, pp. 23–28.

Quality Function Deployment Six sigma and other quality standards are designed to eliminate mistakes. **Quality function deployment (QFD)** is a process of linking the needs of end users (customers) to design, development, engineering, manufacturing, and service functions. The goal is to go beyond not making mistakes to maximizing customer satisfaction. One way to do that is to identify customers' spoken and *unspoken* needs and to meet as many of those needs as possible by constantly improving. QFD came out of Japan but is now used at many leading companies in the United States, including Boeing, NASA, Nike, and 3M. QFD is a subject worth researching—see the second Taking It to the Net exercise at the end of this chapter. The Dealing with Change box on p. 278 explores how quality is changing today.

quality function deployment (QFD)
A process of linking the needs of end users (customers) to design, development, engineering, manufacturing, and service functions.

Quality Standards: The Baldrige Awards In the United States in 1987, a standard was set for overall company quality with the introduction of the Malcolm Baldrige National Quality Awards, named in honor of the late U.S. secretary of commerce. Companies can apply for these awards in each of the following areas: manufacturing, services, small businesses, education, and health care. To qualify, an organization has to show quality in seven key areas: leadership, strategic planning, customer and market focus, information and analysis, human resources focus, process management, and business results. Major criteria for earning the award include whether customer wants and needs are being met and whether customer satisfaction ratings are better than those of competitors. As you can see, the focus is shifting away from just making quality goods and services to providing top-quality customer service in all respects.[16]

One of the recent Baldrige award winners was Sunny Fresh Foods, a small company that makes about 200 different egg products. Sunny Fresh was the first food company to win the award, and one of few small companies. The company used the Baldrige criteria to drive business systems development and business systems redesign. Another recent small-business winner was Texas Nameplate. The company, which makes metal nameplates, etching many of

Dealing with Change

www.qualitydigest.com

Why Is Service Still So Bad?

Are you happy with the service you receive at retail stores, from auto repair facilities, and from businesses and other organizations? One of the improvements that managers need to make, and make quickly, is the betterment of consumer relations. It is one thing to talk about quality function deployment, six sigma quality, and all that in a college class; it is quite another thing to find quality in the real world—especially at the consumer level (you and I shopping at the mall).

Quality Digest has been addressing that issue. One article was called "Why Is Quality Still So Bad?" and the other was called "Mining the TQM Mother Load." TQM stands for total quality management and is a traditional quality approach. Both articles place the blame for poor quality squarely on management. The first article says, "The blame lies not with the humble quality manager, but entirely, and I do mean entirely, with senior management. With very few exceptions, today's CEOs, presidents, and the like just don't give quality as much attention as they should." The article went on to say that all the statistical measures in the world won't help if the company doesn't focus on service to the customer as well.

The second article has a different perspective. It says that quality begins with the managers themselves. They must put quality into their duties: allocating resources, selecting leaders, developing processes, setting priorities, and the like. If these responsibilities are not fulfilled, any total quality effort is likely to fail. Joseph M. Juran, a quality expert, says that 80 to 85 percent of all problems are caused by management. Some 62 percent of those problems could be controlled by first- and second-level managers. But those managers are not always involved in top-level meetings and don't always see the big picture. In short, the change needed in corporations today is for top managers to get serious about quality and then give first- and second-level managers the information and the tools necessary to implement quality initiatives. Will we see such changes soon? Let's go to the mall and find out.

Sources: Scott Madison Paton, "Grading Quality: Why Is Quality Still So Bad?" *Quality Digest,* April 2002, p. 4; and H. James Harrington, "Mining the TQM Mother Load," *Quality Digest,* April 2002, p. 12.

them with chemicals, is a quality company not only when it comes to production but also when it comes to the environment. It has cut its waste dispersal to almost zero.

ISO 9000 and ISO 14000 Standards The International Organization for Standardization (ISO) is a worldwide federation of national standards bodies from more than 140 countries that set the global measures for the quality of individual products. ISO is a nongovernmental organization established in 1947 to promote the development of world standards to facilitate the international exchange of goods and services. (ISO is not an acronym. It comes from the Greek word *isos,* meaning oneness.) **ISO 9000** is the common name given to quality management and assurance standards. The latest standards, called ISO 9001: 2002, were published in 2002.[17] The new standards require that a company must determine what customer needs are, including regulatory and legal requirements. The company must also make communication arrangements to handle issues such as complaints. Other standards involve process control, product testing, storage, and delivery.

ISO 9000
The common name given to quality management and assurance standards.

Prior to the establishment of the ISO standards, there were no international standards of quality against which to measure companies. Now the ISO, based in Europe, provides a common denominator of business quality accepted around the world.

What makes ISO 9000 so important is that the European Union (EU), the group of European countries that have established free-trade agreements, is demanding that companies that want to do business with the EU be certified by ISO standards. Some major U.S. companies are also demanding that suppliers meet such standards. There are several accreditation agencies in Europe and in the United States whose function is to certify that a company meets the standards for all phases of its operations, from product development through production and testing to installation.

ISO 14000 is a collection of the best practices for managing an organization's impact on the environment.[18] It does not prescribe a performance level. ISO 14000 is an environmental management system (EMS). The requirements for certification include having an environmental policy, having specific improvement targets, conducting audits of environmental programs, and maintaining top management review of the processes. Certification in both ISO 9000 and ISO 14000 would show that a firm has a world-class management system in both quality and environmental standards. In the past, firms assigned employees separately to meet both standards. Today, ISO 9000 and 14000 standards have been blended so that an organization can work on both at once.

This photo, from left to right, shows Commerce Secretary Don Evans, David Branch (CEO Branch–Smith Printing), Daniel Hanson (Chief Operating Officer), and Vice President Dick Cheney. Branch–Smith Printing recently won the Baldrige Award for its quality efforts. Why would the government be so interested in rewarding quality improvements by U.S. companies?

ISO 14000
A collection of the best practices for managing an organization's impact on the environment.

Operations Management in the Service Sector

Let's look at the life of an operations manager in the service sector to see how he got to that position and what it entails. Horst Schulze was born in West Germany. He attended a six-month pre-apprenticeship boarding school, emphasizing the hotel industry. He then worked in several fine hotels in Germany and Switzerland, including Le Beau Rivage Palace in Lausanne, Switzerland.

In 1965, Horst Schulze moved to the United States where he began work at the University Club in San Francisco and Chicago as food and beverage manager. The Conrad Hilton offered him the job of catering manager in 1971. He was promoted to assistant food and beverage director of the Palmer House, also managed by Hilton. In 1973, he was promoted to director of food and beverage for two Hilton Hotels in Cincinnati. Under his management, the gourmet restaurant of the Terrace Hilton became the only Mobil Guide Five Star hotel restaurant in the United States. Schulze then worked for the Hyatt Corporation for 9 years.

He joined W. B. Johnson Properties, Inc., in 1983 as vice president of operations in the formation of The Ritz-Carlton Hotel Company. He then served as general manager of The Ritz-Carlton, Buckhead. In July 1987, Mr. Schulze received the appointment of executive vice president, operations. In February 1988 he was subsequently promoted to president and chief operating officer and is responsible for the 30 Ritz-Carlton hotels worldwide.

Mr. Schulze's commitment to quality is apparent in the many innovations and changes that he initiated over the years. These innovations include installation of a sophisticated computerized guest recognition program and a Quality Management Program to ensure that all employees are "certified" in their positions.

Operations management in the service industry is all about creating a good experience for those who use the service. In a Ritz-Carlton hotel, operations management includes restaurants that offer the finest in service, elevators that run smoothly, and a front desk that processes people quickly. It may include placing fresh-cut flowers in the lobbies and dishes of fruit in every room. More important, it may mean spending thousands of dollars to provide training in quality management for every new employee. If you want to learn about the great service at the Ritz, look up the article by Paul Hemp called "My Week as a Room-Service Waiter at the Ritz" in the *Harvard Business Review,* June 2002. It is the equivalent of a small handbook on providing world-class service.

Operations management in luxury hotels is changing with today's new executives. As customers in hotels, executives are likely to want in-room Internet access and a help center with toll-free telephone service. Also, when an executive has to give a speech or presentation, he or she needs video equipment and a whole host of computer hardware and other aids. Foreign visitors would like multilingual customer-support services. Hotel shops need to carry more than souvenirs, newspapers, and some drugstore and food items to serve today's high-tech travelers. The shops may also carry laptop computer supplies, electrical adapters, and the like. Operations management is responsible for locating and providing such amenities to make customers happy.

In short, delighting customers by anticipating their needs has become the quality standard for luxury hotels, as it has for most other service businesses. But knowing customer needs and satisfying them are two different things. That's why operations management is so important: It is the implementation phase of management.

Measuring Quality in the Service Sector

There's strong evidence that productivity in the service sector is rising, but the government simply doesn't have the means to measure it. One problem is that productivity measures don't capture improvements in *quality.* In an example from health care, positron emission tomography (PET) scans are much better than X rays, but the quality difference is not reported in productivity figures. The traditional way to measure productivity involves tracking inputs (worker-hours) compared to outputs (dollars). Notice that there is no measure for quality improvement. When new information systems are developed to measure the quality improvement of goods and services—including the speed of their delivery and customer satisfaction—productivity in the service sector will go up dramatically.

Using computers is one way the service sector is improving productivity, but not the only way. Think about labor-intensive businesses like hospitals and fast-food restaurants, where automation plays a big role in controlling costs and improving service. Today at Burger King, for example, customers fill their own drink cups from soda machines, which allows workers to concentrate on preparing the food. And, because the people working at the drive-up window now wear headsets instead of using stationary mikes, they aren't glued to one spot anymore and can do four or five tasks while taking an order.

Most of us have been exposed to similar productivity gains in banking. For example, people in most towns no longer have to wait in long lines for tellers to help them deposit and withdraw money. Instead, they use automated teller machines (ATMs), which usually involve little or no waiting and are available 24 hours a day. "Enhanced" ATMs sell postage stamps, long-distance phone minutes, and even tickets to sporting events or plays.[19]

British Airways customer service representatives are monitored by software that tracks productivity in sales and customer-complaint resolution. The system also tracks the amount of time spent on things like breaks and personal phone calls. Incentive dollars are associated with effective work. What would be your response to having your work so closely monitored? Would it make a difference if your pay were increased as a result?

Another service that was once annoyingly slow was grocery-store checkout. The system of marking goods with universal product codes enables computerized checkout and allows cashiers to be much more productive than before. Now many stores are setting up automated systems that enable customers to go through the checkout process on their own. Some grocery chains and even some independent companies are implementing Internet services that allow customers to place orders online and receive home delivery. The potential for productivity gains in this area are enormous. Note how Amazon.com has grown over the last few years.[20]

In short, operations management has led to tremendous productivity increases in the service sector but still has a long way to go. Also, service workers are losing jobs to machines just as manufacturing workers did. The secret to obtaining and holding a good job is to acquire appropriate education and training. Such education and training must go on for a lifetime to keep up with the rapid changes that are happening in all areas of business. That message can't be repeated too frequently.

Services Go Interactive

The service industry has always taken advantage of new technology to increase customer satisfaction. Jet travel enabled FedEx to deliver goods overnight. Computer databases enabled AT&T to provide individualized customer service. Cable TV led to pay-per-view services. And now interactive computer networks are revolutionizing services. Interactive services are already available from banks, stockbrokers, travel agents, and information providers of all kinds. More individuals may soon be able to participate directly in community and national decision making via telephone, cable, and computer networks.

You can now buy a greater variety of books and CDs on the Internet than you can in most retail stores. You can also search for and buy new and used automobiles and new and used computers. As computers and modems get faster, the Internet may take over more of traditional retailing. Regardless of what is being sold, however, the success of service organizations in the future will depend greatly on establishing a dialogue with consumers so that the operations managers can help their organizations adapt to consumer demands faster and more efficiently. Such information systems have been developed and should prove highly useful.

Progress Assessment

- Can you name and define three functions that are common to operations management in both the service and manufacturing sectors?
- What are the major criteria for facility location?
- What is involved in implementing each of the following: six sigma, SQC, SPC, QFD, ISO 9000, and ISO 14000?

Operations Management in the Manufacturing Sector

Common sense and some experience have already taught you much of what you need to know about production processes. You know what it takes to write a term paper or prepare a dinner. You need money to buy the materials, you need a place to work, and you need to be organized to get the task done. The same is true of the production process in industry. It uses basic inputs to produce outputs (see Figure 9.2). Production adds value, or utility, to materials or processes. **Form utility** is the value added by the creation of finished goods and services, such as the value added by taking silicon and making computer chips or putting services together to create a vacation package. Form utility can exist at the retail level as well. For example, a butcher can produce a specific cut of beef from a whole cow or a baker can make a specific type of cake out of basic ingredients. We'll be discussing utility in more detail in Chapter 15.

form utility
The value added by the creation of finished goods and services, such as the value added by taking silicon and making computer chips or putting services together to create a vacation package.

FIGURE 9.2

THE PRODUCTION PROCESS

The production process consists of taking the factors of production (land, etc.) and using those inputs to produce goods, services, and ideas. Planning, routing, scheduling, and the other activities are the means to accomplish the objective—output.

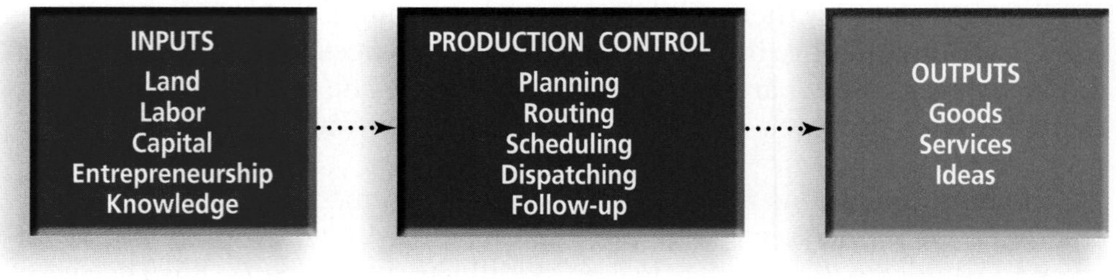

To be competitive, manufacturers must keep the costs of inputs down. That is, the costs of workers, machinery, and so on must be kept as low as possible. Similarly, the amount of output must be relatively high. The question today is: How does a producer keep costs low and still increase output? This question will dominate thinking in the manufacturing and service sectors for years to come. In the next few sections, we explore manufacturing processes and the latest technology being used to cut costs.

Manufacturing Processes

There are several different processes manufacturers use to produce goods. Andrew S. Grove, chairman of computer chip manufacturer Intel, uses a great analogy to explain production:

> *To understand the principles of production, imagine that you're a chef... and that your task is to serve a breakfast consisting of a three-minute soft-boiled egg, buttered toast, and coffee. Your job is to prepare and deliver the three items simultaneously, each of them fresh and hot.*

Grove goes on to say that the task here encompasses the three basic requirements of production: (1) to build and deliver products in response to the demands of the customer at a scheduled delivery time, (2) to provide an acceptable quality level, and (3) to provide everything at the lowest possible cost.

Using the breakfast example, it's easy to understand two manufacturing terms: process and assembly. **Process manufacturing** physically or chemically changes materials. For example, boiling physically changes the egg. (Similarly, process manufacturing turns sand into glass or computer chips.) The **assembly process** puts together components (eggs, toast, and coffee) to make a product (breakfast). (Cars are made through an assembly process that puts together the frame, engine, and other parts.)

process manufacturing
That part of the production process that physically or chemically changes materials.

assembly process
That part of the production process that puts together components.

In addition, production processes are either continuous or intermittent. A **continuous process** is one in which long production runs turn out finished goods over time. As the chef in our diner, you could have a conveyor belt that lowers eggs into boiling water for three minutes and then lifts them out on a continuous basis. A three-minute egg would be available whenever you wanted one. (A chemical plant, for example, is run on a continuous process.)

continuous process
A production process in which long production runs turn out finished goods over time

It usually makes more sense when responding to specific customer orders to use an **intermittent process**. This is an operation where the production run is short (one or two eggs) and the machines are changed frequently to make different products (like the oven in a bakery or the toaster in the diner). (Manufacturers of custom-designed furniture would use an intermittent process.)

intermittent process
A production process in which the production run is short and the machines are changed frequently to make different products.

Today most new manufacturers use intermittent processes. Computers, robots, and flexible manufacturing processes allow firms to turn out custom-made goods almost as fast as mass-produced goods were once turned out. We'll discuss how they do that in detail later in the chapter. For now, let's look at some of the newer techniques being used to make the production process more efficient.

Materials Requirement Planning

Materials requirement planning (MRP) is a computer-based operations management system that uses sales forecasts to make sure that needed parts and materials are available at the right time and place. In our diner, for example, we could feed the sales forecast into the computer, which would specify how many eggs and how much coffee to order and then print out the proper scheduling and routing sequence. The same can be done with the seats and other parts of an automobile.

materials requirement planning (MRP)
A computer-based production management system that uses sales forecasts to make sure that needed parts and materials are available at the right time and place.

MRP is now considered old; it was most popular with companies that made products with a lot of different parts. MRP quickly led to MRP II, an advanced version of MRP that allowed plants to include all the resources involved in the efficient making of a product, including projected sales, personnel, plant capacity, and distribution limitations. MRP II was called manufacturing resource (not materials requirement) planning because the planning involved more than just material requirements.

The newest version of MRP is **enterprise resource planning (ERP)**. ERP is a computer application that enables *multiple* firms to manage all of their operations (finance, requirements planning, human resources, and order fulfillment) on the basis of a single, integrated set of corporate data (see Figure 9.3). The result is shorter time between orders and payment, less staff to do ordering and order processing, reduced inventories, and better customer service for all the firms involved. By entering customer and sales information in an ERP system, a manufacturer can generate the next period's demand forecast, which in turn generates orders for raw materials, production scheduling, and financial projections.

enterprise resource planning (ERP)
A computer application that enables multiple firms to manage all of their operations (finance, requirements planning, human resources, and order fulfillment) on the basis of a single, integrated set of corporate data.

Information technology (IT) has had a major influence on the whole production process from purchasing to final delivery. Many IT advances have been add-ons to ERP. For example, software from BroadVision or Intershop creates a world-class order fulfillment process that includes the handling of returns, partial shipments, and refunds. Ariba, Commerce One, and others provide add-on software that creates a world-class electronic procurement process that not only finds the best supplier but also receives and pays invoices electronically. Getting to know customers better is known as customer relationship marketing (CRM). (We will discuss CRM in more detail when we explore the marketing function later in the text.) Siebel provides an add-on to ERP that handles CRM also. Finally, I2 Techologies and SAP (a German company) provide add-on software that optimizes the linkage among firms. For example, the software signals a company when prices are low so that purchasing costs can be minimized.

ERP software enables the monitoring of quality and customer satisfaction as it is happening. ERP systems are going global now that the Internet is powerful enough to handle the data flows. At the plant level, dynamic performance monitoring enables plant operators to monitor the use of power, chemicals, and other resources and to make needed adjustments. In short, flows to, through, and from plants have become automated.

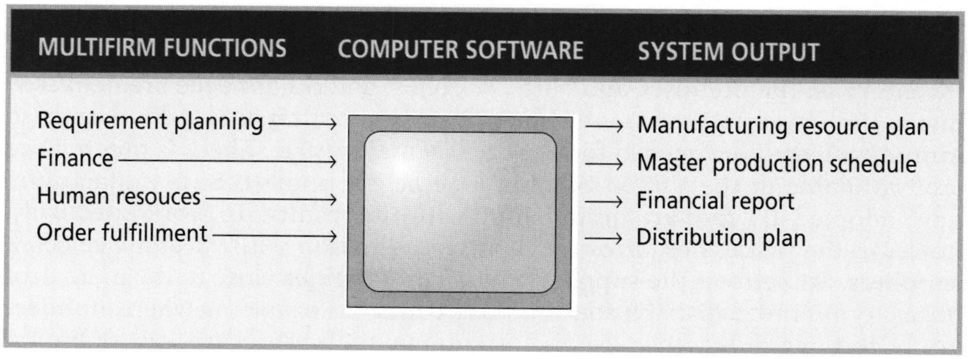

FIGURE 9.3
ENTERPRISE RESOURCE PLANNING

Some firms are providing a service called sequential delivery. These firms are suppliers that provide components in an order sequenced to their customers' production process. For example, Ford's seat supplier loads seats onto a truck such that, when off-loaded, the seats are in perfect sequence for the type of vehicle coming down the assembly line. Companies now using sequential delivery systems include Coors Ceramics (structural products); Phoenix Designs (office systems and furniture); and Red Devil (sealants, caulks, and hand tools).

Progress Assessment

- Can you explain the production process?
- Can you define and differentiate the following: process manufacturing, assembly process, continuous process, and intermittent process?
- What is the difference between materials resource planning (MRP) and enterprise resource planning (ERP)?

Modern Production Techniques

The ultimate goal of manufacturing and process management is to provide high-quality goods and services instantaneously in response to customer demand. As we have stressed throughout this book, traditional organizations were simply not designed to be so responsive to the customer. Rather, they were designed to make goods efficiently (inexpensively). The whole idea of mass production was to make a large number of a limited variety of products at very low cost.

Over the years, low cost often came at the expense of quality and flexibility. Furthermore, suppliers didn't always deliver when they said they would, so manufacturers had to carry large inventories of raw materials and components. Such inefficiencies made U.S. companies subject to foreign competitors who were using more advanced production techniques.

As a result of global competition, largely from Japan and Germany, companies today must make a wide variety of high-quality custom-designed products at very low cost. Clearly, something had to change on the production floor to make that possible. Seven major developments have radically changed the production process in the United States: (1) just-in-time inventory control, (2) Internet purchasing, (3) flexible manufacturing, (4) lean manufacturing, (5) mass customization, (6) competing in time, and (7) computer-aided design and manufacturing.

Just-in-Time Inventory Control

just-in-time (JIT) inventory control
A production process in which a minimum of inventory is kept on the premises and parts, supplies, and other needs are delivered just in time to go on the assembly line.

One major cost of production is holding parts, motors, and other items in storage for later use. Storage not only subjects such items to obsolescence, pilferage, and damage but also requires construction and maintenance of costly warehouses. To cut such costs, the Japanese implemented a concept called **just-in-time (JIT) inventory control**. JIT systems keep a minimum of inventory on the premises and parts, supplies, and other needs are delivered just in time to go on the assembly line. There is a scarcity of land in Japan, so minimizing the area needed for storage is a major issue. There is much more land available in the United States. Nonetheless, some U.S. manufacturers have adopted JIT and are quite happy with the results. To work effectively, however, the process requires excellent coordination with carefully selected suppliers. Sometimes the supplier builds new facilities close to the main producer to minimize distribution time. JIT runs into problems when suppliers are farther away. Weather may delay shipments, for example. Other limitations are that JIT works best with standard products, demand should be high and stable, and suppliers need to be extremely reliable.

Here's how it works: A manufacturer sets a production schedule using ERP or one of the other systems just described (e.g., MRP), and then determines what parts and supplies will be needed. It informs suppliers electronically of what it will need. The suppliers must deliver the goods just in time to go on the assembly line. Naturally, this calls for more effort (and more costs) on the suppliers' part. The manufacturer maintains efficiency by linking electronically to the suppliers so that the suppliers become more like departments in the firm than separate businesses.

ERP and JIT systems make sure the right materials are at the right place at the right time at the cheapest cost to meet both customer and production needs. That's the first step in modern production innovation. Part of that process is rethinking the purchasing process. We shall explore that issue next.

purchasing
The function in a firm that searches for quality material resources, finds the best suppliers, and negotiates the best price for goods and services.

flexible manufacturing
Designing machines to do multiple tasks so that they can produce a variety of products.

Internet Purchasing

Purchasing is the function in a firm that searches for quality material resources, finds the best suppliers, and negotiates the best price for quality goods and services. In the past, manufacturers tended to deal with many different suppliers with the idea that, if one supplier or another couldn't deliver, materials would be available from someone else. Today, however, manufacturers are relying more heavily on one or two suppliers because the firms share so much information that they don't want to have too many suppliers knowing their business. The relationship between suppliers and manufacturers is thus much closer than ever before.

The Internet has transformed the purchasing function in recent years. For example, a business looking for supplies can contact an Internet-based purchasing service and find the best supplies at the best price. Similarly, a company wishing to sell supplies can use the Internet to find all the companies looking for such supplies. The cost of purchasing items has thus been reduced tremendously.

Flexible Manufacturing

Flexible manufacturing involves designing machines to do multiple tasks so that they can produce a variety of products. Flexible manufacturing is one reason that Japanese and German manufacturers of automobiles in the United States are so profitable.[21]

Allen-Bradley (part of Rockwell Automation), a maker of industrial automation controls, uses flexible manufacturing to build motor starters. Orders come in daily, and within 24 hours the company's 26 machines and robots manufacture, test, and package the starters—which are untouched by human hands. Allen-Bradley's machines are so flexible that a special order, even a single item, can be included in the assembly without slowing down the process.

There is no question that reduced supplier costs should lead to more profit, but how, exactly, does one go about cutting these costs? One answer, as this ad suggests, is to use SAS supplier intelligence software. By using this type of software, companies can identify opportunities to cut spending, minimize risk, and maximize profit. Can you see how such software could be part of enterprise resource planning (ERP)?

Lean Manufacturing

lean manufacturing
The production of goods using less of everything compared to mass production.

Lean manufacturing is the production of goods using less of everything compared to mass production: less human effort, less manufacturing space, less investment in tools, and less engineering time to develop a new product. A company becomes lean by continuously increasing its capacity to produce high-quality goods while decreasing its need for resources.

Ford Motor Company's Romeo engine plant recently won an award for lean manufacturing.[22] General Motors (GM) also uses lean manufacturing. To make the Saturn automobile, for example, GM abandoned its assembly line production process. The fundamental purpose of restructuring was to dramatically cut the number of worker-hours needed to build a car. GM made numerous changes, the most dramatic of which was to switch to modular construction. GM suppliers preassemble most of the auto parts into a few large components called modules. Workers are no longer positioned along miles of assembly line. Instead, they're grouped at various workstations, where they put the modules together. Rather than do a few set tasks, workers perform a whole cluster of tasks. Trolleys carry the partly completed car from station to station. Compared to the assembly line, modular assembly takes up less space and calls for fewer workers—both money-saving factors.

Finally, GM greatly expanded its use of robots in the manufacturing process. A *robot* is a computer-controlled machine capable of performing many tasks requiring the use of materials and tools. Robots, for example, spray-paint cars and do welding. Robots usually are fast, efficient, and accurate. Robots and other machines perform routine, repetitive jobs quickly, efficiently, and accurately. This provides opportunities for workers to be more creative.

Critical Thinking

People are being replaced by robots and other machines. On the one hand, that is one way companies compete with cheap labor from other countries. No labor at all is less expensive than cheap labor. On the other hand, automation eliminates many jobs. Are you concerned that automation may increase unemployment or underemployment in the United States and around the world?

Mass Customization

mass customization
Tailoring products to meet the needs of individual customers.

To customize means to make a unique product or provide a specific service to an individual. Although it once may have seemed impossible, **mass customization**, which means tailoring products to meet the needs of a large number of individual customers, is now practiced widely. The National Bicycle Industrial Company in Japan, for example, makes 18 bicycle models in more than 2 million combinations, with each combination designed to fit the needs of a specific customer. The customer chooses the model, size, color, and design. The retailer takes various measurements from the buyer and faxes the data to the factory, where robots handle the bulk of the assembly. Thus, flexible manufacturing, as described above, is one of the factors that makes mass customization possible. Given the exact needs of a customer, flexible machines can produce a customized good as fast as mass-produced goods were once made.

More and more manufacturers are learning to customize their products. For example, some General Nutrition Center (GNC) stores feature machines that enable shoppers to custom-design their own vitamins, shampoo, and lotions. Other companies produce custom-made books with a child's name inserted in key places, and custom-made greeting cards have appeared on the market. The Custom Foot stores use infrared scanners to precisely measure each foot so that shoes can be crafted to fit perfectly. InterActive Custom Clothes offers a wide variety of options in custom-made jeans, including four different rivet colors.[23] You can also buy custom-made sneakers and even M&Ms. Motorola's Pager Division has 30 million possible permutations of pagers.

Mass customization is coming to services as well. Capital Protective Insurance (CPI), for example, sells customized risk-management plans to companies. The latest in computer software and hardware makes it possible for CPI to develop such policies. Health clubs now offer unique fitness programs for individuals, travel agencies provide vacation packages that vary according to individual choices, and some colleges allow students to design their own majors. Actually, it is much easier to custom-design service programs than it is to custom-make goods, because there is no fixed tangible good that has to be adapted. Each customer can specify what he or she wants, within the limits of the service organization—limits that seem to be ever widening.[24]

This photo shows computer-aided design (CAD) in operation. When linked with computer-aided manufacturing (CAM), these software systems can greatly improve the design and production process. What advantages might this technology offer to smaller manufacturing companies?

Competing in Time

Competing in time means being as fast as or faster than competition in responding to consumer wants and needs and getting goods and services to them. Speedy response is essential to competing in a global marketplace.[25] Ford Motor Company estimates that, to match the best, it must be 25 percent faster than it is now in creating new products. Using the latest in technology, Ford should have no problem meeting that goal. The following section explores dramatic changes that are increasing the speed of production processes and otherwise maintaining American competitive strength in manufacturing. Such changes as computer-aided design and manufacturing enable firms to compete in time and in efficiency.

Computer-Aided Design and Manufacturing

The one development in the recent past that appears to have changed production techniques and strategies more than any other has been the integration of computers into the design and manufacturing of products. The first thing computers did was help in the design of products; this is called **computer-aided design (CAD)**. The latest CAD systems allow designers to work in three dimensions. The next step was to involve computers directly in the production process; this is called **computer-aided manufacturing (CAM)**.

CAD/CAM (the use of both computer-aided design and computer-aided manufacturing) made it possible to custom-design products to meet the needs of small markets with very little increase in cost. A manufacturer programs the computer to make a simple design change, and that change can be incorporated directly into the production line.

CAD and CAM are invading the clothing industry. A computer program establishes a pattern and cuts the cloth automatically. Today, a person's dimensions can be programmed into the machines to create custom-cut clothing at little additional cost. In food service, CAM is used to make cookies in fresh-baked cookie shops. On-site, small-scale, semiautomated, sensor-controlled baking makes consistent quality easy to achieve.

CAD has doubled productivity in many firms. But it's one thing to design a product and quite another to set the specifications to make a machine do the work. The problem in the past was that CAD machines couldn't talk to CAM machines directly. Recently, however, software programs have been designed to unite CAD with CAM: the result is **computer-integrated manufacturing (CIM)**. The new software is expensive, but it cuts as much as 80 percent of the time

competing in time
Being as fast as or faster than competition in responding to consumer wants and needs and getting goods and services to them.

computer-aided design (CAD).
The use of computers in the design of products.

computer-aided manufacturing (CAM).
The use of computers in the manufacturing of products.

computer-integrated manufacturing (CIM).
The uniting of computer-aided design with computer-aided manufacturing.

needed to program machines to make parts. The printing company JohnsByrne uses CIM in its Niles, Illinois, plant. It noticed a decreased cost in overhead, reduced outlay of resources, and fewer errors. IBM also uses CIM in a semiconductor facility. You can consult the *International Journal of Computer-Integrated Manufacturing* for other examples.

Critical Thinking

Computer-integrated manufacturing (CIM) has begun to revolutionize the production process. Now everything from cookies to cars can be designed and manufactured much more cheaply than before. Furthermore, customized changes can be made with very little increase in cost. What will such changes mean for the clothing industry, the shoe industry, and other fashion-related industries? What will they mean for other consumer and industrial goods industries? How will you benefit as a consumer?

program evaluation and review technique (PERT)
A method for analyzing the tasks involved in completing a given project, estimating the time needed to complete each task, and identifying the minimum time needed to complete the total project.

critical path
In a PERT network, the sequence of tasks that takes the longest time to complete.

Control Procedures: PERT and Gantt Charts

An important function of an operations manager is to be sure that products are manufactured and delivered on time, on budget, and to specifications. The question is: How can one be sure that all of the assembly processes will go smoothly and end up completed by the required time? One popular technique for maintaining some feel for the progress of production was developed in the 1950s for constructing nuclear submarines: the **program evaluation and review technique (PERT)**. PERT users analyze the tasks involved in completing a given project, estimate the time needed to complete each task, and identify the minimum time needed to complete the total project.

Formally, the steps involved in using PERT are (1) analyzing and sequencing tasks that need to be done, (2) estimating the time needed to complete each task, (3) drawing a PERT network illustrating the information from steps 1 and 2, and (4) identifying the critical path. The **critical path** is the sequence of tasks that takes the longest time to complete. The word *critical* is used in this term because a delay in the time needed to complete this path would cause the project or production run to be late.

Figure 9.4 illustrates a PERT chart for producing a music video. Note that the squares on the chart indicate completed tasks and the arrows leading to the squares indicate the time needed to complete each task. The path from one

FIGURE 9.4

PERT CHART FOR A VIDEO

The minimum amount of time it will take to produce this video is 15 weeks. To get that number, you add the week it takes to pick a star and a song to the four weeks to design a set, the two weeks to purchase set materials, the six weeks to construct the set, the week before rehearsals, and the final week when the video is made. That's the critical path. Any delay in that process will delay the final video.

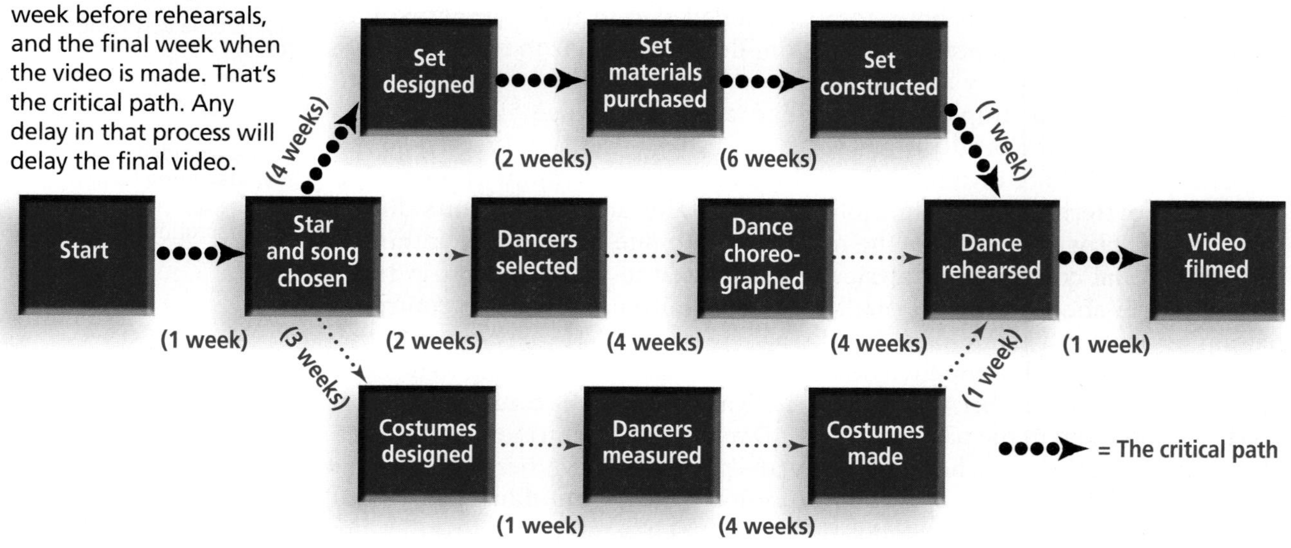

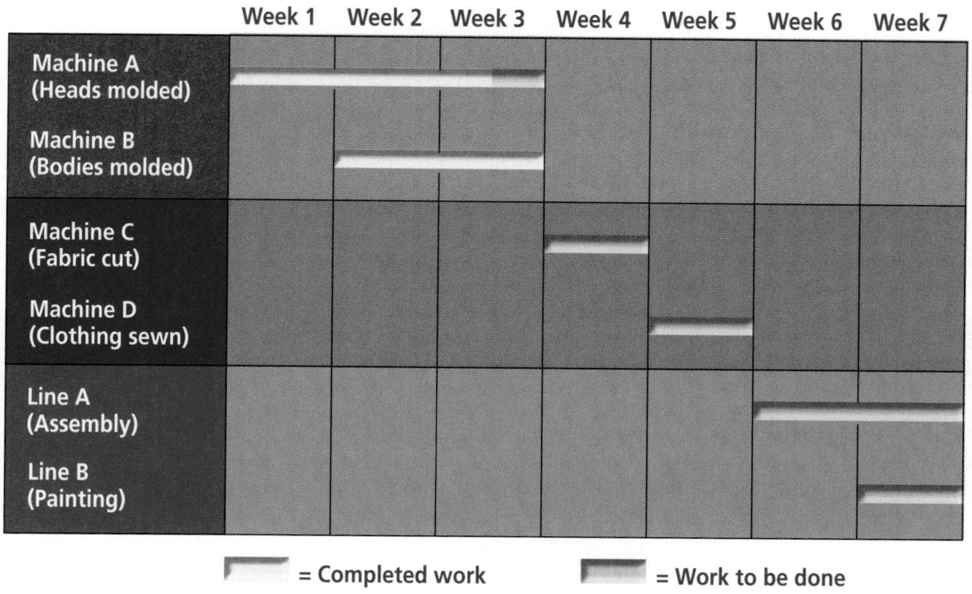

FIGURE 9.5

GANTT CHART FOR A DOLL MANUFACTURER

A Gantt chart enables a production manager to see at a glance when projects are scheduled to be completed and what the status is now. For example, the dolls' heads and bodies should be completed before the clothing is sewn, but they could be a little late as long as everything is ready for assembly in week 6. This chart shows that at the end of week 3, the dolls' bodies are ready, but the heads are about half a week behind.

completed task to another illustrates the relationships among tasks. For example, the arrow from "set designed" to "set materials purchased" shows that designing the set must be completed before the materials can be purchased. The critical path (indicated by the bold black arrows) reflects that producing the set takes more time than auditioning dancers and choreographing dances as well as designing and making costumes. The project manager now knows that it's critical that set construction remain on schedule if the project is to be completed on time, but short delays in the dance and costume preparation shouldn't affect completing the total project on time.

A PERT network can be made up of thousands of events over many months. Today, this complex procedure is done by computer. Another, more basic strategy used by manufacturers for measuring production progress is a Gantt chart. A **Gantt chart** (named for its developer, Henry L. Gantt) is a bar graph that clearly shows what projects are being worked on and how much has been completed at any given time. Figure 9.5 shows a Gantt chart for a doll manufacturer. The chart shows that the dolls' heads and bodies should be completed before the clothing is sewn. It also shows that at the end of week 3, the dolls' bodies are ready, but the heads are about half a week behind. All of this calculation was once done by hand. Now the computer has taken over. Using a Gantt-like computer program, a manager can trace the production process minute by minute to determine which tasks are on time and which are behind so that adjustments can be made to allow the company to stay on schedule.

Gantt chart
Bar graph showing production managers what projects are being worked on and what stage they are in at any given time.

PREPARING FOR THE FUTURE

The United States remains a major industrial country and is likely to become even stronger. This means that there are tremendous opportunities for careers in operations management. Today relatively few college students major in production and operations management, inventory management, and other areas involving manufacturing and operations management in the service sector. That means more opportunities for those students who can see the future trends and have the skills to own or work in tomorrow's highly automated, efficient factories, mines, service facilities, and other production locations.

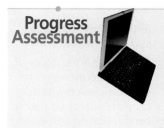

Progress Assessment

- What is just-in-time inventory control?
- How does flexible manufacturing differ from lean manufacturing?
- What are CAD, CAM, and CIM?
- Draw a PERT chart for making a breakfast of three-minute eggs, buttered toast, and coffee. Define the critical path. How could you use a Gantt chart to keep track of production?

Summary

1. Define operations management and describe the evolution of manufacturing in the United States.

1. Operations management is a specialized area in management that converts or transforms resources (including human resources) into goods and services.
   - ***What kind of firms use operations managers?***

   Firms in both the manufacturing and service sectors use operations managers.

2. Describe the operations management planning issues involved in both the manufacturing and service sectors, including facility location, facility layout, and quality control.

2. Functions involved in both the manufacturing and service sectors include facility location, facility layout, and quality control.
   - ***What is facility location and how does it differ from facility layout?***

   Facility location is the process of selecting a geographic location for a company's operations. Facility layout is the physical arrangement of resources (including people) to produce goods and services effectively and efficiently.
   - ***Why is facility location so important, and what criteria are used to evaluate different sites?***

   The very survival of U.S. manufacturing depends on its ability to remain competitive, and that means either making inputs less costly (reducing costs of labor and land) or increasing outputs from present inputs (increasing productivity). Labor costs and land costs are two major criteria for selecting the right sites. Other criteria include whether (1) resources are plentiful and inexpensive, (2) skilled workers are available or are trainable, (3) taxes are low and the local government offers support, (4) energy and water are available, (5) transportation costs are low, and (6) the quality of life and quality of education are high.
   - ***What are the latest quality control concepts?***

   Six sigma quality (just 3.4 defects per million opportunities) detects potential problems before they occur. Statistical quality control (SQC) is the process some managers use to continually monitor all processes in the production process to assure that quality is being built into the product from the beginning. Statistical process control (SPC) is the process of taking statistical samples of product components at each stage of the production process and plotting those results on a graph. Any variances from quality standards are recognized and can be corrected. Quality function deployment (QFD) is a process of linking the needs of end users (customers) to design, development, engineering, manufacturing, and service functions. The goal is to go beyond not making mistakes to maximizing customer satisfaction.
   - ***What quality standards do firms use in the United States?***

   Many firms try for the Malcolm Baldrige National Quality Awards. To qualify for one of these awards, a company has to show quality in seven key areas: leadership, strategic planning, customer and market focus, information and analysis, human resources focus, process management, and business results. International standards U.S. firms strive to meet include ISO 9001:2002 (ISO 9000) and ISO 14000. The first is a European standard for quality and the second is a collection of the best practices for managing an organization's impact on the environment.

3. There's strong evidence that productivity in the service sector is rising, but the government simply doesn't have the means to measure it.
   - ***Why is productivity so hard to measure?***

   The traditional way to measure productivity involves tracking inputs (worker-hours) compared to outputs (dollars). Quality improvements are not weighed. New information systems must be developed to measure the quality of goods and services, the speed of their delivery, and customer satisfaction.
   - ***How is technology creating productivity gains in service organizations?***

   Computers have been a great help to service employees, allowing them to perform their tasks faster and more accurately. ATMs make banking faster and easier, automated checkout machines enable grocery clerks (and customers) to process items faster. In short, operations management has led to tremendous productivity increases in the service sector but still has a long way to go.

3. Discuss the problem of measuring productivity in the service sector, and tell how new technology is leading to productivity gains in service companies.

4. There are several different processes manufacturers use to produce goods.
   - ***What is process manufacturing, and how does it differ from assembly processes?***

   Process manufacturing physically or chemically changes materials. Assembly processes put together components.
   - ***Are there other production processes?***

   Production processes are either continuous or intermittent. A continuous process is one in which long production runs turn out finished goods over time. An intermittent process is an operation where the production run is short and the machines are changed frequently to produce different products.
   - ***What relationship does enterprise resource planning (ERP) have with the production process?***

   ERP is a computer application that enables multiple firms to manage all of their operations (finance, requirements planning, human resources, and order fulfillment) on the basis of a single, integrated set of corporate data. The result is shorter time between orders and payment, less staff to do ordering and order processing, reduced inventories, and better customer service for all the firms involved. It is an advanced form of MRP.

4. Explain manufacturing processes, MRP, and ERP.

5. Companies are using seven new production techniques to become more profitable: (1) just-in-time inventory control, (2) Internet purchasing, (3) flexible manufacturing, (4) lean manufacturing, (5) mass customization, (6) competing in time, and (7) computer-aided design and manufacturing.
   - ***What is just-in-time(JIT) inventory control?***

   JIT involves having suppliers deliver parts and materials just in time to go on the assembly line so they don't have to be stored in warehouses.
   - ***How have purchasing agreements changed?***

   Purchasing agreements now involve fewer suppliers who supply quality goods and services at better prices in return for getting the business. Many new Internet companies have emerged to help both buyers and sellers complete the exchange process more efficiently.
   - ***What is flexible manufacturing?***

   Flexible manufacturing involves designing machines to produce a variety of products.
   - ***What is lean manufacturing?***

   Lean manufacturing is the production of goods using less of everything compared to mass production: less human effort, less manufacturing space, less investment in tools, and less engineering time to develop a new product.
   - ***What is mass customization?***

   Mass customization means making custom-designed goods and services for a large number of individual customers. Flexible manufacturing makes mass customization possible. Given the exact needs of a customer, flexible

5. Describe the seven new manufacturing techniques that have improved the productivity of U.S. companies: just-in-time inventory control, Internet purchasing, flexible manufacturing, lean manufacturing, mass customization, competing in time, and computer-aided design and manufacturing.

machines can produce a customized good as fast as mass-produced goods were once made. Mass customization is also important in service industries.

- ***How does competing in time fit into the process?***

Getting your product to market before your competitors is essential today, particularly in the electronics industry. Thus, competing in time is critical. Computer-aided design and manufacturing enable firms to compete in time and in efficiency.

- ***How do CAD/CAM systems work?***

Design changes made in computer-aided design (CAD) are instantly incorporated into the computer-aided manufacturing (CAM) process. The linking of the two systems—CAD and CAM—is called computer-integrated manufacturing (CIM).

6. Explain the use of PERT and Gantt charts.

6. The program evaluation and review technique (PERT) is a method for analyzing the tasks involved in completing a given project, estimating the time needed to complete each task, and identifying the minimum time needed to complete the total project. A Gantt chart is a bar graph that clearly shows what projects are being worked on and how much has been completed at any given time.

- ***Is there any relationship between a PERT chart and a Gantt chart?***

Figure 9.4 shows a PERT chart. Figure 9.5 shows a Gantt chart. Whereas PERT is a tool used for planning, a Gantt chart is a tool used to measure progress.

Key Terms

assembly process 282
competing in time 287
computer-aided design (CAD) 287
computer-aided manufacturing (CAM) 287
computer-integrated manufacturing (CIM) 287
continuous process 282
critical path 288
enterprise resource planning (ERP) 283
facility layout 273
facility location 270
flexible manufacturing 285
form utility 281
Gantt chart 289
intermittent process 282
ISO 9000 278
ISO 14000 279
just-in-time (JIT) inventory control 284
lean manufacturing 286
mass customization 286
materials requirement planning (MRP) 283
operations management 269
process manufacturing 282
production 268
production management 269
program evaluation and review technique (PERT) 288
purchasing 285
quality 275
quality function deployment (QFD) 277
six sigma quality 276
statistical process control (SPC) 276
statistical quality control (SQC) 276

Developing Workplace Skills

1. Choosing the right location for a manufacturing plant or a service organization is often critical to its success. Form small groups and have each group member pick one manufacturing plant or one service organization in town and list at least three reasons why its location helps or hinders its success. If its location is not ideal, where would be a better one?

2. In teams of four or five, discuss the need for better operations management at airports and with the airlines in general. Have the team develop a three-page report listing (*a*) problems team members have encoun-

tered in traveling by air and (*b*) suggestions for improving operations so such problems won't occur in the future.

3. Discuss some of the advantages and disadvantages of producing goods overseas using inexpensive labor. Summarize the moral and ethical issues of this practice.

4. Think of any production facility (e.g., sandwich shop or woodworking facility) or service center (e.g., library, copy room) at your school and redesign the layout (make a pencil drawing placing people and materials) so that the facility could more effectively serve its customers and so that the workers would be more effective and efficient.

5. Think about some of the experiences you have had with service organizations recently (e.g., the admissions office at your school), and select one incident in which you had to wait for an unreasonable length of time to get what you wanted. Tell what happens when customers are inconvenienced, and explain how management could make the operation more efficient and customer-oriented.

Taking It To The Net 1

Purpose

To illustrate production processes.

Exercise

Take a virtual tour of the Hershey Foods Corporation's chocolate factory by going to www.hersheys.com/tour/index.shtml. If you have a high-speed Internet connection, you can choose the video tour. If not, the picture tour is a faster choice.

1. Does Hershey use process manufacturing or the assembly process? Is the production of Hershey's chocolate an example of an intermittent or continuous production process? Justify your answers.
2. What location factors might go into the selection of a manufacturing site for Hershey's chocolate?

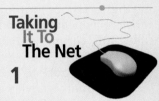

Taking It To The Net 2

Purpose

To learn more about the links between quality function deployment (QFD) and other quality concepts.

Exercise

Go to the Quality Function Deployment Institute website at www.qfdi.org and click on "What is QFD?" Then click on "Frequently Asked Questions about QFD."

1. How does QFD differ from other quality initiatives?
2. Who are the founders of QFD?
3. What are "expected quality" and "exciting quality"?

Casing The Web

To access the case "Griffin Hospital," visit

www.mhhe.com/ub7e

Video Case

Reality On Request—Digital Domain

As Chairman and CEO of Digital Domain in Venice, California, Scott Ross runs one of the largest digital production studios in the world. His studio won an Academy Award for doing the simulation of the sinking of the *Titanic* in the movie with the same name. It also created the digital waves that wiped out the horsemen in *Lord of the Rings*.

Operations management is unique at Digital Domain because no two projects are ever the same. One day they may be making a digital cow (*O Brother, Where Art Thou*), on another a digital spaceship (*Apollo 13*), and on still another digital waves (*Titanic*). Digital is both a production and service provider. How so? In addition to producing digital scenes for movies, the company advises movie producers as to what is possible to do digitally. Still, certain activities, such as facility location and facility layout, are common to both service organizations and production firms.

Since many movies are made in Los Angeles, it's important for Digital Domain to be close to the city. Actors are often chosen from that area, as are workers and specialists at Digital. The company's most important resource, however, is its workers. Thus, facilities layout is designed to make the job of workers easier, yet efficient. For example, there's a combination conference room and cafeteria. Given the company's passion for *quality*, everything is designed to be clean and logical. Facility layout assists workers in developing the highest-quality product possible given time and money constraints.

Materials requirement planning (MRP) is a computer-based operations management system that uses sales forecasts to make needed parts and materials available at the right time and place. Since Digital's primary resource is people, the company lists 54 key disciplines in its database, so it's easy to find the right person for the right job. For example, a project may come up on Wednesday that demands having resources available the next Monday. People have to be contacted and hired *just in time* to keep the project on time and within budget.

The company does much of its purchasing on the Internet. It also uses *flexible manufacturing*. To keep costs down, Digital also used *lean manufacturing*, the production of goods using less of everything: less human effort, less manufacturing space, less investment in tools, and less engineering time for a given project. To keep costs down the company does a lot of pre-visualizing—simulating projects to determine the best way to proceed.

Of course, *mass customization* is basically what Digital Domain is all about: creating new and different scenes that can't be duplicated. However, once the company learns to create artificial waves or some other image, it is easier to duplicate a similar image next time. Since film is very expensive, many ideas are created using pen and pencil first. From such "primitive" tools, the company goes on to use *computer-aided design*.

Making movies is expensive. Everything needs to be done as planned. Scott Ross knows it's show *business*, and the accent is on business, and making a profit. For this reason, Digital uses PERT charts to follow projects and to determine what series of steps is critical to getting things out in time. It also uses computerized GANTT charts to follow goods in process. Getting things done right and on time is the hallmark at Digital Domain.

Thinking It Over

1. Do you have an appreciation for operations management now that you've seen how exciting such a job can be at a company like Digital Domain?
2. Mass customization is critical in the production of movies and special effects. As a consumer, what benefits do you see in being able to buy custom-made shoes, clothes, automobiles, and more?
3. What lessons did you learn from this video that you could apply at any job you might get?
4. This video points out that certain workers are very focused on quality and that there comes a time when you have to stop improving things because time has a cost. Have you had to make a trade-off between perfection and "good enough"? What were the consequences?

Part 3

Business Management

Career Portfolio

Management is the people part of business. Although managers are also responsible for managing finance, information, and various processes, their main responsibility is to the people who work for them. The managers are the people who run the organization. Without managers, there would be no business.

As everything else in the human realm is constantly changing, so is management and our attitudes toward it. Management careers have always been among the most challenging and fulfilling in the field of business. Likewise, the role of managers continues to change rapidly.

SKILLS

The skills managers need today are different from those they needed a generation ago. Today's managers must know how to be both team players and team leaders. They cannot get away with the "jump when I say jump" mentality of the past. More than ever, managers need to be effective communicators. They especially need to know how to listen, to hear, and to understand the needs of both their subordinates and their own managers. They also need the ability to organize and to keep others organized and to possess the know-how to motivate workers.

CAREER PATHS

Today's management opportunities often start out as management training openings that later develop into full-blown management positions. Both government and larger companies have management training programs. Some of these organizations will hire workers through campus recruiters. Others look for skills that can be acquired outside the classroom. Another common way to become a manager is to start as an employee and work your way up the management ladder. College courses and other forms of management training are often available tuition-free to the ambitious employee (the company pays).

Once a manager is hired, the progress into middle and top management is far from automatic. As one gets closer to the top, there are fewer and fewer opportunities. Getting to the top, then, means learning to be competitive and good at what you do. Understanding office politics is also certainly a plus, though some companies are more political than others.

As a manager moves up in an organization, his or her responsibilities and authority increase. Becoming an integral part of planning and running an organization brings excitement as well as rewards.

SOME POSSIBLE POSITIONS IN MANAGEMENT				
JOB TITLE	**SALARY**	**JOB DUTIES**	**CAREER PATH**	**PROSPECTS**
Top executives (general manager, CEO, executive vice president)	Amount varies widely, depending on responsibilities and type and size of firm.	Establish the organizations's general goals and policies. Act as liaison with other companies; direct the individual department or division; direct supervisor in motivation and control of workers.	Most general managers and top CEOs have a bachelor's or higher degree, often in business administration, but qualifications vary widely. Most vacancies are filled by promoting lower-level managers up through the ranks.	Average growth in opportunities through year 2010, but competition is keen.
Health services manager	Varies widely by type and size of facility; median is $56,370.	Manage a health care facility or department, including personnel, finance, and facility operations.	Master's degree in health services administration, public health, health sciences, or related area is required. New grads may start as staff employees and move up from there.	Faster than average growth through 2010.
Industrial production manager	Median is $61,660.	Plan production schedules within time and budgetary limits. Handle staffing, equipment procurement, inventory control, and quality control.	A college degree is required, as are good interpersonal skills. Company-based training programs are often used to teach unique organization plans or production processes.	Outlook through 2010 is slower than average.
Management analyst	Varies greatly, based on experience, education, and employer.	Act as an adviser and analyst of management concerns in host organizations. Propose ways to improve a company's structure, efficiency, or profits.	Degree and work experience help market credibility of the consultant. However, knowledge of the industry and self-confidence are most important qualities.	Faster than average growth through 2010, especially in firms doing business internationally.

Source: Bureau of Labor Statistics, *Occupational Outlook Handbook,* 2002–03 edition.

Central Florida Response & Recovery, Inc.

Name: Matthew D. Meyers

Age: 38

Position/title: CEO/President

Salary range: $80,000–$100,000

Time in this position: 2 years

Major factors in the decision to take this position: After 18 years of working with the government in positions such as Fire Chief and Director of Emergency Management, the opportunity to help others while being independent intrigued me. After years spent climbing the promotional ladder, I had many certificates and no degree, so at the age of 34, I returned to college. I was in my second year at Florida Metropolitan University, taking a small business course, when I realized that forming a disaster consulting company would allow me to have the best of both worlds.

Company description: An emergency and disaster consulting company.

Job description: I provide consultation to both private sector and government agencies in the preparation for, response to, and recovery from both human-caused and natural disasters.

Ideal next job: When I started my company, my only thought was to establish a small firm with one employee. As additional opportunities continue to arise, I have added 12 part-time professionals to assist. I now have visions of substantially increasing the company's net worth over the next three years.

Best part of your job: The best part of my job is the immense pride I feel in having had the opportunities to assist after some of our country's worst disasters. I have had the privilege to meet and work with some of our nation's finest leaders.

Worst part of your job: The worst part of my job is dealing with the personal loss associated with tragedies and disasters. When tragedy strikes, the devastation felt by those affected leaves lingering memories for me.

Educational background: I graduated Summa Cum Laude from Florida Metropolitan University with a Bachelor's of Science Degree in Management/Marketing, then completed a Master's Degree in Organizational Management from the University of Phoenix, also Summa Cum Laude, and have initiated my first steps toward a PhD.

Favorite course/Best course for your career: My favorite course was also the best course for my career. Professor Phil Reffitt's Small Business Management class showed me that all of this was possible.

Recommended by Phillip Reffitt, Florida Metropolitan University

Chapter 10

Motivating Employees and Building Self-Managed Teams

Learning Goals

After you have read and studied this chapter, you should be able to

1. Explain Taylor's scientific management.
2. Describe the Hawthorne studies, and relate their significance to management.
3. Identify the levels of Maslow's hierarchy of needs, and relate their importance to employee motivation.
4. Distinguish between the motivators and hygiene factors identified by Herzberg.
5. Explain how job enrichment affects employee motivation and performance.
6. Differentiate among Theory X, Theory Y, and Theory Z.
7. Explain goal-setting theory and how management by objectives (MBO) exemplifies the theory.
8. Describe the key principles of expectancy, reinforcement, and equity theories.
9. Explain how open communication builds teamwork, and describe how managers are likely to motivate teams in the future.

Getting to Know Herb Kelleher and Colleen Barrett of Southwest Airlines

The skies are not always friendly, but they do seem to smile for one airline. Southwest Airlines has continued flying high while other airlines have struggled to stay aloft. Southwest was the only U.S. airline to remain profitable after the September 11, 2001, tragedies crippled all of the nation's other airlines, and it is the only one that has remained profitable every single year since 1973. It now ranks as the fourth largest in the United States. What makes Southwest so special? Analysts credit much of the airline's achievement to the engaging management style of the company's unconventional cofounder and ex-CEO, Herb Kelleher. In fact, Kelleher was named the 1999 CEO of the Year by *Chief Executive* magazine. Kelleher resigned as president and CEO in 2001, but he continues to serve as chairman of the board. The Board of Directors passed the president position on to Colleen Barrett, who started as Kelleher's personal legal secretary in 1967. She later moved to Southwest when Kelleher started the airline with his friend Rollin King. Kelleher has great faith that Barrett will continue to carry on the traditions Southwest is noted for.

The major role fun plays in motivating Southwest employees shows that it can be more than just having a good time—fun can develop employees who are happy, productive, and intensely loyal.

Known to show up at company events dressed as a woman or King Arthur, Kelleher was the jokemeister of the airline industry. Under his coaching, Southwest was a consistent winner of the service triple crown—highest customer satisfaction, most on-time flights, and best baggage handling. Southwest employees are far more productive than employees of competing airlines. Per worker, Southwest flies more planes and serves more passengers than any other U.S. airline. Southwest employees also pitch in wherever needed. Pilots might work the boarding gate if things back up; ticket agents might haul luggage to get the plane out on time. When fuel prices accelerated during the Gulf War, employees even began a voluntary payroll deduction program to defray costs. Southwest workers (approximately 85 percent of whom are union members) are paid competitively.

The major role fun plays in motivating Southwest employees shows that it can be more than just having a good time—fun can develop employees who are happy, productive, and intensely loyal. A company can promote fun either by organizing events, such as a weekly barbecue, or by simply making it known that a sense of humor is a highly valued trait.

Many analysts believe that the corporate culture is so finely ingrained at Southwest that the airline will continue its success now that Kelleher is no longer president and CEO. While some folks refer to Kelleher as Uncle Herbie, they think of Barrett as the Queen of Hearts. As the woman in charge of Southwest's employee-centered corporate culture, Barrett has been described by Kelleher as having "the wonderful ability to get different people working together cohesively. She gets her troops fired with enthusiasm, and she is fair and firm at the same time." With more than 35,000 employees to look after, Barrett has been called the matriarch of Southwest, since she is so devoted to her corporate family. Birthdays, anniversaries, and other significant events in an employee's life are noted with a card from Barrett's office. She believes that emphasis on employee satisfaction comes more naturally to women than to men. That may help explain why 10 of the top 24 executives at Southwest are women.

According to Kelleher, corporate culture "is the hardest thing for competitors to imitate. You can get an airplane. You can get ticket-counter space, you can get baggage conveyors. But it is our esprit de corps—the culture, the spirit—that is truly our most valuable competitive asset."

Sources: Joyce S. Harris, "Mother of the Flock: What's Behind Colleen Barrett's Success as President of Southwest Airlines?" *Dallas Morning News,* August 4, 2002, p. 3F; Sally Donnelly, "The Sky's the Limit: Women Execs Have Taken Over Top Jobs at Major Airlines, Helping Them Shift Focus from Hardware to Customer Service," *Time,* July 15, 2002, p. Y1; and Wendy Zellner, "Holding Steady," *Business Week,* February 3, 2003, pp. 66–68.

The Importance of Motivation

"If work is such fun, how come the rich don't do it?" quipped comedian Groucho Marx. Well, the rich do work—Bill Gates didn't make his billions playing computer games. And workers can have fun—if managers like Herb Kelleher and Colleen Barrett make the effort to motivate them. As the chapter opening profile of Southwest Airlines shows, the importance of satisfaction among the workforce cannot be overstated. Happy workers lead to happy customers, and happy customers lead to successful businesses.[1] On the opposite side, unhappy workers are likely to leave the company, and when this happens, the company usually loses out. Losing a valuable, highly skilled employee could cost more than $100,000 for such things as exit interviews, severance pay, the process of hiring a replacement worker, and lost productivity while the new employee is learning the job. The "soft" costs are even greater: loss of intellectual capital, decreased morale, increased employee stress, and a negative reputation.[2] Motivating the right people to join and remain with the organization is a key function of managers.

People are willing to work, and work hard, if they feel that their work makes a difference and is appreciated. People are motivated by a variety of things, such as recognition, accomplishment, and status.[3] An **intrinsic reward** is the personal satisfaction you feel when you perform well and complete goals. The belief that your work makes a significant contribution to the organization or society is a form of intrinsic reward. An **extrinsic reward** is something given to you by someone else as recognition for good work. Such things as pay increases, praise, and promotions are examples of extrinsic rewards. Although ultimately motivation—the drive to satisfy a need—comes from within an individual, there are ways to stimulate people that bring out their natural drive to do a good job.[4]

intrinsic reward
The personal satisfaction you feel when you perform well and complete goals.

extrinsic reward
Something given to you by someone else as recognition for good work; extrinsic rewards include pay increases, praise, and promotions.

The purpose of this chapter is to help you understand the concepts, theories, and practice of motivation. The most important person to motivate, of course, is yourself. One way to do that is to find the right job in the right organization—one that enables you to reach your goals in life.[5] The whole purpose of this book is to help you in that search and to teach you how to succeed once you get there. One secret of success is to recognize that everyone else is on a similar search. Naturally, some are more committed than others. The job of a manager is to find that commitment, encourage it, and focus it on some common goal.

This chapter begins with a look at some of the traditional theories of motivation. You will learn about the Hawthorne studies because they created a new interest in worker satisfaction and motivation. Then you'll look at some assumptions about employees that come from the traditional theorists. You will see the names of these theorists over and over in business literature and courses: Taylor, Mayo, Maslow, Herzberg, and McGregor. Finally, you will learn the modern applications of motivation theories and the managerial procedures for implementing them.

Frederick Taylor: The Father of Scientific Management

Several books in the 19th century presented management principles, but not until the early 20th century did there appear any significant works with lasting implications. One of the most well-known, *The Principles of Scientific Management,* was written by American efficiency engineer Frederick Taylor and published in 1911. This book earned Taylor the title "father of scientific management." Taylor's goal was to increase worker productivity in order to benefit both the firm and the worker. The way to improve productivity, ➤P. 15◄, Taylor thought, was to scientifically study the most efficient ways to do things, determine the one "best way" to perform each task, and then teach people those methods. This became known as **scientific management**. Three elements were basic to Taylor's approach: time, methods, and rules of work. His most important tools were observation and the stopwatch. It's Taylor's thinking that is behind today's measures of how many burgers McDonald's expects its flippers to flip and how many callers the phone companies expect operators to assist.

scientific management Studying workers to find the most efficient ways of doing things and then teaching people those techniques.

A classic Taylor story involves his study of men shoveling rice, coal, and iron ore with the same type of shovel. Taylor felt that different materials called for different shovels. He proceeded to invent a wide variety of sizes and shapes of shovels and, with stopwatch in hand, measured output over time in what were called **time-motion studies**—studies of the tasks performed to complete a job and the time needed to do each task. Sure enough, an average person could shovel more (in fact, from 25 to 35 tons more per day) using the most efficient motions and the proper shovel. This finding led to time-motion studies of virtually every factory job. As the most efficient ways of doing things were determined, efficiency became the standard for setting goals.

time-motion studies Studies, begun by Frederick Taylor, of which tasks must be performed to complete a job and the time needed to do each task.

Taylor's scientific management became the dominant strategy for improving productivity in the early 1900s. Hundreds of time-motion specialists developed standards in plants throughout the country. One follower of Taylor was Henry L. Gantt, who developed charts by which managers plotted the work of employees a day in advance down to the smallest detail. (See Chapter 9 for a discussion of Gantt charts.) American engineers Frank and Lillian Gilbreth used Taylor's ideas in a three-year study of bricklaying. They developed the **principle of motion economy,** which showed that every job could be broken down into a series of elementary motions called a *therblig* (Gilbreth spelled backward with the *t* and *h* transposed). They then analyzed each motion to make it more efficient.

principle of motion economy Theory developed by Frank and Lillian Gilbreth that every job can be broken down into a series of elementary motions.

Scientific management viewed people largely as machines that needed to be properly programmed. There was little concern for the psychological or human aspects of work. Taylor felt simply that workers would perform at a high level of effectiveness (that is, be motivated) if they received high enough pay.

Some of Taylor's ideas are still being implemented. Referring to a set of papers supporting ratification of the U.S. Constitution, management guru Peter Drucker even calls Taylor's ideas "the most lasting contribution America has made to Western thought since *The Federalist Papers*."[6] Some companies still place more emphasis on conformity to work rules than on creativity, flexibility, and responsiveness. For example, UPS tells drivers how fast to walk (three feet per second), how many packages to pick up and deliver a day (average of 400), and how to hold their keys (teeth up, third finger). Drivers even wear "ring scanners," electronic devices on their index fingers wired to a small computer on their wrists that shoot a pattern of photons at a bar code on a package to let a customer trolling the Internet know exactly where his or her package is at any given moment. See the Legal Briefcase box for more about scientific management at UPS.

The benefits of relying on workers to come up with solutions to productivity problems have long been recognized, as we shall discover next.

Elton Mayo and the Hawthorne Studies

One of the studies that grew out of Frederick Taylor's research was conducted at the Western Electric Company's Hawthorne plant in Cicero, Illinois. The study began in 1927 and ended six years later. Let's see why it was one of the major studies in management literature.

Elton Mayo and his colleagues from Harvard University came to the Hawthorne plant to test the degree of lighting associated with optimum productivity. In this respect, theirs was a traditional scientific management www.ups.com

Legal Briefcase

Scientific Management Is Alive and Well at UPS

UPS is truly a powerhouse of a company. With over $30 billion in revenues and 350,000 employees, UPS is the world's largest package distribution company. *Fortune* magazine rates UPS as the most admired company in its industry. The company grew from a small bicycle-messenger service in 1907 to today's mammoth delivery service in part by dictating every task for its employees. Drivers are required to step out of their trucks with their right foot, fold their money face up, and carry packages under their left arm. If they are considered slow, a supervisor rides with them, prodding them with stopwatches and clipboards. The need to improve productivity to meet increased competition from other delivery services recently prompted UPS to add 20 new services that require more skill. Drivers had to learn an assortment of new codes and billing systems and deliver an increasing number of time-sensitive packages that have special-handling requirements.

Drivers have long accepted such work requirements, taking comfort in good wages, generous benefits, and an attractive profit-sharing plan. All of this pressure, however, has taken its toll. Many UPS drivers have suffered from anxiety, phobias, or back strain, and at one point UPS had twice the injury rate of other delivery companies. In 1994, UPS settled a $3 million complaint from the Occupational Safety and Health Administration that it did not provide adequate safety for workers who handle hazardous wastes. UPS has spent nearly $1.5 billion since 1995 on improving health and safety programs. The total of days lost to disability has been on the decline.

In August 1997, the Teamsters Union, which represents 210,000 of UPS's employees, called a nationwide strike against the company because workers and managers couldn't reach agreement on a new contract. The Teamsters said they wanted better wages and pensions, and a safer workplace. They also wanted the company to limit its use of part-time workers, who receive limited benefits, and provide more full-time jobs. The 15-day strike ended when the union and UPS managers agreed on a five-year deal that created 10,000 new full-time jobs from existing part-time positions, increased full-time pay by $3.10 an hour, and retained the pension plan. Workers threatened to strike again in 2002 but were successful in negotiating a 25 percent increase over the next six years before the contract deadline.

UPS's CEO Michael Eskew believes the company is using new technologies and better planning to achieve greater productivity without overloading employees. Competition from companies such as FedEx (where workers earn 30 to 50 percent less than UPS workers) also requires greater efficiency. The variety of new UPS services requires drivers to remember more things. Because the jobs require more thinking, the company has begun hiring a new breed of skilled, college-educated workers. Do you think the new breed of UPS workers will be more or less tolerant of the company's rules and demands?

Sources: Gregory Cancelada, "Teamsters, UPS Work to Stave Off a Strike; Sides Worry About the New FedEx Threat," *St. Louis Post-Dispatch,* June 7, 2002, p. C1; Robin Ajello, "In Business This Week: Big Brown's Big Deal with Workers," *Business Week,* July 29, 2002, p. 52; "NAACP Honors UPS for Corporate Diversity Works," Reuters Business Report, February 15, 2002; and Bob Brewin, "UPS Readies Wireless Upgrade in U.S.," *Computerworld,* March 3, 2003, p. 7.

study; the idea was to keep records of the workers' productivity under different levels of illumination. But the initial experiments revealed what seemed to be a problem: The productivity of the experimental group compared to that of other workers doing the same job went up regardless of whether the lighting was bright or dim. This was true even when the lighting was reduced to about the level of moonlight. These results confused and frustrated the researchers, who had expected productivity to fall as the lighting was dimmed.

A second series of experiments was conducted. In these, a separate test room was set up where temperature, humidity, and other environmental factors could be manipulated. In the series of 13 experimental periods, productivity went up each time; in fact, it increased by 50 percent overall. When the experimenters repeated the original condition (expecting productivity to fall to original levels), productivity increased yet again. The experiments were considered a total failure at this point. No matter what the experimenters did, productivity went up. What was causing the increase?

In the end, Mayo guessed that some human or psychological factor was involved. He and his colleagues then interviewed the workers, asking them about their feelings and attitudes toward the experiment. The researchers' findings began a profound change in management thinking that has had repercussions up to the present. Here is what they concluded:

- The workers in the test room thought of themselves as a social group. The atmosphere was informal, they could talk freely, and they interacted regularly with their supervisors and the experimenters. They felt special and worked hard to stay in the group. This motivated them.
- The workers were involved in the planning of the experiments. For example, they rejected one kind of pay schedule and recommended another, which was used. The workers felt that their ideas were respected and that they were involved in managerial decision making. This, too, motivated them.
- No matter what the physical conditions were, the workers enjoyed the atmosphere of their special room and the additional pay they got for more productivity. Job satisfaction increased dramatically.

Elton Mayo and his research team forever changed managers' fixed assumptions about what motivates employees. Mayo and his Harvard University team gave birth to the concept of human-based motivation after conducting studies at the Western Electric Hawthorne plant (pictured here) in Cicero, Illinois. Before the studies at Hawthorne, workers were often programmed to behave like human robots.

Researchers now use the term **Hawthorne effect** to refer to the tendency for people to behave differently when they know they're being studied. The Hawthorne study's results encouraged researchers to study human motivation and the managerial styles that lead to more productivity. The emphasis of research shifted away from Taylor's scientific management and toward Mayo's new human-based management.

Mayo's findings led to completely new assumptions about employees. One of those assumptions, of course, was that pay was not the only motivator. In fact, money was found to be a relatively ineffective motivator. That change in assumptions led to many theories about the human side of motivation. One of the best-known motivation theorists was Abraham Maslow, whose work we discuss next.

Hawthorne effect
The tendency for people to behave differently when they know they are being studied.

Motivation and Maslow's Hierarchy of Needs

Psychologist Abraham Maslow believed that to understand motivation at work, one must understand human motivation in general. It seemed to him that motivation arises from need. That is, people are motivated to satisfy unmet needs; needs that have been satisfied no longer provide motivation. He thought that needs could be placed on a hierarchy of importance.

Figure 10.1 shows **Maslow's hierarchy of needs,** whose levels are as follows:

Maslow's hierarchy of needs
Theory of motivation based on unmet human needs from basic physiological needs to safety, social, and esteem needs to self-actualization needs.

Physiological needs: basic survival needs, such as the need for food, water, and shelter.

Safety needs: the need to feel secure at work and at home.

FIGURE 10.1

MASLOW'S HIERACHY OF NEEDS

Maslow's hierarchy of needs is based on the idea that motivation comes from need. If a need is met, it's no longer a motivator, so a higher-level need becomes the motivator. Higher-level needs demand the support of lower-level needs. This chart shows the various levels of need. Do you know where you are on the chart right now?

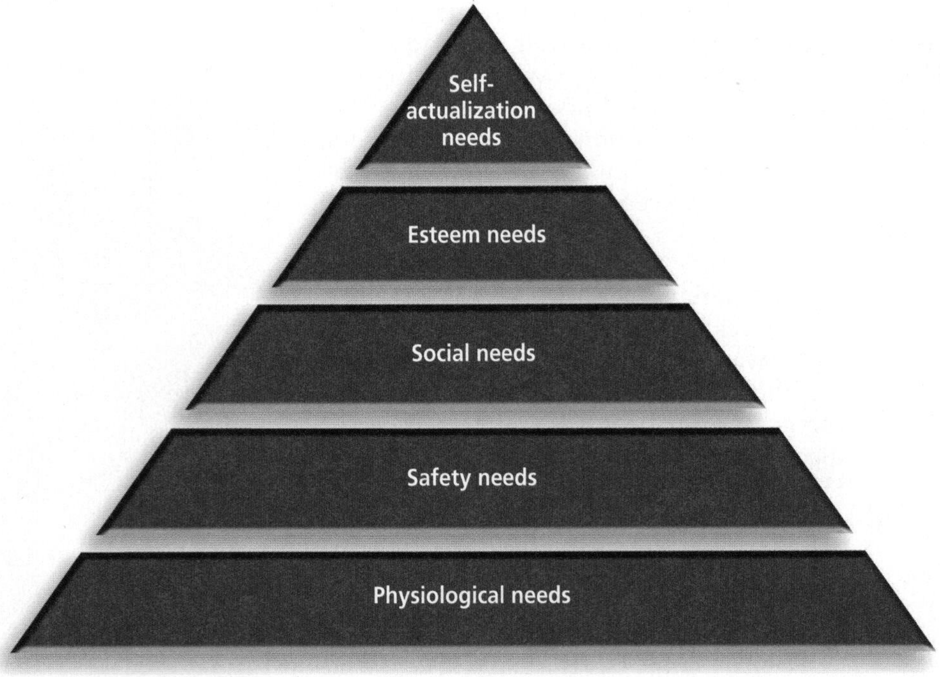

Social needs: the need to feel loved, accepted, and part of the group.

Esteem needs: the need for recognition and acknowledgment from others, as well as self-respect and a sense of status or importance.

Self-actualization needs: the need to develop to one's fullest potential.

When one need is satisfied, another, higher-level need emerges and motivates the person to do something to satisfy it. The satisfied need is no longer a motivator. For example, if you just ate a full-course dinner, hunger would not (at least for several hours) be a motivator, and your attention may turn to your surroundings (safety needs) or family (social needs). Of course, lower-level needs (e.g., thirst) may emerge at any time they are not met and take your attention away from higher-level needs such as the need for recognition or status.

Most of the world's workers struggle all day simply to meet the basic physiological and safety needs. In developed countries, such needs no longer dominate, and workers seek to satisfy growth needs (social, esteem, and self-actualization needs).

To compete successfully, U.S. firms must create a work environment that motivates the best and the brightest workers. That means establishing a work environment that includes goals such as social contribution, honesty, reliability, service, quality, dependability, and unity.

Critical Thinking

Your job right now is to finish reading this chapter. How strongly would you be motivated to do that if you were sweating in a 105-degree room? Imagine now that your roommate has turned on the air-conditioning. Now that you are more comfortable, are you more likely to read? Look at Maslow's hierarchy of needs to see what need would be motivating you at both times. Can you see how helpful Maslow's theory is in understanding motivation by applying it to your own life?

Applying Maslow's Theory

Andrew Grove, former CEO and current chairman of Intel, observed Maslow's concepts in action in his firm.[7] One woman, for example, took a low-paying job that did little for her family's standard of living. Why? Because she needed the companionship her work offered (social/affiliation need). One of Grove's friends had a midlife crisis when he was made a vice president. This position had been a lifelong goal, and when the man reached it he felt unsettled because he had to find another way to motivate himself (self-actualization need). People at a research and development lab were motivated by the desire to know more about their field of interest, but they had little desire to produce marketable results and thus little was achieved. Grove had to find new people who wanted to learn not just for the sake of learning but to achieve results as well.

Once managers understand the need level of employees, it is easier to design programs that will trigger self-motivation. Grove believes that all motivation comes from within. He believes that self-actualized persons are achievers. Personally, Grove was motivated to earn a doctorate from the University of California at Berkeley after surviving a childhood in communist Hungary. He also wrote several best-selling books, including his memoir *Swimming Across*, and designed a managerial program at Intel that emphasized achievement. Now Intel's managers are highly motivated to achieve their objectives because they feel rewarded for doing so.

In addition to being a best-selling author, former Intel CEO Andrew Grove remains one of the most admired business minds in the United States. He believes that managers can use Maslow's concepts to improve workers' job performance. How do you think managers can apply Maslow's theory in the workplace?

Progress Assessment

- What are the similarities and differences between Taylor's time-motion studies and Mayo's Hawthorne studies?
- How did Mayo's findings influence scientific management?
- Draw a diagram of Maslow's hierarchy of needs. Label and describe the parts.
- According to Andrew Grove, what is the ultimate source of all motivation?

Herzberg's Motivating Factors

Another direction in managerial theory is to explore what managers can do with the job itself to motivate employees (a modern-day look at Taylor's research). In other words, some theorists ask: Of all the factors controllable by managers, which are most effective in generating an enthusiastic work effort?

The most discussed study in this area was conducted in the mid-1960s by psychologist Frederick Herzberg. He asked workers to rank various job-related factors in order of importance relative to motivation. The question was: What creates enthusiasm for workers and makes them work to full potential? The results showed that the most important motivating factors were the following:

1. Sense of achievement.
2. Earned recognition.

3. Interest in the work itself.
4. Opportunity for growth.
5. Opportunity for advancement.
6. Importance of responsibility.
7. Peer and group relationships.
8. Pay.
9. Supervisor's fairness.
10. Company policies and rules.
11. Status.
12. Job security.
13. Supervisor's friendliness.
14. Working conditions.

Herzberg noted that the factors receiving the most votes were all clustered around job content. Workers like to feel that they contribute to the company (sense of achievement was number 1). They want to earn recognition (number 2) and feel their jobs are important (number 6). They want responsibility (which is why learning is so important) and want recognition for that responsibility by having a chance for growth and advancement. Of course, workers also want the job to be interesting.

Herzberg noted further that factors having to do with the job environment were not considered motivators by workers. It was interesting to find that one of those factors was pay. Workers felt that the absence of good pay, job security, friendly supervisors, and the like could cause dissatisfaction, but the presence of those factors did not motivate them to work harder; they just provided satisfaction and contentment in the work situation.

motivators
In Herzberg's theory of motivating factors, job factors that cause employees to be productive and that give them satisfaction.

hygiene factors
In Herzberg's theory of motivating factors, job factors that can cause dissatisfaction if missing but that do not necessarily motivate employees if increased.

The conclusions of Herzberg's study were that certain factors, called **motivators,** did cause employees to be productive and gave them a great deal of satisfaction. These factors mostly had to do with job content. Herzberg called other elements of the job **hygiene factors** (or maintenance factors). These had to do mostly with the job environment and could cause dissatisfaction if missing but would not necessarily motivate employees if increased. See Figure 10.2 for a list of both motivators and hygiene factors.

Considering Herzberg's motivating factors, we come up with the following conclusion: The best way to motivate employees is to make the job interesting, help them achieve their objectives, and recognize that achievement through advancement and added responsibility.

FIGURE 10.2

HERZBERG'S MOTIVATORS AND HYGIENE FACTORS

There's some controversy over Herzberg's results. For example, sales managers often use money as a motivator. Recent studies have shown that money can be a motivator if used as part of a recognition program.

MOTIVATORS	HYGIENE (MAINTENANCE) FACTORS
(These factors can be used to motivate workers.)	(These factors can cause dissatisfaction, but changing them will have little motivational effect.)
Work itself	Company policy and administration
Achievement	Supervision
Recognition	Working conditions
Responsibility	Interpersonal relations (co-workers)
Growth and advancement	Salary, status, and job security

Applying Herzberg's Theories

Herzberg believed that motivational factors such as recognition increase worker performance. Managers of the nation's largest company, Wal-Mart, obviously agree with his theory. Here a Wal-Mart employee in Temple, Texas, receives an award for high productivity. How do you think Herzberg's motivational factors encourage workers to a higher level of performance on the job?

Kingston Technology, a manufacturer of computer chips, headquartered in Fountain Valley, California, was identified in 2002 by *Fortune* magazine as one of the 100 best companies to work for in America. Why? You might think that its employees would point to the special annual bonus (which averages $30,000 per worker). Or perhaps they would cite the free lunches once a month or the driving range behind the plant. No, the majority of Kingston employees say what matters most to them is the respect they're paid by the company's founders, John Tu and David Sun.[8]

Pat Blake, an employee of Sunnen Products Company, an industrial supplier in St. Louis, Missouri, says that what makes her happy to work extra hours or learn new skills is less tangible than money or bonuses—it's a kind word from her boss: "When something good happens, like we have a shipping day with so many thousands of dollars going out the door, they let us know about that. It kind of makes you want to go for the gold."

Improved working conditions (such as better wages or increased security) are taken for granted after workers get used to them. This is what Herzberg meant by hygiene (or maintenance) factors: Their absence causes dissatisfaction, but their presence (maintenance) does not motivate. The best motivator for some employees is a simple and sincere "Thanks, I really appreciate what you're doing."[9]

Many surveys conducted to test Herzberg's theories have supported his finding that the number one motivator is not money but a sense of achievement and recognition for a job well done.[10] If you're skeptical about this, think about the limitations of money as a motivating force. Most organizations review an employee's performance only once a year and allocate raises at that time. To inspire and motivate employees to perform at their highest level of capability, managers must recognize their achievements and progress more than once a year. In the National Survey of the Changing Workforce conducted by the Families and Work Institute in New York, salary ranked 16th in a list of items considered very important in rating jobs. A study prepared by Robert Half International, a staffing and recruitment firm in Menlo Park, California, identified lack of enough praise and recognition as the primary reason employees leave their job.

Look back at Herzberg's list of motivating factors and identify the ones that tend to motivate you. Rank them in order of importance to you. Keep these factors in mind as you consider jobs and careers. What motivators do your job opportunities offer to you? Are they the ones you consider important? Evaluating your job offers in terms of what's really important to you will help you make a wise career choice.

A review of Figure 10.3 shows that there is a good deal of similarity in Maslow's hierarchy of needs and Herzberg's theory of factors.

Job Enrichment

Both Maslow's and Herzberg's theories have been extended by job enrichment theory. **Job enrichment** is a motivational strategy that emphasizes motivating the worker through the job itself. Work is assigned to individuals so that they have the opportunity to complete an identifiable task from beginning to end.

job enrichment
A motivational strategy that emphasizes motivating the worker through the job itself.

FIGURE 10.3

COMPARISON OF MASLOW'S HIERARCHY OF NEEDS AND HERZBERG'S THEORY OF FACTORS

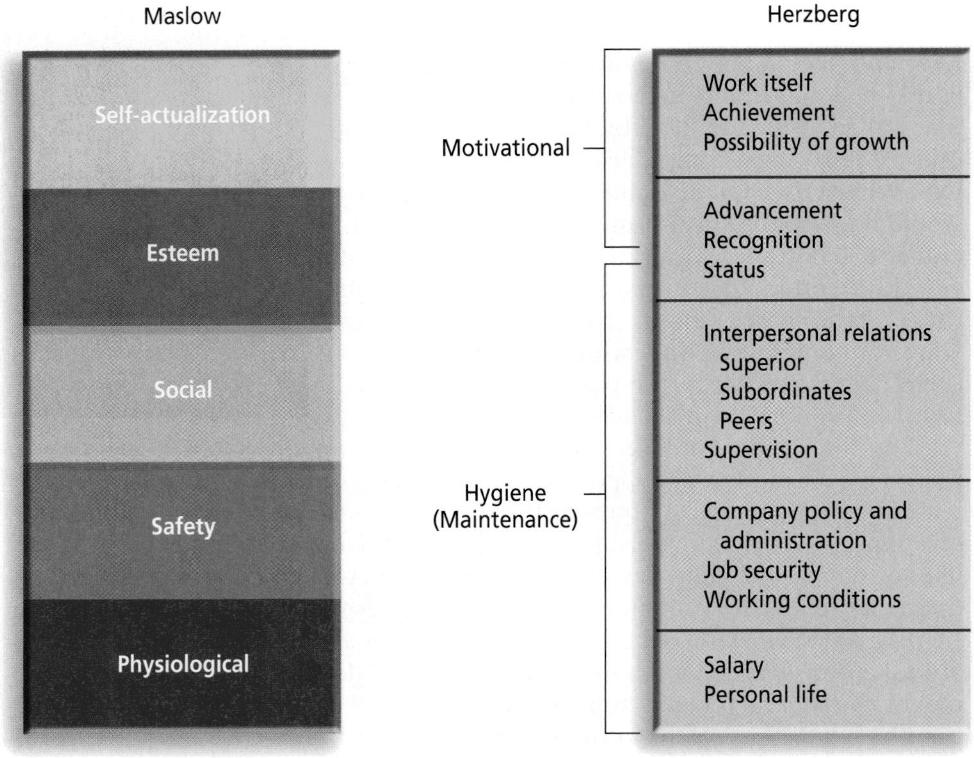

They are held responsible for successful completion of the task. The motivational effect of job enrichment can come from the opportunities for personal achievement, challenge, and recognition. Go back and review Maslow's and Herzberg's work to see how job enrichment grew out of those theories.

Those who advocate job enrichment believe five characteristics of work to be important in affecting individual motivation and performance:

1. **Skill variety.** The extent to which a job demands different skills.
2. **Task identity.** The degree to which the job requires doing a task with a visible outcome from beginning to end.
3. **Task significance.** The degree to which the job has a substantial impact on the lives or work of others in the company.
4. **Autonomy.** The degree of freedom, independence, and discretion in scheduling work and determining procedures.
5. **Feedback.** The amount of direct and clear information that is received about job performance.

Variety, identity, and significance contribute to the meaningfulness of the job. Autonomy gives people a feeling of responsibility, and feedback contributes to a feeling of achievement and recognition.

Job enrichment is what makes work fun. Although it was stressed in the chapter opening profile of Herb Kelleher and Colleen Barrett of Southwest Airlines, the word *fun* can be misleading. We're not talking about having parties all the time. For example, Roger Sant, founder and chairman of the global electricity company AES, says that what makes working at AES fun is that people are fully engaged: "They have total responsibility for decisions. They are accountable for results. What they do every day matters to the company, and it matters to the communities we operate in. We do celebrate a lot—because lots of great things are happening. We just did a billion-dollar deal, for instance, and that called for a party. But it's what happens before the celebrations that's really fun."[11]

Spotlight on Small Business: Motivating Employees in a Small Business

www.pacebutler.com

When you run a small business, every dollar counts. When you waste the intelligence, energy, or skills of your employees, it's like throwing money out the window, according to Rhonda Abrams, author of *Wear Clean Underwear: Business Wisdom from Mom.* Abrams says the surest way to get the best value from your employees is to treat them with respect: "When you allow your employees to think about how to solve problems, not just carry out specific tasks, you can unleash an amazing amount of creativity and energy. To do so, however, they'll need information, patience, and a sense they won't be 'punished' if they make an honest mistake."

To help your employees be more productive, Abrams recommends that you:

- Train your employees to do a wide variety of tasks. In a small business, employees have to pitch in on many jobs, so instead of teaching them specific tasks, you need to teach them about the whole business and encourage problem solving.
- Communicate frequently. Tom Pace of Pace/Butler Corporation in Oklahoma City holds 15-minute motivation sessions each morning. Employees compliment each other for recent behaviors, both minor and major. Then each person shares something they've done well. Pace says, "These meetings raise individual self-esteem and set the tone for the rest of the day."
- Empower your employees to make decisions. Let them use their brains, not just their backs.
- Acknowledge their contributions. The least productive thing you can say is "I don't need to thank employees; I pay them." We all need to be thanked and recognized.

It's difficult for a small company to match the financial benefits of large corporations, so it's even more important for small-business owners to make every employee feel valued, included, and respected. As your employees grow, your business is more likely to grow.

Sources: Rhonda Abrams, "How Small Business Has Grown and Changed," *Arizona Republic,* January 30, 2001, p. D2; and Neal St. Anthony, "Doing Right by Its Employees Pays Off for Reell," *Minneapolis Star Tribune,* January 24, 2003, p. 1D.

As mentioned above, job enrichment is based on Herzberg's higher motivators such as responsibility, achievement, and recognition. It stands in contrast to *job simplification,* which produces task efficiency by breaking down a job into simple steps and assigning people to each of those steps.

Another type of job enrichment used for motivation is **job enlargement,** which combines a series of tasks into one challenging and interesting assignment. For example, Maytag, the home appliance manufacturer, redesigned the production process of its washing machines so that employees could assemble an entire water pump instead of just one part. **Job rotation** also makes work more interesting and motivating by moving employees from one job to another. One problem with job rotation, of course, is having to train employees to do several different operations. However, the resulting increase in employee motivation and the value of having flexible, cross-trained employees offsets the additional costs.

job enlargement
A job enrichment strategy that involves combining a series of tasks into one challenging and interesting assignment.

job rotation
A job enrichment strategy that involves moving employees from one job to another.

Job enrichment is one way to ensure that workers enjoy responsibility and a sense of accomplishment. The Spotlight on Small Business box offers advice on using job enrichment strategies in small businesses.

McGregor's Theory X and Theory Y

The way managers go about motivating people at work depends greatly on their attitudes toward workers. Management theorist Douglas McGregor observed that managers' attitudes generally fall into one of two entirely different sets of managerial assumptions, which he called Theory X and Theory Y.

Theory X managers come in all sizes and shapes. Take Selina Lo of Alteon Websystems, for example. She may not fit the typical Theory X stereotype, but on the job this University of California at Berkeley graduate is a tough and exacting Theory X manager. Her in-your-face style has earned her a reputation as one of the toughest managers in the industry. Would you prefer to work for a Theory X manager or a Theory Y manager?

Theory X

The assumptions of Theory X management are as follows:

- The average person dislikes work and will avoid it if possible.
- Because of this dislike, workers must be forced, controlled, directed, or threatened with punishment to make them put forth the effort to achieve the organization's goals.
- The average worker prefers to be directed, wishes to avoid responsibility, has relatively little ambition, and wants security.
- Primary motivators are fear and money.

The natural consequence of such attitudes, beliefs, and assumptions is a manager who is very "busy" and who watches people closely, telling them what to do and how to do it. Motivation is more likely to take the form of punishment for bad work rather than reward for good work. Theory X managers give workers little responsibility, authority, or flexibility. With his scientific management, Taylor and other theorists who preceded him would have agreed with Theory X. That is why management literature focused on time-motion studies that calculated the one best way to perform a task and the optimum time to be devoted to a task. It was assumed that workers needed to be trained and carefully watched to see that they conformed to the standards.

Theory X management still dominates some organizations. Many managers and entrepreneurs ➤P. 4◄ still suspect that employees cannot be fully trusted and need to be closely supervised. No doubt you have seen such managers in action. How did this make you feel? Were these managers' assumptions accurate regarding the workers' attitudes?

Theory Y

Theory Y makes entirely different assumptions about people:

- Most people like work; it is as natural as play or rest.
- Most people naturally work toward goals to which they are committed.
- The depth of a person's commitment to goals depends on the perceived rewards for achieving them.
- Under certain conditions, most people not only accept but also seek responsibility.
- People are capable of using a relatively high degree of imagination, creativity, and cleverness to solve problems.
- In industry, the average person's intellectual potential is only partially realized.
- People are motivated by a variety of rewards. Each worker is stimulated by a reward unique to that worker (time off, money, recognition, etc.).

Rather than emphasize authority, direction, and close supervision, Theory Y emphasizes a relaxed managerial atmosphere in which workers are free to set objectives, be creative, be flexible, and go beyond the goals set by management. A key technique in meeting these objectives is empowerment ➤P. 20◄.

Pat Croce, owner of the NBA's Philadelphia 76ers, lives by Theory Y management, making him a winner with his players, workers, and fans. His mission statement is three simple words: quality, profit, and fun. The words obviously ring clear since the team's value has increased by 70 percent since his involvement.

Empowerment gives employees the authority to make decisions and the tools to implement the decisions they make. For empowerment to be a real motivator, management should follow these three steps:

1. Find out what people think the problems in the organization are.
2. Let them design the solutions.
3. Get out of the way and let them put those solutions into action.

Often employees complain that although they're asked to become involved in company decision making, their managers fail to actually empower them to make decisions. Have you ever worked in such an atmosphere? How did that make you feel?

The trend in many U.S. businesses is toward Theory Y management. One reason for this trend is that many service industries are finding Theory Y helpful in dealing with on-the-spot problems. Dan Kaplan of Hertz Rental Corporation would attest to this. He empowers his employees in the field to think and work as entrepreneurs. Leona Ackerly of Mini Maid, Inc., agrees: "If our employees look at our managers as partners, a real team effort is built."

OUCHI'S THEORY Z

In addition to the reasons given above for the trend toward Theory Y management, another reason for companies to adopt a more flexible managerial style is to meet competition from foreign firms such as those in Japan, China, and the European Union. Back in the 1980s, Japanese companies seemed to be outperforming American businesses. William Ouchi, a management professor at the University of California–Los Angeles, wondered if the secret to Japanese success was the way Japanese companies managed their workers. The Japanese management approach (what Ouchi called Type J) involved lifetime employment, consensual decision making, collective responsibility for the outcomes of decisions, slow evaluation and promotion, implied control mechanisms, nonspecialized career paths, and holistic concern for employees. In contrast, the American management approach (what Ouchi called Type A) involved short-term

FIGURE 10.4

THEORY Z: A BLEND OF AMERICAN AND JAPANESE MANAGEMENT APPROACHES

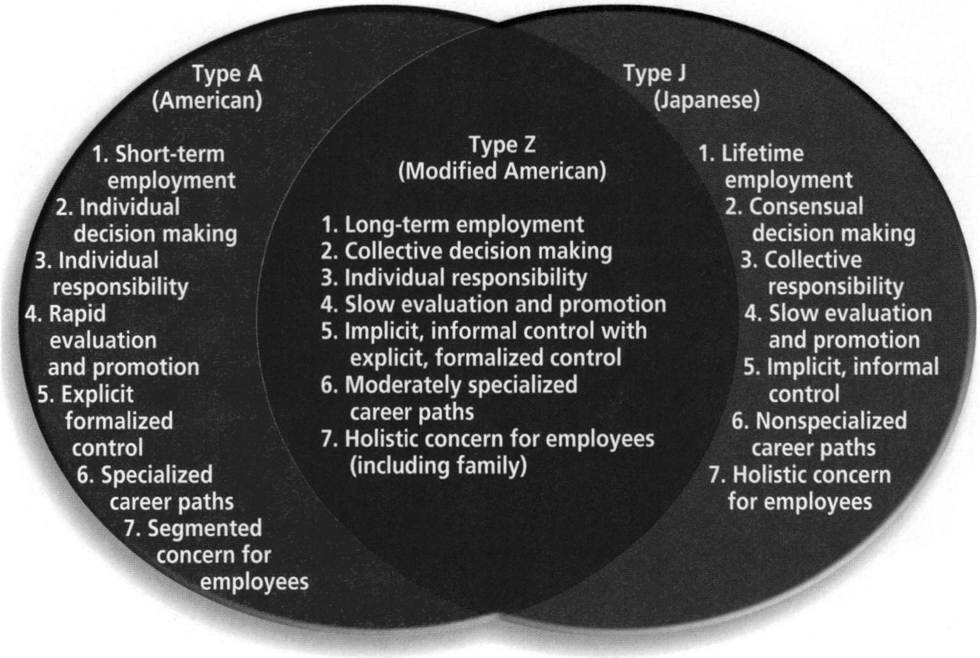

employment, individual decision making, individual responsibility for the outcomes of decisions, rapid evaluation and promotion, explicit control mechanisms, specialized career paths, and segmented concern for employees.

Type J firms are based on the culture of Japan, which includes a focus on trust and intimacy within the group and family. Conversely, Type A firms are based on the culture of America, which includes a focus on individual rights and achievements. Ouchi wanted to help American firms adopt the successful Japanese strategies, but he realized that it wouldn't be practical to expect American managers to accept an approach based on the culture of another country. Judge for yourself. A job for life in a firm may sound good until you think of the implications: no chance to change jobs and no opportunity to move up quickly through the ranks. Therefore, Ouchi recommended a hybrid of the two approaches in what he called Theory Z (see Figure 10.4). Theory Z blends the characteristics of Type J and Type A into an approach that involves long-term employment, collective decision making, individual responsibility for the outcomes of decisions, slow evaluation and promotion, moderately specialized career path, and holistic concern for employees (including family). The theory views the organization as a family that fosters cooperation and organizational values.

Today, economic decline, demographic and social changes, and fierce global competition are forcing Japanese managers to reevaluate the way they conduct business. Whereas a decade ago the Japanese system was admired for its focus on building long-term business relationships, today there is a realization that Japanese firms need to become both more dynamic and more efficient in order to compete effectively in the rapidly changing global economy.[12] Feeling the pain of the worst recession in their country's history, some Japanese managers are changing the way they do business. For example, electronics giant Hitachi was the first major Japanese company to announce it would quit requiring corporate calisthenics—exercises done in groups not only for health but also to foster cohesion among employees. "The idea of getting everyone in one place at the same time to do the same thing is outdated," said a Hitachi spokesperson.[13] Having everyone start the day with group exercises symbolized doing the same thing the same way. It reinforced the cultural belief that em-

THEORY X	THEORY Y	THEORY Z
1. Employees dislike work and will try to avoid it.	1. Employees view work as a natural part of life.	1. Employee involvement is the key to increased productivity.
2. Employees prefer to be controlled and directed.	2. Employees prefer limited control and direction.	2. Employee control is implied and informal.
3. Employees seek security, not responsibility.	3. Employees will seek responsibility under proper work conditions.	3. Employees prefer to share responsibility and decision making.
4. Employees must be intimidated by managers to perform.	4. Employees perform better in work environments that are nonintimidating.	4. Employees perform better in environments that foster trust and cooperation.
5. Employees are motivated by financial rewards.	5. Employees are motivated by many different needs.	5. Employees need guaranteed employment and will accept slow evaluations and promotions.

FIGURE 10.5

A COMPARISON OF THEORIES X, Y, AND Z

ployees should not take risks or think for themselves. Many managers think that such conformity is what has hurt Japanese business.[14] Will Japanese managers move toward the hybrid Theory Z in the future? We'll have to wait and see. The appropriate managerial style is one that matches the culture, the situation, and the specific needs of the organization and its employees. (See Figure 10.5 for a summary of Theories X, Y, and Z.)

GOAL-SETTING THEORY AND MANAGEMENT BY OBJECTIVES

Goal-setting theory is based on the idea that setting ambitious but attainable goals can motivate workers and improve performance if the goals are accepted, accompanied by feedback, and facilitated by organizational conditions. All members of an organization should have some basic agreement about the overall goals of the organization and the specific objectives to be met by each department and individual. It follows, then, that there should be a system to involve everyone in the organization in goal setting and implementation.

goal-setting theory
The idea that setting ambitious but attainable goals can motivate workers and improve performance if the goals are accepted, accompanied by feedback, and facilitated by organizational conditions.

Peter Drucker developed such a system in the 1960s. Drucker asserted, "Managers cannot motivate people; they can only thwart people's motivation because people motivate themselves." Managers, he believed, can only create the proper environment for the seed to grow. Thus, he designed his system to help employees motivate themselves. Called **management by objectives (MBO),** it is a system of goal setting and implementation that involves a cycle of discussion, review, and evaluation of objectives among top and middle-level managers, supervisors, and employees. Large corporations such as the Ford Motor Company have used MBO, as has the U.S. Department of Defense. MBO also spread to other companies and government agencies. MBO calls on managers to formulate goals in cooperation with everyone in the organization, to commit employees to those goals, and then to monitor results and reward accomplishment.

management by objectives (MBO)
A system of goal setting and implementation that involves a cycle of discussion, review, and evaluation of objectives among top and middle-level managers, supervisors, and employees.

MBO is most effective in relatively stable situations in which long-range plans can be made and implemented with little need for major changes. It is also important to MBO that managers understand the difference between helping and coaching subordinates. Helping means working with the subordinate and doing part of the work if necessary. Coaching means acting as a resource—teaching, guiding, and recommending—but not helping (that is, not participating actively or doing the task). The central idea of MBO is that employees need to motivate themselves.

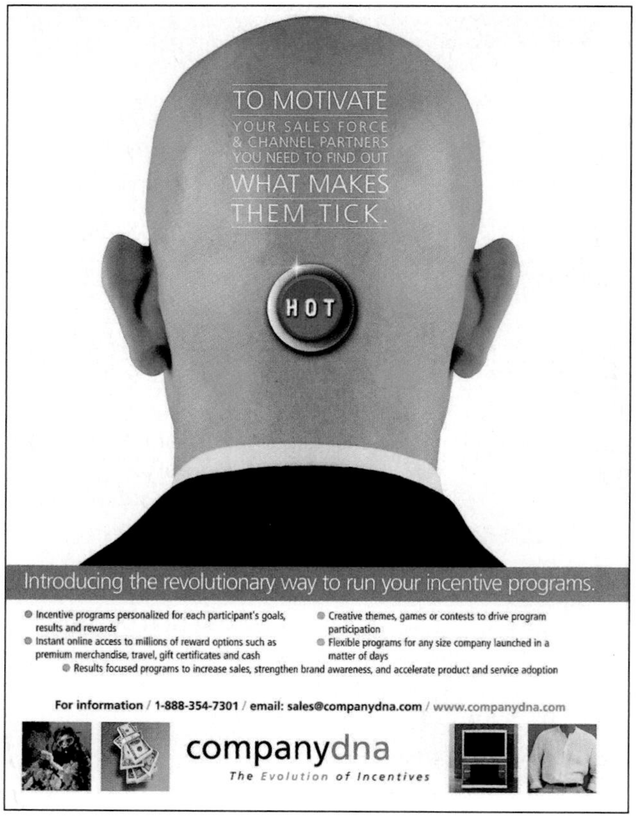

Victor Vroom believed employees can be motivated if they feel enhanced job performance leads to valued rewards. Identifying what rewards are important to employees is not an easy task. Companydna helps managers find out what makes their employees tick and then personalizes incentive programs to ensure employees receive the rewards they value and expect. What incentives would motivate you to improve your job performance?

Problems can arise when management uses MBO as a strategy for forcing managers and workers to commit to goals that are not really agreed on mutually but are instead set by top management. Employee involvement and expectations are important.

Victor Vroom identified the importance of employee expectations and developed a process called expectancy theory. Let's examine this concept next.

Meeting Employee Expectations: Expectancy Theory

According to Victor Vroom's **expectancy theory,** employee expectations can affect an individual's motivation. Therefore, the amount of effort employees exert on a specific task depends on their expectations of the outcome.[15] Vroom contends that employees ask three questions before committing maximum effort to a task: (1) Can I accomplish the task? (2) If I do accomplish it, what's my reward? (3) Is the reward worth the effort? (See Figure 10.6.)

expectancy theory
Victor Vroom's theory that the amount of effort employees exert on a specific task depends on their expectations of the outcome.

Think of the effort you might exert in your class under the following conditions: Your instructor says that to earn an A in the course you must achieve an average of 90 percent on coursework plus jump eight feet high. Would you exert maximum effort toward earning an A if you knew you could not possibly jump eight feet high? Or what if your instructor said any student can earn an A in the course but you know that this instructor has not awarded an A in 25 years of teaching? If the reward of an A seems unattainable, would you exert significant effort in the course? Better yet, let's say that you read in the newspaper that businesses actually prefer hiring C-minus students to hiring A-plus students. Does the reward of an A seem worth it? Now think of the same types of situations that may occur on the job.

Expectancy theory does note that expectation varies from individual to individual. Employees therefore establish their own views in terms of task difficulty and the value of the reward. Researchers David Nadler and Ed-

FIGURE 10.6

EXPECTANCY THEORY

The amount of effort employees exert on a task depends on their expectations of the outcome.

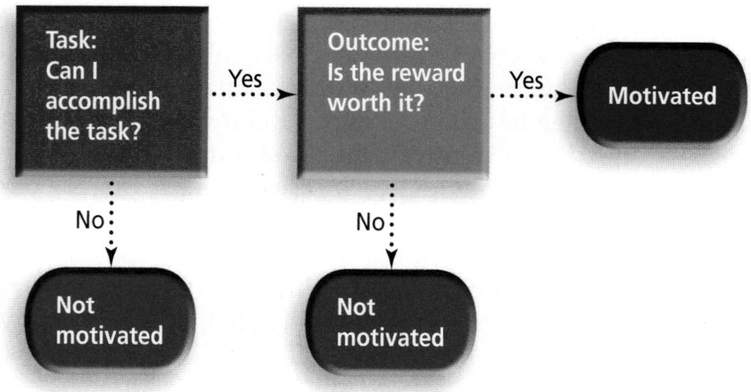

ward Lawler modified Vroom's theory and suggested that managers follow five steps to improve employee performance:

1. Determine what rewards are valued by employees.
2. Determine each employee's desired performance standard.
3. Ensure that performance standards are attainable.
4. Guarantee rewards tied to performance.
5. Be certain that rewards are considered adequate.[16]

Reinforcing Employee Performance: Reinforcement Theory

Reinforcement theory is based on the idea that positive and negative reinforcers motivate a person to behave in certain ways. In other words, motivation is the result of the carrot-and-stick approach (reward and punishment). Individuals act to receive rewards and avoid punishment. Positive reinforcements are rewards such as praise, recognition, or a pay raise. Negative reinforcement includes reprimands, reduced pay, and layoff or firing. A manager might also try to stop undesirable behavior by not responding to it. This is called *extinction* because the hope is that the unwanted behavior will eventually become extinct.[17] Figure 10.7 illustrates how a manager can use reinforcement theory to motivate workers.

reinforcement theory
Theory that positive and negative reinforcers motivate a person to behave in certain ways.

Treating Employees Fairly: Equity Theory

Equity theory deals with the questions "If I do a good job, will it be worth it?" and "What's fair?" It has to do with perceptions of fairness and how those perceptions affect employees' willingness to perform. The basic principle is that employees try to maintain equity between inputs and outputs compared to others in similar positions. Equity comparisons are made from the information that is available through personal relationships, professional organizations, and so on.

When workers do perceive inequity, they will try to reestablish equitable exchanges in a number of ways. For example, suppose you compare the grade

equity theory
The idea that employees try to maintain equity between inputs and outputs compared to others in similar positions.

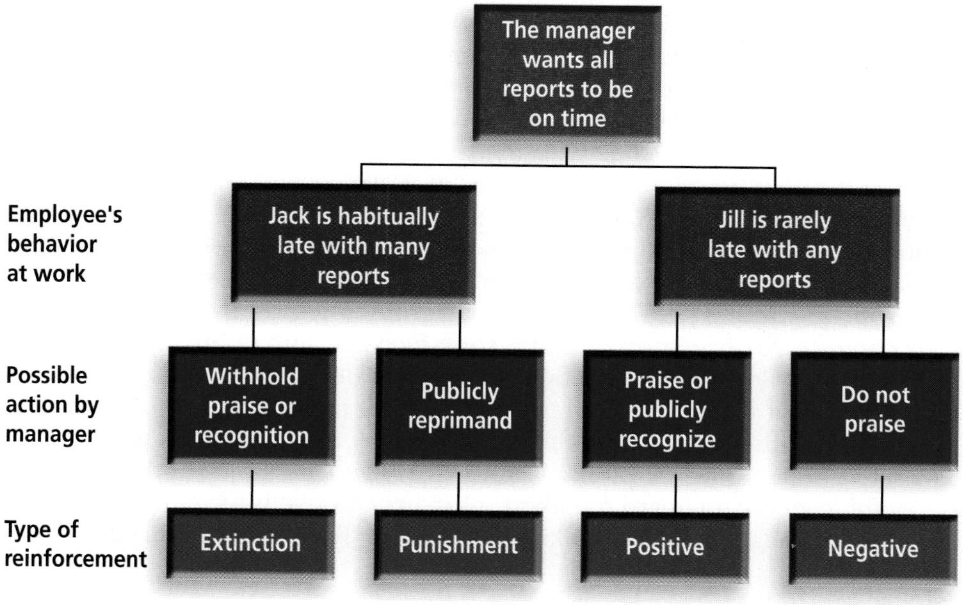

FIGURE 10.7

REINFORCEMENT THEORY

A manager can use both positive and negative reinforcement to motivate employee behavior.

you earned on a term paper with your classmates' grades. If you think you received a lower grade compared to the students who put out the same effort as you, you will probably react in one of two ways: (1) by reducing your effort on future class projects or (2) by rationalizing. The latter may include saying, "Grades are overvalued anyway!" If you think your paper received a higher grade than comparable papers, you will probably (1) increase your effort to justify the higher reward in the future or (2) rationalize by saying, "I'm worth it!" In the workplace, inequity may lead to lower productivity ➤P. 15◄, reduced quality ➤P. 275◄, increased absenteeism, and voluntary resignation.

Remember that equity judgments are based on perceptions and are therefore subject to errors in perception. When workers overestimate their own contributions—as happens often—they are going to feel that any rewards given out for performance are inequitable. Sometimes organizations try to deal with this by keeping employee salaries secret, but secrecy may make things worse; employees are likely to overestimate the salaries of others in addition to overestimating their own contribution. In general, the best remedy is clear and frequent communication. Managers must communicate as clearly as possible both the results they expect and the outcomes that will occur when those results are achieved or when they are not.

Progress Assessment

- Briefly describe the managerial attitudes behind Theories X, Y, and Z.
- Relate job enrichment to Herzberg's motivating factors.
- Evaluate expectancy theory. Can you think of situations in which expectancy theory could apply to your efforts or lack of effort?
- Explain the principles of equity theory.

BUILDING TEAMWORK THROUGH OPEN COMMUNICATION

Companies with highly motivated workforces usually have several things in common. Among the most important factors are open communication systems and self-managed teams. Open communication helps both top managers and team members understand the objectives and work together to achieve them. Communication must flow freely throughout the organization when teams are empowered to make decisions—they can't make these decisions in a vacuum. It is crucial for people to be able to access the knowledge they need when they need it.

Having teams creates an environment in which learning can happen because most learning happens at the peer level—peers who have an interest in helping each other along. Empowerment ➤P. 20◄ works when people volunteer to share their knowledge with their colleagues. For example, when Flora Zhou, a business development manager at global power company AES, was putting together a bid to the Vietnam government, she sent a detailed e-mail about what she was planning to bid and why to about 300 people within AES. She asked for and received lots of advice and comments. Most people thought her proposal was fine, but Sarah Slusser, a group manager in Central America, sent Zhou a three-page response that contained a wealth of information about a similar situation she had encountered with a plant in the Yucatan. Slusser told Zhou what technology issues she needed to pay attention to. A few days later, Zhou made the bid. It was the lowest bid by two-tenths of a percent. Did Slusser tell Zhou the exact dollar to bid? No, but she and many others, including plant leaders and board members, gave her the best information and judgments they had to help her make her decision. They shared everything they knew with her.

Teamwork does not happen by itself. The whole organization must be structured to make it easy for managers and employees to talk to one another. Procedures for encouraging open communication include the following:[18]

- **Create an organizational culture that rewards listening.** Top managers must create places to talk, and they must show employees that talking with superiors counts—by providing feedback, adopting employee suggestions, and rewarding upward communication—even if the discussion is negative. Employees must feel free to say anything they deem appropriate. Jerry Stead, chairman of technology provider Ingram Micro, has his own 24-hour toll-free phone line to take calls from employees. Yes, he really answers it. He says: "If we are doing something right, I love to hear about it. If there's something we should be doing differently, I want to know that too." Stead has also given his home number to all 13,000 Ingram Micro employees.
- **Train supervisors and managers to listen.** Most people receive no training in how to listen, either in school or anywhere else, so organizations must do such training themselves or hire someone to do it.
- **Remove barriers to open communication.** Having separate offices, parking areas, bathrooms, and dining rooms for managers and workers only sets up barriers in an organization. Other barriers are different dress codes and different ways of addressing one another (e.g., calling workers by their first names and managers by their last). Removing such barriers may require imagination and willingness on the part of managers to give up their special privileges.
- **Actively undertake efforts to facilitate communication.** Large lunch tables at which all organization members eat, conference rooms, organizational picnics, organizational athletic teams, and other such efforts all allow managers to mix with each other and with workers.

Let's see how one organization addresses the challenge of open communication in teams.

Applying Open Communication in Self-Managed Teams

Kenneth Kohrs, vice president of car product development at Ford Motor Company, says that an inside group known as "Team Mustang" sets the guidelines for how production teams should be formed. Given the challenge to create a car that would make people dust off their old "Mustang Sally" records and dance into the showrooms, the 400-member team was also given the freedom to make decisions without waiting for approval from headquarters or other departments. The team moved everyone from various departments into cramped offices under one roof of an old warehouse. Drafting experts sat next to accountants, engineers next to stylists. Budgetary walls that divided departments were knocked down as department managers were persuaded to surrender some control over their subordinates.

When the resulting Mustang convertible displayed shaking problems, suppliers were called in, and the team worked around the clock to solve the problem. The engineers were so motivated to complete the program on schedule and under budget that they worked late into the night and slept on the floors of the warehouse when necessary. The senior Ford executives were tempted to overrule the program, but they stuck with their promise not to meddle. The team solved the shaking problem and still came in under budget and a couple of months early. The new car was a big hit in the marketplace, and sales soared.[19]

In fact, the automotive pricing and review website Edmunds.com named it one of the top American muscle cars of 2003.[20]

To implement such teams, managers at most companies must reinvent work. This means respecting workers, providing interesting work, rewarding good work, developing workers' skills, allowing autonomy, and decentralizing authority. In the process of reinventing work, it is essential that managers behave ethically toward all employees. The Making Ethical Decisions box illustrates a problem managers may face when filling temporary positions.

Does seeing this sleek Mustang convertible make you want to put down your text and head for the road? At Ford Motor Company, the 400-member "Team Mustang" was empowered to create a car that does just that. The work team, suppliers, the company, and consumers worked together to make the Mustang a winner in a very competitive market.

Models of Employee Empowerment

Miller Brewing Company and Mary Kay Cosmetics are glowing examples of companies that succeeded at taking a lead in employee motivation, customer service, and establishment of a general partnership with employees. Let's review the experience of these two companies to see what lessons we can learn.

Miller Brewing Company is the second largest brewer in the United States.[21] It opened its brewery of the future in Trenton, Ohio, with a mandate to develop a totally new workplace design that abandoned the rigidity of traditional brewery operations. The company decided to experiment by employing self-directed, cross-functional teams of 6 to 19 employees. It assigned the teams to handle brewing, packaging, and distribution.

To keep communications open, the company established an electronic mailbox for each employee and gave each team its own local area network (linked computers). In the daily operations at the brewery, employees rotated jobs, routinely backed each other up, and learned exactly how their actions affected the other employees. Workers enjoyed the freedom and flexibility offered at the plant, and the Trenton brewery enjoyed a 30 percent increase in productivity in comparison to Miller's other breweries. The top union official at the plant says, "We're partners in the business. We don't just make beer, we manage day-to-day operations. At this facility we have so many different tasks we don't check our brains at the door." According to company officials, "That's what teamwork is all about. Employees can't just say this is my job and my job only."

The late Mary Kay Ash started her billion-dollar cosmetics company in 1963 when the promotion she had been working toward was given to her male assistant, whom she had just spent nine months training. She vowed to run a company that would treat women right, not "ruin their self-esteem," she said, or limit how much money they could make. Developing women's leadership potential was a priority at Mary Kay Cosmetics from the start. Many Mary Kay consultants are refugees from corporate America. There are lawyers, a Harvard MBA, and even a pediatrician in the Mary Kay ranks.

But everyone starts off on the same foot. If you were a rocket scientist in your last job, great—but you still need to buy a beauty case and start calling your friends. Your earnings will increase as your sales do and as you recruit more Mary Kay employees, who are known as consultants. More important, though, is the emotional compensation the job provides.

Every summer, for example, more than 50,000 Mary Kay beauty consultants invade Dallas, Texas, to participate in a three-day sales rally called Seminar—at which there is plenty of emotion. Seminar is part convention, part *Hello, Dolly!* Caught up in the Mary Kay enthusiasm, the women laugh, cry, and sing as the company doles out $6 million in diamonds and pink Cadillacs under enough spotlights and sequins to rival any Broadway musical.

Making Ethical Decisions

www.manpower.com

Motivating Temporary Employees

Say that you work as a manager for the hypothetical Highbrow's, a rather prestigious department store. Each year, in order to handle the large number of shoppers at Christmastime, you must hire temporary employees. Because of store policy and budget constraints, all temporaries must be discharged on January 10. As you interview prospective employees, however, you give the impression that the store will hire at least two new full-time retail salespeople for the coming year. You hope that this will serve to motivate the temporary workers and even foster some competition among them. You also instruct your permanent salespeople to reinforce the falsehood that good work during the Christmas season is the path to full-time employment. Is this an ethical way to try to motivate your employees? What are the dangers of using a tactic such as this?

Color-coded suits, badges, sashes, crowns, and other emblems show how far each person has come—like military insignia, they immediately indicate who's done what. Joan Watson, a former medical secretary now a Mary Kay executive senior director says, "A lot of people really don't understand what we are doing. I still have people say, 'Pink Cadillac?! They're so gaudy.' And I say, 'What color car does your boss give you?' "

Despite the glitter of the diamonds and cars given out at Seminar, the most treasured rewards are the vacations, which often offer consultants special treatment. On one trip to London, Mary Kay got the famous Harrods department store to close for an hour so that only Mary Kay consultants could shop there. Before her death in 2001, Mary Kay Ash herself used to go on many of these trips. Her consultants considered her to be uniquely approachable. Mary Kay consultants are trained to treat their customers with the same kind of interest. They remember their customers' birthdays, send them notes, and find other ways to show concern. Mary Kay is not just a job—it's a way of life. Ash's son, Richard Rogers, who remains the company's chairman and chief executive, said his life's mission is to keep his mother's philosophy alive. "Mary Kay knew what she had started was larger than her life and that enriching women's lives around the world would not end when her life ended," Rogers said.[22]

Learning from Miller Brewing's and Mary Kay's Experiences Understanding what motivates employees is the key to success in companies such as Miller Brewing Company and Mary Kay Cosmetics. Miller learned at its Trenton plant that teamwork promotes a self-starting philosophy among employees that encourages them to be superior. In fact, someone at the plant said the letters in *Team* stand for "together, everyone achieves more."

Mary Kay Ash developed not just a business, but a true American success story. She felt that success in business depends on believing in yourself and showing interest in your employees and your customers. The best way to lead is by example, and Mary Kay was a model for employees and for managers in all types of firms.

The lessons we can learn from the Miller and Mary Kay examples include the following:

- The growth of industry and business in general depends on a motivated, productive workforce.
- Motivation is largely internal, generated by workers themselves; giving employees the freedom to be creative and rewarding achievement when it occurs will release their energy.

- The first step in any motivational program is to establish open communication among workers and managers so that the feeling generated is one of cooperation and teamwork. A family-type atmosphere should prevail.

MOTIVATION IN THE FUTURE

Today's customers expect high-quality, customized goods ➤P. 25◀ and services ➤P. 26◀. This means that employees must provide extensive personal service and pay close attention to details. Employees will have to work smart as well as hard. No amount of supervision can force an employee to smile or to go the extra mile to help a customer. Managers need to know how to motivate their employees to meet customer needs.

Tomorrow's managers will not be able to use any one motivational formula for all employees. Rather, they will have to get to know each worker personally and tailor the motivational effort to the individual. As you have learned in this chapter, different employees respond to different managerial and motivational styles. This is further complicated by the increase in global business and the fact that managers now work with employees from a variety of cultural backgrounds. Different cultures experience motivational approaches differently; therefore, the manager of the future will have to study and understand these cultural factors in designing a reward system. The Reaching Beyond Our Borders box describes how Digital Equipment Corporation dealt with these cultural issues within global teams.

Cultural differences are not restricted to groups of people from various countries. Such differences also exist between generations raised in the same country. Members of generations such as the baby boomers (born between 1946 and 1964); Generation X (born between 1965 and 1980); and Generation Y (born between 1981 and 1994) are linked through shared life experiences in their formative years—usually the first 10 years of life. The beliefs you gather as a child affect how you view risk and challenge, authority, technology, relationships, and economics. If you are in a management position, they can affect even whom you hire, fire, or promote. Boomers were raised in families that experienced unprecedented economic prosperity, parents with secure jobs, and optimism about the future. "Gen Xers" were raised in dual-career families with parents who focused on work. As children, they attended day care or became latchkey kids. Their parents' successive layoffs added to their insecurity about a lifelong job.

How do these generational differences affect motivation in the workplace? For the boomer managers, it means that they will need to be flexible with their Gen X employees or they will lose them. For Gen X employees, it means that they will need to use their enthusiasm for change and streamlining to their advantage. Although many Gen Xers are unwilling to pay the same price for success that their parents and grandparents did, concern about undue stress and long work hours does not mean they lack ambition. Gen Xers' de-

do less have more
REAL SIMPLE.
the magazine for a simpler life, home, body and soul
REAL SIMPLE
Easy storage solutions for every room
For your free preview issue
call 1.800.521.3002 or realsimple.com
AOL keyword realsimple
Also available on newsstands.

There's no magic formula to successfully motivating every worker. Each generation of employees has different attitudes about what's important to them in seeking a balance between a successful career and a happy private life. *Real Simple* is a new magazine that appeals to people yearning for more simplicity in life. What's most important to you in your career and home life?

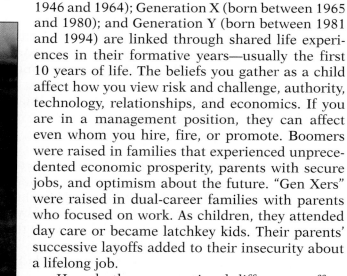

Reaching Beyond Our Borders

www.hp.com

Global Teamwork

The global economy has altered the world landscape by bringing products and services to every corner of the earth and helping many people in less developed countries improve their quality of life. Business globalization has also resulted in the creation of global work teams, a rather formidable task.

Even though the concept of teamwork is nothing new, building a harmonious global work team is a new task and can be complicated. Global companies must recognize differing attitudes and competencies in the team's cultural mix and the technological capabilities among team members. For example, a global work team needs to determine whether the culture of its members is high-context or low-context. In a high-context team culture, members build personal relationships and develop group trust before focusing on tasks. In the low-context culture, members often view relationship building as a waste of time that diverts attention from the task. Koreans, Thais, and Saudis (high-context cultures), for example, often view American team members as insincere due to their need for data and quick decision making.

When Digital Equipment Corporation (now a part of Hewlett-Packard) decided to consolidate its operations at six manufacturing sites, the company recognized the need to form multicultural work teams. Realizing the challenge it faced, Digital hired an internal organization-development specialist to train the team in relationship building, foreign languages, and valuing differences. All team members from outside the United States were assigned American partners and invited to spend time with their families. Digital also flew the flags of each employee's native country at all its manufacturing sites. As communication within the teams increased, the company reduced the time of new-product handoffs from three years to just six months.

Understanding the motivational forces in global organizations and building effective global teams is still new territory for most companies. Developing group leaders who are culturally astute, flexible, and able to deal with ambiguity is a challenge businesses must face in the 21st century.

sire for security typically equals that of older workers, but there is a big difference in their approach to achieving it. Rather than focusing on job security, Gen Xers tend to focus on career security. As they look for opportunities to expand their skills and grow professionally, they are willing to change jobs to do it.[23]

Many Gen Xers are now or soon will be managers themselves and responsible for motivating other employees. What type of management will this generation provide? In general, Gen X managers will be well equipped to motivate people. They understand that there is more to life than work, and they think a big part of motivating people is letting them know you recognize that fact. As a result, Gen X managers may tend to focus more on results than on hours in the workplace. They will tend to be flexible and good at collaboration and consensus building. They may tend to think in broader terms than their predecessors because, through the media, they have been exposed to a lot of problems around the world. They may also have a great impact on their team members because they will likely give the people working for them the goals and the parameters of the project and then leave them alone to do their work.

Perhaps their best asset might be their ability to give their employees feedback, especially positive feedback. One reason they may be better at providing feedback is that they expect more of it themselves. One new employee remarked that he was frustrated because he hadn't received feedback from his boss since he was hired—two weeks earlier. In short, managers will need to realize that young workers demand performance reviews and other forms of feedback more than once or twice a year.

In every generational shift, the old generation says the same thing about the new generation: They break the rules. The generation that lived through the Great Depression and World War II said it of the baby boomers. Now boomers look at Gen Xers and say, "Why are they breaking the rules?" And you can be sure the Gen Xers will look at the next group and say, "What's wrong with these kids?" In fact, Gen Yers are entering the professional workforce now. As a group, Generation Yers tend to share a number of common characteristics: They are considered impatient, skeptical, blunt and expressive, image driven, and inexperienced. Like any generation, what may make Generation Y difficult to deal with on the job is also what could make it uniquely skilled. For example, a number of talents and tendencies dominate the Gen Yers: They are adaptable, tech savvy, able to grasp new concepts, practiced at multitasking, efficient, and tolerant. Perhaps the most surprising attribute many Gen Yers share is a sense of commitment. What do you think are the most effective strategies managers can use to motivate Gen Y workers?

One thing in business is likely to remain constant, though: Motivation will come from the job itself rather than from external punishments or rewards. Managers will need to give workers what they need to do a good job: the right tools, the right information, and the right amount of cooperation.

Motivation doesn't have to be difficult. It begins with acknowledging a job well done. You can simply tell those who do such a job that you appreciate them—especially if you make this statement in front of others. After all, as we said earlier in this chapter, the best motivator is frequently a sincere "Thanks, I really appreciate what you're doing."

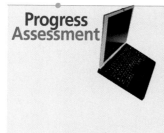

Progress Assessment

- What are several steps firms can take to increase internal communications and thus motivation?
- What problems may emerge when trying to implement participative management?
- Why is it important today to adjust motivational styles to individual employees? Are there any general principles of motivation that today's managers should follow?

Summary

1. Explain Taylor's scientific management.

1. Human efficiency engineer Frederick Taylor was one of the first people to study management.
   - ***What is Frederick Taylor known for?***

   Frederick Taylor has been called the father of scientific management. He did time-motion studies to learn the most efficient way of doing a job and then trained workers in those procedures. He published his book *The Principles of Scientific Management* in 1911. Henry L. Gantt and Frank and Lillian Gilbreth were followers of Taylor.

2. Describe the Hawthorne studies, and relate their significance to management.

2. Management theory moved away from Taylor's scientific management and toward theories that stress human factors of motivation.
   - ***What led to the more human managerial styles?***

   The greatest impact on motivation theory was generated by the Hawthorne studies in the late 1920s and early 1930s. In these studies, Elton Mayo found that human factors such as feelings of involvement and participation led to greater productivity gains than did physical changes in the workplace.

3. Abraham Maslow studied basic human motivation and found that motivation was based on needs; he said that a person with an unfilled need would be motivated to satisfy it and that a satisfied need no longer served as motivation.
   - ***What were the various levels of need identified by Maslow?***
   Starting at the bottom of Maslow's hierarchy of needs and going to the top, the levels of need are physiological, safety, social, esteem, and self-actualization.
   - ***Can managers use Maslow's theory?***
   Yes, they can recognize what unmet needs a person has and design work so that it satisfies those needs.

3. Identify the levels of Maslow's hierarchy of needs, and relate their importance to employee motivation.

4. Frederick Herzberg found that some factors are motivators and others are hygiene (or maintenance) factors; hygiene factors cause job dissatisfaction if missing but are not motivators if present.
   - ***What are the factors called motivators?***
   The work itself, achievement, recognition, responsibility, growth, and advancement.
   - ***What are hygiene (maintenance) factors?***
   Factors that do not motivate but must be present for employee satisfaction, such as company policies, supervision, working conditions, interpersonal relations, and salary.

4. Distinguish between the motivators and hygiene factors identified by Herzberg.

5. Job enrichment describes efforts to make jobs more interesting.
   - ***What characteristics of work affect motivation and performance?***
   The job characteristics that influence motivation are skill variety, task identity, task significance, autonomy, and feedback.
   - ***Name two forms of job enrichment that increase motivation.***
   Job enrichment strategies include job enlargement and job rotation.

5. Explain how job enrichment affects employee motivation and performance.

6. Douglas McGregor held that managers will have one of two opposing attitudes toward employees. They are called Theory X and Theory Y. William Ouchi introduced Theory Z.
   - ***What is Theory X?***
   Theory X assumes that the average person dislikes work and will avoid it if possible. Therefore, people must be forced, controlled, and threatened with punishment to accomplish organizational goals.
   - ***What is Theory Y?***
   Theory Y assumes that people like working and will accept responsibility for achieving goals if rewarded for doing so.
   - ***What is Theory Z?***
   Theory Z comes out of Japanese management and stresses long-term employment; collective decision making; individual responsibility; slow evaluation and promotion; implicit, informal control with explicit, formalized control; moderately specialized career paths; and a holistic concern for employees (including family).

6. Differentiate among Theory X, Theory Y, and Theory Z.

7. Goal-setting theory is based on the notion that setting ambitious but attainable goals will lead to high levels of motivation and performance if the goals are accepted, accompanied by feedback, and facilitated by organizational conditions.
   - ***What is management by objectives (MBO)?***
   MBO is a system of goal setting and implementation that involves a cycle of discussion, review, and evaluation of objectives among top and middle-level managers, supervisors, and employees.

7. Explain goal-setting theory and how management by objectives (MBO) exemplifies the theory.

8. Describe the key principles of expectancy, reinforcement and equity theories.

8. According to Victor Vroom's expectancy theory, employee expectations can affect an individual's motivation.
   - ***What are the key elements involved in expectancy theory?***

   Expectancy theory centers on three questions employees often ask about performance on the job: (1) Can I accomplish the task? (2) If I do accomplish it, what's my reward? and (3) Is the reward worth the effort?
   - ***What are the variables in reinforcement theory?***

   Positive reinforcers are rewards like praise, recognition, or raises that a worker might strive to receive after performing well. Negative reinforcers are punishments such as reprimands, pay cuts, or firing that a worker might be expected to try to avoid.
   - ***According to equity theory, employees try to maintain equity between inputs and outputs compared to other employees in similar positions. What happens when employees perceive that their rewards are not equitable?***

   If employees perceive that they are underrewarded, they will either reduce their effort or rationalize that it isn't important. If they perceive that they are overrewarded, they will either increase their effort to justify the higher reward in the future or rationalize by saying, "I'm worth it!" Inequity leads to lower productivity, reduced quality, increased absenteeism, and voluntary resignation.

9. Explain how open communication builds teamwork, and describe how managers are likely to motivate teams in the future.

9. Companies with highly motivated workforces often have open communication systems and self-managed teams.
   - ***Why is open communication so important in building effective self-managed teams?***

   Open communication helps both top managers and team members understand the objectives and work together to achieve them. Teams establish an environment in which learning can happen because most learning happens at the peer level.
   - ***How are Generation X managers likely to be different from their baby-boomer predecessors?***

   Baby boomers are willing to work long hours to build their careers and often expect their subordinates to do likewise. Gen Xers strive for a more balanced lifestyle and are likely to focus on results rather than on how many hours their teams work. Gen Xers are better than previous generations at working in teams and providing frequent feedback. They are not bound by traditions that may constrain those who have been with an organization for a long time and are willing to try new approaches to solving problems.

Key Terms

equity theory 315
expectancy theory 314
extrinsic reward 300
goal-setting theory 313
Hawthorne effect 303
hygiene factors 306
intrinsic reward 300
job enlargement 309
job enrichment 307
job rotation 309
management by objectives (MBO) 313
Maslow's hierarchy of needs 303
motivators 306
principle of motion economy 301
reinforcement theory 315
scientific management 301
time-motion studies 301

Developing Workplace Skills

1. Talk with several of your friends about the subject of motivation. What motivates them to work hard or not work hard in school and on the job? How important is self-motivation to them?

2. Look over Maslow's hierarchy of needs and try to determine where you are right now on the hierarchy. What needs of yours are not being met? How could a company go about meeting those needs and thus motivate you to work better and harder?

3. One of the most recent managerial ideas is to let employees work in self-managed teams. There is no reason why such teams could not be formed in colleges as well as businesses. Discuss the benefits and drawbacks of dividing your class into self-managed teams for the purpose of studying, doing cases, and so forth.

4. Think of all the groups with which you have been associated over the years—sports groups, friendship groups, and so on—and try to recall how the leaders of those groups motivated the group to action. Did the leaders assume a Theory X or a Theory Y attitude? How often was money used as a motivator? What other motivational tools were used and to what effect?

5. Herzberg concluded that pay was not a motivator. If you were paid to get better grades, would you be motivated to study harder? In your employment experiences, have you ever worked harder to obtain a raise or as a result of receiving a large raise? Do you agree with Herzberg?

Taking It To The Net 1

Purpose

To assess your personality type using the Keirsey Character Sorter and to evaluate how well the description of your personality type fits you.

Exercise

Sometimes understanding differences in employees' personalities helps managers understand how to motivate them. Find out about your personality by going to the Keirsey Temperament Sorter website (www.keirsey.com) and answer the 36-item Keirsey Character Sorter questionnaire or the 70-item Keirsey Temperament Sorter questionnaire. Each test identifies four temperament types: Guardian, Artisan, Idealist, and Rational. (Disclaimer: The Keirsey tests, like all other personality tests, are only preliminary and rough indicators of personality.)

1. After you identify your personality, read the corresponding personality portrait. How well or how poorly does the identified personality type fit?

2. Sometimes a personality test does not accurately identify your personality, but it may give you a place to start looking for a portrait that fits. After you have read the portraits on the Keirsey website, ask a good friend or relative which one best describes you.

Taking It To The Net 2

Purpose

To analyze why employees of the Container Store agree with *Fortune* magazine that their employer is an excellent company to work for.

Exercise

Employees at the Container Store sell boxes and garbage cans for a living. Find out why *Fortune* magazine has rated it at or near the top of its "100 Best Companies to Work For" list for four straight years. Go to the company's website (www.containerstore.com) and click on "About Us."

1. What are the Container Store's foundation principles?
2. Give an example of how the Container Store employees are empowered to please their customers.
3. The national average annual turnover rate for salespeople is 73.6 percent. The Container Store's turnover rate is a mere 28 percent. Many of its employees took pay cuts to join the company. Identify at least five ways the company motivates its employees and explain why they are one of the most motivated workforces in America.

Casing The Web

To access the case "Making Teams Work in a Changing Market," visit

www.mhhe.com/ub7e

Video Case

Working for the Best: The Container Store

Looking for a company where motivational techniques are effectively applied? Look no further than the Container Store. The company was voted "the best company to work for in America" twice and was second two other times. That record demands attention and copying, if possible.

What's the secret to hiring highly motivated people who feel their company is America's best? First, you need good products. Employees are motivated when they know that the products they sell are helpful to consumers and top quality. Second, you have to empower workers to do what they can to exceed customer expectations, even if that means having them go out in the parking lot to give a customer a driving lesson.

One of the cornerstones at the Container Store is: Hire Great People. Management believes that one great person is worth three good people. They cite famed home-run hitter Babe Ruth, who hit 56 home runs in one year; the second-best home-run hitter hit only 13. A great player may be worth over four times what a good player is worth. The challenge is to find and keep great workers. The Container Store often does that by hiring part-time people and then motivating the best of them to stay.

Workers must be taught to provide astonishing levels of customer service. One such case is the worker in Houston who loaned her car to a stranded customer. How do you encourage such outstanding service? Management at the Container Store knows motivational principles. They know, for example, that Frederick Taylor looked at workers as if they were machines to be programmed, and that such a style is no longer effective in most organizations. They also know that Elton Mayo introduced a more human-based form of motivation.

It's clear that the store uses Maslow's needs hierarchy. Wages paid are above the industry standard, meeting the physiological needs of workers. Safety needs are met by tolerating mistakes and urging employees to do what's necessary to please customers. Employees also feel secure because the store emphasizes proper values, including integrity,honesty, and open communications. Good employees are recognized for their contribution and the social atmosphere is one of "family." It's clear the Container Store used McGregor's Theory Y concepts.

Herzberg claims that a good job environment is not a motivator; it is considered a hygiene factor (i.e., it doesn't motivate workers if it is present, but causes dissatisfaction if missing). Container Store employees place a high importance on the job environment, including the quality of their coworkers. This implies that people like to work with others who are equally motivated and responsible. This also fits into Maslow's level of social needs.

The Container Store focuses on job enrichment. Employees are trained to do a variety of jobs that help prepare them to become managers when openings are available. The store uses daily coaching so employees can understand and implement management by objectives. The store also uses open communication to stress that good work will be rewarded. That includes peer-to-peer communication where everyone helps everyone else to do the best job possible.

In short, the Container Store uses a humanistic approach coupled with empowerment, strong values, cross training, and open communication to motivate employees to the point where they will continue to be one of the best companies to work for in America.

Thinking It Over

1. What have you learned from this video that could be used by any firm seeking a motivated workforce that loves working for the business?
2. There is some debate whether or not money is a motivator. If you were offered twice as much pay, would you or could you work twice as hard?
3. What has motivated you to do a great job and what has discouraged you from doing your best?
4. What can you do to increase your self-motivation? Does it always help working with self-motivated people who do quality work?

Chapter 11

Human Resource Management: Finding and Keeping the Best Employees

Learning Goals

After you have read and studied this chapter, you should be able to

1 Explain the importance of human resource management, and describe current issues in managing human resources.

2 Summarize the five steps in human resource planning.

3 Describe methods that companies use to recruit new employees, and explain some of the issues that make recruitment challenging.

4 Outline the six steps in selecting employees.

5 Illustrate the use of various types of employee training and development methods.

6 Trace the six steps in appraising employee performance.

7 Summarize the objectives of employee compensation programs, and describe various pay systems and fringe benefits.

8 Explain scheduling plans managers use to adjust to workers' needs.

9 Describe the ways employees can move through a company: promotion, reassignment, termination, and retirement.

10 Illustrate the effects of legislation on human resource management.

Getting to Know Karen Oman of Certes Financial Pros

Karen Oman, president and founder of Certes Financial Pros, believes that organizations should offer workers their choice of work arrangements. Job security is important to some, flexibility to others. As their staff sizes rise and fall with the global marketplace, many companies say they require a flexible workforce made up of people who can come and go as they are needed. Increasingly, workers are demanding flexible schedules to help balance work and life. Such schedules include nontraditional work arrangements such as part-time and temporary jobs.

That's where Oman comes in. Her company finds financial professionals to fit these flexible work environments. Certes employs the workers and sends them out to companies for temporary assignments. For example, financial officer Scott Eckes's wife is a teacher and his son is a 12-year-old with a full schedule of baseball games throughout the summer. Eckes takes the summer off from his Certes job to share the time with his family. Certes will welcome him back in the fall with no loss of his benefits. In fact, Certes employees can take up to six months off and still retain benefits.

"We work to live, not live to work."

One of Oman's mottos is "We work to live, not live to work." She lives that motto by treating her employees well—she not only gives them generous benefits and above-average wages but also makes three vacation homes available to workers free of charge. Offering such generous benefits is not typical of temporary agencies, but doing so helped Oman attract a loyal workforce. While the average turnover in temporary agencies is over 400 percent, Oman's turnover rate is around 25 percent. Certes Financial Pros' revenue increased from $100,000 when Oman started the company in 1994 to $7.4 million in 2001. Oman managed to increase revenues by 28 percent in 2001, a year that was extremely difficult for personnel supply companies due to a softened demand for employees that is typical during recessions. Such dramatic growth, achieved while cultivating a balanced workplace environment, earned Oman the Best Employer award from *Working Woman* magazine.

Temporary employees who are placed by companies such as Certes are now called *contingent workers.* Today, few workers expect to work at one company their entire careers. Unlike their parents, who could build a career with one skill, today's workers must seek out ongoing education and diverse work experience. The specific job you take is becoming much less important today than the skills you build over time. Contingent workers view their temporary positions as opportunities to build their skills and gain the necessary experience. Many employers also view temporary agencies as excellent training grounds for workers to develop the skills the company needs. Employers say that hiring people for temporary work is an efficient way to "test-drive" employees before committing to hire them full-time.

Many contingent workers find such flexibility liberating. It gives them more time with their families, while giving them opportunities to build skills or switch careers. Not everyone considers this flexibility so positively. Labor leaders fear that such new employer–employee relationships will make it harder for the employees to provide for their families. They fear that the flexibility will actually mean that workers end up with less control of their lives, since part-time workers do not receive the same insurance and pension benefits as full-time employees. A growing number of workers are unable to secure a full-time position. They must try to work two or three jobs, and even then cannot secure paid benefits or a decent income.

As you can see, these new employer–employee relationships are partly good and partly bad. Contingent workers increase companies' flexibility and therefore their competitiveness. However, the drive for cost-cutting and flexibility crashes head-on into another important aspect: the belief that competitive success is based on retaining motivated, creative, empowered workers. Can this goal be met by a largely disposable workforce? That is one of the issues that human resource managers face as they strive to recruit, hire, train, evaluate, and compensate the best people to accomplish the objectives of their organizations.

Sources: Jim Buchta, "Women's Business Group Selects Oman for Top Award," *Minneapolis Star Tribune,* April 15, 2002, p. 1D; Dan Barreirom, "Monday's People," *Minneapolis Star Tribune,* May 20, 2002, p. 3D; Michelle Conlin, "The Workplace: Productivity: The Big Squeeze on Workers," *Business Week,* May 13, 2002, p. 96; and Margaret Webb Pressler, "A Workforce Divided; Rising Use of Temps Is Creating Two Classes of Employees," *Washington Post,* June 23, 2002, p. H1.

WORKING WITH PEOPLE IS JUST THE BEGINNING

Students have been known to say they want to go into human resource management because they want to "work with people." It is true that human resource managers work with people, but they are also deeply involved in planning, record keeping, and other administrative duties. To begin a career in human resource management, you need to develop a better reason than "I want to work with people." This chapter will discuss various aspects of human resource management. **Human resource management** is the process of determining human resource needs and then recruiting, selecting, developing, motivating, evaluating, compensating, and scheduling employees to achieve organizational goals (see Figure 11.1). Let's explore some of the trends in human resource management.

human resource management
The process of determining human resource needs and then recruiting, selecting, developing, motivating, evaluating, compensating, and scheduling employees to achieve organizational goals.

Developing the Ultimate Resource

One reason human resource management is receiving increased attention now is that the U.S. economy has experienced a major shift from traditional manufacturing industries to service ➤P. 26◄ and high-tech manufacturing industries that require highly technical job skills. This shift means that many workers must be retrained for new, more challenging jobs. For example, Sun Microsystems spent $39 million to ready a facility to manufacture one of its newest product lines, StarCat, a large, sophisticated mainframe server used by airports and hospitals. Part of the cost involved sending employees to

FIGURE 11.1

HUMAN RESOURCE MANAGEMENT

As this figure shows, human resource management is more than hiring and firing personnel. All activities are designed to achieve organizational goals within the laws that affect human resource management. (Note that human resource management includes motivation, as discussed in Chapter 10, and employee–union relations, as discussed in Chapter 12.)

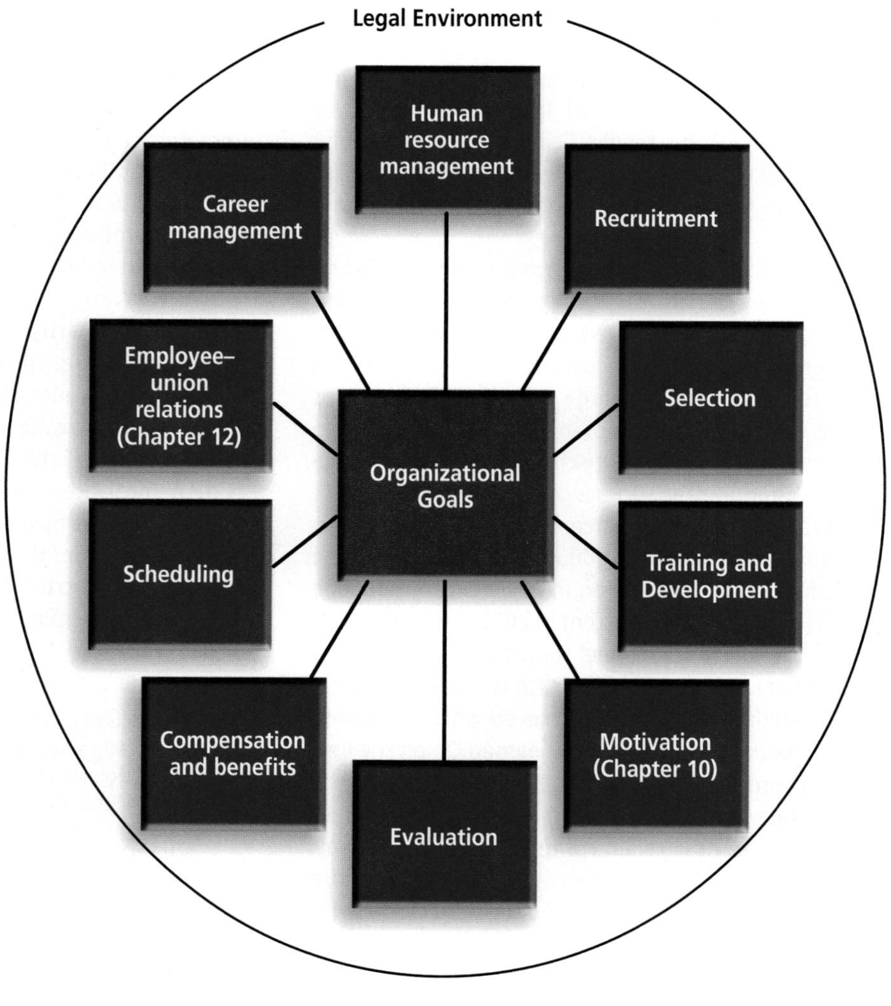

Beaverton, Oregon, for retraining. "Our people now know it's dangerous if they are doing the same job for four years," says Sun spokesperson Hugh Aitken.[1]

Some people have called employees the ultimate resource, and when you think about it, nothing could be truer. People develop the ideas that eventually become the products that satisfy consumers' wants and needs. Take away their creative minds, and leading firms such as IBM, General Electric, Hewlett-Packard, and General Motors would be nothing. The problem is that human resources have always been relatively plentiful, so there was little need to nurture and develop them. If you needed qualified people, you simply went out and hired them. If they didn't work out, you fired them and found others. But *qualified* labor is scarcer today, and that makes recruiting more difficult.

Historically, most firms assigned the job of recruiting, selecting, training, evaluating, compensating, motivating, and, yes, firing people to the various functional departments. For years, the personnel department was more or less responsible for clerical functions such as screening applications, keeping records, processing the payroll, and finding people when necessary.

Today the job of human resource management has taken on an entirely new role in the firm.[2] In the future it may become the most critical function, in that it will be responsible for dealing with all aspects of a business's most critical resource—people. In fact, the human resource function has become so important that it is no longer the function of just one department; it is a function of all managers. Most human resource functions are shared between the professional human resource manager and the other managers. What are some of the challenges in the human resource area that managers face? We'll outline a few of those challenges next.

The Human Resource Challenge

The changes in the American business system that have had the most dramatic impact on the workings of the free enterprise system are the changes in the labor force. The ability of the U.S. business system to compete in global markets depends on new ideas, new products, and new levels of productivity ➤P. 15◀—in other words, on people with good ideas. The following are some of the challenges and opportunities being encountered in the human resource area:

- Shortages in people trained to work in the growth areas of the future, such as computers, biotechnology, robotics, and the sciences. It is estimated that more than half a million U.S. information technology jobs went unfilled in 2002.[3]
- A huge population of skilled and unskilled workers from declining industries, such as steel, automobiles, and garment making, who are unemployed or underemployed and who need retraining. Underemployed workers are those who have more skills or knowledge than their current jobs require.[4]
- A growing percentage of new workers who are undereducated and unprepared for jobs in the contemporary business environment.[5]
- A shift in the age composition of the workforce, including aging baby boomers, many of whom are deferring retirement.[6] The Dealing with Change box on p. 332 discusses the new human resource challenges faced by an aging workforce.
- A complex set of laws and regulations involving hiring, safety, unionization, and equal pay that require organizations to go beyond a profit orientation and be more fair and socially conscious.[7]

www.newamericans.com

Dealing with Change

Who Will Replace the Graying Workers?

Wine connoisseurs believe that most great wines get better with age. Unfortunately, the economies of industrialized countries cannot make the same claim. By 2050, the average age of the world's population is expected to rise from 26 to 36. In Spain the average will be 55. This aging of the population presents huge economic implications. Who will do the work in geriatric societies? Who will support the increasing number of pensioners? What will happen to economic growth with a declining labor force? Nations such as Japan, Russia, and Brazil will have huge numbers of retirees; in Europe only two working-age people will be supporting each European over 65 instead of the four who support each retiree today.

The United States has similar problems but has faced this challenge differently than European and Asian countries. For the past two decades the United States has been importing workers to increase the labor force. Few countries other than the United States have the administrative capabilities or the desire to absorb many foreigners annually. These workers supply important technical and scientific talent, start new companies, and help hold down prices by filling low-wage jobs. Even with this influx of foreign workers, the United States could experience labor shortages by 2010.

Labor unions view immigrant recruitment with mixed emotions. Many labor leaders feel that the growing numbers of immigrants entering the country will fuel future union growth. Some labor leaders also support the immigration of skilled workers to staff growth industries that don't have an adequate supply of qualified workers in the United States. However, labor decries the loss of union jobs to low-paid immigrants in many service industries and the shift of manufacturing jobs to states with growing numbers of immigrants. Overall, the unions agree that an overhaul of the nation's immigration laws is necessary to meet the workforce challenges of the future.

Sources: Moon Ihlwan, Pete Engardio, and Aaron Burnstein, "The Coming Battle for Immigrants," *Business Week,* August 26, 2002, pp. 138–39; and "Groups Urge Overhaul of Immigration," AP Online, March 11, 2002.

- An increasing number of both single-parent and two-income families, resulting in a demand for day care, job sharing, maternity leave, and special career advancement programs for women.[8]
- A shift in employee attitudes toward work. Leisure time has become a much higher priority, as have concepts such as flextime and a shorter workweek.[9]
- Continued downsizing that is taking a toll on employee morale as well as increasing the demand for temporary workers.[10]
- A challenge from overseas labor pools whose members are available for lower wages and subject to many fewer laws and regulations. This results in many jobs being shifted overseas.[11]
- An increased demand for benefits tailored to the individual.[12]
- A growing concern over such issues as health care, elder care, child care (discussed in Chapter 12), equal opportunities for people with disabilities, and special attention given to affirmative-action programs.[13]
- A decreased sense of employee loyalty, resulting in increased employee turnover and increased costs of replacing lost workers.[14]

Given all of these issues, and others that are sure to develop, you can see why human resource management has taken a more central position in management thinking than ever before.

Critical Thinking

Given the complex situations you'd be addressing, does human resource management seem like a career area that interests you? What have been your experiences in dealing with people who work in human resource management?

Determining Your Human Resource Needs

All management, including human resource management, begins with planning. Five steps are involved in the human resource planning process:

1. **Preparing a human resource inventory of the organization's employees.** This inventory should include ages, names, education, capabilities, training, specialized skills, and other information pertinent to the specific organization (e.g., languages spoken). Such information reveals whether or not the labor force is technically up-to-date, thoroughly trained, and so forth.
2. **Preparing a job analysis.** A **job analysis** is a study of what is done by employees who hold various job titles. Such analyses are necessary in order to recruit and train employees with the necessary skills to do the job. The results of job analysis are two written statements: job descriptions and job specifications. A **job description** specifies the objectives of the job, the type of work to be done, the responsibilities and duties, the working conditions, and the relationship of the job to other functions. **Job specifications** are a written summary of the minimum qualifications (education, skills, etc.) required of workers to do a particular job. In short, job descriptions are statements about the job, whereas job specifications are statements about the person who does the job. See Figure 11.2 for hypothetical examples of a job description and job specifications.
3. **Assessing future human resource demand.** Because technology changes rapidly, training programs must be started long before the need is apparent. Human resource managers who are proactive—that is, who anticipate the organization's requirements identified in the forecast process—make sure that trained people are available when needed.
4. **Assessing future supply.** The labor force is constantly shifting: getting older, becoming more technically oriented, attracting more women, and so forth. There are likely to be increased shortages of some

job analysis
A study of what is done by employees who hold various job titles.

job description
A summary of the objectives of a job, the type of work to be done, the responsibilities and duties, the working conditions, and the relationship of the job to other functions.

job specifications
A written summary of the minimum qualifications required of workers to do a particular job.

JOB ANALYSIS	
Observe current sales representatives doing the job. Discuss job with sales managers. Have current sales reps keep a diary of their activities.	
JOB DESCRIPTION	**JOB SPECIFICATIONS**
Primary objective is to sell company's products to stores in Territory Z. Duties include servicing accounts and maintaining positive relationships with clients. Responsibilities include • Introducing the new products to store managers in the area. • Helping the store managers estimate the volume to order. • Negotiating prime shelf space. • Explaining sales promotion activities to store managers. • Stocking and maintaining shelves in stores that wish such service.	Characteristics of the person qualifying for this job include • Two years' sales experience. • Positive attitude. • Well-groomed appearance. • Good communication skills. • High school diploma and two years of college credit.

FIGURE 11.2

JOB ANALYSIS

A job analysis yields two important statements: job descriptions and job specifications. Here you have a job description and job specifications for a sales representative.

workers in the future (e.g., computer and robotic repair workers) and oversupply of others (e.g., assembly line workers).

5. **Establishing a strategic plan.** The plan must address recruiting, selecting, training and developing, appraising, compensating, and scheduling the labor force. Because the previous four steps lead up to this one, this chapter will focus on these elements of the strategic human resource plan.

RECRUITING EMPLOYEES FROM A DIVERSE POPULATION

recruitment
The set of activities used to obtain a sufficient number of the right people at the right time.

Recruitment is the set of activities used to obtain a sufficient number of the right people at the right time; its purpose is to select those who best meet the needs of the organization. One would think that, with a continuous flow of new people into the workforce, recruiting would be easy. On the contrary, recruiting has become very difficult, for several reasons:

- Some organizations have policies that demand promotions from within, operate under union regulations, or offer low wages, which makes recruiting and keeping employees difficult or subject to outside influence and restrictions.
- The emphasis on corporate culture, teamwork, and participative management makes it important to hire people who not only are skilled but also fit in with the culture and leadership style of the organization.[15]
- Sometimes people with the necessary skills are not available; in this case, workers must be hired and then trained internally.[16]

Because recruiting is a difficult chore that involves finding, hiring, and training people who are an appropriate technical and social fit, human resource managers turn to many sources for assistance (see Figure 11.3). These sources

FIGURE 11.3

EMPLOYEE SOURCES

Internal sources are often given first consideration. So it's useful to get a recommendation from a current employee of the firm for which you want to work. College placement offices are also an important source. Be sure to learn about such facilities early so that you can plan a strategy throughout your college career.

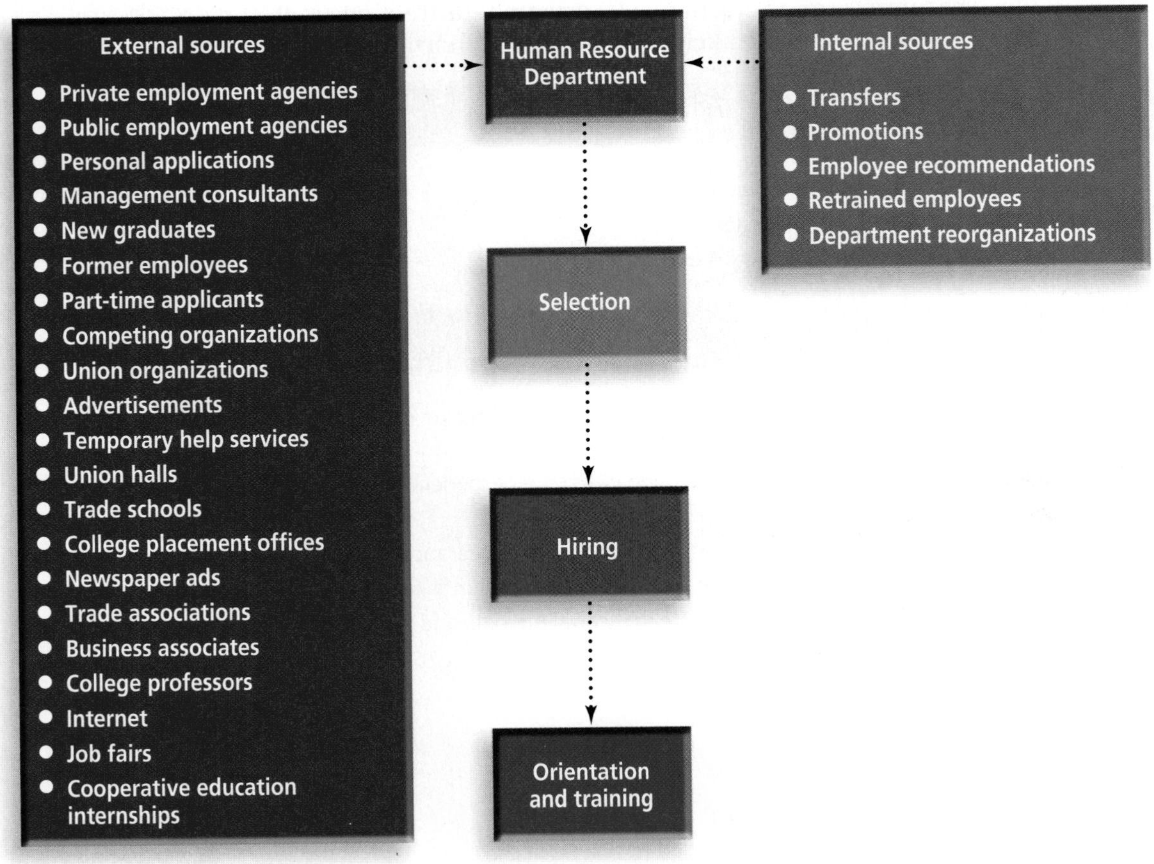

Spotlight on Small Business

Competing for Qualified Workers

www.careerbuilder.com

It's difficult for small-business owners to find qualified employees. Small businesses want top talent but often can't afford corporate-level benefits or expensive recruiters to hunt down the best people. Despite the hurdles, small-business management consultants say there are many ways to lure desirable workers:

- *Transform ads into promotional tools.* For example, Ecoprint, a small print shop in Maryland, brags in its advertisements about the benefits of working for this collegial company.
- *Post job openings on the Internet.* Running a 20-line ad on an online service like CareerBuilder or the Monster Board costs $100 to $150 for 30 days. A comparable ad in the *New York Times* can cost $1,728 for only a week.
- *Let your staff help select hires.* The more staff people involved in the interview process, the better chance you have to find out who has the personality and skills to fit in.
- *Create a dynamic workplace to attract local, energetic applicants.* Sometimes word of mouth is the most effective recruiting tool.
- *Test-drive an employee.* Hiring temporary workers can allow you to test candidates for a few months before deciding whether to make an offer or not.
- *Hire your customer.* Loyal customers sometimes make the smartest employees.
- *Check community groups and local government agencies.* Don't forget to check out state-run employment agencies. The welfare-to-work programs may turn up excellent candidates you can train.
- *Lure candidates with a policy of promotions and raises.* Most employees want to know that they can move up in the company. Give employees an incentive for learning the business.
- *Outsource fringe benefit management to a professional employer organization (PEO).* PEOs may be able to offer lower insurance rates for benefit programs because of greater economies of scale. While this may not bring a small business's benefits program all the way up to the level of those offered by most large companies, it may help close the gap and therefore help attract qualified workers.

Sources: Susan T. Port, "Staff Leasing Firms Help Small Businesses Compete," *Palm Beach Post,* January 27, 2001, p. 2D; Brian S. Klass, John McClendon, and Thomas W. Gainey, "Trust and the Role of Professional Employer Organizations: Managing HR in Small and Medium Enterprises," *Journal of Managerial Issues,* April 1, 2002, p. 31; and "Improving Worker Coverage and Benefits," Government Accounting Office report, April 9, 2002.

are classified as either internal or external. Internal sources include employees who are already within the firm (and may be transferred or promoted) and employees who can recommend others to hire. Using internal sources is less expensive than recruiting outside the company. The greatest advantage of hiring from within is that it helps maintain employee morale. It isn't always possible to find qualified workers within the company, however, so human resource managers must use external recruitment sources such as advertisements, public and private employment agencies, college placement bureaus, management consultants, professional organizations, referrals, and walk-in applications.

Recruiting qualified workers may be particularly difficult for small businesses ➤P. 184◄ that don't have enough staff members to serve as internal sources and may not be able to offer the sort of competitive compensation that attracts external sources. The Spotlight on Small Business box outlines some ways in which small businesses can address their recruiting needs. Newer tools for recruiting employees include Internet services such as CareerBuilder.com and Monster (see the first Taking It to the Net exercise at the end of this chapter).

SELECTING EMPLOYEES WHO WILL BE PRODUCTIVE

selection
The process of gathering information and deciding who should be hired, under legal guidelines, for the best interests of the individual and the organization.

Selection is the process of gathering information and deciding who should be hired, under legal guidelines, for the best interests of the individual and the organization. Selecting and training employees have become extremely expensive processes in some firms. Think of what's involved: interview time, medical exams, training costs, unproductive time spent learning the job, moving expenses, and so on. It's easy to see how selection expenses can amount to over $130,000 for a top-level manager. It can even cost one and a half times the employee's annual salary to recruit, process, and train an entry-level worker.[17] Thus, the selection process is an important element of any human resource program. A typical selection process would involve six steps:

1. **Obtaining complete application forms.** Once this was a simple procedure with few complications. Today, however, legal guidelines limit the kinds of questions that may appear on an application form. Nonetheless, such forms help the employer discover the applicant's educational background, past work experience, career objectives, and other qualifications directly related to the requirements of the job. Large employers like Target and Blockbuster make the application process more effective and efficient by using an artificial intelligence program called Smart Assessment, developed by application-service provider Unicru. An applicant sits down at a computer and spends a half hour answering questions about job experience, time available to work, and personality. Ten minutes later, a report is e-mailed to a hiring manager. The reports tell the manager whether to interview the applicant or not. If an interview is recommended, the report even suggests questions the manager can ask to find the best-fitting position for the applicant. Blockbuster says Unicru's system helped the company cut the hiring process from two weeks to three days and has reduced the employee turnover rate by 30 percent.[18]
2. **Conducting initial and follow-up interviews.** A staff member from the human resource department often screens applicants in a first interview. If the interviewer considers the applicant a potential employee, the manager who will supervise the new employee interviews the applicant as well. It's important that managers prepare adequately for the interview to avoid selection decisions they may regret.[19] Certain mistakes, such as asking an interviewee about his or her family, no matter how innocent the intention, could later be used as evidence if that applicant files discrimination charges.[20]
3. **Giving employment tests.** Organizations use tests to measure basic competencies in specific job skills (e.g., welding, word processing) and to help evaluate applicants' personalities and interests.[21] In using employment tests, it's important that they be directly related to the job. Employment tests have been severely criticized as potential sources of illegal discrimination.[22] For example, several Bell South employees sued the company for discrimination because they were not promoted when they failed math/logic tests. The employees said the tests did not assess the interpersonal skills needed for the job.[23] Many companies test potential employees in assessment centers where applicants perform actual tasks of the real job. Such testing is likely to make the selection process more efficient and will generally satisfy legal requirements.
4. **Conducting background investigations.** Most organizations now investigate a candidate's work record, school record, credit history, and references more carefully than they have in the past.[24] It is simply too costly to hire, train, and motivate people only to lose them and have to start the process over. Background checks help an employer identify which candidates are most likely to succeed in a given position. Websites such as PeopleWise allow prospective employers not only to conduct speedy background checks of criminal records, driving records,

and credit histories but also to verify work experience and professional and educational credentials.

5. **Obtaining results from physical exams.** There are obvious benefits to hiring physically and mentally healthy people. However, medical tests cannot be given just to screen out individuals. (See the discussion of the Americans with Disabilities Act on p. 355.) In some states, physical exams can be given only after an offer of employment has been accepted. In states that allow preemployment physical exams, the exams must be given to everyone applying for the same position. There has been some controversy about preemployment testing to detect drug or alcohol abuse, as well as screening to detect carriers of the virus that causes AIDS. Over 70 percent of U.S. companies now test both current and potential employees for drug use.[25]

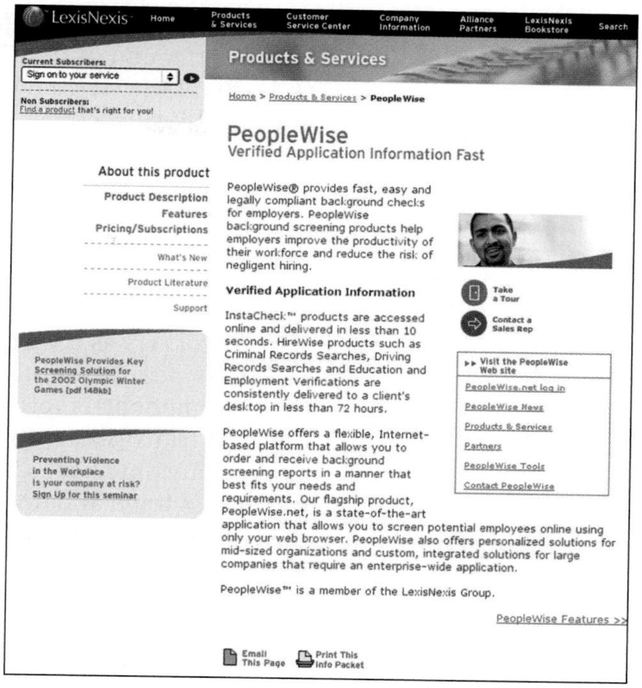

6. **Establishing trial (probationary) periods.** Often an organization will hire an employee conditionally. This enables the person to prove his or her worth on the job. After a specified probationary period (perhaps six months or a year), the firm may either permanently hire or discharge that employee on the basis of evaluations from supervisors. Although such systems make it easier to fire inefficient or problem employees, they do not eliminate the high cost of turnover.

Unfortunately, businesses have learned that hiring the wrong person to fill a job costs valuable time and money. Today, companies like PeopleWise reduce the risk of making a bad choice by offering a flexible means to screen potential employees online. PeopleWise provides carefully screened background checks of potential employees to see who best fits the needs of a company. Visit the company's website at *www.peoplewise.net.*

The selection process is often long and difficult, but it is worth the effort to select new employees carefully because of the high costs of replacing workers. The process helps ensure that new employees meet the requirements in all relevant areas, including communication skills, education, technical skills, experience, personality, and health.

Hiring Contingent Workers

When more workers are needed in a company, human resource managers may want to consider finding creative staffing alternatives rather than simply hiring new full-time employees. A company with varying needs for employees—from hour to hour, day to day, week to week, and season to season—may find it cost-effective to hire contingent workers. **Contingent workers** are defined as workers who do not have the expectation of regular, full-time employment. Such workers include part-time workers (anyone who works 1 to 34 hours per week), temporary workers (workers paid by temporary employment agencies), seasonal workers, independent contractors, interns, and co-op students.

contingent workers
Workers who do not have the expectation of regular, full-time employment.

A varying need for employees is the most common reason for hiring contingent workers. Companies may also look to hire contingent workers when full-time employees are on some type of leave (such as maternity leave), when there is a peak demand for labor, or when quick service to customers is a priority. Companies in areas where qualified contingent workers are available, and in which the jobs require minimum training, are most likely to consider alternative staffing options.

Temporary staffing has evolved into a $40 billion industry. According to the U.S. Bureau of Labor Statistics, about 12.6 million people in the United States

(10 percent of workers) are employed in an alternative working arrangement.[26] At the beginning of the 1990s, half of those jobs were office/clerical positions and one-quarter were industrial (construction, trucking, plumbing, etc.). Now industrial jobs account for more than one-third of all temps. As suggested in the chapter opening profile, an increasing number of contingent workers are educated professionals such as accountants, attorneys, and engineers.

Contingent workers receive few benefits; they are rarely offered health insurance, vacation time, or private pensions. They also tend to earn less than permanent workers do. On the positive side, many of those on temporary assignments are eventually offered full-time positions. Managers see using temporary workers as a way of weeding out poor workers and finding good hires.

Many people find that temporary work offers them a lot more flexibility than permanent employment. For example, student Daniel Butrym found that the transition from student to temp worker was not difficult. Butrym says, "You come back in town. You don't have to interview. You don't have to run across town and do a drug test. You don't have to waste a lot of time looking for a job. The first time you walk into [the temporary staffing] office, they meet you, sit you down and they find out your skills. Once you're in their computer, they have all your stats, they know what you can do and you're done. [Later] I can call from school, say 'I'm going to be home for spring break, I need some money.' " As soon as Butrym calls, he's put into the system for work assignments.

Butrym is not alone. Andy Williams of Randstad North America, the staffing services giant, welcomes college students. "A lot of the college students are computer-literate, and they are familiar with many of the popular software programs that the companies use. And, they are quick to get up to speed on [any] proprietary software an employer might use. . . Every customer is different. Some assignments come for one day. Some assignments are for weeks or for the whole summer," Williams says.[27]

In an era of downsizing and rapid change, some contingent workers have even found that temping can be more secure than full-time employment.[28]

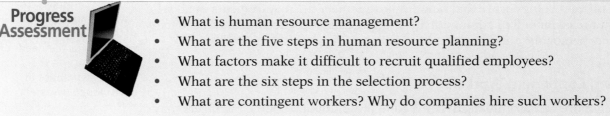

Progress Assessment

- What is human resource management?
- What are the five steps in human resource planning?
- What factors make it difficult to recruit qualified employees?
- What are the six steps in the selection process?
- What are contingent workers? Why do companies hire such workers?

Training and Developing Employees for Optimum Performance

Because employees need to learn how to work with equipment—such as word processors, computers, and robots—companies are finding that they must offer training programs that often are quite sophisticated. Employers find that spending money on training is usually money well spent. A study by the National Center on the Educational Quality of the Workforce found that a 10 percent increase in a workforce's education level led to an 8.6 percent gain in total productivity. By contrast, a 10 percent increase in spending on new equipment boosted productivity by just 3.4 percent.[29]

training and development
All attempts to improve productivity by increasing an employee's ability to perform. Training focuses on short-term skills, whereas development focuses on long-term abilities.

Training and development include all attempts to improve productivity by increasing an employee's ability to perform. Training focuses on short-term skills, whereas development focuses on long-term abilities. But both training and development programs include three steps: (1) assessing the needs of the organization and the skills of the employees to determine training needs; (2) designing training activities to meet the identified needs; and (3) evaluating the effectiveness of the training.[30] Some common training and development activities are employee orientation, on-the-job training, apprenticeship, off-the-job training, vestibule training, job simulation, and management training.

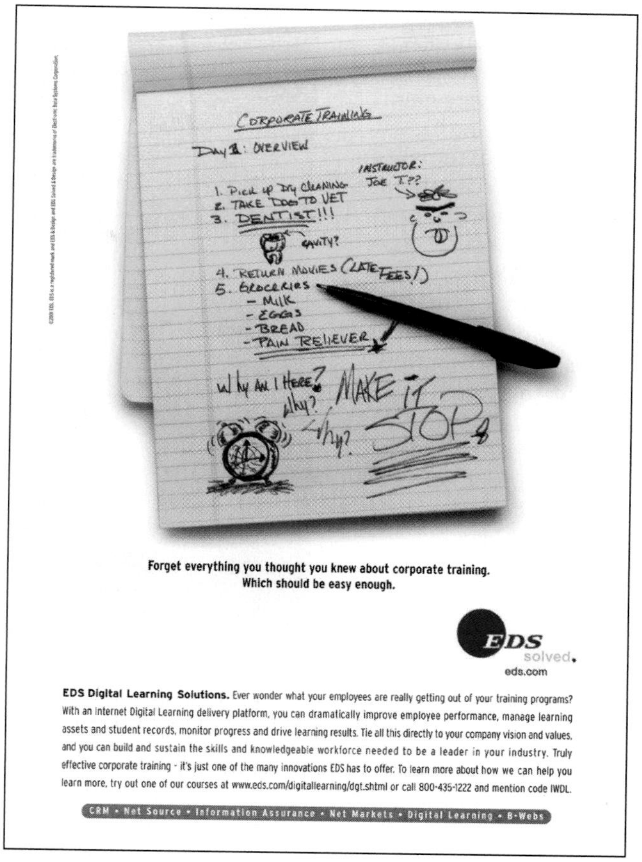

CORPORATE TRAINING
DAY 1: OVERVIEW
1. PICK UP DRY CLEANING
2. TAKE DOG TO VET
3. DENTIST!!!
CAVITY?
INSTRUCTOR: JOE ???
4. RETURN MOVIES (LATE FEES!)
5. GROCERIES
- MILK
- EGGS
- BREAD
- PAIN RELIEVER
Why am I HERE? Why? Why?
MAKE IT STOP
Forget everything you thought you knew about corporate training.
Which should be easy enough.
EDS solved.
eds.com
EDS Digital Learning Solutions. Ever wonder what your employees are really getting out of your training programs? With an Internet Digital Learning delivery platform, you can dramatically improve employee performance, manage learning assets and student records, monitor progress and drive learning results. Tie all this directly to your company vision and values, and you can build and sustain the skills and knowledgeable workforce needed to be a leader in your industry. Truly effective corporate training - it's just one of the many innovations EDS has to offer. To learn more about how we can help you learn more, try out one of our courses at www.eds.com/digitallearning/dgt.shtml or call 800-435-1222 and mention code IWDL.
CRM • Net Source • Information Assurance • Net Markets • Digital Learning • B-Webs

How can companies make sure that their employees are getting the most out of the training they provide? Many companies use electronic delivery systems such as those developed by EDS Digital Learning Systems. EDS helps companies monitor what employees have learned through online training and provides additional help when it is needed. Check out one of their courses at *www.eds.com/digitallearning/*. Do you prefer traditional classroom-type instruction or online training? Why?

- **Employee orientation** is the activity that initiates new employees to the organization; to fellow employees; to their immediate supervisors; and to the policies, practices, and objectives of the firm. Orientation programs include everything from informal talks to formal activities that last a day or more. They may involve such activities as scheduled visits to various departments and required reading of handbooks.[31] For example, at British Airways new employees participate in meetings that provide an education in the company's values and in its brand integrity. Part history lesson, part rules-of-the-road orientation, the training covers everything from principles of customer service to the choice of colors on the aircraft.
- **On-the-job training** is the most fundamental type of training. The employee being trained on the job immediately begins his or her tasks and learns by doing, or watches others for a while and then imitates them, right at the workplace. Salespeople, for example, are often trained by watching experienced salespeople perform. Naturally, this can be either quite effective or disastrous, depending on the skills and habits of the person being watched. On-the-job training is obviously the easiest kind of training to implement when the job is relatively simple (such as clerking in a store) or repetitive (such as collecting refuse, cleaning carpets, or mowing lawns). More demanding or intricate jobs require a more intense training effort. Intranets and other new forms of technology are leading to cost-effective on-the-job training programs available 24 hours a day, all year long. Computer systems can monitor workers' input and give them instructions if they become confused about what to do next. Such an intranet system helped furniture maker Steelcase not only reduce its number of training courseware developers from 20 to 5 but also totally eliminate its $30,000 training material printing budget. The Web allows greater flexibility, but the company believes its greatest advantage is the ability to make changes and updates in real time.[32]
- **Apprentice programs** involve a period during which a learner works alongside an experienced employee to master the skills and procedures of a craft. Some apprenticeship programs also involve classroom training. Many skilled crafts, such as bricklaying and plumbing, require a new

employee orientation
The activity that introduces new employees to the organization; to fellow employees; to their immediate supervisors; and to the policies, practices, and objectives of the firm.

on-the-job training
Training in which the employee immediately begins his or her tasks and learns by doing, or watches others for a while and then imitates them, all right at the workplace.

apprentice programs
Training programs involving a period during which a learner works alongside an experienced employee to master the skills and procedures of a craft.

No, this is not an NBA tryout. Employees of overnight delivery giant FedEx are playing blindfolded basketball, a bonding exercise intended to build trust among workers and managers. FedEx spends six times more than the average company on training, but enjoys a remarkably low 4 percent employee turnover rate. Would a commitment to training similar to FedEx help other companies retain employees? Why?

worker to serve as an apprentice for several years. Trade unions often require new workers to serve apprenticeships to ensure excellence among their members as well as to limit entry to the union. Workers who successfully complete an apprenticeship earn the classification of *journeyman.* In the future, there are likely to be more but shorter apprenticeship programs to prepare people for skilled jobs in changing industries. For example, auto repair will require more intense training as new automobile models include advanced computers and other electronic devices.[33]

off-the-job training
Training that occurs away from the workplace and consists of internal or external programs to develop any of a variety of skills or to foster personal development.

- **Off-the-job training** occurs away from the workplace and consists of internal or external programs to develop any of a variety of skills or to foster personal development. Training is becoming more sophisticated as jobs become more sophisticated. Furthermore, training is expanding to include education (through the Ph.D.) and personal development—subjects may include time management, stress management, health and wellness, physical education, nutrition, and even art and languages.

online training
Training programs in which employees "attend" classes via the Internet.

- **Online training** offers an example of how technology is improving the efficiency of many off-the-job training programs. In such training, employees "attend" classes via the Internet. Many colleges and universities now offer a wide variety of Internet courses.[34] Such programs are sometimes called *distance learning* because the students are separated by distance from the instructor or content source.

vestibule training
Training done in schools where employees are taught on equipment similar to that used on the job.

- **Vestibule training** (near-the-job training) is done in classrooms where employees are taught on equipment similar to that used on the job. Such classrooms enable employees to learn proper methods and safety procedures before assuming a specific job assignment in an organization. Computer and robotics training is often completed in a vestibule classroom.

job simulation
The use of equipment that duplicates job conditions and tasks so that trainees can learn skills before attempting them on the job.

- **Job simulation** is the use of equipment that duplicates job conditions and tasks so that trainees can learn skills before attempting them on the job. Job simulation differs from vestibule training in that the simulation attempts to duplicate the *exact* combination of conditions that occur on the job. This is the kind of training given to astronauts, airline pilots, army tank operators, ship captains, and others who must learn difficult procedures off the job.

Management Development

Managers need special training. To be good communicators, they especially need to learn listening skills and empathy. They also need time management, planning, and human relations skills.

Management development, then, is the process of training and educating employees to become good managers and then monitoring the progress of their managerial skills over time. Management development programs have sprung up everywhere, especially at colleges, universities, and private management development firms. Managers participate in role-playing exercises, solve various management cases, and attend films and lectures.

The dictionary says a mentor is a wise and trusted counselor or teacher. In business, a mentor can be a whole lot more. Mentors not only counsel and teach lower-level employees, they often introduce them to the right people within an organization who can help the employees advance. Firms like Lockheed Martin (shown here) have a formal system of assigning mentors to employees who show strong potential. What types of guidance can mentors offer lower-level employees?

Management development is increasingly being used as a tool to accomplish business objectives. For example, Ford Motor Company is teaching executives how to be more responsive to customers. Most management training programs also include several of the following:

- **On-the-job coaching**. This means that a senior manager will assist a lower-level manager by teaching him or her needed skills and generally providing direction, advice, and helpful feedback.[35]
- **Understudy positions.** Job titles such as *undersecretary* and *assistant* are part of a relatively successful way of developing managers. Selected employees work as assistants to higher-level managers and participate in planning and other managerial functions until they are ready to assume such positions themselves.
- **Job rotation.** So that they can learn about different functions of the organization, managers are often given assignments in a variety of departments. Through job rotation, top managers gain the broad picture of the organization necessary to their success.
- **Off-the-job courses and training.** Managers periodically go to schools or seminars for a week or more to hone their technical and human relations skills. Companies, such as McDonald's Corporation, have their own "colleges" for managers. At McDonald's Hamburger University, managers and potential franchise owners attend six days of classes, a course of study equivalent to 36 hours of college business-school credit.

management development
The process of training and educating employees to become good managers and then monitoring the progress of their managerial skills over time.

Networking

Networking is the process of establishing and maintaining contacts with key managers in one's own organization and in other organizations and using those contacts to weave strong relationships that serve as informal development systems. Of equal or greater importance to potential managers is a **mentor,** a corporate manager who supervises, coaches, and guides selected lower-level employees by introducing them to the right people and generally acts as their organizational sponsor. In reality, an informal type of mentoring goes on in most organizations on a regular basis as older employees assist younger work-

networking
The process of establishing and maintaining contacts with key managers in one's own organization and other organizations and using those contacts to weave strong relationships that serve as informal development systems.

mentor
An experienced employee who supervises, coaches, and guides lower-level employees by introducing them to the right people and generally being their organizational sponsor.

ers. However, many organizations, such as Intel, use a formal system of assigning mentors to employees considered to have strong potential.[36]

It's also important to remember that networking and mentoring can go beyond the business environment. For example, college is a perfect place to begin networking. Associations you nurture with professors, with local businesspeople through internships, and especially with your classmates might provide you with a valuable network you can turn to for the rest of your career.

Diversity in Management Development

As women moved into management, they also learned the importance of networking and of having mentors. But since most older managers are male, women often have more difficulty than men do in finding mentors and entering the network. Women managers won a major victory when the U.S. Supreme Court ruled that it was illegal to bar women from certain clubs, long open to men only, where business activity flows and contacts are made. More and more, women are now entering established networking systems or, in some instances, creating their own.[37]

Similarly, African American managers are learning the value of networking. Working together, African Americans are forming pools of capital and new opportunities that are helping many individuals overcome traditional barriers to success.[38] *Black Enterprise* magazine sponsors several networking forums each year for African American professionals.

Other ethnic groups are networking as well. For example, Mark Shir, a financial and computer specialist from Taiwan, felt that he would never get ahead in the U.S. companies he had worked in for 10 years. When he joined Monte Jade, an association that helps Taiwanese and Chinese assimilate in American business, he met people who helped him start his own successful hardware-packaging company.[39]

Companies that take the initiative to develop female and minority managers understand three crucial principles: (1) grooming women and minorities for management positions isn't about legality, morality, or even morale; it is about bringing more talent in the door—the key to long-term profitability; (2) the best women and minorities will become harder to attract and retain, so the companies that start now will have an edge later; and (3) having more women and minorities at all levels means that businesses can serve their increasingly female and minority customers better. If you don't have a diversity of people working in the back room, how are you going to satisfy the diversity of people coming in the front door?

Appraising Employee Performance to Get Optimum Results

Managers must be able to determine whether or not their workers are doing an effective and efficient job, with a minimum of errors and disruptions. They do so by using performance appraisals. A **performance appraisal** is an evaluation in which the performance level of employees is measured against established standards to make decisions about promotions, compensation, additional training, or firing. Performance appraisals consist of these six steps:

performance appraisal
An evaluation in which the performance level of employees is measured against established standards to make decisions about promotions, compensation, additional training, or firing.

1. **Establishing performance standards.** This is a crucial step. Standards must be understandable, subject to measurement, and reasonable. They must be accepted by both the manager and subordinates.
2. **Communicating those standards.** Often managers assume that employees know what is expected of them, but such assumptions are dan-

gerous at best. Employees must be told clearly and precisely what the standards and expectations are and how they are to be met.

3. **Evaluating performance.** If the first two steps are done correctly, performance evaluation is relatively easy. It is a matter of evaluating the employee's behavior to see if it matches standards.
4. **Discussing results with employees.** Most people will make mistakes and fail to meet expectations at first. It takes time to learn a new job and do it well. Discussing an employee's successes and areas that need improvement can provide managers with an opportunity to be understanding and helpful and to guide the employee to better performance. Additionally, the performance appraisal can be a good source of employee suggestions on how a particular task could be better performed.
5. **Taking corrective action.** As an appropriate part of the performance appraisal, a manager can take corrective action or provide corrective feedback to help the employee perform his or her job better. Remember, the key word is *performance.* The primary purpose of conducting this type of appraisal is to improve employee performance if possible.
6. **Using the results to make decisions.** Decisions about promotions, compensation, additional training, or firing are all based on performance evaluations. An effective performance appraisal system is a way of satisfying certain legal conditions concerning such decisions.

Effective management means getting results through top performance by employees. That is what performance appraisals are for—at all levels of the organization. Even top-level managers benefit from performance reviews made by their subordinates. The latest form of performance appraisal is called the 360-degree review because it calls for feedback from all directions in the organization. Instead of an appraisal based solely on the employee's and the supervisor's perceptions, opinions are gathered from those under, above, and on the same level as the worker. The goal is to get an accurate, comprehensive idea of the worker's abilities.[40] Figure 11.4 illustrates how managers can make performance appraisals more meaningful.

Progress Assessment

- Can you name and describe four training techniques?
- What is the primary purpose of a performance appraisal?
- What are the six steps in a performance appraisal?

FIGURE 11.4

CONDUCTING EFFECTIVE APPRAISALS AND REVIEWS

1. **DON'T** attack the employee personally. Critically evaluate his or her work.
2. **DO** allow sufficient time, without distractions, for appraisal. (Take the phone off the hook or close the office door.)
3. **DON'T** make the employee feel uncomfortable or uneasy. *Never* conduct an appraisal where other employees are present (such as on the shop floor).
4. **DO** include the employee in the process as much as possible. (Let the employee prepare a self-improvement program.)
5. **DON'T** wait until the appraisal to address problems with the employee's work that have been developing for some time.
6. **DO** end the appraisal with positive suggestions for employee improvement.

COMPENSATING EMPLOYEES: ATTRACTING AND KEEPING THE BEST

Companies don't just compete for customers; they also compete for employees. Compensation is one of the main marketing tools companies use to attract qualified employees, and it is one of the largest operating costs for many organizations. The long-term success of a firm—perhaps even its survival—may depend on how well it can control employee costs and optimize employee efficiency. For example, service organizations such as hospitals, airlines, and banks have recently struggled with managing high employee costs. This is not unusual since these firms are considered labor intensive. That is, their primary cost of operations is the cost of labor. Manufacturing firms in the auto, airline, and steel industries have asked employees to take reductions in wages to make the firms more competitive. Many employees have agreed, even union employees who have traditionally resisted such cuts. They know that not to do so is to risk going out of business and losing their jobs forever. In other words, the competitive environment is such that compensation and benefit packages are being given special attention. In fact, some experts believe that determining how best to pay people has replaced downsizing as today's greatest human resources challenge.

A carefully managed compensation and benefit program can accomplish several objectives:

- Attracting the kinds of people needed by the organization, and in sufficient numbers.
- Providing employees with the incentive to work efficiently and productively.
- Keeping valued employees from leaving and going to competitors, or starting competing firms.
- Maintaining a competitive position in the marketplace by keeping costs low through high productivity from a satisfied workforce.
- Providing employees with some sense of financial security through insurance and retirement benefits.

Pay Systems

How an organization chooses to pay its employees can have a dramatic effect on efficiency and productivity. Managers want to find a system that compensates employees fairly. Figure 11.5 outlines some of the most common pay systems.

Many companies still use the pay system devised by Edward Hay for General Foods. Known as the Hay system, this compensation plan is based on job tiers, each of which has a strict pay range. In some firms, you're guaranteed a raise after 13 weeks if you're still breathing. Conflict can arise when an employee who is performing well earns less than an employee who is not performing well simply because the latter has worked for the company longer.

John Whitney, author of *The Trust Factor,* believes that companies should begin with some base pay and give all employees the same percentage merit raise. Doing so, he says, sends out the message that everyone in the company is important. Fairness remains the issue. What do you think is the fairest pay system?

Compensating Teams

Thus far we've talked about compensating individuals. What about teams? Since you want your teams to be more than simply a group of individuals, would you compensate them as you would individuals? If you can't answer

FIGURE 11.5

PAY SYSTEMS

Some of the different pay systems are as follows:

- **Salary:** fixed compensation computed on weekly, biweekly, or monthly pay periods (e.g., $1,500 per month or $400 per week). Salaried employees do not receive additional pay for any extra hours worked.
- **Hourly wage or daywork:** wage based on number of hours or days worked, used for most blue-collar and clerical workers. Often employees must punch a time clock when they arrive at work and when they leave. Hourly wages vary greatly. The federal minimum wage is $5.15, and top wages go as high as $20 to $30 per hour for skilled craftspeople. This does not include benefits such as retirement systems, which may add 30 percent or more to the total package.
- **Piecework system:** wage based on the number of items produced rather than by the hour or day. This type of system creates powerful incentives to work efficiently and productively.
- **Commission plans:** pay based on some percentage of sales. Often used to compensate salespeople, commission plans resemble piecework systems.
- **Bonus plans:** extra pay for accomplishing or surpassing certain objectives. There are two types of bonuses: monetary and cashless. Money is always a welcome bonus. Cashless rewards include written thank-you notes, appreciation notes sent to the employee's family, movie tickets, flowers, time off, gift certificates, shopping sprees, and other types of recognition.
- **Profit-sharing plans:** share of the company's profits over and above normal pay. Ninety-nine percent of the Fortune 500 companies use some sort of performance-based incentives. These companies set goals with the input from employees ahead of time. Bonuses are based on progress in meeting the goals.
- **Stock options:** right to purchase stock in the company at a specific price over a specific period of time. Often this gives employees the right to buy stock cheaply despite huge increases in the price of the stock in the marketplace. For example, Rob Gordon started out at Home Depot 10 years ago as an assistant manager. Today, at 39, he's a general manager—and a millionaire due to the growth of Home Depot's stock price. With his stock options, Gordon was able to buy stock worth $63.75 a share for as little as $15 a share.

that question immediately, you are not alone. While most managers believe in using teams, fewer are sure about how to pay them.[41] This suggests that team-based pay programs are not as effective or as fully developed as managers would hope. Measuring and rewarding individual performance on teams while at the same time rewarding team performance can be tricky. Nonetheless, it can be done. Football players are rewarded as a team when they go to the playoffs and to the Super Bowl, but they are paid individually as well. Companies are now experimenting with and developing similar incentive systems.

Jay Schuster, co-author of an ongoing study of team pay, found that when pay is based strictly on individual performance, it erodes team cohesiveness and makes it less likely that the team will meet its goals as a collaborative effort. Schuster recommends basing pay on team performance.[42] Skill-based pay and profit-sharing are the two most common compensation methods for teams.

Skill-based pay is related to the growth of both the individual and the team. Base pay is raised when team members learn and apply new skills. For example, Baldrige award winner Eastman Chemical Company rewards its teams' proficiency in technical, social, and business knowledge skills. A cross-functional compensation policy team defines the skills. The drawbacks of the skill-based pay system are twofold: the system is complex, and it is difficult to correlate skill acquisition and profit gains.[43]

In most gain-sharing systems, bonuses are based on improvements over a previous performance baseline. For example, Behlen Manufacturing, a diversified maker of agricultural and industrial products, calculates its bonuses by dividing quality pounds of product by worker-hours. *Quality* means no defects; any defects are subtracted from the total. Workers can receive a monthly gain-sharing bonus of up to $1 an hour when their teams meet productivity goals.

It is important to reward individual team players also. Outstanding team players—those who go beyond what is required and make an outstanding individual contribution to the firm—should be separately recognized for their additional contribution. Recognition can include cashless as well as cash rewards. A good way to avoid alienating recipients who feel team participation was uneven is to let the team decide which members get what type of individual award. After all, if you really support the team process, you need to give teams freedom to reward themselves.

Fringe Benefits

fringe benefits
Benefits such as sick-leave pay, vacation pay, pension plans, and health plans that represent additional compensation to employees beyond base wages.

Fringe benefits include sick-leave pay, vacation pay, pension plans, and health plans that provide additional compensation to employees beyond base wages. Fringe benefits in recent years grew faster than wages. In fact, employee benefits can't really be considered "fringe" anymore. While such benefits accounted for less than 2 percent of payrolls in 1929, they account for approximately 30 percent of payrolls today. U.S. companies now spend an average of approximately $13,000 a year per employee for benefits.[44] Many employees request more fringe benefits, instead of more salary, to avoid higher taxes. This has resulted in much debate and much government investigation.

Fringe benefits can include everything from paid vacations to health care programs, recreation facilities, company cars, country club memberships, day care services, and executive dining rooms. Employees want packages to include dental care, mental health care, elder care, legal counseling, eye care, and short workweeks. As the cost of health care continues to spiral higher, many employers are now asking their employees to pay a larger share of their health insurance bill.[45]

Understanding that it takes many attractions to retain the best employees, dozens of companies on *Fortune* magazine's list of the "100 Best Companies to Work For" offer so-called soft benefits. *Soft benefits* help workers maintain the balance between work and family life that is as important to hardworking employees as the nature of the job itself. These perks include things such as on-site haircuts and shoe repair, concierge services, and free breakfasts. Freeing employees from spending time on errands and chores gives them more time for family—and work.

cafeteria-style fringe benefits
Fringe benefits plan that allows employees to choose the benefits they want up to a certain dollar amount.

To counter these growing demands, over half of all large firms offer **cafeteria-style fringe benefits** plans, in which employees can choose the benefits they want, up to a certain dollar amount. Choice is the key to these flexible plans. At one time, most employees' needs were similar. Today, employees are more varied and more demanding. Some employees may need child care benefits, whereas others may need relatively large pension benefits. Rather than giving all employees identical benefits, managers can equitably and cost-effectively meet employees' individual needs by allowing employees some choice.[46]

Managing the benefits package will continue to be a major human resource issue in the future. The cost of administering benefits programs has be-

Less Rest Assured

Is your downtime too far down?

TRAVEL—Americans rank lowest in the world for the average number of vacation days allotted by employers. But not too many of us are complaining. In fact, most Americans don't even use all of their vacation time. Here is how we rank, according to the World Trade Organization, when compared with other countries.

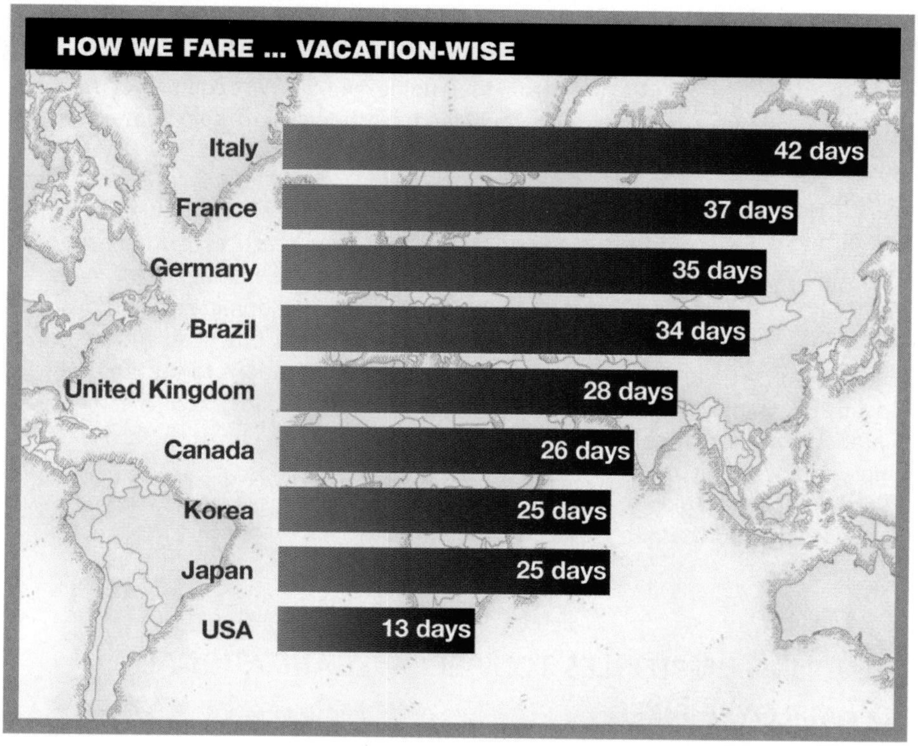

Is vacation time the primary benefit you look for in a job? Well, better check the want ads in Naples or Palermo, Italy. As this illustration shows, Italians take an average of 42 days of vacation per year while the average American worker receives the least time off (13 days)—and many don't even take all of the vacation time coming to them. Why do you think Americans take so little time off?

come so great that a number of companies outsource ➤P. 257◄ this function—that is, they are hiring outside companies to run their employee benefits plans. IBM, for example, decided to spin off its human resources and benefits operation into a separate company, Workforce Solutions, which provides customized services to each of IBM's independent units. The new company saves IBM $45 million each year. Workforce Solutions now handles benefits for other organizations such as the National Geographic Society. In addition to saving them money, outsourcing fringe benefits administration helps companies avoid the growing complexity and technical requirements of the plans.

Managing benefits can be especially complicated when employees are located in other countries. The Reaching Beyond Our Borders box on p. 348 discusses the new human resource challenges faced by global businesses. To put it simply, benefits are as important to wage negotiations and recruitment now as salary. In the future, benefits may become even more important than salary.

www.shrm.org

Reaching Beyond Our Borders

Managing a Global Workforce

Human resource people who manage a global workforce begin by understanding the customs, laws, and local business needs of every country in which the organization operates.

Varying cultural and legal standards can affect a variety of human resource functions:

- *Compensation.* Salaries must be converted to and from foreign currencies. Often employees with international assignments receive special allowances for relocation, children's education, housing, travel, or other business-related expenses.
- *Health and pension standards.* Human resource managers must consider the different social contexts for benefits in other countries. For example, in the Netherlands the government provides retirement income and health care.
- *Paid time off.* Cultural differences can be quite apparent when it comes to paid time off. Employees in other countries enjoy more vacation time than those in the United States. For example, four weeks of paid vacation is the standard of many European employers. But other countries do not have the short-term and long-term absence policies we have in the United States. They do not have sick leave, personal leave, or family and medical leave. Global companies need a standard definition of what time off is.
- *Taxation.* Different countries have varying taxation rules, and the payroll department is an important player in managing immigration information.
- *Communication.* When employees leave to work in another country they often feel a disconnection from their home country. Wise companies use their intranet and the Internet to help these faraway employees keep in direct contact.

Human resource policies will be influenced more and more by conditions and practices in other countries and cultures. Human resource managers will need to move away from the assumed dominance and/or superiority of American business practices and sensitize themselves and their organizations to the cultural and business practices of other nations.

Sources: "Employee Benefits and Ownership Part 1," United Press International, March 16, 2002; and "Employee Benefits and Ownership, Part 2," United Press International, March 17, 2002.

Scheduling Employees to Meet Organizational and Employee Needs

By now, you are quite familiar with the trends occurring in the workforce that result in managers' and workers' demands regarding companies' flexibility and responsiveness. From these trends have emerged several new or renewed ideas such as flextime, in-home employment, and job sharing.[47] Let's see how these innovations affect the management of human resources.

Flextime Plans

flextime plan
Work schedule that gives employees some freedom to choose when to work, as long as they work the required number of hours.

core time
In a flextime plan, the period when all employees are expected to be at their job stations.

A **flextime plan** gives employees some freedom to choose when to work, as long as they work the required number of hours. The most popular plans allow employees to come to work between 7:00 and 9:00 AM and leave between 4:00 and 6:00 PM. Usually, flextime plans will incorporate what is called core time. **Core time** refers to the period when all employees are expected to be at their job stations. For example, an organization may designate core time as between 9:30 and 11:00 AM and between 2:00 and 3:00 PM. During these hours all employees are required to be at work (see Figure 11.6). Flextime plans, like job-sharing plans, are designed to allow employees to adjust to the demands of the times; two-income families find them especially helpful. The federal government has experimented extensively with flextime and found it to be a boost to employee productivity ➤P. 15◄ and morale.[48]

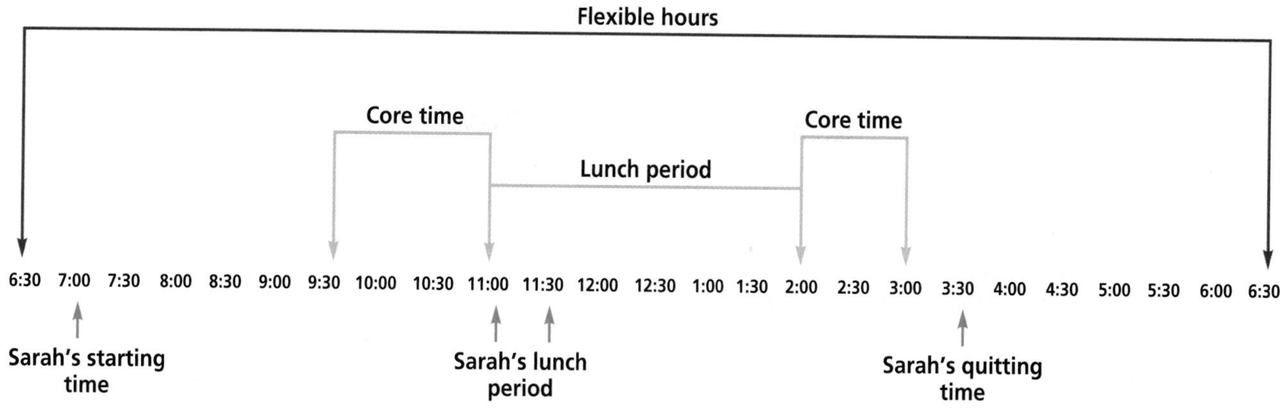

FIGURE 11.6

A FLEXTIME CHART

At this company, employees can start work anytime between 6:30 and 9:30 AM. They take a half hour for lunch anytime between 11:00 AM and 1:30 PM, and can leave between 3:00 and 6:30 PM. Everyone works an eight-hour day. The blue arrows show a typical employee's flextime day.

There are some real disadvantages to flextime as well. Flextime is certainly not for all organizations. For example, it cannot be offered in assembly line processes where everyone must be at work at the same time. It also is not effective for shift work.

Another disadvantage to flextime is that managers often have to work longer days in order to assist and supervise employees. Some organizations operate from 6:00 AM to 6:00 PM under flextime—a long day for supervisors. Flextime also makes communication more difficult; certain employees may not be there when others need to talk to them. Furthermore, if not carefully supervised, some employees could abuse the system, and that could cause resentment among others. You can imagine how you'd feel if half the workforce left at 3:00 PM on Friday and you had to work until 6:00 PM.

Another popular option used in approximately 24 percent of companies is a **compressed workweek.** That means that an employee works a full number of hours in less than the standard number of days. For example, an employee may work four 10-hour days and then enjoy a long weekend instead of working five 8-hour days with a traditional weekend. There are the obvious advantages of working only four days and having three days off, but some employees get tired working such long hours, and productivity could decline. Many employees find such a system of great benefit, however, and are quite enthusiastic about it.

compressed workweek
Work schedule that allows an employee to work a full number of hours per week but in fewer days.

Although many companies offer flexible schedules, few employees take advantage of them.[49] Most workers report that they resist using the programs because they fear it will hurt their careers. Managers signal (directly or indirectly) that employees who change their hours are not serious about their careers.

Home-Based and Other Mobile Work

As we noted in Chapter 1, telecommuting has grown tremendously in recent years. Nearly 10 million U.S. workers now work at least several days per month at home.[50] Home-based workers can choose their own hours, interrupt work for child care and other tasks, and take time out for various personal reasons. Working at home isn't for everyone, however. To be successful, a home-based worker must have the discipline to stay focused on the work and not be easily distracted.[51]

Telecommuting can be a cost saver for employers.[52] For example, IBM used to have a surplus of office space, maintaining more offices than there were employees. Now the company has cut back on the number of offices, with employees telecommuting, "hoteling" (being assigned to a desk through a reservations system), and "hot-desking" (sharing a desk with other employees at different times).[53] When Accenture, a technology and management consulting company, built its new headquarters, it added only 250 seats for 700 workers. By doing away with the concept of one seat per employee, Accenture spent half of what it

Tired of spending time doing your hair or finding a different outfit for work every day? Consider a job with JetBlue Airways. All of JetBlue's 600 reservations agents work from home through the company's virtual reservations center. Working from home or telecommuting can be a cost saver for companies as well as a welcomed option and benefit for employees. What do you think would be the biggest problem working from home?

would have cost for more conventional offices. When employees enter the Accenture office, they check a computer to find out where they've been assigned for the day. Depending on how much space they need, they might be in a cubicle, a small office, or a conference room. If they just need to make a quick phone call or check their e-mail, there are club chairs, phones, and Internet connections. Or they can hang out in the company's Internet café, which features a fireplace, a TV, a snack bar, and an outside terrace with Internet access at each table.[54] Figure 11.7 outlines the benefits and challenges of home-based work to organizations, individuals, and society.

Job-Sharing Plans

job sharing
An arrangement whereby two part-time employees share one full-time job.

Job sharing is an arrangement whereby two part-time employees share one full-time job. The concept has received great attention as more and more women with small children have entered the labor force. Job sharing enables parents to work only during the hours their children are in school. It has also proved beneficial to others with special needs, such as students and older people who want to work part-time before fully retiring. The benefits include

- Employment opportunities for those who cannot or prefer not to work full-time.
- A high level of enthusiasm and productivity.
- Reduced absenteeism and tardiness.
- Ability to schedule people into peak demand periods (e.g., banks on payday) when part-time people are available.
- Retention of experienced employees who might have left otherwise.

However, as you might suspect, disadvantages include having to hire, train, motivate, and supervise twice as many people and to prorate some fringe benefits. Nonetheless, most firms that were at first reluctant to try job sharing are finding that the benefits outweigh the disadvantages.

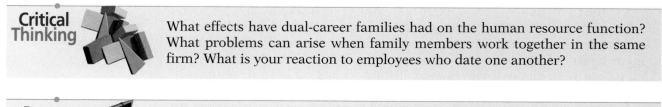

Critical Thinking

What effects have dual-career families had on the human resource function? What problems can arise when family members work together in the same firm? What is your reaction to employees who date one another?

Progress Assessment

- Can you name and describe five alternative compensation techniques?
- What advantages do compensation plans such as profit sharing offer an organization?
- What are the benefits and challenges of flextime? Telecommuting? Job sharing?

	BENEFITS	CHALLENGES
To organization	• Increases productivity due to fewer sick days, fewer absences, higher job satisfaction, and higher work performance ratings • Broadens available talent pool • Reduces costs of providing on-site office space	• Makes it more difficult to appraise job performance • Can negatively affect the social network of the workplace and can make it difficult to promote team cohesiveness • Complicates distribution of tasks (Should office files, contact lists, and such be allowed to leave the office?)
To individual	• Makes more time available for work and family by reducing or eliminating commute time • Reduces expenses of buying and maintaining office clothes • Avoids office politics • Helps balance work and family • Expands employment opportunities for disabled individuals	• Can cause feeling of isolation from social network • Can raise concerns regarding promotions and other rewards due to being "out of sight, out of mind" • May diminish individual's influence within company due to limited opportunity to learn the corporate culture
To society	• Decreases traffic congestion • Discourages community crime that might otherwise occur in bedroom communities • Increases time available to build community ties	• Increases need to resolve zoning regulations forbidding business deliveries in residential neighborhoods • May reduce ability to interact with other people in a personal, intimate manner

FIGURE 11.7

BENEFITS AND CHALLENGES OF HOME-BASED WORK

Home-based work (also known as telecommuting) offers many benefits and challenges to organizations, individuals, and to society as a whole.

Moving Employees Up, Over, and Out

Employees don't always stay in the position they were initially hired to fill. They may excel and move up the corporate ladder or fail and move out the front door. In addition to being moved through promotion and termination, employees can be moved by reassignment and retirement. Of course, employees often choose to move themselves by quitting and going to another company.

Promoting and Reassigning Employees

Many companies find that promotion from within the company improves employee morale. Promotions are also cost-effective in that the promoted employees already familiar with the corporate culture and procedures do not need to spend valuable time on basic orientation.

Due to the prevalence of flatter corporate structures, there are fewer levels for employees to reach now than there were in the past. Therefore, it is more common today for workers to move *over* to a new position than to move *up* to one. Such transfers allow employees to develop and display new skills and to learn more about the company overall. This is one way of motivating experienced employees to remain in a company with few advancement opportunities.

Terminating Employees

As we discussed in previous chapters, downsizing and restructuring, increasing customer demands for greater value, and the relentless pressure of global competition and shifts in technology have human resource managers struggling to manage layoffs and firings. Even companies that regain financial strength, however, are hesitant to rehire new full-time employees. Why? One reason is that the cost of terminating employees is prohibitively high. The cost of firing comes from lost training costs as well as damages and legal fees paid in wrongful discharge suits. To save money, many companies are either using temporary employees or outsourcing certain functions.

At one time the prevailing employment doctrine in the United States was "employment at will." This meant that managers had as much freedom to fire workers as workers had to leave voluntarily. Most states now have written employment laws that limit the at-will doctrine to protect employees from wrongful firing. For example, an employer can no longer fire an employee simply because that person exposed the company's illegal actions, refused to violate a law, or was a member of a minority or other protected group. This well-intended legislation restricted management's ability to terminate employees as it increased workers' rights to their jobs. In some cases, workers fired for using illegal drugs have sued on the ground that they have an illness (addiction) and are therefore protected by laws barring discrimination against the handicapped. See Figure 11.8 for advice about how to minimize the chance of wrongful-discharge lawsuits.

Retiring Employees

In addition to layoffs, another tool used to downsize companies is to offer early retirement benefits to entice older (and more expensive) workers to retire. Such benefits usually involve financial incentives such as one-time cash payments, known in some companies as *golden handshakes*. The advantage of offering early retirement benefits over laying off employees is that early

FIGURE 11.8

HOW TO AVOID WRONGFUL-DISCHARGE LAWSUITS

Consultants offer this advice to minimize the chance of a lawsuit for wrongful discharge:

- Prepare before hiring by requiring recruits to sign a statement that retains management's freedom to terminate at will.
- Don't make unintentional promises by using such terms as *permanent employment.*
- Document reasons before firing and make sure you have an unquestionable business reason for the firing.
- Fire the worst first and be consistent in discipline.
- Buy out bad risk by offering severance pay in exchange for a signed release from any claims.
- Be sure to give employees the true reasons they are being fired. If you do not, you cannot reveal it to a recruiter asking for a reference without risking a defamation lawsuit.
- Disclose the reasons for an employee's dismissal to that person's potential new employers. For example, if you fired an employee for dangerous behavior and you withhold that information from your references, you can be sued if the employee commits a violent act at his or her next job.

Sources: "In Economics Old and New, Treatment of Workers Is Paramount," *Washington Post,* February 11, 2001, p. L1; and www.us/aw.com.

retirement offers increase the morale of the surviving employees. Retiring senior workers also increases promotion opportunities for younger employees.

Losing Employees

In spite of a company's efforts to retain talented workers by offering flexible schedules, competitive salaries, and attractive fringe benefits, some employees will choose to pursue opportunities elsewhere. Learning about their reasons for leaving can be invaluable in preventing the loss of other good people in the future.[55] One way to learn the real reasons employees leave is to have a third party (not the employee's direct manager) conduct an exit interview. Harvard Pilgrim Health Care goes a step further—it offers a "knowledge bounty" of up to $5,000 for departing information left behind in a document or in a conversation with senior-level managers.[56]

LAWS AFFECTING HUMAN RESOURCE MANAGEMENT

Legislation has made hiring, promoting, firing, and managing employee relations in general very complex and subject to many legal complications and challenges. Let's see how changes in the law have expanded the role and the challenge of human resource management.

The U.S. government had little to do with human resource decisions until the 1930s. Since then, though, legislation and legal decisions have greatly affected all areas of human resource management, from hiring to training and working conditions (see the Legal Briefcase box on p. 354). These laws were passed because many businesses would not exercise fair labor practices voluntarily.

One of the more important pieces of social legislation passed by Congress was the Civil Rights Act of 1964. This act generated much debate and was actually amended 97 times before final passage. Title VII of that act brought the government directly into the operations of human resource management. Title VII prohibits discrimination in hiring, firing, compensation, apprenticeships, training, terms, conditions, or privileges of employment based on race, religion, creed, sex, or national origin. Age was later added to the conditions of the act. The Civil Rights Act of 1964 was expected to stamp out discrimination in the workplace. However, specific language in the act often made its enforcement quite difficult. With this in mind, Congress took on the task of amending the law.

In 1972, the Equal Employment Opportunity Act (EEOA) was added as an amendment to Title VII. It strengthened the Equal Employment Opportunity Commission (EEOC), which was created by the Civil Rights Act of 1964. Congress gave rather broad powers to the EEOC. For example, it permitted the commission to issue guidelines for acceptable employer conduct in administering equal employment opportunity. The EEOC also set forth specific recordkeeping procedures as mandatory. In addition, Congress vested the commission with the power of enforcement to ensure that these mandates were carried out. The EEOC became a formidable regulatory force in the administration of human resource management.

Probably the most controversial program enforced by the EEOC concerns **affirmative action;** that is, activities designed to "right past wrongs" by increasing opportunities for minorities and women. Interpretation of the affirmative-action law eventually led employers to actively recruit and give preference to qualified women and minority group members. Interpretation of the law has often been controversial, and enforcement difficult. Questions

affirmative action
Employment activities designed to "right past wrongs" by increasing opportunities for minorities and women.

www.eeoc.gov/welcome.html

Legal Briefcase: Government Legislation

National Labor Relations Act of 1935. Established collective bargaining in labor–management relations and limited management interference in the right of employees to have a collective bargaining agent.

Fair Labor Standards Act of 1938. Established a minimum wage and overtime pay for employees working more than 40 hours a week.

Manpower Development and Training Act of 1962. Provided for the training and retraining of unemployed workers.

Equal Pay Act of 1963. Specified that men and women doing equal jobs must be paid the same wage.

Civil Rights Act of 1964. Outlawed discrimination in employment based on sex, race, color, religion, or national origin. Applies to employers with 15 or more employees.

Age Discrimination in Employment Act of 1967. Outlawed personnel practices that discriminate against people ages 40 and above. An amendment outlaws company policies that require employees to retire by a specific age.

Occupational Safety and Health Act of 1970. Regulated the degree to which employees can be exposed to hazardous substances and specified the safety equipment to be provided by the employer.

Equal Employment Opportunity Act of 1972. Strengthened the Equal Employment Opportunity Commission (EEOC) and authorized the EEOC to set guidelines for human resource management.

Comprehensive Employment and Training Act of 1973. Provided funds for training unemployed workers. (Was known as the *CETA program.*)

Employee Retirement Income Security Act of 1974. Regulated company retirement programs and provided a federal insurance program for bankrupt retirement plans. (Known as *ERISA.*)

Immigration Reform and Control Act of 1986. Required employers to verify the eligibility for employment of *all* their new hires (including U.S. citizens).

Supreme Court ruling against set-aside programs (affirmative action), 1989. Declared that setting aside 30 percent of contracting jobs for minority businesses was reverse discrimination and therefore unconstitutional.

Older Workers Benefit Protection Act, 1990. Protects older people from signing away their rights to things like pensions or to fight against illegal age discrimination.

Civil Rights Act of 1991. Applies to firms with over 15 employees. It extends the right to a jury trial and punitive damages to victims of intentional job discrimination.

Americans with Disabilities Act of 1990 (1992 implementation). Prohibits employers from discriminating against qualified individuals with disabilities in hiring, advancement, or compensation, and requires them to adapt the workplace if necessary.

Family and Medical Leave Act of 1993. Businesses with 50 or more employees must provide up to 12 weeks of unpaid leave per year upon birth or adoption of an employee's child or upon serious illness of a parent, spouse, or child.

reverse discrimination
Discrimination against whites or males in hiring or promoting.

have persisted about the legality of affirmative action and the effect the program could have in creating a sort of reverse discrimination in the workplace. **Reverse discrimination** has been defined as discrimination against whites or males. Charges of reverse discrimination have occurred when companies have been perceived as unfairly giving preference to women or minority group members in hiring and promoting. The term has generated much heated debate.

The Civil Rights Act of 1991 expanded the remedies available to victims of discrimination by amending Title VII of the Civil Rights Act of 1964. Now victims of discrimination have the right to a jury trial and punitive damages. One still-open question is whether or not companies would have to establish "quotas" in hiring. Human resource managers continue to follow court cases closely to see how the law is enforced. This issue is likely to persist for years to come.

Laws Protecting the Disabled and Older Employees

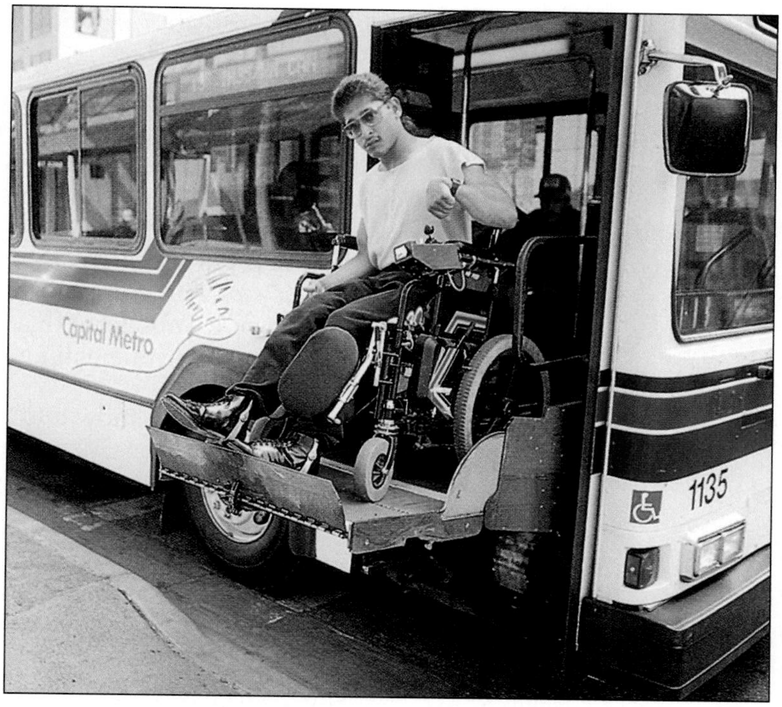

In 1990 the U.S. Congress made certain that all Americans are guaranteed equal opportunity by passing the Americans with Disabilities Act. Businesses, including public transportation systems, are required to make "reasonable accommodations" for persons with disabilities. How do laws like the Americans with Disabilities Act affect businesses?

The courts have continued their activity in issues involving human resource management. As you read above, the courts look carefully into any improprieties concerning possible discrimination in hiring, firing, training, and so forth specifically related to race or sex. The Vocational Rehabilitation Act of 1973 extended the same protection to people with disabilities. Today, businesses cannot discriminate against people on the basis of any physical or mental disability.

The Americans with Disabilities Act of 1990 (ADA) requires employers to give disabled applicants the same consideration for employment as people without disabilities. It also requires that businesses make "reasonable accommodations" for people with disabilities. This means doing such things as modifying equipment or widening doorways. Reasonable accommodations are not always expensive. For example, a company can provide an inexpensive headset that allows someone with cerebral palsy to talk on the phone.[57] The ADA also protects disabled individuals from discrimination in public accommodations, transportation, and telecommunications.[58]

Equal opportunity for people with disabilities promises to be a continuing issue into the next decade. Most companies are not having trouble making structural changes to be accommodating; what they are finding difficult are the cultural changes. Employers used to think being fair meant treating everyone the same. Now a key concept is *accommodation,* which means treating people according to their specific needs. In 1997, the EEOC issued new ADA guidelines that tell employers how they are supposed to treat workers and applicants with mental disabilities. The accommodations include putting up barriers to isolate people readily distracted by noise, reassigning workers to new tasks, and making changes in supervisors' management styles.

Older employees are also guaranteed protection against discrimination in the workplace. Courts have ruled against firms in unlawful-discharge suits where age appeared to be the major factor in the dismissal.[59] The Age Discrimination in Employment Act of 1967 (ADEA) protects individuals who are 40 years of age or older from employment discrimination based on age. The ADEA's protections apply to both employees and job applicants. Under the ADEA, it is unlawful to discriminate against a person because of age with respect to hiring, firing, promotion, layoff, compensation, benefits, job assignments, and training. The ADEA applies to employers with 20 or more employees. Additionally, the ADEA outlawed mandatory retirement in most organizations. It does allow age limits for certain professions if evidence shows the ability to perform a particular job significantly diminishes with age, or imposes a danger to society. This includes professions such as airline pilot and bus driver because research shows ability to perform these occupations decreases with age.

Effects of Legislation

Clearly, legislation affects all areas of human resource management. Such legislation ranges from the Social Security Act of 1935, to the Occupational Safety and Health Act of 1970, to the Employment Retirement Income Security Act of 1974. Human resource managers must read *The Wall Street Journal, Business Week,* and other current publications to keep up with all human resource legislation and rulings.

We have devoted so much space to civil rights and related legislation because such decisions have greatly affected human resource programs and will continue to do so. It's apparent that a career in human resource management offers a challenge to anyone willing to put forth the effort. In summary:

- Employers must know and act in accordance with the legal rights of their employees or risk costly court cases.
- Legislation affects all areas of human resource management, from hiring and training to compensating employees.
- Court cases have made it clear that it is sometimes legal to go beyond providing equal rights for minorities and women to provide special employment (affirmative action) and training to correct discrimination in the past.
- New court cases and legislation change human resource management almost daily; the only way to keep current is to read the business literature and become familiar with the issues.

Progress Assessment

Can you explain what was covered by the following laws?

- The Civil Rights Act of 1964.
- The Civil Rights Act of 1991.
- The Equal Employment Opportunity Act of 1972.
- The Americans with Disabilities Act of 1990.

Summary

1. Explain the importance of human resource management, and describe current issues in managing human resources.

1. Human resource management is the process of evaluating human resource needs, finding people to fill those needs, and getting the best work from each employee by providing the right incentives and job environment, all with the goal of meeting organizational objectives.
   - ***What are some of the current challenges and opportunities in the human resource area?***

   Many of the current challenges and opportunities revolve around the changing demographics of workers: more women, minorities, immigrants, and older workers. Other challenges concern a shortage of trained workers and an abundance of unskilled workers, skilled workers in declining industries requiring retraining, changing employee work attitudes, and complex laws and regulations.

2. Summarize the five steps in human resource planning.

2. Like all other types of management, human resource management begins with planning.

• ***What are the steps in human resource planning?***
The five steps are (1) preparing a human resource inventory of the organization's employees; (2) preparing a job analysis; (3) assessing future demand; (4) assessing future supply; and (5) establishing a plan for recruiting, hiring, educating, appraising, compensating, and scheduling employees.

3. Recruitment is the set of activities used to obtain a sufficient number of the right people at the right time to select those who best meet the needs of the organization.
   • ***What methods do human resource managers use to recruit new employees?***
   Recruiting sources are classified as either internal or external. Internal sources include hiring from within the firm (transfers, promotions, etc.) and employees who recommend others to hire. External recruitment sources include advertisements, public and private employment agencies, college placement bureaus, management consultants, professional organizations, referrals, walk-in applications, and the Internet.
   • ***Why has recruitment become more difficult?***
   Legal restrictions complicate hiring and firing practices. Finding suitable employees can also be made more difficult if companies are considered unattractive workplaces.

3. Describe methods that companies use to recruit new employees, and explain some of the issues that make recruitment challenging.

4. Selection is the process of gathering and interpreting information to decide which applicants should be hired.
   • ***What are the six steps in the selection process?***
   The steps are (1) obtaining complete application forms, (2) conducting initial and follow-up interviews, (3) giving employment tests, (4) conducting background investigations, (5) obtaining results from physical exams, and (6) establishing a trial period of employment.

4. Outline the six steps in selecting employees.

5. Employee training and development include all attempts to improve employee performance by increasing an employee's ability to perform through learning.
   • ***What are some of the activities used for training?***
   After assessing the needs of the organization and the skills of the employees, training programs are designed that may include the following activities: employee orientation, on- and off-the-job training, apprentice programs, online training, vestibule training, and job simulation. The effectiveness of the training is evaluated at the conclusion of the activities.
   • ***What methods are used to develop managerial skills?***
   Management development methods include on-the job-coaching, understudy positions, job rotation, and off-the-job courses and training.
   • ***How does networking fit in this process?***
   Networking is the process of establishing contacts with key managers within and outside the organization to get additional development assistance.

5. Illustrate the use of various types of employee training and development methods.

6. A performance appraisal is an evaluation of the performance level of employees against established standards to make decisions about promotions, compensation, additional training, or firing.
   • ***How is performance evaluated?***
   The steps are (1) establish performance standards; (2) communicate those standards; (3) evaluate performance; (4) discuss results; (5) take corrective action when needed; and (6) use the results for decisions about promotions, compensation, additional training, or firing.

6. Trace the six steps in appraising employee performance.

7. Summarize the objectives of employee compensation programs, and describe various pay systems and fringe benefits.

7. Employee compensation is one of the largest operating costs for many organizations.
   - ***What kind of compensation systems are used?***

   They include salary systems, hourly wages, piecework, commission plans, bonus plans, profit-sharing plans, and stock options.
   - ***What types of compensation systems are appropriate for teams?***

   The most common are gains-sharing and skill-based compensation programs. It is also important to reward outstanding individual performance within teams.
   - ***What are fringe benefits?***

   Fringe benefits include such items as sick leave, vacation pay, pension plans, and health plans that provide additional compensation to employees beyond base wages. Many firms offer cafeteria-style fringe benefits plans, in which employees can choose the benefits they want, up to a certain dollar amount.

8. Explain scheduling plans managers use to adjust to workers' needs.

8. Workers' increasing need for flexibility has generated new innovations in scheduling.
   - ***What scheduling plans can be used to adjust to employees' need for flexibility?***

   Such plans include job sharing, flextime, compressed workweeks, and working at home.

9. Describe the ways employees can move through a company: promotion, reassignment, termination, and retirement.

9. Employees often move from their original positions in a company.
   - ***How can employees move within a company?***

   Employees can be moved up (promotion), over (reassignment), or out (termination or retirement) of a company. Employees can also choose to leave a company to pursue opportunities elsewhere.

10. Illustrate the effects of legislation on human resource management.

10. There are many laws that affect human resource planning.
    - ***What are those laws?***

    See the Legal Briefcase box on page 354 and review the text section on laws. This is an important subject for future managers to study.

Key Terms

affirmative action 353
apprentice programs 339
cafeteria-style fringe benefits 346
compressed workweek 349
contingent workers 337
core time 348
employee orientation 339
flextime plan 348
fringe benefits 346
human resource management 330
job analysis 333
job description 333
job sharing 350
job simulation 340
job specifications 333
management development 341
mentor 341
networking 341
off-the-job training 340
online training 340
on-the-job training 339
performance appraisal 342
recruitment 334
reverse discrimination 354
selection 335
training and development 338
vestibule training 340

Developing Workplace Skills

1. Look in the classified ads in your local newspaper or on the Internet and find at least two positions that you might like to have when you graduate. List the qualifications specified in each of the ads. Identify methods the companies might use to determine how well applicants meet each of those qualifications.

2. Read several current business periodicals to find information on the latest court rulings involving fringe benefits, affirmative action, and other human resource issues. Compose a summary of your findings. What seems to be the trend? What will this mean for tomorrow's college graduates?

3. Recall the various training programs you have experienced. Think of both on-the-job and off-the-job training sessions. What is your evaluation of such programs? Write a brief critique of each. How would you improve them? Share your ideas with the class.

4. Consider these occupations: doctor, computer salesperson, computer software developer, teacher, and assembly worker. Identify the method of compensation you think is appropriate for determining the wages for each of these workers. Explain your answer.

5. Choose one of these positions: a human resource manager notifying employees of mandatory drug testing or an employee representative protesting such testing. Write a memorandum supporting your position.

Taking It To The Net 1

Purpose

To use job-search websites to identify employment options and to compare the services offered by several recruiting-related sites.

Exercise

There are many recruiting-related sites on the Internet. You can find links to such sites at Careers.org. Select three job-search websites. Use the search feature in each site to try to identify a position for which you might qualify after graduation. Find the website for the companies offering the jobs.

1. Do some job-search sites offer services that the others don't? Compare the strengths and weaknesses of each site from the perspective of both job seekers and employers. Include such criteria as variety of occupations in the database, volume of jobs, number of employers, geographical locations, ease of use, supplemental job hunting advice, and unique features.

2. What types of information did the individual companies' websites offer to attract potential employees?

Taking It To The Net 2

Purpose

The purpose of this exercise is twofold. From a manager's perspective, the purpose is to illustrate the types of questions managers typically ask during interviews. From an applicant's perspective, the purpose is to practice answering such questions in a safe environment.

Exercise

Go to Monster Campus at http://campus.monster.com. Answer the sample interview questions in the Virtual Interview section. This interactive section gives you the opportunity to test your answers so that when you do go on an actual interview you are less likely to fumble for an answer.

Casing The Web

To access the case "Dual-Career Planning," visit

www.mhhe.com/ub7e

SAS

Jeff Chambers is vice president of human resources at SAS, the world's largest privately owned software company. At such a company, employees are the most important asset because the company can't produce any software or provide any service without good, quality people. Part of Jeff's job is to find and keep such employees. Finding people who want to work at SAS isn't difficult; there are about 93,000 applicants for 500 jobs. The challenge is to screen those people to find those who fit in best.

The company assesses future labor requirements, prepares job analyses to see what various jobs entail, and then tries to find employees within the firm to meet those future needs. If they are not available, the company must search outside the firm to find the best people. Its strategic plan calls for interviewing, testing, and evaluating prospects. Spending more time in the hiring process means spending less time later trying to replace workers who were not a good fit in the firm.

In the future, there will be a great demand for skilled workers; thus, employee retention is critical at SAS. Evidence of how successfully the company retains people is the fact that turnover each year is about 4 percent, way below the industry average. One way to keep employees is to promote from within, and that means training people to move up within the organization. Such training includes in-house classes, online training, internships, and apprenticeships. Of course, managers get management training to keep them up to date and more qualified for promotion.

Keeping employees means more than providing them with a satisfying job and a good chance for promotion. It also means providing fringe benefits that employees want and need. That includes health care, day care, and an in-house recreation center. Medical insurance carries over to retired workers as well. SAS tries to accommodate the needs of individual workers as much as possible. If someone needs to take off early, he or she can. Employees can work from home (telecommuting) if they prefer. The company also has job sharing and flextime.

At a company like SAS, performance evaluations are very important. That's why the company doesn't use a simple form like so many others do. Instead, the company works closely with each employee to make sure the person understands the goals of the firm and how she or he fits into those goals.

SAS has a great relationship with its customers. The company spends 25 percent of its bottom line on research and development. Its quality products result in customer retention rates in the 98 percent range. The company treats its employees with the same care that it treats its customers. Because employees are so happy and turnover is so low, the company has more funds to invest in R&D and more happy customers. All this leads to more business and therefore the need to hire even more people.

Thinking It Over

1. What skills appear to be most important to getting hired at SAS: technical skills, people skills, team-building skills, or some combination? Which skills would you expect prospective workers to lack the most?
2. After watching this video, do you think that being a human resource manager at a high-tech firm would be an interesting and challenging job? Why or why not?
3. Is there more to human resource management than you first believed? What are some duties you hadn't previously anticipated for this position?

Chapter 12

Dealing with Employee–Management Issues and Relationships

Learning Goals

After you have read and studied this chapter, you should be able to

1. Trace the history of organized labor in the United States.
2. Discuss the major legislation affecting labor unions.
3. Outline the objectives of labor unions.
4. Describe the tactics used by labor and management during conflicts, and discuss the role of unions in the future.
5. Explain some of today's controversial employee–management issues, such as executive compensation; comparable worth; child care and elder care; AIDS testing, drug testing, and violence in the workplace; and employee stock ownership plans (ESOPs).

Getting to Know Paul Tagliabue, Commissioner of the National Football League

Paul Tagliabue learned early in his life about hard work and competition. In high school in Union City, New Jersey, he was an honor student and a highly recruited basketball player. His skill on the court earned him a scholarship to Georgetown University, where he majored in government and captained the basketball team. He was also president of his senior class, a Rhodes Scholar finalist, and a dean's list honor graduate. After Georgetown, he went on to New York University to study law on a public-service scholarship, and graduated with honors in 1965.

As a young lawyer in the mid to late 1960s, Tagliabue worked in the Pentagon on defense issues, specifically counterterrorism. In 1969, he moved on to Covington & Burling, a Washington, D.C., law firm that was the principal outside counsel for the National Football League (NFL). His involvement with the NFL began that same year. Over time, he became a close confidant of NFL commissioner Pete Rozelle. When Rozelle decided to step down as commissioner in 1989, Tagliabue (now a partner at Covington & Burling) was the choice to replace him.

Unfortunately, the NFL commissioner's job in the 1980s was by no means the respectable, glamorous position it once was under Rozelle. The league had to deal with legal difficulties due to antitrust lawsuits filed against it. In 1982 and 1987, the National Football League Players Association (NFLPA) walked out on strike, putting the league and the sport in considerable jeopardy. When Tagliabue assumed the commissioner's job in 1989, there was no promise of teamwork in the huddle.

Today, there is calm in the NFL and both players and owners are prospering. A labor agreement negotiated by Tagliabue in 1993 gave the players the freedom of free agency they had long sought and also provided the owners with a salary cap that kept player salaries from going out of sight as they have in professional baseball and basketball. Tagliabue believed the NFL's health and strength relied on fielding balanced teams. Today, the NFL is considered to have the best team balance in all of professional sports. In 2002, the NFLPA and owners signed a contract extension that will run through the 2007 season. The new agreement improved players' pension benefits, put some limits on off-season workouts, and made salary cap adjustments that should help high-priced veteran players compete more effectively for jobs. Commissioner Tagliabue also hired pro football hall of famer Mike Hayes as the NFL's vice president for player and employee development. His job is to keep players on the right path and prepare them for the often dramatic lifestyle change they experience when their football careers come to an end.

In 2002, Paul Tagliabue was ranked as the most powerful person in sports by the prestigious publication Sporting News *and honored as the Executive of the Year by the* Sports Business Journal.

In 2002, Paul Tagliabue was ranked as the most powerful person in sports by the prestigious publication *Sporting News* and honored as the Executive of the Year by the *Sports Business Journal.* He is heralded as a glowing example of modern professional sports management, in which players and owners can coexist and thrive in an industry often beset with problems. Professional sports, of course, is not the only industry that has problems dealing with labor–management relations, employee compensation, and other work-related issues. Managers in both profit-seeking and nonprofit organizations address these challenges every day. This chapter discusses employee–management issues and relationships such as labor unions, executive pay, comparable worth, elder care, ESOPs, and other issues that promise to dominate headlines and the business environment in the coming years.

Sources: Manny Topol, "A Super Commish: As Other Multi-Billion Corporations Struggle, Paul Tagliabue Has Made the Right Calls for the NFL," *Newsday,* January 25, 2003, p. F06; and Tom Lowry, "The NFL: The NFL Machine," *Business Week,* January 27, 2003, p. 86.

union
An employee organization that has the main goal of representing members in employee–management bargaining over job-related issues.

EMPLOYEE–MANAGEMENT ISSUES

The relationship between managers and employees has never been very smooth. Management has the responsibility of producing a profit through maximum productivity ➤P. 15◄. Managers have to make hard decisions that often do not let them win popularity contests. Labor (the collective term for nonmanagement workers) is interested in fair and competent management, human dignity, and a reasonable share in the wealth its work generates. Many issues affect the relationship between managers and labor: executive compensation, comparable worth, child care and elder care, AIDS testing and drug testing, violence in the workplace, and employee stock ownership plans (ESOPs). This chapter discusses such issues.

Like other managerial challenges, employee–management issues must be worked out through open discussion, goodwill, and compromise. It is important to know both sides of an issue, however, in order to make reasoned decisions. Any discussion of employee–management relations in the United States probably should begin with a discussion of labor unions. A **union** is an employee organization that has the main goal of representing members in employee–management bargaining over job-related issues. Workers originally formed unions to protect themselves from intolerable work conditions and unfair treatment. They also united to secure some say in the operations of their jobs. As the number of union members grew, workers gained more negotiating power with managers and more political power as well. Historically, employees turned to unions for assistance in gaining specific workplace rights and benefits. Labor unions were largely responsible for the establishment of minimum-wage laws, overtime rules, workers' compensation, severance pay, child-labor laws, job safety regulations, and more. Recently, however, union strength has waned. Throughout the 1990s and early 2000s, unions failed to regain the power they once had and membership continued to decline.[1] Business observers suggest that global competition, shifts from manufacturing to service and high-tech industries, growth in part-time work, and changes in management philosophies are some of the reasons for labor's decline. Some analysts also contend the decline is related to labor's success in seeing the issues it championed become law.

While many labor analysts forecast that unions will regain strength in the 21st century, others insist that unions have seen their brightest days.[2] Still, few

Are labor unions still necessary in the workplace? Union critics argue the dangerous conditions labor unions once fought against are no longer present. Many Hispanic workers may disagree. Here five Hispanic workers lost their lives when unsafe scaffolding collapsed in New York. Since 1992, 6,800 Hispanic workers have died on the job, often due to poor work conditions. What do you think the future of labor unions will be in the United States in the 21st century?

doubt that the role and position of unions in the workplace will continue to arouse emotions and opinions that contrast considerably. Let's briefly look at labor unions and then analyze other key issues affecting employee–management relations in the 21st century.

LABOR UNIONS FROM DIFFERENT PERSPECTIVES

Are labor unions essential in the American economy today? This question is certain to evoke emotional responses from various participants in the workplace. An electrician carrying a picket sign in New York might elaborate on the dangers to our free society if employers continue to try to bust, or break apart, authorized unions.[3] Small manufacturers would likely embrace a different perspective and complain about having to operate under union wage and benefit obligations in an increasingly global economy.

Most historians generally agree that today's unions are an outgrowth of the economic transition caused by the Industrial Revolution of the 19th and early 20th centuries. Workers who once toiled in the fields, dependent on the mercies of nature for survival, suddenly became dependent on the continuous roll of the factory presses and assembly lines for their living. Breaking away from an agricultural economy to form an industrial economy was quite difficult. Over time, workers learned that strength through unity (unions) could lead to improved job conditions, better wages, and job security.

Critics of organized labor maintain that few of the inhuman conditions that once dominated U.S. industry still exist in the workplace. They charge that organized labor has in fact become a large industrial entity in itself and that the real issue of protecting workers has become secondary. Critics also maintain that the current legal system and changing management philosophies minimize the chances that the sweatshops (workplaces with unsatisfactory and often unsafe or oppressive labor conditions) of the late 19th and early 20th centuries will reappear in the United States.[4] Unfortunately, sweatshops are present in other countries, and many workers around the world are struggling to gain the right to join unions.[5] A short discussion of the history of labor unions will cast a better light on the issues involved.

The Early History of Organized Labor

The presence of formal labor organizations in the United States dates back almost to the time of the American Revolution. As early as 1792, cordwainers (shoemakers) in Philadelphia met to discuss fundamental work issues of pay, hours, conditions, and job security—many of the same issues that dominate labor negotiations today. The cordwainers were a **craft union,** which is an organization of skilled specialists in a particular craft or trade.[6] They were typical of the labor organizations formed before the Civil War in that they were local or regional in membership. Also, most were established to achieve some short-range goal such as curtailing the use of convict labor as an alternative to available free labor (this is still an issue in some states). Often, after attaining a specific objective, the labor group disbanded. This situation changed dramatically in the late 19th century with the expansion of the Industrial Revolution.[7]

craft union
An organization of skilled specialists in a particular craft or trade.

The Industrial Revolution changed the economic structure of the United States. Enormous productivity increases gained through mass production and job specialization made the United States a true world economic power. This growth, however, brought problems for workers in terms of productivity expectations, hours of work, wages, and unemployment.

Workers were faced with the reality that production was vital. Anyone who failed to produce lost his or her job. People had to go to work even if they were ill or had family problems. Over time, the increased emphasis on production led firms to expand the hours of work. The length of the average workweek in 1900 was 60 hours, but an 80-hour week was not uncommon for some industries.[8] Wages were low, and the use of child labor was widespread. Minimum-wage laws and unemployment benefits were nonexistent, which meant that periods of unemployment were hard on families who earned subsistence wages. As you can sense, these were not short-term issues that would easily go away. The workplace was ripe for the emergence of national labor organizations.

Knights of Labor
The first national labor union; formed in 1869.

American Federation of Labor (AFL)
An organization of craft unions that championed fundamental labor issues; founded in 1886.

industrial unions
Labor organizations of unskilled and semiskilled workers in mass-production industries such as automobiles and mining.

Congress of Industrial Organizations (CIO)
Union organization of unskilled workers; broke away from the American Federation of Labor (AFL) in 1935 and rejoined it in 1955.

The first truly national labor organization was the **Knights of Labor,** formed by Uriah Smith Stephens in 1869. By 1886, the Knights claimed a membership of 700,000. The organization offered membership to all working people, including employers, and promoted social causes as well as labor and economic issues. The intention of the Knights was to gain significant *political* power and eventually to restructure the entire U.S. economy. The organization fell from prominence after being blamed for a bomb that killed eight policemen during a labor rally at Haymarket Square in Chicago in 1886.[9]

A rival group, the **American Federation of Labor (AFL),** was formed that same year. By 1890, the AFL, under the dynamic leadership of Samuel Gompers, stood at the forefront of the labor movement.[10] The AFL was an organization of craft unions that championed fundamental labor issues. It intentionally limited membership to skilled workers (craftspeople), assuming they would have better bargaining power than unskilled workers in attaining concessions from employers. It's important to note that the AFL was never one big union. Rather, it functioned as a federation of many individual unions that could become members yet keep their separate union status. Over time, an unauthorized AFL group, called the Committee of Industrial Organizations, began to organize workers in **industrial unions,** which consisted of unskilled and semiskilled workers in mass-production industries such as automobile manufacturing and mining.[11] John L. Lewis, president of the United Mine Workers, led this committee.

As a member of the Screen Actors Guild, Rob Schneider encouraged the public to boycott Procter & Gamble products when the company used nonunion workers in its commercials in place of striking members of the Screen Actors Guild. Boycotts or strikes are often used by unions if they fail to reach an agreement under collective bargaining. Why do unions and management typically work hard to prevent strikes?

Lewis's objective was to organize both craftspeople and unskilled workers. When the AFL rejected his proposal in 1935, Lewis broke away to form the **Congress of Industrial Organizations (CIO).** The CIO soon rivaled the AFL in membership, partly because of the passage of the National Labor Relations Act (also called the Wagner Act) that same year (see the next section). For 20 years, the two organizations struggled for power in the labor movement. It wasn't until passage of the Taft-Hartley Act in 1947 (discussed on p. 369) that the two organizations saw the benefits of a merger. In 1955, under the leadership of George Meany, 16 million labor members united to form the AFL-CIO. Today, the AFL-CIO includes affiliations with 66 national and international labor unions and has about 13 million members.[12]

Labor Legislation and Collective Bargaining

The growth and influence of organized labor in the United States have depended primarily on two major factors: the law and public opinion. Figure 12.1 out-

Norris-LaGuardia Act, 1932	Prohibited courts from issuing injunctions against nonviolent union activities; outlawed contracts forbidding union activities; outlawed the use of yellow-dog contracts by employers. (Yellow-dog contracts were contractual agreements forced on workers by employers whereby the employee agreed not to join a union as a condition of employment.)
National Labor Relations Act (Wagner Act), 1935	Gave employees the right to form or join labor organizations (or to refuse to form or join); the right to collectively bargain with employers through elected union representatives; and the right to engage in labor activities such as strikes, picketing, and boycotts. Prohibited certain unfair labor practices by the employer and the union, and established the National Labor Relations Board to oversee union election campaigns and investigate labor practices. This act gave great impetus to the union movement.
Fair Labor Standards Act, 1938	Set a minimum wage and maximum basic hours for workers in interstate commerce industries. The first minimum wage set was 25 cents an hour, except for farm and retail workers.
Labor–Management Relations Act (Taft-Hartley Act), 1947	Amended the Wagner Act; permitted states to pass laws prohibiting compulsory union membership (right-to-work laws); set up methods to deal with strikes that affect national health and safety; prohibited secondary boycotts, closed-shop agreements, and featherbedding (the requiring of wage payments for work not performed) by unions. This act gave more power to management.
Labor–Management Reporting and Disclosure Act (Landrum-Griffin Act), 1959	Amended the Taft-Hartley Act and the Wagner Act; guaranteed individual rights of union members in dealing with their union, such as the right to nominate candidates for union office, vote in union elections, attend and participate in union meetings, vote on union business, and examine union records and accounts; required annual financial reports to be filed with the U.S. Department of Labor. One goal of this act was to clean up union corruption.

FIGURE 12.1

MAJOR LEGISLATION AFFECTING LABOR–MANAGEMENT RELATIONS

lines five major federal laws that have had a significant impact on the rights and operations of labor unions. (Take a few moments to read the basics involved in each of these laws in Figure 12.1 before going on.)

The Norris-LaGuardia Act paved the way for union growth in the United States. This legislation prohibited employers from using contracts that forbid union activities such as yellow-dog contracts. A **yellow-dog contract** required employees to agree as a condition of employment not to join a union. However, it was passage of the National Labor Relations Act (or Wagner Act) that provided labor with clear legal justification to pursue key issues that were strongly supported by Samuel Gompers and the AFL.[13] One of these key issues, **collective bargaining**, is the process whereby union and management representatives negotiate a contract for workers. The Wagner Act expanded labor's right to collectively bargain, and obligated employers to meet at reasonable times and bargain in good faith with respect to wages, hours, and other terms and conditions of employment.[14] Gompers believed collective bargaining was critical to attaining a fairer share of the economic pie for workers. He further believed that collective bargaining would enhance the well-being of workers by improving conditions on the job.

yellow-dog contract
A type of contract that required employees to agree as a condition of employment not to join a union; prohibited by the Norris-LaGuardia Act in 1932.

collective bargaining
The process whereby union and management representatives form a labor–management agreement, or contract, for workers.

The Wagner Act also established an administrative agency, the National Labor Relations Board (NLRB), to oversee labor–management relations. Consisting of five members who are appointed by the president, the NLRB provides guidelines and offers legal protection to workers who seek to vote on organizing a union to represent them in the workplace. **Certification** is the formal process whereby a labor union is recognized by the NLRB as the authorized bargaining agent for a group of employees. Figure 12.2 describes the steps involved in a union-organizing campaign leading to certification. After the election, both the union and management have five days to contest the results of an election to the NLRB. The Wagner Act also provided workers with a clear

certification
Formal process whereby a union is recognized by the National Labor Relations Board (NLRB) as the bargaining agent for a group of employees.

FIGURE 12.2

STEPS IN UNION-ORGANIZING AND DECERTIFICATION CAMPAIGNS

Note that the final vote in each case requires that the union receive over 50 percent of the *votes cast.* Note, too, that the election is secret.

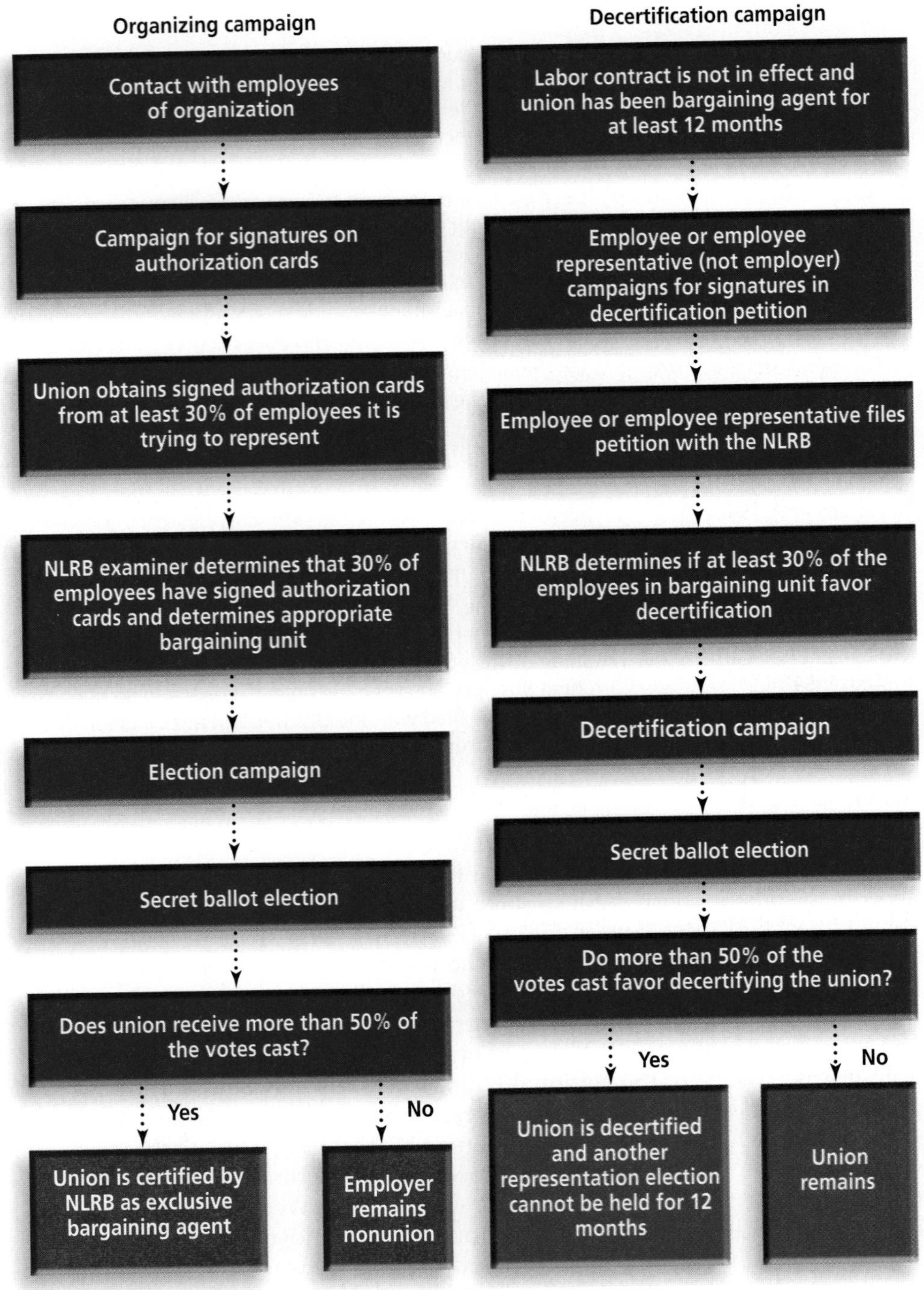

decertification
The process by which workers take away a union's right to represent them.

process to remove a union as the workers' representative. **Decertification,** also described in Figure 12.2, is the process by which workers can take away a union's right to represent them.

Objectives of Organized Labor

The objectives of labor unions frequently change because of shifts in social and economic trends. For example, in the 1970s the primary objective of labor unions was to obtain additional pay and benefits for their members. Throughout the 1980s, objectives shifted toward issues related to job security and union recognition. In the 1990s and early 2000s, unions again focused on job security, but the issue of global competition and its effects often took center stage. The AFL-CIO, for example, was a major opponent of the North American Free

1. Management rights	*d.* Overtime regulations
2. Union recognition	*e.* Leaves of absence
3. Union security clause	*f.* Break periods
4. Strikes and lockouts	*g.* Flextime
5. Union activities and responsibilities	*h.* Mealtime allotments
a. Dues checkoff	8. Job rights and seniority principles
b. Union bulletin boards	*a.* Seniority regulations
c. Work slowdowns	*b.* Transfer policies and bumping
6. Wages	*c.* Promotions
a. Wage structure	*d.* Layoffs and recall procedures
b. Shift differentials	*e.* Job bidding and posting
c. Wage incentives	9. Discharge and discipline
d. Bonuses	*a.* Suspension
e. Piecework conditions	*b.* Conditions for discharge
f. Tiered wage structures	10. Grievance procedures
7. Hours of work and time-off policies	*a.* Arbitration agreement
a. Regular hours of work	*b.* Mediation procedures
b. Holidays	11. Employee benefits, health, and welfare
c. Vacation policies	

FIGURE 12.3

ISSUES IN A NEGOTIATED LABOR–MANAGEMENT AGREEMENT

Labor and management often meet to discuss and clarify the terms that specify employees' functions within the company. The topics listed in this figure are typically discussed during these meetings.

Trade Agreement (NAFTA) passed by Congress in 1994; the organization feared its members would lose their jobs to low-wage workers in other countries. The AFL-CIO also opposed Congress's decision to normalize trade relations with China in 2000, which led to China's acceptance into the WTO.[15] Labor was again on the losing end when it encouraged Congress in 2002 to deny President George W. Bush's request to speed up trade agreements through what is called fast-track legislation; President Bush got his request.[16]

The **negotiated labor–management agreement,** more informally referred to as the labor contract, sets the tone and clarifies the terms and conditions under which management and organized labor will function over a specific period. Negotiations cover a wide range of topics and can often take a long time. Figure 12.3 provides a list of topics commonly negotiated by labor and management during contract talks.

Labor unions generally insist that a contract contain a union security clause. A **union security clause** stipulates that employees who reap benefits from a union must either officially join or at least pay dues to the union. After passage of the Wagner Act, labor unions sought strict security in the form of the closed shop agreement. A **closed shop agreement** specified that workers had to be members of a union before being hired for a job. To labor's dismay, the Labor–Management Relations Act (Taft-Hartley Act) outlawed this practice in 1947 (see Figure 12.4). Today, labor unions clearly favor the union shop agreement as the most effective means of ensuring workers' security. Under the **union shop agreement,** workers do not have to be members of a union to be hired for a job, but must agree to join the union within a prescribed period (usually 30, 60, or 90 days). However, under a contingency called an **agency shop agreement,** employers may hire nonunion workers; these workers are not required to join the union, but must pay a special union fee or pay regular union dues. Labor unions argue that such fees or dues are justified because the union represents all workers in collective bargaining, not just the union's members.

The Taft-Hartley Act recognized the legality of the union shop but granted individual states the power to outlaw such agreements through passage of

negotiated labor–management agreement (labor contract)
Agreement that sets the tone and clarifies the terms under which management and labor agree to function over a period of time.

union security clause
Provision in a negotiated labor–management agreement that stipulates that employees who benefit from a union must either officially join or at least pay dues to the union.

closed shop agreement
Clause in a labor–management agreement that specified workers had to be members of a union before being hired (was outlawed by the Taft-Hartley Act in 1947).

union shop agreement
Clause in a labor–management agreement that says workers do not have to be members of a union to be hired, but must agree to join the union within a prescribed period.

agency shop agreement
Clause in a labor–management agreement that says employers may hire nonunion workers; employees are not required to join the union but must pay a union fee.

FIGURE 12.4

DIFFERENT FORMS OF UNION AGREEMENTS

TYPE OF AGREEMENT	DESCRIPTION
Closed shop	The Taft-Hartley Act made this form of agreement illegal. Under this type of labor agreement, employers could hire only current union members for a job.
Union shop	The majority of labor agreements are of this type. In a union shop, the employer can hire anyone, but as a condition of employment, employees hired must join the union to keep their jobs.
Agency shop	Employers may hire anyone. Employees need not join the union, but are required to pay a union fee. A small percentage of labor agreements are of this type.
Open shop	Union membership is voluntary for new and existing employees. Those who don't join the union don't have to pay union dues. Few union contracts are of this type.

right-to-work laws
Legislation that gives workers the right, under an open shop, to join or not join a union if it is present.

open shop agreement
Agreement in right-to-work states that gives workers the option to join or not join a union, if one exists in their workplace.

right-to-work laws.[17] To date, 22 states have passed such legislation (see Figure 12.5). In a right-to-work state, an **open shop agreement** exists that gives workers the option to join or not join a union, if one is present in the workplace. Furthermore, if they choose not to join the certified union in their workplace, they cannot be forced to pay a fee or dues to the union. (The Casing the Web case at www.mhhe.com/ub7e discusses the Taft-Hartley Act in depth.)

In the future, the focus of union negotiations will most likely shift as issues such as child and elder care, worker retraining, two-tiered wage plans, outsourcing ➤P. 257◀, employee empowerment ➤P. 20◀, and even integrity and honesty testing further challenge union members' rights in the workplace. Unions also intend to carefully monitor immigration policies and global agreements such as NAFTA to see that U.S. jobs are not lost.[18]

Labor unions play a key workplace role in countries other than the United States as well. In Europe organized labor is a major force throughout the continent. Unions in Europe have historically had a good deal more influence in the workplace than unions have in the United States.[19] The Reaching Beyond Our Borders box discusses a formidable challenge the European Union faces with its unions as it works toward the goals of regional unity and a single currency, the euro.

Resolving Labor–Management Disagreements

The rights of labor and management are outlined in the negotiated labor–management agreement. Upon acceptance by both sides, the agreement becomes a guide to work relations between union members and managers. However, signing the agreement doesn't necessarily end the employee–management negotiations. There are sometimes differences concerning interpretations of the labor–management agreement. For example, managers may interpret a certain clause in the agreement to mean that they are free to select who works overtime. Union members may interpret the same clause to mean that managers must select employees for overtime on the basis of employee seniority. If controversies such as this cannot be resolved between the two parties, employees may file a grievance.

grievance
A charge by employees that management is not abiding by the terms of the negotiated labor–management agreement.

A **grievance** is a charge by employees that management is not abiding by or fulfilling the terms of the negotiated labor–management agreement according to how they perceive it. Overtime rules, promotions, layoffs, transfers, job assignments, and so forth are generally sources of employee grievances. Handling such grievances demands a good deal of contact between union officials

Reaching Beyond Our Borders

The Euro Strikes Out with the Unions

www.europa.eu.int

On January 1, 2002, cash registers rang out across Europe officially launching the euro, the new joint currency of 12 member nations of the European Union (EU). Businesses boasted that they would save billions on the currency conversions that had to be made prior to the euro. Other supporters cheered the euro as an economic elixir that would improve European competitiveness and provide an economic edge in the global economy. Well, the cheering has stopped, at least among many of the labor unions in the EU.

The euro lays bare comparative wage costs across Europe. Labor unions (and some economists) believe this will inevitably lead to greater competition among workers in the EU. The problem is that the hourly wage rate varies greatly among the member countries of the EU. Wages in France are about 25 percent below those in Germany but 30 percent above those in Spain. Ireland has labor costs double those of Portugal but one-third lower than those of the Netherlands. It's these wage differences that cause unions to fear that competitive pressures will encourage companies to go from country to country to test how far down they can get wages. Labor unions in high-wage countries such as Germany, the Netherlands, and Belgium view the presence of a single currency as a threat to their members.

Reiner Hoffman, director of the European Trade Union Institute in Brussels, argues, "Labor unions do not want to fall into a trap in which we compete with each other in Europe to undercut wages. This is what the euro could force us to do."

For the first time in European history, there have been discussions of transnational collective bargaining to reach common salary and benefits among union members. However, even the most strident labor leaders admit that common salary and benefit policies would be difficult to implement across national borders. Plus, low-wage nations are less than eager for such talks because they hope that their low wages will help attract new businesses and new jobs.

The unions are firm in their resolve and promise to fight on toward common salaries that would protect current high-wage workers and press countries to compete for new businesses on the basis that their workers are productive rather than cheap.

Sources: Laura D'andrea Tyson, "Why Europe Is Even More Sluggish Than the U.S.," *Business Week,* January 13, 2003, p. 26; "Portugal's Labor Cost Lowest in the EU," Xinhua News Agency, March 6, 2003; Michael Heise, "Europe Misses the Point," *Newsweek International,* January 27, 2003, p. 39.

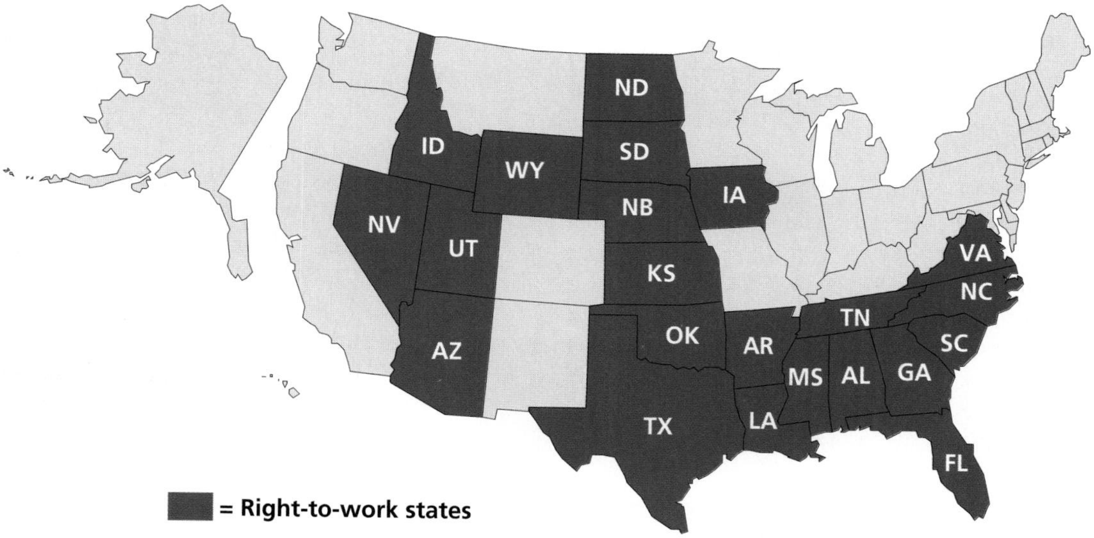

FIGURE 12.5

STATES WITH RIGHT-TO-WORK LAWS

and managers. Grievances, however, do not imply that a company has broken the law or the labor agreement. In fact, the vast majority of grievances are negotiated and resolved by **shop stewards** (union officials who work permanently in an organization and represent employee interests on a daily basis) and supervisory-level managers. However, if a grievance is not settled at this level, formal grievance procedures will begin. Figure 12.6 illustrates the different steps the formal grievance procedure could follow.

shop stewards
Union officials who work permanently in an organization and represent employee interests on a daily basis.

Mediation and Arbitration

During the negotiation process, there is generally what's called a **bargaining zone,** which is a range of options between the initial and final offer that each party will consider before negotiations dissolve or reach an impasse. If labor–management negotiators aren't able to agree on alternatives within this bargaining zone, mediation may be necessary. **Mediation** is the use of a third party, called a mediator, who encourages both sides in a dispute to continue negotiating and often makes suggestions for resolving the dispute. However, it's important to remember that mediators evaluate facts in the dispute and then make suggestions, not decisions. Elected officials (current and past), attorneys, and college professors are often called on to serve as mediators in labor disputes. The National Mediation Board provides federal mediators when requested by both sides in a dispute. America West Airlines and the Allied Pilots Association asked for such assistance in negotiating a new contract after airline demand was slashed after the terrorist attacks of September 11, 2001.[20]

bargaining zone
Range of options between the initial and final offer that each party will consider before negotiations dissolve or reach an impasse.

mediation
The use of a third party, called a mediator, who encourages both sides in a dispute to continue negotiating and often makes suggestions for resolving the dispute.

FIGURE 12.6

THE GRIEVANCE RESOLUTION PROCESS

The grievance process may move through several steps before the issue is resolved. At each step, the issue is negotiated between union officials and managers. If no resolution comes internally, an outside arbitrator may be mutually agreed on. If so, the decision by the arbitrator is binding (legally enforceable).

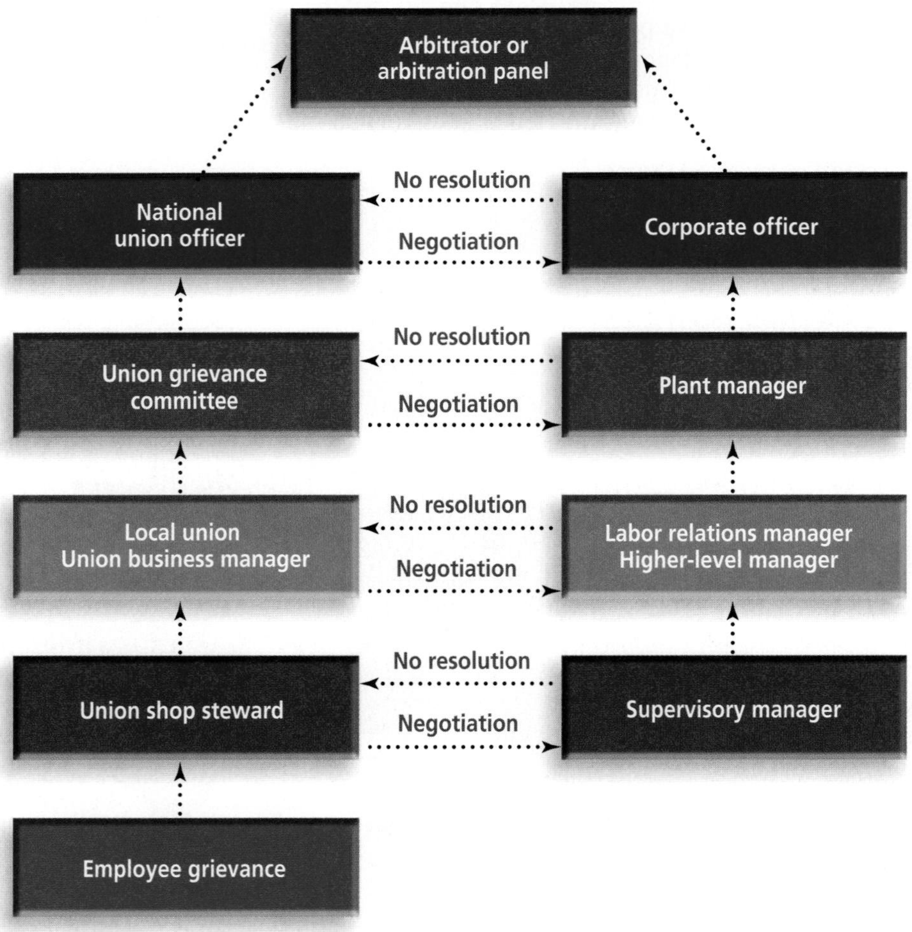

A more extreme option used to resolve labor–management conflicts is arbitration. **Arbitration** is an agreement to bring in an impartial third party (a single arbitrator or a panel of arbitrators) to render a binding decision in a labor dispute.[21] You may have heard of baseball players filing for arbitration to resolve a contract dispute with their teams.[22] Many of the negotiated labor–management agreements in the United States call for the use of an arbitrator to end labor disputes. The arbitrator must be acceptable to both labor and management. The nonprofit American Arbitration Association is the dominant organization used in dispute resolution.

Sometimes, negotiators from labor unions and management fail to reach an agreement and want to snap each other's head off. If that happens, it often makes sense to enlist the services of an arbitrator to resolve the impasse. An arbitrator must be acceptable to both sides and the decision reached is binding. The American Arbitration Association has assisted in dispute resolution for over 75 years. What type of person would make a good arbitrator?

Tactics Used in Labor–Management Conflicts

If labor and management reach an impasse in collective bargaining and negotiations break down, either side or both sides may use specific tactics to enhance their position and perhaps sway public opinion. The primary tactics used by organized labor are the strike and the boycott. Unions might also use pickets and work slowdowns to get desired changes. Management, for its part, may implement lockouts, injunctions, and even strikebreakers. The following sections look briefly at each of these contrasting tactics.

Union Tactics

The strike has historically been the most potent tactic unions use to achieve their objectives in labor disputes. A **strike** occurs when workers collectively refuse to go to work. Strikes can attract public attention to a labor dispute and at times cause operations in a company to slow down or totally cease. You may remember the delivery slowdowns caused by the United Parcel Service (UPS) strike in 1997. You may also recall that things were not too sweet at Hershey Foods when 2,700 members of Chocolate Workers Local 464 walked out on strike in 2002.[23] Besides refusing to work, strikers may also picket the company, which means that they walk around the outside of the organization carrying signs and talking with the public and the media about the issues in the labor dispute. Unions also use picketing as an informational tool before going on strike. The purpose is to alert the public to an issue that is stirring labor unrest even though no strike has been voted.

Strikes have often led to resolution of a labor dispute; however, they also have generated violence and extended bitterness when emotions on both sides reached a boiling point. The United Auto Workers' 17-month strike against Caterpillar in the 1990s, for example, caused a great deal of bitterness, some of which still exists today. Even after the strike was finally settled, both labor and management remained openly hostile toward each other and mutual complaints of violations of the negotiated labor–management agreement continued. The same is true of the Teamsters strike against Overnite Transit Company, which began in 1999 and was not ended until 2003.[24]

arbitration
The agreement to bring in an impartial third party (a single arbitrator or a panel of arbitrators) to render a binding decision in a labor dispute.

strike
A union strategy in which workers refuse to go to work; the purpose is to further workers' objectives after an impasse in collective bargaining.

This crowd on Chocolate Street in Hershey, Pennsylvania, was not very sweet on this day. Hershey workers displayed a large balloon rat they named Lenny (after Hershey CEO Richard Lenny) as they picketed the firm's factory. The workers went on strike to protest the company's decision to increase the cost of employee health insurance. After a six-week strike the union and company reached a compromise. How do you think the strike affected the relationship of employees and managers?

The public often realizes how important a worker is when he or she goes on strike. Imagine what an economic and social disaster it would be if a town's police force or doctors and nurses at a large hospital went on strike. That's why many states prohibit such job actions as strikes even though state and other public safety workers can be unionized. Nonetheless, police officers, firefighters, teachers, and others sometimes exert their frustrations by engaging in "sick-outs" (often called the blue flu)—union members don't strike, but they do refuse to come to work on the pretext of illness. Employees of the federal government, such as postal workers, can organize unions but are also denied the right to strike.

Under the provisions of the Taft-Hartley Act, the president can ask for a cooling-off period to prevent a strike in what's considered a critical industry. During a **cooling-off period,** workers return to their jobs while the union's bargaining team and management continue negotiations. The cooling-off period can last up to 80 days. Bill Clinton became the first U.S. president to use this provision in 19 years when he halted an American Airlines pilots' strike in 1997. In 2002, President George W. Bush ordered cooling-off periods to prevent a strike by disgruntled mechanics at United Airlines and to force locked-out dockworkers to return to work on the West Coast.[25] The Dealing with Change box describes the dockworker union's conflicts with management.

cooling-off period
When workers in a critical industry return to their jobs while the union and management continue negotiations.

Both labor and management seek to avoid strikes if at all possible, and very few labor disputes lead to a strike. Social perceptions and attitudes, however, can also affect the potential for strikes. For example, after President Ronald Reagan fired striking air traffic controllers in 1981 (for violating the Public Employees Relations Act) and broke their union, other unions then hesitated to strike. The Major League Baseball Players strike that canceled the World Series in 1994 was not only unpopular among fans and the general public but also caused additional hostilities toward strikes. Labor unions clearly felt that the mood of the country was against them. The successful UPS strike in 1997, however, changed organized labor's aversion to strike. Since then,

Dealing with Change

Sitting on the Docks

www.ilwu.org

Nobody wants to lose his or her job to new technology. More than 400 jobs were threatened in the fall of 2002 when shipping managers on the West Coast wanted to upgrade container-tracking technology with scanners and other computer-aided devices. Until then, containers being moved onboard ships and on docks were tracked by longshore clerks who manually entered information into the shippers' databases. With their members' jobs at risk, the dockworkers union went into action—or, as the managers saw it, the union went into *inaction*. Shipping managers accused the dockworkers of intentionally slowing work down to a crawl and thus interrupting the flow of goods into the United States. The union denied the claims, saying that they simply told their workers to work at a safer speed since five dockworkers died in work-related accidents earlier in the year.

The management initiated a lockout of all dockworkers in response to the work slowdown. Shipping on the West Coast came to a complete halt. With billions of dollars' worth of perishable goods rotting on ships and countless other goods unable to be delivered to shore, the U.S. economy was in danger of losing \$1–\$2 billion a day. The critical Christmas shopping season was about to begin with literal boatloads of merchandise stranded at sea rather than stocking store shelves. The Bush administration considered this economic loss a risk to national security and therefore invoked the Taft-Hartley Act. Dockworkers were ordered back to work, and both sides were ordered back to the bargaining table under the Taft-Hartley Act's 80-day cooling-off period.

After the 12-day lockout and months of collective bargaining, the International Longshore and Warehouse Union ratified a new six-year contract. The agreement allows shippers to use the new technology. Although 400 jobs will be eliminated, the affected workers will be retrained for other positions rather than being let go. The union maintains control over the remaining positions as well as any new ones created via the technology. While salary increases were not a major issue, the agreement raises salaries approximately 12 percent, making the average dockworker's salary around \$90,000 a year. Pension benefits increased 60 percent, and employers are required to absorb the total bill for the skyrocketing health care costs they had hoped to have the workers help cover.

"I think both sides, in very general terms, got what they wanted to get," said William Gould, former chair of the National Labor Relations Board. "The unions got job security and enhanced income for those who are contemplating retirement, and the employers got technological innovation." And since dockworkers unloaded enough products to stock the nation's stores in time for the Christmas shopping season, most shoppers got what they wanted for Christmas.

Sources: Paul Nyhan, "Dockworkers Vote to Ratify Contract by 89% Margin," *Seattle Post-Intelligencer,* January 23, 2003; David Bacon, "Dockworkers' Contract Postpones Crucial Jurisdiction Questions," *Labor Notes,* February 2003; and "West Coast Dockworkers Vote on Contract," Reuters Business, January 6, 2003.

possible strikes and other labor–management confrontations involving highly visible businesses such as major-league baseball have become news.[26] As technological change, the Internet economy, and reductions in worker benefits such as health insurance continue to alter the traditional workplace, it's unlikely that labor disputes in the 21st century will disappear.[27] Strikes in air and ground transportation, publishing, telecommunications, aerospace and auto manufacturing, overnight delivery, and professional sports have illustrated that the strike is not yet dead as a labor tactic.

Unions also use boycotts as a means to obtain their objectives in a labor dispute. Boycotts can be classified as primary or secondary. A **primary boycott** occurs when organized labor encourages both its members and the general public not to buy the products of a firm involved in a labor dispute. A **secondary boycott** is an attempt by labor to convince others to stop doing business with a firm that is the subject of a primary boycott. For example, a union could initiate a secondary boycott against a supermarket chain because that chain carries goods produced by a company that's the target of a primary boycott. Labor unions can legally authorize primary boycotts, but the Taft-Hartley Act prohibits the use of secondary boycotts.

primary boycott
When a union encourages both its members and the general public not to buy the products of a firm involved in a labor dispute.

secondary boycott
An attempt by labor to convince others to stop doing business with a firm that is the subject of a primary boycott; prohibited by the Taft-Hartley Act.

Longshoreman Steve Christensen waves to supporters while holding a sign expressing his displeasure at being locked out of his job. Steve and other West Coast dockworkers at 29 ports were locked out by the Pacific Maritime Association, which claimed workers were slowing down at their jobs to protest the company's intention to use computerized cargo tracking. What does a company hope to accomplish by locking workers out of their jobs?

Management Tactics

Like labor, management also uses specific tactics to achieve its workplace goals. Historically, to thwart union membership, management used yellow-dog contracts until they were declared illegal. A **lockout** is an attempt by managers to put pressure on union workers by temporarily closing the business. If workers are not working, they are not paid. Today, management rarely uses lockouts as a tactic to achieve its contract objectives. However, the lockout of West Coast dockworkers in 2002 (see again the Dealing with Change box) and the high-profile lockout of National Basketball Association (NBA) players by the owners in 1998–99 remind us the lockout is not dead. Still, management today most often uses injunctions and strikebreakers to defeat labor demands it sees as excessive.

An **injunction** is a court order directing someone to do something or to refrain from doing something. Management has sought injunctions to order striking workers back to work, limit the number of pickets that can be used during a strike, or otherwise deal with actions that could be detrimental to the public welfare. For a court to issue an injunction, management must show a "just cause," such as the possibility of violence or the destruction of property. The use of strikebreakers has been a particular source of hostility and violence in labor relations. **Strikebreakers** (called scabs by unions) are workers who are hired to do the jobs of striking employees until the labor dispute is resolved. Employers have had the right to replace strikers since a 1938 Supreme Court ruling, but it wasn't until the 1980s that this tactic was frequently used. Be sure to read the Making Ethical Decisions box, which deals with this issue.

lockout
An attempt by management to put pressure on unions by temporarily closing the business.

injunction
A court order directing someone to do something or to refrain from doing something.

strikebreakers
Workers hired to do the jobs of striking workers until the labor dispute is resolved.

givebacks
Concessions made by union members to management; gains from labor negotiations are given back to management to help employers remain competitive and thereby save jobs.

The Future of Unions and Labor–Management Relations

Many new labor–management issues have emerged that affect labor unions and management relations. Increased global competition, advancing technology, and the changing nature of work have threatened or altered the jobs of many workers. To save jobs, many unions have granted concessions, or **givebacks,** to management. In such acts, union members give back previous gains from labor negotiations. For example, unions at airlines such as US Airways, United, and American Airlines agreed to give back previous workplace gains just to keep the airlines flying.

To grow, unions will have to include more white-collar, female, and foreign-born workers than they have traditionally included. The AFL-CIO, for example, plans to specifically target membership campaigns to women in relatively low-paying fields, such as health care and garment sewing. The number of women in labor unions increased to slightly over 6.8 million in 2002.[28] Other union efforts are focused on organizing contingent workers ➤P. 337◄ like freelancers, temporary employees, telecommuters, and high-tech consultants. Today, the largest labor organization in the United States is the National Education Association (NEA), which represents almost 2.7 million members.[29] The Spotlight on Small Business box on p. 378 discusses the movement of nurses and doctors toward union membership.

Making Ethical Decisions *www.ethics.ubc.ca/resources/business*

Crossing the Line or Double-Crossing

Assume you read over the weekend that More-4-Less, a local grocery chain in your town, is seeking workers to replace members of the Commercial Food Workers Union who are currently on strike against the company. Some of the students at your college are employed at More-4-Less and are supporting the strike, as are several people employed by the company in your neighborhood. More-4-Less argues that its management has made a fair offer to the union and that the demands of the workers are clearly excessive and could ruin the company. More-4-Less is offering an attractive wage rate and flexible schedules to workers willing to cross the picket line and come to work during the strike. As a student, you could certainly use the job and the extra money for tuition and expenses. What would you do? What will be the consequences of your decision? Is your choice ethical?

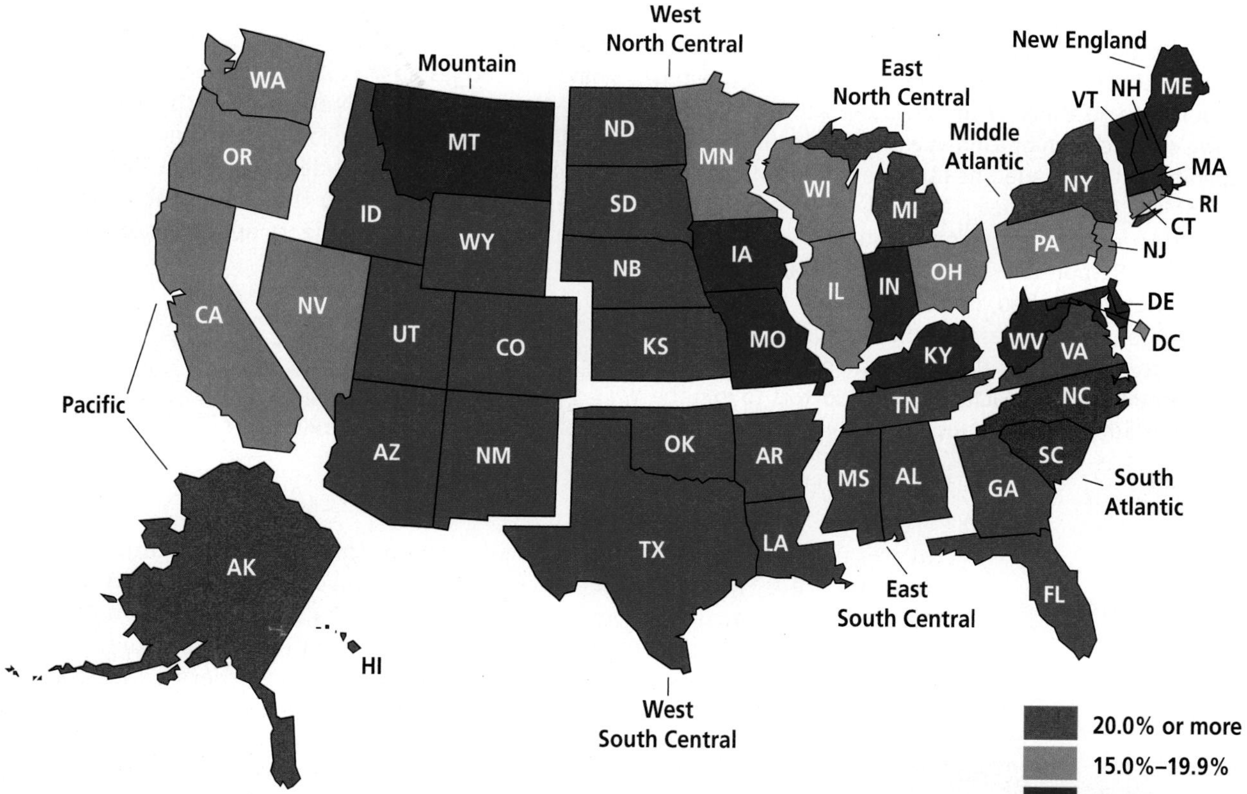

FIGURE 12.7

UNION MEMBERSHIP BY STATE

Source: www.afl.cio.com, 2003.

Organized labor is at a crossroads. Membership in the United Auto Workers has decreased by 60 percent, or 420,000 jobs, since 1979.[30] The unionized share of the workforce has declined from a peak of 35.5 percent in 1945 to just 13.2 percent today.[31] Only 9 percent of workers in the private sector are unionized, and union membership by state varies considerably (see Figure 12.7). It's safe to assume that the role of unions in the 21st century is likely to be quite different from their role in the past. Union leaders and members are aware that U.S. firms must remain competitive with foreign firms. Organized labor knows it must do its best to maintain U.S. competitiveness. In the

Spotlight on Small Business

www.4prn.com

The ER Meets the Teamsters

Last year, a group of workers led by a former Teamsters union representative marched into an office building demanding to see the head of a trade association. The workers roamed through the hallways and made quite a ruckus. Teamster roughnecks, you assume? Hardly. The workers were registered nurses and members of the 38,000-plus-member California Nurses Association. The nurses were upset over cost-cutting at health maintenance organizations (HMOs). Expectations are that nurses at more than 150 U.S. hospitals will petition for union representation this year. The United Nurses Association (UAN) joined the AFL-CIO in 2001.

Ever thought about going to the doctor and asking to see a union card before saying "Ahhh"? This is not as absurd as you think. Many private-practice physicians have embraced unionizing as a means to collective bargaining with managed health care organizations such as HMOs. The American Medical Association (AMA) launched a physicians union in late 1999 called Physicians for Responsible Negotiations (PRN). When the union was established, doctors promised that if physicians organized and bargained collectively, they would never go on strike or threaten patient care. The PRN also promised not to actively solicit doctors to join the union as other labor groups do.

However, in 2002, the AMA's policymaking body decided to cease financial support to the union pending settlement of key legal cases. According to antitrust law, competitors in an industry are prohibited from joining together to set prices and work conditions. Still, medical societies with a combined membership of 75,000 U.S. doctors back the union. With growing pressure from physicians concerning patient treatment and malpractice issues, the possibility of physicians organizing remains strong.

The number of union members in this industry could grow significantly in the years ahead even though federal antitrust provisions currently prohibit many nurses and doctors from unionizing. The AMA has even suggested that it may lobby Congress to lift the antitrust ban for all doctors, which would mean that 500,000 doctors could bargain collectively. Maybe someday the president of the AFL-CIO may be called away from leading the annual Labor Day parade to perform an emergency appendectomy or deliver a baby.

Sources: Lindsey Tanner, "Doctors Union Battles for Survival," AP Online, May 5, 2002; Lindy Washburn, "Doctors Clamor for Reforms," *Bergen County (New Jersey) Record,* February 5, 2003, p. A1; Laura Parker, "Surgeons' Strike Forces Hospitals to Juggle Service," *USA Today,* January 3, 2003, p. 3A.

future, unions and management will face compromises and confrontations. In many ways, labor unions have already taken on a new role in assisting management in training workers, redesigning jobs, and assimilating the 21st century workforce; that is, unions are helping recruit and train foreign workers, unskilled workers, former welfare recipients, and others who need special help in adapting to the job requirements of the new economy. Business has witnessed such cooperation already at companies like Saturn and Southwest Airlines, where unions have taken a leadership role with management in making things happen.

Bruce Raynor, the president of the Union of Needletrades, Industrial & Textile Employees, has been credited with reinvigorating the union and increasing membership by focusing on low-wage industries such as laundry and retail distribution that aren't subject to trade pressure. He feels more funds must be spent on recruiting new members than servicing existing ones. Do you think dynamic leaders like Bruce Raynor will be able to increase organized labor's membership in other industries?

Unions, undoubtedly, will also face confrontations and disagreements with management in the first decade of the 2000s. Organized labor, for example, helped lead the charge for corporate governance reform after the corporate scandals involving Enron, Global Crossing, WorldCom, and other companies in the early 2000s. Unions have also promised to use their economic power, in the form of $3 trillion (that's right, trillion) in pension assets, to prod businesses to adopt worker-friendly, good-governance practices.[32]

The rewards unions can expect for cooperating with management include improved job security, profit sharing, and sometimes increased wages. Management for its part can expect a productive, dedicated workforce to handle the challenges of growing competition. How organized labor and management handle these major challenges may well define the future for labor unions.

Progress Assessment

- What are the major laws that affected union growth, and what does each one cover?
- Why do the objectives of unions change over time?
- What are the major tactics used by unions and by management to assert their power in contract negotiations?
- What kinds of workers are joining unions today, and why are they joining?

Controversial Employee–Management Issues

This is an interesting time in the history of employee–management relations. Organizations are involved in outsourcing ➤P. 257◀, technology change, and global expansion. The government has eliminated some social benefits to workers and is taking a much more active role in mandating what benefits and assurances businesses must provide to workers. In other instances, employees are raising general questions of fairness and workplace security. Let's look at several controversial issues, starting with that of executive compensation.

Today the CEO of a major corporation makes 411 times what the average hourly worker earns. This bounty does not include additional job perks that would make a Roman emperor feel neglected. Pay consultant Graef Crystal places a large part of the blame on boards of directors that routinely act as rubber stamps for CEOs. What do you think would be a fair system of compensation for CEOs? Should workers have input?

Executive Compensation

Tiger Woods putts his way to over $69 million a year, Tom Hanks acts his way to $45 million a year, Oprah Winfrey talks her way to over $150 million a year, and George Lucas "has the force with him" for over $200 million a year.[33] Is it out of line, then, for Howard Solomon, the chief executive of Forest Laboratories, to make $148 million a year? Or for Louis Gerstner to earn almost $127 million for his last year as CEO of IBM?[34] In Chapter 2 we explained that the U.S. free-market system is built on incentives that allow top executives to make such large amounts—or more. Today, however, the government, boards of directors, stockholders, unions, and employees are challenging this principle and arguing that executive compensation has gotten out of line. In fact, way out of line. In 2002, the average total compensation (salary and bonuses) for a CEO of a major company was $34 million; compare this to just $25,467 for the average worker.[35] Even after adjustments for inflation, this represents an enormous increase from the $160,000 average CEO compensation in 1960.

In the past, an executive's compensation and bonuses were generally determined by the firm's profitability or an increase in its stock price. The assumption in using such incentives is that the CEO will improve the performance of the company and raise the price of the firm's stock. Today, most executives receive stock options (the ability to buy company stock at a set price at a later date) as part of their compensation. In fact, 10 years ago options accounted for only 27 percent of CEO compensation. Today they account for 60 percent.[36] Many feel that a problem arises when executives are compensated with stock options and the stockholders or employees are not or, worse, when executives sell their stock at a high price and then the stock collapses, leaving stockholders in a lurch.[37] What's even more confusing, however, is that a CEO whose poor performance forced him or her to resign can still walk away with lofty compensation. For example, CEO Richard McGinn of Lucent Technologies was rewarded $12.5 million for getting fired.[38] Kenneth Lay of Enron received over $67 million after leading Enron into bankruptcy and legal problems.[39] Many CEOs also walked away with fat retainers, consulting contracts, and lavish perks when they retired. Make sure to read the Legal Briefcase box for further discussion of this strange phenomenon.

Noted management consultant Peter Drucker has criticized executive pay levels since the mid-1980s, when he suggested that CEOs should not earn much more than 20 times the salary of the company's lowest-paid employee. Herman Miller, a Michigan producer of office furniture, followed Drucker's advice. At this company, pay for the chief executive is limited to 20 times the average worker's pay. Many companies, however, have ignored this advice, and today the average chief executive of a major corporation makes 411 times as much as the average hourly worker; back in 1980, the average CEO made only 42 times as much.[40] At some companies the numbers can be staggering. For example, a custodian or maintenance worker earning minimum wage at Oracle would have to work 63,468 years to make what CEO Larry Ellison earned in 2001 ($706 million).[41]

As global competition intensifies, looking at what executives in other countries earn provides another point of view. In Japan, CEOs do not generally receive stock options and are paid much less than U.S. executives. American CEOs typically earn two to three times as much as executives in Europe and Canada. It's worth noting that European companies often have workers who sit on the board of directors according to a process called codetermination. Since boards set executive pay, this could be a reason why the imbalance between starting pay and top pay is less for European executives than for their American counterparts.[42] Graef Crystal, a pay consultant and expert on corporate governance, sees a link between executives' pay and handsomely paid boards of directors that turn a blind eye to staggering increases in executive compensation.[43]

It's important to recognize, however, that most U.S. executives are responsible for multibillion-dollar corporations and work 70-plus hours a week. Many can show that their decisions turned potential problems into success and rewards for employees and stockholders. For example, during Lou Gerstner's tenure at IBM, the company prospered and the stock soared. Stockholders said very little about the compensation paid to Gerstner during those growth years. Furthermore, the market is not awash with seasoned, skilled professionals who can manage large companies. This is especially true for troubled companies looking for the right CEO to accomplish a turnaround. Lucent, Gap, and Tyco paid out millions to find CEOs to set them on the right path.[44] Clearly, there is no easy answer to the question of what is fair compensation for executives, but it's a safe bet that many changes are likely to take place in the 2000s.

www.rileyguide.com/execpay.html

Legal Briefcase

Getting the Golden Boot

The early 2000s were tough times. Many workers lost their jobs because of the downturn in the economy. Questions such as "How can I pay the bills if I get sick?" plagued many households. No question about it, losing a job is a financially traumatic, gut-wrenching experience for any employee to endure. For the most part, retirees fared no better. Some had to forgo the traditional gold watch due to cutbacks at their companies. Others saw retirement nest eggs dwindle as the stock market took a nosedive. Many discovered that living without a regular paycheck takes some adjustment. It truly was a tough time for employees. Well, check that—maybe not all employees.

Some corporate executives who exited their companies under fire wound up better off than if they had stayed—at least in monetary terms. Take CEO Jacques A. Nasser, who was behind the wheel of Ford Motor Company's $5.45 billion loss in 2001. Like other workers at Ford, Nasser was let go as a result of the poor performance. Unlike those others, however, he walked off with $20 million in compensation for the year. That same year, Joseph P. Nacchio, chief executive of Qwest Communications, received $1.5 million in bonus, $24 million in cash, and $74 million in exercised stock options the year Qwest posted a $4 billion loss. Nacchio soon left the company under a cloud of accounting irregularities. In what might be the strangest quirk of all, Mark Belnick, general counsel of Tyco International, had a provision in his contract that said he would be paid up to $10.6 million if he were convicted of a felony committed during his tenure at Tyco.

Other CEOs have found the road to retirement a golden path, especially when their companies were the ones paving the road. Former CEO Geoffrey Bible did not get a gold watch upon his retirement from Philip Morris, but he did retain use of the corporate jet at his discretion. Also, in exchange for being "occasionally" available as a consultant, Bible will get perks that include corporate security at both his primary residence and vacation home, a company car and driver or a car allowance of up to $100,000 a year, and an office and secretary near his home. All of this is on top of the $50 million Bible earned at Philip Morris before retiring in 2001. Jack Welch, former CEO of General Electric, also found riches in retirement. Welch received access to GE's corporate aircraft; use of an expensive company-owned Manhattan apartment (complete with staff, wine, and food); floor-level seats to the New York Knicks basketball games; courtside seats at the U.S. Open Tennis tournament; box seats for New York Yankee baseball games; club fees at golf clubs; and box seats at Metropolitan Opera events. Judy Fischer, managing director of Executive Compensation Advisory Services, says such exit packages became common in the mid-1990s. It should be noted that both Bible and Welch had distinguished careers at their companies.

Such "corporate benevolence" is causing stockholders and lower-level employees to question the disparity of treatment for top executives. Lawsuits are possible, and the issue could be decided in the U.S. Congress, where elected officials can debate the merits and logic of bestowing bonus pay and excessive perks to discharged executives and retirees. Stay tuned.

Sources: Nicolas Stein, "America's Most Admired Companies," *Fortune,* March 3, 2003, p. 81; Nanette Byrnes, "At Philip Morris, Perks for Life," *Business Week,* July 15, 2002, p. 12; and Kevin McCoy, "Ex-Tyco Executive Faces New Charges," *USA Today,* February 4, 2003, p. 3B.

Comparable Worth

Another controversial issue is that of pay equity, or comparable worth, for women versus men. **Comparable worth** is the concept that people in jobs that require similar levels of education, training, or skills should receive equal pay. This somewhat thorny issue has become more important as women have become a sizable and permanent part of the labor force. In 1890, for example, women made up only 15 percent of the labor force; in 2003, the rate was close to 60 percent.[45]

comparable worth
The concept that people in jobs that require similar levels of education, training, or skills should receive equal pay.

Comparable worth goes beyond the concept of equal pay for equal work. Federal and state equal-pay laws have been in effect for many years. For example, the Equal Pay Act of 1963 requires companies to give equal pay to men and women who do the same job.[46] Put simply, it's against the law to pay a female nurse less than a male nurse unless factors such as seniority, merit pay, or performance incentives are involved. The issue of comparable worth centers on comparing the value of jobs such as a bank teller or librarian (traditionally women's jobs) with jobs such as truck driver or plumber (traditionally men's jobs). Such a comparison shows that "women's" jobs tend to pay less—sometimes much less.

In the United States today, women earn approximately 76 percent of what men earn, though the disparity varies considerably by profession, job experience and tenure, and level of education.[47] In the past the primary explanation for this disparity was that women only worked 50 to 60 percent of their available years once they left school (experience and tenure), whereas men, on the whole, worked all of those years. This explanation doesn't hold much substance today because fewer women now leave the workforce for an extended time. Other explanations suggest that many working women devote more time to their families than men do. This causes them to fall off the career track or voluntarily choose flexible jobs with low pay, such as retailing, bookkeeping, nursing, or secretarial work.

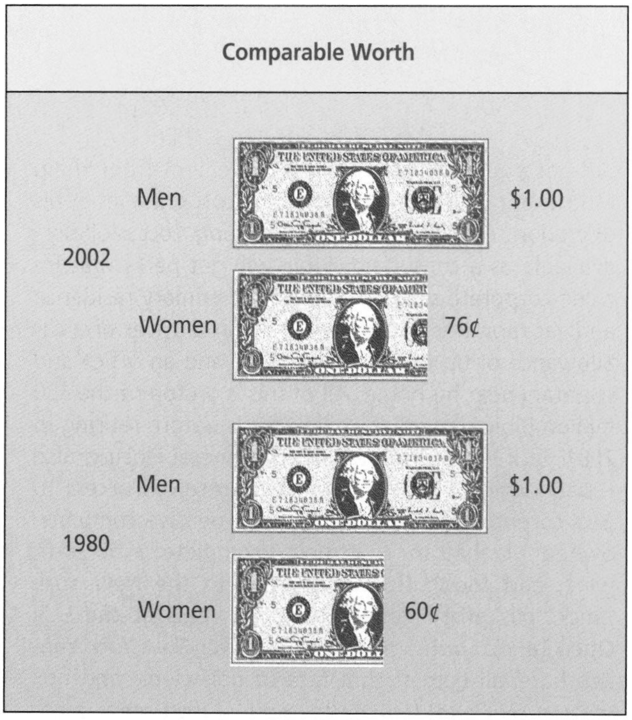

Women have made important strides in business, politics, and sports. They still, however, are a distant second when it comes to getting paid. Today, women earn only 76 percent of what men make in similar positions in the workplace. Such disparities cause many to support the case for comparable worth and a more equitable workplace. What's your opinion concerning this issue?

Evidence, however, shows that it's difficult to determine whether comparable worth would lead to better market equilibrium and fairness or just create more chaos. In today's knowledge-based economy, women appear poised to compete financially with men in growing fields such as health care, telecommunications, biotechnology, and knowledge technology. Studies conducted at the University of Michigan found that earnings of women with baccalaureate degrees were 94 percent of men's. Female engineers earn 98 percent of what their male counterparts are paid. However, Heather Boushey, an economist at the Economic Policy Institute in Washington, D.C., feels that the government puts too much faith in the idea that education will automatically close the pay gap.[48] She and other critics claim that because of the difficulties in implementing and enforcing comparable worth, government and other institutions overlook the pay gaps. As women continue to comprise a large percentage of the labor force, comparable worth promises to be an intriguing issue well into the 21st century.

Critical Thinking

Should college football coaches be paid the same as college volleyball coaches? Should female basketball players in the Women's National Basketball Association be paid the same as their male counterparts in the National Basketball Association? That is, are their jobs of comparable worth? What role should market forces and government play in determining wages?

Sexual Harassment

sexual harassment Unwelcome sexual advances, requests for sexual favors, and other conduct (verbal or physical) of a sexual nature that creates a hostile work environment.

Sexual harassment refers to unwelcome sexual advances, requests for sexual favors, and other conduct (verbal or physical) of a sexual nature that creates a hostile work environment. It became a major issue in the workplace in the 1980s, but the furor over sexual harassment intensified in 1991 during the televised confirmation hearing of Supreme Court Justice Clarence Thomas. At the hearing before the Senate Judiciary Committee, an attorney and college professor named Anita Hill accused Thomas of sexual impropriety.[49] Although the charge did not block Thomas's approval by the U.S. Senate and appointment to the Court, Hill's testimony on national television clearly heightened interest in this issue. During the 1990s, charges of sexual harassment were raised against President Bill Clinton, Senator Bob Packwood, and several high-ranking U.S. military officers.

Legally, both men and women are covered under the Civil Rights Act of 1991, which governs sexual harassment. This fact was reinforced in 1997, when the Supreme Court agreed that same-sex harassment also falls within the purview of sexual harassment law.[50] Women, however, still file the majority of sexual harassment cases. The number of sexual harassment complaints filed annually with the Equal Employment Opportunity Commission (EEOC) grew from 6,000 in 1990 to over 16,000 in 2000. The number of lawsuits seems to be leveling off since 2000.[51] It's also interesting to note that approximately 90 percent of sexual harassment suits are settled out of court.[52]

In evaluating sexual harassment, a person's conduct on the job can be considered illegal under specific conditions:

- The employee's submission to such conduct is made either explicitly or implicitly a term or condition of employment, or an employee's submission to or rejection of such conduct is used as the basis for employment decisions affecting the worker's status. A threat such as "Go out with me or you are fired" or "Go out with me or you will never be promoted here" would constitute *quid pro quo sexual harassment.*
- The conduct unreasonably interferes with a worker's job performance or creates an intimidating, hostile, or offensive work environment. This type of harassment is referred to as *hostile environment sexual harassment.*

The Thomas hearings and subsequent disclosures involving companies such as the Mitsubishi Motor Manufacturing Company of America introduced managers to the concept of a hostile workplace, which is any workplace where particular behavior occurs that would offend a reasonable person.[53] The Supreme Court in 1996 broadened the scope of what can be considered a hostile work environment. In evaluating charges of sexual harassment the keyword seems to be *unwelcome,* a term the courts have hotly debated and will continue to debate in the 21st century.

There's no question that managers and workers are now much more sensitive to sexual comments and behavior than they were in the past. Still, EEOC statistics report that sexual harassment is still a persistent area of employee complaint. A major problem is that workers and managers often know that a policy concerning sexual harassment exists but have no idea what it says. Former U.S. secretary of labor Lynn Martin suggests that companies offer management training, require sexual harassment workshops for all employees, and revamp the human resource department if necessary to ensure compliance. Such efforts may save businesses millions of dollars in lawsuits and make the workplace more productive and harmonious. Many companies have complied and offer training at work or through information on the Internet. Nonetheless, it's a safe bet that sexual harassment will remain an important employee–management issue in the 21st century.

Progress Assessment

- How does top-executive pay in the United States compare with that in other countries?
- What's the difference between comparable worth and equal pay for equal work?
- How is the term *sexual harassment* defined, and when does sexual behavior become illegal?

Child Care

Child care became an increasingly important workplace issue in the 1990s and promises to remain a workplace concern in the 21st century. Questions involving responsibilities for child care subsidies, child care programs, and even parental leave are topics that promise to be debated in the private and public sectors of the economy. Many workers strongly question workplace benefits for parents, and argue that single workers and single-income families should not subsidize child care for dual-income families. Additionally, federal child care assistance has risen significantly since the passage of the Welfare Reform Act of 1996. In 2002, Congress reauthorized the Child Care and Development Fund with $4.8 billion of funding.[54] Still, the issue of child care is an important one to business.

According to the U.S. Census Bureau, a sizable number of today's 50 million working women are likely to bear children during their working years. Such statistics obviously raise concerns among employers. Why? Two key reasons: (1) It's estimated that absences related to child care already cost American businesses billions of dollars annually, and (2) employee child care raises the controversial workplace question of who should pay for child care services.

The number of companies that offer child care as an employee benefit is growing. *Working Mother* magazine highlighted companies such as Bank of America, Colgate-Palmolive, IBM, and General Mills as being particularly sympathetic to working mothers.[55] Other large firms that offer extensive child care programs include Johnson & Johnson, American Express, and Campbell Soup. A few companies even provide emergency child care services for employees whose children are ill or whose regular child care arrangements are disrupted.

Small companies have found that implementing creative child care programs that meet specific employee needs helps them compete with larger organizations in the search to hire qualified employees. For example, Haemonetics Corporation in Braintree, Massachusetts, has a state-of-the-art child care facility called the Kids' Space at Haemonetics. In the summer, the facility includes Camp Haemonetics—the kids come to work with their parents and then get bused off for swimming, hiking, and so forth at a nearby state park. At noon, they come back for lunch with Mom or Dad, and then return for more camp activities until about 5:00 PM.[56] In 1986, entrepreneurs Roger Brown and Linda Mason recognized the emerging power of child care as a benefit in the workplace. The husband and wife team started Bright Horizons Family Solutions, Inc., to provide child care at worksites. Today, the company runs more than 400 child care centers for about 300 employers.[57]

What's obvious to businesses of all sizes is that working parents consider safe, affordable child care an issue on which they will not compromise. Companies have responded by providing

- Discount arrangements with national child care chains.
- Vouchers that offer payments toward whatever type of child care the employee selects.
- Referral services that help identify high-quality child care facilities to employees.
- On-site child care centers at which parents can visit children at lunch or during lag times throughout the workday.
- Sick-child centers to care for moderately ill children.

As the number of single-parent and two-income households continues to grow in the 21st century, child care is certain to remain a hotly debated employee–management issue. However, a new workplace storm is brewing over an issue employees and managers have not faced in times past: elder care.

Stride Rite is not just a leader in the shoe market; it's considered one of the most innovative companies in the United States in the area of employee benefits. Here at the company's intergenerational daycare center, on site daycare programs are provided for children as well as elderly dependents of employees. Are you aware of any companies in your locale that offer employees a similar benefit?

Elder Care

The workforce in the United States is aging. The 2000 census showed that since 1990, the number of people age 65 and over jumped 12 percent, to 35 million. The number is expected to double by 2040, with 77 million Americans over 65.[58] In 2005, 40 percent of all U.S. workers will be 40 to 58 years old. Fortunately, many of these workers will not have to concern themselves with finding child care for their children. However, they will confront another problem: how to care for older parents and other relatives. The number of households with at least one adult providing elder care has tripled since 1992. In 1940, only 13 percent of persons age 60 or over had an elderly parent still alive: today, the total is 44 percent. Over the next five years 18 percent of the U.S. workforce is expected to be involved in the time-consuming and stressful task of caring for an aging relative. Current estimates suggest that companies are presently losing $11 billion a year in reduced productivity, absenteeism, and turnover from employees who are responsible for aging relatives.[59] Denise Talbot-White, a gerontology specialist for MetLife Mature Market Institute, suggests that elder care is the child care of the new millennium.

The U.S. Office of Personnel Management (OPM) found that employees with elder care responsibilities need information on medical, legal, and insurance issues, as well as the full support of their supervisors and company. The OPM also suggested that the issue may require some employees to move to flextime, telecommuting, part-time employment, or job sharing.[60] Some firms have reacted to the effect of elder care on their workforce. At Boeing and AT&T, employees are offered elder care programs that include telephone hot lines workers can call to seek help or counseling for older relatives. Unfortunately, few U.S. companies (large, medium, or small) now provide any type of elder care programs or benefits. Nor does the government provide much relief with this issue. Both Medicare and Medicaid place heavy financial burdens on family caregivers.[61] Some companies are trying to help ease this burden for their employees. A 1999 survey of companies with more than 100 employees found that 23 percent offered elder care referral or resource services, 9 percent were underwriting long-term care insurance for their employees or relatives, and 5 percent had made contributions to elder care programs.

Andrew Scharlach, a professor of aging at the University of California–Berkeley, expects costs to companies to rise even higher as more and more experienced and high-ranking employees become involved in caring for older parents and other relatives. His arguments make sense. Since the jobs older workers hold are often more critical to a company than those held by younger workers (who are most affected by child care problems), many businesses will see the cost of elder care skyrocket. Already some firms note that transfer and promotion decisions are especially difficult for employees whose elderly parents need ongoing care. Unfortunately, as the nation gets older, the elder care situation will grow considerably worse.[62] With an aging workforce, this employee–management issue promises to persist well into the 21st century.

AIDS Testing, Drug Testing, and Violence in the Workplace

Thankfully, the spread of acquired immunodeficiency syndrome (AIDS) has declined considerably in the United States. The disease is, however, still a top national concern. AIDS is a leading cause of death for Americans between the ages of 25 and 44—a group that represents almost half of the nation's workforce.[63] This fact will force businesses to continue focusing on issues related to AIDS, since no one predicts a quick victory over this disease. The U.S. Centers for Disease Control launched a program called Business Responds to AIDS, which explains how companies can teach employees about the basics of AIDS and how to deal with it on the job. Certainly clear-cut policies must be developed to confront this critical issue

One controversial employee–management issue concerns the mandatory testing for the human immunodeficiency virus (HIV), believed to be the virus that causes AIDS. Preemployment medical testing cannot be used selectively to screen out anyone who may be HIV-positive. If administered, the tests must be given to all potential employees across the board. More and more firms are insisting on mandatory HIV testing because AIDS-afflicted employees can cost companies an enormous amount in terms of insurance, losses in productivity, increased absenteeism, and turnover. Many firms have gone beyond preemployment testing and suggested that all existing employees should be tested for the HIV antibody. Managers argue that the information they would gain would allow for the development of a uniform and humanitarian AIDS policy at the workplace. Secretary of State Colin Powell has encouraged businesses with overseas operations to make HIV/AIDS prevention and care a universal workplace principle.[64] Nevertheless, this issue, like others, has no easy answer.

Many companies feel that alcohol and drug abuse are more serious workplace issues than AIDS because substance abuse involves far more workers. An estimated 11 percent of employed adults in the United States are believed to currently use illicit drugs; 8 percent of full-time workers—or 6.3 million Americans—had used illegal drugs within the past month. Overall, approximately 4.7 million Americans ages 12 and older are abusing or dependent on illegal drugs.[65] Individuals who use drugs are three and a half times more likely to be involved in workplace accidents and five times as likely to file a workers' compensation claim than those who do not use drugs. Illegal drug use costs U.S. companies up to $140 billion a year, according to the Partnership for a Drug-Free America.[66] The National Institutes of Health estimates that each drug abuser costs an employer approximately $7,000 annually. Financial and other losses have caused drug testing at work to grow at a rapid pace. Over 60 percent of major companies now test workers and job applicants for substance abuse.[67]

Employers are also struggling with a growing trend toward violence in the workplace. The U.S. Department of Labor now cites homicide as the second leading cause of job-related fatalities. Workplace homicides account for 17 percent of all workplace deaths.[68] The nation faced the shock of large-scale workplace violence in 1986, when a postal service employee in Oklahoma killed 14 fellow workers before taking his own life. Since then, many employees have perished on the job at the hands of fellow employees.[69] Many executives and managers now take workplace violence seriously and have taken action to prevent problems before they occur. For example, at software firm Mindbridge,

EXPECTED BENEFITS OF ESOPs	POTENTIAL PROBLEMS WITH ESOPs
Increased employee motivation	Lack of employee stock voting rights within the firm
Shared profitability through shared ownership of the firm	Lack of communication between management and employees
Improved management–employee relations	Little or no employee representation on the company board of directors
Higher employee pride in the organization	Lack of job security assurances
Better customer relations	

FIGURE 12.8

BENEFITS AND PROBLEMS OF ESOPs

based in Worchester, Pennsylvania, two company officials must be present whenever an employee is disciplined or fired. Nine states presently have passed laws allowing an employer to seek a temporary restraining order on behalf of workers experiencing threats or harassment. Still, some companies believe that reports of workplace violence are primarily overblown by the media. According to an American Management Association study, close to half of its member companies do not provide any formal training for dealing with prevention of violence in the workplace. Unfortunately, organizations such as the U.S. Postal Service, Edgewater Technology, and Xerox can attest that workplace violence is all too real.[70] Many firms now recognize the threat and have begun to hold focus groups for employee input, hire managers with strong interpersonal skills, and employ skilled consultants to deal with the growing employee–management issue of workplace violence.

While issues such as AIDS testing, drug testing, and workplace violence present a somewhat grim picture of the workplace, many employees are assuming new roles within their companies. In fact, many have become owners. Let's see how this is happening.

Employee Stock Ownership Plans (ESOPs)

No matter how hard workers fight for better pay, they will never become as wealthy as the people who actually own the company. At least that is the theory behind **employee stock ownership plans (ESOPs).** An ESOP enables employees to buy part or total ownership of the firm. Louis O. Kelso, a San Francisco lawyer and economist, conceived the idea of ESOPs about 50 years ago.[71] His plan was to turn workers into owners by selling them stock. Using this concept, he helped the employees of a newspaper buy their company. Since then, the idea of employees taking over all or some of the ownership of their companies has gained much favor—there are approximately 11,500 ESOPs today.[72] Employee participation in ownership has emerged as an important issue in many different industries and every type of company.

employee stock ownership plans (ESOPs)
Programs that enable employees to buy part or total ownership of the firm.

Many people consider ESOPs examples of capitalism ➤P. 41◄ at its best. The fact is, however, that not all ESOPs work as planned. Figure 12.8 outlines both the benefits and the problems of ESOPs. When used correctly, ESOPs can be a powerful strategy for improving company profitability and increasing employee satisfaction, participation, and income.

Firms that have healthy employee–management relations have a better chance to prosper than those that don't. As managers, taking a proactive approach is the best way to ensure workable employee–management environments. The proactive manager anticipates potential problems and works toward resolving those issues before they get out of hand—a good lesson to remember.

Progress Assessment

- What are some of the issues related to child care and elder care, and how are companies addressing those issues?
- What are ESOPs, and what are the benefits and drawbacks of ESOPs?

Summary

1. Trace the history of organized labor in the United States.

1. Organized labor in the United States dates back almost to the American Revolution.
   - ***What was the first union?***

   The cordwainers (shoemakers) organized a craft union of skilled specialists in 1792. The Knights of Labor, which was formed in 1869, was the first national labor organization.
   - ***How did the AFL-CIO evolve?***

   The American Federation of Labor (AFL), formed in 1886, was an organization of craft unions. The Congress of Industrial Organizations (CIO), a group of unskilled and semiskilled workers, broke off from the AFL in 1935. Over time, the two organizations saw the benefits of joining together and became the AFL-CIO in 1955. The AFL-CIO is a federation of labor unions, not a national union.

2. Discuss the major legislation affecting labor unions.

2. Legislation has had an important effect on the growth of labor unions.
   - ***What are the provisions of the major legislation affecting labor unions?***

   See Figure 12.1 on page 367.

3. Outline the objectives of labor unions.

3. The objectives of labor unions shift in response to changes in social and economic trends.
   - ***What topics typically appear in labor–management agreements?***

   See Figure 12.3 on page 369.

4. Describe the tactics used by labor and management during conflicts, and discuss the role of unions in the future.

4. If negotiations between labor and management break down, either or both sides may use certain tactics to enhance their position or sway public opinion.
   - ***What are the tactics used by unions and management in conflicts?***

   Unions can use strikes and boycotts. Management can use injunctions and lockouts.
   - ***What will unions have to do to cope with declining membership?***

   In order to grow, unions will have to adapt to an increasingly white-collar, female, and culturally diverse workforce. To help keep American businesses competitive in international markets, unions must soften their historic "us-versus-them" attitude and build a new "we" attitude with management.

5. Explain some of today's controversial employee–management issues, such as executive compensation; comparable worth; child care and elder care; AIDS testing, drug testing, and violence in the workplace; and employee stock ownership plans (ESOPs).

5. Some controversial employee–management issues are executive compensation, comparable worth, child care and elder care, AIDS testing, drug testing, violence in the workplace, and ESOPs.
   - ***What is a fair wage for managers?***

   The market and the businesses in it set managers' salaries. What is fair is open to debate. The top executives of the 100 largest public companies were paid on average $34 million in 2002.

- ***What is comparable worth?***

The Equal Pay Act of 1963 provides that workers receive equal pay for equal work (with exceptions for seniority, merit, or performance). Comparable worth is the demand for pay equity for jobs requiring similar levels of education, training, and skills.

- ***Isn't pay inequity caused by sexism?***

There is some evidence that supports that statement and counter arguments that refute the charge. It's possible some remedial action will be taken by government or business regardless of the root causes.

- ***How are some companies addressing the child care issue?***

Responsive companies are providing child care on the premises, emergency care when scheduled care is interrupted, discounts with child care chains, vouchers to be used at the employee's chosen care center, and referral services.

- ***What is elder care, and what problems do companies face with regard to this growing problem?***

Workers with older parents or other relatives often need to find some way to care for them. It's becoming a problem that will perhaps outpace the need for child care. Workers who need to care for dependent parents are generally more experienced and vital to the mission of the organization than younger workers are. The cost to business is very large and growing.

- ***What are some concerns surrounding AIDS and mandatory HIV testing?***

An employee with AIDS can cost an employer an enormous amount in terms of insurance increases, losses in productivity, increased absenteeism, and employee turnover. Employees may question the accuracy of HIV tests and may see the tests as an infringement on their right to privacy.

- ***Why are more and more companies now testing workers and job applicants for substance abuse?***

Estimates are that 11 percent of employed adults in the United States are believed to be current illicit drug users. Individuals who use drugs are three and a half times more likely to be involved in workplace accidents and five times more likely to file a worker's compensation claim than those who do not use drugs.

- ***How well are employee stock ownership plans (ESOPs) working?***

ESOPs have had mixed results, but the overall trend is favorable. Some 11,500 businesses now have ESOPs. Properly implemented, such plans can increase morale, motivation, commitment, and job satisfaction. The problem is that many firms have used ESOPs as a capital-raising scheme and have not given employees increased participation in management. The issue of the administration of ESOPs will be a major one in the next decade.

Key Terms

agency shop agreement 369
American Federation of Labor (AFL) 366
arbitration 373
bargaining zone 372
certification 367
closed shop agreement 369
collective bargaining 367
comparable worth 381
Congress of Industrial Organizations (CIO) 366
cooling-off period 374
craft union 365
decertification 368
employee stock ownership plans (ESOPs) 387
givebacks 376
grievance 370
industrial unions 366
injunction 376
Knights of Labor 366
lockout 376
mediation 372

negotiated labor–management agreement (labor contract) 369
open shop agreement 370
primary boycott 375
right-to-work laws 370
secondary boycott 375
sexual harassment 382
shop stewards 372
strike 373
strikebreakers 376
union 364
union security clause 369
union shop agreement 369
yellow-dog contract 367

Developing Workplace Skills

1. Many health care professionals, especially doctors and nurses, do not belong to a union. Nurses' pay has fallen behind compensation in industry, and doctors feel they are losing a good deal of control over their patients because of strict rules enforced in many health maintenance organizations (HMOs). Talk with several health care professionals about their feelings of possible unionization in health care professions. List the pros and cons they offer concerning unions advancing in the medical profession.

2. Debate the following statement with several classmates: "Unions are dinosaurs that have outlived their usefulness in today's technological world." Consider such questions as these: Do unions serve a key purpose in some industries? Do unions make the United States less competitive in global markets? To get a better feeling for the other side's point of view, take the opposite side of this issue from the one you normally would. Include information from outside sources to substantiate your position.

3. Find the latest information on federal and state legislation related to child care, parental leave, and elder care benefits for employees. In what direction are the trends pointing? What will be the cost to businesses for these new initiatives? Do you favor such advancements in workplace legislation? Why or why not?

4. Compile a list of two or three employee–management issues not covered in the chapter. Compare your list with those of several classmates and see what issues you selected in common and ones unique to each individual. Collectively select one or two workplace issues you all agree will be important in the first decade of the new millennium and discuss its likely effects and outcomes.

5. Do businesses and government agencies have a duty to provide additional benefits to employees beyond fair pay and good working conditions? Does providing benefits such as child care and elder care to some employees discriminate against those who do not require such assistance? Propose a benefits system that you consider fair and workable for both employees and employers.

Taking It To The Net

Purpose

To understand why workers choose to join unions and how unions have made differences in certain industries.

Exercise

Visit the AFL-CIO website at www.aflcio.com. Navigate through the site and find information regarding why workers join unions and what the benefits have been.

1. There have been many debates about right-to-work laws. Compare the average wages of workers in right-to-work states with those in other states.

Which group of states offers the higher wages? In addition to union pressure, what else could account for the wage differences?

2. What percentage of workers in your state belongs to a union? If the percentage of union workers is higher (or lower) than the national average, explain why unions do (or do not) have strength in your state.
3. Explain how union membership has affected minorities, women, younger and older workers, and part-time workers.
4. The AFL-CIO site presents the union's perspective on labor issues. Choose one of these issues and find other resources that support management's perspective on the issue.

Casing The Web

To access the case "Do Right-to-Work Laws Help States?" visit

www.mhhe.com/ub7e

Video Case

LUV in the Workplace: Southwest Airlines

You feel the difference the first time you fly Southwest Airlines (stock symbol LUV). Employees are friendly and funny. They joke with passengers, but are helpful whenever needed. That's not always the case with airlines these days, especially since September 11, 2001, and the extra security and fall-off in airline revenues. Southwest is the only consistently profitable major airline.

Other carriers try to imitate Southwest, with some success, but Southwest still leads the way. It has the best service record for baggage handling, the fewest customer complaints, the best safety record, the lowest workforce turnover, and the best labor relations. The latter is somewhat surprising because the airline's workforce is 85 percent unionized. Nonetheless, Southwest continues to outshine other companies in the industry. Why? The video offers several explanations, but perhaps the most important is that Southwest focuses as much on pleasing its workers as it does on pleasing its customers.

The relationship between management and workers, historically, has not always been so pleasing. That's the reason there are unions in the United States. Unions fought for improvements in the minimum wage, overtime pay, workers' compensation, severance pay, job safety, and child labor laws. Workers today often forget the debt they owe unions for making such improvements in working conditions.

Today, labor contracts include the terms and conditions under which labor and management will function over a set period of time. If an employee has a grievance, he or she can go to a union representative to have it settled. If settlement is not forthcoming, a formal grievance process is in place to reach a satisfactory conclusion.

Such procedures seem straightforward and mutually satisfying. The truth is, however, that labor and management often fail to reach a labor agreement. In such cases, union workers may resort to a strike—that is, a work stoppage. They may also picket or call for a boycott of a company and its products. Management may lock employees out of their jobs or hire temporary workers (called scabs) to replace union workers while they are on strike. In short, tensions can develop between both sides that become quite heated. In these cases a mediator may be brought in to make suggestions as to a fair and equitable solution. An arbitrator can also be used; both sides are bound by the arbitrator's ruling.

How did Southwest avoid such labor problems? Southwest begins its close cooperation with employees by bringing them to its University for People. The New Hire Training Course gives them a history of Southwest and the importance of employees to that history. The training looks at failed airlines of the past that at one time were large, effective, and profitable. Employees today are less concerned about wage increases and work conditions and are more concerned about employee benefits and job security, the latter being especially important in the airline industry. That does not mean, however, that Southwest does not pay well or provide great benefits. Benefits include child care and elder care referrals, a counseling service, and a catastrophe fund for those who get caught in dire emergencies.

The airline "hires for attitude and trains for skill." Skills can be learned and Southwest helps people attain their goals. Many employees even bring their spouses to work for the firm as well. A good company with good employees is a winner today, even in highly competitive and hard-to-make-money industries like the airlines.

Thinking It Over

1. Many companies would like to have the relationship with employees that Southwest does. What could a company do to build such a relationship?
2. What have you learned from this video that might be helpful to you on the job?
3. About 13.2 percent of workers in America today are union members. Do you think unions have more influence than the numbers suggest? Why or why not?

Part 4

Management of Human Resources

Career Portfolio

Human resources are the people in an organization. How those people are hired, managed, and treated is the responsibility of human resource managers. These key people used to be called personnel managers or directors—and still are in some companies. They are personnel specialists who help to make management more effective in hiring and in overall job satisfaction. Many organizations are too large to allow close contact between top management and most subordinates. In such firms, human resource people provide this link.

Human resource specialists select, interview, and recommend prospective employees for job openings. They are involved in training for both employees and managers. Human resource personnel will often be directly involved in writing training guides, and they keep everyone in the organization informed about training opportunities. A director of human resources may manage several departments in larger companies, including equal employment opportunity specialists and recruitment specialists.

Skills

A human resource manager must have a thorough knowledge of current laws. Since the early 1960s, many new laws affecting employment have been passed, especially in the area of equal employment opportunity. Not knowing the law can damage a company and even cause it to lose credibility with the public.

Like other managers, human resource managers need the ability to organize themselves and to keep others organized. They also need good communications skills, both oral and written. Because human resource planning is an integral part of the job, human resource managers must also be good planners, able to project both long- and short-term needs. Good human resource managers should also like to persuade and influence the actions of others. Often they have to sell their ideas on such issues as creative training programs, changing company traditions, and staffing changes.

Other skills are more specific to the careers in the area. For example, training specialists need skills in teaching and developing training programs. Directors of labor relations need to have extensive training in labor union operations and law. Human resource planning specialists must be adept at forecasting future trends and planning for them.

Career Paths

In today's workplace, most companies want to hire college graduates, even for entry-level human resource positions. An increasing number of colleges offer programs that lead to a human resources management degree. Graduate programs leading to master's and doctoral degrees are also numerous. Human resource management is also one field that hires many women and minorities.

Entry-level jobs include administrative assistant, human resource assistant, or office assistant. Even with the academic training that is required experience in a human resource department is important for success as a human resource manager. Just as in other management positions, promotion to the top in a large organization is likely to be competitive—and even political.

SOME POSSIBLE POSITIONS IN HUMAN RESOURCE MANAGEMENT

JOB TITLE	SALARY	JOB DUTIES	CAREER PATH	PROSPECTS
Training specialist	Median: $40,830	Assess needs for training, plan and implement training programs. Conduct orientation and on-the-job training programs.	A background in teaching or psychology is helpful. Degree in human resource management can also help. Often will be promoted into management within human resource department.	Average growth through 2010.
Employment/ placement specialist	Median: $36,480	Act as broker, bringing job and applicant together.	College degree desirable. Jobs are available in state employment agencies and in private career placement companies.	Average growth through 2010.
Employee benefits specialist	Median: $41,660	Administer programs in health insurance, retirement plans, profit sharing, etc. Apply ever-changing federal laws to the process.	Begin by following orders of human resource manager; given more responsibility with experience.	Average growth through 2010.
Labor relations specialist	Median: $31,963 (to start)	Assist management in conducting negotiations with the union and help in labor–management disputes.	Entry-level specialists deal with minor grievances and other minor labor–management issues. After experience, they become involved in higher-level negotiations.	Average growth through 2010.

Source: Bureau of Labor Statistics, *Occupational Outlook Handbook,* 2002–03 edition.

The Health Alliance

Name: Vanessa J. Niño

Age: 30

Position/title: Translator/Interpreter

Major factors in the decision to take this position: As a Health Alliance Bilingual Hispanic Associate, I have been working for the past two years with Limited English Proficient associates and community groups. Our Hispanic population has grown immensely in the past decade, and our hospital rooms have seen an increase in Hispanic patients.

Company's Web address: www.health-alliance.com

Company description: The Health Alliance covers the entire Greater Cincinnati area. The Health Alliance has six hospital facilities, including teaching and acute care hospitals.

Job description: As an interpreter, I provide interpreting services as needed for Limited English Proficient (LEP) patients and staff throughout the hospitals. As a translator, I translate a wide variety of written information from English to Spanish, such as patient information forms, booklets, information sheets, and any other information as needed.

Career paths: I started working for the Health Alliance as a translator, interpreter, and trainer at the laundry facility for the hospitals; about 50 percent of the employees are Hispanic. After about six months, I transferred into the Business Center as an HR specialist, while still in contact with the laundry facility. This allowed me to work in a similar fashion with the hospitals. One of my goals was to hire bilingual associates for the organization, translate patient materials and other projects related to LEP, as well as other general projects. One thing led to another, and I accepted a position as HR Coordinator in an attempt to have a more direct approach to hiring bilingual associates and other associates as well.

Ideal next job: I just started my ideal next job!

Best part of your job: Patient satisfaction. The smiles on their faces because they know they have all the information they need and were able to ask all the appropriate questions.

Worst part of your job: I love to help people; therefore the worst part of my job is doing too many things at the same time. There is so much I want to do, but so little time.

Educational background: I have associate degrees in Graphic Communications, Flexographic Communications, and International Trade Management. My Bachelor's is in Business Administration/International Business, and I am a certified Medical Translator and Interpreter.

Favorite course: I found "Business in the European Union" fascinating!

Best course for your career: "World Religions." Every patient is different; sometimes the care they require is different as well. Different religions require different approaches, and we need to respect their beliefs.

Recommended by Carolyn Waits, Cincinnati State Technical and Community College

Chapter 13

Marketing: Building Customer and Stakeholder Relationships

Learning Goals

After you have read and studied this chapter, you should be able to

1. Define *marketing* and explain how the marketing concept applies in both for-profit and nonprofit organizations.
2. List and describe the four Ps of marketing.
3. Describe the marketing research process, and explain how marketers use environmental scanning to learn about the changing marketing environment.
4. Explain how marketers meet the needs of the consumer market through market segmentation, relationship marketing, and the study of consumer behavior.
5. List ways in which the business-to-business market differs from the consumer market.
6. Show how the marketing concept has been adapted to fit today's modern markets.
7. Describe the latest marketing strategies, such as stakeholder marketing and customer relationship management (CRM).

Profile

www.ssbtechnologies.com/about/index.php

Getting to Know Marco Sorani of SSB Technologies

Marco Sorani went to Princeton, where he was a swimmer and a water polo player. When he was 24, Sorani broke his fifth cervical vertebra in a body-surfing accident. Sorani lost the use of his legs and the ability to move his fingers. That accident led Sorani in an entirely new direction, one that has benefited him and many others.

Sorani saw a new opportunity and took it. He noticed that many of the 54 million disabled Americans like himself were not able to access websites. That was a sizable market that really needed some help. Sorani became the chief executive at SSB Technologies, a San Francisco firm that helps companies make their websites accessible to the disabled. SSB's software can read captions out loud so that blind people can hear what is on the screen. It can also caption Web audio, enlarge linking buttons, and enlarge the text.

The U.S. government recently released guidelines for compliance with Section 508 of the Rehabilitation Act of 1998. Guess what Section 508 calls for? It says that all information technology systems deployed by federal agencies must be accessible to disabled people. The passage of this act meant that all government websites had to be adapted. SSB was ready to supply the government with the software to do the job.

What Sorani did—noticing that people had needs that weren't being met, finding a solution for those needs, and then providing them with needed goods and services—is called marketing. As people like Sorani go about solving one problem, they are likely to see other needs that call for other products that must be promoted to those in need so they know there is a solution out there. Making websites accessible helps not only the disabled but also anyone else who is in a position where access is difficult—such as people who are in transit or using a cell phone.

What Sorani did—noticing that people had needs that weren't being met, finding a solution for those needs, and then providing them with needed goods and services—is called marketing.

This is an exciting time to be studying business and marketing. New technological innovations—such as voice-activated computers, cell phones that access e-mail, and software that enables individuals to send music and photos and videos to others make life easier and more exciting. They also provide an opportunity for students to find all kinds of marketing careers in the high-tech firms that make such products. Such careers include marketing research to see what people want and need, product design and testing, selling, advertising, public relations, distribution, and follow-up services such as training people how to use products and make repairs.

As you go through the day, you are likely to see market opportunities such as the ones Sorani saw among the disabled. What opportunities await those who, say, provide meals on the road for vegetarians? What other unmet needs have you observed? This chapter and the three that follow will introduce you to all phases of marketing. Someday, you too may be the chief officer of a small company making goods or services for people. If so, you will need to contact suppliers, sell your ideas to investors, advertise your products to consumers, and somehow distribute them.

Sources: Josh McHugh, "A Healthy Niche Market," *Forbes,* February 26, 2001, pp. 36–38; and www.sbbtechnologies.com/index.php, 2003.

What Is Marketing?

marketing
The process of planning and executing the conception, pricing, promotion, and distribution of goods and services to facilitate exchanges that satisfy individual and organizational objectives.

Many people think of marketing as "selling" or "advertising." Yes, selling and advertising are part of marketing, but marketing involves much more. **Marketing** is the process of planning and executing the conception, pricing, promotion, and distribution of goods ➤P. 25◄ and services ➤P. 26◄ to facilitate exchanges that satisfy individual and organizational objectives.

What marketers do at any particular time depends on what needs to be done to fill customers' needs. Consumers' wants and needs continually change. Let's take a brief look at how these changes influenced the evolution of marketing.

The Evolution of Marketing

The evolution of marketing in the United States involved four eras: (1) production, (2) selling, (3) marketing concept, and (4) customer relationship (see Figure 13.1).

The Production Era From the time the first European settlers began their struggle to survive in America until the early 1900s, the general philosophy of business was "Produce as much as you can because there is a limitless market." Given the limited production capability and the vast demand for products in those days, such a philosophy was both logical and profitable. Business owners were mostly farmers, carpenters, and trade workers. There was a need for greater and greater productive capacity, so the goals of business centered on production ➤P. 296◄. This was necessary at the time because most goods were bought as soon as they became available. The greatest marketing need was for distribution and storage.

The Selling Era By the 1920s, businesses had developed mass-production techniques (e.g., automobile assembly lines) and production capacity often exceeded the immediate market demand ➤P. 43◄. Therefore, the business philosophy turned from an emphasis on production to an emphasis on selling. Most companies emphasized selling and advertising in an effort to persuade consumers to buy existing products; few offered service after the sale.

The Marketing Concept Era After World War II ended, in 1945, there was a tremendous demand for goods and services among the returning soldiers who

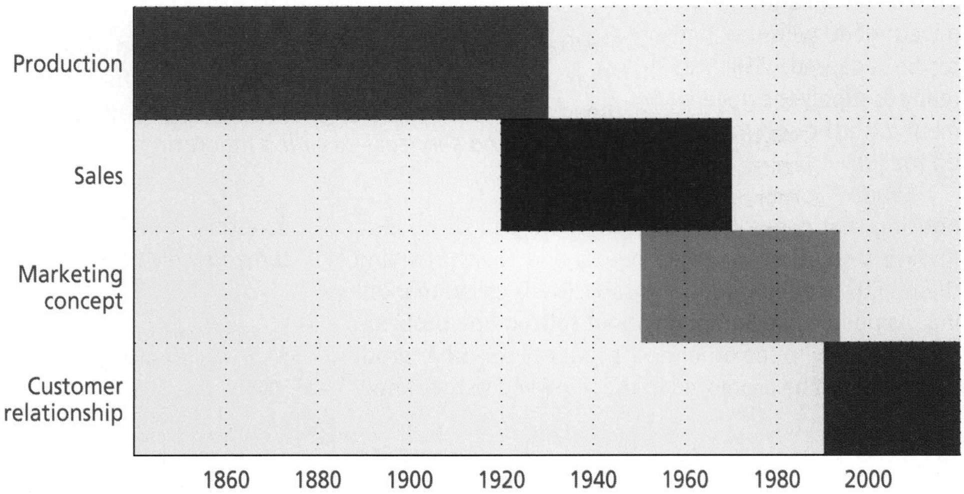

FIGURE 13.1
MARKETING ERAS
The evolution of marketing in the United States involved four eras: (1) production, (2) sales, (3) marketing concept, and (4) customer relationship.

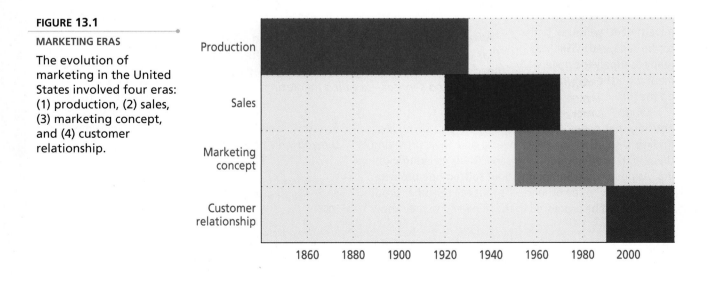

Home Depot's research discovered that women wanted to learn more about home maintenance and repair, including, as this photo shows, learning about such things as how to install bricks for a walkway. The concept of "find a need and fill it" has led Home Depot to begin offering classes for women called "Do It Herself Night." Are there other stores in your area that could increase revenues by being more responsive to the needs of women?

were starting new careers and beginning families. Those postwar years launched the baby boom (a sudden increase in the birthrate) and a boom in consumer spending. Competition for the consumer's dollar was fierce. Businesses recognized the need to be responsive to consumers if they wanted to get their business, and a philosophy emerged in the 1950s called the marketing concept.

The **marketing concept** had three parts:

marketing concept
A three-part business philosophy: (1) a customer orientation, (2) a service orientation, and (3) a profit orientation.

1. **A customer orientation.** Find out what consumers want and provide it for them. (Note the emphasis on consumers rather than promotion or sales.)
2. **A service orientation.** Make sure everyone in the organization has the same objective—customer satisfaction. This should be a total and integrated organizational effort.
3. **A profit orientation.** Focus on those goods and services that will earn the most profit and enable the organization to survive and expand to serve more consumer wants and needs.

It took a while for businesses to implement the marketing concept. That process went slowly during the 1960s and 70s. During the 1980s, businesses began to apply the marketing concept more aggressively than they had done over the preceding 30 years. That led to the focus on customer relationship management (CRM) that has become so important today. We shall explore that concept next.

customer relationship management (CRM)
The process of learning as much as possible about customers and doing everything you can to satisfy them—or even exceed their expectations—with goods and services over time.

The Customer Relationship Era In the 1990s, managers extended the marketing concept by adopting the concept of customer relationship management. **Customer relationship management (CRM)** is the process of learning as much as possible about customers and doing everything you can to satisfy them—or even exceed their expectations—with goods and services over time.[1] The idea is to enhance customer satisfaction and stimulate long-term customer loyalty. For example, most airlines offer frequent-flier programs that reward loyal customers with free flights. We shall explore CRM in more depth later in the chapter.

City Harvest is a nonprofit organization that gathers food for distribution to the poor. This ad features Harrison Ford as a spokesperson for the cause. How would you rate the marketing efforts of the nonprofit organizations in your area? Are they better or worse than marketing efforts for profit-seeking businesses?

Nonprofit Organizations Prosper from Marketing

Even though the marketing concept emphasizes a profit orientation, marketing is a critical part of almost all organizations, whether for-profit or nonprofit. Charities use marketing to raise funds (e.g., to combat world hunger) or to obtain other resources.[2] For example, the Red Cross uses promotion to encourage people to donate blood when local or national supplies run low. Greenpeace uses marketing to promote ecologically safe technologies. Churches use marketing to attract new members and to raise funds. Politicians use marketing to get votes.

States use marketing to attract new businesses and tourists. Many states, for example, have competed to get automobile companies from other countries to locate plants in their area. Schools use marketing to attract new students. Other organizations, such as arts groups, unions, and social groups, also use marketing.[3] The Advertising Council, for example, uses marketing to create awareness and change attitudes on such issues as drunk driving and fire prevention. Marketing, in fact, is used to promote everything from environmentalism (Save a Whale) and crime prevention (Take a Bite Out of Crime) to social issues (Choose Life).

Critical Thinking

Which of your needs are not being met by businesses and/or nonprofit organizations in your area? Are there enough people with similar needs to attract an organization that would meet those needs? How would you find out?

The Marketing Mix

Pleasing customers has become a priority for marketers. Much of what marketing people do has been conveniently divided into four factors, called the four Ps to make them easy to remember and implement. They are

1. Product
2. Price
3. Place
4. Promotion

Dealing with Change

www.autobytel.com

Applying the Four Ps

You can see the four Ps of marketing in action if you closely follow changes that are occurring in the automobile industry. New products are being designed to meet market niches. There are, for example, sports cars designed to compete with the Porsche Boxster and appeal to successful young executives, and sport-utility vehicles (SUVs) for nearly every taste. Pickup trucks have features like four-wheel drive, grocery-bag hooks, and center armrests that double as laptop workstations.

Never before have there been more choices in cars—from small personal cars to large vans to "green" cars that run on a combination of gas and battery power. And in those cars is every conceivable convenience from phones to CD players, cup holders, and global positioning systems. Automobile companies truly seem to be listening to customers and trying to meet their needs. This is the *product* part of the four Ps.

BusinessWeek

When it comes to *pricing,* there is a whole new revolution going on in this industry. On the Web, sites such as Autobytel.com and Autoweb.com provide product and price information and dealer referrals. Customers can thus determine the best price before going to a dealership. To eliminate one of the most annoying parts of buying a car, some dealers are offering no-haggle pricing.

Getting cars to a *place* that is convenient for customers is also being done by auto websites. Autobytel.com and Autoweb.com help customers find the dealer closest to them that will offer the best price for the automobile they choose. Ford and General Motors (GM) are experimenting with websites and factory-owned stores. GM's service, called BuyPower, gives consumers access to every vehicle on participating dealers' lots as well as independent data about competing models. Meanwhile, chains such as AutoNation and CarMax are selling both new and used cars at convenient locations. Consumers can now order almost any car from anywhere in the world via the Internet. The car will be shipped to a nearby port, and all paperwork is handled with ease.

Promotion for new and used cars is also changing. Dealers are trying low-pressure salesmanship because they know that customers are now armed with much more information than in the past. More and more power is being shifted to consumers. They can go on the Internet; learn about various cars and their features, including safety features; pick which features they want; get the best price available; and order the car—all without leaving their homes. In such an atmosphere the marketing task shifts from helping the seller sell to helping the buyer buy. Internet sellers make every effort to help buyers find the car that best meets their needs and minimize the hassle involved in getting that car.

In the future, the real difference among dealers may be in postpurchase (after-sale) service. Those dealers who treat customers best through relationship marketing (discussed later in this chapter) may develop loyalty that can't be matched in any other way. Such relationships are built through service contracts, guarantees, reminder cards telling customers when to come in for various services, parties with customers, and more. The model for such relationships is that set by Harley-Davidson with its motorcycles. No customers are more loyal and more united with each other than Harley buyers. Developing such loyalty will be the goal of most marketers, including automakers and auto dealers.

Sources: Bob Thompson, "If Profit Is the Point, Loyalty Is the Key," *Business Week* (advertisement), July 3, 2000, pp. 67 ff.; Amy Tsao, "Online Retailing Finds Its Legs," *Business Week,* December 20, 2002; Amy Tsao, "Harley: A Good Time for a Ride?" *Business Week Online,* Spring 2003; and Kathleen Kerwin, "Hybrids: How Detroit Can Gun the Engines," *Business Week,* February 17, 2003, p. 80.

Managing the controllable parts of the marketing process, then, involves (1) designing a want-satisfying *product,* (2) setting a *price* for the product, (3) placing the product in a *place* where people will buy it, and (4) *promoting* the product. These four factors are called the **marketing mix** because they are blended together in a marketing program. A marketing manager designs a marketing program that effectively combines the ingredients of the marketing mix (see Figure 13.2). The Dealing with Change box discusses how the automobile industry is adjusting to the market using the four Ps.

marketing mix
The ingredients that go into a marketing program: product, price, place, and promotion.

FIGURE 13.2

MARKETING MANAGERS AND THE MARKETING MIX

Marketing managers must choose how to implement the four Ps of the marketing mix: product, price, place, and promotion. The goals are to please customers and make a profit.

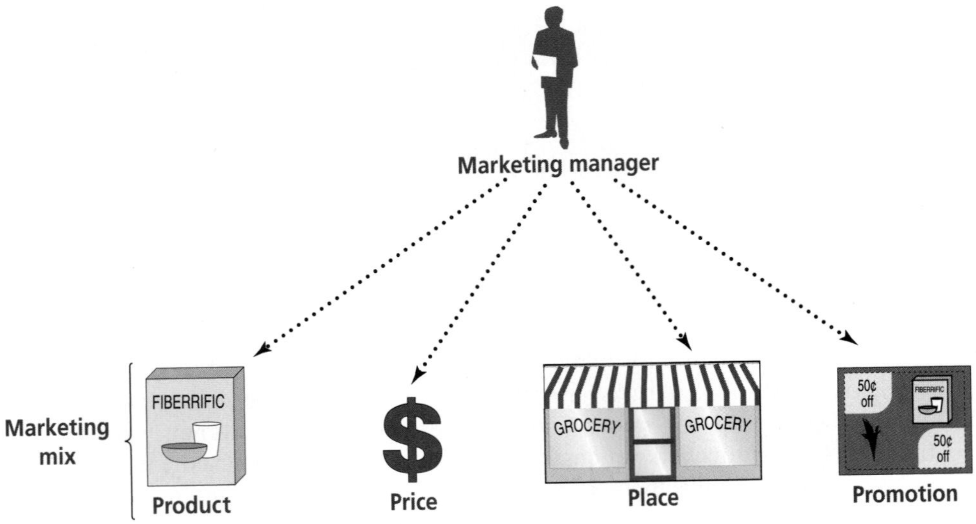

Applying the Marketing Process

The four Ps are a convenient way to remember the basics of marketing, but they don't include everything that goes into the marketing process. One of the best ways for you to understand the entire marketing process is to take a product and follow the process that led to its development and sale (see Figure 13.3). Imagine that you and your friends don't have time to eat big breakfasts. You want something for breakfast that's fast, nutritious, and good tasting. Some of your friends eat a cereal made with 100 percent natural oats and honey, but you and others are not happy with this product. In fact, you know that the Center for Science in the Public Interest placed this cereal at the top of its list of "10 Foods You Should Never Eat!" because of its high sugar and fat content. Furthermore, you've read in a magazine that the cereal industry has been slow to innovate. You sense opportunity. Finding such opportunities is a great first step toward becoming a successful marketer.

You ask around among your acquaintances and find that a huge demand exists for a good-tasting breakfast cereal that's nutritious, high in fiber, and low in sugar. This fact leads you to conduct a more extensive marketing research study to determine whether there's a large enough market for such a cereal. Your research supports your assumption: there is a large market for a high-fiber cereal. You have completed one of the first steps in marketing: researching consumer wants and needs and finding a need for a product that's either not yet available or could be greatly improved. We shall discuss marketing research in detail later in the chapter.

Designing a Product to Meet Needs

product
Any physical good, service, or idea that satisfies a want or need plus anything that would enhance the product in the eyes of consumers, such as the brand.

Once you have researched consumer needs and found a target market (discussed in detail later) for your product, the four Ps of marketing begin. You start by developing a product. A **product** is any physical good, service, or idea that satisfies a want or need plus anything that would enhance the product in the eye of consumers, such as the brand. In this case, your proposed product is a health-enhancing multigrain cereal made with an artificial sweetener. It's a good idea at this point to do *concept testing*. That is, you develop an accurate description of your product and ask people, in person or online, whether the concept (the idea of the cereal) appeals to them. If it does, you might go to a manufacturer that has the equipment and skills to design such a cereal, and begin making prototypes. *Prototypes* are samples of the product that you take to consumers to test their reactions. The process of testing products among potential users is called **test marketing**.

If consumers like the product and agree they would buy it, you may turn the production process over to an existing manufacturer or you may decide to produce the cereal yourself. *Outsourcing* ➤P. 257⮜, remember, is the term used to describe the allocation of production and other functions to outside firms. The idea is to retain only those functions that you can do most efficiently and outsource the rest. The Reaching Beyond Our Borders box on p. 404 discusses the resources available to help you reach global markets.

Once the product meets taste and quality expectations, you have to design a package and think of an appropriate brand name.[4] A **brand name** is a word, letter, or group of words or letters that differentiates one seller's goods and services from those of competitors. Cereal brand names, for example, include Cheerios, Frosted Flakes, and Raisin Bran. Let's say that you name your cereal Fiberrific to emphasize the high fiber content and terrific taste. We'll discuss the product development process, including packaging, branding, and pricing, in detail in Chapter 14. In other chapters, we will follow the Fiberrific case to show you how the concepts apply to one particular product. For now, we're simply sketching the whole process to give you an idea of what the overall marketing picture is all about. So far, we've only covered the first P of the marketing mix: product. Next comes price.

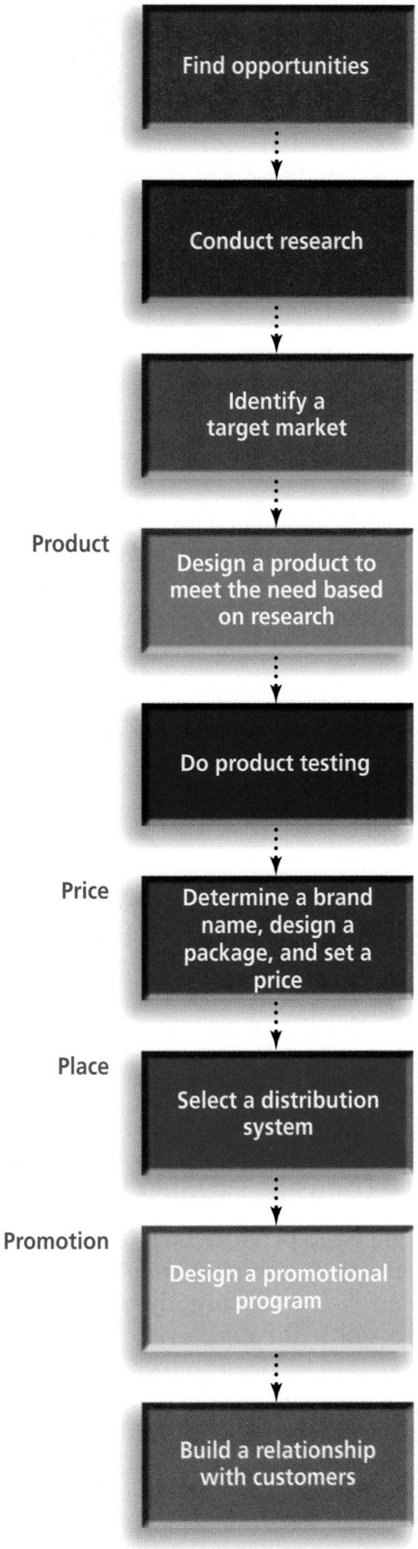

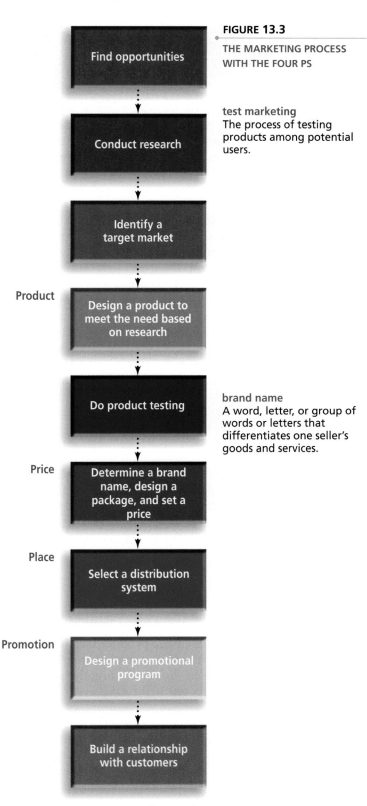

FIGURE 13.3
THE MARKETING PROCESS WITH THE FOUR PS

test marketing
The process of testing products among potential users.

brand name
A word, letter, or group of words or letters that differentiates one seller's goods and services.

Setting an Appropriate Price

After you have developed the product or designed the service you want to offer consumers, you have to set an appropriate price.[5] That price depends on a number of factors. For example, in the cereal business, the price should probably be close to what other cereal makers charge since most cereals are priced competitively. You also have to consider the costs involved in producing, distributing, and promoting the product. You might price the product higher than other cereals to create an image of quality. We shall discuss all of these issues in more detail in Chapter 14.

Reaching Beyond Our Borders

Problems and Solutions

www.landsend.com

Now that Internet companies are selling globally, they have to abide by all the rules of all the countries they are in—and that is not easy. For example, Lands' End got into trouble in Germany by promoting its guarantee on goods purchased. Such guarantees are not legal in Germany. Germany's reasoning is that the cost of offering a guarantee is hidden in a higher sales price. Anyhow, small companies advertising on the Internet must be careful to not break any laws of the countries they reach. The cost of fighting such laws is too high for a small firm. Lands' End may have the money, but most small firms do not. Many companies are now having second thoughts about selling goods and services globally on the Internet. One of the problems that occurs regularly is learning how to ship goods across national boundaries.

How does a firm adapt to the demands of a global market? The answer is that companies have emerged to provide third-party services to help other companies reach and serve foreign customers. Such services include marketing support, e-commerce development, and transportation.

At first, only large companies such as UPS World Wide Logistics provided third-party services to global marketers. But lately smaller companies have emerged to offer more specialized services, such as website development and follow-up services after the sale. Selling in China, for example, has never been easy for U.S. firms. But East-West Equipment and Technology, Inc., now operates as a development and trade management company with offices in Beijing and Wuhan. The company was originally set up to sell secondhand equipment to Chinese buyers. It turned out that Chinese buyers didn't have enough information as they tried to choose from thousands of pieces of used equipment. So East-West began providing guidance and detailed information to Chinese buyers. It now does the same for U.S. buyers who need information about Chinese business practices.

U.S. firms once found it difficult to set up distribution networks in Mexico. Now GATX Corporation has a logistics subsidiary in Mexico that helps U.S. firms reach Mexican consumers. The company also operates in Chile. Many more companies could be cited that provide services to firms wishing to sell internationally. The Internet may provide access to global markets, but there still is the problem of transporting goods. Transportation and logistics services in general (e.g., warehousing) are available in most countries to help finalize the sale.

Sources: "Globalization: Lessons Learned," *Business Week,* November 6, 2000, p. 228; Robert Selwitz, "The Logistics of Geography," *Global Business,* February 2000, pp. 48–56; Krivda, "E-Supply Chain," *Fortune* (advertisement), June 21, 2000, pp. 341 ff.; Keith H. Hammonds, "The New Face of Global Competition," *Fast Company,* February 2003, pp. 91–97; and Sarah Mc Bride, "Kia's Audacious Sorento Plan," *The Wall Street Journal,* April 8, 2003, p. A12.

Getting the Product to the Right Place

Once the product is manufactured, you have to choose how to get it to the consumer. Remember, *place* is the third P in the marketing mix. You may want to sell the cereal directly to supermarkets or health-food stores, or you may want to sell it through organizations that specialize in distributing food products. Such organizations, called *intermediaries,* are in the middle of a series of organizations that distribute goods from producers to consumers. (The more traditional word for such companies is *middlemen.*)[6] Getting the product to consumers when and where they want it is critical to market success. We'll discuss the importance of marketing intermediaries and distribution in detail in Chapter 15.

Developing an Effective Promotional Strategy

promotion
All the techniques sellers use to motivate people to buy their products or services.

The last of the four Ps of marketing is promotion. **Promotion** consists of all the techniques sellers use to inform people and motivate them to buy their products or services. They include advertising; personal selling; public relations; publicity; word of mouth; and various sales promotion efforts, such as coupons, rebates, samples, and cents-off deals. Promotion is discussed in detail in Chapter 16.

Cereal makers have long used discount coupons as a central part of their ongoing strategies to build and promote their brands. Part of their thinking is that if the discount induces you to try a particular cereal you will become a repeat customer. Would you be inclined to use this strategy to launch a new cereal like Fiberrific? Why or why not?

This last step in the marketing process often includes relationship building with customers. That includes responding to suggestions consumers may make to improve the product or its marketing. Postpurchase, or after-sale, service may include exchanging goods that weren't satisfactory and making other adjustments to ensure consumer satisfaction, including recycling. Marketing is an ongoing process. To remain competitive, companies must continually adapt to changes in the market and to changes in consumer wants and needs.

Progress Assessment

- What are the three parts of the marketing concept?
- What are the four Ps of the marketing mix?

Providing Marketers with Information

Every step in the marketing process depends on information that is used to make the right decisions. **Marketing research** is the analysis of markets to determine opportunities and challenges, and to find the information needed to make good decisions.

marketing research
The analysis of markets to determine opportunities and challenges, and to find the information needed to make good decisions.

Marketing research helps determine what customers have purchased in the past and what situational changes have occurred to alter not only what consumers want now but also what they're likely to want in the future. In addition, marketers conduct research on business trends, the ecological impact of their decisions, global trends, and more. Businesses need information in order to compete effectively, and marketing research is the activity that gathers that information. Note, too, that in addition to listening to customers, marketing researchers should pay attention to what employees, shareholders, dealers, consumer advocates, media representatives, and other stakeholders ➤P. 6◀ have to say.

The Marketing Research Process

A simplified marketing research process consists of four key steps:

1. Defining the question (problem or opportunity) and determining the present situation.
2. Collecting data.
3. Analyzing the research data.
4. Choosing the best solution and implementing it.

The following sections look at each of these steps.

Defining the Question and Determining the Present Situation Marketing researchers should be given the freedom to help discover what the present situation is, what the problems or opportunities are, what the alternatives are, what information is needed, and how to go about gathering and analyzing data.

Collecting Data Obtaining usable information is vital to the marketing research process. Research can become quite expensive, so some trade-off must often be made between the need for information and the cost of obtaining that information. Normally the least expensive method is to gather information that has already been compiled by others and published in journals and books or made available online. Such existing data are called **secondary data** since you aren't the first one to gather them. Figure 13.4 lists the principal sources of secondary marketing research information. Despite its name, secondary data should be gathered first to avoid incurring unnecessary expense.

secondary data
Information that has already been compiled by others and published in journals and books or made available online.

primary data
Data that you gather yourself (not from secondary sources such as books and magazines).

Often, secondary data don't provide all the information managers need for important business decisions. To gather additional, in-depth information, marketers must do their own research. The results of such new studies are called **primary data**. One way to gather primary data is to conduct a survey. Telephone surveys, online surveys, mail surveys, and personal interviews are the most common forms. Focus groups are another popular method of surveying individuals.

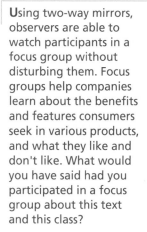

Using two-way mirrors, observers are able to watch participants in a focus group without disturbing them. Focus groups help companies learn about the benefits and features consumers seek in various products, and what they like and don't like. What would you have said had you participated in a focus group about this text and this class?

PRIMARY SOURCES	SECONDARY SOURCES		
Interviews	**Government publications**		
Surveys	*Statistical Abstract of the United States*	*Census of Transportation*	
Observation	*Survey of Current Business*	*Annual Survey of Manufacturers*	
Focus groups	*Census of Retail Trade*		
Online surveys			
Questionnaires	**Commercial publications**		
Customer comments	ACNielsen Company studies on retailing and media		
	Marketing Research Corporation of America studies on consumer purchases		
	Selling Areas–Marketing, Inc., reports on food sales		
	Magazines		
	Entrepreneur	*Journal of Retailing*	*Journal of Advertising Research*
	Business Week	*Journal of Consumer Research*	Trade magazines appropriate to your industry such as *Progressive Grocer*
	Fortune	*Journal of Advertising*	Reports from various chambers of commerce
	Inc.	*Journal of Marketing Research*	
	Advertising Age	*Marketing News*	
	Forbes		
	Harvard Business Review		
	Journal of Marketing		
	Newspapers		
	The Wall Street Journal, Barron's		
	Internal sources		
	Company records	Income statements	
	Balance sheets	Prior research reports	
	General sources		
	Internet searches	Commercial databases	

FIGURE 13.4

SELECTED SOURCES OF PRIMARY AND SECONDARY INFORMATION

You should spend a day or two at the library becoming familiar with these sources. You can read about primary research in any marketing research text from the library.

A **focus group** is a small group of people (8 to 14 individuals, for example) who meet under the direction of a discussion leader to communicate their opinions about an organization, its products, or other given issues. This textbook is updated periodically using many focus groups made up of faculty and students. They tell the authors what subjects and examples they like and dislike, and the authors follow their suggestions for changes.

Marketers can now gather both secondary and primary data online. The authors of this text, for example, do much research online, but also gather data from books, articles, interviews, and other sources.

focus group
A small group of people who meet under the direction of a discussion leader to communicate their opinions about an organization, its products, or other given issues.

Analyzing the Research Data The data collected in the research process must be turned into useful information.[7] Careful, honest interpretation of the data collected can help a company find useful alternatives to specific marketing challenges. For example, by doing primary research, Fresh Italy, a small Italian pizzeria, found that its pizza's taste was rated superior compared to the larger pizza chains. However, the company's sales lagged behind the competition. Secondary research on the industry revealed that free delivery (which Fresh Italy did not offer) was more important to customers than taste. Fresh Italy now delivers—and has increased its market share.

Making Ethical Decisions

www.kelloggs.com

No Kidding

Marketers have long recognized that children can be an important influence on their parents' buying decisions. In fact, many direct appeals for products are focused on children. Let's say that at Fiberrific you've experienced a great response to your new high-fiber, high-protein cereal among health-conscious consumers. The one important group you haven't been able to attract is children. Therefore, the product development team is considering introducing Fiberrific Jr. to expand the product line.

Fiberrific Jr. may have strong market potential if you follow two recommendations of the research department. First, coat the flakes generously with sugar (significantly changing the cereal's nutritional benefits). Second, promote the product exclusively on children's TV programs. Such a promotional strategy should create a strong demand for the product, especially if you offer a premium (a toy or other "surprise") in each box. The consensus among the research department is that kids will love the new taste, plus parents will agree to buy Fiberrific Jr. because of their positive impression of your best-selling brand. The research director commented, "The chance of a parent actually reading our label and noting the addition of sugar is nil."

Would you introduce Fiberrific Jr. according to the recommendations of your research department? What are the benefits of doing so? What are the risks involved in following the recommendations? What would you do if you were the marketing manager for this product?

Choosing the Best Solution and Implementing It After collecting and analyzing data, market researchers determine alternative strategies and make recommendations as to which strategy may be best and why. This final step in a research effort involves following up on the actions taken to see if the results were as expected. If not, the company can take corrective action and conduct new studies in the ongoing attempt to provide consumer satisfaction at the lowest cost. You can see, then, that marketing research is a continuous process of responding to changes in the marketplace and changes in consumer preferences.

Company websites have vastly improved the marketing research process in both domestic and global markets. Businesses can now continuously interact with their customers as they strive to improve products and services. The information exchanged can be useful in determining what customers want. Keeping customer information in a database ➤P. 17◄ enables a company to improve its product offerings over time and to design promotions that are geared exactly to meet the needs of specific groups of consumers.

In today's customer-driven market, ethics ➤P. 102◄ is also important in every aspect of marketing. Companies should therefore do what's right as well as what's profitable. This step could add greatly to the social benefits of marketing decisions. (See the Making Ethical Decisions box.)

The Marketing Environment

environmental scanning
The process of identifying the factors that can affect marketing success.

Marketing managers must be aware of the surrounding environment when making marketing mix decisions. **Environmental scanning** is the process of identifying the factors that can affect marketing success. As you can see in Figure 13.5, those factors include global, technological, sociocultural, competitive, and economic influences. We discussed these factors in some detail in Chapter 1, but it is helpful to review them from a strictly marketing perspective as well.

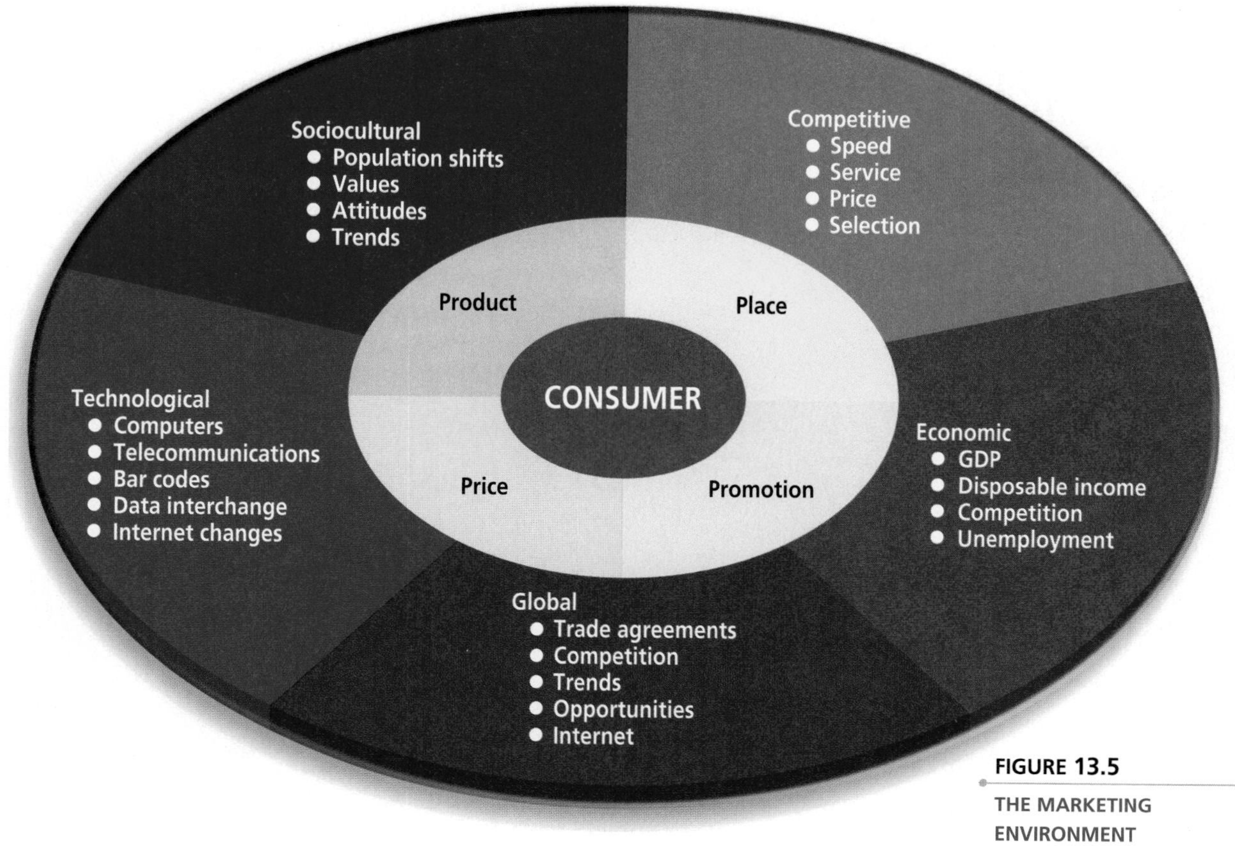

FIGURE 13.5

THE MARKETING ENVIRONMENT

Global Factors The most dramatic global change is probably the growth of the Internet. Now businesses can reach many of the consumers in the world relatively easily and carry on a dialogue with them about the goods and services they want. This globalization of marketing puts more pressure on those whose responsibility is to deliver products. Many marketers outsource that function to companies like FedEx, UPS, and DHL, which have a solid reputation for delivering goods quickly.

Technological Factors The most important technological changes also involve the Internet and the growth of consumer databases. Using consumer databases, companies can develop products and services that closely match the needs of consumers. As you read in Chapter 9, it is now possible to produce customized goods and services for about the same price as mass-produced goods. Thus, flexible manufacturing and mass customization ➤P. 315◄ are also major influences on marketers.

Sociocultural Factors There are a number of social trends that marketers must monitor to maintain their close relationship with customers. Population growth and changing demographics are examples of social trends that can have an effect on sales. For example, one of the fastest-growing segments of the U.S. population in the 21st century is people over 65. The increase in the number of older Americans creates growing demand for nursing homes, health care, prescription drugs, recreation, continuing education, and more. Other shifts in the American population are creating new challenges for marketers as they adjust their products to meet the tastes and preferences of Hispanic, Asian, and other growing ethnic groups.

Demographically, America is growing increasingly multicultural. This change in the environment of marketing has led to many new and interesting developments, including the International Channel. This ad is aimed at the Asian market. Other shows focus on African Americans or Hispanics or smaller segments of those groups. Are you aware of any ethnic segments within the United States that seem to be left out of the attempts by marketers to reach emerging new groups?

Competitive Factors Of course, marketers must pay attention to the dynamic competitive environment. Many brick-and-mortar companies must be aware of new competition from the Internet, including those that sell automobiles, insurance, music videos, and clothes.[8] In the book business, Barnes & Noble and Borders Books are still adjusting to the new reality of Amazon.com's huge selection of books at good prices.[9] Now that consumers can literally search the world for the best buys through the Internet, marketers must adjust their pricing policies accordingly. Similarly, they have to adjust to competitors who can deliver products quickly or provide excellent service.

Economic Factors Marketers must pay close attention to the economic environment. As we began the new millennium, the United States was experiencing unparalleled growth and customers were eager to buy even the most expensive automobiles, watches, and vacations. But as the economy slowed, marketers had to adapt by offering products that were less expensive and more tailored to consumers with modest incomes.[10] Marketers in countries such as Indonesia had already gone through such an economic fall and are now recovering. You can see, therefore, that environmental scanning is critical to a company's success during rapidly changing economic times.

Critical Thinking

What environmental changes are occurring in your community? What environmental changes in marketing are most likely to change your career prospects in the future? How can you learn more about those changes? What might you do to prepare for them?

Two Different Markets: Consumer and Business-to-Business (B2B)

Marketers must know as much as possible about the market they wish to serve. As we defined it in Chapter 6, a market ➤P. 194⮜ consists of people with unsatisfied wants and needs who have both the resources and the willingness to buy. Thus, if there are people who want a high-fiber, low-sugar cereal like Fiberrific, and if those people have the resources and willingness to buy it, then it is said that there's a market for Fiberrific.

There are two major markets in business: the consumer market and the business-to-business market. The **consumer market** consists of all the individuals or households that want goods and services for personal consumption or use and have the resources to buy them. The **business-to-business (B2B) market** consists of all the individuals and organizations that want goods and services to use in producing other goods and services or to sell, rent, or supply goods to others. Oil-drilling bits, cash registers, display cases, office desks, public accounting audits, and corporate legal advice are examples of B2B goods and services. Traditionally, they have been known as industrial goods and services because they are used in industry.

consumer market
All the individuals or households that want goods and services for personal consumption or use.

business-to-business (B2B) market
All the individuals and organizations that want goods and services to use in producing other goods and services or to sell, rent, or supply goods to others.

The important thing to remember is that the buyer's reason for buying—that is, the end use of the product—determines whether a product is considered a consumer product or a B2B product. For example, a box of Fiberrific cereal bought for a family's breakfast is considered a consumer product. However, if Dinnie's Diner purchased the same box of Fiberrific to sell to its breakfast customers, the cereal would then be considered a B2B product. The following sections will outline in more detail consumer and B2B markets.

Progress Assessment

- What are the four steps in the marketing research process?
- What is environmental scanning?
- Can you define the terms *consumer market* and *business-to-business market*?

The Consumer Market

The total potential consumer market consists of the over 6 billion people in global markets. Because consumer groups differ greatly in age, education level, income, and taste, a business usually can't fill the needs of every group. Therefore, it must first decide which groups to serve and then develop products and services specially tailored to their needs.

Take the Campbell Soup Company, for example. You know Campbell for its traditional soups such as chicken noodle and tomato. You may also have noticed that Campbell has expanded its product line to appeal to a number of different tastes. Campbell noticed the population growth in the American South and in the Latino community in cities across the nation, so it introduced a creole soup for the southern market and a red bean soup for the Latino market. In Texas and California, where people like their food with a bit of kick, Campbell makes its nacho cheese soup spicier than in other parts of the country. Campbell is just one company that has had some success studying the consumer market, breaking it down into categories, and then developing products for separate groups of consumers.

market segmentation
The process of dividing the total market into groups whose members have similar characteristics.

The process of dividing the total market into several groups whose members have similar characteristics is called **market segmentation**. Selecting which groups (market segments) an organization can serve profitably is called

Pepsi's latest effort at market segmentation and targeting is illustrated in its new products, which include Pepsi Blue, lemon-lime Sierra Mist, and Mountain Dew Code Red. Pepsi wants to build on its foundation of Pepsi and Mountain Dew to appeal to smaller market segments. Will one or more of these new flavors appeal to you? What, if any, factors might keep Coke or Pepsi from developing many additional brands of soda?

target marketing. For example, a shoe store may choose to sell only women's shoes, only children's shoes, or only athletic shoes. The issue is finding the right target market (the segment that would be most profitable to serve) for the new venture.

Segmenting the Consumer Market

There are several ways a firm can segment the consumer market (see Figure 13.6). For example, rather than trying to sell Fiberrific throughout the United States, you might try to focus on just one or two regions of the country where you might be most successful. One option is to focus on people in southern states such as Florida and North Carolina. Dividing the market by geographic area (cities, counties, states, regions, etc.) is called **geographic segmentation**.

Alternatively, you could aim Fiberrific's promotions toward people aged 25 to 45 who have some college training and have above-average incomes. Automobiles such as Lexus are often targeted to this audience. Segmentation by age, income, and education level are ways of **demographic segmentation**. Also included are religion, race, and profession. This is the most used segmentation variable, but not necessarily the best. The Dealing with Change box on p. 414 explores how a cable television channel successfully used the power of this type of market segmentation.

target marketing
Marketing directed toward those groups (market segments) an organization decides it can serve profitably.

geographic segmentation
Dividing the market by geographic area.

demographic segmentation
Dividing the market by age, income, and education level.

psychographic segmentation
Dividing the market using the group's values, attitudes, and interests.

benefit segmentation
Dividing the market by determining which benefits of the product to talk about.

volume, or usage, segmentation
Dividing the market by usage (volume of use).

You may want Fiberrific ads to portray a group's lifestyle. To do that, you could study the group's lifestyle, values, attitudes, and interests. This segmentation strategy is called **pychographic segmentation**. For example, if you decide to target Generation Y (teenagers), you would do an in-depth study of their values and interests. Such research reveals which TV shows they watch and which actors they like the best. That information could then be used to develop advertisements for those TV shows using those stars. PepsiCo did such a segmentation study for its Mountain Dew brand. The resulting promotion dealt with Generation Y's living life to the limit.

What benefits of Fiberrific might you talk about? Should you emphasize high fiber, low sugar, price, health in general, or what? Determining which benefits are preferred and using those benefits to promote a product is called **benefit segmentation**.

You can also determine who are the big eaters of cereal. Children certainly eat a good deal of cereal, but so do adults. Separating the market by usage (volume of product use) is called **volume, or usage, segmentation**. Most cereal companies seem to target children. Why not go for the adult segment, a less competitive market, and one whose members actually eat more cereal each day than children do?

The best segmentation strategy is to use all the variables to come up with a consumer profile (a target market) that's sizable, reachable, and profitable. On the one hand, that may mean not segmenting the market at all and instead going after the total market (everyone). On the other hand, it may mean going after smaller and smaller segments. We'll discuss that strategy next.

Reaching Smaller Market Segments

niche marketing
The process of finding small but profitable market segments and designing or finding products for them.

Niche marketing is the process of finding small but profitable market segments and designing or finding products for them. Just how small such a segment can be is illustrated by Fridgedoor.com. This company sells refrigerator

MAIN DIMENSION	SAMPLE VARIABLES	TYPICAL SEGMENTS
Geographic segmentation	Region	Northeast, Midwest, South, West
	City or county size	Under 5,000; 5,000–10,999; 20,000–49,000; 50,000–99,999
	Density	Urban, suburban, rural
Demographic segmentation	Gender	Male, female
	Age	Under 5; 5–10; 11–18; 19–34; 35–49; 50–64; 65 and over
	Education	Some high school or less, high school graduate, some college, college graduate, postgraduate
	Race	Caucasian, African American, Indian, Asian, Hispanic
	Nationality	American, Asian, Eastern European, Japanese
	Life stage	Infant, preschool, child, teenager, collegiate, adult, senior
	Income	Under \$15,000; \$15,000–\$24,999; \$25,000–\$44,999; \$45,000–\$74,999; \$75,000 and over
	Household size	1; 2; 3–4; 5 or more
	Occupation	Professional, technical, clerical, sales supervisors, farmers, students, home-based business owners, retired, unemployed
Psychographic segmentation	Personality	Gregarious, compulsive, extroverted, aggressive, ambitious
	Values	Actualizers, fulfillers, achievers, experiencers, believers, strivers, makers, strugglers
	Lifestyle	Upscale, moderate
Benefit segmentation	Comfort	(Benefit segmentation divides an already established market into smaller, more homogeneous segments. Those people who desire economy in a car would be an example. The benefit desired varies by product.)
	Convenience	
	Durability	
	Economy	
	Health	
	Luxury	
	Safety	
	Status	
Volume segmentation	Usage	Heavy users, light users, nonusers
	Loyalty status	None, medium, strong

FIGURE 13.6

MARKET SEGMENTATION

This table shows some of the methods marketers use to divide the market. The aim of segmentation is to break the market into smaller units.

magnets on the Internet. It keeps some 1,500 different magnets in stock and sells as many as 400 a week. Marco Sorani (featured in the chapter opening profile) focuses on a niche market—the disabled—and does quite well.

One-to-one marketing means developing a unique mix of goods and services for *each individual customer.* Travel agencies often develop such packages, including airline reservations, hotel reservations, rental cars, restaurants, and admission to museums and other attractions for individual customers. This is relatively easy to do in B2B markets where each customer may buy in huge volume. But one-to-one marketing is now becoming possible in consumer markets as well. Dell provides a unique computer system for each customer. Automakers are starting to customize cars as well.

one-to-one marketing Developing a unique mix of goods and services for each individual customer.

Moving toward Relationship Marketing

In the world of mass production following the Industrial Revolution, marketers responded by practicing mass marketing. **Mass marketing** means developing products and promotions to please large groups of people. That is,

mass marketing Developing products and promotions to please large groups of people.

Dealing with Change

www.bet.com

Finding New Market Opportunities

One of the most successful African American entrepreneurs in America is Robert L. Johnson of BET. Johnson noticed that African Americans watched more TV than many other groups, and that advertisers wanted to reach them. The market potential was so great that Johnson was able to get funding easily. BET now airs 24 hours a day and reaches about 67 million homes, including almost 100 percent of the 6.8 million African American households with cable.

That's the power of market segmentation—breaking the total market into smaller segments based on age, sex, income, or some other category (such as ethnicity)—and then designing products and services to meet the specific needs of those segments. Once you have found an audience, the idea is to develop new products to meet the changing needs of that market. BET Holdings, for example, has expanded into a billion-dollar enterprise with two movie channels, a jazz channel, BET Weekend (a weekend newspaper insert), a health and fitness magazine called *Heart and Soul,* a financial services company, a clothing line, an airline called DC Air, and more—including a planned chain of music-themed restaurants. Also in the plans are 10 TV movies, a late-night talk show, and a Las Vegas restaurant.

Once you have developed such a market niche, the next step is to develop a close relationship with those customers and develop a loyal following among them. Most of BET's nearly 600 employees are African American. Many of them are young and knowledgeable about their peers. They are able to talk with BET's customers and work with them to develop the new products and services that they want. The African American market segment is made up of some 37 million people, and their incomes are rising fast. Johnson recognizes the fact that there are other market segments that may prove equally profitable. He says, "We're moving toward more market fragmentation, so markets can become sustainable with smaller and smaller numbers, customized down to even one person . . . You can combine strong brand identification with niche marketing if you're nimble."

Media giant Viacom recently bought BET Holdings for $3 billion. Viacom had the money, TV movies, feature films, and other resources to greatly improve BET's offerings. Viacom already owned CBS, UPN, MTV, VH1, Nickelodeon, TNN, Showtime, Country Music Television, and TV Land—and some of the shows from these companies may soon be shown on BET. Johnson has expanded his financial interests by building hotels in some cities. He recently launched an expansion franchise in Charlotte, NC, for the National Basketball Association and is seeking to buy a bank.

There are marketing opportunities available in other market segments, including people over the age of 60, Asian Americans, and teens. You could be the next entrepreneur who develops TV shows, restaurants, and other products to meet the needs of these specialized market segments. Part of managing change is being aware of new market opportunities and then satisfying them.

Sources: Brian Sharp, "BET Executive Robert Johnson, an Icon in the Making," Gannett News Service, June 16, 2000; Neil Irwin, "Deal Means Potential Change for BET.com," *Washington Post,* November 4, 2000, pp. E1–E2; www.BET.com, 2003; and Nicholas Johnston, "BET Founder May Try to Buy Thrift," *Washington Post,* June 13, 2003, pp. E1 and E4.

there is little segmentation. The mass marketer tries to sell products to as many people as possible. That means using mass media, such as TV, radio, and newspapers. Although mass marketing led many firms to success, marketing managers often got so caught up with their products and competition that they became less responsive to the market. Airlines, for example, got so caught up in meeting competition that they often annoyed customers.

relationship marketing
Marketing strategy with the goal of keeping individual customers over time by offering them products that exactly meet their requirements.

Relationship marketing tends to lead away from mass production and toward custom-made goods and services. The goal is to keep individual customers over time by offering them new products that exactly meet their requirements. The latest in technology enables sellers to work with individual buyers to determine their wants and needs and to develop goods and services specifically designed for them (e.g., hand-tailored shirts and unique vacations). One-way messages in mass media give way to a personal dialogue among participants. Relationship marketing, combined with enterprise resource planning (ERP), links firms in a smooth customer-oriented system.[11]

The following are just a couple of examples of relationship marketing:

- Airlines, rental car companies, and hotels have frequent-user programs through which loyal customers can earn special services and awards. For example, a traveler can earn bonus miles good for free flights on an airline. He or she can also earn benefits at a car rental agency (that includes no stopping at the rental desk—just pick up a car and go) and special services at a hotel, including faster check-in and check-out procedures, flowers in the room, free breakfasts, and free exercise rooms.
- The Hard Rock Cafe used customer relationship management software to launch a loyalty program, personalize its marketing campaigns, and provide the contact center with more customer information. The result was that response times to customer inquiries were cut from a week to 24 hours. A recent marketing campaign directed at loyal customers yielded $150,000 in sales.[12]

One-to-one marketing means designing a separate product for each individual customer. An example is Kool Calendars. Using Xerox technology, the company can take pictures that you give them and make a customized calendar from those pictures. It is easier to customize services because you only have to find what a customer wants and then adapt the service accordingly. What other services could be customized to each individual?

Relationship marketing is more concerned with retaining old customers than with creating new ones. Special deals, fantastic service, loyalty programs (e.g., frequent-flier programs), and the like are just the beginning. By maintaining current databases, companies can custom-make products for individuals. Levi-Strauss, for example, tried to recapture lost market share by permitting some stores to sell custom-made Levi's for about $10 more than mass-produced Levi's. Through an agreement with Levi's, once the store has your measurements, you can be assured of a perfect fit every time (as long as you don't gain or lose weight) at a reasonable price. The Spotlight on Small Business box on page 416 shows how a small business can compete with larger firms by using relationship marketing.

Forming Communities of Buyers

Relationship marketing eventually leads to a dialogue with customers, often on the Internet (e.g., consumer chat rooms). As we described earlier, a database is established so that every contact with consumers results in more information about them.[13] For example, whenever a customer buys something, the color, the size, and other important data are recorded in the database. If the consumer sends a letter, that letter is also included. Over time, the seller learns more and more about its customers; the next step is to put that knowledge to use in establishing a community of buyers. Smith & Noble, a direct-to-consumer window-covering company, used such information to set up a website to attract more buyers. The site now brings in 20 percent of total sales, and the orders are 50 percent larger than orders by phone or by mail.[14]

Fly & Field is a small store in Glen Ellyn, Illinois, that sells fly-fishing equipment. Fly fishers are a relatively small market locally, but a nice-sized market nationally. To reach the national audience, Fly & Field has established an interactive website (www.flyfield.com) where customers and prospects can www.zanescycles.com

Spotlight on Small Business

Relationship Marketing of Bicycles

Putting into practice old marketing techniques has enabled small retailers to compete with the giants such as Wal-Mart and Sears. Zane's Cycles in Branford, Connecticut, is a good example. Chris Zane, the owner, began the shop when he was still a teenager. Early on, he learned that to keep customers a store has to offer outstanding service and more. The principle behind such service is a concept now called customer relationship management (CRM). Long before such a concept emerged, however, small stores knew that the secret to long-term success against giant competitors is to give superior service.

Most large stores focus on making the sale; they give follow-up service little thought. The goal is to make the transaction, and that is the end of it; thus, such an approach is called *transactional marketing.*

With CRM, in contrast, the goal is to keep a customer for life. Zane's Cycles attracts customers by setting competitive prices (and providing free coffee). Chris Zane keeps customers by giving them free lifetime service on their bicycles. He also sells helmets to young people at cost to encourage safety.

Zane keeps a database on customers so that he knows what they need and when they will need it. For example, if he sells a bicycle with a child's seat, he knows that soon the customer who purchased that bike may be buying a regular bicycle for the child—and he can send out an appropriate brochure at just the right time. Zane encourages people to give him their names, addresses, and other such information by offering to make exchanges without receipts for those people whose transaction information is in the database.

Zane also establishes close community relationships by providing scholarships for local students. Because of Zane's competitive prices, great service, and community involvement, his customers recommend his shop to others. No large store can compete with Zane's in the areas of friendly service and personal attention to each customer. That is what the new style of marketing is all about.

Sources: Rekha Balu, "Listen Up," *Fast Company,* May 2000, pp. 304–14; Ross Atkin, "Getting Past the Schwinn Mentality," *Christian Science Monitor,* August 8, 2000, p. 16; Donna Fenn, "A Bigger Wheel," *Inc.,* November 2000, pp. 78–88; www.zanes.com, 2003; and Jennifer Monahan, "Why Customers Buy Is More Important than What They Buy," *1 to 1 Magazine,* May/June 2003, pp. 52–53.

chat with each other. Naturally, visitors to the site can also access fly-fishing materials and an online catalog where they can buy what they want.

Fly & Field is not alone. Many companies are using interactive websites as part of the move from relationship marketing to forming communities of buyers. Others are using a wide variety of activities. Harley-Davidson has a 220,000-member club that has its own newsletter, meetings, and rallies. The Wally Byam Caravan Club is made up of owners of Airstream trailers and motor homes; they have events for which the manufacturer sends merchandise, staff, information, giveaway items, and more. Community bonding leads to a strong commitment to the products and the company. Such loyalty is hard to match.

Relationship marketing depends greatly on understanding consumers and responding quickly to their wants and needs. Therefore, knowing how consumers make decisions is important to marketers. An understanding of the consumer decision-making process helps marketers adapt their strategies in reaching customers and developing lasting relationships.

The Consumer Decision-Making Process

A major part of the marketing discipline is called consumer behavior. Figure 13.7 shows the consumer decision-making process and some of the outside factors that influence it. The five steps in the process are often studied in courses on consumer behavior. Problem recognition may occur, say, when your washing machine breaks down. This leads to an information search—you look for ads about washing machines and read brochures about them. You may even

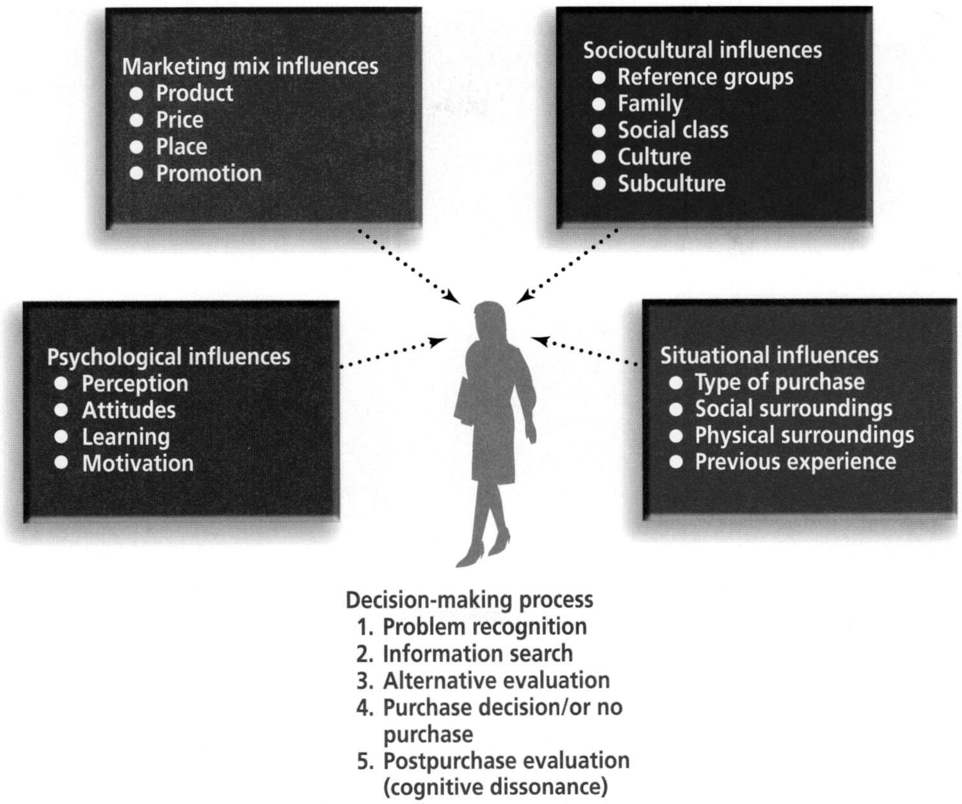

FIGURE 13.7

THE CONSUMER DECISION-MAKING PROCESS AND OUTSIDE INFLUENCES

There are many influences on consumers as they decide which goods and services to buy. Marketers have some influence, but it's not usually as strong as sociocultural influences. Helping consumers in their information search and their evaluation of alternatives is a major function of marketing.

consult a secondary data source like *Consumer Reports* or other information sources. And, most likely, you will seek advice from other people who have purchased washing machines. After compiling all this information, you evaluate alternatives and make a purchase decision. But the process does not end here. After the purchase, you may first ask the people you spoke to previously how their machines perform and then do other comparisons. Marketing researchers investigate consumer thought processes and behavior at each stage to determine the best way to facilitate marketing exchanges.

Consumer behavior researchers also study the various influences that impact on consumer behavior. Figure 13.7 shows several such influences that affect consumer buying: marketing mix variables (the four Ps); psychological influences, such as perception and attitudes; situational influences, such as the type of purchase and the physical surroundings; and sociocultural influences, such as reference groups and culture. Other factors important in the consumer decision-making process whose technical definitions may be unfamiliar to you include the following:

- **Learning** involves changes in an individual's behavior resulting from previous experiences and information. For example, if you've tried a particular brand of shampoo and you don't like it, you may never buy it again.
- **Reference group** is the group that an individual uses as a reference point in the formation of his or her beliefs, attitudes, values, or behavior. For example, a college student who carries a briefcase instead of a backpack may see businesspeople as his or her reference group.
- **Culture** is the set of values, attitudes, and ways of doing things that is transmitted from one generation to another in a given society. The American culture, for example, emphasizes education, freedom, and diversity.

This young lady is doing an alternative evaluation at the Yankee Candle Outlet in Freeport, Maine. There are many, many scents to choose from and many different kinds of candles. How far from a purchase decision do you think she might be?

- **Subculture** is the set of values, attitudes, and ways of doing things that results from belonging to a certain ethnic group, religious group, racial group, or other group with which one closely identifies (e.g., teenagers). The subculture is one small part of the larger culture. Your subculture may prefer rap and hip-hop music, while your parents' subculture may prefer light jazz.
- **Cognitive dissonance** is a type of psychological conflict that can occur after a purchase. Consumers who make a major purchase like a car may have doubts about whether they got the best product at the best price. Marketers must therefore reassure such consumers after the sale that they made a good decision. An auto dealer, for example, may send positive press articles about the particular car a consumer purchased. The dealer may also offer product guarantees and provide certain free services to the customer.

Consumer behavior courses are a long-standing part of a marketing curriculum. Today, colleges are expanding their offerings in marketing to include courses in business-to-business marketing. The following section will give you some insight into that growing and important area.

The Business-to-Business Market

B2B marketers include manufacturers; intermediaries such as retailers; institutions (e.g., hospitals, schools, and charities); and the government. The B2B market is larger than the consumer market because items are often sold and resold several times in the B2B process before they are sold to the final consumer. The marketing strategies often differ from consumer marketing because business buyers have their own decision-making process. Several factors make B2B marketing different; some of the more important are as follows:

1. The number of customers in the B2B market is relatively few; that is, there are just a few construction firms or mining operations compared to the 70 million or so households in the U.S. consumer market.

	BUSINESS-TO-BUSINESS MARKET	CONSUMER MARKET
Market structure	Relatively few potential customers Larger purchases Geographically concentrated	Many potential customers Smaller purchases Geographically dispersed
Products	Require technical, complex products Frequently require customization Frequently require technical advice, delivery, and after-sale service	Require less technical products Sometimes require customization Sometimes require technical advice, delivery, and after-sale service
Buying procedures	Buyers are trained Negotiate details of most purchases Follow objective standards Formal process involving specific employees Closer relationships between marketers and buyers Often buy from multiple sources	No special training Accept standard terms for most purchases Use personal judgment Informal process involving household members Impersonal relationships between marketers and consumers Rarely buy from multiple sources

FIGURE 13.8

COMPARING BUSINESS-TO-BUSINESS AND CONSUMER BUYING BEHAVIOR

2. The size of business customers is relatively large; that is, a few large organizations account for most of the employment and production of various goods and services. Nonetheless, there are many small to medium-sized firms in the United States that together make an attractive market.
3. B2B markets tend to be geographically concentrated. For example, oilfields tend to be concentrated in the Southwest and in Alaska. Consequently, marketing efforts may be concentrated on a particular geographic area and distribution problems can be minimized by locating warehouses near industrial centers.
4. Business buyers are generally thought to be more rational (as opposed to emotional) than ultimate consumers in their selection of goods and services; they use specifications and often more carefully weigh the total product offer, including quality, price, and service.
5. B2B sales tend to be direct. Manufacturers sell products, such as tires, directly to auto manufacturers but tend to use intermediaries, such as wholesalers and retailers, to sell to ultimate consumers.
6. There is much more emphasis on personal selling in B2B markets than in consumer markets. Whereas consumer promotions are based more on advertising, B2B sales are based on selling. That is because there are fewer customers who demand more personal service.

Figure 13.8 shows some of the differences between buying behavior in the B2B market compared to the consumer market. You will learn all about the business-to-business market if you take advanced marketing courses.

UPDATING THE MARKETING CONCEPT

As we noted earlier in the chapter, the marketing concept was developed in the 1950s to meet the consumer needs of the time. Now that we're in the 21st century, marketers have to readjust their strategies to meet the needs of modern

A serviceman will be there sometime between 8am tomorrow & next spring. Please have someone home during that time.
Doan Piraro 7-17-02

Unfortunately, what makes this cartoon so humorous is its reflection of what consumers perceive as everyday reality. Companies often will promise delivery of a product or service on a certain day, but not at a precise time, or even whether it will be morning or afternoon, forcing customers to wait. Have you had such an experience? What was your reaction?

consumers. That means each of the elements of the marketing concept—a consumer orientation, a service orientation, and a profit orientation—all have to be updated. Let's explore each of those changes next.

From Providing Customer Satisfaction to Exceeding Expectations

Marketing's goal in the past was to provide customer satisfaction. Today, the goal of some six sigma quality ➤P. 303◀ firms is to exceed customer expectations by providing goods and services that exactly meet their requirements. One objective of a company's marketing effort, therefore, is to make sure that the response to customer wants and needs is so fast and courteous that customers are truly surprised and pleased by the experience.

You don't have to look far to see that most organizations haven't yet reached the goal of meeting, much less exceeding, customer expectations. Retail stores, government agencies, and other organizations may still irritate customers as often as they please them. Nonetheless, global competition is forcing organizations to adopt quality concepts, which means, above all, adapting organizations to customers.

Businesses have learned that employees won't provide first-class goods and services to customers unless they receive first-class treatment themselves. Marketers must therefore work with others in the firm, such as human resource personnel, to help make sure that employees are pleased. In some firms, such as IBM, employees are called *internal customers* to show the need to treat them well—like customers.

Benchmarking and Uniting Organizations

As we explained in Chapter 8, determining whether organizations are providing world-class service and quality is done through competitive benchmarking ➤P. 256◀. That means that companies compare their processes and products with those of the best companies in the world to learn how to improve them. Xerox Corporation, for example, has benchmarked its functions against corporate leaders such as American Express (for billing), Ford (for manufacturing floor layout), Mary Kay Cosmetics (for warehousing and distribution), and Florida Power & Light (for quality processes).

Manufacturers, unfortunately, cannot always exceed customer expectations on their own. They have to have the cooperation of suppliers to assure customers that they are getting the finest parts. They have to have close relationships with dealers to make sure that the dealers are providing fast, friendly service. We shall discuss the close relationships among marketing intermediaries in Chapter 15.

Maintaining a Profit Orientation

Marketing managers must make sure that everyone in the organization understands that the purpose behind pleasing customers and uniting organizations is to ensure a profit ➤P. 4◀ for the firm. Using that profit, the organization can then satisfy other stakeholders ➤P. 6◀ of the firm such as stockholders, environmentalists, and the local community.

It has been estimated that reducing by 5 percent the number of customers who defect—that is, who switch from buying your products to buying another company's—can increase profit by as much as 85 percent (though this figure varies by industry). Some of that profit comes from increased purchases and some from referrals. Thus, customer relationship management is becoming an intimate part of any organization seeking to maximize profits.

ESTABLISHING RELATIONSHIPS WITH ALL STAKEHOLDERS

The traditional marketing concept emphasized giving *customers* what they want. Modern marketing goes further by recognizing the need to please other stakeholders as well. If you go too far in giving customers what they want, the organization may lose money and hurt other stakeholders, such as investors. Likewise, you could please customers but harm the environment, thus harming relationships with the larger community. Balancing the wants and needs of all the firm's stakeholders—employees, customers, suppliers, dealers, stockholders, media representatives, and the community—is a much bigger challenge than marketing has attempted in the past.

Stakeholder marketing, then, is establishing and maintaining mutually beneficial exchange relationships over time with all the stakeholders of the organization. Organizations that adopt stakeholder marketing take the community's needs into mind when designing and marketing products. For example, many companies have responded to the environmental movement by introducing green products into the marketplace. A **green product** is one whose production, use, and disposal don't damage the environment.[15] For example, Ventura, California–based Patagonia sells many items of outdoor clothing made from organically grown cotton; that means less use of fertilizers to pollute the soil. Patagonia also pledges 1 percent of sales or 10 percent of pretax profit, whichever is greater, to local preservation efforts.

stakeholder marketing
Establishing and maintaining mutually beneficial exchange relationships over time with all the stakeholders of the organization.

green product
A product whose production, use, and disposal don't damage the environment.

"Green marketing" is involved with products that are ecologically safe, clean, and in the case of the "Think" bike, cheap. What could be better ecologically than traveling to work or school on a bicycle rather than in a SUV? This bike, designed by Ford, lets you do that. It will go as fast as 18 mph and when needed to climb hills or to travel longer distances you can switch to its battery power. What hesitation might you have in using such a bike for short errands or travel to school?

Customer Relationship Management (CRM) Goes High Tech

In marketing, the 80/20 rule says that 80 percent of your business is likely to come from just 20 percent of your customers. That's why some companies, like banks, have found it more profitable to discourage some unprofitable customers and put more focus on profitable ones—giving them better, more personal service. Also, it is far more expensive to get a new customer than to strengthen a relationship with an existing one. That is what customer relationship management (CRM) is all about.

One reason CRM is so popular today is that many companies are competing to provide computer software to make the process more effective. These companies have made CRM an all-encompassing business strategy, and a "customer-centric" philosophy of doing business.[16] Top-selling programs include ACT! and Goldmine for small businesses and SalesLogix and Pivotal for midrange companies. We mention these programs because you will be hearing more and more about them as CRM becomes the most profitable way of doing business.[17]

Your Prospects in Marketing

There is a wider variety of careers in marketing than in most business disciplines. Therefore, if you were to major in marketing, an array of career options would be available to you. You could become a manager in a retail store like Saks or Target. You could do marketing research or get involved in product management. You could go into selling, advertising, sales promotion, or public relations. You could get involved in transportation, storage, or international distribution. You could design interactive websites to implement CRM. These are just a few of the possibilities. As you read through the following marketing chapters, consider whether a marketing career would interest you. We'll discuss marketing careers again later, after you have reviewed all the marketing chapters.

Critical Thinking

When businesses buy goods and services from other businesses, they usually buy in large volume. Salespeople in the business-to-business area usually are paid on a commission basis; that is, they earn a certain percentage of each sale they make. Can you see why B2B sales may be a more financially rewarding career area than consumer sales? Industrial companies sell goods such as steel, lumber, computers, engines, parts, and supplies. Where would you find the names of such companies?

Progress Assessment

- Can you name and describe five ways to segment the consumer market?
- What are four key factors that make industrial markets different from consumer markets?
- What is niche marketing, and how does it differ from one-to-one marketing?
- What is stakeholder marketing?

Summary

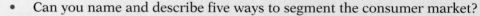

1. Define *marketing* and explain how the marketing concept applies in both for-profit and nonprofit organizations.

1. Marketing is the process of determining customer wants and needs and then providing customers with goods and services that meet or exceed their expectations.

   • ***How has marketing changed over time?***

   During the *production era,* marketing was largely a distribution function. Emphasis was on producing as many goods as possible and getting them to markets. By the early 1920s, during the *selling era,* the emphasis turned to selling and advertising to persuade customers to buy the existing goods produced by mass production. After World War II, the tremendous demand for goods and services led to the *marketing concept era,* when businesses recognized the need to be responsive to customers' needs. During the 1990s, marketing entered the *customer relationship era.* The idea became one of trying to enhance customer satisfaction and stimulate long-term customer loyalty.

   • ***What are the three parts of the marketing concept?***

   The three parts of the marketing concept are (1) a customer orientation, (2) a service orientation, and (3) a profit orientation (that is, market those goods and services that will earn the firm a profit and enable it to survive and expand to serve more customer wants and needs).

- ***What kinds of organizations are involved in marketing?***

All kinds of organizations use marketing, both for-profit and nonprofit organizations (including states, charities, churches, politicians, and schools).

2. The marketing mix consists of the four Ps of marketing: product, price, place, and promotion.
   - ***How do marketers implement the four Ps?***

   The idea is to design a *product* that people want, *price* it competitively, *place* it in a location where consumers can find it easily, and *promote* it so that consumers know it exists.

2. List and describe the four Ps of marketing.

3. Marketing research is the analysis of markets to determine opportunities and challenges and to find the information needed to make good decisions.
   - ***What are the steps to follow when conducting marketing research?***

   (1) Define the problem and determine the present situation, (2) collect data, (3) analyze the research data, and (4) choose the best solution.
   - ***What is environmental scanning?***

   Environmental scanning is the process of identifying the factors that can affect marketing success. Marketers pay attention to all the environmental factors that create opportunities and threats.
   - ***What are some of the more important environmental trends in marketing?***

   The most important global and technological change is probably the growth of the Internet. An important technological change is the growth of consumer databases. Using consumer databases, companies can develop products and services that closely match the needs of consumers. There are a number of social trends that marketers must monitor to maintain their close relationship with customers—population growth and shifts, for example. Of course, marketers must also monitor the dynamic competitive environment and pay attention to the economic environment.

3. Describe the marketing research process, and explain how marketers use environmental scanning to learn about the changing marketing environment.

4. The process of dividing the total market into several groups whose members have similar characteristics is called market segmentation.
   - ***What are some of the ways marketers segment the consumer market?***

   Geographic segmentation means dividing the market into different regions. Segmentation by age, income, and education level are ways of *demographic segmentation.* We could study a group's values, attitudes, and interests; this segmentation strategy is called *psychographic segmentation.* Determining which benefits customers prefer and using those benefits to promote a product is called *benefit segmentation.* Separating the market by usage (volume of use) is called *volume segmentation.* The best segmentation strategy is to use all the variables to come up with a consumer profile (a target market) that's sizable, reachable, and profitable.
   - ***What is the difference between mass marketing and relationship marketing?***

   Mass marketing means developing products and promotions to please large groups of people. Relationship marketing tends to lead away from mass production and toward custom-made goods and services. Its goal is to keep individual customers over time by offering them products or services that meet their needs.

4. Explain how marketers meet the needs of the consumer market through market segmentation, relationship marketing, and the study of consumer behavior.

- ***What are some of the factors that influence the consumer decision-making process?***

See Figure 13.7 on page 417 for some of the major influences on consumer decision making. Some other factors in the process are learning, reference group, culture, subculture, and cognitive dissonance.

5. List ways in which the business-to-business market differs from the consumer market.

5. The B2B market consists of manufacturers, intermediaries such as retailers, institutions (e.g., hospitals, schools, and charities), and the government.
   - ***What makes the business-to-business market different from the consumer market?***

   The number of customers in the B2B market is relatively small, and the size of business customers is relatively large. B2B markets tend to be geographically concentrated, and industrial buyers generally are more rational than ultimate consumers in their selection of goods and services. B2B sales tend to be direct, and there is much more emphasis on personal selling in B2B markets than in consumer markets.

6. Show how the marketing concept has been adapted to fit today's modern markets.

6. Now that we're in the 21st century, marketers have to readjust their strategies to meet the needs of modern consumers. That means each of the elements of the marketing concept—a consumer orientation, a service orientation, and a profit orientation—has to be updated.
   - ***How has the marketing concept been adapted to today's environment?***

   Marketing is becoming more customer-oriented than ever before. Originally, marketing's goal was simply to satisfy customers. Now marketing tries to exceed customer expectations. Rather than relying on their own resources to provide quality service, companies are counting on their suppliers, dealers, and others to help provide world-class service to customers. And profit is being maintained by focusing on present customers rather than finding new customers all the time.

7. Describe the latest marketing strategies, such as stakeholder marketing and customer relationship management (CRM).

7. Stakeholder marketing is establishing and maintaining mutually beneficial exchange relationships over time with all the stakeholders of the organization. Organizations that adopt stakeholder marketing take the community's needs into mind when designing and marketing products.
   - ***What is customer relationship management?***

   Customer relationship management (CRM) is learning as much as possible about customers and doing everything you can to satisfy them with goods and services over time.

Key Terms

psychographic segmentation 412
relationship marketing 414
secondary data 406
stakeholder marketing 421
target marketing 412
test marketing 403
volume, or usage, segmentation 412

Developing Workplace Skills

1. Think of an effective marketing mix for one of the following goods and services: a new electric car, an easy-to-use digital camera, or a car wash for your neighborhood. Be prepared to discuss your ideas in class.
2. Working in teams of five (or on your own if class size is a problem), think of a product or service that your friends want but cannot get on or near campus. You might ask your friends at other schools what's available there. What kind of product would fill that need? Discuss your results in class and how you might go about marketing that new product.
3. Relationship marketing efforts include frequent-flier deals at airlines, special discounts for members at certain supermarkets (e.g., Safeway), and websites that remember your name and what you've purchased in the past and recommend new products that you may like (e.g., Amazon.com). Evaluate any one of these programs (if you have no personal experience with them, look up such programs on the Internet). What might they do to increase your satisfaction and loyalty? Be prepared to discuss these programs in class.
4. Working in teams of four or five (or on your own if teams are difficult to form), list as many brand names of pizza as you can, including brands from pizza shops, restaurants, supermarkets, and so on. Merge your list with the lists from other groups. Then try to identify the "target market" for each brand. Do they all seem to be after the same market or are there different brands for different markets? What are the separate appeals?
5. A "smoke shop" near the Berkeley campus sells bongs and other items related to the use of marijuana. It also sells markers that young people sniff to get a high. People question the ethics of selling such items near campus. Others question the sale of guns, cigarettes, liquor, condoms, and pornography anywhere. Should marketers be allowed to sell anything they want? If not, what do you think the limits should be and why? Write a one-page defense of your position.

Taking It To The Net

Purpose

To demonstrate how the Internet can be used to enhance relationship marketing.

Exercise

Nike wants to help its customers add soul to their soles and express their individuality by customizing their own shoes. See for yourself at www.nike.com. Click on NIKEiD and build a shoe that fits your style.

1. What if you're in the middle of your shoe design and have questions about what to do next? Where can you go for help?

2. How does Nike's website help the company strengthen its relationships with its stakeholders? Give examples to support your answer.
3. How do the elements of the website reflect Nike's target market?
4. Does Nike invite comments from visitors to its website? If so, how does this affect its attempt to build positive relationships with its customers?

Casing The Web

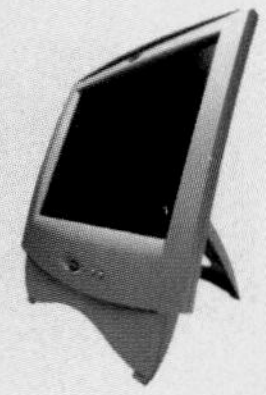

To access the case "Customer-Oriented Marketing Concepts at Thermos," visit

www.mhhe.com/ub7e

Video Case

Racing to Market—NASCAR

The stands are packed with 125,000 enthusiastic fans wearing caps and jackets touting their favorite sports superhero. Many have driven hundreds of miles for the chance to be part of this sport they love so dearly. Welcome to the world of NASCAR.

NASCAR (National Association of Stock Car Auto Racing) started in 1948 in Daytona Beach, Florida. Over the past 50-plus years, it has become a marketing phenomenon. Some refer to NASCAR as a marketing vehicle within a marketing vehicle. One look at a NASCAR event and it's easy to understand why NASCAR is the largest marketing show in America and an excellent example of integrated marketing communication at work. For example, every car is plastered with various company logos. The cars themselves represent specific automobile manufacturers who know that success on the track can lead to success in auto showrooms. Product advertising is almost everywhere—on the cars, on signs, and in the sky. Word of mouth from fans draws even more fans so that auto racing dominates the sports world for fan attention. Publicity about the races and the drivers is in magazines, newspapers, and on TV. Sales promotion strategies and special deals on apparel and auto racing related items are apparent. In short, auto racing is a marketer's paradise.

NASCAR today can boast that 17 of the top 20 largest sports events in America are NASCAR events (soon to be called the NASCAR Nextel Cup Series). The sport is special in that the "stars" (the drivers), are very fan-friendly and draw huge crowds. The drivers travel between venues with brand-loyal fans close on their heels. NASCAR fans are willing to spend a great deal of their discretionary time and money to travel to such events. The price they pay in time and effort greatly exceeds the price they pay for an event ticket.

NASCAR owes a great deal of its popularity to extensive marketing research. Research has helped marketers make crucial marketing decisions such as where to locate tracks. NASCAR decided early on that corporate sponsorship was vital to long-term growth because market research showed that NASCAR fans are three times more likely to buy NASCAR sponsors' products than fans of other sports. For that reason, major companies are willing to sponsor cars and drivers. Today, more Fortune 500 companies are involved in NASCAR than any other sport in the country. NASCAR licensing sales amount to about $2 billion a year.

If you are not already a fan, take a chance and watch a NASCAR event on TV or visit a track in your area. It is a lot of fun watching the drivers manipulate for position on the track. You'll soon learn what a grueling sport it is as nerves and skills are tested for hours at a time—and death may be only a turn away. But it is equally fun, for someone interested in marketing, to watch how marketers have positioned themselves to sell their products. You can see the names of sponsors on the cars, on the driver's helmets and clothes, and throughout the event. Pay attention and you will see an example of integrated marketing at its finest. You will hear the announcers giving publicity to drivers and future events and will see advertising, personal selling, promotions, and publicity everywhere you look. It is all very exciting and interesting. Maybe you too will become a fan and learn something about marketing while you're at it.

Thinking It Over

1. What marketing opportunities are evident at sporting events in general? Can you picture the four Ps of marketing (product, price, place, and promotion) in action at your favorite sports venue? Explain.
2. Which marketing efforts at NASCAR events seem most effective and why?
3. Why are market segmentation and market research important in the planning of NASCAR events?

Chapter 14

Developing and Pricing Products and Services

Learning Goals

After you have read and studied this chapter, you should be able to

1. Explain the concept of a total product offer.
2. Describe the various kinds of consumer and industrial goods.
3. List and describe the functions of packaging.
4. Describe the differences among a brand, a brand name, and a trademark, and explain the concepts of brand equity and brand loyalty.
5. Explain the role of brand managers and the steps of the new-product development process.
6. Draw the product life cycle, describe each of its stages, and describe marketing strategies at each stage.
7. Explain various pricing objectives and strategies.
8. Explain why nonpricing strategies are growing in importance.

Getting to Know Alan G. Lafley of Procter & Gamble

Alan G. Lafley is better known at his company as A. G. Lafley or simply A.G. He served in the navy as a supplies officer during the Vietnam War; that is, he ran a department store for servicepeople. He says about his experience, "I learned there that even when you've got a complex business, there's a core, and the core is what generates most of the cash, most of the profits. The trick was to find the few things that were really going to sell, and sell as many of them as you could."

Lafley took his military experience with him to Procter & Gamble (P&G)—the company that markets Tide, Crest, Pampers, and numerous other well-known consumer products. P&G has almost 110,000 employees in more than 70 countries. Lafley has been working at P&G for over a quarter of a century. He began as brand assistant for Joy dishwashing liquid. Over the years, he has been in charge of laundry and cleaning products, global beauty care, cosmetics, and several other product areas. In 1994 he was sent to run operations in Asia, and by 2000 he had honed his skills sharply enough to become the chief executive officer (CEO). At the time, the company was in crisis. The former CEO had retired under pressure and the company's major brands were dropping in sales relative to the competition. The company's stock was dropping as well; it went from $117 a share in January 2000 to less that $60 a share in March.

Using his military background, Lafley immediately began the process of focusing on profitable products. The message was "big brands, big countries, big customers." In other words, focus on the brands that were successful and go for the largest markets. A dozen brands that were not doing as well as expected, such as Clearasil, were cut. The focus of the company was on adult women, and the slogan was "The consumer is boss."

Lafley had everyone in the company focus on the top 10 brands (e.g., Tide and Pampers), each of which generated over $1 billion in sales. In the hair care group, the focus was on Pantene. Instead of marketing by consumer hair style (fine, normal, oily, dry), P&G focused on what the consumer was trying to achieve (volumizing, smoothing, curls). The company changed the shape, cap, and color of the bottle.

"I learned there that even when you've got a complex business, there's a core, and the core is what generates most of the cash, most of the profits. The trick was to find the few things that were really going to sell, and sell as many of them as you could."

The emphasis on customer wants and needs extended to customers overseas. Lafley toured various countries and went to the stores that sold P&G products. He checked the shelves, listened to the salespeople, and adapted P&G's offerings accordingly. Sales at P&G reached $40.2 billion. *Fortune* magazine reported that Lafley had "turned around P&G in 27 months."

Lafley's experiences at P&G show the importance of choosing the right products to sell and adapting those products to the wants and needs of customers. He learned that packaging and branding were critical. He also understood the need to add new products to grow sales over time. For example, he added powerhouses like Whitestrips, the tooth whitener, and Actonel, the osteoporosis drug. This chapter will explore the basic concepts behind such decisions, including decisions about pricing.

Sources: Cliff Peale, "How A. G. Lafley Turned Procter Around," *Cincinnati Enquirer,* September 9, 2002; Katrina Brooker, "The UnCEO," *Fortune,* September 16, 2002, pp. 88–96; and Robert Berner, "P&G: New and Improved," *Business Week,* July 7, 2003, pp. 52–63.

Product Development and the Total Product Offer

value
Good quality at a fair price. When consumers calculate the value of a product, they look at the benefits and then subtract the cost to see if the benefits exceed the costs.

A. G. Lafley at P&G found that global competition today is so strong that American businesses could lose some part of the market to foreign producers if they are not careful. The only way to prevent such losses is to design and promote better products, meaning products that are perceived to have the best **value**—good quality at a fair price. When consumers calculate the value of a product, they look at the benefits and then subtract the cost to see if the benefits exceed the costs. As we'll see in this chapter, whether consumers perceive a product as the best value depends on many factors, including the benefits they seek and the service they receive.[1] To satisfy consumers, marketers must learn to listen better than they do now and to adapt constantly to changing market demands.[2] Managers must also constantly adapt to price challenges from competitors.[3]

Learning to manage change, especially new-product changes, is critical for tomorrow's managers. That is why Dell Computer is adding printers, storage, and handhelds.[4] An important part of the impression consumers get about products is the price.[5] This chapter will therefore explore two key parts of the marketing mix: product and price.

McDonald's CEO James R. Cantalupo and other marketers have learned that adapting products to new competition and new markets is an ongoing necessity. An organization can't do a one-time survey of consumer wants and needs, design a group of products to meet those needs, put them in the stores, and then just relax. It must constantly monitor changing consumer wants and needs, and adapt products, policies, and services accordingly. That's why many of the McDonald's stores in France look nothing like those in the United States. Half of the 932 French stores have been upgraded, using at least eight different themes, such as "Mountain." Such stores have a wood-beam ceiling like a ski chalet.[6] Elsewhere, McDonald's is adding Golden Arches Hotels to its list of products. Two such hotels have been built in western Switzerland.[7]

In Kokomo, Indiana, McD's is trying waiter service and a more varied menu. In New York, McD's is offering McDonuts to compete with Krispy

How would you like a beer or glass of wine with your Big Mac? You can get both at this McDonald's in Paris. Also, notice how this McDonald's restaurant in Paris fits into the architectural scheme of the city. The same is true of the menu in McDonald's restaurants in countries other than the United States. In Europe, McDonald's frequently adapts its menus and interior restaurant designs to fit into the taste and cultural demands of each country.

Kreme. In Atlanta, McDonald's computer stations link to the Internet. In Hawaii, McD's is trying a Spam breakfast platter (it sold 3,000 the first day; no report on the second day), and in Columbus, Ohio, a Mega McD's has a karaoke booth.[8] And watch out, Starbucks, McDonald's has a McCafe in Chicago's Loop. Of course, it sells premium coffee, pastries, and wrapped sandwiches. There are more than 300 such cafes in other countries. In the United States, McDonald's is now offering salads.[9]

Fast-food organizations must constantly monitor all sources of information for new-product ideas. McDonald's isn't alone in that. KFC put in a new line of chicken sandwiches. Burger King tried a new X-treme Double Cheeseburger. Wendy's added stuffed pitas to its menu. Offerings differ in various locations according to the wants of the local community. In Iowa pork tenderloin is big, but in Oklahoma City it's tortilla scramblers. Overseas, companies must adapt to local tastes. At Bob's Big Boy in Thailand, for example, you can get Tropical Shrimp; at Carl's Junior in Mexico, you can order the Machaca Burrito; and at Shakey's Pizza in the Philippines, you can get Cali Shandy, a Filipino beer.

Product development, then, is a key activity in any modern business, anywhere in the world. There's a lot more to new-product development than merely introducing goods ➤P. 25◀ and services ➤P. 26◀, however. What marketers do to create excitement for those products is as important as the products themselves.

Developing a Total Product Offer

From a strategic marketing viewpoint, a total product offer is more than just the physical good or service. A **total product offer** (also called a *value package*) consists of everything that consumers evaluate when deciding whether to buy something. Thus, the basic product or service may be a washing machine, an insurance policy, or a beer, but the total product offer also may consist of the value enhancers that appear in Figure 14.1.

total product offer
Everything that consumers evaluate when deciding whether to buy something; also called a *value package*.

When people buy a product, they may evaluate and compare total product offers on all these dimensions. Note that some of the attributes are tangible (the product itself and its package) whereas others are intangible (the reputation of the producer and the image created by advertising). A successful marketer must begin to think like a consumer and evaluate the total product offer as a collection of impressions created by all the factors listed in Figure 14.1. It is wise to talk with consumers to see which features and benefits are most important to them, that is, which value enhancers to include in the final offerings.

FIGURE 14.1

POTENTIAL COMPONENTS OF A TOTAL PRODUCT OFFER

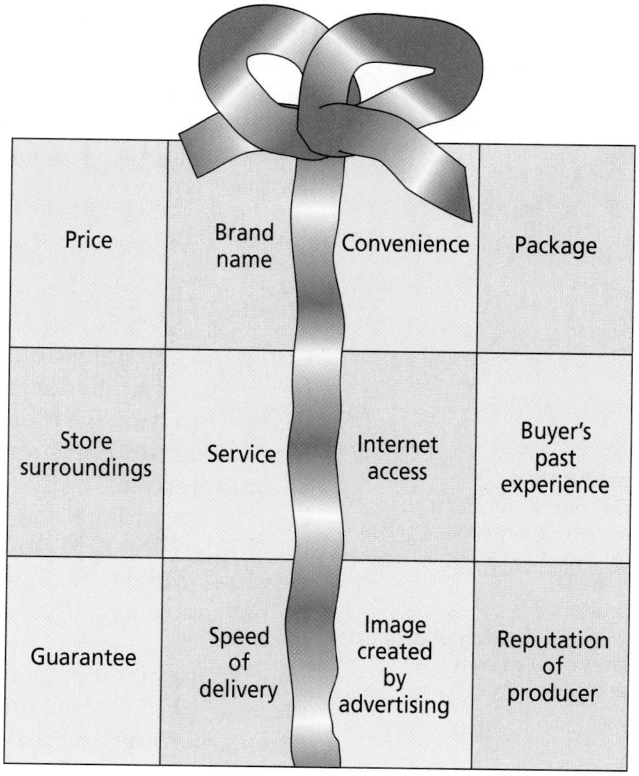

Let's go back and look at the highly nutritious, high-fiber, low-sugar breakfast cereal Fiberrific, which we introduced in Chapter 13. The total product offer as perceived by the consumer is much more than the cereal itself. Anything that enhances a consumer's perceptions about the cereal's benefits and value may determine whether that consumer purchases the cereal. The price certainly is an important part of the perception of product value.

A high price may indicate exceptional quality. The store surroundings also are important. If the cereal is being sold in an exclusive health-food store, it

NEVER HEAR OF ANYONE CURSING OUT THE ON-BOARD MASSEUSE, NOW DO YOU?
Business Class to London
virgin atlantic

What is included in a total product offer? For Virgin Atlantic, in a certain class of service, it may even include a massage. What other services would you enjoy on a long airline flight? What services can you think of that would successfully differentiate the value packages of Virgin Atlantic's competitors—while offering comparable pricing?

takes on many characteristics of the store (e.g., healthy and upscale). A guarantee of satisfaction can increase the product's value in the minds of consumers, as can a well-known brand name.[10] Advertising can create an attractive image, and word of mouth can enhance the reputation. Thus, the Fiberrific total product offer is more than a cereal; it's an entire bundle of impressions.

Sometimes an organization can use low price to create an attractive total product offer. For example, outlet stores often offer brand-name goods for less than regular retail stores do. Shoppers must be careful, however, because outlet stores also carry lower-quality products with similar but not exactly the same features as those carried in regular stores. Consumers like shopping in outlet stores in any case because they believe they are getting quality goods at low prices.

Different consumers may want different total product offers, so the company may develop a variety of offerings. For example, auto companies sometimes offer customers a choice between zero-percent financing and a rebate of thousands of dollars. Of course, the autos themselves may have features such as automatic fold-down seats, cup holders, global positioning systems, VCRs, and more—lots more. The consumer is invited to select from a variety of options. The Dealing with Change box looks at the value enhancers that may be provided by a real estate agent.

Critical Thinking

What value enhancers affected your choice of the school you attend? Did you consider size, location, price, reputation, Internet services, library services, sports, placement, and selection of courses offered? What factors were most important? Why? What schools were your alternatives? Why didn't you choose them?

Product Lines and the Product Mix

Companies usually don't sell just one product. Rather, they sell several different but complementary products. A **product line** is a group of products that are physically similar or are intended for a similar market. They usually face similar competiton. Figure 14.2 shows the 22 product lines for Procter & Gamble (P&G). In one product line, there may be several competing brands. Thus, P&G has many brands in its laundry detergent product line, including Tide, Era, Downy, and Bold. All of P&G's product lines make up its **product mix**, which is the combination of all product lines offered by a manufacturer. Figure 14.3 shows the products within selected P&G product lines.

product line
A group of products that are physically similar or are intended for a similar market.

product mix
The combination of product lines offered by a manufacturer.

Service providers have product lines and product mixes as well. For example, a bank or credit union may offer a variety of services from savings accounts, automated teller machines, and computer banking to money market

Dealing with Change

www.callelizabeth.com

Using the Web to Provide More Information

The real estate market is constantly changing. What can a realtor do to differentiate his or her product from that offered by other realtors? The price of the service is usually about the same. The houses they sell are often similar. So what value enhancements can a realtor make to the process to attract customers to them? The answer, according to Elizabeth Gray-Carr of Prudential Real Estate, is to build relationships with potential sellers and buyers by offering interactive tools and unusually detailed information, including personal Web pages.

All realtors are expected to know information about schools, shopping, religious facilities, recreation, mortgage rates, recent prices in various neighborhoods, and so forth. What makes Gray-Carr stand out from the bunch is that she provides all that information on a website. As she thinks of new information to add, Gray-Carr puts it on the Web. That includes weather information, nearby golf courses and other recreation sites, and so on. For buyers, the site lists all the agency's entire inventory of homes and provides a virtual tour of each of them. Buyers can also access extensive information about the neighborhood, including school districts and the prices of homes recently sold.

Sellers can use similar information to determine the right price for their homes. If a seller signs with Gray-Carr, that seller will have 24/7 information about the process of the sale and will have a lot less paperwork to worry about than usual. When there are settled standards for electronic signatures, buyers and sellers will be able to handle all the paperwork from remote locations, making it possible to buy a home from another country and move in as soon as you arrive. Can you imagine what other value-enhancing information Gray-Carr could add to her total product offer? Can you see how her total product offer can be more valuable than those offered by other real estate agents?

Sources: Lauren Gibbons Paul, "The Site Next Door," *Inc. Tech 2000,* no. 4, p. 63; and www.callelizabeth.com, 2003.

Antiperspirants	Hair Care	Personal Cleansing
Baby Care	Hair Color	Pet Health and Nutrition
Colognes	Health Care	Prescription Drugs
Commercial Products	Household Cleaners	Prestige Fragrances
Cosmetics	Laundry	Skin Care
Deodorants	Oral Care	Snacks and Beverages
Dish Care	Paper Products	Special Fabric Care
Feminine Protection		

FIGURE 14.2

PROCTER & GAMBLE'S 22 PRODUCT LINES

Dish Care:	Cascade, Dawn, Joy, Ivory
Oral Care	Crest (toothpaste, toothbrushes, whitestrips), Scope, Fixodent, Gleem
Household cleaners:	Bounty, Swiffer, Mr. Clean
Baby care:	Pampers, Luvs, Dreft, Charmin Kid Fresh
Laundry:	Tide, Cheer, Febreze, Ivory, Downy, Bounce, Dreft, Bold, Gain, Era, Dryel

FIGURE 14.3

PRODUCTS IN PROCTER & GAMBLE'S VARIOUS PRODUCT LINES

funds, safety deposit boxes, loans (home, car, etc.), traveler's checks, online banking, and insurance. AT&T combines services (telephone) with goods (computers, phones) in its product mix.

Product Differentiation

product differentiation The creation of real or perceived product differences.

Product differentiation is the creation of real or perceived product differences. Actual product differences are sometimes quite small, so marketers must use a creative mix of pricing, advertising, and packaging (value enhancers) to create a unique, attractive image. Various bottled water companies, for example, have successfully attempted product differentiation. The companies made their bottled waters so attractive through pricing and promotion that now restaurant customers often order water by brand name instead of Coke, Pepsi, or other drinks.

There's no reason why you couldn't create an attractive image for your product, Fiberrific. With a high price and creative advertising, it could become the Perrier or Evian of cereals. But different products call for different marketing strategies.

Small businesses ➤P. 184◄ can often win market share with creative product differentiation. For example, yearbook photographer Charlie Clark competes with other yearbook photographers by offering multiple clothing changes, backgrounds, and poses along with special allowances, discounts, and guarantees. He has been so successful that companies use him as a speaker at photography conventions. This is just one more example of how small businesses may have the advantage of being more flexible than big businesses in adapting to customer wants and needs and giving them attractive product differences.

Marketing Different Classes of Consumer Goods and Services

Several attempts have been made to classify consumer goods and services. One classification, based on consumer purchasing behavior, has four general categories—convenience, shopping, specialty, and unsought.

convenience goods and services Products that the consumer wants to purchase frequently and with a minimum of effort.

shopping goods and services Those products that the consumer buys only after comparing value, quality, price, and style from a variety of sellers.

specialty goods and services Consumer products with unique characteristics and brand identity. Because these products are perceived as having no reasonable substitute, the consumer puts forth a special effort to purchase them.

1. **Convenience goods and services** are products that the consumer wants to purchase frequently and with a minimum of effort (e.g., candy, gum, milk, snacks, gas, banking services). One store that sells mostly convenience goods is 7-Eleven. Location, brand awareness, and image are important for marketers of convenience goods and services. The Internet has taken convenience to a whole new level, especially for banks and other service companies, such as real estate firms. Companies that don't offer such services are likely to lose market share to those who do unless they offer outstanding service to customers who visit in person.
2. **Shopping goods and services** are products that the consumer buys only after comparing value, quality, price, and style from a variety of sellers. Shopping goods and services are sold largely through shopping centers where consumers can make comparisons. Sears is one store that sells mostly shopping goods. Because many consumers carefully compare such products, marketers can emphasize price differences, quality differences, or some combination of the two. Examples include clothes, shoes, appliances, and auto repair services.
3. **Specialty goods and services** are consumer products with unique characteristics and brand identity. Because these products are per-

ceived as having no reasonable substitute, the consumer puts forth a special effort to purchase them. Examples include fine watches, expensive wine, fur coats, jewelry, imported chocolates, and expensive cigars, as well as services provided by medical specialists or business consultants. A Jaguar automobile dealer is an example of a specialty-goods retailer. These products are often marketed through specialty magazines. For example, specialty skis may be sold through sports magazines and specialty foods through gourmet magazines. By establishing interactive websites where customers can place orders, companies that sell specialty goods and services can make buying their goods as easy as or easier than shopping at a local mall.

4. **Unsought goods and services** are products that consumers are unaware of, haven't necessarily thought of buying, or find that they need to solve an unexpected problem. Some examples of unsought products are emergency car-towing services, burial services, and insurance.

unsought goods and services
Products that consumers are unaware of, haven't necessarily thought of buying, or find that they need to solve an unexpected problem.

industrial goods
Products used in the production of other products. Sometimes called business goods or B2B goods.

The marketing task varies depending on the category of product; that is, convenience goods are marketed differently from specialty goods, and so forth. The best way to promote convenience goods is to make them readily available and to create the proper image. Some combination of price, quality, and service is the best appeal for shopping goods. Specialty goods rely on reaching special market segments through advertising. Unsought goods such as life insurance often rely on personal selling; car towing relies heavily on Yellow Pages advertising.

Whether a good or service falls into a particular class depends on the individual consumer. A shopping good for one consumer (e.g., coffee) could be a specialty good for another consumer (e.g., flavored gourmet coffee). Some people shop around to compare different dry cleaners, so dry cleaning is a shopping service for them. Others go to the closest store, making it a convenience service. Therefore, marketers must carefully monitor their customer base to determine how consumers perceive their products. Can you see how Fiberrific could be either a convenience good or a shopping good?

Furthermore, the Internet has made it possible for consumers to purchase goods from home. That puts much greater pressure on retailers to offer such outstanding service that consumers will be willing to leave their homes to get it.

Marketing Industrial Goods and Services

Industrial goods (sometimes called business goods or B2B goods) are products used in the production of other products. They are sold in the business-to-business (B2B) market ➤P. 411◄. Some products can be classified as both consumer goods and industrial goods. For example, personal computers could be sold to consumer markets or B2B markets. As a consumer good, the computer might be sold through electronics stores like Best Buy or through computer magazines. Most of the promotional task would go to advertising. As an industrial good, personal computers

The Jill Stuart brand jeans on the left and the Diesel Fanker's on the right sell for over $140. The price for the Mavi brand jeans in the middle is closer to $50. Regular old denim pants are often sold as convenience goods; that is, you can even buy them from a vending machine. Do you think that designer jeans, like these, are shopping goods or specialty goods? Does it depend on the wealth of the shopper?

FIGURE 14.4

VARIOUS CLASSES OF CONSUMER AND INDUSTRIAL GOODS AND SERVICES

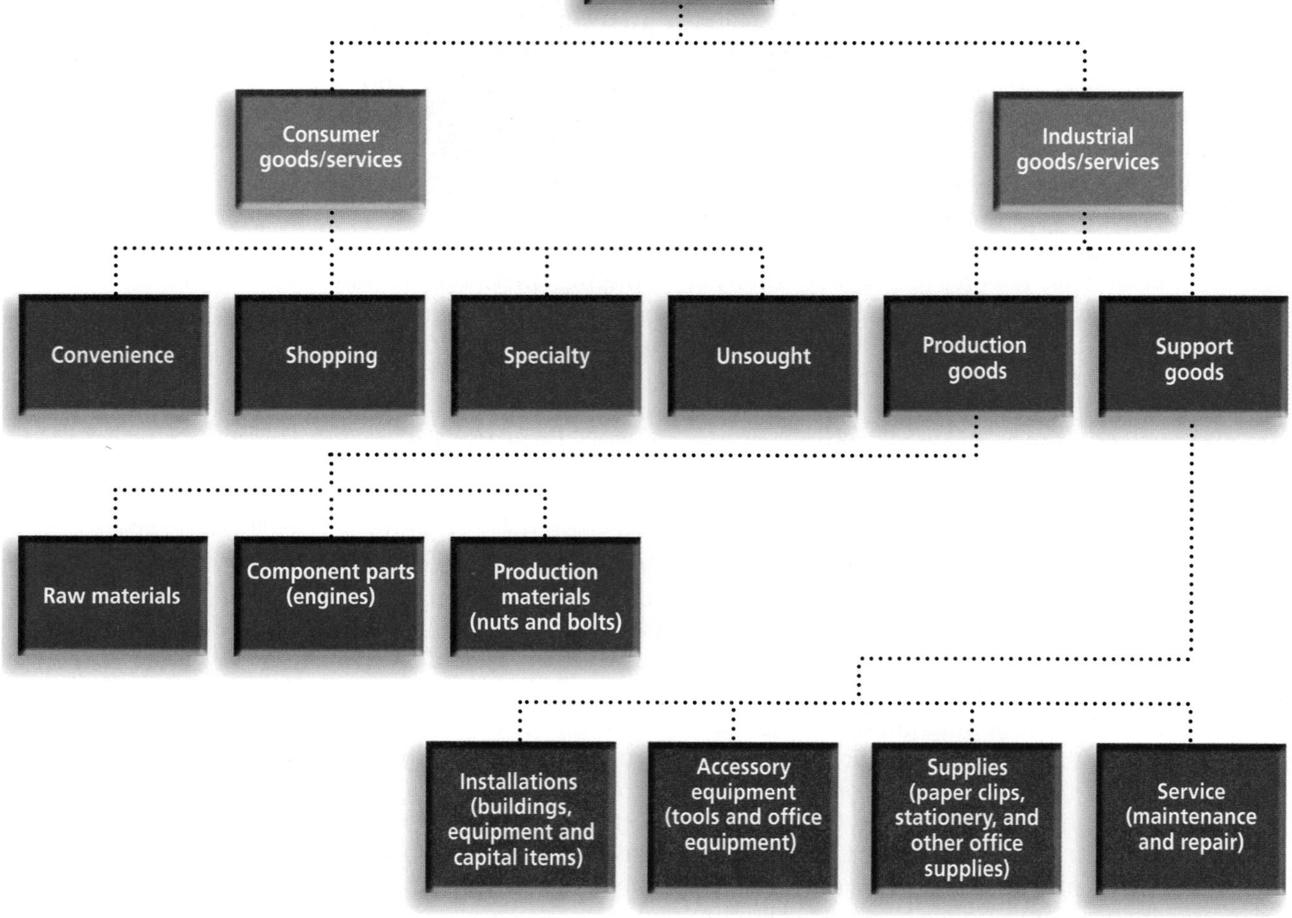

are more likely to be sold by salespeople or on the Internet. Advertising would be less of a factor in the promotion strategy. You can see that classifying goods by user category helps determine the proper marketing mix strategy.

Figure 14.4 shows some categories of both consumer and industrial goods and services. *Installations* consist of major capital equipment such as new factories and heavy machinery. *Capital items* are products that last a long time and cost a lot of money. A new factory building where Fiberrific would be produced would be considered both a capital item and an installation. *Accessory equipment* consists of capital items that are not quite as long lasting or as expensive as installations. Examples include computers, photocopy machines, and various tools. Other industrial goods and examples are labeled in the chart.

Progress Assessment

- What value enhancers may be included in a total product offer?
- What's the difference between a product line and a product mix?
- Name the four classes of consumer goods and services, and give examples of each.
- Describe three different types of industrial goods.

PACKAGING CHANGES THE PRODUCT

We've said that consumers evaluate many aspects of the total product offer, including the brand. It's surprising how important packaging can be in such evaluations. Many years ago people had problems with table salt because it would stick together and form lumps during humid or damp weather. The Morton Salt Company solved that problem by designing a package that kept salt dry in all kinds of weather, thus the slogan "When it rains, it pours." Packaging made Morton's salt more desirable than competing products, and even though other salt companies developed similar packaging, Morton's is still the best-known salt in the United States.

Other companies have also used packaging to change and improve their basic product. Thus, we've had squeezable ketchup bottles that stand upside down on their caps for easier pouring; square paint cans with screw tops and integrated handles; plastic bottles for motor oil that eliminate the need for funnels; toothpaste pumps; packaged dinners and other foods, like popcorn, that can be cooked in a microwave oven; and so forth.[11] In each case, the package changed the product in the minds of consumers and opened large markets.

Packaging can also help make a product more attractive to retailers. For example, the Universal Product Codes (UPCs) on many packages help stores control inventory; the UPC is the combination of a bar code (those familiar black and white lines) and a preset number that gives the retailer information about the product (price, size, color, etc.). In short, packaging changes the product by changing its visibility, usefulness, or attractiveness.

One new technology in tracking products is the radio frequency identification (RFID) chip. Attached to products, these chips send out signals telling a company where the products are at all times. The advantages over bar codes include the fact that more information can be carried in the chips, items don't have to be read one at a time (whole pallets can be read in an instant), and items can be read at a distance.[12] Wal-Mart has been a leader in using such technology.

The Growing Importance of Packaging

Packaging has always been an important aspect of the product offer, but today it's carrying more of the promotional burden than in the past. Many products that were once sold by salespersons are now being sold in self-service outlets, and the package has been given more sales responsibility. The Fair Packaging and Labeling Act was passed so that consumers could get quantity and value comparisons on packaging. As a result, you are now getting much more information on packages now than in the past. The package must perform the following functions:

1. Protect the goods inside, stand up under handling and storage, be tamperproof, deter theft, and yet be easy to open and use.
2. Attract the buyer's attention.
3. Describe the contents and give information about the contents.
4. Explain the benefits of the good inside.
5. Provide information on warranties, warnings, and other consumer matters.
6. Give some indication of price, value, and uses.

CokeM International Ltd. was number one on *Entrepreneur* magazine's list of the Hot 100 companies two years in a row. It packages and sells video games and home entertainment software. The company's growth is due largely to its purchasing a great amount of product from manufacturers and then repackaging or customizing it for stores like Best Buy and Wal-Mart. CokeM's low prices are also a factor. Are you drawn to products because of their unusual or attractive packaging?

brand
A name, symbol, or design (or combination thereof) that identifies the goods or services of one seller or group of sellers and distinguishes them from the goods and services of competitors.

brand name
That part of the brand consisting of a word, letter, or group of words or letters comprising a name that differentiates a seller's goods or services from those of competitors.

trademark
A brand that has been given exclusive legal protection for both the brand name and the pictorial design.

manufacturers' brand names
The brand names of manufacturers that distribute products nationally.

dealer (private-label) brands
Products that don't carry the manufacturer's name but carry a distributor or retailer's name instead.

Packaging of services also has been getting more attention recently. For example, Virgin Airlines includes door-to-door limousine service and in-flight massages in its total package. Financial institutions are offering everything from financial advice to help in purchasing insurance, stocks, bonds, mutual funds, and more. When combining goods or services into one package, it's important not to include so much that the price gets too high. It's best to work with customers to develop value enhancers that meet their individual needs.

Branding and Brand Equity

Closely related to packaging is branding. A **brand** is a name, symbol, or design (or combination thereof) that identifies the goods or services of one seller or group of sellers and distinguishes them from the goods and services of competitors. The word *brand* is sufficiently comprehensive to include practically all means of identification of a product. A **brand name** is that part of the brand consisting of a word, letter, or group of words or letters comprising a name that differentiates a seller's goods or services from those of competitors. Brand names you may be familiar with include QVC, Sony, Del Monte, Campbell, Levi's, Snackwell's, Borden, and Michelob. Such brand names give products a distinction that tends to make them attractive to consumers.

A **trademark** is a brand that has been given exclusive legal protection for both the brand name and the pictorial design. Trademarks such as McDonald's golden arches are widely recognized. Trademarks need to be protected from other companies that may want to trade on the trademark holder's reputation and image. Companies often sue other companies for too-closely matching brand names. McDonald's might sue to prevent a company from selling, say, McDonnel hamburgers.

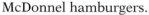

Creating a new brand image is very different from managing a brand that is already well known. These three men created and built a highly successful brand called Tommy Bahama. There is no such person as Tommy, but shoppers still have an image of the kind of guy he is: cool, relaxed, and so on. The brand image is carried over by selling the clothes at specialty stores where customers expect higher quality and can get better service. Are you the Tommy Bahama type?

People are often impressed by certain brand names, even though they say they know there's no difference between brands in a given product category. For example, when people say that all aspirin is alike, put two bottles in front of them—one with the Anacin label and one with the label of an unknown brand. See which they choose. Most people choose the brand name, even when they say there's no difference.

For the buyer, a brand name assures quality, reduces search time, and adds prestige to purchases. For the seller, brand names facilitate new-product introductions, help promotional efforts, add to repeat purchases, and differentiate products so that prices can be set higher.

Brand Categories

Several categories of brands are familiar to you. **Manufacturers' brand names** are the brand names of manufacturers that distribute products nationally—Xerox, Kodak, Sony, and Chevrolet, for example.

Dealer (private-label) brands are products that don't carry the manufacturer's name but carry a distributor or retailer's name instead. Kenmore and Diehard are dealer brands sold by Sears. These brands are also known as house brands or distributor brands.

Many manufacturers fear having their brand names become generic names. A *generic name* is the name for a product category. Did you know that aspirin and linoleum, which are now generic names for products, were once brand names? So were nylon, escalator, kerosene, and zipper. All those names became so popular, so identified with the product, that they lost their brand status and became generic. (Such issues are decided in the courts.) Their producers then had to come up with new names. The original Aspirin, for example, became Bayer aspirin. Companies that are working hard to protect their brand names today include Styrofoam (cups and packaging) and Rollerblade (in-line skates).

Generic goods are nonbranded products that usually sell at a sizable discount compared to national or private-label brands. They feature basic packaging and are backed with little or no advertising. Some are of poor quality, but many come close to having the same quality as the national brand-name goods they copy. There are generic tissues, generic cigarettes, generic peaches, and so forth. Consumers today are buying large amounts of generic products because their overall quality has improved so greatly in recent years that it approximates or equals that of more expensive brand names. What has been your experience trying generic products?

generic goods
Nonbranded products that usually sell at a sizable discount compared to national or private-label brands.

Knockoff brands are illegal copies of national brand-name goods. If you see an expensive brand-name item such as a Polo shirt or a Rolex watch for sale at a ridiculously low price, you can be pretty sure it's a knockoff. Often the brand name is just a little off, like Palo or Bolex. Look carefully.

knockoff brands
Illegal copies of national brand-name goods.

Generating Brand Equity and Loyalty

A major goal of marketers in the future will be to reestablish the notion of brand equity. **Brand equity** is the combination of factors—such as awareness, loyalty, perceived quality, images, and emotions—that people associate with a given brand name. In the past companies tried to boost their short-term performance by offering coupons and price discounts to move goods quickly. This eroded consumers' commitment to brand names. Now companies realize the value of brand equity and are trying to measure the earning power of strong brand names.

brand equity
The combination of factors—such as awareness, loyalty, perceived quality, images, and emotions—that people associate with a given brand name.

The core of brand equity is brand loyalty. **Brand loyalty** is the degree to which customers are satisfied, like the brand, and are committed to further purchases.[13] A loyal group of customers represents substantial value to a firm, and that value can be calculated.

brand loyalty
The degree to which customers are satisfied, like the brand, and are committed to further purchase.

Brand awareness refers to how quickly or easily a given brand name comes to mind when a product category is mentioned. Advertising helps build strong brand awareness. Established brands, such as Coca-Cola and Pepsi, are usually the highest in brand awareness. Event sponsorship (e.g., the Winston-Salem auto races and Virginia Slims tennis tournament) helps improve brand awareness.

brand awareness
How quickly or easily a given brand name comes to mind when a product category is mentioned.

Perceived quality is an important part of brand equity. A product that's perceived as having better quality than its competitors can be priced accordingly. The key to creating a perception of quality is to identify what consumers look for in a high-quality product and then to use that information in every message the company sends out. Factors influencing the perception of quality include price, appearance, and reputation. Consumers often develop *brand preference*—that is, they prefer one brand over another—because of such cues. When consumers reach the point of *brand insistence,* the product becomes a specialty good. For example, a consumer may insist on Goodyear tires for his or her car.

It's now so easy to copy a product's benefits that off-brand products are being developed to draw consumers away from brand-name goods. Brand X disposable diapers, for example, has increased its market share from 7 to 20 percent. Paragon Trade Brands gives retailers higher-than-normal margins (the difference between purchasing cost and selling price) and quickly matches the product innovations of the major companies. Brand-name manufacturers,

Making Ethical Decisions

www.gotagless.com/retires_mj.html

Are We Too Star Struck?

Many producers use brand association to sell their products—often to young people. They use famous people, like Michael Jordan, in their ads to attract the attention of the audience. This is true for many products. An ethical question raised by such ads is: "What if the star in the ad doesn't really use the product?" If young people are lured into trying things like huge soft drinks, too much fast food, overly revealing clothes, and the like because they see their idols on TV or in the movies using them, who is responsible for the harm that may be caused? The producer? The TV show? The network? The person in the ad? Have you been persuaded to buy such products because of celebrity endorsements? Was your experience a positive one? Do you have any feeling of responsibility for your buying behavior? What are the ethical choices?

like Intel Corporation, have to develop new products and new markets faster and promote their names better than ever before to hold off challenges from competitors.

Creating Brand Associations

brand association
The linking of a brand to other favorable images.

The name, symbol, and slogan a company uses can assist greatly in brand recognition for that company's products. **Brand association** is the linking of a brand to other favorable images. For example, you can link a brand to other product users, to a popular celebrity, to a particular geographic area, or to competitors. Note, for example, how ads for Mercedes-Benz and Buick associate those companies' cars with rich people who may spend their leisure time playing or watching golf or polo. Tiger Woods was chosen as a spokesperson for Buick because of his golf popularity. Note, too, the success of associating basketball shoes with stars such as Shaquille O'Neal. What person might we associate with Fiberrific to give the cereal more appeal? The ethical dimensions of using celebrities to sell products is explored in the Making Ethical Decisions box.

The person responsible for building brands is known as a brand manager or product manager. We'll discuss that position next.

Brand Management

brand manager
A manager who has direct responsibility for one brand or one product line; called a product manager in some firms.

A **brand manager** (known as a product manager in some firms) has direct responsibility for one brand or one product line. This responsibility includes all the elements of the marketing mix: product, price, place, and promotion. Thus, the brand manager might be thought of as a president of a one-product firm. Imagine being the brand manager for Fiberrific. You'd be responsible for everything having to do with that one brand. One reason many large consumer-product companies created the position of brand manager is to have greater control over new-product development and product promotion. Some companies have brand-management teams to bolster the overall effort.

Progress Assessment

- What six functions does packaging now perform?
- What's the difference between a brand name and a trademark?
- Can you explain the difference between a manufacturer's brand, a dealer brand, and a generic brand?
- What are the key components of brand equity?

THE NEW-PRODUCT DEVELOPMENT PROCESS

Chances that a new product will fail are overwhelmingly high. About 86 percent of products introduced in one year failed to reach their business objectives. Not delivering what is promised is a leading cause of new-product failure. Other reasons for failure include poor positioning, not enough differences from competitors, and poor packaging. Small firms, especially, may experience a low success rate unless they do proper product planning.

As Figure 14.5 shows, new-product development for producers consists of several stages:

1. Idea generation, based on consumer wants and needs.
2. Product screening.
3. Product analysis.
4. Development (including building prototypes).
5. Testing.
6. Commercialization (bringing the product to the market).

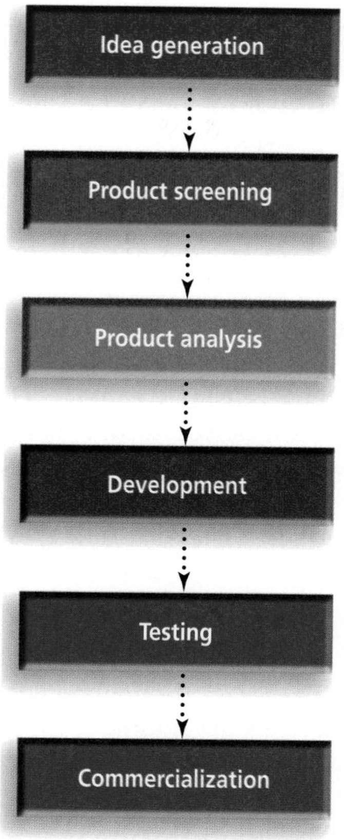

FIGURE 14.5

THE NEW-PRODUCT DEVELOPMENT PROCESS

Product development is a six-stage process. Which stage do you believe to be the most important?

New products continue to pour into the market every year, and the profit potential looks tremendous. Think, for example, of the potential of home video conferencing, interactive TV, large-screen high-definition TV sets, virtual reality games and products, Internet-connected phones, and other innovations. Where do these ideas come from? How are they tested? What's the life span for an innovation? The following material looks at these issues.

Generating New-Product Ideas

A strong point can be made for listening to employee suggestions for new products. The number one source of ideas for new industrial products has been company sources (e.g., employees) other than research and development. Employees are also a major source for new consumer goods ideas. Firms should also listen to their suppliers for new-product ideas.

Product Screening

Product screening is designed to reduce the number of new-product ideas being worked on at any one time. Criteria needed for screening include whether the product fits in well with present products, profit potential, marketability, and personnel requirements. Each of these factors may be assigned a weight, and total scores are then computed. It now takes about seven ideas to generate one commercial product.

product screening
A process designed to reduce the number of new-product ideas being worked on at any one time.

Product Analysis

Product analysis is done after product screening. It's largely a matter of making cost estimates and sales forecasts to get a feeling for profitability of new-product ideas. Products that don't meet the established criteria are withdrawn from consideration.

product analysis
Making cost estimates and sales forecasts to get a feeling for profitability of new-product ideas.

Product Development and Testing

If a product passes the screening and analysis phase, the firm begins to develop it further. A product idea can be developed into many different product concepts, which are alternative product offerings based on the same product idea that have different meanings and values to consumers. For example, a firm that makes packaged meat products may develop the concept of a chicken dog—a hot dog made of chicken that tastes like an all-beef hot dog. A prototype, or sample, may be developed so that consumers can actually try the taste.

concept testing
Taking a product idea to consumers to test their reactions.

Concept testing involves taking a product idea to consumers to test their reactions. Do they see the benefits of this new product? How frequently would they buy it? At what price? What features do they like and dislike? What changes would they make? Different samples are tested using different packaging, branding, ingredients, and so forth until a product emerges that's desirable from both production and marketing perspectives. Can you see the importance of concept testing for Fiberrific?

Commercialization

Even if a product tests well, it may take quite a while before the product achieves success in the market. Take the zipper, for example, the result of one of the longest development efforts on record for a consumer product. After Whitcomb Judson received the first patents for his clothing fastener in the early 1890s, it took more than 15 years to perfect the product—and even then consumers weren't interested. Judson's company suffered numerous financial setbacks, name changes, and relocations before settling in Meadville, Pennsylvania. Finally, the U.S. Navy started using zippers during World War I. Today, Talon Inc. is the leading U.S. maker of zippers, producing some 500 million of them a year.

commercialization
Promoting a product to distributors and retailers to get wide distribution, and developing strong advertising and sales campaigns to generate and maintain interest in the product among distributors and consumers.

The example of the zipper shows that the marketing effort must include **commercialization**. This includes (1) promoting the product to distributors and retailers to get wide distribution and (2) developing strong advertising and sales campaigns to generate and maintain interest in the product among distributors and consumers. New products are now getting rapid exposure to global markets by being promoted on the Internet. Interactive websites enable consumers to view new products, ask questions, and make purchases easily and quickly.[14]

The International Challenge

U.S. marketers have learned through experience that the secret to success in today's rapidly changing environment is to bring out high-quality new products, and to bring them out quickly. This is especially true in light of the rapid development process occurring in other countries.

U.S. automakers (Ford, General Motors, DaimlerChrysler) all formed task forces to cut product development cycles that had swollen to nearly five years. The Japanese cycles were taking about three and a half years. The American firms are now down to less than two years.[15] To stay competitive in world markets, U.S. businesses must develop an entirely new product-development process. To keep products competitive requires continuous incremental improvements in function, cost, and quality. Cost-sensitive design and new process technologies are critical.

More attention in the United States must be given to the product-development process for overseas markets. To implement new-product development, managers must go out into the market and interact closely with their dealers and their ultimate customers in each country. Successful new-product development is an interactive process whereby customers present their needs

Reaching Beyond Our Borders

www.unilever.com

Designing Products for the Poor

When designing products for the world market, it is easy to forget that over 2 billion people in this world make $2 a day or less. They are not necessarily interested in the latest PalmPilot or DVD player. However, in some countries, people are buying cell phones and renting them out to their neighbors. The owners make a few cents a call and everyone in the village is able to communicate better with others. To sell in such villages, other companies must learn to make and sell products that are meant to be shared. That often means helping buyers finance the product and teaching them how to begin a business as a renter of goods.

Unilever, the Anglo-Dutch consumer-goods giant, has taken a lead in developing products for people in less developed countries. The idea was to develop small packages with low prices, thus making it possible for people with very little money to have access to products they want. In India, for example, Unilever sells single-use packages of Sunsilk shampoo for as little as 2 cents. It also has a deodorant stick that sells for 16 cents. The deodorant is a big hit in the Philippines, Bolivia, Peru, and India. There is also a nickel-sized package of Vaseline and a small tube of Close Up toothpaste that sells for 8 cents.

Poor people often cannot afford eyeglasses. Scojo Vision out of Brooklyn now sells glasses in El Salvador, India, Haiti, and Guatemala for $2 a pair. Scojo is training entrepreneurs in those countries to use eye charts so they can prescribe the right correction (there are three different ones). London's Freeplay Energy Group is making radios for countries in which electricity doesn't exist and batteries are too expensive—the radios are powered by cranking a handle.

Microlending firms are giving entrepreneurs loans of $100 to $300 or so to start their own businesses. With a little capital, these entrepreneurs are able to generate money to send their children to school and to buy food and other necessities. They can also buy a few "luxury" goods like soap and deodorant, if the price is right. Doing business globally means learning to adapt to the wants and needs of everyone, and that includes the wants and needs of the very poor. As they learn to become entrepreneurs themselves, they will have the resources to buy other products and someday to trade globally themselves.

Sources: Manjeet Kripalani and Pete Engardio, "Small Is Profitable," *Business Week,* August 26, 2002, pp. 112–14; Pete Engardio, Declan Walsh, and Manjeet Kripalani, "Global Poverty," *Business Week,* October 14, 2002, pp. 108–18; and Chris Prystay, "Companies Market to India's Have-Littles," *The Wall Street Journal,* June 5, 2003, pp. B1 and B12.

and new-product designs are prepared to meet those needs. Changes are made over time to make sure that the total product offer exactly meets the customer's needs. The focus shifts from internal product development to external customer responsiveness.

This development process is particularly important when trying to meet the needs of people in other countries. Billions of potential customers make less than $2 a day. How does one respond to such customers? The Reaching Beyond Our Borders box explores that issue.

The Product Life Cycle

Once a product has been developed and tested, it is placed on the market. Products often go through a life cycle consisting of four stages: introduction, growth, maturity, and decline. This is called the product life cycle (see Figure 14.6). The **product life cycle** is a theoretical model of what happens to sales and profits for a product class (e.g., all dishwasher soaps) over time. However, not all products follow the life cycle, and particular brands may act differently. For example, while frozen foods as a generic class may go through the entire cycle, one brand may never get beyond the introduction stage. Also, some products become classics and never experience much of a decline. Others may be withdrawn from the market altogether. Nonetheless,

product life cycle
A theoretical model of what happens to sales and profits for a product class over time.

FIGURE 14.6

SALES AND PROFITS DURING THE PRODUCT LIFE CYCLE

Note that profit levels start to fall *before* sales reach their peak. This is due to increasing price competition. When profits and sales start to decline, it's time to come out with a new product or to remodel the old one to maintain interest and profits.

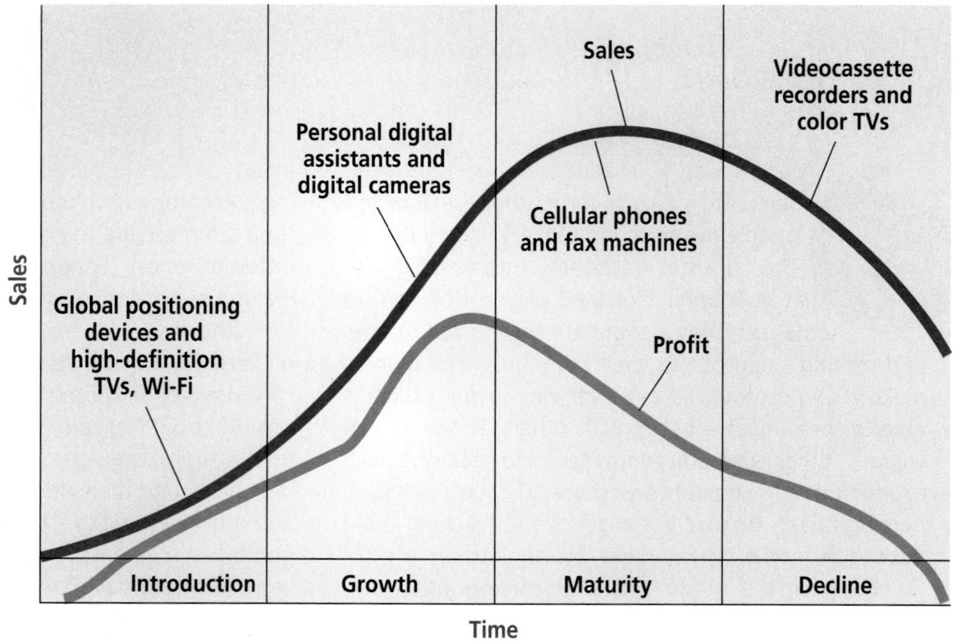

the product life cycle may provide some basis for anticipating future market developments and for planning marketing strategies. Some products, such as microwave ovens, stay in the introductory stage for years. Other products, such as fad clothing, may go through the entire cycle in a few months.

Example of the Product Life Cycle

You can see how the theory works by looking at the product life cycle of instant coffee. When it was introduced, most people didn't like it as well as "regular" coffee, and it took several years for instant coffee to gain general acceptance (introduction stage). At one point, though, instant coffee grew rapidly in popularity, and many brands were introduced (growth stage). After a while, people became attached to one brand and sales leveled off (maturity stage). Sales then went into a slight decline when freeze-dried coffees were introduced (decline stage). Now freeze-dried coffee is, in turn, at the decline stage as consumers are buying fresh specialty beans and grinding them at home. It's extremely important to recognize what stage a product is in because such an analysis may lead to intelligent and efficient marketing decisions.

The Importance of the Product Life Cycle

The importance of the product life cycle to marketers is this: Different stages in the product life cycle call for different marketing strategies. The table in Figure 14.7 outlines the marketing mix decisions that might be made. As you go through the table, you'll see that each stage calls for multiple marketing mix changes. Remember, these concepts are largely theoretical and should be used only as guidelines. The price strategies mentioned in the table will be discussed later in this chapter.

Figure 14.8 shows in table form the theory of what happens to sales volume, profits, and competition during the product life cycle. You can compare this table to the graph in Figure 14.6. For instance, both the table and the graph show that a product at the mature stage may reach the top in sales growth while profit is decreasing. At that stage, a marketing manager may decide to

	MARKETING MIX ELEMENTS			
LIFE CYCLE STAGE	**PRODUCT**	**PRICE**	**PLACE**	**PROMOTION**
Introduction	Offer market-tested product; keep mix small	Go after innovators with high introductory price (skimming strategy) or use penetration pricing	Use wholesalers, selective distribution	Dealer promotion and heavy investment in primary demand advertising and sales promotion to get stores to carry the product and consumers to try it
Growth	Improve product; keep product mix limited	Adjust price to meet competition	Increase distribution	Heavy competitive advertising
Maturity	Differentiate product to satisfy different market segments	Further reduce price	Take over wholesaling function and intensify distribution	Emphasize brand name as well as product benefits and differences
Decline	Cut product mix; develop new-product ideas	Consider price increase	Consolidate distribution; drop some outlets	Reduce advertising to only loyal customers

FIGURE 14.7

SAMPLE STRATEGIES FOLLOWED DURING THE PRODUCT LIFE CYCLE

create a new image for the product to start a new growth cycle. You may have noticed, for example, how Arm & Hammer baking soda gets a new image every few years to generate new sales. One year it's positioned as a deodorant for refrigerators and the next as a substitute for harsh chemicals in swimming pools. Knowing what stage in the cycle a product has reached helps marketing managers decide when such strategic changes are needed.

Critical Thinking

- In what stage of the product life cycle are laptop computers? What does Figure 14.7 indicate firms should do at that stage? What will the next stage be? What might you do at that stage to optimize profits?
- Peanut butter is in the maturity or decline stage of the product life cycle. Does that explain why Skippy introduced a reduced-fat version of its peanut butter? What other variations on older products have been introduced in the last few years?

LIFE CYCLE STAGE	SALES	PROFITS	COMPETITORS
Introduction	Low sales	Losses may occur	Few
Growth	Rapidly rising sales	Very high profits	Growing number
Maturity	Peak sales	Declining profits	Stable number, then declining
Decline	Falling sales	Profits may fall to become losses	Declining number

FIGURE 14.8

HOW SALES, PROFITS, AND COMPETITION VARY OVER THE PRODUCT LIFE CYCLE

Theoretically all products go through these stages at various times in their life cycle. What happens to sales as a product matures?

The product life cycle can give marketers valuable clues as to how to promote a product over time. Some products, like crayons and sidewalk chalk, have very long product life cycles, change very little, and never seem to go into decline. Crayola Crayons has been successful for 100 years! In contrast, the TV show *Who Wants to Be a Millionaire?* had a very short product life cycle, perhaps due to overexposure (ABC elected to put the show on several times a week). Do you think *Millionaire* would still be popular if it had been aired only once a week?

Progress Assessment

- What are the five steps in the new-product development process?
- Can you draw a product life cycle and label its parts?

Competitive Pricing

Pricing is so important to marketing and the development of total product offers that it has been singled out as one of the four Ps in the marketing mix, along with product, place, and promotion. It is one of the most difficult of the four Ps for a manager to control. That is important because price is a critical ingredient in consumer evaluations of the product. In this section, we'll explore price both as an ingredient of the total product offer and as a strategic marketing tool.

Pricing Objectives

A firm may have several objectives in mind when setting a pricing strategy. When pricing Fiberrific, we may want to promote the product's image. If we price it high and use the right promotion, maybe we can make it the Evian of cereals, as we discussed earlier. We also might price it high to achieve a certain profit objective or return on investment. We could also price Fiberrific lower than its competitors because we want poor people and older people to be able to afford this nutritious cereal. That is, we could have some social or ethical goal in mind. Low pricing may also discourage competition because the profit potential is less in this case. A low price may also help us capture a larger share of the market. The point is that a firm may have several pricing objectives over time, and it must formulate these objectives clearly before developing an overall pricing strategy. Popular objectives include the following:

1. **Achieving a target return on investment or profit.** Ultimately, the goal of marketing is to make a profit ➤P. 4◄ by providing goods and services to others. Naturally, one long-run pricing objective of almost all firms is to optimize profit.[16]
2. **Building traffic.** Supermarkets often advertise certain products at or below cost to attract people to the store. These products are called loss leaders. The long-run objective is to make profits by following the short-run objective of building a customer base. Yahoo once provided an auction service for free in competition with eBay. Why give such a service away free? To increase advertising revenue on the Yahoo site and attract more people to Yahoo's other services.
3. **Achieving greater market share.** The U.S. auto industry is in a fierce international battle to capture and hold market share. One way to capture a larger part of the market is to offer low finance rates (e.g., zero-percent financing), low lease rates, or rebates. Recently, many auto companies used such discounts, but the result was a large loss in profits.[17] Computer companies offered free digital cameras and printers, rebates, and daily sweepstakes to capture business from Dell. Dell responded by offering buyers the chance to win $50,000. Such counterattacks have enabled Dell to maintain and even grow its market share.
4. **Creating an image.** Certain watches, perfumes, and other socially visible products are priced high to give them an image of exclusivity and status.
5. **Furthering social objectives.** A firm may want to price a product low so that people with little money can afford the product. The government often gets involved in pricing farm products so that everyone can get basic needs such as milk and bread at a low price.

Note that a firm may have short-run objectives that differ greatly from its long-run objectives. Both should be understood at the beginning and put into the strategic marketing plan. Pricing objectives should be influenced by other marketing decisions regarding product design, packaging, branding, distribution, and promotion. All of these marketing decisions are interrelated.

People believe intuitively that the price charged for a product must bear some relation to the cost of producing the product. In fact, we'd generally agree that prices are usually set somewhere above cost. But as we'll see, prices and cost aren't always related. In fact, there are three major approaches to pricing strategy: cost-based, demand-based (target costing), and competition-based.

Cost-Based Pricing

Producers often use cost as a primary basis for setting price. They develop elaborate cost accounting systems to measure production costs (including materials, labor, and overhead), add in some margin of profit, and come up with a price. The question is whether the price will be satisfactory to the market as well. In the long run, the market—not the producer—determines what the price will be. Pricing should take into account costs, but it should also include the expected costs of product updates, the objectives for each product, and competitor prices.

Product development is often a very expensive process, especially making prescription drugs for specific illnesses. Without the incentive to make substantial profits, some drug companies say they can't afford the costs of research and development. That was a major issue in this protest of GlaxoSmithKline's decision not to sell drugs to Canadian pharmacies and wholesalers who, in turn, resold them to American consumers at much cheaper prices.

Demand-Based Pricing

target costing
Designing a product so that it satisfies customers and meets the profit margins desired by the firm.

An opposing strategy to cost-based pricing is one called target costing. **Target costing** is demand based. It means designing a product so that it satisfies customers and meets the profit margins desired by the firm. Target costing makes the final price an input to the product development process, not an outcome of it. You estimate the selling price people would be willing to pay for a product and subtract the desired profit margin. The result is the target cost of production. Japanese companies such as Isuzu Motors, Komatsu Limited, and Sony all have used target costing.

Competition-Based Pricing

competition-based pricing
A pricing strategy based on what all the other competitors are doing. The price can be set at, above, or below competitors' prices.

price leadership
The procedure by which one or more dominant firms set the pricing practices that all competitors in an industry follow.

Competition-based pricing is a strategy based on what all the other competitors are doing. The price can be at, above, or below competitors' prices. Pricing depends on customer loyalty, perceived differences, and the competitive climate. **Price leadership** is the procedure by which one or more dominant firms set the pricing practices that all competitors in an industry follow. You may have noticed that practice among oil and cigarette companies.

Pricing in the Service Sector

Service industries are adopting many of the same pricing tactics as goods-producing firms. They begin by cutting costs as much as possible. Then they determine what services ➤P. 26◀ are most important to customers; those that aren't important are cut. For example, some airlines have eliminated meals on their flights. Southwest doesn't incur the administrative costs of assigned seats. In return, customers get good value.[18]

Wireless phone services keep cutting their prices to beat competition, but profits are being driven down as fast as prices.[19] Thus, telecommunications companies in general are not doing well in the stock market.

Many luxury hotels cut their prices after the terrorist attacks of September 11, 2001, because business demand fell. Luxury rooms were often as inexpensive as rooms in less luxurious hotels and motels. Such cuts lowered

Spotlight on Small Business www.marcelsdc.com

Going from Low-End to Upscale Restaurants

Dave Thomas was a marketing major at George Washington University who earned a small fortune using his marketing skills to build, grow, and sell Subway sandwich shops. He built his first shop in 1994, just before graduating from college. He went on to build four more stores in the District of Columbia. Thomas learned a lot as a sandwich shop owner. For one thing, he learned how to offer a low-priced value meal. But Thomas dreamed of owning an upscale restaurant where he could charge higher prices and make even more money.

There are many midpriced restaurants in and around Washington, D.C., that were started by small-business owners; Clyde's and the Capitol City Brewing Company are just two of the more popular ones. They attract customers by offering consistent service and fair prices. There are also many upscale restaurants that offer outstanding food and service to customers willing to pay premium prices. It is this latter market that Thomas was after.

The challenge when going upscale is to capture and keep customers by offering them value for their money. One way to do that is to bring in a good chef. Thomas found a chef who had worked at such upscale restaurants as the Four Seasons, the Grand Hotel Café, and the Watergate Hotel's Aquarelle. The chef, Robert Wiedmaier, was eager to become a small-business owner himself and jumped at the idea when Thomas offered him the chance to open a restaurant in a premier Washington, D.C., location. Together, they opened Marcel's on Pennsylvania Avenue. In Thomas's new marketing situation, a nonprice strategy was more important than a low-price strategy. Customers in an upscale restaurant care less about pricing and more about great food, great service, and a pleasant ambience. Thomas's favorite dish at Marcel's is quail stuffed with foie gras. You just can't buy something like that at Subway. The secret to an upscale restaurant, however, is the value added by the waiters and the ambience. Waiters must dress formally, provide wine and meal suggestions in a professional manner, and in general make the meal a memorable event. A good waiter is, as they say in the commercial, "priceless."

Source: www.marcelsdc.com.

the profit for each room but increased the number of customers, thus providing more revenue from other services, such as attached restaurants and spas.

With both goods and services, the idea is to give the consumer value. But trying to give the consumer value while maintaining profits is a challenge.[20] The Spotlight on Small Business box looks at the challenge of going upscale in pricing. When making such a change, break-even analysis (discussed next) can help an organization relate sales, profit, and price to see what the results of such a change might be.

Break-Even Analysis

Before you go into the business of producing Fiberrific cereal, it may be wise to determine how many boxes of cereal you'd have to sell before making a profit. You'd then determine whether you could reach such a sales goal. **Break-even analysis** is the process used to determine profitability at various levels of sales. The break-even point is the point where revenues from sales equal all costs. The formula for calculating the break-even point is as follows:

break-even analysis The process used to determine profitability at various levels of sales.

$$\text{Break-even point (BEP)} = \frac{\text{Total fixed cost (FC)}}{\text{Price of one unit (P)} - \text{Variable cost (VC) of one unit}}$$

Total fixed costs are all the expenses that remain the same no matter how many products are made or sold. Among the expenses that make up fixed costs are the amount paid to own or rent a factory or warehouse and the amount paid for business insurance. **Variable costs** change according to the level of production. Included are the expenses for the materials used in making prod-

total fixed costs All the expenses that remain the same no matter how many products are made or sold.

variable costs Costs that change according to the level of production.

ucts and the direct costs of labor used in making those goods. For producing Fiberrific cereal, let's say you have a fixed cost of $200,000 (for mortgage interest, real estate taxes, equipment, and so on). Your variable cost (e.g., labor and materials) per box of cereal is $2. If you sold the cereal for $4 a box, the break-even point would be 100,000 boxes. In other words, you wouldn't make any money selling cereal unless you sold more than 100,000 boxes of it:

$$\text{BEP} = \frac{\text{FC}}{\text{P} - \text{VC}} = \frac{\$200{,}000}{\$4.00 - \$2.00} = \frac{\$200{,}000}{\$2.00} = 100{,}000 \text{ boxes}$$

Other Pricing Strategies

Let's say a firm has just developed a new line of products, such as high-definition television (HDTV) sets. The firm has to decide how to price these sets at the introductory stage of the product life cycle. One strategy would be to price them high to recover the costs of developing the sets and to take advantage of the fact that there are few competitors. A **skimming price strategy** is one in which a new product is priced high to make optimum profit while there's little competition. Of course, those large profits will attract competitors. That happened when high-priced HDTVs were introduced in the late 1990s.

skimming price strategy
Strategy in which a new product is priced high to make optimum profit while there's little competition.

A second strategy would be to price the new HDTVs low. This would attract more buyers and discourage other companies from making sets because the profit is so low. This strategy enables the firm to penetrate or capture a large share of the market quickly. A **penetration strategy**, therefore, is one in which a product is priced low to attract more customers and discourage competitors. The Japanese successfully used a penetration strategy with videocassette recorders. No U.S. firm could compete with the low prices the Japanese offered.

penetration strategy
Strategy in which a product is priced low to attract many customers and discourage competition.

There are several pricing strategies used by retailers. One is called **everyday low pricing (EDLP)**. That's the pricing strategy used by Home Depot and Wal-Mart. Such stores set prices lower than competitors and usually do not have many special sales. The idea is to have consumers come to those stores whenever they want a bargain rather than waiting until there is a sale, as they do for most department stores.

everyday low pricing (EDLP)
Setting prices lower than competitors and then not having any special sales.

Department stores and other retailers most often use a **high–low pricing strategy**. The idea is to have regular prices that are higher than those at stores using EDLP but also to have many special sales in which the prices are lower than those of competitors. The problem with such pricing is that it teaches consumers to wait for sales, thus cutting into profits. As the Internet grows in popularity, you may see fewer stores with a high–low strategy because consumers will be able to find better prices on the Internet and begin buying more and more from online retailers.

high–low pricing strategy
Setting prices that are higher than EDLP stores, but having many special sales where the prices are lower than competitors'.

Some retailers use price as a major determinant of the goods they carry. For example, there are stores that promote goods that sell for only $1 or only $10. Outlet stores supposedly sell brand-name goods at discount prices, and sometimes they do. Other stores, sometimes called discount stores, sell "seconds," or damaged goods. Consumers must take care to carefully examine such goods to be sure the flaws are not too major.

Bundling means grouping two or more products together and pricing them as a unit. For example, a store might price washers and dryers as a unit. Jiffy Lube offers an oil change and lube, and then checks your car's fluid levels and air pressure and bundles them all into one price. **Psychological pricing** means pricing goods and services at price points that make the product appear less expensive than it is. For example, a house might be priced at $299,000 with the idea that it sounds a lot less than $300,000. Gas stations almost always use psychological pricing—$1.99 per gallon sounds less than $2.00.

bundling
Grouping two or more products together and pricing them as a unit.

psychological pricing
Pricing goods and services at price points that make the product appear less expensive than it is.

How Market Forces Affect Pricing

Ultimately, price is determined by supply ➤P. 43◀ and demand ➤P. 43◀ in the marketplace, as described in Chapter 2. For example, if you charge $3 for Fiberrific and nobody buys your cereal at that price, you'll have to lower the price until you reach a point that's acceptable to customers and to you. The price that results from the interaction of buyers and sellers in the marketplace is called the *market price.*

Recognizing the fact that different consumers may be willing to pay different prices, marketers sometimes price on the basis of consumer demand rather than cost or some other calculation. That's called *demand-oriented pricing* and is reflected by movie theaters with low rates for children and by drugstores with discounts for senior citizens. The Washington Opera Company in Washington, D.C., for example, raised its prices on prime seating and lowered its pricing on less attractive seating; this strategy raised the company's revenues by 9 percent.

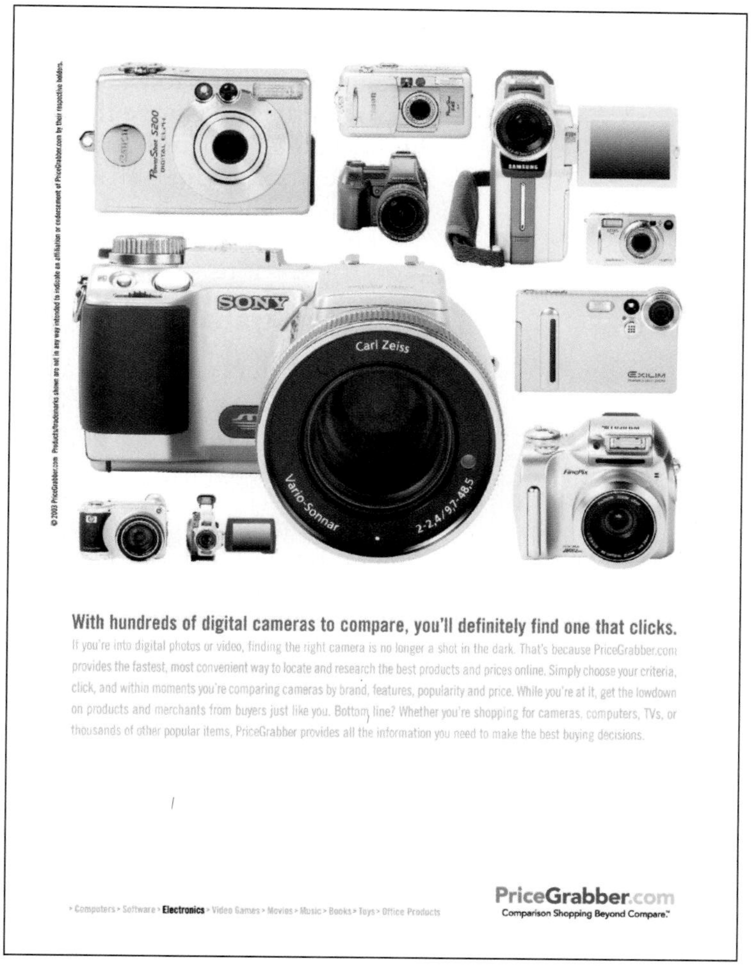
With hundreds of digital cameras to compare, you'll definitely find one that clicks.
If you're into digital photos or video, finding the right camera is no longer a shot in the dark. That's because PriceGrabber.com provides the fastest, most convenient way to locate and research the best products and prices online. Simply choose your criteria, click, and within moments you're comparing cameras by brand, features, popularity and price. While you're at it, get the lowdown on products and merchants from buyers just like you. Bottom line? Whether you're shopping for cameras, computers, TVs, or thousands of other popular items, PriceGrabber provides all the information you need to make the best buying decisions.
> Computers > Software > Electronics > Video Games > Movies > Music > Books > Toys > Office Products
PriceGrabber.com
Comparison Shopping Beyond Compare.™

How much of an impact do you think comparison shopping on the Internet is having on the pricing practices of marketers? PriceGrabber.com enables people to comparison shop quickly and easily for an increasingly wide range of products. From your perspective how important are product descriptions and follow-up service to such sales, or is price the major determinant?

Marketers are facing a new pricing problem: Customers can now compare prices of many goods and services on the Internet. For example, you may want to check out deals on sites such as DealTime.com, BrandsForLess.com, or ICanBuy.com. Priceline.com introduced consumers to a "demand collection system," in which buyers post the prices they are willing to pay and invite sellers to either accept or decline the price. Consumers can get great prices on airlines, hotels, and other products by naming the price they are willing to pay. You can also buy used goods online. Have you or any of your friends bought or sold anything on eBay or Amazon.com? Clearly, price competition is going to heat up as consumers have more access to price information from all around the world.[21] As a result, nonprice competition is likely to increase.

NONPRICE COMPETITION

In spite of the emphasis placed on price in microeconomic theory, marketers often compete on product attributes other than price. You may have noted that price differences are small with products such as gasoline, men's haircuts, candy bars, and even major products such as compact cars and private colleges. Typically, you will not see price used as a major promotional appeal on television. Instead, marketers tend to stress product images and consumer benefits such as comfort, style, convenience, and durability.

Many small organizations promote the services that accompany basic products rather than price in order to compete with bigger firms. The idea is that good service will enhance a relatively homogeneous product. Danny O'Neill, for example, is a small wholesaler who sells gourmet coffee to upscale restaurants. He has to watch competitors' prices and see what services they offer so that he can charge the premium prices he wants. To charge high prices, he has to offer superior service. Larger companies often do the same thing. For example, some airlines stress friendliness, promptness, abundant flights, good meals, and other such services. High-priced hotels stress "no surprises," cable TV, business services, health clubs, and other extras.[22]

Nonprice Strategies

Often marketers emphasize nonprice differences because prices are so easy to match. However, few competitors can match the image of a friendly, responsive, consumer-oriented company. The following are some other strategies for avoiding price wars:

1. **Add value.** Some drugstores with elderly customers add value by offering home delivery. Training videos add value to any product that's difficult to use. Lawn-mower manufacturer Toro gives "lawn parties" during which it teaches customers lawn care strategies.
2. **Educate consumers.** Home Depot teaches its customers how to use the equipment it sells and how to build decks and other do-it-yourself projects. The Iowa Beef Processors educate their customers about the value of buying top-grade beef, which has less waste than low-grade beef.
3. **Establish relationships.** Customers will pay extra for products and services when they have a friendly relationship with the seller. Today many auto dealers, like Saturn, send out cards reminding people when service is needed. They may also have picnics and other special events for customers. Airlines, credit card providers, supermarkets, hotels, and car rental agencies have frequent-buyer clubs that offer all kinds of fringe benefits to frequent users. The services aren't always less expensive, but they offer more value.

As you can see, this chapter begins and ends with one theme: Give customers value and they'll give you their loyalty.

Progress Assessment

- Can you list two short-term and two long-term pricing objectives? Can the two be compatible?
- What's wrong with using a cost-based pricing strategy?
- What's the purpose of break-even analysis?
- Can you calculate a product's break-even point if producing it costs $10,000 and revenue from the sale of one unit is $20?

Summary

1. Explain the concept of a total product offer.

1. A total product offer consists of everything that consumers evaluate when deciding whether to buy something.
   - ***What's included in a total product offer?***

   A total product offer includes price, brand name, satisfaction in use, and more.

- ***What's the difference between a product line and a product mix?***

A product line is a group of physically similar products with similar competitors. A product line of gum may include bubble gum and sugarless gum. A product mix is a company's combination of product lines. A manufacturer may offer lines of gum, candy bars, chewing tobacco, and so on.

- ***How do marketers create product differentiation for their goods and services?***

Marketers use a mix of pricing, advertising, and packaging to make their products seem unique and attractive.

2. Consumer goods are sold to ultimate consumers like you and me and not to businesses.

2. Describe the various kinds of consumer and industrial goods.

- ***What are the four classifications of consumer goods and services, and how are they marketed?***

There are convenience goods and services (requiring minimum shopping effort), shopping goods and services (for which people go searching and compare price and quality), specialty goods and services (which consumers go out of their way to get, and often demand specific brands), and unsought goods and services (which consumers did not intend to buy when they entered the store). Convenience goods and services are best promoted by location, shopping goods and services by some price/quality appeal, and specialty goods and services by specialty magazines and interactive websites.

- ***What are industrial goods, and how are they marketed differently from consumer goods?***

Industrial goods are products sold in the business-to-business market (B2B), and are used in the production of other products. They're sold largely through salespeople and rely less on advertising. Installations are major capital equipment such as new factories and heavy machinery. Accessory equipment is capital items that are not quite as long lasting or as expensive as installations. Examples include computers, photocopy machines, and various tools.

3. Packaging changes the product and is becoming increasingly important, taking over much of the sales function for consumer goods.

3. List and describe the functions of packaging.

- ***What are the six functions of packaging?***

The six functions are (1) to protect the goods inside, stand up under handling and storage, be tamperproof, deter theft, and yet be easy to open and use; (2) to describe the contents; (3) to explain the benefits of the product inside; (4) to provide information on warranties, warnings, and other consumer matters; (5) to indicate price, value, and uses; and (6) to attract the buyer's attention.

4. Branding also changes a product.

4. Describe the differences among a brand, a brand name, and a trademark, and explain the concepts of brand equity and brand loyalty.

- ***Can you give examples of a brand, a brand name, and a trademark?***

One example of a brand name of crackers is Waverly by Nabisco. The brand consists of the name Waverly as well as the symbol (a red triangle in the corner with *Nabisco* circled in white). The brand name and the symbol are also trademarks, since Nabisco has been given legal protection for this brand. Manufacturers need to protect their brand names from competitors who try to steal their name or image.

- ***What is brand equity, and how do managers create brand associations?***

Brand equity is the combination of factors such as awareness, loyalty, perceived quality, images, and emotions people associate with a given brand name. Brand association is the linking of a brand to other favorable images. For example, you can link a brand to other product users, to a popular celebrity, to a particular geographic area, or to competitors.

5. Explain the role of brand managers and the steps of the new-product development process.

5. Brand managers coordinate product, price, place, and promotion decisions for a particular product.
   - ***What are the six steps of the product development process?***

   The steps are (1) generation of new-product ideas, (2) product screening, (3) product analysis, (4) development, (5) testing, and (6) commercialization.

6. Draw the product life cycle, describe each of its stages, and describe marketing strategies at each stage.

6. Once a product is placed on the market, marketing strategy varies as the product class goes through various stages of acceptance called the product life cycle.
   - ***What are the theoretical stages of the product life cycle?***

   They are introduction, growth, maturity, and decline.
   - ***How do marketing strategies theoretically change at the various stages?***

   See Figures 14.7 and 14.8.

7. Explain various pricing objectives and strategies.

7. Pricing is one of the four Ps of marketing.
   - ***What are pricing objectives?***

   Objectives include achieving a target profit, building traffic, increasing market share, creating an image, and meeting social goals.
   - ***What's the break-even point?***

   At the break-even point, total cost equals total revenue. Sales beyond that point are profitable. The break-even point = Total fixed cost ÷ (Price of one unit − Variable cost of one unit).
   - ***What strategies can marketers use to determine a product's price?***

   A *skimming price strategy* is one in which the product is priced high to make optimum profit while there's little competition, whereas a *penetration strategy* is one in which a product is priced low to attract more customers and discourage competitors. *Demand-oriented pricing* is based on consumer demand rather than cost. *Competition-oriented pricing* is based on all competitors' prices. *Price leadership* occurs when all competitors follow the pricing practice of one or more dominant companies. *Bundling* means grouping two or more products into a unit and charging one price for them.

8. Explain why nonpricing strategies are growing in importance.

8. In spite of the emphasis placed on price in microeconomic theory, marketers often compete on product attributes other than price.
   - ***Why do companies use nonprice strategies?***

   Pricing is one of the easiest marketing strategies to copy. Therefore, often it is not a good long-run competitive tool. Instead, marketers may compete using nonprice strategies that are less easy to copy, including offering great service, educating consumers, and establishing long-term relationships with customers.

Key Terms

brand 438
brand association 440
brand awareness 439
brand equity 439
brand loyalty 439
brand manager 440
brand name 438
break-even analysis 449
bundling 450
commercialization 442
competition-based pricing 448
concept testing 442
convenience goods and services 434
dealer (private-label) brands 438
everyday low pricing (EDLP) 450
generic goods 439
high–low pricing strategy 450
industrial goods 435
knockoff brands 439
manufacturers' brand names 438
penetration strategy 450
price leadership 448
product analysis 441
product differentiation 434
product life cycle 443
product line 432
product mix 432
product screening 441
psychological pricing 450

shopping goods and services 434
skimming price strategy 450
specialty goods and services 434
target costing 448
total fixed costs 449
total product offer 431
trademark 438
unsought goods and services 435
value 430
variable costs 449

Developing Workplace Skills

1. Look around your classroom and notice the different types of shoes that students are wearing. What product qualities were they looking for when they chose those shoes? What was the importance of price, style, brand name, and color? Describe the product offerings you would feature in a new shoe store designed to appeal to college students.

2. A total product offer consists of everything that consumers evaluate when choosing among products, including price, package, service, and reputation. Working in teams, compose a list of as many factors that consumers might consider when evaluating the following products: a vacation resort, a college, a new car.

3. Imagine that you are involved in a money-raising activity for your school. You decide to sell large pizzas for $12 each. You buy a used pizza oven for $12,000. That is the only fixed cost. The variable cost per unit is $6.00. Calculate the break-even point and decide whether or not you should go ahead with the project. That is, do you think you could sell enough pizzas to make a sizable profit?

4. How important is price to you when buying the following products: shoes, milk, computers, hair cuts, and auto rentals? What nonprice factors are more important, if ever, in making these choices? How much time does it take to evaluate factors other than price when making such purchases?

5. Determine where in the product life cycle you would place each of the following products and then prepare a marketing strategy for each product based on the recommendations in this chapter:

   a. Alka-Seltzer.
   b. Cellular phones.
   c. Electric automobiles.
   d. Campbell's chicken noodle soup.

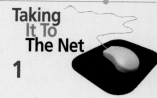

Taking It To The Net 1

Purpose

To assess how the Internet can be used to shop for various goods.

Exercise

Shopbots are Internet sites that you can use to find the best prices on goods you need. No shopbot searches the entire Internet, so it's a good idea to use more than one to get the best deals. Furthermore, not all shopbots figure in shipping and handling. Here are some to try:

mySimon.com
Pricegrabber.com
ShopFind.com
PriceSCAN.com

1. Which of the shopbots seem most comprehensive—offering the most goods or the most information?
2. Which shopbot is the easiest to use? The hardest?
3. Write down some of the prices you find on the Internet and then go to a local discount store, such as Wal-Mart, and compare prices. Which source—the Net or the store—has the lowest prices, or does it depend on the product?
4. Evaluate shopping on the Internet versus shopping in stores. What are the advantages and disadvantages of each?

Taking It To The Net 2

Purpose

To determine the appropriate pricing strategy for specific products.

Exercise

Go to www.marketingteacher.com/Lessons/lesson_pricing.htm and review the various types of pricing strategies.

1. Click on the Exercise button at the top of the page and place the products listed in the appropriate cells of the grid provided.
2. Click on the Answer button at the top of the page to check your work. If you do not agree with the answers, scroll down the screen for an explanation.

Casing The Web

To access the case "Everyday Low Pricing," visit

www.mhhe.com/ub7e

Video Case

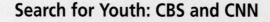

Search for Youth: CBS and CNN

Have you ever thought of the difficulties in developing a product like a newspaper or a TV news show for a particular market? To compound the challenge, imagine that the target market you identified has shown a distinct lack of interest in products related to the news. Readership is down for newspapers; television news is very fragmented. That's the problem facing newspapers and TV news shows in this video.

USA Today has made a determined effort to appeal to those elusive customers between 18 and 34 years old. However, the company realizes that it must be careful not to offend its core market of older readers while it targets this younger group. A first glance at *USA Weekend* magazine shows a clear appeal to a younger market. The magazine uses specific colors to attract attention and features what it calls "youth icons," stories about personalities that attract the attention of consumers between 18 and 34.

Attracting a younger audience has been more difficult for TV news shows. One problem has been competition. Gen Y viewers prefer to go online for information rather than watching TV news. Why, then, do TV executives go to great lengths to reach these unwilling consumers? Simple marketing analysis: Young people, especially those 18 and up, are an attractive target for advertisers. These consumers have yet to establish brand loyalties for most products. Therefore, TV executives are willing to pay two or three times as much to attract these younger viewers because that's what their advertisers want.

Andrew Heyward, president of CBS News, strongly supports structuring his news programming to reach these young consumers. CBS is a unit of Viacom and therefore has access to news content from other Viacom properties such as MTV, VH-1, BET, and UPN. The idea has been to bring youth-oriented material from those channels into CBS News programs (such as *48 Hours*) to attract younger viewers. CBS has also hired younger anchorpersons for news programs like the *CBS Early Show*.

Perhaps the model to follow is *CNN Headline News*. Like CBS, CNN employs younger anchors, but it presents the news in rapid-paced, information-packed segments. Research indicates that young consumers will watch the news for an average of only 15 minutes. CNN obliges by offering screens jammed with graphics and crawls so viewers can grasp as much information as possible in a very short time. Such an overload of information may turn away older viewers, but the process seems to attract the target audience of younger viewers. CNN anchors like Robin Meade and Kris Osborn talk fast, which seems to meet the style preference of the Internet generation.

Developing products for target markets is a challenge for all marketers. News organizations are determined to build awareness with Generation Y to show them that TV news really is for them.

Thinking It Over

1. What has this video taught you about the difficulty of product development in services in general and the challenges of reaching young customers?
2. If you were a news program director, what suggestions would you have to draw viewers in the targeted 18–34 age group to your news program?
3. Evaluate the various media and their response to people in the target group. Consider newspapers, magazines, TV (network and cable), and radio.

Chapter 15

Distributing Products Quickly and Efficiently

Learning Goals

After you have read and studied this chapter, you should be able to

1 Explain the concept of marketing channels and the value of marketing intermediaries.

2 Give examples of how intermediaries perform the six marketing utilities.

3 Describe the various wholesale intermediaries in the distribution system.

4 Explain the ways in which retailers compete and the distribution strategies they use.

5 Explain the various kinds of nonstore retailing.

6 Explain the various ways to build cooperation in channel systems.

7 Describe the emergence of logistics.

8 Outline how intermediaries move goods from producers to consumers through the use of various transportation modes and storage functions.

Getting to Know Gus Pagonis of Sears

Few people in the world have more expertise in logistics (that is, moving goods from here to there—defined in detail later in this chapter) and overall leadership in management than William "Gus" Pagonis. He is widely known for his logistical achievements, particularly during the 1991 Gulf War. During the war, Pagonis kept 250,000 GIs fed, clothed, and equipped for battle. During the peak of the military buildup, 5,000 troops arrived on the front each day. Pagonis was responsible for feeding, sheltering, and equipping each one. He used global positioning technology to track the movement of supplies.

After his success in masterminding the logistics for the Gulf War, Pagonis left the army in 1993 and was appointed executive vice president of logistics for Sears, Roebuck & Company. As head of the Sears Logistics Group, he is the contact person for all of Sears's logistics and is responsible for vendor relations, transportation, home deliveries, outlet stores, international logistics, and the integration of information systems to tie it all together. Sears has millions of dollars' worth of materials on the move daily. The retailer makes 5,000 home deliveries a day and moves 250,000 truckloads of goods each year. It has 30 large distribution centers and 90 smaller outlets. Pagonis must move some 100,000 products to over 2,000 stores through that system.

All of Pagonis's military logistical experience proved invaluable in keeping Sears products moving after terrorists attacked the World Trade Center and the Pentagon on September 11, 2001. You would expect a military man to have a disaster plan ready. Sure enough, following the attacks Pagonis was ready with an effective disaster plan. In each area of the country, one or two employees served as focal points for communications. There was a disaster operations center in the headquarters building in Hoffman Estates, Illinois. The center's walls were covered with system status charts, and computers tracked home deliveries, vendor shipments, and trucks. Delays at U.S. borders had to be handled, and contingency plans had to be made in case of further attacks. The center remained open for 30 days after 9/11.

All of Pagonis's military logistical experience proved invaluable in keeping Sears products moving after terrorists attacked the World Trade Center and the Pentagon on September 11, 2001.

As the head of Sears's everyday logistical operations, Gus Pagonis draws on his military experience to find a balance between minimizing inventory overhead, keeping costs down, and having enough goods on hand to keep store shelves fully stocked. The process of moving goods from producers to distribution centers and on to stores, and then from stores to ultimate consumers, is a major undertaking. It calls for complex computer programs to manage the flows, to keep inventory costs down, and to ensure fast and efficient service to people like you and me. Technology has altered the way customers buy and the way manufacturers sell. More important for this chapter, technology has also changed the way goods are distributed. This chapter will explore these and other changes.

Sources: www.kepplerassociates.com/pagonis.htm, September 9, 2002; www.nuteweb.tpc.edu/public/current/patterson/lectures/pagonis.html, September 9, 2002; Eric Hellweg, "Supply-Chain Hero," *Business 2.0,* January 2002, pp. 74–75; and Nelson D. Schwartz, "Army Stores," *Fortune,* April 28, 2003, p. 40.

The Emergence of Marketing Intermediaries

Look around at the feet of your fellow students. Some of them are probably wearing shoes made by Timberland. Now try to imagine the challenge of getting the raw materials together, making 12 million pairs of shoes, as Timberland does, and then distributing those shoes to stores throughout the world. That's what thousands of manufacturing firms—making everything from automobiles to toys—have to deal with every day. There are hundreds of thousands of marketing intermediaries whose job it is to help move goods from the raw-material state to producers and then on to consumers.

marketing intermediaries Organizations that assist in moving goods and services from producers to industrial and consumer users.

channel of distribution A whole set of marketing intermediaries, such as wholesalers and retailers, that join together to transport and store goods in their path (or channel) from producers to consumers.

agents/brokers Marketing intermediaries who bring buyers and sellers together and assist in negotiating an exchange but don't take title to the goods.

wholesaler A marketing intermediary that sells to other organizations.

retailer An organization that sells to ultimate consumers.

Marketing intermediaries are organizations that assist in moving goods and services from producers to business and consumer users. They're called intermediaries because they're in the middle of a whole series of organizations that join together to help distribute goods from producers to consumers. A **channel of distribution** consists of a whole set of marketing intermediaries, such as agents, brokers, wholesalers, and retailers, that join together to transport and store goods in their path (or channel) from producers to consumers. **Agents/brokers** are marketing intermediaries who bring buyers and sellers together and assist in negotiating an exchange, but don't take title to the goods—that is, at no point do they own the goods. A **wholesaler** is a marketing intermediary that sells to other organizations, such as retailers, manufacturers, and hospitals. They are part of the business-to-business (B2B) ➤P. 411◀ system. A **retailer** is an organization that sells to ultimate consumers (that is, people like you and me).

Channels of distribution ensure communication flows and the flow of money and title to goods. They also help ensure that the right quantity and assortment of goods will be available when and where needed. Figure 15.1 pictures selected channels of distribution for both consumer and industrial (or B2B) goods.

Why Marketing Needs Intermediaries

Manufacturers don't always need marketing intermediaries to sell their goods to consumer and business buyers. Figure 15.1 shows that some manufacturers sell directly to buyers. So why have marketing intermediaries at all? The answer is that intermediaries perform certain marketing tasks—such as transporting, storing, selling, advertising, and relationship building—faster and cheaper than most manufacturers could. A simple analogy is this: You could deliver packages in person to people anywhere in the world, but usually you don't. Why not? Because it's usually cheaper and faster to have them delivered by the U.S. Postal Service or some private firm such as UPS or FedEx.

Similarly, you could sell your home by yourself or buy stock directly from other people, but you probably wouldn't do so. Why? Again, because there are specialists (agents and brokers) who make the process more efficient and easier than it would be otherwise. Agents and brokers are marketing intermediaries. They facilitate the exchange process. In the next section, we'll explore how intermediaries improve the efficiency of various exchanges.

How Intermediaries Create Exchange Efficiency

The benefits of using marketing intermediaries can be illustrated rather easily. Suppose that five manufacturers of various food products each tried to sell directly to five retailers. The number of exchange relationships that would have to be established is 5 times 5, or 25. But picture what happens when a wholesaler enters the system. The five manufacturers would contact one wholesaler to establish five exchange relationships. The wholesaler would have to estab-

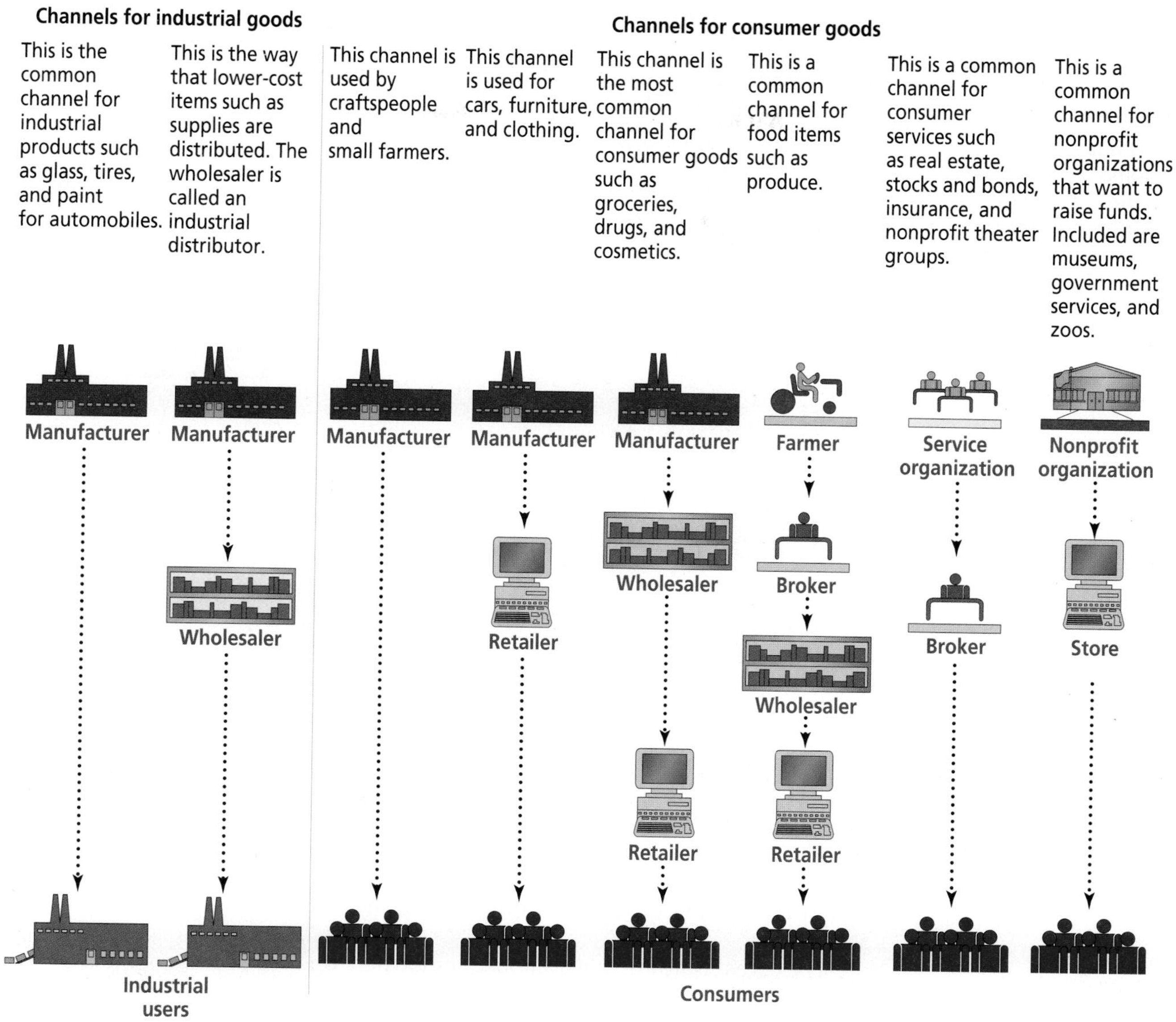

Channels for industrial goods
This is the common channel for industrial products such as glass, tires, and paint for automobiles.
This is the way that lower-cost items such as supplies are distributed. The wholesaler is called an industrial distributor.
Channels for consumer goods
This channel is used by craftspeople and small farmers.
This channel is used for cars, furniture, and clothing.
This channel is the most common channel for consumer goods such as groceries, drugs, and cosmetics.
This is a common channel for food items such as produce.
This is a common channel for consumer services such as real estate, stocks and bonds, insurance, and nonprofit theater groups.
This is a common channel for nonprofit organizations that want to raise funds. Included are museums, government services, and zoos.
Manufacturer
Manufacturer
Manufacturer
Manufacturer
Manufacturer
Farmer
Service organization
Nonprofit organization
Wholesaler
Retailer
Wholesaler
Broker
Broker
Store
Wholesaler
Retailer
Retailer
Industrial users
Consumers

FIGURE 15.1

SELECTED CHANNELS OF DISTRIBUTION FOR INDUSTRIAL AND CONSUMER GOODS AND SERVICES

lish contact with the five retailers. That would also mean five exchange relationships. Note that the number of exchanges is reduced from 25 to only 10 by the addition of a wholesaler. Figure 15.2 on p. 462 shows this process.

Some economists have said that intermediaries add costs and need to be eliminated. Marketers say that intermediaries add value and that the value greatly exceeds the cost. In the next section, we shall explore this debate and show you the value that intermediaries provide.

The Value versus the Cost of Intermediaries

Marketing intermediaries have always been viewed by the public with a degree of suspicion. Some surveys have shown that about half of the cost of the things we buy are marketing costs that go largely to pay for the work of intermediaries. People reason that if we could only get rid of intermediaries, we could greatly reduce the cost of everything we buy. Sounds good, but is the solution really that simple?

Let's take as an example a box of Fiberrific cereal (the extended example we introduced in Chapter 13) that sells for $4. How could we, as consumers, get the cereal for less? Well, we could all drive to Michigan where some of the

FIGURE 15.2

HOW INTERMEDIARIES CREATE EXCHANGE EFFICIENCY

This figure shows that adding a wholesaler to the channel of distribution cuts the number of contacts from 25 to 10. This improves the efficiency of distribution.

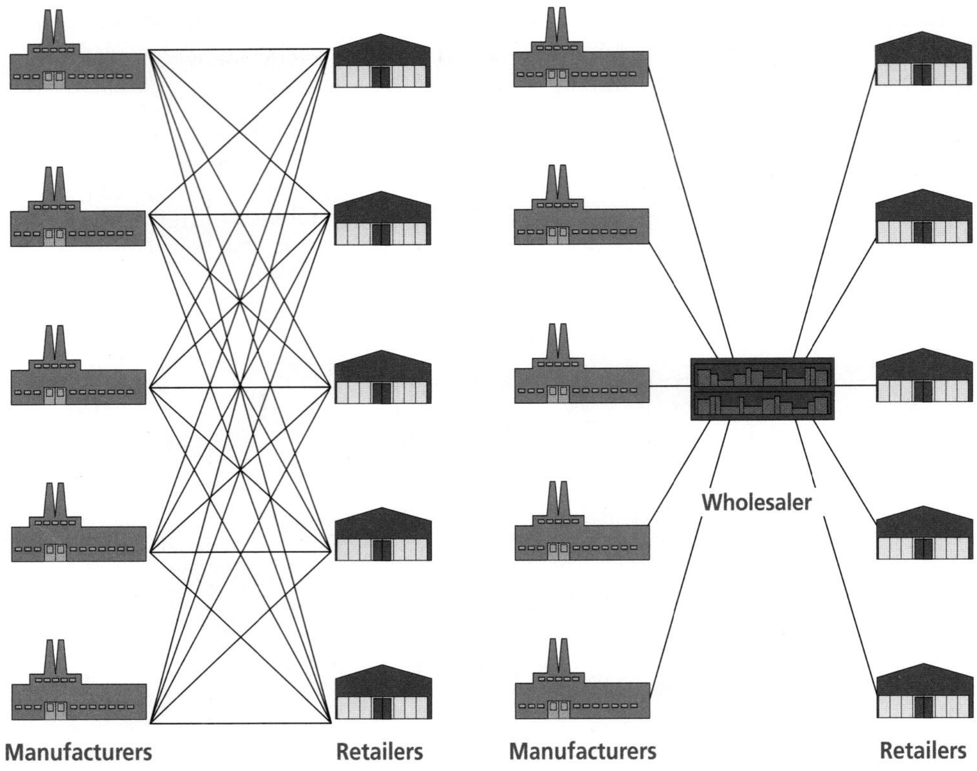

cereal is produced and save some shipping costs. But would that be practical? Can you imagine millions of people getting in their cars and driving to Michigan just to buy some cereal? No, it doesn't make sense. It's much cheaper to have intermediaries bring the cereal to major cities. That might involve transportation and warehousing by wholesalers. These steps add cost, don't they? Yes, but they add value as well, the value of not having to drive to Michigan.

The cereal is now in a warehouse somewhere on the outskirts of the city. We could all drive down to the wholesaler and pick it up. But that still isn't the most economical way to buy cereal. If we figure in the cost of gas and time, the cereal would be too expensive. Instead, we prefer to have someone move the cereal from the warehouse to a truck, drive it to the corner supermarket, unload it, unpack it, price it, shelve it, and wait for us to come in to buy it. To make it even more convenient, the supermarket may stay open for 24 hours a day, seven days a week. Think of the costs. But think also of the value! For $4, we can get a box of cereal when we want it, and with little effort.

If we were to get rid of the retailer, we could buy a box of cereal for slightly less, but we'd have to drive farther and spend time in the warehouse looking through rows of cereals. If we got rid of the wholesaler, we could save a little more money, not counting our drive to Michigan. But a few cents here and a few cents there add up—to the point where marketing may add up to 75 cents for every 25 cents in manufacturing costs.

Figure 15.3 shows where your money goes in the distribution process. Notice that the largest percentage goes to people who drive trucks and work in wholesale and retail organizations. Note also that only 3.5 cents goes to profit. That's probably less than you imagined. Here are three basic points about intermediaries:

- Marketing intermediaries can be eliminated, but their activities can't; that is, you can eliminate some wholesalers and retailers, but then consumers or someone else would have to perform the intermediaries'

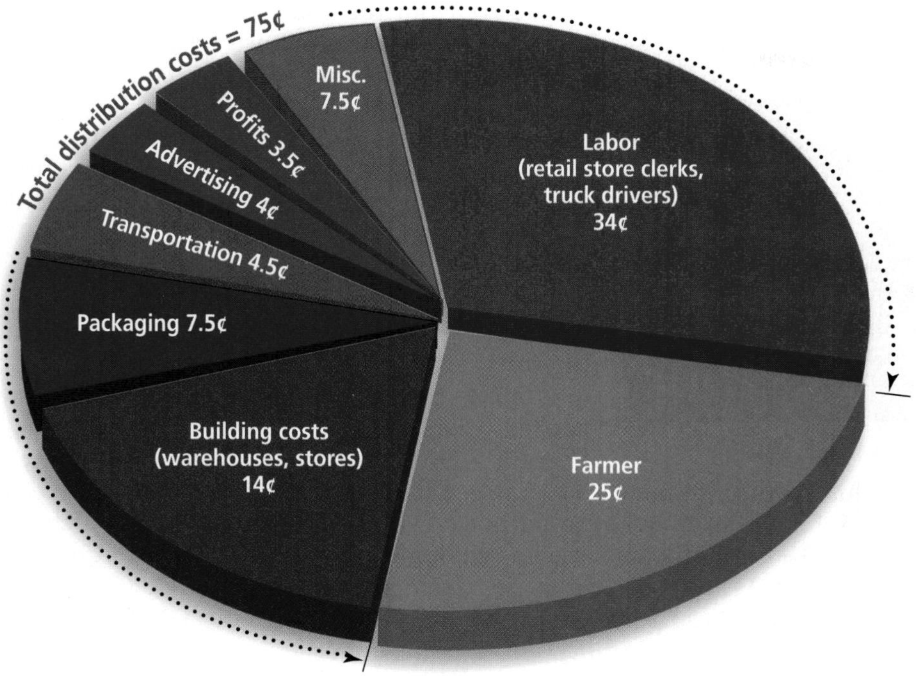

FIGURE 15.3

DISTRIBUTION'S EFFECT ON YOUR FOOD DOLLAR

Note that the farmer gets only 25 cents of your food dollar. The bulk of your money goes to intermediaries to pay distribution costs. Their biggest cost is labor (truck drivers, clerks), followed by warehouses and storage.

tasks, including transporting and storing goods, finding suppliers, and establishing communication with suppliers.[1]

- Intermediary organizations have survived in the past because they have performed marketing functions faster and cheaper than others could. To maintain their competitive position in the channel, intermediaries must adopt the latest in technology.[2]
- Intermediaries add costs to products, but these costs are usually more than offset by the values they create.

Critical Thinking

Imagine that we have eliminated intermediaries and you have to go shopping for groceries and shoes. How would you find out where the shoes and groceries were? How far would you have to travel to get them? How much money do you think you'd save for your time and effort? Which intermediary do you think is most important and why?

The Utilities Created by Intermediaries

Utility, in economics, is the want-satisfying ability, or value, that organizations add to goods ➤P. 25◄ or services ➤P. 26◄ when the products are made more useful or accessible to consumers than they were before. Six utilities are added: form, time, place, possession, information, and service. Although some utilities are performed by producers, most are performed by marketing intermediaries. We shall explore all the utilities next and describe how intermediaries provide each.

utility
In economics, the want-satisfying ability, or value, that organizations add to goods or services when the products are made more useful or accessible to consumers than they were before.

Form Utility

Traditionally, form utility has been provided mostly by producers rather than by intermediaries. It consists of taking raw materials and changing their form so that they become useful products ➤P. 402◄. Thus, a farmer who separates the wheat from the chaff and the processor who turns the wheat into flour are creating form utility. Retailers and other marketers sometimes perform form utility as well. For example, retail butchers cut pork chops from a larger piece of meat and trim off the fat. The servers at Starbucks make coffee just the way you want it. Dell assembles computers according to customers' wishes.

Sometimes, time utility is the critical marketing factor. Note, for example, the Walgreens' sign promoting the fact that its drive-thru pharmacy is open 24 hours a day. Have you ever needed to renew a drug prescription late at night or buy something from a pharmacy at the last minute? Can you see how time utility offers added value?

Time Utility

Intermediaries, such as retailers, add **time utility** to products by making them available when they're needed. For example, Devar Tennent lives in Boston. One winter evening while watching TV with his brother, Tennent suddenly got the urge for a hot dog and Coke. The problem was that there were no hot dogs or Cokes in the house. Devar ran down to the corner delicatessen and bought some hot dogs, buns, Cokes, and potato chips. He also bought some frozen strawberries and ice cream. Devar was able to get these groceries at midnight because the local deli was open 24 hours a day. That's time utility. You can buy goods at any time on the Internet, but you can't beat having them available right around the corner *when you want them.* On the other hand, note the value that an Internet company provides by staying accessible 24 hours a day.

time utility
Adding value to products by making them available when they're needed.

place utility
Adding value to products by having them where people want them.

Place Utility

Intermediaries add **place utility** to products by having them *where* people want them. For example, while traveling through the badlands of South Dakota, Juanita Ruiz got hungry and thirsty. There are no stores for miles in this part of the country. Juanita saw one of many signs along the road saying that Wall Drug with fountain service was up ahead. Lured by the signs, she stopped at the store for refreshments. She also bought sunglasses and souvenir items there. The goods and services provided by Wall Drug are in a convenient place for vacationers. Throughout the United States, 7-Eleven stores remain popular because they are usually in easy-to-reach locations. They provide place utility. As more and more sales become global, place utility will grow in importance.

Possession Utility

possession utility
Doing whatever is necessary to transfer ownership from one party to another, including providing credit, delivery, installation, guarantees, and follow-up service.

Intermediaries add **possession utility** by doing whatever is necessary to transfer ownership from one party to another, including providing credit. Activities associated with possession utility include delivery, installation, guarantees, and follow-up service. For example, Larry Rosenberg wanted to buy a nice home in the suburbs. He found just what he wanted, but he didn't have the money he needed. So he went with the real estate broker to a local savings and loan and borrowed the money to buy the home. Both the real estate broker and the savings and loan are marketing intermediaries that provide possession utility. For those consumers who don't want to own goods, possession utility makes it possible for them to use goods through renting or leasing.

Information Utility

information utility
Adding value to products by opening two-way flows of information between marketing participants.

Intermediaries add **information utility** by opening two-way flows of information between marketing participants. For example, Jerome Washington couldn't decide what kind of TV set to buy. He looked at various ads in the newspaper,

Making Ethical Decisions

Look One Place, Buy Another

After talking with some of your friends, you have discovered a practice that is quite common among them. It goes like this: They go to a local department store or furniture store and shop. They talk to the salespeople and get all kinds of help with the choice of fabrics and other matters. They copy all the information on a piece of paper, including the name of the manufacturer, the model number of the piece they are looking at, and the price. They then call the manufacturer and order the item directly, thus saving the retail markup. Often they simply go online and do the same.

You need a new sofa for your apartment. The retail price at your local furniture store is $2,200. The price directly from the manufacturer is closer to $1,000. You have spent lots of time with the salesperson at the store and she was very helpful. She helped you pick out colors and fabrics. You wonder about the ethical issue of buying the sofa somewhere else. You know lots of others are doing it, why not you? What would you do? What are the ethical consequences?

talked to salespeople at several stores, and read material at the library and on the Internet. He also got some booklets from the government about radiation hazards and consumer buying tips. Newspapers, salespeople, libraries, websites, and government publications are all information sources made available by intermediaries. They provide information utility. Check out the Making Ethical Decisions box. It explores an ethical question involved with getting free information utility from one intermediary with the intention of buying from another.

Service Utility

Intermediaries add **service utility** by providing fast, friendly service during and after the sale and by teaching customers how to best use products over time. For example, Sze Leung bought a personal computer for his office at home. Both the computer manufacturer and the retailer where he bought the computer continue to offer help whenever Leung needs it. He also gets software updates for a small fee to keep his computer up-to-date. What attracted Leung to the retailer in the first place was the helpful, friendly service he received from the salesperson in the store. Service utility is rapidly becoming the most important utility for many retailers because without it they could lose business to direct marketing (e.g., marketing by catalog or on the Internet). Can you see how some of these services could be provided over the Internet?

service utility
Adding value by providing fast, friendly service during and after the sale and by teaching customers how to best use products over time.

The Dealing with Change box on p. 466 illustrates how technology such as the Internet has helped change the way intermediaries create utility.

Progress Assessment

- What is a channel of distribution, and what intermediaries are involved?
- Why do we need intermediaries? Can you illustrate how intermediaries create exchange efficiency? How would you defend intermediaries to someone who said that getting rid of them would save millions of dollars?
- Can you give examples of the utilities created by intermediaries and how intermediaries perform them?

www.madetoorder.com

Dealing with Change: How Technology Helped Change the Way Intermediaries Create Utility

Technology such as the Internet has changed the way intermediaries create utility. For example, imagine how intermediaries can use the Internet to create form utility by making specialized product offerings for business buyers. Business owners can go to a website such as MadeToOrder.com to order customized items (e.g., mugs, key chains, rulers, calendars, shirts) printed with their business's logo on them. The value provided by the intermediary doesn't change; just the means.

Time utility takes on a whole new dimension when you add the Internet to the process. You can buy insurance, put money in the bank, pay your bills, and look for the best car deal online—24/7, which means you can do such things any time you want.

How can the Internet add place utility? Sometimes it is easier to order items without having to go anywhere. Sure, stores are sometimes conveniently placed, but sometimes they are not. What if you live way out in the country? There may not be any stores for miles. Place utility is also provided by companies that deliver goods right to your home. Some companies even make the Web available to shoppers by placing Internet kiosks in their stores. After searching the Net, customers can order items right at the store's counter.

Another issue that emerges when selling goods and services online is payment (possession utility). How can sellers be sure that buyers will pay for what they order? The online auction company eBay bought PayPal to solve that problem. PayPal acts as an online broker that allows people to move money from one person's bank or credit card account into another. PayPal and other financial institutions have emerged to help marketers provide credit and to manage payments; thus, they too can be considered as intermediaries that help in the exchange process.

Perhaps one of the most widely acclaimed benefits of the Internet is the service utility business websites offer. Take, for example, WeddingChannel.com. This company helps people with the complex task of planning a wedding. Multiple vendors are recommended for things like flowers, caterers, wedding gowns, event venues, printers, travel providers, and more. Through Wedding Channel a couple can establish a website that acts as a registry. Once the couple is married, the website directs them to another site having to do with beginning married life. Note that intermediaries have not disappeared; they have merely taken on new tasks, sometimes in new places. What websites have you used to get information about products and places?

BusinessWeek

Sources: Heather Green and Robert D. Hof, "Lessons of the Cyber Survivors," *Business Week*, April 22, 2002, p. 42; and Timothy J. Mullaney, Heather Green, Michael Arndt, Robert D. Hof, and Linda Himelstein, "The E-Biz Surprise," *Business Week*, May 12, 2003, pp. 60–68.

WHOLESALE INTERMEDIARIES

There's often some confusion about the difference between wholesalers and retailers. It's helpful to distinguish wholesaling from retailing and to clearly define the functions performed in each so that companies can design effective systems of distribution. Some producers will deal only with wholesalers and won't sell directly to retailers. Some producers give wholesalers a bigger discount than retailers. What confuses the issue is that some organizations sell much of their merchandise to other intermediaries (a wholesale sale) but also sell to ultimate consumers (a retail sale). The office superstore Staples is a good example. It sells office supplies to small businesses and to consumers as well. Warehouse clubs such as Sam's Club and Costco are also examples.

The issue is really rather simple: A *retail sale* is the sale of goods and services to consumers for their own use. A *wholesale sale* is the sale of goods and services to businesses and institutions (e.g., hospitals) for use in the business or to wholesalers or retailers for resale. Wholesalers make business-to-business (B2B) ➤P. 411◀ sales. Most people are not as familiar with the various kinds of wholesalers as they are with retailers. Let's explore some of these helpful wholesale intermediaries.

A FULL-SERVICE WHOLESALER WILL:	THE WHOLESALER MAY PERFORM THE FOLLOWING SERVICES FOR CUSTOMERS:
1. Provide a sales force to sell the goods to retailers and other buyers.	1. Buy goods the end market will desire and make them available to customers.
2. Communicate manufacturers' advertising deals and plans.	2. Maintain inventory, thus reducing customers' costs.
3. Maintain inventory, thus reducing the level of the inventory suppliers have to carry.	3. Transport goods to customers quickly.
4. Arrange or undertake transportation.	4. Provide market information and business consulting services.
5. Provide capital by paying cash or quick payments for goods.	5. Provide financing through granting credit, which is especially critical to small retailers.
6. Provide suppliers with market information they can't afford or can't obtain themselves.	6. Order goods in the types and quantities customers desire.
7. Undertake credit risk by granting credit to customers and absorbing any bad debts, thus relieving the supplier of this burden.	
8. Assume the risk for the product by taking title.	

Source: Thomas C. Kinnear and Kenneth L. Bernhardt, *Principles of Marketing,* 2nd ed. (Glenview, IL: Scott, Foresman, 1986), p. 369.

FIGURE 15.4

A FULL-SERVICE WHOLESALER

Merchant Wholesalers

Merchant wholesalers are independently owned firms that take title to the goods they handle. About 80 percent of wholesalers fall in this category. There are two types of merchant wholesalers: full-service wholesalers and limited-function wholesalers. *Full-service wholesalers* perform all of the distribution functions (see Figure 15.4). *Limited-function wholesalers* perform only selected functions, but try to do them especially well. Three common types of limited-function wholesalers are rack jobbers, cash-and-carry wholesalers, and drop shippers.

merchant wholesalers
Independently owned firms that take title to (own) the goods they handle.

Rack jobbers furnish racks or shelves full of merchandise to retailers, display products, and sell on consignment. This means that they keep title to the goods until they're sold, and then they share the profits with the retailer. Merchandise such as music, toys, hosiery (L'eggs panty hose), and health and beauty aids are sold by rack jobbers.

rack jobbers
Wholesalers that furnish racks or shelves full of merchandise to retailers, display products, and sell on consignment.

Cash-and-carry wholesalers serve mostly smaller retailers with a limited assortment of products. Traditionally, retailers went to such wholesalers, paid cash, and carried the goods back to their stores—thus the term *cash-and-carry.* Today, stores such as Office Depot and Staples allow retailers and others to use credit cards for wholesale purchases.

cash-and-carry wholesalers
Wholesalers that serve mostly smaller retailers with a limited assortment of products.

Drop shippers solicit orders from retailers and other wholesalers and have the merchandise shipped directly from a producer to a buyer. They own the merchandise but don't handle, stock, or deliver it. That's done by the producer. Drop shippers tend to handle bulky products such as coal, lumber, and chemicals.

drop shippers
Wholesalers that solicit orders from retailers and other wholesalers and have the merchandise shipped directly from a producer to a buyer.

Koen Books of Moorestown, New Jersey, is a highly successful merchant wholesaler. Although they actually charge more than the publishers they compete against, Koen prospers due to its ability to provide extraordinary service that includes, among many things, same-day processing and shipping, free shipping, and author-autographed copies of bestsellers. If you were a book retailer would you prefer the service advantages provided by Koen or a slightly lower price?

Agents and Brokers

Agents and brokers bring buyers and sellers together and assist in negotiating an exchange. However, unlike merchant wholesalers, agents and brokers never own the products they distribute. Usually they do not carry inventory, provide credit, or assume risks. While merchant wholesalers earn a profit from the sale of goods, agents and brokers earn commissions or fees based on a percentage of the sales revenues. Agents and brokers differ in that agents maintain long-term relationships with the people they represent whereas brokers are usually hired on a temporary basis.

Agents who represent producers are known as *manufacturer's agents* or *sales agents*. As long as they do not represent competing products, manufacturer's agents may represent one or several manufacturers in a specific territory. Manufacturer's agents are often used in the automotive supply, footwear, and fabricated steel industries. Sales agents represent a single producer in a typically larger territory. Sales agents are used by small producers in the textile and home furnishing industries.

Brokers have no continuous relationship with the buyer or seller. Once they negotiate a contract between a buyer and seller, their relationship ends. Brokers are used by the producers of seasonal products (e.g., fruits and vegetables) and in the real estate industry.

Retail Intermediaries

Perhaps the most useful marketing intermediaries, as far as you're concerned, are retailers. They're the ones who bring goods and services to your neighborhood and make them available day and night. Next time you go to the supermarket to buy groceries, stop for a minute and look at the tremendous variety of products in the store. Think of how many marketing exchanges were involved to bring you the 18,000 or more items that you see. Some products (e.g., spices) may have been imported from halfway around the world. Other products have been processed and frozen so that you can eat them out of season (e.g., corn and green beans).

A supermarket is a retail store. A retailer, remember, is a marketing intermediary that sells to ultimate consumers. The United States boasts approximately 2.3 million retail stores. This does not include the retail websites on the

TYPE	DESCRIPTION	EXAMPLE
Department store	Sells a wide variety of products (clothes, furniture, housewares) in separate departments	Sears, JCPenney, Nordstrom
Discount store	Sells many different products at prices generally below those of department stores	Wal-Mart, Target
Supermarket	Sells mostly food with other nonfood products such as detergent and paper products	Safeway, Kroger, Albertson's
Warehouse club	Sells food and general merchandise in facilities that are usually larger than supermarkets and offer discount prices; membership may be required	Costco, Sam's Club
Convenience store	Sells food and other often-needed items at convenient locations; may stay open all night	7-Eleven
Category killer	Sells a huge variety of one type of product to dominate that category of goods	Toys "R" Us, Bass Proshops, Office Depot
Outlet store	Sells general merchandise directly from the manufacturer at a discount; items may be discontinued or have flaws ("seconds")	Nordstrom Rack, Liz Claiborne, Nike
Specialty store	Sells a wide selection of goods in one category	Jewelry stores, shoe stores, bicycle shops
Supercenter	Sells food and general merchandise at discount prices; no membership required	Super Kmart

FIGURE 15.5

TYPES OF RETAIL STORES

Internet. Retail organizations employ more than 11 million people and are one of the major employers of marketing graduates. Figure 15.5 lists, describes, and gives examples of various kinds of retailers. Have you shopped in each kind of store? What seems to be the advantages of each? Some retailers seem to compete mostly on price, but others, such as specialty stores, use variety as a competitive tool. The following section discusses the various ways in which retailers compete.

How Retailers Compete

There are five major ways in which retailers compete for the consumer's dollar: price, service, location, selection, and entertainment. Since consumers are constantly comparing retailers on price, service, and variety, it is important for retailers to use benchmarking to compare themselves against the best in the field to make sure that their practices and procedures are the most advanced. The following sections describe the five means of competition.

Price Competition Discount stores such as Wal-Mart, Target, Kmart, and T. J. Maxx/Marshalls—not to mention all the various Internet discount sites—succeed by offering low prices. It's hard to compete with these price discounters over time, especially when they offer good service as well.

Service organizations also compete on price. Note, for example, Southwest Airlines' success with its low-price strategy. The same is true of H&R Block in income tax preparation services, Hyatt Legal Plans for legal services, and Motel 6 or Red Roof Inns for motel-room rentals.

Price competition is getting fiercer as Internet firms like mySimon.com help consumers find the best prices on a wide range of items. Look up BotSpot (www.botspot.com) for other companies that do price searches. As you learned earlier, prices are easy to match, so most retailers have to turn to other strategies—like service—to win and keep customers.

Service Competition A second competitive strategy for retailers is service. Retail service involves putting the customer first. This requires all frontline people to be courteous and accommodating to customers. Retail service also means follow-up service such as on-time delivery, guarantees, and fast installation. Consumers are frequently willing to pay a little more for goods and services if the retailer offers outstanding service.

The benchmark companies in this regard include Dayton's, Lord & Taylor, Dillard's, and Nordstrom. These retailers show that if you hire good people, train them well, and pay them fairly, you will be able to provide world-class service. Service organizations that have successfully competed using service include Scandinavian Airlines, Tokyo's Imperial Hotel, Metropolitan Life Insurance Company, and Florida Power & Light. Sheraton hotels are offering your money back or a free night if you aren't happy with their services.[3] Small service providers, such as The Hair Cuttery, Sam's Auto Repair, and Beautiful Nails, also compete by offering superior service.

Location Competition Many services, especially convenience services like banks and dry cleaners, compete effectively by having good locations. That's why you find automated teller machines in convenient places such as supermarkets and train stations. Many fast-food stores, such as Burger King and Pizza Hut, now have locations on college campuses so that students can reach them quickly. Some dry cleaners pick up and deliver laundry at your home or business.

Often, nothing is more convenient than shopping online: You don't have to go outside at all and fight crowds or traffic. But online retailers have to learn to deliver goods faster and more reliably and handle returns better, or they will lose the advantage of convenience. Also, many consumers are nervous about giving their credit card numbers to online retailers for fear of having them stolen. Each of these problems will be solved someday, but meanwhile competition between brick-and-mortar retailers and online retailers will intensify.

Selection Competition A fourth competitive strategy for retailers is selection. Selection is the offering of a wide variety of items in the same product category. *Category killer stores* offer wide selection at competitive prices. They are called category killers because they are so competitive that they usually overpower smaller competitors that don't offer comparable selection or price and drive them out of business. Toys "R" Us stores carry some 18,000 toys, and the company has over 500 stores around the world. Many small, independent toy stores closed their doors because they simply couldn't compete with the low prices and wide selection found at Toys "R" Us. Tower Records carries over 75,000 titles. Borders Books carries some 150,000 different titles. Sportmart carries over 100,000 sporting goods items. PETsMART and other pet food superstores have some 10,000 items each.

Despite their initial success, many category killer stores are in turn being killed by discount department stores like Wal-Mart.[4] Wal-Mart has become a huge challenge to Toys "R" Us. Consumers are finding it more convenient to shop for multiple items at stores like Costco rather than go out of their way to find stores selling only sports equipment or only pet supplies. Thus, location may be more important than selection for consumer items.

Internet stores can offer products from dozens of suppliers and offer almost unlimited selection (e.g., Amazon.com). Small retailers

You won't believe what you can buy from vending machines these days. This photo, for example, shows a vending machine that sells fish bait, including live worms. What are some of the limitations you perceive for vending machines? Can you see a day when those limitations are overcome and you can buy almost anything small enough to fit into a machine? Can you think of a product that should be but isn't yet offered in vending machines?

sometimes compete by offering wide selection within one or a few categories of items. Thus, you have successful small stores that sell nothing but coffee beans or party products. Small retailers also compete by offering personalized service. Restoration Hardware, with stores in the Bay Area of California and around the country, is one store that has survived the competition with Home Depot and the other giant lumber and hardware stores. Restoration was able to succeed by offering consumers products that couldn't be found in the other stores.

Service organizations that compete successfully on selection include Blockbuster (wide selection of rental videos and DVDs), most community colleges (wide selection of courses), and Schwab Mutual Funds (hundreds of funds).

With over 200 stores, outlets, restaurants, and entertainment sources, "shoppertainment" is thriving at the Arundel Mills mall in Hanover, Maryland. You can do rock climbing, go bowling, or enjoy a movie at a theater with valet parking and a children's playroom. The mall is broken up into "neighborhoods"; one is like being in a giant pinball machine, another a bowling lane. Have you visited a store or a mall with lots of entertainment options? Did it lure you back?

Entertainment Competition The Internet may be a convenient place to shop, but it can't possibly be as much fun as a brick-and-mortar store designed to provide entertainment as well as a place to buy things. When you approach a Jordan's furniture store in New England, for example, you notice that the design team has recreated French Quarter facades like those in New Orleans. As you walk in, you see a Louis Armstrong look-alike playing in a room that resembles Bourbon Street (in New Orleans). There is even a replica of a riverboat that features live music every weekend. You can eat a free fresh-baked cookie and, if it's raining, you can get an umbrella.

One mall calls it "shoppertainment." In any case, it's making it more fun to shop at stores and malls. At Bass Pro Shops, you are treated to giant aquariums, waterfalls, trout ponds, rifle ranges, and classes in everything from ice fishing to conservation. In San Francisco, Sony's Metreon is a Sony Entertainment Center with a restaurant, an IMAX theater, and lots of exciting video games to play. You get to see and experience all the latest high-tech equipment and have fun at the same time. Vans, Inc., a sporting goods retailer, opened a 60,000-square-foot skate park and off-road bicycle track at Ontario Mills Mall near Los Angeles.

Retail Distribution Strategy

A major decision marketers must make is selecting the right retailers to sell their products. Different products call for different retail distribution strategies. There are three categories of retail distribution: intensive distribution, selective distribution, and exclusive distribution.

Intensive distribution puts products into as many retail outlets as possible, including vending machines. Products that need intensive distribution include convenience goods such as candy, cigarettes, gum, and popular magazines.

Selective distribution is the use of only a preferred group of the available retailers in an area. Such selection helps to assure producers of quality sales and service. Manufacturers of appliances, furniture, and clothing (shopping goods) usually use selective distribution.

Exclusive distribution is the use of only one retail outlet in a given geographic area. The retailer has exclusive rights to sell the product and is therefore likely to carry a large inventory, give exceptional service, and pay

intensive distribution
Distribution that puts products into as many retail outlets as possible.

selective distribution
Distribution that sends products to only a preferred group of retailers in an area.

exclusive distribution
Distribution that sends products to only one retail outlet in a given geographic area.

more attention to this brand than to others. Luxury auto manufacturers usually use exclusive distribution, as do producers of specialty goods such as skydiving equipment or fly-fishing products.

Progress Assessment

- Describe the activities of rack jobbers and drop shippers.
- What are some of the ways in which retailers compete? Give examples.
- What kinds of products would call for each of the different distribution strategies: intensive, selective, exclusive?

NONSTORE RETAILING

Nothing else in retailing has received more attention recently than electronic retailing. Internet retailing, however, is just one form of nonstore retailing. Other categories of nonstore retailing include telemarketing; vending machines, kiosks, and carts; direct selling; multilevel marketing; and direct marketing. Small businesses can use nonstore retailing to open up new channels of distribution for their products.

Electronic Retailing

electronic retailing
Selling goods and services to ultimate customers (e.g., you and me) over the Internet.

Electronic retailing consists of selling goods and services to ultimate consumers (e.g., you and me) over the Internet. But getting customers is only half the battle. The other half is delivering the goods, providing helpful service, and keeping your customers. When electronic retailers fail to have sufficient inventory or fail to deliver goods on time (especially at Christmastime and other busy periods), customers give up and go back to brick-and-mortar stores.

Most Internet retailers now offer e-mail confirmation. But sometimes electronic retailers are not so good at handling complaints, taking back goods that customers don't like, and providing personal help. Some websites are trying to improve customer service by adding help buttons that lead customers to almost instant assistance from a real person. Rightstart.com, for example, is a seller of children's toys and products. It has added a live chat function to its online retailing. If you have a problem, you click the Live Help link and a customer-service representative answers within minutes.

Tex-Mex food online? Yep, cowboy, that's what they sell at texmexgourmet.com. You can have an instant fiesta anywhere in the world, munching on tamales and enchiladas, while sipping margaritas. During the holiday season the website gets 65,000 hits a day. Texmexgourmet.com is owned and managed by Rosemary Garbett, who at an age when most folks retire, launched the Internet food shop. What do you think the competitive retail landscape will look like among e-commerce food sellers in another 10 years?

www.inditex.com

Reaching Beyond Our Borders

What You Want, When You Want It

You can find what you want at Zara's and, if you can't, you only have to wait a couple of days and shop again, because Zara's has one of the best supply-chain systems in the world. Zara's, owned by parent Inditex, is an apparel store with a flagship store in Madrid, Spain. You can also find Zara's stores in Germany, Italy, and Great Britain. Stores in the United States are in New York and Miami. There is another one in San Juan, Puerto Rico.

What is special about these stores is the response they make to consumer wants and needs. Few markets change as rapidly as the consumer fashion industry, and no other store is more responsive than Zara's. Store managers use handheld computers to punch in orders as customer demand dictates. Some 200 designers and product managers compile the data from the various stores and decide what to produce next. That information is sent by intranet to a group of nearby factories. Within days, those outfits will be hanging on store shelves. Flexible factories can replace or redesign a pair of jeans faster than a teenager can change her mind.

The clothes are gathered in a huge warehouse that's about nine times bigger than Amazon.com's warehouse (about 90 football fields). The warehouse is connected to 14 factories through a maze of tunnels. Items move into the warehouse and are out the door in a matter of hours. Zara's is thus able to have twice-a-week deliveries that bring in fresh designs all the time. Shoppers can come in weekly and find new merchandise that represents the latest in fashion.

Part of what makes Zara's amazing distribution system so fast is that Zara does not go overseas to manufacture its clothes. The merchandise may cost more as a result, but it is much fresher and more up-to-date than clothing sold in other retail stores.

Source: Miguel Helft, "Fashion Fast Forward," *Business 2.0,* May 2002, pp. 60–66; and Scot J. Paltrow, "Profiting from Impatience," *The Wall Street Journal,* April 28, 2003, p. R5.

Old brick-and-mortar stores are rapidly going online also. The result, sometimes called a brick-and-click store, allows customers to choose which shopping technique suits them best. In any case, most companies that want to compete in the future will probably need both a real store presence and an online presence to provide consumers with all the options they want. Part of that strategy is to include the company's phone number in all Internet promotions so that consumers can call in an order as well as place it online (see the Reaching Beyond Our Borders box to learn more about quick response).

Traditional retailers like Sears (see the chapter opening profile) have learned that selling on the Internet calls for a new kind of distribution system. Sears' warehouses were accustomed to delivering truckloads of goods to the company's retail outlets. But they were not prepared to make deliveries, except for large orders like furniture and appliances, to individual consumers. It turns out, therefore, that both traditional retailers and new Internet retailers have to develop new distribution systems to meet the demands of today's Internet-savvy shoppers.

Telemarketing

Telemarketing is the sale of goods and services by telephone. Some 80,000 companies use telemarketing today to supplement or replace in-store selling and to complement online selling. Many send a catalog to consumers and let them order by calling a toll-free number. As we noted, many electronic retailers provide a help feature online that serves the same function. The federal "do-not-call" registry is expected to eliminate 80 percent of telemarketing calls.[5]

telemarketing
The sale of goods and services by telephone.

Vending Machines, Kiosks, and Carts

A vending machine dispenses convenience goods when consumers deposit sufficient money in the machine. Vending machines carry the benefit of location—they're found in airports, office buildings, schools, service stations, and other areas where people want convenience ➤P. 434◄ items. Vending machines in Japan sell everything from bandages and face cloths to salads and spiced seafood. Vending by machine will be an interesting area to watch as such innovations are introduced in the United States.

Carts and kiosks have lower overhead costs than stores do; therefore, they can offer lower prices on items such as T-shirts and umbrellas. You often see vending carts outside stores on the sidewalk or along walkways in malls; mall owners love them because they're colorful and create a marketplace atmosphere. Kiosk workers often dispense coupons and provide all kinds of helpful information to consumers, who tend to enjoy the interaction. Also, many kiosks serve as gateways to the Internet, so consumers can shop at a store and still have access to all the products available on the Internet in one place.

Direct Selling

direct selling
Selling to consumers in their homes or where they work.

Direct selling involves selling to consumers in their homes or where they work. Major users of this category include cosmetics producers (Avon) and vacuum cleaner manufacturers (Electrolux). Trying to emulate the success of those companies, other businesses are now venturing into direct selling. Lingerie, artwork, and plants are just a few of the goods now sold at "house parties" sponsored by sellers.

Because so many women work outside the home and aren't at home during the day, companies that use direct selling are sponsoring parties at workplaces or in the evenings and on weekends. Some companies, such as those in encyclopedia sales, have dropped most of their direct selling efforts in favor of Internet selling.

Multilevel Marketing

Over 1,000 U.S. companies have had great success using multilevel marketing (MLM). MLM salespeople work as independent contractors. They earn commissions on their own sales and they also create commissions for the "upliners" who recruited them. In turn, they receive commissions from any "downliners" they recruit to sell. When you have hundreds of downliners—that is, people who have been recruited by the people you recruit—the commissions can be quite sizable. Some people make tens of thousands of dollars a month this way.

Multilevel marketing has been successful around the world in selling a wide variety of products. One MLM firm is Rexall Sundown, which sells nutritional and health-related products. Salespeople not only earn commissions at Rexall but may also buy stock options.

The main attraction of multilevel marketing for employees, other than the potential for making money, is the low cost of entry. For a small investment, the average person can start up a business and begin recruiting others. Many people question MLM marketing because there have been some companies that have been unethical. It is true that one must be very careful to examine the practices of such firms. Nonetheless, the success of this form of marketing is revealed by the fact that MLM sales overall have reached $18 billion a year.

Direct Marketing

direct marketing
Any activity that directly links manufacturers or intermediaries with the ultimate consumer.

One of the fastest-growing aspects of retailing is direct marketing. **Direct marketing** includes any activity that directly links manufacturers or intermediaries with the ultimate consumer. Thus, direct retail marketing includes direct mail, catalog sales, and telemarketing as well as online marketing. Popular consumer catalog companies that use direct marketing include Coldwater Creek, L. L. Bean, and Lands' End. Direct marketing has created tremendous competition in some high-tech areas as well. For example, direct sales by Dell Computers, Gateway 2000, and other computer manufacturers have led IBM and Hewlett-Packard to use price-cutting tactics to meet the competition. Hewlett-Packard also decided to go online to compete more directly and to offer its own custom-designed computers.

Direct marketing has become popular because shopping from home or work is more convenient for consumers than going to stores. Instead of driving to a mall, people can "shop" in catalogs and freestanding advertising supplements in the newspaper and then buy by phone, mail, or computer. Interactive online selling is expected to provide increasing competition for retail stores in the near future.

Direct marketing took on a new dimension when consumers became involved with interactive video. Producers now provide all kinds of information on CD-ROMs or websites. The potential of such systems seems almost limitless. Consumers can ask questions, seek the best price, and order goods and services—all by computer. Companies that use interactive video have become major competitors for those who market by regular paper catalogs.

For consumers to receive the maximum benefit from marketing intermediaries, the various organizations must work together to ensure a smooth flow of goods and services to the consumer. Historically, there hasn't always been total harmony in the channel of distribution. As a result, channel members have created certain systems that make the flows more efficient. We'll discuss those systems next.

Harry and David uses a combination of brick-and-mortar stores, catalogs, and a website to sell its gift baskets, fresh fruits, candy, pies, and other goodies. Forget to buy someone a gift? Just go to harryanddavid.com and find something special to send out immediately. What advantages does each option (store, catalog, website) offer consumers?

Building Cooperation in Channel Systems

One way that traditional retailers can stay competitive with online retailers is to make the whole system so efficient that online retailers can't beat them out on cost—given the need for customers to pay for delivery. That means that manufacturers, wholesalers, and retailers (members of the channel of distribution) must work closely together to form a unified system. How can manufacturers get wholesalers and retailers to cooperate in such a system? One way is to somehow link the firms together in a formal relationship. Four systems have emerged to tie firms together: corporate systems, contractual systems, administered systems, and supply chains.

Corporate Distribution Systems

A **corporate distribution system** is one in which all of the organizations in the channel of distribution are owned by one firm. If the manufacturer owns the retail firm, clearly it can maintain a great deal of control over its operations. Sherwin-Williams, for example, owns its own retail stores and thus coordinates everything: display, pricing, promotion, inventory control, and so on. Other companies that have tried corporate systems include General Electric, Firestone, and Xerox.

corporate distribution system
A distribution system in which all of the organizations in the channel of distribution are owned by one firm.

Contractual Distribution Systems

contractual distribution system
A distribution system in which members are bound to cooperate through contractual agreements.

administered distribution system
A distribution system in which producers manage all of the marketing functions at the retail level.

supply chain (or value chain)
The sequence of linked activities that must be performed by various organizations to move goods from the sources of raw materials to ultimate consumers.

If a manufacturer can't buy retail stores, it can try to get retailers to sign a contract to cooperate. A **contractual distribution system** is one in which members are bound to cooperate through contractual agreements. There are three forms of contractual systems:

1. **Franchise systems** such as McDonald's, KFC, Baskin-Robbins, and AAMCO. The franchisee ➤P. 158◀ agrees to all of the rules, regulations, and procedures established by the franchisor. This results in the consistent quality and level of service you find in most franchised organizations.
2. **Wholesaler-sponsored chains** such as Ace Hardware and IGA food stores. Each store signs an agreement to use the same name, participate in chain promotions, and cooperate as a unified system of stores, even though each store is independently owned and managed.
3. **Retail cooperatives** such as Associated Grocers. This arrangement is much like a wholesaler-sponsored chain except that it is initiated by the retailers. The same degree of cooperation exists, however, and the stores remain independent. Normally in such a system, retailers agree to focus their purchases on one wholesaler, but cooperative retailers could also purchase a wholesale organization to ensure better service.

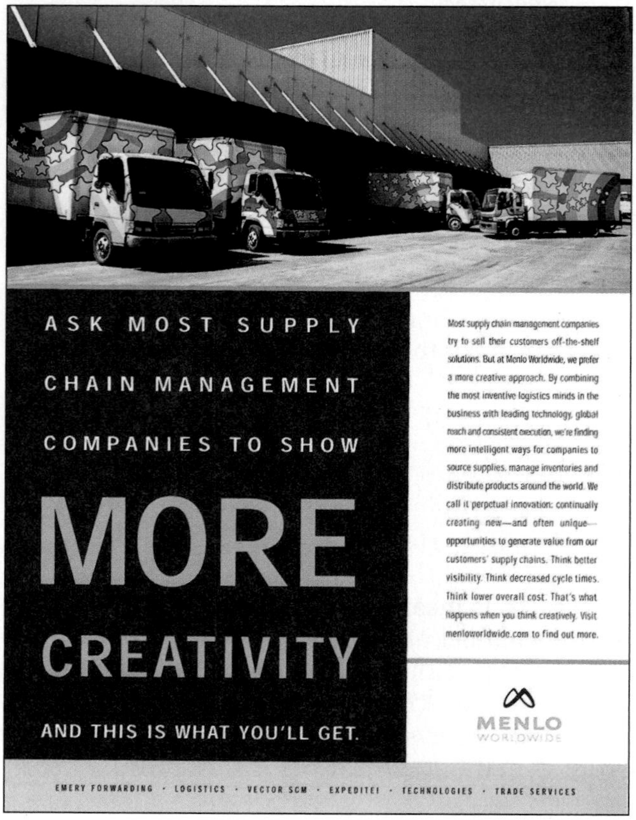

Supply chain management (SCM) ties companies together in a unified system designed to generate efficiencies that are hard for other firms to compete against. But creating an effective SCM system is easier said than done. That's where companies like Menlo come in. They provide a full-service outlet where you can find ways of cutting costs and providing better service at the same time. Do you see any disadvantages to working with companies like Menlo?

Administered Distribution Systems

If you were a producer, what would you do if you couldn't get retailers to sign an agreement to cooperate? One thing you could do is to manage all the marketing functions yourself, including display, inventory control, pricing, and promotion. A system in which producers manage all of the marketing functions at the retail level is called an **administered distribution system**. Kraft does that for its cheeses; Scott does it for its seed and other lawn care products. Retailers cooperate with producers in such systems because they get a great deal of free help. All the retailer has to do is ring up the sale.

Supply Chains

The latest in systems coordination involves the supply chain. The **supply chain** (sometimes called a **value chain**) consists of the sequence of linked activities that must be performed by various organizations to move goods and services from the source of raw materials to ultimate consumers. The supply chain is longer than a channel of distribution because it includes links from suppliers to manufacturers, whereas the channel of distribution begins with manufacturers. Channels of distribution are part of the overall supply chain (see Figure 15.6). Included in the supply chain are farmers, miners, suppliers of all kinds (e.g., parts, equipment, supplies), manufacturers, wholesalers, and retailers.

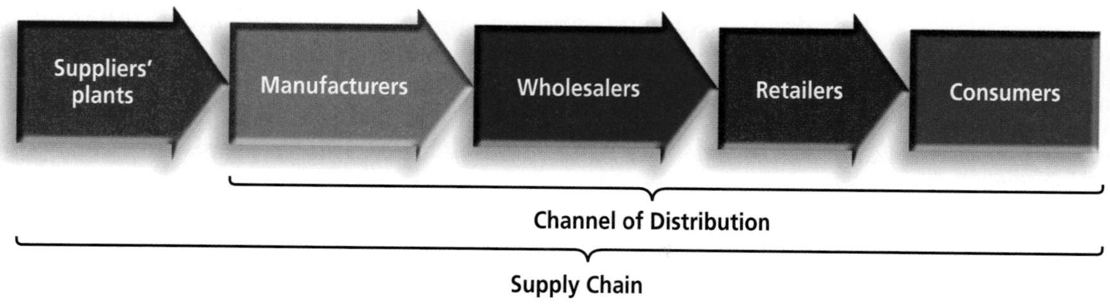

FIGURE 15.6
THE SUPPLY CHAIN

Supply-chain management is the process of managing the movement of raw materials, parts, work in progress, finished goods, and related information through all the organizations involved in the supply chain; managing the return of such goods if necessary; and recycling materials when appropriate.[6]

supply-chain management The process of managing the movement of raw materials, parts, work in progress, finished goods, and related information through all the organizations involved in the supply chain; managing the return of such goods, if necessary; and recycling materials when appropriate.

One example of a complex supply chain is provided by the automaker Kia's model Sorento. It is assembled in South Korea, named after an Italian resort, and made from components from all over the world. The car has over 30,000 parts. The shock and front loading system is from AF Sachs AG, the front-wheel drive is from BorgWarner, and the tires are from Michelin. Airbags are sometimes flown in from Swedish company Autoliv Inc., which makes them in Utah.[7] As you can see, supply-chain management is interfirm and international. Countries involved in making Kia's Sorento include the United States, Mexico, Thailand, China, and, of course, South Korea.

Companies such as SAP, PeopleSoft, i2, and Manugistics have developed software that makes it possible to coordinate the movement of goods and information so that consumer wants can be translated into products with the least amount of materials, inventory, and time.[8] The flows among firms are so smooth that it looks like all of the organizations involved are one firm. Computers make such linkages possible. Naturally, the systems are quite complex and quite expensive, but they pay for themselves in the long run because of inventory savings, customer service improvement, and responsiveness to market changes.[9] It is because such systems are so effective and efficient that they are sometimes called value chains instead of supply chains.

The complexity of supply-chain management often leads firms to outsource ➤P. 257◄ the whole process to experts that know how to integrate it.[10] Richardson Electronics of LaFox, Illinois, for example, does business in 125 countries with 37 different currencies. Richardson relies on PeopleSoft's Supply Chain Management and Financial Management solutions. Note that PeopleSoft also provides financial help, making it easier and easier to ship goods anywhere in the world and be sure of payment. Outsourcing of the distribution function is on the rise as more firms realize the complexities involved.

THE EMERGENCE OF LOGISTICS

Clearly, a major issue in marketing in the future will be: How can I ship goods from city to city or country to country in the fastest way possible and still keep costs low enough to make such exchanges mutually beneficial? When shipping from country to country, it is often impossible to use trucks or trains because the goods have to travel over water. Shipping by air is often prohibitively expensive. That narrows the choice to moving goods by ship. But how do you get the goods to the ship? And from the ship to the buyer? And how do you handle foreign trade duties and taxes? To better manage customs problems, many companies are turning to Web-based trade compliance systems. ClearCross and Xporta, for example, determine what paperwork is needed, cross-checking their databases for information about foreign trade duties and taxes, U.S. labor law restrictions, and federal regulations from the Food and Drug Administration or the Bureau of Alcohol, Tobacco, and Firearms.[11] Distributing goods globally is more complicated than you thought, we'd guess. As transportation and distribution issues got more and more complex, marketers responded by developing more sophisticated systems.

Distribution issues have been at the core of marketing from the very beginning. In fact, the first college courses in marketing had titles like "The Distribution of Farm Products." Those courses focused on distribution (mostly transportation), and marketing was defined as "the business activity that directs the flow of goods and services from producer to consumer." We have come a long way since then, with marketers shifting focus to other issues such as product development, branding, consumer behavior, promotion, and marketing research. But marketing is now coming full circle, and physical distribution is again a major issue. Over time, the term *physical distribution* tended to be replaced by the broader term *logistics*. **Logistics** involves planning, implementing, and controlling the physical flow of materials, final goods, and related information from points of origin to points of consumption to meet customer requirements at a profit.

Inbound logistics brings raw materials, packaging, other goods and services, and information from suppliers to producers. **Materials handling** is the movement of goods within a warehouse, from warehouses to the factory floor, and from the factory floor to various workstations. *Factory processes* change raw materials and parts and other inputs into outputs, such as finished goods (e.g., shoes, cars, clothes). We described such processes in Chapter 9. **Outbound logistics** manages the flow of finished products and information to business buyers and ultimate consumers (people like you and me). **Reverse logistics** involves bringing goods back to the manufacturer because of defects or for recycling materials.[12]

Logistics is as much about the movement of *information* as it is about the movement of goods. Customer wants and needs must flow through the system all the way to suppliers and must do so in real time. Information must also flow down through the system with no hesitation. That, of course, demands sophisticated hardware and software.

Third-party logistics is the term used to describe the use of outside firms to help move goods from here to there. Third-party logistics providers managed $61 billion worth of distribution expenditures in 2001.[13]

logistics
The marketing activity that involves planning, implementing, and controlling the physical flow of materials, final goods, and related information from points of origin to points of consumption to meet customer requirements at a profit.

inbound logistics
The area of logistics that involves bringing raw materials, packaging, other goods and services, and information from suppliers to producers.

materials handling
The movement of goods within a warehouse, from warehouses to the factory floor, and from the factory floor to various workstations

outbound logistics
The area of logistics that involves managing the flow of finished products and information to business buyers and ultimate consumers (people like you and me).

reverse logistics
The area of logistics that involves bringing goods back to the manufacturer because of defects or for recycling materials.

How do you move heavy raw materials like timber from one country to another? This photo shows some of the firms involved in the logistical process. A trucking firm brings the logs to a dock where huge cranes lift the logs into the hold of a ship. The ship must be unloaded and the logs put on another truck to move to a processing plant. Why is successfully managing the logistics process a key to surviving in some industries?

Moving goods from one place to another is a major part of logistics. Next, we explore alternative means of shipment.

Progress Assessment

- What are the four systems that have evolved to tie together members of the channel of distribution?
- How does logistics differ from distribution?
- What are inbound logistics, outbound logistics, and reverse logistics?

Getting Goods from Producer to Consumer Efficiently

How do you get products to people around the world after you have sold the goods? What are your options? You could take the goods to the buyer yourself, but that doesn't seem like the most efficient way of doing things. You could send goods by truck, by train, by ship, or by pipeline. You could use a shipping specialist, such as UPS, FedEx, or the U.S. Postal Service, but often that is too expensive, especially for large items. Nonetheless, some of the most sophisticated marketers outsource the distribution process to such specialists. Seattle-based Groovetech, an online music store catering to DJs, ships 100 time-sensitive orders per day. The company credits UPS OnLine WorldShip with boosting customer satisfaction and cutting order processing time to one minute.[14] The UPS sorting center in Louisville, Kentucky, processes 304,000 packages an hour, but even this number could be increased to 500,000 if UPS could get planes in and out faster.[15] Choosing the most efficient method of getting goods from producer to consumer requires evaluating both transportation and storage strategies.

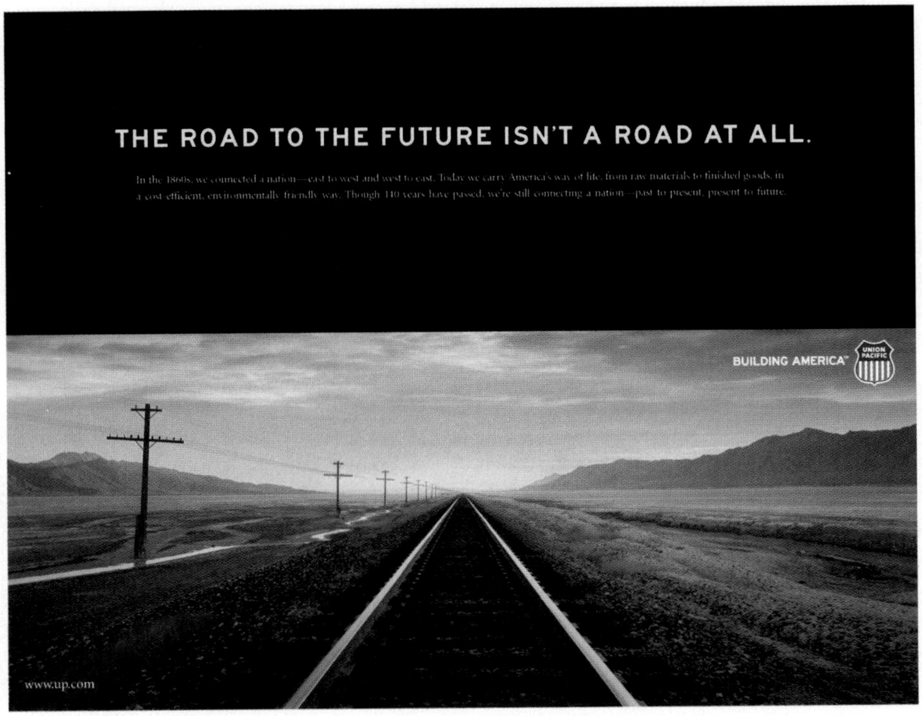
THE ROAD TO THE FUTURE ISN'T A ROAD AT ALL.
In the 1860s, we connected a nation—east to west and west to east. Today we carry America's way of life, from raw materials to finished goods, in a cost-efficient, environmentally friendly way. Though 140 years have passed, we're still connecting a nation—past to present, present to future.
BUILDING AMERICA
UNION PACIFIC
www.up.com

As Union Pacific proclaims, railroads will continue to play a critical role in transportation and logistics. This ad is designed to remind people that railroads are a real competitor to trucks when it comes to long-range shipments. What could the railroads do to compete more successfully with trucks for shorter interstate shipments?

Choosing the Right Transportation Mode

All transportation modes can be evaluated on basic service criteria: cost, speed, dependability, flexibility, frequency, and reach. Figure 15.7 compares the various transportation modes on these criteria.

Trains Are Great for Large Shipments The largest percentage of goods in the United States (by volume) is shipped by rail. Railroad shipment is best for bulky items such as coal, wheat, automobiles, and heavy equipment.[16] For the past 20 years or so, railroads have handled about 35 to 40 percent of the total volume of goods in the United States. In piggyback shipping, a truck trailer is detached from the cab; loaded onto a railroad flatcar; and taken to a destination where it will be offloaded, attached to a truck, and driven to customers' plants. As a result of practices such as piggyback shipments, railroads should continue to hold better than a 38 percent share of the market. Railroad shipment is a relatively energy-efficient way to move goods and could therefore experience significant gains if energy prices continue to climb.

A company may not ship enough goods to even think of using a railroad. However, smaller manufacturers or marketers that don't ship enough products to fill a railcar or truck can get good rates and service by using a freight forwarder. A **freight forwarder** can put many small shipments together to create a single large shipment that can be transported cost-effectively, by truck or train, to the final destination.[17] Some freight forwarders also offer warehousing, customs assistance, and other services along with pickup and delivery. You can see the benefits of such a company to a smaller seller. A freight forwarder is just one of many distribution specialists that have emerged to help marketers move goods from one place to another.

freight forwarder
An organization that puts many small shipments together to create a single large shipment that can be transported cost-effectively to the final destination.

Trucks Are Good for Small Shipments to Remote Locations The second largest surface transportation mode is motor vehicles (trucks, vans, and so forth). Such vehicles handle a little over 25 percent of the volume. As Figure 15.7 shows, trucks reach more locations than trains. Trucks can deliver almost any commodity door-to-door. You could buy your own truck to make deliveries, but for widespread delivery you can't beat trucking specialists. Like freight forwarders, they have emerged to supply one important marketing function—transporting goods. Railroads have joined with trucking firms to further the process of piggybacking. The difference lately is that the new 20-foot-high railroad cars, called double-stacks, can carry two truck trailers, one on top of the other.

Water Transportation Is Inexpensive but Slow When sending goods overseas, often the least expensive way is by ship. Obviously ships are slower than ground or air transportation, so water transportation isn't appropriate for goods that need to be delivered quickly. Ships move a greater volume of goods than you might expect. Over the past 20 years, water transportation has carried

FIGURE 15.7

COMPARING TRANSPORTATION MODES

Combining trucks with railroads lowers cost and increases the number of locations reached. The same is true when combining trucks with ships. Combining trucks with airlines speeds goods over long distances and gets them to almost any location.

MODE	COST	PERCENTAGE OF DOMESTIC VOLUME	SPEED	ON-TIME DEPENDABILITY	FLEXIBILITY HANDLING PRODUCTS	FREQUENCY OF SHIPMENTS	REACH
Railroad	Medium	38%	Slow	Medium	High	Low	High
Trucks	High	25	Fast	High	Medium	High	Highest
Pipeline	Low	21	Medium	Highest	Lowest	Highest	Lowest
Ships (water)	Lowest	15	Slowest	Lowest	Highest	Lowest	Low
Airplane	Highest	1	Fastest	Low	Low	Medium	Medium

15 to 17 percent of the total. Water transport is local as well as international. If you live near the Mississippi River, for example, you've likely seen towboats hauling as many as 30 barges at a time, with a cargo of up to 35,000 tons. On smaller rivers, about eight barges can be hauled, carrying up to 20,000 tons—that's the equivalent of four 100-car railroad trains. Thus, you can see the importance of river traffic. Add to that Great Lakes shipping, shipping from coast to coast and along the coasts, and international shipments, and water transportation takes on a new dimension as a key transportation mode. When truck trailers are placed on ships to travel long distances at lower rates, the process is called *fishyback* (see the explanation of *piggyback*). When they are placed in airplanes, by the way, the process is called *birdyback*.

Pipelines Are Fast and Efficient One transportation mode that's not readily visible to the average consumer is movement by pipeline. About 21 percent of the total volume of goods moves this way. Pipelines are used primarily for transporting water, petroleum, and petroleum products—but a lot more products than you may imagine may be sent by pipeline. One company, for example, sent coal by pipeline by first crushing it and mixing it with water.

Air Transportation Is Really Fast but Expensive Today, only a small part of shipping is done by air. Nonetheless, air transportation is a critical factor in many industries. Airlines carry everything from small packages to luxury cars and elephants, and are expanding to be a competitive mode for other goods. The primary benefit of air transportation is speed. No firms know this better than FedEx and UPS. As just two of several competitors vying for the fast-delivery market, FedEx and UPS have used air transport to expand into global markets.

The air freight industry is starting to focus on global distribution. Emery has been an industry pioneer in establishing specialized sales and operations teams aimed at serving the distribution needs of specific industries. KLM Royal Dutch Airlines has cargo/passenger planes that handle high-profit items such as diplomatic pouches and medical supplies. Specializing in such cargo has enabled KLM to compete with FedEx, TNT, and DHL.[18]

intermodal shipping
The use of multiple modes of transportation to complete a single long-distance movement of freight.

Intermodal Shipping **Intermodal shipping** uses multiple modes of transportation—highway, air, water, rail—to complete a single long-distance movement of freight. Services that specialize in intermodal shipping are known as intermodal marketing companies. Today, railroads are merging with each other and with other transportation companies to offer intermodal distribution.

You can imagine such a system in action. Picture an automobile made in Japan for sale in the United States. It would be shipped by truck to a loading dock where it would be moved by ship to a port in the United States. It may be placed on another truck, taken to a railroad station for loading on a train that will take it across country to again be loaded on a truck for delivery to a local dealer. No doubt you have seen automobiles being hauled across country by train and by truck. Now imagine that all of that movement was handled by one integrated shipping firm. That's what intermodal shipping is all about.

Now you know about the various ways of shipping goods once you have sold them. But that is only the first step in understanding the system that has been developed to move goods from one point to another. Recall from the chapter opening profile about Gus Pagonis that Sears has 30 large distribution centers and 90 smaller outlets. Clearly, an important part of a complex logistics system consists of storage.

Intermodal shipping often involves the use of truck trailers. In this photo you can see truck trailers (containers) being unloaded from a ship and then driven away. Often these containers will be lifted from the truck and put onto a train for a cross-country trip where it will again be attached to another truck. Can you see how intermodal shipping works to move various products around the world?

The Storage Function

People want goods to be delivered quickly when they finally decide to buy them. That means that marketers must have goods available in various parts of the country ready to be shipped locally when ordered. About 25 to 30 percent of the total cost of logistics is for storage. This includes the cost of the storage warehouse (distribution facility) and its operation, plus movement of goods within the warehouse. There are two major kinds of warehouses: storage and distribution. A *storage warehouse* holds products for a relatively long time. Seasonal goods such as lawn mowers would be kept in such a warehouse.

Distribution warehouses are facilities used to gather and redistribute products. You can picture a distribution warehouse for FedEx or UPS handling thousands of packages in a very short time. The packages are picked up at places throughout the country and then processed for reshipment at these centers. General Electric's combination storage and distribution facility in San Gabriel Valley, California, gives you a feel for how large such buildings can be. It is nearly half a mile long and 465 feet wide—that's massive enough to hold almost 27 football fields.

It's hard to imagine the complexity of today's most contemporary distribution warehouses, but this photo will give you a glimpse. This is UPS's new, high-tech distribution center in Louisville, Kentucky. Inside the 4,000,000-square-foot building (yes, that's millions) is a 63-mile maze of conveyor belts that move some 3,304,000 packages an hour (yes, an hour). We can only imagine the technology that sorts all of those packages so that they efficiently end up at the right destinations.

What All This Means to You

The life or death of a firm often depends on its ability to take orders, process orders, keep customers informed about the progress of their orders, get the goods out to customers quickly, handle returns, and manage any recycling issues. Some of the most exciting firms in the stock market are those that assist in some aspect of supply-chain management.

What all this means to you is that there are many new jobs becoming available in the exciting area of supply-chain management. These include jobs with the companies providing the various modes of distribution: trains, airplanes, trucks, ships, and pipelines. It also means new jobs handling information flows between and among companies (e.g., website development). But there are also jobs that involve processing orders, keeping track of inventory, following the path of products as they move from seller to buyer and back, recycling goods, and more—much more.[19]

Critical Thinking

One of the major scarcities in the future will be water. If you could think of an inexpensive way to get water from places of abundance to places where it is needed for drinking, farming, and other uses, you could become very, very rich. Pipelines are an alternative, but you could also freeze the water and ship it by train or truck. You could put the water into huge rubber or plastic containers and roll the containers on railroad tracks. You could tie a rope or chain onto icebergs and tow them to warmer climates. Future wealth is awaiting those who develop the most practical and efficient (read inexpensive) way to move water. Do you have any good ideas?

Summary

1. A channel of distribution consists of a whole set of marketing intermediaries, such as agents, brokers, wholesalers, and retailers, who join together to transport and store goods in their path (or channel) from producers to consumers.
   - ***How do marketing intermediaries add value?***

   Intermediaries perform certain marketing tasks—such as transporting, storing, selling, advertising, and relationship building—faster and cheaper than most manufacturers could. Channels of distribution ensure communication flows and the flow of money and title to goods. They also help ensure that the right quantity and assortment of goods will be available when and where needed.
   - ***What are the principles behind the use of such intermediaries?***

   Marketing intermediaries can be eliminated, but their activities can't; that is, you can eliminate some wholesalers and retailers, but then consumers or someone else would have to perform the retailer's tasks, including transporting and storing goods, finding suppliers, and establishing communication with suppliers. Intermediary organizations have survived in the past because they have performed marketing functions faster and cheaper than others could. Intermediaries add costs to products, but these costs are usually more than offset by the values they create.

1. Explain the concept of marketing channels and the value of marketing intermediaries.

2. Marketing intermediaries perform the following utilities: form, time, place, possession, information, and service.
   - ***How do intermediaries perform the six marketing utilities?***

   A retail grocer may cut or trim meat, providing some form utility. But marketers are more often responsible for the five other utilities. Time utility is provided by having goods available when people want them. Place utility is provided by having goods where people want them. Possession utility is provided by making it possible for people to own things by providing them with credit, delivery, installation, guarantees, and anything else that will help complete the sale. Marketers also inform consumers of the availability of goods and services with advertising, publicity, and other means. That provides information utility. Finally, marketers provide fast, friendly, and efficient service during and after the sale (service utility).

2. Give examples of how intermediaries perform the six marketing utilities.

3. A wholesaler is a marketing intermediary that sells to organizations and individuals, but not to final consumers.
   - ***What are some wholesale organizations that assist in the movement of goods from manufacturers to consumers?***

   Merchant wholesalers are independently owned firms that take title to (own) goods that they handle. *Rack jobbers* furnish racks or shelves full of merchandise to retailers, display products, and sell on consignment. *Cash-and-carry wholesalers* serve mostly small retailers with a limited assortment of products. *Drop shippers* solicit orders from retailers and other wholesalers and have the merchandise shipped directly from a producer to a buyer.

3. Describe the various wholesale intermediaries in the distribution system.

4. A retailer is an organization that sells to ultimate consumers.
   - ***How do retailers compete in today's market?***

   There are five major ways of competing for the consumer's dollar today: price, service, location, selection, and entertainment.
   - ***What are three distribution strategies marketers use?***

   Marketers use three basic distribution strategies: intensive (putting products in as many places as possible), selective (choosing only a few stores in a chosen market), and exclusive (using only one store in each market area).

4. Explain the ways in which retailers compete and the distribution strategies they use.

5. Explain the various kinds of nonstore retailing.

5. Nonstore retailing is retailing done outside a store.
   - ***What are some of the forms of nonstore retailing?***

   Nonstore retailing includes online marketing; telemarketing (marketing by phone); vending machines, kiosks, and carts (marketing by putting products in convenient locations, such as in the halls of shopping centers); direct selling (marketing by approaching consumers in their homes or places of work); multilevel marketing (marketing by setting up a system of salespeople who recruit other salespeople and help them to sell directly to customers); and direct marketing (direct mail and catalog sales). Telemarketing and online marketing are also forms of direct marketing.

6. Explain the various ways to build cooperation in channel systems.

6. One way of generating more cooperation in channels of distribution is to form unified systems.
   - ***What are the four types of distribution systems?***

   The four distribution systems that tie firms together are (1) *corporate systems,* in which all organizations in the channel are owned by one firm; (2) *contractual systems,* in which members are bound to cooperate through contractual agreements; (3) *administered systems,* in which all marketing functions at the retail level are managed by manufacturers; and (4) *supply chains,* in which the various firms in the supply chain are linked electronically to provide the most efficient movement of information and goods possible. Note that the supply-chain system is longer than a channel of distribution because it includes organizations selling to manufacturers while the other systems only merge firms in the channel of distribution *after a product is made.* Supply chains are so efficient that they are sometimes known as value chains.

7. Describe the emergence of logistics.

7. Logistics involves planning, implementing, and controlling the physical flow of materials, final goods, and related information from points of origin to points of consumption to meet customer requirements at a profit.
   - ***What is the difference between logistics and distribution?***

   Distribution is a much more basic concept and involves mostly transportation. Logistics is more complex. *Inbound logistics* brings raw materials, packaging, other goods and services, and information from suppliers to producers. *Materials handling* is the moving of goods from warehouses to the factory floor and to various workstations. *Outbound logistics* manages the flow of finished products and information to business buyers and ultimate consumers (people like you and me). *Reverse logistics* involves bringing goods back to the manufacturer because of defects or for recycling materials.

8. Outline how intermediaries move goods from producers to consumers through the use of various transportation modes and storage functions.

8. Various transportation modes are used to move goods from producers to consumers.
   - ***What are the differences among the various transportation modes?***

   Ships (for slow, inexpensive movement of goods, often internationally); rail (for heavy shipments within the country or between bordering countries); trucks (for getting goods directly to consumers); airplanes (for shipping goods quickly); and pipelines (for moving water and oil and other such goods).
   - ***What is intermodal shipping?***

   Intermodal shipping uses multiple modes of transportation—highway, air, water, rail—to complete a single long-distance movement of freight.
   - ***What costs are involved in storage, and what are the different kinds of warehouses?***

   About 25 to 30 percent of the total cost of physical distribution is for storage. A storage warehouse stores products for a relatively long time. Distribution warehouses are facilities used to gather and redistribute products.

Key Terms

administered distribution system 476
agents/brokers 460
cash-and-carry wholesaler 467
channel of distribution 460
contractual distribution system 476
corporate distribution system 475
direct marketing 474
direct selling 474
drop shippers 467
electronic retailing 472
exclusive distribution 471
freight forwarder 480
inbound logistics 478
information utility 464
intensive distribution 471
intermodal shipping 481
logistics 478
marketing intermediaries 460
materials handling 478
merchant wholesalers 467
outbound logistics 478
place utility 464
possession utility 464
rack jobbers 467
retailer 460
reverse logistics 478
selective distribution 471
service utility 465
supply chain (or value chain) 476
supply-chain management 477
telemarketing 473
time utility 464
utility 463
wholesaler 460

Developing Workplace Skills

1. The six utilities of marketing are form, time, place, possession, information, and service. Give examples of organizations in your area that perform each of these functions.

2. Form small groups and diagram how Dole might get pineapples from a field in Thailand to a canning plant in California to a store near your college. Include the intermediaries and the forms of transportation each one might use.

3. Discuss the merits of buying and selling goods in stores versus over the Internet. What advantages do stores have? Has anyone in the class tried to sell anything on the Internet? How did he or she ship the product?

4. Many students have worked in retailing, and some want to continue such careers after college, yet few students consider similar jobs in wholesaling. Discuss in class the differences between wholesaling and retailing and why retailing has more appeal. Since there are fewer students seeking jobs in wholesaling, do you think such jobs may be easier to get?

5. Recall some of the experiences you have had with telemarketers (those people who tend to call at dinnertime trying to sell you things). How could they change their approach so you would be more responsive and positive about their calls?

Taking It To The Net 1

Purpose

To examine how small businesses can learn to use the Internet to distribute their products directly to customers.

Exercise

Many small businesses have no idea how to begin selling goods over the Internet. Several free websites have been developed to help small businesses get started. Some have links to other sites that provide all kinds of help from setting up the site to doing marketing, handling credit purchases, and more. Many businesses will need help setting up websites of their own. You may be able to help if you learn now all that is involved. Begin by going to www.bigstep.com to learn the steps involved. Take the eight-step tour and learn as much as you can.

Then go to www.workz.com, click on "Build Your Web Site," and answer the following questions:

1. What kind of information were you able to gather about starting a website?
2. What additional information would you like before getting started? Where might you turn for such help?
3. What other advice would you give a small company about trying to sell on the Internet? What would you say about credit cards, answering consumer questions, distribution, and returns?
4. What issues may come up for foreign visitors to the site?

Taking It To The Net 2

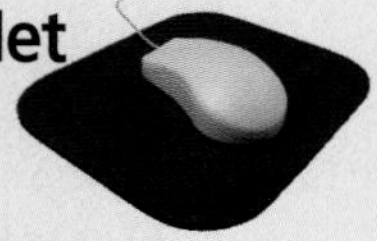

Purpose

To analyze how products move from online retailers to end customers.

Exercise

Let's say that you're a consumer in the market for a particular product. You've done your research and have found the perfect product for your needs at the lowest price available and you've ordered it online. Now what? How does the online merchant get the product to you? One of the most commonly used delivery services is UPS. Go to www.ups.com and use what you find there to answer the following questions.

1. UPS delivers approximately 13 million packages a day. How did UPS grow from a Seattle-based messenger service started by 19-year-old Jim Casey with a borrowed $100 to a worldwide delivery service that invests $1 billion each year in information technology alone?
2. How does UPS work? That is, what happens from the moment a request is made to ship a product to the moment it arrives at the customer's doorstep?
3. In the mid-1980s, UPS shifted its emphasis from an operations focus to a customer needs focus. Today, UPS provides many tools that help its customers meet their shipping needs. What are some examples of such tools?

Casing The Web

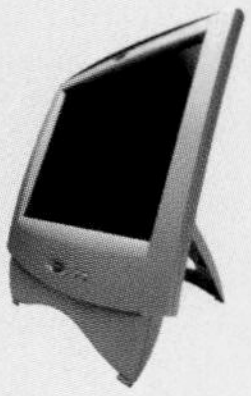

To access the case "Multilevel Marketing," visit

www.mhhe.com/ub7e

Video Case

Bricks & Clicks–Mall of America & Amazon

Did you ever walk out of a store and wonder, "Where did I park the car?" If you've ever been to the Mall of America in Minneapolis, you understand how important it is that you know the answer to that question. If not, you may never find your car among the 13,000 parking spaces. (There are another 7,000 spaces available during peak periods.)

The Mall of America, the largest completely enclosed shopping mall, is home to over 500 stores. It is 4.2 million square feet, the equivalent of 88 football fields. A walk around just one floor is more than a half-mile trip; a walk around all of the store fronts is almost 4.5 miles. Feel like taking a peek in all of the stores? If you spent just 10 minutes browsing in each one it would take you 86 hours, that's more than 3.5 days–without stopping for a snack! And, of course, you couldn't go to the Mall of America and not stop for food in one of the two food courts with 27 restaurants or 30 other restaurants scattered throughout the complex. Other unique features of the Mall of America include: (1) Camp Snoopy, the largest indoor family theme park in the country, with a rollercoaster, Ferris wheel, and 30 other rides in a seven-acre glass-enclosed area; (2) Underwater World, where sharks, stingrays, giant sea turtles, and over 3,000 living sea creatures swim so close, you'll feel like you can reach out and touch them; (3) Upper East Side, a floor with bars, nightclubs, game rooms, comedy club, 14-screen theater and bowling alley; (4) The LEGO Land Imagination Center, a four-story LEGO showplace with more than 30 full-size LEGO models including dinosaurs, astronauts, and the world's largest animated and interactive LEGO clock tower; (5) Jillian's Hi Life Lanes, a state of the art bowling alley that includes a dozen bowling lanes, giant video screens, a video DJ, retro lounge, and 150 of the latest electronic simulation games; and (6) NASCAR Silicon Motor Speedway, high-tech indoor stock car simulation machines.

More than 350 million people have visited the Mall of America since it opened its doors in 1992. Since the Minneapolis–St. Paul area is a market of only 3 million people, where do all of these visitors come from? A survey showed that 43 percent of the shoppers come from outside Minnesota and account for 56 percent of the sales. The Mall of America provides shuttle bus service every half hour to and from the busy international airport only three miles way.

Can the biggest get any bigger? It appears so–Mall of America announced a plan to expand another 5.7 million square feet, that's another 117 football fields. There are plans for three hotels, a performing arts center, a business-office complex, an art museum, and maybe even a television broadcast studio.

Is the Mall of America the place to go to pick up a box of paperclips or buy the latest best-selling novel? Probably not. For those of us who would rather let our fingers do the shopping, there is another monster-size shopping mall where you don't have to worry about where you parked the car, because you don't need to leave home to shop there. Of course, we're talking about Amazon.com. It doesn't have a single inch of storefront floor space, but Amazon boasts the "Earth's Biggest Selection" of products and services, including books, CDs, videos, toys and games, electronics, kitchenware, computers, electronic greeting cards, and auctions.

Amazon maintains seven huge distribution centers where it keeps an inventory of more than 2.7 million products. Amazon must manage the flow of products from its suppliers to its distribution centers and the flow of customer orders from the distribution centers to customers' homes or offices. Amazon uses special software to forecast purchasing patterns and allows it to give its suppliers better information about delivery dates and volumes. Technology is equally essential in increasing the speed at which information is passed back and forth between the company and its customers. The success of Amazon's logistics and supply chain management abilities was illustrated during a recent holiday shopping season. Between November 9 and December 21, Amazon received orders for 37.9 million items–over 99 percent of them were delivered on time!

Whether businesses entice customers with entertainment features like roller coasters or with convenience features like shopping from home, getting products and services to customers when and where they need them is what distribution is all about.

Thinking It Over

1. What role does entertainment play in the success of the Mall of America?
2. How do Amazon's logistics and supply-chain management activities help create value for customers?
3. Where do you think the future growth in retailing lies—in bricks (i.e., Mall of America) or clicks (i.e., Amazon)? Why?

Chapter 16

Today's Promotional Techniques

Learning Goals

After you have read and studied this chapter, you should be able to

1. Define *promotion* and list the four traditional tools that make up the promotion mix.
2. Define *advertising* and describe the advantages and disadvantages of various advertising media, including the Internet.
3. Illustrate the steps of the B2B and B2C selling processes, and discuss the role of a consultative salesperson.
4. Describe the role of the public relations department, and tell how publicity fits in that role.
5. Explain the importance of various forms of sales promotion, including sampling, word of mouth, and viral marketing, and tell how they are affected by new technologies.
6. Describe integrated marketing communication and the role of interactive communications within it.

Getting to Know Dan Wieden of Wieden and Kennedy

You may not know the name Dan Wieden, but you are likely to have seen his work. He is the person who created the "Just Do It" slogan for Nike. His company, Wieden and Kennedy (W&K), is known as one of the most creative advertising agencies in the United States.

One of the most controversial Nike ads from W&K featured a streaker running around a stadium during a soccer game. The filming was so realistic that many people thought that they were witnessing an actual event. In fact, the people in the stands were extras who were hired for the shoot. The commercial took five days to create in near-freezing weather. It's no wonder the man in the commercial ran so fast! With the tagline "MoreGo," the commercial promoted Nike's ShoxNZ.

One of the most controversial Nike ads from W&K features a streaker running around a stadium during a soccer game.

W&K was started in Portland, Oregon, in 1982 with Nike as its sole client. By the 1990s, Nike ads featuring Michael Jordan, Spike Lee, and Tiger Woods were being hailed as industry leaders. Wieden was credited with bringing in a new, postmodern school of advertising that blended influences from the popular culture, the art scene, independent film, and rock and rap music. For example, rapper Snoop Dogg was featured in a disco Nike ad. W&K now has many other clients, including ESPN and Miller Brewing.

As an independent ad agency, W&K is freer to experiment and take risks than traditional agencies are. Part of that risk-taking is to move the agency into entertainment as well as advertising. For example, W&K is putting together a Broadway musical about basketball that is set to a hip-hop beat. Its Tokyo office is launching a record label. You might also see documentary films, a weekly TV series, and MTV music videos coming out of the agency. W&K's first piece of self-funded entertainment was a book about dogs in Portland. It hit the best-seller lists overseas. You can see the appeal of the book by looking at the cover. It says, "Cat Spelled Backward Doesn't Spell God," an obvious dig at cat owners.

Why is an advertising agency getting involved in so many other ventures? Part of the answer is that the ad business was battered by the recession in early 2000, hurt tremendously by the fall of dot-coms, and threatened by new technology. In the early 2000s, companies wishing to promote their products began looking for ways of promotion more creative than the typical 30-second TV commercial. Companies feared, for one thing, that many consumers, armed with TiVo-brand and other personal recorders, would simply skip watching commercials on TV by programming their recorders to avoid them.

Pop-up ads on the Internet have proved too annoying to be a powerful promotional tool. Nonetheless, many companies are using websites packed with product information, entertainment, and branding messages. Promoters are tending toward using a variety of promotional companies rather than one huge agency that promises to do it all for them. That means that companies are hiring public relations firms, Internet specialists, media buying specialists, and international specialists to provide them with variety and expertise. That includes, of course, hiring an agency like W&K to come up with creative ads that people don't soon forget.

This chapter will explore today's promotional techniques—not just in advertising, but in personal selling, public relations, word of mouth, and other areas as well. Promotion is one of the four Ps of marketing. Promotional efforts are needed to keep the economy moving forward when people become more cautious with their spending because of an economic slowdown, terrorism, and war.

Sources: Warren Berger, "Just Do It. Again," *Business 2.0,* September 2002, pp. 77–84; and Gerry Khermouch, "The 5 Rules of the Ad Game," *Business Week,* January 20, 2003, pp. 12–13.

Promotion and the Promotion Mix

promotion
An effort by marketers to inform and remind people in the target market about products and to persuade them to participate in an exchange.

promotion mix
The combination of promotional tools an organization uses.

integrated marketing communication (IMC)
A technique that combines all the promotional tools into one comprehensive and unified promotional strategy.

Promotion is an effort by marketers to inform and remind people in the target market about products and to persuade them to participate in an exchange. Marketers use many different tools to promote their products and services. Traditionally, as shown in Figure 16.1, those tools included advertising, personal selling, public relations, and sales promotion. The combination of promotional tools an organization uses is called its **promotion mix**. The product ➤P. 402◄ is shown in the middle of the figure to illustrate the fact that the product itself can be a promotional tool (e.g., through giving away free samples). We'll discuss all of the promotional tools in this chapter.

Integrated marketing communication (IMC) combines all the promotional tools into one comprehensive and unified promotional strategy. The idea is to use all the promotional tools and company resources to create a positive brand image and to meet the strategic marketing and promotional goals of the firm.[1] Lately, companies have been including Internet promotions in that mix.[2] Figure 16.2 shows the six steps to follow in establishing a promotional campaign.

FIGURE 16.1
THE TRADITIONAL PROMOTION MIX

FIGURE 16.2
STEPS IN A PROMOTIONAL CAMPAIGN

1. Identify a target market. (Refer back to Chapter 13 for a discussion of segmentation and target marketing.)
2. Define the objectives for each element of the promotion mix. Goals should be clear and measurable.
3. Determine a promotional budget. The budgeting process will clarify how much can be spent on advertising, personal selling, and other promotional efforts.
4. Develop a unifying message. The goal of an integrated promotional program is to have one clear message communicated by advertising, public relations, sales, and every other promotional effort.
5. Implement the plan. Advertisements must be scheduled to complement efforts being made by public relations and sales promotion. Salespeople should have access to all materials to optimize the total effort.
6. Evaluate effectiveness. Measuring results depends greatly on clear objectives. Each element of the promotional mix should be evaluated separately, and an overall measure should be taken as well. It is important to learn what is working and what is not.

As we discuss each of the promotional tools in this chapter, we explore the changes that are occurring in those areas. Then, at the end of the chapter, we examine the latest promotional strategies and how they can be combined to build better relationships with customers and other stakeholders. We begin the exploration of promotional tools by looking at advertising.

ADVERTISING: PERSUASIVE COMMUNICATION

Advertising is paid, nonpersonal communication through various media by organizations and individuals who are in some way identified in the advertising message. Figure 16.3 lists various categories of advertising. Take a minute to look it over because there is a lot more to advertising than just TV advertising.

advertising
Paid, nonpersonal communication through various media by organizations and individuals who are in some way identified in the advertising message.

The importance of advertising in the United States is easy to document; just look at the numbers in Figure 16.4. The total ad volume exceeds $231 billion yearly. Television in all its forms is the number one medium (over 23 percent of the total). Direct mail is number two, with 19.3 percent of the total expenditures. Closely following is newspapers, at 19.2 percent. Note that Internet advertising still takes less than 2.5 percent of the total expenditure.[3]

The public benefits greatly from advertising expenditures. First, ads are informative. The number three medium, newspaper advertising, is full of information about products, prices, features, and more. So is direct mail advertising, the number two medium. Advertising not only informs us about products but also provides us with free TV and radio programs: The money advertisers spend

FIGURE 16.3
MAJOR CATEGORIES OF ADVERTISING

Different kinds of advertising are used by various organizations to reach different market targets. Major categories include the following:

- *Retail advertising*—advertising to consumers by various retail stores such as supermarkets and shoe stores.
- *Trade advertising*—advertising to wholesalers and retailers by manufacturers to encourage them to carry their products.
- *Business-to-business advertising*—advertising from manufacturers to other manufacturers. A firm selling motors to auto companies would use business-to-business advertising.
- *Institutional advertising*—advertising designed to create an attractive image for an organization rather than for a product. "We Care about You" at Giant Food is an example. "Virginia Is for Lovers" and "I ❤ New York" are two institutional campaigns by government agencies.
- *Product advertising*—advertising for a good or service to create interest among consumer, commercial, and industrial buyers.
- *Advocacy advertising*—advertising that supports a particular view of an issue (e.g., an ad in support of gun control or against nuclear power plants). Such advertising is also known as cause advertising.
- *Comparison advertising*—advertising that compares competitive products. For example, an ad that compares two different cold care products' speed and benefits is a comparative ad.
- *Interactive advertising*—customer-oriented communication that enables customers to choose the information they receive, such as interactive video catalogs that let customers select which items to view.
- *Online advertising*—advertising messages that appear on computers as people visit different websites.

FIGURE 16.4

ADVERTISING EXPENDITURE BY MEDIA (IN MILLIONS OF DOLLARS)

RANK	MEDIUM	TOTAL U.S. VOLUME	AS % OF TOTAL
1	Direct mail	$ 44.7	19.3
2	Newspapers	44.3	19.2
3	Broadcast TV	38.9	16.8
4	Radio	17.9	7.7
5	Cable TV	15.5	6.7
6	Yellow Pages	13.6	5.9
7	Magazines	11.1	4.8
8	Internet	5.8	2.5
9	Out of home	5.1	2.2
10	Business publications	4.5	1.9
		30.0	13.0
	Total	$231.4	100.0

Source: *Advertising age FACTPACK*, 2002.

Advertising, as this advertisement suggests, is the way brands get to be great brands. How much has the advertising for Coke influenced your choice of Coke over Pepsi? Or did the Pepsi ads win you over? Or don't you drink either? Are you aware of any influence advertising has had on items that you have purchased? Which ads?

for commercial time pays for the production costs. Advertising also covers the major costs of producing newspapers and magazines. When we buy a magazine, we pay mostly for mailing or promotional costs. Figure 16.5 discusses the advantages and disadvantages of various advertising media to the advertiser. Newspapers, radio, and the Yellow Pages are especially attractive to local advertisers.

Television offers many advantages to national advertisers, but it's expensive. For example, the cost of 30 seconds of advertising during the Super Bowl telecast is just over $2 million.[4] How many bottles of beer or bags of dog food must a company sell to pay for such commercials? The answer may seem to be "A lot," but few other media besides television have ever allowed advertisers to reach so many people with such impact. About 40 percent of U.S households are reached by the Super Bowl. That compares with the 26 percent reached by the Academy Awards (at $1.6 million for 30 seconds) and the 17 percent reached by the show *Friends* (at $350,000 for 30 seconds).[5]

TV advertising isn't limited to traditional commercials for products that interrupt TV programming; sometimes the products appear in the programs themselves. **Product placement** means paying to put products into TV shows and movies where they will be seen. Have you noticed products that have been featured in movies and TV shows, like the cars in James Bond movies? The Dealing with Change box on p. 494 offers other examples of product placement.

product placement
Putting products into TV shows and movies where they will be seen.

Marketers must now choose which media can best be used to reach the audience they desire. Radio advertising, for example, is less expensive than TV advertising and often reaches people when they have few other distractions, such as driving in their cars. Radio is especially good, therefore, for

MEDIUM	ADVANTAGES	DISADVANTAGES
Newspapers	Good coverage of local markets; ads can be placed quickly; high consumer acceptance; ads can be clipped and saved.	Ads compete with other features in paper; poor color; ads get thrown away with paper (short life span).
Television	Uses sight, sound, and motion; reaches all audiences; high attention with no competition from other material.	High cost; short exposure time; takes time to prepare ads.
Radio	Low cost; can target specific audiences; very flexible; good for local marketing.	People may not listen to ad; depends on one sense (hearing); short exposure time; audience can't keep ad.
Magazines	Can target specific audiences; good use of color; long life of ad; ads can be clipped and saved.	Inflexible; ads often must be placed weeks before publication; cost is relatively high.
Outdoor	High visibility and repeat exposures; low cost; local market focus.	Limited message; low selectivity of audience.
Direct mail	Best for targeting specific markets; very flexible; ad can be saved.	High cost; consumers may reject ad as junk mail; must conform to post office regulations.
Yellow Pages advertising	Great coverage of local markets; widely used by consumers; available at point of purchase.	Competition with other ads; cost may be too high for very small businesses.
Internet	Inexpensive global coverage; available at any time; interactive.	Relatively low readership.

FIGURE 16.5

ADVANTAGES AND DISADVANTAGES OF VARIOUS ADVERTISING MEDIA

The most effective media are often very expensive. The inexpensive media may not reach your market. The goal is to use the medium that can reach your desired market most effectively and efficiently.

selling services that people don't usually read about in print media—services such as banking, mortgages, continuing education, brokerage services, and the like.

Brothers Robert and Jim Millican learned the benefit of radio advertising when they opened Smoothieville in Chapel Hill, North Carolina. People in that area were not too familiar with fruit smoothies at that time. The brothers had decided to give out free smoothies the first day they were open, but though they used word of mouth and buy-one-get-one-free coupons, not much happened—fewer than 100 customers enjoyed the free fruit shakes. Then the Millicans thought of radio. Putting a few thousand dollars into radio commercials got the business rolling. Profits became so good that Smoothieville now has two locations: one across from the University of North Carolina in Chapel Hill and another in Durham.

Billboards, or outdoor advertising, is a rather ubiquitous and aesthetically controversial form of advertising. When you are traveling, do you read them in search of restaurants, rooms, and entertainment? What other products have you seen on billboards? What advantages and disadvantages do you think signs like this one have over other advertising media?

Dealing with Change

Product Placement Challenges Advertising

Have you ever been watching a TV show or a movie and noticed that the actors are using brand-name products? They drive a certain kind of car, use a certain kind of camera, and drink a certain kind of drink. Most of the time, such product exposure is no accident. As explained in the text, the term for the promotional tool in which marketers pay to have their products featured on TV shows and in the movies is *product placement.* In the TV series *Lost,* you could see the participants drinking Dasani bottled water (a Coke product) and using survival items from crates prominently displaying the Lowe's logo. Nike wasn't identified as the creator of *Road to Paris,* a one-hour documentary about the U.S. cycling team, but you might have guessed had you noticed how often Nike's swoosh showed up. You may also have noticed the Coke cups sitting on the table in front of the judges on *American Idol.* Few viewers missed the Pontiac GTO used in the movie *XXX* with Vin Diesel. The BMW Films series on the Internet called "The Hire" features a BMW and its driver, played by Clive Owen.

The use of product placement is a challenge to traditional advertising agencies and to the networks and studios. They have to adapt to this change in promotional emphasis. Though it is difficult to measure advertising effectiveness, some marketers have found traditional forms of advertising too expensive for the responses they were getting. That is why they turned to product placement. What products have you noticed on TV shows and in the movies? Were you ever tempted to buy a product because you saw actors using it in the course of the program or film?

infomercial
A full-length TV program devoted exclusively to promoting goods or services.

The Growing Use of Infomercials

One growing form of advertising is the infomercial. An **infomercial** is a full-length TV program devoted exclusively to promoting goods or services. Infomercials have been so successful because they show the product in great detail. A great product can often sell itself if there's some means to show the public how it works. Infomercials provide that opportunity. People have said that a half-hour infomercial is the equivalent of sending your very best salespeople to a person's home and allowing them to use everything in their power to make the sale: drama, demonstration, testimonials, graphics, and more. RotoZip Tool Company thought that consumers would never buy its Spiral Saw line unless they saw the saws being used. So RotoZip spent $250,000 for an infomercial. Sales zoomed by 300 percent.[6]

Some products, such as personal development seminars or workout tapes, are hard to sell without showing people a sample of their contents and using testimonials. The Spotlight on Small Business box discusses in more detail the benefit of testimonials in advertising.

The use of infomercials as an advertising medium and strategy continues to grow. Their length typically ranges from two minutes to one hour. All day, five days a week, Kathleen Funchion-McGrenra of Philadelphia is paid to monitor and watch infomercials. In fact, she attempts to watch 13 monitors at a time. What factors about infomercials have led to their popularity among advertisers?

Advertising and Promotion on the Internet

Advertising on the Internet is a relatively new phenomenon in marketing.[7] *Red Herring* magazine reported, "Most ads on the Internet today are like handbills stapled on telephone poles: you walk by them, but don't pay too much attention to them."[8] That report came out a couple of years ago, and things have only gotten worse since. De-

Spotlight on Small Business

www.jwrobel.com/test.html

Using Testimonials to Build Business

Carol Boucher of Valley Forge, Pennsylvania, has a small company called Bridal Event that gives bridal shows. There is a lot of competition for audiences among such shows, and Boucher wanted her company to stand out from the others. She went to an advertising consultant who recommended the following:

1. Top your ads with an attention-capturing headline like "I DO."
2. Put in a series of testimonials from attendees at previous shows. (For example, start with a statement such as "I DO prefer the Bridal Event because . . . " and then list the positive things people have said.)
3. Remember that satisfied customers provide your best ad copy.

Some small companies pay their previous customers to recommend new customers. For example, they may give previous customers $5 for every new customer who comes to the show because of their recommendation.

Small businesses find that an important part of promotion is getting local papers to print stories about them. One way a bridal company can get such free publicity is to take a picture of several brides and grooms and write interesting stories about how each couple met and why they went to a bridal show. Other stories could feature new wedding gowns, fun things to do at wedding receptions, or unusual flower arrangements. The latest thing is to fax the stories to the various papers or to make a short video and mail it to them. If the stories are interesting enough, the local paper will print them as news.

According to *American Demographics,* 83 percent of consumers in the market for a particular product ask for information from those they know already own the product. Gathering testimonials makes the whole process easier because potential customers can see what others are saying without having to search out for themselves someone who can speak about the product. How impressed are you with testimonials from your friends and others?

spite the fact that most people tend to ignore Internet ads, companies continue to use them because they hope to tap into the huge potential that online marketing offers. Ultimately, the goal is to get customers and potential customers to a website where they can learn more about the company and its products—and vice versa. If users click through an ad to get to the website, the company has the opportunity not only to provide information but also to interact with the customer (e.g., gathering names, addresses, opinions, or preferences). Internet advertising thus becomes a means to bring customers and companies together.

Interactive promotion allows marketers to go beyond a monologue, where sellers try to persuade buyers to buy things, to a dialogue in which buyers and sellers work together to create mutually beneficial exchange relationships. For example, Garden.com was an online retailer of garden products and services before its assets were acquired by Burpee. Dionn Schaffner, vice president of marketing, says, "Gardening is an information-intensive activity. Customers obviously want to learn about gardening, but they also seek inspiration by communicating with fellow gardeners and experts." Garden.com's answer was an interactive website through which customers could chat with each other and ask gardening questions. When customers came to the site, the company knew who they were and what they had asked in the past because it kept track of them using cookies (little bits of data that are kept about customers on a database).[9]

interactive promotion
Promotion process that allows marketers to go beyond a monologue, where sellers try to persuade buyers to buy things, to a dialogue in which buyers and sellers work together to create mutually beneficial exchange relationships.

Technology greatly improves the speed and potential of Internet dialogues. Many companies provide online videos, chat rooms, and other services in a virtual store where they are able to talk to other customers, talk to salespeople, examine goods and services, and buy products.

The Internet is changing the whole approach to working with customers. Note that we said "working with" rather than "promoting to." The current

Reaching Beyond Our Borders

www.starbucks.com

Can There Be a Starbucks Inside a Starbucks?

There are 124 Starbucks coffeeshops in Manhattan. Some are only a couple of blocks apart. All together, there are some 4,247 Starbucks locations across the United States and Canada. (Though would you believe that there are eight states with no Starbucks?) Although there is room for some growth in the United States, Starbucks has much more room to grow overseas. But that means learning how to adapt to the culture of each country. There are Starbucks outlets in Kuwait, Lebanon, Oman, Qatar, and Saudi Arabia. There are about 368 stores in Japan, but sales are slipping as the Japanese economy continues to slide sideways and downward. The 310 Starbucks stores in England are doing well, but competition is popping up everywhere. You can imagine the challenge of opening stores in Italy, whose citizens are very proud of their own coffee, which sells for much less than Starbucks charges. Furthermore, Italians like to have food with their coffee and Starbucks has not been as strong as it might be in adding food to its offering. In any case, it is important for Starbucks to continue to expand overseas because the U.S. market is getting saturated—thus the widely circulated joke about the new law prohibiting a Starbucks from opening in the bathroom of another Starbucks.

One of the competitors of Starbucks is Dunkin' Donuts. No grande and venti for coffee sizes at Dunkin' Donuts, just small, medium, and large. And no $8 sandwiches either. Dunkin' Donuts has had some success adapting to the local culture in other countries. It may be one company Starbucks can benchmark as it continues its expansion.

Dunkin' Donuts, for example, has about 127 shops in Thailand, serving more than 300,000 customers a week. In Thailand, Dunkin' Donuts and other fast-food establishments are places where you meet your friends and family and you relax. Thus, most business is conducted in the afternoon and evening, as in a café. The Dunkin' Donuts in Thailand therefore promotes itself as a company that cares for society and believes in the importance of family.

One promotion was called the "Longest Love Message to Moms" for Mother's Day. All Thais were invited to come to a Dunkin' Donuts store and, on a specially made vinyl banner, write a love note to their mother, whether they bought something or not. Eventually the signed pieces were sewn together to form a mile-long banner with more than 50,000 love messages. The whole effort boosted sales by $375,000. This successful effort shows the value of custom-designing promotions to match the social and economic conditions of each country where units are built. It would come as no surprise if Starbucks were to begin such country-oriented promotions as it learns more about marketing in different countries.

Sources: Paula Lyon Andruss, "Thais Sweet on Mom, 'Love' Campaign," *Marketing News,* September 11, 2000, pp. 6–7; and Stanley Holmes, Drake Bennett, Kate Carlisle, and Chester Dawson, "Planet Starbucks," *Business Week,* September 9, 2002, pp. 100–10.

trend is to build relationships with customers over time.[10] That means carefully listening to what consumers want, tracking their purchases, providing them with better service, and giving them access to more information.

Global Advertising

Harvard professor Theodore Levitt is a big proponent of global marketing and advertising. His idea is to develop a product and promotional strategy that can be implemented worldwide. Certainly global advertising would save companies money in research and design. In fact, that is the strategy being used by major companies such as Hewlett-Packard, IBM, and Intel. However, other experts think that promotions targeted at specific countries or regions may be much more successful than global promotions since each country or region has its own culture, language, and buying habits.

The evidence supports the theory that promotional efforts specifically designed for individual countries often work best. For example, commercials for Camay soap that showed men complimenting women on their appearance were jarring in cultures where men don't express themselves that way. A

different campaign is needed in such countries. (See the Reaching Beyond Our Borders box for a discussion of adapting promotions to other countries.)

CHAMPION
KNITWEAR CO. INC.
THE STORY GOES ON.
Dal 1919 Champion si allena con gli atleti di tutto il mondo. Una passione cominciata con le prime felpe e arrivata ai giorni nostri, attraverso innovazioni che hanno cambiato il modo di vestire lo sport.
Champion
AUTHENTIC ATHLETIC APPAREL

Champion Sportswear is a U.S. based company that markets its products internationally. This ad is partially in Italian and appeared in an Italian magazine. It seems to feature a game of inner-city basketball somewhere in the United States. Do you think more Italian consumers would respond to Champion products if they associated their products with an Italian rather than an American image? Why or why not?

In Chapter 3, we listed some problems that well-known companies encountered in global marketing. Others include the following: When a Japanese company tried to use English words to name a popular drink, it called the product Pocari Sweat, not a good image for a beverage in the minds of most English-speaking people. In England, the Ford Probe didn't go over too well because the word *probe* made people think of doctors' waiting rooms and medical examinations. People in the United States may have difficulty with Krapp toilet paper from Sweden. But perhaps even that is not as bad as the translation of Coors' slogan "Turn it loose" that became "Suffer from diarrhea." Clairol introduced its curling iron, the Mist Stick, to the German market, not realizing that *Mist* in German can mean "manure." A T-shirt promoting a visit by the Pope in Miami read *la papa,* which means "the potato." The T-shirt should have said *el Papa.* As you can see, getting the words right in international advertising is tricky and critical. So is understanding the culture.

People in Brazil rarely eat breakfast, but they treat Kellogg's Corn Flakes as a dry snack like potato chips. Kellogg is trying a promotional strategy that shows people in Brazil how to eat cereal with cold milk in the morning. Many more situations could be cited to show that international advertising calls for researching the wants and needs of people in each specific country and then designing appropriate ads and testing them.

In the United States, selected groups are large enough and different enough to call for specially designed promotions. Masterfoods USA, for example, tried to promote dulce de leche (caramel) M&M's to the Hispanic market in cities like Los Angeles, Miami, and San Antonio. The promotion was not successful, however. Knowing the market had potential, Masterfoods changed course and bought a candy company called the Lucas Group, which has had success selling such candies as Felix Sour Fruit and Lucas Hot and Spicy in Mexico.[11] Maybelline, which makes a wide array of cosmetics, is targeting special promotions to African American women. In short, much advertising today is moving from globalism (one ad for everyone in the world) to regionalism (specific ads for each country or for specific groups within a country). In the future, marketers will prepare more custom-designed promotions to reach smaller audiences—audiences as small as one person.

Critical Thinking

Now that there is a greater possibility of interactive communications between companies and potential customers, do you think the importance of traditional advertising will grow or decline? What will be the effect, if any, on the price we consumers must pay for TV programs, newspapers, and magazines?

personal selling
The face-to-face presentation and promotion of goods and services.

prospecting
Researching potential buyers and choosing those most likely to buy.

qualifying
In the selling process, making sure that people have a need for the product, the authority to buy, and the willingness to listen to a sales message.

prospect
A person with the means to buy a product, the authority to buy, and the willingness to listen to a sales message.

Personal Selling: Providing Personal Attention

Personal selling is the face-to-face presentation and promotion of goods ➤P. 25◄ and services ➤P. 26◄. It also involves the search for new prospects and follow-up service after the sale. Effective selling isn't simply a matter of persuading others to buy. In fact, it's more accurately described today as helping others satisfy their wants and needs.

Given that perspective, you can see why salespeople are starting to use the Internet, portable computers, paging devices, fax machines, and other technology. They can use this technology to help customers search the Net, design custom-made products, look over prices, and generally do everything it takes to complete the order. The benefit of personal selling is that there is a person there to help you complete a transaction. The salesperson should listen to your needs, help you reach a solution, and do all that is possible to make accomplishing that solution smoother and easier.

It is costly to provide customers with personal attention, especially since some companies are replacing salespeople with Internet services and information. Therefore, those companies that retain salespeople must train them to be especially effective, efficient, and helpful.

To illustrate personal selling's importance in our economy and the career opportunities it provides, let's look at some numbers. First, U.S. census data show that nearly 10 percent of the total labor force is employed in personal selling. When we add those who sell for nonprofit organizations, we find that over 7 million people are employed in sales.

The average cost of a single sales call to a potential business-to-business (B2B) ➤P. 411◄ buyer is about $400. Surely no firm would pay that much to send out anyone but a highly skilled, professional marketer and consultant. But how does one get to be that kind of sales representative? What are the steps along the way? Let's take a closer look at the process of selling.

Steps in the Selling Process

The best way to understand personal selling is to go through the selling process with a product and see what's involved. Imagine that you are a software salesperson whose job is to show business users the advantages of using various programs. As we noted in Chapter 13, one product that is really hot these days, and one that is becoming critically important to establishing long-term relationships with customers, is customer relationship management (CRM) software.[12] Let's go through the selling process to see what you can do to sell CRM software. Although this is a business-to-business (B2B) example, the process is similar, but less complex, in consumer selling. We shall explore the process for consumer selling later. In both business-to-business and consumer selling, it is critical for the salesperson to know the product well and know how the product compares to competitor products. Such product knowledge is needed before the salesperson begins the selling process. The selling process then consists of seven steps, explained in the following subsections.

Get-Real-Dolls Inc. of San Francisco is a successful producer of sports-action dolls. The owners, shown here, say the trick isn't making the dolls, it is getting companies like Target and Toys "R" Us to carry them. That requires sending out experienced salespeople who know how to promote and persuade the stores' buyers to offer the dolls for sale. Jana Machin and Julz Chavez understood this because both had experience selling for larger manufacturers before starting Get-Real-Dolls.

1. Prospect and Qualify The first step in the selling process is prospecting. **Prospecting** involves researching potential buyers and choosing those most likely to buy. That selection process is called **qualifying**. To qualify people means to make sure that they have a need for the product, the authority to buy, and the willingness to listen to a sales message. A person who meets these criteria is called a **prospect**. You often meet prospects at trade shows, where they come up to booths sponsored by manufacturers and ask questions. Other prospects may visit your website seeking information. But often the best prospects are people at companies who were recommended to you by others who use your product or know all about it. Salespeople often e-mail potential clients with proposals to see if there is any interest before making a formal visit.[13]

2. Preapproach Before making a sales call, you must do further research. In the preapproach phase, you must learn as much as possible about customers and their wants and needs. Before you try to sell the CRM software, you would want to know which people in the company are most likely to buy or use it. What kind of customers do they deal with? What kind of relationship strategies are they now using? All that information should be in a database ➤**P. 17**◀ so that, if one representative leaves the firm, the company can carry information about customers to the new salesperson. Note that the selling process may take a long time and that gathering information before you approach the customer is critical.

3. Approach An old saying goes "You don't have a second chance to make a good first impression." That's why the approach is so important. When you call on a customer for the first time, your opening comments are important. The idea is to give an impression of friendly professionalism, to create rapport, to build credibility, and to start a relationship. Often the decision of whether or not to use a software package depends on reliable service from the salesperson. In selling CRM products, you can make it known from the start that you'll be available to help the prospect company train its employees to use the software and to upgrade the package when necessary.

4. Make Presentation In the actual presentation of the CRM software, the idea is to match the benefits of your value package to the client's needs.[14] Companies such as Ventaso, Inc., and the Sant Group now provide sales proposal software that includes everything from PowerPoint presentations to competitive analysis. Since you've done your homework and know the prospect's wants and needs, you can tailor the presentation accordingly. During the presentation is a great time to use testimonials (letters or statements from users praising the product) to show potential buyers that they are joining leaders in other firms in trying this new software. See the box on p. 495 for more on testimonials.

5. Answer Objections You should anticipate any objections the prospect may raise and determine proper responses. Think of questions as opportunities for creating better relationships, not as challenges to what you're saying. Customers may have legitimate doubts, and you are there to resolve those doubts. Relationships are based on trust, and trust comes from successfully and honestly working with others. Often you can introduce the customer to others in the firm who can answer their questions and provide them with anything they need. Using a laptop computer, you may set up a virtual meeting in which the customer can chat with other members of the firm and begin building a relationship.

6. Close Sale As a salesperson, you have limited time and can't spend forever with one potential customer answering questions and objections. A **trial close** consists of a question or statement that moves the selling process toward the actual close. Questions you might ask in a trial close include, "Would you like the blue one or the red one?" or "Do you want to pay for that with your credit card?" The final step is to ask for the order and show the client where to sign.

trial close
A step in the selling process that consists of a question or statement that moves the selling process toward the actual close.

Once a relationship is established, the goal of the sales call may be to get a testimonial from the customer. As you can see, salespeople must learn to close many times before a long-term relationship is established.

7. Follow Up The selling process isn't over until the order is approved and the customer is happy. The sales relationship may continue for years as you respond to new requests for information. You can see why selling is often described as a process of establishing relationships, not just a matter of selling goods or services. The follow-up step includes handling customer complaints, making sure that the customer's questions are answered, and quickly supplying what the customer wants. Often, customer service is as important to the sale as the product itself. Most manufacturers have therefore established websites where information may be obtained and discussions may take place.

The selling process varies somewhat among different goods and services, but the general idea is the same. Your goals as a salesperson are to help the buyer buy and to make sure that the buyer is satisfied after the sale. Sales force automation (SFA), in fact, includes over 400 software programs that help salespeople design products, close deals, tap into company intranets, and more. With SFA, some salespeople can even conduct virtual reality tours of the manufacturing plant for the customer.

Using Technology to Practice Consultative Selling

Salespeople now have at their fingertips data about the customer, about competitors, about where products are in the supply chain ➤P. 476◀, about pricing and special promotions, and more. You also are aware that B2B customers are increasingly using the Internet to buy goods and services. That means that B2B salespeople will have new roles to play in the future. Here is how Marc Miller, president and CEO of Change Master, a Cleveland-based sales-productivity improvement firm, puts it: "If you're a salesperson who only communicates product value—'This is what we make, let me give you a presentation'—you're gone. But if you know how to add value, you're going to have a nice business as a consultative salesperson."

consultative salesperson
A salesperson who begins by analyzing customer needs and then comes up with solutions to those needs.

What's a consultative salesperson? A **consultative salesperson** is a salesperson who begins by analyzing customer needs and then comes up with solutions to those needs. At Dell Computer, for example, it's the sales team, not tech support, that builds and manages customers' extranet sites. The sales team helps determine what information should be available on such sites and its members generally act as consultants on all matters having to do with computers, software, purchasing issues, and more.

Will selling to the consumer market change as dramatically as selling to the B2B market has? Probably so. Salespeople in retail stores will also see dramatic changes in the way they do things. Imagine an automobile salesperson,

for example. A customer can go to a dealer, sit down with a salesperson at a computer, and design a car custom-made to his or her specifications. Any product information the customer wants is available online, and the salesperson assists customers in finding that information. Often, customers will have searched the Internet to determine what car they want and will have explored most of the options. So what is the role of the salesperson? As in B2B selling, the role of the salesperson is evolving to one of a consultant, that is, one who provides such helpful assistance that the customer feels it is worthwhile to go to the dealership to get help. That means that the salesperson will have to be computer proficient and be able to walk the customer quickly and easily through the whole exchange process—which includes not only getting financing, license plates, and insurance but also ensuring prompt delivery at the customer's convenience.

There will always be a need for the kind of salesperson who directs people to the proper place to find things, discusses product features, and helps buyers complete the sales process. But such salespeople will be fewer and will get paid much less than consultative salespeople who can use computers and other technology to help customers find and buy things quickly.

HOW ARE WE DOING?
STARBUCKS COFFEE
At Starbucks, we work passionately to bring you an enjoyable experience and want to know if we are meeting your expectations. Please take a few moments to share your thoughts with us. Your feedback will help us serve you better.
SKU 144494

Marketers try hard to please you, but they don't always know what you're thinking. You can help marketers to be more responsive to your preferences by filling out customer inquiry forms like this one from Starbucks. A minute of your time may make a significant difference in the service you get next time. Do you have friends who complain about poor products or services but are unwilling to provide businesses with feedback?

The Business-to-Consumer (B2C) Sales Process

Most sales to consumers take place in retail stores, where the role of the salesperson differs somewhat from that in B2B selling. In both cases, knowing the product comes first. However, in business-to-consumer (B2C) sales the salesperson does not have to do much prospecting or qualifying. Except in sales processes involving expensive products such as automobiles and furniture, during which salespeople may have to ask a few questions to qualify prospective customers before spending too much time with them, it is assumed that most people who come to the store are qualified to buy the merchandise.

Similarly, retail salespeople don't usually have to go through a preapproach step, although it is important to understand as much as possible about the type of people who shop at a given store. One thing for sure, though, is that a salesperson needs to focus on the customer and refrain from talking to fellow salespeople—or, worse, talking on the phone to friends—when customers are around.

The first formal step in the B2C sales process, then, is the approach. Too many salespeople begin with a line like "May I help you?" That is not a good opening because the answer too often is "No." A better approach is "What may I help you with?" or, simply, "How are you today?" The idea is to show the customer that you are there to help and that you are friendly and knowledgeable. Also, you need to discover what the customer wants.

According to what the customer tells you, you then make a presentation. You show customers how the products you have meet their needs. You answer questions that help them choose the products that are right for them. The more you learn about the customers' specific wants, the better you are able to help them choose the right product or products to meet those wants.

As in B2B selling, it is important to make a trial close. "Would you like me to put that on hold?" or "Will you be paying

FIGURE 16.6

STEPS IN THE BUSINESS-TO-CONSUMER (B2C) SELLING PROCESS

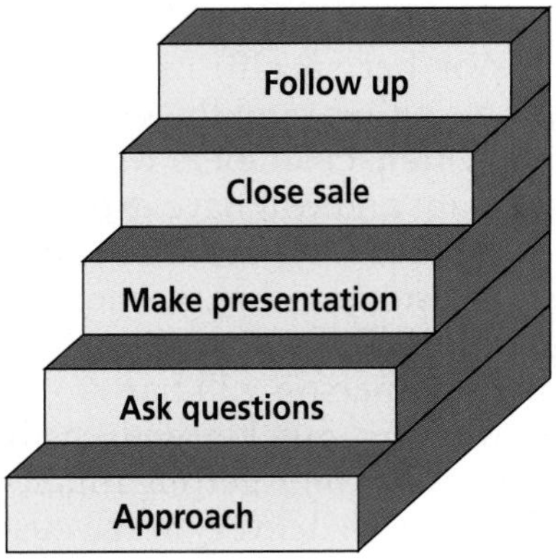

for that with your store credit card?" are two such efforts. A store salesperson walks a fine line between being helpful and being pushy. Selling is an art, and a salesperson must learn just how far to go. Often individual buyers need some time alone to think about the purchase. The salesperson must respect that need and give them time and space, but still be clearly available when needed.

After-sale follow-up is an important but often neglected step in B2C sales.[15] If the product is to be delivered, the salesperson should follow up to be sure it is delivered on time. The same is true if the product has to be installed. There is often a chance to sell more merchandise when a salesperson follows up on a sale. Figure 16.6 shows the whole B2C selling process. You can compare that figure to the seven-step process we outlined earlier for B2B selling.

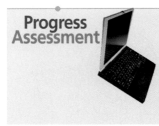

Progress Assessment

- What are the four traditional elements of the promotion mix?
- What are the three most important advertising media in order of dollars spent?
- What are the seven steps in the B2B selling process?
- What is a consultative salesperson?

Public Relations: Building Relationships

public relations (PR)
The management function that evaluates public attitudes, changes policies and procedures in response to the public's requests, and executes a program of action and information to earn public understanding and acceptance.

Public relations (PR) is defined as the management function that evaluates public attitudes, changes policies and procedures in response to the public's requests, and executes a program of action and information to earn public understanding and acceptance. In other words, a good public relations program has three steps:

1. **Listen to the public.** Public relations starts with good marketing research ("evaluates public attitudes").
2. **Change policies and procedures.** Businesses don't earn understanding by bombarding the public with propaganda; they earn understanding by having programs and practices in the public interest. The best way to learn what the public wants is to listen to people often—in different forums, including on the Internet.
3. **Inform people that you're being responsive to their needs.** It's not enough to simply have programs in the public interest. You have to tell the public about those programs so that they know you're being responsive.

Public relations demands a dialogue with customers so that information can be exchanged over time and trust can be developed through responsiveness.[16] Customers today often complain that it is hard to find someone to talk to in a firm. They may spend literally hours on the phone going through automated choices, waiting, and not being satisfied. In desperation, they often call the PR department. In the past, the PR department sent such callers off to someone else in a long and futile chase for someone to handle the problem. Today, however, PR is taking a much more active role in listening to consumers and working with them to handle problems.[17] That means that PR must establish good relationships with production and service people so they can find answers to customer questions quickly.

PR is becoming so critical to a firm's success that many small companies cannot find a PR firm with which to work—most are too busy with large firms. The U.S. Bureau of Labor Statistics reports that PR has become one of the three fastest-growing industries in the country. One firm that has had huge success because of PR is Yahoo. It began its PR campaign when the World Wide Web was just starting to open the Internet to the general public (not just academics) in the early 1990s. The idea was to get stories in the media about the growing importance of the Internet. The second phase of the PR campaign came before Yahoo sold any stock. The idea then was to use the media to promote the head of the company, Tom Koogle, and his professionalism. If investors had not been assured that Yahoo had a good business model, it would not have been able to sell much stock to first-time buyers. Once the company got started, the goal of PR was to show Yahoo as a major Internet company, the equivalent of America Online. Then the goal was to show that Yahoo was as important to Internet commerce as it was in Internet communications. Much of the success of Yahoo, then, is directly attributable to its long-term PR strategy.

It is the responsibility of the PR department to maintain close ties with the media, community leaders, government officials, and other corporate stakeholders ➤P. 6◄. The idea is to establish and maintain a dialogue with all stakeholders so that the company can respond to inquiries, complaints, and suggestions quickly.[18]

Critical Thinking

What kinds of problems can emerge if a firm doesn't communicate with environmentalists, the news media, and the local community? In your area have you seen examples of firms that aren't responsive to the community? What have been the consequences?

Publicity: The Talking Arm of PR

Publicity is the talking arm of public relations. It is one of the major functions of almost all organizations. Here's how it works: Suppose that you want to introduce your new Fiberrific cereal to consumers but you have very little money to promote it. You need to get some initial sales to generate funds. One effective way to reach the public is through publicity. **Publicity** is any information about an individual, product, or organization that's distributed to the public through the media and that's not paid for, or controlled by, the seller. You might prepare a publicity release describing Fiberrific and the research findings supporting its benefits, and send it to the various media. Much skill is involved in writing such releases so that the media will want to publish them. You may need to write different stories for different media. If the stories are published, release of the news about Fiberrific will reach many potential consumers (and investors, distributors, and dealers), and you may be on your way to becoming a wealthy marketer.

publicity
Any information about an individual, product, or organization that's distributed to the public through the media and that's not paid for or controlled by the seller.

Publicity works only if the media find the material interesting or newsworthy. The idea, then, is to write publicity that meets those criteria. Gillette,

Few new products are able to get the publicity that Dean Kamen received with his Segway. Even the president of the United States tried it—and fell! Kamen is shown here demonstrating the Segway on *Good Morning America* the day it was introduced. How important is early and widespread consumer awareness to new products like the Segway?

for example, used publicity to launch its Sensor and Mach III razors.[19] Dean Kamen got a huge amount of publicity for his motorized scooter, the Segway Human Transporter. There were articles in newspapers and magazines and news clips on TV shows in every city. Sales have been slow, but not because people haven't heard of the scooter.[20] Besides being free, publicity has several further advantages over other promotional tools, such as advertising. For example, publicity may reach people who wouldn't read an ad. It may appear on the front page of a newspaper or in some other prominent position, or be given air time on a television news show. Perhaps the greatest advantage of publicity is its believability. When a newspaper or magazine publishes a story as news, the reader treats that story as news—and news is more believable than advertising. That's why Gardenburger and other companies that sell soybean products have been so intent on sending out publicity releases about their health benefits.

There are several disadvantages to publicity as well. For example, marketers have no control over how, when, or if the media will use the story. The media aren't obligated to use a publicity release, and most are thrown away. Furthermore, the story may be altered so that it's not so positive. There's good publicity (IBM comes out with a new supercomputer) and bad publicity (Firestone tires cause accidents). Also, once a story has run, it's not likely to be repeated. Advertising, in contrast, can be repeated as often as needed. One way to see that publicity is handled well by the media is to establish a friendly relationship with media representatives, being open with them when they seek information. Then, when you want their support, they're more likely to cooperate.

Progress Assessment

- What are the three steps involved in setting up a public relations program?
- What are the advantages and disadvantages of publicity versus advertising?

Sales Promotion: Getting a Good Deal

sales promotion
The promotional tool that stimulates consumer purchasing and dealer interest by means of short-term activities.

Sales promotion is the promotional tool that stimulates consumer purchasing and dealer interest by means of short-term activities. These activities include such things as displays, trade shows and exhibitions, event sponsorships, and contests. Figure 16.7 lists some B2B sales promotion techniques. For consumer sales promotion activities, think of those free samples of products that you get in the mail, the cents-off coupons that you clip from newspapers, the contests that various retail stores sponsor, and the prizes in Cracker Jack boxes (see Figure 16.8). Sales promotion programs are designed to supplement personal selling, advertising, and public relations efforts by creating enthusiasm for the overall promotional program. There was a big increase in such promotions as the 21st century began, especially online.

Trade shows	Catalogs
Portfolios for salespeople	Conventions
Deals (price reductions)	

FIGURE 16.7

BUSINESS-TO-BUSINESS SALES PROMOTION TECHNIQUES

Coupons	Bonuses (buy one, get one free)
Cents-off promotions	Catalogs
Sampling	Demonstrations
Premiums	Special events
Sweepstakes	Lotteries
Contests	In-store displays

FIGURE 16.8

CONSUMER SALES PROMOTION TECHNIQUES

Sales promotion can take place both internally (within the company) and externally (outside the company). Often it's just as important to generate employee enthusiasm about a product as it is to attract potential customers. The most important internal sales promotion efforts are directed at salespeople and other customer-contact people, such as complaint handlers and clerks. Internal sales promotion efforts include (1) sales training; (2) the development of sales aids such as flip charts, portable audiovisual displays, and videotapes; and (3) participation in trade shows where salespeople can get leads. Other employees who deal with the public may also be given special training to improve their awareness of the company's offerings and make them an integral part of the total promotional effort.

After generating enthusiasm internally, it's important to get distributors and dealers involved so that they too are eager to help promote the product. Trade shows are an important sales promotion tool because they allow marketing intermediaries to see products from many different sellers and make comparisons among them. Today, virtual trade shows—trade shows on the Internet—enable buyers to see many products without leaving the office. Furthermore, the information is available 24 hours a day, seven days a week.

After the company's employees and intermediaries have been motivated with sales promotion efforts, the next step is to promote to final consumers using samples, coupons, cents-off deals, displays, store demonstrations, premiums, contests, rebates, and so on. Sales promotion is an ongoing effort to maintain enthusiasm, so different strategies must be used over time to keep the ideas fresh.

sampling
A promotional tool in which a company lets consumers have a small sample of a product for no charge.

This International Manufacturing Trade Show in Chicago featured 4,000 booths, giving buyers for other businesses thousands of new products to explore and purchase. Can you see why trade shows in many industries are an efficient and necessary way to stay abreast of the latest developments, your competitors, and consumer reactions and needs?

Sampling Is a Powerful Sales Promotion Tool

One popular sales promotion tool is **sampling**—letting consumers have a small sample of the product for no charge. Because many consumers won't buy a new product unless they've had a chance to see it or try it, grocery stores often have people standing in the aisles handing out small portions of food and beverage products. Sampling is a quick, effective way of demonstrating a product's superiority at the time when consumers are making a purchase decision.

Pepsi introduced its FruitWorks product line with a combination of sampling, event marketing, and a new website. *Event marketing* means sponsoring events such as rock concerts or being at various events to promote your products. In the case of FruitWorks, Pepsi first sent samples to Panama City, Florida, and South Padre Island, Texas, for spring break. Students got free rides on Pepsi trucks and samples of the drinks. Similar sampling and event marketing efforts had been successful for SoBe (herbal-fortified drinks) and Snapple (fruit drinks and iced teas).

Word of Mouth

word-of-mouth promotion
A promotional tool that involves people telling other people about products they've purchased.

Although word of mouth is not normally listed as one of the major promotional efforts, it is often one of the most effective tools and is becoming recognized as such because Internet word of mouth can reach so many people so easily. In **word-of-mouth promotion**, people tell other people about products that they've purchased. The success of movies such as *My Big Fat Greek Wedding* and *Bend It Like Beckham* were largely due to word-of-mouth promotion among friends.[21] Anything that encourages people to talk favorably about an organization may be effective word of mouth. Notice, for example, how stores use clowns, banners, music, fairs, and other attention-getting devices to create word of mouth. Clever commercials can also generate much word of mouth. The whole idea is to get more and more people talking about your products and your brand name so that customers remember them when they go to buy things.

Viral Marketing and Other Word-of-Mouth Strategies

A number of companies have begun creating word of mouth by paying people to promote their products to others. One such strategy encourages people to go into Internet chat rooms and hype (or talk enthusiastically and favorably about) bands, movies, video games, and sports teams.[22] People who agree to hype products in this way may get what the industry calls *swag*—free tickets, backstage passes, T-shirts, and other such merchandise. What do you think of the ethics of paying ordinary people to promote goods and services?

viral marketing
The term now used to describe everything from paying people to say positive things on the Internet to setting up multilevel selling schemes whereby consumers get commissions for directing friends to specific websites.

Viral marketing is the term now used to describe everything from paying people to say positive things on the Internet to setting up multilevel selling schemes whereby consumers get commissions for directing friends to specific websites. Here is how Barnes & Noble does it: You send your friends an e-mail that tells them how much you enjoyed reading a certain book and gives them a link to the Barnes & Noble website. If they follow the link and buy a book, you get a 5 percent commission.

Lee Jeans successfully used viral marketing in its promotions featuring brand icon Buddy Lee. Sales went up 13 percent. In the boating world, word of mouth is huge. It made Boats.com a leader in the field.[23]

One especially effective strategy for spreading positive word of mouth is to send testimonials (remember, these are letters or statements from customers praising a product) to current customers. Most companies use testimonials only in promoting to new customers, but testimonials are also effective in confirming customers' belief that they chose the right company. Positive word of mouth from other users further confirms their choice. Therefore, some companies make it a habit to ask customers for referrals.

It is important to note also that negative word of mouth can hurt a firm badly. Taking care of consumer complaints quickly and effectively is one of the best ways to reduce the effects of negative word of mouth. Today, negative word of mouth can spread faster than ever before. Online forums, chat rooms, bulletin boards, and websites can all be used as means to spread criticism about a product or company. For example, a company angered by insensitive customer service on the part of a major express company posted its complaints on the Internet and thus triggered a chorus of agreements that business managers worldwide read.

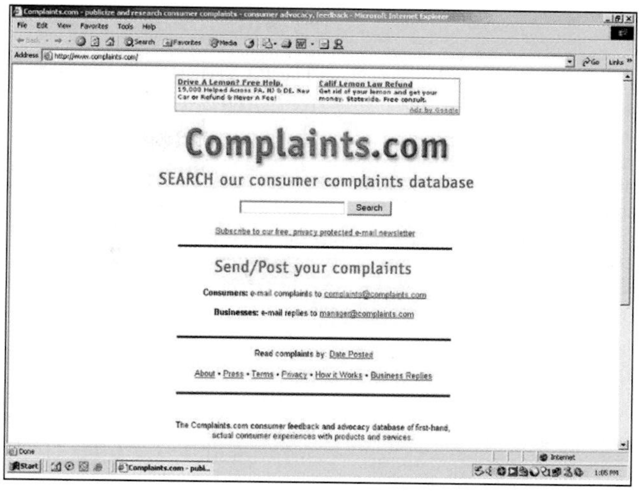

Abuse or mistreat your customers and you and your business may be the one who ultimately gets burned. Thanks to a number of websites like Complaints.com, consumers now have an option to get even, and get even they do. Have you ever consulted one of these sites before buying from or doing business with unfamiliar companies?

How New Technologies Are Affecting Promotion

As people purchase goods and services on the Internet, companies keep track of those purchases and gather other facts and figures about those consumers. Over time, companies learn who buys what, when, and how often. They can then use that information to design catalogs and brochures specifically designed to meet the wants and needs of individual consumers as demonstrated by their actual purchasing behavior. So, for example, a flower company may send you a postcard first reminding you that your spouse's birthday is coming up soon and that you bought a particular flower arrangement last time, and then recommending a new arrangement this time. Because so much information about consumers is now available, companies are tending to use the traditional promotional tools (e.g., advertising) less than before and are putting more money into direct mail and other forms of direct marketing, including catalogs and the Internet. Consumers are reacting favorably to such promotions, so you can expect the trend toward direct sales and Internet sales to accelerate. Promotional programs will change accordingly.

New technology offers consumers a continuous connection to the Internet and enables marketers to send video files and other data to them faster than ever before. Using such connections, marketers can interact with consumers in real time. As you have read in this chapter, that means that you can talk with a salesperson online and chat with other consumers about their experiences with products and services. You can also search the Net for the best price and find any product information you may want in almost any form you want—copy, sound, video, or whatever.

Such technology gives a great deal of power to consumers like you. You no longer have to rely on advertising or other promotions to learn about products. You can search the Net on your own and find as much information as you want, when you want it. If the information is not posted, you can request it and get it immediately. Thus, promotion has become much more interactive than ever before.

Managing the Promotion Mix: Putting It All Together

Each target group calls for a separate promotion mix. For example, large, homogeneous groups of consumers (i.e., groups whose members share specific similar traits) are usually most efficiently reached through advertising. Large organizations are best reached through personal selling. To motivate people to buy now rather than later, sales promotion efforts such as sampling, coupons, discounts, special displays, premiums, and so on may be used. Publicity adds support to the other efforts and can create a good impression among all consumers. Word of mouth is often the most powerful promotional tool and is generated effectively by listening, being responsive, and creating an impression worth passing on to others.

Promotional Strategies

push strategy
Promotional strategy in which the producer uses advertising, personal selling, sales promotion, and all other promotional tools to convince wholesalers and retailers to stock and sell merchandise.

pull strategy
Promotional strategy in which heavy advertising and sales promotion efforts are directed toward consumers so that they'll request the products from retailers.

There are two key ways to facilitate the movement of products from producers to consumers. The first is called a push strategy. In a **push strategy**, the producer uses advertising, personal selling, sales promotion, and all other promotional tools to convince wholesalers and retailers to stock and sell merchandise. If the push strategy works, consumers will then walk into a store, see the product, and buy it. The idea is to push the product through the distribution system to the stores.

A second strategy is called a pull strategy. In a **pull strategy**, heavy advertising and sales promotion efforts are directed toward consumers so that they'll request the products from retailers. If the pull strategy works, consumers will go to the store and order the products. Seeing the demand for the products, the store owner will then order them from the wholesaler. The wholesaler, in turn, will order them from the producer. Products are thus pulled down through the distribution system. When movie producers keep advertising new films on TV, they use a pull strategy, hoping that viewers will ask for those movies at movie theaters.

Dr Pepper has used TV advertising in a pull strategy to increase distribution. Tripledge, a maker of windshield wipers, also tried to capture the interest of retail stores through a pull strategy. Of course, a company could use both push and pull strategies at the same time in a major promotional effort. The latest in pull and push strategies are being conducted on the Internet, with companies sending messages to both consumers and businesses.

It is important to make promotion part of a total systems approach to marketing. That is, promotion should be part of supply-chain management ➤P. 477◀. In such cases, retailers would work with producers and distributors to make the supply chain as efficient as possible. Then a promotional plan would be developed for the whole system. The idea would be to develop a total product offer that would appeal to everyone: manufacturers, distributors, retailers, and consumers.

Creating an Integrated Marketing Communication (IMC) System

As we noted at the start of this chapter, an integrated marketing communication (IMC) system is a formal mechanism for uniting all the promotional efforts in an organization to make them more consistent with each other and more responsive to that organization's customers and other stakeholders.[24] That includes the latest in Internet communications and interactive tools. The result is a unified image of the company in the public's mind. In the past, advertising was created by ad agencies, public relations was created by PR firms, and selling was done in-house. There was little coordination across promotional efforts. As a result, consumers often received conflicting messages about a company and its products.[25] For example, TV advertising may have emphasized quality while the sales promotion people were pushing couponing and discounting. Such conflicting images aren't as effective as a unified image created by multiple promotional means.

Today, more and more companies are trying to create an integrated approach to promotion. Ad agencies are buying direct marketing companies so that they can offer an integrated approach. To implement an IMC system, you start by gathering data about customers and stakeholders and their information needs. Gathering such data and making that information available to everyone in the value chain is a key to future marketing success. All messages reaching customers, potential customers, and other stakeholders would be consistent and coordinated (see Figure 16.9).

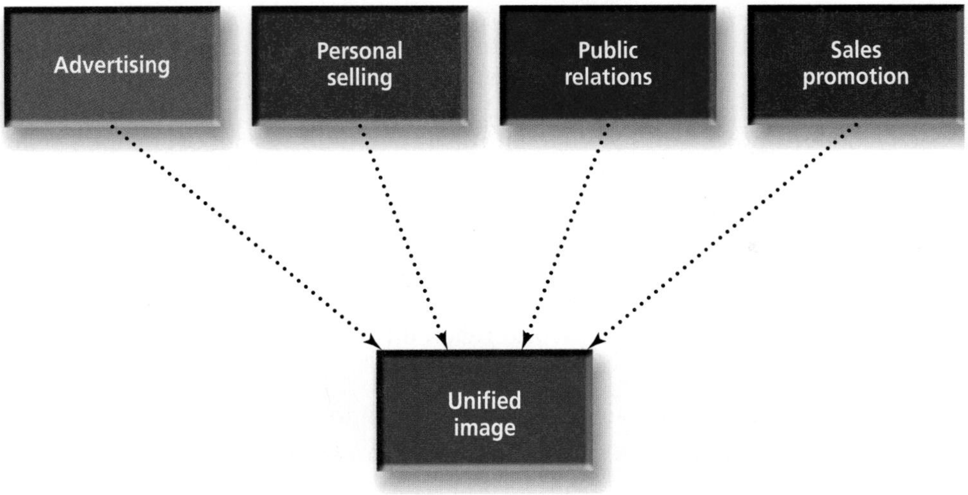

FIGURE 16.9

INTEGRATED MARKETING COMMUNICATION

Building Interactive Marketing Programs

Earlier in this chapter, we described interactive promotion as an exchange between buyers and sellers. Thus, an **interactive marketing program** is one where consumers can access company information on their own and supply information about themselves in an ongoing dialogue. Here are the basic steps for implementing such a program:

interactive marketing program
A system in which consumers can access company information on their own and supply information about themselves in an ongoing dialogue.

1. Constantly gather data about the groups affected by the organization (including customers, potential customers, and other stakeholders) and keep that information in a database ➤P. 17◄. Make the data available to everyone in the value chain. An up-to-date, easily accessible database is critical to any successful program. Today, a company can gather data from sales transactions, letters, e-mail, and faxes. It may also turn to a company that specializes in gathering such data.
2. Respond quickly to customer and other stakeholder information by adjusting company policies and practices and by designing wanted products and services for target markets. A responsive firm adapts to changing wants and needs quickly and captures the market from other, less responsive firms. That's why information is so vital to organizations today and why so much money is spent on computers and information systems. You can also see how important it is for the marketing department to work closely with the information systems department and other departments in the firm to make the process of ordering and delivering goods fast and smooth.
3. Make it possible for customers and potential customers to obtain the information they need to make a purchase. Then make it easy for people to buy your products in stores or from the company directly by placing an order through e-mail, fax, phone, or other means.

The advantages of interactive marketing on the Internet include the fact that information is available 24 hours a day, seven days a week; that ads and catalogs can be updated continually; that buyers and sellers can engage in a dialogue over time; and that it can be used by small as well as large companies.

This is an exciting time to study promotion and marketing in general. Changes are happening daily, and you and your friends will find it easier and easier to purchase whatever you want. Now you may read ads on your cellular phone or portable computer and order products immediately with just a push of a button.

Critical Thinking

How much of your buying behavior has moved from stores to the Internet? If you don't actually buy things on the Internet, do you use it to compare goods and prices? Do you or your friends take advantage of the low prices on used goods from eBay? Do you see yourself turning to the Internet over time for an increasing number of purchases? Why or why not?

Progress Assessment

- What are the sales promotion techniques used to reach consumers? What promotion techniques are used to reach businesses?
- What is viral marketing?
- Describe how to implement a push strategy and a pull strategy.
- What are the three steps used in setting up an interactive marketing communication system?

Summary

1. Define *promotion* and list the four traditional tools that make up the promotion mix.

1. Promotion is an effort by marketers to inform and remind people in the target market about products and to persuade them to participate in an exchange.
   - ***What are the four traditional promotional tools that make up the promotion mix?***

   The four traditional promotional tools are advertising, personal selling, public relations, and sales promotion. The product itself can be a promotional tool: that's why it is shown in the middle of Figure 16.1.

2. Define *advertising* and describe the advantages and disadvantages of various advertising media, including the Internet.

2. Advertising is limited to paid, nonpersonal (not face-to-face) communication through various media by organizations and individuals who are in some way identified in the advertising message.
   - ***What are the advantages of using the various media?***

   You can review the advantages and disadvantages of the various advertising media in Figure 16.5.
   - ***Why the growing use of infomercials?***

   Infomercials are growing in importance because they show products in use and present testimonials to help sell goods and services.
   - ***What are the dangers of using global advertising?***

   Some words and concepts simply don't go over well in other countries. Examples include Pocari Sweat from Japan and Krapp toilet paper from Sweden. In general, it is best to adapt ads to the culture of each country. It is even better to adapt ads to specific groups within each country.

3. Illustrate the steps of the B2B and B2C selling processes, and discuss the role of a consultative salesperson.

3. Personal selling is the face-to-face presentation and promotion of products and services. It also involves the search for new prospects and follow-up service after the sale.
   - ***What are the seven steps of the B2B selling process?***

   The steps of the selling process are (1) prospect and qualify, (2) preapproach, (3) approach, (4) make presentation, (5) answer objections, (6) close sale, and (7) follow up.
   - ***What are the steps in the B2C selling process?***

   The steps are the approach, which includes asking questions; the presentation, which includes answering questions; the closing; and the follow-up.

- ***What does a consultative salesperson do?***

A consultative salesperson begins by analyzing customer needs and then comes up with solutions to those needs. He or she does much more than make sales presentations. Such salespeople are truly business consultants who do things like develop intranets for clients.

4. Describe the role of the public relations department, and tell how publicity fits in that role.

4. Public relations (PR) is the function that evaluates public attitudes, changes policies and procedures in response to the public's requests, and executes a program of action and information to earn public understanding and acceptance.

- ***What are the three major steps in a good public relations program?***

(1) Listen to the public—public relations starts with good marketing research; (2) develop policies and procedures in the public interest—one doesn't earn understanding by bombarding the public with propaganda; rather, one earns understanding by having programs and practices in the public interest; and (3) inform people that you're being responsive to their needs.

- ***What is publicity?***

Publicity is the talking part of sales promotion; it is information distributed by the media that's not paid for, or controlled by, the seller. It's an effective way to reach the public. Publicity's greatest advantage is its believability.

5. Explain the importance of various forms of sales promotion, including sampling, word of mouth, and viral marketing, and tell how they are affected by new technologies.

5. Sales promotion motivates people to buy now instead of later, and word of mouth encourages people to talk about an organization and its products.

- ***How are sales promotion activities used both within and outside the organization?***

Internal sales promotion efforts are directed at salespeople and other customer-contact people to keep them enthusiastic about the company. Internal sales promotion activities include sales training, sales aids, audiovisual displays, and trade shows. External sales promotion (promotion to consumers) involves using samples, coupons, cents-off deals, displays, store demonstrators, premiums, and other such incentives.

- ***How is word of mouth being used in promotion today?***

A number of companies have begun creating word of mouth by paying individuals to promote products. Some pay people to go into Internet chat rooms and hype (talk enthusiastically and favorably about) bands, movies, video games, and sports teams. People who agree to hype products in this way get what the industry calls *swag*—free tickets, backstage passes, T-shirts, and other merchandise. *Viral marketing* is the term now used to describe everything from paying people to say positive things on the Internet to setting up multilevel selling schemes whereby consumers get commissions for directing friends to specific websites.

6. Describe integrated marketing communication and the role of interactive communications within it.

6. Marketers use various promotional strategies to move goods from producers to consumers.

- ***What are the various promotional strategies?***

In a push strategy, the producer uses advertising, personal selling, sales promotion, and all other promotional tools to convince wholesalers and retailers to stock and sell merchandise. In a pull strategy, heavy advertising and sales promotion efforts are directed toward consumers so that they'll request the products from retailers.

- ***How do you set up an integrated marketing communication system?***

An integrated marketing communication system consists of three ongoing parts: (1) Listen constantly to all groups affected by the organization, keep that information in a database, and make that information available to everyone in the organization; (2) respond quickly to customer and other stakeholder information by adjusting company policies and practices and by designing wanted products and services for target markets; and (3) use integrated marketing communication to let all customers and other stakeholders know that the firm is listening and responding to their needs.

- ***How do you set up interactive marketing programs?***

There are three steps in setting up an interactive marketing program: (1) Gather data constantly about the groups affected by the organization, (2) respond quickly to customer and other stakeholder information by adjusting company policies and practices and by designing wanted products and services for target markets, and (3) make it possible for customers and potential customers to obtain the information they need to make a purchase. Then make it easy for people to buy your products in stores or from the company directly by placing an order through e-mail, fax, phone, or other means.

Key Terms

advertising 491
consultative salesperson 500
infomercial 494
integrated marketing communication (IMC) 490
interactive marketing program 509
interactive promotion 495
personal selling 498
product placement 492
promotion 490
promotion mix 490
prospect 498
prospecting 498
public relations (PR) 502
publicity 503
pull strategy 508
push strategy 508
qualifying 498
sales promotion 504
sampling 505
trial close 499
viral marketing 506
word-of-mouth promotion 506

Developing Workplace Skills

1. Choose four ads from at least two different media—a newspaper, magazine, or any other medium—two that you consider good and two that you don't consider good. Be prepared to discuss why you feel as you do about each ad.

2. Scan your local newspaper for examples of publicity (stories about new products) and sales promotion (coupons, contests, sweepstakes). Share your examples and discuss the effectiveness of such promotional efforts with the class.

3. Many students shy away from careers in selling, often because they think that salespeople are dishonest or too pushy or need to be more outgoing than they are. Prepare a one-page document that discusses your experience with salespeople and what you think of selling as a career.

4. In small groups, discuss whether or not you are purchasing more goods using catalogs and/or the Internet and why. Do you look up information on the Internet before buying goods and services? How helpful are such searches? Present your findings to the class.

5. In small groups or individually, make a list of six products (goods and services) that most students own or use and then discuss which promotional techniques prompt you to buy these goods and services: advertising, personal selling, publicity, sales promotion, or word of mouth. Which tool seems to be most effective for your group? Why do you suppose that is?

Taking It To The Net 1

Purpose

To learn about online sales promotion efforts.

Exercise

Many marketers put coupons in magazines and newspapers. Some place tear-coupons in supermarket and other store displays. The latest in couponing is Internet placement. To find such sites, go to www.couponmountain.com and click on various links to explore what is available. Sometimes the best deal is to pay nothing at all. To check out free offers on the Internet, go to www.yesfree.com and explore what is available there.

1. Are you willing to register at these various sites to get free coupons faxed to you? Why or why not?
2. What could these websites do to become more user friendly for you and your friends?
3. Have you become more price conscious now that websites give so much competitive information about price and coupons for so many products that are readily available? Is that a good thing or not for marketers?
4. Integrated marketing communication efforts are designed to create a good image for a firm, one that is consistent. Do sites like these fit into such a scheme? Why or why not?

Taking It To The Net 2

Purpose

To evaluate the promotional effectiveness of two websites.

Exercise

A promotional website is more like a product than an advertisement; that is, it is more like a constantly changing magazine than a brochure. It should have an action-oriented design to pull consumers to the site and be set to move the consumer closer to a sale.

1. How well do the sites for Mountain Dew (www.mountaindew.com) and Rain Forest Café (www.rainforestcafe.com) use the Web to present their messages? Consider these criteria in evaluating the websites:
   a. Achieves marketing objectives (such as consumer awareness, image, trial, accelerating repurchase, attracting job candidates).
   b. Attracts target market.
   c. Is useful to target market.
   d. Is easy to navigate.
   e. Is graphically pleasing.
   f. Loads quickly.
2. Choose one of the websites and offer suggestions for improving the site.

Casing The Web

To access the case "Developing a Promotional Strategy for Biltmore Estate," visit

www.mhhe.com/ub7e

Video Case

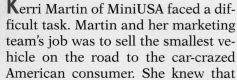

The Art of Motoring: MiniUSA

Kerri Martin of MiniUSA faced a difficult task. Martin and her marketing team's job was to sell the smallest vehicle on the road to the car-crazed American consumer. She knew that competition in the U.S. automobile market was intense, with market giants like General Motors and Ford spending enormous amounts each year on promotion. Her team decided it could compete best by integrating several promotional tools into one integrated program for the Mini. Their promotional tools included billboard advertising, brochures, publicity, sales promotion, personal selling, and more.

The idea for the Mini automobile is anything but new; the car was built in Europe over 40 years ago. Today's version is designed for a younger, more in-tune audience. As it turns out, the target audience is more diverse than just young people. Anyone from 16 to 60 may enjoy the look and feel of this new car. The company made it possible to custom-design the car online so that your Mini won't look like any other on the road. The carefully defined market is described as people who are successful but define success for themselves. They are tech-savvy and comfortable on the Web.

From the beginning of the marketing campaign, MiniUSA wanted to create one singular tone of voice to promote the new car. While competitors focused on "driving," Mini focused on "motoring." It even created a *Book of Motoring* that reached thousands through its website. The book stressed motoring habits like smiling at others and carrying jumper cables to help others in need. While SUV drivers guzzle gas, Mini owners sip theirs.

Mini did a prelaunch e-mail campaign. Mini stresses that you can track your car online from production to delivery. The best thing is the ability to "you-ify" your car: You can choose colors, decorations, hub caps, and other features that together make your car unique. Company promotion is done through booklets at auto shows and special promotions like a carsickness bag ad. Put simply, the whole promotional campaign is designed to be different and special.

Mini decided to put its advertising dollars into print ads and billboards rather than TV, as most other auto companies have done. Publicity was extensive; the car itself is so unique that TV shows, magazines, and other media were eager to picture the car and talk about it—for free. On publicity releases, emphasis was on safety, reliability, and value.

Personal selling techniques are also different for the Mini. Salespeople are called Mini-motoring advisers. Each adviser goes through extensive training before coming to work for the company. Training, however, does not end there. Brand-heavy training continues throughout a salesperson's employment. Dealerships have fun with customers, doing things like sponsoring a scavenger hunt for prizes. Since most customers have some familiarity with the car from their contact on the Internet, the dealer is able to spend more time listening to customers and responding to their needs.

Mini was chosen North American Car of the Year. It's a fun car backed with integrated marketing communication and creative marketing in general. Listening and responding to consumers, along with promotion, is all part of a marketing communication system (MCS) at Mini. The Mini culture is to respond quickly and, most important, let people know the company is listening and responding. You can learn more about the company and the car by going to www.miniUSA.com.

Thinking It Over

1. After watching this video, how would you rate Mini's job in promoting its product to the U.S. consumers? What do you think is the most effective part of the company's promotion program?
2. As part of the target market for the Mini, how would you respond to the firm's overall promotional effort? What else could Mini do that it is not doing now to get you as a buyer?
3. Do you think Mini has done a good job of listening to customers and responding appropriately? Can you think of any auto companies that listen and respond better?

Part 5

Fundamentals of Marketing

Career Portfolio

Marketing is a challenging and dynamic area in which to choose a career. The field is so varied that it can attract people with a tremendous variety of talents, skills, and interest areas. For example, a number-crunching person could choose marketing research; artistic individuals might be attracted to advertising or sales promotion; and entrepreneurial types might choose wholesaling or retailing. There are dozens of other combinations.

Marketing is based on the exchange of goods and services. Like every other area of business, it is dynamic and always changing, especially with the current emphasis on international markets. Anyone who wants to be involved in this exciting area must be able to change with the times as tastes for new products and services change and as new markets open and old ones close. Marketing is an area that remains wide open.

Skills

Although marketing draws on talents from a variety of personality types and skill areas, some realistic generalizations can be made about skills that most marketers have in common. Marketers need to be people oriented, even the number crunchers mentioned above. They also need to be tuned in to the culture of the country or region where they are marketing. They need to sense trends and changing habits of customers. Above all, they must be effective communicators, possessing an ability to be heard and noticed as well as to hear and notice the needs of others. The amount of education required varies widely from position to position, and even firm to firm.

Career Paths

Many marketing careers start out as sales positions. Sales is a challenging area in which individuals can prove themselves, using that success as a means of moving up to sales manager or other positions of responsibility. Advertising is another avenue of interest, especially for those who are attracted to the tantalizing mixture of psychology, communications, and art that advertisers use. Retailing also offers a variety of opportunities, some more marketing-oriented than others.

Not all positions in marketing require a four-year degree, although one is usually a formally stated prerequisite. In many companies, your skill level is the important issue. Marketing skills can often be developed in two-year business programs and in real-world experience. On-campus clubs such as Future Business Leaders of America (FBLA) and Distributive Education Clubs of America (DECA) can help you learn to compete in the world of marketing while still in school.

SOME POSSIBLE POSITIONS IN MARKETING				
JOB TITLE	**SALARY**	**JOB DUTIES**	**CAREER PATH**	**PROSPECTS**
Market researcher	$27,570–$96,360 Median: $51,190	Design surveys, opinion polls, and questionnaires; collect and analyze data using various methods.	Bachelor's degree with marketing courses. Upper-level positions often require a master's degree.	Faster than average growth through 2010.
Sales representative	$27,000–$100,000+ (depends both on the company and initiative of the individual).	Call on customers; fulfill needs; provide follow-up; sometimes deal with credit issues; report regularly to home office.	Training programs usually provided by company. Successful representatives are usually promoted to sales manager.	Slower than average growth through 2010.
Purchasing agent (buyer)	$25,650–$67,980 Median $41,370	Stay informed about buying opportunities; maintain good relations with company sales force. Maintain positive relations with suppliers.	Usually start out as buyer trainee or assistant buyer. Can be promoted to purchasing manager or merchandising manager.	Little or no growth through 2010.
Advertising manager	$27,840 to start Median $53,360	In large firms, oversee in-house media, creative, and account services.	Bachelor's degree is typically required for entry-level position in advertising.	Faster than average growth through 2010.
Public relations specialist	Median $39,580; senior $70,480	Build and maintain a good image for the company. Communicate the goals and purposes of the company to the public and stockholders, if any. Must be good writer and speaker and be comfortable in all areas of the mass media.	Advancement to management level can be slow, particularly in small firms. College degree with entry-level experience, usually gained through an internship. Many PR people started in some other career, such as journalism, but made this career move later. Can be promoted to management, often outside of public relations.	Faster than average growth through 2010.
Marketing manager	Varies greatly	Identify potential markets and determine demand for products or services. Develop the firm's marketing strategy.	Bachelor's or master's degree preferred, particularly with emphasis in marketing. Work in certain industries may require special training.	Faster than average growth through 2010, especially in areas of international and high-tech marketing.

Source: Bureau of Labor Statistics, *Occupational Outlook Handbook*, 2002–03.

TBC Corporation

Name: Gregory V. Ortega

Age: 32

Position/Title: Strategic Marketing Manager

Salary Range: $90,000–$125,000

Major factors in the decision to take this position: Moving to a position at corporate headquarters in Memphis, TN, is allowing me to obtain a broader perspective of our total business and better prepare me for a senior management position at one of our subsidiary companies in the future.

Job description: I coordinate and direct all of our product planning and marketing, and formulate all of our Strategic Product plans. My responsibilities include new-product development, as well as line and brand management.

Career path: Right after college I looked for the best company I could find that would help me build a solid foundation of sales training. I started with the Gallo Wine Company and while it was an entry-level position, the experience and training I gained there benefit me to this day. I then switched industries and obtained a more senior sales position at one of my current company's subsidiary companies. There I managed a sales territory in Southern California and Arizona. Within two years I was promoted to subsidiary headquarters in Denver, CO. During my short stay in Denver, I led several technology projects, including the development of a company website and Extranet www.bigotires.com. A year later I was promoted to TBC headquarters in Memphis, TN.

Best part of your job: The best part of my job is identifying a new market opportunity, bringing that product to market, and watching it grow and contribute to our company's strategic plans.

Educational background: Associate's degree from Riverside City College; bachelor's degree in business administration/marketing from California State University–San Bernardino; MBA in global management from the University of Phoenix.

Favorite course: My favorite courses were always marketing related, but I liked International Marketing best.

Best course for your career: Education is the key to opening up new opportunities. From there I think you need to be very flexible early in your career and seek out challenging new opportunities. Don't be afraid to work outside your major in the short term or to relocate to other parts of the country or departments/divisions within your current company. Take the big projects and work hard. I also think a couple of years in a sales position at a good company is invaluable. No matter what you do or where you go in your career, you are always selling something to someone, so you should learn to do it as professionally as possible.

Recommended by Jose Duran, Riverside Community College.

Chapter 17

Using Technology to Manage Information

Learning Goals

After you have read and studied this chapter, you should be able to

1. Outline the changing role of business technology.
2. List the steps in managing information, identify the characteristics of useful information, and discuss how data are stored and mined.
3. Compare the scope of the Internet, intranets, extranets, and virtual private networks as tools in managing information.
4. Review the hardware most frequently used in business, and outline the benefits of the move toward computer networks.
5. Classify the computer software most frequently used in business.
6. Evaluate the human resource, security, privacy, and stability issues in management that are affected by information technology.
7. Explain the importance of computer literacy and the career opportunities available to people with computing skills and experience.

Getting to Know W. Roy Dunbar of Eli Lilly

Not too long ago, a scientist toiling over a Bunsen burner in one of Eli Lilly's U.S. labs may have enjoyed an "Ah-ha!" moment only to be dragged down by days of researching the company's three different databases to see if other scientists in the mammoth pharmaceutical company had had similar insights about a substance. A greater problem than having to perform multiple searches was that the three different databases didn't store information under the same labels or registration numbers, so it wasn't always clear what Lilly knew or didn't know. For example, a researcher in Belgium might have registered the same substance as the one for which the U.S. scientist was searching—but under a different name or number. This could make the search for information feel like a hunt for a needle in a haystack and in the process slow discoveries to a walk instead of a run.

Well, needle-in-a-haystack searches may have been common at Lilly before W. Roy Dunbar became chief information officer (CIO) in 1999, but they sure aren't now. Dunbar, a Jamaican raised in England, led the information technology (IT) overhaul required to integrate the divergent databases into one smooth system. As a result, the time needed to conduct substance searches was reduced from days to minutes. His team did this by creating what he calls Lilly's Sample Identification Database, a system that registers and stores globally all Lilly compounds under a single digital name. This means that chemists can spend less time calculating and more time doing research. Dunbar's primary mission as CIO is to find new ways to use information technology to shrink the 10 to 15 years it takes to discover new drugs and to successfully deliver them to physicians and patients.

More difficult than replacing old computer systems are, first, getting the scientists to see the value of the new system and, second, getting them to use it. "Legacy behaviors [i.e., old behaviors] are as bad or worse than legacy systems," says Dunbar. "Systems are dumb and can be easily replaced. People are sentimental; they have reasons why they do what they do. And they can't be so easily replaced."

Dunbar found a way to nudge folks who were used to working in relative isolation on specific projects toward sharing information with outsiders. Of course, Dunbar didn't accomplish this feat single-handedly. He doubled his IT team to 2,700 specialists and devoted 600 of them to research and development (R&D). He hired people with dual degrees in computer science and biology or chemistry so that the IT workers could talk more credibly with the scientists. In fact, the communication between the IT team and the scientists was one of the keys to the success of the new technology adoption. "It's never just a question of putting the technology in place," says Dunbar. "I'm intensely focused on results," he says. "[I'm also] very keen on the human side—work really gets done by individuals." Scientists and IT techs met regularly to discuss resources and requirements. Programmers developed a prototype, and then the two sides figured out what had to happen for the new technology to work. All of this talking seems to be working. As more Lilly scientists hear about how the new technology supplies information 10 to 100 times faster, they are actually asking to be trained on the new systems.

"Storage is critical to the future of this industry, as the amount of sheer data that will be available to mine is growing exponentially by the day. Our ability to store it, mine it and access it all in a heartbeat is at the core of our present and future ability to compete."

One of the big challenges in the evolution of information technology is to build the data storage needed to manage all of the new information, and not to simply create data landfills. The challenge is to use IT not only to get more information faster but to get better information as well. Dunbar says: "Storage is critical to the future of this industry, as the amount of sheer data that will be available to mine is growing exponentially by the day. Our ability to store it, mine it and access it all in a heartbeat is at the core of our present and future ability to compete."

Sources: Stephanie Overby, "They Want a New Drug," *CIO*, October 15, 2002, pp. 73–79; Mark D. Uehling, "The Pharma Prophecies," *Bio-IT World*, April 7, 2002; and Perry Glasser, "Eli Lilly: Speedy Recover," *CIO Insight*, October 10, 2002.

The Role of Information Technology

Throughout this text, we have emphasized the need for managing information flows among businesses and their employees, businesses and their suppliers, businesses and their customers, and so on. Since businesses are in a constant state of change, those managers who try to rely on old ways of doing things will simply not be able to compete with those who have the latest in technology and know how to use it.

data processing (DP) Name for business technology in the 1970s; included technology that supported an existing business and was primarily used to improve the flow of financial information.

information systems (IS) Technology that helps companies do business; includes such tools as automated teller machines (ATMs) and voice mail.

information technology (IT) Technology that helps companies change business by allowing them to use new methods.

Business technology has often changed names and roles. In the 1970s, business technology was known as **data processing (DP).** (Although many people use the words *data* and *information* interchangeably, they are different. Data are raw, unanalyzed, and unorganized facts and figures. Information is the processed and organized data that can be used for managerial decision making.) DP was used to support an existing business; its primary purpose was to improve the flow of financial information. DP employees tended to be hidden in a back room and rarely came in contact with customers.

In the 1980s, business technology became known as **information systems (IS).** IS moved out of the back room and into the center of the business. Its role changed from supporting the business to doing business. Customers began to interact with a wide array of technological tools, from automated teller machines (ATMs) to voice mail. As business increased its use of information systems, it became more dependent on them.

Until the late 1980s, business technology was just an addition to the existing way of doing business. Keeping up-to-date was a matter of using new technology on old methods. But things started to change as the 1990s approached. Businesses shifted to using new technology on new methods. Business technology then became known as **information technology (IT),** and its role became to change business.

Obviously, the role of the information technology staff has changed as the technology itself has evolved. The chief information officer (CIO) has moved out of the back room and into the boardroom. Because improved hardware and software keep computers running more smoothly than in the past, the average CIO can spend less time worrying about keeping the systems running and more time finding ways to use technology to boost business by participating in purchasing decisions, operational strategy, even marketing and sales. Today the role of the CIO is to help the business use technology to communicate better with others while offering better service and lower costs.[1]

Thirteenth-century Italian village Colletta di Castelbianco found a new lease on life when an architect gave it a new design and high-speed Internet connectivity. The village is now a haven for mobile knowledge workers who want to live in medieval Italy but remain connected to the rest of the world. Do you think such "televillages" could become a model for future communities?

How Information Technology Changes Business

Time and place have always been at the center of business. Customers had to go to the business during certain hours to satisfy their needs. We went to the store to buy clothes. We went to the bank to arrange for a loan. Businesses decided when and where we did business with them. Today, IT allows businesses to deliver goods ➤P. 25◄ and services ➤P. 26◄ whenever and wherever it is convenient for the customer. Thus, you can order clothes from the Home Shopping Network, arrange a home mortgage loan by phone or computer, or buy a car on the Internet at any time you choose.

Consider how IT has changed the entertainment industry. If you wanted to see a movie 35 years ago, you had to go to a movie theater. Thirty years ago you could wait for it to be on television. Twenty years ago you could wait for it to be on cable television. Fifteen years ago you could go to a video store and rent it. Now you can order video on demand by satellite or cable, or download the movie over the Internet.[2]

As IT breaks time and location barriers, it creates organizations and services that are independent of location. For example, the NASDAQ and the SOFFEX are electronic stock exchanges without trading floors. Buyers and sellers make trades by computer.

Being independent of location brings work to people instead of people to work. With IT, data and information can flow more than 8,000 miles in a second, allowing businesses to conduct work around the globe continuously. We are moving toward what is called **virtualization,** which is accessibility through technology that allows business to be conducted independently of location. For example, you can carry a virtual office in your pocket or purse. Such tools as cellular phones, pagers, laptop computers, and personal digital assistants allow you to access people and information as if you were in an actual office. Likewise, people who otherwise would not have met are forming virtual communities through computer networks.[3]

virtualization
Accessibility through technology that allows business to be conducted independent of location.

The way people do business drastically changes when companies increase their technological capabilities. Electronic communications can provide substantial time savings whether you work in an office, at home, or on the road. E-mail ends the tedious games of telephone tag and is far faster than paper-based correspondence.[4] Instant messaging (IM), best known as the preferred way for millions of teenagers to find out who likes whom, is now a favorite business real-time communication tool. For example, the first thing Steven Kamer does when he gets to work at Totality, a Web service company, is to turn on his laptop and see who else is logged on. Typically Kamer participates in half a dozen IM conversations at once through a cascade of pop-up windows. He might try to fix a hardware problem for a client in one window and agree to meet a colleague for lunch in another. (However, not everyone can tolerate the many interruptions that IM brings, so many people choose to keep IM turned off.)[5]

Internet and intranet communication using shared documents and other methods allow contributors to work on a common document without time-consuming meetings. The Dealing with Change box on p. 523 provides an example of how online collaboration can improve the productivity of meetings. See Figure 17.1 on p. 522 for other examples of how information technology changes business.

Moving from Information Technology toward Knowledge Technology

In the mid-1990s, yet another change occurred in the terminology of business technology as we started moving away from information technology and toward knowledge technology (KT). Knowledge is information charged with enough intelligence to make it relevant and useful. KT adds a layer of intelligence to filter appropriate information and deliver it when it is needed. For example, consider the number 70. Alone, it doesn't mean much. Change it to 70 percent and it means a little more but still doesn't tell us a lot. Make it a 70 percent chance of rain and we have more meaning.

FIGURE 17.1

HOW INFORMATION TECHNOLOGY IS CHANGING BUSINESS

This table shows a few ways that information technology is changing businesses, their employees, suppliers, and customers.

Organization	Technology is breaking down corporate barriers, allowing functional departments or product groups (even factory workers) to share critical information instantly.
Operations	Technology shrinks cycle times, reduces defects, and cuts waste. Service companies use technology to streamline ordering and communication with suppliers and customers.
Staffing	Technology eliminates layers of management and cuts the number of employees. Companies use computers and telecommunication equipment to create "virtual offices" with employees in various locations.
New products	Information technology cuts development cycles by feeding customer and marketing comments to product development teams quickly so that they can revive products and target specific customers.
Customer relations	Customer service representatives can solve customers' problems instantly by using companywide databases to complete tasks from changing addresses to adjusting bills. Information gathered from customer service interactions can further strengthen customer relationships.
New markets	Since it is no longer necessary for customers to walk down the street to get to stores, online businesses can attract customers to whom they wouldn't otherwise have access.

Now let's imagine that you are the first one on your block with a wristwatch featuring KT. As you walk out the door, the watch signals you that it has a message: "70 percent chance of rain in your city today." KT just gave you relevant and useful information at the moment you needed it. Now you can head for class with an umbrella under your arm, knowing that you made an informed decision.

KT changes the traditional flow of information; instead of an individual going to the database ➤P. 17◄, the data comes to the individual.[6] For example, using KT business training software, AT&T can put a new employee at a workstation and then let the system take over everything from laying out a checklist of the tasks required on a shift to answering questions and offering insights that once would have taken up a supervisor's time. Knowledge databases may one day replace the traditional mentors who helped workers up the corporate ladder.

KT "thinks" about the facts according to an individual's needs, reducing the time that person must spend finding and getting information. Businesspeople who use KT can focus on what's important: deciding about how to react to problems and opportunities.

The New Economy, in which technology is the key to growth, is based on brains, not brawn. The businesses that build flexible information infrastructures will have a significant competitive advantage. Constant changes in technology interact with each other to create more change. Maintaining the flexibility to successfully integrate these changes is crucial to business survival. History is filled with stories of once-mighty companies that couldn't keep up with the challenge of change: U.S. Steel, Packard Bell, and RCA once dominated their industries but failed to compete effectively and have lost market share. They had size and money, but not flexibility. Knowledge sharing is at the heart of keeping pace with change.

Dealing with Change www.webex.com

The Next Best Thing to Being There

In the days following September 11, 2001, countless U.S. businesses grounded many of their employees. Fear of flying as well as the need to cut costs drastically reduced the amount of face time between businesspeople and their out-of-town colleagues and clients—at least in-the-flesh face time, that is. Web conferencing has skyrocketed since 9/11 because the technology allows customers to see each other; talk; share PowerPoint presentations, animation, and video; and record and play back meetings—all from their own desks. In fact, one of the few technology companies to flourish since the dot-com bubble burst is the Web-conferencing services company WebEx. In 2002, WebEx's revenue climbed over 80 percent from a year earlier.

Some people might think that Web conferencing is a second choice, that if companies had unlimited time and money, they would choose face-to-face meetings first. Not always. For example, Texas Instruments (TI) found that virtual meetings not only reduce travel costs and save time but are also helpful in generating feedback from international participants. Some foreign participants find it easier to use the online chat feature that allows them to type in English, which they find easier than speaking it.

Even on a local level, many people are finding Web connectivity beneficial. If you've ever crowded around a PC screen with a few other people, you know how difficult it can be to see what is going on. It is much easier if everyone brings his or her own laptop to a meeting, makes a wireless connection, turns on WebEx, and gets a personal view. Not only can everyone see but everyone also shares control of the screen and can enter comments and revisions. When the meeting is over, everyone has the same version of the document and there is no confusion about what decisions were made. It looks like virtual work has finally become a business reality.

Sources: Olga Kharif, "Subrah Iyar and Min Zhu: Meetings on the Web," *Business Week,* October 1, 2002; and Timothy J. Mullaney, "Break Out the Black Ink," *Business Week,* May 13, 2002.

Critical Thinking

What information would you like to receive exactly when and where you need it? If you could design a system to provide this information, what might it look like and what would it do?

Progress Assessment

- How has the role of information technology changed since the days when it was known as data processing?
- How has information technology changed the way we do business?

MANAGING INFORMATION

Even before the use of computers, managers had to sift through mountains of information to find what they needed to help them make decisions. Today, businesspeople are deluged with information from voice mail, the Internet, fax machines, e-mail, and instant messaging. Businesspeople refer to this information overload as *infoglut*. Remember the classic episode of TV's *I Love Lucy* with Lucy and Ethel on the candy line? Everything was going OK until

"The employee handbook... Has anyone seen the freakin' employee handbook?"
CONQUER YOUR MOUNTAIN OF HR, BENEFITS AND PAYROLL PAPERWORK.
With Simpata℠, employees get the information they need when they need it from one central location – the Internet. It keeps information consistent, accurate and easily accessible 24/7, and gives you the tools to help keep your company compliant with employment laws. Bring your HR, Benefits and Payroll information together with a 100% Internet solution.
SIMPATA
Bring It All Together
Call 1-877-HR-SIMPLE
or visit www.nomountain.com
Copyright © 2000. Simpata logo and Bring It All Together are trademarks of Simpata, Inc. All rights reserved.

the candy started coming too fast for them. Then mayhem broke loose. That's what's happening to many managers today. Instead of candy, it is information that is passing by too quickly. Too much information can confuse issues rather than clarify them. How can managers keep from getting buried in the infoglut? Stepping back to gain perspective is the key to managing the flood of information.

The most important step toward gaining perspective is to identify the four or five key goals you wish to reach. Eliminating the information that is not related to those top priorities can reduce the amount of information flowing into your office by half. For example, as we were gathering information to include in this chapter, we collected over 500 journal articles. Feeling the pressure of information overload, we identified the goals we wanted the chapter to accomplish and eliminated all the articles that didn't address those goals. As we further refined our goals, the huge stack of paper gradually dropped to a manageable size.

Obviously, not all of the information that ends up on your desk will be useful. The usefulness of management information depends on four characteristics:

In times past, businesspeople faced the problem of finding useful information; today, the problem is dealing with infoglut, which can confuse issues rather than clarify them. How can you judge the usefulness of the information you access?

1. **Quality**. Quality means that the information is accurate and reliable. When the clerk at a fast-food restaurant enters your order into the cash register, it may be automatically fed to a computer, and the day's sales and profits can be calculated as soon as the store closes. The sales and expense data must be accurate, or the rest of the calculations will be wrong. This can be a real problem when, for example, a large number of calculations are based on questionable sales forecasts rather than actual sales.
2. **Completeness.** There must be enough information to allow you to make a decision but not so much as to confuse the issue. Today, as we have noted, the problem is often too much information rather than too little.
3. **Timeliness.** Information must reach managers quickly. If a customer has a complaint, that complaint should be handled instantly if possible and certainly within no more than one day. In the past, a salesperson would make a report to his or her manager; that report would go to a higher-level manager, and the problem would not be resolved for days, weeks, or months. E-mail, instant messaging, and other developments make it possible for marketing, engineering, and production to hear about a problem with a product the same day the salesperson hears about it. Product changes can be made on the spot using computer-integrated manufacturing, as discussed in Chapter 9.
4. **Relevance.** Different managers have different information needs. Again, the problem today is that information systems often make too much data available. Managers must learn which questions to ask to get the answers they need.

The important thing to remember when facing information overload is to relax. You can never read everything that is available. Set goals for yourself, and do the best you can. Remember, just because there is a public library doesn't mean you should feel guilty about not reading every book in it. And so it is with the information superhighway: You can't make every stop along the route, so plan your trip wisely and you're likely to get where you need to go.

Can a small firm look like an industry giant without spending giant sums of money? Bob Shallenberger of Rug World Oriental Rugs found a software program that specifically fit his firm's needs, for just a few thousand dollars. Due in part to the customer care the software allows, Rug World's annual revenues have grown from $350,000 to over $1 million. "If I want to know how many rugs I have from supplier X, and what I owe them, I can do it in 30 seconds."

Storing and Mining Data

It doesn't matter how interesting your information is if nobody's paying attention or can't get to the information they need when they need it. Storing, sorting, and getting useful information to the right people at the right time are the goals in managing information. How do businesses organize a data glut into useful information? The answer for many companies is a data warehouse. A *data warehouse* stores data on a single subject over a specific period of time.[7]

The whole purpose of a data warehouse is to get data out. *Data mining* is looking for hidden patterns in a data warehouse. Data mining software discovers previously unknown relationships among the data. The legendary example of data mining is a study by a retail chain that revealed a spike in beer sales coincided with a spike in diaper sales between 5 and 7 PM. The conclusion that thirsty dads pick up diapers on the way home from work prompted store managers to consider moving the diapers next to the beer to boost sales. The retail chain never did pair the Heineken with the Huggies, but the story led to a new science of tracking what's selling where and who's buying it.[8] Wal-Mart is the poster child for data mining. The retail giant has massive data warehouses that track sales on a minute-by-minute basis that can reveal regional and local sales trends. Using this information, Wal-Mart customizes each store's offerings on the basis of local demand, keeping it and its suppliers informed about how each of the 70,000 products in the stores is selling.[9]

The success of data mining depends on a number of factors, but perhaps the most important is access to data to mine in the first place. Frequently, organizations have a multitude of data storage systems that run on incompatible platforms. The divergent systems must be integrated in some way before the data can be connected. Such integration is possible today, but getting departments and divisions to hand over the keys to their data can be difficult.[10] The Dealing with Change box on p. 526 illustrates the importance of open information systems.

THE ROAD TO KNOWLEDGE: THE INTERNET, INTRANETS, EXTRANETS, AND VIRTUAL PRIVATE NETWORKS

The importance of business knowledge is nothing new—what is new is the recognition of the need to manage it like any other asset. To manage knowledge, a company needs to learn how to share information throughout the organization and to implement systems for creating new knowledge. This need is leading to new technologies that support the exchange of information among staff, suppliers, and customers. Who wins and who loses in the new economy www.homeland-directory.com

Dealing with Change

IT May Change Everything, but It Doesn't Cure All Ills

The United States may be able to produce more missiles and microwaves than any other country, but our global domination in mass production didn't mean much on September 11, 2001. Armed with low-tech box cutters, terrorists were able to hijack high-tech airlines and fly them into symbols of U.S. high-tech engineering, the World Trade Center and the Pentagon. Ironically, U.S. Special Forces had success in Afghanistan riding on the backs of borrowed horses and using air strikes by 50-year-old B-52 bombers.

Sure, both the United States and the terrorists had a long list of cutting-edge gadgetry, but the critical element for success was something more intangible than rockets and missiles: It was information. The terrorists' box cutters weren't their deadliest weapon on 9/11; it was their understanding of U.S. air transportation. Information technology made manuals and flight schedules readily available to them. Online access to news articles gave them enough information to know that U.S. aircrews are trained to collaborate with rather than confront hijackers in an effort to save passengers' lives. And it was information that allowed U.S. planners to coordinate missions over Afghanistan by way of Central Asian airstrips, aircraft carriers, and U.S. bases. Digital communications devices on the ground transmitted precise coordinates to bombers overhead. Global positioning system satellites in space steered the bombs to those coordinates. Without the information systems, U.S. forces could have been blindly blasting at mountaintops.

But it is not just information that makes the difference between a shot in the dark and a direct hit—it is getting the right information in the right hands at the right time. Obviously, it isn't a matter of having a lot of data. Anyone who has done a Web search knows that quantity of information isn't the key to meeting your goals. "Being submerged in data is not very productive," said Kenneth Watman, director of warfare analysis and research at the Naval War College in Newport, Rhode Island. "You've got to have some sort of intelligent scheme for putting things together."

And that's where the government falls short. There are countless local, state, and federal information networks, but they aren't linked to share information. For example, when Florida state police ticketed alleged terrorist ringleader Mohammed Atta for driving without a license in April 2001, they did not have access to federal intelligence information that would have told them he was on a CIA terrorist watch list. The 9/11 attacks gave new momentum to the call to pool information across government. The technology to do so exists, so what's the holdup? Resistance to change plays a big part. So does the jealous guarding of knowledge. Knowledge is power, and those who have power generally like to keep it. Moving to a more open information system requires both organizational and cultural change, and sometimes change is just too hard. Is the government ready to accept the challenge?

Sources: Sydney J. Freedberg, Jr., "Government: IT Changes Everything," *National Journal*, May 11, 2002; and Jim Krane, "Information Is U.S. Military's Most Lethal Weapon in Future Conflicts," AP Worldstream, February 19, 2002.

will be decided by who harnesses the technology that provides the pipeline of two-way interaction and information flow between individuals and organizations. At the heart of this technology are the Internet, intranets, extranets, and virtual private networks.

You already know that the Internet is a network of computer networks. (If you would like more detailed information about the Internet, you can refer back to the material called "Surfing the Internet" in the Getting Ready for Prime Time section at the beginning of the book.) Internet users can point and click their way from site to site with complete freedom. But what if you don't want just anybody to have access to your website? You might create an intranet.

intranet
A companywide network, closed to public access, that uses Internet-type technology.

An **intranet** is a companywide network, closed to public access, that uses Internet-type technology. To prevent unauthorized outsiders (particularly the competition) from accessing their sites, companies can construct a firewall between themselves and the outside world to protect corporate information from unauthorized users. A firewall can consist of hardware, software, or both.[11] Firewalls allow only authorized users to access the intranet. Some companies use intranets only to publish information for employees, such as phone lists

Neon HOT NOW signs signal us that Krispy Kreme's finest are ready. "Hot now" also describes the company's success. Still, Krispy Kreme leaves little to chance. The firm's Web portal keeps store managers in direct contact with headquarters. Forecasting, ordering, and inventory are all done online. Visit www.krispykreme.com.

and employee policy manuals. These companies do not enjoy as high a return on their investment as other companies that create interactive intranet applications. Such applications include allowing employees to update their addresses or submit company forms such as supply requisitions, timesheets, or payroll forms online. These applications save money or generate revenue increases because they eliminate paper handling and enable decision making. AmeriKing, the largest independent Burger King franchisee in the United States, estimates that it saves about a half a million dollars a year on printing and distribution costs for things such as physician directories, employee profiles, and employee contact information.[12]

Many businesses choose to open their intranets to other, selected companies through the use of extranets. An **extranet** is a semiprivate network that uses Internet technology and allows more than one company to access the same information or allows people on different servers to collaborate.[13] One of the most common uses of extranets is to extend an intranet to outside customers. Extranets change the way we do business. No longer are the advantages of electronic data interchange (EDI) available only to the large companies that can afford such a system. Now almost all companies can use extranets to share data and process orders, specifications, invoices, and payments. Cisco Systems completes 90 percent of its purchasing and sales contracts electronically. Cisco employee Brad Boston says that in the year after he joined the company, he signed only three pieces of paper: his employment contract, his tax return, and one contract with a Cisco supplier that insisted on having a hard copy.[14]

extranet
A semiprivate network that uses Internet technology and allows more than one company to access the same information or allows people on different servers to collaborate.

Notice that we described an extranet as a semiprivate network. This means that outsiders cannot access the network easily; but since an extranet does use public lines, knowledgeable hackers (people who break into computer systems for illegal purposes such as transferring funds from someone's bank account to their own without authorization) can gain unauthorized access. Most companies want a network that is as private and secure as possible. One way to increase the probability of total privacy is to use dedicated lines (lines reserved solely for the network). There are two problems with this method: (1) It's expensive, and (2) it limits use to computers directly linked to those lines. What if your company needs to link securely with another firm or individual for just a short time? Installing dedicated lines between companies in this case would be too expensive and time-consuming. Virtual private networks are a solution.

virtual private network (VPN)
A private data network that creates secure connections, or "tunnels," over regular Internet lines.

A **virtual private network (VPN)** is a private data network that creates secure connections, or "tunnels," over regular Internet lines.[15] The idea of the VPN is to give the company the same capabilities at much lower cost by using shared public resources rather than private ones. This means that companies no longer need their own leased lines for wide-area communication but can instead use public lines securely. Just as phone companies provide secure shared resources for voice messages, VPNs provide the same secure sharing of public resources for data. This allows for on-demand networking: An authorized user can join the network for any desired function at any time, for any length of time, while keeping the corporate network secure.

The Front Door: Enterprise Portals

How do users log on to an organization's network? Frequently, through an enterprise portal that centralizes information and transactions. Portals serve as entry points to a variety of resources, such as e-mail, financial records, schedules, and employment and benefits files. They can even include streaming video of the company's day care center. Portals are more than simply Web pages with links. They identify users and allow them access to areas of the intranet according to their roles: customers, suppliers, employees, and so on. They make information available in one place so that users don't have to deal with a dozen different Web interfaces. The challenge to the CIO is to integrate resources, information, reports, and so on—all of which may be in a variety of places—so that they appear seamless to the user.[16]

The ease of searching and navigating different information systems that is gained by having the information easily accessible in one place saves money as well as time. Compuware, a software developer, estimates that enterprise portals save each employee 30 minutes a day. That calculates to 125 hours an employee a year. Multiply that by the number of employees and the average hourly salary and you can see how much money a company can save.[17]

Broadband Technology

broadband technology
Technology that offers users a continuous connection to the Internet and allows them to send and receive mammoth files that include voice, video, and data much faster than ever before.

As traffic on the Internet increases, the slower the connection becomes. New technologies unlock many of the traffic jams on the information superhighway. For example, **broadband technology** offers users a continuous connection to the Internet and allows them to send and receive mammoth files that include voice, video, and data much faster than ever before. The more bandwidth, the bigger the pipe for data to flow through—and the bigger the pipe, the faster the flow. Whether the broadband connection is by cable modem, digital subscriber lines (DSL), satellite, or fixed wireless, the impact is much the same. With broadband, data can reach you more than 50 times faster than with a dial-up connection using a 56k modem (the kind that came with most computers in the late 1990s and early 2000s).[18] You may want to refer to Figure G.4 in the Getting Ready for Prime Time section at the beginning of the book for a comparison of the various bandwidth connections.

Even with broadband technology, the traffic on the information superhighway has become so intense that early Net settlers—scientists and other scholars—have found themselves being squeezed off the crowded Internet and thus unable to access, transmit, and manipulate complex mathematical models, data sets, and other digital elements of their craft. Their answer? Create another Internet, reserved for research purposes only.

Internet2
The new Internet system that links government supercomputer centers and a select group of universities; it runs more than 22,000 times faster than today's public infrastructure and supports heavy-duty applications.

The new system, **Internet2**, runs more than 22,000 times faster than today's public infrastructure and supports heavy-duty applications such as videoconferencing, collaborative research, distance education, digital libraries, and full-body simulations known as teleimmersion. A key element of Internet2 is a network called very-high-speed backbone network service (vBNS), which was set up in 1995 as a way to link government supercomputer centers and a select group of universities. The power of Internet2 makes it possible for a remote medical specialist to assist in a medical operation over the Internet without having to contend with deterioration of the connection as, say, home users check sports scores.[19]

Although Internet2 became available to only a few select organizations in late 1997, by 2002 there were more than 200 member universities.[20] Whereas the public Internet divides bandwidth equally among users (if there are 100 users, they each get to use 1 percent of the available bandwidth), Internet2 is more capitalistic. Users who are willing to pay more can use more bandwidth.

Cynics say that soon Internet 2 itself will be overrun by networked undergrads engaged in song swapping and other resource-hogging pursuits. But the designers of Internet2 are thinking ahead. Not only do they expect Internet history to repeat itself, but they are counting on it. They are planning to filter the Internet2 technology out to the wider Internet community in such a way that there is plenty of room on the road for all of us—at a price, of course.

THE ENABLING TECHNOLOGY: HARDWARE

We hesitate to discuss the advances that have been made in computer hardware because what is powerful as we write this may be obsolete by the time you read it. In the mid-1970s the chairman of Intel Corporation, Gordon E. Moore, predicted that the capacity of computer chips would double every year or so. This has since been called Moore's law.[21] The million-dollar vacuum-tube computers that awed people in the 1950s couldn't keep up with a pocket calculator today. In fact, a greeting card that plays "Happy Birthday" contains more computing power than existed before 1950.

The speed of evolution in the computer industry has slowed little since Moore's remark, although in 1997 Moore did say that his prediction cannot hold good for much longer because chip makers will sooner or later run into a fundamental law of nature, which is that the finite size of atomic particles will prevent infinite miniaturization. That, however, won't stop computer companies from improving chips in other ways than shrinking them.[22] Rapid advances make one product after another obsolete, helping create demand for newer chips. For example, a three-year-old personal computer is considered out-of-date. So rather than add potentially outdated facts to your information overload, we offer you a simple overview of the current computer technology.

Hardware includes computers, pagers, cellular phones, printers, scanners, fax machines, personal digital assistants (PDAs), and so on. The mobile worker can find travel-size versions of computers, printers, and fax machines that are almost as powerful and feature-laden as their big brothers. All-in-one devices that address the entire range of your communications needs are also available. For example, there are handheld units that include a wireless phone, fax and e-mail capabilities, Web browsers, and a personal information manager (PIM).

All of these tools are great—as long as they work. IBM is working on a solution to computer breakdowns with an approach called SMASH: simple,

There's the right tool for every job. Bigger isn't always better. The first step in choosing the right information technology tool is to identify what it is you want to accomplish and then go from there. For example, there is no need to invest in a screaming, state-of-the-art computer if you only plan to use it for simple word processing.

Love those theme parks but hate those lines? Universal Studios is dealing with the situation. Roaming ticket sellers armed with Wi-Fi-enabled devices and belt-mounted printers become personal hosts and shorten a guest's wait. They can even help plan a guest's entire day at the park. What other services could adapt this technology and assist customers?

many, and self-healing. The hope is to build computers made of many small components that have the ability to monitor their own performance and solve problems. IBM's inspiration was biology. A hangnail doesn't stop you from typing; a software or hardware problem shouldn't stop your computer from working either. After all, we take such semi-intelligent automation for granted in other technology. For example the telephone system, with its vast networks, switches, and services providers, automatically sends signals around a faulty circuit. In other words, it is self-healing. How often do you have to reboot your phone? Someday you might be as lucky with your computer.[23]

Cutting the Cord: Wireless Information Appliances

Some experts think we have entered the post-PC era—that is, they believe we are moving away from a PC-dominant environment and toward an array of Internet appliance options. Internet appliances are designed to connect people to the Internet and to e-mail.[24] They include equipment like PDAs (e.g., PalmPilot and Blackberry), smart phones, two-way paging devices, and in-dash computers for cars.[25]

The standardization of wireless networking has set the common PC free as well. No longer chained to their desks, laptop computer users find it liberating to have the mobility and flexibility to work on the Internet or company network anywhere they can tap into a wireless network. Wireless networks use a technology called Wi-Fi, from the term *wireless fidelity.* (Techies call Wi-Fi by its official name, 802.11, but Wi-Fi will do just fine for us.)[26] Wireless local-area networks in hotel rooms and airport lounges allow users with laptops outfitted with wireless modems to connect to the Web and download at 50 times the speed of typical dial-up connections. Wayport, the largest Wi-Fi operator in the United States, says that 5 percent of business travelers use Wi-Fi in their hotel rooms today. Of course, this is just the beginning—only 1,500 of the 15,000 hotels that could be connected have installed the system. The rest will follow quickly because customers will demand it. As Dave Vucina, Wayport CEO, says, "Once you've used [Wi-Fi], that's just the only way you'll work." Vucina uses Wi-Fi at work and at home, where he likes to check e-mail and sports scores from the porch.[27] The point is that people are taking the Internet with them, tapping in anytime and anywhere to gather information and transact business.

Computer Networks

Perhaps the most dynamic change in business technology in recent years has been the move away from mainframe computers that serve as the center of information processing and toward network systems that allow many users to access information at the same time. In an older system, the mainframe performed all the tasks and sent the results to a "dumb" terminal that could not perform those tasks itself. In a **network computing system** (also called **client/server computing**), personal computers (clients) can obtain needed information from huge databases in a central computer (the server). Networks connect people to people and people to data; they allow companies the following benefits:

network computing system (client/server computing) Computer systems that allow personal computers (clients) to obtain needed information from huge databases in a central computer (the server).

- **Saving time and money.** SynOptics Communications found that electronic delivery of mail and files increased the speed of project development by 25 percent.
- **Providing easy links across functional boundaries.** With networks, it's easy to find someone who can offer insightful solutions to a problem. The most common questions on computer bulletin boards begin, "Does anyone know . . . ?" Usually someone does.
- **Allowing employees to see complete information.** In traditional organizations, information is summarized so many times that it often loses its meaning. For example, a sales representative's two-page summary may be cut to a paragraph in the district manager's report and then to a few numbers on a chart in the regional manager's report. Networks, in contrast, catch raw information.

Here's how networks helped software giant Lotus Development. Instead of waiting for the information gained from 4 million annual phone calls to be summarized by technical support people, Lotus Development now sends the information straight into a database, where it's available on demand. Rather than accepting someone else's idea of what information is needed, any Lotus development employee can access the data and search according to his or her needs. The result is that many more employees than before have direct access to market information and can act accordingly.

Networks have their drawbacks as well. Maintaining a fleet of finicky desktop PCs can be expensive. Studies show that the cost of maintaining one corporate Windows desktop computer can run up to $10,000 a year.[28] The cost of the computer itself is just the down payment. Computing costs go up with productivity losses as you upgrade and troubleshoot equipment and train employees to use it. By the time you've recouped your costs, it's time for another upgrade. A large part of PC support costs comes from adding software that causes conflicts or disables other software on the system. Making upgrades to two or three PCs in a small home office is annoying; making them to dozens or hundreds of PCs in a corporation is daunting. Using networks requires so many organizational changes and incurs such high support and upgrade costs that some companies that tried networking PCs are now looking at other options.

One option is a hybrid of mainframe and network computing. In this model, applications and data reside on a server, which handles all of the processing needs for all the client machines on the networks. The client machines look like the PCs that most people use, but they lack the processing power to handle applications on their own. Called *thin-client networks,* these new networks may resemble the ill-tempered dumb terminals of the 1980s, but the execution is much better. Users can still use the Windows applications that they had been using. In a thin-client network, software changes and upgrades need to be made only on the server, so the cost of ownership can be reduced by 20 percent.

Another option is to rent software and hardware access by way of the Internet as needed instead of trying to maintain your own network. Back in the Web boom, companies called application service providers (ASPs) ran software at data centers and rented access to these functions to customers who didn't want to buy expensive servers and software. Most ASPs went out of business because CIOs were slow to hand over their critical data to companies with no track record or little experience in their specific industries. But the fall of little ASPs didn't stop the flow of outsourcing ➤P. 257◄ IT functions to big service providers like IBM. IBM offers pay-as-you-go computing, even hourly rentals, involving all types of IT, from server access to supply-chain-management software.[29] Boots, a British drugstore chain, outsources the management of its IT to IBM. IBM manages Boots's data center, in-store systems, data networks, and telecommunications. It also manages the point-of-sale systems it installed in the 1,600 Boots stores, saving the company more than $200 million.[30]

Critical Thinking

What are the implications for world trade given the ability firms and government organizations now have to communicate with one another across borders? Could the cooperation needed among telecommunications firms worldwide lead to increased cooperation among other organizations on issues such as world health care and worldwide exchanges of technical information?

SOFTWARE

Computer software provides the instructions that enable you to tell the computer what to do. Although many people looking to buy a computer think first of the equipment, it is important to find the right software before finding the right hardware. The type of software you want dictates the kind of equipment you need.

Some programs are easier to use than others. Some are more sophisticated and can perform more functions than others. A businessperson must decide what functions he or she wants the computer system to perform and then choose the appropriate software. That choice will help determine what brand of computer to buy, how much power it should have, and what other peripherals it needs.

shareware
Software that is copyrighted but distributed to potential customers free of charge.

public domain software (freeware)
Software that is free for the taking.

Although most software is distributed commercially through suppliers like retail stores or electronic retailers, there is some software, called **shareware,** that is copyrighted but distributed to potential customers free of charge. The users are asked to send a specified fee to the developer if the program meets their needs and they decide to use it. The shareware concept has become very popular and has dramatically reduced the price of software. **Public domain software (freeware)** is software that is free for the taking. The quality of shareware and freeware varies greatly. To help you have an idea of the quality of such programs, find a website that rates shareware and freeware programs. For example, Sharewarejunkies.com lists the programs downloaded most often, editors' picks, and links to downloadable programs.

Businesspeople most frequently use software for (1) writing (word processors), (2) manipulating numbers (spreadsheets), (3) filing and retrieving data (databases), (4) presenting information visually (graphics), (5) communicating (e-mail and instant messaging), and (6) accounting. Today's software can perform many functions in one kind of program known as integrated software or a software suite. Another class of software program, called groupware, is used on networks. Figure 17.2 describes these types of software.

Progress Assessment

- What are the four characteristics of information that make it useful?
- How do computer networks change the way employees gather information?
- Can you list and describe the major types of computer software used in business?

Word processing programs	With word processors, standardized letters can be personalized quickly, documents can be updated by changing only the outdated text and leaving the rest intact, and contract forms can be revised to meet the stipulations of specific customers. The most popular word processing programs include Corel WordPerfect, Microsoft Word, and Lotus WordPro.
Desktop publishing (DTP) software	DTP combines word processing with graphics capabilities that can produce designs that once could be done only by powerful page-layout design programs. Popular DTP programs include Microsoft Publisher, Adobe PageMaker Plus, and Corel Print Office.
Spreadsheet programs	A spreadsheet program is simply the electronic equivalent of an accountant's worksheet plus such features as mathematical function libraries, statistical data analysis, and charts. Using the computer's speedy calculations, managers have their questions answered almost as fast as they can ask them. Some of the most popular spreadsheet programs are Lotus 1-2-3, Quattro Pro, and Excel.
Database programs	A database program allows users to work with information that is normally kept in lists: names and addresses, schedules, inventories, and so forth. Using database programs, you can create reports that contain exactly the information you want in the form you want it to appear in. Leading database programs include Q&A, Access, Approach, Paradox, PFS: Professional File, PC-File, R base, and FileMaker Pro for Apple computers.
Personal information managers (PIMs)	PIMs or contact managers are specialized database programs that allow users to track communication with their business contacts. Such programs keep track of everything—every person, every phone call, every e-mail message, every appointment. Popular PIMs include Goldmine, Lotus Organizer, ACT, and ECCO Pro.
Graphics and presentation programs	Computer graphics programs can use data from spreadsheets to visually summarize information by drawing bar graphs, pie charts, line charts, and more. Inserting sound clips, video clips, clip art, and animation can turn a dull presentation into an enlightening one. Some popular graphics programs are Illustrator and Freehand for Macintosh computers, Microsoft PowerPoint, Harvard Graphics, Lotus Freelance Graphics, Active Presenter, and Corel Draw.
Communications programs	Communications software enables a computer to exchange files with other computers, retrieve information from databases, and send and receive electronic mail. Such programs include Microsoft Outlook, ProComm Plus, Eudora, and Telik.
Message center software	Message center software is more powerful than traditional communications packages. This new generation of programs has teamed up with fax/voice modems to provide an efficient way of making certain that phone calls, e-mail, and faxes are received, sorted, and delivered on time, no matter where you are. Such programs include Communicate, Message Center, and WinFax Pro.
Accounting and finance programs	Accounting software helps users record financial transactions and generate financial reports. Some programs include online banking features that allow users to pay bills through the computer. Others include "financial advisers" that offer users advice on a variety of financial issues. Popular accounting and finance programs include Peachtree Complete Accounting, Simply Accounting, Quicken, and QuickBooks Pro.
Integrated programs	Integrated software packages (also called suites) offer two or more applications in one package. This allows you to share information across applications easily. Such packages include word processing, database management, spreadsheet, graphics, and communications. Suites include Microsoft Office, Lotus SmartSuite, and Corel WordPerfect Suite.
Groupware	Groupware is software that allows people to work collaboratively and share ideas. It runs on a network and allows people in different areas to work on the same project at the same time. Groupware programs include Lotus Notes, Frontier's Intranet Genie, MetaInfo Sendmail, and Radnet Web Share.

FIGURE 17.2

TYPES OF POPULAR COMPUTER SOFTWARE

Effects of Information Technology on Management

The increase of information technology has affected management greatly and will continue to do so. Three major issues arising out of the growing reliance on information technology are human resource changes, security threats, and privacy concerns.

Human Resource Issues

By now, you may have little doubt that computers are increasingly capable of providing us with the information and knowledge we need to do our daily tasks. The less creative the tasks, the more likely they will be managed by computers. For example, many telemarketing workers today have their work structured by computer-driven scripts. That process can apply to the work lives of customer service representatives, stockbrokers, and even managers. Technology makes the work process more efficient as it replaces many bureaucratic functions. We talked in Chapter 8 about tall versus flat organization structures. Computers often eliminate middle management functions and thus flatten organization structures.

One of the major challenges technology creates for human resource managers is the need to recruit employees who know how to use the new technology or train those who already work in the company. Often companies hire consultants instead of internal staff to address these concerns. Outsourcing technical training allows companies to concentrate on their core businesses. Even techno-savvy companies outsource technology training. Computer companies such as 3Com, Cisco, and Microsoft often hire a technology training company called Information Management Systems to train employees to use their own systems.

Perhaps the most revolutionary effect of computers and the increased use of the Internet and intranets is that of telecommuting. Mobile employees using computers linked to the company's network can transmit their work to the office, and back, from anywhere as easily as (and sometimes more easily than) they can walk into the boss's office.

Naturally, such work decreases travel time and overall costs, and often increases productivity. Telecommuting helps companies save money by allowing them to retain valuable employees during long pregnancy leaves or to tempt experienced employees out of retirement. Companies can also enjoy savings in commercial property costs, since having fewer employees in the office means a company can get by with smaller, and therefore less expensive, offices than before. At AT&T, managers telecommute at least one day a month and 10 percent of all other employees telecommute full-time, saving the company $25 million a year just in real estate costs.[31]

Like any workplace innovation, telecommuting has good points and bad points. Workers enjoy telecommuting's flexibility but complain that they become disconnected with the office (hopefully not to the extent in this cartoon). They also miss the human interactions on the job. What are other advantages and disadvantages of telecommuting?

Telecommuting enables men and women to stay home with small children. It has also been a tremendous boon for workers with disabilities. Employees who can work after hours on their home computers rather than at the office report lowered stress and improved morale. Studies show that telecommuting is most successful among people who are self-starters, who don't have home distractions, and whose work doesn't require face-to-face interaction with co-workers.

Even as telecommuting has grown in popularity, however, some telecommuters report that a consistent diet of long-distance work gives them a dislocated feeling of being left out of the office loop. Some feel a loss of the increased energy people can get through social interaction. In addition to the isolation issue is the intrusion that work brings into what is normally a personal setting. Often people working from home don't know when to turn the work off. Some companies are pulling away from viewing telecommuting as an either–or proposition: either at home or at the office. Such companies are using telecommuting as a part-time alternative. In fact, industry now defines telecommuting as working at home a minimum of two days a week.

Electronic communication can never replace human communication for creating enthusiasm and esprit de corps. Efficiency and productivity can become so important to a firm that people are treated like robots. In the long run, such treatment decreases efficiency and productivity. Computers are a tool, not a total replacement for managers or workers, and creativity is still a human trait. Computers should aid creativity by giving people more freedom and more time. Often they do, but unfortunately many Americans take the results of their productivity gains not in leisure (as do the Europeans), but in increased consumption, making them have to work even harder to pay for it all. Information technology allows people to work at home, on vacation, and in the car at any time of the day. Now U.S. citizens work longer hours than people in any other nation on earth.

Figure 17.3 illustrates how information technology changes the way managers and workers interact. For additional information about telecommuting and home-based workers, review Chapters 6 and 11.

FIGURE 17.3

WHEN INFORMATION TECHNOLOGY ALTERS THE WORKPLACE

MANAGERS MUST	WORKERS MUST
• Instill commitment in subordinates rather than rule by command and control. • Become coaches, training workers in necessary job skills, making sure they have resources to accomplish goals, and explaining links between a job and what happens elsewhere in the company. • Give greater authority to workers over scheduling, priority setting, and even compensation. • Use new information technologies to measure workers' performance, possibly based on customer satisfaction or the accomplishment of specific goals.	• Become initiators, able to act without management direction. • Become financially literate so they can understand the business implications of what they do and changes they suggest. • Learn group interaction skills, including how to resolve disputes within their work group and how to work with other functions across the company. • Develop new math, technical, and analytical skills to use newly available information on their jobs.

Security Issues

One current problem with computers that is likely to persist in the future is that they are susceptible to hackers. In 1994, officials were unable to find the hackers who broke into Pentagon computers through the Internet and stole, altered, and erased numerous records. Ironically, one of the Pentagon systems to which the hackers gained access was that of computer security research.

Computer security is more complicated today than ever before. When information was processed on mainframes, the single data center was easier to control because there was limited access to it. Today, however, computers are accessible not only in all areas within the company but also in all areas of other companies with which the firm does business.

virus
A piece of programming code inserted into other programming to cause some unexpected and, for the victim, usually undesirable event.

An ongoing security issue involves the spread of computer viruses over the Internet. A **virus** is a piece of programming code inserted into other programming to cause some unexpected and, for the victim, usually undesirable event. Viruses are spread by downloading infected programming over the Internet or by sharing an infected diskette. Often the source of the file you downloaded is unaware of the virus. The virus lies dormant until circumstances cause its code to be executed by the computer. Some viruses are playful ("Kilroy was here!"), but some can be quite harmful, erasing data or causing your hard drive to crash. There are programs, such as Norton's AntiVirus, that "inoculate" your computer so that it doesn't catch a known virus. But because new viruses are being developed constantly, antivirus programs may have only limited success. Therefore, you should keep your antivirus protection program up-to-date and, more important, practice "safe computing" by not downloading files from unknown sources and by using your antivirus program to scan diskettes before transferring files from them.

Existing laws do not address the problems of today's direct, real-time communication. As more and more people merge onto the information superhighway, the number of legal issues will likely increase. Today, copyright and pornography laws are crashing into the virtual world. Other legal questions—such as those involving intellectual property and contract disputes, online sexual and racial harassment, and the use of electronic communication to promote crooked sales schemes—are being raised as millions of people log on to the Internet. Cybercrimes cost the United States billions of dollars in 2002.[32] Read the Legal Briefcase box for more examples of cybercrime.

Until September 11, 2001, corporate and government security officials worried mostly about online theft, credit card fraud, and hackers. Today, however, they are most concerned about cyberterrorism. According to Mike McConnell, former director of the National Security Agency, if 30 terrorists with hacker skills and $10 million attacked the United States today, they could shut down the entire communications, money supply, electricity, and transportation systems.[33] For instance, an attempt to shut down Web browsing in 2002 occurred when a powerful electronic attack crippled 9 of the 13 computers that manage Internet traffic globally. If one more of the critical computers had been hit, it would have disrupted e-mails and Web browsing across many parts of the Internet. It was considered by officials to be the most sophisticated and large-scale assault against the crucial computers in the history of the Internet.[34] Although most Internet users didn't notice the attack (it lasted only one hour, and most Internet providers routinely store or "cache" popular Web directory information), the attack demonstrated the Net's vulnerability.

The Critical Infrastructure Protection Board, a part of the U.S. Office of Homeland Defense, was created after September 11, 2001, to devise a plan for improving the security of America's critical infrastructure. In order to do this, the agency needs the cooperation of businesses across the country because 85 percent of the system it needs to protect is in the private sector. If the government doesn't know what's going on there (e.g., hacker attacks, viruses), how www.norton.com

Legal Briefcase

Fear Factor: Leaky Cybersecurity

The phrase "Point and click, then stick 'em up" may not replace the old favorites "Freeze" or "Spread 'em" on TV crime shows, but cybercrime is becoming a common threat in the wired world of the 21st century. According to FBI crime statistics, losses from computer crime amount to billions of dollars a year.

Cybercriminals do everything from stealing intellectual property and committing fraud to spreading computer viruses. At times, Internet attacks have shaken electronic commerce worldwide. For example, denial-of-service attacks on February 2, 2000, shut down such popular websites as Yahoo!, Amazon.com, and eBay for hours. In the assault, attackers meticulously obtained remote control of many computers around the world. They then used the computers to bombard the targeted websites, flooding them with so much data that legitimate users were temporarily denied access or service. The victim sites lost hundreds of millions of dollars in business.

Companies are acutely aware that computer hackers know the vulnerabilities of the information superhighway. The problems promise to get worse as Web access changes from the intermittent dial-up service connection to the always-on broadband connection. The longer the connection is maintained, the more time hackers have to work on breaking in. The increased use of information appliances and wireless networks has caused the situation to worsen. According to computer analysts, techno-savvy homes will contain Web-browsing televisions, smart refrigerators, and Web telephones that download software from the Net that could be abused by cyberattackers.

Computer networks provide ready access points for anyone from disgruntled employees to spies, thieves, sociopaths, and even bored teenagers (like the 15-year-old alleged to have made the February 2000 denial-of-service attacks). Once hackers penetrate a corporate network, they can pilfer intellectual property, destroy or tamper with company data, sabotage operations, or even subvert a specific deal or cripple someone's career. Any business on the Internet is a target, even those with sophisticated security systems. For example, in the process of evaluating how secure (or insecure) a nuclear power plant was, a team of experts took just three and a half minutes to access the plant electronically.

For its part, the government has committed itself to combating cybercrime and promised quick retaliation and prosecution of cybercriminals. But government alone cannot ensure Internet security. That's why companies spend billions of dollars on Internet security software that includes such protections as firewalls, intrusion-detection programs, digital certificates, and authentication and authorization software. In fact, Internet security is the supergrowth business in the technology revolution today.

Sources: Linda Tischler, "No Security," *Fast Company,* August 2002, pp. 42–44; Jane Black, "Faceless Snoopers Have the Upper Hand," *Business Week,* June 5, 2002; and Brian Krebs, "White House to Fill Cybersecurity Posts; Key Roles Seen in Terrorism Fight," *Washington Post,* January 10, 2003, p. E5.

can it help defend it? You might think that companies would eagerly give this information to the government in exchange for increased protection, but CIOs are reluctant to file such reports for fear that the public will find out about the security breaches and lose faith in their company's ability to protect its assets. Many CIOs have asked Congress to grant an exemption to the Freedom of Information Act that would ensure that the information corporations give the government about computer attacks would not be made public. This issue is still being debated in Congress as of this writing. Whatever is decided, it will only be a start on what is likely to be a long effort to improve security technologies that keep out the bad guys in cyberspace.[35]

Privacy Issues

The increasing use of technology creates major concerns about privacy. For example, e-mail is no more private than a postcard. You don't need to be the target of a criminal investigation to have your e-mail snooped. More than one-fourth of U.S. companies scan employee e-mail regularly and legally. Just as employers can log and listen to employees' telephone conversations, they

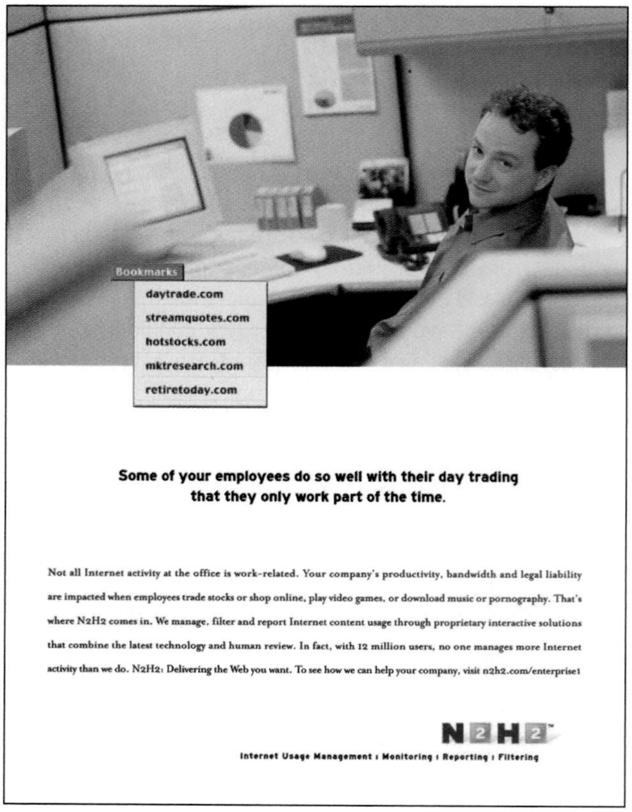

Bookmarks
daytrade.com
streamquotes.com
hotstocks.com
mktresearch.com
retiretoday.com
Some of your employees do so well with their day trading that they only work part of the time.
Not all Internet activity at the office is work-related. Your company's productivity, bandwidth and legal liability are impacted when employees trade stocks or shop online, play video games, or download music or pornography. That's where N2H2 comes in. We manage, filter and report Internet content usage through proprietary interactive solutions that combine the latest technology and human review. In fact, with 12 million users, no one manages more Internet activity than we do. N2H2: Delivering the Web you want. To see how we can help your company, visit n2h2.com/enterprise1
N2H2
Internet Usage Management : Monitoring : Reporting : Filtering

The Internet can add to worker productivity. Unfortunately not all Internet activity is work-related. Workers often trade stocks, play games, or download music on the job. Companies such as N2H2 serve as virtual office tattle-tales as they manage and report employee Internet usage to managers. Do companies like N2H2 violate the privacy of workers on the job?

can track e-mail in a search for trade secrets, non-work-related traffic, harassing messages, and conflicts of interest. Also, most e-mail travels over the Internet in unencrypted plain text. Any hacker with a desire to read your thoughts can trap and read your messages. Some e-mail systems, such as Lotus Notes, can encrypt messages so that you can keep corporate messages private. If you use browser-based e-mail, you can obtain a certificate that has an encryption key from a company such as VeriSign; the cost is about $10 a year. Of course, legitimate users who want to decrypt your mail need to get an unlocking key.[36]

The Internet presents increasing threats to your privacy, as more and more personal information is stored in computers and people are able to access that data, legally or illegally. The Internet allows Web surfers to access all sorts of information about you. For example, some websites allow people to search for vehicle ownership from a license number or to find individuals' real estate property records. One key question in the debate over protecting our privacy is "Isn't this personal information already public anyway?" Civil libertarians have long fought to keep certain kinds of information available to the public. If access to such data is restricted on the Internet, wouldn't we have to reevaluate our policies on public records entirely? The privacy advocates don't think so. After all, the difference is that the Net makes obtaining personal information too easy. Would your neighbors or friends even consider going to the appropriate local agency and sorting through public documents for hours to find your driving records or to see your divorce settlement? Probably not. But they might dig into your background if all it takes is a few clicks of a button.

Average PC users are concerned that websites have gotten downright nosy. In fact, many Web servers track users' movements online. Web surfers seem willing to swap personal details for free access to online information. This personal information can be shared with others without your permission. Websites often send **cookies** to your computer that stay on your hard drive. These are pieces of information, such as registration data or user preferences, sent by a website over the Internet to a web browser that the browser is expected to save and send back to the server whenever the user returns to that website. These little tidbits often simply contain your name and a password that the website recognizes the next time you visit the site so that you don't have to reenter the same information every time you visit. Other cookies track your movements around the Web and then blend that information with a database so that a company can tailor the ads you receive accordingly. Do you mind someone watching over your shoulder while you're on the Web? Tim Berners-Lee, the researcher who invented the World Wide Web, led the development of a way to prevent you from receiving cookies without your permission. His Platform for Privacy Preferences, or P3, allows a website to automatically send information on its privacy policies. With P3 you can set up your Web browser to communicate only with those websites that meet certain criteria.[37] You need to decide how much information about yourself you are willing to give away. Remember, we are living in an information economy, and information is a commodity—that is, an economic good with a measurable value.[38]

cookies
Pieces of information, such as registration data or user preferences, sent by a website over the Internet to a Web browser that the browser software is expected to save and send back to the server whenever the user returns to that website.

Stability Issues

Although technology can provide significant increases in productivity and efficiency, instability in technology also has a significant impact on business. For example, candy maker Hershey discovered the Halloween trick was on it when the company couldn't get its treats to the stores on time. Failure of its new $115 million computer system disrupted shipments, and retailers were forced to order Halloween treats from other companies. Consequently, Hershey suffered a 12 percent decrease in sales that quarter. Every once in a while a computer glitch could work in your favor, though. At least it did for a Swedish woman who checked her bank account to see if her monthly child allowance from the Swedish government had arrived and discovered her balance was more than $10 billion, twice the size of Sweden's defense budget. Apparently, someone had punched in a few too many zeros. When the woman notified her bank, the transaction was canceled and the $1.6 million of interest that accrued over the three days it took to correct the error was taken out of her account. (But she did get a little something—the bank sent her flowers as a thank you for reporting the error quickly.)[39] The list of computer glitches that have caused delays, outages, garbled data, and general snafus could go on and on.

What's to blame? Experts say it is a combination of computer error; human error; malfunctioning software; and an overly complex marriage of software, hardware, and networking equipment. Some systems are launched too quickly to be bug-proof, and some executives are too naive to challenge computer specialists. Industry consultant Howard Rubin says, "This stuff is becoming more critical to big business, yet some of it is built like Lego sets and Tinker Toys. It's not built for rigorous engineering, and people aren't properly trained to use it. As things get more complex, we'll be prone to more errors."[40]

Technology and You

If you are beginning to think that being computer illiterate may be occupational suicide, you are getting the point. Mike Maternaghan, a business development manager for British Telecom, remarked, "It's tempting to say that if you can't use a computer in a couple of years, it will be like not being able to read."[41] Workers in every industry come in contact with computers to some degree. Even fast-food workers read orders on computer screens. The U.S. Department of Commerce estimated that, by 2006, half of all American workers will be employed in IT positions or within industries that use IT products and services intensively. Today 9 out of 10 technology workers are employed in non-technology-based companies such as hospitals, banks, and retail stores.[42] Eight of the 10 occupations projected by the U.S. Bureau of Labor Statistics to grow fastest from 2000 to 2010 are related to computers or IT (see Figure 17.4).[43]

What a difference two or three years made in the technology job market. Back before the dot-com crash in 2000, all that tech workers needed to find a job was a résumé and a way to choose which job offer to accept. Now job searches take longer and salaries are lower. MarketWatch, an online financial news provider, used to pay highly skilled workers $200 an hour; now it's $100 an hour. Technology skills are expected to be in greater demand in the future as the economy rebounds and companies hire more people. Even today, although job possibilities have thinned out, there is still high demand for people with experience in wireless applications and computer security.[44]

If you are still among those considered computer illiterate, do not feel alone. Researchers have found that 55 percent of Americans have some degree of computerphobia (fear of computers). Amazingly, half of all white-collar

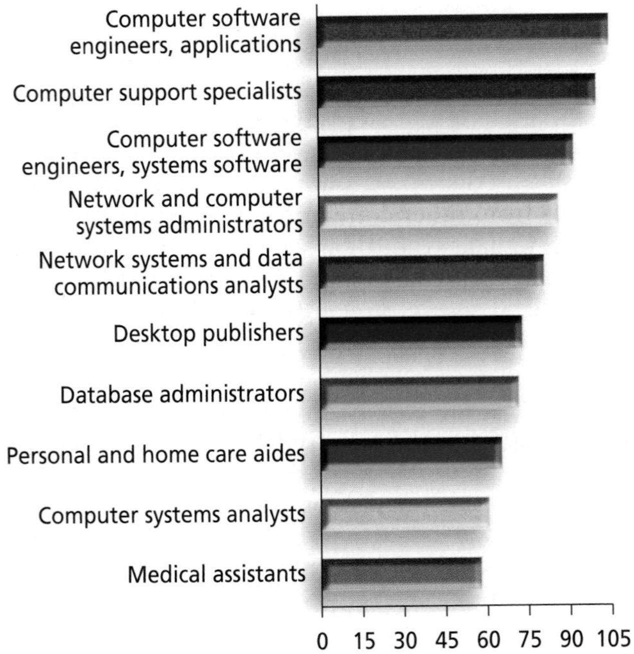

FIGURE 17.4

PERCENT CHANGE IN EMPLOYMENT IN OCCUPATIONS PROJECTED TO GROW FASTEST, 2000–10

Source: U.S. Department of Labor, February 2003.

workers say they are afraid of trying new technologies. Gender, age, and income level don't appear to be linked to computerphobia. The key variable is exposure—that's why Nintendo-era kids take to computers so easily. Computerphobes do not do as well in school as their mouse-clicking classmates. In the workplace, they may get passed up for promotions or lose their jobs. On a psychological level, they often feel inadequate and outdated—sort of like outcasts in a technological, digitized world. Here's the good news: Computerphobia is curable, and computer training (the best medicine) is readily available. You may want to start out with low-tech learning aids such as videos and then gradually move up to training classes or CD-ROMs.

As information technology eliminates old jobs while creating new ones, it is up to you to learn and maintain the skills you need to be certain you aren't left behind.

Progress Assessment

- How has information technology changed the way people work?
- What management issues have been affected by the growth of information technology?
- What career areas are growing as information technology expands?

Summary

1. Outline the changing role of business technology.

1. Business technology is continuously changing names and changing roles.
   - ***What have been the various names and roles of business technology since 1970?***

   In the 1970s, business technology was called data processing (DP) and its role was to support existing business. In the 1980s, its name became information systems (IS) and its role changed to doing business. In the 1990s, business technology became information technology (IT) and its role is now to change business.

- ***How does information technology change business?***

Information technology has minimized the importance of time and place to business. Business that is independent of time and location can deliver products and services whenever and wherever it is convenient for the customer. See Figure 17.1 for examples of how information technology changes business.

- ***What is knowledge technology?***

Knowledge technology adds a layer of intelligence to filter appropriate information and deliver it when it is needed.

2. Information technology multiplies the mountains of information available to businesspeople.

2. List the steps in managing information, identify the characteristics of useful information, and discuss how data are stored and mined.

- ***How can you deal with information overload?***

The most important step in dealing with information overload is to identify your four or five key goals. Eliminate information that will not help you meet your key goals.

- ***What makes information useful?***

The usefulness of management information depends on four characteristics: quality, completeness, timeliness, and relevance.

- ***What are data storage and data mining?***

Data storage is a way businesses organize data into useful information. A *data warehouse* stores data on a single subject over a specific period of time. *Data mining* is looking for hidden patterns in a data warehouse. Data mining software discovers previously unknown relationships among data.

3. To become knowledge-based, businesses must know how to share information and design systems for creating new knowledge.

3. Compare the scope of the Internet, intranets, extranets, and virtual private networks as tools in managing information.

- ***What information technology is available to help business manage information?***

The heart of information technology involves the Internet, intranets, and extranets. The Internet is a massive network of thousands of smaller networks open to everyone with a computer and a modem. An intranet is a companywide network protected from unauthorized entry by outsiders. An extranet is a semiprivate network that allows more than one company to access the same information.

4. Computer hardware changes rapidly.

4. Review the hardware most frequently used in business, and outline the benefits of the move toward computer networks.

- ***What was one of the most dynamic changes in computer hardware in the past decade?***

One of the most dynamic changes was the move away from mainframe computers that serve as the center of information processing toward network systems that allow many users to access information at the same time.

- ***What are the major benefits of networks?***

Networks' major benefits are (1) saving time and money, (2) providing easy links across functional boundaries, and (3) allowing employees to see complete information.

5. Computer software provides the instructions that enable you to tell the computer what to do.

5. Classify the computer software most frequently used in business.

- ***What types of software are used by managers most frequently?***

Managers most often use word processing, electronic spreadsheet, database, graphics, e-mail and instant messaging, and accounting programs. Another class of software, called groupware, allows people to work collaboratively and share ideas.

6. Evaluate the human resource, security, privacy, and stability issues in management that are affected by information technology.

6. Information technology has a tremendous effect on the way we do business.
   - ***What effect has information technology had on business management?***

   Computers eliminate some middle management functions and thus flatten organization structures. Computers also allow employees to work from their own homes. On the negative side, computers sometimes allow information to fall into the wrong hands. Managers must find ways to prevent stealing by hackers. Concern for privacy is another issue affected by the vast store of information available on the Internet. Finding the balance between freedom to access private information and individuals' right to privacy will require continued debate.

7. Explain the importance of computer literacy and the career opportunities available to people with computing skills and experience.

7. Workers in every industry come in contact with computers to some degree. The U.S. Commerce Department estimated that, by 2006, half of all American workers will be employed in IT positions or within industries that use IT products and services.
   - ***What career opportunities are available to people with computer skills and experience?***

   Today 9 out of 10 technology workers are employed in non-technology-based companies. Eight of the 10 occupations projected by the U.S. Bureau of Labor Statistics to grow fastest from 2000 to 2010 are related to IT or computers (see Figure 17.4).

Key Terms

broadband technology 528
cookies 538
data processing (DP) 520
extranet 527
information systems (IS) 520
information technology (IT) 520
Internet2 528
intranet 526
network computing system (client/server computing) 530
public domain software (freeware) 532
shareware 532
virtual private network (VPN) 528
virtualization 521
virus 536

Developing Workplace Skills

1. Imagine that you have $3,000 to buy a computer system or to upgrade a computer you already have. Research the latest in hardware and software in computer magazines and on websites such as www.zdnet.com. Then go to a computer store or to online computer sites such as Dell, Gateway and Micron to find the best value. Make a list of what you would buy, and then write a summary explaining the reasons for your choices.

2. Interview someone who bought a computer system to use in his or her business. Ask why that person bought that specific computer and how it is used. Ask about any problems that occurred during the purchase process or in installing and using the system. What would the buyer do differently next time? What software does he or she find especially useful?

3. If you have worked with computers, you've probably experienced times when the hard drive crashed or the software wouldn't perform as it should have. Describe one computer glitch you've experienced and what you did to resolve it. Analyze and discuss the consequences of the interruption (e.g., decreased productivity, increased stress). If you haven't had a problem with a personal computer, talk with a friend or classmate who has.

4. Choose a topic that interests you and then, on the Internet, use two search engines to find information about the topic. (If you are unfamiliar with

search engines, you can learn about them in the Getting Ready for Prime Time skills section at the beginning of the book.) If the initial result of your search is a list of thousands of sites, narrow your search using the tips offered by the search engine. Did both search engines find the same websites? If not, how were the sites different? Which engine found the most appropriate information?

5. Discuss how technology has changed your relationship with specific businesses or organizations such as your bank, your school, and your favorite places to shop. Has it strengthened or weakened your relationship? On a personal level, how has technology affected your relationship with your family, friends, and community? Take a sheet of paper and write down how technology has helped build your business and personal relationships on one side. On the other side of the paper, list how technology has weakened the relationships. What can you and others do to use technology more effectively to reduce any negative impact?

Taking It To The Net 1

Purpose

To critically evaluate information found on websites.

Exercise

Unlike most print resources, such as magazines and journals, which go through a filtering process (e.g., editing, peer review), information on the Web is mostly unfiltered. The Web has a lot to offer, but not all sources are equally valuable or reliable. Since almost anyone can publish online, accepting information from the Web can be like accepting advice from strangers. It's best to look at all websites with critical eyes.

Let's look at two websites that discuss possible causes of cancer:

- A Star Compendium of Important Tobacco Facts (www.starscientific.com/main_pages/factsheet.htm).
- Power Lines and Cancer: Nothing to Fear (www.quackwatch.com/01QuackeryRelatedTopics/emf.html).

Write a one-paragraph evaluation of each site using the following criteria:

1. *Accuracy.* How reliable and free from error is the information? Are there editors and fact checkers?
2. *Authority.* What is the authority or expertise of the individual or group that created this site? How knowledgeable is the individual or group on the subject matter of the site? Is the site sponsored or co-sponsored by an individual or group that has created other websites? Is contact information for the author or producer included in the document?
3. *Objectivity.* Is the information presented with a minimum of bias? To what extent is the information trying to sway the opinion of the audience?
4. *Currency.* Is the content of the work up-to-date? When was the Web item produced? When was the website last revised? How up-to-date are the links? How reliable are the links—that is, are there blind links or references to sites that have moved?
5. *Coverage.* Are the topics included explored in depth? What is the overall value of the content? What does it contribute to the literature in its field? Given the ease of self-publishing on the Web, this is perhaps even more important in reviewing Web resources than in reviewing print resources. Is

the arrangement appropriate for the topic, and does it facilitate use? Does the site include a search engine? If so, can the user define search criteria?

Taking It To The Net 2

Purpose

To experience the functions and benefits of an enterprise portal.

Exercise

Log on to www.dynamicintranet.com and take the Portal Tour to see what an enterprise portal can do and how that can help businesses and their employees. (Click through the tour to get a general idea of the benefits of enterprise portals; don't try to understand the technical descriptions—you can save that for another course.) B2E (business to employee) portals are not accessible to outsiders, but you can see what one looks like and experiment using some of its tools by logging on to the demo portal of Toasters, Inc., at http://demo.dynamicintra.net/toaster_en.asp.

1. Using the calendar feature in the demo portal, schedule a meeting with three other employees. (Hint: Click "calendar" and then "search public calendar" to get started.) What are the benefits of using this tool rather than calling a meeting personally?
2. Suppose you want to work from home one day a week, but you aren't sure what Toasters' policy is on telecommuting. Find the policy in the human resources directory.
3. You're a team leader for Project 996. What's your reward if your team meets its goal?
4. Some of the folks in marketing have a sick sense of humor. See if you can find why office humor isn't reserved for the water cooler anymore. Obviously, Toasters, Inc., allows individual employees to post information to the portal without supervisory approval. What are the advantages and disadvantages of unmoderated postings?

Casing The Web

To access the case "The Super Bowl of Networks," visit

www.mhhe.com/ub7e

Video Case

As Easy As Riding a Bike–Hoffman Sports Association

There's an old saying, "Once you learn to ride a bike, you never forget." Mat Hoffman took this statement to heart and found a way to make a living riding a bicycle. Mat started his bicycling career at carnivals or anyplace else where young people were gathered. He succeeded in getting growing numbers of daredevils interested in bicycle stunt contests. Today, he is arguably the greatest bicycle freestyle rider in the world. One of his three companies, Hoffman Promotions goes to great lengths to let his sport's followers know just that; the company also does a great deal of work in promoting the sport of freestyle bike riding.

Hoffman found out early that most of the bikes he was using in competition were not strong enough to handle many of the difficult stunts he attempted. He started Hoffman Bikes to take on the challenge of making competition-ready bikes. Unfortunately Mat was beginning to spread himself a bit thin. In addition to riding bikes competitively in the Bicycle Stunts Series which he managed, he now had the added responsibility of designing bikes, finding raw materials, choosing distribution channels, managing inventory, and determining promotional strategies. While he was running three businesses, he was also working hard not to lose touch with his growing young family. Mat knew this was a challenging task, but he found it manageable thanks to modern technology.

Technology makes it possible for someone like Mat to do many things at one time. For example, technology made it possible for him to keep in touch with his family while traveling. On the road, Mat uses a small digital camera to take pictures of everything he is doing. He downloads those photos and posts them daily. He uses his Apple computer to have video conferences with his wife and children. They can see him and he can see them, even though he is hundreds of miles away.

A smart businessperson, as well as a gifted athlete, Mat knows information technology is not very useful unless it has four characteristics: quality, completeness, timeliness, and relevance. Using nothing more than his phone, Mat can surf the Web, get and answer his e-mail, and take photos. The quality of pictures and the timeliness are getting better all the time. Managers like Mat use software programs for word processing, electronic spreadsheets, database management, accounting, graphics, e-mail, and instant messaging. His managers and employees are adept at using such technology so that everyone can communicate with colleagues and customers no matter where they are. The Internet, intranets, and extranets allow companies and employees to stay in touch and manage information from remote points. Wireless communication also frees people to communicate from virtually anywhere.

In a sport known for its risky nature, Mat has broken more bones than anyone cares to count. By surfing the Net, he is able to learn about the latest surgical techniques and where they are performed. Access to such information enables him to stay relatively healthy and able to compete, an important element in any professional sport.

Is it any wonder that Mat Hoffman was named The Small Business Administration's Entrepreneur of the Year? As talented as he is, however, he would be hard pressed to do all that he does without using the latest in technology. Today, there are many career opportunities in information technology. What's important is to motivate yourself to be more technologically prepared to face the business challenges of the 21st century. As a challenge, watch ESPN's X-Games and look for the bicycle stunt events. Imagine yourself competing in such games, creating your own company, doing your own promotions, and starting a family all at the same time. If broken bones don't sound exciting, you may enjoy playing Mat's video game—Mat Hoffman's Pro BMX by Activision. It may motivate you to use your video skills to become an entrepreneur on your own. If you are still not certain, take a bike ride and give it some thought.

Thinking It Over

1. What did this video teach you about using technology to create whole new market opportunities for entrepreneurs?
2. Which of the technologies shown in this video are most familiar to you? What do you anticipate will happen to such technologies in the future?
3. If you are not technologically literate now, what steps could you take now to prepare yourself for the tech careers of the future?

Chapter 18

Understanding Financial Information and Accounting

Learning Goals

After you have read and studied this chapter, you should be able to

1. Describe the importance of financial information and accounting.
2. Define and explain the different areas of the accounting profession.
3. Distinguish between accounting and bookkeeping, list the steps in the accounting cycle, and explain how computers are used in accounting.
4. Explain how the major financial statements differ.
5. Describe the role of depreciation, LIFO, and FIFO in reporting financial information.
6. Explain the importance of ratio analysis in reporting financial information.

Profile

Getting to Know Michael Miller of Goodwill Industries

Back in 1976, when Michael Miller decided to leave a profitable swimming-pool contracting business to accept a position with Goodwill Industries—a thrift-store-based nonprofit organization—many people wondered if he had gone off the deep end. He quickly developed a track record as a turnaround specialist by applying for-profit business management principles in the nonprofit arena. In 1986, Miller accepted a job as CEO of a sleepy, underperforming Goodwill operation in Portland, Oregon. Before he took over, the operation's stores had sales of $4 million and debt of $1 million. By 2002, under his management, the stores were doing $52 million in sales.

Miller knew that to make his stores successful, careful planning and financial management were essential. He reviewed the company's financial records and found that a significant part of Goodwill's funding came from government sources to support Goodwill's services to people with disabilities and other special-needs populations. This concerned Miller because he knew that government funding can swing wildly. Therefore, he set out to make his Goodwill stores as profitable as possible. Today, Miller describes his Goodwill operations as a mission-integrated, enterprise-funded nonprofit business.

To reach his goal, Miller knew that Goodwill's accounting and financial management practices had to change. He analyzed the company's financial position and initiated strategic planning as if he were running a fast-paced, for-profit business. Research of his market found that average donors to Goodwill were women ages 35 to 44 with incomes of approximately $50,000. In contrast, he found the average shoppers at his stores were women ages 25 to 54 who earned $30,000. After a cost analysis of each store, he decided to shut down locations with the lowest sales and open new stores where the groups of donors and shoppers intersected. To date, he's built 30 new stores.

Miller attacked Goodwill's costs with a passion. Under the old system, all donations to Goodwill traveled to distribution branches in Portland and Salem before going to the stores for resale. Miller felt this wasted time and duplicated efforts. He insisted that goods be collected at off-site trailers located near his shops and brought directly to the shop with no detour. He also opened sheltered bays to encourage donations directly at his stores. Those two moves alone cut operating expenses by 30 percent. To increase profitability, Miller felt he needed to make high-profit impulse items available. Today, the stores include Starbucks-like coffee stations where shoppers can purchase high-margin products like coffee and books. In a rather dramatic move, Miller decided to spend 80 percent of his promotion budget advertising on Oregon's TV network affiliates. He knew that potential donors were likely to watch *Friends* or *Oprah.* He recovered most of the cost of this advertising by selling the same ads to 128 Goodwill operations around the country.

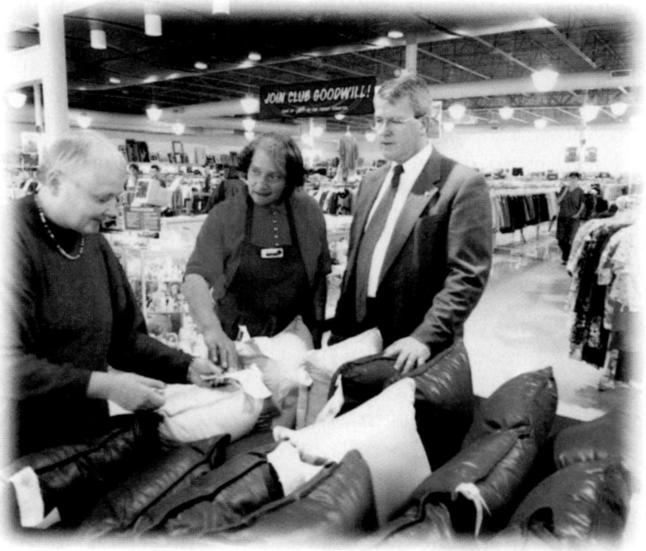

Controlling costs, managing cash flows, understanding profit margins and taxes, and reporting finances accurately are keys to survival for both profit-seeking and nonprofit organizations.

Have his efforts paid off? His employees—mostly people who have disabling conditions such as cerebral palsy or Down's syndrome, or who have long depended on welfare—last year earned $25.9 million in wages, or an average of approximately $12,000 a year for a 28-hour workweek. They earn an average of $8.29 per hour, well above the $6.90 Oregon minimum wage. Miller says he would never lay off someone with a disability but would always encourage his employees to maximize their potential by transitioning to even better jobs in the community. Last year, through the Goodwill network, he placed over 5,000 people in jobs, including those who went through job training classes sponsored by the Goodwill system.

Controlling costs, managing cash flows, understanding profit margins and taxes, and reporting finances accurately are keys to survival for both profit-seeking and nonprofit organizations. This chapter will introduce you to the accounting fundamentals and financial information critical to business success. The chapter also briefly explores the financial ratios that are essential in measuring business performance.

Sources: Tomas Kellner, "One Man's Trash," *Forbes,* March 4, 2002, pp. 96–98; and Melissa B. Robinson, "Goodwill Marks 100th Year," AP Online, March 4, 2002.

The Importance of Financial Information

Stories like that of Michael Miller and Goodwill Industries are repeated hundreds of times every day throughout the business community. Small and sometimes large businesses falter or even fail because they do not follow good financial procedures. Financial information is the heartbeat of competitive businesses. Accounting keeps the heartbeat stable.

Accounting is different from marketing, management, and human resource management in that most of us have limited understanding of accounting principles. As consumers, we have all had some experience with marketing. As workers or students, we have observed and are familiar with many management concepts. But accounting? What is it? Is it difficult to learn? What do accountants do? Is the work interesting? Is this a career path you may wish to pursue?

You have to know something about accounting if you want to succeed in business. Learning some basic accounting terms is mandatory. You also have to understand the relationship of bookkeeping to accounting and how accounts are kept. It's almost impossible to run a business without being able to read, understand, and analyze accounting reports and financial statements.

Accounting reports and financial statements reveal as much about a business's health as pulse rate and blood pressure readings tell us about a person's health. The purpose of this chapter is to introduce you to the process of obtaining needed financial information using basic accounting principles. By the end of this chapter, you should have a good idea of what accounting is, how it works, and why it is important. You should also know some accounting terms and understand the purpose of accounting statements. It's important to understand how accounting statements are constructed, but it's even more important to know what they mean to the business. A few hours invested in learning this material will pay off handsomely as you become more involved in business or investing, or simply in understanding what's going on in the world of business and finance.

accounting
The recording, classifying, summarizing, and interpreting of financial events and transactions to provide management and other interested parties the information they need to make good decisions.

What Is Accounting?

Financial information is primarily based on information generated from accounting. **Accounting** is the recording, classifying, summarizing, and interpreting of financial events and transactions to provide management and other interested parties the information they need to make good decisions. Financial transactions can include such specifics as buying and selling goods ➤P. 25◄ and services ➤P. 26◄, acquiring insurance, paying employees, and using supplies. Once the business's transactions have been recorded, they are usually classified into groups that have common characteristics. For example, all purchases are grouped together, as are all sales transactions. The method used to record and summarize accounting data into reports is called an *accounting system* (see Figure 18.1).

FIGURE 18.1

THE ACCOUNTING SYSTEM

The inputs to an accounting system include sales documents and other documents. The data are recorded, classified, and summarized. They're then put into summary financial statements such as the income statement and balance sheet.

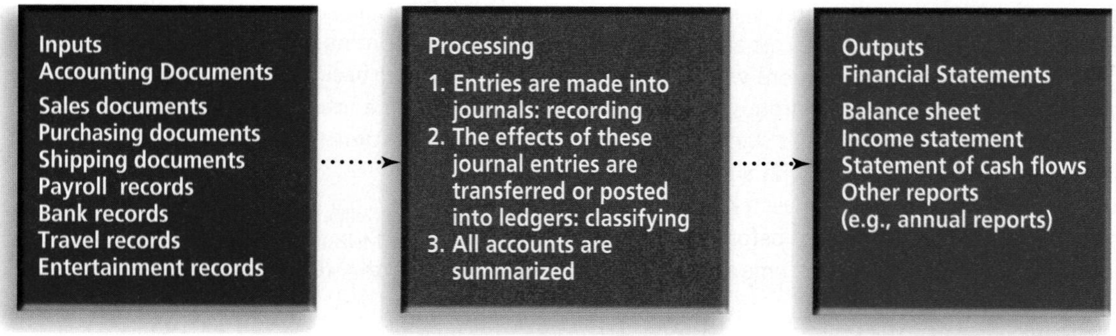

Inputs
Accounting Documents
Sales documents
Purchasing documents
Shipping documents
Payroll records
Bank records
Travel records
Entertainment records
Processing
1. Entries are made into journals: recording
2. The effects of these journal entries are transferred or posted into ledgers: classifying
3. All accounts are summarized
Outputs
Financial Statements
Balance sheet
Income statement
Statement of cash flows
Other reports
(e.g., annual reports)

USERS	TYPE OF REPORT
Government taxing authorities (e.g., the Internal Revenue Service)	Tax returns
Government regulatory agencies	Required reports
People interested in the organization's income and financial position (e.g., owners, creditors, financial analysts, suppliers)	Financial statements found in annual reports (e.g., income statement, balance sheet, statement of cash flows)
Managers of the firm	Financial statements and various internally distributed financial reports

FIGURE 18.2

USERS OF ACCOUNTING INFORMATION AND THE REQUIRED REPORTS

Many types of organizations use accounting information to make business decisions. The reports needed vary according to the information each user requires. An accountant must prepare the appropriate forms.

One purpose of accounting is to help managers evaluate the financial condition and the operating performance of the firm so that they can make well-informed decisions. Another major purpose is to report financial information to people outside the firm such as owners, creditors, suppliers, investors, and the government (for tax purposes). In basic terms, accounting is the measurement and reporting of financial information to various users (inside and outside the organization) regarding the economic activities of the firm (see Figure 18.2). Accounting work is divided into several major areas. Let's look at those areas next.

AREAS OF ACCOUNTING

Accounting has been called the language of business. Without closer scrutiny, you may think that accounting is only for profit-seeking firms. Nothing could be further from the truth; remember the chapter opening profile of Michael Miller from Goodwill Industries. It is also the language used to report financial information about nonprofit organizations such as churches, schools, hospitals, fraternities, and government agencies. The accounting profession is divided into five key working areas: managerial and financial accounting, auditing, tax accounting, and governmental and not-for-profit accounting. All five areas are important, and all create career opportunities for students who are willing to put forth the effort to study accounting.

Managerial Accounting

Managerial accounting is used to provide information and analyses to managers within the organization to assist them in decision making. Managerial accounting is concerned with measuring and reporting costs of production, marketing, and other functions (cost accounting); preparing budgets (planning); checking whether or not units are staying within their budgets (controlling); and designing strategies to minimize taxes (tax accounting).

managerial accounting Accounting used to provide information and analyses to managers within the organization to assist them in decision making.

If you are a business major, it's almost certain you will be required to take a course in managerial accounting. You may even elect to pursue a career as a certified management accountant. A **certified management accountant (CMA)** is a professional accountant who has met certain educational and experience requirements, passed a qualifying exam in the field, and been certified by the Institute of Certified Management Accountants. With growing emphasis on global competition, company rightsizing, outsourcing, and organizational cost-cutting, managerial accounting may be one of the most important areas you study in your college career.

certified management accountant (CMA) A professional accountant who has met certain educational and experience requirements, passed a qualifying exam in the field, and been certified by the Institute of Certified Management Accountants.

Assembling a marine diesel engine involves many tools, parts, raw materials, and other components. Keeping these costs at a minimum and setting realistic production schedules is critical to industry survival. Management accountants team with managers from production, marketing, and other areas to ensure company competitiveness. Visit www.cma.edu to find out more about managerial accounting.

Financial Accounting

financial accounting
Accounting information and analyses prepared for people outside the organization.

annual report
A yearly statement of the financial condition, progress, and expectations of an organization.

private accountants
Accountants who work for a single firm, government agency, or nonprofit organization.

public accountant
An accountant who provides his or her accounting services to individuals or businesses on a fee basis.

certified public accountant (CPA)
An accountant who passes a series of examinations established by the American Institute of Certified Public Accountants.

Financial accounting differs from managerial accounting in that the information and analyses it generates are for people outside the organization. The information goes to owners and prospective owners, creditors and lenders, employee unions, customers, suppliers, government agencies, and the general public. These external users are interested in the organization's profits, its ability to pay its bills, and other important financial information. Much of the information derived from financial accounting is contained in the company's **annual report**, a yearly statement of the financial condition, progress, and expectations of an organization. As pressure builds from stakeholders, companies are pouring more information than ever into their annual reports.[1]

It's critical for firms to keep accurate financial information. Because of this, many organizations employ **private accountants**, who work for a single firm, government agency, or nonprofit organization ➤P. 7◀. However, not all firms or nonprofit organizations want or need a full-time accountant. Therefore, thousands of accounting firms in the United States provide the accounting services an organization needs.

An accountant who provides his or her services to individuals or businesses on a fee basis is called a **public accountant**. Public accountants can provide business assistance in many ways.[2] They may design an accounting system for a firm, help select the correct computer and software to run the system, or analyze the financial strength of an organization right from the start. An accountant who passes a series of examinations established by the American Institute of Certified Public Accountants (AICPA) and meets the state's requirement for education and experience earns recognition as a **certified public accountant (CPA)**.[3] CPAs find careers as private accountants or public accountants, and are often sought out to fill other financial positions within organizations.

It is vital for the accounting profession to ensure users of financial information that the information provided is accurate. The independent Financial Accounting Standards Board (FASB) defines the set of *generally accepted accounting principles (GAAP)* that accountants must follow.[4] If financial reports

Dealing with Change

www.forensisgroup.com

Elementary, Mr. Auditor, Elementary!

Having problems with an audit that's gone awry? Think there's some hidden debt buried in a far corner of your company's books? Who are you going to call? Ghostbusters? No, it's time to call the accounting industry's version of Sherlock Holmes: the forensic accountant.

Forensic accountants have a somewhat sexy job in the normally quiet world of accounting. Forensic accountant Bill Kauppila sums it up well: "Our job is coming up with the story behind the story." Many companies found out the hard way that even the slightest whiff of accounting irregularities can be detrimental to the firm's health. Unfortunately, the pressure to meet earnings expectations caused some companies to play fast and loose with their financial reporting. Enter the accounting supersleuths.

Stealthily uncovering paper trails left behind by company rogues starts the detailed forensic work. Mining computer hard drives, financial papers, and bank records in a search for a smoking gun consumes the attention of the forensic accountant. However, forensic accountants also see part of their job as behavioral, meaning they get out and listen to employees who have concerns about supervisors encouraging them to "cook the books" or "hide some costs." Larry Crumbley, editor of the *Journal of Forensic Accounting,* compares looking for accounting fraud through forensic analysis to taking a metal detector to a garbage dump to find rare coins: "You're going to find a lot of junk out there." As pressures mount on companies to provide accurate financial information, we can expect forensic accountants to stay busy.

Sources: Bill Cramer, "Fraud Squad," *CFO,* April 2003, pp. 36–44; Stan Lomax, "Cooking the Books," *Business and Economics Review,* April–June 2003, pp. 3–8; William Poe, "Forensic Accounting," *St. Louis Commerce,* March 2002, pp. 44–45; and Edward Iwata, "Accounting Detectives in Demand," *USA Today,* February 28, 2003, p. 3B.

are prepared in accordance with GAAP, users can expect that the information is reported according to standards agreed on by accounting professionals.[5]

In the early 2000s, the accounting profession suffered through perhaps the darkest period in its history.[6] Accounting scandals involving high-profile companies such as Enron, WorldCom, and Tyco raised public suspicions and led to the downfall of one of the big five accounting firms: Arthur Andersen.[7] Andersen was convicted of obstruction of justice in 2002 for its actions in the Enron case.[8] It's important for the accounting profession to ensure that the accountants they employ are as professional as doctors or lawyers. Today, scrutiny of the accounting industry is more intense than ever.[9] CPAs on average take 40 hours of continuing education training a year, are subject to recertification, undergo ethics training requirements, and must pass an ethics exam.[10] The Dealing with Change box offers an example of just how intense this scrutiny has become and what some companies are doing about it.

Auditing

The job of reviewing and evaluating the records used to prepare a company's financial statements is referred to as **auditing**. Accountants within the organization often perform internal audits to ensure that proper accounting procedures and financial reporting are being carried out within the company.[11] Public accountants also conduct independent audits of accounting and related records. Financial auditors today not only examine the financial health of an organization but also look into operational efficiencies and effectiveness.[12] An **independent audit** is an evaluation and unbiased opinion about the accuracy of a company's financial statements.

An accountant who has a bachelor's degree and two years of experience in internal auditing, and who has passed an exam administered by the Institute of Internal Auditors, can earn professional accreditation as a **certified internal auditor (CIA)**. Internal financial controls are very important for firms of any size.

auditing
The job of reviewing and evaluating the records used to prepare a company's financial statements.

independent audit
An evaluation and unbiased opinion about the accuracy of a company's financial statements.

certified internal auditor (CIA)
An accountant who has a bachelor's degree and two years of experience in internal auditing, and who has passed an exam administered by the Institute of Internal Auditors.

Ever tried a fish taco from Rubio's Baja Grill? You can learn about the popularity of this culinary delight and find important financial information concerning Rubio's from its annual report. U.S. corporations spend billions on these yearly updates that contain a wealth of accounting information. Did you know *The Wall Street Journal* has a free annual report service?

After accounting scandals such as the ones previously mentioned, the legitimacy of allowing a company to do both auditing and consulting work for the same firm was questioned.[13] To address this issue, the U.S. Securities and Exchange Commission has put in place new rules to take effect in 2004; the U.S. Congress promises to review this relationship further.[14] A firm's annual report often includes a written opinion by an auditor that's important to read for useful information.[15]

Tax Accounting

Taxes are the price we pay for roads, parks, schools, police protection, the military, and other functions provided by government. Federal, state, and local governments require submission of tax returns that must be filed at specific times and in a precise format. A **tax accountant** is trained in tax law and is responsible for preparing tax returns or developing tax strategies. Since governments often change tax policies according to specific needs or objectives, the job of the tax accountant is certainly challenging. Also, as the burden of taxes grows in the economy, the role of the tax accountant becomes increasingly important to the organization or entrepreneur.

tax accountant
An accountant trained in tax law and responsible for preparing tax returns or developing tax strategies.

Government and Not-for-Profit Accounting

Government and not-for-profit accounting involves working for organizations whose purpose is not generating a profit but serving ratepayers, taxpayers, and others according to a duly approved budget. Governments (federal, state, and local) require an accounting system that satisfies the needs of their information users. The primary users of government accounting information are citizens, special interest groups, legislative bodies, and creditors. These users want to ensure that government is fulfilling its obligations and making the proper use of taxpayers' money. Governmental accounting standards are set by the Governmental Accounting Standards Board (GASB). The Federal Bureau of Investigation, the Internal Revenue Service, the Missouri Department of Natural Resources, and the Cook County Department of Revenue are just a few of the many government agencies that offer career possibilities to accountants seeking to work in government accounting.

government and not-for-profit accounting
Accounting system for organizations whose purpose is not generating a profit but serving ratepayers, taxpayers, and others according to a duly approved budget.

Not-for-profit organizations also require accounting professionals. In fact, not-for-profit organizations have a growing need for trained accountants since contributors to nonprofits want to see exactly how and where the funds they contribute are being spent. Charities (like Goodwill), universities and colleges, hospitals, and labor unions all hire accountants to show how the funds they raise are being spent.

As you can see, managerial and financial accounting, auditing, tax accounting, and governmental and not-for-profit accounting each require specific training and skill. Yet some people are confused about the difference between an accountant and a bookkeeper. We'll clarify that difference right after the Progress Assessment.

Progress Assessment

- Could you define accounting to a friend so that he or she would clearly understand what's involved?
- Can you explain the difference between managerial and financial accounting?
- What's the difference between a private accountant and a public accountant?

ACCOUNTING VERSUS BOOKKEEPING

Bookkeeping involves the recording of business transactions. Bookkeeping is an important part of financial reporting, but accounting goes far beyond the mere recording of financial information. Accountants classify and summarize financial data provided by bookkeepers, and then interpret the data and report the information to management. They also suggest strategies for improving the financial condition and progress of the firm. Accountants are especially important in financial analysis and income tax preparation.

If you were a bookkeeper, the first task you would perform is to divide all of the firm's transactions into meaningful categories such as sales documents, purchasing receipts, and shipping documents. The bookkeeper's challenge is to keep the information organized and manageable. Therefore, bookkeepers must begin by recording financial data from the original transaction documents (sales slips and so forth) into record books called journals. A **journal** is the record book or computer program where accounting data are first entered. It's interesting that the word *journal* comes from the French word *jour,* which means "day." A journal is where the day's transactions are kept.

"I'LL TELL YOU HARRIS, THEY DON'T MAKE ACCOUNTANTS LIKE THEY USED TO. THOSE I HAD IN THE 1990'S NEVER BROUGHT ME FIGURES LIKE THESE."

The integrity of a firm's financial statements is vital. Accounting irregularities that occurred in the late 1990s at firms like Enron and WorldCom made the companies look stronger than they actually were. Accountants are now committed to regaining the trust and respect their profession enjoyed in the past. What part should the government play in overseeing the accounting industry?

It is quite possible when recording financial transactions that you could make a mistake. For example, you could easily write or enter \$10.98 as \$10.89. For that reason, bookkeepers record all their transactions in two places. They can then check one list of transactions against the other to make sure that they add up to the same amount. If they don't equal the same amount, the bookkeeper knows that he or she made a mistake. The concept of writing every transaction in two places is called **double-entry bookkeeping**. In double-entry bookkeeping, two entries in the journal and the ledgers (discussed next) are required for each company transaction.

bookkeeping
The recording of business transactions.

journal
The record book or computer program where accounting data are first entered.

double-entry bookkeeping
The concept of writing every business transaction in two places.

To see how this system works, let's suppose a business wanted to determine how much it paid for office supplies in the first quarter of the year. Without a specific bookkeeping tool, that would be difficult even with accurate accounting journals. Therefore, bookkeepers make use of a set of books with pages labeled *office supplies, cash,* and so on. The entries in the journal are transferred, or posted, to these pages, making information about various accounts available quickly and easily.

A **ledger**, then, is a specialized accounting book or computer program in which information from accounting journals is recorded into specific categories and posted so that managers can find all the information about a single account in one place. Today, computerized accounting programs post information from journals into ledgers daily or instantaneously. This way the financial information is readily available whenever the organization needs it.

ledger
A specialized accounting book or computer program in which information from accounting journals is accumulated into specific categories and posted so that managers can find all the information about one account in the same place.

The Six-Step Accounting Cycle

The **accounting cycle** is a six-step procedure that results in the preparation and analysis of the major financial statements (see Figure 18.3). The accounting cycle generally involves the work of both the bookkeeper and the accountant. The first three steps are continual: (1) analyzing and categorizing

accounting cycle
A six-step procedure that results in the preparation and analysis of the major financial statements.

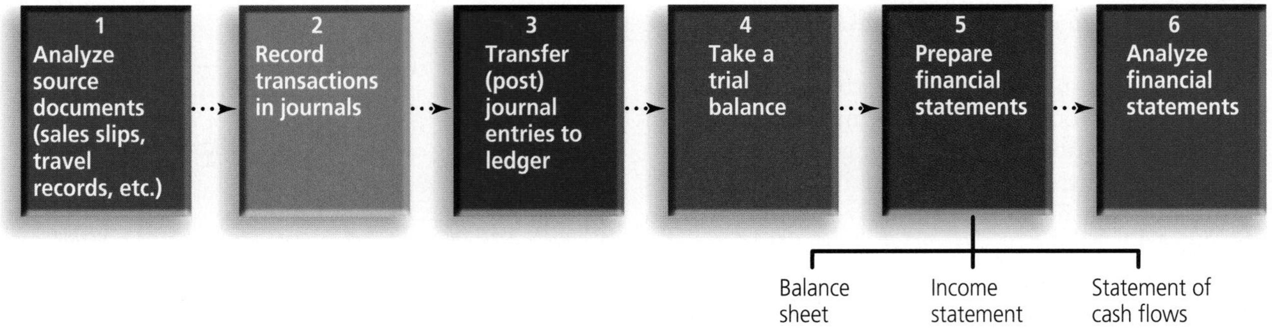
1 Analyze source documents (sales slips, travel records, etc.)
2 Record transactions in journals
3 Transfer (post) journal entries to ledger
4 Take a trial balance
5 Prepare financial statements
6 Analyze financial statements
Balance sheet
Income statement
Statement of cash flows

FIGURE 18.3

STEPS IN THE ACCOUNTING CYCLE

trial balance
A summary of all the data in the account ledgers to show whether the figures are correct and balanced.

documents, (2) putting the information into journals, and (3) posting that information into ledgers. The fourth step involves preparing a trial balance. A **trial balance** is a summary of all the financial data in the account ledgers to check whether the figures are correct and balanced. If the information in the account ledgers is not accurate, it must be corrected before the firm's financial statements are prepared. The fifth step, then, is to prepare the financial statements, including a balance sheet, income statement, and statement of cash flows. The sixth step is when the accountant analyzes the financial statements and evaluates the financial condition of the firm. Computers and accounting software have simplified this process considerably.[16]

The Impact of Computers on Accounting

Financial information and transactions may be recorded by hand or by computer. Computers greatly simplify the mechanical tasks involved in accounting, enabling managers and other interested users to get financial reports exactly when and how they want them. Also, as a business grows, the number of accounts a firm must keep and the reports that need to be generated expand in scope. Because computers can rapidly handle large amounts of financial information, accountants are freed up to do more important tasks such as financial analysis. Computerized accounting programs have been especially helpful to small-business owners, who often lack the strong accounting support within their companies that larger firms enjoy.

Accounting software packages include programs that handle tasks involving general ledgers, sales processing, accounts receivable, purchase orders, accounts payable, cash flow analysis, and inventory control.[17] Tax returns and tax planning can also be performed using tax accounting programs.[18] Many of the latest accounting packages, such as QuickBooks and Peachtree, address the specific needs of small businesses, which are often significantly different from the needs of a major corporation. Large public accounting firms often assist in developing accounting programs for their biggest clients.

Using computers to record and analyze data and to print out financial reports allows managers to obtain up-to-the-minute financial information for the business. It's now possible, thanks to computers, to have continuous auditing, which helps managers prevent cash flow problems and other financial difficulties by allowing them to spot trouble earlier than ever before. Today's software programs allow even novices to do sophisticated financial analyses within days.[19]

It's important to remember, though, that no computer yet has been programmed to make good financial decisions by itself. Granted, a computer is a wonderful tool for businesspeople to use. Yet business owners should understand exactly what computer system and which programs are best suited for their particular needs. That's one reason why it's suggested that before entrepreneurs get started in a small business ➤P. 184◀, they should hire or consult with an accountant to identify the particular needs of their proposed firm.

Then, a specific accounting system can be developed that works with the predesigned accounting software that's been chosen. Today's accounting packages offer ease of use, customization, and efficient interactions with the Internet.

Computers help ease the monotony of bookkeeping and accounting work. Still, the work of an accountant requires training and very specific competencies. It's interesting that beginning business students sometimes assume that opportunities in accounting are rather narrow in scope. Nothing could be further from the truth. Accountants not only provide financial information to the firm but are vital in interpreting and analyzing that information. After the Progress Assessment, we will look at the balance sheet, income statement, and statement of cash flows—and the important information each provides.

Progress Assessment

- Can you explain the difference between accounting and bookkeeping?
- What's the difference between an accounting journal and a ledger?
- Why does a bookkeeper prepare a trial balance?
- What key advantages do computers provide businesses in maintaining and compiling accounting information?

UNDERSTANDING KEY FINANCIAL STATEMENTS

A **financial statement** is a summary of all the transactions that have occurred over a particular period. Financial statements indicate a firm's financial health and stability. That's why stockholders (the owners of the firm), bondholders and banks (people and institutions that lend money to the firm), labor unions, employees, and the Internal Revenue Service are all interested in a firm's financial statements. The following are the key financial statements of a business:

financial statement
A summary of all the transactions that have occurred over a particular period.

1. The *balance sheet,* which reports the firm's financial condition on a specific date.
2. The *income statement,* which summarizes revenues, cost of goods, and expenses (including taxes), for a specific period of time and highlights the total profit or loss the firm experienced during that period.
3. The *statement of cash flows,* which provides a summary of money coming into and going out of the firm that tracks a company's cash receipts and cash payments.

The differences among the financial statements can be summarized this way: The balance sheet details what the company owns and owes on a certain day; the income statement shows what a firm sells its products for and what its selling costs are over a specific period; and the statement of cash flows highlights the difference between cash coming in and cash going out of a business. To fully understand important financial information, you must be able to understand the purpose of an organization's financial statements. We'll explain each statement in more detail next.

The Fundamental Accounting Equation

Imagine that you don't owe anybody money. That is, you don't have any liabilities (debts). In this case, your assets (cash and so forth) are equal to what you *own* (equity). However, if you borrow some money from a friend, you have incurred a liability. Your assets are now equal to what you *owe* plus what you own. Translated into business terms, Assets = Liabilities + Owners' equity.

In accounting, this equation must always be balanced. For example, suppose you have $50,000 in cash and decide to use that money to open a small coffee shop. Your business has assets of $50,000 and no debts. The accounting equation would be:

$$\text{Assets} = \text{Liabilities} + \text{Owners' equity}$$
$$\$50{,}000 = \$0 \qquad + \$50{,}000$$

You have $50,000 cash and $50,000 owners' equity (the amount of your investment in the business—sometimes referred to as net worth). However, before opening the business, you borrow $30,000 from a local bank; the equation now changes. You have $30,000 of additional cash, but you also have a debt (liability) of $30,000. Remember, with each business transaction there is a recording of two transactions. (Recall the discussion of double-entry bookkeeping earlier in this chapter.)

Your financial position within the business has changed. The equation is still balanced but is changed to reflect the transaction:

$$\text{Assets} = \text{Liabilities} + \text{Owners' equity}$$
$$\$80{,}000 = \$30{,}000 \quad + \$50{,}000$$

fundamental accounting equation
Assets = liabilities + owners' equity; this is the basis for the balance sheet.

This formula is called the **fundamental accounting equation** and is the basis for the balance sheet. As Figure 18.4 (a sample balance sheet for Fiberrific, the hypothetical cereal company we introduced in Chapter 13) highlights, on the balance sheet you list assets in a separate column from liabilities and owners' (or stockholders') equity. The assets are equal to or are balanced with the liabilities and owners' (or stockholders') equity. It's that simple. What's often complicated is determining what is included in the asset account and what is included in the liabilities and owners' equity accounts. It's critical that businesspeople understand the important financial information on the balance sheet, so let's take a closer look.

The Balance Sheet

balance sheet
The financial statement that reports a firm's financial condition at a specific time.

A **balance sheet** is the financial statement that reports a firm's financial condition at a specific time. It's composed of three major accounts: assets, liabilities, and owners' equity. It gets its name because it shows a *balance* between two figures: the company's assets on the one hand, and its liabilities plus owners' equity on the other. (These terms will be defined fully in the next sections.)

The following analogy will help explain the idea behind the balance sheet. Let's say that you want to know what your financial condition is at a given time. Maybe you want to buy a new house or car and therefore need to calculate your available resources. One of the best measuring sticks is your balance sheet. First, you would add up everything you own—cash, property, money owed you, and so forth (assets). Subtract from that the money you owe others—credit card debt, IOUs, current car loan, and so forth (liabilities)—and you have a figure that tells you your net worth (equity). This is fundamentally what companies do in preparing a balance sheet. In that preparation, it's important they follow clearly established accounting procedures.[20] The fundamental accounting equation is what sets those procedures.

Assets

assets
Economic resources (things of value) owned by a firm.

Assets are economic resources (things of value) owned by a firm. Assets include productive, tangible items (e.g., equipment, buildings, land, furniture, fixtures, and motor vehicles) that help generate income, as well as intangibles with value

FIBERRIFIC
Balance Sheet
December 31, 2004

Assets			
① Current assets			
Cash		$ 15,000	
Accounts receivable		200,000	
Notes receivable		50,000	
Inventory		335,000	
Total current assets			$600,000
② Fixed assets			
Land		$40,000	
Building and improvements	$200,000		
Less: Accumulated depreciation	−90,000		
		110,000	
Equipment and vehicles	$120,000		
Less: Accumulated depreciation	−80,000		
		40,000	
Furniture and fixtures	$26,000		
Less: Accumulated depreciation	−10,000		
		16,000	
Total fixed assets			206,000
③ Intangible assets			
Goodwill		$20,000	
Total intangible assets			20,000
Total assets			$826,000
Liabilities and Owners' or Stockholders' Equity			
④ Current liabilities			
Accounts payable		$40,000	
Notes payable (due June 2005)		8,000	
Accrued taxes		150,000	
Accrued salaries		90,000	
Total current liabilities			$288,000
⑤ Long-term liabilities			
Notes payable (due Mar. 2009)		$ 35,000	
Bonds payable (due Dec. 2014)		290,000	
Total long-term liabilities			325,000
Total liabilities			$613,000
⑥ Stockholders' equity			
Common stock (1,000,000 shares)		$100,000	
Retained earnings		113,000	
Total stockholders' equity			213,000
Total liabilities & stockholders' equity			$826,000

FIGURE 18.4

SAMPLE FIBERRIFIC BALANCE SHEET

① Current assets: Items that can be converted to cash within one year.

② Fixed assets: Items such as land, buildings, and equipment that are relatively permanent.

③ Intangible assets: Items of value such as patents and copyrights that don't have a physical form.

④ Current liabilities: Payments that are due in one year or less.

⑤ Long-term liabilities: Payments not due for one year or longer.

⑥ Stockholders' equity: The value of what stockholders own in a firm (also called owners' equity.

(e.g., patents, trademarks, copyrights, or goodwill).[21] Think, for example, of the value of brand names ➤P. 403◄ such as Coca-Cola, McDonald's, and Intel. Intangibles such as brand names can be among the firm's most valuable assets. Goodwill is the value that can be attributed to factors such as reputation, location, and superior products.[22] It is included on the balance sheet when a firm acquiring another firm pays more than the value of that firm's tangible assets.[23] Not all companies, however, list intangible assets on their balance sheets.

FIGURE 18.5

CLASSIFICATIONS OF ASSETS

Assets are classified by how quickly they can be turned into cash (liquidity). The most liquid are called *current assets.* Those that are hard to sell quickly are called *fixed assets* or *property, plant, and equipment. Intangible assets* include patents and copyrights.

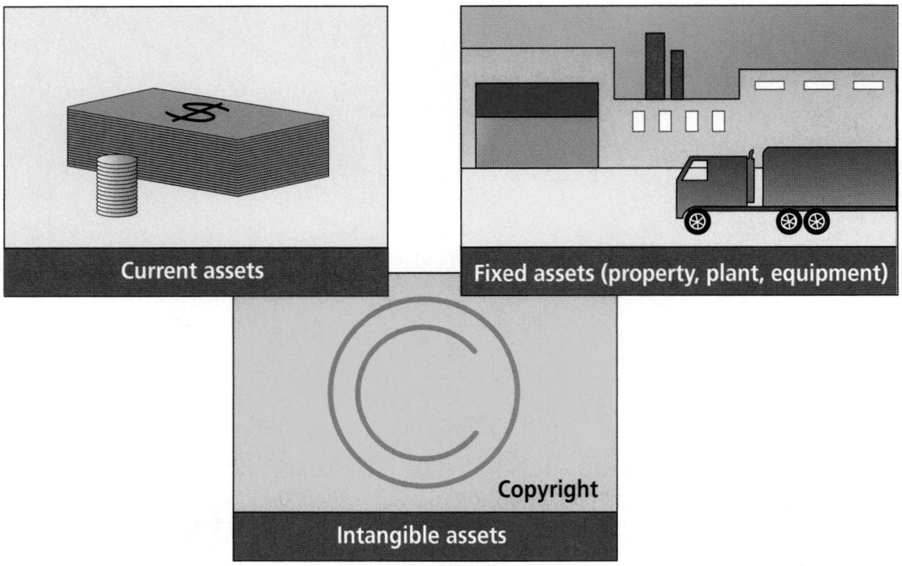

liquidity
How fast an asset can be converted into cash.

Assets are listed on the firm's balance sheet according to their liquidity (see Figure 18.5). **Liquidity** refers to how fast an asset can be converted into cash. For example, an account receivable is an amount of money owed to the firm that it expects to be paid within one year. Accounts receivable are considered liquid assets. Land, however, is difficult to turn into cash quickly because it takes much time and paperwork to sell land; thus, land is a long-term asset (an asset expected to last more than one year) and not considered liquid. Thus, assets are divided into three categories according to how quickly they can be turned into cash:

current assets
Items that can or will be converted into cash within one year.

fixed assets
Assets that are relatively permanent, such as land, buildings, and equipment.

intangible assets
Long-term assets (e.g., patents, trademarks, copyrights) that have no real physical form but do have value.

1. **Current assets** are items that can or will be converted into cash within one year. Current assets include cash, accounts receivable, and inventory.
2. **Fixed assets** are long-term assets that are relatively permanent such as land, buildings, and equipment. (These assets are also referred to on the balance sheet as property, plant, and equipment.)
3. **Intangible assets** are long-term assets that have no real physical form but do have value. Patents, trademarks, copyrights, and goodwill are examples of intangible assets.

Liabilities and Owners' Equity Accounts

liabilities
What the business owes to others (debts).

Another important accounting term is liabilities. **Liabilities** are what the business owes to others (debts). *Current liabilities* are debts due in one year or less; *long-term liabilities* are debts not due for one year or longer. The following are common liability accounts recorded on a balance sheet (see again Figure 18.4):

1. **Accounts payable** are current liabilities involving money owed to others for merchandise or services purchased on credit but not yet paid. If you have a bill you haven't paid, you have an account payable.
2. **Notes payable** are short-term or long-term liabilities (e.g., loans from banks) that a business promises to repay by a certain date.
3. **Bonds payable** are long-term liabilities that represent money lent to the firm that must be paid back. If a firm sells someone a bond, it agrees to repay that person the money he or she lent the company plus interest. (We will discuss bonds in depth in Chapters 19 and 20.)

Spotlight on Small Business

You, Incorporated

www.dinkytown.net/java/NetWorth.html

How do you think You, Inc., stacks up financially? Let's take a little time and find out. You may be pleasantly surprised, or you may realize that you need to think hard about planning your financial future. Remember, your net worth is nothing more than the difference between what you own (assets) and what you owe (liabilities). Be honest, and do your best to give a fair evaluation of your private property's value.

Assets		**Liabilities**	
Cash	$ ________	Installment loans & interest	$ ________
Savings account	________	Other loans and interest	________
Checking account	________	Credit card accounts	________
Home	________	Mortgage	________
Stocks & bonds	________	Taxes	________
Automobile	________	Other debts	________
IRA or Keogh	________		
Personal property	________		
Other assets	________		
Total assets	$ ________	Total liabilities	$ ________

Determine your net worth:

Total assets	$ ________
Total liabilities	– ________
Net worth	$ ________

As the fundamental accounting equation highlighted earlier, the value of things you own (assets) minus the amount of money you owe others (liabilities) is called *equity.* The value of what stockholders own in a firm (minus liabilities) is called *stockholders' equity* (or *shareholders' equity*). Because stockholders are the owners of a firm, stockholders' equity can also be called owners' equity.

Owners' equity is the amount of the business that belongs to the owners minus any liabilities owed by the business. The formula for owners' equity, then, is assets minus liabilities. Differences can exist in the owners' equity account according to the type of organization, however. Businesses that are not incorporated identify the investment of the sole proprietor or partner(s) through a *capital account.* For sole proprietors and partners, then, owners' equity means the value of everything owned by the business minus any liabilities of the owner(s), such as bank loans.

owners' equity
The amount of the business that belongs to the owners minus any liabilities owed by the business.

For corporations, the owners' equity account records the owners' claims to funds they have invested in the firm (such as capital stock), as well as retained earnings. **Retained earnings** are accumulated earnings from the firm's profitable operations that were kept in the business and not paid out to stockholders in dividends (distributions of company profits). We will discuss dividends in depth in Chapter 20. Take a few moments to review Figure 18.4 and see what facts you can determine about Fiberrific from its balance sheet. Then take a few minutes and try to estimate your own personal net worth, following the directions in the Spotlight on Small Business box.

retained earnings
The accumulated earnings from a firm's profitable operations that were kept in the business and not paid out to stockholders in dividends.

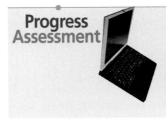

Progress Assessment

- What's the formula for the balance sheet? What do we call this formula?
- What does it mean to list various assets by liquidity?
- What goes into the account called liabilities?
- What is owners' equity and how is it determined?

The Income Statement

income statement
The financial statement that shows a firm's profit after costs, expenses, and taxes; it summarizes all of the resources that have come into the firm (revenue), all the resources that have left the firm, and the resulting net income.

net income or net loss
Revenue left over after all costs and expenses, including taxes, are paid.

The financial statement that shows a firm's bottom line—that is, its profit after costs, expenses, and taxes—is the **income statement** (also called the *profit and loss statement*). The income statement summarizes all of the resources (called *revenue*) that have come into the firm from operating activities, money resources that were used up, expenses incurred in doing business, and what resources were left after all costs and expenses, including taxes, were paid. The resources (revenue) left over are referred to as **net income or net loss** (see Figure 18.6).

The income statement reports the firm's financial operations over a particular period of time, usually a year, a quarter of a year, or a month.[24] It's the financial statement that reveals whether the business is actually earning a profit or losing money. The formula used to prepare an income statement is as follows:

Revenue − Cost of goods sold = Gross profit (or gross margin)
Gross profit − Operating expenses = Net income before taxes
Net income before taxes − Taxes = Net income (or loss)

The income statement includes valuable financial information for stockholders, lenders, investors (or potential investors), and employees. Because of the importance of this financial report, let's take a moment to look at the income statement and learn what each step means. Before we start, however, take a quick look at how the income statement is arranged according to generally accepted accounting principles (GAAP):

Revenue
− Cost of goods sold
Gross profit (gross margin)
− Operating expenses
Net income before taxes
− Taxes
Net income or loss

Revenue

revenue
The value of what is received for goods sold, services rendered, and other financial sources.

Revenue is the value of what is received for goods sold, services rendered, and other financial sources. Note that there is a difference between revenue and sales. Most revenue (money coming into the firm) comes from sales, but there could be other sources of revenue, such as rents received, money paid to the firm for use of its patents, and interest earned, that's included in reporting revenue. Be careful not to confuse the terms *revenue* and *sales,* or to use them as if they were synonymous. Also, a quick glance at the income statement shows you that *gross sales* are the total of all sales the firm completed. *Net sales* are gross sales minus returns, discounts, and allowances.

FIBERRIFIC
Income Statement
For the Year Ended December 31, 2004

① Revenues			
Gross sales		$720,000	
Less: Sales returns and allowances	$12,000		
Sales discounts	8,000	−20,000	
Net sales			$700,000
② Cost of goods sold			
Beginning inventory, Jan. 1		$200,000	
Merchandise purchases	$400,000		
Freight	40,000		
Net purchases		440,000	
Cost of goods available for sale	$640,000		
Less ending inventory, Dec. 31		−230,000	
Cost of goods sold			−410,000
③ Gross profit			$290,000
④ Operating expenses			
Selling expenses			
Salaries for salespeople	$90,000		
Advertising	18,000		
Supplies	2,000		
Total selling expenses		$110,000	
General expenses			
Office salaries	$67,000		
Depreciation	1,500		
Insurance	1,500		
Rent	28,000		
Light, heat, and power	12,000		
Miscellaneous	2,000		
		112,000	
Total operating expenses			222,000
Net income before taxes			$68,000
Less: Income tax expense			19,000
⑤ Net income after taxes			$49,000

FIGURE 18.6

SAMPLE FIBERRIFIC INCOME STATEMENT

① Revenue: Value of what's received from goods sold, services rendered, and other financial sources.

② Cost of goods sold: Cost of merchandise sold or cost of raw materials or parts used for producing items for resale.

③ Gross profit: How much the firm earned by buying or selling merchandise.

④ Operating expenses: Cost incurred in operating a business.

⑤ Net income after taxes: Profit or loss over a specific period after subtracting all costs and expenses, including taxes.

Cost of Goods Sold (Cost of Goods Manufactured)

The **cost of goods sold (or cost of goods manufactured)** is a measure of the cost of merchandise sold or cost of raw materials and supplies used for producing items for resale. It's common sense to calculate how much a business earned by selling merchandise over the period being evaluated, compared to how much it spent to buy the merchandise. The cost of goods sold includes the purchase price plus any freight charges paid to transport goods plus any costs associated with storing the goods. In other words, all the costs of buying and keeping merchandise for sale are included in the cost of goods sold. It's critical that companies accurately report and manage this important income statement item. Remember the problems Michael Miller discovered concerning Goodwill Industries' handling of its costs?

cost of goods sold (or cost of goods manufactured) A measure of the cost of merchandise sold or cost of raw materials and supplies used for producing items for resale.

When you subtract the cost of goods sold from net sales, you get what is called gross profit or gross margin. **Gross profit (gross margin)** is how much a firm earned by buying (or making) and selling merchandise. In a service firm, it's possible there may be no cost of goods sold; therefore, net revenue could

gross profit (gross margin) How much a firm earned by buying (or making) and selling merchandise.

equal gross profit. In a manufacturing firm, however, it's necessary to estimate the cost of goods manufactured. In either case (selling goods or services), the gross profit doesn't tell you everything you need to know about the financial performance of the firm. The financial evaluation of an income statement also includes determining the *net* profit or loss a firm experienced. To get that, you must subtract the business's expenses.

Operating Expenses and Net Profit or Loss

operating expenses
Costs involved in operating a business, such as rent, utilities, and salaries.

In the process of selling goods or services, a business experiences certain expenses. **Operating expenses** are the costs involved in operating a business. Obvious operating expenses include rent, salaries, supplies, utilities, insurance, and even depreciation of equipment (we will look at depreciation a little later). Expenses can generally be classified into two categories: selling and general expenses. *Selling expenses* are expenses related to the marketing and distribution of the firm's goods or services (such as salaries for salespeople, advertising, and supplies.) *General expenses* are administrative expenses of the firm (such as office salaries, depreciation, insurance, and rent). Accountants are trained to help you record all applicable expenses and find other relevant expenses you need to deduct.

After all expenses are deducted, the firm's net income before taxes is determined (see again Figure 18.6). After allocating for taxes, we get to what's called the *bottom line,* which is the net income (or perhaps net loss) the firm incurred from revenue minus sales returns, costs, expenses, and taxes.[25] It answers the question "How much did the business earn or lose in the reporting period?" Net income can also be referred to as net earnings or net profit.

The terms associated with the balance sheet and income statement may seem a bit confusing to you at this point, but you actually use similar accounting concepts all the time. For example, you know the importance of keeping track of costs and expenses when you prepare your own budget. If your expenses (e.g., rent and utilities) exceed your revenues (how much you earn), you are in trouble. If you need more money (revenue), you may need to sell some of the things you own to meet your expenses. The same is true in business. Companies need to keep track of how much money is earned and spent, how much cash they have on hand, and so on. The only difference is that companies tend to have more complex problems and a good deal more information to record than you as an individual do.

Users of financial statements are very interested in handling the flow of cash into and the flow of cash out of a business. Cash flow problems can plague both businesses and individuals. Keep this fact in mind as we look at the statement of cash flows in the next section.

The Statement of Cash Flows

statement of cash flows
Financial statement that reports cash receipts and disbursements related to a firm's three major activities: operations, investments, and financing.

In 1988, the Financial Accounting Standards Board (FASB) required firms to replace the statement of changes in financial position with the statement of cash flows. The **statement of cash flows** reports cash receipts and disbursements related to the three major activities of a firm:

- **Operations** are cash transactions associated with running the business.
- **Investments** are cash used in or provided by the firm's investment activities.
- **Financing** is cash raised from the issuance of new debt or equity capital or cash used to pay business expenses, past debts, or company dividends.

FIBERRIFIC
Statement of Cash Flows
For the Year Ended December 31, 2004

① Cash flows from operating activities		
Cash received from customers	$150,000	
Cash paid to suppliers and employees	(90,000)	
Interest paid	(5,000)	
Income tax paid	(4,500)	
Interest and dividends received	1,500	
Net cash provided by operating activities		$52,000
② Cash flows from investing activities		
Proceeds from sale of plant assets	$4,000	
Payments for purchase of equipment	(10,000)	
Net cash provided by investing activities		(6,000)
③ Cash flows from financing activities		
Proceeds from issuance of short-term debt	$3,000	
Payment of long-term debt	(7,000)	
Payment of dividends	(15,000)	
Net cash inflow from financing activities		(19,000)
Net change in cash and equivalents		$27,000
Cash balance (beginning of year)		(2,000)
Cash balance (end of year)		$25,000

FIGURE 18.7

FIBERRIFIC STATEMENT OF CASH FLOWS

① Cash receipts from sales, commissions, fees, interest, and dividends. Cash payments for salaries, inventories, operating expenses, interest, and taxes.

② Includes cash flows that are generated through a company's purchase or sale of long-term operational assets, investments in other companies, and its lending activities.

③ Cash inflows and outflows associated with the company's own equity transactions or its borrowing activities.

Accountants analyze all of the cash changes that have occurred from operating, investing, and financing to determine the firm's net cash position. The statement of cash flows also gives the firm some insight into how to handle cash better so that no cash flow problems (e.g., having no cash on hand) occur.[26]

Figure 18.7 shows a statement of cash flows, again using the example of Fiberrific. As you can see, this financial statement answers such questions as: How much cash came into the business from current operations? That is, how much cash came into the firm from buying and selling goods and services? Was cash used to buy stocks, bonds, or other investments? Were some investments sold that brought in cash? How much money came into the firm from issuing stock?

These and other financial transactions are analyzed to see their effect on the cash position of the firm. Understanding cash flow can mean success or failure of any business. We will analyze cash flow a bit more in depth in the next section. But first, consider the above and then read the Making Ethical Decisions box on p. 564 to see how accountants can sometimes face some tough ethical challenges in reporting the flow of funds into a business.

The Importance of Cash Flow Analysis

Understanding cash flow is an important part of financial reporting. If not properly managed, cash flow problems can cause a business much concern.[27] Cash flow analysis is really rather simple to comprehend. Let's say you borrow $100 from a friend to buy a used bike and agree to pay your friend back at the end of the week. In turn, you sell the bike for $150 to someone else, who also

Making Ethical Decisions

On the Accounting Hot Seat

www.fasb.gov

You are the only accountant employed by a small manufacturing firm. You are in charge of keeping the books for the company, which has been suffering from an economic downturn that shows no signs of lightening up in the near future.

You know that your employer is going to ask the bank for an additional loan so the company can continue to pay its bills. Unfortunately, the financial statements for the year will not show good results, and your best guess is that the bank will not approve a loan increase on the basis of the financial information you will present.

Your boss approaches you in early January before you have closed the books for the preceding year and suggests that perhaps the statements can be "improved" by treating the sales that were made at the beginning of January as if they were made in December. He also asks you to do a number of other things that will cover up the trail so that the auditors will not discover the padding of the year's sales.

You know that it is against the professional rules of the Financial Accounting Standards Board (FASB), and you argue with your boss. Your boss tells you that, if the company does not get the additional bank loan, there's a very good chance the business will close. That means you and everyone else in the firm will be out of a job. You believe your boss is probably right and you know that with the current economic downturn finding a job will be tough for you and almost impossible for others in the company. What are your alternatives? What are the likely consequences of each alternative? What will you do?

agrees to pay you in a week. Unfortunately, at the end of the week the person who bought the bike from you does not have the money as promised. This person says that he will have to pay you next month. Meanwhile, your friend wants the $100 you agreed to pay her by the end of the week! What seemed like a great opportunity to make an easy $50 profit is a real cause for concern. Right now, you owe $100 and have no cash. What do you do when your friend shows up at the end of the week and demands to be paid? If you were a business, this might cause you to default on the loan and possibly go bankrupt, even though you had the potential for profits.[28]

cash flow
The difference between cash coming in and cash going out of a business.

It's very possible that a business can increase sales and increase profit, and still suffer greatly from cash flow problems. **Cash flow** is simply the difference between cash coming in and cash going out of a business. Poor cash flow constitutes a major operating problem for many companies and is particularly difficult for small businesses. Such problems can also occur in an emerging business or an established one. Careful cash flow analysis is particularly helpful to seasonal businesses (such as ski resorts) in which the flow of cash into the business is sporadic.

What often happens to a business is that, in order to meet the demands of customers, the business buys more and more goods on credit (no cash is involved). Similarly, more and more goods are sold on credit (no cash is involved). This goes on until the firm uses up all the credit it has with its lenders. When the firm requests more money from its bank to pay a crucial bill, the bank refuses the loan because the credit limit has been reached. All other credit sources refuse funds as well. The company desperately needs funds to pay its bills, or it could be forced into bankruptcy. Unfortunately, all too often, the company does go into bankruptcy because there was no cash available when it was most needed.

Cash flow analysis also points out clearly that a business's relationship with its banker(s) is critical. Maintaining a working relationship with a bank is a path to preventing cash flow problems that often develop. The value that accountants provide to businesses in dealing with cash flow is also critical. Accountants can advise the firm whether it needs cash and, if so, how much. They can also offer advice on how a company is managing its cash position, and provide key insights into how, when, and where finance managers can get the money a firm needs. The statement of cash flows is a good barometer of measuring the cash position within a firm.

Even the mighty can fall. Retail giant Kmart proved that careful cash flow management is not just for small businesses. Poor cash flow forced the company to declare bankruptcy when it could not pay its suppliers. Kmart hopes to emerge from bankruptcy a better managed business. How can a large firm like Kmart suffer cash flow problems?

Applying Accounting Knowledge in Business

If accounting consisted of nothing more than repetitive functions of gathering and recording transactions and preparing financial statements, the tasks could be assigned solely to computers. In fact, most medium and large firms as well as growing numbers of small businesses have done just that. The Internet has initiated a new way of managing a firm's finances: online accounting. But the truth is that *how* you record and report financial data is also critically important.

Take a look at Figure 18.4 on p. 557 again. Note that Fiberrific lists accumulated depreciation on its property, plant, and equipment. What exactly does this mean, and how does it affect the company's financial position?

Depreciation is the systematic write-off of the cost of a tangible asset over its estimated useful life. Have you ever heard the comment that a new car depreciates in market value as soon as you drive it off the dealer's lot? The same principle holds true for equipment and other specific assets of the firm that are considered depreciable, such as machinery and equipment. Companies are permitted to recapture the cost of these assets over time using depreciation as an operating expense of the business.[29]

depreciation
The systematic write-off of the cost of a tangible asset over its estimated useful life.

Subject to certain technical accounting rules (set by GAAP and the Internal Revenue Service), which are beyond the scope of this chapter, a firm may use one of several different techniques for calculating depreciation. The key thing to understand right now is that different depreciation techniques could result in a different net income for the firm. Accountants are able to offer financial advice and recommend ways of legally handling questions regarding depreciation, as well as other accounts such as inventory, where different valuation methods can affect a firm's financial performance. Let's look briefly at how accountants can value inventory.

The valuation of a firm's inventory presents another interesting accounting application. Inventories are a key part of many companies' financial statements and are important in determining a firm's cost of goods sold (or manufactured) on the income statement. Look again at Fiberrific's income statement in Figure 18.6 on p. 561. When a firm sells merchandise from its inventory, it can calculate the cost of that item in different ways. In financial reporting, it doesn't matter when a particular item was actually placed in a firm's inventory, but it does matter how an accountant records the cost of the item when it was sold. Sound a bit confusing? Look at the example below.

Let's say that a college bookstore buys textbooks for resale. It buys 100 copies of a particular textbook in July 2004 at a cost of $50 a copy. When classes begin in August, the bookstore sells 50 copies of the text to students for $60 each. The 50 copies not sold are placed in the bookstore's inventory for next term. In late December the bookstore orders 50 additional copies of the same text to sell for the coming term. Unfortunately, the price of the book to the bookstore has increased to $60 a copy due to inflation and other costs. The bookstore now has 100 copies of the same textbook from different purchase cycles in its inventory (same book, but different costs to the bookstore). If the bookstore sells 50 copies of the book to students for a price of $70 at the beginning of the new term in mid-January, what's the bookstore's cost of the book for accounting purposes? It depends.

The books are identical but the accounting treatment would be different. If the bookstore uses a method called **first in, first out (FIFO)**, the cost of goods sold (cost of 50 textbooks sold) would be $50 each, because the textbook that was bought first cost $50. The bookstore, however, could use another method, called **last in, first out (LIFO)**. Using LIFO, the bookstore's last purchase of the textbook that cost $60 each would be the cost of each of the 50 textbooks sold. If the book sells for $70, you can see how the difference in accounting methods affects the bookstore's net income. FIFO would report $10 more of income (per book) before taxes than LIFO would (see Figure 18.8).

first in, first out (FIFO)
An accounting method for calculating cost of inventory; it assumes that the first goods to come in are the first to go out.

last in, first out (LIFO)
An accounting method for calculating cost of inventory; it assumes that the last goods to come in are the first to go out.

What's important to understand about depreciation and inventory valuation is that generally accepted accounting principles (GAAP) can permit an accountant to use different methods of depreciating a firm's long-term assets and valuing a firm's inventory. That's why the American Institute of Certified Public Accountants (AICPA) insists that companies provide readers of their financial statements complete information concerning their financial operations.[30] The Legal Briefcase box highlights changes in the accounting profession that were implemented due to irregularities, and in some cases outright fraud, that surfaced in the early 2000s. In the accounting profession, the accuracy of financial statements cannot be compromised.[31]

Progress Assessment

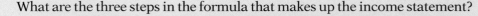

- What are the three steps in the formula that makes up the income statement?
- What's the difference between revenue and income on the income statement?
- Why is the statement of cash flows important in evaluating a firm's operations?
- What's the difference between LIFO and FIFO inventory valuation? How could the use of these methods change financial results?

FIGURE 18.8

ACCOUNTING USING LIFO VERSUS FIFO INVENTORY VALUATION

	FIFO	LIFO
Revenue	$70	$70
Cost of goods sold	50	60
Income before taxes	20	10
Taxes of 40%	8	4
Net income	12	6

Legal Briefcase

www.pcaob.com/firms.php

Auditing the Accounting Profession

When WorldCom disclosed it had uncovered $3.8 billion (that's right, *billion*) in accounting fraud within the company during 2001–2002, everyone from the smallest investor to the president of the United States expressed outrage. When CEOs from Tyco, Adelphia, and Enron were escorted out of their offices in handcuffs by federal marshals after being accused of defrauding investors and looting their companies, it was inevitable that changes would come in the accounting industry. The U.S. Congress responded to the wave of corporate scandals and accounting irregularities by passing the Sarbanes-Oxley Act, which created an accounting oversight board.

Specifically, the Public Company Accounting Oversight Board was charged with overseeing accountants and their professional organization, the American Institute of Certified Public Accountants (AICPA). The primary responsibility of the board, whose establishment ended the industry's practice of regulating itself, is to make auditors more accountable than they have been. The board also agreed to look into possibly tougher accounting standards in reporting stock options and forcing accounting firms doing auditing work for companies to divest themselves of a consulting relationship with the same company.

Legally, the new board is under the Securities and Exchange Commission (SEC). As such, the SEC has the power to override any board decisions. How this new experiment will work and how the accounting industry will fare with new regulation is anyone's guess at this point. However, Rebecca McEnally, an accounting expert at the Association for Investment Management and Research, raised a point with which few CEOs in boardrooms across American could disagree: "Anything that brings daylight to accounting practices at this time . . . has to be good."

Sources: Carrie Johnson Washington, "New Accounting Panel Being Watched for Reform Clues," *Washington Post,* March 4, 2003, p. E1; "Shifting Power: Governance in America," *The Economist,* January 11, 2003, p. 62; and Greg Wright, "Controversy Dogs Board Created to Prevent Accounting Fraud," Gannett News Service, February 6, 2003.

Analyzing Financial Statements: Ratio Analysis

Accurate financial information from the firm's financial statements forms the basis of the financial analysis performed by accountants inside and outside the firm. **Ratio analysis** is the assessment of a firm's financial condition and performance through calculations and interpretation of financial ratios developed from the firm's financial statements. Financial ratios are especially useful in analyzing the actual performance of the company compared to its financial objectives and compared to other firms within its industry. At first glance, ratio analysis may seem complicated. The fact is most of us already use ratios quite often. For example, in basketball, the number of shots made from the foul line is expressed by a ratio: shots made to shots attempted. A player who shoots 85 percent from the foul line is considered an outstanding foul shooter, and suggestions are to not foul him or her in a close game.

ratio analysis
The assessment of a firm's financial condition and performance through calculations and interpretations of financial ratios developed from the firm's financial statements.

Whether ratios measure an athlete's performance or the financial health of a business, they provide a good deal of valuable information. Financial ratios provide key insights into how a firm compares to other firms in its industry in the important areas of liquidity (speed of changing assets into cash), debt (leverage), profitability, and business activity. Understanding and interpreting business ratios is a key to sound financial analysis. Let's look briefly at four key types of ratios businesses use to measure financial performance.

Liquidity Ratios

As explained earlier, the word *liquidity* refers to how fast an asset can be converted to cash. Liquidity ratios measure a company's ability to turn assets into cash to pay its short-term debts (liabilities that must be repaid within one year). These short-term debts are of particular importance to creditors of the firm who expect to be paid on time.[32] Two key liquidity ratios are the current ratio and the acid-test ratio.

The *current ratio* is the ratio of a firm's current assets to its current liabilities. This information can be found on the firm's balance sheet. Look back at Figure 18.4 on p. 557, which details Fiberrific's balance sheet. Fiberrific lists current assets of \$600,000 and current liabilities of \$288,000. The firm therefore has a current ratio of 2.08, which means Fiberrific has \$2.08 of current assets for every \$1 of current liabilities. See below:

$$\text{Current ratio} = \frac{\text{Current assets}}{\text{Current liabilities}} = \frac{\$600{,}000}{\$288{,}000} = 2.08$$

An obvious question to ask is "How well positioned financially is Fiberrific for the short term (less than one year)?" It depends! Usually a company with a current ratio of 2 or better is considered a safe risk for granting short-term credit since it appears to be performing in line with market expectations. However, it's important to compare Fiberrific's current ratio to that of competing firms in its industry. It's also important for the firm to compare its current ratio with its current ratio from the previous year to note any significant changes.

Another key liquidity ratio, called the *acid-test* or *quick ratio,* measures the cash, marketable securities (such as stocks and bonds), and receivables of a firm, compared to its current liabilities:

$$\text{Acid-test ratio} = \frac{\text{Cash} + \text{Accounts receivable} + \text{Marketable securities}}{\text{Current liabilities}}$$
$$= \frac{\$265{,}000}{\$288{,}000} = .92$$

This ratio is particularly important to firms with difficulty converting inventory into quick cash. It helps answer such questions as the following: What if sales drop off and we can't sell our inventory? Can we still pay our short-term debt? Though ratios vary among industries, an acid-test ratio of

Faucets, faucets, and more faucets. Home Depot stores stock over 36,000 items that cover 130,000 square feet of floor space. Maintaining such an enormous inventory is no small task. What financial ratios would help Home Depot make sure it is managing its inventory efficiently?

between 0.50 and 1.0 is usually considered satisfactory, but a ratio under 1.0 could also be a hint of some cash flow problems. Therefore, Fiberrific's acid-test ratio of .92 could raise concerns that perhaps the firm may not meet its short-term debt and may therefore have to go to a high-cost lender for financial assistance.

Leverage (Debt) Ratios

Leverage (debt) ratios measure the degree to which a firm relies on borrowed funds in its operations. A firm that takes on too much debt could experience problems repaying lenders or meeting promises made to stockholders. The *debt to owners' equity ratio* measures the degree to which the company is financed by borrowed funds that must be repaid. Again, we can use Figure 18.4 to measure Fiberrific's level of debt:

$$\text{Debt to owners' equity} = \frac{\text{Total liabilities}}{\text{Owners' equity}} = \frac{\$613{,}000}{\$213{,}000} = 287\%$$

Anything above 100 percent shows that a firm has more debt than equity. With a ratio of 287 percent, Fiberrific has a rather high degree of debt compared to its equity, which implies that the firm may be perceived as quite risky to lenders and investors. However, it's always important to compare a firm's debt ratios to those of other firms in its industry because debt financing is more acceptable in some industries than it is in others.[33] Comparisons with past debt ratios can also identify trends that may be occurring within the firm or industry.

Profitability (Performance) Ratios

Profitability (performance) ratios measure how effectively a firm is using its various resources to achieve profits. Management's performance is often measured by the firm's profitability ratios. Three of the more important ratios used are earnings per share, return on sales, and return on equity.

In 1997, a new Financial Accounting Standards Board rule went into effect that requires companies to report their quarterly earnings per share in two ways: basic and diluted. The *basic earnings per share (basic EPS) ratio* helps determine the amount of profit earned by a company for each share of outstanding common stock. The *diluted earnings per share (diluted EPS) ratio* measures the amount of profit earned by a company for each share of outstanding common stock, but this ratio also takes into consideration stock options, warrants, preferred stock, and convertible debt securities, which can be converted into common stock. For simplicity's sake, we will compute only the basic earnings per share (EPS).

EPS is a very important ratio for a company because earnings help stimulate growth in the firm and pay for such things as stockholders' dividends. Continued earnings growth is well received by both investors and lenders. The basic EPS ratio calculated for Fiberrific is as follows:

$$\text{Basic earnings per share} = \frac{\text{Net income after taxes}}{\text{Number of common stock shares outstanding}}$$

$$= \frac{\$49{,}000}{1{,}000{,}000} = \$.049 \text{ per share}$$

Another reliable indicator of performance is obtained by using a ratio that measures the return on sales. Firms use this ratio to see if they are doing as well as the companies they compete against in generating income from the sales they achieve. *Return on sales* is calculated by comparing a company's net income to its total sales. Fiberrific's return on sales is 7 percent, a figure that must be measured against competing firms in its industry to judge its performance:

$$\text{Return on sales} = \frac{\text{Net income}}{\text{Net sales}} = \frac{\$49{,}000}{\$700{,}000} = 7\%$$

Risk is a market variable that concerns investors. The higher the risk involved in an industry, the higher the return investors expect on their investment. Therefore, the level of risk involved in an industry and the return on investment of competing firms is important in comparing the firm's performance. *Return on equity* measures how much was earned for each dollar invested by owners. It's calculated by comparing a company's net income to its total owners' equity. Fiberrific's return on equity looks reasonably sound:

$$\text{Return on equity} = \frac{\text{Net income after tax}}{\text{Total owners' equity}} = \frac{\$49{,}000}{\$213{,}000} = 23\%$$

It's important to remember that profits help companies like Fiberrific grow. Therefore, these and other profitability ratios are considered vital measurements of company growth and management performance.

Activity Ratios

Converting the firm's resources to profits is a key function of management. Activity ratios measure the effectiveness of a firm's management in using the assets that are available.

The *inventory turnover ratio* measures the speed of inventory moving through the firm and its conversion into sales. Inventory sitting by idly in a business costs money. Think of the fixed cost of storing inventory in a warehouse as opposed to the revenue available when companies sell (turn over) inventory. The more efficiently a firm manages its inventory, the higher the return. The inventory turnover ratio for Fiberrific is measured as follows:

$$\text{Inventory turnover} = \frac{\text{Cost of goods sold}}{\text{Average inventory}} = \frac{\$410{,}000}{\$215{,}000} = 1.9 \text{ times}$$

A lower-than-average inventory turnover ratio in an industry often indicates obsolete merchandise on hand or poor buying practices. A higher than average ratio may signal lost sales because of inadequate stock. An acceptable turnover ratio is generally determined industry by industry. Fiberrific's inventory turnover of 1.9 times would need to be measured with its main competitors to estimate its efficiency in managing its inventory. Managers need to be aware of proper inventory control and expected inventory turnover to ensure proper performance. Have you ever worked as a food server in a restaurant? How many times did your employer expect you to turn over a table (keep changing customers at the table) in an evening? The more times a table turns, the higher the return to the owner.

Accountants and other finance professionals use several other specific ratios, in addition to the ones we have discussed, to learn more about a firm's financial condition. The key purpose here is to acquaint you with what financial ratios are, the relationship they have with the firm's financial statements, and how businesspeople—including investors, creditors, lenders, and managers—use them. If you can't recall where the accounting information used in ratio

BALANCE SHEET ACCOUNTS		
ASSETS	**LIABILITIES**	**OWNERS' EQUITY**
Cash	Accounts payable	Capital stock
Accounts receivable	Notes payable	Retained earnings
Inventory	Bonds payable	Common stock
Investments	Taxes payable	Treasury stock
Equipment		
Land		
Buildings		
Motor vehicles		
Goodwill		

INCOME STATEMENT ACCOUNTS			
REVENUES	**COST OF GOODS SOLD**	**EXPENSES**	
Sales revenue	Cost of buying goods	Wages	Interest
Rental revenue	Cost of storing goods	Rent	Donations
Commissions revenue		Repairs	Licenses
Royalty revenue		Travel	Fees
		Insurance	Supplies
		Utilities	Advertising
		Entertainment	Taxes
		Storage	

FIGURE 18.9

ACCOUNTS IN THE BALANCE SHEET AND INCOME STATEMENT

analysis comes from, see Figure 18.9 for a quick reference. It's also important for you to keep in mind that financial analysis begins where the accounting statements end.

We hope that you can see from this chapter that there is more to accounting than meets the eye. It can be fascinating and is critical to the firm's operations. It's worth saying one more time that, as the language of business, accounting is a worthwhile language to learn.

Progress Assessment

- What's the major benefit of a business performing ratio analysis on the basis of its financial statements?
- What are the four main categories of financial ratios?

Summary

1. Describe the importance of financial information and accounting.

1. Financial information is critical to the growth and development of an organization. Accounting provides the information necessary to measure a firm's financial condition.
   - ***What is accounting?***

   Accounting is the recording, classifying, summarizing, and interpreting of financial events and transactions that affect an organization. The methods used to record and summarize accounting data into reports are called an accounting system.

2. Define and explain the different areas of the accounting profession.

2. The accounting profession covers five major areas: managerial accounting, financial accounting, auditing, tax accounting, and governmental and not-for-profit accounting.

- ***How does managerial accounting differ from financial accounting?***

Managerial accounting provides information and analyses to managers within the firm to assist them in decision making. Financial accounting provides information and analyses to external users of data such as creditors and lenders.

- ***What is the job of an auditor?***

Auditors review and evaluate the standards used to prepare a company's financial statements. An independent audit is conducted by a public accountant and is an evaluation and unbiased opinion about the accuracy of company financial statements.

- ***What is the difference between a private accountant and a public accountant?***

A public accountant provides services for a fee to a variety of companies, whereas a private accountant works for a single company. Private and public accountants do essentially the same things with the exception of independent audits. Private accountants do perform internal audits, but only public accountants supply independent audits.

3. Distinguish between accounting and bookkeeping, list the steps in the accounting cycle, and explain how computers are used in accounting.

3. Many people confuse bookkeeping and accounting.

- ***What is the difference between bookkeeping and accounting?***

Bookkeeping is part of accounting and includes the mechanical part of recording data. Accounting also includes classifying, summarizing, interpreting, and reporting data to management.

- ***What are journals and ledgers?***

Journals are original-entry accounting documents. This means that they are the first place transactions are recorded. Summaries of journal entries are recorded (posted) into ledgers. Ledgers are specialized accounting books that arrange the transactions by homogeneous groups (accounts).

- ***What are the six steps of the accounting cycle?***

The six steps of the accounting cycle are (1) analyzing documents; (2) recording information into journals; (3) posting that information into ledgers; (4) developing a trial balance; (5) preparing financial statements (the balance sheet, income statement, and statement of cash flows); and (6) analyzing financial statements.

- ***How can computers help accountants?***

Computers can record and analyze data and provide financial reports. Software is available that can continuously analyze and test accounting systems to be sure they are functioning correctly. Computers can help decision making by providing appropriate information, but they cannot make good financial decisions independently. Accounting applications and creativity are still human traits.

4. Explain how the major financial statements differ.

4. Financial statements are a critical part of the firm's financial position.

- ***What is a balance sheet?***

A balance sheet reports the financial position of a firm on a particular day. The fundamental accounting equation used to prepare the balance sheet is Assets = Liabilities + Owners' equity.

- ***What are the major accounts of the balance sheet?***

Assets are economic resources owned by the firm, such as buildings and machinery. Liabilities are amounts owed by the firm to others (e.g., creditors, bondholders). Owners' equity is the value of the things the firm owns (assets) minus any liabilities; thus, owners' equity equals assets minus liabilities.

- ***What is an income statement?***

An income statement reports revenues, costs, and expenses for a specific period of time (e.g., for the year ended December 31, 2004). The formula is

Revenue − Cost of goods sold = Gross margin; Gross margin − Operating expenses = Net income before taxes; and Net income before taxes − Taxes = Net income (or net loss). Note that the income statement is sometimes called the profit and loss statement.

- ***What is a statement of cash flows?***

Cash flow is the difference between cash receipts (money coming in) and cash disbursements (money going out). The statement of cash flows reports cash receipts and disbursements related to the firm's major activities: operations, investments, and financing.

5. Applying accounting knowledge makes the reporting and analysis of data a challenging occupation. Depreciation is a key account that accountants evaluate. Also, two accounting techniques for valuing inventory are known as LIFO and FIFO.

5. Describe the role of depreciation, LIFO, and FIFO in reporting financial information.

- ***What is depreciation?***

Depreciation is the systematic writing off of the value of a tangible asset over its estimated useful life. Depreciation must be noted on both the balance sheet and the income statement.

- ***What are LIFO and FIFO?***

LIFO and FIFO are methods of valuing inventory. FIFO means first in, first out; LIFO means last in, first out. The method an accountant uses to value inventory, FIFO or LIFO, can affect its net income.

6. Financial ratios are a key part of analyzing financial information.

6. Explain the importance of ratio analysis in reporting financial information.

- ***What are the four key categories of ratios?***

There are four key categories of ratios: liquidity ratios, leverage (debt) ratios, profitability (performance) ratios, and activity ratios.

- ***What is the major value of ratio analysis to the firm?***

Ratio analysis provides the firm with information about its financial position in key areas compared to comparable firms in its industry and its past performance.

Key Terms

accounting 548
accounting cycle 553
annual report 550
assets 556
auditing 551
balance sheet 556
bookkeeping 553
cash flow 564
certified internal auditor (CIA) 551
certified management accountant 549
certified public accountant (CPA) 550
cost of goods sold (or cost of goods manufactured) 561
current assets 558
depreciation 565
double-entry bookkeeping 553
financial accounting 550
financial statement 555
first in, first out (FIFO) 566
fixed assets 558
fundamental accounting equation 556
government and not-for-profit accounting 552
gross profit (gross margin) 561
income statement 560
independent audit 551
intangible assets 558
journal 553
last in, first out (LIFO) 566
ledger 553
liabilities 558
liquidity 558
managerial accounting 549
net income or net loss 560
operating expenses 562
owners' equity 559
private accountants 550
public accountants 550
ratio analysis 567
retained earnings 559
revenue 560
statement of cash flows 562
tax accountant 552
trial balance 554

1. Visit, telephone, or e-mail a CPA from a local company in your area, or talk with a CPA in your college's business department. Ask what challenges, changes, and opportunities he or she foresees in the accounting profession in the next five years. List the forecasts on a sheet of paper and then compare them with the information in this chapter.

2. Obtain the most recent annual report for a company of your choice. (Hints: *The Wall Street Journal* has a free annual reports service; call to order a report at 1-800-654-2582. Also, many companies post their annual reports on their websites.) Look over the company's financial statements and see if they coincide with the information in this chapter. Read the opinion of the auditing firm (usually at the end of the report). Write down important conclusions the auditors have made about the company's financial statements.

3. Go to the website of the American Institute of Certified Public Accountants (www.aicpa.org), the Institute of Certified Management Accountants (www.imanet.org), and the Institute of Internal Auditors (www.theiia.org). Browse through the sites and find information concerning the requirements for becoming a certified public accountant (CPA), certified management accountant (CMA), and certified internal auditor (CIA). Compare the different requirements of the programs and choose which program is most interesting to you.

4. Place yourself in the role of a small-business consultant. One of your clients, Be Pretty Fashions, is considering opening two new stores. The problem is that the business often experiences cash flow problems due to continuous style changes that occur in the fashion industry. Prepare a formal draft memo to Be Pretty Fashions explaining the problems a firm experiences when it encounters the cash flow problems that typically occur with such growth. Think of a business option Be Pretty Fashions could try to avoid cash flow problems.

5. This chapter describes two ways of accounting for cost of goods sold: first in, first out (FIFO) and last in, first out (LIFO). Compute the net income using FIFO and LIFO with the information listed below. Write down the factors you should consider in deciding which inventory valuation method is best for a firm to use.

Beginning inventory:	25,000 units @ \$20.00
Purchases (new inventory):	25,000 units @ 25.00
Sales:	25,000 units @ 55.00
Tax rate:	33%

Purpose

To calculate and analyze current ratios and quick (acid-test) ratios.

Exercise

Thingamajigs and Things, a small gift shop, has total assets of \$45,000 (including inventory valued at \$30,000) and \$9,000 in liabilities. WannaBees, a specialty clothing store, has total assets of \$150,000 (including inventory valued at \$125,000) and \$85,000 in liabilities. Both businesses have applied for loans. Use the calculators on the Bankrate.com website to answer the following questions:

1. Calculate the current ratio for each company. Comparing the ratios, which company is more likely to get the loan? Why?
2. The quick (acid-test) ratio is considered an even more reliable measure of a business's ability to repay loans than the current ratio. Because inventory is often difficult to liquidate, the value of the inventory is subtracted from the total current assets. Calculate the quick ratio for each business. Do you think either business will get the loan? Why?

Casing The Web

To access the case "Getting Through the Hard Times at Hard Rock," visit

www.mhhe.com/ub7e

Video Case

Talking the Language of Business: AON

Joe Prochaska, senior vice president and comptroller at AON, is familiar with all the names used to describe accountants: bean-counters, pencil-pushers, number-crunchers, to name just a few. Like most accountants, he ignores these unflattering titles because he knows one simple fact: You can't understand business unless you understand accounting, because accounting is the language of business. Whether you operate your own small business from your home or work for a multinational corporation like AON, an understanding of accounting will help you in whatever business career you choose. Prochaska's company is the largest insurance broker in the world, with over 550 offices in 130 countries. If the name AON is not familiar to you, it's because AON actually does most of its business in reinsurance: It sells insurance to insurance companies.

You learned in this chapter that accounting is the process of recording, categorizing, and interpreting financial transactions. You also learned there are several types of accountants. *Managerial accountants* interpret financial data for internal use in a company. *Financial accountants,* such as a certified public accountant (CPA), provide accounting information for persons outside the firm, such as potential investors and the owners themselves. *Auditors* are like financial detectives; they come in and check the accounting records to make sure that the records are accurate and follow all the rules of accounting. *Tax accountants* prepare tax statements and make sure the firm fully complies with tax rules while minimizing the taxes it must pay.

It's important that accountants follow standard procedures so that financial information is similar company by company. The Financial Accounting Standards Board (FASB) created Generally Accepted Accounting Principles (GAAP) for this reason. The Securities and Exchange Commission (SEC) is responsible for making sure companies follow these standards. If a company violates these rules, the penalties may be severe. For example, the SEC has taken strong action against firms such as WorldCom and Enron.

The six-step accounting cycle leads to the preparation of the firm's key financial statements: the balance sheet, income statement, and statement of cash flows. In his role as comptroller at AON, Joe Prochaska is responsible for seeing this process is done correctly. However, the real challenge comes when Prochaska and his staff are called on to analyze what the financial statements mean to AON in terms of how well the firm is doing financially and what improvements it can make to perform even better.

Financial information is crucial to AON as it is to all firms. Being in the reinsurance business, AON helps insurance companies estimate their "catastrophic exposure." In other words, if a disaster hits, such as hurricane Isabella did in 2003, will insurance companies be able to cover the losses suffered by policyholders? The financial data collected will tell the firms, for example, whether they need to raise premiums and, if so, by how much.

Without question, accounting is critical to the long-term success of any organization. Furthermore, it is challenging and interesting work. Most important, accounting is something that everyone needs to understand to comprehend the "language of business."

Thinking It Over

1. If you prepared a balance sheet and income statement for your own finances as the chapter suggested, what did you learn and how could you improve your financial condition in the future?
2. Why is the government concerned with accounting practices? Does the government seem to be less or more involved with accounting procedures in recent years? Why?
3. What group or groups are interested in a company's financial statements? Why would people be interested in compiling financial ratios for a firm?

Part 6

Managing Information (Information Systems)

Career Portfolio

Information management is a major growth industry of the future. To understand either the past or the present conditions of a company, we must have information. The process of getting the right information and processing it efficiently is an important part of staying competitive in today's business world. In a world constantly reshaped by new technology, the field of information management plays a key role.

Changing technologies have created a large number of different job titles in this exciting area. Careers are available in information systems management, computer programming, cost estimating, software engineering, and computer support, just to name a few. All forecasts predict that career opportunities in computer-related businesses and industries will continue to grow more rapidly than the average for other occupations.

Skills

Anyone who chooses to work with information technology should be comfortable with change and have a willingness to keep abreast of changes. Such a person also needs to have an interest in and aptitude for data and information and have an ability to see trends and relationships. People in this area are usually involved in some way with problem solving. An aptitude for seeing possible solutions to problems is important.

Career Paths

In this ever-changing field, up-to-date knowledge is the key. A formal education in computer science, for example, would be almost useless if it was obtained 10 years ago and not updated. Most employers prefer hiring people who have had recent college coursework in software applications, programming, new technologies, and general business. Business knowledge is important because it allows the employee to place his or her work in context.

Computer skills are taught at public and private vocational schools, community colleges, and universities. Many programmers and systems analysts are college graduates, and a degree is helpful in getting hired. However, vocational schools can often provide the knowledge and skill necessary to excel.

SOME POSSIBLE CAREERS IN INFORMATION SYSTEMS				
JOB TITLE	**SALARY**	**JOB DUTIES**	**CAREER PATH**	**PROSPECTS**
Systems analyst	$37,460–$89,040 Median: $59,330	Advise computer programmers on problem solutions. Implement management decision on data processing issues.	In private industry, can start as a trainee and then be promoted into management.	Growth will be much faster than average through 2010.
Computer programmer	$35,020–$93,210 Median: $57,590	Work for systems analyst to write, test, and maintain programs needed by management.	Promotions often mean greater task complexity or supervisory responsibilities. Start out as junior programmer.	Average growth through 2010.
Cost estimator	$27,710–$75,460 Median: $45,800	Prepare specifications using precedent, math, and computer data to predict cost requirements.	Career path varies greatly from company to company and from industry to industry.	Average growth through 2010. Good in construction.
Operations research analyst	$31,860–$88,870 Median: $53,420	Solve problems using computer models and data. Nature of problems varies.	Master's degree or Ph.D. very desirable. High level of computer skills is mandatory. Promotion into management quite possible. Bachelor's degree graduates start as research assistants.	Slower than average growth through 2010. Good opportunities for those with master's degree or Ph.D.

Source: Bureau of Labor Statistics, *Occupational Outlook Handbook*, 2002–03.

Kastle Systems, Inc.

Name: Micky Keener

Age: 50

Position/title: Operations Center Manager

Salary range: $60,000-$85,000

Time in this position: 2½ years

Major factors in the decision to take this position: Flexible hours, opportunity for further advancement, constant challenge, and the opportunity to take the department to a place where employees would enjoy working.

Company name: Kastle Systems, Inc.

Company's Web address: www.kastle.com

Company description: Kastle is a full-service electronic security and access control system provider, with over a quarter century of proven experience providing state-of-the-art outsourced security service to office buildings and their tenants nationwide.

Job description: The Operations Center Manager reports directly to the Vice President of the Operations Department and is responsible for the supervision and management of Operation Center personnel, training, and payroll preparation. The Operations Center Manager is responsible for the 24-hour operation of the Center, the quality of the services provided, and for the physical appearance of the Operations Center. In addition to these unique responsibilities, the Operations Center Manager may be directed to perform special projects as assigned.

Career paths: I have worked for Kastle for 20 years. I started in the Operations Center (3 years), served as shift manager (3 years), assistant manager in Operations Center (7 years), assistant manager in Customer Service (4 years), and now Operations Manager.

Ideal next job: Vice President for the Washington office.

Best part of your job: Since my job is a 24-hour operation, the flexibility of the hours is great. Also, working with the many different personalities is up there, too.

Worst part of your job: Getting people in the Operations Department to come to work on a regular basis. There isn't a lot of commitment from the staff on the importance of a full-time job.

Educational background: Associate's degree in Business Management.

Favorite course: I really enjoyed the business classes. Each was unique and interesting. So many of the topics deal with real-life issues.

Best course for your career: I really can't pick one! I enjoyed all the classes. Each and every one has its benefits in the field of management.

Recommended by Rieann Spence-Gale, North Virginia Community College/Alexandria

Chapter 19

Financial Management

Learning Goals

After you have read and studied this chapter, you should be able to

1. Describe the importance of finance and financial management to an organization, and explain the responsibilities of financial managers.
2. Outline the financial planning process, and explain the three key budgets in the financial plan.
3. Explain the major reasons why firms need operating funds, and identify various types of financing that can be used to obtain these funds.
4. Identify and describe different sources of short-term financing.
5. Identify and describe different sources of long-term financing.

www.krispykreme.com

Getting to Know Randy Casstevens, CFO of Krispy Kreme Doughnuts

When is a doughnut a historical object? When it's on display at the Smithsonian Institution's National Museum of American History. According to Mike Lythgoe, Smithsonian program coordinator, "Krispy Kreme is very much a part of American history; and it's not often you get to eat some of your history." It's true, Krispy Kreme doughnuts have been a part of Americana since 1937, when Vernon Rudolph opened his first store in Winston-Salem, North Carolina.

The challenge of turning a sleepy Southern company, at whose stores old men read the newspaper and traded fishing stories, into a national phenomenon was no easy task. The job of measuring the financial implications of expansion belongs to the company's chief financial officer (CFO) Randy Casstevens. Today the line of people trying to buy a Krispy Kreme franchise seems as long as the lines waiting to buy hot doughnuts in the stores.

When Casstevens analyzed company revenue he found that Krispy Kreme has higher profit margins than other fast-food businesses. In fact, Krispy Kreme's cash-flow margins tend toward the mid-20 percent range compared to 10 to 15 percent for competitors. Casstevens also learned that the average Krispy Kreme generates cash, big cash, from the first day a store opens. After a 12-month honeymoon period, the average Krispy Kreme takes in yearly revenues of approximately $2.4 million, compared to a typical McDonald's $1.5 million, Dunkin' Donuts' $744,000, and Cinnabon's $408,000 a year.

Casstevens considered two questions: How far and how fast should the company expand in the next five years? Should the company expand opportunities for franchisees to get in on the dough (pun intended) or is it best for the company to open only company-owned stores? Casstevens recommended that Krispy Kreme not attempt to become the next Starbucks by opening large numbers of company-owned stores. He also suggested that the company continue its franchising efforts with a few key changes for prospective new franchisees. One, they will have a partner: Krispy Kreme Doughnuts, Inc. Two, the company will push for megafranchisees who will commit to opening at least 10 stores in a given region.

Today the line of people trying to buy a Krispy Kreme franchise seems as long as the lines waiting to buy hot doughnuts in the stores.

Casstevens sees a bright future for the company but is aware of the fact that such popularity could wane. However, with only 250 locations in the country (compared to Dunkin' Donuts' 5,500 stores and McDonald's 30,000), the potential for growth seems limitless. Krispy Kreme (stock symbol KKD) became a public company in 2000 and now offers its stock to investors. The funds obtained from this initial public offering (IPO) helped the company increase its cash position and reduce corporate debt.

Risk, complexity, and uncertainty clearly define the role of financial management, especially in fast-growing firms such as Krispy Kreme. Add to these challenges fluctuations in interest rates, expectations of investors and lenders, budgeting, and managing funds, and the job of the financial manager takes on even more intensity. In this chapter, you'll explore the role of finance in business and learn about the tools financial managers such as Randy Casstevens use to seek financial stability and future growth.

Sources: Ronald Fink, "The Fear of All Sums," *CFO,* August 2002, pp. 34–42; Carlye Adler, "Would You Pay $2 Million for This Franchise?" *Fortune Small Business,* May 1, 2002, pp. 36–41; "Smithsonian to Celebrate Krispy Kreme—A Hole Lot of History," *Washington Times,* March 19, 2002.

The Role of Finance and Financial Managers

finance
The function in a business that acquires funds for the firm and manages those funds within the firm.

financial management
The job of managing a firm's resources so it can meet its goals and objectives.

financial managers
Managers who make recommendations to top executives regarding strategies for improving the financial strength of a firm.

The central goal of this chapter is to answer two major questions: "What is finance?" and "What do financial managers do?" **Finance** is the function in a business that acquires funds for the firm and manages those funds within the firm. Finance activities include preparing budgets; doing cash flow analysis; and planning for the expenditure of funds on such assets as plant, equipment, and machinery. **Financial management** is the job of managing a firm's resources so it can meet its goals and objectives. Without a carefully calculated financial plan, the firm has little chance for survival, regardless of its product or marketing effectiveness. However, before we go any further, let's review the role of an accountant and compare it with that of a financial manager.

An accountant could be compared to a skilled laboratory technician who takes blood samples and other measures of a person's health and writes the findings on a health report (in business, the equivalent of a set of financial statements).[1] A financial manager of a business is the doctor who interprets the report and makes recommendations to the patient regarding changes that will improve the patient's health. In short, **financial managers** examine the financial data prepared by accountants and make recommendations to top executives regarding strategies for improving the health (financial strength) of the firm.

It should be clear that financial managers can make sound financial decisions only if they understand accounting information. That's why we examined accounting thoroughly in Chapter 18. Similarly, a good accountant needs to understand finance. It's fair to say that accounting and finance go together like peanut butter and jelly. In large and medium-sized organizations, both the accounting and finance functions are generally under the control of a chief financial officer (CFO) such as Randy Casstevens, whom you met in the chapter opening profile.[2] However, financial management could also be in the hands of a person who serves as the company treasurer or vice president of finance.

A comptroller is the chief accounting officer. Figure 19.1 highlights a financial manager's tasks. As you can see, the fundamental responsibility is to obtain money and then control the use of that money effectively. That includes managing cash, credit accounts (accounts receivable), and inventory. Where a company invests its cash may have a major impact on profits. Finance, however, is a critical activity in both profit-seeking and nonprofit organizations, no matter what size.[3]

As you may remember from Chapter 6, financing a small business ➤P. 184◄ is a difficult but essential function if a firm expects to survive those important first five years. But the need for careful financial management goes well beyond the first five years and remains a challenge that a business, large or small, must face throughout its existence. Even a market giant cannot afford to ignore finance; Chrysler Corporation, for example, faced extinction in the late 1970s because of severe financial problems. Had it not been for a government-backed loan in 1980 of $1 billion, Chrysler might have joined the ranks of defunct auto companies such as Packard and Hudson instead of becoming part of Daimler-Benz.[4] The following are three of the most common ways for a firm to fail financially:

1. Undercapitalization (lacking enough funds to start the business).
2. Poor control over cash flow.
3. Inadequate expense control.

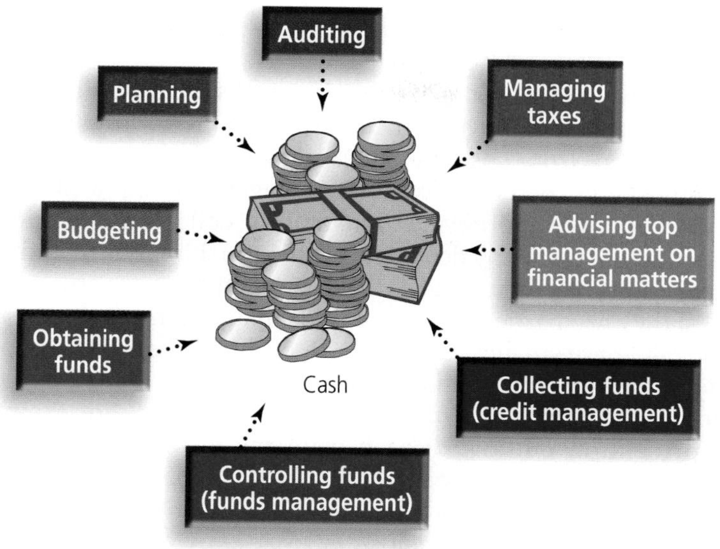

FIGURE 19.1
WHAT FINANCIAL MANAGERS DO

The Importance of Understanding Finance

Consider the financial problems encountered by a small organization called Parsley Patch. Two friends, Elizabeth Bertani and Pat Sherwood, started the company on what can best be described as a shoestring budget. It began when Bertani prepared salt-free seasonings for her husband, who was on a no-salt diet. Her friend Sherwood thought the seasonings were good enough to sell. Bertani agreed, and Parsley Patch, Inc., was born.

The business began with an investment of $5,000, which was rapidly eaten up for a logo and a label design. Bertani and Sherwood quickly learned the importance of capital in getting a business going. Eventually, the two women personally invested more than $100,000 to keep the business from experiencing severe undercapitalization.

The partners believed that gourmet shops would be an ideal distribution point for their product. Everything started well, and hundreds of gourmet shops adopted the product line. But when sales failed to meet expectations, the women decided that the health-food market offered more potential than gourmet shops because salt-free seasonings were a natural for people with restricted diets. The choice was a good one. Sales soared and approached $30,000 a month. Still, the company earned no profits.

Bertani and Sherwood were not trained in monitoring cash flow ➤P. 564◄ or in controlling expenses. In fact, they had been told not to worry about costs, and they hadn't. They eventually hired a certified public accountant (CPA) and an experienced financial manager, who taught them how to compute the costs of the various blends they produced and how to control their expenses. The financial specialists also offered insight into how to control cash coming in and out of the company (cash flow). Soon Parsley Patch earned a comfortable margin on operations that ran close to $1 million a year. Luckily, the owners were able to turn things around before it was too late.

If Bertani and Sherwood had understood finance before starting their business, they may have been able to avoid the problems they encountered. The key word here is *understood.* You do not have to pursue finance as a career to understand finance. Financial understanding is important to anyone who wants to start a small business, invest in stocks and bonds, or plan a retirement fund. In short, finance and accounting are two areas everyone involved in business needs to study. Since accounting was discussed in Chapter 18, let's look at what financial management is all about.

What Is Financial Management?

Financial managers are responsible for seeing that the company pays its bills. Finance functions such as buying merchandise on credit (accounts payable) and collecting payment from customers (accounts receivable) are responsibilities of financial managers. Therefore, financial managers are responsible for paying the company's bills at the appropriate time and for collecting overdue payments to make sure that the company does not lose too much money to bad debts (people or firms that don't pay their bills). While these functions are critical to all types of businesses, they are particularly critical to small and medium-sized businesses, which typically have smaller cash or credit cushions than large corporations.

It's vital that financial managers in any business stay abreast of changes or opportunities in finance and prepare to adjust to them. For example, tax payments represent an outflow of cash from the business. Therefore, financial managers have become increasingly involved in tax management. In keeping with changes in the law, financial managers carefully analyze the tax implications of various managerial decisions in an attempt to minimize the taxes paid by the business.[5] It's critical that businesses of all sizes concern themselves with managing taxes.

short-term forecast
Forecast that predicts revenues, costs, and expenses for a period of one year or less.

cash flow forecast
Forecast that predicts the cash inflows and outflows in future periods, usually months or quarters.

Usually a member of the firm's finance department, the internal auditor, checks on the journals, ledgers, and financial statements prepared by the accounting department to make sure that all transactions have been treated in accordance with generally accepted accounting principles (GAAP).[6] If such audits were not done, accounting statements would be less reliable. Therefore, it is important that internal auditors be objective and critical of any improprieties or deficiencies they might note in their evaluation.[7] Regular, thoroughly conducted internal audits offer the firm assistance in the important role of financial planning, which we'll look at next.

Financial Planning

Planning has been a recurring theme of this book. We've stressed planning's importance as a managerial function and offered insights into planning your career. Financial planning involves analyzing short-term and long-term money flows to and from the firm. The overall objective of financial planning is to optimize the firm's profitability and make the best use of its money. Financial planning is a key responsibility of the financial manager in a business.

Financial planning involves three steps: (1) forecasting both short-term and long-term financial needs, (2) developing budgets to meet those needs, and (3) establishing financial control to see how well the company is doing what it set out to do (see Figure 19.2). Let's look at each step and the role these steps play in improving the financial health of an organization.

Mark Twain said we talk about the weather but can't do a thing about it. Weather derivatives trader and chess champ Anjelina Belakovskala wishes he was wrong. She's in a high stakes game of forecasting weather to businesses affected by any swings in the weather pattern. Forecasting is critical for financial managers even when it involves tough-to-predict problems like the weather.

Forecasting Financial Needs

Forecasting is an important part of any firm's financial plan. A **short-term forecast** predicts revenues, costs, and expenses for a period of one year or less. This forecast is the foundation for most other financial plans, so its accuracy is critical. Part of the short-term forecast may be in the form of a **cash flow forecast,** which predicts the

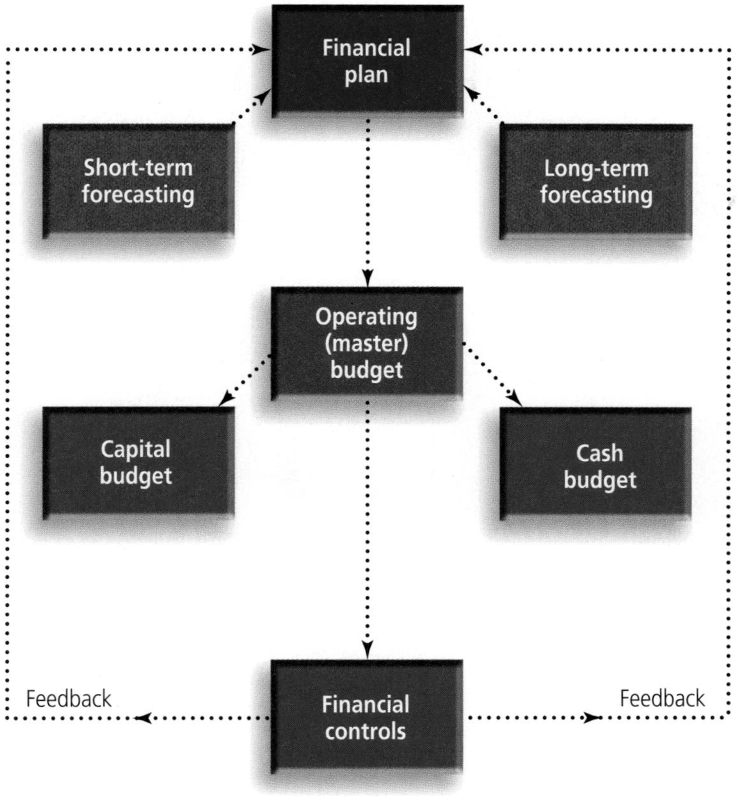

FIGURE 19.2

FINANCIAL PLANNING

Note the close link between financial planning and budgeting.

cash inflows and outflows in future periods, usually months or quarters. The inflows and outflows of cash recorded in the cash flow forecast are based on expected sales revenues and on various costs and expenses incurred and when they'll come due. The company's sales forecast estimates the firm's projected sales for a particular period. A business often uses its past financial statements as a basis for projecting expected sales and various costs and expenses.

A **long-term forecast** predicts revenues, costs, and expenses for a period longer than 1 year, and sometimes as far as 5 or 10 years into the future. This forecast plays a crucial part in the company's long-term strategic plan. Remember, a firm's strategic plan asks questions such as these: What business are we in? Should we be in it five years from now? How much money should we invest in technology and new plant and equipment over the next decade? Will there be cash available to meet long-term obligations? Innovations in Web-based software provide assistance to financial managers in dealing with these long-term forecasting questions.

long-term forecast
Forecast that predicts revenues, costs, and expenses for a period longer than 1 year, and sometimes as far as 5 or 10 years into the future.

The long-term financial forecast gives top management, as well as operations managers, some sense of the income or profit potential possible with different strategic plans. Additionally, long-term projections assist financial managers with the preparation of company budgets.

Working with the Budget Process

The budgeting process depends on the accuracy of the firm's financial statements. Put simply, a budget is a financial plan. To be a bit more specific, a **budget** sets forth management's expectations for revenues and, on the basis of those expectations, allocates the use of specific resources throughout the firm. The key financial statements—the balance sheet, income statement, and statement of cash flows—form the basis for the budgeting process. Financial

budget
A financial plan that sets forth management's expectations, and, on the basis of those expectations, allocates the use of specific resources throughout the firm.

Special processing equipment turns an average potato into the chips and fries we consume by the ton. The firm's capital budget is the financial tool that controls business spending for expensive assets such as this processing equipment. Such major assets are referred to as property, plant, and equipment. What items are in your college's capital budget?

information from the firm's past is what's used as the basis to project future financial needs. A budget becomes the primary guide for the firm's financial operations and financial needs.

Most firms compile yearly budgets from short-term and long-term financial forecasts. It's important that these financial forecasts be as accurate as possible. Therefore, businesses use cost and revenue information derived from past financial statements as the basis for forecasting company budgets.[8] Since budgeting is clearly tied to forecasting, financial managers must take forecasting responsibilities seriously. There are usually several types of budgets established in a firm's financial plan:

- A capital budget.
- A cash budget.
- An operating (master) budget.

capital budget
A budget that highlights a firm's spending plans for major asset purchases that often require large sums of money.

cash budget
A budget that estimates a firm's projected cash inflows and outflows that the firm can use to plan for any cash shortages or surpluses during a given period.

operating (master) budget
The budget that ties together all of a firm's other budgets; it is the projection of dollar allocations to various costs and expenses needed to run or operate the business, given projected revenues.

A **capital budget** highlights a firm's spending plans for major asset purchases that often require large sums of money. The capital budget primarily concerns itself with the purchase of such assets as property, buildings, and equipment.

A **cash budget** estimates a firm's projected cash inflows and outflows that the firm can use to plan for any cash shortages or surpluses during a given period (e.g., monthly, quarterly). Cash budgets are important guidelines that assist managers in anticipating borrowing, debt repayment, operating expenses, and short-term investments. The cash budget is often the last budget that is prepared. A sample cash budget for our continuing example company, Fiberrific, is provided in Figure 19.3.

The **operating (master) budget** ties together all the firm's other budgets and summarizes the business's proposed financial activities. It can be defined more formally as the projection of dollar allocations to various costs and expenses needed to run or operate a business, given projected revenues. How much the firm will spend on supplies, travel, rent, advertising, salaries, and so

FIGURE 19.3

A SAMPLE CASH BUDGET FOR FIBERRIFIC, INC.

FIBERRIFIC, INC.
Monthly Cash Budget

	January	February	March
Sales forecast	$50,000	$45,000	$40,000
Collections			
Cash sales (20%)		$9,000	$8,000
Credit sales (80% of past month)		$40,000	$36,000
Monthly cash collection		$49,000	$44,000
Payments schedule			
Supplies and material		$11,000	$10,000
Salaries		12,000	12,000
Direct labor		9,000	9,000
Taxes		3,000	3,000
Other expenses		7,000	6,000
Monthly cash payments		$42,000	$39,000
Cash budget			
Cash flow		$7,000	$5,000
Beginning cash		−1,000	6,000
Total cash		$6,000	$11,000
Less minimum cash balance		−6,000	−6,000
Excess cash to market securities		$0	$5,000
Loans needed for minimum balance		0	0

forth is determined in the operating (master) budget. The operating budget is generally the most detailed and most used budget that a firm prepares.

Clearly, financial planning plays an important role in the operations of the firm. This planning often determines what long-term investments are made, when specific funds will be needed, and how the funds will be generated. Once a company has forecast its short-term and long-term financial needs and established budgets to show how funds will be allocated, the final step in financial planning is to establish financial controls. But first, the Spotlight on Small Business box on p. 588 challenges you to check your personal financial-planning skill by developing a monthly budget for "You, Incorporated."

Establishing Financial Controls

Financial control is a process in which a firm periodically compares its actual revenues, costs, and expenses with its budget. Most companies hold at least monthly financial reviews as a way to ensure financial control. Such control procedures help managers identify variances to the financial plan and allow them to take corrective action if necessary. Financial controls also provide feedback to help reveal which accounts, which departments, and which people are varying from the financial plans. Finance managers can judge if such variances may or may not be justified. In either case, managers can make some financial adjustments to the plan when needed. The Making Ethical Decisions box on p. 589 details a situation a manager can face related to financial control. After the Progress Assessment we shall explore specific reasons why firms need to have funds readily available.

financial control
A process in which a firm periodically compares its actual revenues, costs , and expenses with its projected ones.

Spotlight on Small Business

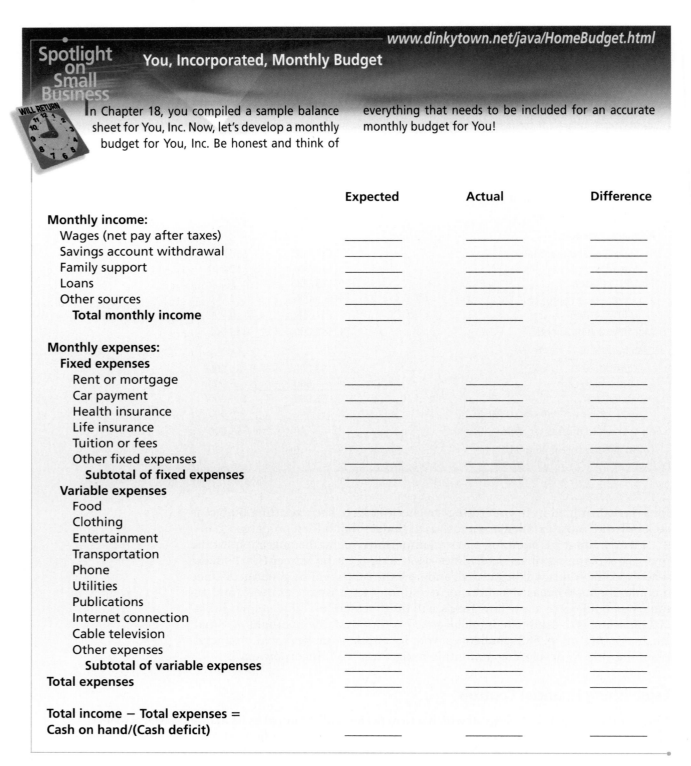

www.dinkytown.net/java/HomeBudget.html

You, Incorporated, Monthly Budget

In Chapter 18, you compiled a sample balance sheet for You, Inc. Now, let's develop a monthly budget for You, Inc. Be honest and think of everything that needs to be included for an accurate monthly budget for You!

	Expected	Actual	Difference
Monthly income:			
Wages (net pay after taxes)			
Savings account withdrawal			
Family support			
Loans			
Other sources			
Total monthly income			
Monthly expenses:			
Fixed expenses			
Rent or mortgage			
Car payment			
Health insurance			
Life insurance			
Tuition or fees			
Other fixed expenses			
Subtotal of fixed expenses			
Variable expenses			
Food			
Clothing			
Entertainment			
Transportation			
Phone			
Utilities			
Publications			
Internet connection			
Cable television			
Other expenses			
Subtotal of variable expenses			
Total expenses			
Total income − Total expenses = Cash on hand/(Cash deficit)			

Progress Assessment

- Name three finance functions important to the firm's overall operations and performance.
- What are the three primary financial problems that cause firms to fail?
- In what ways do short-term and long-term financial forecasts differ?
- What is the organization's purpose in preparing budgets? Can you identify three different types of budgets?

Making Ethical Decisions

http://ethics.acusd.edu/index.html

Playing It Safe

Suppose you are the chairperson of the business administration department at a local community college. Like many other colleges, your campus has been affected financially by cuts in federal and state support and increasing expenses. As the end of the college's fiscal year approaches, you review your departmental budget and note that some unused travel funds, which you lobbied very hard to get for this year, are still available for faculty and staff development. The faculty and staff have not seemed interested in using the travel money for development purposes throughout the year even though it has been readily available. You fear that if the funds are not spent this year, there's a good chance the college's chief financial officer will recommend cutting your travel budget for next year. That means if faculty and staff wish to travel for staff development next year and the needed funds are not available, you will have to limit the number of people who get to use the travel funds.

You consider telling faculty and staff that this money is available for about any type of travel or staff development they desire on a first-come, first-served basis, with no extensive justification needed concerning the educational benefit the college would receive from the travel requested. It's almost certain your superior, the division dean, will not contest any request you put in for travel funds, and you can certainly be a hero in the eyes of your faculty and staff. However, you could just return the unused funds to the dean's office for disbursement to the college's general fund and risk what may happen next year. What will you do? What could result from your decision?

The Need for Operating Funds

In business, the need for operating funds never seems to cease. That's why sound financial management is essential to all businesses. Like our personal financial needs, the capital needs of a business change over time. For example, as a small business grows, its financial requirements shift considerably. (Remember the example of Parsley Patch.) The same is true with large corporations such as AT&T, Johnson & Johnson, and PepsiCo. As they venture into new product areas or markets, their capital needs increase. Different firms need funds available for different reasons. However, in virtually all organizations there are certain operational needs for which funds must be available. Key areas include:

- Managing day-by-day needs of the business.
- Controlling credit operations.
- Acquiring needed inventory.
- Making capital expenditures.

Let's look carefully at these financial needs that affect both the smallest and the largest of businesses.

Managing Day-by-Day Needs of the Business

If workers expect to be paid on Friday, they don't want to have to wait until Monday for their paychecks. If tax payments are due on the 15th of the month, the government expects the money on time. If the interest payment on a business loan is due on the 30th, the lender doesn't mean the 1st of the next month. As you can see, funds have to be available to meet the daily operational costs of the business.

The challenge of sound financial management is to see that funds are available to meet these daily cash needs without compromising the firm's

Collecting accounts receivable from some customers can be time-consuming and costly. Accepting credit cards like Visa, MasterCard, or American Express simplifies transactions, guarantees payment, and provides convenience for both customers and businesses. For what sort of purchases do you use a credit card regularly?

investment potential. Money has what is called a *time value.* In other words, if someone offered to give you $200 today or $200 one year from today, you would benefit by taking the $200 today. Why? It's very simple. You could start collecting interest or invest the $200 you receive today, and over a year's time your money would grow. The same thing is true in business; the interest gained on the firm's investments is important in maximizing the profit the company will gain. That's why financial managers encourage keeping a firm's cash expenditures to a minimum.[9] By doing this, the firm can free up funds for investment in interest-bearing accounts. It's also not unusual for finance managers to suggest that a company pay its bills as late as possible (unless a cash discount is available) but try to collect what's owed to it as fast as possible. This way, they maximize the investment potential of the firm's funds. Efficient cash management is particularly important to small firms in conducting their daily operations because their access to capital is generally much more limited than that of larger businesses.[10]

Controlling Credit Operations

Financial managers know that making credit available helps keep current customers happy and attracts new customers. In today's highly competitive business environment, many businesses would have trouble surviving without making credit available to customers.

The major problem with selling on credit is that as much as 25 percent or more of the business's assets could be tied up in its credit accounts (accounts receivable). This means that the firm needs to use some of its available funds to pay for the goods or services already sold to customers who bought on credit. Financial managers in such firms must develop efficient collection procedures. For example, businesses often provide cash or quantity discounts to buyers who pay their accounts by a certain time. Also, finance managers carefully scrutinize old and new credit customers to see if they have a favorable history of meeting their credit obligations on time.[11] In essence, the firm's credit policy reflects its financial position and its desire to expand into new markets.

One way to decrease the time, and therefore expense, involved in collecting accounts receivable is to accept bank credit cards such as MasterCard or Visa.[12] This is convenient for both the customer and the business. The banks that issue such credit cards have already established the customer's creditworthiness, which reduces the business's risk. Businesses must pay a fee to accept credit cards, but the fees are generally not excessive compared to the benefits the cards provide. In fact, credit card rates are dropping as competition in the industry intensifies, encouraging more people to use them.[13]

Acquiring Needed Inventory

As we noted earlier in the text, effective marketing implies a clear customer orientation. This focus on the customer means that high-quality service and availability of goods are vital if a business expects to prosper in today's markets.[14] Therefore, to satisfy customers, businesses must maintain inventories that often involve a sizable expenditure of funds. Although it's true that firms expect to recapture their investment in inventory through sales to customers, a carefully constructed inventory policy assists in managing the firm's available funds and maximizing profitability. For example, Chips & Dips, a neighborhood ice cream parlor, ties up more funds in inventory (ice cream) in the summer than in the winter. It's obvious why. Demand for ice cream goes up in the summer.

Innovations such as just-in-time inventory help reduce the amount of funds a firm must tie up in inventory. Also, by carefully evaluating its inventory turnover ratio (discussed in Chapter 18 on p. 570) a firm can better control its outflow of cash for inventory. It's important for a business of any size to understand that a poorly managed inventory system can seriously impact cash flow and drain its finances dry.

Making Capital Expenditures

Capital expenditures are major investments in either tangible long-term assets such as land, buildings, and equipment or intangible assets such as patents, trademarks, and copyrights. In many organizations the purchase of major assets—such as land for future expansion, manufacturing plants to increase production capabilities, research to develop new-product ideas, and equipment to maintain or exceed current levels of output—is essential. As you can imagine, these expenditures often require a huge portion of the organization's funds.

capital expenditures Major investments in either tangible long-term assets such as land, buildings, and equipment or intangible assets such as patents, trademarks, and copyrights.

Remember the situation confronting Krispy Kreme Doughnuts discussed in the chapter opening profile? Business expansion into new markets can cost large sums of money with no guarantee that the expansion will be commercially successful. Therefore, it's critical that companies weigh all the possible options before committing what may be a large portion of their available resources.[15] For this reason, financial managers and analysts evaluate the appropriateness of such purchases or expenditures. Consider the situation in which a firm needs to expand its production capabilities due to increases in demand. One option is to buy land and build a new plant from scratch. Another option would be to purchase an existing plant or consider renting. Can you think of financial and accounting considerations that would come into play in this decision?

Obviously, the need for operating funds raises several questions in any firm: How does the firm obtain funds to finance operations and other business necessities? Will specific funds be needed by the firm in the long term or short term? How much will it cost to obtain these needed funds? Will these funds come from internal or external sources? Let's address these questions next.

Alternative Sources of Funds

Earlier in the chapter, you learned that finance is the function in a business that is responsible for acquiring and managing funds within the firm. Determining the amount of money needed for various periods and finding out the most appropriate sources from which to obtain these funds are fundamental steps in sound financial management. **Short-term financing** refers to funds borrowed that will be repaid within one year. In contrast, **long-term financing** refers to funds borrowed for major purchases that will be repaid over a specific period longer than one year.

short-term financing Borrowed capital that will be repaid within one year.

long-term financing Borrowed capital that will be repaid over a specific period longer than one year.

We shall explore different sources of short- and long-term financing fully in the next sections. But first it's important to know that businesses can use different methods of raising money. A firm can seek to raise needed capital through borrowing money (debt), selling ownership (equity), or earning profits (retained earnings). **Debt financing** refers to funds raised through various forms of borrowing that must be repaid. Firms can borrow either

debt financing Funds raised through various forms of borrowing that must be repaid.

Dealing with Change

http://chronicle.com

Financial Crisis in the Classrooms

As the nation's colleges and universities ease into the early years of the new millennium, their report card thus far has good news and bad news. The good news is that enrollment is soaring as the children of the baby-boom generation reach college age. Colleges such as those in the Dallas County Community College District in Texas have experienced a 20 percent jump in enrollment since 2001. The California State University system is growing by 25,000 students per year. The bad news, however, is that American colleges and universities are facing a financial squeeze that could compromise the nation's commitment to higher education for all citizens.

BusinessWeek

The problem is that college costs are increasing faster than any other sector of the economy except health care, and unfortunately college revenues have not kept pace. The many problems colleges are facing include the following:

- State governments are facing their worst budget crisis in 60 years.
- Costs are increasing for expensive new courses and degree programs.
- Growing numbers of students from poor or immigrant families need financial aid.

Some suggest the real problem is that colleges have not had to compete under traditional market conditions and therefore have not practiced good financial management. Well, that's changing in many schools.

Colleges nationwide are implementing financial management practices that save money without sacrificing quality. For example, some schools now use classrooms from 7:30 AM to 10:00 PM instead of leaving them empty for much of the day as they had in the past. Adding Internet courses helps grow enrollment yet cut back on costs. Many schools (including Harvard University) have initiated collective buying among all departments and schools (law, medicine, etc.) to cut costs by being able to buy items at lower bulk rates. Some colleges have even entered into collective buying agreements with nearby schools as well as curriculum agreements that avoid duplication of courses.

The challenges are clear, and the answers are difficult. Should taxpayers pay higher taxes so the government can send more money to colleges? Should college costs be lowered by reducing enrollments (resulting in fewer students getting the opportunity to earn a college degree)? Should colleges employ more financial management techniques to cut costs but preserve quality?

Sources: William C. Symonds, "Colleges in Crisis," *Business Week,* April 28, 2003, pp. 72–78; and Jennifer Merritt, "Should You Go For It?" *Business Week,* March 17, 2003, pp. 104–5.

equity financing
Funds raised from operations within the firm or through the sale of ownership in the firm.

short-term funds, due to be repaid within one year, or long-term funds, due over a period longer than one year. **Equity financing** is money raised from within the firm (from operations) or through the sale of ownership in the firm (e.g., the sale of stock). (For a look at colleges and financing, see the Dealing with Change box.)

We'll look next at methods of acquiring these needed short- and long-term funds from a variety of sources. Before we begin this discussion, however, let's check your understanding with the Progress Assessment.

Progress Assessment

- Money is said to have a time value. What does this mean?
- Why are accounts receivable a financial concern to the firm?
- What's the primary reason an organization spends a good deal of its available funds on inventory and capital expenditures?
- What's the difference between debt and equity financing?

Obtaining Short-Term Financing

The bulk of a finance manager's job does not involve obtaining long-term funds. In fact, in small businesses, long-term financing is often out of the question. Instead, the day-to-day operation of the firm calls for the careful management of short-term financial needs. Firms need to borrow short-term funds for purchasing additional inventory or for meeting bills that come due unexpectedly. Also, as we do in our personal lives, a business sometimes needs to obtain short-term funds when the firm's cash reserves are low. This is particularly true, again, of small businesses.

Most small businesses are primarily concerned with just staying afloat until they are able to build capital and creditworthiness. Firms can obtain short-term financing in several different ways. Also, suppliers of short-term financing can require that the funds provided be secured or unsecured. Let's look at the major forms of short-term financing and what's meant by secured and unsecured financing with regard to different ways of obtaining needed funds.

Trade Credit

The most widely used source of short-term funding, trade credit (an account payable), is the least expensive and most convenient form of short-term financing. Small businesses rely heavily on trade credit from firms, such as UPS, as do large firms such as Kmart.[16] **Trade credit** is the practice of buying goods ➤P. 25◄ or services ➤P. 26◄ now and paying for them later. For example, when a firm buys merchandise, it receives an invoice (a bill) much like the one you receive when you buy something with a credit card.

trade credit
The practice of buying goods and services now and paying for them later.

It is common for business invoices to contain terms such as *2/10, net 30.* This means that the buyer can take a 2 percent discount for paying the invoice within 10 days. The total bill is due (net) in 30 days if the purchaser does not take advantage of the discount. Finance managers need to pay close attention to such discounts because they create opportunities to reduce the cost of financing. Think about it for a moment: If the discount offered to the customer is 2/10, net 30, the customer will pay 2 percent more for waiting an extra 20 days to pay the invoice.

Some uninformed businesspeople feel that 2 percent is insignificant, so they pay their bills after the discount period. In the course of a year, however, 2 percent for 20 days adds up to a 36 percent interest rate (because there are eighteen 20-day periods in the year). If the firm is capable of paying within 10 days, it is needlessly (and significantly) increasing its cost of financing by not doing so.

Promissory Notes

Some suppliers hesitate to give trade credit to organizations with a poor credit rating, no credit history, or a history of slow payment. In such cases, the supplier may insist that the customer sign a promissory note as a condition for obtaining credit. A **promissory note** is a written contract with a promise to pay a supplier a specific sum of money at a definite time. Promissory notes can be sold by the supplier to a bank at a discount (the amount of the note less a fee for the bank's services in collecting the amount due).

promissory note
A written contract with a promise to pay a supplier a specific sum of money at a definite time.

Family and Friends

Many small firms obtain short-term funds by borrowing money from family and friends. Because such funds are needed for periods of less than a year, friends or relatives are sometimes willing to help. Such loans can create

'Tis the season to shop. Ever wonder how retailers get the money to buy all of the items available during the holiday season? Department stores and other large retailers make extensive use of commercial banks and other lenders to borrow the money needed to buy merchandise to stock their shelves.

problems, however, if the firm does not understand cash flow. As we discussed earlier, the firm may suddenly find itself having several bills coming due at the same time with no sources of funds to pay them. It is better, therefore, not to borrow from friends or relatives; instead, go to a commercial bank that fully understands the business's risk and can help analyze your firm's future financial needs.

Entrepreneurs ➤P. 4◄ appear to be listening to this advice. According to the National Federation of Independent Business, entrepreneurs today are relying less on family and friends as a source of borrowed funds than they have in the past.[17] If an entrepreneur does, however, decide to ask family or friends for financial assistance, it's important that both parties (1) agree on specific loan terms, (2) put the agreement in writing, and (3) arrange for repayment in the same way they would for a bank loan. Such actions help keep family relationships and friendships intact.

Commercial Banks and Other Financial Institutions

Banks are highly sensitive to risk and are often reluctant to lend money to small businesses. Nonetheless, a promising and well-organized venture may be able to get a bank loan. If it is able to get such a loan, a small or medium-sized business should have the person in charge of the finance function keep in close touch with the bank. It's also wise to see a banker periodically (as often as once a month) and send the banker all the firm's financial statements so that the bank continues to supply funds when needed.

If you try to imagine the different types of businesspeople who go to banks for a loan, you'll get a better idea of the role of financial management. Picture, for example, a farmer going to the bank to borrow funds for seed, fertilizer, equipment, and other needs. The farmer may buy such supplies in the spring and pay for them after the fall harvest. Now picture a local toy store buying merchandise for Christmas sales. The store may borrow the money for such purchases in the summer and pay it back after Christmas. Restaurants may borrow funds at the beginning of the month and pay by the end of the month. Can you see that how much a business borrows and for how long depends often on the kind of business it is and how quickly the merchandise purchased with a bank loan can be resold or used to generate funds?

You can also imagine how important it is for specialists in a company's finance and accounting departments to do a cash flow forecast. Unfortunately, small-business owners generally lack the luxury of such specialists and must monitor cash flow themselves. By anticipating times when many bills will come due, a business can begin early to seek funds or sell other assets to prepare for the crunch. This is why it's important for a businessperson to keep friendly and close relations with his or her banker.[18] An experienced banker may spot cash flow problems early or be more willing to lend money in a crisis if a businessperson has established a strong, friendly relationship built on openness, trust, and sound management practices. It's important to remember that your banker wants you to succeed almost as much as you do. Bankers can be an invaluable support, especially to small but growing businesses.[19]

Different Forms of Short-Term Loans

Banks and other financial institutions offer different types of loans to customers. A **secured loan** is a loan that's backed by something valuable, such as property. The item of value is called *collateral.* If the borrower fails to pay the loan, the lender may take possession of the collateral. For example, an automobile loan is a secured loan. If the borrower fails to pay the loan, the lender will repossess the car. Collateral takes some of the risk out of lending money.

secured loan
A loan backed by something valuable, such as property.

Accounts receivable are assets that are often used by businesses as collateral for a loan; the process is called *pledging.* Some percentage of the value of accounts receivable pledged (usually about 75 percent) is advanced to the borrowing firm. As customers pay off their accounts, the funds received are forwarded to the lender in repayment of the funds that were advanced.[20] Inventory such as raw materials (e.g., coal, steel), is also often used as collateral or security for a business loan. Other assets that can be used as collateral include buildings, machinery, and company-owned stocks and bonds.

The most difficult kind of loan to get from a bank or other financial institution is an unsecured loan. An **unsecured loan** doesn't require a borrower to offer the lending institution any collateral to obtain the loan. It's basically a loan that's not backed by any specific assets. Normally, a lender will give unsecured loans only to highly regarded customers (e.g., long-standing customers or customers considered financially stable).

unsecured loan
A loan that's not backed by any specific assets.

If a business develops a good relationship with a bank, the bank may open a line of credit for the firm. A **line of credit** is a given amount of unsecured short-term funds a bank will lend to a business, provided the bank has the funds readily available. In other words, a line of credit is not guaranteed to a business. The primary purpose of a line of credit is to speed the borrowing process so that a firm does not have to go through the hassle of applying for a new loan every time it needs funds. The funds are generally available as long as the credit limit set by the bank is not exceeded. As businesses mature and become more financially secure, the amount of credit often is increased. Some firms will even apply for a **revolving credit agreement,** which is a line of credit that's guaranteed. However, banks usually charge a fee for guaranteeing such an agreement. Both lines of credit and revolving credit agreements are particularly good sources of funds for unexpected cash needs.

line of credit
A given amount of unsecured short-term funds a bank will lend to a business, provided the funds are readily available.

revolving credit agreement
A line of credit that is guaranteed by the bank.

If a business is unable to secure a short-term loan from a bank, a financial manager may obtain short-term funds from **commercial finance companies.** These non-deposit-type organizations (often called *nonbanks*) make short-term loans to borrowers who offer tangible assets (e.g., property, plant, and equipment) as collateral. Since commercial finance companies are willing to accept higher degrees of risk than commercial banks, they usually charge higher interest rates than banks. Commercial finance companies often make loans to individuals and businesses that cannot get funds elsewhere. General

commercial finance companies
Organizations that make short-term loans to borrowers who offer tangible assets as collateral.

Electric Capital Corporation is the largest commercial finance company in the United States, with $426 billion in assets in its 28 diversified commercial and consumer finance businesses.[21]

Factoring

factoring
The process of selling accounts receivable for cash.

One relatively expensive source of short-term funds for a firm is **factoring,** which is the process of selling accounts receivable for cash. Factoring dates as far back as 4,000 years, during the days of ancient Babylon. Today, the Internet can help businesses find factors quickly so that they can solicit bids on a firm's accounts receivable.[22] Here's how it works: Let's say that a firm sells many of its products on credit to consumers and other businesses, creating a number of accounts receivable. Some of the buyers may be slow in paying their bills, causing the firm to have a large amount of money due to it. A factor is a market intermediary (usually a financial institution like a commercial bank or commercial finance company) that agrees to buy the accounts receivable from the firm, at a discount, for cash. The factor then collects and keeps the money that was owed the firm when it collects the accounts receivable. How much this costs the firm depends on the discount rate the factor requires. The discount rate, in turn, depends on the age of the accounts receivable, the nature of the business, and the condition of the economy.

Even though factoring can be an expensive way of raising cash, it is popular among small businesses. It's important for you to note that factoring is not a loan; factoring is the sale of an asset (accounts receivable). And while it's true that discount rates charged by factors are usually higher than loan rates charged by banks or commercial finance companies, remember that many small businesses cannot qualify for a loan. Also, a company can reduce the cost of factoring if it agrees to reimburse the factor for slow-paying accounts, and it can reduce them even further if it assumes the risk of those people who don't pay at all.

Factoring can also be used by large firms. Macy's department stores, for example, used factoring during its reorganization. Factoring is very common in the clothing and furniture business and is also popular in financing growing numbers of global trade ventures. Read the Reaching Beyond Our Borders box to see why firms often turn to export factoring as a means of financing global trade.

Commercial Paper

commercial paper
Unsecured promissory notes of $100,000 and up that mature (come due) in 270 days or less.

Sometimes a large corporation needs funds for just a few months and wants to get lower rates of interest than those charged by banks. One strategy is to sell commercial paper. **Commercial paper** consists of unsecured promissory notes, in amounts of $100,000 and up, that mature (come due) in 270 days or less. Commercial paper states a fixed amount of money the business agrees to repay to the lender (investor) on a specific date. The interest rate for commercial paper is stated in the agreement.

Commercial paper is generally sold at a public sale; however, firms like BASF, the world's leading chemical company, have used the Internet to issue commercial paper.[23] Still, because it is unsecured, only financially stable firms (mainly large corporations with excellent credit reputations) are able to sell commercial paper.[24] For these companies it's a way to get short-term funds quickly and for less than the interest charged by commercial banks. Since most commercial paper matures in 30 to 90 days, it's also an investment opportunity for buyers who can afford to put up cash for short periods to earn some interest on their money.

www.factoring.org

Reaching Beyond Our Borders: Making Sure the Check's in the Mail

The 21st century promises to be a time of global economic growth. With over 6 billion customers on planet Earth, the lure is just too enticing for businesses to ignore. Unfortunately, the path of would-be exporters is often blocked by financing constraints such as the complications of trading in foreign currencies and difficulty in collecting money owed from global accounts. Combine these financing challenges with political instability, high loan defaults, threats of terrorism, and unstable currencies, and the prospects of doing business globally look iffy. For example, imagine selling Fiberrific cereal to a foreign buyer who later refuses to pay the bill. What would you do to collect? What legal recourse would you have?

This shaky global environment requires U.S. companies to use creative financing methods for protection in global markets. International factoring (also called forfeiting) is one such method. International factoring involves negotiating with intermediaries who make sure the payment for products gets from the foreign buyer back to the seller.

There are four parties involved in an international factoring transaction: the exporter (seller), the U.S. factor (called the export factor), the foreign factor (called the import factor), and the importer (buyer). It works like this. The exporter and the export factor sign a factoring agreement that transfers the exporter's accounts receivable to the U.S. factor in exchange for coverage against any credit losses that could be incurred globally. In other words, the export factor guarantees the exporter that it will receive the money it is owed (minus fees, of course). The export factor selects an import factor to act on the seller's behalf under the export factor's supervision. The import factor assists in finding local customers in global markets to whom the seller can sell its goods or services.

When an exporter receives an order from a customer, the import factor collects payment from the global buyer. The import factor deducts a fee and gives the remainder to the export factor. The export factor deducts a fee and gives that remainder to the selling company (exporter). By using these agreements, U.S. exporters can do business even in risky global markets minus the possibility of suffering significant credit losses.

Europe is the largest market for international factoring, constituting 65 percent of world volume. The United States accounts for 22 percent. The growing Asia-Pacific region has reached 12 percent. To date, international factoring stands at close to $700 billion. With global networks of factoring organizations emerging, growth prospects look promising.

Sources: Jane Salodof MacNeil, "The Factoring Factor," *Inc.*, September 2002, p. 94; and James O'Brien, "Manufacturing: Exporters Spreading Their Net Yet Wider," *Birmingham (UK) Post,* April 24, 2003, p. 26.

Progress Assessment

- What does the term *2/10, net 30* mean?
- What's the difference between trade credit and a line of credit at a bank?
- What's the difference between a secured loan and an unsecured loan?
- What is factoring? What are some of the considerations involved in establishing a discount rate in factoring?

Obtaining Long-Term Financing

Forecasting helps the firm to develop a financial plan. This plan specifies the amount of funding the firm will need over various time periods and the most appropriate sources of obtaining those funds. In setting long-term financing objectives, financial managers generally ask three major questions:

1. What are the organization's long-term goals and objectives?

2. What are the financial requirements needed to achieve these long-term goals and objectives?
3. What sources of long-term capital are available, and which will best fit our needs?

In business, long-term capital is used to buy fixed assets such as plant and equipment, to develop new products, and to finance expansion of the organization. In major corporations, decisions involving long-term financing normally involve the board of directors and top management, as well as finance and accounting managers. Take pharmaceutical producer Merck, for example. A seven-member chairperson's staff at Merck makes senior policy decisions involving factors such as long-term financing at the company. Merck spends over $3 billion a year researching new products.[25] The actual development of a new innovative medicine can sometimes take 10 years or more and cost $800 million in company funds before the product is ever introduced in the market.

It's easy to see why long-term financing decisions involve high-level managers at Merck. In some instances, a company may even employ an expert like an investment banker (we will look at investment bankers in Chapter 20) to assist with important and risky financing decisions. In small and medium-sized businesses, it's inevitable that the owners are always actively involved in analyzing long-term financing opportunities that affect their company.

As we noted earlier in the chapter, long-term funding comes from two major types of financing, debt financing or equity financing. Let's look at these two important sources of long-term financing next.

Debt Financing

The first type of long-term funding involves borrowing money (debt financing). If a company uses debt financing, it has a legal obligation to repay the amount borrowed. All businesses must keep in mind this legal requirement. Firms can borrow funds by either getting a loan from a lending institution or by issuing bonds.

Debt Financing by Borrowing Money from Lending Institutions Firms that establish and develop rapport with a bank, insurance company, pension fund, commercial finance company, or other financial institution often are able to secure a long-term loan. Long-term loans are usually repaid within 3 to 7 years but may extend to 15 or 20 years. For such loans, a business must sign what is called a term-loan agreement. A **term-loan agreement** is a promissory note that requires the borrower to repay the loan in specified installments (e.g., monthly or yearly). A major advantage of a business using this type of financing is that the interest paid on the long-term debt is tax deductible.

term-loan agreement
A promissory note that requires the borrower to repay the loan in specified installments.

Because they involve larger amounts of funding, long-term loans are often more expensive to the firm than short-term loans are. Also, since the repayment period could be as long as 20 years, lenders are not assured that their capital will be repaid in full. Therefore, most long-term loans require collateral, which may be in the form of real estate, machinery, equipment, stock, or other items of value. Lenders will also often require certain restrictions on a firm's operations to force it to act responsibly in its business practices. The interest rate for long-term loans is based on the adequacy of collateral, the firm's credit rating, and the general level of market interest rates. The greater the risk a lender takes in making a loan, the higher the rate of interest a lender requires. This principle is known as the **risk/return trade-off.**

risk/return trade-off
The principle that the greater the risk a lender takes in making a loan, the higher the interest rate required.

Debt Financing by Issuing Bonds If an organization is unable to obtain its long-term financing needs by getting a loan from a lending institution, it may try to issue bonds. Figure 19.4 is a list of types of organizations that can issue bonds. To put it simply, a bond is like a company IOU with a promise to repay the amount borrowed on a certain date. To be more specific, a bond is a binding contract through which the organization issuing the bond agrees to specific terms with investors in return for the money those investors lend to the company. The terms of the agreement in a bond issue are referred to as the **indenture terms.**

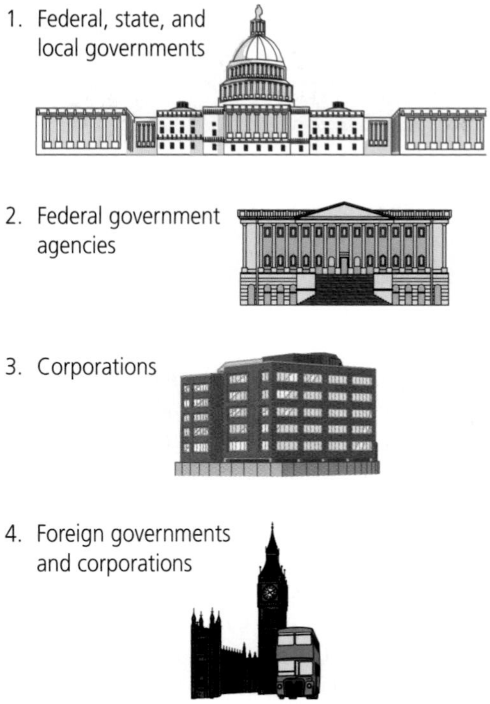

FIGURE 19.4

WHO CAN ISSUE BONDS?

Source: *The Wall Street Journal Guide to Money and Markets.*

A bond is a long-term debt obligation of a corporation or government. You are probably somewhat familiar with bonds. For example, you may own investments like U.S. government savings bonds, or perhaps you have volunteered your time to help a local school district pass a bond issue. Maybe your community is building a new stadium or cultural center that requires selling bonds. It's fair to say that businesses compete with government when issuing bonds. Potential investors (individuals and institutions) in bonds measure the risk involved in purchasing a bond against the return (interest) the bond promises to pay and the company's ability to repay the bond when promised.

indenture terms
The terms of agreement in a bond issue.

Like other forms of long-term debt, bonds can be secured or unsecured. A **secured bond** is issued with some form of collateral, such as real estate, equipment, or other pledged assets. If the bond's indenture terms are violated, the bondholder can issue a claim on the collateral. An **unsecured bond** (called a debenture bond) is a bond backed only by the reputation of the issuer. Investors in such bonds simply trust that the organization issuing the bond will follow through on its financial commitments. Bonds are a key means of long-term financing for many organizations. They can also be valuable investments for private individuals or institutions. Given this importance, we will discuss bonds more in depth in Chapter 20.

secured bond
A bond issued with some form of collateral.

unsecured bond
A bond backed only by the reputation of the issuer; also called a debenture bond.

Equity Financing

If a firm cannot obtain a long-term loan from a lending institution, or if it is unable to sell bonds to investors, it may look for long-term funding from equity financing. Equity financing comes from the owners of the firm. Therefore, equity financing involves selling ownership in the firm in the form of stock, or using earnings that have been retained by the company to reinvest in the business (retained earnings). A business can also seek equity financing by selling ownership in the firm to venture capitalists. Figure 19.5 on p. 600 compares debt and equity financing options.

Equity Financing by Selling Stock Regardless of whether or not a firm can obtain debt financing, there usually comes a time when it needs additional funds. One way to obtain such funds is to sell ownership shares (called *stock*) in the firm to private investors. The key word to remember here is *ownership*. The purchasers of stock become owners in the organization. The number of shares of stock that will be available for purchase is generally decided by the organization's board of directors. The first time a company offers to sell its stock to the general public is called an *initial public offering (IPO).*

FIGURE 19.5

DIFFERENCES BETWEEN DEBT AND EQUITY FINANCING

	TYPE OF FINANCING	
CONDITIONS	DEBT	EQUITY
Management influence	There's usually none unless special conditions have been agreed on.	Common stockholders have voting rights.
Repayment	Debt has a maturity date. Principal must be repaid.	Stock has no maturity date. The company is never required to repay equity.
Yearly obligations	Payment of interest is a contractual obligation.	The firm isn't legally liable to pay dividends.
Tax benefits	Interest is tax deductible.	Dividends are paid from after-tax income and aren't deductible.

Remember, Kripsy Kreme Doughnuts had its initial public offering of stock in 2000. (IPOs are discussed further in Chapter 20.)

Selling stock to the public as a way to obtain equity financing is by no means easy or automatic. U.S. companies can issue stock for public purchase only if they meet requirements set by the Securities and Exchange Commission (SEC) as well as various state agencies. Companies can issue different types of stock, such as common and preferred stock. Both types of stock ownership (common and preferred) are discussed in depth in Chapter 20.

Equity Financing from Retained Earnings Have you ever heard a businessperson say that he or she reinvests the firm's profits right back into the business? You probably remember from Chapter 18 that the profits the company keeps and reinvests in the firm are called retained earnings. Retained earnings often are a major source of long-term funds. This is especially true for small businesses, which have fewer financing alternatives, such as selling bonds or stock, than large businesses do. However, large corporations also depend on retained earnings for needed long-term funding. In fact, retained earnings are usually the most favored source of meeting long-term capital needs since a company that uses them saves interest payments, dividends (payments for investing in stock), and any possible underwriting fees for issuing bonds or stock. Also, if a firm uses retained earnings, there is no new ownership created in the firm, as occurs with selling stock.

The major problem with relying on retained earnings as a source of funding is that many organizations do not have sufficient retained earnings on hand to finance extensive capital improvements or business expansion. If you think about it for a moment, it makes sense. What if you wanted to buy an expensive personal asset such as a new car? The ideal way to purchase the car would be to go to your personal savings account and take out the necessary cash. No hassle! No interest! Unfortunately, few people have such large amounts of cash available. Most businesses are no different. Even though they would like to finance long-term needs from operations, few have the resources on hand to accomplish this.

Equity Financing from Venture Capital The hardest time for a business to raise money is when it is just starting or moving into early stages of expansion. A start-up business typically has few assets and no market track record, so the chances of borrowing significant amounts of money from a bank are slim. **Venture capital** is money that is invested in new or emerging companies that are perceived as having great profit potential. Venture capital has helped dozens of

venture capital
Money that is invested in new or emerging companies that are perceived as having great profit potential.

Marvel Entertainment, home of the Hulk, Spiderman, and Superman, feels pretty strong itself in this photo. The firm is celebrating its IPO (initial public offering) on the New York Stock Exchange. Equity financing by selling shares of ownership is a way to meet a company's long-term financial needs. How does equity financing differ from debt financing?

firms—such as Intel, Apple Computer, Cisco Systems, and Sun Microsystems—get started.[26] Venture capital firms are a possible source of start-up capital for new companies or companies moving into expanding stages of business.

The venture capital industry originally began as an alternative investment vehicle for wealthy families. The Rockefeller family, for example (whose vast fortune came from John D. Rockefeller's Standard Oil Company, started in the 19th century), financed Sanford McDonnell when he was operating his company from an airplane hangar. That small venture grew into McDonnell Douglas, a large aerospace and defense contractor that merged with Boeing Corporation in 1997. The venture capital industry grew significantly in the 1980s, when many high-tech companies such as Intel and Apple were being started. In the 1990s the industry grew immensely, especially in high-tech centers such as California's Silicon Valley, where venture capitalists concentrated primarily on Internet-related companies. In the early 2000s, however, problems in the technology industry and the slowdown in the overall economy reduced venture capital expenditures considerably.[27]

An entrepreneur or finance manager must remember that venture capitalists invest in a company in return for part ownership of the business. Venture capitalists concede that they expect higher-than-average returns and competent management performance for their investment. Therefore, a start-up company has to be careful when choosing a venture capital firm. The dangers of having the wrong venture capital firm can be illustrated by the experience of Jon Birck, who started Northwest Instrument Systems with venture capital. Birck worked until 11:00 or 12:00 each night to build the company. After having dedicated three years to the company, he was asked to leave by the venture capital firm, which wanted a more experienced chief executive officer to protect its investment. Birck had left a secure job, put his marriage on the line, taken out a second mortgage on his house, and given himself a below-average salary to get Northwest on its feet; then, just when the firm was ready for rapid growth, he was asked to resign.

As this story shows, financing a firm's long-term needs through venture capital can involve a high degree of risk. Still, it's obvious there are risks when firms borrow funds from venture capitalists or any lenders. Knowing this, you might be inclined to ask: Why do firms borrow funds at all? Why not just use the other forms of equity funding (selling stock or retained earnings)? The reason involves the use of leverage. Let's look briefly at why companies use leverage next.

Making Decisions on Using Financial Leverage

leverage
Raising needed funds through borrowing to increase a firm's rate of return.

cost of capital
The rate of return a company must earn in order to meet the demands of its lenders and expectations of its equity holders.

Raising needed funds through borrowing to increase the firm's rate of return is referred to as **leverage.** While it's true that debt increases the risk of the firm, it also enhances the firm's ability to increase profits. Remember, two key jobs of the finance manager or CFO are to forecast the need for borrowed funds and to plan how to manage these funds once they are obtained.

Firms are very concerned with the cost of capital. **Cost of capital** is the rate of return a company must earn in order to meet the demands of its lenders and expectations of its equity holders. If the firm's earnings are larger than the interest payments on the funds borrowed, business owners can realize a higher rate of return than if they used equity financing. Figure 19.6 describes an example involving our cereal company, Fiberrific (introduced in Chapter 13). If Fiberrific needed $500,000 in financing, it could consider selling bonds (debt) or stock (equity) to investors. Comparing the two options in this situation, you can see that Fiberrific would benefit by selling bonds since the company's earnings are greater than the interest paid on borrowed funds (bonds). However, if the firm's earnings were less than the interest paid on borrowed funds (bonds), the owners could lose money on their investment. It's also important to remember that bonds, like all debt, have to be repaid at a specific time.

Normally, it's up to each individual firm to determine exactly how to balance debt and equity financing. For example, communications giant America Online (AOL) took on billions of dollars of new debt in its acquisition of Time Warner, as did media power Viacom in its acquisition of CBS, BET, and Comedy Central.[28] Some firms, such as chewing-gum maker Wm. Wrigley Jr. Company and chocolate maker Hershey Foods Corporation, have little long-term debt.

Leverage ratios (which we discussed in Chapter 18) give companies a standard of the comparative leverage of firms in their industries. According to Standard & Poor's and Moody's Investor Services (firms that provide corporate and financial information), the debt of a large industrial corporation typically

FIGURE 19.6

USING LEVERAGE VERSUS EQUITY FINANCING

Fiberiffic Inc. needs to raise $500,000; compare its two options for doing so.

OPTION A			OPTION B		
Raise 10% By Selling Stock (Equity); Raise 90% By Issuing Bonds (Debt).			Raise 100% By Selling Stock (Equity).		
Common Stock	$ 50,000		Common Stock	$500,000	
Bonds (@ 10% interest)	450,000				
	$500,000			$500,000	
Earnings	$125,000		Earnings	$125,000	
Less Bond Interest	45,000				
Net Earnings/Income	$ 80,000		Net Earnings/Income	$125,000	
Return to Stockholders	$ 80,000 / $ 50,000	= 160%	Return to Stockholders	$125,000 / $500,000	= 25%

ranges between 33 and 40 percent of its total assets. Small-business debt varies considerably. As the requirements of financial institutions become more stringent and investors more demanding, it's certain that the job of the finance manager will become more challenging.

Chapter 20 takes a closer look at bonds (debt) and stocks (equity) both as financing tools for businesses and as investment options for private investors. You will learn about bond and stock issues, the securities exchanges, how to buy and sell stock, how to choose the right investment strategy, how to read the stock and bond quotations in *The Wall Street Journal* and other financial publications, and more. Finance takes on a whole new dimension when you see how you can participate in financial markets yourself.

Progress Assessment

- What are the two major forms of debt financing available to a firm?
- How does debt financing differ from equity financing?
- What are the major forms of equity financing available to a firm?
- What is leverage, and why would firms choose to use it?

Summary

1. Describe the importance of finance and financial management to an organization, and explain the responsibilities of financial managers.

1. Finance is that function in a business responsible for acquiring funds for the firm, managing funds within the firm (e.g., preparing budgets and doing cash flow analysis), and planning for the expenditure of funds on various assets.
   - ***What are the most common ways firms fail financially?***

   The most common financial problems are (1) undercapitalization, (2) poor control over cash flow, and (3) inadequate expense control.
   - ***What do financial managers do?***

   Financial managers plan, budget, control funds, obtain funds, collect funds, audit, manage taxes, and advise top management on financial matters.

2. Outline the financial planning process, and explain the three key budgets in the financial plan.

2. Financial planning involves forecasting short- and long-term needs, budgeting, and establishing financial controls.
   - ***What are the three budgets of finance?***

   The capital budget is the spending plan for expensive assets such as property, plant, and equipment. The cash budget is the projected cash balance at the end of a given period. The operating (master) budget summarizes the information in the other two budgets; it projects dollar allocations to various costs and expenses given various revenues.

3. Explain the major reasons why firms need operating funds, and identify various types of financing that can be used to obtain these funds.

3. During the course of a business's life, its financial needs shift considerably.
   - ***What are the major financial needs for firms?***

   Businesses have financial needs in four major areas: (1) managing day-by-day needs of the business, (2) controlling credit operations, (3) acquiring needed inventory, and (4) making capital expenditures.
   - ***What's the difference between short-term and long-term financing?***

   Short-term financing refers to funds that will be repaid in less than one year, whereas long-term financing refers to funds that will be repaid over a specific time period of more than one year.

- ***What's the difference between debt financing and equity financing?***

Debt financing refers to funds raised by borrowing (going into debt), whereas equity financing is raised from within the firm (through retained earnings) or by selling ownership in the company by issuing stock or selling ownership to venture capitalists.

4. Identify and describe different sources of short-term financing.

4. Sources of short-term financing include trade credit, promissory notes, family and friends, commercial banks and other financial institutions, factoring, and commercial paper.

- ***Why should businesses use trade credit?***

Trade credit is the least expensive and most convenient form of short-term financing. Businesses can buy goods today and pay for them sometime in the future.

- ***What's a line of credit?***

It is an agreement by a bank to lend a specified amount of money to the business at any time, if the money is available. A revolving credit agreement is a line of credit that guarantees a loan will be available—for a fee.

- ***What's the difference between a secured loan and an unsecured loan?***

An unsecured loan has no collateral backing it. Secured loans have collateral backed by assets such as accounts receivable, inventory, or other property of value.

- ***Is factoring a form of secured loan?***

No, factoring means selling accounts receivable at a discounted rate to a factor (an intermediary that pays cash for those accounts).

- ***What's commercial paper?***

Commercial paper is a corporation's unsecured promissory note maturing in 270 days or less.

5. Identify and describe different sources of long-term financing.

5. One of the important functions of a finance manager is to obtain long-term financing.

- ***What are the major sources of long-term financing?***

Debt financing involves the sale of bonds and long-term loans from banks and other financial institutions. Equity financing is obtained through the sale of company stock, from the firm's retained earnings, or from venture capital firms.

- ***What are the two major forms of debt financing?***

Debt financing comes from two sources: selling bonds and borrowing from individuals, banks, and other financial institutions. Bonds can be secured by some form of collateral or can be unsecured. The same is true of loans.

- ***What's leverage, and how do firms use it?***

Leverage is raising funds from borrowing. It involves the use of borrowed funds to invest in such undertakings as expansion, major asset purchases, and research and development. Firms measure the risk of borrowing (leverage) against the potential for higher profits.

Key Terms

budget 585
capital budget 586
capital expenditures 591
cash budget 586
cash flow forecast 584
commercial finance companies 595
commercial paper 596
cost of capital 602
debt financing 591
equity financing 592
factoring 596
finance 582
financial control 587
financial management 582
financial managers 582
indenture terms 599
leverage 602
line of credit 595
long-term financing 591

long-term forecast 585
operating (master) budget 586
promissory note 593
revolving credit agreement 595
risk/return trade-off 598
secured bond 599
secured loan 595
short-term financing 591
short-term forecast 584
term-loan agreement 598
trade credit 593
unsecured bond 599
unsecured loan 595
venture capital 600

1. Obtain a recent annual report of a major corporation in your area or a company you admire. (Hint: *The Wall Street Journal* has a free annual reports service; call to order a report at 1-800-654-2582. Also, most companies post their annual reports on their websites.) Read the information provided about the company and review its balance sheet. Check the company's short-term and long-term debt. (Hint: Look under liabilities.) Does the firm appear to be safe in terms of its leverage? Be prepared to defend your opinion.

2. Visit the website of a local bank. Check the bank's current interest rate; then see what rate small businesses would pay for short-term and long-term loans. See if blank forms that borrowers use to apply for loans are available online. Share these forms with your class and explain what type of information the bank is seeking.

3. Go to your campus library and ask the reference librarian for a copy of your college's operating budget for the current year, or check to see if it's available online. Try to identify major capital expenditures planned for the future at the college. Report what you find to the class.

4. A small-business consultant once commented that the most difficult concept to get across to small-business owners is the need to take all the trade credit (e.g., 2/10, net 30) they can get. He could not convince owners that they would save over 36 percent a year by taking advantage of the discount. Work with a small group of classmates and try to build a convincing argument to small-business owners of the benefits of using this concept.

5. Obtain a copy of the financial requirements needed for a franchise of your choice. (Your library most likely has a copy of the *Franchise Opportunities Handbook;* use it as a resource.) Check out the capitalization requirements for the franchise and see if the franchisor offers financial assistance to prospective franchisees. Evaluate the cost of the franchise versus its business potential using the risk/return trade-off.

Purpose

To learn how small-business owners can obtain equity financing by finding investors willing to buy a stake in their companies.

Exercise

When it comes to finding equity capital, many small-business owners have a difficult time finding investors. The Access to Capital Electronic Network (ACE-Net) is an Internet-based listing service developed by the Small Business Administration that allows entrepreneurs to present information about their small, growing company to venture capitalists and institutional and accredited individual investors across the country. ACE-Net encourages entrepreneurs who meet certain criteria to list their businesses and then makes their listing available to qualified investors. Go to https://ace-net.sr.unh.edu/pub/ent/anfe.htm and see if the following businesses qualify for participation on ACE-Net:

1. Growing Like a Weed is a lawn care service business organized as a limited liability company. It needs $25,000 to buy additional equipment in order to expand. Does it meet ACE-Net listing criteria? Why or why not?
2. Allied Technology is a corporation that produces computer chips. It needs $6 million to build a new manufacturing plant. Does it meet ACE-Net listing criteria? Why or why not?
3. Bells 'n Whistles is a pinball refurbishing company. Partners Merv and Marv need $300,000 to buy inventory. Do they meet ACE-Net listing criteria? Why or why not?
4. Lettuce Entertain You is a corporation that needs $500,000 to remodel an old warehouse to house its latest restaurant. Does it meet ACE-Net listing criteria? Why or why not?

Casing The Web

To access the case "Survival of the Financially Fittest," visit

www.mhhe.com/ub7e

Video Case

Financial Management

Students often ask their professors, "Which is more important for me to know as an entrepreneur—finance or accounting?" The answer often is, "You need to know both." They go together like peanut butter and jelly or ham and cheese. Even small businesses need careful financial planning, but there is a difference between small and large businesses when it comes to major financial decisions. For example, a small business doesn't get involved in commercial paper. It is issued when a big company has millions of dollars it wants to invest immediately.

It helps when the financial manager understands fully what information is needed by top management. Naturally, the most important goal is to stay in business. The most common reasons why businesses fail are undercapitalization (not starting with enough money to carry the business through its growth period), poor cash flow (not having enough cash on hand to pay bills), and inadequate expense control (spending more than the company makes). We learned in Chapter 18 about cash flow. Chapter 19 looks at money management (like budgeting), which will help prevent cash flow problems.

Big business and small business have many financial similarities. They both budget, they both pay taxes, and they both audit their books. The major difference is scale. A small business is not going to lose $5 billion as a large business might do. Regardless of size, a business should ask for a budget request from all departments. The capital budget is used for major purchases, like buying a building or truck. The cash budget controls cash flow. The operating budget provides the "big picture"—how much profit a business can expect to make and what to do with the money.

Both small and large businesses sometimes need short-term financing. Sources include trade credit, promissory notes, family and friends, commercial bank loans, factoring, and commercial paper. Trade credit is the most commonly used short-term financing. When a business gets a bill, it will usually have terms such as 2/10, net 30, which means that the bill must be paid within 30 days, but a 2 percent discount can be earned by paying within 10 days. Since the difference is 20 days and there are 18 20-day periods in a year, a business may save about 36 percent by paying within 10 days—a sizable discount. On the other hand, customers don't always pay on time. If a business pays its bills early but its customers pay late, it may run into cash flow problems.

Friends and family are often sources of emergency funds, but businesses must pay them back like any other creditor. Similarly, business owners can borrow from their own savings, but that is dangerous and may ruin their credit rating, which is hard to rebuild. Businesses would like to fund most projects out of retained earnings, but there often isn't enough money there to fund larger projects.

When it comes to longer term financing, companies may issue stock or bonds, but that is more likely to take place in larger firms. Smaller firms often have to turn to commercial banks or other sources for funds. Because the risk is so high, even commercial banks may turn a small business down. You have to have a good credit rating to get a loan. But if you had a good credit rating, you probably would not need a loan. As the video says, "It's a Catch 22 situation." Those who need funds have trouble getting them and those who don't need funds can get them more easily.

The moral of the story is this: All businesspeople need to understand accounting and finance. It is not enough to have a good idea and run out and start making and marketing a product. You need money to make things and to market things. Where do you get that money? How do you budget it? Where should you invest funds? Where should you turn for emergency funds? These are the kinds of questions any businessperson needs to ask and those schooled in finance can readily answer them.

Thinking It Over

1. What insights did you get from this video about the importance of finance to both small and large firms?
2. Which sources of funds are most available to a small business? What additional sources may large businesses tap? Why?
3. Does the management of money look more or less complicated now that you have seen the video? What are some of the trickier concepts?

Chapter 20

Securities Markets: Financing and Investing Opportunities

Learning Goals

After you have read and studied this chapter, you should be able to

1 Identify and explain the functions of securities markets, and discuss the role of investment bankers.

2 Compare the advantages and disadvantages of debt financing by issuing bonds, and identify the classes and features of bonds.

3 Compare the advantages and disadvantages of equity financing by issuing stock, and explain the differences between common and preferred stock.

4 Describe the various stock exchanges where securities are traded.

5 Explain how to invest in securities markets and various investment objectives such as long-term growth, income, cash, and protection from inflation.

6 Analyze the opportunities bonds offer as investments.

7 Explain the opportunities stocks offer as investments.

8 Explain the opportunities in mutual funds as investments and the benefits of diversifying investments.

9 Discuss specific high-risk investments, including junk bonds, buying stock on margin, and commodity trading.

10 Explain securities quotations listed in the financial section of a newspaper, and describe how stock market indicators like the Dow Jones Industrial Average affect the market.

Profile

Getting to Know David and Tom Gardner of the Motley Fool

According to David and Tom Gardner, their interest in stocks and other investments began with chocolate pudding. Sound unusual? It's really quite simple. When the two brothers were young, they would often go to the supermarket with their father, who was both a lawyer and an economist. As the three of them traveled down the various aisles, their dad would tell them, "See that pudding? We own the company that makes it! Every time someone buys that pudding, it's good for our company. Boys, go get some more pudding!"

Those supermarket lessons about investing stuck with David and Tom. After graduating from the University of North Carolina, David became a writer for respected investment guru Louis Rukeyser's *Wall Street* newsletter; brother Tom graduated from Brown University and went on to teach business at the University of Montana. In 1993, the two brothers, along with their friend Erik Rydholm, founded the Motley Fool, with the self-imposed mission "to educate, amuse and enlighten everyday people about the power of investing." Based in Alexandria, Virginia, the company has become one of the most successful multimedia financial-education firms in the nation.

Today, the Motley Fool includes a popular financial website (www.fool.com); five books—*The Motley Fool Investment Guide, You Have More Than You Think, The Motley Fool Investment Workbook, Rule Breakers, Rule Makers,* and *What To Do With Your Money Now*—that have all become bestsellers; a syndicated newspaper column that appears in over 200 papers; and a weekly program carried on National Public Radio.

The mission of the Motley Fool (to provide quality financial information to the masses—regardless of education or income) remains the primary focus of the two founders.

David and Tom chose the name Motley Fool from Shakespeare to reflect the spirit of truthful fun that the company brings to the world of investments. Though they often sport jester hats and are humorous in their analyses, both are intense in their passion to spread the message that securities markets can offer financial opportunity to all. The mission of the Motley Fool (to provide quality financial information to the masses—regardless of education or income) remains the primary focus of the two founders. In 2000, the company took advantage of the interactivity of the Internet and began offering online seminars to assist interested investors or would-be investors in getting specific knowledge of particular investment topics. The Fool also offers in-depth company-specific research reports on companies that are most widely owned by the members of the Fool community. Also, since foolishness has no boundaries, the Motley Fool has expanded its business globally. The company even has a "Foolanthropy" program that invites readers to nominate charities they feel are worthy of the Fool's efforts. Since 1997, the Motley Fool has raised close to $2 million for such charities.

This chapter discusses securities markets and how they assist companies as well as individual investors to achieve their financial goals and objectives. Read this chapter carefully and perhaps you will become a disciple of the Motley Fool in spreading the word of financial freedom for all. When it comes to your finances, be a wise fool.

Sources: Holly Hubbard Preston, "The Motley Fool Investment Guide for TeensBook Report," *International Herald Tribune*, March 8, 2003; David and Tom Gardner, *The Motley Fool Investment Workbook* (New York: Simon & Schuster, 2003); and www.fool.com.

THE FUNCTION OF SECURITIES MARKETS

Securities markets, such as the New York Stock Exchange (NYSE) and the NASDAQ (pronounced *nazz-dak*), are financial marketplaces for stocks and bonds.[1] These institutions serve two major functions: First, they assist businesses in finding long-term funding to finance capital needs, such as beginning operations, expanding their businesses, or buying major goods and services. Second, they provide private investors a place to buy and sell securities (investments), such as stocks, bonds, and mutual funds, that can help them build their financial future. In this chapter, we will look at securities markets such as the NYSE and the NASDAQ from the perspectives of both businesses and private investors.

Securities markets are divided into primary and secondary markets. *Primary markets* handle the sale of new securities. This is an important point to understand. Corporations make money on the sale of their securities only once—when they are first sold on the primary market.[2] The first public offering of a corporation's stock is called an **initial public offering (IPO).** After that, the *secondary market* handles the trading of securities between investors, with the proceeds of a sale going to the investor selling the stock, not to the corporation whose stock is sold. For example, if you, the maker of Fiberrific cereal, offer 2 million shares of stock in your company at $15 a share, you would raise $30 million at this initial offering. However, if Shareholder Jones sells 100 shares of her Fiberrific stock to Investor Smith, Fiberrific collects nothing from this transaction. Smith bought the stock from Jones, not from Fiberrific. However, it's possible for companies like Fiberrific to offer additional shares of stock to raise additional capital.

initial public offering (IPO)
The first public offering of a corporation's stock.

As Chapter 19 implied, the importance of long-term funding to businesses can't be overemphasized. Unfortunately, many new companies start without sufficient capital, and many established firms fail to do adequate long-term financial planning. If given a choice, businesses normally prefer to meet long-term financial needs by using retained earnings ➤P. 600◀ or by borrowing from a lending institution (bank, pension fund, insurance company). However, if such types of long-term funding are not available, a company may be able to raise funds by issuing corporate bonds (debt) or selling stock (ownership). Recall that issuing corporate bonds is a form of debt financing and selling stock in the corporation is a form of equity financing. These forms of debt or equity financing are not available to all companies, especially small businesses. However, many firms use such financing options to meet long-term financial needs.

For example, what if you needed long-term financing to expand your operations at Fiberrific? Your chief financial officer (CFO) explains that the company doesn't have sufficient retained earnings, and it's unlikely the firm can secure the needed funds from a lender. The CFO suggests that you might want to issue corporate bonds or offer shares of stock to private investors to secure the financing needed. She warns, however, that being able to issue corporate bonds or shares of stock in the company is not an automatic right. Getting approval for bond or stock issues requires extensive financial disclosures and detailed scrutiny by the U.S. Securities and Exchange Commission (SEC). Because of such requirements, she recommends that the company turn to an investment banker for assistance. Let's see why.

The Role of Investment Bankers

Investment bankers are specialists who assist in the issue and sale of new securities. Investment banking firms, such as Goldman Sachs, or large financial institutions, like Citigroup and Bank of America, help companies prepare the extensive financial analyses necessary to gain SEC approval for stock or bond issues.

investment bankers
Specialists who assist in the issue and sale of new securities.

www.sec.gov

Dealing with Change: Maintaining the Integrity of Securities Markets

The U.S. financial system is built on the integrity of its information and the trust investors have in the fairness of the system. Investment banking firms have always walked a financial tightrope in this system due to the fact that the same investment banking firm often serves two masters: the companies for which it issues bonds or sells its stock and the investors whom it advises. The cozy relationship between analysts (who advise investors) and their investment banking colleagues is what's raising some eyebrows among regulators and investors.

BusinessWeek

For example, at Merrill Lynch, a leading analyst misled investors by fraudulently promoting stocks of companies with which the firm had an investment banking relationship. Similar accusations were raised against analysts at Salomon Smith Barney, Morgan Stanley Dean Witter, and at least three other investment banking firms. Many feel the problem contaminating the system is that, to an ever-increasing degree, analysts' pay is tied to how much investment banking business they bring into the company.

Another controversy involves the rise of what are referred to as universal banks, brought about by changes in banking laws in the late 1990s. Prior to the changes in law, lending and cash-management services (the specialty of commercial banks) did not exist under the same company roof as stock and bond underwriting (the specialty of investment bankers). Today, financial giants such as Citigroup exist as universal banks that offer financing services that include lending, cash management, investment banking, and brokerage services. Regulators fear that such financial concentration could possibly lead to illegal practices such as *tying*, in which a bank agrees to lend money to a company only if the company agrees to send some lucrative fee-generating business such as bond or stock underwriting its way.

Maintaining the faith and confidence in financial markets is vital to the economic health of the U.S. economy. The Securities and Exchange Commission and the U.S. Congress have pledged that the integrity of this system will not be breached. Felix Rohatyn, a respected financial manager, probably summed it up best when he said, "If Wall Street knows what is good for it and what is good for the country, it will very definitely clean up its act."

Sources: Emily Thornton and Heather Timmons, "Dirty Research: Not Only Analysts Are to Blame," *Business Week,* January 20, 2003, p. 59; and Gary Weiss, "Analysts: Buying Wall Street's Attention," *Business Week,* January 27, 2003, p. 82.

Investment bankers also underwrite new issues of bonds or stocks. In other words, the investment banking firm buys the entire bond or stock issue a company wants to sell at an agreed-on discount, which can be quite sizable, and then sells the issue to private or institutional investors at full price. **Institutional investors** are large organizations—such as pension funds, mutual funds, insurance companies, and banks—that invest their own funds or the funds of others. Because of their vast buying power (these institutions control over 50 percent of U.S. stocks), institutional investors are a powerful force in securities markets.[3]

institutional investors
Large organizations—such as pension funds, mutual funds, insurance companies, and banks—that invest their own funds or the funds of others.

The entire economy depends on the integrity of securities markets to raise and allocate capital.[4] Unfortunately, investment banking came under fire in the early 2000s as questions of conflicts of interest and violations of ethical standards were raised in the securities industry.[5] The Dealing with Change box discusses this issue.

Helping companies raise needed long-term funding using debt financing by issuing bonds is an option many companies pursue. Let's look at issuing bonds as a long-term financing alternative.

Debt Financing by Selling Bonds

A **bond** is a corporate certificate indicating that a person has lent money to a firm. A company that issues bonds has a legal obligation to make regular interest payments to investors and to repay the entire bond principal amount at

bond
A corporate certificate indicating that a person has lent money to a firm.

a prescribed time, called the *maturity date.*[6] Let's explore the language of bonds more carefully so that you understand exactly what's involved.

Learning the Language of Bonds

interest
The payment the issuer of the bond makes to the bondholders for use of the borrowed money.

A more specific definition of a bond than the one just given is that a bond is a contract of indebtedness issued by a corporation or government unit that promises payment of a principal amount at a specified future time. Interest is paid to the holder of the bond until the principal amount is due. Thus, in this context, **interest** is the payment the issuer of the bond makes to the bondholders for use of the borrowed money. The interest rate paid on a bond may also be called the bond's *coupon rate.* This term dates back to when bonds were issued as bearer bonds and the holder, or bearer, was considered the owner. The company issuing the bond kept no accounts of transfers in ownership, and the interest on the bond was obtained by clipping coupons attached to the bond and sending them to the issuing company for payment. Today bonds are registered to particular owners, and changes in ownership are recorded electronically.

The interest rate paid on a bond varies according to factors such as the state of the economy, the reputation of the company issuing the bond, and the going interest rate for government bonds or bonds of similar companies. Once an interest rate is set for a corporate bond issue (except in the case of what's called a floating-rate bond), it cannot be changed. The interest rate being paid by U.S. government bonds clearly affects the interest rate a firm must agree to pay, since government bonds are considered safe investments.[7] (Remember the risk/return trade-off ➤P. 598◄ defined in Chapter 19.) Figure 20.1 lists and describes several types of government bonds that compete in securities markets with U.S. corporate bonds.

maturity date
The exact date the issuer of a bond must pay the principal to the bondholder.

Bonds of all types are evaluated (rated) in terms of their risk to investors by independent rating firms such as Standard & Poor's and Moody's Investors Service.[8] Bond ratings can range from high-quality, gilt-edged bonds to bonds considered junk (which we discuss later in this chapter). Figure 20.2 describes the range of ratings these two firms attach to bond issues.[9] Bonds are issued with a *denomination,* which is the amount of debt represented by one bond. (Bonds are almost always issued in multiples of $1,000.) The *principal* is the face value of a bond. The issuing company is legally bound to repay the bond principal to the bondholder in full on the **maturity date.** For example, if Fiberrific issues a $1,000 bond with an interest rate of 5 percent and a maturity date of 2025, the company is agreeing to pay a bondholder a total of $50 in interest each year

FIGURE 20.1
TYPES OF GOVERNMENT SECURITIES THAT COMPETE WITH CORPORATE BONDS

BOND	DESCRIPTION
U.S. government bond	Issued by the federal government; considered the safest type of bond investment
Treasury bill (T-bill)	Matures in less than a year; issued with a minimum denomination of $1,000
Treasury note	Matures in 10 years or less; sold in denominations of $1,000 and $5,000
Treasury bond	Matures in 25 years or more; sold in denominations of $1,000 and $5,000
Municipal bond	Issued by states, cities, counties, and other state and local government agencies; usually exempt from federal taxes
Yankee bond	Issued by a foreign government; payable in U.S. dollars

RATING		
MOODY'S	STANDARD & POOR'S	DESCRIPTIONS
Aaa	AAA	Highest quality (lowest default risk)
Aa	AA	High quality
A	A	Upper medium grade
Baa	BBB	Medium grade
Ba	BB	Lower medium grade
B	B	Speculative
Caa	CCC, CC	Poor (high default risk)
Ca	C	Highly speculative
C	D	Lowest grade

FIGURE 20.2

BOND RATINGS: MOODY'S INVESTORS SERVICE AND STANDARD & POOR'S INVESTOR SERVICE

until a specified date in 2025, when the full $1,000 must be repaid. Though bond interest is quoted for an entire year, it is usually paid in two installments (semi-annually). Maturity dates for bonds can vary. For example, firms such as Disney and Coca-Cola have issued bonds with 50-year maturity dates.

Advantages and Disadvantages of Issuing Bonds

Bonds offer several long-term financing advantages to an organization. The decision to issue bonds is often based on advantages such as the following:

- Bondholders are creditors, not owners, of the firm and seldom have a vote on corporate matters; thus, management maintains control over the firm's operations.
- Interest paid on bonds is tax deductible to the firm issuing the bond. Chapter 18 explained how certain interest expenses help a firm limit its tax responsibilities to the government.
- Bonds are a temporary source of funding for a firm. They're eventually repaid and the debt obligation eliminated.
- Bonds can be repaid before the maturity date if they contain a call provision, and can also be convertible to common stock (both features are discussed on p. 614).

But bonds also have their drawbacks:

- Bonds increase debt (long-term liabilities) and may adversely affect the market's perception of the firm.
- Paying interest on bonds is a legal obligation. If interest is not paid, bondholders can take legal action to force payment.
- The face value (denomination) of bonds must be repaid on the maturity date. Without careful planning, this repayment can cause cash flow problems when the bonds come due.

Different Classes of Bonds

As mentioned in Chapter 19, corporations can issue two different classes of corporate bonds. The first class is *unsecured bonds,* which are not backed by any collateral (such as equipment). These bonds are usually referred to as **debenture bonds.** Generally, only well-respected firms with excellent credit ratings can issue debenture bonds, since the only security the bondholder has is the reputation and credit history of the company.

debenture bonds
Bonds that are unsecured (i.e., not backed by any collateral such as equipment).

The second class of bonds is *secured bonds,* which are backed by some tangible asset (collateral) that is pledged to the bondholder if bond interest isn't paid or the principal isn't paid back when promised. For example, a mortgage bond is a bond secured by company assets such as land and buildings. In issuing bonds, a company can choose to include different features in the various bond issues. Let's look at some possible special bond features.

Special Bond Features

sinking fund
A reserve account in which the issuer of a bond periodically retires some part of the bond principal prior to maturity so that enough capital will be accumulated by the maturity date to pay off the bond.

By now you should understand that bonds are issued with an interest rate, are unsecured or secured by some type of collateral, and must be repaid at their maturity date. This repayment requirement often leads companies to establish a reserve account called a **sinking fund,** whose primary purpose is to ensure that enough money will be available to repay bondholders on the bond's maturity date. Firms issuing sinking-fund bonds periodically retire (set aside) some part of the bond principal prior to maturity so that enough capital will be accumulated by the maturity date to pay off the bond. Sinking funds can be attractive to issuing firms and potential investors for several reasons:

- They provide for an orderly retirement (repayment) of a bond issue.
- They reduce the risk the bond will not be repaid.
- The market price of the bond is supported because the risk of the firm's not repaying the principal on the maturity date is reduced.

Another special feature that can be included in a bond issue is a call provision. A *callable bond* permits the bond issuer to pay off the bond's principal (i.e., call the bond) prior to its maturity date. Call provisions must be included when a bond is issued, and bondholders should be aware of whether a bond is callable. Callable bonds give companies some discretion in their long-term forecasting. For example, suppose Fiberrific issued $50 million in 20-year bonds in 2005 with an interest rate of 10 percent. The yearly interest expense would be $5 million ($50 million times 10 percent). If market conditions change in 2010, and bonds issued of the same quality are only paying 7 percent, Fiberrific would be paying 3 percent, or $1.5 million ($50 million times 3 percent), in excess interest yearly. Obviously, Fiberrific could benefit if it could call in (pay off) the old bonds and issue new bonds at the lower interest rate. If a company calls a bond before maturity, investors in the bond are often paid a price above the bond's face value.

Another feature sometimes included in bonds is convertibility. A *convertible bond* is a bond that can be converted into shares of common stock in the issuing company.[10] This feature is often an incentive for an investor to buy a bond. Why, you may ask, would bond investors want to convert their investment to stock? That's easy. If the value of the firm's common stock grows sizably over time, bondholders can compare the value of continued bond interest with the possible sizable profit they could gain by converting to a specified number of shares of common stock. When we discuss common stock in the next section, this advantage will become more evident to you.

Progress Assessment

- Why are bonds considered to be a form of debt financing?
- What does it mean when a firm states that it is issuing a 9 percent debenture bond due in 2025?
- Explain the difference between an unsecured and a secured bond.
- Why do companies like callable bonds? Why do investors dislike them?
- Why are convertible bonds attractive to investors?

EQUITY FINANCING BY SELLING STOCK

Equity financing ➤P. 599◄ is the other form of long-term funding first introduced in Chapter 19. One form of equity financing is obtaining funds through the sale of ownership (stock) in the corporation. As we did previously with bonds, let's look first at the language of stock.

Learning the Language of Stock

Stocks are shares of ownership in a company. A **stock certificate** is evidence of stock ownership that specifies the name of the company, the number of shares it represents, and the type of stock being issued (see Figure 20.3). Today stock certificates are generally held electronically for the owners of the stock. Certificates sometimes indicate a stock's *par value,* which is a dollar amount assigned to each share of stock by the corporation's charter. Some states use par value as a basis for calculating the state's incorporation charges and fees; but today, since par values do not reflect the market value of the stock, most companies issue "no-par" stock. **Dividends** are part of a firm's profits that may be distributed to stockholders as either cash payments or additional shares of stock. Dividends are declared by a corporation's board of directors and are generally paid quarterly. Although it's a legal obligation for companies that issue bonds to pay interest, companies that issue stock are not required to pay dividends.[11]

stocks
Shares of ownership in a company.

stock certificate
Evidence of stock ownership that specifies the name of the company, the number of shares it represents, and the type of stock being issued.

dividends
Part of a firm's profits that may be distributed to stockholders as either cash payments or additional shares of stock.

Advantages and Disadvantages of Issuing Stock

The following are some advantages to the firm of issuing stock:

- As owners of the business, stockholders never have to be repaid.
- There's no legal obligation to pay dividends to stockholders; therefore, income (retained earnings) can be reinvested in the firm for future financing needs.

FIGURE 20.3

STOCK CERTIFICATE FOR PET INC.

Examine this certificate for key information about this stock.

- Selling stock can improve the condition of a firm's balance sheet since issuing stock creates no debt. (A corporation may also buy back its stock to improve its balance sheet and make the company appear stronger financially.)

Disadvantages of issuing stock include the following:

- As owners, stockholders (usually only common stockholders) have the right to vote for the company's board of directors. Typically one vote is granted for each share of stock. Hence, the direction and control of the firm can be altered by the sale of additional shares of stock.
- Dividends are paid out of profit after taxes and thus are not tax deductible.[12]
- Management's decisions can be affected by the need to keep stockholders happy.

Companies can issue two classes of stock: preferred and common. Let's see how these two forms of equity financing differ.

Issuing Shares of Preferred Stock

preferred stock
Stock that gives its owners preference in the payment of dividends and an earlier claim on assets than common stockholders if the company is forced out of business and its assets sold.

Owners of **preferred stock** enjoy a preference (hence the term *preferred*) in the payment of dividends; they also have a prior claim on company assets if the firm is forced out of business and its assets sold. Normally, however, preferred stock does not include voting rights in the firm. Preferred stock is frequently referred to as a hybrid investment because it has characteristics of both bonds and stocks. To illustrate this, consider the treatment of preferred stock dividends.

Preferred stock dividends differ from common stock dividends in several ways. Preferred stock is generally issued with a par value that becomes the base for the dividend the firm is willing to pay. For example, if a preferred stock's par value is $100 a share and its dividend rate is 4 percent, the firm is committing to a $4 dividend for each share of preferred stock the investor owns (4 percent of $100 = $4). An owner of 100 shares of this preferred stock is promised a fixed yearly dividend of $400. In addition, the preferred stockholder is also assured that this dividend must be paid in full before any common stock dividends can be distributed.[13]

Preferred stock is therefore quite similar to bonds; both have a face (or par) value and both have a fixed rate of return. Also, like bonds, Standard & Poor's and Moody's Investors Service rate preferred stock according to risk. So how do bonds and preferred stock differ? Remember that companies are legally bound to pay bond interest and to repay the face value (denomination) of the bond on its maturity date. In contrast, even though preferred stock dividends are generally fixed, they do not legally have to be paid; also stock (preferred or common) never has to be repurchased. Though both bonds and stock can increase in market value, the price of stock generally increases at a higher percentage than bonds. Of course, the market value of both could also go down.

Special Features of Preferred Stock

Preferred stock can have special features that do not apply to common stock. For example, like bonds, preferred stock can be callable. This means that preferred stockholders could be required to sell back their shares to the corporation. Preferred stock can also be convertible to shares of common stock.[14] Another important feature of preferred stock is that it can often be cumulative. That is, if one or more dividends are not paid when promised, the missed dividends will be accumulated and paid later to cumulative preferred stockholders. This means that all dividends, including any back dividends, must be paid in full before any common stock dividends can be distributed.

Issuing Shares of Common Stock

Common stock is the most basic form of ownership in a firm. In fact, if a company issues only one type of stock, it must be common. Holders of common stock have the right (1) to vote for company board directors and important issues affecting the company and (2) to share in the firm's profits through dividends, if approved by the firm's board of directors. Having voting rights in a corporation allows common stockholders to influence corporate policy since the elected board chooses the firm's top management and makes major policy decisions. According to Nell Minow of Corporate Library, a firm that tracks stockholder activism (www.thecorporatelibrary.com), common stockholders used this influence in the early 2000s against major companies such as Tyco, Hewlett-Packard, and smaller firms such as Luby's Cafeterias.[15] Common stockholders also have what is called a *preemptive right,* which is the first right to purchase any new shares of common stock the firm decides to issue. This right allows common stockholders to maintain a proportional share of ownership in the company.

common stock
The most basic form of ownership in a firm; it confers voting rights and the right to share in the firm's profits through dividends, if offered by the firm's board of directors.

Now that we have looked at stocks and bonds from a company's perspective as a source of long-term financing, let's look at them from an investor's perspective. Before we do that, though, it's important to discuss stock exchanges—the places where stocks and bonds are traded.

Progress Assessment

- Name at least two advantages and two disadvantages of issuing stock as a form of equity financing.
- What are the major differences between preferred stock and common stock?
- In what ways is preferred stock similar to bonds? How are they different?

STOCK EXCHANGES

As its name implies, a **stock exchange** is an organization whose members can buy and sell (exchange) securities for companies and investors. Brokerage firms such as A. G. Edwards and Merrill Lynch purchase memberships, or seats, on the exchanges, but the number of seats available is limited. The New York Stock Exchange (discussed below), for example, has only 1,366 members, a number that has not changed since 1953. The price of a seat on the NYSE varies with the strength of the market. In August 1999, the price was $2.65 million; by mid-2003 it had fallen to $1.75 million.[16]

stock exchange
An organization whose members can buy and sell (exchange) securities for companies and investors.

U.S. Exchanges

The largest stock exchange in the United States, the New York Stock Exchange (NYSE), was founded in 1792.[17] The NYSE is a floor-based exchange (trades take place on the floor of the stock exchange) that lists about 2,800 companies, mostly very large. For example, in 2002 the 2,800 companies listed on the NYSE had a total market value of about $13.5 trillion.[18] Because of such a

On May 17, 1792, twenty-four commodity merchants and traders signed a pact to trade securities. Since then, excitement is always in the air at the nation's largest stock exchange. The New York Stock Exchange (NYSE) is a floor-based exchange where specialists (like those pictured here) buy and sell over a billion shares of stock each day.

large market value, the NYSE is often referred to as the Big Board. The second largest floor-based U.S. exchange is the American Stock Exchange (AMEX).[19] These two exchanges are considered national exchanges because they handle stocks of companies from all over the United States.

In addition to the national exchanges, there are several regional exchanges in cities such as Chicago, San Francisco, Philadelphia, Cincinnati, Spokane, and Salt Lake City. The regional exchanges deal mostly with firms in their own areas and handle the stock of many large corporations listed on the Big Board. Regional exchanges are often used by big institutional investors to trade stock since their transaction costs are less than those of large exchanges like the NYSE.

Not all securities are traded on registered stock exchanges. The **over-the-counter (OTC)** market provides companies and investors with a means to trade stocks not listed on the national securities exchanges. The OTC market is a network of several thousand brokers that maintain contact with one another and buy and sell securities through a nationwide electronic system.

over-the-counter (OTC) market
Exchange that provides a means to trade stocks not listed on the national exchanges.

The **NASDAQ** stock market (originally known as the National Association of Securities Dealers Automated Quotations) evolved from the OTC market, but is no longer part of it. As of this writing, the SEC is considering NASDAQ's application for exchange registration. Unlike a floor-based exchange like the NYSE, the NASDAQ is a telecommunications network. It links dealers across the nation so that they can buy and sell securities electronically rather than in person. Originally the NASDAQ dealt mostly with small firms. Today, however, well-known companies such as Microsoft, Intel, Starbucks, Cisco, and Dell trade their stock on the NASDAQ. The NASDAQ also handles federal, state, and city government bonds as well. Today, the NASDAQ lists approximately 3,800 companies and its average is reported every business day.

National Association of Securities Dealers Automated Quotations (NASDAQ)
A nationwide electronic system that communicates over-the-counter trades to brokers.

Figure 20.4 lists the requirements for registering (listing) stocks on the various exchanges. It's important to note that stocks can be delisted from an exchange if a company fails to hold to the exchange's minimum requirements.[20] For example, between 1996 and 2001, the NASDAQ delisted 2,116 stocks.[21] Adding a company to an exchange is a highly competitive undertaking, and the battle between the stock exchanges is often fierce.

FIGURE 20.4
REQUIREMENTS FOR LISTING STOCK ON THE NEW YORK, AMERICAN, AND NASDAQ EXCHANGES

EXCHANGE	REQUIREMENTS	TYPE OF COMPANY
New York Stock Exchange (NYSE)	Pretax income of $2.5 million; 2,000 shareholders holding at least 100 shares; market value of $50 million	Oldest, largest, and best-known companies
American Stock Exchange (AMEX)	Pretax income of $750,000; 500,000 shares publicly held at a minimum market value of $3 million; minimum of 400 public shareholders	Midsized growth companies
NASDAQ	Total market value of all shares of $8 million; 400 shareholders holding at least 100 shares	Large, midsized, and small growth companies

The NASDAQ had goals of expanding operations into Europe, Asia, and other global markets by the early 2000s. Frank Zarb, the former chairman and CEO of the NASDAQ exchange, confidently predicted a new stock exchange that spanned the globe and traded securities 24 hours a day. The expectations were a bit premature.[22] The Japanese market was closed in 2002 and European efforts have become very fragmented.[23] Still, despite its challenges, the NASDAQ is the second largest stock exchange in the world and remains profitable.[24]

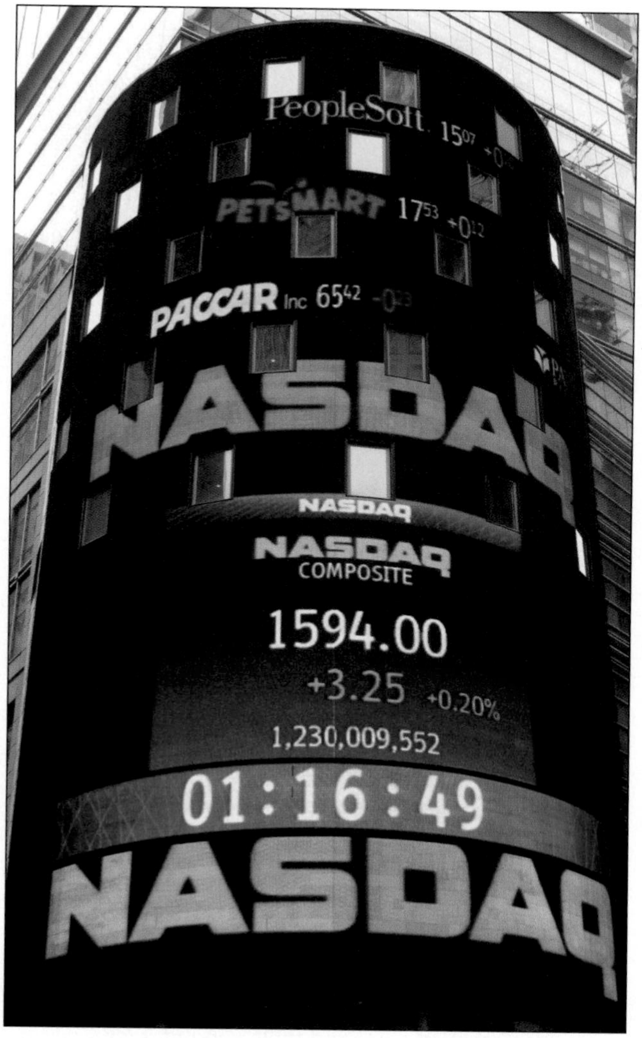

Passersby at New York's Times Square never have to wonder how shares of stock on the NASDAQ exchange are performing. The NASDAQ price wall continually updates prices and number of shares traded. Unlike the NYSE, the NASDAQ doesn't have a trading floor (i.e., there is no chaotic personal interaction by traders).

Securities Regulations and the Securities and Exchange Commission

The Securities Act of 1933 protects investors by requiring full disclosure of financial information by firms selling bonds or stock. The U.S. Congress passed this legislation to deal with the free-for-all atmosphere that existed in the securities markets during the Roaring Twenties and the early 1930s. The Securities and Exchange Act of 1934 created the **Securities and Exchange Commission (SEC),** which has responsibility at the federal level for regulating activities in the various exchanges. Companies trading on the national exchanges must register with the SEC and provide it annual updates.[25] The 1934 act also established specific guidelines that companies must follow when issuing financial securities such as bonds or stock. For example, before issuing either bonds or stock for sale to the public, a company must file a detailed registration statement with the SEC that includes extensive economic and financial information relevant to the firm. The condensed version of that registration document—called a **prospectus**—must be sent to prospective investors.

The 1934 act also established guidelines to prevent company insiders from taking advantage of privileged information they may have. *Insider trading* ➤P. 113◄ involves the use of knowledge or information that individuals gain through their position that allows them to benefit unfairly from fluctuations in security prices.[26] The key words here are *benefit unfairly.* Insiders within a firm are permitted to buy and sell stock in the company they work for so long as they do not take unfair advantage of information.

Originally, the Securities & Exchange Commission (SEC) defined the term *insider* rather narrowly as consisting of a company's directors, employees, and relatives. Today the term has been broadened to include just about anyone with securities information that is not available to the general public.[27] For example, say that the chief financial officer of Fiberrific tells her next-door neighbor that she is finalizing paperwork to sell the company to a major cereal producer. The neighbor buys the stock on this information. A court may well consider the purchase an insider trade. Penalties for insider

Securities and Exchange Commission (SEC)
Federal agency that has responsibility for regulating the various exchanges.

prospectus
A condensed version of economic and financial information that a company must file with the SEC before issuing stock; the prospectus must be sent to prospective investors.

www.sec.gov

Legal Briefcase — Getting the "Inside" Story

The stock market meltdown in the early 2000s reminded market watchers of the "greed-is-good" days of the late 1980s in at least one way: Insider trading raised its ugly head again. Questionable or even dishonest stock trading accusations were leveled against top managers at Enron, Global Crossing, and several other companies. Even Martha Stewart was on the hot seat as the government probed her quick disposal of ImClone stock shortly before the company received bad news from the U.S. Food and Drug Administration. Insider trading involves buying or selling a stock on the basis of company information not available to the investing public. It's sometimes difficult to identify insider trading. The hypothetical examples below will give you an idea of what's legal and what's illegal. See how many of the questions you can answer. The answers are at the bottom of this box.

1. You work in research and development at a large company and have been involved in a major effort that should lead to a blockbuster new product coming to the market. News about the product is not public, and very few other workers even know about it. Can you purchase stock in the company?
2. Pertaining to the above situation, you are in a local coffee bar and mention to a friend about what's going on at the company. Another customer seated at an adjoining table overhears your discussion. Can this person legally buy stock in the company before the public announcement?
3. You work as an executive secretary at a major investment banking firm. You are asked to copy documents that detail a major merger about to happen that will keenly benefit the company being taken over. Can you buy stock in the company before the announcement is made public?
4. Your stockbroker recommends that you buy shares in a little-known company. The broker seems to have some inside information, but you don't ask any questions about his source. Can you buy stock in this company?
5. You work as a cleaning person at a major securities firm. At your job you come across information from the trash cans and computer printers of employees of the firm that provide detailed information about several upcoming deals the firm will be handling. Can you buy stock in the companies involved?

Answers: 1. No; 2. Yes; 3. No; 4. Yes; 5. No.

Sources: Brook A. Masters, "Quattrone, Martha Stewart Cases Follow Very Different Timelines," *Washington Post,* May 9, 2003, p. E1; Curt Anderson, "Government Expands Charges against Enron Execs," AP Online, May 1, 2003; and Monica Roman, "Martha's Lower Standard of Living," *Business Week,* March 17, 2003, p. 48.

trading can include fines or imprisonment. The Legal Briefcase box describes situations that could involve insider trading. See how well you interpret this important legal issue. After that, judge the manager's dilemma in the Making Ethical Decisions box, which could also involve the question of insider actions.

Global Stock Exchanges

It's important to remember that we live in a global economy and that the United States is not the only country offering investment opportunities. Stock exchanges operate globally, even in former communist-bloc countries like Poland and Hungary. Expanded communications and the relaxation of many legal barriers now enable investors to buy securities from companies almost anywhere in the world. For example, if you hear of a foreign company that you feel has great potential for growth, you can obtain shares of its stock with little difficulty from U.S. brokers who have access to foreign stock exchanges. In fact, 470 foreign firms from 51 different countries were listed on the NYSE in 2003 with a market value of $5 trillion.[28] The Reaching Beyond Our Borders box on p. 622 offers advice on how U.S. investors can become active in the global market.

Making Ethical Decisions www.nasdaq.com

What Will It Be: Your Bark or Your Bite?

After 35 years of hard work you finally made it to the post of chief executive officer of Laddie-Come-Home, a large producer of pet foods. As part of your new compensation package, you are entitled to bonuses based on the company's stock performance. If the stock price of Laddie-Come-Home exceeds $50 a share during the current fiscal year, you could realize a windfall of close to $3 million in bonuses. The company's stock is currently selling for $42 per share. It's been brought to your attention by an investment-banking firm that a major competitor, Barking-up-the-Wrong-Tree, has an interest in acquiring your company. The investment banker hinted that Barking-up-the-Wrong-Tree would pay upward of $50 a share for Laddie-Come-Home. Your attorney says the merger is perfectly legal and would have no antitrust problems. You realize the company board of directors would probably follow your recommendation if you suggested selling the company, but you also know that at least half of the current employees (many who have been at the company for over 20 years) would lose their jobs in the takeover.

You plan to retire within the next two years, and $3 million could make life easier. What are the ethical considerations in this situation? What are your alternatives? What are the consequences of each alternative? What will you do?

Foreign investors can also easily invest in U.S. securities. Large exchanges like the London and Tokyo stock exchanges trade large amounts of U.S. securities daily. The number of U.S. companies that are listed on foreign stock exchanges is also growing. In addition to the London and Tokyo exchanges, other major stock exchanges are located in Paris, Sydney, Buenos Aires, Frankfurt, Zurich, Hong Kong, and Taiwan.

The NYSE and NASDAQ are not the only fish in the stock exchange sea. Exchanges like the London Exchange (pictured here) are located throughout the world, even in former communist-bloc countries like Poland and Hungary. If you think a foreign company is destined to be the next Microsoft, call a broker and get in on the opportunity. Does the NYSE exchange trade shares in foreign companies?

How to Invest in Securities

Investing in bonds, stocks, or other securities is not very difficult. First, you decide what bond or stock you want to buy. After that, it's necessary to find a registered representative authorized to trade stocks and bonds who can call a member of the stock exchange to execute your order. A **stockbroker** is a registered representative who works as a market intermediary to buy and sell securities for clients. Stockbrokers place an order with a stock exchange member, who goes to the place at the exchange where the bond or stock is traded and negotiates a price. After the transaction is completed, the trade is reported to your broker, who notifies you to confirm your purchase. Large brokerage firms like Merrill Lynch or A. G. Edwards maintain automated order systems that allow their brokers to enter your order the instant you make it. Seconds later, the order can be confirmed. Online brokers (discussed next), such as Ameritrade or E*Trade, can also confirm investor trades in a matter of seconds.[29]

stockbroker
A registered representative who works as a market intermediary to buy and sell securities for clients.

The same procedure is followed if you wish to sell stocks or bonds. Brokers historically held on to stock or bond certificates for investors to ensure www.ml.com

Reaching Beyond Our Borders

It Really Is a Small World

If first-time investors learned anything about the stock market in the early 2000s, it's that investing is a risky business. The incredible bull market of the 1990s gave way to the bears in the early 2000s. Given the ups and downs of the U.S. stock market, you can understand why investors might question whether investment opportunities in global markets are even worth considering. After all, investing in global markets appears riskier than investing in the U.S. market. Still, financial analysts argue that putting some money overseas might be a good idea. Many believe that global markets in the 21st century could be primed to perform better than the U.S. market.

As an investor, or perhaps a future investor, you may want to consider a few guidelines from experts (whose advice about investing in global markets is not foolproof, of course). Check out these tips, and you may find that global nugget that helps you meet your long-term financial goals:

- Consider mutual funds. In 1990, 116 mutual stock funds held part of their money in multinational stocks. Today, there are over 1,700 mutual funds that invest in international stocks. Mutual funds can offer global portfolios that include U.S. stocks, funds totally international in scope, or funds that invest in individual countries or regions such as Asia or Latin America.
- Look into American depository receipts (ADRs), which can be purchased from American brokers. ADRs represent a set number of shares in a foreign company held on deposit at a foreign branch of an American bank.
- Invest in global companies listed on U.S. stock exchanges. Companies listed on U.S. securities markets must comply with U.S. accounting procedures, and rules of the Securities and Exchange Commission.
- Trade with a domestic broker (such as Merrill Lynch and Morgan Stanley Dean Witter) that has an office abroad. Many U.S. brokers also produce detailed research on foreign companies.
- Invest in stocks of companies in industrialized (developed) countries rather than emerging (less developed) countries. If you do invest in emerging countries, put no more than 5 percent of your portfolio into these markets (lots of high risk here).
- Invest in global companies that have a solid track record like Shell Oil, Nestlé, Sony, and Siemens.
- Be wary of investing in countries that have a history of currency problems or political instability.

As Americans become more global in their perspectives, it's likely that global investments will grow. However, it's important to remember that markets have varying degrees of risk. Keep the risk/return trade-off in mind in considering any investments, especially global ones.

Sources: Elizabeth Sanger, "Accounting Mess at Ahold: Admits Inflating Earnings by at Least $500M in Past 2 Years," *Newsday,* February 24, 2003, p. A59; James Glassman, "We Can See Clearer Now: World of Investing," *International Herald Tribune,* March 29, 2003; and John Waggoner, "Seek Value Manager for International Funds," *USA Today,* February 14, 2003, p. 3B.

safekeeping and to allow investors to sell their securities easily and quickly. Today brokers keep most records of bond or stock ownership electronically, and transactions are almost instantaneous. A broker can be a valuable source of information about what stocks or bonds would best meet your financial objectives. It's important, however, that you learn about and follow stocks and bonds on your own, because investment analysts' advice may not always meet your specific expectations and needs.[30] In fact, several years back, a Stockholm newspaper gave five Swedish stock analysts and a chimpanzee each the equivalent of $1,250 to make as much money as they could in the stock market. The chimp made his selections by throwing darts—and won the competition. *The Wall Street Journal* also periodically compares the predictions of a panel of experts to those of "dart throwers." Make sure to look for these contests in the *Journal.* You might want to compete against the experts to test your knowledge.

Spotlight on Small Business

Getting Your Money's Worth

www.etrade.com

Ten years ago, most small investors did not know how their stocks performed on a particular day until they picked up a copy of the next morning's newspaper. If it was absolutely essential to get a real-time quote on your stocks, the only alternative was to call your broker, who had access to such up-to-the-minute information (if he or she was available). Also, back then, about the only research information small investors could find concerning a company came from the broker's research or the company's annual report. If your community's local library offered publications from Value Line or Standard & Poor's, some additional help might be available.

All this changed with the advent of the Internet. Today, small or budding investors with Internet access have an enormous supply of information about companies right at their fingertips, much of it provided for free. For example, online brokerage firms typically provide their customers with detailed online research as a thank-you for doing business with them (though the level of research available often depends on the trader's account value). Other private investment services can be accessed through the Internet for free or for a small fee. If anything, there's such a wealth of information available today that it could numb the investor's mind. Here's a list of some of the top investor tools (some free, some with a fee) you might want to explore to hone your investing expertise before you get ready to replace Warren Buffett as America's greatest investor:

StreetSmart Pro—Charles Schwab & Company

Moneycentral.com—Microsoft

Yahoo Finance—Yahoo

B4Utrade.com—Lots of material but a $25-a-month cost

Command Center—Ameritrade

Active Trader Pro—Fidelity Investments

RealTick.com—Terra Nova (online broker)

Investors.com—Investors Business Daily

Investor.com—MSNBC

Sources: Murray Coleman, "Brokerage Web Sites Are Touting Advisory Services for Clients," *Investors Business Daily,* February 14, 2003, pp. S1–S3; and Lewis Graham, "Online Trading: Watch Out for Hidden Costs," *Business Week,* May 27, 2002, pp. 98–100.

Investing Online

As we have stressed throughout this book, technology has affected virtually every aspect of business, and trading in investment securities is no exception. Investors can use online trading services to buy and sell stocks and bonds in place of using traditional brokerage services.[31] Ameritrade, E*Trade, and market leader Charles Schwab are a few of the leading providers of Web-based stock trading services. The commissions charged by these trading services are far less than those of regular stockbrokers. Trades that used to cost hundreds of dollars with traditional brokerage firms may cost as low as $5 each on the Web. Traditional brokerage companies, such as Merrill Lynch, introduced their own online capabilities to serve customers who want to trade electronically.[32] It was estimated that, in 2000, one-fifth of all stockholders had an online-brokerage account. However, the technology stock bust and NASDAQ nosedive of the early 2000s reduced the number of online traders significantly. David Pottruck, CEO of Charles Schwab, predicts that trading levels online will never again reach the peak achieved in 2000.

Today, customers interested in online trading services are primarily investors willing to do their own research and make their own investment decisions without the assistance of a broker. The leading online services, however, do provide important market information such as company financial data, price histories of a stock, and consensus analysts' reports. Often the level of information services provided by online brokers depends on the size of your account and level of trading. Read the Spotlight on Small Business box for advice on comparing the services offered by online brokerages. Online brokers are also exploring other financial services alternatives. For example, online broker E*Trade has recast itself as a financial services supermarket. The company offers banking services, checking accounts, mortgages, car loans, credit cards, and insurance.[33]

Whether you decide to trade stocks and bonds using an online broker or decide to invest through a traditional stockbroker, it is important to remember that investing means committing (and risking) your money with the expectation of making a profit.[34] As the market downturn in the early 2000s highlighted, investing is certainly a risky business. Therefore, the first step in any investment program is to analyze such factors as desired income, cash requirements, growth prospects, level of risk, and hedging against inflation. You are never too young or too old to get involved in investments, so let's look at some alternatives and questions you should consider before investing.

Choosing the Right Investment Strategy

As you might suspect, investment objectives change over the course of a person's life. Key investment decisions often center on personal objectives such as growth and income. For example, a young person can afford more high-risk investment options (such as stocks) than a person nearing retirement. Often young investors are looking for significant growth in the value of their investments over time. Therefore, if stocks go into a tailspin and decrease in value, the younger person has time to wait for stocks to rise again. An older person, perhaps on a fixed income, doesn't have the luxury of waiting, and might be prone to invest in bonds that offer a steady return as a protection against inflation. To an elderly investor, additional income is probably more important than potential growth.

What's inherent in any investment strategy is the risk/return trade-off. Investors must evaluate investment strategies related to growth, income, inflation protection, or liquidity. For example, should you consider stocks or bonds? Do you want common or preferred stock? Do you want corporate-issued or government-issued bonds? These are tough questions whose answers vary investor by investor. That's why it's important for investors to consider five key criteria when selecting investment options:

1. **Investment risk.** The chance that an investment will be worth less at some future time than it's worth now.
2. **Yield.** The expected rate of return on an investment, such as interest or dividends, usually over a period of one year.
3. **Duration.** The length of time your money is committed to an investment.
4. **Liquidity.** How quickly you can get back your invested funds if you want them or need them.
5. **Tax consequences.** How the investment will affect your tax situation.

Since new investors are not generally well versed in the world of investing or in choosing proper investment strategies, an investment planner such as a chartered financial analyst (CFA) or a certified financial planner (CFP) can be very helpful.[35] A short course in investments can also be very useful. Setting investment objectives such as growth or income should clearly set the tone for your investment strategy.

Bonds, stocks, and mutual funds all offer opportunities for investors to enhance their financial future. We will look first at the potential of bonds as an investment, then move on to stocks and mutual funds. Before we do that, though, check your understanding by doing the Progress Assessment.

Progress Assessment

- What is the primary purpose of a stock exchange? Can you name the largest stock exchange in the United States?
- What does NASDAQ stand for? How does this exchange work?
- What is the key advantage to online investing? What do investors need to remember if they decide to do their investing online?

Investing in Bonds

For investors who desire low risk and guaranteed income, U.S. government bonds are a secure investment because these bonds have the financial backing and full faith and credit of the federal government. Municipal bonds, also secure, are offered by local governments and often have advantages such as tax-free interest. Some may even be insured. Corporate bonds are a bit more risky and challenging.

Two questions often bother first-time corporate bond investors. The first is "If I purchase a corporate bond, do I have to hold it until the maturity date?" The answer is no, you do not have to hold a bond until maturity. Bonds are bought and sold daily on major securities exchanges (remember the secondary market discussed earlier). However, if you decide to sell your bond to another investor before its maturity date, you are not guaranteed to get the face value of the bond (usually $1,000). For example, if your bond does not have features (high interest rate, early maturity, etc.) that make it attractive to other investors, you may be forced to sell your bond at a *discount,* that is, a price less than the bond's face value. But if your bond is highly valued by other investors, you may be able to sell it at a *premium,* that is, a price above its face value. Bond prices generally fluctuate inversely with current market interest rates. *As interest rates go up, bond prices fall, and vice versa.* Thus, like all investments, bonds have a degree of risk.

"YOU CAN COME BACK IN. IT'S JUST A CORRECTION."

What goes up can also go down. Investing in stock is always a risky venture, as investors found out in the bear market (declining stock prices) of 2000–2002. It's important to set an investment strategy and continuously monitor how your strategy is progressing. What type of investment option (bonds, stocks, mutual funds) is most appealing to you?

The second question is "How can I assess the investment risk of a particular bond issue?" Standard & Poor's and Moody's Investors Service rate the level of risk of many corporate and government bonds (refer back to Figure 20.2). Naturally, the higher the market risk of a bond compared to other bonds, the higher the interest rate the issuer of the bond must offer to investors. This again refers to the risk/return trade-off discussed in Chapter 19. Investors will invest in a bond considered risky only if the potential return to them is high enough. It's important to remember that investors have many investment options besides bonds. One such option is to buy stock.

Investing in Stocks

Buying stock makes the investor an owner of the firm. Stocks provide investors an opportunity to participate in the success of emerging or expanding companies. In fact, since 1925, the average annual return on stocks has been about 12 percent, the highest return of any popular investment. As owners, however, stockholders can also lose money if a company does not do well or the overall stock market is declining. The early 2000s were proof of that. Again, it's up to investors to choose the investment that best fits their overall investment objectives.

capital gains
The positive difference between the purchase price of a stock and its sale price.

According to investment analysts, the market price (and growth potential) of a common stock depends heavily on the overall performance of the corporation in meeting its business objectives. If a company reaches its stated objectives, there are great opportunities for capital gains. **Capital gains** are the positive difference between the price at which you bought a stock and what you sell it for. For example, a $1,000 investment made in Microsoft when its stock was first offered to the public would be worth over $1 million today. Stocks can be subject to a high degree of risk, however. Drops in the stock market such as the ones in 1987, 1997, and 2000–2002 (discussed later in this chapter) certainly caught investors' attention.

Stock investors are often called bulls or bears depending on their perceptions of the market. *Bulls* are investors who believe that stock prices are going to rise, so they buy stock in anticipation of the increase. When overall stock prices are rising, the market is called a bull market. *Bears* are investors who expect stock prices to decline. Bears sell their stocks in anticipation of falling prices. When the prices of stocks decline steadily, the market is called a bear market.[36]

As we discussed previously, setting investment objectives such as growth, income, inflation protection, or cash can set the tone for your investment strategy. Investors may select several different investment opportunities in stock depending on their strategy. *Growth stocks,* for example, are stocks of corporations (often technology, biotechnology, or Internet-related firms) whose earnings are expected to grow at a rate faster than other stocks in the market. While often considered very risky, such stocks offer investors the potential for high returns. Another option is *income stocks.* These are stocks that offer investors a rather high dividend yield on their investment. Public utilities are often considered good income stocks that will generally keep pace with inflation.

The stock of high-quality companies such as Coca-Cola, General Electric, and Gillette are referred to as *blue-chip stocks.* These stocks pay regular dividends and generally experience consistent growth in the company's stock price. However, as the market decline in 2000–2002 proved, even blue-chip stocks are not immune from falling prices. Investors can even invest in a type of stock called a penny stock. *Penny stocks* are stocks that sell for less than $2 (some analysts say less than $5).[37] Such stocks frequently represent ownership in firms, such as mining or oil exploration companies, that compete in high-risk industries. Suffice it to say, penny stocks are considered very risky investments.

It's also interesting to note that investors who buy stock have more options for placing an order than investors buying and selling bonds. Stock investors, for example, can place a *market order,* which tells a broker to buy or to sell a stock immediately at the best price available. This type of order can be processed quickly, and the trade price can be given to the investor almost instantaneously. A *limit order* tells the broker to buy or to sell a particular stock at a specific price, if that price becomes available. Let's say, for example, that a stock is selling for $40 a share; you believe that the price will go up eventually but that it might drop a little before it goes higher. You could place a limit order at $36. The broker will buy the stock for you at $36 if the stock drops to that price. If the stock never falls to $36, the broker will not purchase it.

Stock Splits

stock splits
An action by a company that gives stockholders two or more shares of stock for each one they own.

Companies and brokers prefer to have stock purchases conducted in *round lots,* that is, purchases of 100 shares at a time. However, investors often buy stock in *odd lots,* or purchases of less than 100 shares at a time. The problem is that many investors cannot afford to buy 100 shares of a stock in companies that may be selling for perhaps as high as $100 per share. Such high prices often induce companies to declare **stock splits;** that is, they issue two or more shares for every share of stock that's currently outstanding. For example, if Fiberrific stock were selling for $100 a share, Fiberrific could declare a two-for-one stock split. Investors who owned one share of Fiberrific would now own two shares; each share, however, would now be worth only $50 (one-half as much as before the split). As you can see, there is no change in the firm's ownership structure and no change in the investment's value after the stock split.[38] Investors, however, generally approve of stock splits because often the demand for the stock at $50 per share may be greater than the demand at $100 per share. Thus, the $50 stock price may go up in the near future. It's important to note that a company can never be forced to split its stock. For example, Berkshire Hathaway has never had a stock split and its shares have sold for close to $70,000 for one share.[39]

One of the most popular and simplest ways of investing in bonds and stocks is through mutual funds. Let's see why.

Warren Buffett, who many think is America's most successful investor, is shown here enjoying a Dairy Queen sundae—especially since his firm, Berkshire Hathaway, owns the company. Buffett is now the second richest person in the United States according to *Forbes* magazine's annual list of wealthiest Americans, and the only member on the list who has earned his fortune through investing.

Investing in Mutual Funds

A **mutual fund** buys stocks and bonds and then sells shares in those securities to the public. A mutual fund is like an investment company that pools investors' money and then buys stocks or bonds in many companies in accordance with the specific purpose of the fund. Mutual fund managers are experts who pick what they consider to be the best stocks and bonds available. Investors can buy shares of the mutual funds and thus take part in the ownership of many different companies that they could not afford to invest in individually. Thus, for a normally small fee, mutual funds provide professional investment management and help investors diversify. In 2000, bond and stock mutual funds controlled $7.47 trillion of investors' money. The bear market in 2000–2002 dropped the level to $6.39 trillion.[40]

mutual fund
An organization that buys stocks and bonds and then sells shares in those securities to the public.

Buying shares in a mutual fund is probably the best way for a small or beginning investor to get started. Funds available range in purpose from very conservative funds that invest only in government securities or secure corporate bonds to others that specialize in emerging high-tech firms, Internet companies, foreign companies, precious metals, and other investments with greater risk. Some mutual funds even invest exclusively in socially responsible companies.[41]

For young people, the best choice is usually to buy a few index funds and to diversify those investments among different kinds of stock. An *index fund* is a fund that invests in a certain kind of stock. The most-recommended is an index fund that covers the whole stock market. To *diversify* means to invest in a variety of index funds. For example, you can put your money into an index fund that focuses on large companies, one that focuses on small companies, one that invests in emerging countries, and one that invests mainly in real estate (real estate investment trusts, or REITs). We cannot go into great detail here about the benefits and drawbacks of all the choices. A stockbroker, certified financial planner (CFP), or banker can help you find the mutual fund that best fits your investment objectives. In addition, the newsletter *Morningstar Investor* is an excellent resource for evaluating mutual funds, as are business publications such as *Business Week, The Wall Street Journal, Money,* and *Investor's Business Daily.* Figure 20.5 on p. 628 gives you a list of just some of the options you have in terms of mutual fund investments.

One key advantage of mutual funds is that you can buy most funds directly and save any fees or commissions. The Internet has made access in and out of mutual funds easier than ever. A true no-load fund is one that charges no commission to investors to either buy or sell its shares. A load fund would charge a commission to investors to buy shares in the fund or would charge a commission when investors sell shares in the fund. It's important to check the

FIGURE 20.5

MUTUAL FUND OBJECTIVES

Mutual funds have a wide array of investment categories. They range from low-risk, conservative funds to others that invest in high-risk industries. Listed here are abbreviations of funds and what these abbreviations stand for.

AB	Investment-grade corporate bonds	AU	Gold oriented
BL	Balanced	EI	Equity income
EM	Emerging markets	EU	European region
GL	Global	GM	General municipal bond
GT	General taxable bonds	HB	Health/Biotech
HC	High-yield bonds	HM	High-yield municipal bonds
IB	Intermediate-term corporate bonds	IG	Intermediate-term government bonds
IL	International	IM	Intermediate-term municipal bonds
LC	Large-cap core	LG	Large-cap growth
LT	Latin America	LU	Long-term U.S. bonds
LV	Large-cap value	MC	Mid-cap core
MG	Mid-cap growth	MP	Stock and bond fund
MT	Mortgage securities	MV	Mid-cap value
NM	Insured municipal bonds	NR	Natural resources
PR	Pacific region	SB	Short-term corporate bonds
SC	Small-cap core	SE	Sector funds
SG	Small-cap growth	SM	Short-term municipal bonds
SP	S & P 500	SQ	Specialty
SS	Single-state municipal bonds	SU	Short-term government bonds
SV	Small-cap value	TK	Science & technology
UN	Unassigned	UT	Utility
WB	World bonds	XC	Multi-cap core
XG	Multi-cap growth	XV	Multi-cap value

Sources: *The Wall Street Journal;* and *Investor's Business Daily.*

costs involved in a mutual fund, such as fees and charges imposed in the managing of a fund, because these can differ significantly. It's also important to check the long-term performance record of the fund's management.[42] Some funds, called open-end funds, will accept the investments of any interested investors. Closed-end funds offer a specific number of shares for investment; once a closed-end fund reaches its target number, no new investors can buy into the fund.

The key points to remember about mutual funds is that they offer small investors a way to spread the risk of stock and bond ownership and a way to have their investments managed by a trained specialist for a nominal fee. Most financial advisers put mutual funds high on the list of recommended investments for small or beginning investors.

Diversifying Investments

diversification
Buying several different investment alternatives to spread the risk of investing.

Diversification involves buying several different investment alternatives to spread the risk of investing. For example, an investor may put 20 percent of his or her money into growth stocks that have relatively high risk. Another 30 percent may be invested in conservative government bonds, 15 percent in income stocks, 20 percent in a mutual fund, and the rest placed in the bank for emergencies and possible other investment opportunities. By diversifying investments, investors decrease the chance of losing everything they have invested. This type of investment strategy is often referred to as a *portfolio strategy* or *allocation model.*

Both stockbrokers and certified financial planners are trained to give advice about the portfolio that would best fit each client's financial objectives. However, the more investors read and study the market on their own, the higher their potential for gain. It's also important for investors not to forget the risk/return trade-off and be aware that some investments carry rather heavy risks. Let's take a look at several such high-risk investments.

Investing in High-Risk Investments

At a racetrack some bettors always pick the favorites; others like the long shots. The same thing is true in the investment market. Some investors think that high-rated corporate bonds are clearly the investment of choice; others want to take more market risk. Let's look at three relatively risky investment options: junk bonds, buying stock on margin, and commodities.

Investing in High-Risk (Junk) Bonds

Although bonds are generally considered relatively safe investments, some investors look for higher returns through riskier bonds called **junk bonds.** Standard & Poor's Investment Advisory Service and Moody's Investors Service consider junk bonds as non-investment-grade bonds (bonds rated BB or lower) because of their high risk and high bond-default rates. Junk bonds rely on the firm's ability to pay investors interest as long as the value of the company's assets remains high and its cash flow stays strong.[43] Although the interest rates are attractive and often tempting, if the company can't pay off the bond, the investor is left with a bond that isn't worth more than the paper it's written on—in other words, junk.[44]

junk bonds
High-risk, high-interest bonds.

Buying Stock on Margin

Buying stock on margin involves purchasing stocks by borrowing some of the purchase cost from the brokerage firm. The margin is the amount of money an investor must invest in the stock. The board of governors of the Federal Reserve System sets margin rates in the U.S. market. (You will read about this in more detail in Chapter 21.) Briefly, if the margin rate is 50 percent, an investor who qualifies for a margin account may borrow 50 percent of the stock's purchase price from a broker. Margin debt reached its highest levels ever in early 2000. Although buying on margin sounds like an easy way to buy stocks, the downside is that investors must repay the credit extended by the broker, plus interest. Additionally, if the investor's account goes down in market value, the broker will issue a margin call, requiring the investor to come up with more money to cover the losses the investor's portfolio has suffered. If the investor is unable to make the margin call, the broker can legally sell off shares of the investor's stock to reduce the broker's chance of loss. Margin calls can force the investor to repay a significant portion of his or her account's loss within days or even hours.

buying stock on margin
Purchasing stocks by borrowing some of the purchase cost from the brokerage firm.

Investing in Commodities

Commodities can be high-risk investments for most investors. Investors willing to speculate in commodities hope to profit handsomely from the rise and fall of prices of items such as coffee, wheat, pork bellies (slabs of bacon), petroleum, and other articles of commerce (commodities) that are scheduled for delivery at a given (future) date. Trading in commodities is not for the novice investor; it demands much expertise. Small shifts in the prices of certain items can result in significant gains and losses. It's estimated, in fact, that 75 to 80 percent of the investors who speculate in commodities lose money in the long term.

Trading in commodities, however, can also be used as a means of protecting businesspeople, farmers, and others from wide fluctuations in commodity prices and thus for them can be a very conservative investment strategy. A **commodity exchange** specializes in the buying and selling of precious metals and minerals (e.g., silver, foreign currencies, gasoline) and agricultural goods (e.g., wheat, cattle, sugar). The Chicago Board of Trade (CBOT), with its

commodity exchange
A securities exchange that specializes in the buying and selling of precious metals and minerals (e.g., silver, foreign currencies, gasoline) and agricultural goods (e.g., wheat, cattle, sugar).

60,000-square-foot trading floor, is the largest commodity exchange in terms of floor size. The CBOT is involved with a wide range of commodities, including corn, plywood, silver, gold, and U.S. Treasury bonds.[45]

Commodity exchanges operate much like stock exchanges: Members of the exchange meet on the exchange's floor to transact deals. Yet a commodities exchange looks quite different from a stock exchange, and is interesting to observe. Transactions for a specific commodity take place in a specific trading area, or "pit," that can only be described as an exciting spectacle. Trades result from the meeting of a bid and offer in an open competition among exchange members. The bids and offers are made in a seemingly impossible-to-understand blend of voices, with all participants shouting at once. Today, however, the old color and excitement of the pits are becoming somewhat obsolete. More and more traders and brokers are working electronically at computer screens where millions of contracts are zipping around on global computer networks.[46] In fact, the CBOT has relinquished its long-standing title as the largest trading futures exchange in the world to the Eurex exchange, based in Frankfurt, Germany.[47]

futures markets
Commodities markets that involve the purchase and sale of goods for delivery sometime in the future.

Many companies use commodities markets to their advantage by dealing in the futures market. **Futures markets** involve the purchase and sale of goods for delivery sometime in the future. Take, for example, a farmer who has oats growing in the field. The farmer is not sure what price the oats will sell for at harvest time. To be sure of a price, the farmer could sell the oats on the commodity floor for delivery in the future at a fixed price. Since the price is now fixed, the farmer can plan the farm's budget and expenses accordingly. In contrast, as the producer of Fiberrific, you are worried about the possibility that oat prices will rise. If you buy the oats in the futures market, you know what you will have to pay and, like the farmer, can also plan accordingly. All of this is possible because of commodity exchanges. Figure 20.6 evaluates bonds, stocks, mutual funds, and commodities according to risk, income, and possible investment growth (capital gain).

Progress Assessment

- What services do companies such as Standard & Poor's and Moody's Investors Service provide in bond markets?
- What is a stock split? Why do companies sometimes split their stock?
- What is a mutual fund and how do such funds benefit small investors?
- What is meant by buying stock on margin?
- Why would manufacturers of products such as candy, coffee, and bread be interested in the futures market?

FIGURE 20.6
COMPARING INVESTMENTS

Investment	Degree of risk	Expected income	Possible growth (capital gain)
Bonds	Low	Secure	Little
Preferred stock	Medium	Steady	Little
Common stock	High	Variable	Good
Mutual funds	Medium	Variable	Good
Commodities	Very high	Very volatile	Very volatile

Understanding Information from Securities Markets

You can find a wealth of investment information in newspapers, in magazines, on television, and on websites. Such information is useless, however, until you understand what it means. Look through *The Wall Street Journal, Barron's, Investor's Business Daily, USA Today,* and your local newspaper's business section; listen carefully to business reports on radio and TV for investment analysis and different viewpoints; and visit different sites on the Internet that provide information about companies and markets. But keep in mind that investing is an inexact science and few people are consistently right in predicting future market movements. Every time someone sells a stock believing it will fall, someone else is buying it, believing it will go higher. By reading the following sections carefully, you will begin to understand investment information.

Understanding Bond Quotations

Bonds, remember, are debt issued by corporations and governments. Government issues are covered in *The Wall Street Journal* in a table called Treasury Issues. These issues are traded on the over-the-counter (OTC) market. The price of a bond is quoted as a percentage of $1,000. The interest rate is often followed by an *s* for easier pronunciation. For example, 9 percent bonds due in 2015 are called 9s of 15.

Figure 20.7 gives a sample of bond quotes for corporate bonds. Look at the quotes and note the variation in interest rates and maturity dates. The more you know about the bond market, the better prepared you will be to talk intelligently with investment counselors and brokers. You want to be sure that their advice is consistent with your best interests and investment objectives.

Understanding Stock Quotations

If you look in the Money & Investing section of *The Wall Street Journal,* you will see stock quotations from the NYSE, the AMEX, and the NASDAQ. Look at the top of the columns and notice the headings. To understand the headings better, look carefully at Figure 20.8 on p. 632. This example highlights the information on the NYSE and the AMEX. Stocks are quoted in decimal amounts. The NYSE officially shifted in late August 2000 from trading stocks in fractions to trading in decimals. The NASDAQ converted to the decimal program in the spring of 2001.[48] Preferred stocks are listed separately in *The Wall Street Journal.* If a publication does not list preferred stock issues separately, preferred

Bonds	Yld	Vol	Bond Close	Chg
GMA zr 5	...	27	368.88	...
Hilton 5.06	cv	30	96.13	–0.13
Honywhl zr09	...	5	68.13	...
HousF 6.750,11	6.8	10	99.00	+2.00
IBM 7.500,13	6.5	4	115.00	...
IBM 8.375,19	6.8	94	123.00	...
IBM 6.500,28	6.2	10	104.38	...
JCPL 7.125,04	7.1	10	101.00	...

*This is a zero-coupon bond.

CV means this is a convertible bond

These IBM bonds pay 8.375% interest and mature in 2019

Number of bonds traded this day

The price of this bond increased $20 from the previous day

This bond is currently selling at a premium (1010.00)

This bond is currently yielding 6.2%

FIGURE 20.7

UNDERSTANDING BOND QUOTATIONS

*Zero-coupon bonds pay no interest prior to maturity. The return to the investor comes from the difference between the purchase price and the bond's face value.

Source: *Investor's Business Daily.*

YTD % CHG	52-WEEK HI	52-WEEK LO	STOCK (SYM)	DIV	YLD %	PE	VOL 100s	CLOSE	NET CHG
16.7	22.36	15.05	Mattel MAT	.05	.2	21	9838	20.08	0.13
4.4	19.15	8.21↓	MayrckTube MVK		...	cc	2300	13.52	0.60
−6.2	7.90	1.77	Maxtor MXO		...	dd	28648	5.95	0.05
−36.5	38.86	20.10	MayDeptStrs' MAY	.95	4.0	13	10482	23.47	0.17
−10.9	47.94	18.84	Maytag MYG	.72	2.6	13	5707	27.66	0.56
19.9	65.55	45.10	McClatchy A MNI x	.40	.7	23	1561	56.35	0.52
13.7	27.25	20.67	McCrmkCo MKC s	.44f	1.8	21	3053	23.85	0.05
−70.3	17.29	2.34	McDermint MDR		...	dd	15706	3.65	0.64
−34.3	30.72	15.75	McDonalds MCD	.24f	1.4	14	57791	17.40	0.20
−2.5	69.70	50.71	McGrawH MHP	1.02	1.7	26	6296	59.48	−0.69
−27.8	42.09	24.99	McKesson MCK	.24	.9	17	15741	27.01	0.16
−15.2	6.35	2.54	McMoRanExpl MMR	.35p	...	dd	196	4.91	0.16
21.6	4.14	1.55↓	MdwbrkinsGp MIG		...	20	416	2.42	−0.02
−25.1	36.50	15.57	MeadWVaco MWV	.92	4.0	dd	4169	23.15	−0.43
30.8	4.50	1.57	MediaArts MDA		...	dd	45	3.44	0.14
16.0	69.49	46.55	MediaGen A MEG	.72	1.2	dd	644	57.80	−0.03
−34.7	29.75	9.25	MedStaffNtwk MRN n		...	...	454	14.04	−0.05
−25.0	64.60	33.85	MediclsPhrm MRX		...	31	5997	48.45	−0.42

High and low price for last 52 weeks

Change in stock price for year to date

Symbol for company

599,700 shares of this stock traded today

Price of Mattel stock is 21 times its earnings

Closing price of May Department Stores stock

Stock yields a 1.8% dividend

McKesson went up 16¢ since the previous close

Stock pays a dividend of 72¢

FIGURE 20.8

UNDERSTANDING STOCK QUOTATIONS

Source: *The Wall Street Journal.*

stock is identified by the letters *pf* following the abbreviated company name. Corporations can have several different preferred stock issues.

Let's look at the columns and headings more closely. Moving from left to right, the stock quote tells us the following:

- The percent of change in the stock's price for the year to date (YTD).
- The highest and lowest price the stock has sold for over the past 52 weeks.
- The company name and the company's stock symbol.
- The last dividend paid per share.
- The stock's dividend yield (annual dividend as a percentage of the price per share).
- The price/earnings ratio (P/E) is the price of the stock divided by the firm's per share earnings. (For example, if the price of Fiberrific stock was $50, and the company earnings were $5 per share, Fiberrific's price/earnings ratio would be 10. Take a look again at the discussion of financial ratios at the end of Chapter 18.)
- The number of shares of stock in the company traded that day in 100s.
- The stock's closing price for the day.
- The net change in the stock's price from the previous day.

Look down the columns and find the stock that's had the biggest price change over the past 52 weeks, the stock that pays the highest dividend, and the stock that has the highest and lowest price/earnings ratio. The more you look through the figures, the more sense they begin to make. You might want to build a hypothetical portfolio of stocks and track how they perform over the next six months. (See the Developing Workplace Skills and Taking It to the Net exercises at the end of this chapter for suggested exercises.)

FUND	NAV	NET CHG	YTD %RET	3-YR %RET
American Century Ist				
DivBnd	10.33	-0.01	7.1	8.3
EqIndex	3.62	-0.01	-20.3	-12.9
EqGro	15.58	-0.01	-18.4	-12.0
EqInc	6.58	-0.03	-4.7	9.3
IncGro	22.29	-0.03	-17.6	-10.8
IntlDisc r	9.01	0.04	-12.4	-13.7
IntlGr	6.51	0.02	-18.4	-16.8
Select	29.49	-0.05	-20.7	-15.1
StrMod	5.32	...	-8.6	NS
Ultra	22.05	-0.03	-20.7	-15.8
Value	6.03	-0.02	-11.8	6.6

Name of the fund family

The price at which a fund's shares can be purchased or sold; called net asset value

Name of the specific fund

The rate of percentage return of the fund year to date

Change from the previous day's net asset value (NAV)

Rate of percentage return of the fund for the past 3 years

FIGURE 20.9

UNDERSTANDING MUTUAL FUND QUOTATIONS

Source: *The Wall Street Journal.*

Understanding Mutual Fund Quotations

As we explained earlier, buying mutual funds is a way to get expert investment advice and diversify your investments at a minimum cost. Look up the listing of mutual funds in *The Wall Street Journal* (see Figure 20.9). You will see that many companies offer mutual funds. The various funds offer alternatives to meet investors' objectives. For example, the American Century mutual funds listed in Figure 20.9 highlight many different kinds of funds available from that company. You can learn about the specifics of the various funds by contacting a broker or contacting the fund directly by phone or through its Web page. Business publications can also guide you to free information from various mutual funds.

As you look across the columns in the mutual fund quotations, the information is rather simple to understand. The fund's name is in the first column, followed by the fund's net asset value (NAV), which is the market value of the mutual fund's portfolio divided by the number of shares it has outstanding. The NAV is the price per share of the mutual fund. The next column lists the net change in the NAV from the previous day's trading. The fund's year-to-date (YTD) return is in the next column. Finally, in this example, the fund's three-year return is listed. Publications like *The Wall Street Journal* list a fund's 13-week return, one-year return, and five-year return on different days of the week to provide investors with detailed information about funds that are listed.

It's simple to change your investment objectives with mutual funds. Switching your money, for example, from a bond fund to a stock fund and back is generally no more difficult than calling an 800 number or clicking a mouse. Mutual funds are a great way to begin investing to meet your financial objectives.

Stock Market Indicators

When you listen to news reports on television or on radio, you often hear announcers say things like "The Dow Industrials are up 90 points today in active trading." Wonder what's going on? The **Dow Jones Industrial Average (the Dow)** is the average cost of 30 selected industrial stocks, used to give an indication of the direction (up or down) of the stock market over time. A man named Charles Dow began the practice of measuring stock averages in 1884, using the prices of 12 important stocks. The 12 original stocks and the 30 current stocks in the Dow are illustrated in Figure 20.10 on p. 634. Do you recognize any of the 12 original companies?

Dow Jones Industrial Average (the Dow)
The average cost of 30 selected industrial stocks, used to give an indication of the direction (up or down) of the stock market over time.

THE ORIGINAL DOW 12	THE 30 CURRENT DOW COMPANIES	
American Cotton Oil	Exxon Mobil	Microsoft
American Sugar Refining Co.	McDonald's	Intel
American Tobacco	SBC Communications	Citigroup
Chicago Gas	J. P. Morgan	Home Depot
Distilling & Cattle Feeding Co.	Du Pont	Wal-Mart Stores
General Electric Co.	General Motors	General Electric
Laclede Gas Light Co.	AT&T	International Business Machines (IBM)
National Lead	Coca-Cola	American Express
North American Co.	Minnesota Mining & Manufacturing	Hewlett-Packard
Tennessee Coal, Iron & Railroad Co.	Walt Disney	United Technologies
U.S. Leather	Caterpillar	Alcoa
U.S. Rubber Co.	Boeing	Merck
	International Paper	Procter & Gamble
	Eastman Kodak	Johnson & Johnson
	Altria	Honeywell International

FIGURE 20.10

THE ORIGINAL DOW AND CURRENT DOW

New stocks are substituted on the Dow when it's deemed appropriate. For example, the Dow was broadened in 1982 to include 30 stocks. In 1991, Disney was added to the Dow to reflect the increased importance of the service sector (again, see Figure 20.10). In 1997, the list was again altered with Hewlett-Packard, Johnson & Johnson, Wal-Mart, and Citigroup replacing Texaco, Woolworth, Bethlehem Steel, and Westinghouse. In 1999, the Dow added Home Depot and SBC Communications along with its first NASDAQ stocks, Intel and Microsoft. Chevron, Sears Roebuck, Union Carbide, and Goodyear were eliminated. The 30 current stocks in the Dow Jones Industrial Average also include such long-standing notables as General Electric, IBM, and Coca-Cola. Check out more information about the Dow at www.dow.com.

Critics argue that if the purpose of the Dow is to give an indication of the direction of the broader market over time, the 30-company sample is too small to get a good statistical representation. Many investors and market analysts therefore prefer to follow stock indexes like the Standard & Poor's 500 (S&P 500), which tracks the performance of 400 industrial, 40 financial, 40 public utility, and 20 transportation stocks. Investors also closely follow the NASDAQ average, which is quoted each trading day to show the trends that are occurring in this important exchange.

Staying abreast of what's happening in the market will help you decide what investments seem most appropriate to your needs and objectives. However, it's important to remember two key investment realities: The first is that your personal financial objectives and needs change over time. The second is that markets can be volatile. Let's look at the volatility that's inherent in the market and new challenges in the 21st century that promise to present investors with new risks and opportunities.

The Market's Roller-Coaster Ride

Throughout the 1900s, the stock market had its ups and downs, spiced with several major tremors. The first "crash" occurred on Tuesday, October 29, 1929, when the stock market lost almost 13 percent of its value in a single day. That "Black Tuesday" brought home to investors the reality of market volatility, especially to those who were heavily margined. Many investors lost everything they had invested. On October 19, 1987, the stock market suffered the largest one-day drop in its history: The Dow Jones Industrial Average fell 508 points and lost over 22 percent of the market's value. The loss caused $500 billion to vanish before bewildered investors' eyes. The crash prompted Texas billionaire H. Ross Perot to caution, "It was God tapping us on the shoulder and warning us to get our act together before we get the big shock."

On October 27, 1997, investors felt the fury of the market once again. The Dow fell 554 points, primarily because of investors' fears of an impending economic crisis in Asian markets. Luckily, the market regained its strength after a short downturn. The market was not so fortunate in the early 2000s. The Dow, S&P 500, and NASDAQ all declined significantly in value from 2000 to 2002. Not since 1939–41 had the S&P declined three years in a row, and the NASDAQ had never fallen three consecutive years.[49] All told, investors lost $7 trillion in market value from 2000 through 2002.

What caused the market turmoil of 1929, 1987, 1997, and 2000–2002? Ask a dozen financial analysts and you will probably get a dozen different answers.[50] In 1987, however, many analysts agreed that program trading was a big cause of the disastrous fall. In **program trading,** investors give their computers instructions to sell automatically if the price of their stock dips to a certain point to avoid potential losses. On October 19, 1987, the computers became trigger-happy and sell orders caused many stocks to fall to unbelievable depths on that day.

program trading
Giving instructions to computers to automatically sell if the price of a stock dips to a certain point to avoid potential losses.

The crash of 1987 prompted the U.S. exchanges to create mechanisms to restrict program trading whenever the market moves up or down by a large number of points in a trading day. The two major restrictions are called *curbs* and *circuit breakers.* Program trading curbs are put in effect when the Dow moves up or down more than a certain number of points (2 percent of the previous quarter's average value). Basically this means a key computer is turned off, so program trading must be done "by hand" rather than automatically by computer. When these restrictions are triggered, you'll see the phrase *curbs in* if you watch programming like CNBC or MSNBC.

Circuit breakers are more drastic restrictions that are triggered when the Dow falls 10, 20, or 30 percent in a day. Depending on the rate of decline and the time of day, the circuit breakers will halt trading for anywhere from half an hour to two hours so that traders have time to assess the situation. If the Dow drops 30 percent, however, trading closes for the entire day. Circuit breakers were triggered for the first and only time on October 27, 1997, when the Dow fell 350 points at 2:35 PM and 550 points at 3:30 PM. That reflected an approximate 7 percent overall decline and shut the market for the remainder of the day. Many market watchers believe that the 1997 market drop could have been much worse had it not been for the new rules. Still, it's inevitable that market gyrations will persist, causing investors many headaches and sleepless nights.

Investing Challenges in the 21st-Century Market

It's obvious from the market slides discussed above that in dealing with the stock market, what goes up can also go down. Furthermore, it's a safe bet to presume that 21st-century markets will undergo changes and experience events that will only heighten their risk. The September 11, 2001, terrorist attacks on the World Trade Center and the Pentagon certainly proved that even a superpower like the United States is not immune to outside forces. They also reinforced the fact that today we live in a global market where all the economies of the world are closely linked. As we saw with the Asian financial crisis in 1997, negative events that affect one region economically affect other nation's economies as well.

Investor confidence and trust in corporations and the stock market also eroded in the early 2000s. Investor trust that the real value of companies was fairly reflected in company financial statements was shattered by disclosures of financial fraud at companies such as WorldCom, Enron, and Tyco.[51] Investment analysts also came under fire as information revealed that they often provided wildly optimistic evaluations about companies they knew were not worth their current prices. Dramatic change has impacted the securities exchanges as well. The NYSE and the NASDAQ are intensely competitive in the search for investors' dollars.

Traditional brokers such as Merrill Lynch and A. G. Edwards are changing the way they do business due to challenges from online brokers like E*Trade, which are attracting more and more investors. These challenges and changes, along with the growing influence and activity of institutional investors, promise to make securities markets exciting but not always stable places to be in the 21st century.

The basic lessons to keep in mind are the importance of diversifying your investments and understanding the risks of investing. Taking a long-term perspective is also a wise idea. The 1990s saw the market reach unparalleled heights only to collapse into a deep bear market in 2000–2002. Advertisements by brokerage firms in print and on television could make you think that investing in the market is guaranteed money in the bank. Don't be fooled, and don't be driven by greed. It's critical for you to know that there's no such thing as easy money or a sure thing. Investing is a challenging and interesting field that's always changing. If you carefully research companies and industries, keep up with the news, and make use of investment resources—such as newspapers, magazines, newsletters, the Internet, and TV programs—the payoff can be highly rewarding. You may want to refer to this chapter again when you read about personal finance in Chapter 22.

Progress Assessment

- What exactly does the Dow Jones Industrial Average measure? Why is it important?
- Why do the 30 companies comprising the Dow change periodically?
- Explain program trading and the problems it can create.

Summary

1. Identify and explain the functions of securities markets, and discuss the role of investment bankers.

1. Securities markets provide opportunities for businesses and investors.
   - ***What opportunities are provided to businesses and individual investors by securities markets?***

   Businesses are able to raise much-needed funding to help finance major expenses of the firm. Individual investors can share in the success and growth of emerging firms by having the opportunity of investing in the firm.
   - ***What role do investment bankers play in securities markets?***

   Investment bankers are specialists who assist in the issue and sale of new securities.

2. Compare the advantages and disadvantages of debt financing by issuing bonds, and identify the classes and features of bonds.

2. Companies can raise capital by debt financing, which involves issuing bonds.
   - ***What are the advantages and disadvantages of issuing bonds?***

   The advantages of issuing bonds include the following: (1) Management retains control since bondholders cannot vote; (2) interest paid on bonds is tax deductible; (3) bonds are only a temporary source of financing, and after they are paid off the debt is eliminated; and (4) bonds can be paid back early if they are issued with a call provision and often bonds can be convertible to common stock. The disadvantages of bonds include the following: (1) Because bonds are an increase in debt, they may affect the market's perception of the company adversely; (2) interest on bonds must be paid; and (3) the bond's face value must be repaid on the maturity date.

• ***Are there different types of bonds?***

Yes. There are unsecured (debenture) and secured bonds. Unsecured bonds are not supported by collateral, whereas secured bonds are backed by tangible assets such as mortgages, buildings, and equipment.

3. Companies can also raise capital by equity financing, which involves selling stock.

3. Compare the advantages and disadvantages of equity financing by issuing stock, and explain the differences between common and preferred stock.

• ***What are the advantages and disadvantages of selling stock?***

The advantages of selling stock include the following: (1) The stock price never has to be repaid since stockholders are owners in the company; (2) there is no legal obligation to pay dividends; and (3) no debt is incurred, so the company is financially stronger. Disadvantages of selling stock include the following: (1) Stockholders become owners of the firm and can affect its management by voting for the board of directors; (2) it is more costly to pay dividends, since they are paid after taxes; and (3) managers may be tempted to make stockholders happy in the short term rather than plan for long-term needs.

• ***What are the differences between common and preferred stock?***

Common stockholders have voting rights in the company. Preferred stockholders generally have no voting rights. In exchange for having no voting rights, preferred stocks offer a fixed dividend that must be paid in full before common stockholders receive a dividend. Preferred stockholders are also paid back their investment before common stockholders if the company is forced out of business.

4. Stock exchanges afford investors the opportunity of investing in securities markets through the different investment options that are offered.

4. Describe the various stock exchanges where securities are traded.

• ***What is a stock exchange?***

Stock exchanges are securities markets whose members are involved in buying and selling securities such as bonds and stocks.

• ***What are the different exchanges?***

There are stock exchanges all over the world. The largest U.S. exchange is the New York Stock Exchange (NYSE). It and the American Stock Exchange (AMEX) together are known as national exchanges because they handle stock of companies all over the country. In addition, there are several regional exchanges that deal primarily with companies in their own areas.

• ***What is the over-the-counter (OTC) market?***

The OTC market is a system for exchanging stocks not listed on the national exchanges. It also handles bonds issued by city and state governments.

5. Securities markets provide opportunities to buy and sell investments.

5. Explain how to invest in securities markets and various investment objectives such as long-term growth, income, cash, and protection from inflation.

• ***How do investors normally make purchases in securities markets?***

Investors generally purchase investments through market intermediaries called stockbrokers, who provide many different services. However, online investing is also very popular.

• ***What are the criteria for selecting investments?***

Investors should determine their overall financial objectives. Are they interested in growth, income, cash, or a hedge against inflation? Investments should be evaluated with regard to (1) risk, (2) yield, (3) duration, (4) liquidity, and (5) tax consequences.

- ***How are securities exchanges regulated?***

The Securities and Exchange Commission (SEC) is responsible for regulating securities exchanges. Also, according to SEC rules, companies that intend to sell bonds or stock to the public must provide a prospectus to potential investors.

- ***What is insider trading?***

Insider trading involves the use of information or knowledge that individuals gain through their position that allows them to benefit unfairly from fluctuations in security prices.

6. Analyze the opportunities bonds offer as investments.

6. Bonds present opportunities for investors.

- ***What is the difference between a bond selling at a discount and a bond selling at a premium?***

A bond selling at a premium is a bond that can be sold in securities markets (secondary market) at a price above its face value. A bond selling at a discount is a bond that can be sold in securities markets (secondary market) but at a price below its face value.

7. Explain the opportunities stocks offer as investments.

7. Stocks present opportunities for investors to enhance their financial position.

- ***What is a market order?***

A market order tells a broker to buy or to sell a security immediately at the best price available. A limit order tells the broker to buy or sell at a specific price if the stock reaches that price.

- ***What does it mean when a stock splits?***

When a stock splits, stockholders receive two or more shares of stock for each share they own. Each share is then worth half or less of the original share. Therefore, while the number of the shares in the company increases, the total value of the stockholders' holdings stays the same. The lower price per share may increase demand for the stock.

8. Explain the opportunities in mutual funds as investments and the benefits of diversifying investments.

8. Mutual funds are attractive investments for small or beginning investors.

- ***How can mutual funds help individuals diversify their investments?***

A mutual fund is an organization that buys stocks and bonds and then sells shares in those securities to the public. Individuals who buy shares in a mutual fund are able to invest in many different companies they could not afford to invest in otherwise.

- ***What is diversification?***

Diversification means buying several different types of investments (government bonds, corporate bonds, preferred stock, common stock, etc.) with different degrees of risk. The purpose is to reduce the overall risk an investor would assume by just investing in one type of security.

9. Discuss specific high-risk investments, including junk bonds, buying stock on margin, and commodity trading.

9. Other types of speculative investments are available for investors seeking large returns on their investments.

- ***What is a junk bond?***

Junk bonds are high-risk (rated BB or below), high-interest debenture bonds that speculative investors often find attractive.

- ***What does buying on margin mean?***

It means that the investor borrows up to 50 percent of the cost of a stock from the broker so he or she can get shares of stock without paying the full price of the stock.

- ***What are commodity exchanges?***

Commodity exchanges specialize in the buying and selling of precious metals and minerals (e.g., silver, oil) and agricultural goods (e.g., wheat, cattle, sugar).

10. Security quotations and Dow Jones Industrial Averages are listed daily in newspapers.
    - ***What information do stock quotations give you?***

    The stock quotations give you all kinds of information: the highest price in the last 52 weeks; the lowest price; the dividend yield; the price/earnings ratio; the total shares traded that day; and the close and net change in price from the previous day. Bond quotations give you information regarding trading bonds in securities markets, as do quotations concerning mutual funds.
    - ***What is the Dow Jones Industrial Average?***

    The Dow Jones Industrial Average is the average price of 30 specific stocks traded on the New York Stock Exchange.

10. Explain securities quotations listed in the financial section of a newspaper, and describe how stock market indicators like the Dow Jones Industrial Average affect the market.

Key Terms

bond 611
buying stock on margin 629
capital gains 626
commodity exchange 629
common stock 617
debenture bonds 613
diversification 628
dividends 615
Dow Jones Industrial Average (the Dow) 633
futures markets 630
initial public offering (IPO) 610
institutional investors 611
interest 612
investment bankers 610
junk bonds 629
maturity date 612
mutual fund 627
National Association of Securities Dealers Automated Quotations (NASDAQ) 618
over-the-counter (OTC) market 618
preferred stock 616
program trading 635
prospectus 619
Securities and Exchange Commission (SEC) 619
sinking fund 614
stockbroker 621
stock certificate 615
stock exchange 617
stocks 615
stock splits 626

Developing Workplace Skills

1. Go to your campus library and ask the reference librarian for information from Standard & Poor's and Moody's Investors Service concerning bond ratings. Analyze the process used by these two firms in evaluating and rating corporate bonds, and report what you find to the class.

2. Go to the websites of Charles Schwab (www.schwab.com), E*Trade (www.etrade.com), and Ameritrade (www.ameritrade.com). Investigate each of the brokerage companies and compare what they offer to investors in terms of research and advice and how their price structures work. Evaluate each of the brokers according to specific services they offer and decide which service you consider most appropriate to your investment objectives. Be prepared to defend your choice to the class.

3. Read *The Wall Street Journal, Investor's Business Daily,* or the business section of your local newspaper each day for two weeks and then select three stocks for your portfolio from the New York Stock Exchange and three from the NASDAQ. Track the stocks in your portfolio and use a computer to graphically display the trends of each one on a weekly basis. See how market trends and information affect your stocks and write out a brief explanation of why your stocks were affected.

4. See if anyone is interested in setting up an investment game in your class. Each student should choose one stock (100 shares) and one mutual fund (100 fund shares). Record each student's selections and the corresponding prices

on a chart. In six weeks, look up and chart the prices again. Discuss with your fellow competitors the results on a percentage gain or loss situation.

5. Many businesses try to raise funds by offering new stock offerings called initial public offerings (IPOs). Go to the library, obtain recent financial publications like *The Wall Street Journal* or *Investor's Business Daily,* or go to the websites listed in exercise 1 (www.schwab.com, www.etrade.com, www.ameritrade.com) to find two IPOs that have been offered during the past six months. Track the performance of each IPO from its introduction to its present price.

Taking It To The Net

Purpose

To experience the excitement of the New York Stock Exchange (NYSE) trading floor and to explain the anatomy of a stock trade.

Exercise

Go to the NYSE's website at www.nyse.com.

1. Click on the Trading Floor button to find panoramic views of the NYSE trading floor from a variety of perspectives. How many people work on the trading floor? What roles do the specialists play in stock exchanges?
2. Describe the anatomy of a trade from the moment an investor places an order until the investor receives confirmation that the trade has been made.
3. If you have a high-speed connection (higher than 56k), you can experience the fast pace of the trading floor for yourself by clicking About NYSE, then Education. There you will find a series of videos prepared in conjunction with Cornell University. Click on the segment Broker Technology. How has technology helped brokers keep up with the pace of the trading floor?

Casing The Web

To access the case "Making Dreams Come True," visit

www.mhhe.com/ub7e

Video Case

A Fool and His Money: Motley Fool

Matthew Emmert is no fool, but he loves working for Motley Fool, the company that provides people with financial advice. He enjoys talking about stocks and bonds, and Motley Fool gives him the chance to do that—and make money as well. What a deal! Being a typical broker was not Matt's idea of a good time. The Motley Fool atmosphere is much more relaxed and customer oriented.

David and Tom Gardner started Motley Fool to help people with their investments. They got started by sending out a newsletter and expanded into books, a website, and more. Now they have their own radio show and give seminars. Basically, they do whatever they think might help their clients become better investors.

One investment people can make is to buy stock (ownership of the firm). Stocks are sold on the various exchanges: NYSE, AMEX, and NASDAQ. When you buy a stock, you don't care as much where it is sold; you just want to buy a company that will prosper and grow and earn you money. Most people buy common stock. Others buy preferred stock. That is a kind of stock that pays dividends (a share of the profits) and has a certain preference when it comes to dividing a firm's assets if it fails. You can buy income stocks that pay a large dividend; growth stocks that don't pay a dividend, but are expected to grow faster than most companies; or penny stocks that cost a few dollars, but could rise dramatically if conditions are right.

So how does a person know what stocks to buy and when? That's where the Motley Fool organization comes in. For college students, they would recommend starting with an index fund. An index fund is made up of a bundle of stocks (such as 500 stocks chosen by Standard & Poor's). The idea is to own a whole bunch of companies so that your risk is spread among different companies in different industries. The broader the index, the better. That is, an index of the whole stock exchange is better than one that buys just high-tech stocks or just growth stocks.

Another investment people can make is to buy bonds (lending money to firms). Bonds pay interest, much like the interest you would make by putting your money in a bank. Since a bond is a loan, it states when the loan is due (maturity date) and how much interest it will pay. Some bonds, called junk bonds, are quite risky, but pay high interest. Other bonds are convertible into shares of stock if the price goes up high enough. You are likely to get a better return from investing in stocks rather than bonds. But stocks are said to be more risky, so there is a risk/reward trade-off you have to explore.

To the average investor, there are simply too many choices—too many decisions to make. So Motley Fool tries to help by making the process as simple and as understandable as possible. They wouldn't encourage you, for example, to buy stock on margin (that is, borrow money to buy stock). They wouldn't encourage you to become a day trader either (buying and selling stock often, sometimes within hours). Rather, they would encourage you to buy into an index fund or two and then buy a few shares of stock in companies they recommend. Investing can be fun, especially when you fool around with the "fools" at Motley Fool. But you can lose a lot of money if you are not careful. That's why Matt Emmert and the other employees are there—to help you be a little less foolish with your money.

Thinking It Over

1. What have you learned in this video that might help you to become a better investor in the future?
2. Would you like to receive advice from a company like Motley Fool? Just go to www.fool.com and you can sign up easily.
3. What have you learned about stocks and bonds that would lead you to invest in index funds of stock rather than bonds? Would that be as true for someone just about to retire? Why?
4. Why do you suppose it is important to learn about stocks and bonds now rather than later in your life when you have more money to invest?

Chapter 21

Understanding Money and Financial Institutions

Learning Goals

After you have read and studied this chapter, you should be able to

1. Explain what money is and how its value is determined.
2. Describe how the Federal Reserve controls the money supply.
3. Trace the history of banking and the Federal Reserve System.
4. Classify the various institutions in the U.S. banking system.
5. Explain the importance of the Federal Deposit Insurance Corporation and other organizations that guarantee funds.
6. Discuss the future of the U.S. banking system.
7. Evaluate the role and importance of international banking and the role of the World Bank and the International Monetary Fund.

Profile

Getting to Know Alan Greenspan, Chairman of the Federal Reserve

Alan Greenspan, the head of the U.S. Federal Reserve System (the Fed) since 1987, is one of the most powerful individuals in the United States. *Fortune* magazine recently reported, "As far as the world at large was concerned, if the miracle U.S. economy were a movie, it would have been written, directed, and produced by Alan Greenspan." Earlier, the magazine had said, "It's *his* economy, stupid."

How did one person get to be so powerful? Greenspan went to New York University, where he earned both bachelor's and master's degrees in economics. He then began work as an economist for the Conference Board, a nonprofit research group. Later he started his own consulting firm. After that, he devoted his energies to public service and began a distinguished career in government that included service for six presidents. As one of President Richard Nixon's top economic aides, Greenspan worked on several economic task forces and served as an informal adviser. As chairman of the Council of Economic Advisers under President Gerald Ford, he became an intense inflation fighter. He also argued that government spending must be cut. That's one reason why President Ronald Reagan chose him to be Fed chairman.

In 1991, President George Bush reappointed Greenspan to another term, citing his success in fighting inflation and leading the economic recovery from the recession of 1990. President Bill Clinton retained him for much the same reason, reappointing him in 2000 to keep the economy growing without causing inflation. Now Greenspan is working with President George W. Bush, who has indicated that he will reappoint Greenspan for another term.

Under Greenspan's leadership, the United States enjoyed the longest economic expansion in its history. As chairman of the Federal Reserve, Greenspan has control over the nation's money supply.

Under Greenspan's leadership, the United States enjoyed the longest economic expansion in its history. As chairman of the Federal Reserve, Greenspan has control over the nation's money supply. One tool he uses is interest rates. He raised interest rates several times in 1999–2000 to slow the growth of the economy. He felt it was overheated; that is, he feared inflation. As it turned out, the economy slowed too fast (due to many circumstances, including the higher interest rates), and Greenspan began cutting interest rates to get the economy moving again. He ended up cutting them 13 times. Those cuts were not as effective as hoped, and the stock market stalled. The United States entered a recession. Some people believed that cutting taxes and lowering interest rates together would get the economy moving again. The economy bumped along all through 2002 and began picking up in 2003. The media watched closely to see what Greenspan would do to get the economy moving faster.

Greenspan has led the United States through many ups and downs over the years and has earned a reputation for doing the right thing at the right time. Some people would disagree, but that would be true of any Fed policy. Watch the business page of your local paper to see how Greenspan is doing today.

Sources: Larry Kudlow, "Rx . . . for Economic Anxieties," *Washington Times,* October 7, 2002, p. A18; Justin Fox, "Don't Blame Me," *Fortune,* November 11, 2002, pp. 133–36; William Raspberry, "Not So Fast," *Washington Post,* February 24, 2003, p. A21; and Greg Ip, "Bush Says Greenspan Deserves Another Term as Fed Chairman," *The Wall Street Journal,* April 23, 2003, pp. A1, A8.

Why Money Is Important

The U.S. economy depends heavily on money: its availability and its value relative to other currencies. Economic growth and the creation of jobs depend on money. Money is so important to the economy that many institutions have evolved to manage money and to make it available to you when you need it. Today you can easily get cash from an automated teller machine (ATM) almost anywhere in the world, but in many places cash isn't the only means of payment you can use. Most organizations will accept a check, credit card, debit card, or smart card for purchases.[1] Behind the scenes of this free flow of money is a complex system of banking that makes it possible for you to do all these things.

The complexity of the banking system has increased as the electronic flow of money from country to country has become as free as that from state to state. Each day, more than $1.5 trillion is exchanged in the world's currency markets. Therefore, what happens to any major country's economy has an effect on the U.S. economy and vice versa. Clearly, there's more to money and its role in the economies of the world than meets the eye. There's no way to understand the U.S. economy without understanding global money exchanges and the various institutions involved in the creation and management of money.

We'll explore such institutions in this chapter. Let's start at the beginning by discussing exactly what people mean when they say "money" and how the supply of money affects the prices you pay for goods and services.

What Is Money?

money
Anything that people generally accept as payment for goods and services.

barter
The trading of goods and services for other goods and services directly.

Money is anything that people generally accept as payment for goods and services. In the past, objects as diverse as salt, feathers, stones, rare shells, tea, and horses have been used as money. In fact, until the 1880s, cowrie shells were one of the world's most abundant currencies. **Barter** is the trading of goods and services for other goods and services directly. Though barter may sound like something from the past, many people have discovered the benefits of bartering online. Others still barter goods and services the old-fashioned way—face-to-face. For example, in Siberia two eggs have been used to buy one admission to a movie, and customers of Ukraine's Chernobyl nuclear plant have paid in sausages and milk. Some of the trade in Russia over recent years has been done in barter.

The problem is that eggs and milk are difficult to carry around. People need some object that's portable, divisible, durable, and stable so that they can trade goods and services without carrying the actual goods around with them. One answer to that problem over the years was to create coins made of silver or gold. Coins met all the standards of a useful form of money:

- **Portability.** Coins are a lot easier to take to market than are pigs or other heavy products.
- **Divisibility.** Different-sized coins could be made to represent different values. For example, prior to 1963, a U.S. quarter had half as much silver content as a half dollar, and a dollar had four times the silver of a quarter. Because silver is now too expensive, today's coins are made of other metals, but the accepted values remain.
- **Stability.** When everybody agrees on the value of coins, the value of money is relatively stable. In fact, U.S. money has become so stable that much of the world has used the U.S. dollar as the measure of value.
- **Durability.** Coins last for thousands of years, even when they've sunk to the bottom of the ocean, as you've seen when divers find old Roman coins in sunken ships.

- **Uniqueness.** It's hard to counterfeit, or copy, elaborately designed and minted coins. But with the latest color copiers, people are able to duplicate the look of paper money relatively easily. Thus, the government has had to go to extra lengths to make sure real dollars are readily identifiable. That's why you have new paper money with the picture slightly off center and with new invisible lines that quickly show up when reviewed by banks and stores. Note the blue, peach, and green colors in the new $20 bill.[2] Other denominations of bills also have new colors.

When coins and paper money become units of value, they simplify exchanges. Most countries have their own coins and paper money, and they're all about equally portable, divisible, and durable. However, they're not always equally stable. For example, the value of money in Russia is so uncertain and so unstable that other countries won't accept Russian money (rubles) in international trade.

Electronic cash (e-cash) is the latest form of money.[3] In addition to being able to make online bill payments using software programs such as Quicken or Microsoft Money, you can e-mail e-cash to anyone using websites such as PayPal.com (now owned by eBay). Recipients get an e-mail message telling them they have several choices for how they can receive the money: automatic deposit (the money will be sent to their bank), e-dollars for spending online, or a traditional check in the mail.

Changing the Currency in Europe

The exchange of goods and services among European countries was hindered in the past by the fact that each country had its own currency (money). For example, trading German marks for French francs was a bother at best and, on a larger scale, a hindrance to the free flow of commerce. As mentioned earlier, 12 European countries decided to create one common currency, called the euro.[4] The euro was not as attractive to investors as the U.S. dollar at first, and the value fell for a while (to 83 cents in 2000). But moves by the European Central Bank strengthened the euro, and its value rose (to $1.14 or so in 2003).[5] The value of the euro is expected to keep rising, but expectations are not certainties.[6] You can read all about the euro and see examples of the various bank notes at http://money.howstuffworks.com/euro1.htm.

European bankers now believe that the euro can successfully compete with the U.S. dollar as an international currency of choice. You can check the value of the euro against the dollar yourself to see whether its viability as an international currency has improved. How the euro stands up against the dollar depends greatly on the strength of the U.S. economy versus the European economy.[7] And the strength of the U.S. economy depends partially on its money supply, as you'll see next.

What Is the Money Supply?

This chapter's opening profile says that Fed chairman Alan Greenspan is in control of the money supply. Two questions emerge from that simple statement: (1) What is the money supply? and (2) Why does it need to be controlled?

money supply
The amount of money the Federal Reserve Bank makes available for people to buy goods and services.

M-1
Money that can be accessed quickly and easily (coins and paper money, checks, traveler's checks, etc.).

M-2
Money included in M-1 plus money that may take a little more time to obtain (savings accounts, money market accounts, mutual funds, certificates of deposit, etc.).

The **money supply** is the amount of money the Federal Reserve Bank makes available for people to buy goods and services. There are several ways of referring to the money supply. They're called M-1, M-2, and so on. The *M* stands for money, and the *1* and *2* stand for different definitions of the money supply. **M-1,** for example, includes coins and paper bills, money that's available by writing checks (demand deposits and share drafts), and money that's held in traveler's checks—that is, money that can be accessed quickly and easily. **M-2** includes everything in M-1 plus money in savings accounts, and money in money market accounts, mutual funds, certificates of deposit, and the like—that is, money that may take a little more time to obtain than coins and paper bills. M-2 is the most commonly used definition of money. M-3 is M-2 plus big deposits (e.g., institutional money-market funds and agreements among banks).

Why Does the Money Supply Need to Be Controlled?

Imagine what would happen if governments (or in the case of the United States, the Federal Reserve, a nongovernmental organization) were to generate twice as much money as exists now. There would be twice as much money available, but there would be the same amount of goods and services. What would happen to prices in that case? Think about the answer for a minute. (Hint: Remember the laws of supply ➤P. 43◄ and demand ➤P. 43◄ from Chapter 2.) The answer is that prices would go up because more people would try to buy goods and services with their money and would bid up the price to get what they wanted. This is called inflation ➤P. 54◄. That is why some people define inflation as "too much money chasing too few goods."

Now think about the opposite: What would happen if the Fed took some of the money out of the economy? What would happen to prices? Prices would go down because there would be an oversupply of goods and services compared to the money available to buy them; this is called deflation.[8] If too much money is taken out of the economy, a recession ➤P. 56◄ might occur. That is, people would lose jobs and the economy would stop growing.

Now we come to a second question about the money supply: Why does the money supply need to be controlled? The money supply needs to be controlled because doing so allows us to manage the prices of goods and services somewhat. And controlling the money supply affects employment and economic growth or decline.

The Global Exchange of Money

A *falling dollar value* means that the amount of goods and services you can buy with a dollar decreases.[9] A *rising dollar value* means that the amount of goods and services you can buy with a dollar goes up. Thus, in real terms, the price you paid for a German car 2 years ago was lower than it was 10 years ago because the American dollar rose relative to the euro (Europe's new unit of money). However, as the euro gained strength and rose in value relative to the U.S. dollar, the cost of cars from Germany went up. This was a good sign for American car makers and other manufacturers because prices for their cars would fall in European countries.

What makes the dollar weak (falling dollar value) or strong (rising dollar value) is the position of the U.S. economy relative to other economies. When the economy is strong, the demand for dollars is high, and the value of the dollar rises. When the economy is perceived as weakening, however, the demand for dollars declines, and the value of the dollar falls. The value of the dollar thus depends on a strong economy. Clearly, control over the money supply is important. In the following section, we'll discuss in more detail the money supply and how it's managed. Then we'll explore the U.S. banking system and how it lends money to businesses and individuals, such as you and me.

Critical Thinking

If the value of the dollar declines relative to the euro, what will happen to the price of French wine sold in U.S. stores? Would people in France be more or less likely to buy an American car? Why or why not?

Control of the Money Supply

You already know that money plays a huge role in the American economy and in the economies of the rest of the world. Therefore, it's important to have an organization that controls the money supply to try to keep the U.S. economy from growing too fast or too slow. Theoretically, with the proper monetary policy ➤P. 59◄, you can keep the economy growing without causing inflation. (See Chapter 2 to review monetary policy.) The organization in charge of monetary policy is the Federal Reserve System (the Fed). As we said in the chapter opening profile, the chair of the Federal Reserve is one of the most influential people not only in the country but also in the world because he or she controls the money that much of the world depends on for trade.

Basics about the Federal Reserve

The Federal Reserve System consists of five major parts: (1) the board of governors; (2) the Federal Open Market Committee (FOMC); (3) 12 Federal Reserve banks; (4) three advisory councils; and (5) the member banks of the system. Figure 21.1 shows where the 12 Federal Reserve banks are. Member banks may be chartered by the federal government or by the state in which they're located.

The board of governors administers and supervises the 12 Federal Reserve banks. The seven members of the board are appointed by the president and confirmed by the Senate. The board's primary function is to set monetary policy. The Federal Open Market Committee (FOMC) has 12 voting members and is the policymaking body. The committee is made up of the seven-member

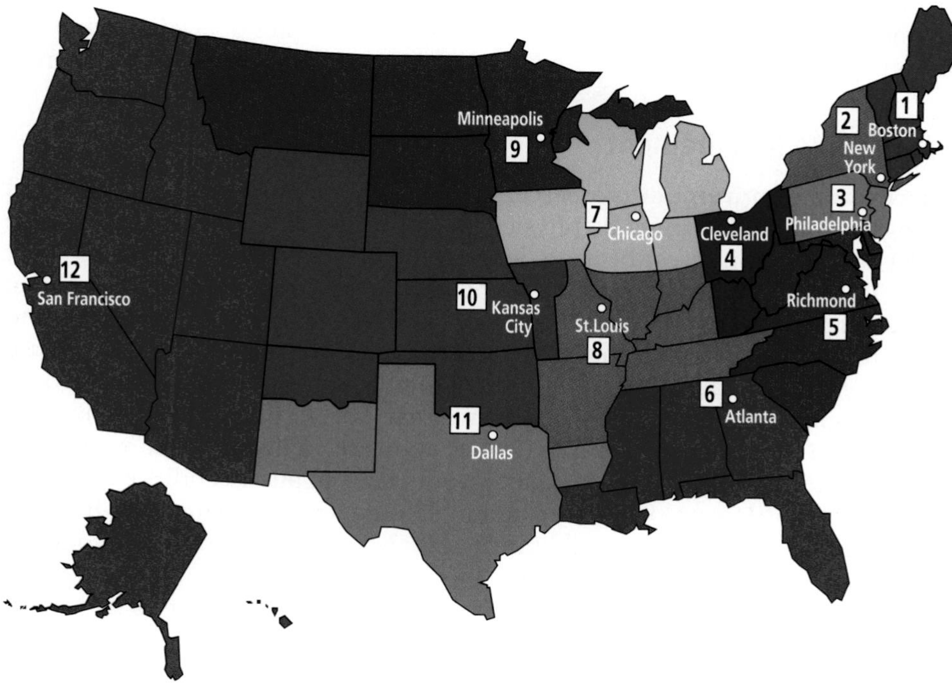

FIGURE 21.1

THE 12 FEDERAL RESERVE DISTRICT BANKS

CONTROL METHOD	IMMEDIATE RESULT	LONG-TERM EFFECT
Reserve Requirements		
A. Increase.	Banks put more money into the Fed, *reducing* money supply; thus, there is less money available to lend to customers.	Economy slows.
B. Decrease.	Banks put less money into the Fed, *increasing* the money supply; thus, there is more money available to lend to customers.	Economy speeds up.
Open-Market Operations		
A. Fed sells bonds.	Money flows from economy to the Fed.	Economy slows.
B. Fed buys bonds.	Money flows into the economy from the Fed.	Economy speeds up.
Managing the Discount Rate		
A. Rate increases.	Banks borrow less from the Fed; thus, there is less money to lend.	Economy slows.
B. Rate decreases.	Banks borrow more from the Fed; thus, there is more money to lend.	Economy speeds up.

FIGURE 21.2

HOW THE FEDERAL RESERVE CONTROLS THE MONEY SUPPLY

board of governors plus the president of the New York reserve bank. Four others rotate in from the other reserve banks. The advisory councils offer suggestions to the board and to the FOMC. The councils represent the various banking districts, consumers, and member institutions, including banks, savings and loan institutions, and credit unions.

The Fed buys and sells foreign currencies, regulates various types of credit, supervises banks, and collects data on the money supply and other economic activity. As part of monetary policy, the Fed determines the reserve requirement, that is, the level of reserves that must be kept at the 12 Federal Reserve banks by all financial institutions. It also lends money to member banks and sets the rate for such loans (called the *discount rate*). Finally, it buys and sells government securities in what are known as open-market operations.[10] It is important to understand how the Fed controls the money supply, so we'll explore that in some depth next. As noted, the three basic tools the Fed uses to manage the money supply are reserve requirements, open-market operations, and the discount rate (see Figure 21.2). Let's explore how each of these is administered.

The Reserve Requirement

reserve requirement
A percentage of commercial banks' checking and savings accounts that must be physically kept in the bank.

The **reserve requirement** is a percentage of commercial banks' checking and savings accounts that must be physically kept in the bank (e.g., as cash in the vault) or in a non-interest-bearing deposit at the local Federal Reserve district bank. The reserve requirement is one of the Fed's most powerful tools. When the Fed increases the reserve requirement, banks have less money for loans and thus make fewer loans. Money becomes more scarce, which in the long run tends to reduce inflation. For instance, if Omaha Security Bank holds deposits of $100 million and the reserve requirement is, say, 10 percent, then the bank must keep $10 million on reserve. If the Fed were to increase the reserve requirement to 11 percent, then the bank would have to put an additional $1 million on reserve, thus reducing the amount it could lend out. Since this increase in the reserve requirement would affect all banks, the money supply would be reduced and prices would likely fall.

A decrease of the reserve requirement, in contrast, increases the funds available to banks for loans, so banks make more loans and money becomes more readily available. An increase in the money supply stimulates the economy to achieve higher growth rates, but it can also create inflationary pressures. That is, the prices of goods and services may go up.

Open-Market Operations

Open-market operations are a commonly used tool by the Fed; they consist of buying and selling government bonds. To decrease the money supply, the federal government sells U.S. government bonds to the public. The money it gets as payment is no longer in circulation, decreasing the money supply. If the Fed wants to increase the money supply, it buys government bonds from individuals, corporations, or organizations that are willing to sell. The money paid by the Fed in return for these securities enters circulation, resulting in an increase in the money supply.

open-market operations
The buying and selling of U.S. government bonds by the Fed with the goal of regulating the money supply.

The Discount Rate

The Fed has often been called the banker's bank. One reason for this is that member banks can borrow money from the Fed and then pass it on to their customers in the form of loans. The **discount rate** is the interest rate that the Fed charges for loans to member banks. When you see in the paper that the Fed is raising or lowering interest rates, it is usually the discount rate that is being discussed. An increase in the discount rate by the Fed discourages banks from borrowing and consequently reduces the number of available loans, resulting in a decrease in the money supply. In contrast, lowering the discount rate encourages member banks to borrow money and increases the funds available for loans, which increases the money supply. The Fed also sets the rate that banks charge each other (the federal funds rate). During the 2003 war with Iraq, the Fed was ready to slash both the discount rate and federal funds rate if a monetary crisis emerged.[11]

discount rate
The interest rate that the Fed charges for loans to member banks.

THE
FED
©02 unitedmedia.com EMAIL: hpayne@detnews.com
"WE RAN OUT OF RATE CUTS."

The Fed can only cut interest rates down to zero. Then some other measure must be taken to get the economy moving forward, such as increasing the money supply. This cartoon shows, in a humorous way, that the Fed in 2003 had just about reached that point.

The Federal Reserve's Check-Clearing Role

One of the functions of the Federal Reserve System is to help process your checks. If you write a check to a local retailer, that retailer will take the check to its bank. If your account is also at that bank, it is a simple matter to reduce your account by the amount of the check and increase the amount in the retailer's account. But what happens if you write a check to a retailer in another state? That retailer will take the check to its bank. That bank will deposit the check for credit in the closest Federal Reserve bank. That bank will send the check to your local Federal Reserve bank for collection. The check will then be sent to your bank and the amount of the check will be withdrawn. Your bank will authorize the Federal Reserve bank in your area to deduct the amount of the check. That bank will pay the Federal Reserve bank that began the process in the first place. It will then credit the deposit account in the bank where the retailer has its account. That bank will then credit the account of the retailer. (See Figure 21.3 for a diagram of such an interstate transaction.) This long and involved process is a costly one; therefore, banks take many measures to lessen the use of checks. Such efforts include the use of credit cards, debit cards, and other electronic transfers of money.

As you can see, the whole economy is affected by the Federal Reserve System's actions. In the following sections, we'll briefly discuss the history of banking to give you some background information on why the Fed came into existence. Then we'll explore what's happening in banking today.

FIGURE 21.3

CHECK-CLEARING PROCESS THROUGH THE FEDERAL RESERVE BANK SYSTEM

Suppose Mr. Brown, a farmer from Quince Orchard, Maryland, purchases a tractor from a dealer in Austin, Texas.

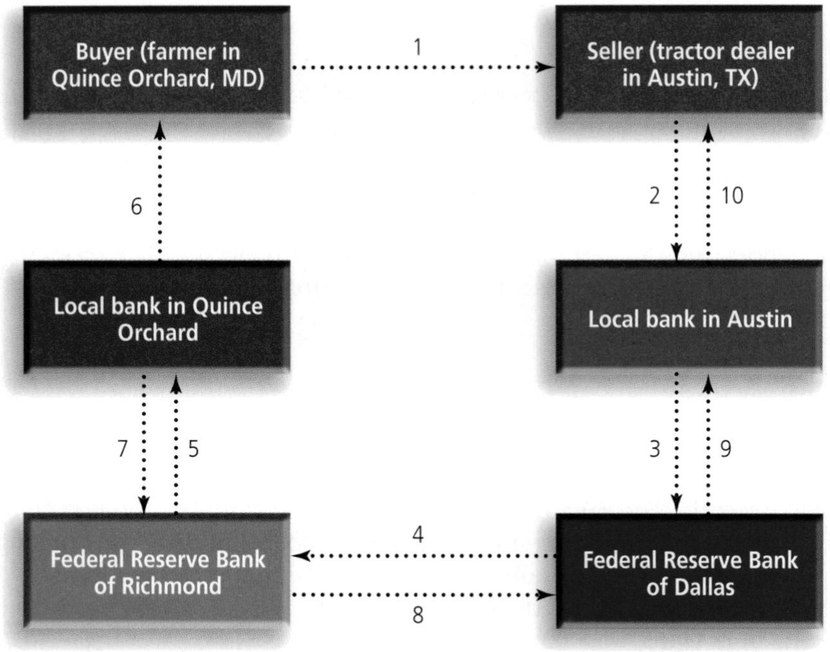

1. Mr. Brown sends his check to the tractor dealer.
2. The dealer deposits the check in his account at a local bank in Austin.
3. The Austin bank deposits the check for credit in its account at the Federal Reserve Bank of Dallas.
4. The Federal Reserve Bank of Dallas sends the check to the Federal Reserve Bank of Richmond for collection.
5. The Federal Reserve Bank of Richmond forwards the check to the local bank in Quince Orchard, where Mr. Brown opens his account.
6. The local bank in Quince Orchard deducts the check amount from Mr. Brown's account.
7. The Quince Orchard bank authorizes the Federal Reserve Bank of Richmond to deduct the check amount from its deposit account with the Federal Reserve Bank.
8. The Federal Reserve Bank of Richmond pays the Federal Reserve Bank of Dallas.
9. The Federal Reserve Bank of Dallas credits the Austin bank's deposit account.
10. The Austin bank credits the tractor dealer's account.

Progress Assessment

- What is money?
- What are the characteristics of useful money?
- What is the money supply, and why is it important?
- What are the various ways the Federal Reserve controls the money supply, and how do they work?
- What are the major functions of the Federal Reserve? What other functions does it perform?

THE HISTORY OF BANKING AND THE NEED FOR THE FED

It will be easier for you to understand why we have a Federal Reserve System and why it is so important to the economy if we trace the history of banking in the United States. At first, there were no banks. Strict laws in Europe limited the number of coins that could be brought to the colonies in the New World.

Thus, colonists were forced to barter for goods; for example, cotton and tobacco may have been traded for shoes and lumber.

The demand for money was so great that Massachusetts issued its own paper money in 1690, and other colonies soon followed suit. But continental money, the first paper money printed in the United States, became worthless after a few years because people didn't trust its value.

Land banks were established to lend money to farmers. But Great Britain, still in charge of the colonies at that point, ended land banks by 1741. The colonies rebelled against these and other restrictions on their freedom, and a new bank was formed in Pennsylvania during the American Revolution to finance the war against England.

Are bank runs a thing of the past? Not if you bank with Abacus Federal Savings in New York City's Chinatown. Rumors of embezzlement and fear of the bank's insolvency triggered this panic in 2003. One of the Federal Reserve Bank's functions is to lend money to banks in case customers lose trust in them—as they did in this case. The Federal Reserve Bank of Philadelphia delivered $1 million in cash the same day, and the crisis was resolved.

In 1791, after the United States gained independence, Alexander Hamilton persuaded Congress to form a *central bank* (a bank at which other banks could keep their funds and borrow funds if needed), over the objections of Thomas Jefferson and others. This first version of a federal bank closed in 1811, only to be replaced in 1816 because state-chartered banks couldn't support the War of 1812. The battle between the Second (Central) Bank of the United States and state banks got hot in the 1830s. Several banks in Tennessee, President Andrew Jackson's home state, were hurt by pressure from the Central Bank. The fight ended when the bank was closed in 1836. You can see that there was great resistance to a central bank through much of U.S. history.

By the time of the Civil War, the banking system was a mess. Different banks issued different kinds of currencies. During the Civil War, coins were hoarded because they were worth more as gold and silver than as coins. The chaos continued long after the war ended, reaching something of a climax in 1907, when many banks failed. People got nervous about the safety of banks and attempted to withdraw their funds. This is now known as a run on the banks. Soon the cash was depleted and some banks had to refuse money to depositors. This caused people to distrust the banking system in general.

Despite the long history of opposition to a central bank, the cash shortage problems of 1907 led to the formation of an organization that could lend money to banks—the Federal Reserve System. It was to be a "lender of last resort" in such emergencies. Under the Federal Reserve Act of 1913, all federally chartered banks had to join the Federal Reserve. State banks could also join. The Federal Reserve became the banker's bank. If banks had excess funds, they could deposit them in the Fed; if they needed extra money, they could borrow it from the Fed. The Federal Reserve System has been intimately related to banking ever since.

Banking and the Great Depression

The Federal Reserve System was designed to prevent a repeat of the 1907 panic. Nevertheless, the stock market crash of 1929 led to bank failures in the early 1930s. When the stock market began tumbling, people hurried to banks to make withdrawals. In spite of the Federal Reserve System, the banks ran out of money and states were forced to close banks. President Franklin D. Roosevelt extended the period of the bank closings in 1933 to gain time to come up with some solution to the problem.

In 1933 and 1935, Congress passed legislation to strengthen the banking system. The most important move was to establish federal deposit insurance, which you'll learn more about later in this chapter. At this point, it's important for you to know that in the 1930s, during the Great Depression, the government started an insurance program to further protect the public from bank failures.

The Federal Reserve and the Banking Industry

The Federal Reserve is frequently in the news as it tries to keep the economy growing at an even pace. In the early 1990s, the Fed increased the money supply and lowered interest rates to get the economy growing. As inflation threatened in the mid-1990s and into the new century, the Fed increased short-term interest rates. That caused bond prices to fall and, along with other events, threatened the stock market. Alan Greenspan became the center of attention as the whole financial community waited for the Fed's next move. When the stock market began falling in the latter part of 2000 and into 2002, Greenspan cut interest rates many times to get the economy growing again. It takes a while for such changes to create an effect, so the economy was still bumping along well into 2003. By then, Greenspan had cut rates 13 times.

In short, the whole world has been watching and will continue to watch the Federal Reserve System to see what direction the U.S. economy will take next. No group of people is more concerned than the nation's bankers. If businesses stop borrowing, then business growth slows, people are fired, and the whole economy stagnates. In fact, it's quite possible to have both slow growth and inflation. (That's called stagflation.) Thus, money and banking, especially the Federal Reserve Bank, are critical to business leaders. You now know about money and the money supply. The following sections explore banking and its importance to businesspeople.

THE AMERICAN BANKING SYSTEM

The American banking system consists of commercial banks, savings and loan associations, credit unions, and mutual savings banks. In addition, there are various financial organizations, often called **nonbanks,** that accept no deposits but offer many of the services provided by regular banks. Nonbanks include pension funds, insurance companies, commercial finance companies, consumer finance companies, and brokerage houses. In the following sections we'll discuss the activities and services provided by each of these institutions, starting with commercial banks.

nonbanks
Financial organizations that accept no deposits but offer many of the services provided by regular banks (pension funds, insurance companies, commercial finance companies, consumer finance companies, and brokerage houses).

Commercial Banks

A **commercial bank** is a profit-seeking organization that receives deposits from individuals and corporations in the form of checking and savings accounts and then uses some of these funds to make loans. Commercial banks have two types of customers: depositors and borrowers (those who take out loans). A commercial bank is equally responsible to both types of customers. Commercial banks try to make a profit by efficiently using the funds depositors give them. In essence, a commercial bank uses customer deposits as inputs (on which it pays interest) and invests that money in interest-bearing loans to other customers (mostly businesses). Commercial banks make a profit if the revenue generated by loans exceeds the interest paid to depositors plus all other operating expenses.

commercial bank
A profit-seeking organization that receives deposits from individuals and corporations in the form of checking and savings accounts and then uses some of these funds to make loans.

Services Provided by Commercial Banks Individuals and corporations that deposit money in a checking account have the privilege of writing personal checks to pay for almost any purchase or transaction. The technical name for a checking account is a **demand deposit** because the money is available on demand from the depositor. Typically, banks impose a service charge for check-writing privileges or demand a minimum deposit. Banks might also charge a small handling fee for each check written. For corporate depositors, the amount of the service charge depends on the average daily balance in the checking account, the number of checks written, and the firm's credit rating and credit history.

Minority businesspeople are often more comfortable dealing with other minorities when they bank. Consequently, more minority banks are emerging all over the country and many of them are experiencing rapid growth. Citizens Trust Bank of Atlanta is just one such bank. Under the leadership of James E. Young, Citizens' assets have more than doubled in the last six years.

In the past, checking accounts paid no interest to depositors, but interest-bearing checking accounts have experienced phenomenal growth in recent years. Most commercial banks offer negotiable order of withdrawal (NOW) and Super NOW accounts to their depositors. A NOW account typically pays an annual interest rate but requires depositors always to maintain a certain minimum balance in the account (e.g., $500) and may restrict the number of checks that depositors can write each month.

A Super NOW account pays higher interest to attract larger deposits. However, Super NOW accounts require a larger minimum balance. They sometimes offer free, unlimited check-writing privileges. Individual banks determine the specific terms for their NOW and Super NOW accounts. The longer you keep your funds in such accounts, the more interest they pay.

In addition to these types of checking accounts, commercial banks offer a variety of savings account options. A savings account is technically called a **time deposit** because the bank can require a prior notice before withdrawal.

A **certificate of deposit (CD)** is a time-deposit (savings) account that earns interest to be delivered at the end of the certificate's maturity date. The depositor agrees not to withdraw any of the funds in the account until the end of the specified period. CDs are now available for periods of three months up to many years; the longer the CD is to be held, the higher the interest. The interest rates also depend on economic conditions and the prime rate at the time of the deposit. In addition to the checking and savings accounts discussed above, commercial banks offer a variety of other services to their depositors, including automated teller machines and credit cards. The Making Ethical Decisions box discusses the kind of situation that led to more automated banking.

Commercial banks also offer credit cards to creditworthy customers, life insurance, inexpensive brokerage services, financial counseling, automatic payment of telephone bills, safe-deposit boxes, tax-deferred individual retirement accounts (IRAs) for qualified individuals and couples, traveler's checks, trust departments, and overdraft checking account privileges. The latter means that preferred customers can automatically get loans at reasonable rates when they've written checks exceeding their account balance.

Automated teller machines (ATMs) give customers the convenience of 24-hour banking at a variety of outlets such as supermarkets, department stores, and drugstores in addition to the bank's regular branches. Depositors can—almost anywhere in the world—transfer funds, make deposits, and get cash at their own discretion with the use of a computer-coded personalized plastic access card. Beyond all that, today's ATMs are doing even more. New ATMs can

demand deposit
The technical name for a checking account; the money in a demand deposit can be withdrawn anytime on demand from the depositor.

time deposit
The technical name for a savings account; the bank can require prior notice before the owner withdraws money from a time deposit.

certificate of deposit (CD)
A time-deposit (savings) account that earns interest to be delivered at the end of the certificate's maturity date.

www.ethics.ubc.ca/resources

Making Ethical Decisions

To Tell the Teller or Not

You have been banking at the same bank for some time, but the tellers at the bank keep changing, so it is difficult to establish a relationship with any one teller. You do not like using the automated teller machine because the bank has decided to charge for each transaction. Therefore, you are working with a teller and withdrawing $300 for some expenses you expect to incur. The teller counts out your money and says: "OK, here's your $300." Before you leave the bank, you count the money once more. You notice that the teller has given you $350 by mistake. You return to the teller and say, "I think you have made a mistake in giving me this money." She replies indignantly, "I don't think so. I counted the money in front of you."

You are upset by her quick denial of a mistake and her attitude. You have to decide whether or not to give her back the overpayment of $50. What are your alternatives? What would you do? Is that the ethical thing to do?

dispense maps and directions, phone cards, and postage stamps. They can sell tickets to movies, concerts, sporting events, and so on. They can even show movie trailers, news tickers, and video ads. Some can take orders for flowers and DVDs, and download music and games.[12] The convenience chain 7-Eleven is testing machines that cash checks and send wire transfers.[13] What next?

Services to Borrowers Commercial banks offer a variety of services to individuals and corporations in need of a loan. Generally, loans are given on the basis of the recipient's creditworthiness. Banks want to manage their funds effectively and are supposed to screen loan applicants carefully to ensure that the loan plus interest will be paid back on time. Small businesses and minority businesses often search out banks that cater to their needs. The Spotlight on Small Business box discusses such banks in more depth.

Savings and Loan Associations (S&Ls)

savings and loan association (S&L)
A financial institution that accepts both savings and checking deposits and provides home mortgage loans.

A **savings and loan association (S&L)** is a financial institution that accepts both savings and checking deposits and provides home mortgage loans. S&Ls are often known as thrift institutions because their original purpose (starting in 1831) was to promote consumer thrift and home ownership. To help them encourage home ownership, thrifts were permitted for many years to offer slightly higher interest rates on savings deposits than banks. Those rates attracted a large pool of funds, which were then used to offer long-term fixed-rate mortgages at whatever the rate was at the time. S&Ls no longer offer better rates than banks.

Between 1979 and 1983, about 20 percent of the nation's S&Ls failed. There are many reasons for these failures, but the largest may be the fact that capital gains taxes were raised, making investments in real estate less attractive. Investors walked away from their real estate loans, leaving S&Ls with lots of property that was worth less than the money they had lent to investors. When those properties were sold, the S&Ls lost money. To improve the financial power of S&Ls, the federal government permitted them to offer NOW and Super NOW accounts, to allocate up to 10 percent of their funds to commercial loans, and to offer mortgage loans with adjustable interest rates based on market conditions. In addition, S&Ls were permitted to offer a variety of other banking services, such as financial counseling to small businesses and credit cards. As a result, S&Ls became much more similar to commercial banks than before.

Spotlight on Small Business

www.nationalbankers.orgwww.pacebutler.com

Where Can Entrepreneurs Go to Get Financing?

Michael Berk, chief executive of H&S Yacht Sales, shifted his account from a large bank to a smaller one when his big bank changed his contact person for the sixth time in four months. In just four days, he got the line of credit he had waited three months for at his old bank.

Susan Ernst is copresident of Royal Electric Company in Columbus, Ohio. She went to two banks, a large national bank and Commerce National Bank, a local bank that specializes in serving small businesses. Ernst says, "It was remarkable how different those two experiences were . . . With the big bank, the employees who dealt with us seemed to treat us like we were not important . . . With the local bank, we got personal attention from the beginning."

Louis E. Prezeau Sr., president and CEO of City National Bank, says that a small-business owner will have a lot more access to somebody who can make decisions in a minority-owned or small bank than in a large bank. That was true for Adetunde Dada when he sought funding for Tunde Dada House of Africa in Orange, New Jersey. He got great service from the African American–owned City National Bank of New Jersey in Newark. Other banks had not turned him down, but they had been really slow in responding to his request.

The National Bankers Association (NBA) is a Washington, D.C.–based trade group that represents some 50 minority- and women-owned banks. Its members are committed to providing employment opportunities, entrepreneurial capital, and economic revitalization in neighborhoods that often have little access to financial services. A large bank may hesitate to make a small loan to a small business, but a small bank can get to know that business and that businessperson well. As a result, a small business can get not only money but financial advice and other services as well.

Sources: Toddi Gutner, "The Sisterhood in Private Banking," *Business Week,* February 4, 2002, p. 98; Emily Thornton, "Revenge of the Boutique Banks," *Business Week,* October 28, 2002, pp. 102–4; Martin Mayer, "A Borrower Be," *Inc.,* January 2003, pp. 84–88; Joyce Rosenberg, "A Small Business Might Need Services of a Small Bank," *Washington Times,* January 24, 2003, p. C12; and "Charles Haddad, "Eyes on the $1 Billion Prize," *Business Week,* April 7, 2003, p. 72.

Credit Unions

Credit unions are nonprofit, member-owned financial cooperatives that offer the full variety of banking services to their members. Today the 10,000 or so credit unions in the United States serve some 83 million clients. Credit unions have grown at four times the rate of the commercial banking industry.[14] Typically, credit unions offer their members interest-bearing checking accounts at relatively high rates, short-term loans at relatively low rates, financial counseling, life insurance policies, and a limited number of home mortgage loans. Credit unions may be thought of as financial cooperatives organized by government agencies, corporations, unions, or professional associations.

credit unions
Nonprofit, member-owned financial cooperatives that offer the full variety of banking services to their members.

As nonprofit institutions, credit unions enjoy an exemption from federal income taxes. You might want to visit a local credit union and see if you are eligible to belong and then compare the rates you get to local banks.

Other Financial Institutions (Nonbanks)

As we explained earlier, *nonbanks* are financial organizations that accept no deposits but offer many of the services provided by regular banks. Nonbanks include life insurance companies, pension funds, brokerage firms, commercial finance companies, and corporate financial services (such as Ford Motor Credit). As competition between these organizations and banks has increased, the dividing line between banks and nonbanks has become less and less apparent. This is equally true in Europe, where U.S. companies such as Fidelity Investment and GE Capital Corporation compete with European banks. The diversity of financial services and investment alternatives offered by nonbanks has led banks to expand the services they offer. In fact, banks today are merging with brokerage firms to offer full-service financial assistance.

Life insurance companies provide financial protection for policyholders, who periodically pay premiums. In addition, insurers invest the funds they receive from policyholders in corporate and government bonds. In recent years, more insurance companies have begun to provide long-term financing for real estate development projects.

pension funds
Amounts of money put aside by corporations, nonprofit organizations, or unions to cover part of the financial needs of members when they retire.

Pension funds are amounts of money put aside by corporations, nonprofit organizations, or unions to cover part of the financial needs of members when they retire. Contributions to pension funds are made either by employees, by employers, or by both employers and employees. A member may begin to collect a monthly draw on this fund upon reaching a certain retirement age. To generate additional income, pension funds typically invest in low-return but safe corporate stocks or in other conservative investments such as government securities and corporate bonds.

Many large pension funds such as the California Public Employees Retirement System (CalPERS) are becoming a major force in U.S. financial markets. Formidable rivals such as the Teachers Insurance and Annuity Association (TIAA) lend money directly to corporations.

Brokerage firms have traditionally offered services related to investments in the various stock exchanges in this country and abroad. However, brokerage houses have made serious inroads into regular banks' domain by offering high-yield combination savings and checking accounts. In addition, brokerage firms offer checking privileges on accounts (money market accounts). Also, investors can get loans from their broker, using their securities as collateral.

Commercial and consumer finance companies offer short-term loans to businesses or individuals who either cannot meet the credit requirements of regular banks or have exceeded their credit limit and need more funds. These finance companies' interest rates are higher than those of regular banks. The primary customers of these companies are new businesses and individuals with no credit history. In fact, college students often turn to consumer finance companies for loans to pay for their education. One should be careful when borrowing from such institutions because the interest rates can be quite high.

Corporate financial systems established at major corporations such as General Electric, Sears, General Motors, and American Express offer considerable financial services to customers. To compete with such nonbank organizations, banks have had to offer something extra—guaranteed savings.

When it comes to car loans banks must compete with credit unions and nonbanks, such as General Motors' financial unit. Shown here is a Chevrolet dealer in Arlington, Texas, touting GM's no-interest loans. How can a bank compete with a 0 percent loan? What other financial institutions (nonbanks) are operating in your area to compete with local banks?

Critical Thinking

Do you keep your savings in a bank, a S&L, a credit union, or some combination? Have you compared the benefits you could receive from each? Where would you expect to find the best loan values?

Progress Assessment

- Why did the United States need a Federal Reserve Bank?
- What's the difference between a bank, a savings and loan association, and a credit union?
- What is a consumer finance company?

How the Government Protects Your Funds

The American economic system learned a valuable lesson from the depression of the 1930s. To prevent investors from being completely wiped out during an economic downturn, several organizations evolved to protect your money. The three major sources of financial protection are the Federal Deposit Insurance Corporation (FDIC); the Savings Association Insurance Fund (SAIF), originally called the Federal Savings and Loan Insurance Corporation (FSLIC); and the National Credit Union Administration (NCUA). All three insure deposits in individual accounts up to $100,000.

The Federal Deposit Insurance Corporation (FDIC)

The **Federal Deposit Insurance Corporation (FDIC)** is an independent agency of the U.S. government that insures bank deposits. If a bank were to fail, the FDIC would arrange to have that bank's accounts transferred to another bank or pay off depositors up to a certain amount ($100,000 per account). The FDIC covers about 13,000 institutions, mostly commercial banks. What would happen if one of the top 10 banks in the United States were to fail? The FDIC has a contingency plan to nationalize the bank so that it wouldn't fail. The idea is to maintain confidence in banks so that others do not fail if one happens to falter.

Federal Deposit Insurance Corporation (FDIC)
An independent agency of the U.S. government that insures bank deposits.

The Savings Association Insurance Fund (SAIF)

The **Savings Association Insurance Fund (SAIF)** insures holders of accounts in savings and loan associations. It's now part of the FDIC. It was originally called the Federal Savings and Loan Insurance Corporation (FSLIC) and was an independent agency. A brief history will show why the association was created.

Savings Association Insurance Fund (SAIF)
The part of the FDIC that insures holders of accounts in savings and loan associations.

Both the FDIC and the FSLIC were started during the Great Depression. The FDIC was begun in 1933, and the FSLIC in 1934. Some 1,700 bank and thrift institutions had failed during the previous few years, and people were losing confidence in them. The FDIC and FSLIC were designed to create more confidence in banking institutions. In the 1980s, to get more control over the banking system in general, the government placed the FSLIC under the Federal Deposit Insurance Corporation (FDIC) and gave it a new name: the Savings Association Insurance Fund. Like the FDIC, it insures accounts for up to $100,000.

The National Credit Union Administration (NCUA)

The National Credit Union Administration (NCUA) provides up to $100,000 coverage per individual depositor per institution. This coverage includes all accounts, including checking, savings or money market accounts, and certificates of deposit. Additional protection can be obtained by holding accounts jointly or in trust. Individual retirement accounts (IRAs) are also separately insured.

THE FUTURE OF BANKING

Banking in the future is likely to change dramatically. One cause of change is the repeal of the Glass-Steagall Act of 1933, which prohibited banks from owning brokerages. The new law—the Gramm-Leach-Bliley Act of 1999—allows banks, insurers, and securities firms (brokers) to combine and sell each other's services. This allows you and other consumers one-stop shopping for all your financial needs. One company can provide you with banking services, including credit and debit cards; mortgages; insurance of all kinds, including life and car; and brokerage services, including the ability to buy stocks, bonds, and mutual funds.[15] Furthermore, since all of your financial records can be kept in the same company, it may be easier for you to compute your taxes. In fact, the financial firm may do much of that work for you.

Ethical Issues Hurt Banking Deeply

As banks formed giant conglomerates offering credit, equity, insurance, fund management, analysis, and more, they began to push the limits of the law and became part of the recent business scandals. Citigroup, J. P. Morgan Chase, Merrill Lynch, and others have been charged with all kinds of misbehavior, and stockholders cut the value of their stocks considerably. Citigroup's Salomon Smith Barney unit gave WorldCom CEO Bernard Ebbers 869,000 shares in initial public offerings. Other WorldCom executives received such shares, which were not made available to the general public. The shares soared on the market and then plunged as the executives sold them. Citigroup's Jack Grubman appears to have promoted WorldCom and other telecommunications stocks to get their investment banking business. Managers at Merrill Lynch, in an apparent conflict of interest, bought shares in a partnership they had structured.[16]

Senate investigators allege that $4.8 billion in Citigroup transactions with Enron were shams, and that the bank knowingly helped the energy company in deceiving investors and the public. Other banks have been caught up in unethical and/or illegal practices that contributed greatly to the downfall of the telecommunications industry and the business scandals in general.[17] As the government concludes its investigations, there could very well be a host of rules and regulations that will greatly affect banking's future. There will also be a challenge to traditional banks from online banking. We'll explore that trend next.

Electronic Banking on the Internet

Not only have banking, insurance, and brokerage services been combined in one company, but they are also available online. All of the nation's top 25 retail banks now allow customers access to their accounts online, and most have bill-paying capacity. Thus, you are now able to do all of your financial transactions from home, using your telephone or your computer. That includes banking transactions such as transferring funds from one account to another (e.g., savings to checking), paying your bills, and finding out how much is in your various accounts.[18] You can apply for a car loan or mortgage online and get a response almost immediately. The company can check your financial records and give you a reply while you wait. Buying and selling stocks and bonds is equally easy. (See the Dealing with Change box for a discussion of the Internet and global banking.)

Dealing with Change

www.ml.com

The Internet and Global Banking

The U.S. market for banking services is relatively mature; therefore, the growth markets of the future will be overseas. Few firms understand the potential of international banking better than Merrill Lynch, a leader in brokering and in financing corporations.

To expand overseas, Merrill Lynch bought the British brokerage Smith New Court; Spain's Iversiones; and stakes in brokerages in India, Thailand, South Africa, Indonesia, and Italy. It is also expanding to Latin America and recently acquired Australia's McIntosh Securities. In all, it is present in over 40 countries. As a consequence, about 30 percent of Merrill Lynch's revenues now come from overseas. Merrill Lynch is using the same concepts it developed in the United States to develop globally. In fact, it was one of the biggest losers during the Asian banking crisis.

Jeff Bahrenburg, global investment strategist at Merrill Lynch, says, "The Internet hastens the speed of financial flows and the pace at which the world is getting smaller." Andrew W. Lo, an economist at MIT, adds, "The most significant effect of the Internet on finance is that it will greatly facilitate the efficient matching of borrowers and investors in the global economy." To give you some idea of the dollar amount involved, consider this: In 1980, the world's stock of equities, bonds, and cash totaled some $11 trillion; by 2000 these financial figures were at $78 trillion.

Other leading U.S. investment firms, insurance companies, and banks are going global as well. Names like Charles Schwab and Travelers Group are becoming familiar all over the world. You can understand the potential when you learn that only 44 percent of the total value of stocks traded worldwide is traded in the United States. Citigroup estimates that total personal loans in Western Europe, which now amount to about $450 billion, could one day rival those in the United States, at about $750 billion. That is an attractive situation for brokers and other financial institutions from all nations. It also means that there will be opportunities for tomorrow's college graduates in finance to work anywhere in the world.

Sources: Daniel Fairlamb and Stanley Reed, "Uber Bank," *Business Week,* March 20, 2000, pp. 52–53; "The Global Giants," *The Wall Street Journal,* October 14, 2002, pp. R10, R11; Stephanie Miles, "What's a Check?" *The Wall Street Journal,* October 21, 2002, p. R5; and Erik Portanger and Paul Beckett, "Banks Vie for Europe's Consumers," *The Wall Street Journal,* Feburary 24, 2003, pp. C1, C5.

New Internet banks (e.g., NetBank) have been created that offer online banking only; they do not have physical branches. Such banks can offer high interest rates and low fees because they do not have the costs of physical overhead that traditional banks have. While many consumers are pleased with the savings and convenience, not all are entirely happy with the service they receive with Internet banks. Why are they dissatisfied? First of all, they are nervous about security. People fear putting their financial information into cyberspace, where others may see it. Despite all the assurances of privacy, people are still concerned. Furthermore, some people want to be able to talk to a knowledgeable person when they have banking problems. They miss the service, the one-on-one help, and the security of local banks.

Because of these issues, the future seems to be with organizations like Wells Fargo, Citigroup, and Bank One, which are traditional banks that offer both online services and brick-and-mortar facilities.[19] Combined online and brick-and-mortar banks not only offer online services of all kinds but also have automated teller machines (ATMs), places to go to deposit and get funds, and real people to talk to in person.

Using Technology to Make Banking More Efficient

The way things have traditionally been done in banking—depositing money, writing checks, protecting against bad checks, and so on—is expensive. Imagine the cost to the bank of approving a check, processing it through the banking system, and mailing it back to you. Bankers have long looked for ways to make the system more efficient.

One step in the past was to issue credit cards. Credit cards reduce the flow of checks, but they too have their costs: There's still paper to process. The future will see much more electronic exchange of money because it is the most efficient way to transfer funds. In an **electronic funds transfer (EFT) system,** messages about a transaction are sent from one computer to another. Thus, funds can be transferred more quickly and more economically than with paper checks. EFT tools include electronic check conversion, debit cards, smart cards, direct deposits, and direct payments.

electronic funds transfer (EFT) system
A computerized system that electronically performs financial transactions such as making purchases, paying bills, and receiving paychecks.

Electronic check conversion (ECC) converts a traditional paper check into an electronic transaction at the cash register (called a point-of-sale terminal) and processes it through the Federal Reserve's Automated Clearing House (ACH). ECC saves time and money while reducing the risks of bounced checks. When a customer makes payment with a check, it is run through a check reader, where magnetic ink character recognition (MICR) information is captured. The check is verified against a database for acceptance. The transaction is electronically transferred through the ACH, where funds are debited directly from the customer's account and deposited automatically into the merchant's account. Since checks are electronically deposited, there are no trips to the bank, deposit slips, or risks of lost or stolen checks.

electronic check conversion (ECC)
An electronic funds transfer tool that converts a traditional paper check into an electronic transaction at the cash register and processes it through the Federal Reserve's Automated Clearing House.

Whereas ECC *reduces* the paper-handling processes of using checks, debit cards *eliminate* them. A **debit card** serves the same function as checks: it withdraws funds from a checking account. Debit cards look like credit cards but work very differently. The difference between a debit card and a credit card is that you can spend no more money than is already in your account. You put the card into a slot in a point-of-sale terminal at a retailer. When the sale is recorded, an electronic signal is sent to the bank, transferring funds from your account to the store's account automatically. A record of transactions appears immediately online. Debit cards are a real challenge to credit cards.[20]

debit card
An electronic funds transfer tool that serves the same function as checks: it withdraws funds from a checking account.

A **smart card** is an electronic funds transfer tool that is a combination of credit card, debit card, phone card, driver's license card, and more. Smart cards replace the typical magnetic strip on a credit or debit card with a microprocessor. The card can then store a variety of information, including the holder's bank balance. Merchants can use this information to check the card's validity and spending limits, and transactions can debit the amount on the card.[21] Visa USA introduced its smart Visa card in 2000. It is embedded with a chip that transmits information online via a card reader plugged into the user's computer. American Express had one of its most successful launches ever with its Blue Card, a smart card with an embedded chip that holds a "certificate of authenticity." That certificate, along with a personal identification number (PIN), secures information that makes Internet shopping safe and convenient.[22]

smart card
An electronic funds transfer tool that is a combination credit card, debit card, phone card, driver's license card, and more.

Some smart cards have embedded radio-frequency antennae that make it possible to access buildings and secure areas within buildings, and to buy gas and other items with a swipe of the card.[23] A biometric function lets you use your fingerprint to boot up your computer. Students are using smart cards to open locked doors to dorms and identify themselves to retailers near campus and on the Internet. The cards also serve as ATM cards.

Visa Buxx and Cobalt-card have new debit cards for teenagers. They work like this: Parents can deposit or withdraw funds from their child's account over the phone or the Internet. That amount is then added to or subtracted from the value on the card. The company then reports where the money is being spent over time. Thus, parents can monitor their children's transactions. Such cards are also made available to employees, nannies, and others. The idea is to have an easy-to-use source of money that can be controlled. It is easier to use such a card than to drive to an ATM every time you need a few dollars.

For many, the ultimate convenience in banking involves automatic transactions such as direct deposit and direct payments. A *direct deposit* is a credit made directly to a checking or savings account. Because of direct deposit, some workers today receive no paycheck. Rather, their employer contacts the bank and orders it to transfer funds from the employer's account to the worker's account. Individuals can use direct deposits to transfer funds to other accounts, such as from a checking account to a savings account.

Not only can you deposit funds directly into bank accounts automatically, but you can also withdraw them automatically. A *direct payment* is a preauthorized electronic payment. Customers sign a separate authorization form for each company they would like the bank to pay automatically. This form authorizes the designated company to collect funds for the amount of the bill from the customer's checking or savings account on the specified date. The customer's financial institution provides information regarding the transaction on the monthly statement.

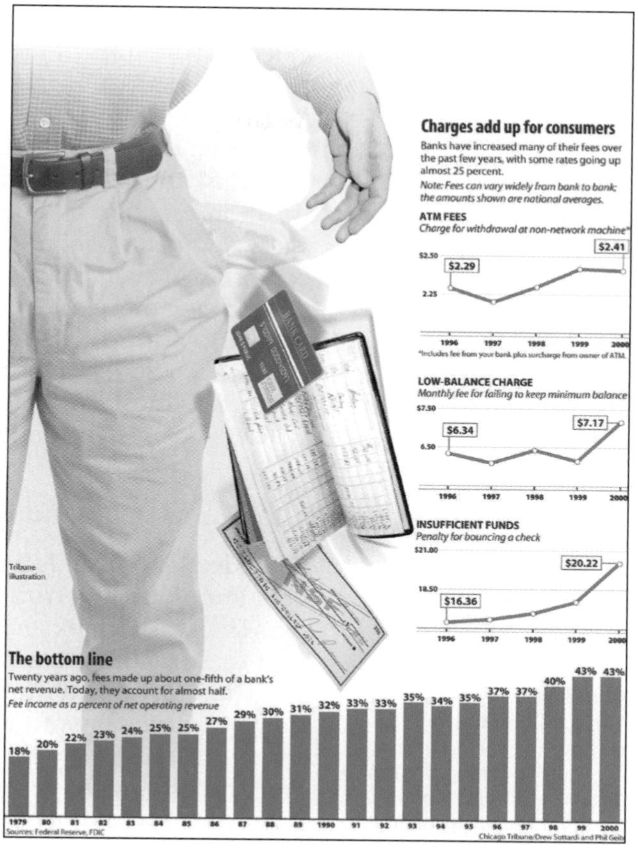

Banks are offering more services to customers, but their fees are growing just as fast, as this illustration shows. What fees are most irritating to you? Does your bank charge you a fee for teller transactions? Do you use or avoid ATMs that charge fees for cash withdrawals?

International Banking and Banking Services

Banks help companies conduct business in other countries by providing three services: letters of credit, banker's acceptances, and money exchange. If a U.S. company wants to buy a product from Germany, the company could pay a bank to issue a letter of credit. A **letter of credit** is a promise by the bank to pay the seller a given amount if certain conditions are met. For example, the German company may not be paid until the goods have arrived at the U.S. company's warehouse. A **banker's acceptance** promises that the bank will pay some specified amount at a particular time. No conditions are imposed. Finally, a company can go to a bank and exchange American dollars for euros to use in Germany; that's called *currency* or *money exchange.*

Banks are making it easier than ever before for travelers and businesspeople to buy goods and services overseas as well. Automated teller machines now provide yen, euros, and other foreign currencies through your personal Visa, MasterCard, Cirrus, Plus, or American Express card.

letter of credit
A promise by the bank to pay the seller a given amount if certain conditions are met.

banker's acceptance
A promise that the bank will pay some specified amount at a particular time.

Leaders in International Banking

This chapter has focused on banking within the United States. In the future, though, it's likely that many crucial financial issues will be international. In today's financial environment, it's foolish to discuss the American economy apart from the world economy. If the Federal Reserve decides to lower interest rates, foreign investors can withdraw their money from the United States in minutes and put it in countries with higher rates. Of course, the Fed's increasing interest rates can draw money to the United States equally quickly.

Today's money markets form a global market system. The United States is just a part of that system. There are banks larger than U.S. banks all over the world. International bankers tend not to be nationalistic in their dealings. That is, they make investments in any country where they can get a maximum return for their money at a reasonable risk. That's how more than $1.5 trillion is traded daily! The net result of international banking and finance has been to link the economies of the world into one interrelated system with no regulatory control. American firms must compete for funds with firms all over the world. An efficient firm in London or Tokyo is more likely to get international financing than a less efficient firm in Detroit or Chicago.

What all this means to you is that banking is no longer a domestic issue; it's an international issue. To understand the U.S. financial system, you must learn about the global financial system. To understand America's economic condition, you'll have to learn about the economic condition of countries throughout the world. What has evolved, basically, is a world economy financed by international banks. The United States is just one player in the game. To be a winning player, America must stay financially secure and its businesses must stay competitive in world markets. The Reaching Beyond Our Borders box shows that ethical issues will be global as well.

The World Bank and the International Monetary Fund (IMF)

To understand what is happening in the global banking world, you have to understand what the World Bank and the International Monetary Fund (IMF) are. The World Bank and the IMF are twin intergovernmental pillars that support the structure of the world's banking community:

World Bank
The bank primarily responsible for financing economic development; also known as the International Bank for Reconstruction and Development.

The **World Bank** (also known as the International Bank for Reconstruction and Development) is primarily responsible for financing economic development. For example, it lent money to countries in Western Europe after World War II so they could rebuild. Today, the World Bank lends most of its money to less-developed nations to improve productivity and help raise the standard of living and quality of life ➤P. 6◄.

Recently, the World Bank has come under considerable criticism, with major protests taking place in Seattle, Washington; Washington, D.C.; and other places. There have been a variety of protestors at such events. Environmentalists charge that the World Bank finances projects that damage the ecosystem, such as China's Three Gorges Dam. Human rights activists and unionists argue that the bank supports countries that restrict religious freedoms and tolerate sweatshops. AIDS activists complain that the bank does not do enough to get low-cost AIDS drugs to developing nations. As a result of such protests, the World Bank is trying to develop strategies that focus more on the poor and do less to damage the environment.[24] Despite its efforts to improve, the World Bank still has many critics.[25]

International Monetary Fund (IMF)
Organization that assists the smooth flow of money among nations.

Protestors have been upset with the IMF as well. In contrast to the World Bank, the **International Monetary Fund (IMF)** was established to assist the smooth flow of money among nations. It requires members (who are voluntary) to allow their own money to be exchanged for foreign money freely, to keep the IMF informed about changes in monetary policy, and to modify those policies on the advice of the IMF to accommodate the needs of the entire membership. The IMF is not supposed to be a lending institution primarily, as is the World Bank. Rather, it is designed to be an overseer of member countries' monetary and exchange rate policies. The IMF's goal is to maintain a global monetary system that works best for all nations. Members of the IMF contribute funds (rich countries pay more, poor countries pay less). Those funds are available to countries when they get into financial difficulty.

The IMF was in the news almost daily in the late 1990s and early part of this century because it was lending money (billions of dollars) to nations whose currencies had fallen dramatically and whose banks were failing (e.g., Asian and Latin American countries and Russia). The most recent IMF failures have taken place in Turkey, Argentina, Uruguay, and Brazil.[26] When Argentina got into financial difficulty, some people believed that it would be better off if the IMF didn't intervene.[27] Many of the protestors in Seattle and Washington were

Reaching Beyond Our Borders

www.hg.org/banking.html

The "Bank of Crooks and Criminals, International"

Many in the banking world feel that the now-defunct Bank of Credit and Commerce, International (BCCI), is a textbook example of what's wrong in international banking. BCCI was fined for laundering drug money in Florida and was involved in a foreign exchange scandal in Kenya. Its customers included former Panamanian strongman Manuel Noriega and Colombian drug lords. The bank was so bad, in fact, that it earned the name "Bank of Crooks and Criminals, International." Yet for almost 20 years, BCCI stayed one step ahead of the law. This financial reign of terror came to a crashing end in the early 1990s when bank regulators from the United States, Britain, and five other countries shut down BCCI. The estimated losses from BCCI's operations amounted to almost $5 billion, making it one of the world's biggest banking failures. How did all this happen, and what can be done to prevent future BCCIs from developing?

Most experts agree that the absence of any type of global regulatory agency permitted BCCI to remain untouchable. For example, the bank's registered home base was Luxembourg, but its managers worked from London. Many of its shareholders were wealthy Persian Gulf oil sheiks, and its assets were tangled in a branch network that included 70 different countries. Many operations were channeled through the Cayman Islands. The complexity of the bank prevented any banking authority from performing regulatory audits. Fraud, corruption, and money laundering became the order of the day. *Time* magazine called the bank the largest corporate criminal enterprise ever.

BCCI's actions have caused many industrialized nations to consider imposing tighter controls on international banks. The U.S. Senate and the Federal Reserve support global actions to control international banking activity. International banks will undergo more intensive scrutiny in the future in an attempt to prevent another BCCI-type scandal.

Sources: "BCCI: Dead and Buried," *The Economist,* April 15, 2000; "Breaking the Bank," *The Wall Street Journal,* August 7, 2001, p. A14; and David Pringle, "BCCI Liquidators Plan to Pay $1.2 Billion to Creditors," *The Wall Street Journal,* May 15, 2003, p. C13.

there to protest actions taken by the World Bank and the IMF. Debt relief advocates want the World Bank and IMF to forgive the debts of poor countries because many of them cannot afford to feed their people, much less pay back huge loans.[28] But the failure of such loans shows that the World Bank and IMF's actions have not been very successful. Therefore, they are both under attack from all directions and are planning to change their policies. Only time will tell what will finally emerge.

Progress Assessment

- What's the difference between the FDIC and the SAIF?
- Describe an electronic funds transfer (EFT) system. What are its benefits?
- What are the limitations of online banking?
- What are the roles of the World Bank and the International Monetary Fund?

Summary

1. Money is anything that people generally accept as payment for goods and services.
   - ***How is the value of money determined?***

   The value of money depends on the money supply; that is, how much money is available to buy goods and services. Too much money in circulation causes inflation. Too little money causes deflation, recession, and unemployment.

1. Explain what money is and how its value is determined.

2. Describe how the Federal Reserve controls the money supply.

2. Because the value of money is so important to the domestic economy and international trade, an organization was formed to control the money supply.
   - ***What's that organization and how does it work?***

   The Federal Reserve makes financial institutions keep funds in the Federal Reserve System (reserve requirement), buys and sells government securities (open-market operations), and lends money to banks (the discount rate). To increase the money supply, the Fed can cut the reserve requirement, buy government bonds, and lower the discount rate.

3. Trace the history of banking and the Federal Reserve System.

3. In the American colonies there were no banks at first and coins were limited. The colonists traded goods for goods instead of using money.
   - ***How did banking evolve in the United States?***

   Massachusetts issued its own paper money in 1690; other colonies followed suit. British land banks lent money to farmers but ended such loans by 1741. After the American Revolution, there was much debate about the role of banking, and there were heated battles between the Central Bank of the United States and state banks. Eventually, a federally chartered and state-chartered system was established, but chaos continued until many banks failed in 1907. The system was revived by the Federal Reserve only to fail again during the Great Depression. The Fed, banks, and S&Ls were in the news during the 1990s because many banks and S&Ls failed and the Federal Reserve kept raising interest rates. The Fed then cut interest rates 13 times.

4. Classify the various institutions in the U.S. banking system.

4. Savings and loans, commercial banks, and credit unions are all part of the banking system.
   - ***How do they differ from one another?***

   Before deregulation in 1980, commercial banks were unique in that they handled both deposits and checking accounts. At that time, savings and loans couldn't offer checking services; their main function was to encourage thrift and home ownership by offering high interest rates on savings accounts and providing home mortgages. Deregulation closed the gaps between banks and S&Ls so that they now offer similar services.
   - ***What kinds of services do they offer?***

   Banks and thrifts offer such services as savings accounts, NOW accounts, CDs, loans, individual retirement accounts (IRAs), safe-deposit boxes, online banking, insurance, stock, and traveler's checks.
   - ***What is a credit union?***

   A credit union is a member-owned cooperative that offers everything that a bank does. That is, it takes deposits, allows you to write checks, and makes loans. It also may sell life insurance and make home loans. Because credit unions are member-owned cooperatives rather than profit-seeking businesses like banks, credit union interest rates are sometimes higher than those from banks, and loan rates are often lower.
   - ***What are some of the other financial institutions that make loans and do other banklike operations?***

   Nonbanks include life insurance companies that lend out their funds, pension funds that invest in stocks and bonds and make loans, brokerage firms that offer investment services, and commercial finance companies.

5. Explain the importance of the Federal Deposit Insurance Coporation and other organizations that guarantee funds.

5. The government has created organizations to protect depositors from losses such as those experienced during the Great Depression.
   - ***What agencies ensure that the money you put into a bank, S&L, or credit union is safe?***

   Money deposited in banks is insured by an independent government agency, the Federal Deposit Insurance Corporation (FDIC). Money in S&Ls is insured by another agency connected to the FDIC, the Savings Association Insurance Fund (SAIF). Money in credit unions is insured by the

National Credit Union Administration (NCUA). These organizations protect your savings up to $100,000 per account.

6. There will be many changes in the banking system in coming years.
   - ***What are some major changes?***

   One important change will be more services offered by banks, including insurance, securities (stocks, bonds, and mutual funds), and real estate sales. This is subject to change given the unethical and illegal behavior of banks in 2001 and 2002. Electronic funds transfer (EFT) systems will make it possible to buy goods and services with no money. Automated teller machines enable you to get foreign money whenever and wherever you want it. Online banking may change the banking process dramatically as people become more used to paying bills and conducting other transactions online. ATMs will offer more services, including the ability to pick up tickets to events and download music.

6. Discuss the future of the U.S. banking system.

7. Today's money markets aren't national; they are global.
   - ***What do we mean by global markets?***

   Global markets mean that banks do not necessarily keep their money in their own countries. They make investments where they get the maximum return.
   - ***What are the roles of the World Bank and the IMF?***

   The World Bank (also known as the International Bank for Reconstruction and Development) is primarily responsible for financing economic development. The International Monetary Fund (IMF), in contrast, was established to assist the smooth flow of money among nations. It requires members (who join voluntarily) to allow their own money to be exchanged for foreign money freely, to keep the IMF informed about changes in monetary policy, and to modify those policies on the advice of the IMF to accommodate the needs of the entire membership.

7. Evaluate the role and importance of international banking and the role of the World Bank and the International Monetary Fund.

Key Terms

banker's acceptance 661
barter 644
certificate of deposit (CD) 653
commercial bank 652
credit unions 655
debit card 660
demand deposit 653
discount rate 649
electronic check conversion (ECC) 660
electronic funds transfer (EFT) system 660
Federal Deposit Insurance Corporation (FDIC) 657
International Monetary Fund (IMF) 662
letter of credit 661
M-1 646
M-2 646
money 644
money supply 646
nonbanks 652
open-market operations 649
pension funds 656
reserve requirement 648
savings and loan association (S&L) 654
Savings Association Insurance Fund (SAIF) 657
smart card 660
time deposit 653
World Bank 662

Developing Workplace Skills

1. In a small group discuss the following: What services do you use from banks and S&Ls? Does anyone use Internet banking? What seem to be the pluses and minuses of such online banking? Use this opportunity to compare the rates and services of various local banks and S&Ls.

2. Poll the class to see who uses banks and who uses a credit union. Have class members compare the services at each (interest rates given on accounts, the services available, and the loan rates). If anyone uses an online service, see how those rates compare. If no one uses a credit union or online bank, discuss the reasons.

3. One role of the Federal Reserve is to help process your checks. Break up into small groups and discuss when and where you use checks versus credit cards and cash. Do you often write checks for small amounts? Would you stop doing that if you calculated how much it costs to process such checks? Discuss your findings with others in the class.

4. While in your small groups, take out some bills ($1 and $5) and look at them closely. Note that it says "Federal Reserve Note" on the top. Look at your $1 notes. You will find a jagged circle in the middle of the left side. What states are they from? Note also the words "This note is legal tender for all debts, public and private." What role does the Fed play in making such money?

5. Write a one-page paper on the role of the World Bank and the International Monetary Fund in providing loans to countries. Is it important for U.S. citizens to lend money to people in other countries through such organizations? Why or why not? Be prepared to debate the value of these organizations in class.

Taking It To The Net

Purpose

To learn a few fun facts about U.S. currency.

Exercise

Your parents always told you money doesn't grow on trees. Other than that what else do you know about money? Go to the website of the Bureau of Engraving and Printing (BEP) at www.moneyfactory.com and answer the following questions:

1. What is currency paper made of?
2. How much ink does the BEP use to print money each day?
3. How much does it cost to produce a paper currency note?
4. Approximately how many times could you fold a piece of currency before it would tear?
5. How long is the life span of a $1 bill?
6. What is the origin of the dollar sign ($)?
7. Why did the BEP print paper notes in 3-, 5-, 10-, 25-, and 50-cent denominations during the Civil War?
8. If you had 10 billion $1 notes and spent one every second of every day, how long would it take you to go broke?
9. Who was the only woman whose portrait appeared on a paper U.S. currency note?
10. When did "In God We Trust" become part of the U.S. currency design?
11. Whose picture is on a $100 bill? (If you're still a kid at heart, you might enjoy playing the money trivia games at the Treasury Dome at www.bep.treas.gov/kids_site/tdome.html.)

Casing The Web

To access the case "Learning about the Federal Reserve System," visit

www.mhhe.com/ub7e

A Reputation You Can Bank On—Bank One

Can you imagine living in an economy where all exchanges are done by barter? That's pretty much the way things were in the United States when it was first colonized. People traded tobacco for corn and corn for shoes. Isn't it convenient that we now have something called money that is portable (easy to carry), divisible (quarters and dollars and such), stable (the value doesn't change if the weather is too hot), and durable (a coin can last for centuries) to use in our exchanges?

Banks were created to store and invest money. Some of the first banks were used to lend money to farmers primarily because most people made their living as farmers back then. Banks were also used to finance wars. Over time, small banks in small towns lent money to start businesses like a local food store or shoe store. The classic movie, *It's a Wonderful Life*, features such a lending institution. Bank One started like the mythical bank in the movie—small. However, small is not the case today. From its beginning in 1863 during the Civil War, Bank One has now become a major financial institution made up of banks and other financial services companies.

Like all federally chartered banks, Bank One is under the jurisdiction of the Federal Reserve System (the Fed). The Fed tries to keep the economy from growing too fast or slowing down too much by controlling the money supply. The Fed, for example, dictates how much money a bank like Bank One must keep at the Fed (reserve requirement). It also determines the interest it charges banks (like Bank One) to borrow money, dropping rates to boost the economy and raising rates to slow the economy. When the Fed sells government bonds (open-market operations), it takes money out of the economy and slows it down.

Banks now face competition from nonbanks such as insurance companies, pension funds, and financial services firms. For example, brokerage firms can offer customers a money market account much like a checking account at Bank One. Similarly, Bank One can sell stocks and bonds. To meet this competition, Bank One offers a variety of services to customers such as credit cards, debit cards, checking accounts, ATMs, Internet banking, and more. It also offers security to its customers since accounts at Bank One are insured by the Federal Deposit Insurance Corporation (FDIC) up to $100,000 per account. The Savings Association Insurance Fund (SAIF) does the same for depositors at savings & loans (S&Ls).

People generally borrow money from banks, S&Ls, or credit unions to buy homes. In 2003, many current borrowers renegotiated how much interest they had to pay on their loans and refinanced them at a lower rate of interest. The rate dropped as low as 5 percent, saving some borrowers hundreds of dollars a month.

The World Bank lends money to developing nations to build their infrastructure—electric plants, water plants, roads, sewers, dams, and the like. It does not compete with Bank One or any other banks in that respect. The International Monetary Fund (IMF) has the role of keeping global currency exchanges in order. Since world trade is important to world economic growth, so is the free trade of currency. It's possible one day there may be just one universal currency for all countries. Or, we all may just use credit cards or debit cards or some other form of "plastic" for exchanges. In any case, there will probably always be a role for banks as a safe haven for money and a source to help people plan for retirement, make home purchases, and more.

Thinking It Over

1. What have you learned from this video and the text that makes you less nervous about putting your money in a bank or S&L or credit union?
2. The economy has been on a roller-coaster ride over the last few years. What role has the Fed played in keeping the economy as stable as possible? How does the Fed do that?
3. How has your experience with banks changed over time? Do you use a credit card, debit card, or ATM? Has the merger of banks into huge banking systems like Bank One affected you?
4. What is the difference between roles of the World Bank and the IMF? What do they have to do, if anything, with banks?

Chapter 22

Managing Personal Finances to Achieve Financial Security

Learning Goals

After you have read and studied this chapter, you should be able to

1. Describe the six steps of learning to control your assets.
2. Explain ways to build a financial base, including investing in real estate, saving money, and managing credit.
3. Explain how buying the appropriate insurance can protect your financial base.
4. Outline a strategy for retiring with enough money to last a lifetime.

Profile

Getting to Know Today's Billionaires

Forbes magazine recently reported on the world's 497 billionaires. They were found in 43 different countries, so becoming a billionaire may not be as impossible as you suspect.

The first question that comes to mind is: How did these people get to be so rich? The rich people most of us read about are movie stars, sports heroes, rock stars, and the like. They make *millions* of dollars. But billions? Who makes billions of dollars? After all, that's 1,000 million!

Nine of the 10 top billionaires in the world live in the United States. The 6th, 7th, 8th, 9th, and 10th on the U.S. billionaire list all have the same last name: Walton. Sam Walton started Wal-Mart and made billions and billions of dollars. So, one way to become a billionaire is to become an entrepreneur and then sell stock in your company. The richest man in the United States, Bill Gates, has over $52 billion. He made his money starting and then selling stock in Microsoft. Another good way to get rich is to find really smart entrepreneurs and then buy their businesses from them. Then you sell stock in those companies. That's how number two on the list, Warren Buffett, made his money. There are female billionaires as well. Oprah Winfrey (United States) is in the media business. Friede Springer (Germany) is in publishing. And Nina Wang (China) made her money in property development.

Forbes *magazine recently reported on the world's 497 billionaires. They were found in 43 different countries, so becoming a billionaire may not be as impossible as you suspect.*

Let's face it, the chances of becoming a billionaire are not really very good; chances of becoming a millionaire are much better, though. There are about 7 million people in the world with more than $1 million in financial assets. More than 2 million of these millionaires live in the United States. One of the best ways to learn how to become a millionaire is to do what companies do: benchmark those who are successful. That is, you should find out what all those millionaires did to make their money. For over 20 years, Thomas Stanley has been doing just that—studying wealthy people. His research is available in a book called *The Millionaire Next Door: The Surprising Secrets of America's Wealthy,* which he co-authored with William Danko.

Stanley and Danko found that the majority of millionaires are entrepreneurs who own one or more small businesses. Self-employed people are four times as likely to be millionaires as people who earn a paycheck working for others. The average income of American millionaires is $131,000 a year. So how did they get to be millionaires? They saved their money. To become a millionaire by the time you are 50 or so, you have to save about 15 percent of your income every year—starting when you are in your 20s. If you start later, you have to save an even larger percentage. The secret is to put your money in a place where it will grow without your having to pay taxes on it. You'll learn how to do that in this chapter.

To save that 15 percent a year, you have to spend less than you earn. Discipline in spending must begin with your first job and stay with you all your life. To save money, the millionaires Stanley studied tended to own modest homes and to buy used cars. In short, becoming a millionaire has more to do with thrift than with how much you earn.

Do you want to be a billionaire or, more plausibly, a millionaire? If so, then you need to do what other rich people have done. You need to get an education, work hard, save your money, and make purchases carefully. This chapter will give you more insight into how to manage your finances. Are you ready to do the hard work it takes to become a millionaire? To reach your goal, your final answer must be "Yes!"

Sources: Tom Fetzer, "Never Say Die," *Success,* December/January 2001, p. 60; "The Global Billionaires," *Forbes,* March 18, 2002, pp. 119–52; "Thomas J. Stanley," *Fast Company,* October 2002, p. 70; "Women and Wealth," *Fast Company,* October 2002, p. 28; "Survival of the Richest," *Forbes,* March 17, 2003, pp. 87–100; and Muoi Tran, "New Money," *Fortune,* July 7, 2003, p. 34.

THE NEED FOR PERSONAL FINANCIAL PLANNING

America is largely a capitalist ➤P. 41◀ country. It follows, then, that the secret to success in such a country is to have capital. With capital, you can take nice vacations, raise a family, invest in stocks and bonds, buy the goods and services you want, give generously to others, and retire with enough money to see you through. Money management, however, is not easy. You have to earn the money in the first place. Then you have to learn how to save money; spend money wisely; and insure yourself against the risks of serious accidents, illness, or death. We shall discuss each of these issues in this chapter so that you can begin making financial plans for the rest of your life. With a little bit of luck, you may be one of the millionaires Stanley and Danko interview for their next book.

Financial Planning Begins with Making Money

A major reason for studying business is that it prepares you for finding and keeping a good job. Today, that usually means learning how to communicate well, how to use a computer, and how to apply some of the skills you have learned in your college classes and in life. It also means staying out of financial trouble.

You already know that one of the secrets to finding a well-paying job is to have a good education. Throughout history, an investment in education has paid off regardless of the state of the economy or political ups and downs. Benjamin Franklin said, "If a man empties his purse into his head, no one can take it away from him. An investment in knowledge always pays the best interest." Education has become even more important since we entered the information age. The lifetime income of families headed by individuals with a bachelor's degree will be about $1.6 million more than the incomes of families headed by those with a high school diploma.[1] One way to begin to be a millionaire, therefore, is to finish college.

The government is eager for you to go to college and is willing to help you by giving you various tax breaks to do so. Figure 22.1 lists some of the incentives the government provides and the conditions you must meet to get them. Many people use their education to find successful careers and to improve their earning potential, but at retirement they have little to show for their efforts. Making money is one thing; saving, investing, and spending it wisely is something else. Less than 10 percent of the U.S. population has accumulated enough money by retirement age to live comfortably. Only slightly more than half of all households have a retirement account.[2] Following the six steps listed in the next section will help you become one of those with enough to live in comfort after retirement.

Six Steps in Learning to Control Your Assets

The only way to save enough money to do all of the things you want to do in life is to make more than you spend! We know you may find it hard to save today, but saving money is not only possible but also imperative if you want to accumulate enough to be financially secure. The following are six steps you can take today to get control of your finances.

Step 1: Take an Inventory of Your Financial Assets To take inventory, you need to develop a balance sheet ➤P. 556◀ for yourself. Remember, a balance sheet starts with the fundamental accounting equation: Assets = Liabilities + Owners' equity. You can develop your own balance sheet similar to the one presented in Chapter 18 by listing your assets (e.g., TV, VCR, DVD, computer,

BENEFIT	ANNUAL LIMIT	EXPENSES THAT QUALIFY	CONDITIONS	MAXIMUM INCOME*
Scholarships				
Generally tax free	NA	Tuition, fees, books, supplies related to course work	Amounts designated specifically for services rendered or to cover living expenses are taxable income	None
Lifetime Learning Credit				
Tax credit	Up to $1,000 per student for first two years	Tuition and fees	Applies to expenses paid for school attendance	$50,000; joint returns: $100,000
Hope Credit				
Tax credit	Up to $1,500 per student for first 2 years of undergraduate study	Tuition and fees	Must be enrolled at least part-time in a degree program	$50,000; joint returns: $100,000
Traditional and Roth IRAs				
No 10% penalty for early withdrawal	Amount of qualifying expenses	Tuition and fees, books, supplies, room and board	Must receive entire balance or begin receiving withdrawals by April 1 of year following year you reach age 70 1/2	$110, 000; joint returns: $160,000
Education Savings Account (ESA)				
Funds grow free of taxes	$2,000 contribution per child under 18	Tuition and fees, books, supplies, room and board, transportation, tutoring, computer equipment	Contributions not deductible; cannot contribute to qualified state tuition program or claim an education credit; must withdraw assets by age 30	$110,000; joint returns: $220,000
Employers' Educational Assistance Program				
Employer benefits are excludable from income	$5,250	Tuition and fees, books, supplies, room and board, equipment	Cannot also claim an education credit; for undergraduate work only	None
Interest Paid on Student Loans				
Deduction from Income	$2,500	Tuition and fees, books, supplies, room and board, transportation	Applies to the first 60 months' interest; must be enrolled at least part time in a degree program	$55,000; joint returns: $75,000
Qualified State Tuition Programs				
Tax on earnings is deferred	None	Tuition and fees, books, supplies, room and board	Earnings are taxed to beneficiary when withdrawn	None
Education as a Miscellaneous Itemized Deduction				
Deduction from income	With other miscellaneous deductions, must exceed 2% of AGI	Tuition, fees, books, supplies. Some costs related to transportation, travel, and research	Must be work related and undertaken to maintain or improve job skills	None
U.S. Savings Bonds				
Interest is not taxed	Amount of qualifying expenses	Tuition, fees, payments to education IRAs and state tuition plans	Applies only to qualified series EE bonds or series I bonds	$68,100; joint returns: $109,650

*Denotes top of an income range in which the benefit is first reduced then eliminated.

FIGURE 22.1

GETTING A TAX BREAK TO PAY FOR COLLEGE

The tax code provides many incentives for higher education. This chart shows the major tax benefits available to people attending college, saving for college, or paying off student loans.

bicycle, car, jewelry, and clothes) on one side and liabilities (e.g., mortgage, credit card debt, and auto loans) on the other. Assets include anything you own. For our purpose, evaluate your assets on the basis of their current value, not purchase price as required in formal accounting statements. If you have no debts (liabilities), then your assets equal your net worth (in a corporation it's called owners' equity). If you do have debts, you have to subtract them from your assets to get your net worth.

If the value of your liabilities exceeds the value of your assets, you aren't on the path to financial security. You may need more financial discipline in your life.

Since we're talking about accounting, let's talk again about an income statement ➤P. 560◄. At the top of the statement is revenue (everything you take in from your job, investments, etc.). You subtract all your costs and expenses to get net income or profit. Software programs such as Quicken and websites such as www.dinkytown.net have a variety of tools that can easily help you with these calculations.

This may also be an excellent time to think about how much money you will need to accomplish all your goals. The more you visualize your goals, the easier it is to begin saving for them.

Crystal Hanlan started with Home Depot as a cashier several years ago. She began buying stock in the company as part of an employee ownership plan and is now worth over a million dollars. There are over a million other employees who got to be millionaires the same way. Are you getting the idea that it is a good idea to participate in such ownership programs and to put the maximum you can into such accounts?

Step 2: Keep Track of All Your Expenses You may often find yourself running out of cash (a cash flow ➤P. 564◄ problem). In such circumstances, the only way to trace where the money is going is to keep track of every cent you spend. Keeping records of your expenses can be a rather tedious but necessary chore if you want to learn discipline. Actually, it could turn out to be an enjoyable task because it gives you such a feeling of control. Here's what to do: Carry a notepad with you wherever you go and record what you spend as you go through the day. That notepad is your journal. At the end of the week, record your journal entries into a record book or computerized accounting program.

Develop certain categories (accounts) to make the task easier and more informative. For example, you can have a category called "Food" for all food you bought from the grocery or the convenience store during the week. You might want to have a separate account for meals eaten away from home because you can dramatically cut such costs if you make your lunches at home. Other accounts could include automobile, clothing, utilities, entertainment, donations to charity, and gifts. Most people like to have a category called "Miscellaneous" where they put expenditures for things like caffe latte. You won't believe how much you fritter away on miscellaneous items unless you keep a detailed record for at least a couple of months.

You can develop your accounts on the basis of what's most important to you or where you spend the most money. Once you have recorded all of your expenses, it is relatively easy to see where you are spending too much money and what you have to do to save more money.

Step 3: Prepare a Budget Once you know your financial situation and your sources of revenue and expenses, you're prepared to make a personal budget.[3] Remember, budgets are financial plans. Items that are important in a household budget include mortgage or rent, utilities, food, clothing, vehicles, furniture, life insurance, car insurance, and medical care. You'll need to make choices regarding how much to allow for such expenses as eating out, entertainment, and so on. Keep in mind that what you spend now reduces what you can save later. For example, spending $3.50 a day for cigarettes adds up to about $25 a week, $100 a month, $1,200 a year. If you can save $4 or $5 a day, you'll have almost $1,800 saved by the end of the year. Keep this up during all four years of college and you'll have saved more than $7,000 by graduation. And that's before adding any interest earned. Cost-saving choices you might consider to reach this goal are listed in Figure 22.2.

You'll learn that running a household is similar to running a small business. It takes the same careful record keeping, the same budget processes and forecasting, the same control procedures, and often (sadly) the same need to periodically borrow funds. Suddenly, concepts such as credit and interest rates become only too real. This is where some knowledge of finance, investments, and budgeting pays off. Thus, the time you spend learning budgeting techniques will benefit you throughout your life.

Step 4: Pay Off Your Debts The first thing to do with the money remaining after you pay your monthly bills is to pay off your debts. Start with the debts that carry the highest interest rates. Credit card debt, for example, may be costing you 14 percent or more a year. Merely paying off such debts will set you on a path toward financial freedom. It's better to pay off a debt that costs 14 percent than to put the money in a bank account that earns, say, only 2 percent or less.[4]

Step 5: Start a Savings Plan It's important to save some money each month in a separate account for large purchases you're likely to make (such as a car or house). Then, when it comes time to make that purchase, you'll have more cash. You should save at least enough for a significant down payment on a loan so you can reduce the finance charges.

The best way to save money is to *pay yourself first.* That is, take your paycheck, take out money for savings, and then plan what to do with the rest. You can arrange with your bank or mutual fund to deduct a certain amount every month. You will be pleasantly surprised when the money starts accumulating and earning interest over time. With some discipline, you can eventually reach

FIRST CHOICE COST PER MONTH	ALTERNATE CHOICE COST PER MONTH	SAVINGS PER MONTH
Starbucks caffe latte $3.00 for 20 days = $60.00	Quick Trip's Cappuccino $.60 for 20 days = $12.00	$48.00
Fast-food lunch of burger, fries, and soft drink $4.00 for 20 days = $80.00	Lunch brought from home $2 for 20 days = $40.00	40.00
Evian bottled water $1.50 for 20 days = $30.00	Generic bottled water $.50 for 20 days = $10.00	20.00
CD = $15.00	Listen to your old CDs = $0.00	15.00
Banana Republic T-shirt = $34.00	Old Navy T-shirt = $10.00	24.00
	Total savings per month	$147.00 × 48 months
	Total savings through 4 years of college	$7,056.00

FIGURE 22.2

POSSIBLE COST-SAVING CHOICES

The effect of the choices you make today can have a dramatic impact on your financial future. Compare the differences these few choices you can make now would mean to your future net worth. If you would make the lower-cost choices every month during your four years of college, and invest the savings in a mutual fund earning 6 percent compounded annually, you would double your money every 12 years.

FIGURE 22.3

HOW MONEY GROWS

This chart illustrates how $5,000 would grow at various rates of return. Recent savings account interest rates were very low (less than 2 percent), but in earlier years they've been over 5 percent. Annual rates of return of the S&P 500 have varied widely, but the average annual return between 1970 and 2003 was 11 percent.

	ANNUAL RATE OF RETURN			
TIME	2%	5%	8%	11%
5 years	$5,520	$ 6,381	$ 7,347	$ 8,425
10 years	6,095	8,144	10,795	14,197
15 years	6,729	10,395	15,861	23,923
20 years	7,430	13,266	23,305	40,312
25 years	8,203	16,932	34,242	67,927

your goal of becoming a millionaire. It's not as difficult as you may think. Figure 22.3 shows how $5,000 grows over various time periods at different rates of return. If you start at age 40, you'll have 25 years in by the time you reach 65.

Step 6: Borrow Money Only to Buy Assets That Have the Potential to Increase in Value or Generate Income Don't borrow money for ordinary expenses; you'll only get into more debt that way. If you have budgeted for emergencies, such as car repairs and health care costs, you should be able to stay financially secure. Most financial experts will tell you to save about six months of earnings for contingency purposes. That means keeping the money in highly liquid ►P. 558◄ accounts, such as the bank or money market fund.

Only the most unexpected of expenses should cause you to borrow. It is hard to wait until you have enough money to buy what you want, but learning to wait is a critical part of self-discipline. Of course, you can always try to produce more income by working overtime or by working on the side for extra revenue. If you must borrow, consider seeking alternative sources—see the Spotlight on Small Business box for a source of credit for women.

If you follow all six of these steps, you'll not only have money for investment but you'll have developed most of the financial techniques needed to become financially secure. At first you may find it hard to live within a budget. Nonetheless, the payoff is well worth the pain.

Critical Thinking

How would your life change if you were to implement the six steps outlined above? Would it be worth the time and effort if you knew you could become a millionaire by following them? What advice would you give college students who are not sure they should follow such a program?

BUILDING YOUR FINANCIAL BASE

The path to success in a capitalist system is to have capital (money) to invest, yet the trend today for graduates is to be not only capital-poor but also in debt. As you've read, accumulating capital takes discipline and careful planning. With the money you save, however, you can become an entrepreneur, one of the fastest ways to wealth. As you read in the chapter opening profile, that often means living frugally.

Living frugally is extremely difficult for the average person. Most people are eager to spend their money on a new car, furniture, CDs, clothes, and the like. They tend to look for a fancy apartment with all the amenities. A capital-generating strategy may require forgoing most (though not all) of these purchases to accumulate investment money. The living style required is similar to the one adopted by most college students: a relatively inexpensive apartment furnished in hand-me-downs from parents, friends, and resale shops.

Spotlight on Small Business

www.count-me-in.org

Financing for Tom, Dick, but Not Mary

Women-owned businesses are America's fastest-growing employers. That is good for the women and good for the community because small businesses provide both jobs and wealth to help a community grow. Yet at a White House women's economic summit, Iris Burnett and Nell Merlino found that women were having a serious problem getting access to credit. Often, their work and their family lives did not conform to the standard credit-rating scores. They found, for example, that women may be out of the workforce for years or they may get a bad credit rating because they were once married to men who had bad credit ratings. In any case, getting money from the bank or other standard sources was very difficult for some women.

Merlino is the woman who started Take Our Daughters and Sons to Work Day. She and Burnett decided that it would be a good idea to create a fund that would lend money to women who were starting or expanding a small business. The fund drive is called Count Me In for Women's Economic Independence. They developed a website as well: www.count-me-in.org. The idea is for lots of people to donate $5 or more to create a fund. That fund would make loans of $500 to $10,000 to women. (First-time loans can't exceed $5,000.) If the women repaid a $5,000 loan on time, they could get a loan of up to $10,000. The goal is to show banks that women are good risks in the hope that banks will make more such loans themselves. Meanwhile, the founders of the fund are working to rewrite the conventional credit-scoring system to reflect the realities of women's lives. "Even if women aren't in the workforce, they often have been doing volunteer work on the side, such as fund-raising for a homeless shelter," Burnett says. That experience should count toward getting funds.

While women own 38 percent of the businesses in the United States, only 1.7 percent of the $12 billion in venture capital committed to new businesses went to projects owned by women in a recent year. Count Me In now has $1 million available that women can use to start more businesses and help themselves and their communities.

Source: www.count-me-in.org/press/newsletter.html.

For five or six years, you can manage with the old sound system, a used car, and a few nice clothes. The necessary living style is one of sacrifice, not luxury. It's important not to feel burdened by this plan; instead, feel happy knowing that your financial future will be more secure. That's the way the majority of millionaires got their money. If living frugally seems too restrictive for you, you can still save a little. It's better to save a smaller amount than none at all.

People are wise to plan their financial future with the same excitement and dedication they bring to other aspects of their lives. When you get married, it is important to discuss financial issues with your spouse. Conflicts over money are a major cause of divorce, so agreeing on a financial strategy before marriage is very important. A great strategy is to try to live on one income and to save the other. The longer you wait before marriage, the more likely it will be that one or the other of you can be earning enough to do that—as college graduates. If the second spouse makes $18,000 a year after taxes, saving that income for five years quickly adds up to $90,000 (plus interest).

What do you do with the money you accumulate? The first investment might be a low-priced home. You should make this investment as early as possible. The purpose of this investment is to lock in payments for your shelter at a fixed amount. This is possible by owning a home, but not by renting. Through the years, home ownership has been a wise investment.

Real Estate: A Relatively Secure Investment

Homes provide several investment benefits. First, a home is the one investment that you can live in. Second, once you buy a home, the payments are relatively fixed (though taxes and utilities go up). As your income rises, the house payments get easier and easier to make, but renters often find that rents tend to go

Some see mortgage payments as a form of forced savings. Government helps by giving you tax breaks for the interest and taxes you pay. By buying a duplex, living on one side and renting the other, you can even generate income. Have you compared the cost of owning versus renting in your area?

up at least as fast as income. Paying for a home is a good way of forcing yourself to save. Every month you must make the payments. Those payments are an investment that prove very rewarding over time for most people.

Some couples have used the seed money accumulated from saving one income (in the strategy outlined above) to buy a duplex home (two attached homes). They live in one part of the duplex and rent out the other. The rent covers a good part of the payments for both homes, so they can be housed very cheaply while their investment in a home appreciates. They learn that it's quite possible to live comfortably, yet inexpensively, for several years. In this way they accumulate capital. As they grow older, they see that such a strategy has put them years ahead of their peers in terms of financial security. As capital accumulates and values rise, they can sell and buy an even larger apartment building or a single-family home. Many fortunes have been made in real estate in just such a manner. Furthermore, a home is a good asset to use when applying for a loan.

Once you understand the benefits of home ownership versus renting, you can decide whether those same principles apply to owning the building if you set up your own business—or owning versus renting equipment, vehicles, and the like. Furthermore, you may start thinking of real estate as a way to earn a living. You could, for example, buy older homes, fix them up, and sell them—a path many millionaires have taken to attain financial security. Figure 22.4 will give you some idea of how expensive a house you can afford, given your income. You can find current mortgage interest rates and mortgage calculators at www.interest.com.

Tax Deduction and Home Ownership Buying a home is likely to be the largest and perhaps the most important investment you'll make. It's nice to know that the federal government is willing to help you with that investment. Here's how: Interest on your home mortgage payments is tax deductible. So are your real estate taxes. Since during the first few years, virtually all the mortgage payments go for interest on the loan, almost all the early payments are tax deductible—a tremendous benefit for home owners and investors. If, for

INCOME	MONTHLY PAYMENT	INTEREST RATES 5%	6%	7%	15%
$ 30,000	$ 700	$106,263	$ 98,303	$ 91,252	$ 56,870
50,000	1,167	180,291	167,081	155,376	98,606
80,000	1,867	287,213	266,056	247,308	155,916
100,000	2,333	361,240	334,832	311,433	198,013

Source: Federal Housing Finance Board.

FIGURE 22.4

HOW MUCH HOUSE CAN YOU AFFORD?

Monthly mortgage payments—including interest, principal, real estate taxes, and insurance—generally shouldn't amount to more than 28 percent of monthly income. Here's how much people in various income categories can afford to pay for a home if they use a 30-year mortgage and make a 10 percent down payment. How do you think the changes in mortgage interest rates affect the average price of homes?

example, your payments are $1,000 a month and your income is in the 25 percent tax bracket, then during the early years of your mortgage Uncle Sam will, in effect, give you credit for about $250 of your payment, lowering your real cost to $750. This makes home ownership much more competitive with renting than it may appear on the surface.

Experienced real estate investors will tell you that there are three keys to getting the optimum return on a home: location, location, and location. A home in the best part of town, near schools, shopping, and work, is usually a sound financial investment. Often young people tend to go farther away from town, where homes are less expensive, but such homes may appreciate in value much more slowly than homes in the city or town center. It's important to learn where the best place to buy is. It's usually better, from a financial viewpoint, to buy a small home in a great location than a large home in a not-so-great setting.

Progress Assessment

- What are the six steps you can take today to control your finances?
- What steps should a person follow to build capital?
- Why is real estate a good investment?

Where to Put Your Savings

You have learned that one place to invest the money you have saved is in a home. What are some other good places to save your money? For a young person, one of the worst places to keep long-term investments is in a bank or savings and loan. As noted earlier, it is important to have about six months' savings in the bank for emergencies, but the bank is not the best place to invest.

One of the best places to invest over time has been the stock market. The stock market does tend to go up and down, but over a longer period of time it has proved to be one of the best investments. That's important because about half of U.S. households own stock and roughly the same percentage own mutual funds.[5] Most financial experts believe that the stock market will grow more slowly in the future than it has over the last 50 years, but that may not be true. The U.S. economy has always managed to rise up after a crisis like the stock market fall of recent years.

The future always looks gloomy during a financial crisis, but that doesn't mean you shouldn't take risks. Remember, the greater the risk, the greater the return. When stocks are low, that is the time to *buy*. Actually, when stocks collapse, as they did in recent years, that is an opportunity to get into the stock market, not avoid it. The average investor buys when the market is high and sells when it is low. Clearly, that is not a good idea. It takes courage to buy when everyone else is selling. That is called a **contrarian approach** to investing. In the long run, however, that's the way the rich get richer.

contrarian approach
Buying stock when everyone else is selling or vice versa.

Chapter 20 gave you a foundation for starting an investment program. That chapter also talked about bonds, but bonds have traditionally lagged behind stocks as a long-term investment.

Learning to Manage Credit

Known as *plastic* to young buyers, credit cards are no doubt familiar to you. Names like Visa, MasterCard, American Express, Discover, and Diners Club are well known to most people. In a credit card purchase, finance charges usually amount to anywhere from 12 to 20 percent annually. This means that if you finance a TV, home appliances, and other purchases with a credit card, you may end up spending much more than if you pay with cash. A good manager of personal finances, like a good businessperson, pays on time and takes advantage of savings made possible by paying early. People who've established a capital fund can tap that fund to make large purchases and pay the fund back (with interest if so desired) rather than pay a bank finance charges.

Credit cards are an important element in a personal financial system, even if they're rarely used. First, some merchants request credit cards as a form of identification. It may be difficult to buy certain goods or even rent a car without owning a credit card because businesses use them for identification and assured payment. Second, credit cards can be used to keep track of purchases. A gasoline credit card, for example, gives you records of purchases over time for income tax and financial planning purposes. It's sometimes easier to write one check at the end of the month for several purchases than to carry cash around. Besides, when cash is stolen or lost, it is simply gone; a stolen credit card can be canceled to protect your account.

Finally, a credit card is simply more convenient than cash or checks. If you come upon a special sale and need more money than you usually carry, paying by credit is quick and easy. You can carry less cash and don't have to worry about keeping your checkbook balanced as often.

Many consumers, especially first time credit card owners, are unable to properly manage them and often end up with severely damaged credit ratings, or worse, in bankruptcy. That's why it may be a good idea for you to pass up the free T-shirt or other offer made by credit card companies.

Dealing with Change www.debtwizards.com/college.htm

Give Me Credit or Give Me Death

College students today use cash for only 42 percent of their purchases. The rest are bought with credit, debit, or ATM cards or even their college IDs. Over 35 percent of freshmen and 60 percent of seniors have their own credit cards. The change from paying cash to buying things on credit is often a traumatic one for students. Often, they simply don't have the experience, or sometimes the self-control, to manage such freedom to buy what they want. Some students are taking on "substantial debt loads that will clearly affect them for the rest of their lives," says a law professor at the University of Houston. A student with a balance of $3,000 on a credit card with an 18 to 20 annual percentage rate who pays the minimum 3 percent monthly payment would take about 15 years to pay off the debt (and that's without using the card again to purchase so much as a candy bar). In addition, the student would end up paying *double* the initial amount of the purchases.

Students are nearly three times as likely to be at least 90 days delinquent on their credit card payments as older adults. Yet credit card issuers don't experience large losses because parents often bail students out. Nonetheless, the need for students to better manage credit cards is clear. One college junior was forced to drop out of school when her credit card charges got out of hand. She still has $10,000 in credit card debt and $23,000 in student loans taken out to pay down debt. Some students are better off with a debit card or stored-value card that sets limits on the amount that can be spent. In fact, debit cards and ATM cards are more popular on campus than credit cards.

Many adults have similar problems handling the freedom of having credit cards available. Often that results in debt from buying expensive new cars and other over-the-top items. Changing from a lifestyle where one spends freely to one where one carefully watches every dime is a major undertaking. Do you know people who suffer from credit card debt? How hard does it seem for them to get rid of that debt? Wouldn't it be a lot easier not to get into such debt in the first place?

Source: Ruth Simon and Christine Whelan, "The New Credo on Campus: Just Charge It," *The Wall Street Journal,* September 3, 2002, pp. D1, D4; "College Students Rake in Too Much Credit Card Debt," U-Wire, Chicago, May 13, 2002 (northernlight.com); and "By the Numbers," *Washington Times,* February 12, 2003, p. A3.

If you do use a credit card, you should pay the balance in full during the period when no interest is charged. Not having to pay 14 percent interest is as good as earning 14 percent tax free. Also, you may want to choose a card that pays you back in cash, like the Discover card, or others that offer paybacks like credits toward the purchase of a car, free long-distance minutes, or frequent-flier miles. The value of these givebacks can be from 1 to 5 percent. Rather than pay 14 percent, you earn a certain percentage—quite a difference. Some cards have no annual fees; others have lower interest rates. To compare credit cards, check out www.cardratings.com or www.angelfire.com/ny/erte2001/cardinfo.html.

The danger of a credit card is the flip side of its convenience. Too often, consumers buy goods and services that they wouldn't normally buy if they had to pay cash or write a check on funds in the bank. Using credit cards, consumers often pile up debts to the point where they're unable to pay. If you aren't the type who can stick to a financial plan or household budget, *it may be better not to have a credit card at all.* The Dealing with Change box explores alternatives to credit card use, such as debit cards. Debit cards are like credit cards, but they won't let you spend more than a predetermined amount, a great benefit for those who are not as careful with their spending as they should be.

Credit cards are a helpful tool to the financially careful buyer. They're a financial disaster to people with little financial restraint and tastes beyond their income. College students take note: Of the debtors seeking help at the National Consumer Counseling Service, more than half were between 18 and 32. The Making Ethical Decisions box on p. 680 discusses giving free gifts to students to get them to apply for credit cards.

www.abiworld.org

Making Ethical Decisions

Giving Credit Cards to Students

They seem to be everywhere—people eager to give away free gifts, like T-shirts and pennants. They are free for the asking. All you have to do is fill out an application for a credit card. Do you want an extra 10 percent off on a store purchase? Just fill out the application for a store credit card. The offers come in the mail and over the Internet. Get a credit card now!!

Students in high school are also targeted for such free offers. More than 70 percent of students in college now have at least one credit card. Others have debit cards. The average balance is $3,066. For many students, the balance is a lot higher.

You have a chance to work part-time for a credit card company passing out free gifts and urging students to sign up. You have noticed that many students abuse such cards and build up debt way beyond what they can afford. The pay is pretty good, however, and it's not your fault that students don't always handle credit cards well. Would you accept the job? What are the ethical issues involved? What might be the consequences of doing such work?

PROTECTING YOUR FINANCIAL BASE: BUYING INSURANCE

One of the last things young people think about is the idea that they may get sick or have an accident and die. It is not a pleasant thought. Even more unpleasant, though, is the reality of young people dying every day in accidents and other unexpected ways. You have to know only one of these families to see the emotional and financial havoc such a loss causes.

Today, with so many husbands and wives both working, the loss of a spouse means a sudden drop in income. To provide protection from such risks, a couple or business should buy life insurance.

term insurance
Pure insurance protection for a given number of years.

Today, the least expensive and simplest form of life insurance is **term insurance**. It is pure insurance protection for a given number of years that typically costs less the younger you buy it (see Figure 22.5). Every few years, however, you might have to renew the policy, and the premium could go higher. It's helpful to check out prices for term insurance through a Web-based service. For example, try www.quickeninsurance.com or www.insweb.com. Be sure to give them as much information as possible to get the most accurate and best rates.

How much insurance do you need? *Newsweek* magazine posed this question: We just had our first baby; how much life insurance should we have? Answer: Seven times your family income plus $100,000 for college. To be fair, apportion it so that a spouse earning 60 percent of the income carries 60 percent of the insurance.[6]

It is a good idea before buying life insurance to check out the insurance company through a rating service such as A. M. Best (www.ambest.com) or Moody's Investors Service (www.moodys.com). One of the newer forms of term insurance is something called multiyear level-premium insurance. It guarantees that you'll pay the same premium for the life of the policy. Recently, 40 percent of new term policies guaranteed a set rate for 20 years or more. Some companies allow you to switch your term policy for a more expensive whole or universal life policy.

whole life insurance
Life insurance that stays in effect until age 100.

Whole life insurance is another type of life insurance. Some part of the money you pay for whole life insurance goes toward pure insurance and another part goes toward savings, so you are buying both insurance and a savings plan. This may be a good idea for those people who have trouble saving money. A universal life policy lets you choose how much of your payment should go to insurance and how much to investments. The investments traditionally were very conservative but paid a steady interest rate.

INSURANCE NEEDS IN EARLY YEARS ARE HIGH.	INSURANCE NEEDS DECLINE AS YOU GROW OLDER.
1. Children are young and need money for education. 2. Mortgage is high relative to income. 3. Often there are auto payments and other bills to pay. 4. Loss of income would be disastrous.	1. Children are grown. 2. Mortgage is low or completely paid off. 3. Debts are paid off. 4. Insurance needs are few. 5. Retirement income is needed.

FIGURE 22.5

WHY BUY TERM INSURANCE?

Variable life insurance is a form of whole life insurance that invests the cash value of the policy in stocks or other high-yielding securities. Death benefits may thus vary, reflecting the performance of the investments. Some people, seeing the stock market go up for so many years, switched out of whole life policies to get the higher potential returns of variable life insurance. When the stock market plunged, they were not so certain of the wisdom of their choice. In the long run, however, stocks should rise again.

variable life insurance
Whole life insurance that invests the cash value of the policy in stocks or other high-yielding securities.

Life insurance companies recognized the desire that people had for higher returns on their insurance (and for protecting themselves against running out of money before they die) and began selling annuities. An **annuity** is a contract to make regular payments to a person for life or for a fixed period. With an annuity, you are guaranteed to have an income until you die. There are two kinds of annuities: fixed and variable. *Fixed annuities* are investments that pay the policyholder a specified interest rate. They are not as popular as *variable annuities,* which provide investment choices identical to mutual funds. Such annuities are gaining in popularity relative to term or whole life insurance. Clearly, people have been choosing more risk to get greater returns when they retire. This means, however, that people must be more careful in selecting an insurance company and what investments are made with their money.

annuity
A contract to make regular payments to a person for life or for a fixed period.

Because life insurance is getting much more complex, before buying any insurance, it may be wise to consult a financial adviser who is not an insurance agent. He or she can help you make the wisest decision about insurance.

Health Insurance

Individuals need to consider protecting themselves from losses due to health problems. You may have health insurance coverage through your employer. If not, you can buy insurance from a health insurance provider (e.g., Blue Cross/Blue Shield), a health maintenance organization (HMO), or a preferred provider organization (PPO). For quick online help in picking a health insurance provider, try www.EHealthInsurance.com or www.healthaxis.com (not available in all areas). You may be able to buy health insurance for less by buying it through a professional organization. Be sure to do a careful search to find the best program for you and your family.

It's dangerous financially not to have any health insurance. Hospital costs are simply too high to risk financial ruin by going uninsured. In fact, it's often a good idea to supplement health insurance policies with **disability insurance** that pays part of the cost of a long-term sickness or an accident. Your chances of becoming disabled at an early age are much higher than your chances of dying from an accident. Therefore, it's important to have the proper amount of disability insurance. Call an insurance agent or check the Internet for possible costs of such insurance. The cost is relatively low to protect yourself from losing your income for an extended period.

disability insurance
Insurance that pays part of the cost of a long-term sickness or an accident.

Homeowners or Renter's Insurance

As you begin to accumulate possessions, you may want to seriously consider getting insurance to cover their loss. You may be surprised to see how much it would cost to replace all the clothes, furniture, pots and pans, appliances, sporting goods, electronic equipment (e.g., computers, VCRs, and the like), and the other things you own. Apartment insurance or homeowners insurance covers such losses. But you must be careful to specify that you want *guaranteed replacement cost*. That means that the insurance company will give you whatever it costs to buy all of those things new. Such insurance costs a little bit more than a policy without guaranteed replacement, but you will get a lot more if you have a loss.

The other option is to buy insurance that covers the depreciated cost of the items. For example, a sofa you bought five years ago for $600 may only be worth $150 now. The current value is what you would get from insurance, not the $700 or more you may need to buy a brand-new sofa. The same is true for a computer you paid $950 for a few years ago. If it were to be stolen, you would get only a few hundred dollars for it rather than the replacement cost.

Most policies don't cover expensive items like engagement and wedding rings and silver pieces of all kinds. You can buy a *rider* to your insurance policy that will cover such items at a very reasonable cost. Ask your agent about such coverage.

Other Insurance

You should buy insurance for your car. In fact, most states require that drivers have automobile insurance. Get a large deductible of $500 or so to keep the premiums lower, and cover small damages on your own. Be sure to include insurance against losses from uninsured motorists.

You'll also need liability insurance to protect yourself against being sued by someone accidentally injured by you. Often you can get a discount by buying all your insurance (life, health, homeowners, automobile, etc.) with one company. This is called an **umbrella policy**. Also, look for other discounts. GEICO, for example, gives discounts for safe driving, good grades, and more.

umbrella policy
A broadly based insurance policy that saves you money because you buy all your insurance from one company.

PLANNING YOUR RETIREMENT

It may seem a bit early to be planning your retirement; however, not doing so would be a big mistake. Successful financial planning means long-range planning, and retirement is a critical phase of life. What you do now could make a world of difference in your quality of life after age 65 or whenever you retire.

Social Security

Social Security
The term used to describe the Old-Age, Survivors, and Disability Insurance Program established by the Social Security Act of 1935.

Social Security is the term used to describe the Old-Age, Survivors, and Disability Insurance Program established by the Social Security Act of 1935. There's little question that by the time you retire, there will have been significant changes in the Social Security system. There is even talk today of making part of the system private.[7] Although the media talk about it all the time, there really is no Social Security trust fund.[8] The money you receive when you retire comes directly from the Social Security taxes being paid by others. The problem is that the number of people retiring and living longer is increasing dramatically, though the number of workers paying into Social Security per retiree is declining. The results are likely to include serious cuts in benefits, a much later average retirement age, reduced cost-of-living adjustments (COLAs), and/or much higher Social Security taxes.

The moral of the story is: Don't count on Social Security to provide you with ample funds for retirement.[9] Rather, plan now to save funds for your nonworking years. Recognizing Social Security's potential downfall, the government has established incentives for you to save money now for retirement. The following section gives the specifics.

Individual Retirement Accounts (IRAs)

Traditionally, an **individual retirement account (IRA)** has been a tax-deferred investment plan that enables you (and your spouse, if you are married) to save part of your income for retirement. A traditional IRA allows people who qualify to deduct from their reported income the money they put into an account. **Tax-deferred contributions** are those for which you pay no current taxes, but the earnings gained in the IRA are taxed as income when they are withdrawn from your IRA after retirement.[10]

individual retirement account (IRA)
A tax-deferred investment plan that enables you (and your spouse, if you are married) to save part of your income for retirement; a traditional IRA allows people who qualify to deduct from their reported income the money they put into an account.

tax-deferred contributions
Retirement account deposits for which you pay no current taxes, but the earnings gained are taxed as regular income when they are withdrawn at retirement.

Let's see why a traditional IRA is a good deal for an investor. The tremendous benefit is the fact that the invested money is not taxed. That means fast, and good, returns for you. For example, say you put $3,000 into an IRA each year. (The maximum IRA contribution was $3,000 in 2004 and will gradually increase to $5,000 by 2008. If you're 50 or older, you can make an additional $500–$1,000 "catch-up" contribution.) Normally, you'd pay taxes on that $3,000 when you receive it as income. But because you put the money into an IRA, you won't have to pay those taxes. If you're in the 25 percent tax bracket, that means you save $750 in taxes! Put another way, the $3,000 you save only costs you $2,250—a huge bargain.

The earlier you start saving the better because your money has a chance to double and double again. If you save $3,000 a year for 35 years in an IRA and earn 11 percent a year, you'll accumulate savings of more than $1 million. If you start when you are just out of school, you'll be a millionaire by the time you're 55. All you have to do is save $3,000 a year and earn 11 percent. If you increase your contribution to the maximum allowable each time it is raised, you can reach your million-dollar goal even earlier. The actual rate of return depends on the type of investments you choose. It is important to remember that future rates of return can't be predicted with certainty and that investments that pay higher rates of return also have higher risk and volatility. For example, the stock market was booming in the mid to late 1990s and then plummeted for several years starting in 1999. The actual rate of return on investments can vary widely over time, but the average for the S&P 500 between 1970 and 2003 was 11 percent a year.[11]

The earlier you start the better. Consider this: If you were to start contributing $3,000 to an IRA earning 11 percent when you're 22 years old and do so for only five years, you'd have nearly $21,000 by the time you're 27. Even if you *never added another penny* to the IRA, by the time you're 65 you'd have a little more than $1 million. If you waited until you were 30 to start saving, you would need to save $3,000 every year for 35 years to have the same nest egg. And what would you have if you started saving at 22 *and* continued nonstop every year until 65? More than $2.6 million! Can you see

More and more women in the United States are becoming financially independent—and in need of sound financial planning. This ad is a direct appeal to women in general to seek and use help from a financial advisor. Are the financial planning needs of women somehow different from men, as this ad may suggest?

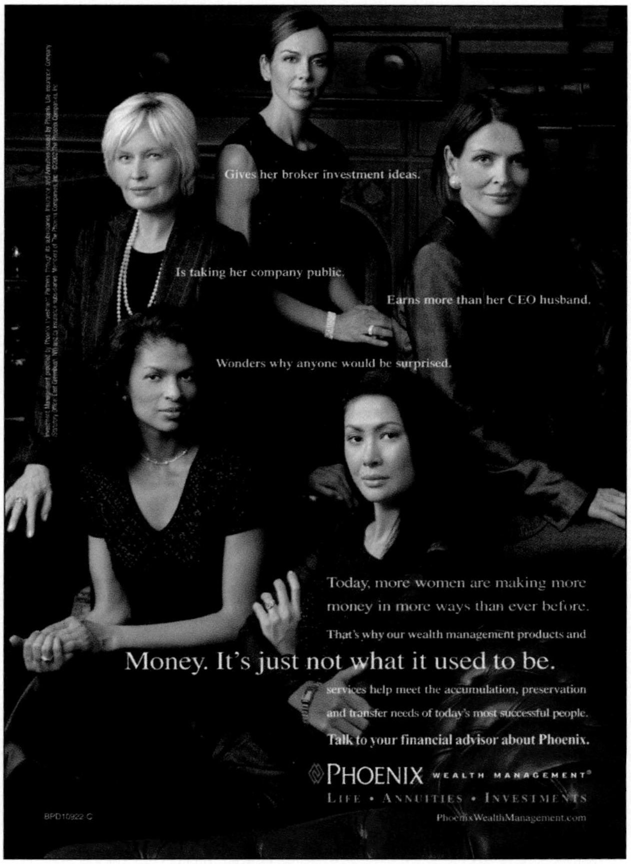

why investment advisers often say that an IRA is the best way to invest in your retirement?

Roth IRA
An IRA where you don't get up-front deductions on your taxes as you would with a traditional IRA, but the earnings grow tax-free and are also tax-free when they are withdrawn.

A more recent kind of IRA is called a **Roth IRA.** People who invest in a Roth IRA don't get up-front deductions on their taxes as they would with a traditional IRA, but the earnings grow tax-free and are also tax-free when they are withdrawn. So in sum, traditional IRAs offer tax savings when they are deposited and Roth IRAs offer tax savings when they are withdrawn. Financial planners highly recommend IRAs, but they differ as to which kind is best. Both have advantages and disadvantages, so you should check with a financial adviser to determine which would be best for you.[12] You may decide to have both kinds of accounts. For more details about IRAs, check out the MoneyChimp website (www.moneychimp.com), run by a group of self-proclaimed amateur investors. See Figure 22.6 for a brief comparison of Roth versus traditional IRAs.

One key point to remember is you can't take the money out of either type of IRA until you are 59 1/2 years old without paying a 10 percent penalty and paying taxes on the income. On the one hand, that's a benefit for you, because it can keep you from tapping into your IRA when an emergency comes up or you're tempted to make a large impulse purchase. On the other hand, the money is there if a real need or emergency arises. For example, the government now allows you to take out some funds to invest in an education or a first home. But check the rules; they change over time.

A wide range of investment choices is available when you open an IRA. Your local bank, savings and loan, and credit union all have different types of IRAs. Insurance companies offer such plans as well. You may prefer to be a bit aggressive with this money to earn a higher return. In that case, you can put your IRA funds into stocks, bonds, mutual funds, or precious metals. Some mutual funds have multiple options (gold stocks, government securities, high-tech stocks, and more). You can switch from fund to fund or from investment to investment with your IRA funds. You can even open several different IRAs as long as the total amount invested doesn't exceed the government's limit. You might consider contributing to an IRA through payroll deductions to ensure that the money is invested before you're tempted to spend it. Opening an IRA may be one of the wisest investments you make.

Simple IRAs Companies with 100 or fewer employees can provide their workers with a simple IRA. Basically, that means that employees can contribute a larger part (up to $9,000 in 2004; $10,000 in 2005) of their income annually than they can with the regular IRAs ($3,000–$5,000). The company matches the contribution.[13] This new plan enables people to save much more money over time and makes for a good employee benefit for smaller companies. Simple IRAs can help companies with 100 or fewer employees compete for available workers.

401(k) Plans

401(k) plan
A savings plan that allows you to deposit pretax dollars and whose earnings compound tax free until withdrawal, when the money is taxed at ordinary income tax rates.

A **401(k) plan** is a savings plan that allows you to deposit pretax dollars and whose earnings compound tax free until withdrawal, when the money is taxed at ordinary income tax rates. 401(k) plans now account for 49 percent of America's private pension savings. More than 220,000 companies now offer 401(k) retirement plans covering some 55 million workers.[14] For 28 percent of these employees, a 401(k) or similar defined-contribution plan is their only pension.[15] One problem is that only 72 percent of eligible employees make any contributions.[16] That is a huge mistake, as you will see.

These plans have three benefits: (1) The money you put in reduces your present taxable income, (2) tax is deferred on the earnings, and (3) employers often match part of your deposit. More than 80 percent of 401(k) plans offer a

	TRADITIONAL IRA	ROTH IRA
Maximum Contributions	$3,000 per person for the 2002–2004 tax years; $3,500 if age 50 or over. Contributions must be from earned income.	$3,000 per person for the 2002–2004 tax years; $2,500 if age 50 or over. Contributions must be from earned income.
Eligibility	No income-based limits for nondeductible contributions, but you must be under age 70½.	Anyone with an AGI subject to the following income limits. **Single filers:** Up to $95,000 for a full contribution; $95,000 to $110,000 for a partial contribution. **Joint filers:** Up to $150,000 for a full contribution; $150,000 to $160,000 for a partial contribution. (If you're married and filing separately, the eligibility phase-out range is between $0 and $10,000.)
Contribution Deductibility	For the 2002 tax year, contributions are fully tax deductible for single filers with an adjusted gross income (AGI) of up to $34, 000 and joint filers with an AGI of up to $54,000. Deductibility phases out for single filers with an AGI over $44,000 and for joint filers with an AGI over $64,000. Contributions are also tax-deductible for anyone not covered by an employer sponsored retirement plan, regardless of their AGI.	Contributions are not tax-deductible.
Taxation on Earnings	Earnings are tax-deferred until withdrawn. You can take withdrawals prior to age 59½ without facing the IRS's 10 percent penalty tax on early withdrawals (although you'll owe income taxes) for certain qualified reasons, which include: a first-time home purchase (up to $10,000); qualified higher education expenses; deductible medical expenses that exceed 7.5 percent of your AGI; death; or disability. Other withdrawals prior to age 59½ are generally subject to the 10 percent IRS penalty tax in addition to regular income tax.	Earnings are tax-deferred until withdrawn. You can withdraw earnings *completely tax-free* provided the IRA has been in place for at least five years and the withdrawal meets at least one of the additional requirements: It's made after age 59½; the taxpayer becomes disabled; the distribution goes to a beneficiary of the taxpayer's estate after the taxpayer's death; the withdrawal is used to pay for first-time homebuyer expenses (up to $10,000). Otherwise, earnings are subject to ordinary income taxes and, if applicable, the IRS's 10 percent early withdrawal penalty. To avoid this penalty tax, the taxpayer must meet one of the IRS's qualifying events, which include: reaching age 59½; using the funds for qualified higher education expenses or a first-time home purchase; deductible medical expenses that exceed 7.5 percent of AGI; disability; or death.
Advantages	• Tax-deferred earnings. • Tax-deductible contributions, if you qualify. • You can take early withdrawals penalty-tax free (but not income-tax free) if you withdrawals qualify (see above).	• Tax-deferred earnings. • You can withdraw contributions penalty-tax and income-tax free whenever you wish. • Earnings can be withdrawn completely tax-free if your withdrawals qualify (see above). • No required minimum distribution rules at age 70½. You can also contribute past age 70½.
Disadvantages	• The ability to deduct contributions is not available to everyone. • You must take required minimum distributions at age 70½, and you cannot contribute past age 70½.	• Contributions are never tax-deductible.

FIGURE 22.6

TRADITIONAL VERSUS ROTH IRA

Source: *TIAA-CREF Participant,* FEBRUARY 2003, P. 8.

The value of Roy Rinard's 401(k) plunged from $475,000 to $2,800 when his company, Enron, collapsed. Enron's stock had been rising at a rapid rate, encouraging him to hold it rather than diversify into a variety of stocks and bonds. Rinard, who had planned to retire at age 58, now thinks he will have to work until he dies. If you've already started to save for your retirement, is your portfolio well diversified?

match, sometimes 50 cents on a dollar. No investment will give you a better deal than an instant 50 percent return on your money. You should deposit at least as much as your employer matches, often up to 15 percent of your salary. You normally can't withdraw funds from this account until you're 59 1/2, but often you can borrow from the account. You can usually select how the money in a 401(k) plan is invested: stocks, bonds, and in some cases real estate. Be careful not to invest all your money in the company where you work. Although the company may be doing quite well, it could collapse and leave you with almost nothing. During the scandals of the early 2000s, many employees, such as those at Enron, lost their 401(k) money.[17] It is always best to diversify your funds among different companies and among stocks, bonds, and real estate investment trusts.

Like the simple IRA, there is a simple 401(k) plan for those firms that employ 100 or fewer employees. Employees again are allowed to invest an amount (maximum of $9,000 in 2004; $10,000 in 2005) that is matched by the employer. This is a rather new program, but it should also prove popular among small businesses in attracting new workers.

Keogh Plans

Millions of small-business owners don't have the benefit of a corporate retirement system. Such people can contribute to an IRA, but the amount they can invest is limited. The alternative for all those doctors, lawyers, real estate agents, artists, writers, and other self-employed people is to establish their own Keogh plan. It's like an IRA for entrepreneurs ➤P. 4◀. You can also check into simplified employee pension (SEP) plans, which are the best types of IRAs for sole proprietors.

The advantage of Keogh plans is that the maximum that can be invested is $40,000 per year. The original amount was much lower, but the government wanted to encourage self-employed people to build retirement funds.

Like traditional IRAs, Keogh funds aren't taxed until they are withdrawn, nor are the returns the funds earn. Thus, a person in the 25 percent tax bracket who invests $10,000 yearly in a Keogh saves $2,500 in taxes. That means, in essence, that the government is financing 25 percent of his or her retirement fund. As with an IRA, this is an excellent deal.

As with an IRA, there's a 10 percent penalty for early withdrawal. Also like an IRA, funds may be withdrawn in a lump sum or spread out over the years. However, the key decision is the one you make now—to begin early to put funds into an IRA, a Keogh plan, or both so that the "magic" of compounding can turn that money into a sizable retirement fund.

Financial Planners

If the idea of developing a comprehensive financial plan for yourself or your business seems overwhelming, relax; help is available. The people who assist in developing a comprehensive program that covers investments, taxes, insurance, and other financial matters are called financial planners.[18] Be careful, though—anybody and his brother or sister can claim to be a financial planner today. It's often best to find a person who has earned the distinction of being a certified financial planner (CFP). To earn the distinction of CFP, a person must complete a curriculum on 106 financial topics and a 10-hour examination. In the United States today there are about 36,000 planners with the CFP distinction. Unfortunately, many so-called financial planners are simply life insurance salespeople or mutual fund salespeople. Businesspeople often turn to their accountants or finance department for legitimate financial planning help.

In the past few years, there has been an explosion in the number of companies offering financial services. Such companies are sometimes called one-stop financial centers or financial supermarkets because they provide a variety of financial services, ranging from banking service to mutual funds, insurance, tax assistance, stocks, bonds, and real estate. It pays to shop around for financial advice. Ask around among your friends and family. Find someone who understands your situation and is willing to spend some time with you.

Most financial planners begin with life insurance. They feel that most people should have basic term insurance coverage. They also explore your health insurance plans. They look for both medical expense and disability coverage. They may also recommend major medical protection to cover catastrophic illnesses.

Financial planning covers all aspects of investing, all the way to retirement and death. Financial planners can advise you on the proper mix of IRAs, stocks, bonds, real estate, and so on.

Estate Planning

It is never too early to begin thinking about estate planning, although you may be far from the time when you may retire. You may even help your parents or others to do such planning. If so, you need to know some basics. An important first step is to select a guardian for your minor children. That person should have a genuine concern for your children as well as a parental style and moral beliefs that you endorse. As part of the process you should ensure that you leave sufficient resources to rear your children, not only for living expenses, but for medical expenses, college, and other major expenses. Often life insurance is a good way to assure such a fund. Be sure to discuss all these issues with the guardian and choose a contingent guardian in case the first choice is unable to perform the functions.

A second step is to prepare a will. A **will** is a document that names the guardian for your children, states how you want your assets distributed, and names the executor for your estate. An **executor** assembles and values your estate, files income and other taxes, and distributes assets.

A third step is to prepare a durable power of attorney. This document gives an individual you name the power to take over your finances if you become incapacitated. A durable power of attorney for health care delegates power to a person named to make health decisions for you if you are unable to make such decisions yourself.

will
A document that names the guardian for your children, states how you want your assets distributed, and names the executor for your estate.

executor
A person who assembles and values your estate, files income and other taxes, and distributes assets.

Tim Ulbrich is an investment broker with A. G. Edwards & Sons. In today's complex economic environment, almost everyone could use some investment advice. Be careful to find someone who understands your wants and needs and can meet them effectively. Begin by determining the most reputable firms in your area. Then interview several investment professionals, finding the one that matches your personality and investment objectives.

There are other steps to follow that are beyond the scope of this text. You may need to contact a financial planner/attorney to help you prepare the paper work and do the planning necessary to preserve and protect your investments for your children and spouse (and others). There are whole books on estate planning, so we can only give you a hint as to what is involved. But it all begins with a strong financial base.

As you have read thus far, accumulating enough funds to be financially secure is a complex and difficult matter. Investing that money and protecting it from loss makes the process even more involved. It is never too early to start a saving and investment program. As you have learned, there are many, many millionaires in the United States and around the world. They have taken various paths to their wealth, but the most common ones are entrepreneurship and wise money management. We hope this chapter helps you join their ranks.

Progress Assessment

- What are three advantages of using a credit card?
- What kind of life insurance is recommended for most people?
- What are the advantages of investing through an IRA? A Keogh account? A 401(k) account?
- What are the main steps to take in estate planning?

Summary

1. Describe the six steps of learning to control your assets.

1. There are six steps you can take today to get control of your finances.
   - ***What are the six steps to managing personal assets?***

   (1) Take an inventory of your financial assets. That means that you need to develop a balance sheet for yourself: Assets − Liabilities = Net Worth, (2) Keep track of all your expenses, (3) Prepare a budget, (4) Pay off your debts, (5) Start a savings plan (the best way to save money is to pay yourself first; that is, take your paycheck, take out money for savings, and then plan what to do with the rest), and (6) If you have to borrow money, bor-

row only when it's to buy assets that have the potential to increase in value or generate income, such as a house or business.

2. You can build a financial base so that you feel financially secure.

2. Explain ways to build a financial base, including investing in real estate, saving money, and managing credit.

- ***How can I accumulate funds?***

First, find a job. Try to live as frugally as possible. The savings can then be invested to generate even more capital. One such investment is a duplex home where the renter helps pay the mortgage.

- ***Why is real estate such a good investment?***

First, a home is the one investment that you can live in. Second, once you buy a home, the payments are relatively fixed (though taxes and utilities go up). As your income rises, the house payments get easier and easier to make, but renters often find that rents tend to go up at least as fast as income.

- ***How does the government help you buy real estate?***

The government allows you to deduct interest payments on the mortgage, which allows you to buy more home for the money than you could otherwise.

- ***Where is the best place to keep savings?***

It is not wise to keep long-term savings in a bank or savings and loan. It is best, in the long run, to invest in stock. It is a good idea to diversify among mutual funds and other investments. Bonds have not traditionally been as good an investment. Although stocks go up and down, in the long run they earn more than most other investments.

- ***What is a good way to handle credit cards?***

You should pay the balance in full during the period when no interest is charged. Not having to pay 14 percent interest is as good as earning 14 percent tax free. Often a debit card is better than a credit card because it limits you to the amount you can spend.

3. It is as important to preserve capital as it is to accumulate it.

3. Explain how buying the appropriate insurance can protect your financial base.

- ***What is the the role of insurance in protecting capital?***

Insurance protects you from loss. For example, if you were to die, you would lose the income that you would have earned. You can buy life insurance that will make up for some or all of that loss. Term insurance is pure insurance protection for a given number of years.

- ***Why is term insurance preferred?***

You can buy much more term insurance than whole life insurance for the same amount of money.

- ***Do I need other insurance?***

It is important to have health insurance to protect against large losses. You also need car insurance (get a large deductible—$500 or so) and liability insurance in case you injure someone. You should also have homeowner's or rental insurance. Often an umbrella policy will provide all your insurance protection for a lower cost.

4. It may seem too early to begin planning your retirement, but not to do so would be a big mistake. Successful financial planning means long-range planning, and retirement is a critical phase of life.

4. Outline a strategy for retiring with enough money to last a lifetime.

- ***Can I rely on Social Security to cover my retirement expenses?***

You cannot rely on Social Security to cover your retirement expenses. Social Security depends on payments from young people to cover the needs of retired people. The problem is that there are fewer and fewer young people paying into the system.

- ***What are the basics of saving for retirement?***

Supplement Social Security with savings plans of your own. Everyone should have an IRA or some other retirement program. A Roth IRA is especially good for young people because your money grows tax-free and it is tax-free when you withdraw it. For entrepreneurs, a Keogh plan or a simplified employee pension (SEP) plan is wise. An IRA-SEP is a savings plan for entrepreneurs. If you work for someone else, check out the 401(k) plan. Find a financial adviser who can recommend the best savings plan and help you make other investments.

- ***What are the basics of estate planning?***

You need to choose a guardian for your children. You need to prepare a will. You need an executor for your estate. You need to sign a durable power of attorney to enable someone else to handle your finances if you are not capable. The same is true of a health durable power of attorney. Estate planning is complex and often calls for the aid of a financial planner/attorney, but the money is well spent to protect your assets.

Key Terms

annuity 681
contrarian approach 678
disability insurance 681
executor 687
401(k) plan 684
individual retirement account (IRA) 683
Roth IRA 684
Social Security 682
tax-deferred contributions 683
term insurance 680
umbrella policy 682
variable life insurance 681
whole life insurance 680
will 687

Developing Workplace Skills

1. Check your local paper or use an online realtor to gather information regarding the cost to rent a two-bedroom apartment and to buy a two-bedroom condominium in your area. Go to www.dinkytown.net and use the site's "rent-versus-buy calculator" to compare the costs. How do the costs compare? Discuss your findings in small groups.

2. Talk with your parents or others you know who have invested in a family home. What appreciation have they gained on the purchase price? What other benefits has the home brought? Compose a list of the benefits and the drawbacks of owning a home and real estate in general as an investment. Be prepared to give a one-minute presentation on what you learned.

3. Check with your family or others in your area to determine the cost of major medical/hospital treatments. Ask them about medical insurance and the dangers of not having any. What insurance program would they recommend? Discuss your results with the class.

4. The best time to start saving for the future is *now*. To prove this point to yourself, calculate how much you will have at age 65 if you begin saving $100 a month now versus $100 a month 10 years from now. You can go onto the Internet to find such calculations. Just type in "compound interest" in Google and find an appropriate site.

5. Check out the benefits and drawbacks of both traditional and Roth IRAs. Be prepared to make a two-minute presentation on the benefits of each and to discuss your findings in class.

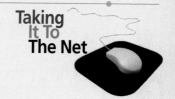

Taking It To The Net

Purpose

To use online resources to make smart personal finance decisions.

Exercise

Use the calculators on the FinanCenter website (www.financenter.com) to answer the following questions:

1. You need $5,000 for a trip to Europe in two years. How much would you have to deposit monthly in a savings account paying 3 percent in order to meet your goal?
2. Investing $1,000 at 6 percent for five years, what is the difference in purchasing power of your savings if inflation increases by 2 percent annually during that time? By 4 percent?
3. Starting today, how much would you need to save each month in order to become a millionaire before you retire?
4. You need a new car. What car can you afford if you have $1,500 for a down payment, can make monthly payments of $300, and get $1,000 for trading in your old clunker?
5. How much house can you afford if you earn $36,000 a year and have $10,000 savings for a down payment, a $6,000 car loan balance, and no credit card debts?

Casing The Web

To access the case "Becoming Financially Secure," visit

www.mhhecom/ub7e

Video Case

So You Want To Be A Millionaire—Edward Jones

It may seem a bit early to plan your retirement, especially since you probably have yet to start your career. Still, there's no better time than today to begin thinking about money matters so you can live a full life and enjoy retirement whenever it rolls around. One key to a secure financial future can be summed up in one word: *discipline*. It takes discipline not to overspend, and it takes discipline to put money away for important milestones in life like the purchase of a home or retirement. Unfortunately, discipline is a trait many people lack. Fortunately, companies like Edward Jones are available to guide us on the right path.

Edward Jones is the oldest financial firm west of the Mississippi, dating back to 1871. The company's strong values and history have helped secure the firm's high level of success. At Edward Jones, personalized service has always been the trademark. Investment representatives do not encourage investors to trade fast and furiously; rather, they help individuals learn how to control and manage their finances. At Edward Jones, investors are encouraged to buy and hold, then hold some more, and finally hold even longer.

Edward Jones financial managers teach clients that sticking to financial goals is the ticket to wealth. Company financial planners like Greg Gaither believe the first step toward building financial security is sitting down face to face with clients and finding out exactly what they want to accomplish before setting specific financial goals. He warns clients that today building wealth takes time and requires them to live frugally. Translation: "Big cars and homes will have to wait." However, the sooner you start saving and investing, the better. Like other company planners, Gaither advises clients to begin the journey to financial independence by following the six steps identified in the chapter:

1. Take an inventory of your financial assets.
2. Keep track of all your expenses.
3. Prepare a budget.
4. Pay off all your debts.
5. Start a savings plan.
6. Borrow money only to buy assets that have the potential to appreciate in value (e.g., a home).

It's also important to keep the rule of 72 firmly in mind. The rule of 72 helps you calculate how long it takes for investments to double over time. You simply divide the growth rate of your investments (for example, 8 percent) into 72; at 8 percent, your money doubles every 9 years. Think about that for a minute. If you are about 20 years old and are fortunate enough to have $10,000, you could double your money five times before you reach age 65. Your $10,000 would be worth $320,000 at retirement ($20,000, $40,000, $80,000, $160,000, and, finally, $320,000).

Edward Jones is truly a great company to work with in planning your financial future. However, the company's notoriety does not stop there. Based on strong employee satisfaction levels, *Fortune* magazine has identified Edward Jones as the best company to work for in the United States the past two years running. So whether you are hoping to find help building your own nest egg or want to pursue a career helping others plot their course to financial freedom, Edward Jones is a valuable stop on that road to financial security.

Thinking It Over

1. What are some of your financial goals? How did the information in the video help you in planning toward achieving those goals?
2. Can you see the benefits of the rule of 72? What is the advantage of starting your personal savings plan now rather than waiting until later?
3. What are some financial pitfalls that could prevent you from reaching your financial goals?

Appendix

Managing Risk

The Increasing Challenge of Risk Management

The management of risk is a major issue for businesses throughout the country. The destruction of the World Trade Center's twin towers and the attack on the Pentagon on September 11, 2001, caused severe economic as well as emotional loss in the United States. Another terrorist attack on the Indonesian island resort of Bali had similar results, driving away tourists and causing economic chaos.[1] Other attacks in Saudi Arabia and other parts of the world have had a major effect on tourism and life in general. The Department of Homeland Security periodically puts the United States on high alert. What effects do such warnings have on you and your fellow students?

Severe acute respiratory syndrome (SARS) had similar results in China, Hong Kong, Canada, and other countries.[2] Operation Iraqi Freedom and its aftermath affected many countries. Relationships between the United States and France, Germany, and Russia became strained. There were threats of war coming from North Korea. In short, the world has become a riskier and riskier place. Such risks cut down on international travel, international trade, and economic growth in general.

Almost every day you hear about another terrorist attack somewhere in the world, or an earthquake, flood, fire, airplane crash, riot, or car accident that destroyed property or injured someone. Such reports are so much a part of the news that we tend to accept these events as part of everyday life. But events involving loss mean a great deal to the businesspeople involved. They must pay to restore the property and compensate those who are injured.

In addition to the news-making stories, thousands of other incidents involve businesspeople in lawsuits. Lawsuits in recent years have covered everything from job-related accidents to sexual harassment and product liability. For example, you may have heard about the people who are suing fast-food companies for making them fat, brokers for losing their money, and landlords for not taking care of mold.

Search and rescue workers survey the damage at a Toys "R" Us store in Lanham, Maryland, after its roof collapsed in a snow storm. Such damage and the personal injuries that occurred are just two of the many risks retailers and other businesses face and should insure against. What differences do you see, if any, in the way a small, independent retailer should manage risk versus a large corporation such as Toys "R" Us?

How Rapid Change Affects Risk Management

Changes are occurring so fast in the business world that it is difficult to keep up with the new risks involved. For example, who in the organization can evaluate the risks of selling products over the Internet?[3] As companies reach global markets over the Internet, who watches for fluctuations in the world's currencies and how they may affect profits? For example, the value of the euro went up 38 percent against the dollar from February 2002 to May 2003.[4] Will global warming affect weather conditions, and how will that affect farms and cattle raising? What will be the long-term effects of the discovery of mad cow disease in Canada? Canadian farmers have already lost millions of dollars. Will there be another anthrax attack in the United States or somewhere else in the world? What would happen to businesses if they could no longer rely on the post office?[5] As you can see, risk management is getting more complex and more critical for all businesses. Those who do business in other countries face increasing risk from social and political unrest. Given such risks, let's explore how companies go about managing risk.

MANAGING RISK

The term **risk** refers to the chance of loss, the degree of probability of loss, and the amount of possible loss. There are two different kinds of risk:

- **Speculative risk** involves a chance of either profit or loss. It includes the chance a firm takes to make extra money by buying new machinery, acquiring more inventory, and making other decisions in which the probability of loss may be relatively low and the amount of loss is known. An entrepreneur takes speculative risk on the chance of making a profit. In business, building a new plant is a speculative risk because it may result in a loss or a profit. One of the causes of the economic slump in the United States in the early 2000s was the slowdown in buying new equipment because of the perceived economic risks.
- **Pure risk** is the threat of loss with no chance for profit. Pure risk involves the threat of fire, accident, or loss. If such events occur, a company loses money; but if the events do not occur, the company gains nothing.

risk
The chance of loss, the degree of probability of loss, and the amount of possible loss.

speculative risk
A chance of either profit or loss.

pure risk
The threat of loss with no chance for profit.

The risk that is of most concern to businesspeople is pure risk. Pure risk threatens the very existence of some firms. Once such risks are identified, firms have several options:

1. Reduce the risk.
2. Avoid the risk.

3. Self-insure against the risk.
4. Buy insurance against the risk.

We'll discuss the option of buying insurance in detail later in this appendix. In the next sections, we will discuss each of the other alternatives for managing risk. These steps should be taken to lower the need for outside insurance.

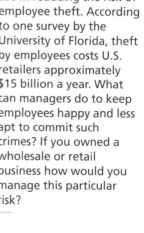

This man is assembling monitoring equipment for use in reducing the risk of employee theft. According to one survey by the University of Florida, theft by employees costs U.S. retailers approximately $15 billion a year. What can managers do to keep employees happy and less apt to commit such crimes? If you owned a wholesale or retail business how would you manage this particular risk?

Reducing Risk

A firm can reduce risk by establishing loss-prevention programs such as fire drills, health education programs, safety inspections, equipment maintenance, accident prevention programs, and so on. Many retail stores, for example, use mirrors, video cameras, and other devices to prevent shoplifting. Water sprinklers and smoke detectors are used to minimize fire loss. In industry, most machines have safety devices to protect workers' fingers, eyes, and so on. Hospital employees and others are wearing masks, gloves, and other protective devices to prevent the spread of SARS and other contagious diseases.[6]

Employees, as well as managers, can reduce risk. For example, truck drivers can wear seat belts to minimize injuries from accidents, operators of loud machinery can wear earplugs to reduce the chance of hearing loss, and those who lift heavy objects can wear back braces. Have you noticed any workers not wearing protective gear when using loud equipment? Such examples show you that loss-prevention programs can be greatly improved.

The beginning of an effective risk management strategy is a good loss-prevention program. However, high insurance rates have forced some people to go beyond merely preventing risks to the point of avoiding risks, and in extreme cases by going out of business.

Avoiding Risk

Many risks cannot be avoided. There is always the chance of fire, theft, accident, or injury. But some companies are avoiding risk by not accepting hazardous jobs and by outsourcing shipping and other functions.[7] Some companies are having second thoughts about building high-rise buildings because of the destruction of the World Trade Center's twin towers and the fear of another such attack.

The threat of lawsuits has driven away some drug companies from manufacturing vaccines, and some consulting engineers refuse to work on hazardous sites. Some companies are losing outside members of their boards of directors for lack of liability coverage protecting them from legal action against the firms they represent. New laws resulting from recent scandals have made it even more risky to be part of the management team, so some managers are refusing to accept positions on boards of directors.

Self-Insuring

Many companies and municipalities have turned to **self-insurance** because they either can't find or can't afford conventional property/casualty policies. Such firms set aside money to cover routine claims and buy only "catastrophe" policies to cover big losses. Self-insurance, then, lowers the cost of insurance by allowing companies to take out insurance only for larger losses.

self-insurance
The practice of setting aside money to cover routine claims and buying only "catastrophe" policies to cover big losses.

Self-insurance is most appropriate when a firm has several widely distributed facilities. The risk from fire, theft, or other catastrophe is then more manageable. Firms with huge facilities, in which a major fire or earthquake could destroy the entire operation, usually turn to insurance companies to cover the risk.

One of the more risky strategies for self-insurance is for a company to "go bare," paying claims straight out of its budget. The risk here is that the whole firm could go bankrupt over one claim, if the damages are high enough. A less risky alternative is to form risk retention group-insurance pools that share similar risks. It is estimated that about one-third of the insurance market is using such alternatives. Another alternative is to buy insurance, but include a very high deductible (the portion of the claim costs that you must pay). In that way, companies cut way back on the cost of insurance, but are covered if they incur huge losses.

Buying Insurance to Cover Risk

Although well-designed, consistently enforced risk-prevention programs reduce the probability of claims, accidents do happen. Insurance is the armor individuals, businesses, and nonprofit organizations use to protect themselves from various financial risks. For this protection, such organizations spend about 10 percent of GDP on insurance premiums. Some insurance protection is provided by the federal government (see Figure A.1), but most risks must be covered by individuals and businesses on their own.

uninsurable risk
A risk that no insurance company will cover.

What Risks Are Uninsurable? Not all risks are insurable, even risks that once were covered by insurance. An **uninsurable risk** is one that no insurance company will cover. Examples of things that you cannot insure include market risks (e.g., losses that occur because of price changes, style changes, or new products that make your product obsolete); political risks (e.g., losses from war or government restrictions on trade); some personal risks (e.g., loss of a job); and some risks of operation (e.g., strikes or inefficient machinery).

FIGURE A.1
PUBLIC INSURANCE
State or federal government agencies that provide insurance protection.

TYPE OF INSURANCE	WHAT IT DOES
Unemployment Compensation	Provides financial benefits, job counseling, and placement services for unemployed workers.
Social Security	Provides retirement benefits, life insurance, health insurance, and disability income insurance.
Federal Housing Administration (FHA)	Provides mortgage insurance to lenders to protect against default by home buyers.
National Flood Insurance Association	Provides compensation for damage caused by flooding and mud slides to properties located in flood-prone areas.
Federal Crime Insurance	Provides insurance to property owners in high-crime areas.
Federal Crop Insurance	Provides compensation for damaged crops.
Pension Benefit Guaranty Corporation	Insures pension plans to prevent loss to employees if the company declares bankruptcy or goes out of business.

What Risks Are Insurable? An **insurable risk** is one that the typical insurance company will cover. Generally, insurance companies use the following guidelines when evaluating whether or not a risk is insurable:

insurable risk
A risk that the typical insurance company will cover.

1. The policyholder must have an **insurable interest,** which means that the policyholder is the one at risk to suffer an economic loss. You cannot, for example, buy fire insurance on your neighbor's house and collect if it burns down.
2. The loss should be measurable.
3. The *chance* of loss should be measurable.
4. The loss should be accidental.
5. The risk should be dispersed; that is, spread among different geographical areas so that a flood or other natural disaster in one area would not bankrupt the insurance company.
6. The insurance company can set standards for accepting risks.

insurable interest
The possibility of the policyholder to suffer a loss.

The Law of Large Numbers An **insurance policy** is a written contract between the insured (an individual or organization) and an insurance company that promises to pay for all or part of a loss. A **premium** is the fee charged by the insurance company or, in other words, the cost of the insurance policy to the insured.

As in all private businesses, the objective of an insurance company is to make a profit. To ensure that it makes a profit, an insurance company gathers data to determine the extent of the risk. What makes the acceptance of risk possible for insurance companies is the law of large numbers.

The **law of large numbers** states that if a large number of people or organizations are exposed to the same risk, a predictable number of losses will occur during a given period of time. Once the insurance company predicts the number of losses likely to occur, it can determine the appropriate premiums for each policy it issues. The people who calculate the chance of loss and the premiums necessary to cover such losses are called **actuaries.** The premium is supposed to be high enough to cover expected losses and yet earn a profit for the firm and its stockholders. Today, many insurance companies are charging high premiums, not for past risks but for the anticipated costs associated with the increasing number of court cases and high damage awards. They also need to cover the losses they incurred by investing their funds in the stock market during the decline. You can imagine the increased cost of insurance on high-rise buildings as a result of the terrorist attacks in New York. Clearly, there is a need to spread the risk somehow.

insurance policy
A written contract between the insured and an insurance company that promises to pay for all or part of a loss.

premium
The fee charged by an insurance company for an insurance policy.

law of large numbers
Principle that if a large number of people are exposed to the same risk, a predictable number of losses will occur during a given period of time.

actuaries
The people who calculate the chance of loss and the premiums necessary to cover losses.

Spreading the Risk: Reinsurance Reinsurance companies supply risk capital to life and property and casualty insurers. You may think of them as insurance companies for insurance companies. More than half of such insurers are in Europe, and U.S. insurers rely heavily on them to spread their risks. Reinsurance companies have suffered huge setbacks as a result of terrorist attacks, widespread floods in Europe, and asbestos settlements. Furthermore, since insurance companies invest in stocks and other investments, the stock market collapse hurt them deeply. In short, the insurance industry, including the reinsurance companies, are suffering financially and the consequences are yet to be known.[8]

The future has its own dangers. More than 8,000 companies have faced lawsuits because they had something to do with asbestos. As of 2002, there were 67 bankruptcies caused by such suits and 750,000 claimants. The cost to companies and their insurers is over $54 billion and may reach over $200 billion.[9]

The tendency for insurance companies is to avoid huge risks, such as those raised by asbestos companies and losses due to terrorist attacks, or to raise

Shown here are workers from Asbestos Maintenance of Amarillo, Texas, removing asbestos-based siding from a building prior to demolition. Asbestos was a widely used fire retardant building material before research discovered its link to cancer. Could the dangers of the use of asbestos have been better anticipated? How?

premiums dramatically. In some cases, the government might step in to back up the insurance industry. If it did not, much construction would be put on hold and the whole economy would slow. Thus, you can see the importance of insurance to the whole economy.

When the Government Gets Involved In November 2002, President George W. Bush signed the Terrorism Risk Insurance Act of 2002. The idea was to lessen the risk that builders had from claims caused by terrorist attacks. Billions of dollars of construction had been put on hold because the builders could not get insurance coverage. The government lessened the risk by making sure that victims would be compensated but that losses due to punitive damages and high lawyer fees would be held down.[10] The government also stepped in to prevent huge losses to pharmaceutical companies that make vaccines.[11] Without such protection, it is possible that no companies would produce the vaccines we may need in time of war or terrorist attack. Such moves by the government make some risks more insurable.

Rule of Indemnity The **rule of indemnity** says that an insured person or organization cannot collect more than the actual loss from an insurable risk. One cannot gain from risk management; one can only minimize losses. One cannot, for example, buy two insurance policies and collect from both for the same loss. If a company or person carried two policies, the two insurance companies would calculate any loss and divide the reimbursement.

Sources of Insurance There are two major types of insurance companies. A **stock insurance company** is owned by stockholders, just like any other investor-owned company. A **mutual insurance company** is owned by its policyholders. A mutual insurance company, unlike a stock company, does not earn profits for its owners. It is a nonprofit organization, and any excess funds (over losses, expenses, and growth costs) go to the policyholders/investors in the form of dividends or premium reductions.

rule of indemnity
Rule saying that an insured person or organization cannot collect more than the actual loss from an insurable risk.

stock insurance company
A type of insurance company owned by stockholders.

mutual insurance company
A type of insurance company owned by its policyholders.

Types of Insurance

As we have discussed, risk management consists of reducing risk, avoiding risk, self-insuring, and buying insurance. There are many types of insurance that cover various losses: property and casualty, marine, business interruption, liability, health, and life insurance. Property losses result from fires, accidents, theft, or other perils. Liability losses result from property damage or injuries suffered by others for which the policyholder is held responsible. Let's begin our exploration of insurance by looking at health insurance.

Health Insurance

Businesses and nonprofit organizations may offer their employees an array of health care benefits to choose from. Everything from hospitalization to physician fees, eye exams, dental exams, and prescriptions can be covered.

Often, employees may choose between options from health care providers (e.g., Blue Cross/Blue Shield); health maintenance organizations (e.g., Kaiser Permanente); preferred provider organizations (PPOs), or consumer-driven plans.

Health Maintenance Organizations (HMOs) **Health maintenance organizations (HMOs)** offer a full range of health care benefits. Emphasis is on helping members stay healthy instead of on treating illnesses. Two nice features typical of HMOs are that members do not receive bills and do not have to fill out claim forms for routine service. HMOs employ or contract with doctors, hospitals, and other systems of health care, and members must use those providers. In other words, they cannot choose any doctor they wish but can select one doctor from the approved list to be their primary care physician. That doctor will then recommend specialists, if necessary. The HMO system is called *managed care.*

HMOs are less expensive than comprehensive health insurance providers, but members sometimes complain about not being able to choose doctors or to get the care they want or need. Some physicians also complain that they lose some freedom to do what is needed to make people well and often receive less compensation than they feel is appropriate for the services they provide. To save money, HMOs usually must approve treatment before it is given. People who prefer to have their doctor make such decisions often choose a PPO, as we shall see next.

Ultimately, many small-business owners turn to insurance to cover risks that they can't assume on their own. Large insurers like State Farm can assist in assessing and identifying potential risks as well as provide a broad array of coverage options.

Preferred Provider Organizations (PPOs) **Preferred provider organizations (PPOs)** also contract with hospitals and physicians, but unlike an HMO, a PPO does not require its members to choose only from those physicians. However, members do have to pay more if they don't use a physician on the preferred list. Also, members usually have to pay a deductible (e.g., $250) before the PPO will pay any bills. When the plan does pay, members usually have to pay part of the bill. This payment is called *co-insurance.* Some people feel that the added expense of PPOs over HMOs is worth the freedom to select their own physicians.

Since both HMOs and PPOs can cost as much as 80 percent less than comprehensive individual health insurance policies, most businesses and individuals choose to join one.

health maintenance organizations (HMOs)
Health care organizations that require members to choose from a restricted list of doctors.

preferred provider organizations (PPOs)
Health care organizations similar to HMOs except that they allow members to choose their own physicians (for a fee).

Consumer-Driven Plans **Consumer-driven plans** work like this. You have a fixed "spending account," funded by your employer, which you can use to pay for office visits, prescription drugs, and routine medical procedures. You can choose any provider you wish from the network you've selected, but you'll pay the full cost of your visits from your account. Annual checkups and mammograms are free. The accounts range from $500 to $1,000 for an individual (double for families), and are replenished annually. If you choose this plan, you agree to a managed care plan that comes with a high deductible (about $1,000 to $2,000). If you spend everything in your account and need more care, you have to pay the deductible before you receive any more money.

The benefit of such plans is that healthy people can save the money in their accounts year after year and use that money later when they have care needs.

consumer-driven plans
A plan where you have a fixed "spending account," funded by your employer, which you can use to pay for office visits, prescription drugs, and routine medical procedures.

Furthermore, consumers have more choice in doctors and facilities. They are expected to be more careful with the care they receive, thus saving money for them and the insurer.[12]

Disability Insurance

Disability insurance replaces part of your income (50 to 70 percent) if you become disabled and unable to work. There usually is a period of time you must be disabled (e.g., 60 days) before you can begin collecting. Many employers provide this type of insurance, but some do not. In either case, insurance experts recommend that you get this type of insurance because the chances of becoming disabled by a disease or accident are much higher than the chance of dying. The premiums for such insurance vary depending on your age, occupation, and income. You can lower the premiums by agreeing to a 180-day waiting period from when you start receiving care to when the policy starts to cover the care cost, but the cost of care for that long makes such a decision a risky one. Also, for an additional premium, you can add *lifetime* sickness and accident coverage, while the traditional policy has limits in years covered.

workers' compensation insurance
Insurance that guarantees payment of wages, medical care, and rehabilitation services (e.g., retraining) for employees who are injured on the job, regardless of fault.

Workers' Compensation

Workers' compensation insurance guarantees payment of wages, medical care, and rehabilitation services (e.g., retraining) for employees who are injured on the job, regardless of fault. Employers in all 50 states are required to provide this insurance. This insurance also provides benefits to the survivors of workers who die as a result of work-related injuries. The cost of insurance varies by the company's safety record, its payroll, and the types of hazards faced by workers. For example, it costs more to insure a steelworker than an accountant.

Liability Insurance

Professional liability insurance covers people who may be found liable for professional negligence. For example, if a lawyer gives advice carelessly and the client loses money, the client may then sue the lawyer for an amount equal to that lost. This type of insurance is also known as malpractice insurance. While you may think of doctors and dentists when you hear the word *malpractice,* the fact is that many professionals, including mortgage brokers, rental firms (for mold), and real estate appraisers, are buying this insurance because of large lawsuits their colleagues have faced.[13]

Medical malpractice insurance costs have gone so high that many doctors are quitting their practices rather than pay the premiums.[14] Legislation has been proposed to limit the right to sue or the amount plaintiffs can collect from doctors, but meanwhile there is a crisis of medical care in some states because needed doctors have left the state or are no longer practicing there.[15] The situation became so serious that changes in the law had to be made.[16]

Dr. Joel Ledbed of Philadelphia gave up his obstetrics practice due to the doubling of his malpractice insurance costs. Other doctors in other cities are doing the same. What can be done to assure citizens that the medical care they need will be available when fewer doctors are working due to their inability to cover escalating insurance costs? Should the government help?

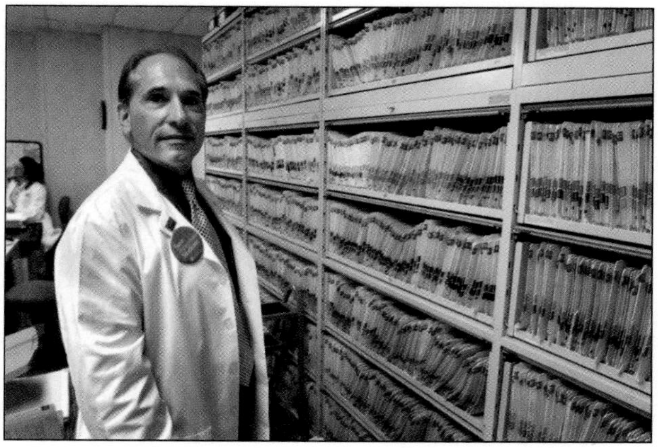

Companies have their own concerns about liability. *Product* liability insurance, for example, provides coverage against liability arising out of products sold. If a person is injured by a ladder or some other household good, he or she may sue the manufacturer for damages. Insurance usually covers such losses.

Critical Thinking

Many swimming pools no longer have high diving boards and playgrounds have taken out swings, merry-go-rounds, and other equipment—all because people may sue the manufacturers. People are also suing cigarette companies, fast-food restaurants (for making them fat), and amusement parks (for dangerous rides). There may come a day when you cannot afford to go horseback riding or ride on a roller coaster because the liability insurance may be too high for the provider. Do you think it is time for consumers like you and me to assume more of the risk of using goods and services we want? Should it be possible to waive the right to sue so that you can take risks on your own—such as skydiving or riding on a roller coaster? Should the courts put a cap on the amount that one person can get from being hurt? How much is enough? How would you decide?

Other Business Insurance

It is impossible in an introductory course like this to discuss in detail all the insurance coverage that businesses may buy. Naturally, businesses must protect themselves against property damage, and they must buy car and truck insurance and more. Figure A.2 will give you some idea of the types of insurance available. As we mentioned in Chapter 22, an umbrella insurance policy covering all kinds of risk is usually less costly and involves less negotiation and paperwork.

The point to be made in this appendix is that risk management is critical in all firms. That includes the risk of investing funds and the risk of opening your own business (speculative risk). Remember from Chapter 1, though, that risk is often matched by opportunity and profits. Taking on risk is one way for an entrepreneur to prosper. Regardless of how careful we are, however, we all face the prospect of death. To ensure that those left behind will be able to continue the business, entrepreneurs often buy life insurance (for key executives) that will pay partners and others what they will need to keep the business going. We'll explore that next.

Life Insurance for Businesses

We discussed life insurance in Chapter 22. There, the focus was on life insurance for you and your family. Everything said there applies to life insurance for business executives as well. The best kind of insurance to cover executives in the firm is term insurance, but dozens of new policies with interesting features have been emerging recently.[17]

Insurance Coverage for Home-Based Businesses

Homeowners' policies usually don't have adequate protection for a home-based business. For example, they may have a limit of $2,500 for business equipment. For more coverage, you may need an endorsement (sometimes called a *rider*) to your homeowners' insurance. For a small amount, you can increase the coverage to $10,000. Check with your insurance agent for details. If you have clients visit your office and receive deliveries regularly, you may need home office insurance. It may cost approximately $150 a year, but it protects you from slip-and-fall lawsuits and other risks associated with visitors. For more elaborate businesses, such as custom cabinetmakers and others who do manufacturing and inventory keeping, a business owner policy may be needed. That costs $300 a year or more. Few of us are experts on insurance, so we need to consult our insurance agent about the best insurance for our home-business needs.

FIGURE A.2
PRIVATE INSURANCE

TYPES OF INSURANCE	WHAT IT DOES
Property and Liability	
Fire	Covers losses to buildings and their contents from fire.
Automobile	Covers property damage, bodily injury, collision, fire, theft, vandalism, and other related vehicle losses.
Homeowners	Covers the home, other structures on the premises, home contents, expenses if forced from the home because of an insured peril, third-party liability, and medical payments to others.
Computer coverage	Covers loss of equipment from fire, theft, and sometimes spills, power surges, and accidents.
Professional liability	Protects from suits stemming from mistakes made or bad advice given in a professional context.
Business interruption	Provides compensation for loss due to fire, theft, or similar disasters that close a business. Covers lost income, continuing expenses, and utility expenses.
Nonperformance loss protection	Protects from failure of a contractor, supplier, or other person to fulfill an obligation.
Criminal loss protection	Protects from loss due to theft, burglary, or robbery.
Commercial credit insurance	Protects manufacturers and wholesalers from credit losses due to insolvency or default.
Public liability insurance	Provides protection for businesses and individuals against losses resulting from personal injuries or damage to the property of others for which the insured is responsible.
Extended product liability insurance	Covers potentially toxic substances in products; environmental liability; and, for corporations, director and officer liability.
Fidelity bond	Protects employers from employee dishonesty.
Surety bond	Covers losses resulting from a second party's failure to fulfill a contract.
Title insurance	Protects buyers from losses resulting from a defect in title to property.
Health Insurance	
Basic health insurance	Covers losses due to sickness or accidents.
Major medical insurance	Protects against catastrophic losses by covering expenses beyond the limits of basic policies.
Hospitalization insurance	Pays for most hospital expenses.
Surgical and medical insurance	Pays costs of surgery and doctor's care while recuperating in a hospital.
Dental insurance	Pays a percentage of dental expenses.
Disability income insurance	Pays income while the insured is disabled as a result of accident or illness.
Life Insurance	
Group life insurance	Covers all the employees of a firm or members of a group.
Owner or key executive insurance	Enables businesses of sole proprietors or partnerships to pay bills and continue operating, saving jobs for the employees. Enables corporations to hire and train or relocate another manager with no loss to the firm.
Retirement and pension plans	Provides employees with supplemental retirement and pension plans.
Credit life insurance	Pays the amount due on a loan if the debtor dies.

Global Risks

Risk management now goes far beyond the protection of individuals, businesses, and nonprofit organizations from known risks. It means the evaluation of worldwide risks such as global warming; AIDS, SARS, and other diseases; and terrorism and wars. It also means prioritizing these risks so that international funds can be spent where they can do the most good. No insurance company can protect humanity from such risks. These risks are the concern of international governments throughout the world, with the assistance of the international scientific community. They should also be your concern as you study risk management in all its dimensions.

Key Terms

actuaries 697
consumer-driven plans 699
health maintenance organizations (HMOs) 699
insurable interest 697
insurable risk 697
insurance policy 697
law of large numbers 697
mutual insurance company 698
preferred provider organizations (PPOs) 699
premium 697
pure risk 694
risk 694
rule of indemnity 698
self-insurance 695
speculative risk 694
stock insurance company 698
uninsurable risk 696
workers' compensation insurance 700

Part 7

Financial Management (Finance and Accounting)

Career Portfolio

Accounting and finance are career areas that have existed for many centuries. Records discovered in the ruins of ancient Babylon dating back to 300 B.C. show that financial records were kept by the ancients. European monarchs, particularly in the 18th and 19th centuries, relied on bankers and other professional financiers to recover from wars and to build the new industrial revolution.

Today, accountants and financial managers are as much in demand as ever. Computerization has enriched both career areas immensely. Because of changing laws and regulations, companies and their personnel in these positions must place a greater emphasis than ever on accurate reporting of financial data. This field, like so many others, is dynamic and changing.

Nearly 2 million people work in some area of finance or accounting, most as accountants, financial managers, banking personnel, or financial consultants. Nearly every company—whether in manufacturing, transportation, retailing, or a variety of services—employs one or more financial managers. Accountants and bookkeepers are equally in demand.

SKILLS

Anyone who enters these areas must have a mathematical aptitude, an interest in numbers, and a considerable amount of patience. As with nearly every other area, speaking and writing skills are a must, because the financial information must be communicated to people. Good ethical judgment is also essential, because areas of finance and accounting both contain more gray areas than many of us imagine.

CAREER PATHS

A bachelor's degree in accounting or finance is usually a prerequisite, although accountants with two-year degrees and outstanding abilities have been hired as bookkeepers and accounting assistants. In some states, tax preparers do not need formal degrees, only mastery of current tax law. In all cases, though, continuing education is becoming increasingly important because of the growing complexity of global commerce, changing federal and state laws, and the constant introduction of new, complex financial instruments.

A well-trained, experienced financial manager is a prime candidate for promotion into top management. Junior public accountants usually advance to semisenior positions within two to five years and to senior positions within six to eight years. Although advancement can be rapid for well-prepared accountants, especially in public accounting, employees without adequate college preparation are often dead-ended in routine jobs. Also, even CPAs must constantly be reeducated in today's changing environment.

SOME POSSIBLE CAREERS IN FINANCE AND ACCOUNTING				
JOB TITLE	**SALARY**	**JOB DUTIES**	**CAREER PATH**	**PROSPECTS**
Accountant	Entry level: $39,397 (bachelor's degree) Senior level:1 Median: $49,250	Depends on size and nature of firm as well as specific job title. Public accountants work independently on a fee basis. Management accountants handle financial records in the company where they are salaried employees. The cost accountant determines unit costs of products and services. The auditor examines and vouches for the accuracy of records.	Start with either an accounting degree or many courses in accounting. A certified public accountant must take a comprehensive exam, then intern as auditor for two years. Able accountants, especially CPAs, can be promoted rapidly. By specializing in certain accounting areas, an accountant can often be promoted.	Openings in all accounting areas are expected to be average through 2010.
Financial Manager	$36,000–$131,120 Median: $67,020	As with accountants, duties depend on size and nature of firm as well as specific job title. Titles include treasurer, controller, credit manager, cash manager. Controllers direct preparation of financial reports; cash and credit managers monitor and control the flow of receipts and disbursements; risk and insurance managers work to minimize risk and cut risk costs.	Most start with a degree in finance or accounting. A master of business administration degree (MBA) is becoming increasingly required by some companies. Often promoted into top management.	Average growth through 2010.
Securities and financial services sales workers	$24,770–$145,600 $124,800 Once established, changes to commission only. Median: $56,080	Open accounts for new customers, execute buy and sell orders based on information from the securities exchange. Get information on company's progress from the research dept. Must be able to anticipate buying and selling trends in the markets.	Many brokerage concerns hire trainees, then place them on a probationary track that includes extensive on-the-job training. Depending on ability and ambition, promotion can be rapid. Bank employees make much less.	Faster than average growth through 2010, though level of growth will depend on the state of the economy.

Source: Bureau of Labor Statistics, *Occupational Outlook Handbook*, 2002–03 edition:1.

Title Check, LLC, and First Draft, Inc.

Name: Michael Hopwood

Age: 31

Position/title: Accountant, Human Resources

Salary range: $32,000–$60,000

Time in this position: 15 months

Major factors in the decision to take this position: I had left a dead-end job to pursue my college education, and found myself working for Kmart when their restructuring under bankruptcy listed the store I worked for as closing. Members of the Business Department at Glen Oaks Community College recommended me to the owner of Title Check, LLC, and First Draft, Inc.

Company's Web address: www.Title-Check.com

Company description: Title Check, LLC, is a property research company. Working in conjunction with the state of Michigan by contractual agreement, we research property ownership and party interest in an attempt to inform property owners of the need to pay past due property taxes.

First Draft, Inc., is the corporate name for a local restaurant and bar. Doing business as Paisano's Ristorante, we offer the Three Rivers, Michigan, area a full-service dining establishment, bar, and dance club. New to our offering are live musical performances by established local and national blues performers.

Job description: I am responsible for all areas of accounting for both businesses (accounts receivable, accounts payable, general accounting, financial statement preparation, end-of-month/end-of-year reporting, revenue/expense analysis, and internal system/procedural auditing).

Ideal next job: I am hoping that my next job will be in the realm of senior accountant or accounting controller for a large corporation in the service or manufacturing industry.

Best part of your job: The best part of my job is the responsibilities inherent in the position. My employer and my workmates trust in my ability to perform my job.

Educational background: After graduating high school in Buhl, Idaho, as covaledictorian, I spent seven years serving in the U.S. Army. After my service, I spent three years driving a tractor-trailer. In 2001, I enrolled at Glen Oaks Community College. I graduated with my Associate of Business degree in 2003. I received a Business Department Award for academic excellence.

Favorite course: My favorite classes have been in the areas of accounting and economics.

Recommended by Larry Hass, Glen Oaks Community College

Chapter Notes

Prologue

1. www.census.gov; Genaro C. Armas, "College Degree Worth Millions, Survey Finds," *Toronto Star,* July 18, 2002; and John Gallagher, "Profiting from Knowledge," *Bergen County, NJ Record,* January 20, 2003, p. L05.
2. John Morley, "The Real Value of a College Education," University Wire, April 29, 2002.
3. "Postsecondary Education," *Education Statistics Quarterly,* Spring 2000.
4. Bill Lodge, "Career-Minded Students Get a Message: Manners Matter," *Dallas Morning News,* April 11, 2002, p. 12T.
5. Callie Buys, "Etiquette Key in Job Field, Experts Say," University Wire, January 15, 2002.
6. Lyndsey Sage, "Students Should Practice Etiquette When Job Hunting," University Wire, April 8, 2003.
7. Cynthia Rodriguez, "Attire Indicates Motivation to Future Employers," University Wire, May 2, 2003.
8. Andrea Kay, "Dressing for Success Can Get Confusing," Gannett News Service, February 27, 2003.
9. Judie Schwartz, "Get That Job by Dressing and Dining for Interview Success," *Denver Rocky Mountain News,* June 1, 2002, p. 1C.
10. Ashley Smith, "Manners Matter in World of Business" University Wire, March 3, 2003.
11. Steven Levy, "The Killer Browser," *Newsweek,* April 21, 2003.
12. Jeff Morrison, "The Swift Rise and Tragic Decline of Netscape," University Wire, March 13, 2003.
13. Steven J. Vaughan-Nichols, "News You Can Choose," *Washington Post,* April 6, 2003, p. H7.
14. "Going Google," *St. Louis Post-Dispatch,* March 17, 2003, p. C4.
15. "The Search Continues . . .," *Toronto Star,* March 29, 2003.
16. Michael Shapiro, "Code Web: Stay or Go?" *Washington Post,* March 2, 2003, p. E1.
17. Julie Claire Diop, "Uncle Sam's Aid for Job Hunters," *Newsday,* April 5, 2003, p. F2.
18. Anita Bruzzese, "Odds Low That Job Searching on Web Will Net Results," Gannett News Service, January 30, 2003.
19. "Posting Résumés May Lead to Privacy Pitfalls, ID Theft," *Palm Beach Post,* February 23, 2003, p. 5F.

Chapter 1

1. "Riders on the Storm," *Forbes,* March 18, 2002, p. 101.
2. "Did You Know That?" *Bottom Line Personal,* January 1, 2003, p. 7.
3. Steve Forbes, "Ignorance Is Not Bliss," *Forbes,* December 23, 2002, p. 45.
4. "My Big Fat Greek Wedding," *Fortune,* December 30, 2002, p. 174.
5. James R. Campbell, "Wealth and Income in America," *Washington Post,* December 27, 2002, p. A24.
6. W. Michael Cox and Richard Alm, "Off the Books," *Reason,* August/September 2002, pp. 47–53.
7. Robert Simons, Henry Mintzberg, and Kunal Basu, "Five Half-Truths of Business," *Fast Company,* June 2002, pp. 117–21.
8. Ibid.
9. Shahrzad Elghanayan, "Loan Ranger," *Worth,* January/February 2003, p. 46.
10. "The 2001 B.E. 100s," *Black Enterprise,* June 2001.
11. David Kirkpatrick, "Where the Action Is," *Fortune,* May 12, 2003, pp. 78–84.
12. Brook Manville and Josiah Ober, "Beyond Empowerment," *Harvard Business Review,* January 2003, pp. 48–53.
13. Jack Anderson, "Companies Hate Misery," *Forbes,* June 23, 2003, p. 58.
14. "Tax-Cut Endgame," *The Wall Street Journal,* May 21, 2003, p. A12.
15. Mark Brzezinski, "Poland: A Democratic Success," *Washington Times,* July 16, 2002, p. A21.
16. W. Chan Kim and Renee Mauborgne, "Fair Process: Managing in the Knowledge Economy," *Harvard Business Review,* January 2003, pp. 127–36.
17. Mark Athitakis, "How to Make Money on the Net," *Business 2.0,* May 2003, pp. 83–84.
18. David Kirkpatrick, "Stupid-Journal Alert: Why HBR's View of Tech Is Dangerous," *Fortune,* June 9, 2003, p. 190.
19. Brad Wieners, "Escape from L.A.," *Business 2.0,* July 2002, p. 63.
20. Owen Thomas, "Farmer on a Dell," *Business 2.0,* July 2002, p. 29.
21. Robert J. Samuelson, "The Spirit of America," *Newsweek,* January 13, 2003, p. 47.
22. Sheila Muto, "Clicks Vs. Bricks," *The Wall Street Journal,* June 11, 2003, p. B8.
23. Maryanne Murray Buechner, "Cruising the Online Mall," *Time,* April 2003, Inside Business section.
24. "The 21st Century Corporation," *Business Week,* August 28, 2000, p. 79.
25. Karen Raugust, "Multicultural Guide," *Advertising Age,* November 2, 2002, pp. M1–M13, and Steve Miller, "Hispanics Now No. 1 Minority in U. S.," *Washington Times,* January 22, 2003, pp. A1 and A13.
26. "Leveraging Diversity," an ad in *Fortune,* November 13, 2000, p. 14.
27. "Too Diverse for Our Own Good?" *Fortune,* July 9, 2001, p. 116.
28. Geoff Williams, "Stop-Gap Measures," *Entrepreneur,* September 2000, p. 90.
29. Claire Raines, Ron Zemke and Bob Filipzak, *Generations at Work* (AMACOM, 1999).
30. Donna DeMarco, "AARP Helps Seniors Cash in on Golden Years," *Washington Times,* June 17, 2002, pp. A1 and A10.
31. Joyce Howard Price, "Specialists to Swap Knowledge of Aging," *Washington Times,* June 15, 2002, p. A2.
32. Robert Levering and Milton Moskowitz, "100 Best Companies to Work for," *Fortune,* January 20, 2003, pp. 127–152.
33. Helen Jung, "Boeing Struggles," *Washington Times,* January 1, 2003, pp. C8, C9.
34. Renae Merle, "Homeland Security Challenge: Make 22 Agencies Work As One," *Washington Post,* January 6, 2003, pp. E1, E9.
35. Phillip Longman, "Squeezed in a Service Economy," *Washington Post,* January 14, 2003, p. A19.

Chapter 2

1. Moon Ihlwan and Brian Bremmer, "The Other Korean Crisis," *Business Week,* January 20, 2003, pp. 44–52.
2. Justin Gillis, "Old Laws, New Fish," *Washington Post,* January 15, 2003, p. E1.
3. "Brute Force," *Washington Times,* July 30, 2002, p. A7.
4. Gautam Naik, Vanessa Fuhrmans, Jonathan Karp, Joel Millman, Farnaz Fassihi, and Joanna Slater, "Global Baby Bust," *The Wall Street Journal,* January 24, 2003, pp. B1 and B4, and Gene Koretz, "Demographic Time Bomb," *Business Week,* April 21, 2003, p. 30.
5. Robert D. McTeer, Jr., "The Dismal Science? Hardly!" *The Wall Street Journal,* June 4, 2003, p. A16.
6. "Charitable Pursuits," *American Demographics,* March 2001, p. 24.
7. Claudia Rosett, "A Toast to Liberty," *The Wall Street Journal,* May 14, 2002, p. A18.
8. Mark Buchanan, "Wealth Happens," *Harvard Business Review,* April 2002, pp. 49–54.
9. Sebastian Mallaby, "A Worm at the Core of Capitalism," *Washington Post,* June 10, 2002, p. A21.
10. Geoffrey Colvin, "Shareholders Are No Fools—Anymore," *Fortune,* July 7, 2003, p. 42.
11. Jack Anderson, "Companies Hate Misery," *Fortune,* June 23, 2003, p. 58.
12. Figures are from the year 2000.
13. Arthur B. Laffer, "California Drainin," *The Wall Street Journal,* January 13, 2003, p. A10.
14. Peter Robinson, "Europe Migrates to the Right," *Washington Times,* January 3, 2003, p. A19.
15. "Adieu, European Left," *The Wall Street Journal,* June 10, 2002, p. A16, and Brian M. Carney, "What's French for 'Tax Cut'," *The Wall Street Journal,* January 10, 2003, p. A10.
16. Moon Ihlwan and Brian Bremmer, "The Other Korean Crisis," *Business Week,* January 20, 2003, pp. 44–52.
17. Daniel J. Mitchell, "Tax Cuts? Da!" *Forbes,* December 9, 2002, p. 38.
18. Jeanne Cummings and Greg Hitt, "Aiming High," *The Wall Street Journal,* January 7, 2003, pp. A1, A8.
19. "Tax Cuts for Growth," *Washington Times,* January 6, 2003, p. A18.
20. "Deflation Warning," *Washington Times,* January 9, 2003, p. A16.
21. Neil Weinberg, "Hot Commodities," *Forbes,* January 20, 2003, pp. 97–99.
22. Robert D. McTeer, "Productive America," *The Wall Street Journal,* January 13, 2003, p. A10.
23. Rich Miller, Peter Coy, Rob Hof, Peter Burrows, and Robert Berner, "Productivity's Second Wind," *Business Week,* February 17, 2003, pp. 36–37.
24. Laura D'Andrea Tyson, "Why Europe Is Even More Sluggish Than the U.S.," *Business Week,* January 13, 2003, p. 26.
25. Phillip Longman, "Squeezed in a Service Economy," *Washington Post,* January 14, 2003, p. A19.
26. Patrice Hill, "Sell-Off Sends Stocks Plunging," *Washington Times,* July 20, 2002, pp. A1, A4.
27. Alan Reynolds, "Improvements . . . and Horror Replays," *Washington Times,* January 12, 2003, p. B8.
28. Richard Rahn, "War Against the Stock Market," *Washington Times,* June 11, 2002, p. A14.
29. Jeremy J. Siegel, "We're Rolling Along," *Kiplinger's,* February 2003, p. 54.

Chapter 3

1. Erin Kelly, "Sanders Going to China to Battle Trade Imbalance," Gannett News Service, January 8, 2003.
2. Michael Luo, "Rocket's Yao Ming Carries Asians in America to New Heights," AP Worldstream, February 7, 2003.
3. Jeremy Laurence, "The Habit Hollywood Just Can't Stub Out," *Independent,* January 5, 2002.
4. Peter Coy, "The Payoff from Free Trade," *Business Week,* June 24, 2002, p. 26.
5. Pete Engardio, Aaron Bernstein, and Manjeet Kripalani, "The New Global Job Shift," *Business Week,* February 3, 2003, p. 50.
6. Ibid.
7. Stacie Driebusch, "Washington U–St. Louis Professor Aims for Understandable Economics," University Wire, January 14, 2003.
8. John J. Wild, Kenneth L. Wild, and Jerry C. Y. Han, *International Business,* 2nd ed. Englewood Cliffs, NJ: Prentice Hall, 2003.
9. Paul Craig Roberts, "Globalism's Offshore Undercurrents," *Washington Times,* January 9, 2003.
10. Jackson Kubl, "Tempest in a Coffeepot," *Reason,* January 1, 2003, p. 55.
11. Mark Pendergast, "Starbucks Goes to Europe . . . with Humility and Respect," *The Wall Street Journal,* April 9, 2002, p. B16.
12. Christopher Lawton, "Anheuser-Busch, China's Tsingtao Plan an Alliance," *The Wall Street Journal,* July 31, 2002, p. B6.
13. David Nicklaus, Gregory Cancelada, and Chern Yeh Kwok, "New A-B Chief Faces a Global Challenge; International Mergers May Threaten Domestic Beer King," *St. Louis Post Dispatch,* April 28, 2002, p. A1.
14. Dermot McGrath, "The High Price of Setting Up or Not Setting Up, a Global Net Presence," *International Herald Tribune,* June 24, 2002.
15. Peter Koy, Jack Ewing, and Laura Cohn, "Soggy and Still Sliding," *Business Week,* January 13, 2003, p. 32.
16. Sue Kirchhoff, "Trade Deficit Sets Record," *USA Today,* January 29, 2003, p. 2B; and "Trade Gap Widens to a Record," United Press International, January 17, 2003.
17. Donald Ratajczak, "U.S. Trade Deficit Not a Concern—Right Now Dollar Instability Could Result If Gap Gets Wider," *Atlanta Journal & Constitution,* April 28, 2002, p. Q3.
18. Paul Magnusson, "A U.S. Trade Ploy That Is Starting to Boomerang," *Business Week,* July 29, 2002, pp. 64–65.
19. Naomi Koppel, "Fifteen Countries Call for Tightening of Anti-Dumping Rules in World Trade Organization," AP Worldstream, February 5, 2003.
20. "Eluding Tariffs, Firms Look at Options in Steel, Lumber Trade," *Washington Times,* January 20, 2003; and George Hager, "Bush Plays the Free Trade Game," *USA Today,* May 5, 2002, p. C1.
21. Marc Gunther, "Has Eisner Lost the Disney Magic?" *Fortune,* January 7, 2002, pp. 64–69.
22. Toshifumi Kitamura, "Japan-Disneyland Anniversary," Agence France Presse, January 25, 2003.
23. Thomas Crampton, "Disney Punches Ticket for Mickey Mouse's Entry into China," *International Herald Tribune,* January 14, 2003.
24. www.usatrade.gov.
25. www.buyusa.com.
26. Courtney Fingar, "The ABCs of EMCs," *Global Business,* May 2002, pp. 51–56.
27. www.buyusa.com
28. "Global Markets-U.S. Stocks Surge on Cisco; Bonds Drop," Reuters, May 18, 2002.
29. "Business: The Great Leap Forward; Cars in China," *The Economist,* February 1, 2003, p. 62.
30. "Daimler, Mitsubishi, Hyundai Ink Car Engine Pact," Reuters, May 4, 2002.
31. Ron Ameln, "Strategic Alliances as a Growth Strategy," *St. Louis Small Business Monthly,* July 2002, p. 36.

32. Eric Krell, "The Alliance Advantage," *Business Finance,* July 2002, pp. 16–23.
33. Matthew Fordahl, "Häagen-Dazs Scoops Up Dreyer's in Cool Deal for Shareholders," Associated Press, June 18, 2002, Business Edition.
34. "India: Losing Sheen for U.S. Multinationals," United Press International, January 27, 2003.
35. Geert Hofstede, *Culture and Organizations: Software of the Mind* (New York: McGraw-Hill, 1997), pp. 3–19.
36. Chang-Ran Kim, "Toyota, Again, Sees Growth in U.S. Market," Reuters Business, January 5, 2003.
37. Manjeet Kripalani and Mark Clifford, "India: Coke Finally Gets It Right," *Business Week,* February 10, 2003, p. 18.
38. Anne Tergesen, "Bucking a Weaker Buck," *Business Week,* June 3, 2002, p. 88.
39. Daniel Bases, "Dollar Hits 3-Year Low Versus the Euro," Reuters Business, January 20, 2003.
40. Steve H. Hanke, "The Strong Dollar Charade," *Forbes,* February 3, 2003, p. 122.
41. Kevin Gray, "Nearly One Year after Devaluation, Inflation in Argentina at 41 Percent," AP Worldstream, January 6, 2003.
42. www.nestle.com.
43. Matt Krantz, "Regulators Look Closely at Bartering," *USA Today,* May 21, 2002, p. 35.
44. Alan O. Sykes, "New Directions in Law and Economics," *American Economist,* April 1, 2002, p. 10.
45. Takure Yhangazha, "AIPPA Fosters Corrupt Environment," Africa News Service, January 23, 2003.
46. Selichi Kondo, "Little Cheats Will Have to Repent Uncooperative Tax Havens," *International Herald Tribune,* May 19, 2002.
47. Alma Olaechea, "Globalization Is Best for All," University Wire, February 13, 2002.
48. Jeffrey H. Birnbaum, "Business to Bush: Let Us into Cuba!" *Fortune,* May 27, 2002, p. 36.
49. Sandra Sobieraj, "Bush Acts to Ease Cold War Restrictions on Computer Exports," AP Worldstream, January 2, 2002.
50. Chester Dawson and Katie Kerwin, "Japan: Mitsubishi Moves into High Gear," *Business Week International,* February 10, 2003, p. 16.
51. Ernesto Zedillo, "Will the Doha Round Implode in 2003?" *Forbes,* February 3, 2003, p. 29.
52. Dan Ikenson, "Bull in a China Shop," *Washington Times,* January 13, 2003.
53. Dexter Roberts and Paul Magnusson, "International Business: China: The Tricks of Trade," *Business Week,* July 15, 2002, p. 52.
54. Anders Aslund, "Russia Must Join the WTO as Soon as Possible," *The St. Petersburg Times* (Russia), February 4, 2003.
55. George Melloan, "Europe Builds an Edifice, but Will It Stand?" *The Wall Street Journal,* December 17, 2002, p. A17; and "Enlargement: EU Finalizes Accession Treaty for Candidate Countries," *European Report,* February 8, 2003.
56. Steve H. Hanke, "The Strong-Dollar Charade," *Forbes,* February 3, 2003, p. 122.
57. John Cavanagh, Sarah Anderson, Jaime Serra, and J. Enrique Espinosa, "Happily Ever NAFTA," *Foreign Policy,* September 1, 2002, p. 58.
58. Ibid.
59. Eric Rubin, "The Case against Globalization," *Tampa Tribune,* July 22, 2002, p. 9.
60. Ibid.
61. "All Americas Trade Agreement Endangered," *The Worldpaper* (USA), January 8, 2003.
62. Dexter Roberts, "Clear Sailing for Pirates," *Business Week,* July 15, 2002, p. 53.

Chapter 4

1. Pallavi Guniganti, "Ethics' Place in Education," University Wire, April 16, 2002.
2. Jack Kemp, "A Golden Age to Sustain," *Washington Times,* January 3, 2001, p. A13; and Anne Papmehl, "Do Green Firms Mirror Market?" *Toronto Star,* June 3, 2002.
3. Lauren Wiener, "Half of College Students Have Cheated, Study Says," University Wire, February 23, 2000; Kelly Simmons, "Student Cheating Taking New Tack: Some May Be Honest Mistakes," *Atlanta Journal and Constitution,* January 20, 2002, p. C1; "Cheating Epidemic Must Be Stopped," University Wire, February 19, 2002; and "Lessons in Integrity Prove Hard to Teach," *Newsday,* February 9, 2002, p. A23.
4. Jamie Reno, "Need Someone in Creative Accounting?" *Newsweek,* May 17, 1999.
5. Kenneth Blanchard and Norman Vincent Peale, *The Power of Ethical Management* (New York: William Morrow, 1996).
6. "Small Business Owners Doing Little to Promote Ethics," Ascribe Newswire, June 25, 2002.
7. Peter Worthington, "Ethics: Either You Have Them or You Don't," *Edmonton Sun,* June 1, 2002, p. 11.
8. John McCormick, "The Sorry Side of Sears," *Newsweek,* February 22, 1999, pp. 36–39.
9. Ethics Resource Center, 2000 National Business Ethics Survey (www.ethics.org/2000survey.html).
10. "The Best & Worst Managers: The Whistle Blower," *Business Week,* January 13, 2003, p. 90.
11. Craig Savoye, "Workers Say Honesty Is Best Company Policy," *Christian Science Monitor,* June 15, 2000, p. 3; and Andrea Kay, "Tread Carefully Before Becoming a Whistleblower," Gannett News Service, February 21, 2002.
12. Fara Warner, "Going Once, Going Twice," *Fast Company,* March 2002.
13. Matthew Murray and Anna Ossipova, "Code Could Have Done Enron Some Good," *St. Petersburg Times,* February 26, 2002; and "Shameful Antics of Some Give the Business Calling a Bad Rap," *Tampa Tribune,* January 3, 2003, p. 12.
14. Ted Jackovics, "Corporate Gifts Exceed Trend," *Tampa Tribune,* July 11, 2002; and "Charities' Post-Attack Fears Fail to Materialize; Donations Rise," *Washington Times,* July 7, 2002.
15. Gia Fenoglio, "Politics: Helping Hands," *National Journal,* March 23, 2002.
16. Heather R. Taylor, "Think Globally, Click Locally: Volunteers Looking to Make a Difference Can Find Plenty of Opportunities Online," *Washington Post,* March 14, 2002, p. C10; and Leslie Miller, "Volunteerism Gets a Web Boost, Too," *USA Today,* March 19, 2002, p. 4D.
17. Anita Lienhart, "She Drove, He Drove Mercedes C320," Gannett News Service, January 9, 2001; Menke-Gluckert, "Baby Benz Faces the Moose," *Europe,* February 2, 1998, pp. 40–44; and Earle Eldridge, "Luxury Sales Up: 'Move Up' Market Strong," *Edmonton Sun,* June 21, 2002, p. DR16.
18. "Charity Is Good Business," AAP General News, June 28, 2002.
19. Del Jones, "Ethics Don't Always Pay, but Lack of Them Always Hurts," *USA Today,* July 5, 2002, p. 8B.
20. Devlin Barrett, "Ex-ImClone CEO Arrested for Trading," AP Online, June 13, 2002; Keith Naughton, "More 'Ridiculousness,' " *Newsweek,* July 8, 2002, p. 46; and John Porretto, "Chrysler Does Not Extend Stewart Deal," AP Online, January 7, 2003.
21. Charles Haddad, Dean Foust, and Steve Rosenbush, "WorldCom's Sorry Legacy," *Business Week,* July 8, 2002, p. 38; and "WorldCom Seeks New Deadline in Bankruptcy Court," *Toronto Star,* January 10, 2003.

22. Teresa M. McAleavy, "How Big Companies Lose Millions When Their Good Workers Defect," *The Record,* May 31, 2002.
23. David D. Perlmutter, "Business Ethics Should Be Part of the Bottom Line," *Newsday,* July 9, 2002, p. A27.
24. www.rhino.com/about/support.html.
25. James Graff, "Business/World Economic Forum: Giving Some of It Back," *Time International,* February 15, 1999, p. 40; and "Samsung Thrives on People, Technology, Future," *Korea Times,* January 30, 2000.
26. By Russ Wiles, "Shareholder Resolutions Boom: Social Responsibility a Top Concern," *Arizona Republic,* June 10, 2002, p. D1; Laurent Belsie, "Tough Times Test Firms' Lofty Standards," *Christian Science Monitor,* January 28, 2002, p. 20; and Susan Scherreik, "Following Your Conscience Is Just a Few Clicks Away," *Business Week,* May 13, 2002, p. 116.
27. Laurent Belsie, "Spotting Links to Terrorism, Inc.," *Christian Science Monitor,* April 22, 2002, p. 15; and Manuel Roig-Franzia, "Florida Arrest Renews Debate over Muslim Charities; Entrepreneur's Donations Linked to Supporting Terrorism," *Washington Post,* January 4, 2003, p. A1.
28. "Nike, Adidas Under Fire for Low Wages," United Press International, March 8, 2002;"Vietnam Labour Body Defends Nike After Court Ruling," Reuters, May 3, 2002;"Nike and Adidas 'Have Failed to Stop Sweatshop Abuses,' " *Independent,* March 8, 2002, p. 17; and Don Cronin, "Nike, Adidas Do Better but Lag, Study Says," *USA Today,* March 8, 2002.
29. "Social Responsibility: Commission Presents Ideas for Special Forum," *European Report,* June 29, 2002.

Chapter 4 Appendix

1. Marc Kaufman and Jeff Adler, "RJ Reynolds Fined for Ads in Youth Magazines; Ruling by California Judge Is First for Violation of Tobacco Settlement Terms," *Washington Post,* June 7, 2002, p. A 12.
2. Michael Barone, "The Common Good," *U.S. News & World Report,* March 25, 2002, p. 22.
3. Dave Barry, "Caution: Flammable; What the Manly Consumer Really Wants in An Owner's Manual," *Washington Post,* July 7, 2002, p. W32.
4. Ira Sager and Jay Greene, "Information Technology: The Best Way to Make Software Secure: Liability," *Business Week,* March 18, 2002, p. 61.
5. Roger LeRoy Miller and Gaylord A. Jentz, *Fundamentals of Business Law,* Cincinnati,Ohio (West Publishing, 2002), p. 104.
6. Benjamin J. Stein, "How to Ruin American Enterprise in 12 Steps," *Bergen County (New Jersey) Record,* January 15, 2003.
7. Richard Lehmann, "The Uncertainty Factor," *Forbes,* February 3, 2003, p. 118; and "Policy-Makers Force Tort Reform," *Washington Times,* February 6, 2003.
8. Geoffrey Cowley, Ken Shulman, Anne Underwood, and Karen Springen, "Getting the Lead Out," *Newsweek,* February 17, 2003, p. 54.
9. "New Jersey City Sues Gun Manufacturers," AP Online, March 29, 2002.
10. Melanthia Mitchell, "Sniper Victims' Families Sue Gun Makers, Gun Store over Assault Rifle," AP Online, January 16, 2003.
11. Fred Bayles, "Boston Becomes 1st City to Drop Its Lawsuit Against Gun Industry," *USA Today,* March 29, 2002, p. 4A.
12. "Judge Throws Out Suit vs. McDonald's," *Newsday,* January 23, 2003, p. A7.
13. Roger Parloff, "Is Fat the Next Tobacco?" *Fortune,* February 3, 2003, pp. 50–54.
14. Ilaina Jonas, "McDonald's Suit May Be Only First Nibble," Reuters Business, January 28, 2003.
15. Lorraine Woellert, "Tort Reform: A Little Here, a Little There," *Business Week,* January 20, 2003, p. 60.
16. Kevin McAbee, "Prescription Drug Innovation: Profit vs. Affordability," University Wire, January 29, 2003; and www.uspto.gov.
17. Quentin Hardy, "Search 500,000 Documents, Review 160,000 Pages in 20 Hours, and Then Do It All Over Again," *Forbes ASAP,* June 24, 2002, pp. 51–56.
18. Ibid.
19. Ibid.
20. Ruth Walker, "Whose Idea Is It Anyway? Bounty Hunters Track the Validity of Patents," *Christian Science Monitor,* January 17, 2002, p. 11.
21. Ibid.
22. Eric Pfeiffer, "Setting Patent Traps," *Forbes ASAP,* June 24, 2002, p. 65.
23. Janet Rae Dupree, "Powers of Invention," *U.S. News & World Report,* February 11, 2002, p. 66.
24. Charles Lane, "Justices Back Congress in Win for Artists, Entertainment Firms," *Washington Post,* January 16, 2003, p. A1.
25. U.S. Copyright Office.
26. "High Court to Hear Victoria's Secret Trademark Suit," *USA Today,* April 16, 2002, p. 1C.
27. Geoffrey. A. Fowler, "Copies 'R' Us," *The Wall Street Journal,* January 31, 2003, pp. B1, B4; and Fred Weir, "Brand Name No Guarantee in Russia," *Christian Science Monitor,* January 14, 2003, p. 7.
28. Frank Hayes, "UCITA: Not Dead Yet," *Computerworld,* February 17, 2003, p. 50.
29. Christine Dugas, "A Win for Retailers in Credit Card Battle," *USA Today,* June 11, 2002, p. 1B; and Jay Greene, Steve Hamm, and Jim Kerstetter, "Ballmer's Microsoft," *Business Week,* June 17, 2002, p. 66.
30. Michael McCarthy and Jayne O'Donnell, "FTC Idea Could Get Telemarketers to Stop Calling," *USA Today,* June 15, 2002, p. 1B.
31. Carolyn E. Mayer, "Justice, FTC Split Duties on Antitrust," *Washington Post,* March 6, 2002, p. E1.
32. Catherine Yang and Jay Greene, "Information Technology: Lawsuits: Has Microsoft Met Its Match?" *Business Week,* February 4, 2002, p. 7
33. Andrew J. Glass, "More to Come on Microsoft; McCain Vows Senate Hearings; Appeals Could Take Years," *Atlanta Journal and Constitution,* April 4, 2000, p. A1; and D. Ian Hopper, "Feds Defend Microsoft Judge," AP Online, January 12, 2001.
34. Jonathan Krim, "Judge Accepts Settlement in Microsoft Case; Call for Tougher Curbs Rejected," *Washington Post,* November 2, 2002, p. A1; and Robert A. Levy, "Big Court Wins by Microsoft Haven't Ended States' Suits," *Investors Business Daily,* January 17, 2003, p. A15.
35. David Ho, "Judge Denies Appeal in Microsoft Ruling," AP Online, January 13, 2003; and David Ho, "Judge Rejects Request by Computer Trade Groups in Microsoft Case," AP Worldstream, January 13, 2003.
36. Tim Dobbyn, "New SEC Chief Takes Oath, Promises to Be Tough," Reuters Business, February 18, 2003.
37. "Finance and Economics: Wishy-Washy; the Sarbanes-Oxley Act," *The Economist,* February 1, 2003, p. 66.
38. Bill Husted, "Cigarette Tax: Plan May Bring Unintended Results," *Atlanta Journal and Constitution,* February 15, 2003, p. F1; and Robert Tanner, "State Budget Gaps Jumped 50 Percent," AP Online, February 5, 2003.

39. Scott Feitell, "Internet Tax Hurts Commerce, Students," University Wire, February 19, 2003.
40. Jim Krane, "EU Plans to Tax Internet," AP Online, May 8, 2002.
41. Richard Newman, "Bankruptcies at All Time High and Rising," *Bergen County (New Jersey) Record,* February 4, 2003.
42. David R. Francis, "Bankruptcy Fix: A Tightening, or an Unfair Squeeze?" *Christian Science Monitor,* May 6, 2002, p. 21.
43. Christine Dugas, "Bankruptcy Filings Set Record in 2002," *USA Today,* February 17, 2003, p. 6B.
44. Kris Frieswick, "What's Wrong with This Picture?" *CFO,* January 2003, pp. 41–46; Brian Deagon, "UAL's Inexorable Slide Toward Chapter 11 Offers Hope to a Beleaguered Industry," *Investors Business Daily,* December 6, 2002, p. A1; Erik Ahlberg, "Kmart Can Close Stores, Proceed with Financing," *The Wall Street Journal,* January 29, 2003, p. B2; and Christine Dugas, "Bankruptcy Filings Set Record in 2002," *USA Today,* February 17, 2003, p. 6B.
45. Jesse J. Holland, "Tougher Bankruptcy Laws Likely," AP Online, July 26, 2002.
46. Josh Roska, "Changes in Bankruptcy Law May Have Chance of Passage," *St. Louis Post Dispatch,* January 23, 2003, p. 2.
47. Mark Hendricks, "Turnaround Tactics," *American Way,* June 15, 2002, pp. 66–69.
48. Sheridan Prasso, "Wow Are They That Good?" *Business Week,* August 5, 2002, p. 14; and "Southwest Airlines Posts Quarterly Profit," Reuters Business, January 22, 2003; and Nicolas Stein, "America's Most Admired Companies," *Fortune,* March 3, 2003, p. 81.
49. Steven Rosenbush, Heather Timmons, Roger Crockett, Christopher Palmeri, and Charles Haddad, "Inside the Telecom Game," *Business Week,* August 5, 2002, pp. 34–40.
50. Ibid.
51. Doug Abrams, "Other States See Repercussions of California's Failed Deregulation Experiment," Gannett News Service, July 24, 2002; and "United States: Utility Executives Lose Confidence in Deregulation," *Transmission and Distribution World,* February 1, 2003.
52. "Deregulating Energy the Right Way," *Business Week,* May 27, 2002, p. 114.

Chapter 5

1. U.S. Internal Revenue Service.
2. Yvette Armendariz, "Corporations Are Popular; But Getting Set Up Has Disadvantages," *Arizona Republic,* July 15, 2002, p. D3.
3. Yvette Armendariz, "Sole Ownership a Mixed Bag," *Arizona Republic,* July 1, 2002, p. D3.
4. Rudy Fichtenbaum and Paulette Olson, "The Impact of Unionization on Health Insurance Benefits," *Journal of Economic Issues,* June 1, 2002, p. 323.
5. John Brown and Ned Minor, "Business at Risk When Owner Dies," *Denver Rocky Mountain News,* March 8, 2002, p. 5B.
6. Daniel Fisher, "Pipeline for Profits," *Forbes,* March 18, 2002, p. 188.
7. Yvette Armendariz, "Partnership Structure Easy to Form, but Not So Popular," *Arizona Republic,* July 8, 2002, p. D4; and "LLP," *Washington Post,* March 17, 2002, p. H3.
8. Simone Kaplan, "The Right Fit," *CIO,* December 1, 2001.
9. Paul Edwards and Sarah Edwards, "Should You INC or Not?" *Entrepreneur,* June 2002.
10. Renee Montagne, "Delaware as a Haven to Businesses Looking to Incorporate," *Morning Edition* (National Public Radio), March 7, 2002; and John Maggs, "Business: Out of the Loop," *National Journal,* March 9, 2002.
11. Armendariz, "Corporations Are Popular."
12. U.S. Internal Revenue Service.
13. Joyce Rosenberg, "Consider Tax Status, Control Level While Deciding Business," *Washington Times,* April 30, 2001, p. D6.
14. Joyce M. Rosenberg, "Should You Incorporate?" AP Online, April 17, 2002.
15. Karen Lowry Miller, "The Giants Stumble," *Newsweek,* July 8, 2002, p. 14.
16. David M. Schweiger, "Merge Right," *Business & Economic Review,* April–June 2002.
17. Rob Longley, "Bucks and Pucks: So, Who Calls the Shots at Maple Leaf Sports and Entertainment Ltd?." *London Free Press,* July 15, 2002, p. B6.
18. Gene G. Marcial, "Inside Wall Street: Just Idling at DaimlerChrysler," *Business Week,* April 29, 2002, p. 124.
19. "Foreign Investment in U.S. Down by 60 Percent Last Year," Xinhua News Agency, June 5, 2002.
20. "Entrepreneur's 22nd Annual Franchise 500," *Entrepreneur,* January 2002.
21. Devlin Smith, "Want Franchise with That?" *Entrepreneur,* May 2002.
22. "Subway Passes McDonald's as the Biggest Chain," *St. Louis Post-Dispatch,* February 4, 2002, p. BP5.
23. Julie Bennett, "Inspired by America's Consumer Boom, Entrepreneurs Pursue New Markets," *The Wall Street Journal,* June 17, 1999, p. B18.
24. Carlye Adler, "Would You Pay $2 Million for This Franchise?" *Fortune Small Business,* May 1, 2002.
25. Cynthia E. Griffin, "Mixing It Up," *Entrepreneur,* November 2001.
26. Ellen Paris, "A Franchise of Her Own," *Entrepreneur,* June 2000, pp. 163–70; and Cynthia E. Griffer, "Fair Financing," *Entrepreneur,* January 2001.
27. Susan Salisbury, "Temporary Agencies in Area See Increase in Demand for Workers," *Palm Beach Post,* June 30, 2002, p. 1F.
28. Cora Daniels, "The Most Powerful Black Executives in America Meet 50 Black Business Men and Women Who Wield Unprecedented Clout," *Fortune,* July 22, 2002, p. 60.
29. "Click Point Pours Efforts into Coffee," *South American Business Information,* January 25, 2002.
30. Dan Morse, "Individual Outlet Owners Set Up E-Commerce Sites," *The Wall Street Journal,* March 28, 2000.
31. Todd D. Maddocks, "Catch the Wave: How to Harness the Power of the Internet and Find a Franchise That's Right for You," *Entrepreneur,* January 2000, pp. 169–73.
32. www.mcdonalds.com/corporate/investor/financialinfo/systemrest/index.html.
33. Phuong Ly, "Immigrants Find a Taste of Home; Foreign Food Shops Expand to U.S. to Serve Old Customers—and New," *Washington Post,* January 22, 2002, p. B1.
34. "January 2002 Web News," *Electrical Construction & Maintenance,* January 1, 2002.
35. Gretchen Schlosser, "Processing Begins in Producers' New Plant," *National Hog Farmer,* January 15, 2002.

Chapter 6

1. Ellen McCarthy, "Entrepreneurial Students More Grounded; As Dot-Com Dreams Fade, Business Basics Come to Fore," *Washington Post,* March 19, 2002, p. E5.
2. U.S. Internal Revenue Service.
3. Ellen McCarthy, "New Wave of Entrepreneurs Runs Start-Ups with Restraint," *Washington Post,* May 31, 2002, p. E1.
4. Angie C. Marek, "Disabled—and Flying Solo: Self-Employment Is an Increasingly Attractive Option for Legions of Disabled People Who Can't Find a Workplace That Accommodates Their Needs," *Fortune Small Business,* July 25, 2002.

5. Chris Gray, "Meet the Modern-Day Medicis Who Dominate the Art World for Profit," *Independent,* July 22, 2002, p. 3.
6. Christina McCarroll, "Beyond Babysitting," *Christian Science Monitor,* June 24, 2002, p. 15.
7. Bret Schulte, "No Fat Cats Allowed; Members of the 'New Boys Club' Are in Town to Take a Meeting, Firmly Closing the Door on the Old Breed of Corporate Executive," *Washington Post,* August 17, 2002, p. C1.
8. Samuel Fromartz, "Newbiz: Entrepreneurs Not Braking for Economic Slowdown," Reuters Business Report, March 20, 2002; Kathy Wagstaff, "Pointers Offered for Small Businesses," *Atlanta Journal and Constitution,* May 30, 2002, p. J3.
9. Amy Joyce, "After the Pink Slip, a Rosier Outlook; Laid-Off Workers Take Chances as Entrepreneurs," *Washington Post,* July 4, 2002, p. T5.
10. Laura Koss-Feder, "Office, Sweet Office," *Newsday,* February 21, 2002, p. C6.
11. "US Census Bureau: 9.3 Million People Worked at Home in 1997, Census Bureau Reports," M2 PressWIRE, January 17, 2002.
12. "Home-Office Costs and Tax Deductions," *Washington Times,* April 12, 2002.
13. "A Home Office Works," *Washington Times,* January 16, 2002.
14. Karen E. Spaede, "Know the Law: Understanding Zoning and Other Restrictions Before You Start Your Business Will Save You Big Headaches (and Money) Later," Entrepreneur.com, February 18, 2002.
15. "E-Stats," U.S. Department of Commerce, March 18, 2002.
16. Bill Husted, "Dot-Com Success: Camera Dealer Develops a Niche," *Atlanta Journal and Constitution,* September 1, 2002, p. Q1.
17. Jerry Useem, "[3M] + [General Electric] = ? Jim McNerney Thinks He Can Turn 3M from a Good Company into a Great One—With a Little Help from His Former Employer, General Electric," *Fortune,* August 12, 2002, p. 127.
18. "Incubators Assist Start-Ups with Subsidies," *Washington Times,* January 21, 2002; and Jenni Smith, "Technology Project Names Its Director: Former Mayor to Head High-Tech Team Forged by UTA," *Dallas Morning News,* March 22, 2002, p. 1Y.
19. Teresa M. McAleavy, "Business Ownership Among Women Rises," *Bergen County (New Jersey) Record,* July 26, 2002, p. B1; Dianne Solis, "Business Boot Camps Help Women Cash In: Female Entrepreneurs Discover Springboard to Venture Capital," *Dallas Morning News,* April 14, 2002, p. 1A; Jim Hopkins, "Big Business Can't Swallow These Little Fish," *USA Today,* March 27, 2002, p. 1B; Julie Rose, "The New Risk Takers Meet the Gutsy Entrepreneurs Who, Even in These Tough Times, Are Breaking Open Markets, Launching Hot Products—And Starting Companies from Scratch," *Fortune Small Business,* March 1, 2002, p. 28; Heather Draper, "Official Says Minority Firms Must Be More Entrepreneurial," *Denver Rocky Mountain News,* March 14, 2002, p. 4B; and Jim Hopkins, "Financial Firms Cater to Powerful Women," *USA Today,* June 19, 2002, p. 3B.
20. Elizabeth Lee Brown, "Against the Odds," *Tampa Tribune,* June 8, 2002, p. 1.
21. Nathan Vardi, "No Free Lunch," *Forbes,* February 3, 2003, pp. 70–71.
22. Solis, "Business Boot Camps."
23. Janet Forgrieve, "Boulder Company Offers 'Angels' Tips, Would-Be Invertors in Startups Get Advice on Making Choices," *Denver Rocky Mountain News,* July 26, 2002, p. 4B; and David Nicklaus, "Angel Investors Won't Take Many Flying Leaps Today," *St. Louis Post-Dispatch,* April 3, 2002, p. C1.
24. Linda Himelstein, "Entrepreneurs: VCs Turn the Screws," *Business Week,* May 27, 2002, p. 82.
25. "U.S. Department of Labor and Small Business Administration Launch Project Gate, a One-Stop Service for Entrepreneurs," Regulatory Intelligence Data, August 28, 2002.
26. "Kerry Urges Finance Committee to Back Tax Incentives for America's Entrepreneurs," US Newswire, June 4, 2002.
27. Keith Lowe, "Why You Need an Accountant," Entreprenuer.com, June 3, 2002.
28. Keith Lowe, "Developing a Solid Relationship with Your Attorney," Entrepreneur.com, May 6, 2002.
29. Keith Lowe, "Keep Your Banker Informed," Entrepreneur.com, April 1, 2002.
30. Andrea Kay, "Older Workers Still a Necessary Part of the Workforce," Gannett News Service, August 15, 2002.
31. "US SBA: SBA and My Own Business, Inc., to Provide Free Online Course to Help Small Businesses," M2 PressWIRE, March 20, 2002.
32. Sara Kehaulani Goo, "Going from Larval Stage to Success; Firms Emerge from Cocoon with Help of MBA Students," *Washington Post,* August 15, 2002, p. T5.
33. "SBA to Bring More Export Financing to Small Business Through Enhanced Export Express Loan Program," US Newswire, September 3, 2002.

Chapter 7

1. Walter B. Wriston, "A Code of Our Own," *The Wall Street Journal,* January 16, 2003, p. A12.
2. "A Bullet Partially Dodged," *The Wall Street Journal,* July 31, 2002, p. A14.
3. Robert J. Samuelson, "The Spirit of America," *Newsweek,* January 13, 2003, p. 47.
4. www.thq.com.
5. Ian Wylie, "There Is No Alternative to . . . TINA," *Fast Company,* July 2002, pp. 106–10.
6. Deborah Ancona, Henrik Bresman, and Katrin Kaeufer, "The Comparative Advantage of X-Teams," *Sloan Management Review,* Spring 2002, pp. 33–39.
7. Jack Otter, "Memo to Imperial CEOs: Party's Over," *SmartMoney,* September 2002, pp. 32–35.
8. W. Chan Kim, "Fair Process: Managing in the Knowledge Economy," *Harvard Business Review,* January 2003, pp. 127–36.
9. Ibid.
10. Darrell Rigby, "Don't Get Hammered by Management Fads," *The Wall Street Journal,* May 21, 2001, p. A22.
11. Sarah Kaplan and Eric D. Beinhocker, "The Real Value of Strategic Planning," *Sloan Management Review,* Winter 2003, pp. 71–76.
12. Robert Barker, "The Art of Brainstorming," *Business Week,* August 26, 2002, pp. 168–69.
13. Michael Goold and Andrew Campbell, "Do You Have a Well-Designed Organization?" *Harvard Business Review,* March 2002, pp. 117–24.
14. Don Steinberg, "The Ultimate Technology Survival Guide," *SmartBusiness,* February 2002, pp. 37–49.
15. Laura Rock Kopczak and M. Eric Johnson, "The Supply-Chain Management Effect," *Sloan Management Review,* Spring 2003, pp. 27–34.
16. Kathleen M. Eisenhardt, "Has Strategy Changed?" *Sloan Management Review,* Winter 2002, pp. 88–91.
17. Lauren Keller Johnson, "The Organizational Identity Trap," *Sloan Management Review,* Summer 2002, p. 11.
18. Bob Weinstein, "What We Can Learn About Leadership from Sam Walton," *Washington Times,* February 25, 2002, p. E2.
19. Elizabeth Wasserman, "A Race for Profits," *mbajungle.com,* March / April 2003, pp. 40–41.

20. H. James Harrington, "Knowledge Management Takes Us from Chance to Choice," *Quality Digest,* April 2003, pp. 14–16.
21. Lori Ioannou, "Corporate America's Social Conscience," *Fortune,* May 26, 2003, pp. S1–S10.

Chapter 8

1. Linda Teschler, "Is Your Company up to Speed?," *Fast Company,* June 2003, pp. 81–111.
2. Scott M. Paton, "Customer Satisfaction Vs. Customer Service," *Quality Digest,* May 2003, p. 4.
3. Jim Keary, "Drivers Steam over DMV Wait," *Washington Times,* August 1, 2002, pp. B1, B2.
4. Brook Manville and Josiah Ober, "Beyond Empowerment: Building a Company of Citizens," *Harvard Business Review,* January 2003, p. 139.
5. Jon E. Hilsenrath, "Retailers Score Points in Keeping Consumers Happy," *The Wall Street Journal,* February 19, 2002, p. A2.
6. Carol Matlack and Pallavi Gogoi, "What's This? The French Love McDonald's?" *Business Week,* January 13, 2003, p. 50.
7. Mark Athitakis, "How to Make Money on the Net," *Business 2.0,* May 2003, pp. 83–90.
8. Fara Warner, "Microsoft Eats the Dog Food," *Fast Company,* September 2002, pp. 46–48.
9. Fara Warner, "GM Goes Off-Road," *Fast Company,* February 2003, pp. 40–42.
10. Michael F. Corbett, "An Inside Look at Outsourcing," *Fortune,* June 9, 2003, pp. S1–S6.
11. Pete Engardio, Aaron Bernstein, and Manjeet Kriplani, "Is Your Job Next?," *Business Week,* February 3, 2003, pp. 50–60.
12. Darlene Superville, "Washington Increasingly Outsources Work," *Washington Times,* February 8, 2003, pp. C8 & C9.
13. Paul Craig Roberts, "Lethal Outsourcing," *Washington Times,* February 27, 2003, p. A19.
14. Pip Coburn, "China's Magic Number," *Red Herring,* February 2003, p. 67.
15. Daniel Eisenberg, "There's a New Way to Think @ Big Blue," *Time,* January 20, 2003, pp. 49–53.
16. Paul J. Kampas, "Shifting Cultural Gears," *Sloan Management Review,* Winter 2003, pp. 41–48.
17. Lauren Keller Johnson, "The Organizational Identity Trap," *Sloan Management Review,* Summer 2002, p. 11.
18. George Anders, "The Carly Chronicles," *Fast Company,* February 2003, pp. 66–72.
19. Mary Kwak, "The True Value of a Lost Customer," *Sloan Management Review,* Winter 2003, p. 9.
20. Walter R. Wreston, "A Code of Our Own," *The Wall Street Journal,* June 16, 2003, p. A12.
21. "Will CEO Pain Lead to Labor Gains?" *Business Week,* September 16, 2002, p. 6.

Chapter 9

1. Joanne Gordon, "Calling Dr. Demetria," *Forbes,* June 12, 2000, pp. 212–14.
2. Kathryn Jones, "The Dell Way," *Business 2.0,* February 2003, pp. 61–66.
3. Spencer E. Ante, "The New Blue," *Business Week,* March 17, 2003, pp. 80–88.
4. Daniel Eisenberg, "There's a New Way to Think @ Big Blue," *Time,* January 20, 2003, pp. 49–53.
5. Pete Engardio, Aaron Bernstein, and Manjeet Kripalani, "Is Your Job Next?" *Business Week,* February 3, 2003, pp. 50–60.
6. Timothy J. Mullaney, "What's Glowing Online Now?" *Business Week,* September 2, 2002, pp. 94–95.
7. Mary Ellen Mark, "The New Fabric of Success," *Fast Company,* June 2000, pp. 252–70.
8. Laura Rock Kopzak and M. Eric Johnson, "The Supply-Chain Management Effect," *Sloan Management Review,* Spring 2003, pp. 27–34.
9. Jerry Flint, "Too Much Globalism," *Forbes,* January 17, 2003, p. 96.
10. Michael F. Corbett, "An Inside Look at Outsourcing," *Fortune,* June 9, 2003, pp. S1–S6.
11. May Wong, "Anytime, Anyplace: Telework Flourishing," *Washington Times,* June 21, 2002, p. A2.
12. Paul Keegan, "The Architect of Happy Customers," *Business 2.0,* August 2002, pp. 85–87.
13. Mary Set-Du Vall, "From the Pot to the Kettle," *Houston Chronicle,* March 9, 2003, pp. D4 and D7.
14. David Dorsey, "Change Factory," *Fast Company,* June 2000, pp. 209–24.
15. "SPC Software," *Quality Digest,* January 2003, p. 165.
16. Richard J. Schonberger, "Is the Baldrige Award Still about Quality?" *Quality Digest,* December 2001, pp. 25–30.
17. Russell T. Westcott, "Overlooked and Underutilized," *Quality Digest,* July 2003, pp. 49–52.
18. Russell Y. Thornton, "Going Green: A Step-by-Step Guide to ISO 14001 Compliance," *Quality Digest,* March 2003, pp. 31–34.
19. Kristina Stefanova, "Want Cash with That?" *Washington Times,* June 18, 2002, pp. C7–C8.
20. Michael Totty, "The Masses Have Arrived . . . ," *The Wall Street Journal,* January 27, 2003, p. R8.
21. Daren Fonda, "Why the Most Profitable Cars Made in the U.S.A. are Japanese and German," *Time,* June 2003, A9–A13.
22. The press release from August 12, 2002 can be found at http://media.ford.com/newsroom/release_display_test.cfm?article
23. Mila D'Antonio, "Finally Taking Off," *1to1 magazine,* May 2003, pp. 25–30.
24. Faith Keenan, Stanley Holmes, Jay Greene, and Roger O. Crockett, "A Mass Market of One," *Business Week,* December 2, 2002, pp. 68–72.
25. "Is Your Company Up to Speed?," *Fast Company,* June 2003, pp. 81–86.

Chapter 10

1. Vicky Uhland, "Cooking Up a Rare Approach: Springs Consultants Help Restaurant Hire, Keep Good Employees," *Denver Rocky Mountain News,* January 4, 2002, p. 8B; Donna Rosato, "Service Training Gets Emphasis," *USA Today,* September 17, 2002, p. 7E; and Jamie Herzlich, "Hospitality Lessons for Hospital Staff," *Newsday,* February 8, 2003, p. A44.
2. Teresa M. Mcaleavy, "How Big Companies Lose Millions When Their Good Workers Defect," *The Bergen County (New Jersey) Record,* May 31, 2002, p. B1.
3. "Workforce: Challenges Keep Staff from Curse of Boredom," *Birmingham Post,* May 30, 2002, p. 26; Bruce Rosenstein, "Experts: Leaders Can Motivate If They Exude the Right Vibes," *USA Today,* March 25, 2002, p. 9B; and Karen Howe, "What Makes an Employee Tick?" *Toronto Sun,* January 4, 2003, p. 35.
4. "The 'Motivation' Myth? Part 1," Africa News Service, July 15, 2002; Sherri Cruz, "Gearworks Strives to Be a Motivating Place to Work," *Minneapolis Star Tribune,* May 22, 2002, p. 2D; and Michelle Conlin, "The Workplace: Productivity: The Big Squeeze on Workers," *Business Week,* May 13, 2002, p. 96.
5. Ellen Goldhar, "Working the Right Job," *London Free Press,* May 27, 2002, p. 6.

6. Geoffrey Colvin, "Capitalist Century: Managing in the Info Era," *Fortune,* March 6, 2000.
7. John A. Byrne, "The 21st Century Corporation: Back to the Future: Visionary vs. Visionary," *Business Week,* August 28, 2000, p. 210.
8. Robert Levering, Milton Moskowitz, Lisa Munoz, and Paola Hjelt, "The 100 Best Companies to Work For in a Tough Year: These Companies Tried to Do Right by Their Employees," *Fortune,* February 4, 2002, pp. 72 ff.
9. J. C. Conklin, "High Praise Often Produces Whale of a Job: Management Technique Emphasizes Importance of Encouraging Words," *Dallas Morning News,* February 26, 2002, p. 2D; and Kerry Hannon, "A Little Praise Goes Long Way Toward Success," *USA Today,* January 6, 2003, p. 6B.
10. "Personal Satisfaction More Important Than Money: Survey," AAP General News (Australia), January 11, 2002; and John A. Byrne, "How to Lead Now," *Fast Company,* August 2003, pp. 62–70.
11. "Organizing for Empowerment: An Interview with AES's Roger Sant and Dennis Bakke," *Harvard Business Review,* January 1, 1999, p. 110.
12. "Bush Faces Less Confident Japan," Kyodo World News Service, February 18, 2002; and Douglas McGray, "Japan's Gross National Cool," *Foreign Policy,* May 1, 2002, p. 44.
13. Michael A. Lev, "Recession Forcing Japanese to Rethink Business Methods," *Arizona Republic,* May 5, 1999, p. E5.
14. Yuri Kageyama, "Eckrodt Heading Mitsubishi, Third Japanese Automaker under Foreign Leadership," AP Worldstream, March 27, 2002; and "Heading Down: Japan's Wage Round," *The Economist,* March 8, 2003, p. 72.
15. Jamie Talan, "A Neuron Link to Motivation, Reward," *Newsday,* June 10, 2002, p. D3; and U.S. General Accounting Office, "Actions and Plans to Build a Results-Oriented Culture," www.gao.gov, January 17, 2003.
16. David Nadler and Edward Lawler, "Motivation—a Diagnostic Approach," in *Perspectives on Behavior in Organizations.* (New York: McGraw-Hill, 1977).
17. Conklin, "High Praise." ed. Richard Hackman, Edward Lawler, and Lyman Porter.
18. Donde P. Ashmos and Maria L. Nathan, "Team Sense-Making: A Mental Model for Navigating Uncharted Territories," *Journal of Managerial Issues,* July 1, 2002, p. 198; Minda Zetlin, "Pulse of the Organization," *Computerworld,* June 3, 2002, p. 40;"Teckchek: Skills Assessment Tool Launched for Project Managers; Online Adaptive Skills Assessment Application Developed for IT Project Teams," M2 PressWIRE, June 25, 2002; Keith L. Alexander, "Cultivating a Culture; and Companies See Strong Link Between Worker Attitudes, Profits," *Washington Post,* April 21, 2002, p. H1.
19. Tom Incantalupo, "Road Test/Mustang Cobra: An Iconic, Affordable, Muscular Car," *Newsday,* September 19, 2002, p. D9; and Tom Incantalupo, "Ford's Lightly Pumped-Up Version of Its Muscle Car," *Newsday,* January 23, 2003, p. D5.
20. Karl Brauer, "F-Body Dies; Mustang Dances on Grave," www.edmunds.com, July 7, 2002.
21. Todd Richmond, "Miller Brewing Gets New Parent Co.," AP Online, May 31, 2002; and Jessica Wohl, "Philip Morris Co. Is Now Altria Group," Reuters Business, January 27, 2003.
22. Ieva M. Augstums, "Mary Kay Convention Opens Today: Sales Reps to Remember Company's Late Founder and Look to the Future," *Dallas Morning News,* July 18, 2002, p. 2D.
23. Ellen Goldhar, "How to Manage Gen X Workers," *London Free Press,* August 19, 2002, p. 7; Ellen Goldhar, "Gen-Xers Require Whole New Management Style," *Toronto Sun,* August 14, 2002, p. C8; Lisi de Bourbon, "Business Watercooler Stories," AP Online, January 22, 2002; "Overtime: When Generations Collide," United Press International, May 21, 2002; Andrea Sachs, Generation Hex? A New Book Identifies Four Age Groups Warring at Work," *Time,* March 11, 2002, p. Y22; Toddi Gutner, "Businessweek Investor: A Balancing Act for Gen X Women," *Business Week,* January 21, 2002, p. 82.

Chapter 11

1. Kerry Capell, "Clouds over Silicon Glen," *Business Week,* September 2, 2002.
2. Steve Bates, "Facing the Future," *HR Magazine,* July 2002.
3. "Survey Sees Demand Returning for Information-Tech Workers," AP Worldstream, May 6, 2002; Victor Godinez, "IT Job Market: Set for a Thaw?" *Dallas Morning News,* May 26, 2002, p. 7L; and Eve Epstein, "Mastering the Moment," *InfoWorld,* June 3, 2002.
4. Jim Abrams, "Senate Trade Bill to Go Well Beyond President's Request for Trading Authority," AP Worldstream, April 3, 2002; and Jim Abrams, "Senate Democrats Unveil Trade Plan," AP Online, May 1, 2002.
5. John J. Casson, "Nickel and Dimed," *American Economist,* April 1, 2002, p. 78; and Sherwood Ross, "Workplace: Labor Day Bleak for Poor," Reuters Business, August 31, 2002.
6. David Nicklaus, "Labor's Pain," *St. Louis Post-Dispatch,* September 2, 2002, p. A1; Andrea C. Poe, "Tapping a Silver Mine," *HR Magazine,* March 2002; and Brian Tumulty, "Aging Workers Seek to Phase in Their Retirement," *Gannett* News Service, September, 22, 2002.
7. Stephen Barr, "EEOC Weighs Changes in Bias Complaint Procedures," *Washington Post,* June 13, 2002, p. B2.
8. Paul Glader, "Day Care Becomes a Growth Industry; Big Companies Move into Prince William," *Washington Post,* June 30, 2002, p. C1; and Rebecca R. Kahlenberg, "When Stay-at-Home Moms Want a Second Job," *Washington Post,* February 7, 2002, p. C10.
9. Sarah Godinez, "Success Story," *Dallas Morning News,* June 2, 2002, p. 22.
10. Michelle Conlin, "The Workplace: Productivity: The Big Squeeze on Workers," *Business Week,* May 13, 2002, p. 96.
11. Mike Allen and Juliet Eilperin, "Health Care Debate Prompts Standoff on Trade Legislation; Senate Democrats Back Subsidies for Displaced Workers," *Washington Post,* May 2, 2002, p. A2; and Paul Magnusson, "Washington Outlook: Fast Track May Be Just a Horse Trade Away," *Business Week,* April 22, 2002, p. 47.
12. Jerome R. Stockfisch, "Profiting from Benefits," *Tampa Tribune,* July 1, 2002, p. 10; and Stephen Barr, "House Panel to Sample Opinion on Cafeteria-Style Benefits," *Washington Post,* May 21, 2002, p. B2.
13. David Stires, "The Coming Crash in Health Care," *Fortune,* October 14, 2002, p. 205; Katherine Yung, "Child Care Slips on Corporate Agenda: Some Firms Easing Burden, but Most Working Parents on Their Own," *Dallas Morning News,* February 3, 2002, p. 1A; Pamela Yip, "Caring Concerns: Struggles to Help Elderly Can Put Kin in Financial Need," *Dallas Morning News,* August 26, 2002, p. 1D; Steny H. Hoyer, "Not Exactly What We Intended, Justice O'Connor," *Washington Post,* January 20, 2002, p. B1; and "Excellence and Diversity," *St. Louis Post-Dispatch,* May 20, 2002, p. B6.
14. Andrea Kay, "How to Encourage Loyalty at Work," Gannett News Service, August 1, 2002.
15. Mark Albright, "Matching Up the Stripes: Some Retailers Apply Personality Testing to Find 'Corporate Fit,' " *Edmonton Sun,* March 30, 2002, p. 56.
16. "Prepares Youths for Careers in Automotive Technology; Ford Supports Training Centers," *Washington Times,* June 21, 2002.

17. "Log On to the Virtual Reality of Top-Flight Job Opportunities," *Birmingham Post,* February 6, 2001, p. 23; and Monty Phan, "Businesses Keep Tabs on Talent Via Alumni Sites," *Newsday,* November 25, 2001, p. C9.
18. Alison Overholt, "True or False: You're Hiring the Right People," *Fast Company,* February 2002, p. 110.
19. "Jobs: How to Survive 'Killer Questions,' " *Evening Telegraph,* March 14, 2002, p. 45.
20. Keith L. Alexander, "Cultivating a Culture; Companies See Strong Link Between Worker Attitudes, Profits," *Washington Post,* April 21, 2002, p. H1.
21. Steve Bates, "Personality Counts," *HR Magazine,* February 2002.
22. Gillian Flynn, "A Legal Examination of Testing," *Workforce,* June 2002, pp. 92–94.
23. Justin Bachman, "Black BellSouth Workers Allege Bias," AP Online, May 2, 2002; and Kathy Brister, "BellSouth Faces Bias Suit: 5 African-Americans Challenging Policies on Testing, Promotions," *Atlanta Journal and Constitution,* May 3, 2002, p. F1.
24. Anne Fisher, "I Got Caught Smoking Pot. Who's Going to Hire Me Now?" *Fortune,* September 16, 2002, p. 224.
25. Shane Sakae, "Survey Finds Most Employers Test for Drug Use," University Wire, May 3, 2002; and Dana Hawkins, "Tests on Trial," *U.S. News & World Report,* August 12, 2002, p. 46.
26. Margaret Webb Pressler, "A Workforce Divided; Rising Use of Temps Is Creating Two Classes of Employees," *Washington Post,* June 23, 2002, p. H1; Caroline Wilbert, "Increase in Temp Jobs Signals Gradual Rebound," *Atlanta Journal and Constitution,* April 26, 2002, p. F2; and Sherwood Ross, "Workplace: Temporary Work Firms Hoping for Upturn in 2nd Half," Reuters Business Report, January 14, 2002.
27. Maria Mallory White, "Student Gives Temp Work 'A' Experience, Pay Found Rewarding," *Atlanta Journal and Constitution,* July 14, 2002, p. R1.
28. Barbara A. Wiens-Tuers and Elizabeth T. Hill, "How Did We Get Here from There? Movement into Temporary Employment," *Journal of Economic Issues,* June 1, 2002, p. 303; Clecia Thompson, "When Workers Opt for Impermanence," *The Bergen County (New Jersey) Record,* July 19, 2002, p. B1; and Stephen Barr, "Looking for a More Permanent Solution to Extended Use of Temporary Workers," *Washington Post,* April 5, 2002, p. B2.
29. Anne Fisher, "Help! My Best People Keep Leaving for Greener Pastures!" *Fortune,* December 4, 2001.
30. Julekha Dash, "The ROI of Training," *Computerworld,* March 18, 2002, p. 58.
31. Sharlene Massie, "Training Key for Success," *Calgary Sun,* May 19, 2002, p. CC3.
32. Brian Sullivan, "Steelcase Streamlines SAP Training," *Computerworld,* September 2, 2002, p. 26.
33. "Apprenticeship Program Wins Federal Approval," *Sound & Video Contractor,* February 1, 2002.
34. Judy A. Serwatka, "Improving Student Performance in Distance Learning Courses," *Technological Horizons in Education,* April 1, 2002, p. 46; Lucinda Kimsel, "Distance Learning Gives U. Hawaii Students More Options," University Wire, September 4, 2002; Colleen Brandao and Julie Young, "Teaching Online: Harnessing Technology's Power at Florida Virtual School," *Technological Horizons in Education,* May 1, 2002, p. 37; Karen Paulson, "FIPSE: Thirty Years of Learning Anytime and Anywhere," *Change,* September 1, 2002, p. 36; and Adrienne Moore, "Merits of Web, TV Classes Stir Debate," University Wire, April 3, 2002.
35. " 'The Coaching Manager': New Business Book by Babson College Professors Helps Managers Develop Top Talent," Ascribe Newswire, June 17, 2002; and Andrea C. Poe, "Establish Positive Mentoring Relationships," *HR Magazine,* February 2002.
36. Fara Warner, "Inside Intel's Mentoring Movement," *Fast Company,* March 15, 2002, p. 116.
37. "Women and Development," *WIN News,* July 1, 2002, p. 8; Chris Sewell, "Strength in Numbers," *Telephony,* March 4, 2002; Debbe Geiger, "To Boost Their Careers and Their Families, Working Moms Turn to Others Like Themselves," *Newsday,* September 22, 2002, p. B17.
38. Victor Godinez, "Sales Networking Group's Dallas Chapter Aims High," *Dallas Morning News,* August 18, 2002, p. 22L.
39. Dean Takahashi, "Ethnic Network Helps Immigrants Succeed," *The Wall Street Journal Interactive Edition,* July 28, 1999.
40. John Kirkpatrick, "Talent Too Often Goes Unrecognized at Firms: Evaluation Systems May Not Identify the Quiet Hidden Stars," *Dallas Morning News,* April 30, 2002, p. 2D; and Bruce Pfau and Ira Kay, "Does 360-Degree Feedback Negatively Affect Company Performance?" *HR Magazine,* June 2002.
41. Donde P. Ashmos and Maria L. Nathan, "Team Sense-Making: A Mental Model for Navigating Uncharted Territories," *Journal of Managerial Issues,* July 1, 2002, p. 198.
42. Perry Pascarella, "Compensating Teams," *Across the Board,* February 1997, pp. 16–23.
43. Stephanie Sandoval, "City Implements New Pay Plan for Dispatchers: Rather Than Length of Service, Raises Will Be Based on Skill Levels," *Dallas Morning News,* October 12, 2001, p. 4Y.
44. Jerome R. Stockfisch, "Profiting from Benefits," *Tampa Tribune,* July 1, 2002, p. 10.
45. Leslie Haggin Geary and Michael J. Powers, "Corporate America's Best Benefits," *Money,* December 1, 2001, p. 140; Larry Lipman, "Employers Pass Along Rising Health Care Costs," *Palm Beach Post,* June 16, 2002, p. 1F; Jim Hertel, "Health Care Woes: Two Views; Is There an End in Sight to the Ever Increasing Spiral of Employee Health Costs?" *Denver Rocky Mountain News,* March 2, 2002, p. 2C.
46. Jennifer Hutchins, "How to Make the Right Voluntary Benefit Choices," *Workforce,* March 2002, pp. 42–48.
47. Suzanne Koudsi, "You Want More but Your Company Doesn't Have It: Suzanne Koudsi Finds Out How to Get a Raise When the Well Has Run Dry," *Fortune,* April 29, 2002, p. 177; "Analysis: The Future of Work," United Press International, June 27, 2002; James P. Burton, Thomas W. Lee, and Brooks C. Holtom, "The Influence of Motivation to Attend, Ability to Attend, and Organizational Commitment on Different Types of Absence," *Journal of Managerial Issues,* July 1, 2002, p. 181; and Brian Tumulty, "Many Working Moms Lack Flexibility in Workplace," Gannett News Service, May 10, 2002.
48. "Pentagon Policy-Makers Battle with Waning Morale," *Washington Times,* August 12, 2002.
49. Matt Moore, "Business Watercooler Stories," AP Online, September 3, 2002.
50. "Census Studies Home-Based Workers," AP Online, January 17, 2002; Heather Draper, "More Are Working at Home; Boulder/Longmont Ranks No. 1 in Percentage Who Do," *Denver Rocky Mountain News,* June 5, 2002, p. 1B.
51. Amy Martinez, "New Technology Helps Some Avoid the Office," *Palm Beach Post,* May 24, 2002, p. 13A; "A Home Office Works," *Washington Times,* January 6, 2002.
52. Owen S. Good, "Commuters Get Perks Employers Aim to Soften Impact of Traffic with Pools, Odd Shifts, Working at Home," *Denver Rocky Mountain News,* April 8, 2002, p. 22A; "Telecommuters Could Solve Traffic Problems," *Toronto Star,* August 31, 2002.
53. Mark Harrington, "Stand By for IBM's 'Office of the Future': At Big Blue, Adjustable Space, Electronic Sensors, No Cubicle Walls," *Newsday,* March 31, 2002, p. D7.

54. Vicky Uhland, "Accenture Workers Have No Office to Call Their Own," *Denver Rocky Mountain News,* January 12, 2002, p. 5C.
55. Victor Godinez, "Positive Exit Interview Can Pay Dividends Later Staying Rational and Cordial Is Key When Facing Job Loss, Outplacement Expert Says," *Dallas Morning News,* February 10, 2002, pp. 11L; and Anne Fisher, "Break All the Rules: after Polling Thousands of Companies, Gallup Created a New Approach to Managing That Has Helped It and Many Others Grow," *Fortune Small Business,* September 1, 2002, p. 52.
56. Dave D. Buss, "Be Ready When Employees Walk out the Door," www.startup.wsj.com, June 30, 1999.
57. Sacha Cohen, "High-Tech Tools Lower Barriers for Disabled," *HR Magazine,* October 2002.
58. Nathan L. Essex, "Americans with Disabilities: Are They Losing Ground?" *The Clearing House,* January 1, 2002, p. 151; and Michael Barrier, "A Line in the Sand," *HR Magazine,* July 2002.
59. Gina Holland, "Court Hears Age Discrimination Case," AP Online, March 20, 2002.

Chapter 12

1. Leigh Strope, "Union Membership in U.S. Hits New Low," AP Online, February 26, 2003.
2. Aaron Bernstein, "Labor: Palace Coup at the AFL-CIO," *Business Week,* March 17, 2003, p. 78.
3. Stephanie Armour, "Wal Mart Takes Hit on Worker Treatment," *USA Today,* February 10, 2003, p. 1B.
4. Diana Fu, "Sweatshops Provoke More Than a Moral Outcry," University Wire, January 29, 2003.
5. Nicholas Stein, "No Way Out: Competition to Make Products for Western Companies Has Revived an Old Form of Abuse—Debt Bondage," *Fortune,* January 20, 2003, p. 102.
6. Liz Fedor, "Union Leader Forsees Consolidated Airline Industry," *Minneapolis Star Tribune,* January 19, 2003, p. 1D.
7. Andrew Curry, "Why We Work," *U.S. News & World Report,* February 24, 2003, p. 49.
8. Marlon Manuel, "Warped Speed: Where Has All the Time Gone?" *Atlanta Journal and Constitution,* May 12, 2002, p. A1.
9. Michael Barone, "A Big Stick," *U.S. News & World Report,* February 25, 2002, p. 52.
10. www.aflcio.com.
11. Leigh Strope, "12 Unions Join to Boost Political Power," AP Online, February 4, 2003.
12. www.aflcio.com.
13. Lawrence L. Knutson, "Two New Portraits Will Grace Senate," AP Online, January 13, 2003.
14. Thomas I. Palley, "The Child Labor Problem and the Need for International Labor Standards," *Journal of Economic Issues,* September 1, 2002, p. 601.
15. Ted Anthony, "China Plans to Resume Rights Talks," AP Online, July 31, 2002.
16. Raju Chebium, "Union Workers Lobby for More U.S. Manufacturing Jobs," Gannett News Service, February 4, 2003.
17. Oren M. Levin-Waldman, "The Minimum Wage and Regional Wage Structure: Implications for Income Distribution," *Journal of Economic Issues,* September 1, 2002, p. 635.
18. Wendy Zellner, "Hiring Illegals: The Risk Grows," *Business Week,* May 13, 2002, p. 94.
19. Jack Ewing, "The Decline of Germany," *Business Week International,* February 17, 2003, p. 46.
20. Ananda Shorey, "America West Pilots Reject Labor Contract," AP Online, March 18, 2003.
21. Carolyn Mayer, "No Suits Allowed; Increasingly Arbitration Is the Only Recourse," *Washington Post,* July 14, 2002, p. H1.
22. Paul Newberry, "Braves' Maddux Seeks $16 Million in Arbitration," AP Online, January 18, 2003.
23. Marc Levy, "Hershey Strike a Sign of the Times," AP Online, May 29, 2002.
24. Noel Holston, "Hard Pitches in the Strike Zone: 'American Standoff' Eyes Nasty Labor Strife," *Newsday,* June 9, 2002, p. B23.
25. Stephen Moore, "Union Tactics Cost Jobs," *Washington Times,* March 13, 2003.
26. Thomas Heath, "Baseball Strike Averted: In Last Hours, Owners and Players Agree on New Economic Structure," *Washington Post,* August 31, 2002, p. A1.
27. David Stires, "The Breaking Point: Worker Health Costs Will Rise a Staggering 24% This Year," *Fortune,* March 3, 2003, p. 104.
28. www.aflcio.com.
29. Herb London, "Outside View: Brainwashing Students?" United Press International, January 21, 2003.
30. Joann Muller, Kathleen Kerwin, and David Welch, "Autos: A New Industry," *Business Week,* July 15, 2002, pp. 98–108.
31. Kristin Downey, "Unions Angry After Chao's Visit: Labor Faults Secretary's Remarks," *Washington Post,* February 28, 2003, p. E1.
32. Amy Borrus and Paula Dwyer, "Getting the Boss to Behave," *Business Week,* July 15, 2002, p. 110.
33. Peter Kafka, "The Wages of Fame: The Celebrity 100," *Forbes,* July 8, 2002, pp. 97–120.
34. Louis Lavelle, Frederick F. Jespersen, and Michael Arndt, "Executive Pay," *Business Week,* April 15, 2002, pp. 80–86.
35. Gary Strauss and Barbara Hansen, "Bubble Hasn't Burst Yet on CEO Salaries Despite the Times," *USA Today,* March 31, 2003, p. 1B.
36. Tim McElligott and Toby Weber, "Drum Beat of Reform Grows Louder," *Telephony,* September 23, 2002.
37. Del Jones, "CEO Pay Takes Another Hit," *USA Today,* March 10, 2003, p. 5B.
38. Joann S. Lublin, "As Their Companies Crumbled, Some CEOs Got Big Money Payouts," *The Wall Street Journal,* February 26, 2002, p. B1.
39. Kathryn Kranhold and Mitchell Pacelle, "Enron Paid Top Managers $681 Million, Even as Stock Slid," *The Wall Street Journal,* June 17, 2002, p. B1.
40. Amy Borrus and Dean Foust, "Compensation: A Battle Royal against Regal Paychecks," *Business Week,* February 24, 2003, p. 127.
41. Strauss and Hansen, "Bubble Hasn't Burst Yet."
42. Meg Richards, "Troubled Companies Wrestle with Issue of CEO Pay," AP Worldstream, February 11, 2003.
43. Neal St. Anthony, "Pressure's On to Punish the Corporate Evildoers," *Minneapolis Star Tribune,* July 9, 2002, p. 1D.
44. Gary Strauss, "Troubled Times Entice CEOs with Platinum Pay," *USA Today,* February 21, 2003, p. 1B.
45. Patrick Reddy, "The New Democratic Majority," United Press International, January 21, 2003.
46. David H. Ciscel, "Living Wages, Equal Wages: Gender and Labor Market Policies in the United States," *Journal of Economic Issues,* March 1, 2003, p. 221.
47. David R. Francis, "Behind a Surge in Firms Owned by Women," *Christian Science Monitor,* September 9, 2002, p. 17.
48. Toddi Gutner, "How to Shrink the Pay Gap," *Business Week,* June 24, 2002, p. 151.
49. Charles Lane, "Clarence Thomas Sells Memoirs: Harper Collins Agrees to Pay Justice Seven-Figure Advance," *Washington Post,* January 9, 2003, p. C1.
50. Raymond L. Hogler, Jennifer H. Frame, and George Thornton, "Workplace Sexual Harassment Law: An Empirical Analysis of Organizational Justice and Legal Policy," *Journal of Managerial Issues,* July 1, 2002, p. 234.

51. Sherwood Ross, "Sexual Harassment Cases Leveling Off—EEOC," Reuters Business Report, February 18, 2002.
52. Ralph Ellis, "Effects of Harassment Widespread," *Atlanta Journal and Constitution,* January 20, 2002, p. C4.
53. Rachel Krier, "Harassment Illegal Regardless of Legal Ignorance or Intentions," University Wire, March 4, 2003.
54. "Who Cares? Working Parents Cry Out for Help," *Washington Times,* May 8, 2002.
55. Ann Merrill, "General Mills Lauded for Aid to Working Mothers," *Minneapolis Star Tribune,* September 24, 2002, p. 1D.
56. www.haemonetics.com.
57. William C. Symonds, "Hot Growth Companies: Providing the Killer Perk," *Business Week,* June 10, 2002, p. 101.
58. Dennis Camire, "Reforms Proposed to Care for Aging Population," Gannett News Service, June 21, 2002.
59. Laura Koss-Feder, "Providing for Parents the 'Sandwich Generation' Looks for New Solutions," *Time,* March 17, 2003, p. G8.
60. Stephen Barr, "Elder Care Becoming Major Issue for Many Workers," *Washington Post,* August 20, 2002, p. B2.
61. Lynn Brenner, "Only Poor People Are Eligible for Medicaid," *Newsday,* February 1, 2003, p. F7.
62. Janet Kornblum, "Many Unprepared to Care for Aged," *USA Today,* March 17, 2003, p. 6D.
63. George Johnson, "Combination Drug Buys Time but Is Not a Cure," *St. Louis Post-Dispatch,* September 9, 1999; and John Carey, "Rethinking the AIDS Arsenal," *Business Week,* July 17, 2000.
64. "Powell Urges Business Leaders Not to Discriminate against Those with AIDS," AP Worldstream, June 24, 2002.
65. Donna Leinwand, "Study Shows That Youth Need More Drug Programs," *USA Today,* February 8, 2002, p. 3A.
66. Christine L. Romero, "Elder Bush Aids Fight against Drugs at Work," *Arizona Republic,* March 19, 2002, p. D1.
67. Dana Hawkins, "Tests on Trial," *U.S. News & World Report,* August 12, 2002, p. 46.
68. Liese Hutchison, "Crime Doesn't Pay for Organizations," *St. Louis Commerce,* March 2002, p. 12.
69. Stephanie Armour, "Employers' New Measures Fight Workplace Violence," *USA Today,* May 9, 2002, p. 3B.
70. Carrie Coolidge, "Risky Business," *Forbes,* January 6, 2003, p. 54.
71. Daphne Eviator, "Exiting Stage Left," *Newsweek International,* March 17, 2003, p. 50.
72. Ibid.

Chapter 13

1. Jerry Bowles, "Customers for Life," *Forbes,* June 9, 2003, pp. 119 ff.
2. Danna Harman, "Aid Workers Seek to Break Hunger Cycle," *Washington Times,* January 30, 2003, p. A14.
3. Jacqueline Trescott, "Nonprofit Arts Groups Say They Generate $134 Billion Annually," *Washington Post,* June 11, 2002, p. C4.
4. Larry Yu, "The Global-Brand Advantage," *Sloan Management Review,* Spring 2003, p. 13.
5. Charles Fishman, "Which Price Is Right?," *Fast Company,* March 2003, pp. 92–102.
6. Scott McMurray, "Return of the Middleman," *Business 2.0,* March 2003, pp. 52–54.
7. Gary Loveman, "Diamonds in the Data Mine," *Harvard Business Review,* May 2003, pp. 109–113.
8. Michael Totty, "The Masses Have Arrived," *The Wall Street Journal,* January 27, 2003, p. R8.
9. Jonathan Krim and Dina ElBoghdady, "Amazon Posts Profit for Second Time," *Washington Post,* January 24, 2003, pp. E1, E3.
10. Gregory L. White and Joseph B. White, "Luxury Lite," *The Wall Street Journal,* February 7, 2003, pp. W1, W7.
11. Bill Millar, "ERP Meets CRM . . . and Neither Blinks," *1to1 Magazine,* January/February 2002, p. 42.
12. Jo Bennett, "Hard Rock Cafe Pumps Up the Volume on CRM," *1to1 Magazine,* March 2002, p. 5.
13. Cheryl Krivda and Michael Krivda, "The Book of ROI," (advertisement), *Business 2.0,* June 2002, pp. S24–S26.
14. Jo Bennett, "One to One Dresses Up the Bottom Line for Custom Window-Covering Company," *1to1 Magazine,* April 2002, p. 5.
15. Marc Gunther, "Tree Huggers, Soy Lovers, and Profits," *Fortune,* June 23, 2003, pp. 98–104.
16. Mark Eisenberg, "Difficult Relationship," *Red Herring,* September 2002, p. 12.
17. Bill Millar, "How Transport Giant JB Hunt Got Its Customer-Relationship ROI Rolling," *1to1 Magazine,* April 2003, pp. 10–13.

Chapter 14

1. Kate Macarthur, "McDonald's Tests Ads That Focus on Service," *Advertising Age,* January 6, 2003, p. 3.
2. Mohanbir Sawhney, Emanuela Prandelli, and Gianmario Verona, "The Power of Innomediation," *Sloan Management Review,* Winter 2003, pp. 77–82.
3. Joann Muller, "Outpsyching the Car Buyer," *Forbes,* February 17, 2003, p. 52.
4. Andrew Park, Faith Keenan, and Cliff Edwards, "Whose Lunch Will Dell Eat Next?" *Business Week,* August 12, 2002, pp. 66–67.
5. Mila D'Antonio, "Targeted Mailings Help BFS Migrate Customers into Higher Spending Brackets," *1to1,* January/February 2003, p. 11.
6. Shirley Leung, "McHaute Cuisine," *The Wall Street Journal,* August 30, 2002, pp. A1, A6.
7. Fred Bernstein, "Want Fries with That McDonald's Room?" *Washington Post,* September 1, 2002, p. E5.
8. "McMarketing," *Business Week,* August 12, 2002, p. 8.
9. Nick Pachette, "Back in the Kitchen," *Money,* July 2003, pp. 44–45.
10. Douglas B. Holt, "What Becomes an Icon Most?" *Harvard Business Review,* March 2003, pp. 43–49.
11. "Dutch Boy Twist & Pour Delivery System," *Business Week,* July 7, 2003, p. 72.
12. "On the Cutting Edge," *Kiplinger's,* September 2003, pp. 21–22.
13. Andy Serwer, "The Hole Story," *Fortune,* July 7, 2003, pp. 52–62.
14. Otis Port, "The Next Web," *Business Week,* March 4, 2002, pp. 96–102.
15. Greg Schneider, "Coming to Showrooms: A New Car Just for You," *Washington Post,* July 13, 2003, pp. A1 and A8.
16. Faith Keenan, "The Price Is Really Right," *Business Week,* March 31, 2003, pp. 62–67.
17. Dan McGinn, "Low Riders," *bajungle.com,* March/April 2003, pp. 16–18.
18. Wendy Zellner and Michael Arndt, "Holding Steady," *Business Week,* February 3, 2003, pp. 66–68.
19. Dean Foust, Michael Arndt, Robert Berner, and Amy Barrett, "Raising Prices Won't Fly," *Business Week,* June 3, 2002, pp. 34–36.
20. Jon E. Hilsenrath, "America's Pricing Paradox," *The Wall Street Journal,* May 16, 2003, pp. B1 and B4.
21. Charles Fishman, "Which Price Is Right?" *Fast Company,* March 2003, pp. 92–102.
22. Keith L. Alexander, "Hotels Try Personal Touch to Lure Guests," *Washington Post,* November 20, 2002, p. E1.

Chapter 15

1. Scott McMurray, "Return of the Middleman," *Business 2.0,* March 2003, pp. 53–54.
2. Mila D'Antonio, "Supply Chain Management Becomes Larger Priority," *1to1 Magazine,* April 2003, p. 46.
3. Stephanie Paterik, "Sheraton Plans to Pay Guests for Bad Service," *The Wall Street Journal,* September 6, 2002, pp. B1, B4.
4. Jim Collins, "Bigger, Better, Faster," *Fast Company,* June 2003, pp. 75–78.
5. Anna Bakalis, "Do-Not-Call Registry Gets Millions as Phones Open," *Washington Times,* July 8, 2003, p. C8.
6. Laura Rock Kopczak and M. Eric Johnson, "The Supply-Chain Management Effect," *Sloan Management Review,* Spring 2003, pp. 27–34.
7. Sarah McBride, "Kia's Audacious Sorento Plan," *The Wall Street Journal,* April 8, 2003, p. A12.
8. Darryl K. Taft, "Cutting Fat from Supply Chain," *eWEEK,* February 11, 2002, p. 26.
9. Julia Kirby, "Supply Chain Challenges: Building Relationships," *Harvard Business Review,* July 2003, pp. 65–73.
10. Lynn Russo, "The Technological Ecosystem Will Rule," *1to1 Magazine,* April 2003, p. 4.
11. Carolyn Abate and Lane Anderson, "Ship Shape," *Smart Business,* January 2002, p. 66.
12. Daniel R. Guide and Luk N. Van Wassenhove, "The Reverse Supply Chain," *Harvard Business Review,* February 2002, pp. 25–26.
13. "Supply Chain: Focus on the Future" (advertisement), *Business Week,* October 7, 2002, pp. 77 ff.
14. "Smarter Shipping through Technology," *Smart Business,* February 2002, p. 60.
15. Daniel Fisher, "Free Flight," *Forbes,* February 3, 2003, pp. 74–76.
16. Don Phillips, "Digital Railroad," *Technology Review,* March 2002, pp. 74–78.
17. Christopher Helman, "The Big Tune-Up," *Forbes,* April 14, 2003, pp. 99–100.
18. Rick Brooks, "Package Delivery Battle Hinges on DHL Ruling," *The Wall Street Journal,* May 18, 2003, pp. B1 and B4.
19. A. Blanton Godfrey, "Déjà Vu All Over Again," *Quality Digest,* June 2003, p. 16.

Chapter 16

1. Jack Neff, "Ad Buyers: 'Show Us the GRPs,' " *Advertising Age,* March 3, 2003, p. S14.
2. Robyn Meredith, "From Rocks to Riches," *Forbes,* August 12, 2002, pp. 101–2.
3. "Total U.S. Ad Spending by Media," *Advertising Age Fact Pack, 2002 Edition,* Crain Communications, 2002, p. 19.
4. Donna De Marco, "Super Ads," *Washington Times,* January 23, 2003, p. C11.
5. Vanessa O'Connell, "Super Bowl Gets Competition," *The Wall Street Journal,* January 28, 2002, pp. B1, B3.
6. "RotoZip: You Have to See It to Believe It," *Marketing News,* March 27, 2000, p. 17.
7. Scott Hays, "Online Media Slowly Discovers Its Fair Share," *Advertising Age,* January 13, 2003, p. M1.
8. Peter Schwartz, "Internet Advertising Is Going to Change. But How?" *Red Herring,* February 2000, pp. 76–78.
9. Mark Athitakis, "How to Make Money on the Internet," *Business 2.0,* May 2003, pp. 83–90.
10. James C. Anderson and James A. Narus, "Selectively Pursuing More of your Customer's Business," *Sloan Management Review,* Spring 2003, pp. 42–49.
11. Stephanie Thompson, "Sweet Nothings," *Advertising Age,* October 7, 2002, p. 37.
12. Jerry Bowles, "Customers for Life," *Forbes,* June 9, 2003 (advertisement), pp. 119ff.
13. "Making the Sale," *The Wall Street Journal,* January 27, 2003, p. R9.
14. Bob Thompson, "CRM: Improving Demand Chain Intelligence for Competitive Advantage," *Business Week,* October 21, 2002 (advertisement) pp. 75ff.
15. Marji McClure, "A Perfect Fit," *1to1 Magazine,* January/February 2003, pp. 23–27.
16. Claire Atkinson, "Edelman at 50," *Advertising Age,* September 23, 2002, pp. C2–C10.
17. Claire Atkinson, "Comstock Took the PR Path to Reach Top Destination at GE," *Advertising Age,* April 14, 2003, p. 40.
18. Clark S. Judge, "PR Lessons from the Pentagon," *The Wall Street Journal,* April 1, 2003 p. B2.
19. Jack Neff, "Ries' Thesis: Ads Don't Build Brands, PR Does," *Advertising Age,* July 15, 2002, p. 14.
20. Jennifer Tanaka, "Believe the Hype," *Newsweek,* April 14, 2003, p. 64.
21. Gene Edward Veith, "The Marriage Craving," *World,* March 8, 2003, p. 13.
22. L. C. Smith, "Wordofmouth," www.mbajungle.com, January 2003, pp. 22–23.
23. Annette Cardwell, "Killer Buzz," *Smart Business,* January 2002, p. 71.
24. Claire Atkinson, "Integration Still a Pipe Dream for Many," *Advertising Age,* March 10, 2003, pp. 1 and 47.
25. Daniel Klein, "Disintegrated Marketing," *Harvard Business Review,* March 2003, pp. 18–19.

Chapter 17

1. Alan Goldstein, "Techies Are Seeing, Being Seen: As Computing Has Changed, So Has Former Basement Dwellers' Role," *Dallas Morning News,* March 20, 2002, p. 1D; Kathleen Melymuka, "35 Years of IT Leadership: The Evolution of the IT Leader," *Computerworld,* September 30, 2002, p. 28; John J. Ciulla, "Step Up and Lead, *CIO,* June 15, 2002, pp. 48–50; and Jean Consilvio, "Q&A: A CIO's First Year on the Job," *Computerworld,* February 10, 2003, p. 46.
2. Jeff Sauer, "The Thriving Streaming Media Sector," *Video Systems,* February 1, 2003.
3. Laura Koss-Feder, "Providing for Parents, the 'Sandwich Generation' Looks for New Solutions," *Time,* March 17, 2003, p. G8.
4. Megan Santosus, "The Doctor Is In—Always," *CIO,* June 15, 2002, pp. 16–18; and Daniel J. Horgan, "You've Got Conversation," *CIO,* October 15, 2002, p. 38.
5. Yudhijit Bhattacharjee, "A Swarm of Little Notes," *Time,* July 16, 2002; and "Change Agent," *InfoWorld,* February 10, 2003.
6. Jim Kerstetter, "The Web at Your Service," *Business Week e.biz,* March 18, 2002.
7. Lynn Greiner, "The House That Data Built," *Computing Canada,* August 9, 2002, p. 12; Tommy Peterson, "Data Scrubbing," *Computerworld,* February 10, 2003, p. 32; and Robert L. Scheier, "How Will You Automate Your Enterprise?" *Computerworld,* January 6, 2003, p. 18.
8. "Debunking Myths over a Few Beers," *Computing Canada,* August 23, 2002, p. 22; and Susan Pigg, "Diapers, Drinking, and Data," *Toronto Star,* August 16, 2002.
9. Bill Saporito, "Can Wal-Mart Get Any Bigger?" *Time,* January 13, 2003, p. 38; and Jerry Useem, "One Nation under Wal-Mart," *Fortune,* March 3, 2003, p. 64.
10. Dan Verton, "Congressman Says Data Mining Could Have Prevented 9–11," *Computerworld,* August 26, 2002, p. 5.

11. Lea Goldman, "A Fortune in Firewalls," *Forbes,* March 18, 2002, p. 102; and Wayne Rash and P. J. Connolly, "Zone Labs Simplifies Personal-Firewall Management," *InfoWorld,* February 10, 2003.
12. Pimm Fox, "Plugging Into Portal Returns," *Computerworld,* April 8, 2002, p. 38.
13. Steve Alexander, "How Will You Build Business on the Web?" *Computerworld,* January 6, 2003, p. 21; and "Attenda Has Appetite for IT Contract," M2 PressWIRE, February 19, 2003.
14. Olga Kharif, "Brad Boston: No Paper," *BusinessWeek Online,* October 1, 2002.
15. James Cope, "Outsourcing VPNS: Privacy for Hire," *Computerworld,* February 11, 2002, p. 36; and "IP Virtual Private Networks Increasingly Outsourced," *Europemedia,* February 4, 2003.
16. Steve Burrell, "The New Digital Campus," *Technological Horizons in Education,* September 1, 2002, p. 20; Luisa Kroll, "R-E-S-P-E-C-T," *Forbes,* July 22, 2002, p. 184; Samuel Greengard, "Get the Most Out of Your HR or Enterprise Portal," *Workforce,* April 2002, p. 38; and "Sun ONE Portal Virtualizes Manufacturing Processes, Supplier Management and Collaboration," M2 PressWIRE, March 5, 2003.
17. "Enterprise Portals: Measurable Productivity and ROI Tools," Africa News Service, May 6, 2002.
18. Alex Salkever, "Ready to Supercharge Your Surfing," *Business Week Online,* September 17, 2002; Anick Jesdanun, "Will Speedy Connections Improve Life?" AP Online, March 11, 2002; and Toby Weber, "Premium Fuel for Wireless," *Wireless Review,* March 1, 2003.
19. Joe Licavoli, "High Speed Internet2 on the Move in the Cal State System," University Wire, February 27, 2002; "World's First Long-Distance Super HD Transmission over IP Network," *TV Meets the Web,* October 30, 2002; Stephanie DeMoor, "Louisiana State U. Acquires Videoconferencing Technology," University Wire, July 16, 2002; "Brain Images from Patients with Schizophrenia Will Be Shared in First Nationwide Imaging Network," Ascribe Newswire, October 29, 2002; and Mark Hall, "Internet2 and You," *Computerworld,* January 20, 2003, p. 32.
20. Peter Shinkle, "Internet2 Attracts Research Centers, Universities," *St. Louis Post-Dispatch,* April 17, 2002, p. E1; and "Sun Microsystems Laboratories Contributes XACML Security Standard Implementation to Open Source Project," M2 PressWIRE, February 19, 2003.
21. "Intel to Roll Out Billion-Transistor Chip in 2007," Xinhua, October 16, 2002; and Tom Walker, "Already a Legend, Turner Graces a Timely Cover," *Atlanta Journal and Constitution,* February 4, 2003, p. D2.
22. David Hamilton, "Hewlett-Packard Scientists Present Tiny Memory Chip," *The Wall Street Journal,* September 10, 2002; "Future UnPlugged," *CIO,* November 2002; and "Feeling the Heat," *The Economist,* March 15, 2003, p. 33.
23. Charles Fishman, "How to S + M + A + S + H Your Strategy," *Fast Company,* August 2002, pp. 90–95; and Ed Scannell, "Microsoft Rolls Out Autonomic Plan," *InfoWorld,* March 24, 2003.
24. Jim Krane, "For Las Vegas Gadget Show, Technology Boom Never Went Bust," *AP Worldstream,* January 7, 2003.
25. Harry Wessel, "Efficiency in Hand," *Bergen County (New Jersey) Record,* March 10, 2003, p. L5; Carlos A. Soto, "2002's Top Products Hint at Future; Bigger, Smaller, Safer, Faster, Cheaper, Friendlier, Better," *Washington Post,* January 9, 2003, p. E7; and Jefferson Graham, "Hello, Tech Designers? This Stuff Is Too Small," *USA Today,* March 4, 2003, p. 1D.
26. "Mobility, Flexibility, and Security," M2 PressWIRE, May 8, 2002; Amey Stone, "How Wi-Fi Can Remake the Workplace," *Business Week Online,* April 1, 2002; and Kevin Fitchard, "Carriers, Vendors Warm Up to Wi-Fi," *Telephony,* January 27, 2003.
27. Olga Kharif, "Dave Vucina: Wi-Fi Everywhere," *Business Week Online,* October 1, 2002.
28. Barry Kipnis, "Technology 2001: A Glimpse to the Future," *National Real Estate Investor,* January 1, 2001.
29. Alex Salkever, "Dev Mukherjee: IT Service, à la Carte," *Business Week Online,* October 1, 2002; and Thomas Hoffman, "All or Nothing," *Computerworld,* March 10, 2003, p. 42.
30. Steve Pain, "Boots Hands Over Key IT Role to IBM," *Birmingham Post,* October 8, 2002, p. 25.
31. "The ROI of Collaboration Technologies," *CIO,* October 1, 2002.
32. "Exploding Cybercrime Costs US Billions a Year," Agence France Presse English, April, 8, 2002; and Pat Currie, "Plugging Holes in Online Armor," *London Free Press,* January 27, 2003, p. S8.
33. Christine Canabou, "Security Check," *Fast Company,* June 2002, pp. 69–78.
34. "Electronic Attack Causes Net Traffic Managers to Fail," *St. Louis Post-Dispatch,* October 23, 2002, p. A12.
35. Sarah D. Scalet, "They Want You for a Safer Infrastructure," *CIO,* June 15, 2002, pp. 76–82; Linda Tischler, "No Security," *Fast Company,* August 2002, pp. 42–44; Yochi J. Dreazen, "Lock Your Doors," *The Wall Street Journal,* September 23, 2002; Sarah D. Scalet, "Fear Factor," *CIO,* October 15, 2002, pp. 63–68; Alex Salkever, "Cybersecurity's Leaky Dikes," *Business Week Online,* July 2, 2002; Alex Salkever, "The Keys to a More Secure Future," *Business Week Online,* July 2, 2002; "Lure of the Homeland," *Washington Times,* June 10, 2002; Pete Engardio, "Who Protects the Nation's Infrastructure?" *Business Week Online,* June 7, 2002; and Brian Krebs, "White House to Fill Cybersecurity Posts," *Washington Post,* January 10, 2003, p. E5.
36. Jane Black, "Faceless Snoopers Have the Upper Hand," *Business Week,* June 5, 2002; and Don Oldenburg, "Identity Theft: It Pays to Be Diligent," *Washington Post,* January 7, 2003, p. C9.
37. Patrick Thibodeau, "IBM Automates Privacy Compliance," *Computerworld,* September 30, 2002, p. 1; and Tyler Hamilton, "Web's Privacy Protocol Needs Big-Name Boost." *Toronto Star,* January 6, 2003.
38. Kevin Demarrais, "Swindlers Find Easy Pickings on Web," *Bergen County (New Jersey) Record,* February 9, 2003, p. B1; "How the FTC Is Policing Privacy," *Business Week,* June 5, 2002; and Ellen McCarthy "Firm Identifies Insurance Risks—and Ways to Reduce Them," *Washington Post,* February 17, 2003, p. E5.
39. "Swedish Woman Receives 93 Billion Kronor (US$10 Billion) in Child Benefits after Computer Glitch," AP Worldstream, October 22, 2002.
40. Strauss, "When Computers Fail," *USA Today,* December 7, 1999, p. A2; Fara Warner, "Microsoft Eats the Dog Food," *Fast Company,* September 2002, pp. 46–48; "Computer Kills 8,500," *The Mirror,* January 10, 2003, p. 19.
41. Meg Mitchell, "Children of the Revolution," *CIO,* January 1, 2000, pp. 159–68.
42. Gregary A. Patterson, "Dismal Tech Outlook," *Minneapolis Star Tribune,* May 27, 2002, p. 1D.
43. "Tomorrow's Jobs," Bulletin 2540-1, U.S. Department of Labor Bureau of Labor Statistics, February 2002.
44. Maria Mallory, "Security Field the Best Bet in Tech Sector Experts Predict Niche Will Lead IT Workplace Recovery," *Atlanta Journal and Constitution,* February 17, 2002, p. R1.

Chapter 18

1. Mike McNamee, "Finance: Annual Reports: Still Not Enough Candor," *Business Week,* March 24, 2003, p. 74.
2. Michael Connor, "Accountants Group Sees Continued Role," Reuters Business, March 20, 2003.

3. David Nicklaus, "Number Crunchers Are Coming Out into the Light Once Again," *St. Louis Post Dispatch,* March 5, 2003, p. C1.
4. David Henry, "The Business Week 50: Investing for Growth: Cleaning Up the Numbers," *Business Week,* March 25, 2003, p. 126.
5. David Henry and Robert Berner, "Finance: Accounting: Ouch! Real Numbers," *Business Week,* March 24, 2003, p. 72.
6. Greg Farrell, "CPAs Look for an Ad Agency to Rebuild Images," *USA Today,* February 26, 2003, p. 2B.
7. Paul Craig Roberts, "Unintended Consequences of Earlier Reforms Bit Market Hard," *Washington Times,* March 16, 2003.
8. Kristen Hays, "Andersen OKs $40 Million for Enron Claims," AP Online, August 27, 2002.
9. "SEC Acts to Keep Companies Honest/Bar Those That Don't Follow New Audit Rules," *Newsday,* April 1, 2003, p. A53.
10. Sandra Block, "Paying Someone to Do Your Taxes? Check Them Out First," *USA Today,* March 11, 2003, p. 3B.
11. Stacy A. Teicher, "Job of 'Policing' Companies May Fall More to Auditors," *Christian Science Monitor,* March 31, 2003, p. 18.
12. Carrie Johnson Washington, "Corporate Audit Panels to Gain Power; SEC Passes New Rules," *Washington Post,* April 2, 2003, p. E2.
13. Jackie Spinner, "Ease Up on Accounting Curbs, Pitt Says," *Washington Post,* March 21, 2002, p. E1.
14. "Shifting Power; Governance in America," *The Economist,* January 11, 2003, p. 62.
15. Matt Krantz, "More Annual Reports Delayed," *USA Today,* April 2, 2003, p. 1B; and Mike McNamee, "Finance: Annual Reports: Still Not Enough Candor," *Business Week,* March 24, 2003, p. 74.
16. Jeffrey Battersby, "QuickBooks Pro 5.0," *MacWorld,* April 1, 2003, p. 34.
17. Ibid.
18. Larry Blasko, "Feds Push Tax-Preparation Software," AP Online, January 27, 2003.
19. Timothy J. Mullaney, "Information Technology: Software: The Wizard of Intuit," *Business Week,* October 28, 2002, p. 60.
20. Robert Barker, "A Cloud Clears for a Gene Mapper," *Business Week,* March 3, 2003, p. 134.
21. Samuel Greengard, "Get a Grip on Assets," *Business Finance,* January 2002, pp. 39–42.
22. Anne Tergesen, "The Fine Print: How Much Is the Goodwill Worth?" *Business Week,* September 16, 2002, p. 83.
23. Ann Harrington, "Honey, I Shrunk the Profits: Accounting Made a Bad Year Look a Whole Lot Worse," *Fortune,* April 14, 2003, pp. 197–99.
24. "Fortune 5 Hundred Notes," *Fortune,* April 14, 2003, p. F-22.
25. Elizabeth MacDonald, "The Ebitda Folly," *Forbes,* March 17, 2003, p. 165.
26. Michael Sivy, "Stocks for a Muddled Market," *Money,* April 1, 2003, p. 67.
27. Deepa Babington, "Cash Flow Numbers Scarce Despite Scandals," Reuters Business, October 27, 2002.
28. Gary Anthes, "Net Present Value," *Computerworld,* February 17, 2003, p. 30.
29. Leonard Wiener, "Gimme a Break," *U.S. News & World Report,* March 10, 2003, p. 40; and Elizabeth MacDonald, "The EBITDA Folly," *Forbes,* March 17, 2003, p. 165.
30. Mike McNamee, "Annual Reports: Still Not Enough Candor," *Business Week,* March 24, 2003, p. 74.
31. Deepa Babington, "Accounting Trade Group Stumbles," Reuters Business, March 2, 2003.
32. Lewis Braham, "Stocks: Weighting the Balance Sheet," *Business Week,* April 1, 2002, p. 84.
33. Dee Depass, "Moody's Downgrades St. Paul Company's Debt," *Minneapolis Star Tribune,* April 4, 2003, p. 3D.

Chapter 19

1. J. Edward Ketz, "Just Say No," *MBA Jungle,* March/April 2002, p. 10.
2. Joseph Weber, Michael Arndt, Emily Thornton, Amy Barrett, and Dean Foust, "CFOs on the Hot Seat," *Business Week,* March 17, 2003, pp. 66–70.
3. Stan Hinden, "Transition at the Top," *Washington Post,* February 23, 2003, p. H1.
4. Martin Hutchinson, "The Bear's Lair: Bye Ford, We'll Miss You," United Press International, March 17, 2003.
5. Nanette Byrnes and Louis Lavelle, "The Corporate Tax Game," *Business Week,* March 31, 2003, pp. 78–83.
6. Stacy A. Teicher, "Job of Policing Companies May Fall More to Insiders," *Christian Science Monitor,* March 31, 2003, p. 18.
7. Carrie Johnson Washington, "Corporate Audit Panels to Gain Power: SEC Passes New Rules," *Washington Post,* April 2, 2003, p. E2.
8. Tad Leahy, "Birth of a New Budget Culture," *Business Finance,* April 2002, pp. 31–34.
9. Mara Der Hovanesian, "Cash: Burn, Baby, Burn," *Business Week,* April 28, 2003, pp. 82–83.
10. Anne Tergesen, "Cash-Flow Hocus-Pocus," *Business Week,* July 16, 2002, pp. 130–32.
11. Paul Katzeff, "Manage Accounts Receivable Upfront before There's a Problem," *Investors Business Daily,* January 27, 2003, p. A4.
12. Krissah Williams Washington, "How Stores Play Their Cards: They'll Give Discounts and Awards to Get Interest and Bigger Sales," *Washington Post,* February 2, 2003, p. H5.
13. Linda Stern, "Credit Card Issuers Offer Some Good Deals," Reuters Business, March 1, 2003.
14. David Skrobot, "Customer Service A-to-Z," *Ward's Dealer Business,* January 1, 2003, p. 35.
15. Lisa McLaughlin, "New Brew on the Block," *Time,* January 20, 2003, p. 143.
16. Lorrie Grant, "Kmart Food Supplier Resumes Shipments," *USA Today,* January 25, 2002, p. 7B; and "Winning the Old-Fashioned Way," *Business Week,* March 25, 2003, p. 176.
17. "Small Firms Finding Money Comes Easier," *Washington Times,* January 7, 2002, p. B1.
18. Courtney McGrath, "Bankers You Can Love," *Kiplinger's,* April 2003, pp. 46–48.
19. Donna Fenn, "Getting a Purchase on Inventory," *Inc.,* April 2003, p. 36.
20. Janice Revell, "How Debt Triggers Can Sink a Stock," *Fortune,* March 18, 2002, pp. 147–51.
21. www.gecapital.com.
22. Jane Salodof MacNeil, "The Factoring Factor," *Inc.,* February 2002, p. 93.
23. "BASF Group: Selling Commercial Paper via the Internet Reduces Costs; Expectations Exceeded," M2 PressWIRE, April 8, 2002.
24. John M. Berry, "Low Interest Rates Are Allowing Corporations to Boost Profit," *Washington Post,* April 19, 2003, p. D12.
25. Toni Clarke and Jed Stelzer, "Merck Profit Rises on Higher Drug Sales," Reuters Business, April 21, 2003.
26. Linda Himelstein, "Venture Capital Catches a Smaller Wave," *Business Week,* March 3, 2003, p. 114.
27. Robert A. Mamis, "The Dry Season," *CFO,* April 2003, pp. 49–52.
28. Ellen Florian, "More Funny Business at Viacom: Full Ownership of Comedy Central Should Have the Media Giant's Investors Smiling," *Fortune,* May 12, 2003, p. 156.

Chapter 20

1. Kathleen Day, "Senators Cast Doubt on Self-Policing Wall Street; Shelby, Sarbanes Say More Has to Be Done," *Washington Post,* May 8, 2003, p. E1.

2. "The Case for Going Private: Corporate Ownership," *The Economist,* January 25, 2003, p. 67.
3. Jeffrey E. Garten, "Economic Viewpoint: Put Your Mouth Where Your Money Is," *Business Week,* January 27, 2003, p. 22.
4. Kathleen Day, "Independent Firms See Payoff: Scandals Boost Business for Untainted Stock Analysis," *Washington Post,* May 8, 2003, p. E1.
5. Ben White, "A Crisis of Trust on Wall Street," *Washington Post,* May 4, 2003, p. F1.
6. Richard Lehman, "How to Buy Corporates," *Forbes,* May 26, 2003, p. 186.
7. Ibid.
8. Kevin Duchschere, "Bond Houses Still Like St. Paul: Standard & Poor's and Moody's Renew the City's High Ratings Despite Cuts in State Aid," *Minneapolis Star Tribune,* February 25, 2003, p. 3B.
9. Scott Herhold, "Wait! Can It Be? Divine Inspiration from an Analyst?" *Business 2.0,* October 2002, pp. 146–48.
10. Adrienne Carter and Penelope Wang, "These 10 All-Weather Stock and Bond Funds Have Shown They Can Prosper in Good Times as Well as Bad," *Money,* February 1, 2003, pp. 80–88.
11. Justin Fox, "Show Us the Money," *Fortune,* February 3, 2003, pp. 76–78.
12. Walter Updegrave, "Dividend Mania, What the Bush Dividend Plan Would Really Mean for You," *Money,* March 1, 2003, pp. 69–74.
13. "The Preferred Route to Income Preferred Stocks Offer the Most Sumptuous Dividend Payments Around," *Money,* March 1, 2003, p. 54B.
14. Michael Barbaro, "Primus Agrees to Sell Convertible Preferred Stock," *Washington Post,* January 1, 2003, p. E5.
15. "The Prime of Ms. Nell Minow," *CFO,* March 2003, pp. 56–62.
16. "Price for NYSE Seat Sees Another Decline," Reuters Business, February 10, 2003.
17. Susan Harrigan, "New 'Defining Moment' for Grasso? NYSE Chair Slow to Respond to Conflicts-of-Interest Issues," *Newsday,* May 14, 2003, p. A47.
18. www.nyse.com.
19. www.amex.com.
20. Jeff Ostrowski, "Proposal Would Cut Flood of Delistings," *Palm Beach Post,* February 6, 2003, p. 4D.
21. Paul Farhi, "Nasdaq 'Casino' Had Few Safeguards," *Washington Post,* November 11, 2002, p. A1.
22. "Rocky Road for the NASDAQ in Germany," *Toronto Star,* March 21, 2003.
23. Alix Nyberg, "The Power of Balance," *CFO,* January 2003, pp. 30–32.
24. Amy Baldwin, "New CEO Faces Question on NASDAQ's Role," AP Online, April 23, 2003.
25. Floyd Norris and Patrick McGeehan, "NYSE and NASDAQ Resist New Governance Rules," *International Herald Tribune,* May 16, 2003.
26. Brook A. Masters, "Quattrone, Martha Stewart Cases Follow Very Different Timelines," *Washington Post,* May 9, 2003, p. E1.
27. Ken Kurson, "Insider Trading: Is It Really So Bad?" *Money,* September 2002, p. 26; and Elizabeth Sanger, "Lawyer Settles SEC Charges/Accused of Insider Trading," *Newsday,* May 12, 2003, p. A49.
28. www.NYSE.com.
29. www.etrade.com.
30. Ben White and Kathleen Day, "SEC Approves Wall Street Settlement; Conflict of Interest Targeted," *Washington Post,* April 29, 2003, p. A1.
31. Mara Der Hovanesian, "The Market's Closed—Wake Up," *Business Week,* March 3, 2003, p. 132.
32. Louise Lee and Emily Thornton, "Schwab v/s Wall Street," *Business Week,* June 3, 2002, pp. 64–69; and Greg Cresci, "Schwab Move Addresses Corporate Governance," Reuters Business, January 31, 2003.
33. Louise Lee, "Finance: Brokerages: Did E-Trade Just Trade Up?" *Business Week,* February 10, 2003, p. 68.
34. Ben White, "A Crisis of Trust on Wall Street," *Washington Post,* May 4, 2003, p. F1.
35. Paul J. Lim, "Finance," *U.S. News & World Report,* February 24, 2003, p. 83; and Walter Updegrave, "Advice on Advice; Not Evey Relationship Has to Be a Long-Term Commitment," *Money,* January 2003, pp. 53–57.
36. Eric Troseth, "Finding a Rally in Bearish Times," *Christian Science Monitor,* May 5, 2003, p. 14.
37. Jyoti Thottam, "Are Penny Stocks Worth a Look?" *Time,* August 12, 2002, p. 46.
38. Matt Krantz, "Microsoft Stock Splits into 10 Billion Shares," *USA Today,* February 19, 2003, p. 1B.
39. Daniel Kadlec and Julie Rawe, "Comeback Crusader Investing Legend Warren Buffett Has Regained His Golden Touch, and His Call for Reform Has CEOs Running Scared . . . or Taking Notes," *Time,* March 10, 2003, pp. 42–47.
40. Bill Deener, "Bear Market Savaging Mutual Funds: Industry Pulls in the Reins, Awaits a Turnaround," *Dallas Morning News,* October 21, 2002, p. 1D; and Sandra Block, Christine Dugas, Thomas Fogarty, and John Waggoner, "Farewell to a Bad Year," *USA Today,* January 8, 2003, p. 3B.
41. Martha Graybow, "Do Good Mutual Funds Gain in Rough Market?" Reuters Business, February 9, 2003.
42. John Rekenthaler, "When Mutual Funds Die, Companies Bury Their Mistakes, Distorting Returns," *Money,* April 2003, pp. 49–53.
43. John Waggoner, "No Stock Treasures, So Pick at Bond Trash," *USA Today,* March 7, 2003, p. 3B.
44. Michelle Singletary, "Mistakes to Avoid When Investing in Bonds," *Washington Post,* April 17, 2003, p. E3.
45. "CME, CBOT Reach Definitive Agreement on Clearing Services," M2 PressWIRE, April 17, 2003.
46. Melissa Goldfine, "CBOT Faces Decision on Electronics System," Reuters Business, January 1, 2003.
47. "Finance and Economics: Ferscha's Leap: Derivatives Exchanges," *The Economist,* January 18, 2003, p. 72.
48. Bruce Stanley, "Electronic Exchanges Face Competition," AP Online, May 16, 2002.
49. "Putting the Market in Perspective," *Washington Times,* January 5, 2003.
50. David Kotz, "Neoliberalism and the U.S. Economic Expansion of the '90s," *Monthly Review,* April 1, 2003, p. 15.
51. Kathleen Day and Carrie Johnson Washington, "New Strength at the SEC's Helm; Donaldson Surprises Consumer Advocates," *Washington Post,* May 7, 2003, p. E1.

Chapter 21

1. Evan I. Schwartz, "How You'll Pay," *Technology Review,* January 2003, pp. 50–56.
2. Guy Gugliotta, "Another Day, Another Dollar," *Washington Post,* May 14, 2003, p. C16.
3. Catherine Siskos, "Cash in a Flash," *Kiplinger's,* October 2002, pp. 30–31.
4. Michael R. Sesit and Nicholas Hastings, "How High Can the Euro Climb?," *The Wall Street Journal,* May 28, 2003, pp. C1, C16.

5. Michael M. Phillips, "Ship Those Boxes; Check the Euro!" *The Wall Street Journal,* February 7, 2003, pp. C1, C7.
6. Steve Pearlstein, "The Dollar Finally Loses Its 1990s Luster," *Washington Post,* May 14, 2003, p. E1.
7. Jack Ewing, Gail Edmondon, David Fairlamb, John Rossant, and Christina Passariello, "Beware the Super Euro," *Business Week,* May 19, 2003, pp. 52–53.
8. "Deflation Warning," *Washington Times,* May 14, 2003, p. A20.
9. Patrick Barta and Michelle Higgins, "Dollar's Fall Could End Many Bargains," *The Wall Street Journal,* January 9, 2003, pp. D1, D4.
10. Rich Miller, "Inside the Fed's First-Aid Kit," *Business Week,* March 31, 2003, p. 39.
11. Rich Miller, Marcia Vickers, Heather Timmons and David Fairlamb, "The Fed's Plans for Dousing the Fire," *Business Week,* March 24, 2003, p. 44.
12. Julie Rawe, "A Mini-Mall in Your ATM," *Time,* April 8, 2002, p. 61.
13. Michelle Higgins, "ATMs to Go Far Beyond Cash," *The Wall Street Journal,* June 6, 2002, pp. D1, D2.
14. Daren Fonda, "Big Little Lenders," *Time,* June 2003, Inside Business section.
15. Scott Kirsner, "Would You Like a Mortgage with Your Mocha?" *Fast Company,* March 2003, pp. 111–14.
16. "Flawed Financial Giants," *Business Week,* September 9, 2002, p. 156.
17. Heather Timmons, Laura Cohn, Mike McNamee, and John Rossant, "Citi's Sleepless Nights," *Business Week,* August 5, 2002, pp. 42–43.
18. Stephanie Miles, "What's a Check?" *The Wall Street Journal,* October 21, 2002, p. R5.
19. Pallavi Gogoi, "The Hot News in Banking: Bricks and Mortar," *Business Week,* April 21, 2003, pp. 83–84.
20. Roger Parloff, "The $50 Billion Card Game" *Fortune,* May 12, 2003, pp. 108–119.
21. Janet Bodnar, "Small Change, Big Fees," *Kiplinger's,* March 2003, p. 92.
22. Evan I. Schwartz, "How You'll Pay," *Technology Review,* December 2000/January 2003, pp. 50–56.
23. Sara Kehaulani Goo, "An ID with a High IQ," *Washington Post,* February 23, 2003, p. H1.
24. Robert Chapman Wood and Gary Hamel, "The World Bank's Innovation Market," *Harvard Business Review,* November 2002, pp. 104–13.
25. Ken Ringle, "Bank Shot," *Washington Post,* March 20, 2002, pp. C1, C4.
26. Pete Engardio and Rich Miller, "The IMF Mess," *Business Week,* September 30, 2002, pp. 54–56.
27. Martin Feldstein, "Argentina Doesn't Need the IMF," *The Wall Street Journal,* May 28, 2002, p. A18.
28. Paul Blustein, "IMF, World Bank Short on Global Solutions," *Washington Post,* September 30, 2002, p. A16.

Chapter 22

1. Katherine Hansen, "What Good Is a College Education Anyway?" www.Quintcareers.com/college_education_value.html, November 4, 2002.
2. "Household Finances," *Kiplinger's,* April 2003, p. 28.
3. Anne D'Innocenzio, "College Students Need Education about Credit," *Washington Times,* February 21, 2002, p. C11.
4. Kimberly Lankford and Catherine Siskos, "Kick the Debt Habit," *Kiplinger's,* February 2003, pp. 69–74.
5. "Numbers Are What You Make of Them," *Kiplinger's,* May 2003, p. 18.
6. *Newsweek,* March 24, 2003, p. 62.
7. Nancy M. Pfotenhauer, "Social Security for Her," *Washington Times,* April 25, 2003, p. A19.
8. Doug Bandow, "Pushing Prosperity for All," *Washington Times,* February 14, 2003, p. A20.
9. Walter Updegrave, "Your Greatest Retirement Fear," *Money,* Fall 2002, pp. 112–18.
10. "Look to the Future: Invest in an IRA," *TIAA-CREF Participant,* February 2002, pp. 6–7.
11. www.motleyfool.com and www.dinkytown.net.
12. "IRAs Can Help Keep Your Plans for Retirement on Track," *TIAA-CREF Participant,* February 2003, pp. 6–9.
13. Roger W. Lusby III, "Simple Retirement Plans," *Tax Hotline,* September 2002, pp. 7–9.
14. Kristina Stefanova, "Workers' Financial Literacy Seen Low," *The Washington Times,* February 25, 2002, pp. D8–D9.
15. Pat Regnier and Joan Caplin, "Can We Fix the 401(k)?" *Money,* April 2003, pp. 86–98.
16. Ibid.
17. "The New Look of Pensions," *Kiplinger's,* April 2002, pp. 23–24.
18. Ron Liber, "Advice for Sale: How to Pick a Financial Planner," *The Wall Street Journal,* May 13, 2003, pp. D1, D2.

Chapter 22 Appendix

1. Scott Neuman, Constance Mitchell Ford, and Erika Lederman, "Altready Battered by Terror, Tourism Gets Double Blow," *The Wall Street Journal,* April 8, 2003, pp. A1, A9.
2. James Hookway, "Increasingly Global Work Force Helps Spread a Dread Disease; Circling the World, Via Toronto," *The Wall Street Journal,* May 2, 2003, pp. B1, B5.
3. Ileana Ros-Lehtinen, "Internet Safety Woes and Remedy," *Washington Times,* January 12, 2003, p. B3.
4. David McHugh, "Euro at New High Against Dollar," *Washington Post,* May 28, 2003, p. E3.
5. Rod Kurtz, "War: Who Is It Good For?" *Inc.,* February 2003, pp. 42–43.
6. Pete Engardio, Bruce Einhorn, Alysha Webb, and Irene M. Kunii, "Sales Take a Holiday," *Business Week,* May 12, 2003, pp. 44–45.
7. Jerry Bowles, "Why Outsourcing Is Becoming a Strategic Tool," *Forbes,* November 11, 2002, pp. 87 ff.
8. "Doomsday and Reinsurance," *The Wall Street Journal,* November 29, 2002, p. A14.
9. Susan Warren, "Asbestos Quagmire," *The Wall Street Journal,* January 27, 2003, pp. B1, B3.
10. "President Signs Terrorism Insurance Act," www.whitehouse.gov/news/releases/2002/11/20021126–1.html , December 2, 2002.
11. "Politicizing Vaccines," *The Wall Street Journal,* November 18, 2002, p. A22.
12. Ellen McGirt, "Insurance: Less Costs More," *Money,* November 2002, pp. 146–48.
13. "Very Expensive Suits," *Fortune,* March 3, 2003, p. 40.
14. "Malpractice Insurance Madness," *Washington Times,* January 6, 2003, p. 18.
15. Lorraine Woellert, "Tort Reform: A Little Here, a Little There . . . ," *Business Week,* January 20, 2003, pp. 60–62.
16. Lorraine Woellert and Mike France, "Tort Reform Has Friends in High Places," *Business Week,* April 21, 2003, p. 78.
17. Richard Newman, "Life Insurance Checkup Time," *Bottom Line Personal,* January 1, 2003, pp. 3–4.

Glossary*

401(k) plan (p. 684) A savings plan that allows you to deposit pretax dollars and whose earnings compound tax free until withdrawl, when the money is taxed at ordinary income tax rates.

a deal *A special price or some other benefit that not all people get.*

absolute advantage (p. 70) The advantage that exists when a country has a monopoly on producing a specific product or is able to produce it more efficiently than all other countries.

accounting (p. 548) The recording, classifying, summarizing, and interpreting of financial events and transactions to provide management and other interested parties the information they need to make good decisions.

accounting cycle (p. 553) A six-step procedure that results in the preparation and analysis of the major financial statements.

acquisition (p. 156) One company's purchase of the property and obligations of another company.

actuaries (p. 697) The people who calculate the chance of loss and the premiums necessary to cover losses.

administered distribution system (p. 476) A distribution system in which producers manage all of the marketing functions at the retail level.

administrative agencies (p. 125) Federal or state institutions and other government organizations created by Congress or state legislatures with delegated power to pass rules and regulations within their mandated area of authority.

advertising (p. 491) Paid, nonpersonal communication through various media by organizations and individuals who are in some way identified in the advertising message.

affirmative action (p. 353) Employment activities designed to "right past wrongs" by increasing opportunities for minorities and women.

agency shop agreement (p. 369) Clause in a labor-management agreement that says employers may hire nonunion workers; employees are not required to join the union but must pay a union fee.

agents/brokers (p. 460) Marketing intermediaries who bring buyers and sellers together and assist in negotiating an exchange but don't take title to the goods.

American Federation of Labor (AFL) (p. 366) An organization of craft unions that championed fundamental labor issues; founded in 1886.

annual report (p. 550) A yearly statement of the financial condition, progress, and expectations of an organization.

annuity (p. 681) A contract to make regular payments to a person for life or for a fixed period.

apprentice programs (p. 339) Training programs involving a period during which a learner works alongside an experienced employee to master the skills and procedures of a craft.

arbitration (p. 373) The agreement to bring in an impartial third party (a single arbitrator or a panel of arbitrators) to render a binding decision in a labor dispute.

assembly process (p. 282) That part of the production process that puts together components.

assets (p. 556) Economic resources (things of value) owned by a firm.

auditing (p. 551) The job of reviewing and evaluating the records used to prepare a company's financial statements.

autocratic leadership (p. 226) Leadership style that involves making managerial decisions without consulting others.

automatically fed to a computer *Standard procedure of inputting specific information into a computer on a regular basis.*

balance of payments (p. 72) The difference between money coming into a country (from exports)

*Terms and definitions printed in italics are considered business slang, or jargon.

and money leaving the country (for imports) plus money flows from other factors such as tourism, foreign aid, military expenditures, and foreign investment.

balance of trade (p. 72) A nation's ratio of exports to imports.

balance sheet (p. 556) The financial statement that reports a firm's financial condition at a specific time.

ballyhooed *Talked about in an exaggerated way.*

banker's acceptance (p. 661) A promise that the bank will pay some specified amount at a particular time.

bankruptcy (p. 136) The legal process by which a person, business, or government entity unable to meet financial obligations is relieved of those obligations by a court that divides any assets among creditors, allowing creditors to get at least part of their money and freeing the debtor to begin anew.

bargaining zone (p. 372) Range of options between the initial and final offer that each party will consider before negotiations dissolve or reach an impasse.

barter (p. 644) The trading of goods and services for other goods and services directly.

bear market *Situation where the stock market is declining in value and investors feel it will continue to decline.*

been there, done that *Prior experience.*

benchmarking (p. 256) Comparing an organization's practices, processes, and products against the world's best.

benefit segmentation (p. 412) Dividing the market by determining which benefits of the product to talk about.

bond (p. 611) A corporate certificate indicating that a person has lent money to a firm.

bookkeeping (p. 553) The recording of business transactions.

bottom line *The last line in a profit and loss statement; it refers to net profit.*

bottom line *Net income or loss a firm incurred from operations.*

brain drain (p. 48) *The loss of the best and brightest people to other countries.*

brainstorming (p. 219) Coming up with as many solutions to a problem as possible in a short period of time with no censoring of ideas.

brand (p. 438) A name, symbol, or design (or combination thereof) that identifies the goods or services of one seller or group of sellers and distinguishes them from the goods and services of competitors.

brand association (p. 440) The linking of a brand to other favorable images.

brand awareness (p. 439) How quickly or easily a given brand name comes to mind when a product category is mentioned.

brand equity (p. 439) The combination of factors—such as awareness, loyalty, perceived quality, images, and emotions—that people associate with a given brand name.

brand loyalty (p. 439) The degree to which customers are satisfied, like the brand, and are committed to further purchase.

brand manager (p. 440) A manager who has direct responsibility for one brand or one product line; called a product manager in some firms.

brand name (p. 403) A word, letter, or group of words or letters that differentiates one seller's goods and services.

brand name (p. 438) That part of the brand consisting of a word, letter, or group of words or letters comprising a name that differentiates a seller's goods or services from those of competitors.

breach of contract (p. 131) When one party fails to follow the terms of a contract.

break-even analysis (p. 449) The process used to determine profitability at various levels of sales.

brightest days *The best of times for a person or organization.*

broadband technology (p. 528) Technology that offers users a continuous connection to the Internet and allows them to send and receive mammoth files that include voice, video, and data much faster than ever before.

budget (p. 585) A financial plan that sets forth management's expectations, and, on the basis of those expectations, allocates the use of specific resources throughout the firm.

bull market *Situation where the stock market is increasing in value and investors feel it will continue to grow.*

bundling (p. 450) Grouping two or more products together and pricing them as a unit.

bureaucracy (p. 243) An organization with many layers of managers who set rules and regulations and oversee all decisions.

business (p. 4) Any activity that seeks to provide goods and services to others while operating at a profit.

business cycles (p. 56) The periodic rises and falls that occur in all economies over time.

business environment (p. 12) The surrounding factors that either help or hinder the development of businesses.

business law (p. 125) Rules, statutes, codes, and regulations that are established to provide a legal framework within which business may be conducted and that are enforceable by court action.

business plan (p. 189) A detailed written statement that describes the nature of the business, the target market, the advantages the business will have in relation to competition, and the resources and qualifications of the owner(s).

business-to-business (B2B) market (p. 411) All the individuals and organizations that want goods and services to use in producing other goods and services or to sell, rent, or supply goods to others.

buying stock on margin (p. 629) Purchasing stocks by borrowing some of the purchase cost from the brokerage firm.

cafeteria-style fringe benefits (p. 346) Fringe benefits plan that allows employees to choose the benefits they want up to a certain dollar amount.

cannibalize a business *One franchise pulls business away from another franchise.*

capital budget (p. 586) A budget that highlights a firm's spending plans for major asset purchases that often require large sums of money.

capital expenditures (p. 591) Major investments in either tangible long-term assets such as land, buildings, and equipment or intangible assets such as patents, trademarks, and copyrights.

capital gains (p. 626) The positive difference between the purchase price of a stock and its sale price.

capitalism (p. 41) An economic system in which all or most of the factors of production and distribution are privately owned and operated for profit.

cash budget (p. 586) A budget that estimates a firm's projected cash inflows and outflows that the firm can use to plan for any cash shortages or surpluses during a given period.

cash flow (p. 564) The difference between cash coming in and cash going out of a business.

cash flow forecast (p. 584) Forecast that predicts the cash inflows and outflows in future periods, usually months or quarters.

cash-and-carry wholesalers (p. 467) Wholesalers that serve mostly smaller retailers with a limited assortment of products.

celebrity stargazers *Customers who attend the opening of a new business hoping to see or meet a celebrity.*

center stage *A very important position.*

centralized authority (p. 245) An organization structure in which decision-making authority is maintained at the top level of management at the company's headquarters.

certificate of deposit (CD) (p. 653) A time-deposit (savings) account that earns interest to be delivered at the end of the certificate's maturity date.

certification (p. 367) Formal process whereby a union is recognized by the National Labor Relations Board (NLRB) as the bargaining agent for a group of employees.

certified internal auditor (CIA) (p. 551) An accountant who has a bachelor's degree and two years of experience in internal auditing, and who has passed an exam administered by the Institute of Internal Auditors.

certified management accountant (CMA) (p. 549) A professional accountant who has met certain educational and experience requirements, passed a qualifying exam in the field, and been certified by the Institute of Certified Management Accountants.

certified public accountant (CPA) (p. 550) An accountant who passes a series of examinations established by the American Institute of Certified Public Accountants.

chain of command (p. 243) The line of authority that moves from the top of a hierarchy to the lowest level.

channel of distribution (p. 460) A whole set of marketing intermediaries, such as wholesalers and retailers that join together to transport and store goods in their path (or channel) from producers to consumers.

climbed the ladder *Promoted to higher-level jobs.*

closed shop agreement (p. 369) Clause in a labor-management agreement that specified workers had to be members of a union before being hired (was outlawed by the Taft-Hartley Act in 1947).

collective bargaining (p. 367) The process whereby union and management representatives form a labor-management agreement, or contract, for workers.

command economies (p. 49) Economic systems in which the government largely decides what goods and services will be produced, who will get them, and how the economy will grow.

commercial bank (p. 652) A profit-seeking organization that receives deposits from individuals and corporations in the form of checking and savings accounts and then uses some of these funds to make loans.

commercial finance companies (p. 595) Organizations that make short-term loans to borrowers who offer tangible assets as collateral.

commercial paper (p. 596) Unsecured promissory notes of $100,000 and up that mature (come due) in 270 days or less.

commercialization (p. 442) Promoting a product to distributors and retailers to get wide distribution, and developing strong advertising and sales campaigns to generate and maintain interest in the product among distributors and consumers.

commodity exchange (p. 629) A securities exchange that specializes in the buying and selling of precious metals and minerals (e.g., silver, foreign currencies, gasoline) and agricultural goods (e.g., wheat, cattle, sugar).

common law (p. 125) The body of law that comes from decisions handed down by judges; also referred to as unwritten law.

common market (p. 90) A regional group of countries that have a common external tariff, no internal tariffs, and a coordination of laws to facilitate exchange; also called a *trading bloc*. An example is the European Union.

common stock (p. 617) The most basic form of ownership in a firm; it confers voting rights and the right to share in the firm's profits through dividends, if offered by the firm's board of directors.

communism (p. 49) An economic and political system in which the state (the government) makes all economic decisions and owns almost all the major factors of production.

comparable worth (p. 381) The concept that people in jobs that require similar levels of education, training, or skills should receive equal pay.

comparative advantage theory (p. 69) Theory that states that a country should sell to other countries those products that it produces most effectively and efficiently, and buy from other countries those products that it cannot produce as effectively or efficiently.

competing in time (p. 287) Being as fast as or faster than competition in responding to consumer wants and needs and getting goods and services to them.

competition-based pricing (p. 442) A pricing strategy based on what all the other competitors are doing. The price can be set at, above, or below competitors' prices.

compliance-based ethics codes (p. 108) Ethical standards that emphasize preventing unlawful behavior by increasing control and by penalizing wrongdoers.

compressed workweek (p. 349) Work schedule that allows an employee to work a full number of hours per week but in fewer days.

computer-aided design (CAD) (p. 284) The use of computers in the design of products.

computer-aided manufacturing (CAM) (p. 287) The use of computers in the manufacturing of products.

computer-integrated manufacturing (CIM) (p. 287) The uniting of computer-aided design with computer-aided manufacturing.

concept testing (p. 442) Taking a product idea to consumers to test their reactions.

conceptual skills (p. 221) Skills that involve the ability to picture the organization as a whole and the relationship among its various parts.

conglomerate merger (p. 157) The joining of firms in completely unrelated industries.

Congress of Industrial Organizations (CIO) (p. 366) Union organization of unskilled workers; broke away from the American Federation of Labor (AFL) in 1935 and rejoined it in 1955.

consideration (p. 131) Something of value; consideration is one of the requirements of a legal contract.

consultative salesperson (p. 500) A salesperson who begins by analyzing customer needs and then comes up with solutions to those needs.

consumer market (p. 411) All the individuals or households that want goods and services for personal consumption or use.

consumer price index (CPI) (p. 54) Monthly statistics that measure the pace of inflation or deflation.

consumer-driven plans (p. 699) A plan where you have a fixed "spending account," funded by your employer, which you can use to pay for office visits, prescription drugs, and routine medical procedures.

consumerism (p. 134) A social movement that seeks to increase and strengthen the rights and powers of buyers in relation to sellers.

contingency planning (p. 218) The process of preparing alternative courses of action that may be used if the primary plans don't achieve the organization's objectives.

contingent workers (p. 337) Workers who do not have the expectation of regular, full-time employment.

continuous process (p. 282) A production process in which long production runs turn out finished goods over time.

contract (p. 130) A legally enforceable agreement between two or more parties.

contract law (p. 130) Set of laws that specify what constitutes a legally enforceable agreement.

contract manufacturing (p. 78) A foreign country's production of private-label goods to which a domestic company then attaches its brand name or trademark; also called *outsourcing.*

contractual distribution system (p. 476) A distribution system in which members are bound to cooperate through contractual agreements.

contrarian approach (p. 678) Buying stock when everyone else is selling or vice versa.

controlling (p. 214) A management function that involves establishing clear standards to determine whether or not an organization is progressing toward its goals and objectives, rewarding people for doing a good job, and taking corrective action if they are not.

convenience goods and services (p. 434) Products that the consumer wants to purchase frequently and with a minimum of effort.

conventional (C) corporation (p. 149) A state-chartered legal entity with authority to act and have liability separate from its owners.

cookies (p. 538) Pieces of information, such as registration data or user preferences, sent by a website over the Internet to a Web browser that the browser software is expected to save and send back to the server whenever the user returns to that website.

cooking the books *Making accounting information look better than it actually is to outside observers and users of financial information of a company.*

cooling-off period (p. 374) When workers in a critical industry return to their jobs while the union and management continue negotiations.

cooperative (p. 165) A business owned and controlled by the people who use it—producers, consumers, or workers with similar needs who pool their resources for mutual gain.

copyright (p. 129) A document that protects a creator's rights to materials such as books, articles, photos, and cartoons.

core competencies (p. 257) Those functions that the organization can do as well as or better than any other organization in the world.

core time (p. 348) In a flextime plan, the period when all employees are expected to be at their job stations.

corporate distribution system (p. 475) A distribution system in which all of the organizations in the channel of distribution are owned by one firm.

corporate philanthropy (p. 110) Dimension of social responsibility that includes charitable donations.

corporate policy (p. 110) Dimension of social responsibility that refers to the position a firm takes on social and political issues.

corporate responsibility (p. 110) Dimension of social responsibility that includes everything from hiring minority workers to making safe products.

corporate social responsibility (p. 110) A business's concern for the welfare of society.

corporation (p. 142) A legal entity with authority to act and have liability separate from its owners.

cost of capital (p. 602) The rate of return a company must earn in order to meet the demands of its lenders and expectations of its equity holders.

cost of goods sold (or cost of goods manufactured) (p. 561) A measure of the cost of merchandise sold or cost of raw materials and supplies used for producing items for resale.

couch potatoes *People who sit and watch TV for hours at a time.*

countertrading (p. 85) A complex form of bartering in which several countries may be involved, each trading goods for goods or services for services.

counting on it *Expecting it.*

craft union (p. 365) An organization of skilled specialists in a particular craft or trade.

credit unions (p. 665) Nonprofit, member-owned financial cooperatives that offer the full variety of banking services to their members.

critical path (p. 288) In a PERT network, the sequence of tasks that takes the longest time to complete.

cross-functional self-managed teams (p. 254) Groups of employees from different departments who work together on a long-term basis.

current assets (p. 558) Items that can or will be converted into cash within one year.

customer relationship management (CRM) (p. 399) The process of learning as much as possible about customers and doing everything you can to satisfy them—or even exceed their expectations—with goods and services over time.

damages (p. 131) The monetary settlement awarded to a person who is injured by a breach of contract.

data processing (DP) (p. 520) Name for business technology in the 1970s; included technology that supported an existing business and was primarily used to improve the flow of financial information.

database (p. 7) An electronic storage file where information is kept; one use of databases is to store vast amounts of information about consumers.

dealer (private-label) brands (p. 438) Products that don't carry the manufacturer's name but carry a distributor or retailer's name instead.

debenture bonds (p. 613) Bonds that are unsecured (i.e., not backed by any collateral such as equipment).

debit card (p. 660) An electronic funds transfer tool that serves the same function as checks: it withdraws funds from a checking account.

debt financing (p. 591) Funds raised through various forms of borrowing that must be repaid.

decentralized authority (p. 245) An organization structure in which decision-making authority is delegated to lower-level managers more familiar with local conditions than headquarters management could be.

decertification (p. 368) The process by which workers take away a union's right to represent them.

decision making (p. 218) Choosing among two or more alternatives.

deflation (p. 54) A situation in which prices are declining.

demand (p. 43) The quantity of products that people are willing to buy at different prices at a specific time.

demand deposit (p. 653) The technical name for a checking account; the money in a demand deposit can be withdrawn anytime on demand from the depositor.

demographic segmentation (p. 412) Dividing the market by age, income, and education level.

demography (p. 21) The statistical study of the human population with regard to its size, density, and other characteristics such as age, race, gender, and income.

departmentalization (p. 248) The dividing of organizational functions into separate units.

depreciation (p. 565) The systematic write-off of the cost of a tangible asset over its estimated useful life.

depression (p. 56) A severe recession.

deregulation (p. 138) Government withdrawal of certain laws and regulations that seem to hinder competition.

devaluation (p. 84) Lowering the value of a nation's currency relative to other currencies.

direct marketing (p. 474) Any activity that directly links manufacturers or intermediaries with the ultimate consumer.

direct selling (p. 474) Selling to consumers in their homes or where they work.

disability insurance (p. 681) Insurance that pays part of the cost of a long-term sickness or an accident.

discount rate (p. 649) The interest rate that the Fed charges for loans to member banks.

disinflation (p. 54) A situation in which price increases are slowing (the inflation rate is declining).

diversification (p. 628) Buying several different investment alternatives to spread the risk of investing.

dividends (p. 615) Part of a firm's profits that may be distributed to stockholders as either cash payments or additional shares of stock.

double-entry bookkeeping (p. 553) The concept of writing every business transaction in two places.

Dow Jones Industrial Average (the Dow) (p. 633) The average cost of 30 selected industrial stocks, used to give an indication of the direction (up or down) of the stock market over time.

drop shippers (p. 467) Wholesalers that solicit orders from retailers and other wholesalers and have the merchandise shipped directly from a producer to a buyer.

dumping (p. 74) Selling products in a foreign country at lower prices than those charged in the producing country.

e-commerce (p. 16) The buying and selling of goods and services over the Internet.

e-mail snooped *When someone other than the addressee reads e-mail messages.*

economic pie *The money available in the economy.*

economics (p. 36) The study of how society chooses to employ resources to produce goods and services and distribute them for consumption among various competing groups and individuals.

economies of scale (p. 241) The situation in which companies can reduce their production costs if they can purchase raw materials in bulk; the average cost of goods goes down as production levels increase.

electronic check conversion (ECC) (p. 660) An electronic funds transfer tool that converts a traditional paper check into an electronic transaction at the cash register and processes it through the Federal Reserve's Automated Clearing House.

electronic funds transfer (EFT) system (p. 660) A computerized system that electronically performs financial transactions such as making purchases, paying bills, and receiving paychecks.

electronic retailing (p. 472) Selling goods and services to ultimate customers (e.g., you and me) over the Internet.

embargo (p. 88) A complete ban on the import or export of a certain product or stopping all trade with a particular country.

employee orientation (p. 339) The activity that introduces new employees to the organization; to fellow employees; to their immediate supervisors; and to the policies, practices, and objectives of the firm.

employee stock ownership plans (ESOPs) (p. 387) Programs that enable employees to buy part or total ownership of the firm.

empowerment (p. 20) Giving frontline workers the responsibility, authority, and freedom to respond quickly to customer requests.

enabling (p. 229) Giving workers the education and tools they need to make decisions.

enterprise resource planning (ERP) (p. 283) A computer application that enables multiple firms to manage all of their operations (finance, requirements planning, human resources, and order fulfillment) on the basis of a single, integrated set of corporate data.

enterprise zones (p. 183) Specific geographic areas to which governments try to attract private business investment by offering lower taxes and other government support.

entrepreneur (p. 4) A person who risks time and money to start and manage a business.

entrepreneurial team (p. 187) A group of experienced people from different areas of business who join together to form a managerial team with the skills needed to develop, make, and market a new product.

entrepreneurship (p. 174) Accepting the risk of starting and running a business.

environmental scanning (p. 408) The process of identifying the factors that can affect marketing success.

equity financing (p. 592) Funds raised from operations within the firm or through the sale of ownership in the firm.

equity theory (p. 315) The idea that employees try to maintain equity between inputs and outputs compared to others in similar positions.

ethics (p. 102) Standards of moral behavior, that is, behavior that is accepted by society as right versus wrong.

everyday low pricing (EDLP) (p. 450) Setting prices lower than competitors and then not having any special sales.

exchange rate (p. 84) The value of one nation's currency relative to the currencies of other countries.

exclusive distribution (p. 471) Distribution that sends products to only one retail outlet in a given geographic area.

executor (p. 687) A person who assembles and values your estate, files income and other taxes, and distributes assets.

expectancy theory (p. 314) Victor Vroom's theory that the amount of effort employees exert on a specific task depends on their expectations of the outcome.

exporting (p. 68) Selling products to another country.

express warranties (p. 130) Specific representations by the seller that buyers rely on regarding the goods they purchase.

external customers (p. 232) Dealers, who buy products to sell to others, and ultimate customers (or end users), who buy products for their own personal use.

extranet (p. 527) A semiprivate network that uses Internet technology and allows more than one company to access the same information or allows people on different servers to collaborate.

extrinsic reward (p. 300) Something given to you by someone else as recognition for good work; extrinsic rewards include pay increases, praise, and promotions.

facility layout (p. 273) The physical arrangement of resources (including people) in the production process.

facility location (p. 270) The process of selecting a geographic location for a company's operations.

factoring (p. 596) The process of selling accounts receivable for cash.

factors of production (p. 10) The resources used to create wealth: land, labor, capital, entrepreneurship, and knowledge.

Federal Deposit Insurance Corporation (FDIC) (p. 657) An independent agency of the U.S. government that insures bank deposits.

finance (p. 582) The function in a business that acquires funds for the firm and manages those funds within the firm.

financial accounting (p. 550) Accounting information and analyses prepared for people outside the organization.

financial control (p. 587) A process in which a firm periodically compares its actual revenues, costs, and expenses with its projected ones.

financial management (p. 582) The job of managing a firm's resources so it can meet its goals and objectives.

financial managers (p. 582) Managers who make recommendations to top executives regarding strategies for improving the financial strength of a firm.

financial statement (p. 555) A summary of all the transactions that have occurred over a particular period.

first in, first out (FIFO) (p. 566) An accounting method for calculating cost of inventory; it assumes that the first goods to come in are the first to go out.

fiscal policy (p. 56) The federal government's efforts to keep the economy stable by increasing or decreasing taxes or government spending.

fixed assets (p. 558) Assets that are relatively permanent, such as land, buildings, and equipment.

flat organization structure (p. 247) An organization structure that has few layers of management and a broad span of control.

flexible manufacturing (p. 285) Designing machines to do multiple tasks so that they can produce a variety of products.

flextime plan (p. 348) Work schedule that gives employees some freedom to choose when to work, as long as they work the required number of hours.

focus group (p. 409) A small group of people who meet under the direction of a discussion leader to communicate their opinions about an organization, its products, or other given issues.

foreign direct investment (p. 74) The buying of permanent property and businesses in foreign nations.

foreign subsidiary (p. 80) A company owned in a foreign country by another company (called the *parent company*).

form utility (p. 281) The value added by the creation of finished goods and services, such as the value added by taking silicon and making computer chips or putting services together to create a vacation package.

formal organization (p. 260) The structure that details lines of responsibility, authority, and position; that is, the structure shown on organization charts.

franchise (p. 158) The right to use a specific business's name and sell its products or services in a given territory.

franchise agreement (p. 158) An arrangement whereby someone with a good idea for a business sells the rights to use the business name and sell a product or service to others in a given territory.

franchisee (p. 158) A person who buys a franchise.

franchisor (p. 158) A company that develops a product concept and sells others the rights to make and sell the products.

free trade (p. 69) The movement of goods and services among nations without political or economic obstruction.

free-for-all atmosphere *A situation where all order seems to be lost in conducting business.*

free-market economies (p. 49) Economic systems in which the market largely determines what goods and services get produced, who gets them, and how the economy grows.

free-rein leadership (p. 227) Leadership style that involves managers setting objectives and employees being relatively free to do whatever it takes to accomplish those objectives.

freight forwarder (p. 480) An organization that puts many small shipments together to create a single large shipment that can be transported cost-effectively to the final destination.

fringe benefits (p. 346) Benefits such as sick-leave pay, vacation pay, pension plans, and health plans that represent additional compensation to employees beyond base wages.

from scratch *From the beginning.*

fundamental accounting equation (p. 556) Assets = liabilities + owners' equity; this is the basis for the balance sheet.

futures markets (p. 630) Commodities markets that involve the purchase and sale of goods for delivery sometime in the future.

Gantt chart (p. 289) Bar graph showing production managers what projects are being worked on and what stage they are in at any given time.

General Agreement on Tariffs and Trade (GATT) (p. 89) A 1948 agreement that established an international forum for negotiating mutual reductions in trade restrictions.

general partner (p. 145) An owner (partner) who has unlimited liability and is active in managing the firm.

general partnership (p. 145) A partnership in which all owners share in operating the business and in assuming liability for the business's debts.

generic goods (p. 439) Nonbranded products that usually sell at a sizable discount compared to national or private-label brands.

geographic segmentation (p. 412) Dividing the market by geographic area.

get in on the dough *Take the opportunity to make some money.*

Ghostbusters *Popular film of the 1980s in which characters chase and capture ghosts. Inspired the song "Who You Going to Call? Ghostbusters!"*

givebacks (p. 376) Concessions made by union members to management; gains from labor negotiations are given back to management to help employers remain competitive and thereby save jobs.

go for the gold *To work to be the very best (figuratively winning a gold medal).*

go out with me *Go with me to dinner or to a movie or some other entertainment.*

goals (p. 215) The broad, long-term accomplishments an organization wishes to attain.

goal-setting theory (p. 313) The idea that setting ambitious but attainable goals can motivate workers and improve performance if the goals are accepted, accompanied by feedback, and facilitated by organizational conditions.

gone off the deep end *Doing something risky, almost crazy—like jumping into the deep end of a swimming pool when you can't swim.*

goods (p. 25) Tangible products such as computers, food, clothing, cars, and appliances.

goofing off *Doing things at work not associated with the job, such as talking with others at the drinking fountain.*

government and not-for-profit accounting (p. 552) Accounting system for organizations whose purpose is not generating a profit but serving ratepayers, taxpayers, and others according to a duly approved budget.

green product (p. 421) A product whose production, use, and disposal don't damage the environment.

grievance (p. 370) A charge by employees that management is not abiding by the terms of the negotiated labor-management agreement.

gross domestic product (GDP) (p. 53) The total value of goods and services produced in a country in a given year.

gross profit (gross margin) (p. 561) How much a firm earned by buying (or making) and selling merchandise.

hard copy *Copy printed on paper.*

Hawthorne effect (p. 303) The tendency for people to behave differently when they know they are being studied.

health maintenance organizations (HMOs) (p. 669) Health care organizations that require members to choose from a restricted list of doctors.

heart *The most important part of something; the central force or idea.*

helped turn around *Helped reverse the downward trend.*

hierarchy (p. 243) A system in which one person is at the top of the organization and there is a ranked or sequential ordering from the top down of managers who are responsible to that person.

high-low pricing strategy (p. 450) Setting prices that are higher than EDLP stores, but having many special sales where the prices are lower than competitors'.

horizontal merger (p. 157) The joining of two firms in the same industry.

hot second *Immediately.*

human relations skills (p. 221) Skills that involve communication and motivation; they enable managers to work through and with people.

human resource management (p. 330) The process of determining human resource needs and then recruiting, selecting, developing, motivating, evaluating, compensating, and scheduling employees to achieve organizational goals.

hygiene factors (p. 306) In Herzberg's theory of motivating factors, job factors that can cause dissatisfaction if missing but that do not necessarily motivate employees if increased.

If it isn't broken, don't fix it *Don't risk making things worse by changing things that don't need to be changed.*

implied warranties (p. 130) Guarantees legally imposed on the seller.

import quota (p. 87) A limit on the number of products in certain categories that a nation can import.

importing (p. 68) Buying products from another country.

inbound logistics (p. 478) The area of logistics that involves bringing raw materials, packaging, other goods and services, and information from suppliers to producers.

income statement (p. 560) The financial statement that shows a firm's profit after costs, expenses, and taxes; it summarizes all of the resources that have come into the firm (revenue), all the resources that have left the firm, and the resulting net income.

incubators (p. 183) Centers that offer new businesses low-cost offices with basic business services.

indenture terms (p. 599) The terms of agreement in a bond issue.

independent audit (p. 551) An evaluation and unbiased opinion about the accuracy of a company's financial statements.

individual retirement account (IRA) (p. 683) A tax-deferred investment plan that enables you (and your spouse, if you are married) to save part of your income for retirement; a traditional IRA allows people who qualify to deduct from their reported income the money they put into an account.

industrial goods (p. 435) Products used in the production of other products. Sometimes called business goods or B2B goods.

industrial unions (p. 366) Labor organizations of unskilled and semiskilled workers in mass-production industries such as automobiles and mining.

inflation (p. 54) A general rise in the prices of goods and services over time.

infomercial (p. 494) A full-length TV program devoted exclusively to promoting goods or services.

informal organization (p. 260) The system of relationships and lines of authority that develops spontaneously as employees meet and form power centers; that is, the human side of the organization that does not appear on any organization chart.

information systems (IS) (p. 520) Technology that helps companies do business; includes such tools as automated teller machines (ATMs) and voice mail.

information technology (IT) (p. 520) Technology that helps companies change business by allowing them to use new methods.

information utility (p. 464) Adding value to products by opening two-way flows of information between marketing participants.

initial public offering (IPO) (p. 610) The first public offering of a corporation's stock.

injunction (p. 376) A court order directing someone to do something or to refrain from doing something.

insider trading (p. 113) An unethical activity in which insiders use private company information to further their own fortunes or those of their family and friends.

institutional investors (p. 611) Large organizations—such as pension funds, mutual funds, insurance companies, and banks—that invest their own funds or the funds of others.

insurable interest (p. 697) The possibility of the policyholder to suffer a loss.

insurable risk (p. 697) A risk that the typical insurance company will cover.

insurance policy (p. 697) A written contract between the insured and an insurance company that promises to pay for all or part of a loss.

intangible assets (p. 558) Long-term assets (e.g., patents, trademarks, copyrights) that have no real physical form but do have value.

integrated marketing communication (IMC) (p. 490) A technique that combines all the promotional tools into one comprehensive and unified promotional strategy.

integrity-based ethics codes (p. 108) Ethical standards that define the organization's guiding values, create an environment that supports ethically sound behavior, and stress a shared accountability among employees.

intensive distribution (p. 471) Distribution that puts products into as many retail outlets as possible.

interactive marketing program (p. 509) A system in which consumers can access company information on their own and supply information about themselves in an ongoing dialogue.

interactive promotion (p. 495) Promotion process that allows marketers to go beyond a monologue, where sellers try to persuade buyers to buy things, to a dialogue in which buyers and sellers work together to create mutually beneficial exchange relationships.

interest (p. 612) The payment the issuer of the bond makes to the bondholders for use of the borrowed money.

intermittent process (p. 282) A production process in which the production run is short and the machines are changed frequently to make different products.

intermodal shipping (p. 481) The use of multiple modes of transportation to complete a single long-distance movement of freight.

internal customers (p. 232) Individuals and units within the firm that receive services from other individuals or units.

International Monetary Fund (IMF) (p. 662) Organization that assists the smooth flow of money among nations.

Internet2 (p. 528) The new Internet system that links government supercomputer centers and a select group of universities; it runs more than 22,000 times faster than today's public infrastructure and supports heavy-duty applications.

intranet (p. 526) A companywide network, closed to public access, that uses Internet-type technology.

intrapreneurs (p. 181) Creative people who work as entrepreneurs within corporations.

intrinsic reward (p. 300) The personal satisfaction you feel when you perform well and complete goals.

inverted organization (p. 258) An organization that has contact people at the top and the chief executive officer at the bottom of the organization chart.

investment bankers (p. 610) Specialists who assist in the issue and sale of new securities.

invisible hand (p. 39) A phrase coined by Adam Smith to describe the process that turns self-directed gain into social and economic benefits for all.

involuntary bankruptcy (p. 136) Bankruptcy procedures filed by a debtor's creditors.

IOUs *Debt; abbreviation for "I owe you."*

ISO 14000 (p. 279) A collection of the best practices for managing an organization's impact on the environment.

ISO 9000 (p. 278) The common name given to quality management and assurance standards.

job analysis (p. 333) A study of what is done by employees who hold various job titles.

job description (p. 333) A summary of the objectives of a job, the type of work to be done, the responsibilities and duties, the working conditions, and the relationship of the job to other functions.

job enlargement (p. 309) A job enrichment strategy that involves combining a series of tasks into one challenging and interesting assignment.

job enrichment (p. 307) A motivational strategy that emphasizes motivating the worker through the job itself.

job rotation (p. 309) A job enrichment strategy that involves moving employees from one job to another.

job sharing (p. 350) An arrangement whereby two part-time employees share one full-time job.

job simulation (p. 340) The use of equipment that duplicates job conditions and tasks so that trainees can learn skills before attempting them on the job.

job specifications (p. 333) A written summary of the minimum qualifications required of workers to do a particular job.

joint venture (p. 79) A partnership in which two or more companies (often from different countries) join to undertake a major project.

journal (p. 553) The record book or computer program where accounting data are first entered.

judiciary (p. 124) The branch of government chosen to oversee the legal system through the court system.

jumped headfirst *Began quickly and eagerly without hesitation.*

junk bonds (p. 629) High-risk, high-interest bonds.

just-in-time (JIT) inventory control (p. 284) A production process in which a minimum of inventory is kept on the premises and parts, supplies, and other needs are delivered just in time to go on the assembly line.

key player *Important participant.*

kick back and relax *To take a rest.*

Knights of Labor (p. 366) The first national labor union; formed in 1869.

knockoff brands (p. 439) Illegal copies of national brand-name goods.

know-how *A level of specific expertise.*

knowledge management (p. 229) Finding the right information, keeping the information in a readily accessible place, and making the information known to everyone in the firm.

last in, first out (LIFO) (p. 566) An accounting method for calculating cost of inventory; it assumes that the last goods to come in are the first to go out.

latchkey kids *School-age children who come home to empty houses since all of the adults are at work.*

law of large numbers (p. 697) Principle that if a large number of people are exposed to the same risk, a predictable number of losses will occur during a given period of time.

leading (p. 214) Creating a vision for the organization and guiding, training, coaching, and motivating others to work effectively to achieve the organization's goals and objectives.

lean manufacturing (p. 286) The production of goods using less of everything compared to mass production.

ledger (p. 553) A specialized accounting book or computer program in which information from accounting journals is accumulated into specific categories and posted so that managers can find all the information about one account in the same place.

letter of credit (p. 661) A promise by the bank to pay the seller a given amount if certain conditions are met.

level playing field *Treating everyone equally.*

leverage (p. 602) Raising needed funds through borrowing to increase a firm's rate of return.

leveraged buyout (LBO) (p. 157) An attempt by employees, management, or a group of investors to purchase an organization primarily through borrowing.

liabilities (p. 558) What the business owes to others (debts).

licensing (p. 76) A global strategy in which a firm (the licensor) allows a foreign company (the licensee) to produce its product in exchange for a fee (a royalty).

limited liability (p. 145) The responsibility of a business's owners for losses only up to the amount they invest; limited partners and shareholders have limited liability.

limited liability company (LLC) (p. 153) A company similar to an S corporation but without the special eligibility requirements.

limited liability partnership (LLP) (p. 145) A partnership that limits partners' risk of losing their personal assets to only their own acts and omissions and to the acts and omissions of people under their supervision.

limited partner (p. 145) An owner who invests money in the business but does not have any management responsibility or liability for losses beyond the investment.

limited partnership (p. 145) A partnership with one or more general partners and one or more limited partners.

line of credit (p. 595) A given amount of unsecured short-term funds a bank will lend to a business, provided the funds are readily available.

line organization (p. 251) An organization that has direct two-way lines of responsibility, authority, and communication running from the top to the bottom of the organization, with all people reporting to only one supervisor.

line personnel (p. 251) Employees who are part of the chain of command that is responsible for achieving organizational goals.

liquidity (p. 558) How fast an asset can be converted into cash.

lockout (p. 376) An attempt by management to put pressure on unions by temporarily closing the business.

logistics (p. 478) The marketing activity that involves planning, implementing, and controlling the physical flow of materials, final goods, and related information from points of origin to points of consumption to meet customer requirements at a profit.

long-term financing (p. 591) Borrowed capital that will be repaid over a specific period longer than one year.

long-term forecast (p. 585) Forecast that predicts revenues, costs, and expenses for a period longer than 1 year, and sometimes as far as 5 or 10 years into the future.

loss (p. 5) When a business's expenses are more than its revenues.

M-1 (p. 646) Money that can be accessed quickly and easily (coins and paper money, checks, traveler's checks, etc.).

M-2 (p. 646) Money included in M-1 plus money that may take a little more time to obtain (savings accounts, money market accounts, mutual funds, certificates of deposit, etc.).

macroeconomics (p. 36) The part of economics study that looks at the operation of a nation's economy as a whole.

management (p. 213) The process used to accomplish organizational goals through planning, organizing, leading, and controlling people and other organizational resources.

management by objectives (MBO) (p. 313) A system of goal setting and implementation that involves a cycle of discussion, review, and evaluation of objectives among top and middle-level managers, supervisors, and employees.

management development (p. 341) The process of training and educating employees to become good managers and then monitoring the progress of their managerial skills over time.

managerial accounting (p. 549) Accounting used to provide information and analyses to managers within the organization to assist them in decision making.

managing diversity (p. 224) Building systems and a climate that unite different people in a common pursuit without undermining their individual strengths.

manufacturers' brand names (p. 438) The brand names of manufacturers that distribute products nationally.

market (p. 194) People with unsatisfied wants and needs who have both the resources and the willingness to buy.

market price (p. 44) The price determined by supply and demand.

market segmentation (p. 411) The process of dividing the total market into groups whose members have similar characteristics.

marketing (p. 398) The process of planning and executing the conception, pricing, promotion, and distribution of goods and services to facilitate exchanges that satisfy individual and organizational objectives.

marketing concept (p. 399) A three-part business philosophy: (1) a customer orientation, (2) a service orientation, and (3) a profit orientation.

marketing intermediaries (p. 460) Organizations that assist in moving goods and services from producers to industrial and consumer users.

marketing mix (p. 401) The ingredients that go into a marketing program: product, price, place, and promotion.

marketing research (p. 405) The analysis of markets to determine opportunities and challenges, and to find the information needed to make good decisions.

marriage of software, hardware, etc. *Combination of various technologies.*

Maslow's hierarchy of needs (p. 303) Theory of motivation based on unmet human needs from basic physiological needs to safety, social, and esteem needs to self-actualization needs.

mass customization (p. 286) Tailoring products to meet the needs of individual customers.

mass marketing (p. 413) Developing products and promotions to please large groups of people.

master limited partnership (MLP) (p. 145) A partnership that looks much like a corporation (in that it acts like a corporation and is traded on a stock exchange) but is taxed like a partnership and thus avoids the corporate income tax.

materials handling (p. 478) The movement of goods within a warehouse, from warehouses to the factory floor, and from the factory floor to various workstations.

materials requirement planning (MRP) (p. 283) A computer-based production management system that uses sales forecasts to make sure that needed parts and materials are available at the right time and place.

matrix organization (p. 252) An organization in which specialists from different parts of the organization are brought together to work on specific projects but still remain part of a line-and-staff structure.

maturity date (p. 612) The exact date the issuer of a bond must pay the principal to the bondholder.

measuring stick *Tool used to evaluate or compare something.*

mediation (p. 372) The use of a third party, called a mediator, who encourages both sides in a dispute to continue negotiating and often makes suggestions for resolving the dispute.

mentor (p. 341) An experienced employee who supervises, coaches, and guides lower-level employees by introducing them to the right people and generally being their organizational sponsor.

merchant wholesalers (p. 467) Independently owned firms that take title to (own) the goods they handle.

merger (p. 156) The result of two firms forming one company.

Mickey D's *Nickname for McDonald's.*

microeconomics (p. 36) The part of economics study that looks at the behavior of people and organizations in particular markets.

micropreneurs (p. 178) Entrepreneurs willing to accept the risk of starting and managing the type of business that remains small, lets them do the kind of work they want to do, and offers them a balanced lifestyle.

middle management (p. 220) The level of management that includes general managers, division managers, and branch and plant managers who are responsible for tactical planning and controlling.

mine the knowledge *Make maximum use of the knowledge employees have.*

mission statement (p. 215) An outline of the fundamental purposes of an organization.

mixed economies (p. 50) Economic systems in which some allocation of resources is made by the market and some by the government.

monetary policy (p. 59) The management of the money supply and interest rates.

money (p. 644) Anything that people generally accept as payment for goods and services.

money supply (p. 646) The amount of money the Federal Reserve Bank makes available for people to buy goods and services.

monopolistic competition (p. 45) The market situation in which a large number of sellers produce products that are very similar but that are perceived by buyers as different.

monopoly (p. 46) A market in which there is only one seller for a product or service.

more than meets the eye *More than one can see with his or her own eyes; much is happening that is not visible.*

motivators (p. 306) In Herzberg's theory of motivating factors, job factors that cause employees to be productive and that give them satisfaction.

mouse-click away *Ease of doing something by using the computer or Internet.*

muddy the water *Making things even more difficult than they currently are.*

multinational corporation (p. 80) An organization that manufactures and markets products in many different countries and has multinational stock ownership and multinational management.

mutual fund (p. 627) An organization that buys stocks and bonds and then sells shares in those securities to the public.

mutual insurance company (p. 699) A type of insurance company owned by its policyholders.

National Association of Securities Dealers Automated Quotations (NASDAQ) (p. 618) A nationwide electronic system that communicates over-the-counter trades to brokers.

national debt (p. 57) The sum of government deficits over time.

negligence (p. 126) In tort law, behavior that causes unintentional harm or injury.

negotiable instruments (p. 130) Forms of commercial paper (such as checks) that are transferable among businesses and individuals and represent a promise to pay a specified amount.

negotiated labor-management agreement (labor contract) (p. 369) Agreement that sets the tone and clarifies the terms under which management and labor agree to function over a period of time.

net income or net loss (p. 560) Revenue left over after all costs and expenses, including taxes, are paid.

network computing system (client/server computing) (p. 530) Computer systems that allow personal computers (clients) to obtain needed information from huge databases in a central computer (the server).

networking (p. 255) Using communications technology and other means to link organizations and allow them to work together on common objectives.

networking (p. 341) The process of establishing and maintaining contacts with key managers in one's own organization and other organizations and using those contacts to weave strong relationships that serve as informal development systems.

niche marketing (p. 412) The process of finding small but profitable market segments and designing or finding products for them.

nonbanks (p. 652) Financial organizations that accept no deposits but offer many of the services provided by regular banks (pension funds, insurance companies, commercial finance companies, consumer finance companies, and brokerage houses).

nonprofit organization (p. 7) An organization whose goals do not include making a personal profit for its owners or organizers.

North American Free Trade Agreement (NAFTA) (p. 91) Agreement that created a free-trade area among the United States, Canada, and Mexico.

objectives (p. 215) Specific, short-term statements detailing how to achieve the organization's goals.

off-the-job training (p. 340) Training that occurs away from the workplace and consists of internal or external programs to develop any of a variety of skills or to foster personal development.

oligopoly (p. 46) A form of competition in which just a few sellers dominate the market.

one-to-one marketing (p. 413) Developing a unique mix of goods and services for each individual customer.

online training (p. 340) Training programs in which employees "attend" classes via the Internet.

on-the-job training (p. 339) Training in which the employee immediately begins his or her tasks and learns by doing, or watches others for a while and then imitates them, all right at the workplace.

open shop agreement (p. 370) Agreement in right-to-work states that gives workers the option to join or not join a union, if one exists in their workplace.

open-market operations (p. 649) The buying and selling of U.S. government bonds by the Fed with the goal of regulating the money supply.

operating (master) budget (p. 586) The budget that ties together all of a firm's other budgets; it is the projection of dollar allocations to various costs and expenses needed to run or operate the business, given projected revenues.

operating expenses (p. 562) Costs involved in operating a business, such as rent, utilities, and salaries.

operational planning (p. 218) The process of setting work standards and schedules necessary to implement the company's tactical objectives.

operations management (p. 289) A specialized area in management that converts or transforms resources (including human resources) into goods and services.

organization chart (p. 219) A visual device that shows relationships among people and divides the organization's work; it shows who is accountable for the completion of specific work and who reports to whom.

organizational (or corporate) culture (p. 259) Widely shared values within an organization that provide unity and cooperation to achieve common goals.

organizing (p. 213) A management function that includes designing the structure of the organization and creating conditions and systems in which everyone and everything work together to achieve the organization's goals and objectives.

out of the office loop *Out of the line of communication that occurs in the workplace.*

outbound logistics (p. 478) The area of logistics that involves managing the flow of finished products and information to business buyers and ultimate consumers (people like you and me).

outsourcing (p. 257) Assigning various functions, such as accounting, production, security, maintenance, and legal work, to outside organizations.

over-the-counter (OTC) market (p. 618) Exchange that provides a means to trade stocks not listed on the national exchanges.

owners' equity (p. 559) The amount of the business that belongs to the owners minus any liabilities owed by the business.

participative (democratic) leadership (p. 226) Leadership style that consists of managers and employees working together to make decisions.

partnership (p. 142) A legal form of business with two or more owners.

patent (p. 128) A document that gives inventors exclusive rights to their inventions for 20 years.

pave the way *Process of making a task easier.*

peanut butter and jelly *Popular combination for sandwich; the two are seen as perfect complementary products.*

penetration strategy (p. 450) Strategy in which a product is priced low to attract many customers and discourage competition.

pension funds (p. 656) Amounts of money put aside by corporations, nonprofit organizations, or unions to cover part of the financial needs of members when they retire.

perks *Short for* perquisites; *compensation in addition to salary, such as day care or a company car.*

perfect competition (p. 45) The market situation in which there are many sellers in a market and no seller is large enough to dictate the price of a product.

performance appraisal (p. 342) An evaluation in which the performance level of employees is measured against established standards to make decisions about promotions, compensation, additional training, or firing.

personal selling (p. 498) The face-to-face presentation and promotion of goods and services.

place utility (p. 464) Adding value to products by having them where people want them.

planning (p. 213) A management function that includes anticipating trends and determining the best strategies and tactics to achieve organizational goals and objectives.

piece of the action *A share in the opportunity.*

pink slip *A notice that you've lost your job.*

pitch in *To help as needed.*

PMI (p. 219) Listing all the pluses for a solution in one column, all the minuses in another, and the implications in a third column.

possession utility (p. 464) Doing whatever is necessary to transfer ownership from one party to another, including providing credit, delivery, installation, guarantees, and follow-up service.

poster child *Best example.*

precedent (p. 125) Decisions judges have made in earlier cases that guide the handling of new cases.

preferred provider organizations (PPOs) (p. 699) Health care organizations similar to HMOs except that they allow members to choose their own physicians (for a fee).

preferred stock (p. 616) Stock that gives its owners preference in the payment of dividends and an earlier claim on assets than common stockholders if the company is forced out of business and its assets sold.

premium (p. 694) The fee charged by an insurance company for an insurance policy.

price leadership (p. 448) The procedure by which one or more dominant firms set the pricing practices that all competitors in an industry follow.

primary boycott (p. 375) When a union encourages both its members and the general public not to buy the products of a firm involved in a labor dispute.

primary data (p. 406) Data that you gather yourself (not from secondary sources such as books and magazines).

principle of motion economy (p. 301) Theory developed by Frank and Lillian Gilbreth that every job can be broken down into a series of elementary motions.

private accountants (p. 550) Accountants who work for a single firm, government agency, or nonprofit organization.

problem solving (p. 219) The process of solving the everyday problems that occur. Problem solving is less formal than decision making and usually calls for quicker action.

process manufacturing (p. 282) That part of the production process that physically or chemically changes materials.

producer price index (PPI) (p. 54) An index that measures prices at the wholesale level.

product (p. 402) Any physical good, service, or idea that satisfies a want or need plus anything that would enhance the product in the eyes of consumers, such as the brand.

product analysis (p. 441) Making cost estimates and sales forecasts to get a feeling for profitability of new-product ideas.

product differentiation (p. 434) The creation of real or perceived product differences.

product liability (p. 126) Part of tort law that holds businesses liable for harm that results from the production, design, sale, or use of products they market.

product life cycle (p. 443) A theoretical model of what happens to sales and profits for a product class over time.

product line (p. 432) A group of products that are physically similar or are intended for a similar market.

product mix (p. 432) The combination of product lines offered by a manufacturer.

product placement (p. 492) Putting products into TV shows and movies where they will be seen.

product screening (p. 441) A process designed to reduce the number of new-product ideas being worked on at any one time.

production (p. 268) The creation of finished goods and services using the factors of production: land, labor, capital, entrepreneurship, and knowledge.

production management (p. 269) The term used to describe all the activities managers do to help their firms create goods.

productivity (p. 15) The amount of output you generate given the amount of input.

profit (p. 4) The amount of money a business earns above and beyond what it spends for salaries and other expenses.

program evaluation and review technique (PERT) (p. 288) A method for analyzing the tasks involved in completing a given project, estimating the time needed to complete each task, and identifying the minimum time needed to complete the total project.

program trading (p. 635) Giving instructions to computers to automatically sell if the price of a stock dips to a certain point to avoid potential losses.

promissory note (p. 593) A written contract with a promise to pay a supplier a specific sum of money at a definite time.

promotion (p. 404) All the techniques sellers use to motivate people to buy their products or services.

promotion (p. 490) An effort by marketers to inform and remind people in the target market about products and to persuade them to participate in an exchange.

promotion mix (p. 490) The combination of promotional tools an organization uses.

pros and cons *Arguments for and against something.*

prospect (p. 498) A person with the means to buy a product, the authority to buy, and the willingness to listen to a sales message.

prospecting (p. 498) Researching potential buyers and choosing those most likely to buy.

prospectus (p. 619) A condensed version of economic and financial information that a company must file with the SEC before issuing stock; the prospectus must be sent to prospective investors.

provided the spark *Supplied the energy that motivated others.*

psychographic segmentation (p. 412) Dividing the market using the group's values, attitudes, and interests.

psychological pricing (p. 450) Pricing goods and services at price points that make the product appear less expensive than it is.

public accountant (p. 550) An accountant who provides his or her accounting services to individuals or businesses on a fee basis.

public domain software (freeware) (p. 532) Software that is free for the taking.

public relations (PR) (p. 502) The management function that evaluates public attitudes, changes policies and procedures in response to the public's requests, and executes a program of action and information to earn public understanding and acceptance.

publicity (p. 503) Any information about an individual, product, or organization that's distributed to the public through the media and that's not paid for or controlled by the seller.

pull strategy (p. 508) Promotional strategy in which heavy advertising and sales promotion efforts are directed toward consumers so that they'll request the products from retailers.

pump up the profits *Making profits in a company appear larger than they actually are under recognized accounting rules.*

purchasing (p. 285) The function in a firm that searches for quality material resources, finds the best suppliers, and negotiates the best price for goods and services.

pure risk The threat of loss with no chance for profit.

push strategy (p. 508) Promotional strategy in which the producer uses advertising, personal selling, sales promotion, and all other promotional tools to convince wholesalers and retailers to stock and sell merchandise.

qualifying (p. 498) In the selling process, making sure that people have a need for the product, the authority to buy, and the willingness to listen to a sales message.

quality (p. 275) Consistently producing what the customer wants while reducing errors before and after delivery to the customer.

quality function deployment (QFD) (p. 277) A process of linking the needs of end users (customers) to design, development, engineering, manufacturing, and service functions.

quality of life (p. 6) The general well-being of a society in terms of political freedom, a clean natural environment, education, health care, safety, free time, and everything else that leads to satisfaction and joy.

quid pro quo *Latin phrase meaning "something given in return for something else."*

quite a stir *Something that causes a feeling of concern.*

rack jobbers (p. 467) Wholesalers that furnish racks or shelves full of merchandise to retailers, display products, and sell on consignment.

ratio analysis (p. 567) The assessment of a firm's financial condition and performance through calculations and interpretations of financial ratios developed from the firm's financial statements.

real time (p. 255) The present moment or the actual time in which something takes place.

recession (p. 56) Two or more consecutive quarters of decline in the GDP.

recruitment (p. 334) The set of activities used to obtain a sufficient number of the right people at the right time.

reengineering (p. 258) The fundamental rethinking and radical redesign of organizational processes to achieve dramatic improvements in critical measures of performance.

reinforcement theory (p. 315) Theory that positive and negative reinforcers motivate a person to behave in certain ways.

relationship marketing (p. 414) Marketing strategy with the goal of keeping individual customers over time by offering them products that exactly meet their requirements.

reserve requirement (p. 648) A percentage of commercial banks' checking and savings accounts that must be physically kept in the bank.

resource development (p. 37) The study of how to increase resources and to create the conditions that will make better use of those resources.

restructuring (p. 257) Redesigning an organization so that it can more effectively and efficiently serve its customers.

retailer (p. 460) An organization that sells to ultimate consumers.

retained earnings (p. 559) The accumulated earnings from a firm's profitable operations that were kept in the business and not paid out to stockholders in dividends.

revenue (p. 5) The total amount of money a business takes in during a given period by selling goods and services.

revenue (p. 560) The value of what is received for goods sold, services rendered, and other financial sources.

reverse discrimination (p. 354) Discrimination against whites or males in hiring or promoting.

reverse logistics (p. 478) The area of logistics that involves bringing goods back to the manufacturer because of defects or for recycling materials.

revolving credit agreement (p. 595) A line of credit that is guaranteed by the bank.

right-to-work laws (p. 370) Legislation that gives workers the right, under an open shop, to join or not join a union if it is present.

risk (p. 5) The chance an entrepreneur takes of losing time and money on a business that may not prove profitable.

risk (p. 694) The chance of loss, the degree of probability of loss, and the amount of possible loss.

risk/return trade-off (p. 598) The principle that the greater the risk a lender takes in making a loan, the higher the interest rate required.

Roth IRA (p. 684) An IRA where you don't get upfront deductions on your taxes as you would with a traditional IRA, but the earnings grow tax-free and are also tax-free when they are withdrawn.

rule of indemnity (p. 698) Rule saying that an insured person or organization cannot collect more than the actual loss from an insurable risk.

rules-of-the-road orientation *Introduction to the proper procedures within an organization.*

S corporation (p. 152) A unique government creation that looks like a corporation but is taxed like sole proprietorships and partnerships.

sales promotion (p. 504) The promotional tool that stimulates consumer purchasing and dealer interest by means of short-term activities.

sampling (p. 505) A promotional tool in which a company lets consumers have a small sample of a product for no charge.

savings and loan association (S&L) (p. 654) A financial institution that accepts both savings and checking deposits and provides home mortgage loans.

Savings Association Insurance Fund (SAIF) (p. 657) The part of the FDIC that insures holders of accounts in savings and loan associations.

scientific management (p. 301) Studying workers to find the most efficient ways of doing things and then teaching people those techniques.

sea of information *Lots of information, often too much to process.*

secondary boycott (p. 375) An attempt by labor to convince others to stop doing business with a firm that is the subject of a primary boycott; prohibited by the Taft-Hartley Act.

secondary data (p. 406) Information that has already been compiled by others and published in journals and books or made available online.

secured bond (p. 599) A bond issued with some form of collateral.

secured loan (p. 595) A loan backed by something valuable, such as property.

Securities and Exchange Commission (SEC) (p. 619) Federal agency that has responsibility for regulating the various exchanges.

selection (p. 335) The process of gathering information and deciding who should be hired, under legal guidelines, for the best interests of the individual and the organization.

selective distribution (p. 471) Distribution that sends products to only a preferred group of retailers in an area.

self-insurance (p. 695) The practice of setting aside money to cover routine claims and buying only "catastrophe" policies to cover big losses.

Service Corps of Retired Executives (SCORE) (p. 196) An SBA office with volunteers from industry, trade associations, and education who counsel small businesses at no cost (except for expenses).

service utility (p. 465) Adding value by providing fast, friendly service during and after the sale and by teaching customers how to best use products over time.

services (p. 26) Intangible products (i.e., products that can't be held in your hand) such as education, health care, insurance, recreation, and travel and tourism.

sexual harassment (p. 382) Unwelcome sexual advances, requests for sexual favors, and other conduct (verbal or physical) of a sexual nature that creates a hostile work environment.

shaky ground *Idea that possible problems lie ahead.*

shareware (p. 532) Software that is copyrighted but distributed to potential customers free of charge.

Sherlock Holmes *A famous fictional detective who was particularly adept at uncovering information to solve very difficult mysteries.*

shoestring budget *A budget that implies the company is short on funds and only includes a minimal amount of financial expenditures (i.e., it's as thin as a shoestring).*

shop stewards (p. 372) Union officials who work permanently in an organization and represent employee interests on a daily basis.

shopping goods and services (p. 434) Those products that the consumer buys only after comparing value, quality, price, and style from a variety of sellers.

short-term financing (p. 591) Borrowed capital that will be repaid within one year.

short-term forecast (p. 584) Forecast that predicts revenues, costs, and expenses for a period of one year or less.

sift through mountains of information *Sort through large volumes of information.*

sinking fund (p. 614) A reserve account in which the issuer of a bond periodically retires some part of the bond principal prior to maturity so that enough capital will be accumulated by the maturity date to pay off the bond.

six sigma quality (p. 276) A quality measure that allows only 3.4 defects per million opportunities.

skimming price strategy (p. 450) Strategy in which a new product is priced high to make optimum profit while there's little competition.

small business (p. 184) A business that is independently owned and operated, is not dominant in its field of operation, and meets certain standards of size (set by the Small Business Administration) in terms of employees or annual receipts.

Small Business Administration (SBA) (p. 192) A U.S. government agency that advises and assists small businesses by providing management training and financial advice and loans.

Small Business Investment Company (SBIC) Program (p. 192) A program through which private investment companies licensed by the Small Business Administration lend money to small businesses.

smart card (p. 660) An electronic funds transfer tool that is a combination credit card, debit card, phone card, driver's license card, and more.

smoking gun *An issue or other disclosure that proves a person or organization has done something wrong.*

social audit (p. 116) A systematic evaluation of an organization's progress toward implementing programs that are socially responsible and responsive.

Social Security (p. 682) The term used to describe the Old-Age, Survivors, and Disability Insurance Program established by the Social Security Act of 1935.

socialism (p. 47) An economic system based on the premise that some, if not most, basic businesses should be owned by the government so that profits can be evenly distributed among the people.

sole proprietorship (p. 142) A business that is owned, and usually managed, by one person.

span of control (p. 246) The optimum number of subordinates a manager supervises or should supervise.

specialty goods and services (p. 434) Consumer products with unique characteristics and brand identity. Because these products are perceived as having no reasonable substitute, the consumer puts forth a special effort to purchase them.

speculative risk (p. 694) A chance of either profit or loss.

squeezing franchisees' profits *Tightening or reducing profits.*

staff personnel (p. 257) Employees who advise and assist line personnel in meeting their goals.

staffing (p. 223) A management function that includes hiring, motivating, and retaining the best people available to accomplish the company's objectives.

stakeholder marketing (p. 421) Establishing and maintaining mutually beneficial exchange relationships over time with all the stakeholders of the organization.

stakeholders (p. 6) All the people who stand to gain or lose by the policies and activities of a business.

standard of living (p. 5) The amount of goods and services people can buy with the money they have.

start-up business *A new company.*

state-of-the-art *The most modern type available.*

statement of cash flows (p. 562) Financial statement that reports cash receipts and disbursements related to a firm's three major activities: operations, investments, and financing.

statistical process control (SPC) (p. 276) The process of taking statistical samples of product components at each stage of the production process and plotting those results on a graph. Any variances from quality standards are recognized and can be corrected if beyond the set standards.

statistical quality control (SQC) (p. 276) The process some managers use to continually monitor all phases of the production process to assure that quality is being built into the product from the beginning.

statutory law (p. 125) State and federal constitutions, legislative enactments, treaties of the federal government, and ordinances—in short, written law.

staying afloat *Staying in business during tough times.*

stock certificate (p. 615) Evidence of stock ownership that specifies the name of the company, the number of shares it represents, and the type of stock being issued.

stock exchange (p. 617) An organization whose members can buy and sell (exchange) securities for companies and investors.

stock insurance company (p. 698) A type of insurance company owned by stockholders.

stock splits (p. 626) An action by a company that gives stockholders two or more shares of stock for each one they own.

stockbroker (p. 621) A registered representative who works as a market intermediary to buy and sell securities for clients.

stocks (p. 615) Shares of ownership in a company.

strategic alliance (p. 79) A long-term partnership between two or more companies established to help each company build competitive market advantages.

strategic planning (p. 216) The process of determining the major goals of the organization and the policies and strategies for obtaining and using resources to achieve those goals.

strict product liability (p. 126) Legal responsibility for harm or injury caused by a product regardless of fault.

strike (p. 373) A union strategy in which workers refuse to go to work; the purpose is to further workers' objectives after an impasse in collective bargaining.

strikebreakers (p. 376) Workers hired to do the jobs of striking workers until the labor dispute is resolved.

supervisory management (p. 220) Managers who are directly responsible for supervising workers and evaluating their daily performance.

supply (p. 43) The quantity of products that manufacturers or owners are willing to sell at different prices at a specific time.

supply chain (or value chain) (p. 476) The sequence of linked activities that must be performed by various organizations to move goods from the sources of raw materials to ultimate consumers.

supply-chain management (p. 477) The process of managing the movement of raw materials, parts, work in progress, finished goods, and related information through all the organizations involved in the supply chain; managing the return of such goods, if necessary; and recycling materials when appropriate.

SWOT analysis (p. 216) A planning tool used to analyze an organization's strengths, weaknesses, opportunities, and threats.

tactical planning (p. 217) The process of developing detailed, short-term statements about what is to be done, who is to do it, and how it is to be done.

tall organization structure (p. 247) An organizational structure in which the pyramidal organization chart would be quite tall because of the various levels of management.

target costing (p. 448) Designing a product so that it satisfies customers and meets the profit margins desired by the firm.

target marketing (p. 412) Marketing directed toward those groups (market segments) an organization decides it can serve profitably.

tariff (p. 87) A tax imposed on imports.

tax accountant (p. 552) An accountant trained in tax law and responsible for preparing tax returns or developing tax strategies.

tax-deferred contributions (p. 683) Retirement account deposits for which you pay no current taxes, but the earnings gained are taxed as regular income when they are withdrawn at retirement.

taxes (p. 134) How the government (federal, state, and local) raises money.

technical skills (p. 221) Skills that involve the ability to perform tasks in a specific discipline or department.

technology (p. 15) Everything from phones and copiers to computers, medical imaging devices, personal digital assistants, and the various software programs that make business processes more efficient and productive.

telecom *Short for telecommunications.*

telemarketing (p. 473) The sale of goods and services by telephone.

telephone tag *To leave a telephone message when you attempt to return a message left for you.*

term insurance (p. 680) Pure insurance protection for a given number of years.

term-loan agreement (p. 598) A promissory note that requires the borrower to repay the loan in specified installments.

test marketing (p. 403) The process of testing products among potential users.

thorny issue *An issue that can cause pain or difficulty (as a thorn on a rose bush may).*

through the grapevine *Information communication; stories told by one person to the next.*

time deposit (p. 653) The technical name for a savings account; the bank can require prior notice before the owner withdraws money from a time deposit.

time in the trenches *Working with the other employees and experiencing what they contend with as opposed to managing from an office and relying solely on reports about what is happening in the workplace.*

time utility (p. 464) Adding value to products by making them available when they're needed.

time-motion studies (p. 301) Studies, begun by Frederick Taylor, of which tasks must be performed to complete a job and the time needed to do each task.

to take a break *To slow down and do something besides work.*

top management (p. 219) Highest level of management, consisting of the president and other key company executives who develop strategic plans.

tort (p. 126) A wrongful act that causes injury to another person's body, property, or reputation.

total fixed costs (p. 449) All the expenses that remain the same no matter how many products are made or sold.

total product offer (p. 431) Everything that consumers evaluate when deciding whether to buy something; also called a *value package.*

trade credit (p. 593) The practice of buying goods and services now and paying for them later.

trade deficit (p. 72) An unfavorable balance of trade; occurs when the value of a country's imports exceeds that of its exports.

trade protectionism (p. 87) The use of government regulations to limit the import of goods and services. Advocates of trade protectionism believe that it allows domestic producers to survive and grow, producing more jobs.

trademark (p. 438) A brand that has been given exclusive legal protection for both the brand name and the pictorial design.

trademark (p. 129) A legally protected name, symbol, or design (or combination of these) that identifies the goods or services of one seller and distinguishes them from those of competitors.

training and development (p. 358) All attempts to improve productivity by increasing an employee's ability to perform. Training focuses on short-term skills, whereas development focuses on long-term abilities.

transparency (p. 255) A concept that describes a company being so open to other companies working with it that the once-solid barriers between them become see-through and electronic information is shared as if the companies were one.

trial balance (p. 554) A summary of all the data in the account ledgers to show whether the figures are correct and balanced.

trial close (p. 499) A step in the selling process that consists of a question or statement that moves the selling process toward the actual close.

trigger-happy *Term that refers to people reacting too fast to the circumstances facing them in a difficult situation.*

turn a blind eye *Ignore something of importance.*

turn the work off *Stop working.*

umbrella policy (p. 682) A broadly based insurance policy that saves you money because you buy all your insurance from one company.

unemployment rate (p. 53) The number of civilians at least 16 years old who are unemployed and tried to find a job within the prior four weeks.

Uniform Commercial Code (UCC) (p. 129) A comprehensive commercial law, adopted by every state in the United States, that covers sales laws and other commercial laws.

uninsurable risk (p. 696) A risk that no insurance company will cover.

union (p. 364) An employee organization that has the main goal of representing members in employee-management bargaining over job-related issues.

union security clause (p. 369) Provision in a negotiated labor-management agreement that stipulates that employees who benefit from a union must either officially join or at least pay dues to the union.

union shop agreement (p. 369) Clause in a labor-management agreement that says workers do not have to be members of a union to be hired, but must agree to join the union within a prescribed period.

unlimited liability (p. 143) The responsibility of business owners for all of the debts of the business

unsecured bond (p. 599) A bond backed only by the reputation of the issuer; also called a debenture bond.

unsecured loan (p. 595) A loan that's not backed by any specific assets.

unsought goods and services (p. 435) Products that consumers are unaware of, haven't necessarily thought of buying, or find that they need to solve an unexpected problem.

utility (p. 463) In economics, the want-satisfying ability, or value, that organizations add to goods or services when the products are made more useful or accessible to consumers than they were before.

value (p. 430) Good quality at a fair price. When consumers calculate the value of a product, they look at the benefits and then subtract the cost to see if the benefits exceed the costs.

variable costs (p. 449) Costs that change according to the level of production.

variable life insurance (p. 681) Whole life insurance that invests the cash value of the policy in stocks or other high-yielding securities.

venture capital (p. 600) Money that is invested in new or emerging companies that are perceived as having great profit potential.

venture capitalists (p. 192) Individuals or companies that invest in new businesses in exchange for partial ownership of those businesses.

vertical merger (p. 156) The joining of two companies involved in different stages of related businesses.

vestibule training (p. 340) Training done in schools where employees are taught on equipment similar to that used on the job.

viral marketing (p. 506) The term now used to describe everything from paying people to say positive things on the Internet to setting up multilevel selling schemes whereby consumers get commissions for directing friends to specific websites.

virtual corporation (p. 256) A temporary networked organization made up of replaceable firms that join and leave as needed.

virtual private network (VPN) (p. 528) A private data network that creates secure connections, or "tunnels," over regular Internet lines.

virtualization (p. 521) Accessibility through technology that allows business to be conducted independent of location.

virus (p. 536) A piece of programming code inserted into other programming to cause some unexpected and, for the victim, usually undesirable event.

vision (p. 215) An encompassing explanation of why the organization exists and where it's trying to head.

volume, or usage, segmentation (p. 412) Dividing the market by usage (volume of use).

voluntary bankruptcy (p. 136) Legal procedures initiated by a debtor.

walk out the door *Leave the company; quit your job.*

watching over your shoulder *Looking at everything you do.*

whistleblowers (p. 108) People who report illegal or unethical behavior.

whole life insurance (p. 680) Life insurance that stays in effect until age 100.

wholesaler (p. 460) A marketing intermediary that sells to other organizations.

will (p. 687) A document that names the guardian for your children, states how you want your assets distributed, and names the executor for your estate.

word-of-mouth promotion (p. 506) A promotional tool that involves people telling other people about products they've purchased.

workers' compensation insurance (p. 700) Insurance that guarantees payment of wages, medical care, and rehabilitation services (e.g., retraining) for employees who are injured on the job, regardless of fault.

World Bank (p. 662) The bank primarily responsible for financing economic development; also known as the International Bank for Reconstruction and Development.

World Trade Organization (WTO) (p. 89) The international organization that replaced the General Agreement on Tariffs and Trade, and was assigned the duty to mediate trade disputes among nations.

yellow-dog contract (p. 367) A type of contract that required employees to agree as a condition of employment not to join a union; prohibited by the Norris-LaGuardia Act in 1932.

Photo Credits

Table of Contents

TOC-01, page v, Courtesy of Monster.com
TOC-02, page vi, Wolfgang Schmidt
TOC-03, page vii, Courtesy of Learning Leaders
TOC-04, page viii, Courtesy of Principal Technical Services, Inc.
TOC-05, page ix, Harley L. Schwadron
TOC-06, page x, Pablo Bartholomew
TOC-07, page xi, Frederick J. Brown/Agence France Press
TOC-08, page xii, Michael S. Wirtz/Phila. Inquirer
TOC-09, page xiii, AP Wide World Photo
TOC-10, page xiv, April Saul/Phila. Inquirer
TOC-11, page xv, Ann Farrell

Prologue

P01, page P-4, PhotoDisc
P02, page P-5, Courtesy of McGraw-Hill
P03, page P-6, Photo Disc
P04, page P-8, Virginia Kamsky
P05, page P-9, B. Mahoney/The Image Works
P06, page P-11, Bob Thaves
P07, page P-12, PhotoDisc
P08, page P-14, Rosemary Hedger
P09, page P-16, McGraw-Hill
P10, page P-17, Coneyl Jay/Tony Stone Images
P11, page P-23, AOL screenshots © 2002 America Online, Inc. Used with permission.
P12, page P-24, AOL screenshots © 2002 America Online, Inc. Used with permission.
P13, page P-26, Courtesy of McGraw-Hill
P14, page P-27, April Saul/Phila. Inquirer
P15, page P-29, Courtesy of Hoover's, Inc. (www.hoovers.com)
P16, page P-31, South Carolina Department of Parks, Recreation and Tourism
P17, page P-34, William F. Steinmetz/Philadelphia Inquirer

Chapter 1

P01-01, page 3, AP Wide World Photos
P01-02, page 4, Henry Ray Abrams/Agence France-Presse
P01-03, page 7, Monika Graff/The Image Works
P01-04, page 9, Courtesy of National Assembly of Health & Human Service Organizations
P01-05, page 10, David M. Warren/Philadelphia Inquirer
P01-06, page 14, Dave Bartruff/Stock Boston
P01-07, page17, Kelly Culpepper
P01-08, page 18, AP Wide World Photos
P01-09, page 20, James Smolka © 2002
P01-10, page 22, Mike Greenlar/The Image Works
P01-11, page 23, © 2002 SAS Institute Inc. All Rights Reserved.
P01-12, page 25, USA Today
P01-13, page 26, David Frazier/Stock Boston

Chapter 2

P02-01, page 35, Rosemary Hedger
P02-02, page 36, Lee/Kpix
P02-03, page 36, AP Wide World Photos
P02-04, page 39, The Bettmann Archive
P02-05, page 40, Courtesy of the Gates Foundation
P02-06, page 41, AP Wide World Photos
P02-07, page 43, Chien-Chi Chang/Magnum Photos
P02-08, page 46, Courtesy of Green Mountain Energy
P02-09, page 48, Francis Dean/The Image Works
P02-10, page 48, Ilene Perlman/Stock Boston
P02-11, page 53, AP Wide World Photos
P02-12, page 56, James Marshal/The Image Works
P02-13, page 58, AP Wide World Photos

Chapter 3

P03-01, page 67, Mr. Shi Xiaobing
P03-02, page 70, Courtesy of Burrston House
P03-03, page 71, AP Wide World Photos
P03-04, page 72, Robbie McClaran
P03-05, page 74, Mauricio Lima/Agence France-Presse
P03-06, page 77, Barbara Slavin/USA Today
P03-07, page 78, Courtesy of Domino's Pizza
P03-08, page 79, AP Wide World Photos
P03-09, page 80, Al Anderer
P03-10, page 82, Courtesy of Systems Union
P03-11, page 84, AP Wide World Photos
P03-12, page 86, Scott Olson/WirePix/The Image Works
P03-13, page 89, AP Wide World Photos

Chapter 4

P04-01, page 101, Chip Pankey/Courtesy of Storage USA
P-04-02, page 102, AP Wide World Photos
P04-03, page 107, AP Wide World Photos
P04-04, page 110, Courtesy of Xerox Corporation
P04-05, page 112, Courtesy of Rhino Entertainment
P04-06, page 113, AP Wide World Photos
P04-07, page 114, Justin Sullivan/Getty Images
P04-08, page 115, Courtesy of Green Mountain Energy
P04-09, page 116, Courtesy of Ford Motor Company
P04-10, page 118, AP Wide World Photos

Chapter 4 Appendix

P04App-01, page 124, AP Wide World Photos
P04App-02, page 127, AP Wide World Photos
P04App-03, page 129, Courtesy of McDonald's Corporation
P04App-04, page 133, AP Wide World Photos
P04App-05, page 134, Hartford Current
P04App-06, page 137, AP Wide World Photos

Chapter 5

P05-01, page 141, Courtesy of Auntie Anne's Pretzels
P05-02, page 143, Chris Navin
P05-03, page 147, Ron Ceasar
P05-04, page 149, John Costello/Philadelphia Inquirer
P05-05, page 150, V. Craig Sands
P05-06, page 157, David Bashaw
P05-07, page 159, The Crown Plaza Hotel, Edinburgh
P05-08, page163, Courtesy of Mompreneurs
P05-09, page 164, V.C.L./Getty Images

Chapter 6

P06-01, page 173, Photo provided by Leaping Lion Photography
P06-02, page 174, USA Today/Robert Deutsch
P06-03, page175, Chris Navin
P06-04, page178, Courtesy of L.A. Times/Photo by Carlos Chavez
P06-05, page 179, Courtesy of KEH Camera
P06-06, page183, Kate Swan
P06-07, page 185, Courtesy of Organica Foods
P06-08, page 189, Courtesy of The Advocate/Kevin Graff
P06-09, page 190, Piranha Illustrations/ Krzysztof Palonka
P06-10, page192, Courtesy of the Philadelphia Inquirer/Ron Tarver
P06-11, page 195, Rosemary Hedger
P06-12, page 196, Patrick Hood © 1999

Chapter 7

P07-01, page 211, AP Wide World Photos
P07-02, page 212, AP Wide World Photos
P07-03, page 213, Courtesy of Monster
P07-04, page 218, Tim Matsui/USA Today
P07-05, page 221, © 2002 Thaves. Reprinted with permission.
P07-06, page 222, Courtesy of Texas Instruments
P07-07, page 224, Courtesy of Eastman Kodak Company
P07-08, page 232, Charles Barsotti

Chapter 8

P08-01, page 239, AP World Wide Photo
P08-02, page 242, Darr Beiser/USA Today
P08-03, page 243, Courtesy of German Information Center, NY
P08-04, page 245, Courtesy of Burrston House
P08-05, page 249, Courtesy of Expedia Inc.
P08-06, page 254, Courtesy of Rubbermaid Inc.
P08-07, page 255, Joe Vaughan
P08-08, page 256, Angela Wyantt/Courtesy of K2 Corp.
P08-09, page 257, Bob Riha Jr./USA Today
P08-10, page 259, Scogin Mayo
P08-11, page 260, AP Wide World Photos

Chapter 9

P09-01, page 267, AP Wide World Photos
P09-02, page 268, Knight-Ridder Tribune/Charles Osgood
P09-03, page 269, Courtesy of Demetria Giannisis
P09-04, page 271, Ann States
P09-05, page 273, Courtsey of Empire State Development
P09-06, page 274, Courtesy of Rainer Holz
P09-07, page 276, Jeff Sciortino
P09-08, page 279, Courtesy of Branch-Smith Printing Co.
P09-09, page 280, Ben Van Hook
P09-10, page 285, Courtesy of SAS Institute
P09-11, page 287, CORBIS

Chapter 10

P10-01, page 299, Courtesy of Southwest Airlines
P10-02, page 303, Courtesy of AT&T Corporate Archives
P10-03, page 305, Rosemary Hedger
P10-04, page 307, Bob Daemmrich/Stock Boston
P10-05, page 310, Jason Grow/SABA
P10-06, page 311, Getty Images
P10-07, page 311, Getty Images
P10-08, page 318, Ford Motor Corporation
P10-09, page 320, Courtesy of Real Simple

Chapter 11

P11-01, page 329, Courtesy of Certes Financial Pros
P11-02, page 337, Courtesy of PeopleWise.com
P11-03, page 339, Courtesy of EDS
P11-04, page 340, 1995-2000 FedEx. All Rights Reserved.
P11-05, page 341, KRP/Knight Ridder Tribune
P11-06, page 347, AAA World, Sept/Oct '01, Vol.3, No.5, p. 13
P11-07, page 350, Courtesy of Avaya, Inc. and JetBlue Airways
P11-08, page 355, Bob Daemmrich/The Image Works

Chapter 12

P12-01, page 363, AP Wide World Photos
P12-02, page 364, AP Wide World Photos
P12-03, page 366, AP World Wide Photos
P12-04, page 373, Courtesy of the American Arbitration Association
P12-05, page 374, AP Wide World Photos
P12-06, page 376, AP Wide World Photos
P12-07, page 378, Nelson Chenault
P12-08, page 379, Universal Press Syndicate/Toles
P12-09, page 382, Courtesy of Institute for Women's Policy Research
P12-10, page 385, Dorothy Littell Greco/The Image Works

Chapter 13

P13-01, page 397, Andrea Sorani
P13-02, page 399, Rose Howerter/Inquirer Suburban Staff
P13-03, page 400, © 2003 City Harvest. A partner of America's Second Harvest. Special Thanks to Harrison Ford. Photo: Timothy White
P13-04, page 405, Courtesy of Kellogg's
P13-05, page 406, Spencer Grant/Photo Edit
P13-06, page 410, Courtesy of International Cable Channel
P13-07, page 412, Rosemary Hedger
P13-08, page 415, William Steinmetz/Philadelphia Inquirer
P13-09, page 418, Peter Hvizdak/The Image Works
P13-10, page 420, © Dan Piraro. Reprinted with Special Permission of King Features Syndicate.
P13-11, page 421, Christopher Harting

Chapter 14

P14-01, page 429, AP Wide World Photos
P14-02, page 430, Ray Reiss Photography
P14-03, page 432, © Virgin Atlantic Airways
P14-04, page 435, Bonnie Weller/Inquirer Staff Photographer
P14-05, page 437, Sal Skog Photography
P14-06, page 438, © Dennis Kleiman Photography 2002
P14-07, page 446, Scott S. Hamrick/Inquirer Suburban Staff
P14-08, page 446, Copyright 2003 ABC Photography Archives
P14-09, page 448, Eric Mencher/Inquirer Staff Photographer
P14-10, page 451, PriceGrabber.com, LLC

Chapter 15

P15-01, page 459, Courtesy of Sears Roebuck & Co.
P15-02, page 464, Al Anderer
P15-03, page 468, Rosemary Hedger
P15-04, page 470, Elizabeth Robertson/Inquirer Suburban Staff
P15-05, page 471, ErhardPfeiffer/Courtesy of MillsServices Corp.
P15-06, page 472, Steve Campbell/Chronicle
P15-07, page 475, Courtesy of Harry and David
P15-08, page 476, © 2003 Menlo Worldwide, LLC
P15-09, page 478, © Gary Braasch/Woodfin Camp & Associates
P15-10, page 479, Courtesy of Union Pacific
P15-11, page 481, David Alan Harvey/Magnum Photos
P15-12, page 482, Michael Vaughn

Chapter 16

P16-01, page 489, Sam Jones
P16-02, page 492, Reprinted with permission of the AAF
P16-03, page 493, © Eastcott,Momatiuk/Woodfin Camp & Associates
P16-04, page 494, Michael S. Wirtz/Phila. Inquirer
P16-05, page 497, Courtesy of Champion
P16-06, page 498, Peter Ross
P16-07, page 500, Scott Adams
P16-08, page 501, Courtesy of Burrston House
P16-09, page 504, AP Wide World Photos
P16-10, page 507, Courtesy of complaints.com
P16-11, page 517, Gregory V. Ortega

Chapter 17

P17-01, page 519, Courtesy of Eli Lilly
P17-02, page 520, Brian Doben
P17-03, page 524, Christoph Rehben/SI International
P17-04, page 525, Kate Swan
P17-05, page 527, © 2003 Ofer Wolberger
P17-06, page 530, Amanda Marsalis
P17-07, page 531, Courtesy of Veritas
P17-08, page 534, Dilbert reprinted by permission of United Feature Syndicate, Inc.
P17-09, page 538, Courtesy of N2H2/Photo by Greg Sweney

Chapter 18

P18-01, page 547, AP Wide World Photos
P18-02, page 550, Michael Rosenfeld/Getty Images
P18-03, page 552, Rosemary Hedger
P18-04, page 553, Dave Carpenter
P18-05, page 565, AP Wide World Photos
P18-06, page 568, Courtesy of Home Depot

Chapter 19

P19-01a, page 579, Micky Keener
P19-01, page 581, Courtesy of Krispy Kreme
P19-02, page 584, David Crenshaw
P19-03, page 586, Jeff Greenberg/PhotoEdit
P19-04, page 590, Courtesy of nextcard.com
P19-05, page 594, Vic Bider/PhotoEdit
P19-06, page 601, AP Wide World Photos

Chapter 20

P20-01, page 609, Peter Sterling
P20-02, page 618, AP Wide World Photos
P20-03, page 619, Robert Brenner/PhotoEdit
P20-04, page 621, Christian Lagereek/Getty Images
P20-05, page 625, Mick Stevens
P20-06, page 627, AP Wide World Photos

Chapter 21

P21-01, page 643, AP Wide World Photos
P21-02, page 645, AP Wide World Photos
P21-03, page 649, unitedmedia.com
P21-04, page 651, Eric Mencher/Philadelphia Inquirer
P21-05, page 653, Ann States
P21-06, page 656, Paul Moseley/Fort Worth Star Telegram
P21-07, page 661, © 2003, Chicago Tribune Company. All rights reserved. Used with permission.

Chapter 22

P22-01, page 669, AP Wide World Photo
P22-02, page 672, AP WideWorld Photo
P22-03, page 676, Photo Disc
P22-04, page 678, Courtesy of Citi-Card
P22-05, page 683, Courtesy of The Phoenix Companies, Inc.
P22-06, page 686, John Gress
P22-07, page 688, Courtesy of A.G. Edwards

Chapter 22 Appendix

P22A-01, page 694, AP Wide World Photos
P22A-02, page 695, Sarah J. Glover/Philadelphia Inquirer
P22A-03, page 698, AP Wide World Photos
P22A-04, page 699, © State Farm Mutual Automobile Insurance Company, 1996. Used by permission.
P22A-05, page 700, Jonathan Wilson/Philadelphia Inquirer

Name Index

L

M

Y

Z

Organization Index

D

E

F

G

H

I

J

K

L

M

Subject Index

C

F

G

N

T

U

V

W

Y

Z